ビジネス実務
総合英和辞典

Dictionary of
Practical Business English

菊地義明 ▶著

三省堂

© 2009 菊地義明

Dictionary of Practical Business English
ビジネス実務総合英和辞典

Printed in Japan

装幀・組版設計　———　宗利淳一

組版　———　原島康晴（エディマン）

はじめに

　この『ビジネス実務総合英和辞典』は，経済（景気動向，経済指標，経済統計），経営（M&A，経営管理），金融（証券，銀行，保険），財務・会計，Eビジネス，国際取引，契約，法律（会社法，ビジネス法，英米商法），マーケティングや各種産業など各専門分野の基本用語と重要語句をまとめたものです。

　これらは，英字新聞，経済・ビジネス専門誌等のビジネス関連記事やビジネス文書，ビジネス・レポートなどを読み解くうえで，また日常のビジネス活動を円滑に進めるうえでも必須とされるものばかりです。

　本書は，基本的に見出し語とその語義，見出し語の関連語句と文例とで構成されています。見出し語には，語義の後に見出し語の同意・反意語や参照項目のほか，必要に応じて適宜，簡単な説明も加えてあります。関連語句としては，一般の学習用語辞典には掲載されていないビジネス用語が多数収録されています。また，最新性と実用性を考慮してカレントなトピックを豊富に盛り込んだ文例も，この辞典の特長です。そのため，時事用語辞典として本書を利用することもできます。

　さらに文例にはその的確な訳例が付してあり，訳例として同意表現が可能な場合には日本語の同意表現も加えてあるため，専門用語辞典のほかに「翻訳事典」として利用することもできます。

　このように本書は，ビジネス分野で多用される見出し語，関連語句，文例が選定されているため，ビジネスピープルにとって真の実用辞典として活用することができます。

　なお，財務・会計用語については，既刊の『財務情報英和辞典』（三省堂）で詳しく触れてありますので，あわせてご活用ください。

2009年6月
菊地義明

目次

はじめに ——————————————————————————— iii

凡例 ——————————————————————————— iv–v

A—Z ——————————————————————————— 001–680

和英索引 ——————————————————————————— 681–806

凡例

1. 見出し語

単一の語のほかに，2語以上からなる語句（分離複合語）も重要なものは見出し語として立てた。同じつづりで語源が異なるもの，複数の品詞を持つもののうち重要なものはそれぞれを見出し語としたが，番号などで区別することはしていない。

1.1 配列

見出し語の配列は原則としてアルファベット順としたが，分離複合語およびハイフンで結合された複合語は，構成要素の最初の語を基準としてひとまとまりで示した。数字は，アルファベットとは別種の文字として扱い，アルファベットよりも前に昇順で置いた。

1.2 品詞

単一の語には品詞を略記した。
- **名**　名詞
- **形**　形容詞
- **動**　動詞
- **副**　副詞
- **前**　前置詞
- **接**　接続詞

2. 語義

語義の区分はカンマで示した。

2.1 括弧類

括弧類を次の原則に基づいて使用した。
- (　)　注記，参照，略語の成り立ちなどを示す。
- 〈　〉　他動詞の目的語や語の内包的意味を補助的に示す。
- [　]　交換可能であることを示す。
- 《　》《略　》の形で略語を示す。

2.2 その他記号類
- ＝　ほぼ同義で用いられる語句を示す。
- ⇒　当該の見出し語を含む例文が参照先に存在することを表す。

3. 副見出し

分離複合語および文の形をとっていない用例を副見出しとして示した。
配列と語義の書式は見出し語と同様の規則に基づく。

4. 用例

用例は原則として完全文の形で示した。見出し部分を斜字体で示した。

A

a

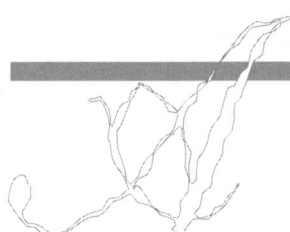

A$ 名　豪ドル
AAA　米国仲裁協会（American Arbitration Associationの略）
AAA　アメリカ自動車協会（American Automobile Associationの略）
AAA 名 形　トリプルA, トリプルAの格付け
　AAA company　トリプルAの会社, トリプルAの格付けの会社, 超一流企業
　AAA-rated borrower　トリプルA格の発行体
　AAA rating　トリプルAの格付け
▶We are a *AAA* company.　当社は, トリプルAの超一流企業です。
ABA　米国銀行協会（American Bankers' Associationの略）
ABA　米国法曹協会（American Bar Associationの略）
abandon 動　〈権利や財産を〉放棄する,〈船舶や積み荷を〉委付する,〈訴訟を〉取り下げる
▶We *abandon* to you our interest in the undermentioned shipments.　当社は, 下記積み荷に対する当社の権利を御社に委付する。
abandonment 名　除却, 放棄, 遺棄, 廃棄, 引渡し, 中断, 中止, 委付, 保険委付, 委付保険,〈訴訟の〉取下げ
　abandonment of a cargo　積み荷の委付
　abandonment of application　特許などの出願放棄
　abandonment of mark　登録商標の放棄
　abandonment of vessel　船舶の委付
　abandonment value　廃棄価値
　asset abandonment　資産除却
　equipment abandonment　設備の廃却

property abandonment　財産放棄
▶These provisions include $110 million for closing facilities, lease terminations and asset *abandonments* associated with centralizing customer support services.　この引当金には, 顧客支援サービス部門の集中化に関連した施設閉鎖費, リース解約費と資産除却費用の1億1,000万ドルも含まれています。
ABC　活動基準原価計算, ABC管理（⇒activity based costing）
ABC agreement　ABC契約（米国の証券会社が, ニューヨーク証券取引所の会員資格を得るために自社従業員と結ぶ契約）
abend 名　〈コンピュータ・プログラム実行中の〉異常終了,〈コンピュータ自体の〉異常停止, アベンド（＝abnormal end）
ability 名　能力, 力
　ability to buy back shares　自社株を買い戻す能力, 自社株買戻し能力, 買戻し能力
　ability to control costs　コスト管理能力
　ability to finance　資金調達力
　ability to generate cash　収益力, キャッシュ・フロー生成能力, キャッシュ・フローを生み出す能力
　ability to meet cash capital requirements　資金需要を賄う能力
　ability to pay down debt　債務返済能力（＝ability to meet debt payments due）
　ability to refinance　借換え能力
　debt-paying ability　債務返済能力（＝debt servicing capacity）
▶This company has demonstrated its *ability* to

deal with change and challenge throughout all of its history. 当社は，創立以来こんにちに至るまで，変革と課題に対応する当社の能力を示してきました。

ABM 活動基準管理 (⇒**activity based management**)

about-face 名 方向転換, 方針転換, 180度転換 [転向, 転回], 180度方向転換, 急転換, 回れ右 (= about-turn)
▶The bank's serious financial difficulties have forced it to do an *about-face*. 同行は深刻な経営難で，方針転換を迫られている。

About Us 会社案内, 会社概要 (= Company Fact Sheet, Corporate Profile)

above 前 …を上回る, …より上の, …以上の, アバブ
  above-average 平均を上回る
  above par 額面超過, 額面以上, 額面以上の状態, 割増
  above the market 市価 [時価] を上回る, アバブ・ザ・マーケット注文
  above the market strategy 市価以上戦略, 高価格市場戦略
  above trend growth トレンドを上回る成長率

above the line 経常損益計算, 経常収支, 経常支出, 範囲内, アバブ・ザ・ライン (「アバブ・ザ・ライン」は事業の経常的な収益と費用を指し，lineは損益計算書の経常利益または当期純利益を指す)
  above the line profit 経常利益

ABS 資産担保証券, アセットバック証券 (⇒**assetbacked securities**)

absence 名 不在, 欠勤, 欠席, 不出頭 (⇒**evidence**)

absentee 名 不在者, 欠席者, 意図的欠勤者, 長期欠勤者, 職務離脱者

absenteeism 名 無断欠勤

absolute 形 絶対の, 完全な, 純粋な, 無条件の, 絶対的な, 全面的な
  absolute advantage 絶対優位, 絶対的優位性
  absolute contract 無条件契約
  absolute cost 絶対的費用, 絶対原価, 絶対的生産費
  absolute disadvantage 絶対劣位
  absolute error 絶対誤差
  absolute income 絶対所得
  absolute inflation 絶対的インフレーション
  absolute insolvency 絶対的債務超過
  absolute level of credit risk 信用リスクの絶対水準
  absolute level of leverage 負債の絶対水準
  absolute liability 絶対責任, 無過失責任
  absolute majority 絶対多数, 過半数
  absolute monopoly 完全独占, 絶対独占
  absolute profit 純益
  absolute rate 絶対値
  absolute sale 絶対売買
  absolute share 絶対的分け前
  absolute standard of living 最低生活水準, 最低生活費
  absolute total loss 絶対全損
  absolute value 絶対値, 絶対価値
  average [mean] absolute deviation 平均絶対偏差
  in absolute terms 金額ベースで, 絶対ベースで, 絶対値で
  on an absolute basis 絶対水準で, 絶対値で

absorb 動 吸収する, 吸収合併する, 配賦する, 塡補（てんぽ）する, 〈税金などを〉負担する, 解消する (⇒**after-tax loss**)
  absorb losses 損失を吸収する
  absorb fixed overhead as a cost of product 固定間接費を製品原価の一部として配賦する
  absorb the withholding tax 源泉課税を負担する
  absorbed cost 全部原価, 配賦済み原価, 配賦原価
  absorbed overhead 製造間接費配賦額 (= absorbed burden, applied overhead)
▶Nippon Oil Corp. will *absorb* Kyushu Oil Co. on Oct. 1, 2008. 新日本石油は，2008年10月1日に九州石油を吸収合併する。
▶We will *absorb* the company as a wholly owned subsidiary. 当社は，同社を完全子会社として吸収する [同社を完全子会社化する] 方針です。

absorption 名 吸収, 吸収合併, 配賦, 賦課, 塡補
  absorption cost 全部原価 (=full cost: 製品の製造過程で生じる原価をすべて製品原価に算入する計算方法)
  absorption income 全部原価計算に基づく損益
  actual absorption costing 実際全部原価計算
  mergers and absorptions 吸収・合併
  overhead absorption 間接費の配賦
  tax absorption fee 課税負担手数料
▶All mergers are regarded as *absorption* in the United States, even if some are effectively on an equal basis. 実際には対等の立場での合併であっても，米国では合併はすべて吸収合併と見なされる。

abstract of title 権原要約書 (土地の所有権・使用権に生じた変動を要約した書類)

accelerate 動 加速する, 加速させる, 促進する, 推進する, 拍車をかける
　accelerated amortization 加速償却, 加速減価償却, 加速なし崩し償却
　accelerated disposal of bad loans 不良債権処理の加速
　accelerated method 加速償却法（＝accelerated depreciation method）
　▸A series of accounting scandals and delays in the recovery of corporate performance are *accelerating* falls in stock prices on the U.S. markets, along with the weakening of the dollar. 一連の［相次ぐ］企業会計の不祥事と企業業績回復の遅れで, 米国の株安とドル安が加速している。

accept 動 承諾する, 受諾する, 受け入れる, 同意する,〈手形や注文などを〉引き受ける, 認める, 容認する
　accept a bill 手形を引き受ける
　accept a risk 危険を引き受ける, リスクをとる
　accept an offer 申込みを受諾する
　generally accepted 一般に認められた, 一般に公正妥当と認められた
　▸Applications have been *accepted* with few exceptions as long as necessary documents are submitted. 必要な書類が提出されていれば, 申請はほぼ例外なく受理されてきた。
　▸TCI, a British investment fund, asked J-Power to *accept* two TCI executives as board members. 英投資ファンドのTCIは, Jパワーに TCI役員2人の取締役受入れを求めた。
　▸The consolidated financial statements have been prepared in accordance with accounting principles generally *accepted* in Canada. 連結財務書類［連結財務諸表］は, カナダで一般に公正妥当と認められた会計基準に従って［会計基準に準拠して］作成されています。

acceptable 形 一般に認められている, 公正妥当と認められている, 認められている, 許容できる, 容認できる, 許容範囲の, 採択可能な
　acceptable actuarial cost method 一般に認められている保険数理上の原価計算法
　acceptable actuarial cost method for financial purposes 財務会計上認められている保険数理上の原価計算法
　acceptable actuarial method 一般に認められている［認められている］保険数理法
　acceptable use policy ネットワークやコンピュータ・システムを利用する際の方針や約束事《略 **AUP**》

acceptance 名〈申し込み［オファー］に対する〉承諾, 承認,〈手形の〉引受け, 引受済み手形, 商品の受領, 検収
　acceptance commission 手形引受手数料
　acceptance of bill 手形引受け
　acceptance of goods 商品の受領, 商品の引受け
　acceptance of import bill 輸入手形引受け
　acceptance of offer 申込みの承諾, オファーの承諾
　acceptance of order 注文の受諾
　accommodation acceptance 融通手形引受け
　bank acceptance 銀行引受手形《略 **BA**》（＝banker's acceptance）
　brand acceptance ブランド受容
　clean acceptance 単純引受け
　consumer acceptance 消費者受容, 需要者承認
　documentary against acceptance 引受渡し（＝documents against acceptance）
　eligible acceptance 適格手形
　inspection, testing and acceptance 検査, 試験と検収
　prime banker's acceptance 一流銀行引受手形
　qualified acceptance 手形の条件引受け, 制限引受け
　written acceptance 承諾書
　▸The seller shall be liable for latent defects of the products at any time after delivery to the purchaser of the products or any subsequent purchaser, notwithstanding the inspection and *acceptance* of the products by the purchaser or any subsequent purchaser. 売り主は, 本製品の隠れた瑕疵（かし）については, 買い主またはその後の購入者による本製品の検収［検査］にかかわらず, 本製品の買い主またはその後の購入者への引渡し後, いつでも責任を負うものとする。

access 動 接続する, 利用する, データを検索する, 閲覧する, 入手する, 参加する, 参入する, 加入する, 立ち入る, 接近する
　access cash 資金を調達する
　access external sources of cash 外部から資金調達する（＝access external sources of funding, access external funding sources）
　access foreign technology 海外技術を導入する
　access information on …の情報を入手する, …の情報を閲覧する
　access the capital markets 資本市場で資金を調達する, 資本市場で調達する
　access the market 起債する, 市場で資金を調達する

▶Yahoo Japan Corp. provides free detailed disaster information via its Web site that can be *accessed* by cell phone. ネット検索大手のヤフーが，携帯電話でアクセスできる気象サイトで詳しい災害情報を，無料で提供している。

access 名 参入，参入機会，市場アクセス，加入，参加，利用，閲覧，〈コンピュータ・システムやネットワークへの〉接続，アクセス

- **access line** 加入回線，接続回線，端末回線，アクセス回線
- **access right** 参照権，アクセス権（端末，中央処理装置，データ，OSやファイルの利用権などがある）
- **access route** 進入路
- **access to assets** 資産の取扱い （⇒**authorization**）
- **access to capital** 資金調達，資金調達力
- **access to funding** 資金調達，資金源の確保
- **access to information** 情報の入手，情報の閲覧
- **access to markets on an unsecured basis** 無担保ベースでの資金調達
- **access to records and books of account** 会計記録と会計帳簿の閲覧
- **access to the market** 市場への参入，市場への参入機会，市場進出，市場アクセス，市場へのアクセス （＝market access）
- **have access to** …に立ち入る，…に面会する，…に参加する，…を入手する，…が利用できる，…を閲覧できる，…に接することができる （＝get access to）
- **Internet access service** インターネット接続サービス （＝Internet connection service）
- **market access** 市場への参入，市場への参入機会，市場進出，市場アクセス，市場へのアクセス （＝access to the market）
- **market-access barriers** 市場参入障壁

▶The shareholders' auditors have full *access* to the audit committee, with and without management being present. 経営者の同席の有無にかかわらず，監査委員会とは会計監査人が密接に連絡を取っています［監査委員会には会計監査人が毎回参加することができます］。

access charge 接続料金，通信事業者間接続料金，アクセス料金，ネットワーク利用料金 （＝access fee）

▶Contributing to the widespread use of the Net is a decline in *access charges* and the growth of high-speed, high-capacity broadband communication networks. インターネットの広範な普及に寄与しているのが，接続料金の低下と高速大容量（ブロードバンド）通信網の伸びである。

access to financing 資金調達，資金源の確保 （⇒**access to funding**）

▶We have easy *access to financing* when we need it. 資金調達については，当社は必要な時にたやすく資金調達ができます。

accomplishment 名 業績，成果，達成，成就，遂行，完了，完遂，熟練技術，技能

▶This *accomplishment* is especially gratifying given the current climate. この業績［成果］は，とくに現在の経営環境を考えますと，まことに喜ばしい限りです。

accord 名 合意，同意，合意書，合意文書，協定，意見の一致，和解，代物弁済

▶Under the *accord*, the banking, trust and brokerage units of the financial group will be the surviving companies, respectively. 合意書によると，同金融グループの銀行，信託，証券会社がそれぞれ存続会社となる。

account 名 口座，預金，勘定，勘定書，計算，計算書，収支，決算，決算書，会計，取引関係，取引先，投資家，説明，報告，理由，考慮，重要性 《略 a/c》 （⇒**impair, settle, window-dress, withdrawal**）

- **account books** 会計帳簿，売掛債権帳，売掛帳，決算書 （＝accounting books, books of account, financial books; ⇒**books of account**）
- **account due** 未収金
- **account executive** 広告会社の営業責任者，証券会社のセールスマン《略 AE》
- **account holder** 口座名義人
- **account number** 口座番号
- **account of business** 営業報告書
- **bank account** 銀行口座，銀行勘定，預金
- **branch account** 支店勘定
- **call ... to account** …に釈明を求める，…に責任を問う
- **fund account** 資金勘定
- **head office account** 本店勘定
- **off-the-book account** 簿外口座
- **open account** 当座預金，当座勘定，交互計算
- **open an account** 口座を開設する
- **ordinary account** 普通口座
- **settlement account** 決済口座
- **specified account** 特定口座
- **trade account** 貿易収支
- **two sets of account books** 二重帳簿
- **Web account** ウェブ口座

▶Customers can choose a settlement-specific or a savings deposit when they open an *account*. 口座を開設する際，顧客は普通預金か決済用預金か

を選択することができる。
▶The brokerage firm manages client assets of ¥520 billion in about 150,000 *accounts*. この証券会社は，口座数約15万で顧客預り資産は5,200億円に達する。

account balance 差引残高，勘定残高，銀行口座の残高，口座残高
▶*Account balance* can be checked on the Internet. 口座の残高は，インターネットでチェックできる。

account for 計上する，処理する，会計処理する，…を占める，説明する（⇒**distribute**, **financial services**, **total cost**)
▶In the past, the finance subsidiaries of the Corporation were *accounted for* by the equity method. これまで，当社の金融事業を営む子会社は，持ち分法で会計処理していました。
▶Intellectual assets *account for* about 70 percent of the total market value of all corporate assets in the United States. 知的資産は，米国では全企業資産の総時価評価額の約70%を占めている。

account payable 買掛金，未払い金，支払い勘定，支払い債務，買入れ債務，購入債務，仕入債務
▶*Accounts payable* are lower because of reduced access and other interconnection costs. 買掛金は，アクセス料とその他の中間接続原価の減少に伴って減少します。

account receivable 売掛金，未収金，未収入金，受取勘定，売掛債権，売上債権，受取債権（＝account due, sales credit)
▶The growth in *accounts receivable* comes from our higher sales levels. 売掛金の増加は，当社の販売額の増加によるものです。

account settlement 決算（＝settlement of accounts; ⇒**confidence**, **end**)
　account settlement term 決算期
　account settlement term ending in March 3月決算期，3月期
　March account settlement 3月決算
　midyear account settlement 中間決算（＝midterm account settlement)
　the first-half account settlement 上半期決算，中間決算
　the latest account settlement 今決算
▶In the latest *account settlements*, some banking groups gave up including sizable deferred tax assets in their equity capital. 今決算では，一部の銀行グループが，巨額の繰延べ税金資産の自己資本への計上を見送った。

accountability 名 義務，責任，実施義務，説明責任，報告責任，会計責任，企業責任，アカウンタビリティ
　accountability of assets 資産に対する企業責任
　accountability to customers 顧客への説明責任
　business accountability 独立採算
　corporate accountability 企業の説明責任
　management accountability 経営の説明責任，経営の説明責任能力
　operational accountability 経営責任
　stewardship accountability 受託責任
▶Corporation's internal controls are designed to adequately safeguard, verify and maintain *accountability* of assets. 当社の内部統制は，資産に対する企業責任を十分に保証・確認・維持するよう図られています。

accountable 形 …する責任がある
　accountable for …に対して責任がある，…の責任がある
　be held accountable for …の責任を問われる，…について責任がある
　hold accountable for …に責任を持たせる
▶Executives will be held *accountable* if the low-rated government bonds they have purchased fail to produce profits. 経営者が購入した格付けの低い国債が利益を生み出さなかったら［経営者が格付けの低い国債への投資で失敗したら］，経営者が(株主から)その責任を問われることになる。
▶The bank's investigation committee is compiling a report that holds several former executives *accountable* for the enormous losses. 同行の調査委員会は，旧経営陣数名に多額の損失の責任を問う内容の報告書をまとめている。

accountant 名 会計士，会計［経理］担当者，会計専門家，監査人（⇒ **accounting fraud**, **independent**)
　accountant general 経理部長
　accountant's certificate 監査報告書
　accountant's fee 監査報酬
　accountant's office 会計事務所
　certified accountant 公認会計士
　certified management accountant 公認管理会計士
　certified public accountant 公認会計士《略 CPA》
　chartered accountant 勅許会計士
　chief accountant 会計主任，経理課長，主任会計審査官
　continuing accountant 継続会計士
　public accountant 公認会計士，公共会計士，職

業会計士［会計人］
reporting accountant 報告会計士
tax accountant 税理士
▶Four certified public *accountants* at ChuoAoyama PricewaterhouseCoopers were involved in the window dressing. 中央青山監査法人の4人の公認会計士が，粉飾決算に関与していた。

accounting 名 会計，会計処理，決算処理，会計処理方法，会計学，経理，計算，算定 (⇒**mark-to-market**)
accounting audit 会計監査
accounting date 決算日
accounting department 経理部，経理部門，会計部門 （＝accounting division, accounting section）
accounting income 会計上の利益 (⇒**provide**)
accounting malpractice 不正会計
accounting policy 会計方針
accounting profit 会計上の利益
accounting scandal 不正経理や粉飾決算などの企業会計疑惑，会計疑惑，会計処理疑惑，会計不祥事，会計スキャンダル，不正会計事件
accounting term ending in September 2009 2009年9月期，2009年9月中間決算，2009年9月に終了する会計期間
accounting year 会計年度 （＝accounting period, business year, fiscal year, operating period）
consolidated accounting 連結決算
corporate accounting 企業会計，企業の会計処理，企業の会計処理方法，企業の経理，会社会計 (⇒**collapse**)
current value accounting 現在価値会計，時価主義会計《略 **CVA**》（＝mark-to-market accounting, market value accounting）
false accounting 不正経理
financial accounting 財務会計
manufacturing accounting 製造原価計算
mark-to-market accounting 時価会計 （＝fair value accounting, market value-based accounting）
product cost accounting 製品別原価計算
tax accounting 税務会計
uniform accounting system 統一会計制度
value accounting 価値会計

accounting books 会計帳簿
▶The *accounting books* and other data have been leaked. 会計帳簿や他のデータが，流出してしまった。

accounting change 会計処理の変更，会計基準の変更，会計上の変更，会計処理方法の変更，会計見積りの変更 (⇒**change**)
▶We made three *accounting changes* this past year. 当社は，当年度に三つの会計処理の変更を行いました。

accounting firm 会計事務所，会計士事務所，監査法人
▶International Business Machines Corp. will buy the consulting and technology services arm of PricewaterhouseCoopers, the world's largest *accounting firm*, for $3.5 billion in cash and stock. 米IBMは，世界最大手の会計事務所「プライスウォーターハウス・クーパース」（PwC）のコンサルティング業務と技術サービス部門を，現金と株式交換により35億ドルで買収することになった。

accounting for income taxes 法人税等に関する会計処理
▶In 2008, the Company adopted SFAS No. 109, "*Accounting for Income Taxes*." 2008年度に当社は，財務会計基準書（SFAS）第109号「法人税等に関する会計処理基準」を採用しました。

accounting fraud 会計操作，不正会計処理，粉飾決算 （＝accounting manipulation）
▶A certified public accountant took part in an *accounting fraud* for the company. 公認会計士が，同社の粉飾決算に加担していた。

accounting irregularities 不正経理，不正会計
▶The *accounting irregularities* were carried out by all of the firm's seven branch offices. 不正経理は，同社の7支店全店で行われていた。

accounting manipulation 会計操作
▶Such an *accounting manipulation* can be done simply by doctoring the books. このような会計操作は，帳簿に手を加えるだけで簡単にできる。

accounting method 会計処理方法，会計方法
▶We sometimes decide to change our *accounting methods* because of trends in our business or industry. 当社は，当社の事業や業界の動向に応じて会計処理方法の変更を決定することもあります。

accounting mistake 経理ミス （＝accounting error）
▶The amount that the company failed to declare totaled about ¥2 billion if *accounting mistakes* are included. 同社の申告漏れの額は，経理ミスを含めると総額で約20億円にのぼった。

accounting period 会計期間，会計年度，事業年度 （＝financial period, financial year, fiscal period, fiscal year: 財務書類［財務諸表］の基本会

計期間は1年となっている。⇒**books of account**)
▶Major corporations' percentage of the drop in after-tax gains significantly exceeded that of the fall in recurring profits during the latest *accounting period*.　当期は，大手企業の税引き後利益の減率が経常利益の減少率を大きく上回った。

accounting principle　会計原則，会計基準，会計処理基準，会計処理の方法　（⇒ **generally accepted accounting principles**）
▶The financial statements have been prepared in accordance with Canadian generally accepted *accounting principles*.　この財務書類は，カナダの会計基準に準拠して［カナダの一般に認められた会計基準に従って］作成されています。

accounting rule　会計規則，会計基準
▶Nonbank firms are forced to raise provisions by a recent *accounting rule* change.　今回の会計規則の変更で，ノンバンク（銀行以外の金融機関）各社は引当金の積み増しを迫られている。

accounting standards　会計基準，会計原則　（＝accounting criteria；⇒ **current value accounting standard**）
▶For the business year ending in March 2009, we will post more than ¥3 trillion in consolidated operating profits based on U.S. *accounting standards*.　2009年3月期連結決算で，米国会計基準に基づく当社の連結営業利益は3兆円を上回る見通しだ。

accounting system　会計制度，会計組織，会計システム，計算制度，計算体系
▶Internal auditors continually review the *accounting* and control *systems*.　内部監査人は，継続して当社の会計処理システムと管理システムを検討しています。

accounts 名　財務書類，財務諸表，計算書類，勘定，会計記録，決算　（＝financial statements：⇒ **audit firm, group accounts, majority-owned subsidiary**）
　accounts settlement ending in March　3月期決算
　annual accounts　年次財務諸表，年次財務書類，年次計算書類　（＝annual financial statements, final accounts）
　book of accounts　会計帳簿，財務帳簿　（＝accounts book）
　closing of accounts　決算　（＝closing of books）
　corporate accounts　会社財務諸表
　final accounts　決算報告書，決算，年次財務書類，年次財務諸表

　income and expenditure accounts　収支計算書
　individual accounts　個別財務諸表
　interim accounts　中間財務諸表，中間財務書類，半期財務書類　（＝interim financial statements, interim statements）
　midyear accounts　中間決算
　profit and loss accounts　損益計算書
　statement of accounts　決算，決算報告，決算報告書
　the half-year closing of fiscal 2009 accounts　2009年度中間決算
　the last period of settlement of accounts　最終決算期
▶The consolidated financial statements include the *accounts* of the corporation and all subsidiary companies.　連結財務書類には，当社と当社の全子会社の財務書類（経営成績と財政状態に関する情報）が含まれています。
▶This midranked general contractor is said to have window-dressed *accounts* for four years.　この中堅ゼネコンは，4年間，決算を粉飾したといわれている。

accrual 名　〈利子や権利などの〉発生，未払い金，未払い費用，未払い額見越し，見越し額，見越し項目，引当金，見積り額，増加額，増加部分
　accrual basis　発生主義，発生基準　（＝accrual concept, accrual method, accrual principle）
　accrual expense　発生費用，見越し費用
　accrual rate　経過金利
▶Current liabilities increased due primarily to increased *accruals* resulting from the restructuring and other actions taken in the fourth quarter.　流動負債の増加は，主に第4四半期に実施したリストラクチャリング［事業再編成］などの施策に伴って発生した引当金の増加によるものです。

accrue 動　生じる，発生する，付加する，付与する，増加する，計上する，見越し計上する　（⇒**current service cost**）
　accrued basis　発生主義，発生基準
　accrued bonuses　賞与引当金，未払い賞与
　accrued charges　未払い費用　（＝accrued expenses, accrued payables, accrued liabilities）
　accrued compensation　未払い報酬
　accrued expenses and liabilities　未払い費用および負債
　accrued income　未収収益　（＝accrued receivables, accrued revenues）
　accrued payroll　未払い給与
　accrued receivables　未収収益，見越し債権

(＝accrued income, accrued revenues)

accrued revenues 未収収益（＝accrued income, accrued receivables）

fully accrue 全額計上する

running royalty accruing under this agreement 本契約により生じるランニング・ロイヤルティ

▶The Corporation has fully *accrued* on its books all income taxes for any period which is not yet due. 当社は、まだ支払い期日が到来していない期間のすべての法人税等を、当社の会計帳簿に全額計上しています。

▶The right to exercise options generally *accrues* over a period of four years of continuous employment. オプションを行使する権利は、原則として勤務期間[在任期間, 勤続年数]が4年を経過した時点で発生します。

accrued interest 発生済み利息, 発生利息, 未払い利息, 未収利息, 経過利息（＝interest accrued）

▶This amount includes the appropriate *accrued interest*. この金額には、適切な未収利息が含まれています。

accrued liabilities 未払い負債, 未払い債務, 未払い費用, 見越し負債

▶Interest expense is the interest on short-term and long-term debt and *accrued liabilities*. 支払い利息は、短期および長期負債と未払い債務に対する利息です。

accumulated 形 蓄積した, 累積した

accumulated deficit 累積赤字（＝accumulative deficit）

accumulated depreciation and amortization 減価償却累計額, 減価償却引当金

accumulated dividend 累積配当, 累積利益配当, 累積未払い配当

accumulated earnings 利益剰余金, 留保利益, 累積利益, 積立利益（＝accumulated income, accumulated profit）

accumulated plan benefits 年金未支給額, 年金給付累積額, 累積給付額, 累積給付債務額（⇒ **net of**）

accumulated profit 利益剰余金, 留保利益（＝accumulated income）

▶When we sell or retire plant that was depreciated using the group method, we deduct the original cost from the plant account and from *accumulated* depreciation. グループ償却法を用いて償却した工場を売却もしくは除却する場合、当社は当該工場の取得原価を当該資産勘定と減価償却累計額から控除します。

accumulated liability 累積債務

▶When we adopted the new standard, we had an *accumulated liability* related to past service from retirees and active employees. 当社が新基準を採用した時点で、当社には退職者と現従業員の過去勤務に関する累積債務がありました。

accumulated losses 累積損失

▶The amount of the bank's *accumulated losses* over the period up to the end of its 2008 business year was five times the level of its operating revenue. 同行の2008年度末までの累積損失額は、経常収益の水準の5倍となった。

accumulation 名 蓄積, 増加, 累積, 蓄財, 積み増し, 増殖, アキュムレーション

accumulation plan 積立プラン

capital accumulation 資本蓄積（＝accumulation of capital）

cost accumulations 原価累積額

debt accumulation 累積債務

inventory accumulation 在庫の増加, 在庫増, 在庫の積み増し（＝accumulation of inventories）

property accumulation savings 財形貯蓄

accuse 動 告発する, 告訴する, 起訴する, 訴える, 非難する, 責める, 指摘する

▶A major credit guarantor company has been *accused* of concealing taxable income by the Tokyo Regional Taxation Bureau. 大手の信用保証会社が、東京国税局から課税所得隠しを指摘された。

achieve 動 達成する, 完了する, 獲得する, 確保する, もたらす（＝rack up; ⇒**action**）

achieve improved results 業績が改善する

achieve one's planned growth 成長目標を達成する

achieve profitability 黒字転換を果たす

▶This improvement in revenues was *achieved* despite a lower rate of growth in the number of network access services. この収益改善は、ネットワーク・アクセス・サービス利用件数の伸び率が低下したにもかかわらず達成しました。

achievement 名 成績, 業績, 達成, 成果

achievement value 業績価値

actual achievement 実績

corporate achievements 企業の業績

employee achievements 従業員の功績

financial achievement 業績

performance achievement 業績達成

▶The company, aiming to expand its financial

acid test | **across the board**

achievement, will open a new factory in Texas in May 2009. 業績拡大を目指す同社は，2009年5月に米テキサスの新工場を稼働させる。

acid test 厳しい検査，最終的な厳しい考査，厳しい試験，酸性試験，吟味，厳しい試練，試金石，正念場 （＝severe test）
▸All major banking groups now face the *acid test* of whether they can regain profitability this fiscal year. 大手銀行・金融グループは，すべて今期の収益力回復に向けて正念場を迎えている。

acid test ratio 当座比率，酸性試験比率 （＝quick ratio: 企業の短期的な支払い能力を示す財務指標の一つで，流動負債に対する当座資産（現金・預金，受取勘定，市場性有価証券などの合計額）の割合）

ACLI 全米保険業協会，アメリカ生命保険協会（**American Council of Life Insurance**の略）

ACM アラブ共同市場（**Arab Common Market**の略）

acquire 動 取得する，購入する，引き受ける，買収する （＝buy, purchase; ⇒**controlling stake, veto**）
　　acquired company 被買収会社，被買収企業 （＝acquiree company, acquired firm）
　　after-acquired property 事後取得財産
　　recently acquired business 最近買収した事業，最近取得した事業
　　year acquired 取得年度，買収年度，購入年度
▸Sumitomo Heavy Industries Ltd. offered to *acquire* Axcelis Technologies of U.S. for $544 million. 住友重機械工業が，米国のアクセリス・テクノロジー社を5億4,400万ドルで買収する提案を行った。
▸We *acquired* shares in the company. 当社は，同社の株式を取得しました。

acquirer 名 買収会社，買収企業，買収者，取得者，購入者，買取り手 （⇒**antitakeover method, control**）
▸A foreign *acquirer* of a Japanese company is allowed to pay shareholders of the Japanese entity "merger consideration" in the form of cash and the parent company's shares. 日本企業を買収する外国企業は現在，「合併の対価」を，現金や親会社の株式の形で日本企業の株主に支払うことができる。

acquisition 名 取得，購入，買取り，買付け，買収，企業取得，企業買収，事業買収
　　acquisition and development アクイジッション・アンド・ディベロプメント《略 **A&D**》（買収により新技術や商圏を取り込み，成長戦略の武器にすること）
　　acquisition cost 取得原価，買収コスト，新契約費
　　acquisition of businesses 事業の買収
　　acquisition of fixed assets 固定資産購入，固定資産の取得
　　acquisition offer 買収の申込み，買収提案
　　acquisition price 取得価格，買付け価格，取得原価，買取価格
　　acquisition strategy 買収戦略
　　corporate acquisition 企業買収，企業取得 （＝acquisition of business, business acquisition, corporate buyout）
　　discount on acquisition 買入のれん
　　friendly acquisition 友好的買収
　　hostile acquisition 敵対的買収
　　major acquisition 大型買収
　　neutral acquisition 中立的買収
　　share-swap acquisition 株式交換による買収
　　stock acquisition 株式取得，株式購入 （＝share acquisition）
▸We made some important adjustments and *acquisitions* in the area of telecommunications in 2008. 2008年度は，通信事業の分野で，重要な調整と買収をいくつか実施しました。

across-the-board 形 一括の，一律の，全面的，総括的，全業種一律の，全社の
　　across-the-board agreement 全面的合意，全面的同意
　　across-the-board compliance 法令・規則の全社的順守
　　across-the-board cut 一括引下げ （＝across-the-board decrease）
　　across-the-board drop 全面安，一斉下落
　　across-the-board increase 一括引上げ，一律昇給，一律賃上げ
　　across-the-board pay hike 一律賃上げ，一律昇給
　　across-the-board selling 売り一色
　　across-the-board tax cut 一律減税
　　across-the-board testing for BSE infection 狂牛病(BSE)感染の全頭検査
　　across-the-board wage hike 一律値上げ

across the board 全面的に，全般的に，軒並み，一括して，すべてに公平に （⇒**appreciate**）
　　appreciate across the board 全面高となる
　　improve across the board 全面高となる
　　plunge across the board 全面安となる
　　retreat across the board 全面安となる （＝fall across the board）

soar across the board 全面高となる (＝go up across the board)
tumble across the board 全面安となる
widen across the board 全面的に拡大する
▶The yen dropped *across the board*. 円は，全面安になった。
▶Tokyo stocks dropped *across the board*. 東京株［東京株式市場の株価］は，全面安となった。

act 名 行為, 行動, 法律, 条令, 制定法
Act Against Unfair Competition 不正競争防止法
act [Act] of God 天災, 不可抗力, 不測の事態
Banking Act of 1933 1933年銀行法
Community reinvestment Act 地域社会再投資法
Companies Act 会社法
Comprehensive Trade Act 包括通商法
Consumer Credit Protection Act 消費者信用保護法
Depository Institution Act of 1982 1982年預金金融機関法
Equal Employment Opportunity Act 平等雇用機会法
Export Administration Act 米国の輸出管理法
Financial Service Act 金融サービス法
judicial act 法律行為
Model Business Corporation Act 模範事業会社法
Omnibus Trade Act 包括通商法
Section 301 of the Trade Act of 1974 米通商法301条
Securities Exchange Act 証券取引所法
Social Security Act 社会保障法

action 名 行動, 活動, 実行, 動き, 行政上の処分, 措置, 対応, 決議, 決定, 訴え, 訴訟,〈裁判の〉判決, 行為, 作為, アクション (⇒class action suit, legal action)
action holiday 報償休暇
action level 限界水準
action point 行動提案
administrative action 行政処分
affirmative action 積極的優遇措置, 積極的是正措置, 差別修正措置, 差別撤廃措置, 少数民族の優遇措置, アファーマティブ・アクション
antidumping actions 反ダンピング措置
business action 業務行為
class action 集団訴訟, 集団代表訴訟
disciplinary actions 懲戒処分
industrial action 争議行為, 労働争議, ストライキ

line of action 行動方針
price action 値動き
rating action 格付け見直し, 格付け変更
unofficial action 非公認活動, 非公式活動
▶Officials of many leading companies encouraged employees to take *action* and achieve results. 多くの主要企業の経営者は，実行に移して成果を出すよう社員に求めた。
▶We have taken many *actions* in the last five years to streamline our business and reduce the number of employees. 事業の合理化と従業員数削減のため，当社はここ5年間に多くの施策を講じてきました。

action program 行動計画, 実行計画, アクション・プログラム (＝action plan)
▶We have a written *action program* which includes everything posing a threat to the environment: plant, use of products and even their journey to the rubbish tip. 当社の文書化したアクション・プログラムには，生産設備や製品の使用から製品の廃品処理に行き着くまでの過程にいたるまで，環境を脅かすあらゆる要因が盛り込まれています。

active 形 活発な, 活動的な, 活況を呈している, 取引量の多い, 積極的な, 現役の, 現職の, 勤続中の, アクティブ
active job-opening ratio 有効求人倍率
active management 積極的運用, アクティブ運用, 積極的な経営陣
active market 活発な市況, 活況市場, 好況市場, 好況市況, 好況
active stock 人気株, 花形株
▶Companies continue to be *active* in plant and equipment investment. 企業の設備投資が，引き続き活発だ。

activity 名 活動, 動き, 働き, 活動範囲, 活動度, 操業, 事業, 業務, 業務活動, 取引, 活気, 活況, 景気, 好景気 (⇒corporate activities, economic activity)
activity analysis 業務活動分析
activity level 操業度
activity method 生産高比例法 (＝production method)
activity report 業務活動報告
advertising activities 広告宣伝活動
banking activity 銀行業務
business activities 事業活動, 企業活動, 営業活動, 経営活動, 景気, 商況, 業況
core activities 中核事業, 主力事業 (＝core business, main activities)

credit activities 与信業務
financial activity 資金調達活動
financing activities 財務活動, 資金調達活動, 金融活動, 資金調達と返済に関する活動
international activities 国際事業
investing activities 投資活動
lending activities 貸出業務
local citizenship activities 社会貢献活動
main activities 主力事業
off-balance sheet activity オフバランス取引
operating activities 営業活動
pick-up in activity 景気回復
principal areas of activity 中核事業
profit or loss from [on] ordinary activities 経常損益
quality control activity QC運動
regional activity 地域活動
statement of activity 営業報告書, 活動報告書
trading activities 業務展開

▶Miscellaneous other *activities* include the distribution of computer equipment through retail outlets. その他の各種事業には, 小売店によるコンピュータ機器の販売も含まれています。

▶Much of the financing *activity* shown on our statement of cash flows relates to these refinancing activities. 当社のキャッシュ・フロー計算書に示した資金調達活動の大半は, これら負債の借換え関連です。

▶This amount of cash was provided by business *activities*. この現金額は, 営業活動で得られたものだ。

activity based costing 活動基準原価計算, 活動基準原価管理, ABC管理《略 **ABC**》(一つの作業にかかった時間を計測して, かかった時間に応じて人件費などの間接コストを配賦し, 製品の正確な原価を割り出す手法。隠れた不採算製品の洗い出しなどに効果があるとされている)

activity based management 活動基準管理《略 **ABM**》(活動基準原価計算(ABC)を利用して業務改革につなげる取組み)

actuarial 形 年金数理計算上の, 年金数理上の, 保険数理上の
　actuarial asset value 保険数理による資産価値
　actuarial cost method 保険数理原価法, 保険数理による原価計算法, 年金数理計算方式
　actuarial gains and [or] losses 保険数理上の損益, 年金数理上の誤差, 数理計算上の差異(年金基金の運用時に生じる見積り額と実際額との差額)
　actuarial liability 保険数理上の債務
　actuarial measurement of pension cost and obligation 年金費用および年金債務額の統計的手法による測定
　actuarial method 年金数理法, 保険数理法
　actuarial valuation 保険数理評価, 保険数理価値

actuarial assumption 年金数理計算上の仮定, 保険数理上の計算基礎, 年金数理計算上の基礎率

▶Pension cost in 2008 was lower than in 2007 principally due to *actuarial assumption* changes in the U.S. and several non-U.S. plans. 2008年度の年金費用は, 主に米国内制度と一部の米国外制度の年金数理上の仮定の変更により, 前年度より減少しました。

actuarial present value 年金数理上の現在価値, 保険数理上の現在価値

▶The *actuarial present value* of the accrued plan benefits and the net assets available to discharge these benefits at December 31 are as follows: 12月31日現在の年金給付債務額の年金数理現価と年金給付債務に充当可能な年金純資産は, 以下のとおりです。

actuarially computed value 保険数理上の計算価値

actuary 名 保険数理士, 保険計理士, 保険数理専門家, 年金数理人, アクチュアリー

▶An *actuary* applies the theory of probability to the business of insurance and is responsible for the calculation of premiums, policy reserves and other values. 保険数理士は, 保険業に確率論を適用して, 保険料, 保険契約準備金やその他の価値を計算するのが仕事だ。

A/D [a/d] 振出日後 (after dateの略)

added value 付加価値, 付加価値額 (=value added)
　added value per employee 従業員1人当たりの付加価値額 (⇒manpower)
　added value statement 付加価値計算書
　added value tax 付加価値税

▶Our affiliate program offers your Web site the opportunity to generate profit while providing *added value* to your customers. 当社のアフィリエイト・プログラムは, あなたの顧客に付加価値を提供しながら利益を生み出す機会を, あなたのウェブ・サイトに提供します。

addition 名 追加, 追加投資, 付加, 加算, 増築, 増設, 増加, 拡張 (⇒reliability)
　addition to reserves 積立金繰入れ
　additions and betterments [improvements] reserves 増改築積立金, 増設改良積立金
　additions to long-term debt 長期債務の増加

capital additions 追加資本, 追加投資, 追加設備投資

plant additions 工場の増設

▶We had lower depreciation expense because we reduced plant *additions*. 工場の増設を手控えたため、減価償却費は低下しました。

additional 形 追加的な, 付加的な, 特別の
　additional allowance 割増手当
　additional charge 追加料金, 追加費用, 割増料金
　additional equity capital 増資 (＝additional equity)
　additional expense 追加費用
　additional fund 追加資金
　additional paid-in capital 株式払込み剰余金, 払込み資本剰余金, 資本剰余金, 払込み剰余金, 付加的払込み資本, 追加払込み資本 (＝capital surplus)
　additional shares 追加株式, 増資株, 増資, 株式数の増加
　additional tax 追徴税, 加算税, 増税
　additional working capital 追加的運転資金

additional capital 増加資本

▶As in the past, the Corporation and its subsidiaries raised *additional capital* during this year's first half. 従来どおり、当社と子会社は当上半期も追加資本を調達しました。

additional investment 追加投資

▶The principal requirement for funds is for capital expenditures and to acquire new and *additional investments*. 資金需要は、主に資本的支出と新規および追加投資を行うにあたって発生します。

add-on equipment 追加機器, 付属設備, アタッチメント

add-on rate アドオン金利(当初元本に基づいて利息を計算)

adequacy 名 充実, 充実度, 妥当性, 適切性, 適正, 適応性
　adequacy of disclosure 開示の適切性
　BIS capital adequacy standards BIS (国際決済銀行)の自己資本比率基準
　capital adequacy 資本充実度, 自己資本の充実, 資本要件, 自己資本比率
　loan loss reserve adequacy 貸倒れ準備金の適切性

adjust 動 修正する, 調整する, 調節する, 補正する, 織り込む
　adjust to the rise in inflation インフレ率上昇率を織り込む
　adjusted current earnings 調整後当期利益《略 ACE》
　adjusted earnings per share 調整後1株当たり利益
　adjusted for inflation and taxes インフレと税金修正後の
　be adjusted downward 下方修正される
　in seasonally adjusted dollar terms 季節調整済みのドル表示額で
　in seasonally adjusted GDP 季節調整済みGDPの
　not seasonally adjusted 季節調整前の
　risk-adjusted yield [returns] リスク調整後の利回り
　seasonally adjusted annual rate 季節調整済み年率
　the value of assets adjusted to market 時価に修正した資産価額

▶We recognized a $80 million benefit from *adjusting* our deferred tax assets for the new tax rate. 新税率を適用して当社の繰延べ税金資産を調整した結果、8,000万ドルの利益を認識しました。

adjustable peg 調整可能な固定為替相場制度, アジャスタブル・ペッグ

adjustable rate convertible note 変動利付き転換社債《略 ARCN》

adjustable rate mortgage 変動金利型抵当貸付け《略 ARM》

adjustment 名 調整, 修正, 照合, 整理, 査定, 精算, 期末整理, 決算整理 (⇒upward)
　adjustment bond 整理社債
　adjustment for fractional differences 四捨五入による調整
　adjustment for taxable income 税務調整, 申告調整
　adjustment inflation 調整インフレ
　adjustment of complaint 苦情処理
　adjustment of financial statements of prior periods 過年度の財務諸表修正
　backlog adjustment 遡及修正 (＝catch-up adjustment)
　capital adjustment 資本修正
　closing adjustment 決算整理, 決算整理事項 (＝close adjustment)
　currency translation adjustment 外貨換算調整勘定
　downward adjustment 下方修正, 減額修正, 下方調整
　exchange rate adjustment 為替レートの調整
　experience adjustment 実績による修正

administer | 013 | advance

　inventory adjustment　在庫調整
　prior period adjustment　過年度修正, 過年度損益修正, 前期損益修正
　production adjustment　生産調整
　seasonal adjustment　季節調整
▸We make all the *adjustments* needed to catch up with these new accounting methods.　これらの新会計処理方法に対応するにあたって, 必要な修正はすべて行っています。

administer　動　管理する, 処理する, 手当てする, 執行する, 運用する

administration　名　経営, 経営管理, 管理, 運営, 事務, 事務管理, 業務, 執行, 政権, 政府, 行政
　administration cost　一般管理費　(＝administration expense, administration overhead)
　administration of shares　株式事務　(⇒consign)
　administration process　社内手続き, 事務手続き
　board of administration　理事会
　business administration　企業経営, 商工経営, 経営管理, 経営学　(＝business management)
　capital and administration　資本と経営
　department administration　部門管理
　financial administration　財務管理, 財政
　general administration cost　一般管理費
　human resources and administration department　人事・総務部
　personnel administration　人事管理
▸We continued to consolidate support activities for manufacturing, development and *administration*.　当社は, 引き続き製造, 開発と事務部門に対する支援活動を統合しました。

administrative　形　経営管理上の, 経営上の, 運営上の, 管理上の, 管理的, 行政の
　administrative ability　経営能力, 経営手腕, 管理能力, 行政手腕
　administrative and maintenance expenses　維持管理費, 維持管理費用
　administrative and selling expenses　一般管理費および販売費
　administrative control　管理統制, 業務統制, 運営管理コントロール, 行政管理
　administrative cycles　管理サイクル
　administrative expenses　一般管理費, 管理費, 経費　(＝administration costs, administration overhead, administrative and general expense)
　administrative guidance　行政指導
　administrative policy　業務方針
　administrative process　運用過程
　administrative services　行政サービス

▸Operating profit, or sales minus the cost of goods sold and *administrative* expenses, rose 1.4 percent to ¥161 billion from ¥159 billion a year ago.　売上高から販売した製品の製造原価［売上原価］と一般管理費を差し引いた収益を示す営業利益は, 前期の1,590億円に対して1.4%増の1,610億円でした。

admission　名　入場, 入会, 入学, 入学許可, 入場料, 承認, 許容

adopt　動　採用する, 採択する, 可決する, 〈計画などを〉実施する, 選出する, 指名する
▸We *adopt* SFAS No.106, "Employers' Accounting for Postretirement Benefits Other Than Pensions."　当社では, 財務会計基準書(SFAS)第106号「年金以外の退職後給付に関する事業主の会計処理」を採用しています。

adoption　名　採用, 採択, 管理引受け, 公認

ADR　米国預託証券　(American Depository Receipt の略)

ADSL　非対称デジタル加入者回線, 非対称デジタル加入者線　(＝asymmetric digital subscriber line: asymmetrical digital subscriber lineの略)
　ADSL connection provider　ADSL接続業者
　ADSL service provider　ADSLサービス・プロバイダー
▸The company entered the telecommunications business in 2001 and currently offers *ADSL* and a low-cost fixed line phone service.　同社は2001年に通信事業に参入して, 現在はADSL(非対称デジタル加入者回線)と格安の固定電話サービスを提供している。

ad valorem　従価方式の, 従価方式で, 価格に準じた
　ad valorem duties [taxes]　従価税
　ad valorem freight [rate]　従価運賃
　ad valorem goods　従価課税品
　ad valorem property tax　不動産従価税
　ad valorem tariff　従価関税

advance　動　進歩する, 発展する, 前進する, 進出する, 増加する, 上昇する, 向上する, 値上がりする, 進める, 促進する, 〈提出する予定を〉繰り上げる, 前渡しする, 前払いする, 提供する
　advance funds　資金を提供する
　advance strongly　力強く伸びる, 力強く値上がりする, 大幅に伸びる, 大幅な伸びを示す, 力強い伸びを示す
▸The firm's consolidated sales *advanced* 13.4 percent to ¥21.04 trillion.　同社の連結売上高は, 前期比13.4%増の21兆400億円となった。

advance　名　進歩, 発展, 進展, 革新, 前進, 進出,

advanced ... advantage

増加, 上昇, 騰貴, 向上, 値上がり, 前払い, 前渡し, 前貸し, 融資, 借入れ, 前払い金, 前渡し金, 前貸金, 前受金, 前金, 仮払い金, 借入金

advance copy 予定原稿, 新刊見本, アドバンス・コピー

advance corporation tax 前払い法人税, 予納法人税《略 ACT》

advance-decline line 騰落株線 （＝A-D line）

advance from customers 顧客からの前受金

advance in profits 増益

advance in productivity 生産性の伸び, 生産性の向上

advance notice 事前通告

advance of funds 資金の提供

advance payment 前払い, 前渡し補償金

advance premium 前払い保険料

advance refunding 〈社債の〉満期日前償還［期中償還］,〈借換え債務の〉事前負担, 期前借換え

advance sales 予約販売, 前売り

advances from customers 顧客からの前受金, 顧客前受金, 得意先前受金

advances payable 借入金, 前受金

advances receivable 貸付け金, 前渡し金

bank advance 銀行貸出

cash advance 頭金

economic advance 経済進展

export advance system 輸出前貸し制度

generate a strong advance 業績を大幅に伸ばす

make a liquidity advance 資金を提供する, 流動性を供与する

royalty advance 著作権, 特許権などの前払い使用料

strong advance 力強い伸び, 大幅な伸び

technical advances 技術革新, 技術の進歩 （＝advances in technology）

technological advance 技術革新

▸Another strong *advance* will be seen. 今後は, もう一段の力強い伸び［もう一段の上げ相場］が期待されます。

▸Deferred tax assets are essentially taxes paid in *advance* that are expected to be refunded when the bank incurs losses, for instance by writing off bad loans resulting from the bankruptcy of corporate borrowers. 繰延べ税金資産は本質的に前払いした税金で, 例えば融資先企業の倒産などで不良債権を処理して, 銀行が損失を被った時点で戻ってくる。

advanced 形 進んだ, 進歩［発達］した, 先端の, 最先端の, 最新の, 最新鋭の, 高度な, 高等の, 上級レベルの, 前渡しの, 期限前の, 繰上げの

advanced degree 博士号

Advanced Communications Technology Satellite 実験通信衛星《略 ACTS》

advanced composite material 先端複合材料, 先進複合材料《略 ACM》

advanced country 先進国

advanced developing nation 先進開発上国

advanced economy 先進経済

advanced information communications society 高度情報通信社会

advanced information society 高度情報化会, 高度情報社会《略 AIS》

advanced materials 新素材

advanced payments 前払い金

advanced piloting system 先進的操縦システム

advanced processed goods 高度加工品

advanced processing 二次加工, 川下部門

advanced redemption 繰上げ償還 （＝early redemption）

advanced technology 最新技術, 先進技術, 先端技術, 高度技術, 高度な技術, 技術革新, ハイテク （＝high technology, sophisticated technology, state-of-the-art technology）

advanced technology industry 先端技術産業, 先進技術産業

advanced television 高品位テレビ

advanced thermal reactor 新型転換炉《略 ATR》

advanced traffic information system 高度交通情報システム

advanced turbo-prop 先進ターボプロップ《略 ATP》

products of advanced technology 先端技術製品, ハイテク製品

▸NTT Docomo Inc. will remove *advanced* functions and services from its cell phones' operating software (OS). NTTドコモは, 同社の携帯電話の基本ソフト (OS) から高度な機能とサービスを切り離す方針だ。

advantage 名 有利, 利点, 強み, メリット, 利益, 優勢, 優位, 優位性, 競争力, 優遇措置 （⇒ **competitive advantage**）

absolute advantage 絶対優位, 絶対的優位性

comparative advantage 比較優位, 比較優位性 （＝relative advantage）

cost advantage コスト面での競争力

gross advantage 総利益

net advantage 正味利益

tax advantages 税制上の優遇措置, 節税効果

▶An urgent task facing each financial group is to improve its financial conditions and profitability on the strength of *advantages* gained from merger.　合併・統合で得られる相乗効果を生かして，財務内容と収益力を向上させることが，各金融グループの現在の急務だ．

▶We hope to retain our *advantages* by slowing down the technology drain.　当社としては，技術流出を遅らせて当社の優位性を保ちたい．

adverse effect 逆効果, 不利な影響, 悪影響, マイナス影響, 悪材料

▶To the best knowledge of the Corporation, no litigation, proceeding or controversy which would have a materially *adverse effect* on the Corporation has been threatened against the Corporation.　当社の知るかぎり，当社に重大な悪影響を及ぼすような訴訟，訴訟行為または紛争は，これまでのところ当社に対しては起こりそうにない．

adverse wind 逆風, 向かい風

▶*Adverse winds* have begun blowing for the Japanese economy lately, such as uncertainty over the prospects for both the U.S. and Chinese economies and soaring crude oil prices.　米中両国経済の先行き不透明や原油価格の高騰など，このところ日本経済に逆風が吹き始めた．

advertise 動 広告する, 宣伝する

advertisement 名 広告, 広告宣伝 （＝ad, advertising)
　advertisement exposure 広告の露出, 広告露出（＝advertising exposure)
　banner advertisement バナー広告
　e-mail advertisement メール広告
　image advertisement 印象広告, イメージ広告
　Internet advertisement ネット広告, インターネット広告
　keyword search advertisement キーワード・サーチ広告
　mobile phone advertisement 携帯広告, 携帯電話広告
　online advertisement オンライン広告
　point-of-purchase advertisement 小売店頭広告, 購買時点広告, POP広告
　pop-up advertisement ポップアップ広告
　sponsorship advertisement スポンサーシップ広告
　tombstone advertisement 墓石広告, 墓碑広告（証券の発行広告)
　video advertisement ビデオ広告
　Web advertisement ウェブ広告

▶The *advertisements* of the three companies were deemed to be less malicious.　この3社の広告は，悪質性がやや低いと判断された．

▶The Net *advertisement* business is expected to grow rapidly in Japan as well.　ネット広告事業は，日本でも急成長が見込める．

advertiser 名 広告主

advertising 名 広告, 広告宣伝, 広告宣伝費 （＝ad, advertisement; ⇒ **Web advertising business**)
　advertising agency 広告代理店
　advertising allowance 広告援助金
　advertising and promotion costs 広告宣伝費
　advertising balloon アドバルーン
　advertising budget 広告予算
　advertising campaign 広告キャンペーン, 広告・宣伝活動 （＝advertising drive)
　advertising e-mail 広告メール
　advertising expense 広告宣伝費
　advertising jingle 宣伝文句, 宣伝のかけ声
　advertising materials 広告材料, 広告資料, 宣伝資料, 宣伝広告資料, 広告宣伝用品
　advertising media 広告媒体
　advertising on the Internet インターネット広告
　advertising revenue 広告収入
　advocacy advertising 主張広告, 擁護広告, 意見広告, アドボカシ広告
　B2B advertising ビー・ツー・ビー広告 （＝B to B advertising: 広告主も広告の受け手も企業である広告活動)
　business advertising 企業広告, ビジネス広告
　classified advertising 案内広告, 求人・求職広告
　comparative advertising 比較広告
　corporate advertising 企業広告, 会社の広告
　direct mail advertising ダイレクトメール広告, DM広告
　drip advertising ドリップ式広告（長期間にわたって繰り返し流す広告)
　editorial advertising 記事広告, 意見広告
　floor advertising フロア広告
　full page advertising 全面広告
　Internet advertising インターネット広告, ネット広告
　issue advertising 意見広告 （＝advocacy advertising, opinion advertising)
　mass media advertising マス・メディア広告
　new product advertising 新製品広告
　opinion advertising 意見広告 （＝protest advertising)

response advertising レスポンス広告
retail advertising 小売広告
sales promotion advertising SP広告
sizzle advertising シズル広告
subliminal advertising サブリミナル広告
teaser advertising ティーザー広告
tie-up advertising タイアップ広告
trade advertising 流通広告
virtual advertising バーチャル広告
▶The firm depends entirely on *advertising* revenue. 同社は, 完全に広告収入に依存している.

advice 名 忠告, 助言, 報告, 通知, 案内
advice note 発送通知書, 小包送り状

adviser [advisor] 名 顧問, 顧問業務, 顧問業, 顧問会社, 諮問, 相談役, 助言者, 米大統領補佐官, アドバイザー
adviser system 顧問制度, 顧問制(退任役員を全員, 自動的に顧問とする制度で, 顧問は現役役員の指導や社外活動にあたる)
Council of Economic Advisers 経済諮問委員会
financial adviser 財務顧問, 資金調達のアドバイザー, フィナンシャル・アドバイザー
investment adviser 投資顧問, 投資顧問業, 投資顧問会社
security adviser 証券顧問業者
special adviser 特別顧問
supreme adviser 最高顧問

advisory 形 諮問の, 顧問の, 投資顧問の, 助言の, 勧告の
advisory board 諮問委員会, 諮問機関, アドバイザリー・ボード
advisory council 理事会, 参事会, 諮問委員会, 諮問評議会
advisory director 相談役, 顧問重役
advisory income 投資顧問収益
advisory service 顧問業務, 投資顧問業, 助言サービス, アドバイザリー業務 (=advisory business)
advisory specialist for consumer's affairs 消費生活アドバイザー《略 ASCA》
financial advisory service 財務顧問サービス
investment advisory service 投資顧問業務, 投資顧問サービス
▶An *advisory* report by Sumitomo Mitsui Banking Corp. said "both tie-up plans are almost the same." 三井住友銀行の意見書は, 「両社の提携案は優劣つけがたい」としていた.
▶The *advisory* board composed of external experts convenes regularly and reports to the executive committee. 社外の有識者を委員とす

るアドバイザリー・ボード(諮問委員会)は, 委員会を定期的に開催して, 経営委員会に報告書を提出しています[社外の有識者を委員とするアドバイザリー・ボードは, 経営委員会の諮問機関として, 委員会を定期的に開催しています].

AE 〈広告会社の〉営業責任者,〈証券会社の〉セールスマン (**account executive**の略)

affair 名 仕事, 業務, 事務, 事業, 事態, 情勢, 状況, 事柄, 問題, 事件, 出来事, 事項, 関心事, 関係 (⇒**blank bill, ethical standard**)
affairs entrusted 委任事項
affairs of state 国事, 政務
as affairs stand 現状では
business affairs 仕事, 業務, 企業事象
community affairs 社会事業
financial affairs 財務内容, 財務状態, 財務状況 (=financial position)
get one's affairs straight 財務を整理する
international affairs 国際問題, 国際関係, 対外関係, 国際情勢
on business affairs 商用で, 所用で (=on business)
public affairs 公務, 公報
state of affairs 事態, 形勢, 財政状態
statement of affairs 状況報告書
wind up one's affairs 店じまいをする
world affairs 国際問題, 国際社会
▶Companies disclose their financial *affairs* through financial statements. 企業は, 財務諸表[財務書類]で企業の財務内容を開示する.

affect 動 影響を及ぼす, 影響を与える, …に影響する, …を対象とする
affect the stock market 株式相場に影響を与える
most seriously affected countries 最も[特に]深刻な被害国, 最貧国《略 MSAC》
negatively affect マイナス影響を与える, 悪影響を及ぼす
unfavorably affect 不利な影響を与える, マイナス影響を与える, 悪影響を及ぼす
▶This accounting change does not *affect* cash flows. この会計処理の変更は, キャッシュ・フローには影響しません.

affiliate 動 提携する, 合併する, 傘下入りする, 加入する, 加盟する, 友好関係を結ぶ, 提携させる, 合併させる, 系列[傘下]に置く, 加入させる
affiliated advertising agency 専属広告代理店
affiliated agency 提携代理店
affiliated card 提携カード, 共用カード
affiliated company 関連会社, 関係会社, 系列会

affiliate

社, 系列企業, 傘下企業 （＝affiliate firm, associated company）
- **affiliated loan** 提携ローン
- **affiliated nonbank** 系列ノンバンク
- **affiliated person** 利害関係者
- **affiliated supermarket** 系列スーパー
- **affiliated transaction** グループ内取引
- **bank-affiliated securities subsidiary** 銀行系証券子会社
- **foreign-affiliated company** 外資系企業
- **government-affiliated financial institution** 政府系金融機関

▸Both companies are *affiliated* with Mizuho Financial Group. 両社は, みずほフィナンシャルグループの系列会社だ。

affiliate 图 関係会社, 関連会社, 系列会社, 子会社, 関係者, 提携者, 加入者, 参加者, アフィリエイト （＝affiliate firm, affiliated company, associate; ⇒**added value, consolidated affiliate**）

関係会社とは➡20％以上, 50％以下の議決権株式を所有され, 持ち分法を適用される会社のことを関係会社という。これに対して, 50％超の議決権株式を所有されている会社が子会社で, 米国の会計実務では親会社が連結財務諸表（連結財務書類）を作成する際に原則として連結の範囲に含められる。

▸*Affiliates* can earn a 10% commission on every item sold through their websites. アフィリエイトのウェブサイトを通じて販売した商品については, アフィリエイトはすべて10％のコミッションを受け取ることができます。

▸Due to the brand's popularity, the number of shops of the company's *affiliate* in Japan has grown to about 70 as of the end of 2008. ブランドの人気で, 同社の日本子会社の店舗数は, 2008年末現在で約70店にまで拡大した。

AFL-CIO 米国［アメリカ］労働総同盟産業別組合会議 （American Federation of Labor and Congress of Industrial Organizationsの略）

afloat 形 流通する, 浮動する, 副 流通して, 浮動して

aforesaid 形 前述の, 上記の

AFTA アセアン自由貿易圏, アセアン自由貿易地域（Association of South-East Asian Nations Free Trade Areaの略）

after 前 …差引き後, …控除後, …を控除した［差し引いた］うえで, 事後の, 事後的, …後, …以後, 以降
- **after bill date** 手形振出日後
- **after cost** 事後費用, 事後経費, アフター・コスト（売上収益計上後に発生する費用）
- **after date** 振出日後
- **after dividends on preferred shares** 優先株式配当額を控除したうえで （⇒**dividends on preferred shares**）
- **after effect of advertising** 広告の事後的効果
- **after sight** 一覧後
- **after sight bill** 一覧後定期払い手形
- **after the fact control** 事後管理
- **three days after sight** 一覧後3日払い（提示の日を含まないで, 次の日から数えて3日）
- **within 30 days after the date of the invoice** 請求書の日付けの翌日から起算して30日以内に, 請求書の日付け後30日以内に

▸The provisions, *after* giving effect to taxes and minority interest, reduced 2008 earnings by $200 million. これらの引当金繰入れで, 関連税額と少数株主持ち分利益控除後の2008年度の純利益は, 2億ドル減少しました。

after-hours 形 定時を過ぎた, 時間外の
- **after-hours trading** 時間外取引 （⇒**off-hours trading**）

after-sales service 購買後サービス, 販売後サービス, アフター・サービス （＝afterservice）

▸We will do our best to continue offering *after-sales services*, even after halting the sales of Opel models. オペル車の販売中止後も, 引き続きアフター・サービスに万全を尽くす方針だ。

after tax 税引き後で, 手取りで

▸*After taxes*, this charge was $1,200 million. 税引き後で, この費用は12億ドルでした。

after-tax 形 税引き後の, 手取りの
- **after-tax balance** 税引き後利益
- **after-tax earnings** 税引き後利益 （＝earnings after tax）
- **after-tax effect** 税引き後の影響
- **after-tax gain** 税引き後利益, 税引き後の手取り額 （⇒**accounting period**）
- **after-tax income** 税引き後所得, 税引き後利益

after-tax loss 税引き後損失, 税引き後赤字

▸Three leading shipbuilding and machinery companies recorded *after-tax losses* because they failed to absorb increases in the value of the yen against the dollar and rising prices of steel products. 造船・重機大手3社は, 円高と鋼材価格の上昇分を吸収できなかったため, 税引き後で赤字となった。

after-tax margin 税引き後利益率

▸Worldwide net earnings for the nine months were $3 billion in 2008, with *after-tax margins* of 7.5 percent. 2008年度1～9月期の世界全体で

の純利益は30億ドルで，税引き後利益率は7.5%でした。

after-tax profit 税引き後利益，税引き後黒字（「税引き後利益」は，決算書上では一般に「当期純利益」と表記され，企業の収益から諸費用や税金を差し引いて残った最終的な利益のこと）
▶The state-funded Japan Post Holdings' *after-tax profits* are expected to be ¥508 billion in fiscal 2008. 政府出資の持ち株会社，日本郵政グループの2008年度の税引き後利益は，5,080億円が見込まれている。

aftercare 名 事後処理，販売後の保証・修理，アフター・サービス，病後保護

aftermarket 名 〈有価証券の〉流通市場（= secondary market），販売後市場，補修部品市場，関連ハードウエア／ソフトウエア／周辺装置の市場，アフター・マーケット（= after market, aftermath market: 新規発行株式が取引される発行市場に対して，「流通市場」は証券取引所や店頭市場など，いったん発行された株式が二次的に売買される市場をいう）

AG ドイツの株式会社（Aktiengesellschaftの略）
AG以外のドイツの4企業形態

Gesellschaft mit beschränkter Haftung	有限会社, GmbH
GmbH & Co. KG	合資会社の特殊形態
Kommanditgesellschaft	合資会社, KG
Offene Handelsgesellschaft	合名会社, OHG

age of globalization グローバル時代
age of people decline 人口減少社会
▶Japan is entering the *age of people decline*. 日本は，人口減少社会に突入している。

aged society 高齢社会，長寿社会
agency 名 代理，代理権，代理行為，代理業，代理店，代理関係，行政機関，行動，行為，作用，働き，仲介，世話
　advertising agency 広告代理店，広告代理業
　agency agreement 代理店契約，代理契約
　agency commission 代理店手数料
　agency of record 指定代理店
　agency relationship 代理関係
　exclusive selling agency 一手販売代理店
　general agency 総代理店
　granting agency 認可機関
　hold agency for …の代理をする，…の代理店をする
　human agency 人間の行為
　maker's export agency 輸出代理店
　news agency 通信社
　online ad agency オンライン広告代理店，ネット広告代理店，オンライン広告代理業
　paying and conversion agency agreement 支払い・転換代理契約
　principal paying agency agreement 主支払い代理人契約
　secure agency 代理権を獲得する
　sole selling agency 一手販売代理店
　special advertising agency 特殊広告代理店
　undertake exclusive agency for …の代理業を一手に引き受ける
▶Distributor shall not be given any *agency*, express or implied, by Company for any purpose whatsoever. 販売店［代理店］に対して，会社は明示・黙示を問わずどんな目的であれいかなる代理権も付与しないものとする。

agenda 名 議題，課題，協議事項，予定，予定表，予定案，政策，覚書，備忘録，アジェンダ（⇒**distribution industry**）
　be high on the agenda 重要議題に挙げられる，最重要課題となる，主要議題になる
　fiscal agenda 財政政策
　humanitarian agenda 人道的政策
　item on the agenda 議題
　lending agenda 融資案件
　on the agenda 議事日程に載っている
▶The issue of how to curb crude prices is expected to be high on the *agenda* at the upcoming G-7 talks. 近く予定されているG7の会議では，原油価格の抑制策が主要議題になる見通しだ。

agent 名 代理店，代理機関，代理人，代行業者，仲介業者，斡旋業者，担当者，保険外交員，セールスマン，捜査官，工作員，手先，スパイ，主因，動因，要因，作用物質，薬剤，エージェント
　agent bank 幹事銀行，エージェント行（= lead bank, lead manager）
　agent service エージェント・サービス（希望する情報の分野やキーワードを登録すると，電子メールなどで希望する情報が得られるサービス）
　advertising agent 広告代理店，広告代理人
　blood-clotting agents 血液凝固因子
　cleaning agent 洗剤
　clearing agent 通関代理店
　enrolled agent 米国の税理士
　estate agent 不動産仲介業者，不動産斡旋業者
　exclusive import agent 輸入総代理店
　FBI agent FBI（米連邦捜査局）捜査官
　forwarding agent 通運業者
　insurance agent 保険外交員，保険代理店
　intelligent agent 情報の代理店

land agent 不動産会社, 土地ブローカー
listing agent 上場代理人
literary agent 著作者代理人
management agent 運営代理人, 幹事行
personal agent 購買代理店型企業
process agent 送達受領代理人, 送達受取人（＝agent for service of process）
sales agent 保険などの営業職員, 保険外交員
sole agent 総代理店, 一手販売店
shopping agent ショッピング・エージェント
user agent ユーザー・エージェント

▶The Local Autonomy Law authorizes local governments to conduct extraordinary inspections of financial institutions that they have designated as *agents*. 　地方自治体法で, 地方自治体は, 代理機関に指定した金融機関に対して特別検査を行う権限が与えられている。

▶To boost business performance, the company's sales *agents* obtained contracts by telling would-be policyholders that they did not need to detail health conditions. 　業績を伸ばすため, 同社の保険外交員は, 保険契約希望者に「健康状態の詳細の告知は必要ない」といって契約を獲得していた。

aggregate 動 総計…になる （⇒**cancelation**）
aggregate 名 総計, 総額, 合計, 総体, 集合体, 集団
　broad liquidity aggregate 広義流動性
　industry aggregates 業界平均
　money aggregates マネー・サプライ, マネー・サプライ伸び率
aggregate 形 総計の, 合計の, 総体の, マクロの, 集計的
　aggregate demand 総需要
　aggregate guarantee 総合保証
　aggregate income 総所得
　aggregate limits 総額規制
　aggregate supply 総供給
　aggregate wage measures マクロの賃金指標
aggregate market value 時価総額 （＝aggregate market price, market valuation, total market value; ⇒**represent**）

▶An *aggregate market value* represents a corporate value in terms of stock price. 　時価総額は, 株価による企業価値を示す。

aging 名 高齢化, 加齢, 老化, 老朽, 老朽化, 熟成, 年齢調べ, 年数調べ, 経過期間, エイジング
　accounts-receivable aging 売掛金の年齢調べ, 未収金の経過期間 （＝aging of accounts receivable）
　aging of receivables 債権の経過期間

aging of society 高齢化, 高齢化社会 （＝a graying of the population, an aging society, an aging population, the graying of society）
aging society and declining birthrate 少子高齢化
rapid aging of the population 急速な高齢化

▶The *aging* of small business owners may prove to be a turn of events in the Japanese economy. 　中小企業事業主の高齢化は, 日本経済の一つの転機になる可能性がある。

aging population 高齢化 （＝a graying of the population, the graying of society）

▶Due to the rapidly *aging population* and the diminishing number of children, the stability of Japan's entire social security system is in danger. 　少子高齢化の急激な進展のため, 日本の社会保障制度全体の安定性が崩れかかっている。

aging society 高齢化, 高齢化社会 （＝a graying of the population, an aging population, the graying of society）

▶The key to economic growth for an *aging society* with a declining birthrate lies in how to put the abilities of women and elderly people into full play. 　少子高齢化社会での経済成長のカギは, 女性と高齢者の能力活用の仕方にある。

agio 名 打歩（うちぶ）, アジオ
AGM 年次株主総会, 定例株主総会, 定時株主総会, 年次社員総会 （＝shareholder AGM: **annual general meeting**の略）
agreement 名 契約, 契約書, 合意, 合意書, 合意事項, 同意, 同意書, 協定, 協約, 取決め （⇒**basic agreement, commitment, swap agreement**）
　affiliate agreement アフィリエイト契約 （⇒**affiliate**）
　agreement among underwriters 引受団契約
　agreement on recruitment 就職協定
　basic agreement 基本的合意, 基本合意, 大筋合意, 基本合意書, 基本契約, 基本契約書
　broad agreement 大筋合意 （⇒**agricultural negotiations**）
　by mutual agreement 相互の同意により, 合意の上で
　credit agreement 借入契約 （＝financing agreement）
　currency swap agreement 通貨スワップ契約
　customer agreement 顧客合意書
　debt agreement 借入契約 （＝financing agreement）
　draft agreement 契約案文
　interest rate swap agreement 金利スワップ

契約
loan agreement 借入契約, 融資契約, 貸付け契約
make and enter into an agreement 契約を締結する, 契約書を作成する
master agreement 標準契約, 基本契約, 基準協定, マスター契約
memorandum of general agreement 一般取引条件協約書
original agreement 原契約
prior agreement 事前の合意
reach an agreement 合意に達する, 合意する
revolving loan agreement 回転融資契約
sign an agreement 契約を締結する, 契約書[合意書]に署名する, 基本合意する
software license agreement ソフトウエア使用許諾契約
terms of service agreement 利用規約
underwriting agreement 引受契約
written agreement 書面による合意, 合意書, 契約書
▶GM reached a tentative contract *agreement* with the United Auto Workers. GMは，全米自動車労組(UAW)と暫定協定で合意した。

agribusiness 名 農業関連産業, アグリビジネス
agricultural 形 農業の, 農産物の
Agricultural Adjustment Act 米国の農業調整法, 農事調整法
agricultural chemicals 農薬, 基礎化学品
agricultural commodity 農業製品, 農産物
Agricultural Credits Act 米国の農業信用法
agricultural disarmament 保護主義的農業政策の撤廃
agricultural import 農産物輸入
agricultural location 農業立地
agricultural output 農業生産高
agricultural resources 農業資源
agricultural sector 農業分野
agricultural system 農法

agricultural negotiations 農業交渉 (= farm talks)
▶The *agricultural negotiations* at the World Trade Organization aim at reaching a broad agreement by the end of the month. 世界貿易機関(WTO)の農業交渉は，今月末の大枠合意を目指している。

agricultural product 農産品, 農産物, 農業製品
▶The government has so far protected domestic farmers by levying steep tariffs on imported *agricultural products* while distributing subsidies to those growing rice, wheat and other *agricultural products*. 政府はこれまで，輸入農産品に高い関税をかける一方，米や麦などの農産品の栽培者に補助金を配って，国内農家を保護してきた。

agriculture 名 農業, 農法
agriculture and forestry 農林業
estate agriculture 農園農業
intensive agriculture 集約農業
multiple agriculture 多角的農業
organic agriculture 有機農法
paddy agriculture 水田農業
plantation agriculture 水田農業
subsistence agriculture 零細農業 (= minute agriculture)
tray agriculture 水耕法
agri-power 名 農業大国
agronomics 名 農業経営, 農業経済学
agrotechnology 名 農業技術
agrotype 名 栽培品種
AID 米国国際開発局 (Agency for International Developmentの略)
ailing 形 経営不振の, 〈業績が〉悪化している, 〈経営が〉行き詰まった, 不調の, 不況の, 病める
ailing business 経営難の事業, 経営不振の企業
ailing company 経営不振の会社
ailing economy 病める経済, 不況の経済
▶When *ailing* businesses are revamped, those who invested in them benefit. 経営不振企業を再建すると，出資者が利益を得られる。

AIM 代替投資市場 (Alternative Investment Marketの略。ロンドン証券取引所のベンチャー株式市場。1995年6月創設)
AIPPI 国際工業所有権保護協会 (Association Internationale pour la Protection de la Propriété Industrielleの略)
air 名 空気, 大気, 放送, エア
air cargo 航空貨物, 航空荷物, 空輸貨物
air carrier 航空会社 (airline), 航空運送業者
air cleaner 空気清浄器, エア・クリーナー
air conditioner 冷房装置 空気調節装置, エアコン
air conditioning 冷房, 空気調節, エアコン
air contaminant 大気汚染物質
air contamination 大気汚染 (= air pollution)
air disaster 航空機事故
air duct 通風管, 送風管
air pocket 株式急落, 急落銘柄
air pollutant 大気汚染物質
air pollution 大気汚染

airbag ／ **allocate**

021

Air Pollution Control Law　大気汚染防止法, 大気汚染規制法
air quality　大気性状, 大気の質
air right　空中権
air time　放送開始時刻
air-to-ground telephone services　航空機用対地電話サービス
air transport industry　航空運送業
air waves　放送電波
▶The Company provides cellular telecommunications, private and shared mobile radio voice and data communications, and *air-to-ground telephone services*.　当社は, 自動車電話(セルラー通信機器), 私設・共用音声／データ移動無線通信システムと航空機用の空対地電話サービスを提供しています。

airbag [**air bag**] 名　空気袋, エアバッグ(車の安全装置)
▶The device will automatically send details of the car's location and license plate number if its *airbag* is activated.　この装置は, 車のエアバッグが作動すると, 車の現在位置や車体番号などの詳しい情報を自動的に発信する。

air-cooling effects　冷却効果
▶In New York and Paris, spacious parks and rivers generate *air-cooling effects*.　ニューヨークやパリでは, 広々とした公園や川が冷却効果を生んでいる。

aircraft 名　航空機
　aircraft financing　航空機融資, 航空機ファイナンス
　aircraft industry　航空機産業
　aircraft leasing　航空機リース
　commercial aircraft　民間航空機
　general aviation aircraft　小型機

airline [**air line**] 名　航空路線, 航路, 定期航空路, 航空会社
　airline credit card　エアライン・カード
　airline industry　航空業界
　commuter airline　短距離定期便会社
▶Delta and Northwest *airlines* may announce a merger as early as next week.　デルタとノースウエストの米航空2社は, 来週にも合併を発表する見通しだ。

airliner 名　定期旅客機

algorithm trading　アルゴリズム取引 (コンピュータのアルゴリズム(問題解決のための処理手順)を株式売買の執行に応用したもので, あらかじめ組み込まれたプログラムに基づき, 株の値動きに応じてコンピュータが自動的に大量の売買注文を実行する)

all-time high　過去最高, 過去最高値, 史上最高値, 上場来の高値, 過去最多, 過去最悪
▶Crude oil prices have exceeded $100 a barrel in London and New York, setting *all-time highs* on these markets.　ニューヨークとロンドン市場で原油価格が1バレル＝100ドルを上回って, 両市場最高値を記録した。

all-time low　過去最安値, 史上最安値, 上場来の安値, 過去最低
▶Stock prices have set new *all-time lows*.　株価は, 史上最安値を更新した。

allegation 名　主張, 陳述, 申立て, 弁明, 申し開き, 容疑
▶Our in-house investigation into the *allegations* is under way.　容疑についての当社の社内調査は現在, 進行中です。

allfinanz 名　総合保険, オールファイナンス, 銀行兼保険業務

alliance 名　提携, 提携関係, 連携, 連合, 統合, 同盟, 同盟関係, 同盟国 (＝tie-up; ⇒business alliance, capital alliance, strategic alliance)
　alliance pact　提携契約
　alliance strategy　提携戦略
　capital and business alliance　資本・業務提携, 資本提携を含む業務提携
　comprehensive alliance　包括的提携, 包括提携 (＝broad alliance)
　equity alliance　資本提携関係
　producer-retailer alliance　製販同盟
　three-way alliance　3社提携
▶*Alliances* between securities houses and banks are likely to gain momentum.　証券界と金融界の連携の動きが, 一層加速しそうだ。
▶The Nissan-Renault *alliance* and GM has called off alliance talks.　日産・仏ルノー連合とGMは, 提携協議を取り止めた。

alliance partner　提携先, 提携相手
▶GM has sold shares in its *alliance partners* including Fuji Heavy Industries Ltd., Isuzu Motors Ltd., and Suzuki Motor Corp. to help balance its books.　GMは, 富士重工業やいすゞ自動車, スズキなど提携先の保有株式を売却して, 財務体質の改善に取り組んでいる。

allocate 動　割り当てる, 配分する, 配賦する, 割り振る (＝allot; ⇒plan participant)
　amounts allocated to income tax liabilities　未払い税金に配分された額
　fully allocated cost　全部配賦原価 (＝fully distributed cost)

allocation — amortization

tax effects allocated to stockholders' equity 資本勘定に配分される税効果額

▶Hokuetsu Paper Mills Ltd. decided to *allocate* 50 million new shares to trading house Mitsubishi for ¥607 per share and form a business tie-up with the trading house. 北越製紙は、三菱商事に1株607円で新株5,000万株を割り当て、三菱商事と業務提携することを決めた。

allocation 名 割当て, 配分, 期間配分, 配賦, 原価配賦, 割振り, 割当 （=allotment）
  allocation of burden 製造間接費の配賦, 間接費の配分
  allocation of capital 資本の投入
  allocation of cost 原価配分, 費用配分, 原価の配賦 （=cost allocation）
  allocation of income taxes 所得税[法人税]の期間配分
  allocation of new shares to a third party 第三者割当て, 第三者割当増資 （=third party allocation, third-party share allotment）
  allocation of revenue 収益の配分
  allocation of shares 株式割当て （=share allocation）
  asset allocation 資産配分, 資金の割当て
  foreign exchange allocation 外貨割当て, 外貨資金割当て
  fund allocation 資金配分
  liquidity allocation 資金の供給
  private allocation 縁故者割当て
  resource allocation 資源配分
  systematic and rational allocation 体系的で合理的な配分

▶We intend to rebuild its financial structure by a large-scale *allocation* of the new shares to the third parties. 当社は、大規模な第三者割当増資で資本構成を再構築する考えだ。

allot 動 割り当てる, 分配する

allotment 名 〈株式の〉割当て, 株式割当, 配分, 割当金 （=allocation; ⇒recapitalize, third-party allotment）
  allotment of new shares 新株割当て （=new share allotment）
  final allotments 最終割当額
  over-allotment option 超過引受オプション

▶With a fair and balanced *allotment* of shares, the corporation laid the foundation for a stable and long-term shareholder securities. 公正でバランスのとれた株式割当てにより、当社は安定した長期株主構成の基盤を据えることとなりました。

allow 動 許す, 割り当てる, 支給する, 見込む, 斟酌(しんしゃく)する, 考慮する

allowable 形 許される, 許容できる, 合法な （⇒Internal Revenue Code）

allowance 名 引当金, 見込み額, 値引き, 控除, 手当, 承認, 許可, 排出権, 排出割当て （⇒retirement allowances）
  allowance for credit losses 貸倒れ引当金 （=allowance for bad debts, allowance for doubtful debts, allowance for uncollectible debts）
  allowance for depreciation 減価償却累計額減, 減価償却引当金 （=accrued depreciation, accumulated depreciation, depreciation allowance, reserve for depreciation）
  allowance for investment losses 投資損失引当金
  allowance market 排出権市場, 排出割当ての取引市場
  assignment allowance 職務手当
  child care allowance 育児手当
  commuter allowance 通勤手当
  earned income allowance 勤労所得控除
  extra allowance 特別手当, 臨時手当
  overtime allowance 残業手当
  sustenance allowance 扶養手当

▶We use the *allowance* method based on credit sales to estimate bad debts. 当社は、不良債権の見積りに掛売りをもとにした引当金設定法を採用しています。

alternative 名 代案, 代替策, 選択肢, 代わるべき手段
  alternative demand 代替需要, 選択需要
  alternative director 代理取締役
  alternative energy source 代替エネルギー源
  alternative fuels 代替燃料
  alternative liquidity 代替流動性
  alternative planning 代替計画, 代替案
  alternative technology 代替技術

▶We looked for *alternatives* that would improve prospects for longer-term profits and growth. 私ども経営陣は、長期的な利益と成長見通しの好転につながる代替策を模索しました。

amalgamation 名 合併（一般に新設合併を consolidation, 吸収合併を merger というが, amalgamation は両方の意味で使われる）

amortization 名 償却, なし崩し償却, 減価償却, 定額償却, 償却額, 償還, 年賦償還, 割賦償還, 減算, アモチゼーション （⇒depreciation）
  amortization of bond discounts 社債発行差金償却
  amortization of deferred asset 繰延べ資産の

償却
amortization of [on] goodwill 営業権の償却
amortization of past service cost 原始過去勤務原価の償却
amortization of principal 元本の返済
amortization of software ソフトウエア償却費
amortization of transition asset 移行時資産の償却, 移行時差額の償却
amortization of unrecognized prior service costs 未認識過去勤務債務の償却
amortization period 元利払い期間
▶*Amortization* of the excess of cost over the net assets acquired is to be recorded over sixty months. 取得した純資産に対する取得価額超過額の償却は, 60か月にわたって行う予定です。

amortize 名 償却する,〈負債などを〉割賦償還する, 定期的に返済する,〈不動産を〉譲渡する
▶For financial reporting purposes, we *amortize* investment tax credits as a reduction to the provision for income taxes over the useful lives of property that produced the credits. 財務報告上, 投資税額控除については, 当社は対象資産の耐用期間にわたって法人税繰入れ額の減少項目として償却しています。

amount 動 総計…に達する, 名 量, 金額, 総額, 元利合計

ample liquidity 高い流動性, 流動性の高さ, 豊富な資金, 大量の資金, 潤沢な資金
▶The Bank of Japan decided to continue providing *ample liquidity* to financial markets. 日本銀行は, 金融市場に大量の資金供給を続けることを決定した。

AMU アジア通貨単位 (Asian Monetary Unitの略)

analysis 名 分析, アナリシス
　break-even analysis 損益分岐点分析, 採算点分析
　competitor analysis 競争相手分析, 競争者分析
　cost-benefit analysis 費用便益分析《略 CBA》
　cost-volume-profit analysis 原価・営業量・利益分析, 原価・操業度・利益分析, CVP分析
　decision analysis 意思決定分析, 決定分析
　multiple regression analysis 多重回帰分析
　quantitative analysis 定量分析, 数量分析, 量的分析
　risk analysis リスク分析, 危険分析
　sales analysis 売上分析, 売上高分析, 販売分析
　sensitivity analysis 感応分析, 感度分析
　skills analysis 技能分析
　variance analysis 差異分析(予算数値と実際の数値との差異分析), 分散分析(統計学)

analyst 名 分析家, 情勢分析家, 解説者, アナリスト
　analysts' earnings estimate アナリスト収益予想
　analysts' opinions アナリスト評価
　bond market analyst 債券アナリスト
　credit analyst 信用アナリスト
　current analysts' consensus estimates 最新アナリスト予想
　economic analyst 経済アナリスト, 経済情勢分析家
　equity analyst 証券アナリスト
　Financial Analysts Federation 全米証券アナリスト協会
　fundamental analyst ファンダメンタル・アナリスト
　industry analyst 業界アナリスト, 産業アナリスト
　investment analyst 投資アナリスト
　securities analyst 証券アナリスト
　Society for Investment Analysts 証券アナリスト協会
　stock analyst 株式アナリスト
　technical analyst テクニカル・アナリスト
▶The preliminary GDP figures released by the Cabinet Office are significantly higher than *analysts'* predictions. 内閣府が発表した国内総生産(GDP)速報値は, アナリストの事前予想を大幅に上回っている。

anchor tenant アンカーテナント(ショッピングセンターに客や他店舗をひきつける店)

anchorman 名 総合司会者, ニュースキャスター, 校閲者, 原稿を最終的にまとめる編集者, 最終走者, 最強打者, アンカーマン

ANCOM アンデス共同市場, アンコム (Andean Common Marketの略)

and/or 接 および/または, かつ/または, 両方またはいずれか一方 (一般にA and/or Bは, (A and B) or (A or B)を意味するといわれる。例文で示すように, A and/or Bは, AまたはB(またはその両方)と訳すこともできる)
▶The savings plans allow employees to contribute a portion of their pretax *and/or* after-tax income in accordance with specified guidelines. この貯蓄制度では, 従業員は従業員の税引き前所得または税引き後所得(あるいはその両方)の一部を, 特定の基準に従って拠出することができます。

angel 名 ベンチャー企業への個人投資家, 資金提供者, 新興企業への後援者, エンジェル (=busi-

announce

ness angel: 主にベンチャー企業に出資の形で資金を提供し、経営の助言なども行って株式公開時に大きな利益が得られることを期待するハイリスク・ハイリターン型投資の個人投資家を「エンジェル」という。ベンチャー企業育成のため、ベンチャー企業に個人投資家が投資をしやすくする税制を「エンジェル税制」という）

angel-funded start-up エンジェルが出資したベンチャー企業 [新興企業]

angel investment エンジェルの投資

business angel 企業後援者, 企業 [新興企業] への資金提供者, 新事業への個人投資家

announce 動 発表する, 公表する, 告示する, 表明する, 知らせる, 告知する

▶The firm's share prices declined after it *announced* an antitakeover measure in May. 同社が5月に買収防衛策を発表した後、同社の株価は下落した。

announcement 名 発表, 公表, 告示, 告知, 声明, 表明, お知らせ

announcement advertising 告知広告
announcement day 募集開始日, 募集発表日
dividend announcement 配当発表
earnings announcement 利益発表, 業績発表
official announcement 政府声明, 公示
pre announcement 予告
results announcement 業績発表, 決算発表 (=announcement of business results)

annual 形 年間の, 年次の, 通期の, 年1回の, 毎年の, アニュアル

annual accounting 年次決算
annual audit 年次監査
annual consolidated financial statements 年次連結財務書類, 年次連結財務諸表
annual earnings 年次利益, 年間所得
annual financial report 年次財務報告
annual financial statements 年次財務諸表, 年次財務書類, 年次報告書, 年次有価証券報告書 (=annual accounts)
annual growth rate 年成長率, 年間伸び率 [成長率]
annual loss 年間赤字, 通期での赤字
annual income 年収
annual paid holiday 年次有給休暇
annual production 年間生産台数
annual profit and loss 年次損益
annual results 通期決算, 通期業績, 年間業績, 年間成績
annual return 年次報告書, 年次届け出書 (英国の会社が会社登記官に届け出る財務報告書)

annual securities report

annual statement 年次報告書 (米国の保険会社が州保険局長官に提出する財務報告書), 年次営業報告書

annual accounts settlement 年次決算

▶A large majority of First Section-listed companies close their books at the end of March for their *annual accounts settlement*. 東証1部上場企業の大半が、年次決算のため3月末に帳簿を締める。

annual general meeting of shareholders 年次株主総会, 定例株主総会, 定時株主総会, 年次社員総会《略 AGM》(=annual general meeting, annual general shareholders meeting, annual shareholders meeting, annual shareholders' meeting)

▶In Japan, *annual general meetings of shareholders* are generally held in June. 日本では、一般に年次株主総会は6月に開かれる [6月に集中する]。

annual meeting 定時総会, 年次総会, 定時株主総会, 年次株主総会

annual meeting of policyholders' representatives 総代会 (⇒policyholders' representative meeting)
annual meeting of shareholders [stockholders] 年次株主総会, 定例株主総会, 定時株主総会 (=annual shareholders meeting)

▶The *annual meeting* of the shareholders of this corporation will be held on May 15, 2009. 当社の年次株主総会は、2009年5月15日に開催します。

annual report 年次報告書, 年次決算報告書, 年次営業報告書, 有価証券報告書, 年報, アニュアル・レポート (⇒form 10-K, quarterly report)

annual report and accounts 年次報告書
annual report on Form 10-K 様式10-Kに基づく年次報告書 (⇒available)
annual report to stockholders [shareholders] 株主向け年次報告書, 年次報告書

▶Form 10-K is our *annual report* to the Securities and Exchange Commission. 様式10-Kは、当社が米証券取引委員会に提出する年次報告書です。

annual salary system 年俸制

▶Our annual salary system does not pay bonuses. 当社の年俸制では、ボーナスが支給されません。

annual securities report 年次有価証券報告書

▶The presence of investment funds on the share register is generally unknown until their names are listed in *annual securities reports*. 株主名簿上の投資ファンドの存在は、一般にそのファンド

名が年次有価証券報告書に記載されるまで分からない。

annual shareowners [shareholders, stockholders] meeting 年次株主総会
▶The 69th *Annual Shareowners Meeting* will be held 10:30 a.m., April 20, 2009 at the World Congress Center.　第69回年次株主総会は, 2009年4月20日, ワールド・コングレス・センターで午前10時30分から開催されます。

annualized [annualised] 年率換算の, 年換算の, 年率の
　annualized growth 年率の伸び, 年率の伸び率
　on an annualized basis 年率換算で, 年換算で, 年率で
　quarter on quarter annualized rate 前期比年率
　seasonally adjusted annualized rate 季節調整済み年率

annualized rate 年率 (⇒real terms)
▶The real-term gross domestic product in the fourth quarter grew at an *annualized rate* of 3 percent over the same period of the previous year.　第4四半期の実質国内総生産 (GDP) の成長率は, 前年同期比で年率3%だった。

annualized terms [basis] 年率換算, 年換算, 年率
▶The real growth in *annualized terms* was 5.6 percent, showing clear signs of an economic recovery.　年率換算での実質成長率は5.6%で, 明らかに景気回復基調を示した。

annuitant 名 年金受給者, 年金受給権者
annuity 名 年金, 年金保険制度, 年金受領権, 年賦金, 出資金, 掛金
　amount of annuity 年金終価
　annuity cost 年金費用
　annuity due 期首払い年金 (=annuity in advance)
　annuity in arrears 期末払い年金
　annuity scheme 年金制度 (⇒defined-contribution annuity scheme)
　fixed annuity 定額年金
　occupational annuity 企業年金
　present value of annuity 年金現価
　retirement annuity 退職年金
　variable annuity 変額年金
▶In the corporate type of defined-contribution pension plans, companies pay *annuities* for employees.　企業型の確定拠出年金制度では, 企業が従業員のために掛金を支払う。

ANSI 米国国家規格協会, アンシー (American National Standards Institute の略)

answering service 電話取次ぎ代行業, テレホン・サービス

ante-date 動 …より前に起こる, …に先立つ, 実際より前の日付を付ける, 名 前日付
antenna shop 実験店舗, アンテナ・ショップ (=pilot shop)
anticipate 動 予想する, 見込む, 見越す, 期待する, 予定する
　anticipate a rise in interest rate 金利上昇を見越す
　anticipated loss 見込み損失, 予想損失 (=anticipatory loss)
　anticipated profit 見込み利益, 予想利益, 期待利益 (=anticipatory profit)
　anticipated shipping date 出荷予定日
　be tougher than originally anticipated 当初予想より厳しい
▶This letter of credit shall be opened not less than 30 calendar days before the first *anticipated* or scheduled shipping date for each order.　この信用状は, 各注文の最初の出荷予定日から30暦日以上前に開設するものとする。

antideflationary measures デフレ対策 (=antideflationary package)
▶What the *antideflationary measures* lack is steps to boost demand.　今回のデフレ対策に欠けているのは, 需要拡大のための対策だ。

antidumping 名形 反ダンピング (不当廉売), ダンピング防止, アンチダンピング《略AD》 (⇒dumping, probe)
　antidumping duties 反ダンピング関税, ダンピング防止関税
　antidumping measures 反ダンピング措置
antidumping investigation 反ダンピング調査, アンチダンピング調査 (=antidumping probe)
▶China has started an *antidumping investigation* into steel imports from South Korea and Russia.　中国は, 韓国やロシアからの輸入鉄鋼製品を対象にアンチダンピング調査を開始した。

antidumping probe 反ダンピング調査
▶In the United States, a provisional ruling on dumping is usually issued about six months after launching *antidumping probes*.　米国では, ダンピング (不当廉売) の仮決定をするのは通例, 反ダンピング調査の開始から半年程度である。

Antimonopoly Law 独占禁止法
▶Prosecutors arrested seven employees of seven firms on suspicion of violating the *Anti-mono-*

poly Law by rigging bids in eight public works projects.　検察当局は，8件の公共事業入札で不正があったとして，独占禁止法違反容疑で7社の従業員7人を逮捕した。

antitakeover measure　買収防衛策，買収への対抗措置
▸More than 100 companies are expected to seek shareholder approval of their *antitakeover measures*.　100社を超える企業が，買収防衛策の株主承認を求める見通しだ。

antitakeover method　買収防衛方式，買収防衛策，買収への対抗策
▸The company's poison pill scheme is inappropriate as an *antitakeover* before a potential acquirer emerges.　同社のポイズン・ピル防衛策は，買収候補が現われる前の買収への対抗策[買収への事前の対抗策]としては相当性を欠いている。

antitrust 形　独占禁止の，反トラストの，トラストを規制する
　Antitrust Act　米国の独占禁止法
　antitrust cooperation accord　独占禁止法協力協定
　antitrust law　独占禁止法，反トラスト法
　antitrust legislation　独占禁止法，反トラスト法

antivirus software　ウイルス対策ソフト，ウイルス駆除ソフト（＝virus protection software）

AOB [a.o.b.]　その他（議題にない項目，議題にない項目を話し合う時間。**any other business**の略）

APEC　アジア太平洋経済協力会議，エイペック（**Asia-Pacific Economic Cooperation**の略）
▸*APEC* groups 21 economies, including Japan, the United States, China, South Korea, Russia, Southeast Asian countries, Canada and some Latin American nations.　APECには，日本，米国，中国，韓国，ロシア，東南アジア諸国，カナダ，中南米諸国など21の国・地域が参加している。

applicable 形　適用される，適用できる，適用可能な，応用できる，配賦可能な，妥当な，適当な，適切な，適格な，対応する
　amounts applicable to　…に配分された額
　applicable Federal rate　適格連邦税率
　applicable fees　適用料金
　applicable income taxes　適用所得税，当該所得税
　applicable law　適用法，準拠法，適用される法律（＝governing law）
　applicable percentage　該当率，適格割合
　applicable tax law　適用される税法
　applicable tax rate　適用税率
　applicable taxes　租税公課

consolidated net income applicable to common shares　普通株式に帰属する連結純利益
▸Licensor shall bear any tax to be levied under *applicable* tax laws on the income of Licensor arising under this agreement.　ライセンサーは，適用される税法に基づき，本契約に基づいて生じるライセンサーの所得に課される税金を負担する。

applicant 名　応募者，志願者，申請者，申込者

application 名　申込み，申請，出願，申請者，申込み者，願書，信用状開設依頼書，運用，適用，応用，使途，配賦，予定配賦，割賦適用業務，アプリケーション・ソフト，応用ソフト，応用システム，適用業務，アプリケーション（⇒**accept, full cost, International Financial Reporting Standards**）
　application for registration　登録申請
　application form　申込み書，申請書，願書
　application of funds　資金運用，資金の使途，資金の適用
　application software　応用ソフト[ソフトウエア]，市販ソフト（＝application, application package, application program）
　applications satellite　実用衛星
　applications technology satellite　応用技術衛星
　commercial application　商用化，実用化，商用アプリケーション
　computer application　コンピュータ利用技術
　electronic application　電子出願
　license application　免許申請
　listing application　上場申請
　patent application　特許出願
　preliminary application for listing　上場の仮申請
▸At the time of its *application* for court protection under the Civil Rehabilitation Law, the firm had debts amounting to ¥2.2 billion.　民事再生法の適用申請時に，同社は総額22億円の負債をかかえていた。
▸We have completed the transformation into an *application*-oriented high-tech group.　当社は，アプリケーション志向のハイテク・グループへの変革を成し遂げました。

apply 動　適用する，応用する，利用する，当てはめる，配賦する
　applied cost　配賦原価，原価配賦額，賦課済み原価，適用原価
　applied research　応用研究
　apply for protection from creditors　会社更生手続きを申請する，破綻申請する，資産保全を請求する（＝file for protection from creditors）

apply for protection from creditors under the bankruptcy reform law 民事再生法の適用を申請する (=file for protection from creditors under the Civil Rehabilitation Law)
▸New accounting rules *apply* to all U.S. companies. 新会計規則は，米国企業にすべて適用されている。
▸The firm was forced to *apply* to the Financial Services Agency for protection from creditors. 同社は，金融庁への破綻申請を迫られた。

appoint 動 指名する，任命する，選任する，指定する，定める
▸In the proposal, the investment fund requests nine people be *appointed* board members. この提案で，同投資ファンドは，9人を取締役に選任するよう求めている。
▸The FSA *appointed* three administrators to take charge of the failed bank's administration, operations and asset management. 金融庁は，破綻した銀行の経営，業務と資産の管理に当たる金融整理管財人3名を指名した。

appointment 名 任命，指名，指定，官職，地位，役職，取決め，約束，予約，アポイントメント
  appointment and removal of …の任免
  appointment of a trustee 管財人の指名
  appointment of representative 代表者の選任
▸A majority of the votes cast is required to ratify the *appointment* of auditors. 監査役指名の承認を得るには，投票総数の過半数の賛成投票が必要です。
▸Recently, shareholders' proposals have come from investment funds seeking higher dividends and the *appointment* of outside directors. 最近の株主提案は，増配や社外取締役選任などを求める投資ファンドから出されている。

apportion 動 配分する，割り当てる，配当する
apportionment 名 配賦，分配，割当て，配当
appraisal 名 評価，査定，鑑定，見積り
  appraisal of asset 資産の鑑定
  appraisal profit 含み益，評価益 (=appraisal gain, latent profit)
  appraisal profits and losses 含み損益，評価損益 (=latent profits and losses, unrealized profits and losses)
  appraisal value 評価額，評価価値，鑑定評価額，査定価値 (=appraised value, assessed value)
  performance appraisal 業績評価
appraisal gain 含み益，評価益 (=appraisal profit, latent gain)
▸The nine insurers booked about ¥5 trillion in combined *appraisal gains* on their shareholdings. 生保9社の保有株式の含み益は，総額で約5兆円となった。

appraisal loss 含み損，評価損，保有株の評価損を損失に計上する減損処理額 (=latent loss, valuation loss)
▸The nine nonlife insurers suffered total *appraisal losses* on securities of ¥360 billion. 損保9社が，9社合計で3,600億円の有価証券評価損を計上した。

appreciate 動 上昇する，騰貴する，高く評価する (⇒negative effect)
▸If the yen starts to *appreciate*, this will have a negative effect on the revenues of exporting companies. 円高に転じれば，輸出企業の収益は円高のマイナス影響を受けることになる。
▸Tokyo stocks *appreciated* across the board. 東京株[東京株式市場の株価]は，全面高となった。

appreciation 名 〈価格・相場の〉上昇，騰貴，急騰，増価(資産価値の増加を意味する)，平価切上げ，正当な評価，評価増，評価切上げ，評価益，増加額
  appreciation of the yen against the U.S. dollar 円高・ドル安，円の対ドル相場の上昇，米ドルに対する円相場の上昇
  appreciation surplus 評価剰余金，評価替剰余金，再評価積立金 (=appraisal surplus)
  benefits of the yen's appreciation 円高差益
  capital appreciation キャピタル・ゲイン
  equity appreciation 株価上昇
  sharp yen appreciation 急激な円高
  yen's appreciation against the dollar 円高・ドル安，ドルに対する円相場の上昇
▸A rapid *appreciation* of the yen is not desirable to the U.S. economy. 急激な円高は，米国経済には好ましくない。

approach 名 主義，方法，方式，手法，取組み，取組み方，姿勢，政策，路線，研究，研究法，解決法，進入，接近，アプローチ (⇒cooperative approach)
  analytic approach 分析的アプローチ，分析手法
  asset-liability approach 資産負債法
  commodity approach 商品研究
  cooperative approach 協調路線
  cost approach 原価法
  full cost approach 全部原価法
  functional approach 機能研究，機能の研究，関数論的方法 (=functional analysis: 機能的分析)
  management approach 経営方法，意思決定論的アプローチ
  mark-to-market approach 値洗い方式

net-of-tax approach 税額控除法
net profit approach 純利益法
pragmatic approach 現実路線, 現実的な政策
product approach 商品研究
probusiness approach 企業寄りの政策
rating approach 格付け方法
rule-based approach 細則主義 (=cook book approach)
system approach システム・アプローチ
top-down approach トップ・ダウン型アプローチ
value added approach 付加価値接近法
▶BHP sweetened its initial *approach* by 13 percent, offering 3.4 of its shares for every Rio share. 英豪系資源最大手のBHP社は, 最初の提示条件を13%引き上げ, リオ1株に対してBHPの株式3.4株の株式交換比率を提示した。

appropriate 動 充当する, 当てる[充てる], 支出する, 〈予算に〉計上する, 〈支出を〉承認する, 占有する, 私物化する, 私用に供する, 着服する, 横領する, 盗用する
　appropriate a common interest 公共の利益を独占する
　appropriate public money for one's own use 公金を横領する
　appropriated goods 収用品
　appropriated retained earnings [income] 処分済み利益剰余金 (=appropriated earned surplus)
　appropriated surplus 処分済み剰余金
　retained earnings appropriated for bond 減債積立金

appropriate 形 適切な, 適正な, 特有の
　appropriate credit protections 適切な信用補強
　appropriate example 適例
　appropriate interest rate 適正な利率, 適正な金利
　appropriate medical treatment 適切な医療
　appropriate technology 適正技術

approval 名 承認, 承諾, 是認, 賛成, 賛同, 同意, 支持, 認可, 許可
　approval rating 支持率 (=approval rate, popularity rating, support rate)
　blanket approval 一括承認
　conditional approval 条件付き認可
　conversion approval 転用認可
　credit approval 与信承認, 信用供与承認 (⇒exposure)
　investment approvals 投資承認額, 投資認可額
　official approvals 許認可

▶Companies should obtain shareholder *approval* when introducing methods to counter hostile takeover attempts. 敵対的買収への対抗策を導入する場合, 企業は株主の承認を得なければならない。
▶The Tokyo Stock Exchange has canceled its *approval* for the company's plan to go public on the Mother's market. 東京証券取引所は, 同社の東証マザーズへの上場計画承認を取り消した。

approve 動 承認する, 承諾する, 賛成する, 賛同する, 同意する, 支持する, 認可する, 許可する
▶The executive compensation committee of the board of directors *approves* the compensation of all executive officers. 取締役会の役員報酬委員会は, 業務執行役員全員の報酬について承認しております。

approved pension scheme 適格年金制度
approximate 形 おおよその, 概算の, 近似の, 動 近づく, 近づける, 概算する
April-June quarter 4-6月期(3月決算企業の第1四半期, 12月決算企業の第2四半期)
▶In the *April-June quarter*, major high-tech companies suffered losses or profit declines. 4-6月期は, 主要ハイテク企業が赤字や減益に苦しんでいる。
April-September period 4-9月期, 9月中間決算 (=the six months to September 30)
▶The firm posted a net profit of ¥1.5 billion for the *April-September period*. 同社は, 9月中間決算で15億円の税引き後利益を計上した。

arbiter 名 仲裁人, 調停者, 裁決[決定]者, 権威
arbitrage 名 裁定, 仲介, 裁定取引, 鞘取り売買
arbitration 名 仲裁, 裁定, 仲裁機関, 国際裁判 (⇒award)
　American Arbitration Association 米国仲裁協会《略 AAA》
　China International Economic and Trade Arbitration Commission 中国国際経済貿易仲裁委員会《略 CIETAC》
　Court of Arbitration, International Chamber of Commerce 国際商業会議所仲裁裁判所《略 ICC》
　Japan Commercial Arbitration Association 日本商事仲裁協会《略 JCAA》(旧称: 国際商事仲裁協会。2003年1月1日から名称変更)
　London Court of International Arbitration ロンドン国際仲裁裁判所

▶All disputes arising in relation to this agreement shall be referred to *arbitration* by one or more arbitrators. 本契約に関して生じた紛争は, すべて1人またはそれ以上の仲裁人による仲裁に付すも

arbitrator 名 仲裁人 （⇒arbitration）
  a panel of three arbitrators　3名の仲裁人団
  commercial arbitrator　商事仲裁人
  Panel of Arbitrators　仲裁委員会
  sole arbitrator　単独仲裁人
  third arbitrator　第三仲裁人
▸The award of the *arbitrators* shall be final. 仲裁人の仲裁判断は、最終的なものとする。

architecture 名 〈コンピュータ・システムの〉設計、基本的な設計思想、基本設計、〈ハードウエアとソフトウエアの〉仕様と構成、構造、構造物、構築、建築、建築物、建築技術、建築様式、建築学、産物、アーキテクチャー
  bus architecture　バス構成
  computer communications network architecture　コンピュータ間通信ネットワーク・アーキテクチャー
  database architecture　データベースの設計思想・構造
  network architecture　網構成、ネットワーク・アーキテクチャー
  open network architecture　ネットワーク仕様公開
  system architectures　システム構成
  the architecture of the cold war　冷戦の産物
▸Products such as cellular telephones and personal communicators require low power consumption, efficient packaging, information compression and advanced system *architecture*. 携帯電話やパーソナル・コミュニケーターなどの製品には、低消費電力、効率的パッケージ、情報圧縮や高度なシステム構成などが求められている。

area 名 地域、領域、部門、分野、圏、エリア
  area headquarters　地域本部
  area network　地域通信網、地域ネットワーク
  area organization　地域別組織
  area superintendent　地域担当管理部長
  bonded area　保税地域
  diversify into related areas　関連分野への多角化を進める、関連分野に多角化する
  free trade area　自由貿易地域
  geographic area information　地域別情報、地域セグメント情報
  key areas　主要分野、中核業務
  leading-edge area　先端分野
  market area　市場地域、営業地域、商圏
  planted area　栽培面積
  trade area　商圏、商勢圏、貿易圏
  trade-area size　商圏規模、商圏の大きさ
  U.S. dollar area　米ドル圏
  waterfront industrial areas　臨海工業地帯
▸Aeon Co. now owns a number of large stores in suburban *areas*, such as Jusco. イオンは現在、ジャスコなど郊外で展開する大型店を多く所有している。

arithmetic mean　等差中項、相加平均、算術平均

ARM　変動金利型抵当貸付け（adjustable rate mortgageの略）

arm 名 子会社、部門、部局、支店（＝unit）
  brokerage arm　証券子会社、証券会社、証券部門
  consulting arm　コンサルティング部門、コンサルティング会社
  financing arm　金融子会社、金融部門
  long-arm jurisdiction　域外適用管轄権
  research arm　研究所、研究部門
  treasury arm　財務部門
▸General Motors Acceptance Corp. (GMAC), GM's finance *arm*, is giving the boost to the struggling automaker's bottom line. GMの金融子会社GMACが、経営再建に取り組む米自動車メーカーGMの業績の後押しをしている。

arm's length [arm's-length]　公正な、独立した、独立当事者間の、独立企業間の、独立第三者間の、第三者間取引にかかわる、商業ベースの
  arm's length bargaining　公正な取引、独立当事者間の取引
  arm's length basis　純然たる商業ベース、商業ベース
  arm's length price　独立当事者間の価格、独立企業間価格、第三者間との取引価格
  arm's length pricing basis　第三者に対する取引価格基準
  arm's length relationship　商業ベースの取引関係
  arm's length transaction　第三者間の公正な取引、独立当事者間の取引、独立第三者間取引、対等取引、商業ベースの取引
▸In the case of sale by the licensee to an affiliated company thereof, such royalties shall be calculated based upon the price which would be charged if the transaction were an *arm's length* transaction. ライセンシーの関係会社に対するライセンシーの販売の場合、ロイヤリティは、その取引が第三者間の公正な取引［純然たる商業ベースの取引］であった場合に請求する価格に基づいて計算するものとする。

arrange 動 手配する、取り決める、手はずを整える、取りまとめる、準備する、打ち合わせる、解決す

る, 同意する, アレンジする
arrange an initial public offering 株式公募を取りまとめる
arrange interim financing つなぎ融資をアレンジする
arrange with …と打ち合わせる
arranged total loss 妥協全損 (＝agreed total loss)
sell at an arranged price 同意した価格で売却する, 取り決めた価格で販売する
▸Please *arrange* for the transportation of Products. 本製品の運送の手配をお願い致します。

arrangement 名 手配, 準備, 打合せ, 取決め, 協定, 合意, 契約, 取りまとめ, 調整, 解決
agency arrangement 取引約定書
arrangement plan 設備配置計画
business arrangement 業務協定, 業務契約, 業務提携
correspondent arrangement コルレス契約
formal arrangement 正式取決め
insurance arrangements 保険契約
joint clearing arrangements 共同決済協定
licensing arrangements ライセンス契約
market sharing arrangement 市場協定
reciprocal arrangement 相互協定
standby arrangement スタンドバイ協定, スタンドバイ取決め, 借入予約協定
substitute arrangement 代替契約
supply arrangements 供給契約, 原材料の供給契約
technology licensing arrangements 技術ライセンス契約
trade arrangements 貿易協定
▸The two firms have built a relationship during a three-year business *arrangement*. 両社は, 3年前からの業務提携で信頼関係を築いた。

arrears 名 延滞, 遅滞, 遅延, 滞納, 延滞金, 滞納金, 未納金, 未払い金
arrears on loan repayments 延滞債権
in arrears 延滞している, 未払いの, 未納の, 遅れが出ている
interest for arrears 延滞利息
▸The bank has about ¥2.6 trillion in loans to firms that are in *arrears* on principal and interest payments. 同行には, 元利の返済に遅れが出ている企業向け融資額[債権]が約2兆6,000億円ある。

articles of association 〈米国の会社の〉基本定款(articles of incorporation)〈英国の会社の〉通常定款(英国の会社の基本定款＝memorandum of association), 団体規約

articles of incorporation 〈会社の〉基本定款, 設立定款, 定款 (＝articles of association: 会社の方針を定めたもの。日本は単一定款制度をとっているのに対して, 欧米では基本定款(articles of association, articles of incorporation)と付属款(bylaws)の二つの定款制度をとっている)
initial articles of incorporation 設立時の定款, 設立定款
revised articles of incorporation 変更定款
▸We will amend our *articles of incorporation* at our shareholders meeting in June to shift to the new management system. 当社は6月の株主総会で基本定款を改定して, 新経営システムに移行する。

articles of partnership 組合定款, 組合規約, 合名会社定款, パートナーシップ定款

as is, where is 無保証の

as of …現在で, …の時点で, …現在の, …の日付で, …の日付に
▸The bank reported a capital adequacy ratio of 4.54 percent *as of* the end of fiscal 2008. 同行の2008年度末現在[時点]の自己資本比率は, 4.54%だった。

ASEAN アセアン, 東南アジア諸国連合 (Association of South-East Asian Nationsの略)

ASEM アジア欧州会議, アジア欧州首脳会議 (Asia-Europe summit meetingの略。1996年3月, アジアと欧州の関係強化を目的としてバンコクで第一回首脳会議を開いて発足。日本, 中国, 韓国, 東南アジア7か国と欧州連合(EU), 欧州委員会が参加)

Asia-Pacific Economic Cooperation アジア太平洋経済協力会議, エイペック 《略 APEC》

asking price 提示価格, 募集価格

assemble 動 組み立てる, 生産する
assemble products 製品を組み立てる
assembling parts 組立部品 (＝assembly parts)
assembling plant 組立工場 (＝assembly plant)
assembling production 組立生産 (＝assembly production)

assembly line 組立ライン, 組立作業ライン
▸If wind turbines are mass-produced on *assembly lines* like automobiles, the cost of wind-generated electricity could drop to 1 to 2 cents per kilowatt-hour. 風力タービンが車のように組立ラインで大量生産されるようになれば, 風力発電のコストは, 1キロワット時当たり1−2セントにまで下がる可能性がある。

assembly plant 組立工場 (＝assembling

plant, assembly factory）
▶The firm's car *assembly plant* in St. Petersburg is planned to go on stream in December 2008. ロシアのサンクトペテルブルクにある同社の自動車組立工場は，2008年12月から生産を開始する．

assertive shareholder もの言う株主
▶The pension fund association is an *assertive shareholder* that makes tough demands on corporate managements. 企業年金連合会は，企業の経営姿勢に厳しい注文をつける「もの言う株主」でもある．

assess 動 評価する，査定する，審査する，算定する，判断する（⇒brand）
assessed value 査定価額，査定評価額，査定価値，課税価額
assessed value of fixed assets 固定資産税評価額
▶Managers must continuously *assess* their resource needs and consider further steps to reduce costs. 経営陣は，つねに資源の必要性を評価して，コスト削減のための一段と進んだ方法を考える必要がある．

assessment 名 評価，事前評価，鑑定，査定，審査，算定，課税，賦課，更正，判断，評価額，鑑定額，査定額，賦課金，追徴金，アセスメント
assessment of taxes 税の賦課
assessment plan 賦課方式
asset assessment 資産査定，資産評価（＝asset appraisal, asset evaluation）
basis of assessment 課税標準
collateral assessment 担保評価
credit assessment 信用評価，信用分析
damage assessment 損害査定
official assessment method 賦課課税方式
rating assessment 格付け評価
self-assessment 申告納税
▶Outstanding nonperforming loans held by banks are increasing due to poor business results of borrowers and the strict asset *assessment* methods. 金融機関が抱える不良債権残高は，貸出先［融資先］の業績不振や資産の査定方法の厳格化で増加している．

asset 名 資産，財産，アセット（⇒assessment）
asset deficiency 債務超過
asset disposition 資産処分
asset investment 資産運用
asset liability management 資産負債総合管理，資産負債管理，バランス・シート管理《略 ALM》
asset management company 資産管理会社，資産運用会社
asset provision 資産評価損引当金，資産評価損引当金繰入れ額
asset swap 資産交換，アセット・スワップ
asset turnover 資産回転率
assets acquired 取得資産
assets and liabilities 資産と負債
bad assets 不良資産
capital asset 資本資産，資本的資産，固定資産（＝fixed asset, fixed capital, long-lived asset, permanent asset）
commercial assets 商業資産
customer assets 預り資産，顧客からの預り資産
foreign assets 対外資産，海外資産
freezing terrorist-related assets テロ関連資産の凍結
hidden assets 含み資産
intangible assets 無形資産，無形固定資産
out-of-book assets 簿外資産
quick assets 当座資産
real assets 不動産
securitized assets 証券化資産，証券化した資産
tangible assets 有形資産，有形固定資産
wasting assets 減耗資産，消耗資産，減耗性資産，涸渇性資産
▶The Corporation will put all its efforts into increasing its profitability and promptly selling its unnecessary *assets*. 当社は，利益水準の向上や不要資産の即時売却などに全力を挙げる方針です．

asset-backed commercial paper 資産担保コマーシャル・ペーパー，資産担保CP，アセットバックCP《略 ABCP》
▶*Asset-backed commercial paper* refers to commercial paper whose creditworthiness is guaranteed by sales credit that the corporate issuer has with its debtors. 資産担保CPとは，企業発行体がその債務者に対して保有する売掛金によって信用度が保証されるコマーシャル・ペーパーを指す．

asset-backed securities 資産担保証券，商業用不動産証券，アセットバック証券《略 ABS》（銀行の貸出債権や企業の売掛債権などを担保に発行される証券．⇒CBO, CDO, CLO, RMBS）
▶The Bank of Japan decided to relax the rules under which it buys *asset-backed securities*. 日銀は，資産担保証券の買入れ基準を緩和することを決めた．

asset base 資産基盤，資産構成
▶A steady annual improvement in earnings of five percent or more is a reasonable goal given the weight of regulated companies in our *asset*

base. 当社の資産構成で規制対象企業が大きな比重を占めていることを考えると，毎年5%以上の利益率増加の安定確保は，妥当な目標と言えるでしょう。
▸ABC Inc. management took vigorous steps during 2008 to reinforce the performance of ABC's *asset base*. ABCの経営陣は，資産運用実績を強化するため，2008年度に思い切った措置をとりました。
▸We sold some assets in return for an interest in a larger entity with greater potential for growth and a more diversified *asset base*. 当社は，大きな潜在成長力と一段と多様化した資産基盤をもつ大規模企業の株式を取得する対価として，一部資産を売却しました。

asset impairment accounting 減損会計（＝accounting for the impairment of assets: 企業が保有する土地やビル，工場，店舗などの固定資産から生じる収益が，投資額に見合うかどうかを判断する会計基準）
▸This extraordinary loss of ¥581.06 billion stems partly from the write-offs of appraisal losses in fixed assets under an *asset impairment accounting* rule. この5,810億6,000万円の特別損失の一因は，減損会計基準に基づく固定資産の減損処理によるものだ。

asset management 資産管理，資産運用，投資顧問
▸All these events are part of a larger strategy of our *asset management*. これらの措置は，当社の資産運営戦略拡大の一環としてとられたものです。

asset management services 資産運用サービス
▸The new firm will offer *asset management services* to individual investors whose net worth is ¥100 million or more. 新会社は，純資産が1億円以上の個人投資家に資産運用サービスを提供する。

asset value 資産価値，資産価格，純資産
▸A certified public accountant evaluated the *asset value* of the advertising agency. 公認会計士が，この広告会社の資産価値を評価［算定］した。

assign 動 割り当てる，任命する，指定する，与える，譲渡する，委託する
▸The pension fund association *assigns* other institutional investors to manage the rest of its funds for domestic equity investment. 年金基金連合会は，国内株式投資資金の残りの運用を，他の機関投資家［外部の運用機関］に委託している。

assignable 形 譲渡可能な

assignment 名 割当て，割当量，譲渡，譲渡証書
▸The Corporation acknowledges the *assignment* and other terms and provisions included in the *assignment* agreement. 当社は，この譲渡契約書に定められた譲渡とその他の条件および規定を確認する。

associate 名 関連会社，関係会社，系列会社，同系会社，半数所有会社，持ち分法適用会社 （＝affiliated company, associated company）

associated company 関連会社，関係会社，系列会社
▸The Group's share of reported income in *associated companies* is included in the consolidated income statement. 関連会社の公表利益に対する当グループの持ち分は，連結損益計算書に表示されています。

association 名 社団，団体，協会，組合，連合，連合体
　American Bankers Association アメリカ銀行協会
　Association of Consumer Affairs Professionals 米消費者関連専門家会議, エイキャップ《略 ACAP》
　Association of International Bond Dealers 国際債券取引業者協会, 国際債券ディーラーズ協会《略 AIBD》
　commercial and industrial association 商工組合
　consumer's association 消費者組合
　cooperative association 協同組合
　credit association 信用金庫
　employees' association 従業員組合
　employers association 経営者団体, 事業者団体, 使用者団体
　friendly association 共済組合, 友愛組合
　handicraft association 職人組合
　industry association 業界団体
　National Association of Manufacturers 全米製造業協会
　producers' association 生産者組合
　public relations association PR団体, ピーアール団体
　savings association 貯蓄組合
　trade association 同業組合, 産業団体, 事業者体, 同業者団体, 商工団体
　voluntary association 任意団体

assume 動 〈任務や義務・債務を〉引き受ける，〈債務などを〉肩代わりする，負担する，就任する，就く，責任を負う，責任をとる，引き継ぐ，継承する，占有する，…と仮定する，推定する，想定する，予想する，予定する，見込む，考慮する
　assume A to be B AをBとみなす，AをBと仮定

assume liquidity risk 流動性リスクを負担する
assume office 就任する
assume responsibility for …の責任を負う，…の責任を取る
assume the risk リスクを負う，リスクを引き受ける
assumed bond 保証社債
assumed liability 引継ぎ負債，債務引受未払い金
assumed loans 債務の肩代わり
assumed rate of interest 予定利率
assumed rate of return 予想収益率，予想運用利益率
assumed rates of return on pension funds 予想年金基金運用収益率
assumed trend rate 予想傾向値
assumed yield 予想利回り
earnings per common share—assuming full dilution 普通株1株当たり利益—完全希薄化［希釈化，希釈効果］を考慮した場合，完全希薄化後普通株1株当たり利益

▶We *assumed* that the growth in the per capita cost of covered health care benefits (the health care cost trend rate) would gradually decline after 2008. 当社は，計上済み医療給付費用の1人当たりの伸び率（医療費用の傾向値）は，2008年度以降はゆるやかに減少するものと予想しています。

assumption 名 〈義務や債務の〉引受け，〈債務などの〉肩代わり，負担，就任，引継ぎ，継承，占有，仮定，前提，公準，想定，予想，考慮
actuarial assumption 保険数理上の仮定
assumption of accounting 会計上の仮定
assumption of going concern 継続企業の前提
basic assumption 基礎的仮定
debt assumption 債務引受け，債務引受契約，債務履行引受け，債務の肩代わり，債務引受契約に基づく債務譲渡，デット・アサンプション
economic assumptions 経済見通し
going concern assumption 継続企業の公準，継続企業の前提
risk assumption business リスク負担型ビジネス

▶To use the new accounting method, we made *assumptions* about trends in health care costs, interest rates and average life expectancy. 新会計処理方法を採用するにあたって，当社は医療給付コスト，金利と平均寿命の傾向について仮定を設けました。

▶We made the following *assumptions* in valuing our postretirement benefit obligation at December 31, 2008. 2008年12月31日現在の退職後給付債務の評価にあたって，当社は以下の仮定を行いました。

assurance 名 保証，確約，確信，確実性，自信，言質（げんち），保険（insurance） (⇒**audit** 名)
assurance of bill 手形保証
firm assurance 確信
life assurance business 生命保険事業
quality assurance 品質保証
verbal assurance 言質

asymmetrical digital subscriber line 非対称デジタル加入者回線《略 ADSL》
ATL 現実全損 (actual total loss の略)
ATM 非同期転送モード (asynchronous transfer mode の略)
ATM 現金自動預け払い機，現金自動預入引出機 (automated teller machine の略で，automatic teller machine ともいう)
ATM charges ATM利用手数料（＝ATM fees）
ATM network ATMネットワーク
withdraw deposits via ATM ATM（現金自動預け払い機）を利用して預金を引き出す

▶Under the bank's monthly fixed-charge system, customers are able to make transactions at the bank's *ATMs* free of individual charges even outside the bank's office hours. 同行の月額固定料金制では，利用者は時間外でもATMの利用手数料が無料になる。

ATM card ATMカード，キャッシュ・カード (⇒**biometric identification function**)

▶The bank issues new *ATM cards* that also function as credit cards and electronic money. 同行は，クレジット・カードと電子マネーの機能を加えた新型キャッシュ・カードを発行している。

attach 動 取り付ける，貼付する，添付する，付属させる，所属させる
attached e-mail 添付したEメール
attached file 添付ファイル

▶Political organizations are required to *attach* receipts to their funds reports for every operating expense except personnel costs. 政治団体は，人件費を除くすべての経常経費について，政治資金収支報告書への領収書添付が求められている。

attachment 名 付属部品，付属文書，付属装置，連結装置，差押さえ，配属，出向，愛着，添付ファイル
attachment of a file to one's e-mail Eメールへのファイル添付
attachment of property 財産差押さえ
execution [service] of attachment 差押さえ執行
order of attachment 差押さえ命令

preservative attachment 債権保全
provisional [auxiliary] attachment 仮差押さえ
release from attachment 差押さえ解除

attitude 名 態度, 姿勢, 考え方, 通念, 意見, 主張, 判断, 外観, アティテュード
  attitude change 態度変容
  attitude control 姿勢制御
  attitude measurement 態度測定, 態度調査
  attitude survey 態度調査
  financial institutions' lending attitude 金融機関の貸出態度
  our company's longstanding attitude 当社の長年の姿勢
  risk neutral attitude リスク中立的態度
  risk seeking attitude リスク選好的態度
  social attitudes 社会通念
  "you" attitude 相手の身になって考える姿勢 [態度], 広告メッセージの制作態度, ユー・アティテュード
  youthful attitude 若年消費者の態度
  wait-and-see attitude 様子見

attorney 名 代理人, 弁護士, 弁理人, 法律家, 検事, 法務官
  associate attorney 副代理人
  attorney at law 弁護士
  attorney fee 弁護士費用, 弁護士報酬, 仲裁などの代理人費用 (＝attorney's fee)
  attorney in fact 代理人
  Attorney General 米国の司法長官, 英国の法務長官《略 AG》
  letter of attorney 委任状
  patent attorney 弁理士, 特許弁理士, 特許弁護士
  power of attorney (代理)委任状 (＝letter of attorney)
  tax attorney 税理士

attract 動 引きつける,〈顧客などを〉取り込む,〈資金などを〉集める, 興味を持つ [引く], 呼び寄せる, 誘引する, 誘致する
  attract companies 企業を誘致する
  attract customers 顧客を引きつける, 顧客を取り込む
  attract foreign capital 外国資本を誘致する, 外資を誘致する (＝attract foreign investment)
  attract industries 産業を誘致する
  attract investment 投資を促す
▶Reducing corporate tax is not rare as a measure to *attract* companies. 企業誘致の手段として, 法人税を引き下げるのは珍しくない。

attribute 動 …を原因とする, …に帰する
▶The recent high growth is *attributed* to growing capital spending for digital electric appliances and the rise in exports to Asian countries. 最近の高成長の要因は, デジタル家電の設備投資拡大とアジア向け輸出の伸びにある。
▶The major securities house *attributed* the poor earnings to sharp drops in brokerage fees and trading profits amid the extended slump in the domestic stock market. この大手証券会社は, 減益の要因として, 国内株式市場の長期低迷による株売買手数料と売買益の大幅減を挙げた。

attribute 名 属性, 特質, 特性, 表象, 象徴
  attribute discovery 属性の発見
  attribute measured 測定属性
  attribute of assortment 品揃え属性
  attribute preference 属性選択
  product attribute 製品特性

attrition 名 磨耗, 摩滅, 自然減, 人員漸減 (⇒deposit)
  natural attrition 自然減
  war of attrition 消耗戦, 持久戦

auction 名 競売, 競り売り, 公売, 入札, 公募入札, オークション (⇒online auction)
  30 year auction 30年物入札
  auction market 競売市場, 競争売買市場
  auction price 入札価格
  auction site オークション・サイト, 競売サイト (売り手が出品した物品を, 買い手が落札するホームページのこと。⇒auction items)
  competitive auction 競争入札
  e-auction eオークション
  Net auction ネット・オークション (＝Internet auction)
  open auction 公開競売
  reverse auction 逆オークション, リバース・オークション
▶Dealers are allowed to bid for Treasury bonds by a quarterly *auction*. ディーラーは, 四半期ごとの入札 [四半期入札] で米財務省証券への入札が認められている。

auction business オークション事業, オークション・ビジネス
▶NTT DoCoMo will take a 40 percent stake for about ¥4.2 billion in a new company to be set up by splitting off Rakuten's *auction business*. 楽天のネットオークション・ビジネスを分社化して設立される新会社に, NTTドコモは4割(約42億円)出資する。

auction items オークション出品物
▶Companies that operate auction sites and

collect charges from users should monitor *auction items* more thoroughly. オークション・サイトを運営して(落札時に)利用者から手数料を徴収する会社が，オークション(競売)に出品される品物を十分監視すべきだ．

auctioneer 名 競売人
audio 名 形 音声, 音, 録音, オーディオ
  audio auto-response system 音声自動応答システム
  audio book オーディオブック
  audio communications 音声通信
  audio performance 音声性能
  audio tape [audiotape] 録音テープ
  audio teleconferencing 音声会議, 電話会議
▶ Japan Telecom has been hard-hit by sluggishness in its core business of *audio* communications, due to the increase in the number of cell phones and broadband users. 日本テレコムは，携帯電話やブロードバンド(高速大容量通信)利用者の増加で，主力事業である音声通信事業の低迷に苦しんでいる．

audiographic conference 電話会議
audiographic teleconferencing service 音声画像会議通信サービス
audiovisual 形 視聴覚の, 音響・映像の《略 AV》
  audiovisual aids 視聴覚教材
  audiovisual communication products AVC(音響・映像・情報)機器
  audiovisual device 視聴覚機器, AV機器 (= audiovisual apparatus, audiovisual equipment)
  audiovisual equipment 音響・映像機器, 視聴覚機器, AV機器
  audiovisual technology AV技術
  audiovisual works 視聴覚著作物
▶ The development, manufacturing and distribution of the company's *audiovisual* communication products will be transferred to the tentatively named AVC Networks Co. 同社のAVC機器の開発・製造と販売が，AVCネットワークス社(仮称)に移管される．

audit 動 監査する, 会計検査する
▶ The auditing firm *audited* the accounts of failed companies Yamaichi Securities Co. and Yaohan Japan Corp. この監査法人は，経営破綻した山一証券やヤオハンジャパンの財務書類の監査を担当した．

audit 名 監査, 会計検査 (= auditing)
  accounting audit 会計監査
  audit certificate 監査証明, 監査証明書, 監査報告書
  audit opinion 監査意見
  audit procedure 監査手続き (= auditing procedure)
  audit year 監査年度
  book audit 帳簿監査
  external audit 外部監査
  final audit 期末監査
  interim audit 期中監査, 中間監査
  internal audit 内部監査
  operation audit 業務監査 (= operational audit)
  site audit 現場監査
  statutory audit 法定監査
▶ We plan and perform the *audit* to obtain reasonable assurance about whether the financial statements are free of material misstatements. 私どもは，監査を計画・実施して，財務書類に重大な虚偽記載がないかどうかについての合理的な確証を得ます．

audit firm 監査法人 (= audit corporation, auditing firm)
▶ The FSA gave an official warning to this *audit firm* under the Certified Public Accountants Law over negligence in its checking of the bank's accounts. 金融庁は，同行の財務書類の監査内容が不十分であったとして，公認会計士法に基づきこの監査法人に対して正式に戒告処分を出した．

auditing 名 監査, 会計監査
  auditing officer 監査役
  auditing report 監査報告書
  auditing services 監査業務 (= auditing business, auditing work; ⇒ **auditing contract**)
  auditing standards 監査基準 (= audit standards)
  auditing technique 監査技術
▶ *Auditing* is the practice of checking financial statements, such as balance sheets and income statements, confirming that annual securities reports have been properly written, and proving that those statements and reports are accurate. 監査とは，貸借対照表や損益計算書などの財務書類[財務諸表]をチェックし，年次有価証券報告書が適正に記載されていることを確認して，財務書類や有価証券報告書が正確であることを証明することを言う．

auditing company 監査法人 (= auditing firm)
▶ Listed companies are perplexed over one of the

country's biggest *auditing companies* being ordered to suspend business. 国内最大手の監査法人の一角が業務停止命令を受けるという事態に，上場企業各社は戸惑っている．

auditing contract 監査契約（＝audit engagement)
▸Once the auditing services are suspended, *auditing contracts* become void under the Corporate Law. 監査業務がいったん停止されると，会社法の規定で監査契約は無効になる．

auditing firm 監査法人（＝audit corporation, audit firm, auditing house, auditor:「監査法人」は，5人以上の公認会計士が共同で設立する法人）
▸Certified public accountants and *auditing firms* are responsible for preventing corporate managers from window-dressing business results. 公認会計士や監査法人には，企業経営者の粉飾決算を止めさせる責任がある．

auditor 名 監査人，監査役，監査法人，会計検査官，監査機関（⇒independent)
　auditor's certificate 監査証明書，監査報告書（＝auditor's report)
　auditor's [auditors'] report 監査報告，監査報告書（＝audit report, auditor's certificate, auditors' report)
　auditors' opinion 監査意見（＝audit opinion)
　certified internal auditor 公認内部監査人《略 CIA》
　external auditor 外部監査人
　outside auditor 社外監査人，社外監査役（＝nonexecutive internal auditor)
　primary auditor 持ち株会社の監査人，親会社の監査人
　shareholders' auditors 会計監査人
　statutory auditor 法定監査人，常勤監査役，監査役
　system auditor システム監査人
▸An independent *auditor* found problems with the way Time Warner accounted for a number of transactions. タイム・ワーナーの一部取引の会計処理方法に問題があることに，独立監査人が気づいた．
▸*Auditors* conduct unannounced site inspection after ISO certification each year. ISO（国際標準化機構）の認定後も，監査機関が毎年，予告なしの現場検査を実施します．

austere fiscal policy 緊縮財政政策，緊縮財政
▸The government needs to shift from an *austere fiscal policy* as soon as possible, in view of its issuance of no-interest-bearing, tax-exempt government bonds. 政府は，無利子非課税国債などの発行を視野に入れて，早急に緊縮財政から転換する必要がある．

austerity 名 耐乏生活，緊縮財政
　austerity budget 緊縮予算
　austerity drive [measures] 緊縮政策
　austerity policy 耐乏政策

authentication 名〈インターネットの〉利用者認証，認証，オーセンティケーション
　authentication number 認証番号
　authentication service 認証サービス
　entity authentication 個人認証
　user authentication system ユーザー認証システム
▸This bank requires users to provide special *authentication* numbers to transfer money. この銀行は，振込みの際に専用の認証番号の入力を利用者に義務付けている．

authorities 名 当局，その筋
　authorities concerned 関係当局，関係官庁，当該官庁，その筋
　customs authorities 税関当局
　financial authorities 金融当局
　government authorities 政府当局
　law enforcement authorities 警察当局
　legal authorities 法務当局
　local authorities 地方当局，地方自治体
　military authorities 軍当局
　monetary authorities 金融当局，通貨当局
　municipal authorities 市当局
　relevant authorities 関係機関，関係当局
　tax authorities 税務当局
　U.S. authorities 米政府当局
▸The Financial Stability Forum comprises financial *authorities* of major nations. 金融安定化フォーラムは，主要国の金融当局で構成されている．
▸The nation's tax *authorities* have no authority to tax foreign corporations whose core business is not conducted in this country. 主力事業を日本で行っていない外国法人に対しては，日本の税務当局に課税権はない．

authority 名 権限，権能，代理権，権力，権威，権威者，専門家，公共機関，当局，根拠，その筋，…筋，許可，先例
　authority and duties of officers 役員の権限と職責
　authority by ratification 追認による代理権限
　authority to pay 手形支払い授権書，支払い授

権書
authority to purchase 手形買取り授権書, 買取り授権書
decision-making authority 意思決定権
delegation of authority 権限委譲
express authority 明示の代理権限
full authority 全権限
implied authority 黙示の代理権限
local authority bond 地方債
regulatory authority 規制機関
statutory authority 法的権限
▸To assist it in carrying out its duties, the Board has delegated certain *authority* to several committees. 取締役会は，その職務遂行を補佐する機関として，複数の委員会に特定の権限を委譲しています。

authorization [**authorisation**] 名 承認, 承諾, 認可, 許可, 公認, 権限, 授権, 検定, 委任, 委任状
authorization code 承認番号
credit authorization network 信用照会ネットワーク
credit authorization terminal 信用照会端末装置, 加盟店端末機, クレジット専用端末《略 CAT》
credit card authorization クレジット・カードの認証
governmental authorization 政府の承認, 政府の認可
interim authorization 仮認可
legal authorization 法的裏付け
letter of authorization 授権書
prior authorization 事前の許可
written authorization 書面による権限付与, 授権書
▸Access to assets occurs only in accordance with management's *authorization*. 資産の取扱いは，かならず経営陣の承認に基づいて行われています。

authorize 動 権限を与える, 許可する, 認可する, 認定, 公認する, 検定する
authorized agent 指定代理人
authorized capitalization 授権株式総数
authorized dealer 認可業者
authorized distributor 指定販売店, 正規販売店
authorized foreign exchange bank 外国為替公認銀行
authorized merchant 加盟販売店
authorized minimum 必要最低資本額
authorized representative 授権された代表者, 権限のある代表者, 正当な代表者
authorized signatory 正当な署名人
authorized signature 権限のある者の署名, 署名
authorized source 権威筋
authorized capital 授権資本, 授権株式, 授権株式数, 公称資本, 株式発行可能枠（＝authorized capital stock, authorized share capital: 株式会社がその基本定款に基づいて株式発行により調達できる資本の限度額）
authorized shares [**stock**] 授権株式, 授権株式数
▸We have 100 million *authorized shares* of preferred stock at $1 par value. 当社には，額面1ドルの優先株式1億株の授権株式があります。

automate 動 自動化する, 省力化する, コンピュータ化する, オートメ化する, オートメーション化する
automated billing service system 自動料金請求処理システム
automated clearing house 自動手形交換機構, 自動決済機構
automated guided vehicle 無人搬送者
automated screen trading 証券の自動画面取引, 自動スクリーン取引
automated trading and order-matching system 自動取引・注文執行システム
automated trading system 自動取引システム, コンピュータ売買システム, 自動売買システム
automated teller machine 現金自動預け払い機《略 ATM》（＝automatic teller machine）
▸Cash withdrawals and deposits are made through *automated teller machines*. 現金の入出金は，現金自動預け払い機で行われている。

automatic 名 自動的な, 自動の, 自動式の, 自動装置の, 無意識の, 反射的な, オートマチック
automatic bank transfer 銀行自動振込み
automatic call distribution system 自動着信分配システム, コール自動配分《略 ACD》
automatic data processing 自動データ処理, 自動データ処理法《略 ADP》
automatic fund transfer 口座自動振替え, 自動引落し
automatic liquidation 自動決済
automatic operation 自動操作
automatic ordering 自動発注
automatic payment 自動引落し, 自動支払い
automatic reinvestment 自動再投資
automatic renewal 自動更新
automatic settlement 自動決済
automatic stay 自動停止, 自動的停止
automatic transfer service 自動振替サービス
automatic vending machine 自動販売機

automatic warehouse system 自動倉庫
automation 名 自動化, 省力化, 自動操作, オートメ化, 自動装置, 自動機械, ロボット, 〈コンピュータの〉抽象モデル, オートメーション
  business automation 事務処理の自動化・省力化, ビジネス・オートメーション《略 BA》
  corporate automation コーポレート・オートメーション《略 CA》
  credit automation system 自動与信システム, 自動審査システム (=automated credit decision system: 信用情報の入手から与信限度額の設定, 与信管理判断などを自動的に行うシステムやソフトウエア)
  design automation 設計自動化, デザイン・オートメーション《略 DA》
  factory automation 工場の自動化, ファクトリー・オートメーション《略 FA》
  home automation ホーム・オートメーション《略 HA》
  laboratory automation ラボラトリ・オートメーション《略 LA》
  marketing automation マーケティング・オートメーション《略 MA》
  mechanical automation 機械・加工の自動化《略 MA》
  office automation 事務機械化, 事務作業の機械化, 事務処理の自動化《略 OA》
  office automation design 事務処理自動化設計《略 OAD》
  process automation 生産工程の自動化・自動制御《略 PA》
  sales automation 販売の自動化, セールス・オートメーション《略 SA》
  sales force automation 営業支援システム, セールス・フォース・オートメーション《略 SFA》
  store automation 店舗の自動化《略 SA》

Automobile [Automotive] Recycling Law 自動車リサイクル法
▶The *Automobile Recycling Law* took effect in January 2005. 自動車リサイクル法は, 2005年1月から施行された。

availability 名 有効性, 効力, 利用可能度, 可用性, 可用度, 使用可能度, 提供可能性, 提供, 確保, 稼働率, アベイラビリティ
▶Linux will be unable to acquire a bigger market share than the Windows operating system due to limited *availability* of application software. リナックスは, 入手可能な応用ソフトが限られているため, マイクロソフトの基本ソフト(OS)「ウインドウズ」より高いシェアを確保できないだろう。

available 形 有効な, 利用可能な, 使用可能な, 処分可能な, 充当可能な, 入手可能な, 調達可能な, 配送可能な, 閲覧可能な
  available asset 利用可能資産
  available earned surplus 利用可能利益剰余金, 処分可能利益剰余金
  available for investment 投資に運用可能な
  available profit 処分可能利益
  available time 使用可能時間, 可用時間, 納品期間, 納期
  be commercially available 実用化される
  make available to …に提供する
  net assets available for plan benefits 年金給付債務に充当可能な純資産
  net income available for common stock 普通株主に帰属する当期利益
  profit available for dividend 配当可能利益
  publicly available 公然と入手できる
▶In the event the seller should have quantities of the products *available* for sale, the seller shall notify the purchaser of such quantities. 売り主が販売に提供できる本製品の余裕数量を持ち合わせている場合, 売り主は買い主に当該数量を通知するものとする。
▶The Annual Report on Form 10-K is *available* from the date of its filing with the Securities and Exchange Commission in the United States. 様式10-Kに基づく当社の年次報告書は, 米国の証券取引委員会(SEC)への提出日以降に入手できます。

average 動 …の平均をとる, …の平均値を出す, 平均して…になる, 相殺する, 合算する
  average down ナンピン(難平)買いする, (証券などを売買して)平均値を下げる
  average out 売り抜ける, 売買して逃げる, 利益ありまたは損失なしの結果で終わる
  average out to …に落ち着く, 平均して…になる
  average up ナンピン売りする, (証券などを売買して)平均値を上げる
▶Corporate profits will *average* out to positive growth. 企業収益は, 横ばいを脱して積極的な増加[プラス成長]に転じるだろう。
▶Under the new securities taxation system, gains and losses on stocks and investment trusts will be *averaged* before being taxed. 新証券税制では, 株式の損益[株式譲渡損益]と投信の損益[投資信託の償還・解約に伴う損益]を合算[相殺]して課税する。

average 名 平均, 海損, 形 平均の
  arithmetic average [mean] 算術平均
  arithmetic weighted average 加重平均

average common shares outstanding 発行済み普通株式の平均数, 発行済み普通株式の平均株式数

average number of listed stocks [shares] 平均上場株式数, 上場株式総数の平均(「平均上場株式数」は(期初の上場株式数＋期末の上場株式数)÷2で算出する)

average rate of profit 平均利益率

average rate of return 平均資本利益率

average remaining service period of employees 従業員の平均残存勤続[勤務]期間

average return on investment 平均投資収益率, 平均投資収益

average shares outstanding 期中平均発行済み株式総数

compound yield based on weighted average 加重平均利回り

moving average 移動平均

return on average equity 平均株主資本利益率

stock price average 平均株価

weighted average price 加重平均株価

weighted average share 加重平均株式数

▶The *average* market price of the company's common stock was $20 per share during 2008. 同社の普通株式の平均株価は, 2008年度は1株当り20ドルであった。

average daily balance 平均残高, 1日平均残高 (⇒CD)

▶The *average daily balance* of domestic bank lending grew 0.5 percent in January 2008 from a year before to ¥392.78 trillion. 国内銀行の2008年1月の貸出平均残高は, 前年同月比で0.5%増の392兆7,800億円となった。

average number of shares outstanding 期中平均発行済み株式数, 平均発行済み株式数[株式総数] (＝average shares outstanding)

▶For the nine months ended September 30, 2008, the *average number of shares outstanding* was 582.8 million. 2008年1-9月期の平均発行済み株式総数は, 5億8,280万株でした。

average return on capital 平均資本利益率

▶The *average return on capital* of Britain's businesses rose 26 basis points to 4.95 percent in this year's first quarter. 今年第1四半期の英国企業の平均資本利益率は, （前年同期比）0.26％増の4.95％だった。

award 動 与える, 授与する, 査定する, 裁定する

▶Supplier will pay all damages and costs *awarded* therein against Distributor or its customers. 供給者は, これについて裁定された損害賠償額と費用を全額, 販売店またはその顧客に支払う。

award 名 判断, 裁定, 仲裁判断, 仲裁裁定, 裁定額, 裁定金, 報奨金, 賞与, 昇給, 賞品, 賞金 (⇒ **arbitration**)

accept the arbitration award 仲裁裁定を受け入れる

arbitral award 仲裁判断, 仲裁裁定 (＝arbitration award)

award of attorney fess 弁護士報酬裁定額

award of subcontracts 下請契約の発注

award of the arbitrators 仲裁人の仲裁判断

bonus awards ボーナス支給額

cash awards 奨励金

contract awards 契約額

damage award 損害賠償裁定金

foreign arbitral awards 外国仲裁判断

stock award plan 株式報奨制度

▶The *award* of the arbitration shall be binding upon the parties. 仲裁判断は, 両当事者を法的に拘束するものとする。

ax [axe] 動 大ナタを振るう, 解雇する, 削減する, 廃止する

▶The company *axed* 30,000 jobs worldwide in a sweeping restructuring plan. 抜本的な再建策として, 同社は全世界の人員3万人を削減した。

ax [axe] 名 解雇, 首切り, 人員[経費]削減, 縮小

▶Surplus workers fell a victim to the *axe*. 過剰人員が, 人員削減の犠牲になった。

B / b

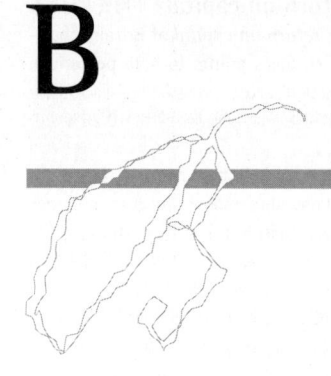

b 企業 (=business)
  b to b 企業対企業の取引［電子商取引］, 企業間, ビー・ツー・ビー (=B2B, business to business, business to business EC)
  b to b EC 企業対企業の電子商取引 (=b to b, B2B, business to business EC)
  b to c 企業対消費者の取引［電子商取引］, 消費者向け電子商取引, ビー・ツー・シー (=B2C, business to consumer, business to consumer EC)
  b to c EC 企業対消費者の取引［電子商取引］, 企業と一般顧客との取引 (=B2C, business to consumer EC)
  b to e 企業対従業員の取引［電子商取引］, ビー・ツー・イー (=B2E, business to employee, business to employee EC)
  b to e EC 企業対従業員の取引［電子商取引］ (=B2E, business to employee EC)
  b to g 企業対政府の取引［電子商取引］, 政府調達, ビー・ツー・ジー (=B2G, business to government, business to government EC)
B of E イングランド銀行 (⇒**Bank of England**)
B2B 企業対企業の取引, 企業対企業の電子商取引, 企業間の取引, 企業間, ビー・ツー・ビー (=b to b, business to business, business to business EC)
  B2B advertising ビー・ツー・ビー広告 (=B to B advertising: 広告主も広告の受け手も企業である広告活動)
  B2B e-commerce service 企業間eコマース・サービス, 企業間eビジネス・サービス
  ▸Internet-based commerce has been rapidly expanding both in terms of *B2B* and B2C transactions, covering a wide variety of merchandise, including books, compact discs and financial products. ネット取引は, 書籍やCD, 金融商品など広範な商品を対象に, 企業対企業の取引や企業対消費者の取引で急激に拡大している.
B2C 企業対消費者の取引［電子商取引］, ビー・ツー・シー (=b to c, business to consumer, business to consumer EC)
  B2C companies 企業対消費者間の取引をしている企業
B2E 企業対従業員の取引［電子商取引］, ビー・ツー・イー (=b to e, business to employee, business to employee EC)
B2G 政府調達, ビー・ツー・ジー (=b to g, business to government, business to government EC)
baby bond 小額債券
baby boomers ベビー・ブーマー, 団塊の世代
  ▸With their advanced technical skills, *baby boomers* have long been a driving force behind firms' research and development efforts. 高い技能を持つ団塊の世代は, 企業の研究開発の原動力［牽引役］となってきた.
baby busters ベビー・バスター世代（1960年代半ばの出生率急低下時代の人）
baby sharks retailing コバン鮫［コバンザメ］商法（集客力のある店のそばに出店して売上増を図る商法）
back 副 隠して, 抑えて, 滞って
back burner 後回し, 先送り, 二の次, 棚上げ状態, 保留
  ▸The current reconstruction plan was put on the *back burner*. 現在の再建計画は, 先送りされた.

back end 最終, 後端, 後端部, 終末処理, 後処理, バックエンド
 back-end cost バックエンド費用
 back-end load 解約手数料 (＝deferred sales charge, redemption charge)
 back-end processor 後処理装置, 後置き型処理装置, 後置プロセッサー, バックエンド・プロセッサー
 back-end promotion 抱き合わせ販売促進
 back-end right 最終権, バックエンド・ライト (乗っ取りの対象となった企業が, 株主の利益を守るために株主に付与する, 株式を現金・優先株や債券に転換する権利のこと)
▶The *back-end* costs for generating nuclear power refer to expenses that arise after the energy has been generated, including the cost of extracting plutonium from spent nuclear fuel. 原子力発電のバックエンド費用とは, 使用済み核燃料からプルトニウムを取り出す費用を含めて, 原子力発電を行った後に生じる費用のことだ。

back-in 名 バックイン (敵対的買収に対する防衛策の一つで, 株主に取締役会が定めた価格で持ち株を売り戻す権利を与えるもの)

back number 時代遅れのもの, 旧式のもの, 〈定期刊行物の〉旧号[既刊号], バック・ナンバー

back office 事務部門, 後方部門, 事務処理, ディーリング管理業務, バック・オフィス業務, バック・オフィス
 back-office operation バック・オフィス業務
 back-office procedures 事務処理手続き

back order 受注残
back pay [salary] 未払い給料
back room 裏舞台
back-to-back [back to back] 形 連続の, 続けざまの, 相次ぐ, 背中合わせの, 見返り信用状の
 back-to-back credit 同時発行信用状, 同時開設信用状, バック・ツー・バック信用状, 見返り信用状, バック・ツー・バック融資
 back-to-back loan 異通貨相互貸付け, バック・ツー・バック・ローン
▶Japan's industrial output climbed for a second straight month in June, the first *back-to-back* rise in two years. 日本の6月の鉱工業生産高は, 2か月連続で増加し, 2年ぶりに2か月連続の増加となった。

backbone 名 中軸, 主力, 中心的存在, 重要要素, 〈ネットワークの〉基幹回線 (backbone network), LAN接続ケーブル
 backbone cable 主線ケーブル
 backbone LAN バックボーンLAN
 backbone network 基幹ネットワーク, ネットワークの基幹回線
 backbone networking 基幹ネットワーク

backdate 動 遡って日付を入れる, 遡及して適用する

backdoor financing 裏口資金調達, 裏口金融

backdrop 名 背景, 事情
▶Against this *backdrop*, we reported a 4% increase in total revenues in 2008. これを受けて[こうした事情から], 2008年度の当社の総営業収益は4％の伸びを示しました。

-backed …が支持する, …が後押し[後援]する, …を裏付けとする, …を担保とする (⇒**asset-backed securities**)
 asset-backed preferred stock アセットバック優先株
 mortgage-backed securities モーゲージ担保証券, モーゲージ証券《略 MBS》
 retail receivables-backed lending 債権担保融資

backer 名 裏書人, 支持者, 保証人, 支援者
backfire 動 裏目に出る, 期待はずれに終わる, 思わぬ悪い結果を生む, 逆効果になる
▶The firm's makeover could *backfire* badly. 同社のイメージ・チェンジは, 大いに裏目に出る可能性がある。

background 名 背景, 背後事情, 遠因, 経歴, 学歴, 環境, 予備知識, バックグラウンド (⇒**baragaining power**)
 background and history of the company 会社の沿革と組織
 background briefing 背景説明
 background graphics 背景画像
 background of the invention 発明の背景
 background printing バックグラウンド印刷 (コンピュータで, ある仕事をしながら同時に印刷すること)
 background program バックグラウンド・プログラム (多重プログラミング・システムで優先順位が最も低いプログラム)

backing 名 支持, 後援, 援助, 保証, 裏書き, 後援者, 後援者団体
 backing activities 店舗後方活動
 backing sore 補助記憶装置
 backing up 両面印刷
 financial backing 経済援助
 strong asset backing 強力な資産基盤, 強力な資産の裏付け

backlist 名 既刊書目録, 在庫目録

backlog 名 未処理, 未処理部分, 残務,〈仕事の〉やり残し, 在庫, 残高, 受注残高(backlog figure), 注文残高, 手持ち注文, 予備貯蔵, 蓄積, 山積, 積み残した(ソフトウエア開発の)案件, バックログ (=backlogging)

backlog adjustment 遡及修正 (=catch-up adjustment)

backlog depreciation 遡及償却額, 取戻し償却額, バックログ償却 (=catch-up depreciation)

factory backlog 製造業の受注残高

order backlog 受注残高 (=backlog of unfilled orders)

▸The continuing global acceptance of our products and our record *backlog* indicate an improved second half of the year. 当社の製品が引き続きグローバル市場で受け入れられ, 受注残高も過去最高であることから, 下半期[下期]の業績は改善する見込みです。

backlogged money transfer 未処理の口座振替え, 口座振替未処理部分

▸The bank is trying to process about 500,000 *backlogged money transfers*. 同行は, 約50万件の口座振替未処理部分の処理作業を急いでいる。

backlogged transaction 未決済取引

backorder item 在庫のない商品, 在庫のない品

backup 名 複製, 予備, 代役, 代替, 代案, 別計画, 別方針, 支持, 後援者,〈金利などの〉上昇, バックアップ機能, バックアップ

backup copy バックアップ・コピー (不測の事態に備えて複製するデータやプログラムのこと)

backup file 複製したファイル (=backup copy)

backup funding 代替流動性, バックアップ資金

backup in long rates 長期債利回りの上昇

backup in U.S. rates 米国金利の上昇

yield backup 利回りの上昇 (=backup in yields)

bad debt 不良債権, 不良貸付け, 貸倒れ, 焦げ付き, 貸倒れ損失 (=bad loan, doubtful debt, nonperforming loan, uncollectible loan, unrecoverable loan:「不良債権」は, 銀行などが融資して回収困難となった貸出金のこと)

bad-debt clean-up charge 不良債権処理額

bad debt expense 貸倒れ費用, 貸倒れ損失, 貸倒償却

bad debt loss 貸倒れ損失

bad debt provision 貸倒れ引当金, 貸倒れ準備金 (=bad debt reserve)

bad debt recovery 償却債権の回収

bad debts written off 貸倒れ償却

▸The major financial and banking groups achieved the *bad-debt* reduction goals six months earlier than initially planned. 大手金融・銀行グループは, 当初の計画より半年早く不良債権削減の目標を達成した。

bad loan 不良債権, 不良貸付け, 不良貸出, 不良融資, 貸倒れ (=bad debt, nonperforming loan, uncollectible loan)

bad loan charges 不良債権処理額

bad loan costs 不良債権処理費用, 貸倒れ損失, 貸倒償却

bad loan disposal 不良債権処理 (=disposal of bad loans, disposal of nonperforming loans, writing off bad loans)

bad loan securitization 不良債権の証券化

bad loan write-offs 不良債権処理 (⇒**accounting period**)

losses from bad loan disposals 不良債権処理に伴う損失額

▸The accelerated disposal of *bad loans* will augment deflationary pressures on the economy. 不良債権処理の加速は, デフレ圧力を強める。

bad loan ratio 不良債権比率

▸Major banks were ordered to cut their *bad loan ratios* to less than 5 percent of all lending by next March. 大手銀行は, 来年3月までに不良債権比率を融資全体の5%以下に下げるよう行政命令を受けた。

bail 名 保釈, 保釈金, 動 保釈する, 委託する

bail bond 出廷等担保金証書

bailout 名 救済, 緊急援助, 金融支援, 債務棚上げ, 救済措置

▸We withdrew from a *bailout* of the company. 当社は, 同社への金融支援を打ち切りました。

balance 名 収支, 差額, 残高, 勘定残高, 残金, 残り, 貸借勘定, 帳尻, 不足額, 繰越金残存価額, 均衡, 釣り合い, 貸借勘定, バランス (⇒**cash balance**)

account balance 勘定残高口座残高

balance at beginning of year 期首残高 (=balance at the beginning of the period)

balance at end of year 期末残高 (=balance at the end of the period, balance at the term-end)

balance of payments 国際収支 (=balance of international payments, international balance of payments)

balance of supply and demand 需給バランス

balance sheet / **ban**

　（＝supply-demand balance）
bank balance 銀行残高, 銀行預金残高 （＝balance at the bank）
cash balance 現金残高, キャッシュ・バランス
certificate of bank balance 預金残高証明書
clearing balance 交換尻
clearing house balance 手形交換尻
credit balances 貸方残高, 預金残高
debt balance 融資残高
declining balance 定率法
financial balance 金融収支
fiscal balance 財政収支
invisible trade balance 貿易外収支
merchandise trade balance 貿易収支
outstanding balances 残存元本
overall balance of payments 総合収支 （＝overall balance）
service balance 貿易外収支
the beginning balance 期首残高
the closing balance 期末残高
total balance 総合収支
unpaid balance 未払い額

▶The consortium intends to raise funds to cover one-third of its development costs and expects the government will pay the *balance*. この共同事業体は、開発費の三分の一は独自に資金調達する方針で、残りは政府の支援を見込んでいる。

▶The worsening *balance* of supply and demand is mainly due to the surplus of production equipment. 需給バランス悪化の主因は、過剰設備である。

balance sheet 貸借対照表, 財務基盤, 財務体質, 財務内容, 財務状況, 財務状態, 財務, 資産, バランス・シート《略 BS, B/S》（＝position statement, statement of financial condition, statement of financial position；「貸借対照表」は、企業の一定時点（貸借対照表日）の総資産と負債、資本など企業の財政状態を示す財務表（計算書）で、損益計算書とともに財務書類［財務諸表］の中心をなす）
　balance sheet adjustment バランス・シート調整（収益力向上のため、企業が過剰な設備や雇用の調整を進めること）
　balance sheet date 貸借対照表日, 決算日 （＝closing date；⇒monetary assets）
　balance sheet growth 資産の増加
　balance sheet management 財務管理, バランス・シート管理
　balance sheet ratio 財務指標, 貸借対照表比率
　consolidated balance sheet 連結貸借対照表
constant dollar balance sheet 恒常ドル貸借対照表
damaged balance sheet 資産の質の悪化
improve one's balance sheet 財務体質を改善する, 資金ポジションを改善させる
post-balance sheet date 決算日後
post-balance sheet event 後発事象
preparation of balance sheet 貸借対照表の作成
strengthen one's balance sheet 財務体質を強化する
strong balance sheet 健全な財務内容, 健全な財務状態
trim the balance sheet 資産を減らす

▶We first figure out what our *balance sheet* would look like if we had always used the new accounting methods. 新会計処理方法を常時採用した場合、私どもはまず貸借対照表がどのような影響を受けるかを考えます。

balance sheet items 貸借対照表の項目
▶All *balance sheet items* are translated at exchange rates at the respective year-ends of foreign subsidiaries. 貸借対照表の項目は、すべて各外国子会社の期末の為替レートで換算されています。

balanced scorecard バランスト・スコアカード（財務会計的な項目のほかに、顧客満足度や業務プロセスなどの非財務的な項目を数値化して評価する業績評価法）

ballot 名 新株割当て抽選

ban 動 禁止する, 停止する （⇒bankcard, banned ingredient）
▶Japan *banned* U.S. beef imports immediately after the first case of BSE was reported in the United States. 米国で初の狂牛病（BSE）発生例が公表された直後に、日本は米国産牛肉の輸入を禁止した。

ban 名 禁止, 停止, 廃絶, 禁止令
　ban on imports 輸入停止, 輸入禁止 （＝import ban）
　blanket ban 全面禁止
　lift the ban on …を解禁する, …の禁止を解除する, …の規制を解除する
　put a ban on …を禁止する （＝impose a ban on, place a ban on）

▶The company considered switching purchases of chicken from Thailand to China following the *ban* on imports of Thai chicken. 同社は、タイ産鶏肉の輸入停止で、鶏肉の調達先をタイから中国に切り替えることを検討した。

bank 名 銀行，バンク （⇒**Internet bank, Net bank**）
agent bank 幹事銀行
bank card 銀行発行のクレジット・カード，バンク・カード （=bankcard: キャッシュ・カードと同義）
bank charge 銀行手数料，銀行諸費用
bank credit 銀行借入れ，銀行貸出，銀行融資，銀行当座貸し，銀行信用，銀行信用状
Bank for International Settlements 国際決済銀行《略 BIS》（⇒**capital adequacy ratio, minimum**）
bank interest 銀行利子
bank loan [loans] payable 銀行借入金
Bank of Japan 日本銀行，日銀《略 BOJ》
bank prime rate 銀行プライム・レート（一流企業に対する最優遇貸出金利）
bank rate 公定歩合，銀行利率，金利 （=official discount rate: 中央銀行が定める貸出金の基準金利）
bank refinancing 銀行融資の借換え
bank service fee 銀行手数料 （⇒**discount**）
bank stock prices 銀行株価
bank stocks 銀行株
bank transfer 銀行振替え，口座振替え，銀行間振替え，銀行送金，銀行決済，銀行振込み （=credit transfer）
commercial bank 商業銀行，民間銀行，都市銀行，都銀
core bank 主力取引銀行
custodian bank 保管銀行，カストディ銀行
financially healthy bank 健全行
funding bank 貸出銀行，貸出行
leading banks 大手銀行 （=major banks）
main bank 主要取引銀行，主力取引銀行，主力銀行，メインバンク
merchant bank マーチャント・バンク，引受銀行
mortgage bank 住宅金融会社
national bank 国法銀行(米国)，国立銀行，全国銀行
nonbank ノンバンク （=nonbank financial institution: 銀行以外の金融機関）
one bank policy 一行取引主義
prime bank 一流銀行，有力銀行
retail bank リテール・バンク
state bank 州法銀行(米国)，国営銀行
top banks 上位行，上位銀行
trust bank 信託銀行
wholesale bank 法人向けの銀行
▶Several major banks have recently received upgraded ratings. 大手銀行数行の格付けが最近，上方修正されている。

bank account 銀行口座，銀行預金口座，銀行勘定，預金
▶*Bank accounts* are bought and sold on the Internet. 銀行口座が，インターネット上で売買されている。

bank agent system 銀行代理店制度 （= **banking agent system**）
▶A *bank agent system* obliges business corporations acting as bank agents to offer time-consuming and costly staff training programs. 銀行代理店制度では，代理店になる事業会社は，人材育成にかなりの手間とコストをかけなければならない。

bank holiday 銀行休日，銀行休業日，法定休日，〈英国の〉祝祭日
▶Fearing a massive run, a *bank holiday* was declared for Friday. 大規模な取付け騒ぎを恐れて，金曜日を銀行休日にする宣言がなされた。

bank lending 銀行貸出，銀行融資 （=bank accommodation, bank advance, bank credit, bank loan）
▶The average daily balance of domestic *bank lending* expanded 1.8 percent to ¥390.95 trillion in January from a year earlier. 国内銀行(民間銀行)の1月の貸出平均残高は，前年同月比1.8%増の390兆9,500億円となった。

bank line of credit 銀行与信枠，銀行信用枠，銀行与信限度額，銀行借入れ枠，利用限度額 （= **bank line**）
▶At December 31, 2008, we had available unused *bank lines of credit* with a number of U.S. and non-U.S. banks permitting borrowings up to an aggregate of $4,000 million. 2008年12月31日現在，当社が米国内および米国外の多数の銀行から与えられた銀行借入限度枠の未使用分は，総額で40億ドルでした。

bank loan 銀行貸付け，銀行融資，銀行貸付け金，銀行借入れ，銀行借入金，銀行間借款，銀行ローン，バンク・ローン （=bank lending）
▶Germany's financial sector used to rely on *bank loan*-centered indirect financing. ドイツの金融業界は，以前は銀行融資中心の間接金融に頼っていた。

Bank of England 〈英中央銀行の〉イングランド銀行《略 BOE》
▶The *Bank of England* lowered its key interest rate to 5.25 percent from 5.5 percent. 英中央銀行のイングランド銀行(BOE)は，政策金利を現

行の年5.5%から5.25%に引き下げた。

bankcard 名 預金通帳, 銀行通帳
▸The revised law bans the sale or transfer of bankbooks and *bankcards* without a legitimate reason. この改正法(改正本人確認法)は, 正当な理由がなく預金通帳とキャッシュ・カードを売買, 譲渡することを禁じている。

banking 銀行業, 銀行業務, 金融, 預金, バンキング
- **Banking Act of 1987** 1987年銀行法
- **banking crisis** 金融危機, 銀行の経営危機
- **Banking industry** 銀行業, 銀行業界 (＝banking sector, banking world)
- **banking operations** 銀行業務, 資金運用
- **banking services** 銀行業務, 銀行サービス, 決済サービス
- **commercial banking** 商業銀行業務 (＝commercial banking services)
- **Competitive Equality Banking Act of 1987** 1987年公正競争銀行法, 1987年競争的公正銀行法
- **consumer banking** 消費者金融業務
- **core banking business** 本業の銀行業務
- **corporate banking** 企業向け銀行業務
- **correspondent banking** コルレス銀行
- **electronic banking** エレクトロニック・バンキング
- **Federal Banking Commission** 連邦銀行委員会
- **firm banking** ファーム・バンキング (銀行のコンピュータと企業のコンピュータを通信回線を介して接続して, 銀行振込み・口座振替えや情報を提供するシステム)
- **home banking** ホーム・バンキング
- **international banking** 国際銀行業務
- **Internet banking** インターネット・バンキング (＝Net banking)
- **interstate banking** 州際銀行業務
- **investment banking** 投資銀行業務
- **mortgage banking** 不動産担保銀行業務, 不動産担保金融業務, 不動産担保貸付け
- **mortgage banking services** 不動産担保金融業務
- **offshore banking** オフショア金融
- **online banking** オンライン・バンキング
- **online branch banking** オンライン支店銀行業務
- **private banking** プライベート・バンキング(個人資産を管理・運用する銀行業務)
- **remote banking** リモート・バンキング(通信手段による銀行業務)
- **retail banking** 小売銀行業務, リテール銀行業務, 小口金融, リテール・バンキング
- **Senate Banking Committee** 米上院銀行委員会
- **telephone banking** テレホン・バンキング
- **TV banking** テレビ・バンキング
- **twenty-four-hour banking** 24時間銀行業務体制
- **unit banking** 単一銀行, 単独銀行
- **unit banking system** 支店を持たない単一銀行制度
- **universal banking** 総合銀行業, ユニバーサル・バンキング (銀行業務と証券業務の併営)
- **wholesale banking** 卸売銀行業務, ホールセール銀行業務, 大口金融

banking business 銀行業務, 金融業, 金融業務 (＝banking activities, banking operations, banking services)
▸The UFJ financial group transferred the corporate *banking business* of UFJ Trust to UFJ Bank. UFJ金融グループは, UFJ信託の企業向け信託業務をUFJ銀行に移管した。

banking group 銀行グループ, 金融グループ, 銀行・金融グループ
▸Many of the *banking groups* will have to use a portion of their legally required reserves to pay their shareholders' dividends. 銀行グループの多くは今後, 株主配当の原資に充てるため, 法定準備金の一部の取り崩しを迫られることになる。

bankrupt 形 破産した, 倒産した, 経営破綻した, 破綻した, 支払い不能の, 名 破産者, 破綻者, 破産宣告を受けた者, 債務支払い不能者
- **be declared bankrupt** 破産宣告を受ける
- **be nearly bankrupt** 倒産寸前
- **go bankrupt** 破産する, 倒産する, 破綻する (＝go under)

▸An increasing number of publishing houses have declared themselves *bankrupt* in the past few years. ここ2, 3年, 自己破産を宣告する出版社が増えている。
▸The company was officially declared *bankrupt* by the Tokyo District Court. 同社は, 東京地裁から正式に破産宣告を受けた。

bankruptcy 名 倒産, 破産, 経営破綻, 破産手続き (＝business failure, insolvency; ⇒ corporate bankruptcy)
- **act of bankruptcy** 破産行為
- **adjudication of bankruptcy** 破産宣告 (＝declaration of bankruptcy)
- **bankruptcy filing** 破産申請
- **bankruptcy petition** 破産申立て (＝filing for bankruptcy, petition of [in] bankruptcy)

bankruptcy procedure 破産手続き (⇒Bankruptcy Law)
Bankruptcy Reform Act of 1978 1978年米連邦改正破産法, 1978年改正破産法
chain-reaction bankruptcy 連鎖倒産 (=chain bankruptcy)
involuntary bankruptcy 強制破産
large-scale bankruptcies 大型倒産
trustee in bankruptcy 破産管財人
US Bankruptcy Code 米国破産法
voluntary bankruptcy 自己破産, 任意破産
▶The number of large-scale *bankruptcies* with debts exceeding ¥1 billion surged 50 percent to 81 in January 2008. 債務額が10億円を超える大型倒産の件数は, 2008年1月に(前年同月比)50%増の81件となった。
▶U.S. subprime mortgage lender New Century Financial filed for *bankruptcy* protection. 米住宅ローン会社のニューセンチュリー・フィナンシャルが, 会社更生手続きの適用を申請した。

Bankruptcy Law 破産法
▶The new *Bankruptcy Law* is aimed at simplifying and quickening bankruptcy procedures. 新「破産法」のねらいは, 破産手続きの簡素化と迅速化にある。

bankruptcy proceedings 破産手続き (=bankruptcy procedures; ⇒Bankruptcy Law)
▶MTS Inc., the parent company of Tower Records, will sell itself through *bankruptcy proceedings*. タワーレコード(米CD・レコード販売大手)の親会社のMTSが, 破産手続きをして身売りすることになった。

banned ingredient 無認可添加物 (=illegal ingredient)
▶The use of *banned ingredients* in a flavoring agent is forcing more than 30 domestic food manufacturers to recall products they had exported. 香料の原料に無認可の添加物を使用していたため, 国内食品メーカーの30社以上が, 輸出した商品の回収を迫られている。

bar code バーコード (光学式走査機で商品を識別する縞状の記号)
bar code reader バーコード読取り装置, バーコード・リーダー

bare 動 露出する, 暴露する, さらけだす, 発表する, 公表する
bare A [lay A bare A] Aを暴露する, Aを公にする, Aを明らかにする, Aを打ち明ける
bare one's feelings 感情をさらけだす
bare one's heart 心中を打ち明ける
bare one's soul 告白する, 心情を吐露する
bare restructuring plan [package] リストラ[経営再建, 事業再編, 人員整理]計画を発表する

bare 形 裸の, むきだしの, 素手の, ありのまま, 赤裸々, 公然の, 空(から)の, 最も基本的な, ほんの, 単なる, 〈賠償の〉保険をかけていない
a bare boat [bareboat] charter 裸用船
a bare boat charter hire purchase agreement 裸用船分割購入計画
a bare desire 露骨な要求, 露骨な欲望
a bare majority ぎりぎりの過半数, かろうじて過半数
a bare possibility ごくわずかな可能性
at the bare thought of …と考えただけでも
bare accounts ありのままの説明
be bare of credit 信用がない
go bare 賠償保険なしで営業する, 無保険で営業する
the bare [barest] minimum 最低限の量
the bare [barest] necessities 最低限必要なもの
the bare bones 要点, 骨子
the bare facts 単なる事実

bargain 動 契約する, 契約で取り決める, 取引する, 交渉する
▶We have no intention of sitting down and *bargaining* again. われわれは, 再び席に着いて交渉するつもりはない。

bargain 名 取引, 交渉, 協議, 取引契約, 売買契約, 契約, 協定, 取決め, 特価品, 格安品, 掘り出し物, バーゲン
at a good bargain 格安の値段で
bargain basement [counter] 値引商品特設売場, 特売場, 特価品売場
bargain buying 押し目買い
bargain hunter 割安株ねらいの投資家, 特売品を買いあさる人
bargain-hunting 安値拾い
bargain sale 特売, バーゲン・セール
drive a hard bargain 有利に交渉を進める, 有利な取引契約を結ぶ
forward bargain 先物取引, 先渡し取引
strike a bargain with …と契約[協定]を結ぶ (=make a bargain with)
▶Consumers are looking for *bargains* even if the economy is improving. 景気が回復しているものの, 消費者は格安品を求めている。

bargain-basement price 格安価格, 安い価格, 安値
▶Acceptance of orders at *bargain-basement prices* just to maintain sales results has become

chronic amid intensified competition. 過当競争のなかで，単に売上高確保のための安値受注が，日常化している。

bargaining 名 交渉, 取引, 労使の契約, 団体交渉
　bargaining cost 契約費用
　bargaining leverage 交渉力
　bargaining partner 交渉相手
　bargaining representative 交渉代表 (=bargaining agent)
　bargaining rights 団体交渉権, 交渉権
　bargaining table 交渉のテーブル
　bargaining unit 交渉単位
　collective bargaining 団体交渉
　have a bargaining session with …と交渉する
　industry-wide bargaining 産業別交渉

bargaining chip 交渉の切り札, 取引の切り札, 有利な取引材料
▶Such brinkmanship diplomacy, with North Korea using its nuclear development program as a *bargaining chip*, will simply deepen its isolation. 核開発計画を交渉の切り札に使う北朝鮮のこのような瀬戸際外交は，北朝鮮の一層の孤立化を招くだけだ。

bargaining power 交渉力, 購買取引力
▶In the background of the global steel industry's consolidation is the intention of steelmakers to enhance their *bargaining power* against both upstream and downstream industries by increasing their size. 世界的な鉄鋼業界の再編成の背景には，巨大化で川上・川下産業［上・下流部門］との交渉力を強めたい，という鉄鋼メーカーの思惑が働いている。

barometer stock 基準株

barrel 名 バレル(石油の単位：米国では42ガロンで159リットル, 英国では42ガロンで191リットル), 政治資金
▶OPEC will carry out a plan to slash 1.5 million *barrels* a day from its daily crude production in an effort to firm up sagging oil prices. 石油輸出国機構(OPEC)は，原油価格の下落に歯止めをかけるため，1日の原油生産枠から日量150万バレル削減する計画を実施する。

barrel per day 日量…バレル, 日産…バレル《略 bpd》
▶The OPEC has agreed an oil output cut of 500,000 *barrels per day*. 石油輸出国機構(OPEC)は，日量50万バレルの原油生産削減に合意した。

barrier 名 障害, 障壁, 壁, 制約, 問題, バリア

barriers to entry 参入障壁
foreign trade barriers 外国貿易障壁
import barriers 輸入障壁
investment barriers 投資障壁
market barriers 市場障壁, 市場への参入障壁
nontariff barriers 非関税障壁
psychological barrier 心理的な壁
regulatory barriers 規制上の障壁, 規制上の障害
tariff barrier 関税障壁
trade barriers 貿易障壁
▶The Japanese economy continues to underperform largely as a result of structural rigidities, excessive regulation and market *barriers*. 日本経済が低迷を続けているのは，構造的硬直性や過剰規制, 市場への参入障壁が大きい。

barter 動 交換する, 物々交換する, 提供する
barter 名 物々交換, バーター
　barter agreement バーター協定
　barter arrangement バーター取引(barter transaction), バーター協定(barter agreement)
　barter change 物々交換 (=exchange and barter)
　barter economy 物々交換経済, 現物交易経済
　barter effect 実物効果
　barter joint 石油会社間の製品相互融通, バーター・ジョイント
　barter syndication バーター企業連合組織, バーター・シンジケーション
　barter system 物々交換制, 交換貿易制, バーター方式, バーター制
　barter terms of trade 交易条件(terms of trade), バーター交易条件
　barter trade バーター貿易

base 動 拠点を置く, …を拠点とする, 根拠を置く, …を根拠に据える, …をベースにする
　be based in [at] …に拠点[本部・本店・本社]を置く, …を拠点とする, …を活動の基盤とする
　be based on [upon] …に基づく, …に基づいて算出[算定]される, …を根拠に置く, …に基づいて構築する
▶Earnings per share for the third quarter were *based* on 305 million average common shares outstanding. 第3四半期の1株当たり純利益は，発行済み普通株式の平均株式数3億500万株に基づいて計算されています。

base 名 基準, 基本, 基礎, 基盤, 拠点, 基地, ベース (⇒asset base, capital base, customer base, revenue base)
　at the parent base 単独ベースで
　base case 規範事例

base lending rate 基準貸出金利
base of taxation 課税標準
base period 基準期間, 基準時, 基準年次
base rate 基本料金, 基準金利, 基準貸出金利, 基準利率, 最低貸出利率, 基本給, 基礎賃金
base rate cuts in corporate taxes 法人税の基本税率引下げ
base stock inventory valuation 基準棚卸し法, 正常在り高[有り高]法, 基礎在り高法 (= base stock inventory, base stock method)
base year 基準年, 基準年度, 基準年次
business base 営業基盤, 経営基盤
capital base 資本基盤
core deposit base コア預金基盤, 中核となる預金基盤
data base データベース, 基礎資料, 基本資料
earnings base 収益基盤
equity base 株主資本基盤
export base 輸出基盤, 輸出拠点
funding base 資金調達源
industrial base 産業基盤, 工業基盤
investor base 投資家基盤, 投資家層
liabilities base 債務の範囲
manufacturing base 生産拠点 (= production base)
production base 生産拠点
tax base 課税基準, 課税標準, 税収基盤
▸Domestic airports serve as *bases* for this nation's air traffic and commodity distribution. 国内空港は, 日本の交通[航空機の発着]と物流の拠点としての役割を担っている。
▸The firm tries to swiftly establish a *base* for further growth. 同社は, 新たな成長の基盤づくりを急ごうとしている。
base money ベースマネー, 基礎貨幣 (= monetary base: 「ベースマネー」は, 通貨供給の量を量るのに用いられる指標で, 現金と金融機関が中央銀行に預けている準備預金の合計)
▸*Base money* refers to the total of cash and reserves that financial institutions deposit in the central bank. 「ベースマネー」とは, 現金と金融機関の中央銀行預金の合計をいう。
base pay 基本給 (= base salary, basic pay)
▸The special *base pay* increase system is applied to employees with outstanding work records. この(公務員の)特別昇給制度[退職時特別昇給制度]は, 勤務成績が特に良好な職員に適用される。
base station 基地局, ベース・ステーション
▸Depending on the place, LAN radio waves can reach as much as 100 meters from the LAN *base station*. 場所によっては, LAN（構内情報通信網）の電波はLAN基地局から100メートルほども届く。

-based [based] …を(営業)基盤とする, …を基軸とする, …基準の, …に本部[本社, 本店]を置く, …駐在の, …型の, …をベースにした, …に基づく, …主義の, …建ての, …密着型の (⇒ community-based, Internet-based banking venture, performance-based)
ability-based classification system of public servants 公務員の能力等級制
broad-based stock index 総合株価指数
broader-based TOPIX index 全体の指数を示す東証株価指数(TOPIX)
cost-based pricing 原価に基づく価格決定
credit-based financial institutions 貸出を基本業務とする金融機関
customer-based 顧客基盤の
dollar-based costs ドル建てのコスト
dollar-based investor ドル・ベースの投資家
IC-based card ICカード (= IC card)
Internet-based commerce ネット商取引, ネット取引 (= e-business, e-commerce, electronic commerce, Internet commerce)
market-based 市場に基づく, 市場原理に基づく
merit- and achievement-based system 能力・実績主義
merit-based pay plan 業績連動[業績連動型の]報酬制度, 成果主義型の報酬制度[賃金制度]
narrow-based stock index 業種別株価指数
risk-based capital リスク基準の自己資本, リスク・ベースの自己資本
strategy-based approach 戦略ベースのアプローチ
technology-based company ハイテク関連企業
yuan-based bond 人民元建て債
zero-based budget ゼロ・ベース予算
▸U.S.-*based* Wal-Mart Stores Inc. suggested a merger with Daiei and Seiyu to create a unified brand in the future. 米ウォルマート・ストアーズは, ダイエーと西友を経営統合して, 将来は統一ブランドに一本化する案を示した。

basic 形 基本的な, 基本の, 基礎的な, 初歩的な, 重要な, 簡素な, 必要最小限の, ベーシック
basic balance of payments 基礎収支
basic deduction 基礎控除
basic element 重要な要素
basic guarantee 根(ね)保証 (= initial guarantee)
basic human needs 基本的人間ニーズ《略

BHN》
basic industry　基礎的産業, 基幹産業
basic item　定番商品, ベーシック商品（常時, 品揃えしている商品）
basic material industry　素材産業
basic net earnings per common share　基本的普通株式1株当たり純利益
basic pay hike　ベア, ベースアップ　（=basic pay increase, basic salary hike）
basic pension　基礎年金
basic profit　基礎利益　（=fundamental profit）
basic technology　基礎技術
basic agreement　基本的合意, 基本合意, 大筋合意, 基本合意書, 基本契約, 基本契約書
　conclude a basic agreement　基本契約を結ぶ, 基本契約を締結する
　reach a basic agreement　基本合意に達する, 基本合意する
　▸The three companies reached a *basic agreement* to sell a 25 percent stake in Sakhalin Energy to Gazprom in July 2005.　3社は, 2005年7月に, ガスプロムにサハリン・エナジー社の株式の25％を譲渡することで基本合意していた。
basic fund　基金（保険会社の資本金に相当）
　▸*Basic fund* is equivalent to the capital of a joint-stock company.　基金は, 株式会社の資本金に当たる。
basic material　原材料, 素材
　▸Factors that could damage corporate performance are creeping up on industrial firms, including higher prices of oil and *basic materials* and increasingly intense end-product price competition.　石油や原材料の値上がり, 最終製品の価格競争など, 企業の業績を悪化させる要因が製造業に忍び寄っている。
basis　名　方針, 基準, 根本原理, 主義, 方式, 基礎, 根拠, 論拠, 土台, 主成分, ベース　（⇒**consolidated basis**）
　accrued basis　発生主義, 発生基準
　basis of consolidation　連結方針, 連結の基準
　basis of recognition　認識基準
　constant dollar basis　実質ベース, 恒常ドル基準
　cost basis　原価主義
　customs basis　通関ベース
　delivery basis　出荷基準
　denominated basis　ドル表示で
　equity basis　持ち分法
　first-in, first-out basis　先入れ先出し法
　full cost basis　全部原価法
　fully diluted basis　完全希薄化法
　historical cost basis　取得原価法
　lower of cost or market basis　低価法, 低価主義, 低価基準
　market price [value] basis　時価主義
　on a consolidated basis　連結ベースで, 一括して
　on a dollar denominated basis　ドル表示で
　on a full year basis　通年で, 通期で
　on a group basis　連結ベースで　（=on a consolidated basis）
　on a moment-to-moment basis　瞬間瞬間ベースで
　on a monthly basis　単月で
　on a nominal basis　名目で
　on a preliminary basis　暫定段階で
　on a same-store basis　既存店ベースで
　on a seasonally adjusted basis　季節調整済みで
　on an all-store basis　全店舗ベースで
　on an annualized basis　年率換算で, 年換算で
　on an optional basis　選択制で
　on the basis of IMF formula　IMF方式で
　parent-basis earnings outlook　単独ベースの収益見通し
　production basis　生産基準
　profitable basis　収益基盤
　settlement date basis　決済日ベース
　straight line basis　定額法
　tax basis　課税標準, 税法基準　（=tax base）
　▸The efforts of our employees are the *basis* for the success we will achieve in the years to come.　当社従業員の努力こそ, 今後の当社発展を支える礎です。
　▸Toyota became Japan's first manufacturer to post sales of more than ¥10 trillion on a half-year *basis*.　売上高が半期ベースで10兆円を突破したのは, 日本企業でトヨタが初めてだ。
basis point　ベーシス・ポイント《略 **b.p.**》（為替・金利変動の基準単位で, 1ベーシス・ポイント=0.01％, 100ベーシス・ポイント=1％。⇒**average return on capital, percentage point**）
　▸Spending on research and development dipped by 10 *basis points*.　研究開発費は, 10ベーシス・ポイント(0.1％)減少しました。
b/e　為替手形　（**bill of exchange**の略）
bear　名　弱気筋, 売り方, 軟派, 形　下向きの, 下がり気味の, 弱気の
　bear bond　ベア・ボンド　（償還時の債券利回りが最初に決めた水準より高い場合に償還元本が増加する債券）

bear covering 買戻し
bear hug ベア・ハッグ（条件のよい株式公開買付けなどの買収提案）
bear interests 弱気筋, 売り方, 軟派
bear market 弱気市場, 弱気相場, 下げ相場, 売り相場（＝bearish market）
bear operator 軟派仕手
bear position 売り持ち, 投機的売り持ち, 空売り, ベア・ポジション（＝short position）
bear raid 売り崩し, 売りたたき（＝bear raiding）
bear seller 弱気筋
bear speculation 投機売り
bear spread ベア・スプレッド（価格が下がれば利益が得られる組合せのオプション取引）
bear squeeze 踏み上げ, 踏み上げ相場（＝bear panic:「踏み上げ」は踏みによる値上がりのことで,「踏み」は信用取引で売った人が, その後相場が上がったため, 損を覚悟で買い戻すこと）
bears over 売り方過多
bearer 名 運搬人, 所持人, 持参人, 形 無記名方式の
bearish 形 弱気の, 弱気含みの, 下落気味の, 下がり気味の, 見通しが暗い, 悲観的な見方の, 全面安の展開, 売り優勢の展開
　be bearish on the economy 景気の見方が悲観的, 景気の先行きを悲観的に見る
　bearish factor 弱気材料, 弱材料, 売り材料, 安材料, 軟化材料
　bearish flurry 気崩れ
　bearish market 下げ相場, 売り相場, 落勢
　bearish mood 先行き不安, 全面安の展開, 弱気の地（じ）合い, 弱気ムード
　bearish outlook 弱気見通し, 弱気な見方
　bearish overtone 悪材料
　bearish sentiment 弱気の地（じ）合い, 売り人気, 弱気（＝bearish market condition, bearish mood）
　bearish stock market 株価低迷, 株価低迷局面
　bearish tone 弱気ムード, 弱含み基調, 安気配, 弱気, 気崩れ
　turn bearish 弱気に転じる
▸A *bearish* mood enveloped the Tokyo market Tuesday from the start of the day's trading.　火曜日の東京市場[東京株式市場]は取引開始から全面安の展開となった。
▸Market players turned *bearish*.　市場関係者は, 弱気に転じた。
beef up 強化する, 増強する, 補強する, 拡充する, 向上させる, 食肉処理する（＝strengthen）
▸We will *beef up* overseas production capacity.　当社は, 海外での生産能力を強化[拡充]する方針です。
beef-up 名 強化, 増強, 補強, 食肉処理
▸The *beef-up* of the early warning system is expected to enable insurers to make decision on the decrease of guaranteed yields before the companies fail.　早期警戒制度の強化で, 生保は破綻前に予定利率引下げを決断できるようになる。
before 前 …前, …考慮前, …差引き前, …控除前（⇒income before income taxes）
　before cumulative effect of accounting change 会計処理変更に伴う累積的影響額考慮前, 会計処理変更の累積効果控除前
　before extraordinary items 異常項目前
　before interest and taxes 利子・税金控除前
　income before income taxes 税引き前利益, 税引き前当期利益, 法人税控除前利益
　income before minority interests 少数株主持ち分控除前利益
　income before provisions 引当金繰入れ前利益, 引当金前の利益
　income before taxes 税引き前利益
▸The U.S. and foreign components of income *before* income taxes and the provision for income taxes are presented in this table.　この表に示すのは, 米国と外国の税引き前利益と法人税繰入れ額の内訳です。
behavior 名 行動, 行為, 動向, 動き, 変動
　behavior of inflation インフレ動向
　business behavior 企業行動
　buying behavior 購買行動
　consumer behavior 消費者行動, 消費者動向（＝consumer's behavior）
　economic behavior 経済行為, 経済行動, 相場の動き
　interest rate behavior 金利動向
　market behavior 市場行動, 市場動向, 市場の動き
　price behavior 価格動向, 物価動向
behind-the-scenes 形 舞台裏の, 秘密裏の, 水面下の
　behind-the-scenes involvement 不明朗な関与, 舞台裏の関与
　behind-the-scenes negotiations 舞台裏での交渉
　behind-the-scenes preparatory sessions 水面下の事前折衝
▸All the *behind-the-scenes* preparatory sessions were held in total secrecy.　水面下の事前折衝は,

すべて外に漏れることなく進められた。

beige book 米地区連銀経済［景況］報告書，ベージュ・ブック（＝tan book）

Beijing 名 中国，中国政府，北京

bellwether 〈市場動向の目安となる〉指標銘柄，〈金利などの〉誘導目標，先導者［主導者，指導者］
▸The Fed cut its *bellwether* federal funds rate for overnight loans between banks by a quarter of a percentage point to 1 percent. 米連邦準備制度理事会（FRB）は，銀行同士の翌日物のフェデラル・ファンド（FF）金利の誘導目標を0.25引き下げて年1％とした。

below-par company 赤字会社

below the line 異常損益項目，利益処分，範囲外（line＝損益計算書の経常利益）

belt-tightening policy 緊縮政策
▸Should the government forge ahead with its *belt-tightening policy*, the budding economic recovery may be reduced to a short-lived upturn. 政府が緊縮路線をひた走れば，景気回復の芽も，薄命の景気回復に終わりかねない。

benchmark 動 基準にする，尺度とする
▸These performance objectives are *benchmarked* and evaluated against companies within industries similar to the Corporation, and with similar internal objectives. これらの業績目標は，当社と類似の業界にあって当社と類似の社内目標を掲げている会社を基準として評価されています。

benchmark 名 基準，尺度，基準値，測定基準，基準指数，基準銘柄，指標，指標銘柄，節目，ベンチマーク
  benchmark corporate lending 基準法人貸出金利
  benchmark federal funds rate 短期金利の指標であるフェデラル・ファンド（FF）金利
  benchmark five-year U.S. Treasury bonds 指標となる5年物財務省証券
  benchmark interest rate 基準金利，指標金利，政策金利（＝benchmark rate）
  benchmark Nikkei Stock Average 日経平均株価
  benchmark price 基準価格
  benchmark reserves 基準準備金
  benchmark short-term federal funds rate 短期金利の指標となるフェデラル・ファンド（FF）金利，短期金利の指標となるFF金利の誘導目標
  benchmark short-term interest rate 短期金利の誘導目標，短期金利の指標
  benchmark year 基準年
  benchmark yield 指標銘柄利回り，指標利回り

▸The Fed raised the *benchmark short-term federal* funds rate a quarter percentage point to 4.75 percent per annum. 米連邦準備制度理事会（FRB）は，短期金利の指標となるフェデラル・ファンド（FF）金利を［短期金利の指標となるFF金利の誘導目標を］0.25％引き上げて年4.75％とした。

benchmark rate 基準金利，指標金利，政策金利（＝benchmark interest rate）
▸The recent interest rate increase of the People's Bank of China was a modest one—the *benchmark rate* on one-year yuan loans was raised by 0.27 percentage point. 中国人民銀行の今回の利上げは小幅にとどまり，指標となる人民元の期間1年の貸出金利は0.27％引き上げられた。

benefactor 名 後援者

beneficial 形 役に立つ，有益な，有利な，利益を受ける，収益を受けるべき，好材料の，プラスの
  beneficial effects プラス効果
  beneficial interest 受益者の利益，受益権
  beneficial owner 受益者，実質所有者

beneficiary 名 〈年金や保険金，為替などの〉受取人，〈信用状の〉受益者，受給者
  beneficiary right to the trust 信託受益権
  contingent beneficiary 偶発受益者
  letter of credit beneficiary 信用状の受益者
  pension beneficiary 年金受給者
  pension fund beneficiary 年金基金の受益者

benefit 動 利益を与える，…の利益になる，…のプラスになる，…に貢献する，利益を得る，恩恵を受ける，利益が発生する
  benefit existing shareholders 株主の利益になる
  benefit from …から利益を得る，…の恩恵を受ける，…のメリットを受ける，…が追い風になる
▸Automobile and electric appliance industries have *benefited* from these windfalls. 自動車と電機業界は，これらの追い風の恩恵を受けた。
▸Goodwill is amortized on a straight-line basis over the periods estimated to be *benefited*, currently not exceeding five years. 営業権は，その効果が及ぶと見込まれる期間にわたり，現在は5年を超えない期間で定額法で償却されています。
▸If agricultural imports become cheaper due to the lowered tariffs, consumers will greatly *benefit*. 関税の引下げで輸入農産品が安くなれば，消費者の利点も大きい。

benefit 名 利益，利得，便益，利点，効果，給付，給付金，給付額，年金，手当，受益，受益金，税減額効果，ベネフィット（⇒**defined benefit plan**, employee benefit, health care benefits, insur-

ance benefits, pension benefits)
accumulated benefit 累積給付
benefit cost 給付コスト
benefit-cost [benefit/cost] analysis 費用便益分析, 便益・費用分析, 効果・費用分析, 収益原価分析 （=cost benefit analysis）
benefit formula 給付額計算方式
benefit obligation 給付債務
benefit plan 給付制度
benefit-related liabilities 給付関連債務
benefit security 給付保障
benefits earned during the period 当期に発生した給付
benefits from declining interest rates 金利低下の効果, 金利低下の恩恵
benefits of cost cutting [reduction] 経費削減効果, コスト削減効果
fringe benefit 付加給付, 給与外給付, 賃金外給付, 追加給付, 福利厚生費
noncontributory defined benefit pension plan 非拠出型確定給付制度
non-vested benefit 受益権非確定給付
retirement benefit 退職給付, 退職給与
right to benefits 受給権
▶If people lose their jobs, they are entitled to *benefits* under the national unemployment insurance system. 失業すれば, 雇用保険制度で失業給付を受けることができる。
▶We estimated the future payments for *benefits* to all present retirees and for accumulated benefits of active employees. 現在の全退職者に対する給付と現職従業員の累積給付の将来支払い額については, 予測を行いました。

benefits of shareholders 株主の利益, 株主利益
▶Japanese companies tend to attach greater importance to favorable relations with customers than to boosting *benefits of shareholders*. 日本企業は, 株主の利益を高めることより, 顧客との好ましい関係を重視する傾向がある。

best-before date 賞味期限
▶The firm discovered that the sauce used in the firm's processed food products had already exceeded its *best-before date*. 同社は, 同社の加工食品に使用していたタレがすでに賞味期限を過ぎていることが分かった。

best-efforts 形 最善の努力をする条件の
beta 名 ベータ係数（株式・投資ポートフォリオの危険率の係数）
BI 企業経営情報, 企業情報 （business intelli-gence の略）

biannual 形 年2回の
bid 名 入札, 申込み, 入札の付け値, 落札価格, 競り, 提案, 買収提案, 買収案件, 買収, 株式公開買付け, 買い注文, 買い呼び値, 買い気配, 買い唱え（証券などの売買で買い手が希望する値段）, ビッド （=bidding, tendering; ⇒bidding, hostile takeover, takeover bid）
accepted bid 落札価格
agreed bid 合意による株式公開買付け
bid for a company 企業買収, 企業買収案
bid price 買い手の指し値, 買い値, 買い呼び値, 買い気配, 入札価格, せり値, 付け値 （=buying price; ⇒buy order）
bid target 買収の標的
competitive bid 競争入札 （=competitive bidding）
hostile bid 敵対的買収提案, 敵対的株式公開買付け （=hostile bid offer）
make a successful bid 落札する, 受注する
submit bids 入札に応じる （=send in a bid）
win the bid 受注する, 落札する
▶A Tokyo-based association of construction firms, to which about 20 small and midsize companies belonged, won the *bid* for ¥430.5 million. 中小の建設会社約20社が加盟する都内の建設業協同組合が, 4億3,050万円で落札した。
▶Aoki Holdings Inc. made a *bid* to take over Futata on Aug. 7, 2006. AOKIホールディングス（アオキ）は, フタタに対して2006年8月7日にTOB（株式公開買付け）を提案した。
▶The company's winning *bid* is subject to the approval of AT&T Wireless shareholders. 同社が獲得した買収案件は, AT&Tワイヤレス株主の承認を得なければならない。

bid-rigging 名 談合, 入札談合, 不正工作, 不正入札 （=bid fixing; ⇒bidding system）
bid-rigging on public works projects 公共工事の談合
proactive involvement in the bid-rigging 談合への主体的関与
the law preventing bid-rigging involving government officials 官製談合防止法
▶The FTC suspects the four companies engaged in *bid-rigging* to keep contract prices artificially high. 4社は落札価格を意図的に高く維持するため[落札価格の下落を意図的に防ぐため]談合を行った, と公正取引委員会は見ている。

bid winner 落札業者, 落札予定会社, 受注業者, 受注会社

▶The four companies negotiated and agreed in advance the *bid winner* and the bidding price. 4社は，事前に談合を行って落札予定会社や入札価格を決めていた．

bidder 名 入札者，入札業者，入札参加企業，入札行，競り手，〈参加などの〉申込み国
　bidder for a contract 請負仕事の入札
　designated bidder 指名入札業者
　highest bidder 最高入札者，最高入札企業
　lowest bidder 最低入札者，最低入札企業
　postpone the bidding 入札を延期する
　potential bidder 入札参加予定者
　preferential bidder 一番札
　preferred bidder 優先入札者
　select bidders 入札業者を選定する，入札参加業者を選定する
　star bidder 最有力の入札参加企業
　successful bidder 落札業者

bidding 名 入札，競り，申込み，買収提案，命令 (＝bid, tender, tendering)
　bidding among designated companies 指名競争入札 (＝designated bidding)
　bidding expense 入札費，入札経費
　bidding procedures 入札手続き
　bidding war 競り，競争，買収戦争，買収提案戦争
　collusive bidding 馴れ合い入札
　competitive bidding 競争入札 (⇒bidding price)
　designated bidding 指名競争入札
　e-bidding 電子入札 (＝Net bidding)
　interfering in the bidding process for …の入札妨害をする
　Net bidding ネット入札，電子入札 (＝e-bidding)
　noncompetitive bidding 非競争入札
　open bidding 公開入札，一般競争入札
　open bidding anew 入札をやり直す
　participate in the bidding 入札に参加する
　postpone the bidding 入札を延期する
　public bidding 公開入札，一般競争入札
　unsolicited bidding 直接入札
　winner of the bidding 落札業者，受注者，受注業者

▶Before *biddings*, the construction firms decided which firm would win the bid. 入札前に，これらの建設会社は受注業者を決めていた．

▶The *bidding* for the public works project was held in July 2008 among designated construction firms. この公共工事の入札は，2008年7月に指名建設会社間で行われた［この公共工事の競争入札は，2007年7月に行われた］．

bidding price 入札価格
▶Each bid was submitted during competitive bidding, with the *bidding price* being between 95 percent and 99 percent of the estimated winning price. 入札はいずれも競争入札で行われ，入札価格は予定落札価格の95-99％だった［落札率（予定落札価格に占める落札価格の割合）は95-99％だった］．

bidding system 入札方式，入札制度
▶To prevent bid-rigging, the Niigata municipal government introduced a new *bidding system*. 談合防止策として，新潟市は新入札方式を導入した．

bilk 動 〈代金などを〉踏み倒す，…から詐取する，…をごまかして金を巻き上げる，だまし取る
▶Individual investors were *bilked* out of about ¥30 billion. 個人投資家が，300億円ほどだまし取られた．

bill 動 〈代金を〉請求する，〈代価を〉請求する，請求書を送る
▶Products shall be considered "sold" hereunder when *billed*. 製品は，代金の請求をした時点で，本契約により「販売された」ものと見なす．

bill 名 手形，証券，証書，紙幣，札（さつ），料金，請求額，勘定書，〈クレジット・カードなどの〉利用明細書，明細書，請求書，法案 (⇒blank bill)
　accept a bill 手形を引き受ける，手形の支払いを引き受ける
　accommodation bill 融通手形
　back a bill 手形の裏書きをする (＝endorse a bill)
　bank bill 銀行券，銀行手形，銀行引受手形 (＝bank note)
　banker's acceptance bill 銀行引受手形，BA手形
　bill holder 手形所持人
　bill of exchange 為替手形
　clean bill 裸手形
　clear a bill 手形を交換する，手形を清算する
　commercial bill 商業手形
　customer's bill 顧客の利用明細書
　demand bill 要求払い手形，一覧払い手形 (＝demand draft, demand note)
　discount a bill 手形を割り引く
　dishonor a bill 手形の支払いを拒否する，手形を不渡りにする
　documentary bill 荷為替手形
　draw a bill on …に手形を振り出す
　due bill 借用証書
　exchequer bill 英大蔵省証券
　export bill 輸出手形

fictitious bill 空(から)手形
first class bill 一流手形 (＝gilt-edged bill)
foot the bill 勘定をする, 合計する
foreign bill 外国為替手形
foul bill 故障手形
government bills 短期国債
import settlement bill 輸入決済手形
interest bill 利付き手形
kite a bill 融通手形を振り出す
long bill 長期手形 (＝long sighted bill, long term bill)
negotiable bill 流通手形
negotiate a bill 手形を買い取る
pass a bill 法案を可決する
pay a bill 手形を支払う (＝honor [meet, take up] a bill)
presentation bill 一覧払い手形, 呈示払い手形
receive a bill for …の請求書を受け取る
renew a bill 手形を書き換える
renewal bill 書換え手形
short bill 短期手形 (＝short sighted bill, short term bill)
sight bill 一覧払い手形
take up a bill 手形を支払う, 手形の支払いを引き受けて支払う, 手形を引き受ける (＝honor a bill)
throw out a bill 法案を否決する
time bill 期限付き手形
trade bill 商業手形
treasury bill 米財務省短期証券, 英大蔵省証券, 政府短期証券, 短期国債, Tビル
usance bill 期限付き手形
way-bill 貨物引換証

▶The *bill* is intended to promote foreign investment in Japan. 同法案は, 外国資本の対日投資を促すのが狙いだ。

▶Unpaid *bills* have emerged as a major structural problem in Chinese business. 中国との取引では, 代金の踏み倒しが大きな構造的問題として浮上している。

bill of lading 船荷証券, 積み荷証券, 貨物引換証, 運送証券, 積み荷証 《略 B/L》
船荷証券(B/L)の種類:

charter party B/L	用船契約船荷証券
claused B/L	条項付き船荷証券
custody B/L	保管付き船荷証券
domestic B/L	国内輸送証券
foul B/L	故障付き船荷証券
on board B/L	船積船荷証券
on-carriage B/L	貨車輸送証券
overseas B/L	海外船荷証券
prepaid B/L	運賃前払い船荷証券
railroad B/L	鉄道貨物引換証
received-for-shipment B/L	船積式船荷証券
red B/L	赤字船荷証券
stale B/L	時期経過船荷証券
straight B/L	(荷受人)指名直送船荷証券, 記名式船荷証券
sub-B/L	口別船荷証券
transshipment B/L	積替え船荷証券
truck B/L	自動貨車積送証券

▶The date of the *bill of lading* shall be conclusive evidence of the date of the delivery. 船荷証券の日付は, 引渡し日の最終的な証拠とする。

bioengineering 名 生体工学, 生物工学, 遺伝子の利用技術, バイオエンジニアリング

▶*Bioengineering* is expected to help drastically improve the conservation of the environment and boost food production. バイオエンジニアリングは, 環境保全と食糧増産の促進に大いに寄与するものと期待されている。

bioethics 名 生命倫理
biofuel 名 バイオ燃料
bioinformatics 名 生命情報工学, 生命情報科学, バイオインフォマティクス (＝bioinformatics: 分子生物学と情報科学が融合した学問分野)

biomass 名 生物資源, 量的生物資源, 生物量, 生物現存量, 生物体総量, バイオマス (「バイオマス」は, 石炭や石油などの化石燃料以外で, 木材や動物のふん尿, 生ゴミなど植物や動物から発生するエネルギー源)

▶*Biomass* energy is derived from plant material and animal waste. バイオマス・エネルギーは, 木材や動物のふん尿から発生する。

biometric authentication system 生体認証システム (＝biometric identification system, biometric recognition system, biometric system)

> **生体認証システムとは** ⇒ 個人差のある身体の特徴, 例えば手のひらや指の静脈の形状, 指紋, 瞳の虹彩(こうさい)などを使って, 本人かどうかを確認するシステム。キャッシュ・カードの場合は, 暗証番号を盗まれても, 本人でないとATMで預金を引き出せない。

biometric identification function 生体認証機能

▶Major banks are introducing new types of ATM cards, some of which feature *biometric identification functions* and others that can be used as electronic money or credit cards. 大手銀行が，生体認証機能や，電子マネーやクレジット・カードにも使える機能などの特長を備えた新型のキャッシュ・カードを導入している。

biometric integrated circuit card 生体認証機能付きICカード

biometric technology 生体認証技術
▸The *biometric technology* is used in addition to personal identification numbers at ATMs. ATM（現金自動預け払い機）には，暗証番号［個人の識別番号］のほかに生体認証技術が採り入れられている。

biometric timecard machine 生体認証タイムレコーダー
▸Fujitsu Ltd. has developed a *biometric timecard machine* that can identify an employee by scanning his or her palm upon arrival at, or departure from, the workplace. 富士通が，出社時や退社時に従業員が手のひらをかざすと本人を識別できる生体認証タイムレコーダーを開発した。

biometrics 名 個人識別法，本人証明技術，生体認証，生物統計学，バイオメトリクス
▸*Biometrics* enables identification of individuals according to their physical characteristics, such as voice or fingerprint. バイオメトリクスは，音声や指紋など身体の特徴によって個人を識別する技術だ。

biotechnology 名 生命工学，生物工学，生命技術，バイオテクノロジー

bird flu 鳥インフルエンザ（=avian flu, avian influenza）
▸Thailand's first probable case of human-to-human transmission of *bird flu* is raising concern among health experts. 鳥インフルエンザの「人から人」への最初の感染例がタイで発生したことに対して，保健衛生の専門家の間で懸念が高まっている。

BIS 国際決済銀行（Bank for International Settlementsの略。⇒**capital adequacy ratio**）
　BIS capital adequacy requirements BISの自己資本規制
　BIS guidelines BIS基準，BIS規制
　BIS regulation BIS規制
　BIS requirements BIS基準，BIS規制，BISの自己資本比率基準（=BIS equity standards, BIS standard）

B/L 船荷証券，積み荷証券，ビーエル（⇒**bill of lading**）
　air B/L 空輸証券（=aircraft B/L）
　clean B/L 無故障船荷証券
　Customs B/L 税関用船荷証券
　export B/L 輸出品船荷証券
　negotiable B/L 流通性船荷証券，流通船荷証券，譲渡可能船荷証券
　ocean B/L 海洋船荷証券（=marine B/L）
　order B/L 指図式船荷証券，指図人式船荷証券
　original B/L 船荷証券原本
　port B/L 積出港船荷証券
　received B/L 受取船荷証券
　shipped B/L 船積船荷証券
　short form B/L 略式船荷証券
　summary B/L 積荷明細書
　through B/L 通し船荷証券

black 名 黒字（=black figure; ⇒**red**）
　in the black 黒字で
　keep one's balance in the black 黒字を確保する
　operate in the black 黒字経営する
　return to the black 黒字に戻る，黒字に転換する，黒字に転じる
　swing back into the black 黒字に転換する
▸The company's after-tax profit returned to the *black* for the first time in six years. 同社の税引き後利益は，6期ぶりに黒字に転換した。

black market ヤミ市，ヤミ市場，アングラ市場，ヤミ取引，ブラック・マーケット
▸Unlike China and other Asian countries, Japan does not have a major *black market* for pirated music. 中国など他のアジア諸国と異なり，日本には海賊版音楽のヤミ市場が少ない。

black knight 黒い騎士，ブラックナイト（買収される企業の意に反する敵対的買収を支援する者［機関］）

blackmail 名 ゆすり，恐喝

blank bill 白紙の請求書
▸Officials in charge of general affairs at each section obtained *blank bills* from restaurants. 各課の庶務担当職員が，料亭や飲食店から白紙の請求書をもらっていた。

blank check 金額未記入の白紙小切手，自由行動権

blanket 形 一括の，包括的な

blastoff 名 〈ロケットなどの〉発射［打上げ］
▸The company asked the government to pay for the cost of inspecting launch facilities and repairing the damaged launch pad after *blastoff*. 同社は，ロケット打上げ時の発射設備の点検費と打上げで傷んだ発射台の修理費の負担を，政府に要請した。

bloc 名 圏

block booking 座席の一括予約

blog 名 ブログ, ウエブログ （=Web log: webとlog（記録）の合成語であるweblogの略. 手軽に開設できてだれでも書き込みが可能な日記風のホームページで, 双方向の交流が可能）, 動 ブログを運営する, ブログに記事を書く
▸About 1 million people are registered as users of the company's *blog* service.　同社のブログ・サービスの会員として, 約100万人が登録されている.

blow 名 打撃, 衝撃, ショック
　deal a blow to　…に打撃を与える, …に難問を抱えさせる
　strike a blow against　…のために反対する, …に反抗する
　strike a blow for　…のために努力する, …に加勢する
▸Overseas economic growth will slow, which could deal a *blow* to exports.　今後は海外の経済成長率が鈍化して, 輸出に打撃を与える可能性がある.

blue book　ブルー・ブック（米連邦準備制度理事会(FRB)とニューヨーク連邦準備銀行(Federal Reserve Bank of New York)が作成して, 連邦公開市場委員会(FOMC)の会議資料となる金融情勢の判断資料）, 公式報告書, 青書, 職員録, 紳士録

blue chip　優良株, 主要銘柄
　blue-chip company [corporation, firm]　優良企業
　blue-chip issues　優良銘柄, 優良企業の銘柄 （=blue-chip stocks）
　blue-chip subsidiary　優良子会社
▸The stock prices of Japan's *blue-chip* companies have declined due to the crisis of U.S. subprime mortgage loans.　日本の優良企業の株価が, サブプライム・ローン（米低所得者向け住宅融資）問題で下落した.

Blue House　青瓦台 （=Cheonwadae, Cheon Wa Dae: 韓国の大統領官邸）

Bluetooth　ブルートゥース（近距離無線の通信規格）
▸The information beacon is installed in buildings and underground passages and transmits information to mobile phones via a *Bluetooth* wireless system.　この情報標識は, 建物の中や地下街に設置し, ブルートゥースという無線システムを使って携帯電話に情報を送る.

blurb 名 （書籍の）宣伝文

BM　ビジネス・モデル （**business model**の略. コンピュータやインターネットによる情報技術を活用したビジネスの方法の仕組み）

BM patent　ビジネス・モデル特許, BM特許, ビジネス方法の特許 （=business model patent: ビジネスの手法を対象にした特許）

bn　10億（**billion**の略）

board 名 取締役会(board of directors), 重役会, 理事会, 審議会, 委員会, 会議, 省[庁, 局, 部], 掲示板, ボード （⇒**authority**）
　Big Board　ニューヨーク証券取引所, ビッグ・ボード
　bill board　広告掲示板, ビル・ボード
　board meeting　取締役会, 取締役会会議, 役員会, 評議会
　board minutes　取締役会議事録
　board of corporate auditors　監査役会
　board of executive officers　常務会
　board of managing directors　常務会
　board of statutory auditors　監査役会
　board of trade　商業会議所
　board of trustees　理事会
　chairman of the board　取締役会会長, 取締役会長 （=chairman of board of directors）
　Chicago Board of Trade　シカゴ商品取引所
　committee of the board　理事会
　executive board　重役会, 常務会, 理事会, 執行委員会
　extraordinary board meeting　臨時取締役会 （=extraordinary meeting of the board of directors）
　fall across the board　全面安になる, 全面的に下落する
　full board　取締役会の全体会議 （⇒**submission**）
　go on the board　上場する
　independent oversight board　独立監視委員会
　management board　取締役会, 重役会
　managing board　運営委員会, 運営理事会
　rise across the board　全面高になる, 全面的に上昇する
　second board companies　二部上場企業
　Securities and Investments Board　英国の証券投資委員会
　sit on the board　取締役を務める, 役員[委員]を務める
　special precinct board　特別委員会
　staggered board　スタガー取締役会 （会社の取締役の任期期間をずらして構成されている取締役会のことで, 敵対的買収への防衛手段として利用されることがある）
　supervisory board　監査役会
　U.S.-style board structure　米国型の取締役会

- General Motors Corp.'s *board* has decided to explore an alliance with Renault SA and Nissan Motor Co.　ゼネラル・モーターズ（GM）の取締役会は，仏ルノー・日産自動車連合との提携について調査することを決めた。

board member　取締役，役員，重役，理事，執行委員（＝board director）
　board members' bonus　役員賞与
　board members' pay [salaries]　役員報酬（＝board members' compensation）
- At the general meeting of shareholders, *board members* are required to hold earnest dialogues with shareholders and clarify their strategies to win their approval.　株主総会では，経営陣は株主と真剣に対話し，経営陣の経営方針を明らかにして株主の承認[賛同]を得なければならない。

board of directors　〈会社の〉取締役会，役員会，重役会，〈財団などの〉理事会《略 BOD》
　取締役会とは➡アメリカの会社の場合，取締役は会社経営の最高意思決定機関で，株主総会で選任された取締役数名で構成される。会社役員（corporate officer）の選任，株式の発行，配当宣言などについての決定権がある。また，社内取締役（inside director）と社外取締役（outside director）を含めて取締役（director）は株主が選任し，役員は取締役が選任することになっている。
　the extraordinary meeting of the board of directors　臨時取締役会
　the permanent committees of the board of directors　取締役会の常設委員会，常設の取締役会付属委員会
　the regular meeting of the board of directors　取締役会の定例会議，定例取締役会
- The *Board of Directors* is responsible for the overall affairs of the Corporation.　取締役会は，当社の全体的な問題に関して全責任を負っています。
- The *board of directors'* audit committee consists solely of outside directors.　取締役会の監査委員会は，社外取締役だけで構成されています。

board proposal　取締役会の提案
- We will oppose every *board proposal* for an increase in the authorized capital scale.　われわれとしては，取締役会の株式発行可能枠（授権株式数）の拡大提案には，全部反対します。

boardroom　〈証券取引所の〉立会場，立会所，役員室，会議室

bolster 動　促進する，伸ばす，〈地位などを〉向上させる，立場を強める，強化する，〈経済を〉増強する，〈景気を〉浮揚させる，〈ドルなどを〉支える，支持する，補強する，救済する
　bolster competitiveness　競争力をつける
　bolster the position　地位を向上させる，立場を強める
　measures to bolster the economy　景気浮揚策
- Exports played a leading role in *bolstering* the economy in the initial phase of its recovery.　景気回復の初期の段階で，輸出が景気浮揚の牽引役を果たした。
- Strategic alliances with and investments in other high-tech firms *bolster* our position in emerging technologies and developing markets.　他のハイテク企業との戦略的業務提携とハイテク企業への投資により，新技術と急成長市場における当社の地位は向上しています。

bond 名　債券，社債，公社債，債務証書，借用証書，保証証書，支払い保証契約，保証，保証金，保釈金（「債券」には，国や地方公共団体が発行する公債と，事業会社が発行する社債があり，これを一括して公社債という。⇒convertible bond, corporate bond, government bond）
　accrued bond interest to date of sale　外部発行時までの社債経過利息
　active bond　利付き債券
　blank bond　無記名債券
　bond authorized　授権社債
　bond expenses　社債発行費
　bond holder　社債権者，社債保有者，債券保有者（＝bondholder, debenture holder）
　bond holdings　債券保有，債券所有，保有債券
　bond interest paid　支払い社債利息
　bond interest received　受入社債利息
　bond issue expenses　社債発行費，債券発行費（＝bond issue costs, bond issuing expenses, issue costs on bonds）
　bond issued at a discount　割引発行社債（社債の発行価額が額面金額[額面価格]より低い社債）
　bond issued at a premium　割増発行社債，プレミアム発行された社債（社債の発行価額が額面金額より高い社債）
　bond outstanding　債券発行残高，発行済み社債，未償還債券，流通社債
　bond payable　未償還社債，社債，社債勘定（＝bonds payable, corporate bond）
　bond price　債券価格
　bond redemption　社債償還，発行済み社債の買戻し，債券の償還（＝redemption of bonds）
　bond refunding　社債借換え（発行済み社債と新規社債を交換すること）
　bond yield　債券利回り，長期国債利回り，長期債

利回り
collateral bond 担保付き社債
collateral for bonds 社債の担保
consolidated bond 整理社債
convertible bond 転換社債
debenture bond 無担保社債
discount bond 割引発行債, 割引債
discount on bonds payable 社債発行差金 （＝premium on bonds payable）
high yield bond 高利回り債
interest bearing bond 利付き債
issue of bonds 社債発行, 社債の発行 （＝issuance of bonds）
mortgage bond 担保付き社債
premium on bonds payable 社債発行差金
private placement bond 私募債
public bond 公債
U.S. longer-term bond 米国の長期国債
yuan-based bond 人民元建て債
zero coupon bond ゼロクーポン債（割引債の一種）
▶ We raised ¥100 billion from the *bond* issue to finance our restructuring. 当社は, 社債発行で 1,000億円を調達して, リストラの資金に充てました。

bond insurance 社債保険, 債券保険, 金融保証保険, 保証保険
▶ FGIC Corp. lost its Aaa *bond insurance* rating at Moody's Investors Service. 米金融保証会社の「FGIC（ファイナンシャル・ギャランティー・インシュランス）」は, ムーディーズ・インベスターズ・サービスの保証保険格付け「Aaa」の格付けを失った。

bond insurer 金融保証専門会社, 金融保証会社, 米国のモノライン（債券など金融商品の保証を専門に行う米国の保険会社。⇒**monoline, reinsure, write a policy**）
▶ The New York-based FGIC Corp. is the fourth-largest *bond insurer*. FGIC（ニューヨーク）は, 米国第4位の金融保証会社（モノライン）だ。

bond issuance 社債発行, 債券発行 （＝bond issue）
▶ Livedoor planned to raise about ¥80 billion, about half the value of all outstanding shares of Nippon Broadcasting System's shares, through *bond issuance*. ライブドアは, 社債を発行して, ニッポン放送株の時価総額の約半分にあたる約800億円の資金を調達する計画だった。

bond market 債券市場, 公社債市場
▶ Plunges in U.S. stock prices caused investment money to flee from the stock market to the *bond market*. 米国の株価低迷で, 投資資金が株式市場から債券市場に流れた。

bond with stock purchase warrant 株式買取り権付き社債, 新株予約権付き社債
▶ The investment fund converted *bonds with stock purchase warrants* into shares. 同投資ファンドは, 新株予約権付き社債を株式に転換した。

bonded 形 保税品の, 保税倉庫に預けられた, 債券によって保証された
bonded area 保税地域
bonded debt 長期負債
bonded display area 保税展示場
bonded goods 保税貨物
bonded manufacturing warehouse 保税工場 （＝bonded factory）
bonded shed 保税上屋（うわや）
bonded transportation 保税運送
bonded warehouse 保税倉庫（輸入手続きの済んでいない貨物の保管倉庫）
bonded zone 保税地区

bonus 名 手当, 賞与, 特別配当, 助成金, ボーナス （⇒**corporate earnings**）
bonus dividend 特別配当 （＝capital dividend）
bonus issue 特別発行, 無償新株発行, 無償増資 （特別配当株の発行）
bonus payment reserve 賞与引当金
bonus payments 賞与支給額
bonus plan 賞与制度, 課業賞与制度
bonus share [stock] 特別配当株, 無償株式, ボーナス株, 景品株
bonus system 報奨制度
bonus to directors 役員賞与
bonus to employees 従業員賞与
bonuses payable 未払い賞与, 未払いボーナス
capital bonus 株式配当 （＝stock dividend）
directors' bonuses 役員賞与
employee's bonus 従業員ボーナス
export bonus 輸出助成金
incentive bonus 奨励手当, 奨励特別手当
officer's bonus 役員賞与
premium bonus 割増手当, 割増賞与
reserve for bonuses 賞与引当金 （＝reserve for bonus payment）
stock bonus plan 株式賞与制度
▶ Since *bonuses* directly reflect corporate performance, most companies have announced reductions in bonus payments. 賞与は企業の業績を直接反映するので, 大半の企業が賞与支給額の削減をすでに打ち出している。

BOO 建設・運営・所有, BOO方式 （**build, operate and own**の略）

BOO scheme 建設・運営・所有方式，BOO方式（＝BOO formula）

book 動 計上する，会計処理する，帳簿に載せる，記入する，記帳する，記録する，〈資産や債権を〉積み増す，予約する （＝post, record; ⇒**recall**)
- **book a special profit** 特別利益を計上する
- **book assets** 資産を積み増す，債権を積み増す
▶KDDI *booked* a group net profit of ¥136.03 billion in the fiscal first half. KDDIは，今年度上期に1,360億3,000万円の連結税引き後利益を計上した。
▶New accounting rules changed the way we *book* expenses for retiree benefits, separation payments and income taxes. 新会計規則により，当社の退職者給付，中途退職金と法人税の各費用の会計処理方法が変わりました。

book 名 帳面，…帳，〈従業員などの〉名簿，帳簿，会計簿，ブック（⇒**alliance partner, close the [one's] books, cook books**)
- **assets out of book** 簿外資産
- **beige book** ベージュ・ブック （⇒見出し語）
- **blue book** ブルー・ブック （⇒見出し語）
- **book-closing period** 決算期
- **book income** 帳簿上の利益，会計上の利益
- **book loss** 帳簿上の損失，含み損，評価損
- **book profit** 帳簿上の利益，帳簿利益，紙上利益，含み益，評価益
- **book surplus** 帳簿上の剰余金，帳簿剰余金
- **closing of books** 決算，帳簿の締め切り（＝book-closing, closing of accounts, closing the books)
- **financial books** 会計帳簿，帳簿
- **green book** グリーン・ブック（米連邦準備制度理事会（FRB）のスタッフが作成して，連邦公開市場委員会（FOMC）の会議資料となる経済見通し）
- **liability off the book** 簿外負債
- **make up the books** 帳簿を締め切る
- **stock transfer book** 株主名簿
- **tan book** 米地区連銀経済報告，ベージュ・ブック（＝beige book)
▶The nation's big four auditing firms audit the *books* of about 80 percent of listed companies. 国内の4大監査法人が，上場企業の約8割の会計監査をしている。

book building method ブックビルディング方式（株式や債券などの新規発行や売出しの際，機関投資家などの意見をもとに投資家の需要を見ながら市場動向に見合った発行・売出額や価格を決定する方式。「需要予測方式」とも呼ばれている）

book-closing 決算
▶We will disclose our earnings forecasts on a consolidated basis, starting with our March 2010 *book-closing*. 当社は，2010年3月期決算から，連結ベースの業績予想を開示する方針だ。

book runner ブック・ランナー（＝bookrunner: シンジケート・ローンなどの国際金融取引で参加銀行の募集事務を行う幹事銀行）
- **equity book runner** 株式引受幹事会社
- **joint book runner** 共同ブック・ランナー

book-to-bill ratio 受注／出荷比，BBレシオ（出荷額に対する受注額の割合で，米半導体業界の景気指標として重視されている。BBレシオが1を超えると，受注が出荷を上回って景気上昇の目安となる。⇒**chipmaking equipment**)

book value 簿価，帳簿価額［価格］，帳簿上の価格，純資産額，取得価格，純資産（＝book price, carrying amount, effective book value)
- **asset book value** 資産簿価（＝book value of assets)
- **be below book value** 取得価格を下回る
- **book value approach** 帳簿価額方式
- **book value at beginning of year** 期首簿価
- **book value method** 簿価法
- **book value per common share [stock]** 普通株式1株当たり純資産，普通株式1株当たり持ち分額，普通株式1株当たり帳簿価額，普通株1株当たり簿価
- **book value per share** 1株当たり純資産，1株当たり純資産額，1株当たり簿価《略 **BPS**》（企業の純資産を発行済み株式数で割った指数。BPSの数値が高いほど，企業の安定性も高いといわれる）
- **book value stock plan** 帳簿価格株式プラン
- **book value stock purchase plan** 帳簿価格株式購入制度
- **books of account** 会計帳簿（＝account books, financial books)
- **excess of cost over book value** 簿価に対する原価超過額
- **fixed percentage of book value method** 定率法
- **net book value** 正味簿価
- **price book-value ratio** 株価純資産倍率
▶We sold equipment costing $50,000, with a *book value* of $25,000, for $20,000 cash on October 15, 2008. 当社は，2008年10月15日に，原価5万ドル（簿価2万5,000ドル）の設備を2万ドルの現金で売却しました。

boom 名 急騰，高騰，急成長，急拡大，急増，景気，好景気，ブーム
- **boom-and-bust** にわか景気

boom-bust dividing line 景気不景気分割線, 景気判断の分かれ目 （＝boom-or-bust line）
boom caused by a strong yen 円高景気
boom town 新興都市, 人口急成長の町
consumption boom 消費景気, 消費ブーム （＝spending boom）
economic boom 好景気, 経済的好況, 経済の活況
housing boom 住宅建設ブーム
inflation boom インフレ景気
property boom 不動産ブーム
takeover boom 企業買収ブーム, 買収ブーム
technology boom ハイテク・ブーム
the recent boom on the Tokyo Stock Exchange 最近の株式市場の活況
wartime boom 戦争景気
▸The economic *boom* in Middle Eastern oil-producing countries on the back of high crude oil prices has led to a jump in Japanese exports of steel products to those countries. 原油高による中東産油国の好景気で, 日本の中東諸国向け鉄鋼製品の輸出が伸びている。

boom-or-bust line
景気判断の分かれ目, 景気の上向き・下向きの分かれ目 （＝boom-bust dividing line, boom-bust threshold, boom-or-bust threshold）
stay below the boom-or-bust line of 50 percent 景気判断の分かれ目となる50％を下回る
top the boom-or-bust line of 50 percent 景気判断の分かれ目となる50％を上回る
▸The coincident indicator, the nation's key gauge of the state of the economy, topped the *boom-or-bust line* of 50 percent in March. 国内の景気の現状を示す一致指数[景気一致指数]が, 3月は景気判断の分かれ目となる50％を上回った。

boost 動 推進する, 引き上げる, 増加させる, 拡大する, 押し上げる, 積み増す, 高める, 向上させる, 増強する, 強化する, 拡充する, 〈需要などを〉喚起する, 活気づかせる, 活性化する, 刺激する
boost domestic demand 内需を拡大する, 内需を喚起する, 内需を刺激する
boost productivity 生産性を高める, 生産性を向上させる
boost profits 利益を押し上げる
boost the economic growth 景気のテコ入れをする, 経済成長率を高める
boost the economy 経済を発展させる, 経済[景気]を刺激する
boost wages 賃金を引き上げる
▸The company will be split into a food supermarket chain and a real estate company to *boost* profitability. 同社は, 収益力を高めるため, 食品スーパーと不動産会社の2社に分割される。
▸The increase in exports *boosted* corporate profits substantially. 輸出拡大で, 企業収益が大幅に増えた。

boost 名 押し上げ, 後押し, 増強, 活気づけ, 景気刺激, 発展, 向上, 増大, 急増, 上昇, 急上昇 （⇒arm）
capital boost 増資
fiscal boost 財政面からの景気刺激策
▸The strong performance was supported by a *boost* in sales, mainly in the U.S. market. この好業績の要因は, 主に米国内市場での販売急増です。

borrow 動 借り入れる, 融資を受ける, 資金を調達する, 借金する （⇒carry trade）
borrowed capital 他人資本, 借入資本
borrowed money 借入金, 借金
borrowed security 借入有価証券
borrowed stock 借り株
▸The company will *borrow* ¥56 billion to fund the introduction of new models. 同社は, 新型車導入の資金を調達するため, 560億円の融資を受ける。
▸The syndicated loan is part of our plan to *borrow* about ¥80 billion. 協調融資は, 当社の約800億円の資金調達計画の一環です。

borrower 名 借り手, 資金の借り手, 貸付け先, 貸出先, 融資先, 融資先企業, 債務者, 発行体, ボロワー （⇒business conditions）
AAA rated borrower トリプルA格の発行体
borrower limit 与信限度
corporate borrowers 融資先, 融資先企業
major borrower 大口融資先, 主要発行体 （＝large borrower）
premium borrower 優良発行体
▸Japan's economic recovery helped improve the business conditions of corporate *borrowers*. 日本の景気回復で, 融資先企業の業況が改善した。
▸The banks have categorized *borrowers* based on their financial health. 銀行は, 経営の健全度に基づいて融資先[債務者]を区分している。

borrowing 名 借入れ, 資金調達, 借入金, 借金, 負債, 債務
banking borrowing 銀行借入れ （＝bank borrowing）
borrowing capacity 資金調達能力, 借入れによる資金調達能力, 借入能力 （＝borrowing power）

borrowing facilities 信用枠
borrowing needs 借入需要, 資金調達需要
borrowing power 借入能力, 資金調達能力 (= borrowing capacity)
interest rate on borrowings 借入金の金利, 借入金の利率
long-term borrowings 長期借入金
net short-term borrowings 短期借入金純額
securitized borrowings 借入れの証券化
unsecured borrowing 無担保借入れ
▶Interest rates on *borrowings* would vary from country to country depending on local market conditions. 借入金の利率は, 各国の市場の状況に左右され, 国によって異なります。

borrowing cost 資金調達コスト, 借入コスト, 借入費用
▶The sale of car and truck loans may lower *borrowing costs* for General Motors Acceptance Corp. 自動車ローン債権の売却は, GMAC (GMの金融子会社) の資金調達コストを低減するねらいもある。

BOT 建設・運営・譲渡, BOT方式 (**build, operate and transfer**の略)
BOT scheme 建設・運営・譲渡方式, BOT方式 (= BOT formula)

bottom 名 底, 最低, 下限, 底値, 大底, 底入れ, 景気の谷, ボトム, 動 底に届く
be close to touching bottom 底入れが近い
bottom fishing 安値拾い, 底値を拾う動き
bottom income 最低所得
bottom management 下部階層の管理職, 下位管理者層, 下級管理層, ボトム・マネジメント (= lower management)
bottom of the cycle 底入れ, 景気の谷
bottom price 底値
buy at the bottom 底値で買いを入れる
close at the bottom of the day's trading 安値引けとなる
double bottom 二番底 (= second bottom)
first bottom 一番底
hit bottom 底を打つ, 谷になる
major bottom 大底
reach bottom 底に達する, 底に届く, 底を打つ
rock bottom price 底値, 最低価格
rock bottom salary 最低賃金
touch the bottom 底入れする, 底をつく
▶The Japanese economy is believed to have hit *bottom*. 日本の景気は底を打った, と思われている。

bottom line (損益計算書の最終行の意味から) 純損益, 純利益, 利益, 当期利益, 純損失収益性, 取引の収支, 業績, 最終損益, 総決算, 最終結果 [成果], 結論, 最終決定, 最重要事項, 要点, カギ, 問題の核心, ぎりぎりの線, 本音 (⇒**arm**)
bottom line results 純利益
bottom lines 業績, 収益
company's bottom line 企業 [会社] の損益
contribute to the bottom line 利益 [当期利益] に貢献する, 利益に寄与する
corporate [corporations'] bottom lines 企業収益
enhance the bottom line 利益を押し上げる, 利益を増やす
flow through to the bottom line 利益に直結する
▶Our *bottom line* shows a loss of $2.80 a share. 当社の最終損益は, 1株当たり2.80ドルの損失を示しています。
▶This is a *bottom-line* confirmation of the improvements of efficiency and competitiveness. これは, 効率性の改善と競争力の向上を決算で確認したことになります。

bottom out 底をつく, 底を打つ, 底入れする, 大底に達する, 底値に達する, 下げ止まる, 底打ちする, 最低レベルに達する, どん底まで下がる
▶Car manufacturers' inventories have *bottomed out* due to the steelworks' suspended operations. 同製鉄所の操業停止で, 自動車メーカーの在庫が底をついた。
▶The decline in capital investment is likely to *bottom out* in the future. 設備投資の減少も, 先行き下げ止まりの気配が見られる。
▶The U.S. economy will *bottom out* soon. 米国景気は, 底入れが近い。

bottom-up 形 下位 [下層] から上位 [上層] への, 下から上に向かっている, 参加型の, ボトム・アップ型の, 名 下からの意見具申, 意見上申, 下意上達, ボトムアップ経営, ボトムアップ (⇒**top-down**)
bottom-up approach ボトムアップ方式, ボトムアップ・アプローチ
bottom-up decentralization 下からの分権化, 下からの分権的組織
bottom-up decision 下からの意思決定, 参加型意思決定, 参加的意思決定
bottom-up forecast ボトムアップ型予測
bottom-up management 下から上への経営管理, 下からの経営管理, 参加型経営, 下意上達経営, ボトムアップ経営, ボトムアップ・マネジメント

bottom-up planning 顧客のニーズに応じた品揃え計画, ボトムアップ計画
bottom-up society ボトムアップ社会(政治・経済の分野で下部が大きい役割を担う社会)
bottom-up strategy 現場意見採用戦略, 意見上申戦略
bottom-up technique ボトムアップ技法

bottoming out [bottoming-out] 底入れ, 底打ち, 底離れ, 下げ止まり
▸Signs of *bottoming out* can be seen in some areas. 一部に, 下げ止まりの兆しが見られる。

bounce 動 〈小切手などが〉不渡りとして戻ってくる, 〈eメールが宛先不明で〉戻ってくる

bourse 名 証券取引所, 取引所, 株式市況, 株式相場 (=securities exchange)
▸A company listed on the Fukuoka *bourse* is subject to delisting after two straight years of negative net worth. 福岡証券取引所に上場している企業は, 2年連続債務超過になると, 上場廃止の対象になる。

bovine spongiform encephalopathy
狂牛病《略 BSE》(=mad cow disease)

BOY 年初 (beginning of year の略)
bp ベーシス・ポイント (basis pointの略)
bpd 日量…バレル, 日産…バレル (barrels per dayの略)
▸The Organization of Petroleum Exporting Countries agreed to cut its crude oil output by 1.2 million *bpd*. 石油輸出国機構(OPEC)は, 原油の生産量を日量120万バレル削減することで合意した。

BPR 業務革新, ビジネス・プロセスの再設計 (business process reengineeringの略)
BPS 1株当たり純資産, 1株当たり純資産額 (book value per shareの略)

bracket 名 階層, 層, グループ, 区分, 等級, ブラケット
  age bracket 年齢層
  five year bracket 5年物
  income tax bracket 所得区分
  low income brackets 低所得者層
  progressive income tax brackets 累進税率区分
  tax bracket 税率区分, 税率等級

branch 名 支店, 支社, 支部, 支局, 出張所, 分野, 部門
  branch business 支店業務
  branch-free bank 無店舗銀行, 店舗を持たない銀行
  branch network 支店網
  branch of industry 業種, 産業部門
  branch office 支店支社, 支所, 支部
  branchless bank オンライン銀行, 店舗を持たない銀行
  domestic branch network 国内支店網
  foreign branch 在外支店, 海外支店
  joint branch 共同店舗
  overseas branch 海外支店
  resident branch 現地支店

branch out 手を広げる, 活動範囲を広げる, 新分野に発展する, 進出する
▸Companies were keen until recently to *branch out* overseas. 企業は最近まで, 海外進出に躍起になっていた。

brand 名 商標, 銘柄, 特定の銘柄品, ブランド, ブランド品, ブランド商品, ブランド店
  barnacle brand バーナクル・ブランド(製品ライフサイクルの後半段階で市場に参入する競合ブランド)
  brand acceptance ブランド受容, 需要者承認
  brand awareness ブランド認知
  brand equity ブランド・エクイティ(ブランドを企業資産として評価するという考え方)
  brand identity 商標の存在価値, 商品の独自性, ブランド・アイデンティティ《略 BI》
  brand label ブランド・レーベル
  brand loyalty 商標忠実性, ブランドに対するこだわり, 銘柄忠実度, 商標信頼度, ブランド・ロイヤルティ
  brand manager 商標管理者, ブランド管理者, ブランド・マネージャー
  brand-named item 銘柄品, メーカー品
  brand new and state-of-the-art 最新技術の粋を集めた新製品
  brand portfolio 有価証券一覧表, ブランド・ポートフォリオ
  brand positioning 商標品の位置付け, ブランド・ポジショニング
  brand preference 商標選好, ブランド選好
  brand recognition ブランド認知
  brand reputation 商標の名声, 商標の評判
  brand strength ブランド競争力
  brand switching 商標変更, ブランド遷移, ブランド・スイッチング
  character brand キャラクター・ブランド(大手メーカーの個性や特徴を強く打ち出した製品)
  consumer brand preference 消費者ブランド選好
  control brand コントロール・ブランド (=double chop: メーカー名と流通業者名を併記したブランドのこと)

corporate brand 企業ブランド, コーポレート・ブランド
designer's brand デザイナーズ・ブランド (デザイナーの名を付した商標)
domestic brand 国産ブランド
factory brand 生産工場独自の商標, ファクトリー・ブランド
family brand 統一ブランド, 代表商標, 共通ブランド, ファミリー・ブランド
fashion brand ファッション・ブランド
fighting brand 競争的ブランド, 競争的商標
generic brand 非銘柄商品, 無印商品, ジェネリック・ブランド (ノーブランド商品, ジェネリック・ラベルともいう)
global brand 世界的なブランド
individual brand 個別ブランド, 個別商標
luxury foreign brands 海外高級ブランド
manufacturer's brand 製造業者商標
multibrand strategy 複数ブランド戦略, マルチブランド戦略
name brand product 有名ブランド品, 有名銘柄品
national brand 全国ブランド, 製造元商標, ナショナル・ブランド
own brand 自社製品ブランド
private brand プライベート・ブランド, 自家商標, 商業者商標 (=store brand)
private brand product 自主開発(プライベート・ブランド)商品 (⇒private brand product)
store brand ストア・ブランド, 自社ブランド, 自店独自のブランド (=private brand)
unified brand 統一ブランド (⇒-based [based])
well-established brand 有名ブランド
▶Microsoft's takeover offer does not properly assess Yahoo's global *brand*. 米マイクロソフトの買収提案は, 米ヤフーの世界的なブランドを適正に評価していない。

brand image ブランド・イメージ (ブランドに対する全体的な知覚)
▶We will promote efficiency in production, distribution and research without damaging *brand image*. ブランド・イメージを損なわない範囲で, 当社は製造と物流, 研究面で効率化を進める方針だ。

brand name 商標名, 商品名, ブランド名, ブランド力, ブランド・ネーム
brand name products ブランド品, ブランド商品 (=branded goods, designer goods)

brand name right 商標権 (=trademark right)
▶With the expanding market in mind, IBM Japan Ltd. started collecting and recycling IBM-made PCs to sell under the *brand name* "IBM Refreshed PC." 市場の拡大をにらんで, 日本IBMは, 同社製の中古パソコンを「IBMリフレッシュPC」のブランド名で販売するため, 中古パソコンの回収と再生利用を開始した。

brand strategy ブランド戦略, 商標戦略
▶Leading childcare product manufacturer Combi Corp. increased its childbirth allowance system as part of a *brand strategy*. ベビー用品大手のコンビは, 出産祝い金制度をブランド戦略の一環として拡充した。

brand value ブランド価値
▶It's important for the two firms to enhance their *brand values* and originality by working off each other. 両社が刺激しあいながら, 両社のブランド価値や独自性を高めることが重要だ。

branding 名 ブランド戦略, ブランディング
breach 名 違反, 侵害, 不履行
break 動 壊す, ばらにする, 暴落する, 展開する
break even 損得なしになる, 収支がとんとんになる, 五分五分になる, 辛うじて採算が取れる, 採算ラインになる
▶If the price of naphtha, which currently is about ¥35,000 per kiloliter, rises ¥1,000, the company's profit and costs will fail to *break even*. 現在1キロ・リットル当たり約35,000円のナフサ(粗製ガソリン)が, 1,000円値上がりすると, 同社の利益とコストは採算が取れなくなる。

break-even (point) 名 損益分岐点, 採算ライン, 採算点, 収支とんとん (=breakdown point)
break-even price 損益分岐点価格
break-even time 損益分岐期間
break-even yield 損益分岐点利回り
profit and loss break-even point 損益分岐点
return to break-even 収支とんとんに戻る, 採算ラインに戻る, 赤字を解消する

breakage 名 破損, 破損箇所, 破損物, 破損賠償
breakdown 名 〈機械の〉故障, 〈交渉の〉決裂, 中断, 崩壊, 倒壊, 内訳, 構成, 分類, 分析, 好機, 見込み
breakdown by industry group 業種別内訳, 業種別分類
breakdown of revenue 売上構成, 売上の内訳
economic breakdown 経済の崩壊
nervous breakdown 神経衰弱
sales breakdown by segment セグメント別売

上構成

▶According to a *breakdown* of the statistics, 190,000 fewer people quit their jobs of their own accord compared with a year earlier.　統計の分析によると、自己都合による退職者は前年同月比で19万人減少した。

breakthrough 名　画期的な出来事、輝かしい成果、難関突破、突破、打開、打破、前進、躍進、重大発見、大発見

▶Toyota's *breakthrough* is partly due to strategic blunders by European and U.S. automakers.　トヨタ躍進の一因は、欧米の自動車メーカーの戦略ミスだ。

bribe 名　賄賂（わいろ）、動　賄賂を贈る、買収する
　bribe-giving　贈賄
　bribe-taking　収賄
　pay ¥30 million as bribes　賄賂として3,000万円を支払う
　receive ten million yen in bribes　賄賂として1,000万円を受け取る

▶Bridgestone gave about ¥150 million in *bribes* to government officials of countries in South East Asia and Central and South America.　ブリヂストンが、東南アジア、中南米諸国の政府職員［政府幹部］に賄賂として約1億5,000万円を支払っていた。

bribery 名　贈収賄、贈収賄行為、贈賄、収賄、汚職

BRICs　有力新興国、ブリックス　（高い経済成長を続けるBrazil（ブラジル）, Russia（ロシア）, India（インド）とChina（中国）の頭文字による造語）

bridge 動　つなぐ、〈溝や意見の違いなどを〉埋める、〈困難を〉乗り越える

▶Differences among the Security Council members can be *bridged*.　（国連）安全保障理事会理事国の意見の相違は、埋めることができる。

bridge bank　つなぎ銀行、承継銀行、ブリッジ・バンク　（「承継銀行」は、破綻した銀行の受け皿銀行が見つかるまで、破綻銀行の金融業務を引き継ぐための公的機関）

▶The *Bridge Bank* of Japan temporarily took over the operation of the collapsed bank.　日本承継銀行が、この破綻銀行の営業を一時的に引き継いだ。

bridge financing　つなぎ融資　（=bridging finance）

bridge loan　つなぎ金融、つなぎ融資、ブリッジ・ローン　（=bridging loan）

brief 名　摘要、指示、任務、権限、動　簡潔な指示を与える、要約する、摘要を作成する

briefing 名　説明会、投資家向け説明会、投資家説明会、経過報告、概要報告、概況・状況説明、背景説明、要約書、セミナー

▶After the *briefing* for foreign investors, a fund manager showed interest in investing in Japanese government bonds.　海外投資家向け説明会の後、あるファンド・マネージャーが日本国債への投資に関心を示した。

brisk 形　活発な、好調な、活気のある、活況の、繁盛している
　brisk demand　活発な需要
　brisk economic recovery　急速な景気回復
　brisk market　活発な市場、活発な市況、上景気、市場活況

brisk business　活発な取引、商売繁盛

▶The index of tertiary industry activity rose 2.2 percent in September from August due to *brisk business* in the leasing sector.　9月の第三次産業活動指数は、リース部門の活発な取引で前月比2.2%の上昇となった。

brisk business performance　好業績、好決算　（=brisk performance, buoyant performance）

▶Buoyed with *brisk business performance*, one in every two companies will increase or resume dividends.　好決算を受けて、2社に1社は増配や復配［配当の再開］に踏み切る見通しだ。

brisk performance　好業績

▶The firm that best represents the *brisk performances* of Japanese companies is Toyota Motor Corp.　日本企業の好業績の代表格は、トヨタ自動車だ。

brisk sales　好調な売れ行き、販売好調

▶Honda Motor Co. and Nissan Motor Co. enjoyed *brisk sales* in the key U.S. market.　ホンダや日産自動車は、主力の北米市場での販売が好調だった。

broadband 名　高速大容量通信、広帯域、広帯域通信網、ブロードバンド
　broadband access　ブロードバンド接続　（=broadband connection）
　broadband communication　高速大容量通信、広帯域通信、ブロードバンド通信　（=broadband）
　broadband Internet service　ブロードバンド・インターネット・サービス
　broadband network　高速大容量通信網、広帯域ネットワーク、高速大容量通信ネットワーク、ブロードバンド・ネットワーク　（=broadband communication network）
　broadband service　高速大容量通信サービス、大容量高速通信サービス、広帯域サービス

▶Japan ranked ninth in the world in terms of the

percentage of the population using *broadband communications*. 高速通信［高速大容量通信］の普及率では，日本が世界で第9位だった。

broadcasting 名 放送
  Broadcasting Culture Award 放送文化賞
  BS digital broadcasting BSデジタル放送
  CS broadcasting 通信衛星放送, CS放送
  data broadcasting データ放送
  digital broadcasting service デジタル放送サービス
  ground-wave broadcasting 地上波放送
  multichannel broadcasting 多チャンネル放送
  private broadcasting corporation 民間放送局

broadly defined liquidity 広義の流動性, 広義流動性 （広義流動性＝M2＋CD＋郵便貯金, 農協・漁協・信用組合・労働金庫の預貯金＋金銭信託・貸付け信託＋債券現先, 金融債, 国債, 投資信託, 外債. M2＋譲渡性預金(CD)を補完する日銀のマネー・サプライ統計）
  ▶*Broadly defined liquidity* is the widest money supply measure that also includes investment trusts, bank debentures and domestic and foreign government bonds. 広義流動性は，最も広範囲なマネー・サプライの指標で，これには投資信託や金融債, 国内外の国債なども含まれる。

brochure 名 〈案内, 広告などの〉パンフレット
  ▶The explanations in the *brochures* are difficult to understand. このパンフレットの説明文は, 分かりにくい。

broke 形 破産した
broker 名 委託販売業者, 仲介人, ブローカー
brokerage 証券業, 証券会社, 仲介, 仲介業, 仲買, 仲買業, 証券仲買会社, 仲介手数料, ブローカー
  brokerage commissions 委託手数料, 委託売買手数料, 株式委託手数料, 仲介手数料, ブローカー手数料 （＝brokerage fees; ⇒**commodity futures**）
  brokerage firm 証券会社 （＝brokerage house, securities company）
  brokerage services 売買仲介業務
  stock brokerage business 証券仲介業務
brokerage business 仲介事業, 仲介業務
  ▶The firm has been trying to expand its *brokerage business* for mergers and acquisitions beyond national boundaries. 同社は，国境を越えたM&A（合併・買収）の仲介事業を活発化している。
brokerage fees 仲介手数料, 株式買手数料, 株式売買手数料, 仲買手数料 （＝brokerage commissions）
  ▶The poor earnings are mainly due to sharp drops in *brokerage fees* and trading profits. この減益の大きな要因は，株売買手数料と売買益の大幅減です。
  ▶There are no *brokerage fees* or other service charges. 仲介手数料やサービス料は, 不要です。
brokerage house 証券会社 （＝brokerage firm, securities firm）
  ▶Many banks and *brokerage houses* have formed business alliances in launching stock brokerage business at the banks. 銀行での証券仲介業務を開始するにあたって，銀行や証券会社の多くは業務提携している。

broking 名 証券売買取引, 株式仲買い, 委託取引
  broking function 証券業務
  broking house 証券会社
  cross-broking 証券売買の相互取引
  international broking 国際委託取引
  stock broking 証券売買仲介

BSE 牛海綿状脳症, 狂牛病 （**bovine spongiform encephalopathy**の略）

BTO 受注生産, 受注生産方式 （**build to order**の略）

bubble 名 バブル, 泡沫
  asset bubble 資産のバブル
  bubble consumption バブル消費
  bubble years バブル期 （＝bubble economic era, bubble period, bubble economy period）
  bursting of the yen bubble 円のバブルがはじけること （＝burst of the yen bubble）
  collapse of the IT bubble IT（情報技術）バブルの崩壊
  down bubbles バブルがしぼむこと, バブルの縮小
  economic bubble burst バブル崩壊
  high-tech bubble ハイテク関連株の狂乱バブル, ハイテク・バブル
  Net bubble ネット株バブル, ネット・バブル
  postbubble closing low バブル崩壊後の終値での最安値 （＝post-bubble closing low）
  postbubble record low バブル崩壊後の最安値
  up bubbles バブルが膨らむこと, バブルの成長

bubble economy バブル経済, バブル景気
  the collapse of the bubble economy バブル経済の崩壊, バブル経済の破綻 （＝bubble economy's collapse）
  the legacy of the bubble economy バブル経済の後遺症, バブル景気の後遺症
  ▶Though stock prices remain low, the number of transactions has already outpaced that during the *bubble economy*. 株価はまだ低いものの, 株

取引の件数はすでにバブル期を超えている。

bubble economy burst バブル経済の崩壊, バブル崩壊（＝bubble burst, bubble collapse, bursting of the bubble economy, collapse of the bubble economy)
▶Since the *bubble economy burst*, low interest rates have been the norm. バブル崩壊以降, 低金利が続いている。

bubble economy era バブル期（＝bubble economy period, bubble years）
▶We had about 10,000 people at our *bubble economy era* peak. 当社には, バブル期のピーク時に約1万人の従業員がいました。

bubble economy period バブル期（＝bubble economic era, bubble period, bubble years）
▶The company followed an aggressive business strategy during the *bubble economy period* of the late 1980s. 同社は, 1980年代終わりのバブル期に積極的な事業戦略を展開した。

budget 名 予算, 財政, 動 予算に計上する
　additional budget 追加予算
　annual budget 年度予算
　balanced budget 均衡予算
　belt-tightening budget 緊縮型予算
　budget appropriation 予算支出, 予算の割当て, 予算の計上, 予算の承認
　budget constraint 予算的制約, 予算の制限
　budget cut 予算削減
　budget deficit 財政赤字, 予算の赤字, 赤字財政（＝budget gap）
　budget-deficit spending 赤字財政支出
　Budget Message 予算教書（＝budget documents, budget plan, spending plan: 一般教書 (the State of the Union address), 経済報告 (Economic Report of the President) と合わせて三大教書と呼ばれている）
　budget numbers 財政収支の数字
　capital budget 資本予算, 資本支出予算, 投資予算, 設備投資計画額
　Congressional Budget Office 米議会予算局
　deficit budget 赤字予算
　draft budget 予算原案, 予算案
　general account budget 一般会計予算
　provisional budget 暫定予算
　quarterly budget 四半期予算
　sales budget 販売予算, 売上高予算
　supplementary budget 補正予算（＝additional budget）
　working budget 実行予算

zero-base budget ゼロベース予算, ゼロベース予算管理

budget 形 安い, 格安の, 予算に合った
　budget airline 格安航空会社
　budget car 大衆車, 格安の車
▶Owners of *budget* Opel cars are not likely to buy luxury cars such as the Cadillac. 大衆車オペルのオーナーが, キャディラックなどの高級車に乗り換える可能性は小さい。

budget year 会計年度
▶The U.S. government's 2009 *budget year* runs through Sept. 30. 米政府の2009会計年度は,（2008年10月から）2009年9月までとなっている。

build to order 受注生産, 受注生産方式, 注文生産方式《略 BTO》(顧客の注文を受けてから顧客の好みの仕様に応じて生産する方式)

bulk 名 大きさ, 容積, かさ, 大量, 大半, 船倉, 積荷, 動 増大する, かさばる, 船荷の容積を評価する

bull 名 強気筋, 強気, 買い方, 形 上向きの, 強気の, 強気筋の, 買い方の
　be stable in the bull market 上げ相場で安定している
　bull account 信用買い, 買い玉
　bull bear bond 強気弱気債
　bull buying 強気買い
　bull campaign 買い策動
　bull clique 強気筋
　bull interests 強気筋
　bull market 強気市場, 強気相場, 強気市況, 上げ相場, 買い相場（＝strong market）
　bull position 買い持ち, 投機的買い持ち, 空買い
　bull speculation 買占め商略
　bull spread ブル・スプレッド（価格が上がると利益が得られる組合せのオプション取引）
▶Personal investors have made profits in the recent *bull* market. 個人投資家は, 最近の上昇相場で利益を上げている。

bullish 形 強気の, 上がり気味の, 見通しが明るい, 楽観的見方の, 積極的な
　bullish factor 強気材料, 強材料, 好材料, 高材料（＝bullish influence, bullish support）
　bullish influence 強気材料, 強材料, 好材料（＝bullish factor, bullish news）
　bullish market 上昇相場, 上げ相場, 買い相場, 強気市況
　bullish news 好材料, 強材料
　bullish sentiment 強気の地(じ)合い, 勢い, 強気心理, 買い気, 上げ相場
　bullish stock market 堅調な株式市場, 株式相場

の上昇, 株高
bullish tone 強気ムード, 強気
▶The domestic economy is *bullish*. 国内景気は, 見通しが明るい。
▶The *bullish* stock market in the past six months has led the unrealized value of bank-held stocks to swell by about ¥3 trillion. 株式市場が過去半年間, 堅調に推移したことで, 銀行保有株式の含み損益が約3兆円増加した。
bullet 名 満期全額一括償還, 満期一括償還型債券
bullying 名 いじめ, 弱い者いじめ
▶There are numerous problems facing this nation's education, including *bullying*, truancy and a decline in the scholastic ability. いじめ, 不登校や学力低下など, いま日本の教育が抱えている問題は多い。
bullying in the workplace 職場でのいじめ, 職場のいじめ, 職場いじめ (＝workplacebullying: 「職場のいじめ」の事例として, 一般にパワー・ハラスメント (職権による人権侵害) や容赦ない叱責 (のしる・どなる・威嚇する), 暴行, 無視, 冷遇, 仲間はずれ, 長時間の時間外労働, 休日出勤, サービス残業などが挙げられている。⇒**harassment**)
▶About 80 percent of industrial counselors have been consulted on *bullying in the workplace*. 産業カウンセラーの約8割が,「職場のいじめ」に関する相談を受けている。
bundle 動 束ねる, 包む, 〈ソフトウェアを〉同梱する, 名 束, 大金, 抱き合わせ販売, セット販売, 同梱ソフトウェア
　bundled product セット商品
bundling 名 〈ソフトウェアなどの〉セット販売, 抱き合わせ販売, バンドリング
▶*Bundling* combines several products for one price. バンドリングとは, 製品を数個組み合わせて, 単一価格で販売することを言う。
buoy 動 活気づかせる, 浮揚させる, 支える
　be buoyed by …で活気づく, …に支えられる
　buoy the economy 景気を浮揚させる
▶Sharp Corp. posted a 14 percent gain in quarterly profit, *buoyed* by robust demand for its liquid crystal display TVs. シャープの四半期利益は, 同社製液晶テレビの需要の大幅な伸びに支えられて, 14％増加した。
buoyant 形 活況の, 好調の, 上昇傾向の, 上がり気味の
　buoyant consumer spending 好調な消費支出, 消費支出の好調
　buoyant demand 需要の拡大, 需要の盛り上がり
　buoyant investment income 投資収益の増大

buoyant market 市場の活況, 騰貴市場
buoyant performance 好業績, 好決算 (＝brisk performance)
▶The high growth rate of GDP is attributable mainly to an increase in companies' capital investment backed by *buoyant* exports to other Asian countries. 国内総生産 (GDP) の高い成長率の主因としては, 好調なアジア向け輸出を背景に企業の設備投資が増加したことが挙げられる。
burden 名 負担, 費用負担, 重荷, 間接費, 製造間接費, 経費
　absorbed burden 製造間接費配賦 (はいふ) 額, 配賦済み製造間接費 (＝absorbed overhead, applied burden, applied overhead)
　debt burden 債務負担, 債務超過
　burden charge 負担金
　burden of debt service 金利負担
　burden of disposing of bad loans 不良債権処理の負担, 不良債権処理損失
　burden rate 間接費配賦率, 製造間接費配賦率, 配賦率
　factory burden 製造間接費
　interest payment burden 金利負担, 利払い負担 (＝the burden of interest payment)
　overhead burden 経費
　tax burden 租税負担
　wage burden 人件費
▶Major banking groups reported after-tax losses for the second consecutive business year due to the *burden* of disposing of bad loans and slumping stock markets. 不良債権処理の負担 [不良債権処理損失] や株式不況の低迷で, 大手銀行は2期連続の税引き後赤字となった。
bureau 名 局, 事務局, 机
burn 動 焼く, 焼ける, 燃やす
burn rate バーン・レート, 資本燃焼率 (新規企業が営業キャッシュ・フローを生み出す前に経費支弁のために資本を消費する率)
burnout 名 燃え尽き, 燃え尽き症候群, 虚脱感, 心身の衰弱
▶More multinational firms' workers are experiencing *burnout* as they work longer hours. 多国籍企業の社員の場合, 労働時間の増加に伴って燃え尽き症候群の経験者が増えている。
business 名 事業, 商売, 商業, 取引, 営業, 業務, 業容, 職務, 職業, 実務, 実業, 実業界, 会社, 企業, 経営, 業績, ビジネス (⇒**core business**)
　banking business 銀行業, 銀行業務
　big business 大企業, 巨大企業
　branch business 支店業務

business activities　事業活動, 企業活動, 営業活動, 経営活動, 景気, 商況, 業況
business affairs　業務, 事業
business area　商圏
business base　営業基盤, 事業基盤, 経営基盤
business body　経済団体　(=business group)
business day　営業日, 就業日, 平日, 銀行営業日
business decision　経営判断
business development　ビジネス開発, ビジネスの展開, 業務展開
business dispute　ビジネス上の紛争　(⇒dispute)
business equipment　事務機器, ビジネス機器, 企業設備
business foundation　事業基盤, 経営基盤, 経営の根幹, 経営体力
business improvement administrative order　業務改善行政命令, 業務改善命令　(=business improvement order)
business integration proposal　事業統合案, 経営統合案　(⇒business integration)
business integrity　商業道徳
business leaders　実業界の指導者, 財界の指導者, 財界首脳経済界の首脳, 企業経営者, 企業のトップ
business line　業務分野, 事業分野, 事業部門, 事業の種類, 業種, 営業品目, 営業項目, 営業科目, 事業ライン　(⇒line of business)
business logistics　企業のトータル物流管理, ビジネス・ロジスティクス
business management　企業経営, 企業管理, 経営管理, 業務管理, 経営　(⇒corporate executive officer)
business manager　企業経営者, 経営者, 業務管理者, 営業部長
business merger　経営統合, 企業の合併　(=merger of businesses)
business operator　事業者
business opportunity　事業機会, 商機会, 商機, ビジネス・チャンス　(=business chance)
business outlook　景気見通し, 企業見通し, 業績見通し　(=business projection)
business partnership　業務提携　(=business tie-up)
business planning　経営計画, 経営企画, 事業計画, ビジネス・プランニング
business planning head office　経営企画本部
business policy　経営方針, 経営政策, 営業政策, 営業方針
business process model　ビジネス・プロセス・モデル
business profit　企業収益, 企業利益, 業務利益　(=business income)
business school　経営学大学院ビジネス・スクール　(⇒MBA)
business sector　事業分野, 業種, 企業セクター, 企業, 産業界, 業界
business sentiment DI of major firms　大企業の業況判断指数(DI), 大企業の業況判断DI
business settlement　取引決済　(⇒checking account)
business solution　ビジネス・ソリューション(ITシステムによる問題解決策)
business statistics　経営統計, 経営分析
business strength　経営体力, 経営力, 事業での成功
business to business　企業対企業, 企業間取引　(=b to b, B2B, business to business EC)
business to consumer　企業対消費者, 企業対消費者間の取引　(=b to c, B2C, business to consumer EC)
business to government　政府調達　(=b to g, B2G)
credit business　信用業務, 信用事業, 与信業務
deterioration in the business situation　経営悪化
dot com business　ドットコム・ビジネス, IT関連ビジネス
e-business　eビジネス, Eビジネス
exchange business　為替業務
expanding business　事業拡大
extension of business　業務拡張
failed business　経営破綻した企業
fashion business　ファッション事業
financial business　金融業務, 金融ビジネス
food business　食品事業
forward business　先物取引
global business strategy　グローバル経営戦略, 企業の世界戦略, 世界的企業戦略
government-business cooperation　官民協調
investment advisory business　投資顧問業
IT business　ITビジネス, IT企業
leading business　先導企業
life and reinsurance business　生保・再保険事業
mortgage business　住宅ローン事業, 不動産担保金融
Net business　ネット・ビジネス
niche business　得意分野
noncore business　非中核事業, 非主力事業

online business オンライン業務, オンライン・ビジネス
scope of business 業務範囲
securities business 証券業務
solution business 問題解決型営業, ソリューション・ビジネス
start-up business 新規企業, 新興企業, ベンチャー企業, ベンチャー分野 (＝start-up, start-up company, start-up firm)
suspension of business 取引停止, 営業停止
tax on business 企業課税
transfer of business 営業譲渡
troubled business 経営の行き詰まり, 経営難, 行き詰まった経営, 経営危機の企業, 経営不振企業
volume of business 取引高
water treatment business 水処理事業
▸Revenues increased across our *business*. 当社の事業全般にわたって, 収益は増加しました。

business alliance 業務提携 (＝business tie-up), 経済団体
▸If the two companies join hands, it would create the nation's largest retail *business alliance*, with more than ¥6 trillion in sales. 両社が提携すれば, 売上高で6兆円を超える国内最大の流通グループ[流通業連合]が誕生する。

business capacity 営業力
▸We are strengthening the *business capacity* of other stores located outside Tokyo. 当社は, 東京以外の地方店舗の営業力を強化している。

business climate 事業環境, 企業環境, 経営環境, 企業風土, 経営風土, 企業の体質, 景況, 商況, 景気 (＝business environment)
▸This accomplishment is especially gratifying given the current business climate. この成果は, 現在の経営環境を考えますと, まことに喜ばしい限りです。

business conditions 景気, 商況, 業況, 業況判断(DI), 業態, 事業環境経営の実態
▸Japan's economic recovery helped improve the *business conditions* of corporate borrowers. 日本の景気回復で, 融資先企業の業況が改善した。

business confidence 景況感, 業況感, 業況判断, 企業マインド, 企業心理, ビジネス・コンフィデンス (＝business mind, business sentiment)
▸*Business confidence* among major manufacturers improved marginally in the three months to December. 10－12月期の大企業・製造業の景況感が, 小幅ながら改善した。
▸The diffusion index (DI) of *business confidence* refers to the percentage of companies that feel business conditions to be favorable, minus the ratio of firms that think otherwise. 業況判断指数(DI)は, 景気が「良い」と感じている企業の割合(%)から, 「悪い」と感じている企業の割合を差し引いた指数だ。

business cost 経費, 事業コスト
▸The payment is not a *business cost* but constitutes a social expense which should be taxed. 支払った金は, 経費ではなく, 課税対象の交際費にあたる。

business cycle 景気循環, 景気 (＝trade cycle)
▸The economy still remains in a recovery phase in the *business cycle*. 景気は, まだ回復局面にある[景気の回復基調はまだ続いている]。

business diversification 事業多角化, 経営多角化 (⇒diversification)
▸Rising debts are mainly due to our business diversification. 借入金の増大は, 主に事業多角化によるものです。

business environment 経営環境, 企業環境, 事業環境, 景気 (＝business climate)
▸The publishing industry's *business environment* has been getting increasingly tough. 出版業界の経営環境[事業環境]は, 厳しさを増している。

business group 企業グループ, 企業集団 (＝corporate group)
▸Hankyu will work with Hanshin to create a new *business group* that can contribute to shareholders and local communities. 阪急は, 株主や地域社会に貢献できる新しい企業集団になれるよう, 阪神と力を合わせて行く方針だ。

business improvement order 業務改善命令 (＝business improvement administrative order)
▸The Financial Services Agency issued *business improvement orders* to the bank. 金融庁は, 同行に対して業務改善命令を出した。

business integration 事業統合, 経営統合 (＝integration of business, merger)
▸We have submitted a *business integration* proposal to the firm to acquire all of its ordinary shares through a takeover bid. 株式公開買付け(TOB)で同社の普通株式を全株取得するため, 当社は同社に経営統合案を提出した[経営統合を申し入れた]。

business line 事業分野, 事業部門, 事業の種類, 業種, 営業品目, 営業項目, 営業科目, 事業ライン (⇒line of business)
▸The firm has been diversifying its *business lines*.

同社は，事業分野の多角化を進めている。

business method 経営手法
▸Many corporate managers often praise *business methods* used in the United States. とかく，米国流の経営手法をもてはやす経営者が多い。

business model ビジネス手法, 事業モデル, 事業計画, ビジネス・モデル
business model patent ビジネス・モデル特許
information-technology business model 情報技術(IT)を活用したビジネス手法特許［ビジネス・モデル特許］
▸Japan Post and Lawson will build a new *business model* to provide goods and services at post office and use post office sites for the operation of convenience stores. 日本郵政とローソンは，郵便局での物品・サービスの提供とコンビニ化のための郵便局のスペース活用を目指して，新事業計画を策定する。

business operating company 事業会社
▸The firm will be split into a *business operating company* and an asset management firm. 同社は，事業会社と資産管理会社に分割される。

business operation 業務運営, 企業運営, 企業経営, 経営, 営業活動, 営業運転, 業務, 事業, 業容
▸The new Nikko president will announce a concrete strategy for integration of Citigroup and Nikko's *business operations* by mid-March. 日興の新社長は，3月中旬までにシティグループと日興の経営統合の具体的な戦略を発表する。

business organization 企業組織, 実業団体, 経済団体, 財界団体
▸Nippon Keidanren (the Japan Business Federation) is the most powerful of the nation's three major *business organizations*. 日本経団連の影響力は，日本の主要財界3団体のなかでは最も強い。

business partner 取引先企業, 取引先
▸Opposition from the company's labor union and *business partners* emerged as obstacles to the signing of an agreement. 同社の労働組合や取引先の反発が，契約調印の障害となった。

business performance 営業成績, 業績, 決算, 経営 (=business results)
▸*Business performance* has improved since the latter half of last year. 昨年後半から，業績は向上しています。

business plan 事業計画, 経営計画, 経営構想 (=business planning)
long-term business plan 長期事業計画, 長期経営計画, 長期経営構想

midterm business plan 中期事業計画, 中期経営計画, 中期経営構想
▸Our midterm *business plan* includes 4,300 job cuts and pay cuts of up to 60% for executives. 当社の中期経営計画には，社員の4,300人削減と役員報酬の最大60%カットが含まれている。

business practice 商慣習, 商慣行, 企業慣行, 取引慣行, 取引方法, 営業手法, 業務
▸The Financial Services Agency ordered the firm to suspend part of its operations as punishment for the major insurance company's illegal *business practices*. 金融庁は，保険大手の同社に業務で法令違反があったとして，同社に一部業務停止命令を出した。

business process reengineering 業務改革, ビジネス・プロセスの再設計, ビジネス・プロセス・リエンジニアリング《略 BPR》(事業全体の業務内容やその流れを分析し,再構築して組織の変更, 意思決定や事務の迅速化, 顧客サービスの向上などを図ること)

business projection 業績見通し
▸The company revised downward its *business projection* for the business year ending in August this year. 同社は，本年8月期決算の業績見通しを下方修正した。

business quarter 四半期
▸The company will hold a press conference every *business quarter* to explain its business results. 同社は今後，四半期ごとに記者会見を開いて業績内容について説明する。

business resources 経営資源
▸Outsourcing is a strategic method that effectively uses *business resources*. アウトソーシングは，経営資源を有効に活用するための戦略的手法です。

business restructuring 事業再編成, 事業再編, 企業のリストラ
business restructuring activities 事業再編成作業
business restructuring costs [charge] 事業再編成費用 (=restructuring costs)
▸We are undertaking a major *business restructuring* which will improve our competitive position. 当社は現在，競争力強化をめざして大規模な事業再編に着手しています。

business results 営業成績, 企業業績, 業績, 決算 (=business performance, operating results; ⇒auditing firm, business quarter)
improved business results 業績向上
poor business results 業績の落ち込み, 業績不

振, 業績低迷
unprecedentedly good business results 空前の好決算
▶Many listed companies announce their midterm consolidated *business results* for the six months up to September in October. 上場企業の多くは, 10月に9月中間連結決算[4-9月期の中間連結決算]を発表する。

business right 営業権
▶Studio Ghibli will take over relevant *business rights* from Tokuma Shoten Publishing Co. for between ¥15 billion and ¥20 billion. スタジオジブリが, 徳間書店から関連営業権を150億-200億円で取得する[徳間書店から150億-200億円で関連営業権の譲渡を受ける]。

business sentiment 景況感, 企業の景況感, 企業の業況感, 業況判断, 企業マインド, 企業心理 (=business confidence, business mind; ⇒ **diffusion index of business sentiment [confidence]**)
▶Corporate *business sentiment* improved in the three months to September for the sixth consecutive quarter. 7-9月の企業の景況感は, 6期連続で改善した。

business sentiment index 業況判断指数, 業況判断DI (=diffusion index of business sentiment)
▶The *business sentiment index* represents the percentage of companies reporting favorable business conditions minus the percentage of those reporting unfavorable conditions. 業況判断指数は, 景気が良いと答えた企業の割合(%)から景気が悪いと答えた企業の割合(%)を差し引いた指数だ。

business soundness 経営の健全性
▶Banks' capital adequacy ratio is an index that shows their *business soundness*. 銀行各行の自己資本比率は, 銀行の経営の健全性を示す指標である。

business strategy 経営戦略, 事業戦略, 企業戦略, ビジネス戦略
▶The company's figures are the fruit of its global *business strategy*. 同社の業績は, 同社のグローバル経営戦略の成果である。

business structure 企業構造, 企業体質, 事業構造, 産業構造
▶The firm aims to improve its *business structure* by focusing on these profitable sectors. 同社は, これらの収益力のある事業分野に的を絞って, 企業体質の改善を目指している。

business suspension 業務停止
▶During the period of *business suspension*, the company is not allowed to extend new loans, solicit new customers or call in loans. 業務停止期間中, 同社は新規の融資や新規顧客の勧誘, 貸出の回収などの業務はできない。

business term 事業期間決算期
business term ending in December 12月終了事業年度, 12月期, 12月期決算, 12月決算期
business term ending in March 3月期, 3月決算期
business term ending in September 9月期, 9月決算期, 9月中間決算
business terms [terms and conditions] 取引条件
▶Toyota's consolidated sales, which surpassed ¥10 trillion in the *business term* ending in March 1997, doubled to ¥21 trillion in the following nine years. トヨタの連結売上高は, 1997年3月期に10兆円を突破した後, 9年間で21兆円に倍増した。

business tie-up 業務提携, 事業の提携, 事業連携 (=business alliance; ⇒**allocate, convenience, float, refinery, upmarket**)
▶Through the multilateral *business tie-up*, the three leading newspapers of Japan will bolster their ability to disseminate information as news media. この多角的な事業連携により, 日本の大手新聞3社は, 報道機関としての情報発信力を強化する。

business tie-up plan 業務提携計画
▶The firm withdrew the capital increase and *business tie-up plans* during the tender offer. 同社は, TOB(株式公開買付け)期間中に増資と業務提携計画を撤回した。

business world 経済界, 産業界, 実業界, 業界 (=business circles, business community)
▶The Cultural Affairs Agency started collecting opinions from the *business world* and experts this year. 文化庁は, 今年から業界や有識者[専門家]の意見の集約を図っている。

business year 営業年度, 事業年度, 会計年度, 年度, 会計期間 (=accounting year, financial year, fiscal year; ⇒**business projection, cut**)
during the business year 期中
the business year ending in March 2010 2010年3月期, 2010年3月期決算, 2010年3月終了事業年度, 2009年度
the business year that ended in December 2009 2009年12月期決算, 2009年12月終了事

業年度, 2009年度
the next business year　来期, 来年度
the settlement of accounts for the business year ending March 31　3月期決算, 3月31日終了事業年度の決算
the whole business year　通期（＝the entire business year）
this business year　今期, 今年度
▶The brokerage firm inflated its consolidated earnings for its *business year* through March 2009.　同証券会社は, 2009年3月期の連結利益を水増ししていた。

businesspeople　ビジネスマン, ビジネスピープル

bust 動　破産する

buy 動　買う, 購入する, 取得する, 買い取る, 買収する,〈株などを〉引き受ける（＝acquire, purchase）
▶Mitsui Fudosan will *buy* 9.85 million shares in Imperial Hotel from current top shareholder Kokusai Kogyo Co.　三井不動産は, 現在の筆頭株主の国際興業から帝国ホテルの株式985万株を取得する。

buy back　買い戻す, 買い取る（＝repurchase）
▶The company plans to *buy back* its own shares in a bid to completely control its subsidiaries.　同社は, 子会社の100％経営支配権を得るため, 自社株買いをする方針だ。
▶To date, we *have bought back* about 26 million shares—close to 4.5 percent of the outstanding shares of the company.　これまで当社は, 約2,600万株（当社の発行済み株式総数の約4.5％）を買い戻しました。

buy into　…に投資する（＝invest in）
▶Investors *bought into* prospects for growth in the M&A market.　投資家は, M&A（企業の合併・買収）市場の成長力に投資した。

buy or sell order　売買注文
▶Nonresident securities houses without TSE membership are obliged to get Financial Services Agency approval for each *buy or sell order* to be placed in Tokyo.　東証の参加資格がない［東証の会員でない］海外の証券会社が東証に売買注文を出す場合には, 個別に金融庁の許可を得なければならない。

buy order　買い注文
▶No deals were struck and the issue ended at a bid price of ¥3.15 million due to a massive wave of *buy orders*.　売買が成立せず, 大量の買い注文が殺到したため, 同銘柄は315万円の買い気

配で終了した。

buy out　〈権利などを〉買い取る, 買い占める, 買い上げる, 買収する, 乗っ取る, 手に入れる, 金で手を引かせる, 金を払って退職させる
▶Oji Paper Co.'s bid to *buy out* Hokuetsu Paper Mills Ltd. did not succeed.　王子製紙が実施している北越製紙株の株式公開買付け（TOB）は, 成立［成功］しなかった。
▶We plan to *buy out* the firm's semiconductor division.　当社は, 同社の半導体事業部門を完全買収する方針だ。

buy up　買い占める, 買い取る
▶The former head of the Murakami Fund instructed Livedoor Co. to *buy up* the radio broadcaster's shares during after-hours trading.　村上ファンドの元代表が, 同ラジオ放送株を時間外取引で買い占めるようライブドア側に指南していた。

buyback 名　買戻し, 買い取り, 買上げ, 自社株買戻し, 自社株買い, 自社株取得, 早期退職勧奨, 退職奨励金（＝buyout）
　buyback limits　自社株の取得枠, 自社株取得枠（＝share buyback limits, stock buyback limits; ⇒**decide**）
　equity buyback　株式の買戻し, 自社株の買戻し
　share [stock] buyback　自社株買戻し, 自社株買い, 株式買戻し（「自社株買い」は, 配当を支払わなければならない会社の株主数が減ることを意味する）
▶GM is making a new round of *buyback* offers to U.S. hourly workers.　GMは現在, 時間給労働者［工場従業員］に対して新たに早期退職勧奨の申し入れを行っている。
▶Stock *buybacks* are commonly aimed at raising profits per share and enhance dividend payouts to shareholders.　株式買戻しのねらいは, 一般に1株当たり利益の引上げと株主への配当支払いの増額にある。

buyback scheme for beef　牛肉買上げ制度（＝beef buyback system）
▶Nippon Meat Packers, Inc. misused the government's *buyback scheme for beef*.　日本ハムは, 政府［国］の牛肉買上げ制度を悪用した。

buyer 名　〈株などの〉引受先, 買い主, 買い手, 売却先, 購買者, 仕入担当者, 海外の輸入者, バイヤー
　buyer awareness　購買者意識, 買い手の意識
　buyer behavior　購買者行動
　buyer segmentation　購買者細分化
　buyer's market　買い手市場
　buyer's monopoly　買い手独占
　buyer's option　買い主の選択

institutional buyer　機関投資家
prospective buyer　見込み客
▶As the firm is offering three types of preferred shares, potential *buyers* will be able to choose stocks depending on their own circumstances.　同社は3種類の優先株を発行するため，引受先はその事情に応じて株を選択できることになる。

buyout [buy-out] 名
買取り，買占め，買収，営業権［経営権］の取得，乗っ取り，株式の買付け，金を払って引き取らせること，金を払って退職させること(buyback)，早期退職勧奨，早期退職奨励金 (⇒**early retirement and buyout packages**)

buyout fund　買収ファンド
buyout of minorities　少数株主持ち分の買取り
corporate buyout　企業買収 (＝corporate acquisition)
corporate buyout strategy　企業買収戦略
employee buyout　従業員の会社買取り，従業員の経営権買取り (＝worker buyout)
leveraged buyout　レバレッジド・バイアウト《略 **LBO**》
management buyout　マネジメント・バイアウト《略 **MBO**》(経営陣による自社株式の公開買付け)
strategic buyout　戦略的買収 (経営戦略に基づいて行われる企業買収)
worker buyout　従業員の経営権買取り

▶Ford Motor Co. will cut about $5 billion in operating costs mainly by offering early retirement and *buyout* packages to all hourly workers and to white-collar employees.　米フォード・モーターは，主に工場従業員［時間給労働者］とホワイトカラー従業員を対象に早期退職優遇制度を導入して，営業経費約50億ドルを削減する方針だ。

buyout firm　企業買収(M&A)専門会社
▶Sony Corp. and two U.S. *buyout firms* are in talks to buy U.S. film studio Metro-Goldwyn-Mayer Inc. for about $5 billion.　ソニーと米国の企業買収専門会社2社が共同で，米国の映画会社MGM（メトロ・ゴールドウィン・メイヤー）を約50億ドルで買収する交渉を進めている。

buyout offer　買収提案
▶Tribune Co. has accepted a *buyout offer* from a real estate investor.　米トリビューン（米新聞業界2位）は，不動産投資家による買収提案を受け入れた。

buyout plan　買収計画
▶We will accept a *buyout plan* proposed by the company.　当社は，同社が提案した買収計画を受け入れる方針です。

buyout strategy　買収戦略
▶The firm's corporate *buyout strategy* took full advantage of the effect of stock splits.　同社の企業買収戦略は，株式分割の効果を最大限，利用した。

bylaws　会社の付属定款，通常定款，準則，付則，細則，規則，業務規則，内規，規約，〈地方自治体の〉条例，地方法 (＝by-laws, byelaws)
▶The officers of the corporation shall consist of a President, one or more Vice-Presidents as may be prescribed by the *Bylaws*, a Secretary, a Treasurer, and such other officers as may be prescribed by the *Bylaws*.　会社の役員は，社長，付属定款で定める1名以上の副社長，秘書役，会計役と，付属定款で定めるその他の役員とで構成するものとする。

Byrd Amendment　米バード修正法，バード法，米国の反ダンピング(不当廉売)関税分配法，反ダンピング・相殺関税分配法 (米政府がダンピング(不当廉売)と認定した輸入製品に対して課す関税の収入を，ダンピング被害を申し立てた企業に救済金として分配することを定めた法律。正式名称はContinued Dumping and Subsidy Offset Actで，2000年10月に成立)
▶The *Byrd Amendment* stipulates that Washington distribute revenues from antidumping tariffs to affected companies.　米国のバード法の規定に基づき，米国政府は反ダンピング関税の収入を被害企業に分配している。

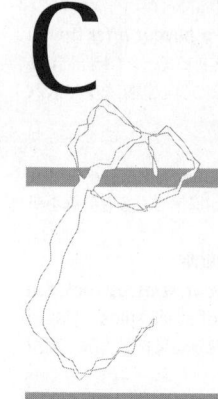

C

c 消費者 （=consumer; ⇒b）
  c to b to c ブローカーを仲介したオークション（=C2B2C, consumer to business to consumer）
  c to c 消費者対消費者の取引［電子商取引］，一般消費者同士の取引，一般顧客同士の取引，消費者対消費者（=C2C, consumer to consumer, consumer to consumer EC）

cable 名 有線，電線，ケーブル（⇒**communication capacity**）
  cable radio broadcasting 有線放送（=cable broadcasting）
  cable network 有線テレビ網，CATV網
  cable transmission ケーブル伝送
  fiber cable 光ファイバー・ケーブル（=fiber optic cable, optical fiber cable）
  local cable 市内ケーブル
  subscriber cable 加入者ケーブル
  toll cable 市外ケーブル
▶Usen Corp. controls about 80 percent of the ¥100 billion *cable* radio broadcasting market. 「有線」は，1,000億円の有線放送市場の約8割を支配している。

CACM 中米共同市場（Central American Common Marketの略）

CAD コンピュータによる設計，コンピュータを利用した設計の自動化システム，コンピュータ支援設計，コンピュータ援用設計（computer-aided designの略）

CAE コンピュータ援用エンジニアリング（computer-aided engineeringの略）

calendar year 暦年，年度，12月期決算（「暦年」1月1日から12月31日までの1年で，a full calendar yearは1暦年，満1暦年を指す。⇒**business year, quarter**）
▶*Calendar year* means a twelve-month period commencing on January 1 and expiring on December 31. 暦年とは，1月1日に始まり12月31日に終わる12か月の期間をいう。

call 動 償還する，貸付け金の返済［返還］を求める
  call in loans 貸付け金を回収する，貸出を回収する
  call the existing bonds 既発債を償還する
  call the loan 貸付け金の返済を請求する，ローンの償還を請求する
  call the preferred issue at a premium プレミアムを払って優先株式を償還する
▶During March 2009, the Corporation *called*, at a rate of 101%, its 11.5% Eurodollar notes due 2012 with a carrying value totaling $93 million. 2009年3月に当社は，帳簿価格総額が9,300万ドルで2012年満期11.5%のユーロドル債を101%で償還しました。

call 名 要求，請求，支払い請求，払い込み請求，短期資金（コール・ローン），買う権利，買付け選択権，繰上げ償還，任意償還，随時償還，電話，通話，訪問，コール
  call account 未払い勘定
  call date 繰上げ償還日
  call detail recording 通話明細記録
  call letter 払い込み請求書
  call loan コール貸付け金，銀行相互間の当座貸付け金，コール・ローン（銀行相互間の要求払い短期貸付け金）
  call money コール借入金，銀行相互間の当座借入金，コール・マネー
  call option 株式買付け選択権，買いオプション，

コール・オプション

call price 償還価格, 繰上げ償還価格, 任意償還価格, 期前償還価格, 買入れ価格, 買戻し価格, コール価格 (＝redemption price)

call protection 据え置き期間, 任意償還権不行使期間

call sales 訪問販売

call salesman 訪問販売員

cash call 増資, 株主割当て発行増資

long call コールの買い, ロング・コール

money at call コール・マネー (＝call money, money on call)

overnight call 翌日物コール

put and call 特権付き売買, プット・アンド・コール

short call コールの売り, ショート・コール

yield to call コール利回り, 繰上げ償還利回り

call center 電話での顧客対応窓口業務, コール・センター

▸The new customer management system will establish a network connecting the head office with the firm's sales offices and *call centers*, allowing the different branches to track customers. 新顧客管理システムでは, 同社の本社と営業拠点およびコール・センターをネットワーク化して, 個々の営業所で顧客情報を追跡できるようにする。

call market 短期市場, 短期資金市場, コール市場 (＝call money market)

コール市場とは➡金融機関や証券会社相互間の短期資金の貸借を行う場が「コール市場」で, 資金の貸し手から見た場合をコール・ローン, 資金の借り手から見た場合をコール・マネーという。コール取引には当日中に資金決済される半日物, 翌日決済の無条件物と, 翌々日決済の2日物や7日物などの期日物がある。

call premium 任意償還プレミアム, 償還プレミアム, 繰上げ償還時に支払われる割増金, コール・オプションを買うときに支払うオプション料, コール・プレミアム

▸The benefits of refinancing were partly offset by cost of that refinancing such as *call premiums*. 借換えの効果は, 償還プレミアムのような資金再調達関連費用によって, 一部相殺されています。

callable 形 償還できる, 償還可能な, 繰上げ償還可能な

callable bond 任意償還可能社債, コーラブル債

callable preferred stock 償還優先株

non-callable 繰上げ償還不能, 期限前償還のない

non-callable US government obligations 期限前償還のない米国国債

▸These notes are *callable* by the Company at the carrying value at any time. これらの債券は, 当社がいつでも帳簿価格で繰上げ償還することができます。

CalPERS カルパース, カリフォルニア州公務員退職年金基金 (California Public Employees' Retirement Systemの略)

CALS 瞬時電子取引, キャルス (Commerce at Light Speedの略)

CALS 生産・調達・運用支援統合情報システム, 継続的調達と製品のライフサイクルの支援, キャルス (Continuous Acquisition and Lifestyle Supportの略)

CAM コンピュータによる製造, コンピュータを利用した製造自動化システム, コンピュータ支援製造, コンピュータ援用製造 (computer-aided manufacturingの略)

CAMEL 資本(capital), 資産内容(asset quality), 経営(management), 収益(earnings), 流動性(liquidity)

campaign 名 活動, 運動, 販売促進運動, 販促キャンペーン, 選挙運動, 作戦, キャンペーン

advertising campaign 広告キャンペーン, 広告・宣伝活動

anti-pollution campaign 公害反対運動

campaign finance law 選挙資金規制法

information campaign 広報活動

presidential campaign 大統領選挙運動

productivity campaign 生産性向上運動

promotional campaign 販促キャンペーン

sales campaign 商戦, 売出し, 販売キャンペーン, セールス・キャンペーン

sales promotion campaign 販売促進運動, 販売促進キャンペーン

▸During the latest summer sales *campaign*, one leading retailer offered a 32-inch liquid crystal display television at less than ¥200,000. 今夏の商戦で, ある量販店は32型の液晶テレビを20万円以下で提供した。

▸The bank ran a *campaign* to increase deposits by introducing a five-year time deposit with a high interest rate of 1.7 percent. 同行は, 年1.7％の高金利の5年定期を導入して預金量を増やすキャンペーンを実施した。

▸The progress in Japan's anti-global warming *campaign* is largely attributable to energy saving efforts by corporations and ordinary households. 日本の地球温暖化対策が進んでいる大きな要因として，企業や一般家庭の省エネ努力が挙げられる。

cancel 動 〈株式を〉償却［消却］する，取り消す，解除する，解約する，中止する，キャンセルする
▶If the delay lasts more than thirty days, the other party may immediately *cancel* the order without liability. 履行遅延が30日以上続く場合，相手方は責任を負うことなく直ちにこの注文を取り消すことができる。
▶The creditor banks are considering having the company reduce its capital by *canceling* a portion of its preferred shares held by them. 同社の取引銀行は現在，各行が保有する同社の優先株（議決権がない代わりに配当が高い株式）の償却による同社の資本金引下げ［減資］を検討している。

cancelable [cancellable] 形 解約可能な
　cancelable lease 解約可能リース，解約可能賃貸借，解約可能賃貸借契約
　non-cancelable lease 中途解約不能リース
　unconditionally cancelable 無条件解消可能な
▶We lease equipment to others through operating leases, the majority of which are *cancelable*. 当社はオペレーティング・リース方式で設備を他社にリースしており，その大部分は解約可能です。

cancelation [cancellation] 名 〈株式の〉消却，〈契約の〉解除，解約，免除，破棄，抹消，中止
　cancelation agreement 解除契約
　cancelation before maturity 中途解約
　cancelation money 解約金
　cancellation of contract 契約の解除（＝contract cancelation）
　cancelation of indebtedness 負債の免除
　cancellation of insurance 保険の解約
　cancelation of license 実施権の解除
　cancelation of stocks 株式消却（＝cancellation of shares, stock cancellation）
　cancelation policy キャンセル規定
　debt cancelation 負債の帳消し，負債の棒引き（＝write-off）
　mark down cancelation 値下げ取消高
　mark up cancelation 値上げ取消高
　policy cancelation 保険の解約
▶The Company repurchased for *cancelation* its own common shares for an aggregate amount of $300 million. 当社は，消却の目的で，総額3億ドルの自社普通株式を買い戻しました。

cancer treatment drug 抗がん剤
▶Foreign-affiliated pharmaceutical makers are targeting the Japanese *cancer treatment drug* market. 外資系製薬会社が，日本の抗がん剤市場に攻勢をかけている。

cannibalism 名 共食い，カニバリズム
canvass 動 勧誘する
CAO 財務統括役員，最高財務担当役員（**chief accounting officer**の略）
CAP コンピュータ援用生産，コンピュータ支援生産（**computer-aided production**の略）
cap 名 上限，最高限度，最高，上限金利，キャップ
　interest rate cap 金利キャップ
　life-of-loan cap 貸出期間中の上限金利
　market cap 時価総額
　set a cap on …に上限を設ける
　small cap index 小型株指数
▶The new law of California imposes a first-in-the-nation emissions *cap* on utilities, refineries and manufacturing plants. 米カリフォルニア州の新法は，発電所［公共事業体］や製油所，製造工場などの温室効果ガス排出量に米国内で初めて上限を設けている。

cap and collar 金利変動幅固定の
cap-and-dollar mortgage 金利変動幅固定住宅ローン，金利変動幅固定型の担保貸付け
cap-and-trade system 排出量取引制度，キャップ・アンド・トレード制度（企業が出す二酸化炭素など温室効果ガスの排出量に上限を設け，その過不足分（排出量）を市場で売買する仕組みのこと）
▶Full-fledged discussions have started over *cap-and-trade system*. 排出量取引制度をめぐって，本格的な議論がスタートした。

capability 名 能力，潜在能力，力，可能性，将来性，才能，素質，手腕，技術，機能，通信機能
　bond redemption capability 社債償還能力
　capital management capabilities 資産運用力
　debt service capability 債務返済能力（＝debt servicing capability）
　export capability 輸出能力
　fabrication capability 製造技術
　operating capability 操業能力（＝operation capability）
　profit-making capability 収益力
　servicing capability 事務処理能力
　technological capability 技術力
▶We are adding dramatic *capabilities* to the network, while simplifying network operations and containing network operating costs. 当社では，ネットワーク運営の簡素化とネットワーク運営コストの節減に取り組む一方，ネットワークに画

期的な機能を付加する方針です。

capacity 名 能力, 資本, 資金, 設備, 生産能力, 操業度, 発電容量, 収容力, 収容能力, 地位, 資格, 立場, キャパシティ (⇒**communication capacity, production capacity**)
 annual capacity 年間生産能力
 average capacity 平均操業度
 business capacity 営業力
 capacity building 能力開発
 capacity ratio 設備稼動率, 稼動率, 創業率, 操業度比率 (=capacity usage ratio)
 capacity utilization 設備利用, 設備稼働, 設備稼動率, 操業, 操業度
 capacity yield 最大産出高
 debt capacity 借入余力
 debt servicing capacity 債務返済能力
 deficient capacity 設備不足
 dividend capacity 配当支払い能力
 dividend paying capacity 配当支払い能力
 excess capacity 過剰設備, 超過設備, 過剰能力
 expand capacity 設備を拡張する
 full capacity 完全操業度, 全能力, 完全能力, 完全利用
 funding capacity 資金調達能力
 idle capacity 遊休設備, 遊休施設, 遊休生産能力
 increase production capacity 生産能力を拡大する
 industrial capacity 工業生産能力, 工業能力, 工業設備
 installed capacity 稼動発電能力
 manufacturing capacity 生産能力, 製造能力
 operate at full capacity フル稼働する, フル稼働状態にある
 operating capacity 操業能力, 操業度
 output capacity 生産能力, 生産設備 (=manufacturing capacity, production capacity, productive capacity)
 plant capacity 工場設備能力, 設備能力, 生産設備
 produce at full capacity フル生産体制を取る
 production capacity 生産能力, 生産設備
 service capacity サービス能力, 供給能力
 spare capacity 設備余力, 遊休設備
 supply capacity 供給能力
 transport capacity 輸送能力
▶By going digital, the company could triple the *capacity* of its existing network. デジタル化により, 同社はその既存のネットワーク容量を3倍に拡大することができた。
▶Technological advances permit us to use existing *capacity* more efficiently. 技術の進歩で, 既存の設備を一段と効率的に使用することが可能になっています。

capex 設備投資, 資本的支出, 資本支出 (=capital spending)
▶The fall in *capex* is a little surprising. 設備投資の減少は, ちょっと意外だ。

capital 名 資本, 自己資本, 資本金, 資金, 元金, 出資金, 〈保険会社の〉基金 (株式会社の資本金に相当), 正味財産, 純資産, キャピタル (⇒**equity capital, paid-in capital, return on capital employed, venture capital**)
 bank capital 銀行の自己資本
 bank capital requirements 銀行の自己資本比率規制 (=bank capital standards)
 borrowed capital 借入資本, 他人資本, 外部資本
 capital affiliation 資本提携 (⇒**cooperation**)
 capital and liabilities ratio 資本負債比率
 capital-asset ratio 自己資本比率 (=capital adequacy ratio, capital-to-asset ratio, net worth ratio)
 capital authorized 公称資本金
 capital constraints 自己資本比率規制 (=capital adequacy rule, capital requirements)
 capital deficit 資本不足, 債務超過 (=net capital deficiency)
 capital demand 資金需要, 資本需要
 capital efficiency 資本効率
 capital employed 使用資本, 投下資本
 capital equipment company 資本財メーカー
 capital expansion 増資, 資本増強 (=capital increase, increase of capital)
 capital export 資本輸出, 資本供給
 capital finance 資本調達
 capital flows in 資本流入
 capital flows out 資本流出
 capital formation 資本形成, 資本構成
 capital import 資本輸入, 外資導入
 capital input 資本拠出, 資本投入量
 capital introduced 拠出資本, 出資金, 資本金
 capital issue 株式発行, 増資, 株券, 株式
 capital movement 資本移動
 capital-output ratio 資本・産出量比率, 資本・産出高比率, 資本係数
 capital preservation 資産の保全
 capital raising 資本調達, 資金調達
 capital resources 資本の源泉, 資本調達源泉, 資本源泉
 capital subscription 出資, 出資金
 capital transaction 資本取引

capital transfer 資本移動, 資本移転
capital turnover 資本回転率
debt capital 借入資本, 固定負債 (＝borrowed capital, loan capital)
declared capital 公示資本, 表示資本, 法定資本
development capital 開発資金
enlarged capital 増資後の資本金
increase in capital at the market price 株式の時価発行
increase of capital 増資 (＝capital increase)
influx of foreign capital 外資流入
initial capital 当初資金
invested capital 投下資本
issued share capital 発行済み株式資本 (＝issued capital)
loan capital 借入資本, 他人資本, 負債, 借入金
outflow of capital 資本の流出, 資本の海外流出
reduction of capital 減資 (＝reduction in capital)
return on capital 資本利益率, 資本収益率, 自己資本利益率
risk capital 危険負担資本, 危険投下資本
short-term working capital 短期運転資金
stated capital 表示資本, 確定資本
subscribed capital 公募資本

▸The company aims to achieve its rehabilitation by asking its largest shareholder and group companies to increase its *capital* by ¥200 billion. 同社は，筆頭株主とグループ企業に2,000億円規模の増資引受けを仰いで，再建を目指している。

▸The company plans to increase its *capital* with help from Mitsubishi UFJ Financial Group. 同社は，三菱UFJフィナンシャル・グループの支援を得て，資本増強を計画している。

capital adequacy 資本充実度, 自己資本の充実, 自己資本比率, 資本要件, 適正資本量

capital adequacy requirements 自己資本比率規制

capital adequacy requirements against market risk BISマーケット・リスク規制, BIS第二次規制

capital adequacy ratio 自己資本比率 (＝capital-asset ratio, capital-to-asset ratio, net worth ratio)

自己資本比率とは➡ 銀行の融資残高などの総資産に対する資本金などの比率で，金融機関の経営健全性［財務の健全性］を判断するのに用いられる。国際銀行業務の銀行の自己資本比率はBIS（国際決済銀行）基準で8％以上，国内銀行業務の銀行の自己資本比率は4％以上とされている。

▸Internationally active banks are required to have *capital adequacy ratios* of at least 8 percent under rules stipulated by the Bank for International Settlements (BIS). 国際業務を行う銀行［金融機関］の自己資本比率は，国際決済銀行（BIS）が定める規則で8％以上が義務付けられている。

capital alliance 資本提携 (＝capital tie-up)

資本提携とは➡ 企業が提携関係を強化するため，株式を互いに取得したり，交換したりすること。業務関係だけの提携に比べて，一段と強い関係を構築できる。新株を発行して割り当てる第三者割当増資や，新株予約権の引受けなどの手法も使われる。

capital and business alliance 資本・業務提携 (＝capital and business links)

▸Sumitomo Mitsui Financial Group Inc. is close to reaching an agreement with moneylender Promise Co. to form a *capital and business alliance*. 三井住友フィナンシャルグループは近く，消費者金融会社のプロミスと資本・業務提携することで合意に達する見込みだ。

capital and business partnership 資本・業務提携 (＝capital and business alliance, capital and business links, capital and business tie-ups, capital and business ties)

▸Yamato Holdings Co. and Nippon Yusen K.K. will launch a *capital and business partnership*. ヤマトホールディングスと日本郵船が，資本・業務提携する方針だ。

capital base 資本基盤, 自己資本, 資本金 (⇒ **capital increment**, **equity procurement**)

▸The G-7 statement called on financial institutions to disclose losses incurred in the subprime mortgage crunch and reinforce their *capital bases* if necessary. G7声明は，金融機関にサブプライム問題関連の損失額の開示と必要に応じた資本増強をを求めた。

capital boost plan 増資計画

▸The share purchase price of Oji Paper Co.'s hostile tender offer will be raised to ¥860 per share if Hokuetsu Paper Mills ltd. drops its *capital boost plan*. 王子製紙の敵対的TOB（株式公開買付け）の株の買付け価格［TOB価格］は，北越製紙がその増資計画を撤回した場合には，1株860円に引き上げられる。

capital decrease 減資 (＝capital reduction, reduction of capital)

▸The Corporation's restructuring plan includes a

capital decrease of more than 50 percent. 当社の再建案には，50%超の減資も盛り込まれている。

capital expenditure 設備投資，固定資産投資，資本支出，資本的支出，資本投資，設備投資額，固定資産投資額，資本支出額，資本投資額 （＝capital investment, capital spending）
▶We reduced *capital expenditures* for the network in 2008. 2008年度は，通信ネットワーク向けの資本的支出額を削減しました。

capital gain 資本利得，資産売却益，資産譲渡益，株式売買益，譲渡所得，値上がり益，キャピタル・ゲイン

　capital gain tax 資本利得税，キャピタル・ゲイン税《略 CGT》

　capital gain taxation 資本利得課税，キャピタル・ゲイン税

　capital gain yield 資本利得率

　capital gains and losses 資本利得および損失，資産譲渡損益，株式譲渡損益，譲渡損益，株式売買損益
▶The bank can expect large *capital gains* from the listing of Mizuho Securities. 同行としては，（みずほ証券に出資することで）みずほ証券の上場により多額の株式譲渡益を期待することができる。
▶The tax rate on *capital gains* from stock sales and on dividend income was lowered to 10 percent from 20 percent. 株式譲渡益［株式売却益］と受取配当金の税率は，20%から10%に引き下げられた。

capital increase 増資，資本増強，〈保険会社の〉基金の積み増し［増額］，基金増資 （＝capital expansion, capital increment, capital injection）
　増資とは➡会社が資本金を増やすことを増資という。これには，払込み金を取って新株を発行する有償増資と，株主から払込み金を取らない増資がある。
▶The *capital increase* will bring the insurer's solvency margin ratio by about 25 percentage points. 基金の積み増し［基金増資］で，この保険会社のソルベンシー・マージン（支払い余力）比率は25%ほど上昇する。
▶The corporation is planning a ¥30 billion *capital increase* to reconstruct itself and rebuild its brand. 同社は，経営再建とブランド（ブランド・イメージ）回復のため，300億円の増資を計画している。

capital inflow 資本流入，資金の流入，流入資金，買い越し
▶*Capital inflows* from abroad have suddenly decreased. 海外からの資本流入が突然，減少した。

capital increment 増資 （＝capital increase）

▶Through 83 rounds of *capital increment* since the listing of its stocks in 2000, Livedoor swelled its capital base from ¥60 million to ¥86.2 billion. 2000年の株式上場以来，83回に及ぶ増資で，ライブドアは資本金を6,000万円から862億円まで膨らませた。

capital injection 資本の注入，資本の増強，増資，〈保険会社への〉基金拠出，〈保険会社の〉基金増資 （＝capital increase）
▶We are considering the tie-ups with other companies, including a *capital injection* into the parent company. 当社は現在，親会社への資本注入も含めて，他企業との提携を検討しているところです。

capital-intensive 資本集約型，資本集約的
▶The list of major Japanese corporations operating in China is dominated by *capital-intensive* businesses, including consumer electronics, information technology and car manufacturers. 中国に進出している主要日本企業は，家電，情報技術（IT）や自動車メーカーなど資本集約型の企業が中心だ。

capital-intensive industry 資本集約型産業
▶An airline is a *capital-intensive industry* that needs a massive amount of funds to expand its business. 航空会社は，業容拡大に巨額の資金が必要な資本集約型産業だ。

capital investment 設備投資，資本投資，公共投資，資本投下，出資，出資金 （＝capital expenditure, capital spending, investment in plant and other facilities）
▶Corporate *capital investment* and individual consumption are healthier than expected. 企業の設備投資や個人消費は，予想以上に好調だ。

capital lease 資産型リース，資本化リース，資本リース，キャピタル・リース
▶Lower long-term debt, including *capital leases*, was the net result of our refinancing and redemption activities. キャピル・リースを含めて長期負債の減少は，最終的に当社が負債の借換えと償還を実施した結果です。

capital link 資本提携 （＝capital tie-up）
▶The two firms are also eyeing a *capital link*. 両社は現在，資本提携も視野に入れている。

capital loss 資本損失，資産売却損，資産譲渡損，譲渡損失，固定資産処分損，キャピタル・ロス
▶For individuals to be able to invest on equal terms with business corporations, they should be allowed to make a deferred deduction of *capita losses* made through stock transactions.

個人が法人と同じ条件で投資できるようにするため，個人の株式売買による譲渡損失[個人の株式譲渡損]の繰延べ控除を認めるべきだ．

capital management capabilities 資産運用力
▶This financial group will send an outside board member to the bank to boost the unit's *capital management capabilities*. この金融グループは，同行に社外取締役を送り込んで，同行の資産運用力を高める方針だ．

capital market 資本市場, 長期金融市場, キャピタル・マーケット (「資本市場」は，一般的には株式・債券の発行市場(primary market: 新規発行の株式や債券が，発行者から投資家に売り渡される市場)と流通市場(secondary market: すでに発行された株式や債券が投資家間で売買される市場)を含めた証券市場とほぼ同義．⇒**money market, securities market**)
▶The Japanese *capital market* is not transparent enough. 日本の資本市場は，透明とは言いがたい．

capital outflow 資本の流出, 資本流出 (= outflow of capital)
▶To stop *capital outflow*, peso-denominated debts worth $13 billion were swapped with U.S. dollar-denominated short-term debts. 資本流出を食い止めるため，130億ドルのペソ建て債務が，米ドル建て短期債務にスワップされた．

capital outlay 資本的支出, 資本設備, 資本投資, 設備投資 (=capital expenditure, capital spending)
▶*Capital outlays* marked the third consecutive quarterly slip for the first time in about five years. 設備投資額は，約5年ぶりに3四半期(9か月)連続で減少した．

capital ownership 出資比率
▶We increased our *capital ownership* of the firm from 35 percent to 51 percent. 当社は，同社への出資比率を現在の35%から51%に引き上げました．

capital raising 資金調達
▶Japan's equity and equity-linked *capital raising* volume for the six months to June slipped 46.7 percent from a year earlier. 日本の1－6月期の株式と株式リンク債の発行による資金調達の取引高は，前年同期に比べて46.7%減少した．

capital ratio [rate] 自己資本比率 (=capital adequacy ratio, capital-asset ratio, net worth ratio; ⇒**capital adequacy ratio**)
▶The bank's *capital ratio* as of Sept. 30, 2008 stood at 11.01 percent, above the international standard of 8 percent. 同行の2008年9月30日現在の自己資本比率は11.01%で，国際基準[国際銀行業務のBIS基準]の8%を上回っている．

capital reduction 減資, 資本の削減 (=capital decrease, reduction of capital: 「減資」とは，資本金を減らして捻出した資金を企業再建に使う措置のことをいう)
▶The *capital reduction* will allow the company to raise the ¥15 billion needed to implement its restructuring plan. 減資を行うことで，同社は会社再建案の実施に必要な150億円を調達[捻出]することができる．

capital requirements 資金需要, 資金の必要額, 自己資本規制, 自己資本比率規制
▶These *capital requirements* will continue growing in 2009. これらの資金需要は，2009年度も増大するものと思われます．

capital reserve 資本準備金, 資本剰余金 (=additional-paid in capital, legal capital reserve)
▶The bank transferred about ¥500 billion in *capital reserves* to retained earnings. 同行は，資本準備金[法定準備金]のうち約5,000億円を剰余金に振り替えた．

capital shortage 資本不足, 資金不足 (=capital shortage, shortage of funds)
▶Currently, no major banks have serious *capital shortages*. 今のところ，深刻な資本不足に陥った大手銀行は見当たらない．

capital shortfall 資本不足, 資金不足, 自己資本不足 (=capital shortage, shortfall in capital)
▶Some major banks have *capital shortfalls*. 大手行の一部は，自己資本不足に陥っている．

capital spending 設備投資, 資本的支出 (=capex, capital investment)
▶*Capital spending* by Japanese companies shrank 7.7 percent in the October-December period of 2007 from a year earlier. 日本企業の2007年10－12月期の設備投資は，前年同期に比べて7.7%減少した．

capital stock 株式資本, 株式資本金, 資本金, 資本ストック, 法定資本, 総株式数, 資本株式, 株式, 普通株, 外部の人々が所有する株式
　capital stock authorized 授権資本, 授権資本金
　capital stock cut 減資 (=capital decrease, capital reduction)
　capital stock issued 発行済み資本金
　capital stock issued under employee plans 従業員プランによる株式の発行
　capital stock of subsidiary and affiliated companies 従属会社および関係会社出資金

capital stock outstanding 発行済み株式数, 流通株式, 社外資本金
capital stock, par value $1.25 per share 資本金, 額面1株当たり1.25ドル
capital stock premium 株式発行差金, 株式割増金
capital stock subscribed 引受済み資本金, 引受済み資本金勘定
capital stock unissued 未発行資本金, 資本未発行分
distribution of capital stock 株式資本の分配
full-paid capital stock 全額払込済み株式
increase in capital stock 資本ストックの増加
increase of capital stock 増資 (＝increase of capital)
large capital stock 大型株
premium on share stock 株式発行差金
reduction of capital stock 減資 (＝reduction of capital)
▸The *capital stock* of the Corporation is its only class of voting security. 当社の資本株式[当社株式]は, 当社の唯一の議決権付き証券です。

capital structure 資本構成, 資本構造, 財務基盤 (「資本構成」「資本構造」は, 総資本に占める自己資本と他人資本(負債)の割合で, バランス・シート上の資本(純資産(net worth)＋優先株式)と長期債務(long term debt)の合計額を指す)
▸The upgrade reflects Moody's expectation that the company will continue to exhibit an excellent operating performance and outstanding *capital structure*. この格上げは, 同社が引き続き好業績と際立った財務基盤を示すとのムーディーズの期待感を反映している。

capital surplus 資本剰余金, 資本準備金, 資本積立金, 差益
capital surplus reserve 資本積立金
capital surplus statement 資本剰余金計算書
▸Profits generated through selling shares of an owned company are included in the amount of capital or *capital surplus* shown on a company's balance sheet. 自社株の売却益は, 会社の貸借対照表上の資本金や資本剰余金に計上される。

capital tie-up 資本提携 (＝capital alliance, capital link, capital ties)
▸The *capital tie-up* of Nissin Food Products and Myojo Foods aims at thwarting a U.S. investment fund's hostile takeover bid for Myojo. 日清食品と明星食品の資本提携は, 明星に対する米系投資ファンドの敵対的TOB(株式公開買付け)阻止が狙いだ。

capital-to-asset ratio 株主資本比率, 自己資本比率 (＝capital adequacy ratio, capital-asset ratio, net worth ratio)
▸The *capital-to-asset* ratios at Japanese major banks are above an 8 percent global standard. 日本の大手銀行の自己資本比率は, グローバル・スタンダードの8％を上回っている。

capitalization 名 資本構成, 資本総額, 資本化, 株式資本化, 資本調達, 収益の資本還元, 資本組入れ, 発行済み株式の時価総額, 長期資本, 資産計上, 資産化, 〈会社[事業]などへの〉投資, 資本基盤 (＝capitalisation; ⇒**market capitalization**)
asset capitalization 資産計上
authorized capitalization 授権株式総数
capitalization issue 資本組入れ発行, 資本組入れ株式発行, 無償発行
capitalization of earnings 収益の資本還元, 収益力の資本還元
capitalization of interest 利息の資産化, 利息の資産計上 (＝interest capitalization)
capitalization period 資産化期間, 資産計上の期間
capitalization requirements 必要資本金額, 資本金制度 (＝capital requirements)
core capitalization コア資本
direct capitalization 直接収益還元法
improved capitalization 資本基盤の改善
large capitalization stock 大型株
low capitalization 資本基盤が弱いこと, 脆弱な資本基盤 (＝weak capitalization)
overall market capitalization 市場の時価総額, 株式時価総額 (＝total market capitalization)
strengthen capitalization 資本の充実化, 資本を充実させる
▸Depreciation expenses increased due to higher average depreciable plant and the effect of the change in the *capitalization* and amortization policy for switching machine software. 減価償却費の増加は, 減価償却の対象となる有形固定資産の平均残高が高水準に達したほか, 交換機ソフトウエアの資産化と償却方針の変更の影響によるものです。

capitalize 動 資本化する, 資産化する, 資産に計上する, 現価計上する, 資本として使用する, 資本に組み入れる, 資本を投入する, 出資する, 投資する
amounts capitalized 資産化金額
capitalized costs 資産に計上した費用, 資産化費用, 費用の資産化 (＝capitalized expenses)
capitalized interest 資産化利息, 利息資産化

capitalized leases 資産に計上したリース，資産化リース，資本化リース，リースの資産化
capitalized surplus 組入れ資本金，資本化された剰余金
poorly capitalized 資金力の乏しい
well capitalized 資金力の豊富な，自己資本の充実した
▶The new company will be *capitalized* at ¥100 billion. 新会社の資本金は，1,000億円になる見通しだ。
▶We *capitalize* the remaining software production costs as other assets. 当社は，残りのソフトウエア製作費用については，その他の資産として資産化しています。

capitalize on 利用する，活用する，生かす，つけ込む，〈需要などを〉見越す
capitalize on a market opportunity 市場機会をとらえる，市場機会を生かす
capitalize on one's market share 市場シェアを生かす，シェアを生かす
▶Japan's major automakers are *capitalizing on* improved quality at production plants overseas as part of their global strategies. 日本の大手自動車メーカーは，自動車各社の世界戦略の一環として，海外生産拠点での品質向上を活用している。

CAPP コンピュータによる工程設計 (**computer-automated process planning**の略)
caption 名 写真説明文，キャプション
captive 形 支配下の，親会社専用の，専属の
carbon 名 炭素，カーボン
  carbon dioxide emissions 二酸化炭素排出量 (=**carbon emissions**)
  carbon emissions 炭素排出量
  carbon monoxide 一酸化炭素
  carbon taxes 炭素税，二酸化炭素税(二酸化炭素の排出量に応じて課税される)
car 名 乗用車，自動車，車，カー (⇒**hybrid car**)
  alternatively-fueled car 代替燃料車
  car dealer 自動車販売業者，カー・ディーラー
  car loan 自動車ローン
  car maker 自動車メーカー
  car navigation system 自動車経路誘導システム，カーナビ，カー・ナビゲーション・システム
  clean car 低公害車，クリーン・カー
  commercial car 商用車
  electric car 電気自動車
  hydrogen fueled car 水素自動車
  new car sales 新車販売台数
  solar car ソーラー・カー
carbon dioxide 二酸化炭素
▶The Construction and Transport Ministry plans to reduce *carbon dioxide* emitted from automobiles by 3 percent annually by 2010 through road improvements. 国土交通省は，道路を改善して，自動車が排出する二酸化炭素を2010年までに年間で3％削減する計画だ。

carbon monoxide poisoning 一酸化炭素中毒 (=**CO poisoning**)
▶The executives of the two companies did not recognize the danger of a *carbon monoxide poisoning* from their products. 両社の幹部は，自社製品が引き起こす一酸化炭素中毒の危険性を認識していなかった。

carbon nanotube カーボン・ナノチューブ (超微細の炭素の管)
▶*Carbon nanotubes* were discovered in 1991 by Meijo University Prof. Sumio Iijima. カーボン・ナノチューブは，飯島澄男・名城大教授が1991年に発見した。

card 名 カード，クレジット・カード，プリント回路基板，プリント基板 (⇒**ATM card, cash card, credit card, IC ATM card, IC card**)
  access card アクセス・カード (クレジット・カードのこと)
  affiliated card 提携カード
  all purpose card 汎用カード (利用する加盟店の範囲，種類が限定されていないクレジット・カード)
  bank card バンク・カード (=**bank credit card**：主に銀行が発行するクレジット・カードで，キャッシュ・カードと同義)
  calling card 名刺
  card-holic クレジット・カード中毒
  card loan カード・ローン
  card phone カード式電話
  card reader カード読取り機《略 CR》
  card replacement カード再発行
  card shopping カード・ショッピング
  card theft and counterfeiting カードの盗難や偽造
  credit card call クレジット・カード通話
  gate card 出勤票
  green card グリーン・カード，米国での労働許可証，永住許可書
  integrated circuit card IC (集積回路) カード (=**IC card**)
  payment by card カード決済
  telephone card テレホン・カード，テレカ
  wild card 波乱材料，予測できない要因，未知数
▶In addition to being ATM *cards*, the new *cards*

can also be used as credit *cards* and to receive loans.　新型カードは，キャッシュ・カードであるほか，クレジット・カードとしても使えるし，ローンの利用にも使える。

card issuer　カード会社（クレジット・カード発行会社）
▶Retail outlets that suffer loss as a result of fraud can also claim compensation from *card issuers*.　不正使用により損害を被っている小売加盟店側も，カード会社に賠償金を請求できる。

cardholder [card holder]　カード会員（＝card member）
▶*Cardholders* verify their identity by holding their palms over a scanner on the ATM.　カード会員は，ATM（現金自動預け払い機）の読取り機に手のひらをかざして本人確認をする。

care 名　注意，注意義務，配慮，保護，看護，世話，管理，医療，医療保険，関心事，ケア
- **acute-care hospital** 救急病院（＝emergency hospital）
- **care label** 衣類などの注意ラベル
- **care of the works** 工事の管理
- **due care** 相当の注意
- **health care** 医療，医療保険，医療サービス，ヘルス・ケア
- **health care benefits** 健康保険給付，医療保険給付
- **home care** 在宅医療，在宅ケア
- **managed care** 管理医療，マネージド・ケア
- **medical care** 医療，保健医療
- **ordinary care** 通常の注意
- **reasonable care** 相当の注意
- **universal health care coverage** 国民皆医療保険制度

▶Recipient shall maintain in confidence and not disclose Confidential Information, using the same degree of *care* as it uses to protect its own confidential information of like nature.　受領者は，本「秘密情報」については，受領者が受領者自身の同じ性質の秘密情報を保護する際に払うのと同程度の注意を払ってその秘密保持に当たり，これを開示しないものとする。

care service　介護サービス，ケア・サービス
▶Our family care development fund improves the quality and supply of child- and elder-*care services* by funding community-based organizations.　当社の家族介護開発基金は，地域密着型組織地域社会ベースの組織に資金を提供することにより，幼児・高齢者介護サービスの質と量の向上を図っています。

career 名　経歴，履歴，職業，専門的職業，仕事，生活手段，生涯，成功，出世，昇進，全速力，キャリア
- **career-average pay** 職歴平均給与方式
- **career break** 育児などのための求職期間
- **career bureaucrats** キャリア組
- **career change** 転職
- **career choice** 職業選択
- **career compensation** 職務給
- **career consumer** 専業主婦
- **career counselor** 職業指導官
- **career development program** 社員の経歴開発計画，職歴開発計画，キャリア開発計画
- **career education** キャリア教育
- **career employee** 常雇い従業員，常備従業員
- **career-high** 自己最多の，自己最高の
- **career labor** 専門職労働
- **career-long employment** 終身雇用，終身雇用制
- **career opportunity** 就業機会，就業チャンス
- **career-oriented** 本格的職業志向の，学歴中心の
- **career-oriented society** 学歴中心の社会
- **career path** キャリア・パス（社員の能力や要望を考慮した人事管理制度）
- **career planning** 経歴計画，生涯計画，キャリア・プラン（＝career plan）
- **career woman** 職業婦人，働く女性，キャリア・ウーマン, OL
- **in full [mad] career** 全速力で（＝at full speed）
- **make a career** 出世する，成功する
- **midcareer plateau** 昇進停滞点，昇進停滞段階
- **move up the career ladder** 出世の階段を上る，昇進する（＝climb the corporate ladder）
- **political career** 政治家人生
- **pursue a career in** …の職業に進む

▶Benefits for management employees are principally based on *career*-average pay.　管理職に対する給付は，主に職歴平均給与方式に基づいています。

careerism 名　立身出世主義，出世第一主義
careerist 名　立身出世主義者，出世第一主義者
cargo 名　貨物，貨物便，積み荷
- **air cargo** 航空貨物
- **cargo airline** 貨物航空便
- **cargo arrival notice** 着荷通知
- **cargo boat [ship, vessel]** 貨物船
- **cargo distributor** 貨物輸送業者（＝terminal operator）
- **cargo handling gear** 荷役装置
- **cargo in bulk** 散荷（ばらに）

cargo insurance 貨物保険, 貨物海上保険, 積み荷保険
cargo liner 貨物定期船
cargo measurement 貨物容積
cargo owner 荷主
cargo plane 貨物輸送機
cargo to abandon 委付貨物
cargo tonnage 載貨トン数
institute cargo clauses 保険協会貨物約款
international cargo 国際貨物便
optional cargo 揚地選択貨物
CARICOM カリブ共同体, カリコム (Caribbean Communityの略)
carnet 名 一時持込み許可証, カルネ (欧州域内の無関税許可証)
carrier 名 運送人, 運送業者, 航空[バス, トラック, 鉄道]会社, 持参人, 保険会社, 保険業者, 保険者, 通信業者, 通信事業者, 電気通信事業者, 保菌者, キャリア
　carrier's haulage コンテナ輸送で船会社が行う内陸輸送サービス
　carrier's note 運送目録
　common carrier 公衆電気通信事業者, 運送業者, 一般運送人, コモン・キャリア
　contract carrier 契約運送人
　global carrier グローバル・キャリア, 国際通信事業者 (＝international carrier)
　grain carrier 穀物専用船
　industrial carrier 自社専用船
　mega carrier 巨大通信会社, メガキャリア
　mobile carrier 携帯電話会社, 携帯電話事業者
　premium carrier 一流航空会社
　private carrier 専属運送業者, 契約運送業者
　type I carrier 第一種事業者, 第一種電気通信事業者
　type II carrier 第二種事業者, 第二種電気通信事業者
▶Delivery of goods to a common *carrier* shall constitute delivery to Buyer. 運送業者に商品を引き渡した時点で, 買い主に引き渡したこととする。
▶JAL is the Japanese flagship *carrier*. 日本航空は, 日本を代表する航空会社だ。
▶The company is the world's largest mobile *carrier*. 同社は, 世界最大の携帯電話会社[携帯電話事業者]だ。
carry back 繰り戻す, 欠損[欠損金]を前期に[前年度以降に]繰り戻す
▶Allowing banks to claim a tax refund by *carrying* a loss *back* to the previous year has not been allowed since fiscal 1992 in Japan, due chiefly to the fiscal plight of the central government. 銀行が欠損金を前年度に繰り戻して税金還付を請求できるようにする制度(欠損金の繰戻し還付)は, 主に国の財政難を理由に, 日本では1992年度から凍結されてきた。
carry forward 繰り越す, 欠損[欠損金]を次期に[翌年度以降に]繰り越す(carry over)
▶Currently, companies are allowed to *carry forward* their losses for up to five years and offset part of any profit incurred in following fiscal years with the losses. 企業は現在, 欠損金を最高5年繰り越し, 翌年度以降に生じた利益の一部をこの欠損金と相殺することができる。
carry over 繰り越す(carry forward), 持ち越す, 引き継ぐ, 延期する
▶To hide losses, the firm *carried over* part of the expenses used for construction projects to the next business year. 損失を隠すため, 同社は工事費用の一部を翌年度[翌決算期]に繰り越していた。
carry trade キャリー取引, キャリー・トレード
▶In yen-*carry trades*, hedge funds borrow yen at low interest rates to invest into financial assets of other major currencies at higher interest rates. 円キャリー取引では, ヘッジ・ファンドが低金利で円を借りて, 円以外の高金利の外貨建て資産に投資している。
carrying amount 帳簿価額, 簿価 (＝book value, carrying value)
▶The Company's finance subsidiary purchases customer obligations under long-term contracts from the Company at net *carrying amount*. 当社の金融子会社は, 当社との長期契約によって, 顧客の債務を当社から帳簿価格で購入しています。
carrying value 帳簿価額, 簿価, 繰越し価額, 未償却残高 (＝book value, carrying amount; ⇒ **book value**, **contract value**)
▶We reduced the *carrying value* of this investment by $70 million because of a sustained decline in its market value. 当社は, この投資の市場価格が長期にわたって下落しているため, その帳簿価額を7,000万ドル引き下げました。
cartel 名 企業連合, カルテル (価格形成やマーケット・シェア, 生産水準など競争を排除するために結ばれる協定や協定に基づく結合)
　anti-recession cartel 不況カルテル
　conditional cartel 条件[生産条件]付きカルテル
　depression cartel 不況カルテル (＝depressed cartel)
　export cartel 輸出カルテル

export-import cartel 輸出入カルテル
form [run] a cartel カルテルを結ぶ
international cartel 国際カルテル
price fixing cartel 価格カルテル
price cartel 価格カルテル, 価格協定
profit-sharing cartel 利益配当カルテル
quantity cartel 生産数量カルテル
quotas cartel 割当カルテル
supply restriction cartel 供給制限カルテル
▶The firm is alleged to have formed an international *cartel* in the sale of its marine hoses used to transfer oil from tankers to storage facilities. 同社は, 石油をタンカーから貯蔵施設に移送するのに使われるマリン・ホースの販売にあたって, 国際カルテルを結んでいたとされる.

CASE コンピュータ支援ソフトウエア技術, コンピュータを利用したソフトウエア工学, コンピュータ支援のソフトウエア開発 (**computer-aided [computer-assisted] software engineering**の略)

case 名 事例, 問題, 事件, 件数, 見方, 論拠, 主張, 陳述, 申立て, 訴訟, 判例, 症例, 患者, 場合, 実情, 真相, ケース (⇒**tier**)
　bullish case 強気の見方
　case-based reasoning 事例に基づく推論《略 CBR》
　case history 事例史, 病歴
　case mark 荷印
　case method 事例研究法
　case study 事例研究, ケース・スタディ
　court case 裁判所の判例
　make a case against …に反対の論拠を示す, …に反対論を唱える
　make a case for …に賛成の論拠を示す, …の擁護論を唱える
　on a case-by-case basis 個別ベースで, 個々の事例に従って, ケース・バイ・ケースで

cash 動 現金に換える, 換金する
▶Quasi money refers to savings at banks that cannot be immediately *cashed*. 準通貨とは, 即時に換金できない[現金に換えられない]銀行預金のことをいう.

cash 名 現金, 預金, 現金預金, 現預金, 通貨, 資金, キャッシュ
　解説➡ 会計上, 「現金」は銀行預金のほかに小切手, 手形, 郵便為替なども含むが, 流動資産(current assets)に含まれるcashは手元現金と銀行の要求払い預金を指す
　cash and carry 現金払い持ち帰り方式
　cash and short term investments 現金預金[現金・預金]および短期投資

cash at bank and in hand 要求払い預金と手元現金
cash basis 現金基準, 現金主義 (＝receipts and payments basis)
cash capital requirements 資金需要
cash from operations 営業収益
cash in hand 手元現金 (＝cash on hand)
cash income 現金収入
cash management service 資金管理サービス
cash on hand and in banks 手元現金および銀行預金, 現金および預金
Cash paid during the year for: 当期現金支払い額:
cash provided from (used for) financing activities 財務活動に伴う資金の調達(使途), 財務活動から生じた(財務活動に使用した)資金
cash provided from (used for) investing activities 投資活動に伴う資金の調達(使途), 投資活動から生じた(投資活動に使用した)資金
cash provided from (used for) operating activities 営業活動[事業活動]に伴う資金の調達(使途), 営業活動[事業活動]から生じた(営業活動に使用した)資金
cash transfer 現金振込み
▶We used the *cash* from operations to pay dividends and to invest in R&D. 配当の支払いと研究開発投資には, 営業活動により生じたキャッシュを充てました.

cash and cash equivalents 現預金および現金同等物[現金等価物], 現金預金および現金等価物, 現金および現金同等物(「現預金および現金同等物」とは, 短期間に現金化できるような投資資産で, 財務省証券やマネー・マーケット・ファンド, 他社発行のコマーシャル・ペーパーなど3か月以内に現金化できる短期の有価証券も含まれる)
▶*Cash and cash equivalents* consist of cash and temporary investments with maturities of three months or less when purchased. 現金預金および現金等価物は, 現金と, 購入時点で3か月以内に満期日が到来する短期投資から成っています.

cash balance 現金預金残高, 現預金残高, 現金残高
▶We raised our *cash balance* in 2008 so that we could act quickly on new opportunities outside the U.S. 当社は2008年度の現預金残高を増やしましたが, これは米国外での新たな事業機会に即応できるようにするためです.

cash card キャッシュ・カード (⇒**charge** 動)
▶The new *cash card* is intended to counter the increase in thefts and counterfeiting of ATM

cards. この新型キャッシュ・カードは，キャッシュ・カードの盗難や偽造事件の多発に対応したものだ．

cash dividend 現金配当，配当金
▶The Corporation declared a *cash dividend* of $0.07 per common share in the first two quarters of 2009. 2009年第1四半期と第2四半期に，当社はそれぞれ普通株式1株当たり0.07ドルの現金配当を宣言しました．

cash equivalents 現金同等物，現金等価物，現金預金同等物，現金等価額
▶The Corporation considers all highly liquid investments purchased with an original maturity of three months or less to be *cash equivalents*. 当社は，取得日から満期日までの期間が3か月以内の流動性の高い投資を，すべて現預金等価物としています．

cash flow 現金の収入と支出，現金収支，資金収支，資金の流出入，資金の運用・調達，資金繰り，現金資金，純収入，キャッシュ・フロー（「キャッシュ・フロー」は現金収入と現金支出の総称で，企業の一定期間の現金などの流れを指す）
　annual cash flow 年間資金収入
　cash flow situation 資金繰り（＝cash situation)
　cash flows from financing activities 金融[財務]から生じた資金フロー，財務活動によるキャッシュ・フロー，財務活動に伴う資金収支[現金収支]
　cash flows from investing activities 投資活動から生じた資金フロー，投資活動によるキャッシュ・フロー
　cash flows from operating activities 営業活動から生じた資金フロー，営業活動によるキャッシュ・フロー
　current cash flow 手元流動性
　excess cash flow 余剰キャッシュ・フロー，超過キャッシュ・フロー
　expected cash flow 期待キャッシュ・フロー
　generate cash flow 現金収入を得る
　future cash flows 将来の資金繰り，将来のキャッシュ・フロー
　internal cash flows 内部キャッシュ・フロー
　net cash flow 純キャッシュ・フロー，正味キャッシュ・フロー，純収入
　tightened cash flow 資金繰りの悪化
▶These accounting changes do not affect *cash flows*; they only change the expenses we report. これらの会計処理方法の変更は，キャッシュ・フローには影響しません．当社が計上する費用の額が，変動するだけです．

cash flow problem 資金繰りの問題，資金難
▶The nonprofit foundation faced *cash flow problems*, such as repayment of the debt and meeting personnel costs. この公益法人は，借入金の返済や人件費のやりくりなど，資金繰りの問題に行き詰まった．

cash in circulation 貨幣流通高，現金通貨
▶The average daily balance of the monetary base—*cash in circulation* plus current-account deposits held at the central bank by private financial institutions—expanded 6.4 percent in April. 4月のマネタリー・ベース[貨幣流通高と日銀当座預金（民間金融機関の中央銀行預け金）との合計]の1日平均残高は，6.4％増加した．

cash merger 現金合併，キャッシュ・マージャー（企業の買収・合併の手段として，存続会社が，合併で吸収される会社の少数株主に対して存続会社の株式ではなく現金を交付する方法．⇒**stock exchange**)

cash provided by operations 営業活動[事業活動]で得られる現金，営業活動[事業活動]によって得られる現金収入，営業活動[事業活動]による資金の調達
▶In 2009, we will meet our cash requirements through *cash provided by operations*, refinancing of $158 million of long-term debt maturing in 2009 and external financing. 2009年度は，事業活動[営業活動]によって得られる現金収入と，2009年に満期[期日]が到来する長期債務1億5,800万ドルの借換えのほか，外部資金の調達で必要資金をまかなう予定です．

cash requirements 必要資金，現金必要[所要]量，現金必要見込み額，資金必要額
▶We will meet our *cash requirements* in 2009 by refinancing debt maturing in 2009. 当社は，2009年に満期が到来する債務の借換えで，2009年度の必要資金を賄う方針です．

cash withdrawals and deposits 現金の入出金
▶*Cash withdrawals and deposits* are made through automated teller machines. 現金の入出金は，ATM（現金自動預け払い機）で行われている．

cashless 形 現金不要の，現金のない，現金を用いないで済ます，キャッシュレスの，キャッシュレス
　cashless account settlement system キャッシュレス決済システム
　cashless payment system キャッシュレス支払いシステム
　cashless society 現金不要の社会，キャッシュレ

ス社会

cast 動 投げる，〈票を〉投じる
casual clothing retailer カジュアル衣料量販店 （＝casual clothing store）
casual clothing store カジュアル衣料店，カジュアル衣料量販店
▶Fast retailing Co. operates *casual clothing stores* under the Uniqlo brand name. ファーストリテイリングは，「ユニクロ」のブランド名でカジュアル衣料量販店を展開している。
casualty 名 損害，災害，障害，不慮の事故
catalog request form カタログ請求書，カタログ請求フォーム
catalog shopping カタログ・ショッピング
Catch-all or End-use Controls キャッチオール規制 （＝catch-all regulations）
　キャッチオール規制とは➡外為法で輸出規制品目のリストに記載されていなくても，最終用途が大量破壊兵器に使用される可能性がある輸出品はすべて規制する制度で，1991年に米国が初めて導入。その後，欧州連合（EU）が1995年に，日本は外為法の輸出貿易管理令を改正して2002年4月に導入した。
▶The *Catch-all or End-use Controls* ban the exports of certain non-contraband goods. キャッチオール規制は，一部の輸出入非禁製品の輸出を禁止している。
category 名 部類，種類，部門，分野，範疇，分類，区分，項目，カテゴリー
　category width カテゴリーの幅
　emerging growth categories 急成長分野
　product category 製品分野，製品カテゴリー
　rating category 格付けの分類
　special category company 特別区分会社
▶A growing number of women and elderly people have been starting business in such *categories* of industry as the service, wholesale and retail sectors. サービス業や卸売り・小売業などの業種で，女性や高齢者層の開業が増加している。
category killer 専門型大量販売店，カテゴリー・キラー（特定の商品分野に専門特化して低価格販売をする小売業態）
▶Specialty stores called *category killers* for home appliances and clothing providing unique items at low prices became more popular in the latter half of 1990s. 個性的な商品を手ごろな価格で提供する家電製品や衣料品の「カテゴリー・キラー」と呼ばれる専門店が，1990年代後半から人気を集めるようになった。
catering service 出前サービス，ケータリング・サービス

cattle industry 畜牛産業，畜牛業界
caution 名 保証書，保証人
CBA 費用便益分析 （**cost-benefit analysis**の略）
CBO 社債担保証券 （**collateralized bond obligation**の略。複数の社債を担保にして発行される資産担保証券（asset-backed securitiesの一種）
CBT コンピュータを使った訓練，コンピュータ利用訓練 （**computer-based training**の略）
CCS 二酸化炭素の回収・貯留 （**Carbon dioxide Capture and Storage**の略）
CD 現金自動支払い機，キャッシュ・ディスペンサー （**cash dispenser**の略）
CD 譲渡性預金，譲渡可能定期預金証書，定期預金証書 （**certificate of deposit**の略）
▶The average daily balance of M2 plus certificates of deposit (*CDs*) came to ¥734.4 trillion in January 2008. M2と譲渡性預金（CD）の2008年1月の1日平均残高は，734兆4,000億円となった。
CD コンパクト・ディスク （**compact disc**の略）
C/D [c/d] 次期繰越し （**carried down**の略）
CDO 債務担保証券 （**collateralized debt obligation**の略。証券化商品で，社債やローン（貸出債権）などで構成される資産を担保にして発行される資産担保証券(asset-backed securities)の一種
CEA 米大統領経済諮問委員会 （**Council of Economic Advisers**の略）
ceiling 名 限界，限度，上限，天井，最高，〈予算の〉概算要求基準，シーリング （下限＝floor）
　ceiling price 最高価格，最高限度価格，シーリング・プライス
　ceiling rate 天井相場
　credit ceiling 貸出限度額，融資限度額
　interest rate ceiling 金利の上限
　wage ceiling 賃金の上限
▶Investment Law sets legal *ceilings* on interest rates and prohibits the laundering of illegally earned profits. 出資法は，金利に上限を設けて，違法収益の洗浄（出所偽装工作）を禁止している。
cell phone 携帯電話 （＝cellular phone, mobile phone; ⇒**electronic money, infrastructure, lithium ion rechargeable battery, MVNO**)
　camera-equipped cell phone カメラ付き携帯電話
　card-shaped, camera-equipped cell phone カード型カメラ付き携帯電話
　cell phone business 携帯電話事業
　cell phone service 携帯電話サービス
　cell-phone Web site 携帯電話のサイト
　cell phone with electronic money functions 電子マネー機能付き携帯電話

▶Customers are now able to use *cell phones* to complete payments at family restaurants, pubs, and beauticians.　顧客は現在，携帯電話を使って，ファミリー・レストランやパブ，美容院などでの支払いを済ませるようになった．

▶NEC unveiled the world's smallest, slimmest camera-equipped *cell phone*.　NECが，世界最小，最薄型のカメラ付き携帯電話を初公開した．

cell phone handset　携帯電話機，携帯電話の端末機，携帯電話端末

▶Mitsubishi Electric Corp. will stop developing and making *cell phone handsets* due to falling profitability in the domestic market.　三菱電機は，国内市場の収益性が低いため，携帯電話端末の開発・生産を中止する．

cell phone number portability system
携帯電話番号持ち運び制度（＝mobile number portability system, number portability system）

▶Under the *cell phone portability system* introduced on Oct. 24, 2006, cell phone users are allowed to use the same phone numbers even after switching to different cell phone service providers.　2006年10月26日から導入された携帯電話番号持ち運び制度では，携帯電話の利用者は，別の携帯電話会社に乗り換えても，同じ電話番号を使うことができる．

cell phone service provider　携帯電話会社，携帯電話の加入会社

▶*Cell phone service providers* are in fierce competition with one another, offering such services as ring-tone melodies and the transmission and reception of images.　携帯電話会社は，着信メロディーや画像送受信などのサービス提供で，厳しい競争を展開している．

cell production system　セル生産方式，セル生産管理方式，屋台生産方式（＝cell manufacturing system, cellular manufacturing system; ⇒**production efficiency**）

▶Canon changed its conveyer belt system to a *cell production system* in autumn 2002.　キャノンは，2002年秋にベルトコンベヤー方式をセル生産方式に変えた．

center [centre] 名　中心，中央，中枢，中心地，中心点，拠点，本場，中心人物，花形，指導者，中間派，穏健派，重点地区，商業地区，繁華街，都市，総合施設，的，対象，センター（⇒**distribution center**）

　business center　取引の中心地，ビジネス・センター

　center of excellence　中核の研究センター，中核的研究機関，世界的研究拠点，センター・オブ・エクセレンス《略 COE》

　commercial center　商業中心地，商業区域，商品センター

　commercial distribution center　流通センター

　computer center　コンピュータ・センター

　cost center　原価中心点，原価部門，コスト・センター

　distribution-center warehouse　流通センター倉庫

　economic and cultural centers　経済と文化の中心地

　financial center　金融センター，金融中心地

　industrial centers　工業都市，工業施設

　information center　案内所，情報センター

　metropolitan centers　都市圏

　process center　生鮮加工センター，プロセス・センター

　production center　生産中心点

　profit center　利益センター，利益中心点，利益責任単位，プロフィット・センター

　R&D center　研究開発センター

　service center　補助部門，サービス・センター

　trade center　貿易センター，商業の中心

　venture enterprise center　研究開発型企業育成センター

　visit center　見学者受付

-centered　…中心の，…を主体とする
　export-centered industry　輸出中心の産業
　U.N.-centerd policies　国連中心主義

central 形　中央の，中心の，中心的な，主要な，重要な，基本的な
　central business district　商業中心地区
　central bankers　中央銀行総裁
　central buying　本部仕入れ，集中仕入れ，一括購入
　central government　中央政府，政府，国
　central processing unit　中央処理装置，中央演算処理装置《略 CPU》
　central parity　中心レート
　Central Reserve Bank　米中央準備銀行《略 CRB》
　Central service　本部管理業務
　Central Standard Time　米中部標準時
　central theme　重要なテーマ
　central wholesale market　中央卸売市場

central bank　中央銀行（日本の場合は日本銀行（日銀）を指す．⇒Bank of England）

　アメリカの中央銀行について➡アメリカには単一の中央銀行が存在せず，連邦準備制度（Federal

Reserve System) のもと連邦準備区 (Federal Reserve district) に設置された全米12の連邦準備銀行 (Federal Reserve Banks) が実際の中央銀行業務をしている。ただし、the U.S. central bankといえば米連邦準備制度理事会 (FRB) を指す。

▶While minimizing possible adverse effects on the stock market, private consumption and corporate performances, the U.S. *central bank* will ensure the United States' economic recovery. 株式市場や個人消費、企業業績などへの考えられる悪影響を最小限に抑えながら、米連邦準備制度理事会 (FRB) は、米国の景気回復を確実なものにしていく方針だ。

central business district 商業中心地区
central bankers 中央銀行総裁
central buying 本部仕入れ、集中仕入れ、一括購入
central processing unit 中央処理装置、中央演算処理装置《略 CPU》
Central Reserve Bank 米中央準備銀行《略 CRB》
central wholesale market 中央卸売市場
CEO 最高業務執行役員、最高経営責任者、最高業務執行理事（＝chief executive: chief executive officerの略）
certificate 名 証明書、証書、報告書、券
　allotment certificate 株式割当証
　beneficiary certificate 受益証券
　bond certificate 社債券、債券
　certificate of authority 許可証明書
　certificate of bank balances 銀行預金残高証明書
　certificate of deposit 譲渡性預金、預金証書、有価証券預り証（⇒CD）
　certificate of exemption 会社法要件免除証明書
　certificate of incorporation 米国の会社設立定款、英国の会社設立証明書
　certificate of incumbency 在職証明
　certificate of insurance 保険証明書、保険承認状
　certificate of necessity 必要施設証明書
　certificate of one's seal impression 印鑑証明
　certificate of origin 原産地証明
　certificate of signature サイン証明
　certificate of the auditor 監査報告書（＝audit certificate, auditor's certificate）
　certificate of title 権原登記証書
　debenture certificate 債券
　deposit certificate 預金証書
　inspection certificate 検査証明書
　money market certificate 市場金利連動型定期預金
　sanitary certificate 衛生証明書
　share certificate 株券（＝certificate of share, stock certificate）
　Treasury certificate 財務省証券
　trust certificate 信託受益証券
　warehouse certificate 倉庫証券

▶Shares shall be represented by *certificates*. 株式は、株券で表象されるものとする。

certificate of share [stock] 株券、記名株券
▶All the *certificates of shares* shall be consecutively numbered or otherwise identified. 株券には、すべて一連番号か他の特定符号を付すものとする。

certified public accountant 公認会計士《略 CPA》
▶*Certified public accountants* and auditing firms are responsible for preventing corporate managers from window-dressing business results. 公認会計士や監査法人には、企業経営者の粉飾決算を止めさせる責任がある。

certify 動 認証する、証明する、認定する、保証する
CESR 欧州証券規制委員会（Committee of European Securities Regulatorsの略）
cf, c/f 次期繰越し（carried forwardの略）
CFO 最高財務担当役員、最高財務担当者、最高財務責任者、財務担当責任者（chief financial officerの略）
chain 名 系統、連鎖、連鎖店、チェーン・ストア、チェーン店、チェーン
　chain buying office チェーン・ストアの仕入本部
　chain discount 連鎖式割引き（＝series discount）
　chain of command 命令系統、指揮系統
　chain of distribution 流通の連鎖
　chain office チェーン・ストア本部
　chain operation 多店舗展開、多店舗展開の経営手法、チェーン・オペレーション（＝chain store operation）
　chain retailer チェーン・ストア小売業（＝chain store）
　cold chain system コールドチェーン・システム（生産地から消費地まで低温のまま輸送する方式）
　cooperative chain 小売店のグループ化・チェーン化、コーペラティブ・チェーン（＝cooperative retail chain, retailer cooperative chain,

retailer cooperative）
corporate chain 会社チェーン，チェーン・ストア
demand chain management デマンドチェーン・マネジメント《略 DCM》
drugstore chain ドラッグストア・チェーン
fast-food chain ファースト・フード・チェーン
franchise chain フランチャイズ・チェーン
menswear retail chain 紳士服小売りチェーン，紳士服チェーン
national chain ナショナル・チェーン（全国的にチェーン店を持つ小売業）
regional chain リージョナル・チェーン（地域限定型の小売店網）
restaurant chain レストラン・チェーン
retail computer distribution chain コンピュータの小売販売チェーン店
specialty store chain 専門店チェーン
super chain スーパー・チェーン
value chain 価値連鎖，バリュー・チェーン
voluntary chain 任意連鎖店，ボランタリー・チェーン

▸Daiei wants the five supermarket *chains* under Daiei's umbrella to maintain their separate listings on the stock market. ダイエーは，傘下の食品スーパー5社の上場を維持する考えだ。

▸Marubeni Corp. plans to choose a partner to assist in the rehabilitation of Daiei after negotiations with major retail *chain* operators such as Aeon Co. and Wal-Mart Stores Inc. 丸紅は，イオンや米ウォルマート・ストアーズなどの流通大手と交渉の上，ダイエー再建に協力する事業提携先を選ぶ方針だ。

▸Toyoko Inn has aggressively expanded its *chain* of budget hotels which do not have restaurants. 東横インは，レストランを持たないビジネスホテル・チェーンを積極的に展開してきた。

chain store 連鎖店，チェーン店，チェーン・ストア（11店舗以上の店舗を所有する小売業）
chain store contract チェーン店契約
Chain Store Law チェーン・ストア法
chain store operation チェーン・ストア経営，チェーン・ストア運営，チェーンストア・オペレーション（多店舗展開の経営手法）

▸The retail stores which form *chain store* contracts with a large manufacturing firm deal with all the products of the manufacturer and receive various services such as design of stores, store arrangement and free supply of samples. ある大手メーカーとチェーン店契約を結ぶ小売店は，そのメーカーの全製品を取り扱い，そのメーカーから店舗のデザインや店舗配列，サンプルの無料提供などの各種サービスを受ける。

chairman 名 会長，委員長，議長，社長，司会者（＝chairperson）
　Chairman and CEO 会長兼最高経営責任者
　chairman emeritus 名誉会長
　chairman of board of directors 取締役会長
　chairman of the board 取締役会長，取締役会議長
　chairman's report [review] 会長報告書
　chairman's statement 会長報告書，社長報告書，社長声明
　Fed Chairman 米連邦準備制度理事会（FRB）議長

▸Sony Corp. named Vice *Chairman* Howard Stringer as the company's new *chairman* and group chief executive officer. ソニーは，ハワード・ストリンガー副会長を，同社の新会長兼グループ最高経営責任者（CEO）に任命した。

chalk up 収益を上げる，…を記録する，計上する，獲得する，達成する（⇒consolidated net loss）

▸At the height of its success, the publisher *chalked up* about ¥4 billion in sales. 同出版社の最盛期に，同社は約40億円の売上を計上した。

challenge 名 挑戦，課題，難題，難問，脅威，やりがいのある仕事，任務，要求，〈競技などへの〉参加勧誘［参加呼びかけ］，〈陪審員に対する〉拒否，忌避，異議，異議申立て，チャレンジ（⇒raise）

▸The *challenge* in monetary policy for countries now is shifting toward finding a way to move away from ultra-loose money policies. 現在，各国の金融政策の課題は，超金融緩和政策からいかに転換するかに移りつつある。

chamber of commerce and industry 商工会議所（商工会議所法に基づいて，原則として市ごとに設置される地域的な総合経済団体で，一定地域の商工業者で構成される。地域経済の調査や経済政策の建議を行う）

▸In principle, each city has a *chamber of commerce and industry.* 原則として，市ごとに商工会議所が一つある。

Chamber of Commerce and Industry Law 商工会議所法

change 名 変動，変化，変更，改革，改正，増減，釣銭，小銭，チェンジ（⇒accounting change）
　adjustment for the change 変更による修正
　capital change 資本の変動，資本の増減
　change in accounts receivable 受取債権の増減

change in cash and cash equivalents 現金および現金同等物の増減
change in other operating assets and liabilities その他の営業資産および営業負債の増減
change in investment securities 投資有価証券の増減
change in short-term debt 短期債務増減
change in value 評価換え
change in accounts payable, accrued and other liabilities 買掛金, 未払い費用およびその他の負債増減
changes during the year 期末の増減
changes in capital 資本の増減, 資金勘定の変動, 資本の変動 (=capital change)
currency changes 為替相場の変動
dividend change 配当変更
financial change 金融改革
interest rate change 金利変動, 金利の変更
rating change 格付け変更
structural change 構造的な変化, 構造的変化
▶Income taxes for 2008 have not been restated for this accounting *change*. 2008年度の法人所得税額は, この会計処理の変更による修正・再表示を行っていません。

change in consciousness 意識改革
▶What is important for Japan now is to bring about a *change in consciousness* in the industrial sector and among business managers. いま日本にとって重要なことは, 産業界や経営者の意識改革だ。

change of control 資本拘束, 経営権の変更
▶The firm is currently negotiating with its domestic capital partners to conclude *change-of-control* agreements. 同社は現在, 国内の資本提携先とチェンジ・オブ・コントロール(資本拘束)条項の契約を結ぶ交渉を進めている。

change of control clause 資本拘束条項, チェンジ・オブ・コントロール条項 (ライセンス契約や代理店契約を結ぶ際, 買収などで一方の会社の支配権が変わった場合には, 相手方の会社が契約を破棄できるとする条項)

channel 名 経路, 筋道, 方向, 通信路, 通話路, 回線, チャネル
  analog channel アナログ回線
  channel captain 経路の統率者, 経路の指導者, チャネル・キャプテン (=channel commander, channel leader)
  communication channel コミュニケーション経路, コミュニケーション・チャネル, コミュニケーションの回線 (=channel of communication)
  digital channel デジタル回線
  distribution channel 流通経路, 流通チャネル, 販売経路
  information channel 情報路, 情報チャネル
  interchannel system competition チャネル・システム間競争
  marketing channel 販売チャネル, 販売経路, 流通チャネル, マーケティング・チャネル (ある商品・サービスがメーカーから最終消費者に渡るまでの取引の流れの経路。主に, メーカーの営業所, 卸売り業者, 小売業者, 配送業者などによって構成される)
  online channel オンライン・チャネル
  sales channel 販売経路, 販売チャネル
▶Noevir Co. specializing in door-to-door sales is adding telephone, fax, cell phone, mail and Internet *channels* to sell its cosmetic products. 訪問販売専門のノエビアが, 同社の化粧品販売チャネルに, 電話, ファクス, 携帯電話, 郵便(はがき)とインターネットを加えている。

Chapter 7 of the National Bankruptcy Act 米連邦破産法第7章 (破綻した企業を再生させずに清算する手続きを定めた法律)

Chapter 11 米連邦改正破産法第11章, 米連邦破産法11章, チャプター・イレブン, 会社更生手続き (=Chapter 11 bankruptcy, Chapter 11 of the U.S. Bankruptcy Code, Chapter 11 of the U.S. Bankruptcy Reform Act: 日本の民事更生法に相当)

Chapter 11 bankruptcy 米連邦破産法第11章による破産

Chapter 11 of the U.S. Bankruptcy Code 米連邦破産法11章

characteristics of the market 市場特性
▶Company executives must strengthen their firms' competitiveness, adapting them to suit the *characteristics of the market* at the time and place in which they are operating. 経営者は, 業務展開している時間と場所の市場特性に応じて, 企業の競争力を強化しなければならない。

charge 動 請求する, 課する, 要求する, 支払わせる, 負担させる, 借方に記入する, 借記する, 計上する, クレジット・カードで買う, 告発する
  be charged to cost of sales 売上原価に計上される
  be charged to expenses as incurred 発生時に費用に計上される, 発生基準で費用に計上される
  be charged to income 費用として計上される, 費用計上される (=be charged to earnings)
  charge against 費用として差し引く, 損失とみ

loans and leases charged off 償却された貸出金とリース, 貸出とリースの償却額
▶Research and development costs are *charged* to earnings in the periods in which they are incurred. 研究開発費は, それが発生した期間に費用として計上されています。
▶The bank stopped *charging* its cash-card holders remittance fees when they send money from its ATMs to accounts at its head and regional branches. 同行は, キャッシュ・カード会員を対象に, 現金自動預け払い機(ATM)から同行の本支店の口座に金を振り込む場合の振込み手数料を無料化した。

charge 名 費用, 料金, 税金, 課税金, 手数料, 代価, 代金, 請求金額, 借方記入, 借記, 負債, 借金, 責任, 義務, 任務, 担保, 担保権, 管理, 監督, 保管, 運営, 処理, 告発, 訴追, 〈陪審に対する裁判官の〉説示, チャージ (⇒**device**)
  accrued charge 未払い費用
  advising charge 通知手数料
  capital charge 資本費, 資本費用, 資本コスト
  charge against revenues 損金
  charge off 貸倒れ償却 (不良債権を決算で損失として処理すること)
  charge sales 掛売り, 掛売上 (＝credit sales)
  charge to income 損失の計上, 費用の計上
  charges for special pension options 特別退職勧奨制度の費用
  deferred charges 繰延べ費用, 繰延べ資産
  discount charge 割引料
  eligible charges 給付額
  estimated charge 見積り費用
  finance charge 金融費用, 融資手数料, 金利
  first legal charge 第一順位の抵当権
  fixed charge 固定費, 固定費用, 固定経費, 固定担保, 金融費用
  floating charge 浮動担保
  interest charges 支払い利息
  lifting charge 取扱い手数料
  maintenance charge 維持費
  management charge 管理費
  one-off charge 一括処理 (⇒**pension obligations**)
  one-time charge 一時的費用
  repair charge 修繕費
  surrender charge 解約手数料
  taxes and public charges 公租公課
  transferring charge 振替手数料
▶Our bottom line includes company-wide *charges* that we took for accounting *changes*. 当社の業績[最終損益]には, 会計処理方法の変更のために計上した全社的な費用も含まれています。

charging system 課金制度, 課金システム
▶With technical improvement, there are more new *charging systems* on the way, such as online music distribution services. 技術上の進歩で, インターネットを通じた音楽配信サービスなど, 新たな課金システムがさらに出来つつある。

chart 名 図, 図表, 予定表, グラフ, チャート
  activity chart 業務活動表
  bar chart 棒グラフ
  break even chart 損益分岐点図表
  control chart 品質管理図
  flow chart 流れ図, 業務運行図, 作業工程図, フロー・チャート
  flow process chart 工程流れ図
  high-low chart 高値・安値チャート
  organization chart 組織図, 会社機構図
  pie chart 円形図表, 円形グラフ, パイ図, パイ図表
  process chart 工程図, プロセス・チャート
  profit planning chart 利益計画図表
  profit-volume chart 利益分岐点図表
  repayment chart 償還予定表

charter 名 貸借契約(書), 用船契約(書), 基本定款, 特許状, チャーター, 動 …に特許を与える, 借り上げる, チャーターする

check [cheque] 名 小切手, 照合, 検査, 点検, チェック (⇒**current deposit**)
  bank check 銀行小切手
  certified check 支払い保証小切手, 銀行支払い保証小切手, 預金手形
  check drawer 小切手振出人
  check list 点検表
  credit checks 信用調査
  payroll check 給与・賃金支払い小切手
▶The Liberal Democratic Party faction received a *check* for ¥100 million from top executives of the Japan Dental Association. 自民党の派閥が, 日本歯科医師会の最高幹部から1億円の小切手を受け取っていた。
▶The purchase price shall be U.S. $50,000 payable in full at the closing by certified *check*. 買取価格は5万米ドルとし, クロージング時に全額, 銀行支払い保証小切手で支払うものとする。

checking account 当座預金, 当座預金口座, 小切手勘定 (⇒**checking transaction**)
▶*Checking accounts* are mainly used by companies for business settlements. 当座預金は, 主

に企業の取引決済に利用されている。

checking transaction 小切手取引 (=check trading)
▶If a financial institution goes under, companies that have checking accounts at that financial institution will become unable to conclude *checking transactions* or settle bills and will go bankrupt. 金融機関が破綻すれば，そこに当座預金を持つ企業は，小切手取引の決済や手形の決済ができなくなり，倒産してしまうことになる。

checkoff 名 〈給料からの〉組合費(union dues)の天引き，チェックオフ

chemical 形 化学の，化学上の，化学的な，ケミカル
  chemical agent 化学薬品
  chemical component 化学成分
  chemical engineering 化学工学，化学工業
  chemical fertilizers 化学肥料
  chemical industry 化学工業
  chemical medicine 化学薬品
  chemical oxygen demand 化学的酸素要求量《略 COD》
  chemical plant 化学工場
  chemical pollutant 化学汚染物質
  chemical product 化学製品 (=chemical goods)
  chemical substance 化学物質
  chemical waste 化学廃棄物
▶Shipments of raw materials, such as steel and *chemical* products, as well as construction equipment have been growing. 鉄鋼や化学製品などの素材のほか，建設機械などの輸出も伸びている。

chemicals 名 化学製品，化学薬品，薬品，化学物質
  agricultural chemicals 農薬，基礎化学品
  commodity chemicals 汎用化学品
  fine chemicals 精製薬品
  heavy chemicals 農工業薬品
  industrial chemicals 工業薬品
  specialty chemicals 精密化学品
▶Commodity loans are used to import commodities such as industrial machinery, industrial raw materials, fertilizer, agricultural *chemicals* and machinery which are agreed upon beforehand between the Japanese and recipient governments. 商品借款は，日本政府と借入国政府が前もって合意した商品(工業資本財，工業用原材料，肥料・農薬や農機具など)の輸入のために使用される。

chief 形 主な，主要な，第一の，最高位の，最大の，主任の，主席の (chief executive officerやchief operating officer等についてはofficerの項参照)
  chief accountant 会計課長，会計係長，会計責任者，主任会計審査官
  chief actuary 保険計理人
  chief competitor 最大の競争相手，最大のライバル
  chief economist 主任エコノミスト，チーフ・エコノミスト
  chief editor 編集長
  chief engineer 主任技師
  chief executive 最高経営責任者(CEO)，企業のトップ，米国の州知事
  Chief Executive 米大統領 (chief executive=州知事)
  chief packager 主幹事
▶The *chief* executives of major U.S. corporations urged Bush to support reductions in climate-changing pollution. 米主要企業のトップは，ブッシュ米大統領に対して，気候変動をもたらす汚染物質の排出削減支持を迫った。

Child-rearing and Nursing Care Leave Law 育児・介護休業法
▶The revised *Child-rearing and Nursing Care Law* requires corporations to extend the length of child-care leave given to employees with children under 3 and reduce their working hours. 改正育児・介護休業法は，3歳未満の子をもつ従業員に与えられる育児休業期間の延長と勤務時間の短縮を企業に義務付けている。

chilled transport チルド輸送

China risk チャイナ・リスク
▶Lax business regulations and ethics are the main factors of the so-called *China risk* faced by foreign companies. 手ぬるいビジネス・ルールや道徳の乏しさなどが，海外企業が直面するいわゆる「チャイナ・リスク」の主な要因となっている。

Chinese wall 情報の障壁，越えがたい障壁，〈企業の各部門間に設けられる〉情報の隔壁，チャイニーズ・ウォール

chip 名 〈珪素の〉記憶素子，小型集積回路，〈パソコンの〉中央処理装置，半導体，シリコン・チップ，チップ
  bio chip 生物化学素子，バイオチップ
  computer chips 集積回路，コンピュータ・チップ
  custom chips 特注IC
  micro chip [microchip] マイクロチップ
  semiconductor chip 半導体チップ
  silicon chip シリコン・チップ (=IC chip)

violence chip Vチップ (=V chip)
▸Elpida Memory Inc. is a *chip* joint venture by Hitachi Ltd. and NEC Corp.　エルピーダメモリは, 日立製作所とNECが共同出資して設立した半導体メーカーだ.

chipmaker 名　半導体メーカー, 半導体製造業者 (=semiconductor manufacturer)
▸Shares in *chipmaker* Elpida Memory Inc. gained 7.14 percent on their Monday debut.　半導体メーカー, エルピーダメモリの株価は, 月曜日の上場で7.14%上昇した.

chipmaking equipment 半導体製造機器 (=chipmaking machinery)
▸The December book-to-bill ratio of Japanese *chipmaking equipment* was 1.19 in a clear sign of steady recovery.　安定した景気回復の明らかな兆しとして, 日本の半導体製造機器のBBレシオは, 12月は1.19だった.

choice 名　選択, 選定, 選択権, 特選品, 逸品
　a fine choice of 精選された, えり抜きの (=well-chosen)
　a wide choice of 各種さまざまな (=a great choice of, a large choice of)
　at one's choice 随意に, 自由選択で
　choice article 精選品, 優良品, 特選品, 極上品 (=choice goods)
　choice of law 準拠法の選定, 適用法の選定, 法の選択, 法律選択
　consumer's choice 消費者選択
　investment choice 投資先
　managerial choice 経営判断
　optimal choice 最適選択
　portfolio choice 資産選択, ポートフォリオ選択
　producer's choice 生産者行動
　technology choice 技術選択
▸This agreement shall be governed by and construed in accordance with the laws of England without reference to its *choice* of law rules.　本契約は, 適用法[準拠法]選択のルールにかかわりなくイングランド法に準拠し, 同法に従って解釈する.

CI コーポレート・アイデンティティ, 企業イメージ統合戦略, 企業認識 (**corporate identity**の略)

CIF 運賃・保険料渡し, 運賃・保険料込み値段 (**cost, insurance and freight**の略で, FOB価格に輸入港までの海上運賃(ocean freight)と海上保険料(in-surance premium)を加えたものがCIF価格)
　CIF basis CIF条件
　CIF contract CIF契約
　CIF New York Port basis CIFニューヨーク港条件
　CIF value CIF価格
　on the basis of CIF Los Angeles CIFロサンゼルス港条件で, ロサンゼルスを仕向地とするCIF条件で
　the amount of 110 percent of CIF value of the shipments of the products 本製品発送品のCIF価格の110%の保険金額
▸The price for the products payable by the purchaser for the first year shall be U.S. $38.00 per set *CIF* San Francisco, U.S.A.　買い主が初年度に支払う本商品の価格は, CIFサンフランシスコ(米国)条件で1セット当たり38.00米ドルとする.

CIM コンピュータ統合生産, コンピュータ統合生産システム, シム (**computer integrated manufacturing (system)**の略)

CIO 最高情報担当役員, 最高情報責任者, 情報戦略統括役員 (**chief information officer**の略)

circles 名　団体, グループ, …界, …社会, サークル
　business circles 経済界, 産業界, 実業界, 業界 (=business community, business world)
　financial circles 金融界, 財界 (=financial sector)
　industrial circles 産業界, 工業会
　political circles 政界

circulate 動　流通させる, 循環させる, 配布する, 広める, 回覧する, 流通する, 出回る, 普及する
　circulate funds 資金を循環させる
　circulate the notice 通達を回覧する
▸Not enough money is *circulating* in the economy.　市中に, 金が出回らなくなっている.
▸The bank's aim is to help *circulate* dormant individual assets in the local economy.　眠れる個人の金融資産を地域経済に循環させるのが, 同行の目的だ.

CIS 独立国家共同体 (**Commonwealth of Independent States**の略)

civil 形　市民の, 一般市民の, 民間の, 民事の
　civil lawsuit 民事訴訟
　civil organization 市民団体
　civil procedure code 民事訴訟法
　civil rehabilitation law 民事再生法
　civil servant 公務員, 役人, 文官
　civil service system 公務員制度
▸Soshisha Publishing Co. filed an application with the Tokyo District Court for protection from creditors under the *Civil* Rehabilitation Law.　草思社は, 民事再生法に基づく資産保全[民事再生法の適用]を東京地裁に申請した.

civil fine 民事制裁金

▸American International Group, one of the largest U.S. insurance companies, agreed to pay a $10 million *civil fine* to settle federal regulators' allegations that it fraudulently helped another company falsify its earnings report and hide losses.　米保険最大手のAIG（アメリカン・インターナショナル・グループ）は，同社が他社の業績報告書改竄と損失隠しに不正に手を貸したとする米証券取引委員会（SEC）の告発を受け，この問題を解決するために民事制裁金1,000万ドルを支払うことに同意した。

CKO　知識統括役員，最高知識担当役員，ナレッジ統括役員　（**chief knowledge officer**の略）

claim 動　〈権利を〉要求する，請求する，〈権利や事実を〉主張する，訴える，〈責任などを〉認める
▸Buyer has the right to extend the period for shipment without prejudice to the right to *claim* damages arising out of such delay in shipment.　買い主には，船積みの遅延で生じた損害の賠償を請求する権利を損なわないで，積み期を延期する権利がある。

claim 名　請求，請求権，請求事項，特許請求の範囲，信用，未収の債権，債権の届出，保険金，権利，権利の主張，苦情，苦情の申立て，クレーム
　amount of claim　請求額
　asset claim　資産請求権
　categorization of loan claims　債権区分
　claim adjustment expense　保険金支払い費
　claim cost recognition　保険金費用の認識
　claim for a refund　還付請求
　claim for reimbursement　未収払戻し金，償還請求
　claims for damages　損害賠償請求，求償権
　claims paid　保険金
　housing loan claim　住宅ローンの債権
　information concerning customer claims　顧客からのクレーム情報
　initial unemployment claims　新規失業保険申請件数
　junior claim　劣後請求権
　money claim　金銭債権
　policy claims　保険金請求，保険金
　refund claim　還付申請書
　senior claim　上位請求権
　warranty claim　保証債務，品質保証に基づくクレーム
▸The Japan Housing Finance Agency plans to securitize housing loan *claims* bought from financial institutions.　住宅金融支援機構（独立行政法人で，旧住宅金融公庫が2007年4月1日に改称）は，金融機関から買い取った住宅ローンの債権を証券化する方針だ。

class action suit　集団代表訴訟，集団訴訟，クラス・アクション　（＝**class action, class action lawsuit**:「株主代表訴訟」は，取締役が法令や定款に違反して会社に損害を与えた場合，株主が会社に代わって取締役を相手取り会社に損害を賠償するよう求める訴訟; ⇒**compensation**）
▸In a *class action suit*, 20 plaintiffs demanded that seven private universities refund about ¥18 million in tuition and entrance fees that had been paid in advance.　集団訴訟で，20人の原告側は，前納した入学金や授業料約1,800万円の返還を私立7大学に求めた。

classification 名　分類，類別，区分，格付け
　classification of economic activities　経済活動別分類
　classification scheme　分類基準
　classification society　船級協会
　commodity classification　商品分類
　functional classification　機能別分類
　industrial classification　産業分類
　industry classification　業種分類，業種別分類，産業別分類
　job classification　職務分類，職業分類，職階制
　land classification　土地区分
　market classification　市場分類
　multiple classification　多重分類
　position classification system [plan]　職階制
　socio-economic classification　社会経済分類
　Standard Industrial Trade Classification　標準国際貿易分類
　statistical classification　輸出入統計品目表
　tariff classification　関税分類

classified 形　分類した，機密扱いの，極秘の，非公開の，高度の軍事機密に属する，名　求人広告，求職広告（**classified ad, want ad**）
　classified ad　求人［求職］広告，項目別案内広告，分類広告，案内広告，3行広告　（＝**classified advertisement [advertising], small ad, want ad**）
　classified balance sheet　分類貸借対照表，区分式貸借対照表
　classified financial statements　区分式財務諸表
　classified fund　機密費
　classified civil service　（米国の）公務員職階制度
　classified common stock　分類普通株
　classified defense information　極秘防衛情報
　classified depreciation　分別償却
　classified documents　機密書類，機密文書

classified information 機密情報, 極秘情報, 高度の軍事機密情報
classified statement of profit and loss 区分式損益計算書
classified stock 発行別分類株, 分類株式
classified telephone directory 職業別電話帳 (=Yellow Pages)
▶Washington suspects that China stole *classified information* on U.S. nuclear weapons technology. 米政府は，米国の核兵器技術の極秘情報を中国が盗用したと見ている。

classify 動 分類する，等級に分ける，〈文書を〉機密扱いにする
　classify as capital 資本資産として扱う，資本資産として分類する
　classify as current 流動資産として扱う，流動資産として分類する

clause 名 〈法律や契約などの〉条項，規定，約款，箇条，項，事項，文言，〈文法の〉節 (⇒contention, contractual clause)
　arbitration clause 仲裁条項
　average clause 分損担保約款
　clause by clause 条項ごとに
　exception clause 免責条項
　clause of definite undertaking 明確な約束の文言
　contract clause 契約条項
　guarantee clause 保証文言
　Institute Cargo Clauses 協会貨物約款
　protective clauses 保護規定
　saving clause 留保条項
　transit clause 運送約款
　whereas clauses 前文，説明条項

claw 動 〈金を〉かき集める

clean 形 公正な，瑕疵(かし)のない，無条件の，担保権が付いていない，安全な，清浄な，クリーン
　Clean Air Act of 1970 1970年大気汚染防止法, マスキー法
　clean bill クリーン手形，信用手形，健康証明書
　clean bill of draft 信用手形 (=clean draft)
　clean bill of health (機械や建物の)安全証明, 完全健康証明書, 太鼓判
　clean bill of lading 無故障船荷証券 (=clean B/L)
　clean copy 清書
　clean credit 荷落ち為替信用状，無担保信用状，クリーン信用状
　clean float 中央銀行が介入しない変動相場制, きれいな変動相場制, クリーン・フロート (中央銀行が介入する変動相場制を「dirty float (汚い変動相場制)」という)
　clean fuels クリーン燃料
　clean loan 無担保借入れ
　clean room 完全無菌室, 無菌室, 無塵(むじん)室
　clean sheet [slate] 汚点のない経歴
　clean sweep 〈組織の〉全面的改革, 全勝
　documentary clean bill 荷落ち為替手形
　documentary clean (letter of) credit 荷落ち為替信用状

clean energy industry クリーン・エネルギー産業, クリーンなエネルギー産業
▶The scale of a new *clean energy industry*, based on solar, wind and biomass energy, is expected to reach about ¥3 trillion in 2030. 太陽光や風力, バイオマスなどを基盤とするクリーンな新エネルギー産業の市場規模は, 2030年には約3兆円に達する見込みだ。

cleaning equipment rental 清掃用品レンタル

cleanup costs 浄化費用, 環境の浄化整備費
▶There are other "potentially responsible parties (PRPs)" who can be expected to contribute to the *cleanup costs*. 浄化費用を分担するものと思われる「潜在責任当事者」は, 当社以外にも存在します。

clear 形 明確な, 正味の, 純粋な, 動 〈船が積荷を〉下ろす, 〈税関などの〉検査を通る, 清算する, 支払う, 認可する

clearance 名 通関手続き, 出港[出国]手続き, 離陸[着陸]許可, 〈在庫品の〉一掃, 除去, 撤去, 手形交換, 手形交換高, 〈証券取引所の〉手じまい, すき間, 間隔, 空(あ)き, クリアランス
　blanket clearance 包括出入港許可
　check clearance 小切手決済, 手形交換
　clearance agent 通関代理店
　clearance from customs 通関 (=customs clearance)
　clearance goods 見切り品
　clearance inwards 入港手続き
　clearance notice 出港通知書
　clearance outwards 出港手続き
　clearance (papers) 船舶出港[入港]証明書
　clearance sale 在庫品一掃大売出し, 蔵払い, クリアランス・セール
　clearance work 障害物除去作業
　exchange clearance 為替交換, 為替の清算
　port clearance 出港手続き, 通関手続き, 出港許可

clearing 名 除去, 手形交換, 清算, 決済, クリアリング

amount of clearings 手形交換高
bill clearing 手形交換
clearing balance 交換尻
clearing bank 決済銀行
clearing house 手形交換所, 清算機関, 決済機関, クリアリング・ハウス
clearance house balance 手形交換尻
clearing operation 清算業務
clearing procedure 決済手続き
clearing system 決済方式, 決済制度, 決済機関, 決済機構
exchange clearing 為替清算
export clearing 輸出通関
incoming clearings 交換持ち帰り手形
international clearing systems 国際決済機構
online clearing オンライン決済
stock clearing 株式清算

clerical 形 書記の, 事務員の, 事務上の, 記載上の
clerical error 事務上の誤り, 記帳上の誤り, 記帳ミス, 誤記
clerical staff 事務職員
clerical work 事務的な[事務の]仕事, 事務職
clerical work measurement 事務量測定《略CWM》
clerical worker 事務員, 事務系労働者, 書記従業者

clerk 名 〈会社の〉事務員, 〈官庁の〉職員, 事務官, 〈銀行の〉行員, 〈ホテルの〉フロント係, 店員, 〈裁判所などの〉書記官 [事務官]
bank clerk 行員, 銀行員
hotel clerk ホテルのフロント係[受付係]
night clerk 夜勤係
office clerk 事務員
reservations clerk 受付係
salesclerk 販売員, 店員

click 動 クリックする
click a mouse button マウス・ボタンをクリックする
click on an icon アイコンをクリックする
▶Click for more information. さらに情報をお求めの方は, クリックしてください。

click 名 クリック
at click protection クリック補償
click rate クリック・レート (=clickthrough [click-through] rate: インプレッションに占めるクリックスルーの割合のこと)
click through [clickthrough] クリックスルー (バナー広告をクリックして広告主のサイトを訪れること)
click-through rate クリック率, クリックスルー・レート (=click rate)
▶While one director makes a presentation using his computers at a board meeting, the others follow on their own computers, turning pages with the *click* of a mouse. 役員会で役員がパソコンを使ってプレゼンテーション(説明)をする間, 他の役員は各自のパソコンの画面を追い, マウスを動かしてページをめくっていく。

click wrap agreement クリック・ラップ・アグリーメント
ウェブ・サイト上でのライセンス契約には, コンピュータ・ソフトをダウンロードしようとすると表示端末装置(ディスプレー)上の契約条件に応答しなければならない方式と, コンピュータ・ソフトウエアのダウンロードは契約しないでできるが, フォーマットが圧縮されているため, これを開くにはユーザーに契約条件が提示される方式がある。この方式を"clip wrap agreement"という。これに対して, 一般の市販ソフトを購入すると, その利用の前提条件としてプラスチック・フィルムの外装(ラップ: wrap)を通して契約条件が読めるようにプリントされ, この条件に同意できない場合はラップを破らないで返品するよう記載されている。これを"シュリンク・ラップ・アグリーメント(shrink-wrap agreement)"や"テア・オープン・ライセンス・アグリーメント(tear open license agreement)"という。

client 名 顧客, お得意, 得意先, 得意客, 取引先, 依頼人, 依頼者, ユーザー, 相談者, 監査依頼会社, 被監査会社(examinee corporation), クライアント (=customer)
attract clients 顧客を引きつける, 顧客を開拓する
client company 取引先, 顧客企業
client control 顧客管理
client defection 顧客離れ
client information 顧客情報
client license クライアント・ライセンス (ネットワークOSに付属する一定数のクライアント使用権)
client management 顧客管理, 得意先管理 (=customer management)
client money 顧客資金
client solicitation 顧客の勧誘 (=solicitation of clients)
corporate client 法人顧客, 取引先, 顧客企業, 銀行の融資先企業 (=corporate customer)
individual client 個人顧客
major client 大口顧客
new client 新規顧客
solvent client 支払い能力のある顧客

▶Banks are allowed to sell insurance policies to *clients*. 銀行は，顧客に保険を販売することができる。

▶Domestic nonlife insurance companies usually renew contracts with most of their corporate *clients* each April. 国内の損保各社は通常，毎年4月に大半の顧客企業と（保険）契約の更新を行っている。

▶The two major securities companies cut brokerage fees further for major *clients*. 大手証券会社2社は，大口顧客に対して株式売買手数料をさらに引き下げた。

client assets 顧客預り資産
▶The brokerage firm manages *client assets* of ¥520 billion in about 150,000 accounts. この証券会社は，口座数約15万で顧客預り資産は5,200億円に達する。

climate 名 気候，風土，条件，環境，状況，情勢，傾向，風潮，思潮，雰囲気，空気，地方，地帯（⇒ business climate）
  changing climate 環境の変化
  Climate Change Levy 気候変動税
  climate-changing pollution 気候変動をもたらす汚染物質（⇒chief）
  climate for acquisition 買収条件
  climate of opinion 世論
  economic climate 経済環境，経済情勢，景況，景気
  financial climate 金融環境
  investment climate 投資環境
  management climate 経営環境
  organizational climate 組織風土，組織環境，経営風土（＝organization climate）

▶The declining income and sales result from the changing *climate* in the mobile phone and digital camera businesses. この減収減益は，携帯電話事業とデジタル・カメラ事業の環境の変化によるものです。

▶Those corporations that will succeed and flourish will be those that create a *climate* encouraging exploration of new business possibilities and encouraging active listening to new ideas. これから成功して繁栄する企業は，新規事業の可能性を積極的に追求し，新しいアイデアの導入を積極的に進める企業風土を創出できる企業でしょう。

clinch 動 勝取る，獲得する，…を決定的［確定的］にする，固定する，〈取引などを〉まとめる
▶Toyota Motor Corp. *clinched* the top spot in corporate income declared to tax authorities for the fourth consecutive year. トヨタ自動車が，法人申告所得（ランキング）で，4年連続トップとなった。

CLO ローン担保証券（**collateralized loan obligation**の略。資産担保証券（asset-backed securities)の一種。金融機関が企業などに貸し出しているローン（貸出債権）を証券化したもので，ローンの元利金を担保にして発行される債券のこと）

cloning 名 人口増殖，クローン作製術，コピー人間作製術，分枝系，クローニング
▶The birth of a cloned sheep named Dolly sparked anxiety throughout the world about future human *cloning*. クローン羊ドリーの誕生が，将来のクローン人間作りに対する不安を世界に広げた。

cloning technology クローン技術
▶Reckless attempts have been made to apply *cloning technology* to reproductive medicine. これまでに，クローン技術を生殖医療に応用する無謀な試みが行われた前例がある。

close 動 〈取引を〉終える，引ける，取り決める，決める，締め切る，閉鎖する，整理する，清算する，解散する
  close a factory 工場を閉鎖する
  close off 勘定などを締め切る
  close out 処分する，締め切る
  close to [into] …に振り替える
  close the day at …で取引を終える
  close the day lower 下落して引ける
  close unprofitable stores 不採算店舗を閉鎖する（⇒restructuring plan）
  closed company 非公開会社，非上場会社（＝ private company, privately held company）
  closed corporation 閉鎖会社，非公開会社（＝ closing corporation）
  closed-end company 閉鎖式投資信託会社，クローズドエンド型投資信託会社

▶Mother Rock, a U.S. hedge fund, *closed* in August due to losses incurred due from the plunge in the natural gas prices. 米国のヘッジ・ファンド「マザーロック」は，天然ガス相場の下落に伴う損失で，今年の8月に解散した。

▶The company plans to *close* or consolidate 46 stores by the end of this fiscal year. 同社は，今年度末までに46店舗の統廃合を計画している。

close 名 終値，引け値，引け，終了
  close of business 営業終了，営業時間の終了
  market on close 引け注文

▶The corporation's regular quarterly dividend will be payable June 30, 2009 to shareholders of record at the *close* of business on June 9,

close | 099 | **CME**

2009．当社の通常四半期配当は，2009年6月9日営業終了時の登録株主に対して2009年6月30日に支払われます．

close 形 密接な，親しい，精密な，周到な，互角の，接戦の，僅差の，非公開の，限られた
　close company 閉鎖会社（基本的に，株主やパートナーなどの構成員が5名以下の会社）
　close cooperation and coordination 密接な協力体制
　close corporation 株式非公開会社，非公開会社，閉鎖会社（＝**closed corporation**）
　close money 金づまり，逼迫した金融
close the [one's] books（決算などのために）帳簿を締める，株式名義の書換えを停止する，申込みを締め切る（＝close one's accounts；⇒**annual accounts settlement**）
▶These companies *close their books* between April and June. これらの企業は，4－6月期決算だ[これらは，4－6月期決算企業だ]．
closed-end 形 〈投資信託が〉クローズドエンド型の，資本額固定の，閉鎖式の，〈担保が〉貸付金額を固定した
closely held company 少数株主支配会社，閉鎖的会社
closing 名 決済，期末，決算，締切り，取引完了，終値，〈正式契約書の〉調印式，〈正式契約書の〉作成・署名，〈不動産売買の〉最終手続き，〈株式の〉譲渡手続きと代金の払込み手続きの同時履行，〈工場などの〉閉鎖，休会，結語，クロージング（⇒**sale and purchase**）
　annual closing 年次決算，年度決算，年度締切り（＝annual closing of accounts）
　closing account for the half year ending March 2009 2009年3月中間決算
　closing accounts for the year 年次決算
　closing balance 期末残高
　closing procedures 決算手続き（＝closing process）
　closing rate 終値，引け値，決算日レート（＝current rate），クロージング・レート《略 **CR**》
　closing statements 決算書類
　interim closing 中間決算
　plant closing 工場閉鎖（＝plant closure）
▶GM's plant *closings* and job cuts in the United States will generate annual savings of roughly $2.5 billion. GMの米国での工場閉鎖と人員削減で，年間約25億ドルのコストが削減される．
closing balance sheet クロージング貸借対照表，クロージング時現在の貸借対照表
▶The *closing balance sheet* fairly presents the financial position of the Corporation at the closing date in conformity with United States GAAP. クロージング時現在の貸借対照表は，米国の一般に認められた会計原則[米国の会計基準]に従って，クロージング日の「会社」の財政状態を適正に表示している．
closing date 払込み日，払込み期日，締切り日，売上締切り日，決算日，〈証券の〉引渡し日，クロージング日（＝closing day）
▶The *closing date* shall be the date of execution of this agreement. クロージング日は，本契約の締結日とする．
closing price 終値，引け値（＝closing market price）
▶Based on the its *closing price*, the firm's market capitalization stands at ¥219 billion, making the second-largest issue on the Mothers market. 終値ベースで同社の時価総額は2,190億円で，新興企業向け市場の東証マザーズ上場銘柄としては第2位となった．
closure 名 〈工場や店舗，事業などの〉閉鎖，封鎖，閉幕，閉会（⇒**money-losing store**）
▶This restructuring program includes streamlining marketing and selling organizations, *closure* and consolidation of several manufacturing facilities and a general streamlining of operations throughout the Corporation. この事業再編計画には，マーケティング組織と販売組織の効率化，一部製造工場の閉鎖・統合や全社レベルでの業務全般の効率化が含まれています．
clout 名 権威，権力，支配力，実力，影響力，リーダーシップ
　financial clout 資金力，資金の影響力
　political clout 政治力
　pricing clout 価格指導力，プライス・リーダーシップ（＝price leadership）
　wield a political clout 政治力を振るう
▶Foreign government-affiliated investment funds, including those of Russia, China and oil producers in the Middle East, wield increasing financial *clout*. ロシア，中国や中東産油国など，海外の政府系投資ファンドが資金の影響力を強めている．
CME シカゴ・マーカンタイル取引所（**Chicago Mercantile Exchange**の略．世界最大の先物取引所）
▶*CME* Group Inc. is the operator of the Chicago Mercantile Exchange (*CME*). CMEグループは，シカゴ・マーカンタイル取引所（CME）を運営している．

CMO 抵当証書担保付き債券, 不動産抵当証書担保債券, モーゲージ担保債務証書 (**collateralized mortgage obligation**の略)

coal 名 石炭
  anthracite coal 無煙炭
  bituminous coal 瀝青(れきせい)炭
  coal burning 石炭消費量
  coal gas 石炭
  coal gasification 石炭ガス化
  coal gasification combined cycle ガス化複合サイクル発電
  coal liquefaction 石炭液化
  coal mine 炭鉱 (=coalmine)
  coal slurry pipeline 石炭スラリー・パイプライン
  coal washing 洗炭
  sub-bituminous coal 亜瀝青炭
  ▶World *coal* burning peaked in 1996 and has fallen 2 percent since then. 世界の石炭消費量は, 1996年にピークに達し, それ以来2%低下している。

code 名 規則, 規約, 基準, 規範, 法, 略号, 暗号, 符号, 情報, コード (⇒**come up with**)
  approval [authorization] code 承認番号
  area code 電話の市外番号 (=dialing code)
  Bankruptcy Code 米連邦破産法
  binary code 2進符号
  card discrimination code カード識別コード
  code name 暗号名
  code of behavior 行動基準
  code of ethics 倫理規程 (=code of conduct)
  code of honor 社交儀礼
  code of practice 服務規程
  code of professional ethics 職業倫理規程
  commercial code 商法
  computer code 機械語 (=machine code)
  distribution code 流通コード《略 DC》
  dumping code ダンピング綱領
  ethical code 倫理綱領, 倫理規程
  Federal Securities Code 米連邦証券法典
  genetic code 遺伝コード, 遺伝暗号, 遺伝子情報
  Internal Revenue Code 内国歳入法
  international codes 国際規約
  telegraphic code 電信符号
  television code テレビ基準
  Uniform Commercial Code 統一商事法典, 統一商法典
  zip code 郵便番号 (=postal code)

code of conduct 行動規範, 行動準則, 倫理綱領, 倫理規定, 取引慣行, コード (=code of ethics)
  ▶The *code of conduct* for battery manufacturers will stipulate the methods of production, including process management, to protect consumers. 電池メーカーに対する行動規範では, 消費者保護のため, 工程管理など電池の製造方法を定めることになった。

code-sharing 名 共同運航 (=code-share)
  ▶The two airlines have agreed to enter into a *code-sharing* arrangement on international routes. 両航空会社は, 国際線の共同運航協定を結ぶことで合意した。

cogeneration system コージェネレーション(熱電併給)システム
  ▶This power station will use a natural gas based *cogeneration system* that will reduce carbon dioxide emissions 30 percent compared with conventional methods of generating power. この発電所では, 天然ガスを使ったコージェネレーション(熱電併給)システムを採用して, 従来の発電方式と比べて二酸化炭素の排出量を3割減らす。

coincident index 景気一致指数, 一致指数 (=coincident indicator: 鉱工業生産指数, 百貨店販売額, 所定外労働時間指数など, 現状の景気の動きと同時期に並行して動く経済指標で, 景気の現状を示す)
  ▶A reading of below 50 percent in the *coincident index* is considered a sign of economic contraction and a figure above that is viewed as a sign of expansion. 一致指数で50%以下の数値は景気収縮[景気後退]を示す指標と見られ, それ以上の数字は景気回復[景気拡大]を示す指標と見なされる。

co-insurance 名 共同保険, 付保割合条件付き保険, コインシュランス

collaborative planning, forecasting and replenishment 需要予測と在庫補充のための共同事業《略 CPFR》

collaborative work 提携作業
  ▶*Collaborative work* that is a premise for the tie-up is already in place. 経営統合の前提である提携作業は, すでに進んでいる。

collapse 動 経営破綻する(fail), 破綻する, 倒産する, 暴落する, 急減する, 崩壊する
  ▶Ashikaga Bank *collapsed* and was temporarily placed under state control. 足利銀行は, 経営破綻して一時国有化された。
  ▶U.S. stock markets *collapsed* following huge sell-offs in overseas markets. 米国の株式相場[株式市場]が, 海外株式市場の株価急落に続いて

急落した。

collapse 名 経営破綻, 破綻, 倒産, 崩壊, 暴落, 急落, 下落, 急減, 悪化
  collapse of financial institutions 金融破綻, 金融機関の経営破綻
  collapse of the dollar ドルの下落
  collapse of the economic bubble バブル崩壊
  collapse of the stock market 株式市場の急落, 株式相場の下落 （=stock market collapse）
  corporate collapse 企業倒産, 企業の経営破綻 （=corporate failure）
  credit collapse 信用崩壊 （=the collapse of credit）
  earnings collapse 業績悪化, 大幅減益, 収益の落ち込み
  ▶Distrust of corporate accounting was ignited by the *collapse* of major energy trader Enron. 企業会計への不信感は, 米エネルギー大手エンロンの経営破綻に端を発した。

collateral 名 担保, 担保物件, 担保品, 担保財産 （=mortgage, security）
  collateral assessment 担保評価
  collateral bond 担保付き社債
  collateral value 担保価値
  fixed collateral 根（ね）抵当, 根抵当権
  foreclosed collateral 担保権の実行, 担保権の行使
  offer ... as collateral …を担保として提供する
  pledge ... as collateral …を担保として差し出す
  post collateral 担保を差し入れる, 担保を設定する, 担保を積む
  ▶We usually do not require *collateral* or other security from other parties to these financial instruments. これらの金融商品については, 当社は通常, 相手方に当該商品に対する担保その他の保証を要求してはいません。

colleague 名 同僚

collect 動〈債権や代金, 資源などを〉回収する,〈年金や保険料, 税金などを〉徴収する,〈預金などを〉獲得する
  ▶*Collecting* receivables helps us to pay our suppliers. 売掛債権を回収すると, 当社の納入業者への支払いが楽になります。

collectible 名 集金, 取立て, 徴収

collection 名〈債権や代金などの〉回収, 代金取立て, 集金,〈年金や保険料, 税金などの〉徴収,〈預金などの〉獲得
  bill for collection 代金取立手形
  cash collection 現金回収, 回収額
  collection and distribution services 集配業務
  collection expense 回収費, 集金費, 代金回収費 （=collection cost）
  collection fee 回収費用
  collection of debts 債権の回収, 債権回収 （=debt collection）
  collection of premiums 保険料の徴収
  collection of principal 元本の回収
  collection of receivables 売掛金[売掛債権]の回収
  collections from customers and others 顧客その他からの回収
  debt collection 債権回収, 貸金取立て, 借金取り （=collecting the debt, collection of debts）
  loan collection 債権回収
  tax collection 徴税, 税の徴収 （=collection of taxes）
  transfer of collections 回収金の送金
  ▶Under the revised law for the promotion of efficient utilization of resources, PC users must pay electronic manufacturers a *collection* fee of several thousand yen when discarding PCs purchased on Sept. 30, 2003 and before. 資源有効利用促進法の改正で, パソコン利用者は, 2003年9月30日以前に購入したパソコンを廃棄する際に, 数千円の回収費用を電機メーカーに支払わなければならない。

collision 名 衝突

collude 動 談合する, 結託する, 共謀する
  collude on a bid 入札について談合する
  collude on prices 価格で談合する, 価格で不正を行う
  ▶Nine European and U.S. consumer products makers are suspected of *colluding* on prices in France. フランスで, 欧米の消費財メーカー9社が価格で談合した疑いが持たれている。

collusion 名 談合, 不正, 共謀, 結託, なれ合い
  collusion on contract bidding 入札での不正
  obtain a contract by way of collusion 談合で契約を獲得する
  price collusion 価格談合
  private-sector collusion 企業の談合
  ▶The suspected price *collusion* is believed to have begun toward the end of 2005. 疑いが持たれている価格談合は, 2005年末頃から始まった。

combination 名 合併, 連結, 企業結合, 企業連合, 相互利益協定, 結合, 組合せ, 関連性
  business combination 企業結合, 企業合同, 合併, 統合, 企業買収 （=combination of business）
  combination of cap and swap キャップとスワップの組合せ

combinations of companies 企業結合, 企業グループ
combination of factors 要因の関連性
deferred taxes in a purchase combination パーチェス法による合併での繰延べ税金
industrial combination 企業結合
▶Goodwill is the difference between the purchase price and the fair value of net assets acquired in business *combinations* treated as purchases. 営業権は, パーチェス法により会計処理した企業買収で取得した純資産の購入価格と公正価格との差異です。

combined 形 合算した, 結合した, 統合した, 連結した, …の合算, …の合計 [合計額]（⇒**customer service**）
combined group net profit 連結税引き後利益の合計額, 連結純利益の合計額
combined losses 赤字合計額
combined net loss 純損失の合計, 税引き後損失の合計額, 全社合わせての赤字
combined net profit 税引き後利益の合計額, 純利益の合計額
combined pretax profit 経常利益合計
combined profits or losses 損益の合算, 損益の通算（＝combined profits and losses）
combined revenue 連結収益総合収益
combined sales 売上高の合計, 全社合計の売上高, 全社合わせての売上高, 総売却額
▶The consolidated tax system calculates taxes based on *combined* profits or losses. 連結税制は, 企業グループの損益を合算［結合］して税額を算定するシステムだ。

combined-cycle power-generation system コンバインドサイクル発電システム
▶In *combined-cycle power-generation system*, liquefied natural gas is combusted to activate gas turbines to produce a high-temperature environment in which steam to power the turbines is generated. コンバインドサイクル発電システムの場合は, 液化天然ガスを燃やしてガス・タービンを回し, そこから生じた高温の空気で蒸気タービンを回す蒸気を作る。

come up with 提出する, 提案する, 打ち出す, 考え出す, 思いつく, 策定する, 発表する, 生産する, 用意する, 見つける
▶The IMF will *come up with* a draft of a code of best practices for sovereign wealth funds by August 2008. 国際通貨基金 (IMF) が, 2008年8月までに政府系投資ファンドの最善の投資指針の原案を策定する。

comfort letter 財務内容に関する会計監査人の意見書［調査報告書］, コンフォート・レター（＝letter of comfort：一種の保証状で「指導念書」ともいわれる）
comfort letter for underwriter 証券引受業者［幹事証券会社］に対する調査報告書（＝letter for underwriter：企業が株式上場や増資などで新規証券を発行する際, 提出する有価証券届出書の記載事項などについて, 証券引受業者の依頼に基づき, 発行会社の監査人が作成する調査報告書）

commerce 名 商取引, 商業, 通商, 貿易, コマース（⇒**e-commerce**）
B2B e-commerce service 企業間eコマース・サービス, 企業間eビジネス・サービス
census of commerce 商業統計
commerce and industry 商工業
commerce and navigation 通商航海
Commerce at Light Speed 瞬時電子取引《略 CALS》
commerce business 商い, 商売
Commerce Department 米商務省
electronic commerce Eコマース, 電子商取引《略 EC》
international commerce arbitration 国際商事仲裁
Internet commerce インターネット・コマース
mobile commerce モバイル・コマース, Mコマース（携帯電話や携帯情報端末などのモバイル機器を利用した商取引）
treaty of commerce 通商条約

commercial 形 商業の, 商業上の, 商業的な, 商業ベースの, 通商の, 営利の, 民間の, 民放の, 大量生産型の, 量産型の, 市販の, 消費者向けの, 名 宣伝, 広告放送, コマーシャル
banker's commercial credit 銀行信用状
commercial agency 商業興信所
commercial arbitration 商事仲裁
commercial artist 商業デザイナー
commercial aviation 民間航空事業
commercial base 商業採算性, 商業採算, 商業ベース, コマーシャル・ベース
commercial break コマーシャルの時間
commercial building オフィス・ビル
Commercial Code 商法（⇒**divestiture**）
commercial company [enterprise] 営利企業
commercial concerns 経済的利益
commercial correspondence 商業通信文
commercial credit 商業信用, 商業信用状, 民間融資
commercial customers 事業法人顧客

commercial document　商業書類
commercial draft　商業手形
commercial exhibition　展示会
commercial farm　営利農場, 商品生産農家
commercial feasibility　商業的実行可能性
commercial flight　民間航空機, 民間の定期航空便
commercial industry　流通業
commercial invoice　商業送り状, 仕切り書
commercial jingle　コマーシャル・ソング
commercial lending　商業貸付け, 民間融資
commercial lines　商業保険, 企業保険
commercial loan　商業貸付け, 商業貸出金, 民間融資, 短期銀行融資
commercial manufacture　大量生産, 量産
commercial message　コマーシャルの宣伝文句, コマーシャル・メッセージ《略 CM》
commercial office space　賃貸用オフィス・ビル
commercial paper outstanding　CP発行残高
commercial production　商業生産
commercial real estate　商業用不動産
commercial securitization　商業用不動産の証券化
commercial standards　商業規格
commercial transaction　商取引, 商業取引, 商行為, 商業活動
commercial traveller　販売外交員, 外交販売員, 行商人 (＝representative, traveling salesman)
commercial treaty　通商条約
commercial TV [television]　民放テレビ
commercial use　商業利用, 商業上の使用
commercial vehicle　営業車, 商用車 (＝commercial car)
International Commercial Terms　国際貿易条件基準, インコタームズ (⇒Incoterms)
program commercial　番組コマーシャル
TV commercial　テレビ・コマーシャル

commercial activities　営業活動
▶Access to the basic residents registers should not be permitted for commercial activities.　住民基本台帳の閲覧は, 営業活動が目的の場合は認めるべきでない。

commercial bank　商業銀行 (米国の場合は, 連邦法または州法により認可を受けた銀行), 都市銀行, 都銀, 市中銀行, 市銀, 銀行 (商業銀行の主な業務は, 融資, 預金の受入れと外国為替)
national commercial bank　国法商業銀行
private commercial bank　民間銀行
state commercial bank　州立商業銀行, 州法商業銀行

state-owned commercial bank　国営商業銀行

commercial paper　商業証券, 商業手形, コマーシャル・ペーパー《略 CP》(「コマーシャル・ペーパー」は, 為替手形 (bill of exchange, draft), 約束手形 (note, promissory note), 小切手 (check) や預金証書 (certificate of deposit) などを指し, 米国では資金調達のために優良企業が発行する通常2日–270日以内の短期約束手形のことをいう。⇒ asset-backed commercial paper)
▶Higher debt maturing within one year chiefly reflects commercial paper we issued to support financial services.　1年以内返済予定の負債の増加は, 主に金融サービス部門の支援のため, 当社がコマーシャル・ペーパーを発行したことを反映しています。

commercial whaling　商業捕鯨
▶The approval of a nonbinding pro-whaling declaration by the International Whaling Commission does not immediately threaten the moratorium on commercial whaling.　国際捕鯨委員会による拘束力のない捕鯨支持宣言の承認は, 商業捕鯨一時禁止措置を直ちに脅かすものではない。

commercial utilization　商業利用, 商業化, 実用化 (＝commercial use)
▶The basic marine development plan includes the commercial utilization of methane hydrate.　海洋開発基本計画には, メタンハイドレートの商業化も含まれている。

commercialism 名　商業主義, 営利主義, コマーシャリズム

commercialization 名　商品化, 商業化, 実用化, 営利化, 産業化
▶In the commercialization of developed technology, the United States is promoting the proliferation of genetically modified seeds for corn and soy beans.　開発された技術の産業化の面では, 米国はトウモロコシや大豆などの遺伝子組換え種子の普及を促進している。
▶The government has boosted spending on science and technology, supporting businesses to realize the commercialization of their technologies.　政府は, 科学技術予算を増やし, 企業の技術製品化実現に向けて企業を支援している。

commission 名　手数料, 株式引受手数料, 報酬, 口銭, 委任, 委任状, 委託, 代理業務, 授与, 授権, 任命, 任命書, 委員会, 実務, 任務, 権限, 職権, 過失, 作為, コミッション (⇒commodity futures, liberalization)
acceptance commission　手形引受手数料

accrued commission 未払い手数料
accrued commission receivable 未収手数料
agent commission 代理店手数料（＝agency commission）
amount of commission charged 請求手数料額
commission and expenses on capital shares 株式発行費用
commission and fee 報酬
commission expense 手数料費用
commission income and expense 受入手数料および支払い手数料
commission payable 未払い手数料
commission receivable 未収手数料
commission revenue 手数料収入
discount commission 割引手数料
fee and commission received 受入手数料
opening commission 発行手数料
placement commission 販売手数料
prepaid commission 前払い手数料
selling commission 販売手数料（＝sales commission）
underwriting commission 引受手数料
▸Securities firms are free to set the price for all *commissions*. 売買委託手数料は，すべて証券各社が自由に設定できる。
▸The inflated part of the *commissions* was handed to officials from foreign governments and other official bodies through the firm's overseas arm. 手数料の上乗せ分は，同社の海外子会社を通じて外国政府や他の公的機関の幹部に渡されていた。

commit 動 約束する，公約する，確約する，取り組む，専念する，全力を挙げる，引き受ける，委託する，委任する
　committed bank facilities 契約に基づく銀行借入枠
　committed bank lines of credit 銀行の信用供与枠
▸We *commit* to these values to guide our decisions and behavior. 私たちは，私たちの意思決定と行動の基準としてこれらの価値観を大切にしています。

commitment 名 委任，委託，公約，誓約，約束，約定，立場の明確な表明，〈協調融資団への〉参加意思表示，〈融資参加の〉意向表明，〈銀行の〉融資承認，融資先，売買約定，売買契約，取引契約，契約債務，契約義務，未履行債務，姿勢，取組み，コミットメント（⇒business model）
　acceptance commitment 引受債務
　brokerage commission 株式委託売買手数料，委託売買手数料，委託手数料，仲介手数料，ブローカー手数料（＝brokerage fee）
　capital commitments 出資，資本参加
　commitment fee 約定料，契約手数料，保証手数料，コミットメント・フィー
　commitments and contingent liabilities 契約債務および偶発債務
　commitments to extend credit 信用供与契約
　customer financing commitments 顧客融資契約
　financial commitment 資金協力，金銭の支払い
　firm commitment 確定契約，成約済み取引
　lease commitment 賃貸借契約，リース契約
　loan commitments 貸出約定，融資契約，融資確約
　new loans commitments 新規融資契約，新規融資承認額
　underwriting commitment 引受額
　unused portions of commitments 貸出枠未実行残高
▸These lease *commitments* are principally for the rental of office premises. これらのリース契約は，主に事務所施設の賃借を対象としています。
▸We are continuing our *commitment* to the Corporation's research and development programs. 当社は，当社の研究開発計画にも引き続き取り組んでいます。

commitment line 融資枠の設定，コミットメント・ライン
　コミットメント・ラインとは▪銀行から一定の範囲で自由に借入れができる融資枠の設定のこと。コミットメント・ラインを設定すると，金融機関は安定した手数料収入が得られるほか，優良企業との取引拡大を期待できる。また，企業にとっては，手数料を払う代わりに金利ゼロで融資を受けられるメリットがある。緊急の資金需要に備えられるほか，資金効率の改善効果もある。最近は，経営不振の企業が，信用不安を解消するため主力取引銀行とコミットメント・ライン契約を結ぶことが多い。

committed to …に取り組む，…に専念する，…に心する，…に入れ込む，…すると言明する，明言する，…する決意である，…（の確保）に努める（⇒ corporate citizen [citizenship]）
▸The leaders of the Group of Eight major nations are *committed to* transparency in the energy sector. 主要8か国の指導者は，エネルギー分野の透明性確保に努めている。

commodity 名 商品，市況品，日用品，物品，生産物，財貨，財
　commodity agreement 商品協定

commodity aid 商品援助
commodity approach 商品研究
commodity composition 商品構成
commodity demand 商品需要
commodity export 商品輸出
commodity fund 商品ファンド
commodity goods 生活必需品
commodity item 品目
commodity-like 差別化が難しい
commodity loans 商品借款 (⇒chemicals)
commodity preservation 商品保全
commodity product 汎用品
commodity structure 商品構造
commodity supply 商品供給
commodity tax 物品税
consumption commodity 消費財 (=commodity consumed, consumer commodity)
domestic commodity prices 国内物価
household commodity 家庭用品
industrial commodity 工業製品
industrial commodity industry 素材産業
marketable commodity 市場性のある商品
marketed commodity 市販品, 市販商品
nonmarketed commodity 非市場性商品
perishable commodity 消耗品
primary commodity 第一次産品, 一次産品, 基本財
taxed commodity 課税品, 課税商品
traded commodity 貿易財

commodity exchange 商品取引所, 商品取引
  Commodities Exchange Commission 商品取引所委員会
  Commodity Exchange Authority 商品取引所監督局
  Commodity Exchanges Center 商品取引所センター
  Commodity Exchange Law 日本の商品取引所法
  U.S. Commodity Exchange Act 米国商品取引所法, 米国商品取引法
▸CME Group Inc. will become the world's biggest *commodity exchange* through its acquisition of NYMEX Holdings Inc. NYMEXホールディングス(ニューヨーク商業取引所を運営)の買収により, CMEグループ(シカゴ・マーカンタイル取引所を運営)は, 世界最大の商品取引所になる。

commodity futures 商品先物, 商品先物契約
▸Brokerage commissions on *commodity futures trading* are completely liberalized. 商品先物取引の委託手数料は, 完全自由化されている。

commodity futures market 商品先物市場
▸Foreign players also are expected to enter the *commodity futures market* in line with the improvement in investment conditions. 投資の環境改善で, 外資[海外企業]の商品先物市場への参入も見込まれる。

commodity futures trading 商品先物取引(金や石油などの商品について, 一定の値段で将来売買することを約束して行う取引で, 価格は取引契約を結ぶ時点で決める)
▸Moves toward a full-scale realignment have been accelerating in the *commodity futures trading* industry, involving companies from other business fields. 商品先物取引業界では, 異業種の企業を巻き込んだ総力を挙げての再編の動きが加速している。

commodity market 商品市場
▸Primary factors behind the buoyant performances were price increases in *commodity markets* such as steel, and increased exports. 好業績[好決算]の主因は, 鉄鋼など商品相場の上昇と輸出の増大である。

commodity market of crude futures 原油先物の商品市場
▸The *commodity market of crude futures* has become increasingly speculative. 原油先物の商品市場は, 次第に投機色を強めている。

commodity prices 市況品価格, 物価
▸Continuing appreciation of the yen has effectively helped companies offset the negative effects of higher *commodity prices*. 円高の進行で事実, 市況商品価格の上昇に伴う企業への悪影響が吸収されている。

common 形 共通の, 共有の, 共同の, 普通の, 通常の
  common cost 共通費, 共通原価
  common dividend 普通株配当金, 普通株配当金
  common equity 普通株式
  common interests 共通の利益
  common knowledge 周知の事実
  common market 共同市場
  common ownership 共同所有, 共有
  common purpose 共通の目的
  common stockholder 普通株主
  common stockholders's equity 普通株主資本, 普通株主資本の部
  common voting stock 普通議決権株式

common control 共通の支配
▸In 2008, no single customer or group under *common control* represented 10% or more of

the Company's sales. 2008年度は，共通の支配下にある単一顧客またはグループで，当社売上高の10%以上を占めるものはありません。

common currency 共通通貨
▸European countries are deepening and expanding economic union by introducing a *common currency* and welcoming East European countries into the European Union. 欧州は，共通通貨の導入や東欧諸国のEU（欧州連合）への取り込みなどで，経済統合の深化と拡大を続けている。

common holding company [firm] 共同持ち株会社
▸The two companies are in talks about integrating their business under a *common holding firm*. 両社は現在，共同持ち株会社方式による経営統合に向けて交渉している。

common share 普通株，普通株式，普通株資本金，資本金（＝common equity, common stock, ordinary share, ordinary stock：普通株は，優先株(preferred share, preferred stock)や後配株(deferred share, deferred stock)のように特別の権利内容を持たない一般の株式のこと）
▸The increase in the number of *common shares* was due mainly to conversion of the $2.70 preferred shares in March. 普通株式数が増加したのは，主に3月に行われた額面2.70ドルの優先株式の転換によるものです。

common shares outstanding 発行済み普通株式，発行済み社外流通株式，普通株式発行総数
▸First quarter earnings per share were based on 320 million average *common shares outstanding*. 第1四半期の1株当たり純利益は，発行済み普通株式の平均株式数3億2,000万株に基づいて計算されています。

common stock 普通株［普通株式］，普通株資本金，資本金（＝common share, ordinary share, ordinary stock）
　authorized common stock　授権普通株式数
　common stock at par　額面普通株資本
　common stock in treasury　自己普通株式，自己株式
　common stock issued and outstanding　普通株式発行済み株式数
　common stock outstanding　発行済み社外流通普通株式（＝common shares outstanding）
　common stock with par value　額面株式（「par value（額面金額）」は，株主が払い込んだ金額のうち法定資本金(legal capital)に組み入れる金額）
　common stock without par value　無額面株式

　junior common stock　劣後普通株式
　outstanding common stock　発行済み普通株式
▸On November 1, 2008, the Company's Board of Directors approved a 43% increase in the quarterly dividend on *common stock*. 2008年11月1日，当社取締役会は，普通株式の四半期配当金の43%増額を承認しました。

common stock equivalents 普通株式相当証券，普通株式等価物，準普通株式（⇒**convertible bond**）
▸*Common stock equivalents* are stock options that we assume to be exercised for the purposes of computing earnings per common share. 普通株式等価物とは，1株当たり純利益を計算するにあたって行使されると仮定したストック・オプションです。

communication 名　通信，伝達，通達，意思疎通，相互理解，やり取り，協議，連絡，手紙，コミュニケーション（⇒**conduct, task**）
　bottom-to-top communication　下から上への意思疎通
　broadband communication network　広帯域通信網《略 BCN》
　business communication　ビジネス・コミュニケーション
　communication at work　職場でのコミュニケーション
　communication barrier　コミュニケーションの障害
　communication by things　物コミ
　communication channel　通信チャネル，コミュニケーション経路，コミュニケーション・チャネル（＝channel of communication）
　communication components　コミュニケーションの構成要素（「送り手，メッセージ，媒介物，受け手，効果」の5要素）
　communication engineering　情報工学
　communication media　コミュニケーション媒体
　communication skills　自己表現能力，自己表現技術
　confidential communication　内密情報
　corporate communication　企業内通信，コーポレート・コミュニケーション
　corporate communication network　企業内通信ネットワーク
　fiber optics communication　光ファイバー通信
　mass communication media　報道機関，マスコミ媒体
　mini communication　ミニコミ
　nonverbal communication　非言語コミュニケ

-ション
oral communication 口頭伝達, オーラル・コミュニケーション
personal communication パーソナル通信, 人的コミュニケーション, 個人のコミュニケーション
pull communication 引くコミュニケーション（消費者から企業側へ情報を引き上げるコミュニケーション）
push communication 押すコミュニケーション（企業側から消費者への積極的な情報提供）
skin communication 皮膚コミュニケーション
two-way communication 両面貿易, 双方向通信, ツーウェイ・コミュニケーション
verbal communication 言葉による意思疎通, 言語コミュニケーション
visual communication 画像通信, ビジュアル・コミュニケーション
▶Reasons given for workplace bullying included deterioration or lack of personal *communication* and a lessening sense of nurturing. 「職場のいじめ」の理由としては, 個人のコミュニケーション能力の低下・欠如や人を育てる意識の希薄化などが挙げられた。

communication capacity 通信容量
▶This submarine cable network has substantially increased *communication capacity* in the Asian market. この海底ケーブル・ネットワークで, アジア市場の通信容量が大幅に増加した。

communication line 通信回線
▶The volume of domestic data flow per second through *communication lines* increased 2.5 times over the past three years. 国内の通信回線を流れるデータ量（毎秒）は, 過去3年で2.5倍に増えた。

communication program コミュニケーション・プログラム
▶Our efforts for environmental improvement include environmental cleanup costs and *communication programs*. 当社の環境改善策には, 環境の浄化整備費や住民とのコミュニケーション・プログラムも含まれています。

communications 名 通信, 通信手段, 通信機器, 報道機関, 交通の便, 意思の疎通 (⇒broadband)
　advanced information communications society 高度情報通信社会
　business communications network ビジネス通信ネットワーク
　cellular communications 移動電話, セルラー通信
　commercial communications satellite 商用通信衛星
　Communications Decency Act 通信品位法, 通信品格法《略 CDA》
　communications gap 相互理解の欠如, 意思疎通の断絶, 意思疎通のずれ, 伝達欠如, コミュニケーション・ギャップ
　communications industry 通信業界
　communications market 通信市場
　communications service provider 通信サービス事業者
　communications standards 通信規格
　data communications service データ通信サービス
　Federal Communications Commission 米連邦通信委員会
　global communications system グローバル通信システム
　intelligent communications 知的通信, 知能通信, 高度通信
　mass communications マスコミ, 大衆伝達, マスコミ媒体
　multimedia communications business マルチメディア通信事業
　network communications ネットワーク通信
　optical communications 光通信, 光ファイバー通信
　satellite communications 衛星通信
　voice communications 音声通信
　wireless communications 無線通信, 無線通信機器

communications circuit 通信回線
▶Telecoms are permitted to operate *communications circuits*, together with such related services as the Internet. 通信会社は, 通信回線の運営とネット接続などの関連業務の展開を認められている。

communications facilities 通信設備
▶NTT dominates the domestic *communications facilities* with its subscribers' cable network. NTTは, その加入者回線網と国内通信設備を支配している。

communications satellite 通信衛星《略 CS》
▶The new *communications satellite* is in a stationary orbit located 110 degrees east latitude. 新CS(通信衛星)は, 東経110度上の静止軌道にある。

community 名 地域社会, 共同社会, 社会, 共同体, 団体, 業界, …界, コミュニティ
　business community 経済界, 財界, 産業界, 実

業界 (=business circles, business world)
community activities 地域社会活動
community center 公民館, 公会堂, 地域社会事業センター, コミュニティ・センター
community development 地域開発
community organization 社会事業団体
community relations 地域社会との関係, 対地域社会関係, 地域社会との良好な関係維持, 地域社会PR, 地域社会関連活動, 地域社会活動《略 CR》
community products コミュニティ製品
community service 地域社会サービス
community shopping center コミュニティ型ショッピング・センター
community site コミュニティ・サイト (掲示板やチャットルームなど, 同じ興味や関心のある人たちが集うインターネット上のサイト)
economic community 経済界, 財界, 経済圏
financial community 金融界, 金融業界
global community 国際社会 (=international community)
industrial community 経済界, 産業界, 実業界
international community 国際社会
investment community 投資業界
legal community 法曹界
local community 地域社会, 地方公共団体
medical community 医学界
Net community ネット社会
virtual community 仮想現実社会
Web-based community ウェブ上のコミュニティ
world community 世界共同体, 国際社会
▶Rakuten's attempt to demand its business integration by purchasing a massive number of shares in TBS drew strong objections from the business *community*. TBSの株を大量に取得して経営統合を要求する楽天の手法は, 経済界の強い反発を招いた。
▶We are responsible to our people and to the *community* where they live and work. 当社は, 従業員に対して責任を負うと同時に, 従業員が生活し働いている地域社会に対しても責任を負っています。

community-based 形 地域社会ベースの, 地域密着型の
community-based sales 地域密着型の営業
community-based services 地域密着型のサービス, 地域密着型の営業活動
▶The Company will enhance *community-based* sales. 当社は今後, 地元密着型の営業を強化し

ます。
community of interest 関心の一致, 利害の一致, 利害の調整, 利益共同体
▶The alliance is a *community of interest* based on new growth opportunities in the global telecommunications equipment markets. この提携は, 世界の通信機器市場で新たな成長の機会をめざす両社の関心が一致したことによるものです。
commutation 名 通勤[通学], 代替(substitution), 交換(exchange), 変換, 換算, 振替え, 代替え, 代償, 代償金, 〈債務などの〉軽減, 〈刑罰の〉減刑, 整流
apply for a commutation of the sentence 減刑を願い出る
commutation ticket 定期券[定期乗車券], 回数券[回数乗車券] (=commuter ticket, season ticket)
commuter 名 通勤者, 通学者, コミューター
commuter belt 通勤圏, 通勤者居住区域, ベッドタウン (=commuterland, commuterville)
commuter bus 通勤バス, 路線バス
commuter car 通勤用自動車
commuter pass 定期券 (=commuter's ticket)
commuter train 通勤電車
comp compensationの略
company 名 会社, 企業, 社団, カンパニー (⇒ holding company, limited liability company, listed company, publicly held company, target company)
acquiring company 買収会社
blue-chip company 優良企業 (=successful company)
business company 事業会社
Companies Act 会社法
company credit quality 企業の信用の質, 企業の信用力
company fact sheet 会社概要 (=company facts, company overview, company profile)
company history 会社の沿革, 会社の歴史, 社史 (=corporate history)
company limited by guarantee 英国の保証有限会社 (=guarantee company)
company objective 会社目標, 企業目標 (=company goal)
company philosophy 企業理念, 企業方針, 会社方針, 経営方針, 企業哲学, 経営哲学
company policy 会社方針, 会社の政策, 企業政策
company profile 会社概要, 会社案内 (=company backgrounder, company description, company facts)

company profit 企業利益, 法人利潤, 企業収益
company results meeting 決算発表時の記者会見
company spokesperson 企業の広報担当者
comparable company 類似会社, 類似企業
fifty-percent-owned company 半数所有会社, 50％所有会社
friendly company 友好的な企業
majority owned company 過半数所有会社
mutual company 相互会社
nonpublic company 非公開企業 (＝private company)
offeree company 買付け対象会社
open company 公開会社 (＝open corporation)
operating company 事業会社 (＝business company)
outstanding company 超優良会社
parent company 親会社
peer companies 同業他社
private company 非公開会社, 株式非公開会社, 非上場会社, 民間企業 (＝privately held company)
public company 株式公開会社, 株式公開企業, 上場会社, 上場企業 (＝publicly held company)
quoted company 上場企業, 上場会社 (＝listed company)
regulated company 規制対象企業
stand alone company 独立企業
subsidiary company 子会社
unquoted company 非上場会社, 非上場会社 (＝unlisted company)
utility company 公益事業会社

▶A targeted *company* demanded a *company* trying to acquire its stocks to present a business plan. 買収の標的企業は, 買収企業[標的企業の株式を取得しようとしている企業]に事業計画の提出を求めた。

▶We are a *company* ever-strengthening its customer partnerships, product line and efficiency. 当社は, つねにお客さまとの連携および製品ラインの強化と効率性改善に取り組んでいる会社です。

company executive 企業経営者, 経営者, 会社重役

▶Japanese *company executives* appear to be faced with an unprecedentedly difficult problem at present. 日本の経営者は現在, いまだかつてないほど厳しい問題に直面しているようだ。

company size 企業規模

▶A breakdown of the employment statistics by *company size* reveals that the number of people working for companies with fewer than 500 employees continued to decline in August. 雇用統計の企業規模別分析では, 500人未満の中小企業の雇用者数は前月に続いて8月も減少している。

company system カンパニー制, 社内企業制 (企業の事業部制に市場原理を導入して, 独立の会社に近づけた形態の擬似会社制。そのメリットとして, 意思決定と実施の迅速化, 組織の活性化, 本業の責任の明確化などが挙げられている)

▶*Company system* of independent divisions is a management system that Sony pioneered as a major company in Japan. 独立事業部門のカンパニー制は, ソニーが日本の大手企業として初めて導入した経営システムである。

company's value 企業価値

▶The market capitalization of a company determines the *company's value*. 企業価値の決定要因は[企業価値を決めるのは], 企業の時価総額だ。

comparable 形 同等の, 類似の, 似通った, 匹敵する, 相当する, 比較可能な, 共通点がある, コンパラブル

comparable analysis 類似企業分析
comparable basis 比較ベース, 継続事業ベース
comparable figures 比較可能数値
comparable performance 同等の性能
comparable size 同等の大きさ[規模, サイズ]
comparable store sales 既存店ベースの売上
comparable worth 男女同一賃金原則, 同一価値原則, 同一労働同一価値原則, コンパラブル・ワース
other comparable companies 同業他社

comparables 名 類似物件

compatibility 名 互換性, 適合性, 両立性, 両立, 共存, コンパチビリティ

backward compatibility 下位互換性下位互換 (＝downward compatibility, lower compatibility)
data compatibility データ互換
electro-magnetic compatibility 電磁環境両立 《略 EMC》
equipment compatibility 装置の互換性
forward compatibility 上位互換性, 上位互換 (＝upper compatibility, upward compatibility)
product compatibility 製品の互換性 (＝the compatibility of products)
upper compatibility 上位互換性, 上位互換 (＝forward compatibility, upward compatibility)

compatible 形 互換性がある, 適合性がある, …対応の, コンパチブル[コンパティブル]

backward compatible 下位互換性がある, 下位互換性
compatible format of data データ互換フォーマット （=data exchange format）
compatible machine 互換機, コンパチブル・マシン, コンパチ
full compatible 完全互換性がある, 完全互換性, フルコンパチ
IC card-compatible vending machine ICカード対応の自動販売機
ISDN-compatible terminal ISDN規格の端末
software compatible ソフトウエア・コンパチブル
upward compatible 上位互換性がある, 上位互換性

▸Customers expect our products to have an attractive design and be user-friendly, reliable and *compatible* at a fair price. 顧客が当社製品に期待しているのは, 適正価格で優れたデザインと簡単な操作性, 信頼性, それに互換性が得られることです。

compensation 名 報酬, 対価, 給与, 手当, 報償, 補償, 賠償, 代償, 減殺, 報償金, 補償金, 賠償金, 慰謝料 《略 comp》 （⇒approve）
　claim compensation from …に賠償金を請求する
　compensation and benefits 給与および給付金
　compensation expense 報償費用
　compensation for losses [damages] 損害賠償, 損害賠償金
　compensation for technical services 技術サービスの対価
　compensation system 給与体系
　employee compensation 雇用者所得, 勤労者所得, 従業員給与 （=compensation of employees）
　executive compensation 役員報酬
　incentive compensation 奨励報償, インセンティブ報酬
　net compensation amount 差額決済金額
　seek compensation from …に補償を求める, …に賠償請求する （=claim compensation from）
　total compensation 給与総額
　unemployment compensation 失業給付
　welfare compensation plan 福利厚生費制度
　worker's compensation insurance 労災保険

▸The *compensation* to the individual was taken care of largely out of our pension fund. 個人に支払われた退職金は, 主に当社の年金基金から拠出しました。

▸Victim firms have entered into talks to file a class action suit for *compensation*. 被害企業が, 損害賠償に向けて集団訴訟のための協議を開始した。

compensatory plan 報酬制度
compete 動 競争する, 競う, 争う, 張り合う, 渡り合う, 競合する

▸The best way to *compete* is to get closer to each customer. 競うための最良の方法は, お客さまにそれぞれもっと近づくことです。

competence 名 敵性, 能力, 能力の高さ, 力量, 資格, 適格性, 権限, 権能, 法的権限, 管轄権, 裁判権, 知的範囲, 言語能力, 資産, かなりの収入
　competence for a task 仕事の遂行能力
　competence of evidence 証拠力
　core competence 中核的業務, 中核能力, 企業固有の技術［スキルや技術］, 企業固有の競争力の核, 自社ならではの強み, コア・コンピテンス
　exceed [go beyond] one's competence 越権行為をする
　industrial competence 工業力

competency model コンピテンシー・モデル （人や組織の行動特性をキャッチする仕組み）

competition 名 競争, 競合, 競業, 競争相手, ライバル （⇒international competition）
　cost reduction competition コスト削減競争
　cutthroat competition 熾烈な競争, 激烈な競争, 激しい競争, のど元をかき切る競争
　demands competition 需要間競争, 需要競争
　excessive competition 過当競争 （=excess competition）
　export competition 輸出競争
　fair competition 公正競争
　global competition 国際競争 （=international competition）
　growing competition 競争激化
　imperfect competition 不完全競争
　intensifying competition 激しさを増す競争, 競争の激化
　inter-industry competition 産業間競争
　market competition 市場での競争, 市場競争
　non-price competition 非価格競争
　open competition 公開競争
　price competition 価格競争
　quality competition 品質競争
　sales competition 販売競争
　unfair competition 不正競争

▸All our business units face stiff *competition*. 当社の事業部門は, すべて苛烈な競争に直面しています。

competitive 形 競争力のある，競争的，競争上の，他社に負けない，安い，低コストの （⇒**cost-competitive**）
  competitive dynamics 競争環境 （＝competitive environment）
  competitive moves 競争力
  competitive position 競争力，競争上の地位，競争上のポジション
  competitive pressure 競争圧力
  competitive strength 競争力
  cost-competitive 価格競争力がある，価格競争力が高い，コスト競争力がある
  highly competitive 競争力が高い
  hold a competitive advantage 競争上の優位性を維持する，競争上の優位性を保つ
  improve competitive position 競争力を高める
  international competitive position 国際競争力
  remain [stay] competitive 競争力を維持する，競争力を保つ
▶Our customers rely on vast amounts of business information to thrive in *competitive* environments. 当社の顧客は，競争環境にあって勝ち残るため，膨大な量のビジネス情報に依存しています。

competitive advantage 競争上の優位，競争上の優位性，競争力，比較優位，比較優位性，競争有利性
▶We believe our new, patented technology gives us a *competitive advantage* that will help us attract and keep customers. 当社の特許取得済みの新技術は，当社に競争力を与え，当社の今後の顧客獲得と顧客離れを防ぐのに役立つと考えています。

competitive edge 競争力，競争上の優位，競争上の優位性，競争力での優位
  add additional competitive edge さらに競争力を高める
  lose competitive edge 競争力を失う
▶The hollowing-out of the pension system may increase companies' personnel costs so much that it could negatively affect their international *competitive edge*. 年金の空洞化で企業の人件費が上昇し，企業の国際競争力に悪影響を及ぼす恐れがある。

competitive environment 競争環境
▶The *competitive environment* inside and outside the nation has been changing drastically. 国内外の競争環境は，激変している。

competitive price 競争価格，競争値段，低価格，安い価格［値段］

▶The sales of South Korean carmakers are increasing due to *competitive prices* and improved quality. 韓国の自動車メーカーの販売台数は現在，低価格と品質向上で伸びている。

competitive product 競争力のある製品
▶In our drive for more *competitive products* and services, we are making essential investments in research, development and engineering. 一段と競争力のある製品とサービスの提供をめざして，当社は研究，開発とエンジニアリングに重要な投資を行っています。

competitiveness 名 競争力，競争 （⇒**characteristics of the market, global competitiveness, international competitiveness**）
  corporate competitiveness 企業競争力
  cost competitiveness コスト競争力，費用競争力
  economic competitiveness 経済競争力
  export competitiveness 輸出競争力 （＝trade competitiveness）
  external competitiveness 対外競争力
  industrial competitiveness 産業競争力，企業の競争力
  market competitiveness 市場競争力
  non-price competitiveness 非価格競争力
  price competitiveness 価格競争力 （＝competitiveness in prices; ⇒**shift**）
  product competitiveness 製品競争力
  trade competitiveness 輸出競争力
▶Major U.S. and European banks have been strengthening their market *competitiveness*. 欧米の大手銀行は，市場競争力を強化してきた。
▶Oji Paper Co. plans to build paper factories in Southeast Asia to enhance its production efficiency and *competitiveness*. 王子製紙は，同社の生産効率と競争力を高めるため，東南アジアに製紙工場を建設する方針だ。

competitor 名 競争相手，競合他社，同業者，ライバル企業，ライバル （⇒**disadvantage**）
▶We won many contracts from our *competitors*. 当社は，競争相手から多くの契約を勝ち取りました。

complaint 名 苦情，苦情の申立て，不平，不満，抗議，クレーム，告訴
  consumer complaint 消費者からの苦情，消費者からのクレーム
  cross-complaint 逆提訴
  customer complaint 顧客からの苦情，顧客からのクレーム
  file [lodge] a complaint with …に苦情を申し立てる，…に告訴する，…に提訴する，…に訴えを

起こす （=make a complaint to）
file a criminal complaint against A with B AについてBに告訴状を提出する，AをBに刑事告発する
lodge [make] a complaint A with B AをBに告訴する
▶Japan has filed a petition with the WTO over the sanctions, and the U.S. has promised a cross-*complaint*. 日本は，制裁措置に対して世界貿易機関(WTO)に提訴し，米国は逆提訴する見込みだ［逆提訴する構えを見せている］.
▶The company lodged the *complaint* with the Tokyo District Court. 同社が，東京地裁に提訴した．
▶There were repeated consumer *complaints* that the company's mobile phones were malfunctioning. 同社の携帯電話がうまく作動しないとの苦情が，消費者から多数寄せられた．

compliance 名 承諾，受諾，遵守［順守］, 遵守性，準拠性，適合，服従，コンプライアンス
affirmative action compliance program 積極的優遇措置遵守プログラム
compliance of financial statements 財務諸表［財務書類］の準拠性，財務諸表の会計原則準拠性
legal compliance 法令遵守 （=regulatory compliance）
compliance officer 法令・規則遵守担当役員，業務監査役，コンプライアンス・オフィサー
compliance program 法遵守プログラム，規制遵守プログラム （⇒planning）
compliance with rules 規則の遵守
▶The company will push ahead with "across-the-board *compliance*" as its most urgent task. 同社は，社の最緊急課題として「法令・規則の全社的順守」を推進する．

component 名 構成部品，部品，構成要素，成分，内訳，部分，項目，コンポーネント
auto-component 自動車部品
chip component チップ部品
component of stockholders' equity 資本の部
component percentage 構成比率 （=component proportion ratio）
component plant 中間組立工場
component ware コンポーネント・ウエア （ソフトウエア部品を組み合わせてアプリケーションを設計・実装する考え方）
debt component 債券部分
electronic component 電子部品 （=electronics component）
interest component 金利部分，利息部分

separate component 独立した構成要素
separate component companies 傘下企業
▶Lasers are critical *components* in optoelectronic transmitter modules that convert electrical signals to light pulses and so allow digital information to be carried over optical fiber cables. レーザーは，電気信号を光のパルスに変換して，デジタル情報を光ファイバー・ケーブルで伝送するオプトエレクトロニクス伝送モジュールを構成する重要な要素です．

composite 形 合成の，混成の，複合の，総合の，モンタージュの
composite currency 複合通貨
composite demand 複合需要
composite depreciation 総合償却
composite index 総合指数, CI
composite index of leading indicators 景気先行指数(CI)
composite materials 合成素材, 複合材料
composite picture 合成写真, モンタージュ写真
composite stock price 総合株価
composite supply 複合供給
Composite Tape of transactions 平均値(コンポジット・テープ・オブ・トランザクション)値
composite transaction 複合取引
composite (useful) life 総合耐用年数
composite works 複合著作物
NYSE [New York Stock Exchange] Composite Index NYSE総合株価指数

compound 形 合成の，混成の，複合の，混合の，複式の
compound duties [tariff] 複合関税
compound industry 複合産業
compound interest 複利
compound pollution 複合汚染 （=combined pollution）
compound rate 複合金利
compound transaction 複合取引
compound yield 複合利回り

comprehensive 形 総合的な，包括的な，広範な，幅広い
comprehensive annual financial report 包括的年次財務報告
comprehensive antideflationary measures 総合デフレ対策
comprehensive economic package plan 総合経済対策
Comprehensive Employment and Training Act 包括的雇用・訓練法 《略CETA》
comprehensive financial services 総合金融サ

ービス

comprehensive income 包括利益, 包括的利益

comprehensive income tax allocation 完全税効果会計, 所得税の完全期間配分, 総合的繰延べ課税 (=comprehensive tax allocation)

comprehensive loss 包括損失, 包括的損失

comprehensive package of economic measures 包括的経済対策

comprehensive settlement 包括的解決

comprehensive tie-up 包括提携, 包括的提携 (=broad alliance, comprehensive alliance)

comprehensive business alliance 包括的な業務提携
▶Japan Post Holdings Co. and convenience store chain Lawson Inc. have signed an agreement on a *comprehensive business alliance*. 日本郵政(株)とコンビニエンス・ストア大手のローソンは, 包括的業務提携で合意した。

comprehensive financial services 総合金融サービス
▶The nation's mega banking groups have been realigning their securities units to offer *comprehensive financial services*. 国内の大手金融グループは, 総合金融サービスを提供するため, グループ各社の証券会社を再統合している。

comptroller 名 経理部長, コントローラー (⇒**controller**)

computer 名 電算機, 電子計算機, コンピュータ

computer aided design コンピュータによる設計, コンピュータを利用した設計の自動化システム, コンピュータ利用設計, コンピュータ支援設計, コンピュータ援用設計, キャド《略 **CAD**》 (=computer-aided design system; ⇒**design**)

computer-mediated communication コンピュータ・ネットワークを介したコミュニケーション《略 **CMC**》

computer network コンピュータ網, コンピュータ・ネットワーク

computer networking コンピュータによるネットワーク化

computer operating system コンピュータの基本ソフト (OS)

computer peripherals コンピュータ周辺機器

computer problems コンピュータの故障 (=computer glitch)

computer screen コンピュータの画面

computer security コンピュータの機密保持, 安全性・信頼性の確保

computer supplies コンピュータ用品

computer system's breakdown コンピュータ・システムの障害, システム障害 (=computer failure, computer malfunction; ⇒**breakdown**)

computer tomography image コンピュータ断層撮影画像, CT画像

computer virus inventor ウイルス作成者 (=computer virus creator)

computer failure コンピュータの障害[誤作動], コンピュータ・システムの障害, システム障害 (=computer malfunction, computer system failure, computer system's breakdown)
▶The TSE's Jasdaq market for start-up firms has repeatedly suspended trading because of *computer failures*. 東証の新興企業向け株式市場ジャスダックは, システム障害による取引停止を繰り返している。

computer malfunction コンピュータの障害[誤作動], コンピュータのシステム障害
▶These troubles were caused by the *computer malfunction*. これらのトラブルは, コンピュータの障害・誤作動で生じた。

computer system コンピュータ・システム
▶Financially troubled Shinginko Tokyo spent ¥12.4 billion on *computer systems* for deposit and loan services, ATMs and the call center. 経営難の新銀行東京は, 預金・融資業務やATM (現金自動預け払い機), コール・センター用コンピュータ・システムの費用として124億円を投入していた。

computer virus コンピュータ・ウイルス, ウイルス (=online virus; ⇒**copyright**)
▶A *computer virus* infected a PC owned by an employee of the subsidiary, leading to the data's distribution via the Net. コンピュータ・ウイルスが, 子会社の社員の私物パソコンに感染して, パソコン内のデータがネットで流れた。

computerization [computerisation] 電算化, 電算機化, 電算機使用, 電子化, 情報化, コンピュータ化, コンピュータの普及, コンピュータリゼーション

computerize [computerise] 動 電算化する, コンピュータ化する, コンピュータ処理する, 電子計算機で自動化する, 情報化する

computerized accounting system コンピュータ利用会計情報システム, コンピュータ化会計システム (=computer-based accounting information system)

computerized administrative services 行政サービスの電子化

computerized axial tomography X線体軸断層撮影, X線CT《略 **CAT**》 (=computed tomo-

graphy, computer-assisted tomography)
computerized numerical control コンピュータ数値制御《略 **CNC**》
computerized reservation system コンピュータ予約システム, コンピュータによる予約・発券システム《略 **CRS**》
computerized society コンピュータ社会, コンピュータ化された社会
computerized typesetting system 電算写植システム, コンピュータを利用した写真植字システム《略 **CTS**》
▶Fujitsu's biometric timecard machine works in combination with a *computerized* salary system, automatically performing payroll calculations. 富士通の生体認証タイムレコーダー(手のひら静脈認証打刻システム)は, コンピュータ給与システムとも連動して, 自動給与計算も自動的に行う。

concentrate 動 集中する, 集中させる, 全力を傾ける, 力を注ぐ, …に照準を合わせる (⇒**best-selling product**, **concept**)
▶The firm plans to *concentrate* its resources on priority areas, such as products related to next-generation telecommunications networks. 同社は, 次世代通信網関連製品などの優先分野に, 同社の資源を集中する方針だ。

concept 名 基本的な考え方, アイデア, 基本思想, 主義, 構想, 概念, 理念, 観念, 基準, 公準, コンセプト
　accounting concept 会計概念
　attributable concept 帰属主義
　auditing concepts 監査上の諸概念
　business concept 企業理念
　cash concept 現金主義
　concept business コンセプト・ビジネス(独自の考え方でトータルなビジネスを展開すること)
　concept of matching costs with revenues 費用対収益対応の概念
　cost concept 現価概念
　founding concept 会社設立構想
　fundamental accounting concepts 会計の基礎概念
　going concern concept 継続企業の公準, 継続企業の概念
　management concept 経営理念
　marketing concept マーケティング理念, マーケティング・コンセプト
　money measurement concept 貨幣[貨幣的]測定の公準
　one-year concept 1年基準
　periodicity concept 会計期間の公準
　product development concept 商品開発のコンセプト, 製品開発コンセプト
　time period concept 会計期間の概念
▶We work with a clear business *concept* geared toward innovation and concentrating on special fields. 当社は, 革新と特定分野への集中に照準を合わせた明確な企業理念を掲げて事業を行っています。

concern 名 関心, 関心事, 関係, 利害関係, 心配, 懸念, 懸念材料, 不安, 不安材料, 配慮, 問題, 会社, 企業, 企業体, 事業, 業務, 責務, 任務, 重要性, 動 …に関係する, 利害関係がある, 重要である (⇒**downside**, **going concern**)
　commercial concerns 経済的利益
　concern for employees 従業員への配慮
　concern interested 関係会社
　concerns over oil supplies 原油供給不安, 原油供給への懸念 (⇒**crude oil futures**)
　credit concerns 信用リスクに対する懸念, 信用不安
　going concern 継続企業, 営業している企業, 企業の存続可能性, ゴーイング・コンサーン (= ongoing concern)
　industrial concern 生産会社, 工業会社
　inflationary concerns インフレに対する懸念, インフレ懸念
　internal concerns 国内問題
　long term concerns 長期的な不安材料
　media concern メディア企業
　political concerns 政局不安, 政局に対する不安
　quitting concern 非継続企業, 終了企業
▶*Concerns* grow over the possibility of a decelerating world economy. 世界経済が減速する可能性に対する懸念が, 増大している。

conciliation 名 調停, 和解, 斡旋(あっせん)
　conciliation committee 調停委員会
　conciliation plan 調停案, 斡旋案
　the rules and conciliation and arbitration 調停・仲裁規則
▶All disputes, controversies or differences arising in connection with this agreement shall be finally settled under the rules of *conciliation* and arbitration of the American Arbitration Association. 本契約に関して生じた紛争, 論争や意見の相違は, すべてアメリカ仲裁協会の調停・仲裁規則に従って最終的に解決するものとする。

conclude 動 決着をつける, 決定する, 結論づける, 結論に達する, 断定[推論]する, 終わらせる, 終える, 締めくくる, まとめる, 完了する (⇒

checking transaction)
conclude an agreement [treaty, deal]　協定［条約, 協議］に合意する
conclude the agreement between A and B　AとBの間で本契約を締結する, AとBが本契約を締結する
conclude checking transactions　小切手取引の決済をする

condition 名　条件, 状態, 状況, 情勢, 動向, 環境（⇒**business conditions, financial condition**）
　business conditions　景気, 商況, 業況, 業況判断（DI）, 業態, 事業環境, 経営の実態, 営業状況
　business condition index　景気動向指数
　credit conditions　信用状態
　economic conditions　経済状態, 経済情勢, 景気
　financial terms and conditions　財務条件
　market conditions　市場環境, 市況
　monetary conditions　金融情勢, 金融環境
　operating conditions　事業環境
　qualifying conditions　年金受給資格
　technical conditions　技術的条件, テクニカル要因
▶Many major customers demand ISO certification as a *condition* of doing business.　主要顧客の多くは, 取引の条件としてISO（国際標準化機構）の認定を求めます。
▶The company's financial statements did not correctly reflect its financial *condition*.　同社の財務諸表は, 財務状況を適正に表示していなかった。

conduct 名　行為, 行動, 遂行, 実施, 活動, 管理, 運営, 処理, 運営方法, 規範, 指針, 紀律
　business conduct　業務活動, 業務遂行, 業務, 営業上の指針
　codes of conduct　行動規範, 行動基準, 倫理規定
　ethical business conduct　倫理的業務活動, 倫理的営業活動, 倫理的業務遂行, 倫理的企業行動
　professional conduct　職業行為, 職業倫理
　rules of conduct　紀律規則
▶The internal accounting control process includes management's communication to employees of policies which govern ethical business *conduct*.　会計に関する内部統制の手順には, 経営者の従業員に対する倫理的業務遂行［倫理的企業行動］に関する方針の通達［通知・伝達］も含まれています。

conference 名　会議, 会談, 協議, 打ち合せ, 相談（＝conferencing）
　academic conference　学術会議
　conference call　電話会議, 会議電話
　conference committees　米上下両院協議会
　conference room　会議室
　conference management　会議運営
　electronic conference　電子会議, 遠隔会議, テレコンファレンス
　joint labor-management conference　労使協議
　news [press] conference　記者会見
　summit conference　首脳会談, トップ会談
　teleconference　電子会議, 遠隔会議, テレビ会議, テレコンファレンス
　video conference　ビデオ会議, テレビ会議
▶Acting in an emergency *conference* call, the U.S. Federal Reserve moved to bolster the flagging economy by cutting interest rates by half a point.　緊急電話会議を開いて, 連邦準備制度理事会（FRB）は, 金利を0.5％引き下げて, 景気減速に歯止めをかけることを決めた。

conferencing 名　会議, 双方向通信機能
　internet conferencing　インターネット会議, ネット会議
　teleconferencing　電子会議, テレビ会議（＝electronic conference, teleconference）
　video conferencing　ビデオ会議, テレビ会議（＝video conference）

confidence 名　信頼, 信用, 信認, 信任, 信頼度, 自信, 消費者マインド, 秘密, 内密, 秘密保持（⇒**business confidence, consumer confidence**）
　business and consumer confidence　企業・消費者マインド, 企業心理と消費者心理
　confidence coefficient　信頼係数
　confidence-sensitive short-term debt markets　信認に敏感な短期金融市場
　investor confidence　投資家の地合（じあ）い, 投資家の信認
　lender confidence　貸手の信認
　rise [increase] in confidence　消費者マインドの向上, 消費意欲の向上（＝improvement in consumer confidence）
　the market's confidence　市場の信認
　weak confidence　消費者マインドの冷え込み（＝depressed [lower] consumer confidence）
▶An improvement in business *confidence* is seen in the automobile and electric machinery industries.　自動車や電機業界では, 業況感の改善が見られる。
▶The firm reviewed its account settlement in an attempt to regain consumer *confidence*.　同社は, 消費者の信頼回復に向けて決算の洗い直しをした。

confidential information　秘密情報, 機密情報

▸The *confidential information* shall not include information which is or becomes generally known or available through no act or failure to act by ABC. この秘密情報は，公知であるか一般に入手することができる情報，またはABCの作為または不作為によらずに公知となるか一般に入手することができる情報を含まないものとする。

confidentiality 名 機密性，秘密性，秘密保持，秘密遵守[順守]，守秘義務
　confidentiality agreement 秘密保持契約(書)，秘密遵守契約(書)，守秘義務合意書
　confidentiality period 秘密保持期間
▸Each party shall take all reasonable steps to ensure the *confidentiality* of all the confidential information. 各当事者は，すべての秘密情報を維持するため，あらゆる合理的な措置を取るものとする。

configuration 名 地形，形式，形状，外形，概観，配置，配列，構成，機器構成，〈プログラムの〉設定
　computer configuration コンピュータ構成
　configuration block 構成ブロック
　configuration file 環境設定ファイル，構成ファイル
　configuration management 環境設定管理，構成管理，コンフィギュレーション管理
　configuration state 構成状態
　redundant configuration 冗長構成
　system configuration システム構成，システムの機器構成
▸With the digital congress network, choosing even the smallest system *configuration* does not mean compromising on functionality. このデジタル・コングレス・ネットワークでは，どんなに小規模なシステムの機器構成でも，機能性に関しては妥協を許しません。

configure to order 受注仕様生産《略 CTO》（受注生産方式の一種。メーカーの販売代理店が注文を受け，自らメーカー・ブランドの製品を組み立てて販売する方式）

confirmation 名 確認，確証，認証，証拠，批准，承認，追認，納品引受書，受注確認書，取引確認通知，売買報告書，確認書
　affirmative [positive] confirmation 積極的保証
　confirmation letter 確認書，取引確認書，確認回答書（＝letter of confirmation）
　confirmation note [sheet] 確認書，確認通知書
　confirmation of balance 残高確認
　confirmation of L/C 信用状の確認
　confirmation of order 注文確認，注文確認書
　confirmation order 確認指図書
　confirmation procedure 確認手続き
　confirmation of purchase 買約確認(書)
　confirmation of sale 売約確認(書)
　external confirmation 外部確認
　negative confirmation 消極的確認
　trade confirmation 売買確認

conflict 名 〈利害，意見などの〉衝突，対立，矛盾，不一致，抵触
　conflict of interest 利害の対立，利害の衝突，利益相反，利益相反行為 （⇒**consulting**）
　conflict of laws 法の抵触，抵触法，衝突法，国際私法，州際私法
　conflict of risk 利害関係
　conflict with the memorandum and the articles of association 基本定款と通常定款との抵触
▸As the economy matured, *conflicts* of interests between individual corporations and industrial organizations intensified. 経済の成熟に伴って，個別企業と業界との利害対立が先鋭化した。

conglomerate 名 コングロマリット，巨大複合企業，複合企業，複合企業体，複合体，多角化企業，企業グループ （＝conglomerate company）
　conglomerate company 多角化企業，コングロマリット
　conglomerate financial statements 複合企業財務諸表
　conglomerate integration 多角的統合
　conglomerate merger 複合的合併，コングロマリット合併
▸The FSA's guideline for supervising financial *conglomerate* is aimed at urging operators of financial *conglomerates* to reinforce their corporate governance to prevent irregularities. 金融庁の金融コングロマリット（複合体）監督指針の狙いは，不正防止に向けて，金融コングロマリットの経営者に経営監視の強化を促すことにある。

consensus 名 合意，総意，同意，一致した意見，意見の一致，大多数の意見，コンセンサス （⇒ **stalemate**）
　consensus ad idem 合意
　consensus building コンセンサス作り，根回し
　consensus estimate コンセンサス予測，コンセンサス予想
　consensus forecast 市場予想，市場予測，コンセンサス予想，コンセンサス予測
　consensus politics 合意政治
　economic consensus エコノミストのコンセン

サス予測
- **general consensus** 一般的な見方, 国民の合意
- **market consensus** 市場予想, 市場予測, 市場のコンセンサス, 市場のコンセンサス予想
- **national consensus** 国民の合意, 国民的合意, ナショナル・コンセンサス

consent 名 同意, 承諾, 承認, 合意, 意見の一致, 許可, 同意書, コンセント・レター
- **at the mutual consent** 相互の話し合いで, 相互の同意で
- **by [with] one consent** 満場一致で
- **consent agreement** 同意書
- **consent decree** 同意審決, 同意判決
- **consent letter** 同意書簡, コンセント・レター (= consent statement in published prospectuses)
- **consent settlement** 同意解決
- **informed consent** 十分な説明に基づく同意, インフォームド・コンセント
- **with prior written consent of** …の書面による事前の承諾を得て
▶This agreement may be terminated at any time upon written *consent* of all the Parties hereto. 本契約は, 本契約当事者全員の書面による合意が得られたときはいつでも解除することができる。

consent 形 同意した

conservatism 名 保守主義, 慎重性の原則, 安全性の原則

consgt 委託, 委託販売, 託送, 委託販売品, 積送品 (**consignment** の略)

consideration 名 対価, 代金, 手付け金, 契約の約因, 考慮
- **as consideration for the services rendered pursuant to this agreement** 本契約に従って提供されたサービスの対価として
- **good consideration** 有効な約因
- **in consideration for the license of the trademark** 商標の使用許諾の対価として, 商標使用許諾の対価として
- **in consideration of the payment of** …の支払いを約因として
- **sufficient consideration** 十分な約因, 有効な約因
▶We acquired 100 percent of the common shares outstanding of the company for a total *consideration* of $850 million. 当社は, 対価総額8億5,000万ドルで, 同社の発行済み普通株式を100%取得しました。

consign 動 委託する, 任せる, 委ねる, 引き渡す, 割り当てる

▶Since July 1971, all newly listed companies must *consign* the administration of their shares to third parties, such as trust banks. 1971年7月以降, 新規上場企業はすべて株式事務を信託銀行などの第三者に委託しなければならない。

consignment 名 委託, 委託販売, 託送, 委託販売品, 積送品

consol 名 〈英国の〉整理公債, コンソル公債, コンソル (英政府発行の償還期限なしの永久公債の一種)
- **consol accounting day** 整理公債受渡しの日
- **consol market** コンソル公債市場, コンソル市場
- **consols [Consols]** コンソル公債 (= bank annuities, consolidated annuities)
- **interest on consols** コンソル公債利子

consolidate 動 連結する, 連結計上する, 連結対象にする, 整理統合する, 統廃合する, 統合する, 合併する, 一元化する, 一体化する, 整理する, 集約する, 強化する (⇒**consolidation**, **contoractual obligation**, **full year**)
▶Steps to reduce costs include *consolidating* facilities, disposing of assets, reducing workforce or withdrawing from markets. コスト削減策としては, 施設の統合, 資産の処分, 人員削減や市場からの撤退などが考えられています。
▶When we raise our ownership in 2009, we will fully *consolidate* this venture in our financial statements. 2009年度に当社の持ち株比率が増加した時点で, 当社はこの事業を当社の財務書類に全部連結[100%連結]する方針です。

consolidated 形 連結対象の, 連結した, 整理統合した, 統合した, 一本化した, 一元化した
- **companies consolidated** 連結対象子会社
- **consolidated accounting period figures** 連結決算 (= group accounting period figures)
- **consolidated after-tax deficit** 連結税引き後赤字 (= consolidated after-tax loss)
- **consolidated after-tax profit** 連結税引き後利益, 連結税引き後黒字
- **consolidated business profits** 連結経常利益 (= consolidated pretax business profits)
- **consolidated company** 連結対象会社, 連結会社
- **consolidated earnings report for the April-September period** 3月期決算企業の9月連結中間決算, 4−9月期の連結決算
- **consolidated equity** 連結持ち分, 親会社持ち分 (= majority interest)
- **consolidated first-half net profit** 上半期[上期]の連結税引き後利益, 上半期の連結純利益
- **consolidated net capital expenditures** 連結

資本的支出純額

consolidated pretax profit 連結経常利益, 連結税引き前利益

consolidated profit 連結利益

consolidated recurring profit 連結経常利益, 企業グループの経常利益

consolidated ratio 合併比率

consolidated return 連結納税申告, 連結納税申告書 (＝consolidated tax return)

consolidated statement 連結計算書

consolidated tax system 連結税制, 連結納税制 (＝consolidated tax payment system, consolidated tax return system, corporate group tax system)

consolidated accounts 連結決算(consolidated accounting period figures), 連結財務書類, 連結財務諸表(consolidated financial statements, group accounts), 財務書類の連結

▸In its *consolidated accounts*, the Toyota group posted ¥21 trillion in sales with a net profit of ¥1.37 trillion, marking a record high for the fourth consecutive year. トヨタの連結決算で, トヨタ・グループの売上高が21兆円, 税引き後利益が1兆3,700億円となり, 4年連続で過去最高を記録した。

consolidated affiliate 連結対象の関連会社, 連結対象関連会社, 連結対象の持ち分法適用会社

▸We made the company our *consolidated affiliate*. 当社は, 同社を連結対象の関連会社としました。

consolidated basis 連結ベース (＝group basis)

▸We posted a record net profit of ¥1.18 trillion on a *consolidated basis* for the year ending March 31. 当社の3月期連結決算は, 税引き後利益[純利益]が過去最高の1兆1,800億円になりました[当社の3月期決算は, 連結ベースで税引き後利益が過去最高の1兆1,800億円になりました]。

consolidated earnings 連結利益, 連結純利益, 連結当期利益

▸Last fiscal year, earnings at the parent company accounted for 56 percent of Toyota's *consolidated earnings*. 前期[前年度]は, トヨタ本体の利益[トヨタの単独ベースの利益]が, 連結利益の56%を占めた。

consolidated earnings forecasts 連結業績予想

▸Toyota has refrained from releasing *consolidated earnings forecasts* as its earnings tend to be susceptible to fluctuations in exchange rates. トヨタの業績は為替変動の影響を受けやすいため, トヨタは連結業績予想の発表を控えてきた。

consolidated earnings report 連結決算報告, 連結決算報告書, 連結業績報告書, 連結決算

▸The Corporation posted an operating profit of ¥2 billion in a *consolidated earnings report* for fiscal 2008. 当社は, 2008年度連結決算で20億円の営業利益を計上しました。

consolidated financial statements 連結財務書類, 連結財務諸表, 合併財務諸表 (＝consolidated accounts, group accounts)

> 連結財務書類について➡アニュアル・レポートや四半期報告書などで公表される米国企業の財務書類[財務諸表]は, ほぼ連結財務書類である。これは, 親会社(他の会社の発行済み株式の50%超を直接・間接に所有している会社)の財務書類と子会社の財務書類を合算して, 親会社を中心とした企業グループとしての経営成績と財政状態を表したものである。なお, 英国では, 連結財務書類[連結財務諸表]のことをgroup accountsと呼んでいる。

▸The *consolidated financial statements* include the accounts of all majority owned subsidiaries, either direct or indirect. 連結財務書類には, 直接所有と間接所有を問わず, 過半数所有の全子会社の財務書類が含まれています。

consolidated income 連結利益

▸The proportional contribution to *consolidated income* of individual ABC Inc. companies was somewhat skewed this year, largely due to the various provisions. 連結利益に対するABC各社の比例貢献度は, 主に各種引当金の繰入れで, 当期[当年度]はいくぶん片寄った結果となりました。

consolidated interest-bearing debt 連結有利子負債

▸We will reduce our *consolidated interest-bearing debts* to less than ¥1 trillion by the business term ending in March 2010. 当社は, 2010年3月期までに連結有利子負債を1兆円以下に削減する方針です。

consolidated net income 連結純利益, 連結当期純利益 (連結損益計算書上の利益)

▸These provisions, after deducting the related tax and minority interest, reduced *consolidated net income* by $150 million. これらの引当金繰入れ額により, 関連税額と少数株主持ち分利益控除後の連結純利益は, 1億5,000万ドル減少しました。

consolidated net loss 連結純損失, 連結税引き後赤字, 連結税引き後損失

▸The firm chalked up a *consolidated net loss* of ¥91.58 billion for the April-June quarter. 同社

は，4-6月期は915億8,000万円の連結税引き後赤字となった。

consolidated net profit 連結純利益，連結税引き後利益，連結ベースの税引き後利益 （=consolidated net income, group net profit）
▶Sony's *consolidated net profit* rose 60.2 percent from a year earlier to ¥33.97 billion on sales of ¥3.60 trillion. ソニーの連結税引き後利益は，3兆6,000億円の売上高に対して，前年同期比60.2％増の339億7,000万円となった。

consolidated operating profit 連結営業利益，連結業務利益，金融機関の業務純益
▶In the year through March 31, the Corporation's *consolidated operating profit* plummeted 38 percent. 3月期決算で，当社の連結営業利益は38％減少しました。

consolidated operating profit margin 連結営業利益率
▶The firm expects to post more than 8 trillion in consolidated sales and to mark a *consolidated operating profit margin* of 5 percent by the end of fiscal 2009. 同社は，2009年度末までに，連結売上高8兆円超と連結営業利益率5％の達成を目指している。

consolidated payout ratio 連結配当性向
▶Toyota is planning to bolster its *consolidated payout ratio* to around 30 percent on a net profit basis under its midterm business strategy. トヨタは，中期経営戦略に従って，税引き後利益ベースで連結配当性向を約30％まで高める方針だ。

consolidated revenues 連結売上高，連結収益 （親会社と子会社とで構成されている連結企業グループ全体としての売上高［収益］のこと）
▶*Consolidated revenues* in 2008 were $5.41 billion, up 10 percent from $4.91 billion in 2007. 2008年［2008年度］の連結売上高は54.1億ドルで，前年［前年度］の49.1億ドルから10％増加しました。

consolidated sales 連結売上高，連結ベースの売上高 （⇒**consolidated operating profit margin**）
▶Toyota's *consolidated sales*, which surpassed ¥10 trillion in the business term ending in March 1997, doubled to ¥21 trillion in the following nine years. トヨタの連結売上高は，1997年3月期に10兆円を突破した後，9年間で21兆円に倍増した。

consolidated subsidiary 連結子会社，連結対象子会社
▶Hanshin became Hankyu's *consolidated subsidiary* on June 27. 阪神は，6月27日付けで阪急の連結子会社になった。

consolidated taxation 連結納税 （=consolidated tax payment）
▶In this *consolidated taxation*, losses from one company in a group are subtracted from the profits of another group company in calculating taxable income, reducing the group's overall tax burdens. この連結納税では，グループ内の会社の損失［赤字］を同じグループ内の別会社の利益［黒字］から差し引いて［控除して］課税所得を算出するため，グループ企業全体の税負担が軽くなる。

consolidation 名 新設合併，統合，企業統合，整理，再編，強化，地固め，連結，連結決算，混載輸送 （⇒**full consolidation**）

連結について➡会計用語の「連結(consolidation)」とは，簡単にいえば，親会社を中心とする企業グループを一つの企業とみなして，親会社(parent company)と子会社(subsidiary)の損益を合算することをいう。米国企業の場合は，親会社が保有する子会社の株式保有の割合によって連結の範囲が決まり，連結の対象になった子会社を連結対象子会社・連結子会社(consolidated subsidiary)，連結の対象から外された子会社を非連結子会社(unconsolidated subsidiary)という。連結の範囲の基準としては，基本的に「他社の発行済み議決権株式(outstanding voting stock)の50％超(過半数)を直接間接に所有している場合，その会社を連結の範囲に含める」ことになっている。

accounting for consolidation 連結決算
budget consolidation 財政建て直し
capital consolidation 資本連結
consolidation and closure 統廃合，統合と閉鎖
consolidation basis 連結の基準，連結の方針 （=basis of consolidation）
consolidation criteria 連結の範囲，連結範囲の基準 （=scope of consolidation）
consolidation date 連結決算日
consolidation goodwill 連結のれん （=consolidated excess, consolidated goodwill）
consolidation group 連結企業グループ，連結対象の会社グループ，連結集団 （=consolidated group）
consolidation of corporations 会社の新設合併
consolidation of shares [stocks] 株式併合
consolidation policy 連結方針，連結の方針 （=principles of consolidation）
consolidation surplus 連結剰余金
debt consolidation fund 国債整理基金
economic consolidation 経済調整

facility consolidation 工場統廃合
in consolidation 連結上, 連結決算上
industrial consolidation 産業再編成, 産業再編
market consolidation 市場再編, 市場統合
staff consolidation 人員整理
scope of consolidation 連結の範囲 （＝consolidation criteria)
stock consolidation 株式併合 （＝share consolidation)

▶The company will be urged to pursue a large-scale *consolidation* of its stores and cut its workforce. 同社は今後, 大規模な店舗の統廃合やリストラ（人員削減）を迫られるのは必至だ。

▶The summarized financial information includes transactions with the company that are eliminated in *consolidation*. 要約財務情報には, 連結では消去されている同社との取引が含まれています。

consolidation within the industry 業界再編, 業界の再編成

▶Previous *consolidation within the industry* has been done in a friendly manner. これまでの業界再編は, 友好的に行われてきた。

consortium 名 国際借款団, 銀行の協調融資団, 債権国会議, 共同事業体, 共同連合体, 企業連合, 企業連合体, 組合, コンソーシアム （⇒balance）
a consortium of companies 合弁企業
a consortium of financial interests 金融関係者の借款団
a consortium of lenders 融資団, 融資グループ
consortium bank 国際投資銀行, 多国籍銀行, 国際銀行連合 （＝multinational bank)
consortium bid 共同入札
consortium loans 国際借款
international banking consortia 国際銀行借款団
investment consortium 投資組合
loan consortium 借款団

▶The Japanese *consortium* will be responsible for production of nearly 50 percent or more than 10 million cubic meters of natural gas per day in the Pars South gas field. 日本の企業連合体は, イランの南パルス・ガス田については, 約50%, 日量1,000万立方メートル以上の生産に当たることになっている。

constant dollar 統一ドル, 恒常ドル, 一定ドル （＝constant purchasing power)
constant dollar accounting 統一ドル会計, 恒常ドル会計, 一般購買力会計, 安定価値会計 （＝constant purchasing power accounting)
constant dollar reporting 統一ドルによる報告, 実質ベースの報告

constituent company 構成会社 （連結グループに含まれる会社)

construction 名 建設, 工事, 建造物, 構築物, 〈契約や条項の〉解釈 （「解釈」の意味の動詞はconstrue; ⇒chemical)
advance on construction 建設工事前渡し金
construction and erection contract 建設・据え付け契約
Construction and Transport Ministry 日本の国土交通省
Construction Business Law 建設業法
construction in progress 建設仮勘定, 未成工事支出金 （＝construction in process)
construction loan 建設借入金, 建設融資, 建設ローン
construction material supplier 建材メーカー
construction of completion 完成工事高
construction of cost 原価構成
construction revenue 工事収益 （＝construction in progress)
construction-type contract 請負工事契約
construction work account receivable 建設工事未収金
estimated cost of construction work 見積り工事原価
income on construction 工事利益
interest on construction 建設中の支払い利息
public construction 公共工事
reserve for construction work guarantee 工事補償引当金

▶The Company has executed two contracts with the firm for the *construction* and operation of the global communications system. 当社は, 国際通信システムの建設と運用のために同社と2件の契約を結びました。

▶The *construction*, validity and performance of this agreement shall be governed in all respects by the laws of Japan. 本契約の解釈, 有効性と履行は, 日本の法律に全面的に準拠するものとする。

construction contract 工事契約, 建設契約

▶Most of the *construction contracts* were made in a dishonest manner. 工事契約の大半は, 不正な形で行われた［工事契約の大半は, 不正な契約だった］。

construction project 建設工事

▶Bidding for part of the *construction project* was opened on Sept. 29-30. 建設工事の一部の入札は, 9月29, 30の両日実施された。

▶The Tokyo metropolitan government and the

company concluded an agreement on the *construction project*. 東京都と同社が，この建設工事の契約［協定］を締結した。

construe 動 解釈する （=interpret; ⇒**choice**）
consultant 名 顧問，相談役，相談相手，顧問医師，コンサルタント
　business consultant 経営管理士，ビジネス・コンサルタント
　computer consultant コンピュータ・コンサルタント
　financial consultant 財務コンサルタント
　management consultant 経営コンサルタント
　marketing consultant マーケティング・コンサルタント
　risk consultant 保険コンサルタント
▶Any inventions conceived by the *Consultant* or its employees in the course of the project covered by this agreement shall be the property of Client. 本契約により引き受けたプロジェクトの過程でコンサルタントまたはその従業員が考案した発明は，依頼者の所有権とする。
consultation 名 相談，諮問，協議，コンサルティング・サービス，審議，協議会，審議会，会議，参考，参照，調査，診察，弁護士の鑑定，コンサルテーション
　consultation body 協議機関，諮問機関
　consultation papers 公開諮問文書
　legal consultation 訴訟協議
　prior consultation 事前協議
consultation fees コンサルタント料
▶The *consultation fees* were, in fact, a rebate. コンサルタント料は事実上，リベートだった。
consultation services コンサルティング・サービス
▶The details of the contract for *consultation services* have not been disclosed. コンサルティング・サービス契約［コンサルタント契約］の詳しい内容は，明らかにされていない。
consulting 名 相談，助言，諮問，診断，コンサルティング
　consulting agreement コンサルティング契約
　consulting service コンサルタント業務，コンサルティング業務
　management consulting 経営診断，企業診断，経営コンサルティング
　management consulting service 経営コンサルタント業務，経営コンサルティング業務
▶The auditing firm's independent oversight board ordered the firm to split its auditing and *consulting services* to eliminate any conflicts of interest. 同監査法人の独立監視委員会は，業務上の利害の対立を排除するため，監査業務と経営コンサルタント業務の分離を同社に命じた。

consumer 名 消費者，コンシューマー
　consumer advertising 消費者広告，消費者向け広告
　consumer advocate 消費者運動家，消費者保護主義者，消費者団体，消費者擁護
　consumer affairs 対消費者活動，消費者問題，コンシューマー・アフェアズ
　consumer boycott 消費者不買運動
　consumer budget 消費者家計
　consumer buying power 消費者購買力
　consumer center 消費者センター （=consumer advice center)
　Consumer Contract Law 消費者契約法 （⇒**door-to-door**)
　consumer counseling services 消費者相談サービス，消費者相談業務，消費者相談窓口
　consumer electronics 家電，家電製品，情報家電，民生用電子機器
　consumer excise tax 消費税
　consumer finance company 消費者金融会社
　consumer financing 消費者金融
　consumer goods 消費財，消費物資，消費者用品 （=consumers' goods)
　consumer group 消費者団体
　consumer lending business 消費者ローン事業，消費者金融業務 （=consumer loan business)
　consumer life 消費生活
　consumer needs 消費者ニーズ，消費者の欲求，消費者の必要
　consumer organization 消費者団体，消費者組織
　consumer orientation 消費者志向，消費者優先，消費者重視
　consumer protection 消費者保護
　consumer resistance 消費者拒否，消費者不買運動，消費者抵抗，購買拒否，買い渋り （=consumer sales resistance)
　consumer sentiment 消費者マインド，消費者態度指数
　consumer satisfaction 消費者満足
　durable consumer goods 耐久消費財
　fast-moving consumer goods 高回転消費財 《略 FMCG》
　loan to consumers 消費者金融
　National Consumer Affairs Center of Japan 国民生活センター
　real consumer outlays 実質個人消費支出

▸Companies should recycle their profits to *consumers.* 企業は，利益を消費者に還元すべきだ。
▸If agricultural imports become cheaper due to the lowered tariffs, *consumers* will greatly benefit. 関税の引下げで輸入農産品が安くなれば，消費者の利点も大きい。
▸The new tariff on beef imports favors producers rather than *consumers.* 牛肉の輸入に対する新関税は，消費者ではなく生産者寄りの対応だ。

consumer confidence 消費者マインド，消費意欲，消費者信頼感，消費者心理
▸U.S. *consumer confidence* improved for the second consecutive month in March. 米国の3月の消費者心理は，2か月連続好転した。

consumer confidence index 消費者信頼感指数，消費者態度指数
▸*Consumer confidence index* is an indicator of consumption trends for the next six months. 消費者態度指数は，今後半年間の消費動向[消費意欲]を示す指標だ。

consumer consumption 個人消費
▸Domestic *consumer consumption* accounts for about half of the nation's GDP. 国内の個人消費は，日本のGDP（国内総生産）の約半分を占めている。

consumer credit 消費者金融，消費者信用，消費者信用残高
  consumer credit industry 消費者信用産業，クレジット産業
  Consumer Credit Protection Act of 1968 米国の1968年消費者信用保護法（信用条件の開示，強要的信用取引や信用情報などに関する規定がある）
  consumer credit service 消費者信用サービス，消費者金融サービス
▸Part-time workers tend to use *consumer credit* services when they run short of cash before payday. パート社員などは，給与の支給日前にお金がなくなると，消費者金融サービス[消費者金融]を利用する傾向がある。

consumer demand 消費者需要，消費需要，民間需要，需要，実需，消費者ニーズ
▸The severe employment, wages and corporate profit situation are putting downward pressure on *consumer demand* and corporate investment. 厳しい雇用・賃金環境と企業収益の動向が，民間需要[消費者需要]と企業の設備投資を下押ししている。

consumer electronics 家電製品，民生用電子機器，情報家電，家電 （⇒capital-intensive）

consumer electronics industry 家電産業，家電業界，消費者向けエレクトロニクス産業

consumer electronics market 家電市場
▸NEC's first-quarter net loss narrowed as it sold more semiconductors used in *consumer electronics.* NECの第1四半期の税引き後赤字 は，家電製品に用いられる半導体の販売増で縮小した。

consumer loan 消費者金融，消費者貸出金，消費者ローン
  consumer loan delinquency ratio 消費者貸出金延滞率
  consumer loan firm 消費者金融会社，消費者金融業者 （=consumer finance company, consumer loan company）
▸*Consumer loan* lender Aiful Corp. will raise ¥120 billion through equity and bond issues to enhance its financial base. 消費者金融のアイフルは，財務基盤[経営基盤]を強化するため，株式と社債の発行で1,200億円を調達する。

consumer market 消費者市場，消費市場
▸Mexico with a population of more than 100 million represents a huge *consumer market.* 人口が1億人を超すメキシコは，巨大な消費市場だ。

consumer price index 消費者物価指数《略 CPI》 （=the key gauge of consumer prices: 米国の消費者物価指数は，全都市消費者物価指数 (Consumer Price Index for All Urban Consumers: CPI-U) と都市賃金労働者消費者物価指数 (Consumer Price Index for Urban Wage Earners and Clerical Workers: CPI-W) に分類される。⇒ **core consumer price index**）
▸The U.S. Labor Department's *Consumer Price Index* is the most widely used gauge of inflation. 米労働省が発表する消費者物価指数は，最も広く使用されているインフレ(物価上昇率)の基準だ。

consumer prices 消費者物価，消費者物価指数
▸Eurozone June *consumer prices* were flat compared with the previous month. ユーロ圏の6月の消費者物価指数は，前月比で横ばいだった。

consumer product 消費者製品，消費者財，民生用製品，民生機器
  Consumer Product Safety Act 消費者製品安全法《略 **CPSA**》
  consumer products company 消費財メーカー
▸The company plans to make drugs and other *consumer product* operations the company's core business. 同社は，医薬品などの消費者製品事業を同社の主力事業にする方針だ。

consumer requirements 消費者のニーズ

▶The handicap between Japanese and European and U.S. companies will become larger in terms of mobility, personnel costs and research into *consumer requirements* for the Chinese market. 機動性や人件費，中国市場の消費者ニーズの研究などで，今後は日本企業と欧米企業とのハンデは開くばかりだ．

consumer spending 消費者支出，個人消費
(=consumer expenditure, consumption expenditure; ⇒**consumption expenditure**)
▶Price increases in food and petroleum-related products will dampen already weak *consumer spending*. 食品や石油関連製品の価格上昇で，個人消費は一段と冷え込むものと思われる．

consumer trust 消費者の信頼
▶The restructuring plan is intended to restore *consumer trust* in the group by implementing aggressive cost cuts. 再生計画の狙いは，コスト削減を積極的に行って同グループに対する消費者の信頼を回復することにある．

Consumers Union 全米消費者同盟
▶*Consumers Union* publishes the influential product review magazine. 全米消費者同盟は，製品に関する書評の有力誌を発行している．

consumers' interests 消費者の利益
▶Government policies to date have emphasized promoting industries and tended to neglect the protection of *consumers' interests* and safety. これまでの政府の政策［行政］は，産業振興に力点が置かれ，消費者の利益や安全の確保は軽視される傾向があった．

consumption 名 消費，個人消費，消費量，消費高，消費額，消費支出，消耗，減耗，肺結核 (⇒ **individual consumption, personal consumption**)
 bubble consumption　バブル消費
 capital consumption　資本減耗
 consumption boom　消費景気
 consumption trend　消費動向 (⇒**consumer confidence index**)
 domestic consumption　国内消費
 electrical consumption　電力消費
 energy consumption　エネルギー消費
 mass consumption society　大衆消費社会
 sluggish consumption　消費低迷，個人消費の低迷
 weak consumption　消費低迷，個人消費の低迷
▶The Japanese economy still has a problem with deflation and weak *consumption* despite signs of recovery. 日本経済は，回復の兆しが見えるものの，デフレと消費低迷で依然，困難な状況にある．

consumption expenditure 消費支出
▶*Consumer spending* or final *consumption expenditure* accounts for more than 50 percent of the GDP. 個人消費（民間最終消費支出）が，国内総生産（GDP）の5割以上を占める．

consumption tax 消費税
 consumption tax hikes　消費税の引上げ，消費税率の引上げ
 consumption tax rate　消費税率
▶The *consumption tax* may be raised to double-digits. 消費税率が二けたに引き上げられる可能性がある．

contain 動 抑える，抑制する，阻止する，歯止めをかける，削減する，含む，…に等しい (⇒**capability**)
▶The Company's increased profitability continued to be primarily affected during 2008 by significant volume increases combined with its efforts to *contain* costs. 当社の2008年度の収益向上は，前年度に続いて主に経費削減努力と大幅な販売数量の増加によるものです．

Container and Packaging Recycle Law 容器包装リサイクル法
▶The *Container and Packaging Recycle Law* formulated in 1995 requires businesses to recycle product packaging. 1995年に制定された容器包装リサイクル法は，製品包装のリサイクルを義務付けている．

contango 名 〈ロンドン証券取引所の〉株式決済引取り猶予金，決済引取り猶予金，引取り猶予金，株式決済猶予金，〈買い手が支払いを遅らせたときに払う〉繰越し日歩（ひぶ），順日歩，遅延金利，先物価格のほうが直物価格よりも高い状態（forwardation），コンタンゴ
 contango business [dealing]　繰越し取引
 contango day　決算繰越し日，繰越し決算日
 contango rate　株式決済猶予金のレート，コンタンゴ・レート
 normal contango　順ざや先物価格

contender 名 競争相手，対抗馬，候補，ライバル

content 名 情報の内容，情報の中身，情報，著作物，〈ラジオやテレビの〉番組，番組の内容，コンテンツ
 content distributor　情報配信事業者，コンテンツ配信事業者
 content industry　コンテンツ産業
 content manager　コンテンツ担当マネージャー
 content partnership　コンテンツ提携
 content production　コンテンツ作成［制作］

content provider 出店企業, コンテンツ・プロバイダー
contents [content] business コンテンツ・ビジネス
contents supplier コンテンツ・サプライヤー
digital content デジタル著作物, デジタル・コンテンツ
electronic content 電子機器
home page contents ホームページの内容
illegal and harmful contents 違法有害コンテンツ
joint information content 結合情報量
killer content キラー・コンテンツ (大衆に人気の高いソフトウエアや番組のこと)
online content オンライン・コンテンツ
popular content 有力なコンテンツ
table of contents 内容目次, 目次
▸The spread of fiber optic and other broadband networks means that ordinary households can easily access online video and radio *content*. 光ファイバーなど高速大容量通信網の普及で, 一般の家庭でも, ネット上でテレビの画像やラジオ番組に簡単にアクセスできるようになった。
▸Yoshimoto Kogyo Co. and Intel Corp. of the United States have agreed to cooperate in the business of producing *contents* for digital home appliances and personal computers. 吉本興業と米半導体最大手のインテルが, デジタル家電やパソコン向けコンテンツ(情報内容)の制作などで業務提携することで合意した。

contention 名 争い, 論争, 論点, 議論, 口論, 主張, 意見, 意見の対立
▸The main point of *contention* in court was whether this clause was legally binding. 法廷での主な争点は, この条項の法的拘束力の有無であった。

contingency 名 偶発事象, 偶発事項, 不測の事態, 緊急事態, 臨時費用
  accounting for contingencies 偶発事象の会計, 偶発事象の会計処理
  contingency fund 偶発資金, 偶発危険準備金 (=contingent fund)
  contingency reserve 偶発損失引当金[準備金], 偶発損失積立金
  disclosure of loss contingencies 偶発損失の開示
  gain contingencies 偶発利益事象
  loss contingencies 偶発損失事象
  off-balance-sheet contingencies オフバランスの偶発債務
  reserve for contingencies 偶発損失引当金, 偶発損失積立金 (=reserve for possible future losses)
  transaction-related contingencies 取引関連偶発債務
▸We provided $30 million for legal *contingencies* in 2008. 2008年度は, 法的偶発債務費として3,000万ドルを計上しました。

contingent 形 偶発の, 不確定の, 不確かな, 臨時の, …を条件とする, …に付随する
  contingent annuity 不確定年金, 臨時払い年金
  contingent charge [cost] 偶発費用 (=contingent expense)
  contingent fee 成功報酬
  contingent gain 偶発利益, 偶発利得 (=contingent profit)
  contingent issues 臨時発行証券, 条件付き証券
  contingent liability 偶発債務 (現時点で債務は発生していないが, 係争事件で賠償義務が生じるとか保証付きで商品を販売する場合など, 将来発生する可能性がある未確定の債務のこと)
  contingent loss 偶発損失
  contingent profit 偶発利益 (=contingent gain)
  contingent reserve 偶発損失引当金, 偶発損失積立金 (=contingency reserve, reserve for contingencies, special contingency reserve)
▸The Company is likely to suffer *contingent* liabilities as it will face a damages suit. 当社は今後, 損害賠償訴訟を起こされるので, 偶発債務が生じる可能性がある。

contra account 相殺勘定, 評価勘定, 対照勘定
contract 名 契約, 契約書, 規約, 協定, 協定書, 請負, 契約商品, 契約品, 約定品 (⇒**construction contract**)
  agency contract 代理店契約 (=agent contract)
  business tie-up contract 業務提携契約
  conclude a contract 契約を結ぶ, 契約を締結する
  contract ad libitum 随意契約 (=free contract)
  contract amount 契約高
  contract charge 契約手数料
  contract construction 請負工事
  contract deposit paid 契約前渡し金
  contract winner 元受業者, 契約獲得企業, 受注者, 施工業者 (=the winner of a contract)
  contract worker 契約社員
  exchange contract 為替契約

export contract 輸出契約
formal contract 正式契約
futures contract 先物契約
group insurance contract 団体保険契約
joint contract 連帯契約
labor contract 労働契約
loan contract 融資契約, 貸付け契約
marine insurance contract 海上保険契約
master contract 基本契約
provisional contract 仮契約
purchasing contract 購入契約
reinsurance contract 再保険契約
renew a contract 契約を更新する
sales contract 売買契約
supply contract 供給契約
system contract システム契約
union contract 組合契約
written contract 書面契約, 成文契約, 契約書

▶Companies have been entering into *contracts* with the temporary staffing agency that can offer the lowest dispatch fees. 企業は, いちばん安い派遣料を提示できる人材派遣会社と契約［派遣料契約］を結んでいる。

contract price 契約価格［価額］, 契約値段, 契約金額, 協定価格, 契約料, 受注金額, 落札価格

▶The general constructors had held talks before tenders were opened for civil engineering projects to determine the *contract prices*. ゼネコン各社は, 土木工事の入札前に談合で落札金額を決めていた。

contract value 契約価格, 契約金額, 契約価値

▶The fair values of these financial instruments were not materially different than their carrying or *contract values*. これらの金融手段［金融資産］の公正価格は, 実質的に帳簿価格または契約価格とほぼ同じでした。

contract pricing 契約価格, 契約価格［価額］の決定, 契約価格算定

▶The total *contract pricing* for construction of the building is $5,000,000. この建物建設の総契約価格は, 500万ドルだ。

contraction 名 縮小, 収縮, 減少, 減退, マイナス成長, 景気［業況の］悪化, 景気縮小, 景気後退, 不況, 短縮語 (⇒**coincident index**)
  credit contraction 信用の収縮
  demand contraction 需要の減退
  economic contraction 景気の悪化, 景気収縮, 景気縮小, 景気後退, 不況, マイナス成長
  expansion and contraction in the factory sector 製造業の景気拡大と景気後退［景気縮小］

▶The Dow Jones industrials plunged 370 points after an unexpected *contraction* in the service sector. 予想しなかったサービス業の業況悪化を受けて, ダウ平均株価（工業株30種）は, 前日比で370ドル急落した。

contractual clause 契約条項

▶The *contractual clause* is a violation of the Antimonopoly Law. この契約条項は, 独占禁止法違反である。

contractual obligation 契約義務, 契約上の義務

▶Provisions for business restructuring include the estimated costs of specific plans to close offices, consolidate facilities, relocate employees and fulfill *contractual obligations*. 事業再編成引当金には, 事業所の閉鎖や施設統合, 従業員の再配置, 契約義務の履行など特定の計画に対する見積り費用が含まれています。

contribute 動 出資する, 払い込む, 納付する, 拠出する, 寄与する, 貢献する, 協力する, 支援する, …に一役買う, …の要因になる (⇒**guideline**)
  contribute to the bottom line 利益に貢献する
  contributed capital 払込み資本, 拠出資本（= paid-in capital: 株主が払い込んだ資本）
  contributed surplus 払込み剰余金, 資本準備金

▶The company *contributed* ¥10 billion of the capital. 同社は, 資本金のうち100億円を出資した。

▶The worldwide digital boom and the company's steady efforts *contributed* to this achievement. 世界的なデジタル・ブームと同社の地道な取組みが, この業績に貢献した。

contributing factor 貢献要因, …をもたらした要因

▶Another *contributing factor* of the increase in operating expenses was an increase in salaries wages for employees. 営業費用の増加をもたらした他の要因としては, 従業員の給与・賃金の引上げを挙げることもできます。

contribution 名 出資, 拠出, 寄与, 貢献, 寄付, 協力, 支援, 貢献額, 寄付金, 拠出金, 負担金, 掛け金, 分担金, 共同海損分担金, 負担部分, 求償権, 保険料, 納付金 (⇒ **consolidated income, defined contribution pension plan**)
  additional contribution 追加拠出
  associate contribution 関連会社の利益寄与
  capital contribution 資本拠出, 出資
  contribution profit or loss 貢献損益
  contribution to capital 出資金, 資本への拠出額
  contribution to affiliated companies 関係会

社出資金
contributions and equity 出資と持ち分
contributions to retirement funds 退職基金への拠出金
defined contribution plan 確定拠出制度, 拠出建て年金制度, 保険料建て方式
divisional contribution 事業部貢献利益 (= divisional contribution margin)
employee contributions 従業員の拠出金 (⇒ match)
equity contribution 出資
national contribution ratio 国民負担率 (所得に関して個人と企業が支払う税金と社会保険料の割合)
profit contribution 利益貢献度, 利益寄与
proportional contribution 比例貢献度
social insurance contribution 社会保険料
▶Our *contributions* to the savings plans amounted to $330 million in 2008. 当社の貯蓄制度に対する会社側の拠出額は, 2008年度は3億3,000万ドルでした。
▶The company plans to discuss the ratio of capital *contribution* to the holding company and the selection of top executives. 持ち株会社への出資比率やトップ人事については, 同社が今後協議する。
▶The company's *contributions* to our net income in the third quarter were $250 million ($230 million in 2007). 当社の第3四半期の純利益に対する同社の貢献額は, 2億5,000万ドル(前年同期は2億3,000万ドル)でした。

contributor 名 貢献要因, 貢献[寄与]したもの (= contributing factor)
▶The main *contributors* to revenue growth were increased product and system sales outside the U.S. 収益の伸びに主に貢献したのは, 米国外での製品とサービスの売上の増加です。

contributory plan 拠出型制度, 拠出型年金制度, 拠出制年金制度

control 動 支配する, 経営権を握る, 経営支配権を得る, 掌握する, 管理する, 抑制する, 抑える, 操作する
completely control one's subsidiaries 100％経営支配権を得る, 完全に経営権を握る
control quality 品質管理をする
control working capital 運転資金を抑える
controlled company 被支配会社, 傘下企業, 従属会社, 子会社 (= subsidiary)
controlled economy 統制経済
controlled firm 傘下企業
controlled foreign corporation 在外子会社, 在外従属会社《略 CFC》
controlled label コントロールド・ラベル (= private brand, store brand)
controlled nonsubsidiary 従属的非子会社
▶Stock swaps allow the acquirer to purchase the company it wants to *control* without preparing a large sum of cash. 株式交換だと, 買収企業は多額の現金を用意しなくても, 相手先企業[経営権を握りたいと思う企業]を買収することができる。

control 名 支配, 統制, 管理, 経営支配権, 経営権, 規制, 抑制, 制御, コントロール (⇒**internal control, quality control**)
administrative control 管理統制, 管理上の統制, 業務統制, 行政監査, 運営管理コントロール
capital control 資本規制, 資本取引規制
change of control 経営権の変更
common control 共通の支配
control environment 統制環境
control of ownership 経営権
corporate control 企業経営
credit control 与信管理, 信用管理, 信用規制, 信用限度, 信用統制 (= credit management)
export control 輸出管理, 輸出規制
family control 同族支配
inventory control 在庫管理
majority control 過半数所有支配, 過半数子会社
management control 経営支配, 経営支配権, 経営管理
marketing control マーケティング統制
material control 資材管理
minority control 少数支配, 少数派支配
monetary control 金融調節 (= monetary adjustment)
operating control 業務管理
process control 工程管理
purchase control 購買管理
separation of ownership and control 所有と経営の分離
stock control 在庫管理, 在庫調整
take control of …の経営権を握る[掌握する], …の経営権を支配する, …の主導権を握る
take full control of …の経営権を完全に掌握する, …を完全子会社化する
under state control 国の管理下にある, 国有化されている
▶The firm plans to take full *control* of a Chinese unit and build a new factory in 2010. 同社は, 中国の子会社を完全子会社化し, 2010年に新工場を建設する計画だ。

▶The purpose of issuing a sizable amount of new shares is to maintain the *control* of a specific stockholder over the company. 新株の大量発行は，同社に対する特定株主の支配権[経営支配権]確保が目的だ。
▶We will focus on even more rigorous credit *control* to avoid risks. 当社は，一段と厳しい与信管理を徹底して，リスク回避を図る方針です。

controller 名 経理部長，財務部長，管理部長，会計監査役，会計検査役，コントローラー（＝comptroller: 米大手企業の「コントローラー (controller)」は，会社の資金調達や運用などの財務部門を統括する役員の「トレジャラー (treasurer)」と違って，会社の経理や会計監査など経理部門の統括者。中小企業の場合は，トレジャラーがコントローラーを兼務することもある。⇒ **treasurer**)
 chief controller [comptroller] 財務部長，経理部長
 controller of audit 監査責任者

controlling 形 支配する，優先する，支配している，支配できる，支配的な，管理する
 controlling company 支配会社，親会社
 controlling families 経営者一族
 controlling function 管理機能
 controlling shareholder 支配株主
▶Both parties agree that the English version of this Agreement shall be *controlling*. 両当事者は，本契約書の英語版が優先することに合意する。

controlling interest 支配(的)持ち分，支配株主持ち分，経営支配権，経営支配株 （＝controlling stake:「経営支配権」とは，一般には他社を支配できる議決権株式(voting stock)の過半数 (50％超)を所有することをいう）
▶GM may sell a *controlling interest* in its profitable finance arm, General Motors Acceptance Corp. (GMAC). GMは，同社の収益性の高い金融子会社GMACの経営支配株を売却する可能性もある。

controlling stake 支配持ち分，支配株主持ち分，経営支配権，経営支配株 （＝controlling interest）
▶The tender offer to acquire a *controlling stake* of more than 50 percent in the company will last through December 10. 同社の50％超の経営支配権[支配持ち分]取得をめざした株式公開買付け(TOB)の期限は，12月10日までの予定だ。

convenience 名 便利，便利さ，利便，利便性，便宜，便益，打算，コンビニエンス
 convenience cost 便益コスト
 convenience food インスタント食品，パッケージ食品，調理済み食品，コンビニエンス・フード
 convenience goods 最寄り品，便宜品，手近品（日曜雑貨品，タバコ，菓子類，雑誌などを指す）
 convenience of location 立地の便宜性
 convenience sample 恣意(しい)的標本，便宜的標本
▶Through the business tie-up, the company aims to increase *convenience* for its clients across the United States. 業務提携により，全米規模で顧客の利便性を向上させるのが同社の狙いだ。

convenience store コンビニエンス・ストア，コンビニ
▶Existing *convenience stores* had too narrow product lineups. 既存のコンビニは，商品数を絞り込みすぎた。

convenience store chain コンビニエンスストア・チェーン
▶Aeon Co. has invited *convenience store chain* operator Lawson Inc. to enter into a broad business tie-up. イオンが，コンビニエンスストア・チェーンのローソンに対して，広範な業務提携を申し入れている。

convention 名 大会，定期大会，党大会，集会，会議，総会，約束事，協定，協約，条約，慣例，慣行，コンベンション
 accounting convention 会計慣行
 annual convention 年次大会，年次総会
 convention hall 会議場，コンベンション・ホール
 convention industry コンベンション産業，コンベンション業界
 Convention on the Law of the Seas 海洋法条約
 Democratic national convention 米民主党全国大会
 national convention 全国大会，全国党大会
 Republican convention 米共和党大会
 tax convention 租税条約

conversion 名 転換，換算，両替，交換，借換え，〈公債などの〉切替え，加工（⇒**right**）
 about 6 million tons (in liquefied natural gas conversion) of natural gas 約600万トン(液化天然ガス換算)の天然ガス
 bond conversion 社債転換，社債の転換，転換社債の株式への転換
 conversion issue 借換え発行
 conversion of convertible debentures 転換社債の転換，転換社債の株式への転換
 conversion of stock 株式転換
 conversion of warrants ワラントの権利行使

conversion planning 移行計画
conversion premium 転換プレミアム
conversion price 転換価格 (転換証券を普通株式に転換する場合の株式1株当たり価格のこと)
conversion rate [ratio] 外貨換算率, 交換比率, 転換比率, 転換割合 (=convertible rate [ratio]:「転換比率」は, 転換証券を普通株式に転換する場合に何株と交換できるかを示す比率)
conversion value 転換価値 (転換によって入手できる普通株式の時価)
date of conversion 転換日, 転換時
debt-equity conversion 債務の株式化
effective conversion price 実効転換価格
interest rate conversion agreement 利率[利子率]変更契約
▸On May 10, 2009, individuals holding $50,000 face value of the Corporation's bonds exercised their *conversion* privilege. 2009年5月10日に, 当社の社債権者が, 額面5万ドル分の転換権を行使しました[額面5万ドル分の株式への転換を行いました]。

convert 動 転換する, 変える, 加工する, 改造する, 流用する, 〈公債などを〉切り替える, 振り替える, 換算する, 両替する, 〈元金に〉繰り入れる (⇒ **inflate**)
convert bonds into shares 社債を株式に転換する
convert to a market economy 市場経済に移行する
▸Securities were *converted* into cash. 有価証券は, 現金化された。
▸The shares were *converted* into approximately 18 million shares of our common stock upon consummation of the merger. この株式は, 合併完了時に約1,800万株の当社普通株式に転換されました。
▸The weak yen has also inflated the firm's profit, which were *converted* into Japanese currency from dollars. 円安も, ドルから円に換算した同社の利益を押し上げた。

convertible 形 転換可能な, 転換できる, 転換性のある, 変換[交換]可能な
convertible class A preferred stock 転換権付きクラスA優先株式
convertible preferred stock 転換優先株式, 転換権付き優先株式
convertible stock 転換株式 (=convertible share)
▸All the first preferred shares are *convertible* into common shares. 第一優先株式は, すべて普通株式への転換が可能です。
convertible bond 転換社債《略 CB》 (=convertible debenture, convertible debt, convertible loan stock)
convertible bond payable 転換社債
convertible bonds with put option プット・オプション付き転換社債
▸These *convertible bonds* are not considered common stock equivalents. これらの転換社債は, 準普通株式とは考えられていません。
convertible note 転換社債, 兌換(だかん)券
▸Ford increased the amount of *convertible notes* it is offering to $4.5 billion from $3 billion announced previously. フォードは, 転換社債の発行規模を当初計画の30億ドルから45億ドルに引き上げた。
convertible subordinated debenture 転換劣後社債, 劣後転換社債, 後順位転換社債
▸The Company completed a $100 million 8% *convertible subordinated debenture* issue during 2008. 当社は, 2008年に利率8%の転換劣後社債1億ドルの発行を完了しました。

conveyance 名 運送, 運搬, 輸送, 輸送機関, 乗り物, 財産移転, 財産移転証書, 譲渡, 不動産譲渡, 譲渡証書, 伝達, 伝言
conveyance by land 陸上輸送
conveyance of know-how [knowhow] ノウハウの譲渡
deed of conveyance 譲渡証書
estate conveyance 財産譲渡 (=conveyance of estate)
fraudulent conveyance 詐欺的譲渡
public conveyance 公共輸送機関
voluntary conveyance 任意譲渡, 無償譲渡

conveyer [conveyor] system コンベヤー[コンベア]方式, コンベヤー[コンベア]による流れ作業
conveyer belt system ベルト・コンベヤー[コンベア]方式 (=conveyer system)
▸*Conveyer belt system* had been used for mass production. ベルト・コンベヤー方式は, かつては大量生産に使われていた。

COO 最高業務運営役員, 最高業務運営責任者, 最高執行責任者 (chief operating officerの略)

cook books 帳簿に手を加える, 帳簿をごまかす, 帳簿を改竄する, 粉飾する (=cook the books)
▸The company *cooked books* to cover loss. 同社は, 帳簿を改竄して損失(赤字)を補塡した。

cool money インターネット取引で動く投資資金, クール・マネー

▸*Cool money* flew away from low-interest America toward the higher interest euro-zone. ネット取引で動く投資資金は，金利の低いアメリカから金利の高いユーロ圏に流れた．

cooling off 冷却期間，クーリング・オフ （＝cooling-off period: 消費者保護制度の一つで，消費者が商品を購入する契約を結んでも，契約後20日以内なら無条件で解約できる）

cooperation 名 協力，協同，協調，協業，提携，提供，援助
　business cooperation 事業提携，業務提携
　capital cooperation 資本提携 （＝cooperation by holding capital）
　cooperation among various industries 異業種交流
　cooperation and competition 協調と競争
　cooperation and coordination 協力・協調関係，協力・協調，協調
　cooperation between firms 企業間協力
　patent cooperation 特許協力
　simple cooperation 単純協業
　technical cooperation 技術提携，技術提供
▸Mitsui Fudosan and Imperial Hotel are considering *cooperation* in redeveloping Tokyo's Hibiya area. 三井不動産と帝国ホテルは，東京・日比谷地区の再開発での提携を検討している．
▸There is a chance that the technological *cooperation* will develop into a capital affiliation. 技術協力が資本提携に発展する可能性がある．

cooperation between management and labor 労使協調
▸Corporations should do their best to secure jobs through *cooperation between management and labor*. 企業は，労使協調して雇用の確保に全力を上げるべきである．

cooperative approach 協調路線
▸The company's management traditionally has taken a *cooperative approach* toward the company's labor union. 同社の経営陣は，伝統的に労使協調路線を取っている．

coordinate 動 調整する，協調する，一元化する，調和させる，連携させる，連携を取る，連携する
　coordinated interest rate cuts 協調利下げ
　coordinated intervention 協調介入
　coordinated terrorist attacks of Sept. 11 9月11日(2001年)の米同時多発テロ （＝Sept.11 terrorist attacks）
▸The TSE president is required to *coordinate* with the securities industry and the Financial Services Agency. 東京証券取引所の社長[東証社長]は，証券界や金融庁との調整を図らなければならない．

coordination 名 調整，調節，すり合わせ，一元化，統一，協調，連携，整合，足並み，同等，対等，対等関係
　lack of coordination 足並みの乱れ
　policy coordination 政策協調
▸*Coordination* between the two groups is expected to be a big issue in future. 両グループ間の調整が，今後の大きな課題になりそうだ．
▸Policy *coordination* efforts between Japanese and U.S. currency authorities are genuine. 日米通貨当局の政策協調努力は，本物だ．

COP 国連気候変動枠組み条約締約国会議 （the Conference of the Parties to the U.N. Framework Convention on Climate Changeの略）

copy 動 複写する，複製する，模倣する，コピーする
▸You may not *copy* any documentation. 文書のコピー[複製]は，一切禁止する．

copy 名 複写，転写，写し，謄本，抄本，副本，複製，模倣，まね，…部，…通，…冊，原稿，コピー
　carbon copy 電子メールのカーボン・コピー《略cc》
　certified copy 認証謄本
　copy desk 新聞社のデスク，原稿整理部，整理部
　copy editor 原稿整理係，編集者
　copy food コピー食品
　copy machine 複写機，コピー機 （＝copier, photocopier）
　copy paper 複写紙，コピー用紙
　duplicate copy 副本
　enclosed copy 同封の副本
　hard copy 印刷物，データやプログラムを紙に印刷したもの，ハード・コピー
　original copy 正本
　soft copy ソフト・コピー （ディスプレーの表示画面のこと）
▸Licensee shall make no *copies* of the Program or any materials supplied to Licensee pursuant to the agreement. ライセンシーは，このコンピュータ・プログラムまたは本契約に従ってライセンシーに提供された資料のコピー[複製]を作成しないものとする．

copyright 動 著作権を取得する，版権を取得する，…の著作権を保護する
　Copyrighted. 著作権所有，版権所有
　copyrighted animation footage 著作権があるアニメ画像
　copyrighted material 版権のある著作物

copyrighted music 著作権のある音楽, 著作権を有する音楽
▶A graduate school student spread a computer virus on the Internet using *copyrighted* animation footage. 大学院生が, 著作権のあるアニメ画像を使って, インターネット上にコンピュータ・ウイルスを流出させた.

copyright 名 著作権, 版権, 形 著作権所有の, 版権所有の
  copyright application 著作権出願
  copyright holder 著作権所有者, 版権所有者, 著作者
  copyright in works 著作物上の著作権
  copyright industry 著作権業
  Copyright Law 著作権法
  copyright notice 著作権表示, 著作権の告知
  copyright on Internet ネット著作権
  copyright piracy 著作権侵害 (＝copyright violation)
  copyright protection 著作権保護
  copyright registration 著作権登録
  Copyright reserved. 著作権所有, 版権所有
  Copyright Royalty Tribunal 米著作権使用料裁定委員会
  copyright violation 著作権侵害 (＝copyright infringement, copyright piracy)
  infringe the copyright 著作権を侵害する, 版権を侵害する
  out of copyright 著作権期限が切れた, 版権の期限が切れた
▶*Copyright* on a song usually belongs to the composer and lyricist who wrote it. 曲の著作権は, その著作にかかわった作曲家や作詞家が持つ.
▶The book is still *copyright*. この本は, まだ版権が生きている.

copyright-related rights 著作隣接権
▶*Copyright-related rights* on a song belong to those who publicize the song, such as the singer, performers and the record label. 曲の著作隣接権は, 歌手や演奏家, レコード会社などその作品を世に送り出した人たちが持つ.

copyright royalty 著作権料, 著作権使用料
▶With videos of Japanese movies, video rental shop operators buy the videos for three to four times the market price to cover the cost of *copyright royalties* paid to film companies and scriptwriters. 邦画ビデオの場合, レンタル店は, 映画会社や脚本家への著作権料の費用を賄うため, 市販品の3−4倍の価格で(メーカーから)ビデオを買い取る.

core 名 核, 中心, 核心, 芯, 中核, 中枢, 主力, 主軸, 基本モデル, 基本設計, 原子炉の炉心, コア, 形 核となる, 軸となる, 中心的な, 中核的な, コアな, 基本的な, 本業の
  core activities 主力事業, 中核事業, 主力業務 (＝core business)
  core bank 主力銀行, 主力行
  core capital 中核的自己資本, 自己資本の基本的項目, 基本的資本項目, コア資本
  core capitalization コア資本
  core competence 中核的業務, 中核能力, 企業固有の技術[スキルや技術], 企業固有の競争力の核, 自社ならではの強み, コア・コンピテンス (**noncore competence**＝非中核業務, ノンコア業務)
  core deposit intangibles コア預金無形資産
  core element 中核的要素
  core ideology 基本理念
  core inflation 基礎インフレ率, コア・インフレ率, コア指数 (＝core rate of inflation)
  core issue 核心的な問題
  core operation 中核事業, 主力事業, 基幹事業, 本業 (＝core business)
  core producer prices 生産者物価のコア部分の指数, 生産者物価指数コア部分
  core product lines 主要製品
  core profitability 主力事業の収益性, コア収益性, コア収益
  core profitable business 収益の柱
  core time コア・タイム (時差出勤で, 社員が全員顔をそろえる時間帯)
  core values 基本的価値観
▶The firm's *core* aviation business posted an operating loss of ¥3.4 billion in the six months through September 2008. 同社の本業の航空事業は, 2008年9月の中間決算で, 34億円の営業損失[営業赤字]を計上した.

core business 中核事業, 中核業務, 中核企業, 主力事業, 基幹事業, 根幹業務, 本業, コア・ビジネス (＝core activities, core operation)
▶Our *core business* is to meet the communications and computing needs of our customers by using networks to move and manage information. 当社の中核事業は, 情報の伝送と処理にネットワークを利用して, 顧客のコミュニケーションとコンピューティングの必要性に応えることです.

core capital rate [ratio] 中核的自己資本比率 (＝Tier 1 capital rate, tier-one capital ratio)
▶The bank's *core capital rate* falls behind those

of many major European and U.S. banks. 同行の中核的自己資本比率は, 欧米の多くの大手銀行より下回っている.

core consumer price index コア物価指数, 消費者物価指数のコア指数, コア指数
▶The *core Consumer Price Index*, which strips out volatile food and energy costs, moved up just 0.1 percent in August. 変動の激しい[変動幅の大きい]食品とエネルギー価格を除いたコア物価指数[消費者物価指数のコア指数]は, 8月は0.1%の上昇にとどまった.

core earnings 中核事業収益, 主力事業の収益, コア収益
▶Group operating profit shows a company's *core earnings* strength. 連結営業利益は, 企業の主力事業の収益力[本業のもうけ]を示す.

core firm 中核会社, 中核企業, 主力企業 (= core company)
▶Under the group's reconstruction plan, its *core firm* will be split into a business operating firm and an asset management company. 同グループの再建計画によると, グループ中核会社のコクドは, 事業会社と資産管理会社に分割される.

core operating profit (生命保険会社の本業のもうけに当たる)基礎利益 (=core profit; ⇒ **dividend income**)
▶The increase in seven insurers' *core operating profits* is due to appraisal gains in their stockholdings. 生保7社の基礎利益(本業のもうけに当たる)の増加は, 保有株式の含み益によるものだ.

core portion of one's capital base 中核的自己資本, 自己資本
▶Mizuho Financial Group Inc. will float preferred securities to domestic institutional investors to enhance the *core portion of its capital base*. みずほフィナンシャルグループ(FG)は, 自己資本[中核的自己資本]を増強するため, 機関投資家向けに優先出資証券を発行する.

core profit コア利益, 主力事業の利益, 生命保険会社の基礎利益
▶*Core profits* increased at major life insurers in the first half of the current fiscal year from a year earlier. 主要生保の今年度上半期(4-9月)の基礎利益(本業のもうけに当たる)は, 前年同期比で増加した.

core strategy 基本戦略, 主力戦略, 中核戦略
▶Customer focus is our *core strategy* for weathering the forces of competition. 顧客志向は, 競争圧力に対応するための当社の基本戦略です.

corner 動 買い占める, 独占する
　corner in commodities 品物を買い占める
　corner the market 市場を独占する, 株などを大量に買い占める
　cornering of the market in stocks and real estate 株と不動産[土地]の買占め
　stock cornering group 仕手グループ

corner 名 〈株や商品の〉買占め, 独占, 地域, 分野, 窮地, 苦境, 苦しい立場
　corners and manipulation 買占めと相場の操作
　cut corners 経費などを切詰める, 節約する, 手抜きをする, 手を抜く, 近道をする
　establish [make] a corner in [on] the shares of …の株を買い占める
　have a corner on the market 市場を独占する, 市場を一手に握っている
　turn the corner 峠を越す・越える, 最悪を脱する, 窮地・危機を脱する

cornerstone laying ceremony 建築物の定礎式

corpocracy 名 企業官僚主義, 大企業の官僚的体質, コーポクラシー (corporateとbureaucracyの合成語)

corporate 形 企業の, 会社の, 法人の, 共通の, 共同の, コーポレート
　corporate accounting 企業会計, 企業の会計処理, 企業の会計処理方法, 企業の経理
　corporate accounting system 企業会計制度, 企業会計組織, 企業会計システム
　corporate advertising 企業広告, 会社広告
　corporate America 企業国家アメリカ
　corporate and non-operating 本社および非営業部門
　corporate body 企業体
　corporate brand management コーポレート・ブランド経営
　corporate breakup 企業分割
　corporate business 法人企業, 法人
　corporate color 企業色, 企業カラー, コーポレート・カラー
　corporate conscience 企業良心
　corporate control 企業経営
　corporate costs 企業経費, 一般管理費
　corporate credit quality 企業の信用力, 企業の信用の質
　corporate defensive measure 企業防衛策 (⇒**defensive measure**)
　corporate deposit 企業預金
　corporate enterprise tax 法人事業税, 法人税 (=corporate tax)

corporate entity 企業実体, 法人実体, 企業体 (=business entity)
corporate equity 企業持ち分
corporate executives 会社経営者, 経営者 (=company executives)
corporate financial health 企業の財務健全性
corporate financial statements 会社財務諸表
corporate giant 大企業
corporate goods price index 企業商品価格指数
corporate hospitality コーポレート・ホスピタリティ (上得意の顧客に対する企業の接待やもてなし)
corporate investment 企業投資, 企業の設備投資, 民間設備投資
corporate institution 企業
corporate irregularities 企業不祥事
corporate ladder 企業の出世街道
corporate loans 法人向け融資, 企業向け融資, 企業向け貸出
corporate rebuilding plan 企業再建計画, 経営再建計画, 再建計画
corporate reconstruction 企業再建, 企業再生
corporate reconstruction fund 企業再生ファンド (=corporate turnaround fund)
corporate safeguards 企業防衛策
corporate social report 企業社会報告
corporate spending 企業の支出, 設備投資
corporate turnaround fund 企業再生ファンド (=corporate reconstruction fund)

corporate activities 企業活動
▶Uncertainties are growing over how long strong exports and corresponding brisk *corporate activities* will last. 輸出の好調とそれに支えられた活発な企業活動がいつまで続くかについて, 不透明感が増している。

corporate assets 全社一般資産, 本社資産, 会社資産, 企業資産, 本部資産
▶*Corporate assets* are principally cash and temporary cash investments. 本社資産は, 主に現金と短期投資です。

corporate bankruptcy 企業倒産 (=corporate failure)
▶The number of *corporate bankruptcies* jumped 7.6 percent in January 2008 from a year earlier to 1,174. 2008年1月の企業倒産件数は, 前年同月比7.6%増の1,174件となった。

corporate bond 社債 (=corporate debenture)
| 社債とは➡企業の資金調達の手段として企業が発行する債券。企業の資金調達の方法としては, 銀行などの金融機関から借り入れる間接金融と, 株式や社債などを発行して投資家から資金を集める直接金融の二つがある。
▶The risk of *corporate bonds* is low if you stick to investment-grade securities. 投資適格債にあくまでも限定すれば, 社債のリスクは低い。

corporate borrowers 融資先, 融資先企業
▶The bank was found to have forced *corporate borrowers* to buy financial products in violation of the Antimonopoly Law. 同行は, 独占禁止法に違反して融資先企業に金融商品を無理に購入させていたことが判明した。

corporate buyout [buy-out] 企業買収 (=corporate acquisition)
▶In a *corporate buyout* through stock swapping, a company that buys another company assesses the corporate value of the latter. 株式交換による企業買収では, 他社を買収する企業が買収相手の企業価値を査定する。

corporate [corporation] charter 会社定款
▶The power of a veto is used to make important management decisions such as mergers or revision of *corporate charters* at shareholders meetings. 拒否権は, 株主総会で合併や会社定款などの重要な経営の意思決定を行う際に行使される。

corporate citizen [citizenship] 企業市民, 市民としての企業, 社会の一員としての企業, コーポレート・シティズン
▶We are committed to being a good *corporate citizen* and a responsible neighbor in the communities in which we live and work. 当社は, 生活や労働の場としている地域社会の善良な企業市民であると同時に責任感の強い隣人でありたいと考えています。

corporate culture 企業文化, 企業の体質, 企業風土, 社風, コーポレート・カルチャー (⇒**customer safety, short term profits**)
▶*Corporate culture* can be a hurdle in a merger. 統合では, 企業風土がハードル(障害)になる場合もある。
▶There appears to be fundamental problems with the *corporate culture* at the company. 同社の場合は, 企業体質に根本的な問題があるようだ。

corporate debt securities 債券
▶The assets of the various plans include corporate equities, government securities, *corporate debt securities* and income-producing real estate.

各種制度の年金資産は，株式，政府証券，債券や収益を稼得する不動産でなどで構成されています。

corporate earnings 企業収益，企業業績
  corporate earnings growth 企業収益の改善
  corporate earnings performance 企業収益
  ▶A rise in *corporate earnings* will stimulate private spending, as it will boost individual income through wage raises and bigger bonuses. 企業業績の上昇は，賃上げやボーナス増で個人所得を増大させ，個人消費を刺激することになる。

corporate employee pension insurance 厚生年金保険
  ▶The Pension Fund Association restarted operations as a special privately owned corporation based on a law on *corporate employee pension insurance* in 2005. 企業年金連合会(旧特殊法人「厚生年金基金連合会」)は，厚生年金保険法に基づく特別民間法人として2005年に再スタートした。

corporate employee pension plan 厚生年金制度，厚生年金
  ▶The Employees Pension Fund supports the public *corporate employee pension plan*. 厚生年金基金は，公的な厚生年金制度を支えている。

corporate employee pension system 厚生年金制度，厚生年金
  ▶The Social Insurance Agency paid out less in *corporate employee* and basic *pension system* benefits to elderly subscribers. 社会保険庁が，高齢加入者に厚生年金や基礎年金(国民年金)の給付金を少なく支給していた。

corporate executive officer 業務執行役員
  ▶The transparency and accountability of business management are generally symbolized by outside directors, *corporate executive officers*, independent auditors and compliance officers. 経営の透明性と説明責任は，一般に社外重役や業務執行役員，独立監査人(外部監査)，コンプライアンス・オフィサー(法令・規則遵守担当役員)などで象徴される。

corporate failure 企業倒産 (＝corporate bankruptcy)
  ▶*Corporate failures* among smaller firms increased in January 2008, accounting for 64.6 percent of the total. 2008年1月の中小企業の企業倒産件数は，増加して全体の64.6％を占めた。

corporate goal 企業目標，会社目標
  ▶When we look to our quarterly results, we are always reminded of our longer term *corporate goals*. 各四半期の業績を検討するにあたって，私たちがつねに想起するのは，当社の長期的な企業目標です。

corporate governance 会社の管理・運営，会社管理法，企業統治，企業支配，経営監視，コーポレート・ガバナンス (株主や取締役，監査役などによる経営チェック・システム; ⇒**conglomerate**)
  ▶The system of U.S. *corporate governance* has been a model for other countries. アメリカの企業統治(コーポレート・ガバナンス)のシステムは，これまで他国が手本としてきた。
  ▶We have developed a *corporate governance* framework based on a system comprising corporate auditors, directors and outside directors and a system of voluntary committees. 当社は，監査役，取締役と外部取締役を置く制度と任意の委員会制度に基づくコーポレート・ガバナンス体制を構築しています。

corporate governance system コーポレート・ガバナンス体制
  ▶We regard the establishment and operation of properly functioning *corporate governance systems* as an important management issue. 当社は，適切に機能するコーポレート・ガバナンス体制の確立と運営を経営の重要課題の一つと位置付けています。

corporate identity 企業イメージ統合戦略，企業認識，企業の存在意義，コーポレート・アイデンティティ，CI (CI計画には，一般に企業理念の確立，社名のロゴタイプや社章，シンボルマーク，社用封筒，便箋，名刺などの統一，企業理念に基づく企業活動などが含まれる)

corporate image 企業イメージ (⇒**growth prospects**)
  ▶Japanese companies have been introducing more sophisticated recycling environmental technologies to their plants in China to improve their *corporate images*. 日本企業は，最新鋭のリサイクル環境技術を中国の現地工場に導入して，企業イメージを高めている。

corporate income 法人所得，企業所得
  corporate income tax 法人所得税，法人税，企業所得税
  corporate income taxes payable 未払い法人税等
  ▶China's *corporate income* tax is similar to Japan's corporate tax. 中国の企業所得税は，日本の法人税に相当する。
  ▶*Corporate income* tax is levied on the basis of companies' net business profits. 法人事業税[法

人所得税］は，企業の業務上の純利益［業務純益］に応じて課税される。

corporate management 企業経営, 会社経営
▶Under the Commercial Code, to gain approval for an important resolution that directly affects *corporate management*, shareholders holding at least 50 percent of shares with voting rights must cast ballots, and two-thirds must back the motion.　商法で，企業の経営に直接影響を及ぼす重要決議の承認を得るには，議決権株式の少なくとも50％を保有する株主が投票し，提案に対してその3分の2の支持を得る必要がある。

corporate manager 企業経営者, 経営者, 企業の管理職, 管理職
▶*Corporate managers* are cautious about wage hikes for fear of the adverse effects on business performances of the recent fall in stock prices and the yen's appreciation.　最近の株安と円高により企業業績に悪影響が出るとの懸念から，経営側は賃上げに警戒感を示している。

corporate officer 企業の業務執行役員, 執行役員
▶The firm will introduce a *corporate officer* under a new system.　同社は，新たに執行役員制度を導入する。

corporate pension plan 企業年金制度, 厚生年金制度
▶Companies are responsible for the pension fund investment under conventional *corporate pension plans*.　従来からの企業年金制度では，企業が年金積立金の運用に責任を負っている。

corporate performance 企業収益, 企業業績, 会社業績, 決算
▶*Corporate performance* has improved at varying rates in different industries and companies.　企業の業績回復には，業種間，企業間で差がある。

corporate philanthropy 企業の慈善行為, 企業の慈善活動, 企業のフィランソロピー活動, 企業の慈善事業, 企業の文化・社会への貢献, コーポレート・フィランソロピー
▶At first, the rapid growth of Japanese *corporate philanthropy* was called to be short-term schemes by Japanese companies to improve their public image.　当初，日本企業のフィランソロピー活動の急速な伸びは，消費者のイメージ・アップを図るための日本企業の短期的な企てだ，といわれた。

corporate profits 企業収益, 企業利益
▶Steady increases in *corporate profits* are the largest factor behind the economic expansion.　企業収益の順調な伸びが，景気拡大の最大の要因だ。

corporate purchase 企業買収
▶The firm's former president spread false information about *corporate purchases* with the aim of inflating the stock prices of its affiliate.　同社の前社長は，関連会社の株価をつり上げるため，虚偽の企業買収情報を公表していた。

corporate reform 企業改革
▶There also is a growing trend for shareholders to press for *corporate reform*.　株主が企業改革への圧力を高める傾向も，強まっている。

corporate rehabilitation 企業再建, 経営再建
　corporate rehabilitation fund 企業再建ファンド, 企業再建基金
　Corporate Rehabilitation Law 会社更生法
　corporate rehabilitation plan 経営再建計画, 企業再建計画

corporate report 会社報告書, コーポレート・レポート（「コーポレート・レポート」は，英国の会社の営業報告書と財務諸表の総称）

corporate sector 企業部門
▶Economic expansion led by the *corporate sector* was firm until the end of last year.　企業部門主導の景気拡大は，昨年末までは堅調に推移した。

corporate social responsibility 企業の社会的責任《略 CSR》（企業の社会的責任には，地域社会に対する責任のほかに，環境や法令遵守，社員の権利尊重などが含まれる）
▶The Corporation is responsible for its people and to the communities where they live and work as a *corporate social responsibility*.　当社は，企業の社会的責任として，従業員のみならず従業員が生活して働いている地域社会に対しても責任を負っています。

corporate strength 企業体質, 企業力, 企業の強み
▶Businesses need to reinforce their *corporate strength*.　企業は，企業体質を強化する必要がある。

corporate takeover 企業買収
▶The Japanese financial institutions are more vulnerable to *corporate takeovers* as stocks held by them have lower aggregate market values than those held by their U.S. and European counterparts.　日本の金融機関は，保有する株式の時価総額が欧米の金融機関の株式に比べて低いため，企業買収の標的になりやすい。

corporate tax 法人税, 法人事業税（企業の利潤に対して課される国税）

corporate tax on gross operating profit 外形標準課税, 業務粗利益への法人事業税[法人税]の課税

corporate tax rate 法人税率

corporate tax revenue 法人税収

▶The shortfall of the current fiscal year's tax revenues was due mostly to plunges in *corporate tax* revenue. 今年度の税収不足は、主に法人税収の落ち込みによるものだった。

corporate value 企業価値 （⇒corporate buyout [buy-out]）

corporate value assessment 企業価値の評価

raise corporate value 企業価値を高める

▶Market capitalization is the only fair indicator of *corporate value* for stock companies. 時価総額は、株式会社の企業価値を示す唯一の公正な指標である。

corporation 名 会社, 企業, 法人, 株式会社, 団体, コーポレーション （米国では、株式会社(stock corporation)などの営利法人(business corporation)を「コーポレーション」という）

audit corporation 監査法人

business corporation 事業会社, 法人企業, 営利法人, 株式会社(stock company), 商社(trading corporation), 会社

corporation income 法人所得, 法人利益, 会社の利益

corporation income tax 法人税

Corporation Tax Act 法人税法

mutual corporation 相互会社

open corporation 公開会社, 株式公開会社

ordinary corporation 普通法人

profit corporation 営利企業, 営利会社, 営利法人会社 （＝profit organization）

public corporation 株式公開企業, 特殊法人, 公共企業体, 公共団体, 公益法人

special purpose corporation 特別目的会社 （＝special purpose company）

stock corporation 株式会社 （＝joint stock company, stock company）

twenty percent corporation 20%所有法人

▶Japanese *corporations* are now fighting a cross-border war against their foreign competitors. 日本企業は現在, 外国のライバル企業[外国勢]と国境を越えた競争を続けている。

▶The power of a veto is used to make important management decisions such as mergers or revision of *corporation* charters at shareholders meetings. 拒否権は、株主総会で合併や会社定款などの重要な経営の意思決定を行う際に行使される。

correct 動 訂正する, 是正する, 補正する, 調整する

▶The company *corrected* financial statements on its portfolio since March 2006. 同社は、2006年3月以降の有価証券報告書の財務諸表を訂正した。

correspondence 名 通信, 往復文書, 書簡, 手紙, 書状, コレポン(貿易通信文・商業英語), 調和, 符号, 一致, 類似, 関連

be in correspondence with …と取引関係がある

business correspondence 商業通信文, 貿易通信文

commercial correspondence 商業通信文

correspondence department 文書課

correspondent 名 特派員, 通信員, 記者, 海外取引先, 取引店, コルレス先, 為替取組み先

correspondent account 代理口座

correspondent agreement [arrangement] コルレス契約

correspondent bank 取引銀行, 取引先銀行, コルレス銀行, 代理銀行

foreign correspondent 海外特派員

corrupt 形 堕落した, 不正の, 汚職の, 賄賂のきく

corrupt practice 不正慣行

▶The FTC ordered construction firms to stop bid-riggings on public works projects in an effort to reform the *corrupt practice* involving the city government. 公正取引委員会(FTC)は, 同市が絡んだ不正慣行を改めるための動きとして, 建設会社に公共工事談合の排除命令を出した。

cosmetic 形 化粧の, ささいな, とるに足らない

cost 動 〈費用などが〉かかる, 必要とする, 要する, 原価計算をする, 原価を見積もる

▶The recall and replacement would *cost* as much as ¥50 billion. 今回のリコール(自主回収と無償交換)の負担額は, 500億円規模に達する。

cost 名 原価, 費用, 経費, 原価法, コスト （⇒borrowing costs, credit cost, personnel, procurement, production cost）

business costs 事業コスト

capital cost 資本費用, 資本コスト （＝cost of capital, cost of equity: 資金調達にかかった費用で, 借入金の金利や株主への配当などが含まれる）

cost allocation 原価配分, 原価配賦(はいふ), 費用配分 （＝cost assignment, cost distribution）

cost basis 原価基準, 原価主義, 取得原価基準

cost-benefit analysis 費用便益分析, 費用対

効果分析 (=benefit-cost analysis, cost and benefit analysis)
cost center 原価中心点, 原価部門, コスト・センター
cost control 原価統制, 原価管理, コスト管理, コスト削減, コスト・コントロール
cost depletion 取得原価に基づく減耗償却, 減耗償却費
cost depreciation 減価償却
cost-efficient 費用効率がよい, 費用効率が高い, コスト効率がよい (=cost-effective)
cost method 原価法, 原価基準, 原価主義 (=cost basis, cost convention, valuation at cost)
cost of debt 借入コスト, 借入資本の調達費用
cost or market, which is lower 低価主義, 低価法 (=lower of cost or market (basis[method], cost or market principle)
cost of sales 売上原価 (=cost of goods sold)
cut operating costs 営業費用を削減する, 営業コスト削減する
cost saving 原価節約, 原価節減, 経費節減, コスト削減, コストの節約
cost-volume-profit analysis 原価・営業量[売上高]・利益関係, 原価・操業度・利益分析, CVP分析 (原価・販売量・利益の関係を分析するCVP分析)
current cost 現在原価, 時価, 現在取替原価, 再調達原価, 当期原価, 当期費用, カレント・コスト 《略 CC》
lower cost of funds 資金調達コストの軽減
managing cost 経営コスト
reduce overhead costs 経費を削減する, 経費を軽減する, 経費を切り詰める
unit labor cost 単位労働コスト

▶A lower *cost* of funds due to lower interest rates also contributed to the improved margin percentage. 金利の低下で資金コストが下がったことも, 利益率の改善に貢献しました。

▶*Costs* related to the conceptual formulation and design of licensed programs are expensed as research and development. ライセンス・プログラムの概念形成と設計に要した原価は, 研究開発費として費用処理されています。

cost calculation 原価計算

▶Pension *cost calculations* were based on a value of assets adjusted to market over periods ranging from 3 to 5 years. 年金原価の計算は, 過去3-5年間の時価に修正した資産価額に基づいています。

cost-competitive 価格競争力がある, 価格競争力が高い, コスト競争力がある

▶Countries, including China, are supplying *cost-competitive* merchandise. 中国などは, 価格競争力の高い製品を供給している。

cost cut 経費削減, 費用削減, コスト削減 (=cost cutting)

▶Continued *cost cuts* and sales promotion efforts offset a ¥70 billion loss generated by the yen's appreciation against the dollar. 引き続き行ったコスト削減と営業努力で, 円高ドル安で生じた700億円の為替差損は相殺された。

▶The firm eyes additional ¥72.6 billion *cost cut* in two years. 同社は, 2年で726億円の追加コスト削減を見込んでいる。

cost cutting 経費削減, 費用削減, コスト削減 (=cost reduction)

cost cutting measures 経費削減策, 経費削減措置
cost cutting competition コスト削減競争

▶Most of the domestic electronics manufacturers have faced increasingly tight *cost cutting* competition. 国内電機メーカーの大半は, 厳しいコスト削減競争にさらされている。

cost effective 費用効果が高い, 費用効率がよい, コスト効率がよい (=cost efficient)

▶To us, our approach of partnering with national carriers and upgrading existing networks is the most *cost-effective* way. 当社にとって, 世界各国の通信事業者と提携して既存のネットワークの向上を図るという当社のアプローチの仕方が, 最も費用効果の高い手段です。

cost effectiveness 費用効果, 費用効率, コスト効率 (=cost efficiency)

▶It is difficult, in terms of *cost effectiveness*, to have fiber optic networks spread to every corner of the nation. 光ファイバー網を全国にくまなく張り巡らすのは, コスト効率の面で難しい。

cost efficiency コスト効率 (=cost effectiveness)

▶Japan Highway Public Corporation has treated its crony families preferentially and has provided benefits only to them regardless of *cost efficiency*. 日本道路公団は, ファミリー企業を優先的に扱い, コスト効率を無視してファミリー企業にだけ利益を与えてきた。

cost of goods sold 売上原価 (=cost of sales: 卸売り・小売業の場合は販売した商品に対応する原価, 製造業の場合は販売した製品の製造原価)

▶The company's operating loss, or sales minus

the *cost* of goods sold and administrative expenses, totaled ¥31.9 billion in the first quarter. 第1四半期（決算）は，売上高から売上原価と一般管理費を差し引いた同社の営業赤字が，総額で319億ドルだった．

cost-plus 形 コストプラス方式の，原価に一定割合の利益を上乗せする方式の

cost reduction コスト削減，経費削減，費用削減，原価削減[低減]，原価引下げ，原価控除（＝cost cutting）
▶The increase in gross profit was mainly due to the success of *cost-reduction* and improved productivity programs. 売上総利益の増加の主な要因は，コスト削減計画と生産性向上計画の成功です．

counselor [counselor] 名 相談員，助言者，相談役，顧問，法律顧問，弁護士，顧問弁護士，指導教官，〈大使館[公使館]の〉参事官，カウンセラー
　counselor-at-law 弁護士
　guidance counselor 進路指導などの相談員
　industrial counselor 産業カウンセラー
　investment counselor 投資カウンセラー
　juridical counselor 法律顧問
▶Industrial *counselors* deal with the psychological welfare of employees at companies and other organizations. 産業カウンセラーは，企業などの組織で，社員の心のケアに携わっている．

countercyclical 形 景気対策の
counterfeit 形 偽造の，模造の
counterfeit brand product 偽ブランド品
▶The exports of *counterfeit* brand products and industrial products that infringe on patents have been banned since January 2007. 偽ブランド品や特許侵害の工業製品の輸出は，2007年1月から禁止されている．

counterpart 名 取引相手，同じ立場[地位]にある人，同等物，同業者，片方，副本，正副2通のうちの1通（⇒**corporate takeover**）
▶In terms of profitability, Japanese companies have been lagging far behind their U.S. and Western European *counterparts*. 収益力の点では，日本企業は欧米企業に大きく水をあけられている．
▶The Corporation is exposed to credit-related losses if *counterparties* to financial instruments fail to perform their obligations. 金融手段の取引相手がその債務履行を怠った場合，当社は信用関連の損失を被ります．
▶We must execute this agreement in two *counterparts*. 本契約書は，副本を2部作成しなければならない．
▶When you meet a business *counterpart*, you can give off a great impression when you are well groomed, and it may even lead to increased credibility. 仕事で誰かに会う場合，きれいにしていたほうが好感度は高いし，信頼度も高まる．

counterparty 名 相手方当事者，当事者，取引相手，取引相手方，カウンターパーティー
▶The process of termination requires the agreement of both *counterparties*. 解約手続きをするには，両当事者の合意が必要である．
▶We do not expect any *counterparties*, which presently have high credit ratings, to fail to meet their obligations. 現在のところ，信用格付けが高い取引相手が債務を履行しないとは，当社は考えていません．

countervailing duty 相殺関税（外国政府の輸出補助金や奨励金を受けた製品が，不当に低い価格で輸入された場合に，国内産業保護のための報復措置としてかける関税）
▶In response to the petition, the government is expected to impose a *countervailing duty* on Hynix's DRAMs. 申請に応じて，政府は，ハイニックスのDRAM（記憶保持動作が必要な随時書込み読出しメモリ）に相殺関税をかける見通しだ．

country of origin 原産地，原産国
▶Generally speaking, every imported article must be marked in a conspicuous place as legibly, indelibly and permanently as the nature of the article will permit so as to indicate to an ultimate purchaser in the United States the English name of the *country of origin* of such article. 一般に，輸入品にはすべて輸入品の性質に応じてできるだけ永続的に消えない形で，また識別できる形で目立つ箇所にマークをつけて，当該輸入品の原産地の英語名を米国の最終購入者に示さなければならない．

coupling 名 連結，結合，連動化，連動すること，関連付けること，継ぎ手，連結器，カップリング

coupon 名 〈債券の〉利息，表面利率，利率，利札，商品券，景品引換え券，クーポン
　coupon bearing securities 利付き債
　coupon bond 利付き債，固定利付き債，クーポン付き社債，クーポン債
　coupon interest クーポン金利
　coupon rate 表面利率
　cum coupon 利付き，利札付き（＝coupon on）
　deferred coupon bond 金利繰延べ債
　discount coupon 割引券

ex coupon 利落ち, 利札落ち (＝coupon off)
exchange coupon 商品券 (＝coupon for goods)
high coupon 高利回り, 表面利率が高い, 高クーポン
issue bonds with a coupon of 3.25 percent 利率3.25%の社債を発行する
offer a coupon premium クーポン・プレミアムを付ける
reprice the coupon 表面利率の再設定をする
short coupons 短期債
zero coupon bond ゼロ・クーポン債

▶At December 31, 2007, the fair value of the convertible zero *coupon* notes due 2012 was $135 million compared to the carrying value of $55 million. 2007年12月31日現在, 2012年満期の転換ゼロ・クーポン債の公正価格は, 1億3,500万ドルで, その帳簿価格は5,500万ドルでした。

courier 名 急使, 特使, 密輸商

court protection from creditors 資産保全

▶An increasing number of publishers have sought *court protection from creditors* under the Civil Rehabilitation Law in the past few years. ここ2, 3年, 民事再生法に基づく資産保全[民事再生法の適用]を申請する企業が増えている。

covenant 名 捺印契約, 捺印証書, 契約, 協約, 約款, 約定, 誓約, 約束
additional covenants 付帯条件
covenant maker 協約締結者
covenant of title 権限担保約款
covenants and warranty 誓約と保証
covenants not to compete 競業禁止特約
debt covenant 債務担保条項
dividend covenant 配当制限条項
negative covenants 消極的約定条項
violation of covenant 契約違反

▶In the event that the Licensee shall breach any of the *covenants* contained in this Agreement, the Licensor shall have the right to terminate this Agreement. ライセンシーが本契約に定める約束に違反した場合, ライセンサーは本契約を解除する権利を持つものとする。

cover 動 保険をかける[付ける], 〈費用や金額などを〉賄う, 損失の穴埋めをする, 〈損失などを〉補塡する, …を抵当とする, …を担保に入れる, 〈問題などを〉取り扱う, …を対象とする, 含む, 表示する, 報道する, 取材する, カバーする (⇒consultant)

▶We expect operating cash flows to continue *covering* capital expenditures and dividends in 2008. 当社は, 営業活動によるキャッシュ・フローで2008年度も資本的支出と配当をカバーできるものと思います。

▶We sponsor noncontributory defined benefit plans *covering* the majority of our employees. 当社は, 従業員の大多数を対象とする非拠出型確定給付年金制度を設けています。

cover up 隠蔽する, 隠匿する, 隠す, もみ消す

▶The company said it had never *covered* up auto part defects. 同社では, 自動車部品の欠陥隠しはないとしていた。

cover-up 名 もみ消し, もみ消し工作, 隠蔽, 隠蔽工作, 隠し立て, …隠し
bad debt cover-up operations 不良債権の隠蔽工作
beef labeling cover-up 牛肉偽装工作隠し
loss cover-up 損失隠し
recall cover-up リコール情報隠し, リコール隠し

▶The company's large-scale *cover-up* of defects surfaced in 2006. 同社の大規模な欠陥隠しは, 2006年に発覚した。

coverage 名 保険の担保, 担保範囲, 付保範囲, 適用範囲, 範囲, 負担能力, カバレッジ
benefit coverage 給付内容
debt coverage 返済余力
earning coverage 収益カバレッジ
extended coverage 拡張担保
fixed charge coverage 金融費用カバレッジ, 固定費カバレッジ
life insurance coverage 保険金額, 保険契約金額, 生命保険給付
loan loss coverage 債券損失カバレッジ
insurance coverage 保険担保, 保険の付保, 保険の担保範囲

▶Major nonlife insurers have introduced terrorism *coverage* exemption clauses for new contracts and contract renewals. 大手損保は, 新規契約と契約の更改分について「テロ免責条項」を導入した。

▶Our postretirement benefits include health care benefits and life insurance *coverage*. 当社の退職後給付には, 医療給付と生命保険給付が含まれています。

CPFR 需要予測と在庫補充のための共同事業 (collaborative planning, forecasting and reple-nishmentの略)

CPA 公認会計士 (certified public accountantの略)

CPI 消費者物価指数 (consumer price index

の略)

CPI-U (米国の)全都市消費者物価指数 (**Consumer Price Index for All Urban Consumers**の略)

CPI-W (米国の)都市賃金労働者消費者物価指数 (**Consumer price Index for Urban Wage Earners and Clerical Workers**の略)
▶Including perishables, the nationwide *CPI* shrank 0.2 percent to 98.1, down for the fifth year. 全国の消費者物価指数(生鮮食品を含む)は98.1と前年度に比べて0.2%縮小し,5年連続の下落となった。

cr creditの略
craftsman 名 職人, 熟練工, 名工, 名匠
▶With the advent of the machine age, many jobs shifted from *craftsmen* to machines. 機械化の時代になって,仕事の多くは職人から機械にに移った。

cramdown 形 強制的な
create 動 創造する, 創出する, 創作する, 作り出す, 開発する, 生み出す, 引き起こす, 発生させる,〈会社などを〉設立する, 新設する, 設ける,〈担保権などを〉設定する, 構築する, 伸ばす, 高める (⇒**climate**)
　create a market 市場を開拓する
　create a portfolio of securities 証券ポートフォリオを構築する
　create a security interest 担保権を設定する
　create an idea アイデアを生み出す
　create deals 案件を組成する
　create jobs 雇用を創出する, 職場[仕事]を作る
　create sales 売上を伸ばす
　create value for shareholders 株主の価値を創出する, 株主の価値を高める, 株主の利益を高める, 株主に対する資産価値を創出する
　create value in diverse markets 広範な市場で収益を生み出す
▶We want to *create* Japan's first media group that will pass as a global player. われわれとしては、グローバル企業として通用する日本初のメディア・グループを設立したい。
▶The restructuring will allow us to continue to *create* value for our shareholders. この事業再編によって,当社は,当社の株主価値を今後とも高めることができます。

creativity 名 創造性, 創作性, 独創性, 創造力, 独創力, 制作, クリエイティビティ (⇒**culture**)
▶Through enhancing the skills of our people and our portfolio of technologies, we draw on the *creativity* and wealth of experience of our people in all cultures. 社員の技能と当社の各種製品技術を高めることによって,当社は多様な文化背景をもつ社員の創造性と豊かな経験を引き出しています。

credit 動 貸方に記入する, 計上する, 差し引く, 控除する
　credit A against B AをBから差し引く, AをBに充当する, AとBを相殺する
　credit to …に計上する, …に貸記する, …に入金する, …に充当する
▶Any unpaid balance will be *credited* to outstanding receivables between the two companies. 一切の未払い残高は,両社間の未収売掛金扱いとします。
▶Under the offset provisions, depositors at a failed bank can have their deposits *credited* against outstanding loans, including mortgages. 相殺規定によると,破綻した銀行の預金者は,預金と住宅ローンなどの借入金残高を相殺してもらえる。

credit 名 信用, 与信, 債権, 貸方, 貸金, 融資, 預金, 利息, 信用状, 支払い猶予期間, 税額控除, 金融, クレジット (⇒**revolving credit**)
　bank credit 銀行信用, 銀行信用状, 銀行貸出, 銀行融資, 銀行借入れ (=bank lending, bank loan, banker's credit)
　banker's credit 銀行信用状 (=bank credit, banker's letter of credit)
　credit agency 信用格付け機関, 信用調査機関, 格付け会社 (=credit rating agency, rating agency)
　credit approval 信用供与承認, 与信承認 (⇒**delinquent balances**)
　credit criteria 与信基準
　credit crunch 貸し渋り, 信用危機, 信用不安, 信用逼迫, 金融逼迫, 金融危機, クレジット・クランチ (=credit crisis)
　credit demand 資金需要
　credit department 債権管理部門, 債権管理部, 信用調査部
　credit easing measures 金融緩和政策, 金融緩和措置 (=credit easing steps)
　credit fear 信用不安 (⇒**fear**)
　credit insecurity 信用不安
　credit limit 信用限度, 与信限度, 信用貸出限度, 貸出限度額, 信用供与限度額 (⇒**credit risk**)
　credit period 与信期間, 支払い期限
　credit profile 信用力, 信用情報
　credit standing 信用状態, 信用度, 信用力 (=credit strength, creditworthiness)

credit strength 信用力, 信用度, 信用の質
credit validation クレジット・カードの確認
debit and credit 借方・貸方
direct credit 直接控除
documentary credit 荷為替信用状
extend credit 信用を供与する
outstanding credits 融資残高
raise credit 資金を調達する
relaxation of credit 金融緩和
reserve for credit losses 貸倒引当金
revolving credit 回転信用, 回転信用状, 回転クレジット, リボルビング・クレジット (⇒**credit facilities**)
revolving credit agreement 自動更新借入契約
tightening in the credit policy 金融引締め
trade credit 企業間信用, 企業信用, 輸出・輸入延払い
uncommitted line of credit 未使用信用枠

▶A large amount of *credit* cannot be removed from the balance sheets of banks even though loan-loss reserves have been set aside.　貸倒引当金を積んでも, 多くの債権は銀行のバランス・シートから切り離せない状況にある[銀行で最終処理できない債権が多い]。

▶Should *credit* not be tightened enough, inflation may accelerate.　金融引締めが不十分だと, インフレが加速しかねない。

▶The firm's debt has been issued using its own *credit*.　同社の負債[債券]は, 同社の信用で調達しています。

credit card　クレジット・カード
credit card authorization クレジット・カードの認証
credit card business クレジット・カード事業
credit card company クレジット・カード会社, 信販
credit card fraud クレジット・カードの不正使用, カード不正
credit card holder クレジット・カード会員
credit card information クレジット・カード情報
credit card misuse クレジット・カードの悪用・不正使用
credit card number クレジット・カード番号
retailer's credit card 流通系カード

▶We also offer a general-purpose *credit card* and financial and leasing services.　当社は, 汎用のクレジット・カードや金融サービス, リース・サービスも提供しています。

credit card transaction　クレジット・カードの取引

▶The growth in costs of financial services and leasing over the last two years came from the higher volume of financing and *credit card transactions*.　過去2年間の金融サービスとリース部門のコスト増の要因は, 資金調達とクレジット・カード取引量の増加です。

credit cost　与信費用, 債権処理費用, 不良債権処理額 (＝loan loss charge)

▶Increases in interest payments on deposits outweighed *credit cost* falls.　預金の利払い増加のほうが, 与信費用の低下より大きかった。

credit facilities　信用枠, 信用供与枠, 与信枠, 融資枠

▶These revolving *credit facilities* are intended for general corporate purposes.　これらの回転融資枠は, 一般の事業目的に使用する予定です。

credit guarantee　信用保証, 信用保証制度

▶Some borrowers have taken advantage of lax screening of *credit guarantee* corporations.　信用保証協会の手薄な審査に便乗している借り手もいる。

credit line　貸出限度(額)貸付け限度(額), 与信限度(額), 信用限度, 信用保証枠, 信用供与限度, 信用供与枠, 融資枠, 融資限度額, 利用限度額, クレジット・ライン (＝ credit limit, line of credit)

▶At December 31 2008, the corporation and certain subsidiaries companies had unused *credit lines*, generally available at the prime bank rate of interest, of approximately $400.　2008年12月31日現在, 当社と一部の子会社が一般にプライム・レートで利用できる銀行与信枠未使用残高は, 約4億ドルとなっています。

credit loss　貸倒れ, 貸倒れ額, 貸倒れ予想額

▶This accounting standard requires us to compute present values for impaired loans when determining our allowances for *credit losses*.　この会計基準は, 貸倒れ引当金を決定するにあたって, 不良債権の現在価値を計算するよう要求しています。

credit rating　信用格付け, 企業の信用等級, 格付け評価, 格付け (＝rating)

格付けとは➡民間の格付け機関[格付け会社]が, 債券を発行する企業や国, 公社などの財務を分析して債務返済能力を判定し, トリプルA (AAA)やB, Cなどとランク付けする仕組み。投資家はこのランク付けに基づいて投資判断をすることができるのに対して, 企業にとっては高い格付けが得られれば低利で債券を発行できるといった利点がある。

bank letter-of-credit ratings 銀行信用状の格

付け
- **long-term credit ratings** 長期格付け
- **credit rating agency** 格付け機関, 信用格付け機関, 格付け会社, 信用調査機関 (=credit agency, rating agency)
- **credit rating service** 信用格付けサービス
▶Declines in *credit ratings* will prevent businesses from acquiring capital from the market or financial institutions. 信用格付けが低下すると、企業は市場や金融機関から資金を引き出せなくなる。

credit risk 信用リスク
▶We control our exposure to *credit risk* through credit approvals, credit limits and monitoring procedures. 当社は、信用供与承認や信用限度、監視手続きを通じて信用リスクを管理しています。

creditor 图 債権者, 債権国, 債権保有者, 資金供与者, 取引銀行, 取引金融機関, 貸主, 貸方, 仕入先, クレディター (⇒civil)
▶*Creditors* of Yamaichi Securities Co. held their last meeting to complete bankruptcy procedures for the major brokerage house, which collapsed in 1997. 山一証券の債権者が最後の集会を開いて、1997年に破綻したこの大手証券会社の破産手続きを完了した。

creditor bank 債権保有銀行, 融資銀行, 取引銀行, 信用供与銀行, クレディター・バンク
▶The firm's *creditor banks* agreed on the bailout plan. 同社の取引銀行は、金融支援策で合意した。
▶The three major *creditor banks* plan to retire preferred shares totaling ¥120 billion that they purchased last year. 債権を保有する主力取引銀行3行は、昨年取得した総額1,200億円の優先株式を消却する方針だ。

creditworthiness 图 信用力, 信用度, 信用の質 (⇒asset-backed commercial paper)

creditworthy [**credit-worthy**] 形 信用度[信用力]の高い, 信用力がある, 優良な
- **creditworthy borrower** 優良な貸出先, 信用力の高い借り手[借入人], 信用貸しする価値のある借り手
- **less-creditworthy** 信用度の低い
▶The long-term prime rate is charged on loans of one year or longer to to the bank's most *creditworthy* corporate clients. 長期プライム・レートは、最も信用力がある銀行の顧客企業に対する1年超の貸付け金に適用される。

crisis 图 危機, 経営危機, 重大局面, 暴落, 恐慌, 不安, 不足, 問題, リスク (⇒currency crisis)
- **bank crisis** 銀行恐慌 (取付け騒ぎで銀行閉鎖を迫られる事態のこと)
- **cash flow crisis** 資金繰りが苦しくなること, 資金繰りがつかないこと
- **credit crisis** 金融恐慌, 信用恐慌, 信用危機 (=credit crunch)
- **crisis center** 災害対策本部
- **crisis management** 危機管理
- **crisis-stricken** 経営危機に陥っている
- **debt crisis** 債務危機, 累積債務危機
- **economic crisis** 経済危機
- **energy crisis** エネルギー危機
- **financial crisis** 金融危機, 金融恐慌
- **liquidity crisis** 流動性危機, 資金繰りの悪化 (=crisis of liquidity)
- **monetary crisis** 通貨危機, 金融危機, 貨幣恐慌
- **oil crisis** 石油危機, 石油ショック
- **power supply crisis** 電力不足
- **sense of crisis** 危機意識
- **stock crisis** 株価暴落
- **stock market crisis** 株式市場の暴落, 株式市場の混乱
- **subprime mortgage crisis** サブプライム・ローン(米低所得者向け住宅融資)問題
- **thrift crisis** 貯蓄金融業界の危機
▶A U.S. financial *crisis* would undoubtedly trigger a global crisis. 米国の金融危機は、間違いなく地球規模の(同時)危機を誘発するものと思われる。
▶The world financial market has been hurt by the subprime mortgage *crisis* in the United States. 世界の金融市場は、サブプライム・ローン(低所得者向け住宅融資)問題で傷(いた)んでいる。

criterion 图 基準, 標準, 尺度
▶At the firm, curbing repayment amounts is regarded as a *criterion* for in-house personnel evaluation. 同社では、返還額を抑えることが、社内の人事評価基準と見なされている。

critical mass 最低限の経済規模, 採算の取れる規模, 望ましい成果を十分得るための確固たる基盤, 限界質量, 臨界質量, 限界量, 臨界量, 臨界, クリティカル・マス
▶This strategic alliance is a major step toward building *critical* mass that will benefit both companies in the highly competitive and rapidly growing global telecommunications markets. この戦略的提携は、クリティカル・マス(望ましい成果を十分得るための確固たる基盤)を構築するための大きなステップで、競争が激しく急成長を見せるグローバル通信市場での両社の事業展開に有利に働くものと思われます。

CRM 顧客関係維持, 顧客関係管理, カスタマー・リレーションシップ・マネジメント (**customer relationship management**の略)

cross licensing [license] agreement クロス・ライセンス契約, 特許相互利用契約, 交互実施許諾契約 (=cross licensing contract)
▸*Cross licensing agreements* are expected to help forestall patent disputes that could delay the development of new products. クロス・ライセンス契約には, 新製品の開発を遅らせる可能性がある特許紛争を未然に防ぐ効果がある。

cross licensing contract クロス・ライセンス契約 (⇒**cross licensing agreement**)
▸Toshiba Corp. and U.S. software giant Microsoft Corp. have signed a comprehensive *cross licensing contract* for mutual use of patents. 東芝と米ソフトウエア最大手のマイクロソフトが, 特許を相互に利用する包括的クロス・ライセンス契約を結んだ。

cross-sectoral tie-up 業態を超えての統合, 業態超え統合

cross selling クロス・セリング (顧客が商品やサービスを購入したとき, 関連商品やサービスの購入を同時に勧めること)

crossheld shares 持ち合い株, 持ち合い株式 (=cross-held shares, crossheld stocks)

crosshold [cross-hold] shares 株式を持ち合う
▸The Corporation *crossholds shares* with other two steel companies. 当社は, 他の鉄鋼2社と株式を持ち合っています。

crossholding [cross-holding] 株式持ち合い (=cross-holding shares, cross shareholding, crossholding of shares)
▸*Crossholding* is a practice in which financial institutions and their client companies own a large amount of stock in each other. 株式持ち合いは, 金融機関とその取引先企業が相互に大量の株式を保有する慣行である。

crown jewels クラウン・ジュエル(王冠の宝石) (買収される会社の特に魅力のある重要資産)

crown jewels defense クラウン・ジュエル防衛, 有望資産売却戦略, 重要資産売却作戦

crude 形 天然の, 天然のままの, 精製[加工]していない, 処理されていない, 補正されていない, 粗末な, 粗雑な, 粗い, 大雑把な, 洗練されていない, 未熟な, みだらな, 名 原油

crude oil 原油 (=crude petroleum)
▸In response to *crude oil* price hikes, Mitsubishi Chemical Corp. will raise the prices of polyethylene and polypropylene by 20-30 percent. 原油高を受けて, 三菱化学がポリエチレンとポリプロピレンを20-30%値上げする。

crude oil futures 原油先物
▸*Crude oil futures* soared in New York due to concerns over oil supplies. ニューヨーク(ニューヨーク・マーカンタイル取引所)の原油先物が, 原油供給不安[原油供給への懸念]から急騰した。

crude oil prices 原油価格
▸Due to soaring *crude oil prices*, oil distributors have a hard time trying to pass the rise in costs on to gasoline stations. 原油価格の高騰で, 石油元売り各社は, ガソリン・スタンド側へのコスト上昇分の転嫁も進んでいない。

crunch 名 危機, 危機的状況, 急場, 土壇場, 経済危機, 経済上の引締め, 財政難, クランチ (⇒**capital base**)
 credit crunch 貸し渋り, 信用危機, 信用逼迫, 信用不安, 信用規制, 信用収縮, 金融危機, 金融逼迫, 金融ピンチ, クレジット・クランチ
 energy crunch エネルギー危機
 gas crunch ガソリン危機
 liquidity crunch 流動性逼迫, 信用逼迫
 oil crunch 石油危機, 石油逼迫
▸The U.S. subprime mortgage *crunch* is becoming more and more serious. 米国のサブプライム・ローン(米低所得者向け住宅融資)問題が, 深刻化している。

CS 顧客満足, 顧客の満足, 顧客の満足度 (**customer satisfaction**の略)

CSR 企業の社会的責任 (⇒**corporate social responsibility**)

CTO 最高技術責任者 (**chief technology officer**の略)

CTO 受注仕様生産 (**configure to order**の略。受注生産方式の一種。メーカーの販売代理店が注文を受け, 自らメーカー・ブランドの製品を組み立てて販売する方式)

cultural product 文化商品
▸Japanese *cultural products* include manga, anime, video games, TV dramas, pop music, fashion magazines and adult movies. 日本の文化商品には, マンガ, アニメ, テレビ・ゲーム, テレビ・ドラマ, ポップス, ファッション雑誌, アダルト映画などが含まれる。

culture 名 文化, 風土, 体質, 耕作, 培養, 養殖, カルチャー (⇒**corporate culture**)
 enterprise culture 企業文化, 企業社会, 起業文化, 起業社会, 起業精神
 fish culture 養殖漁業 (=fish farming)

management culture 経営体質, 経営文化
risk-tolerance culture リスク許容度
▸Our *culture* embraces creativity, seeks different perspectives and risks pursuing new opportunities. 創造性を積極的に受け入れ, さまざまな物の見方を求めて, 新たな事業機会の追求に果敢に挑戦するのが, 当社の企業文化です。

cum 前 …付きの, …付きで, …兼, 直結した (=along with, together with, with)
  cum all 諸権利付き, 全利得付き
  cum bonus 特別配当権付き
  cum call 〈株式の〉払込み付き
  cum coupon 利札付き, 金利付き
  cum distribution 次期所得配当付き
  cum dividend 配当付き, 配当付きで (配当落ち =ex dividend)
  cum interest 利付き
  cum new 新株付き, 子株付き, 権利付き (cum rights)
  cum rights 権利付き, 新株引受権付き
  cum warrants ワラント付き, カム・ワラント
  dwelling-cum-workshop 住宅兼工場, 工場兼住宅, 工場直結の住宅
  garage-cum-workshop 仕事場兼ガレージ[車庫], 仕事場付きガレージ, ガレージ兼仕事場
  souvenir shop-cum-restaurant 食堂兼レストラン, レストラン兼食堂
  study-cum-drawing room 書斎兼応接間, 応接間兼書斎

cumulative dividend 累積配当, 累加配当, 積置き配当
▸The first preferred shareholders are entitled to *cumulative* annual *dividends* per share in the amount set out in the titles of each series. 第一優先株式の株主には, シリーズごとに規定された[各シリーズの証券に記載された]レートで1株当り年間累積配当を受ける権利が与えられています。

curb 動 抑える, 制御する, 抑制する, 制限する, 食い止める, 防止する, 束縛する, 拘束する (=kerb)
  curb credit demand 信用需要を抑える
  curb inflation インフレを抑制する
  curb the imports of foreign cars 外車の輸入を食い止める

currency 名 通貨, 為替, 為替相場, 流通, 流行, カレンシー (⇒carry trade)
  currency authorities 通貨当局 (=monetary authorities; ⇒coordination)
  currency changes 為替相場の変動, 為替変動 (=currency exchange fluctuation, currency fluctuation, currency movements, currency swings, exchange fluctuation)
  currency movements 為替相場の動き, 為替相場の変動, 為替変動 (=currency changes, exchange fluctuation)
  currency policy 通貨政策, 為替政策
  currency translation 通貨換算, 外貨換算
  currency translation adjustments 為替換算調整, 外貨換算調整, 為替換算調整勘定, 外貨換算調整勘定
  foreign currency loan 外貨建て借入金
  hard currency 交換可能通貨, ハード・カレンシー (=hard money: 米ドルや金と交換できる通貨)
  home currency 自国通貨
  key currency 基軸通貨, 国際通貨, キー・カレンシー (=key money)
  local currency 現地通貨(建て), 国内通貨(建て), 自国通貨(建て), ローカル・カレンシー
  major currencies 主要通貨
  soft currency 交換不能通貨, 軟貨, ソフト通貨, ソフト・カレンシー (米ドルやその他の主要通貨と直接交換できない通貨)
  strong dollar against other currencies ドル全面高
▸Non-U.S. subsidiaries operate in a local *currency* environment. 米国外の子会社は, 現地通貨を用いる経済環境で事業を展開しています。
▸The Japanese *currency* is about ¥5 lower than its initial projection of ¥110 to the dollar. 円は, 当初想定した1ドル=110円より5円程度安く推移している。

currency crisis 通貨危機
▸To prevent another *currency crisis*, the G-7 statement spelled out various measures to reform the international financial systems. 通貨危機の再発を防ぐため, 主要7か国の声明は, 国際金融システム改革の施策をいくつか明確にした。

currency exchange rate 為替相場, 為替レート, 通貨交換レート (=exchange rate)
▸We enter into foreign currency exchange contracts, including forward, options and swap contracts, to manage our exposure to changes in *currency exchange rates*. 当社は, 為替相場の変動によるリスクを管理するため, 先物予約, オプションやスワップなどの契約を含めて, 外国為替予約を締結しています。

currency market 為替市場, 外国為替市場, 通貨市場 (=foreign exchange market)
▸Joint intervention by Japan and European countries in the *currency markets* is possible as

the dollar rapidly weakens.　ドル安が急速に進んでいることから，為替市場への日欧協調介入もあり得る．

current 形　現在の，当座の，当期の，短期の，臨時の，経常的，流動的，名　流動，流動性，1年以内返済予定額，当期分
　current balance　当座残高
　current bank loan　短期借入金
　current deposit　当座預金　（＝checking account, current account, current account deposit）
　current fair value　現在公正価格［価額］，現在公正価値
　current loan receivable　短期貸付け金
　current maturities of long-term debt　1年以内返済長期借入金
　current maturity　残存期間，当期支払い額
　current net income　当期純利益　（＝current earnings, current income）
　current operating basis [concept]　当期業績主義
　current operating income　当期営業利益，当期操業利益
　current operating performance theory [basis, concept]　当期業績主義
　current operating profit　当期営業利益，当期操業利益
　current proceeds　当期収入，当期収益，当期売上高，現在現金受領額
　current rate　決算日レート，カレント・レート（＝closing rate）
　current revenue　当期収益，収入，歳入
　current term net loss　当期純損失
　current term settlement　当期決算
　deferred tax asset/current　繰延べ税金資産・短期
　deferred tax liabilities/current　繰延べ税金負債・短期

current account　経常収支，経常勘定，当座預金　（「経常収支」は，モノやサービスの出入りのバランスを示す国際収支のことで，貿易収支（trade balance）とサービス収支（services balance）などから成る）
　current account and trade surpluses　貿易黒字と経常黒字
　current account balance　経常収支　（＝current balance）
　current account deposit　当座預金　（＝current deposit）
▶In general, a *current account* surplus is accompanied by capital and financial account deficits.　一般に，経常収支が黒字だと，資本収支は赤字になる．

current account deficit　経常赤字，経常収支の赤字，経常収支の赤字額
▶The *current account deficit* posted a record quarterly deficit in the January-March quarter.　経常赤字は，1－3月期は四半期ベースで過去最高を記録した．

current account profit　経常利益
▶The Corporation's consolidated *current account profits* stood at ¥80 billion for the current year.　当社の連結経常利益は，今期は800億円でした．

current account surplus　経常黒字，経常収支の黒字，経常収支の黒字額
▶The nation's *current account surplus* increased 26 percent from the previous year to a fraction more than ¥25 trillion.　（モノやサービスの取引を示す）経常収支の黒字は，前年より26％増えて25兆円をいくぶん上回った．
▶We recorded a *current account surplus* of about ¥2 billion in the fiscal period ending December 2008.　当社は，2008年12月期決算で，約20億円の経常黒字を計上しました．

current assets　流動資産　（＝floating assets, near-cash assets, liquid assets：比較的流動性が高く，1年以内に現金化される可能性がある資産）
▶*Current assets* refer to those assets that are relatively liquid and are likely to be turned into cash within the next year.　流動資産は，比較的流動性が高く，次年度以内に現金化される可能性がある資産のことをいう．

current business year　今年度，今期，当年度，当事業年度　（＝current fiscal year, current year）
▶For the *current business year*, the Company anticipates rises in consolidated sales and operating profit, but a fall in group net profit.　今期は，当社の連結売上高と営業利益は増加するが，連結税引き後利益［連結純利益］は減少する見込みです．

current deposit　当座預金　（＝checking account, current account）
▶The existing *current deposit* is mainly used by corporate depositors who withdraw money in the form of drafts or checks.　これまでの当座預金は，主に手形や小切手の形で預金を引き出す法人顧客が利用している．

current fiscal year　今年度，今期，当会計年度，当事業年度，当年度　（＝current business year,

current year)
▶Net profit per share fell as a result of a 2-for-1 stock split carried out at the beginning of the *current fiscal year*. 1株当たり純利益は，今年度の初めに実施した1対2の比率による株式分割のため，減少しました。

current income 当期利益(current earnings, current net income)，経常収益，経常収入，インカム・ゲイン
▶The costs of these benefits are paid out of *current income*, as benefits are received. これらの給付費用は，実際の給付時にその期間の経費として処理されています[実際の給付時に当期利益から支払われています].

current liabilities 流動負債，短期負債 （1年以内に返済期限が到来する債務）
▶Other *current liabilities* declined because some restructuring reserves were reclassified to postemployment liabilities. その他の流動負債は，事業再編成引当金の一部が雇用後債務に振り替えられたため，減少しました。

current net earnings 当期純利益 （＝current net income)
▶There is no change in the *current* or previously reported *net earnings*. 当期純利益と過年度に計上した純利益に，変動はありません。

current profit 経常利益 （＝current account profit, pretax profit, recurring profit)
▶Listed companies saw double-digit growth in their sales and *current profits* from a year earlier. 上場企業の売上高と経常利益は，前年比[前年同期比]で二ケタ増加した。

current ratio 流動比率
▶*Current ratio* shows the relationship between current assets and current liabilities. 流動比率は，流動資産と流動負債との関係を示します。

current results 当期業績
▶Many investors set aside the cumulative effects of changes in accounting when looking at *current results*. 当期業績を見る場合，多くの投資家は，会計処理の変更による累積的影響を除外して考えます。

current service cost 現在勤務費用，当期の勤務費用
▶*Current service costs* of retirement plans are accrued currently. 退職金制度の当期勤務費用は，当期に処理されています。

current value accounting standard 時価主義会計基準
▶The Financial Services Agency's Business Accounting Council adopted a U.S.-style *current value accounting standard* for corporate mergers to increase transparency of accounting rules. 金融庁の企業会計審議会は，会計規則の透明性を高めるため，会社合併については米国式の時価主義会計基準を採用した。

current year 今年度，今期，当年度，当期 （＝current fiscal year)
▶Both *current* and prior *year* results conform with Statement of Financial Accounting Standards Number 94, "Consolidation of All Majority-Owned Subsidiaries." 当年度と過年度の業績は，いずれも財務会計基準書第94号の「すべての過半数株式所有子会社の連結」に適合しています。

current yield 直接利回り，直利 （債券の償還時に発生する額面と購入価格との差益・差損を考慮しないで，1年間の利息を購入価格で割り，100を掛けて算出。債券の購入価格に対する年間利息の割合を示す）

curtail 動 〈費用などを〉削減する，切り詰める
curtailment 名 短縮，縮小，削減，切り詰め，節減
　curtailment in [of] nuclear armament 核兵器の削減
　curtailment of expenditure 経費削減，経費節減
　curtailment of operation 操業短縮，操短 （＝operation curtailment)
　production curtailment 生産削減，操業短縮 （＝curtailment of production)
　self-active curtailment 自主的操業短縮
　settlements, curtailments and termination benefits 清算，削減[縮小]と退職給付
custodial 形 管理の，保守の
custodian 名 証券保管機関，保管人，管理人
custody 名 保護，管理
custody service 証券代行業務，資産管理業務
custom 名 習慣，慣習，愛顧，顧客，得意先，カスタム （⇒customs)
　commercial customs 商慣習
　custom-built 注文製の，あつらえで作った，特別注文の，注文生産の，注文建築の
　custom house 税関
　custom integrated circuit 特注IC，カスタムIC
　custom-made 特別注文の，特注の，別あつらえの，注文生産の，オーダー・メード
　custom-made house 持ち家
　custom order 特別注文
　custom selling 注文販売，あつらえ品販売

custom software 特注ソフトウエア, カスタム・ソフト, ユーザー固有のソフトウエア

custom production 特注生産, カスタム生産
▸Mass production is being replaced by *custom production*. 特注生産が, 大量生産に代わろうとしている。

custom system 特注システム
▸We design and install *custom systems* which incorporate hardware, application software, and mobile computer terminals. 当社は, ハードウエア, 応用ソフトと移動コンピュータ端末を組み合わせて, 顧客の特注による通信システムの設計と設置を行っています。

customer 名 顧客, 得意先, 得意客, 取引先, 需要家, 加入者, ユーザー (⇒carrying amount)
　business customer 法人顧客, 企業ユーザー, 事務用(電話)加入者, 企業取引先
　commercial customer 事業法人顧客
　customer engineer 顧客サービス担当エンジニア, 派遣技術者, カスタマー・エンジニア
　customer management system 顧客管理システム
　customer parking 顧客駐車場
　customer profile 顧客構成, 顧客プロフィール
　customer relationship management 顧客関係維持, 顧客関係管理, カスタマー・リレーションシップ・マネジメント《略 CRM》(顧客情報や顧客との折衝記録を統合的に維持・管理して, 営業活動やマーケティングに利用できる)
　customer sovereignty 消費者主義
　customer support 顧客支援
　customer-tailored service 顧客の個々の要求に応じたサービス, 顧客の特別要求に応えるサービス
　customer value 顧客の価値水準
　customer's personal information 顧客の個人情報
　customers database 顧客データベース
　know your customer 顧客熟知
　large customer 大口顧客
　major customer 主要顧客, 主要得意先, 大口顧客
　potential customer 見込み客, 見込み顧客 (= prospective customer)
　prospective customer 見込み客
　residential customer 個人顧客, 住宅用(電話)加入者
　retail customer 小口顧客, 個人投資家
　small customer 小口顧客, 小企業の顧客
▸Our strategy of listening to our *customers* and improving the competitiveness of our products and services is working. お客さまのご意見を取り入れ, 製品とサービスの競争力強化に取り組んでいる当社の経営戦略が, 功を奏しています。

customer base 顧客基盤, 顧客層
▸The biggest advantage for the bank in entering the venture will be to increase its *customer base* without having to open expensive new branch offices. 同行にとってこの新規事業への参入の最大の利点は, コストのかかる新店舗を開設するまでもなく, 顧客基盤を拡大できることだ。

customer data 顧客情報
▸Osaka-based travel agency's *customer data* were leaked. 旅行会社(大阪)の顧客情報が, 外部に流出した。

customer information 顧客情報
▸Each credit card company possesses a large amount of *customer information*. クレジット・カード会社各社は, 大量の顧客情報を抱えている。

customer loyalty 顧客ロイヤルティ, 顧客の忠誠度, 顧客の忠誠心
▸For the company, terminal equipment represents a key factor in maintaining *customer loyalty*, since it provides the customers with the visible and tangible access to the network. 同社にとって端末機は, 顧客が目と手で直接触れることができる商品なので, 顧客のロイヤルティをつなぎとめる主力商品となっている。

customer needs 顧客のニーズ, 顧客の要求 (= customer requirements)
▸We are required to become a global company in order to meet *customer needs* in a world where companies do business around the globe. 世界全域で事業を展開している企業社会にあって, お客さまのニーズを満たすには, 当社自体がグローバルな企業にならなければなりません。

customer relationship 顧客関係, 顧客との良好な取引関係
▸We gained share in most of our markets, based on the strength of our product line and *customer relationships*. 当社は, 強力な製品ラインとお客さまとの緊密な取引関係に支えられ, 当社市場の大半でシェアを拡大しました。

customer safety 顧客の安全
▸Fujiya Co.'s suspension of confectionery production revealed a corporate culture in which cost-cutting measures are given priority over *customer safety*. 不二家の洋菓子製造停止は, 顧客の安全よりも経費削減策を優先させる企業風土を露呈させた。

customer satisfaction 顧客の満足, 顧客満足度《略 CS》
▶ *Customer satisfaction* is giving customers what they want. 顧客の満足を得るということは, 顧客が欲しいものを提供することである.

customer service 顧客サービス, 顧客への奉仕, 顧客へのサービス, 接客, カスタマー・サービス
▶ Seven & I and Millennium Retailing plan to increase their revenues by taking advantage of the combined effect of their product development and *customer services*. セブン＆アイとミレニアムリテイリングは, 両社の商品開発や接客［顧客サービス］などの面での統合効果を発揮して, 収益力強化を図る計画だ.

customer support services 顧客支援サービス, 顧客支援業務
▶ To provide consistent, coordinated solutions and *customer support services*, regional and branch offices have been created. 一貫性と整合性のあるソリューションと顧客支援サービスを提供するため, 地域営業本部と営業所を設置しました.

customize 動 特別注文に応じて作り変える, 注文に応じて作る, 顧客の要求に応じて特注化する, 特注化する, 注文生産する, 変造する, 変更する, あつらえる, 個別化する

customized 形 特別注文に応じて作った, 顧客の要求に応じて特注化した, オーダーメードの, 特注の, 注文生産した （＝build-to-order）
　customized and integrated offers 顧客の要求に応じて特注化した提案と統合化した提案
　customized manufacturing 特注化製造
　customized PC selling 特注PC販売 （＝build-to-order PC）
　customized solution 顧客の要求に応じて特注化したソリューション, ソリューションの特注化
▶ Besides technical expertise, we have the skills to provide *customized*, integrated offers either alone or in concert with partners. 技術的な専門知識のほかに, 当社は顧客の要求に応じて特注化した提案や統合化した提案を, 単独でもしくはパートナーと共に提供することができます.

customizing 名 特注化, 個別化 （＝customization）

customs 名 関税, 税関 （⇒distribution）
　Customs and Excise 英国の関税消費税庁 （＝Board of Customs and Excise）
　customs barrier 関税障壁
　customs basis 通関ベース （＝customs clearance basis）
　customs [custom] broker 税関貨物取扱い人, 通関業者 （＝custom house broker）
　customs clearance 通関, 通関手続き
　customs clearance record 通関実績
　customs declaration 関税申告
　Customs Declaration Form 税関申告書
　customs duties 関税
　customs entry 通関申告, 通関手続き
　customs invoice 税関送り状
　Customs Law 関税法
　customs post 税関
　customs statistics 通関統計 （＝外国貿易統計）
　customs tariff 関税表, 関税率表
　Customs Tariff Law 関税定率法
　customs tariff table 関税率表
　customs union 関税同盟
　customs valuation 関税評価
　customs warehouse 保税倉庫
　go through customs 税関を通る, 通関する
　U.S. Customs Service 米国税関
▶ The *Customs Tariff Law* bans imports that infringe on patent, design and commercial brand rights. 関税定率法で, 特許, 意匠権, 商標権などの侵害品の輸入は禁止されている.

cut 動 削減する, 縮小する, 減らす, 引き下げる, 下げる
　cut inventories 在庫を削減する, 在庫を取り崩す
　cut labor costs 人件費を引き下げる
　cut operating costs 営業コストを削減する, 営業経費を削減する
　cut payrolls 人員を削減する
　cut production 生産を削減する
　cut spending 支出を減らす, 支出を削減する
▶ The company succeeded in *cutting* costs by jointly purchasing some of the products with its group firm. 同社は, グループ企業と一部商品の仕入れを共通化して, コスト削減に成功した.

cut 名 削減, 節減, 縮小, 値引き, 引下げ, 切下げ, 配給停止, 中断, 停電, 〈利益の〉取り分, 分け前, 傷口, カット （⇒**cost cut, job cut**）
　aid cut 援助削減, 援助カット
　budget cuts 予算の引下げ
　budget deficit cut 財政赤字の削減
　cut in headline rate 利下げ （＝cut in interest rates, rate cut）
　cut in working hours 労働時間の短縮
　cuts in expenditures 歳出カット, 歳出削減 （＝cutting government outlays）
　cuts in spending 支出削減
　defense [defence] cut 国防費の削減, 防衛費の削減

expenditure cut 支出削減, 経費削減
dividend cut 配当引下げ, 減配
Fed cut 米連邦準備制度理事会(FRB)による利下げ
further rate cut 追加利下げ, 一層の利下げ, もう一段の利下げ
income tax cut 所得税減税
interest rate cut 利下げ, 金利引下げ, 利率引下げ (＝rate cut)
key rate cut 政策金利の引下げ (＝discount rate cut, official discount rate cut)
open cut 露天掘り
parity cut 平価切下げ
price cut 値下げ, 価格引下げ
production cut 減産 (＝output cut)
take one's cut of the profits 利益の取り分[分け前]をもらう
tax cut 減税 (＝tax reduction)
wage cut 賃金引下げ, 賃下げ, 賃金の削減, 賃金カット (⇒wage cuts)
▶FRB's policymakers waged war against economic weakness last year with 11 interest rate *cuts*. 米連邦準備制度理事会(FRB)の政策決定者は, 昨年は11回利下げを行って景気低迷と戦った。

cutback 名 削減, 縮小, 圧縮, 短縮 (複数形で使われることが多い)
  cutback in work hours 労働時間の短縮
  cutback [cutbacks] in jobs 雇用削減
  cutback [cutbacks] in output 生産削減, 減産 (＝production cutback)
  inventory cutback 在庫削減
  personnel cutbacks 人員削減
  power cutbacks 電力削減
  production cutback 生産削減
▶Buttressed by buoyant exports and the effect of restructuring moves, such as personnel *cutbacks*, major firms are substantially improving their earnings. 好調な輸出と人員削減などのリストラ策の効果に支えられて, 大手企業の収益は大幅に改善している。

cutoff 名 締切日

cutthroat competition 激しい競争, 熾烈な競争, 激烈な競争
▶The firm's bold move speaks volumes about the *cutthroat competition* for survival among IT businesses. 同社の大胆な動きは, IT(情報技術)業界の熾烈な勝ち残り競争を浮き彫りにしている。

cutting edge 最前線, 最先端, 最新式, 最新型, 最新鋭, 先頭, 主導的地位, 鋭利な刃物 (＝leading edge, sophisticated, state-of-the-art, top of the line)

cutting-edge 形 最前線の, 最先端の, 最新式の
  cutting-edge research 最先端の研究
  cutting-edge semiconductor 最先端の半導体
  cutting-edge technology 最先端技術, 最新技術, 先進技術
▶We are continuously developing and striving to provide *cutting-edge* software that our end-users can use without worry. 当社は, エンドユーザーが安心して利用できる最先端のソフトウエア製品の開発と提供に取り組んでいます。

CWM 事務量測定(clerical work measurementの略)

CWO 現金注文, 注文時支払い条件 (cash with orderの略)

cyberbusiness 名 サイバービジネス (＝e-business: インターネットを使ってホームページを開設して, 消費者に直接販売するビジネス)

cycle 名 周期, 循環, 動向, 景気, 景気サイクル, 景気循環, サイクル
  budget cycle 予算編成手順
  business cycle 景気循環, 景気変動, 景気 (＝trade cycle)
  buying cycle 仕入サイクル
  credit cycle 信用サイクル
  cycle of fashion 流行周期
  cycle stock 運転在庫 (＝fashion cycle, operating stock, working stock)
  down cycle 景気悪化
  economic cycle 経済循環, 景気循環, 景気動向, 景気変動
  industrial cycle 産業循環
  inventory cycle 在庫循環, 在庫サイクル
  investment cycle 投資サイクル
  life cycle 生活循環, 製品寿命, 製品ライフサイクル, ライフサイクル
  operating cycle 営業循環, 営業サイクル
  ordering cycle 発注間隔
  output cycle 生産動向
  product development cycle 製品開発サイクル
  product life cycle 商品[製品]ライフサイクル
  production cycle 生産サイクル
  replacement cycle 買換えサイクル
  silicon cycle 半導体産業の景気循環波動, シリコン・サイクル (⇒semiconductor industry)
  virtuous cycle 好循環
▶The publishing industry is said to be almost immune from the hardships of the business *cycle*. 出版業界はほとんど不況の影響を受けな

い，といわれている。
▸We continue to make essential investments in our drive for more competitive products and services, delivered on ever shorter *cycles*. 当社は，一段と競争力のある製品とサービスを従来より短いサイクルで納入する取組みに対して，極めて重要な投資を継続しています。

cyclical 形 周期的な，循環的な，景気循環の，景気サイクルの，景気[景気変動]に敏感な
  be historically cyclical 好不況を繰り返す，これまで景気サイクルに左右されてきた
  counter-cyclical 景気循環に逆行する，反循環的，景気循環の波を抑える
  cyclical activities 景気循環型事業
  cyclical adjusted 景気循環調整済みの
  cyclical downturn 景気低迷，景気後退
  cyclical ecological system 循環的生態系
  cyclical effects 景気循環要因 (＝cyclical element, cyclical reason)
  cyclical fluctuation 景気変動，周期的景気変動，循環変動 (＝cyclical variation)
  cyclical indication 景気指標
  cyclical peak 景気循環のピーク，サイクルのピーク，景気の頂上
  cyclical pickup 景気回復，景気の上昇局面
  cyclical recovery 景気回復
  cyclical stock 景気循環，株循環株 (＝cyclicals)
  cyclical trough 景気の谷景気サイクルの底
  cyclical upturn 景気回復 (＝cyclical upturn in the economy)
  cyclical weakness 景気低迷，景気の下降局面
  highly cyclical 景気循環の影響が大きい，景気循環色が強い，景気変動に敏感な
  reach a cyclical trough 景気が底入れする
▸Japan's economy was expected to gain *cyclical* momentum for a recovery in the second half of fiscal 2007. 日本経済は，2007年度下期には景気回復の循環にはずみがつく見通しだった。

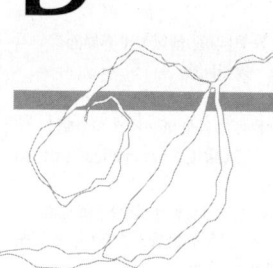

D-day 予定行動開始日
DA 設計自動化, デザイン・オートメーション (design automationの略)
daily 形 毎日の, 日々の, 日常の, 1日当たりの, 日刊の
 daily allowance 日当 (=absence fee)
 daily average for the Nikkei index 日経平均の月中平均株価
 daily-breader 勤労者
 daily essentials 生活必需品
 daily execution 日常業務
 daily foods 乳製品や豆腐などの日配品
 daily periodic rate 日歩(ひぶ) (=interest per diem, per diem rate: 現金100円に対する1日当たりの利息発生率。日歩×3.65=実質年率(%)となる)
 daily price limit 値幅制限 (=daily limit: 株価の乱高下を防ぐため, 証券取引所や日本証券業協会が制限している1日の株価変動幅のこと)
 daily satellite feed 定時衛星伝送, 定時国際テレビジョン伝送
 daily trading limit 日々取引限度, 値幅制限 (=trading limit)
 daily wage 日給
daily average for a month 月中平均
 ▶In the term-end settlement of accounts at the end of September, most companies use the *daily average for a month* of the share prices in gauging the value of latent gains or losses in their stockholdings. 9月末の期末決算で[9月中間決算で], 大半の企業は, 保有株式の含み損益を算出する際に株価の月中平均を使っている。
daily business 日常業務

▶The countries and communities in which the Corporation carries out its *daily business* face many complex economic and social issues—employment, education and environmental concerns. 当社が日常業務を行っている国々と地域社会は, 雇用, 教育や環境など数多くの複雑な経済・社会問題に直面しています。

daily turnover 1日当たりの取引高
▶Average *daily turnover* on the Tokyo Stock Exchange grew 86 percent year-on-year to ¥663 billion during the April-June quarter. 東京証券取引所の4-6月期の1日当たり平均取引高[売買代金]は, 前年同期に比べて86%増の6,630億円に達した。

damage 名 損害, 損害賠償, 被害 (複数形damagesには「損害賠償金, 損害賠償額, 損害額, 被害額」の意味もある)
 actual damages 現実的損害賠償[損害賠償金], 実損
 bring a suit for damages 損害賠償請求の訴えを起こす
 claim damages 損害賠償を請求する, 損害賠償を求める
 compensation for damages 補償の損害賠償
 consequential damages 派生的損害賠償
 damage assessment 損害査定
 damage payments 損害賠償金
 damages suit 損害賠償請求訴訟, 損害賠償訴訟 (=damages lawsuit)
 exemplary damages 懲罰的損害賠償
 incidental damages 付随的損害, 付随的損害賠償, 偶発的損害
 indirect damages 間接的損害, 間接的損害賠償

liquidated damages 予定損害賠償, 約定損害賠償
nominal damages 名目的損害賠償
passive damages 逸失利益
punitive damages 懲罰的損害賠償
special damages 特別損害賠償
▸California's Attorney General Bill Lockyer has sued the six largest U.S. and Japanese automakers for *damages* related to greenhouse gas emissions.　米カリフォルニア州のビル・ロッキャー司法長官は, 自動車が排出する温室効果ガスについて日米の大手自動車メーカー6社に損害賠償を求める訴訟を起こした。
▸Nonlife insurers are exempted from paying for *damages* caused by war or civil strife.　損害保険会社は現在, 戦争や内乱による被害に対する(保険金の)支払いを免除されている。
▸The trust bank claimed ¥100 billion in *damages*.　同信託銀行は, 100億円の損害賠償を求めた。

damage compensation　損害賠償
▸Toshiba may demand *damage compensation* from Sony, and others may follow suit.　東芝はソニーに対する損害賠償請求を検討しており, 他社もこれに追随する可能性がある。

damage costs　損害費用
▸The liability insurance fell short in covering *damage costs*.　この損害賠償責任保険で, 損害費用を賄(まかな)いきれませんでした。

damages lawsuit　損害賠償訴訟, 損害賠償請求訴訟 (=damages suit)
▸The bank reached an out-of-court settlement in a *damages lawsuit* with a bankruptcy administrator of a borrower company.　同行は, 融資先企業の破産管財人との損害賠償訴訟で示談による和解に達した。

data 名　情報, 文書, 資料, 指標, 統計, データ
　backup data データ待避, バックアップ・データ
　customer data 顧客情報 (=customer information)
　data acquisition データ取得, データ収集
　data base management system データ・ベース管理システム
　data clearinghouse データ・クリアリングハウス, スキャンデータ・サービス会社 (POS(販売時点情報管理)データの収集・処理・分析を行う会社)
　data collection データ収集, 情報収集 (=data acquisition, data gathering)
　data leak 情報漏洩, 情報漏れ, 情報流出, データ漏洩 (=data leakage)
　data network データ通信ネットワーク
　data networking products データ通信ネットワーキング製品
　data on transactions 取引データ
　data protection データ保護
　data resource management データ資源管理
　data retrieval データ検索
　data service ventures データ通信サービス事業
　data storage devices データ記憶装置
　data terminal データ端末, データ通信端末
　data terminal equipment データ端末装置, 端末機器, 宅内装置《略 DTE》
　data warehouse データの倉庫, データ・ウエアハウス《略 DWH》(日常業務で発生した大量のデータを蓄積・検索して瞬時にデータを分析するための情報システム)
　digital data デジタル・データ
　economic data 景気指標, 経済指標, 経済データ
　electronic data 電子データ
　employment data 雇用統計 (=labor market data)
　financial data 財務データ, 財務情報, 財務資料
　geographic area data 地域別データ
　image data 画像データ
　input data 入力データ
　key economic data 主要景気指標
　market data 市場統計, 市場データ, 市場資料, 相場の動き
　numeric data 数値データ
　personal data 個人情報 (=personal information)
　public data on issuer 発行体に関する公表データ
　raw data 生のデータ
　stock price data 株価資料
　trade data 貿易統計
　voice, data and video 音声, データと画像
　wireless data industry 無線データ通信業界
　wireline data communications 有線データ通信, 電話回線のデータ通信
▸An architect fabricated earthquake-resistance *data* for a number of condominium buildings and hotels.　1人の建築士が, 多くのマンションやホテルの耐震強度のデータを改竄した。
▸Business operators that handle personal data on 5,000 or more individuals are obliged in principle not to pass on *data* for use other than the original purpose for which it was obtained without the consent of the persons in question.　5,000人超の個人情報を扱う事業者は, 入手した当

初の目的以外に使用するために当該人物の同意を得ないで個人情報を外部に提供するのを基本的に禁じられている。
▸*Data* on other geographic areas pertain to operations that are located outside of the U.S. 「その他の地域」に関する数値は，米国外に拠点を置く事業の数値です。

data center データ・センター (=datacenter, Internet data center: 電子商取引やウェブ・サイト運営事業者，ASP (アプリケーション・サービス・プロバイダー) など，インターネット上のサービスに欠かせない企業のサーバーを預かって，その企業のインターネット事業を代行して運用する施設あるいは業者のこと)

data communication [**communications**] データ通信，データ通信機器《略 DC》
　data communication charges データ通信専用料金
　data communication terminal データ通信端末
　data communications service データ通信サービス
　data communications system データ通信システム
▸When building *data communications* systems, we first develop an in-depth understanding of the business issues facing its clients. データ通信システムを構築するにあたって，当社はまず顧客企業が抱えている業務上の問題点を十分に把握します。

data mining データ・マイニング (=knowledge discovery in database)
　データ・マイニングとは➡膨大な生データから経営やマーケティングに有用な商品の相関関係を発見したり，顧客の購買動向を分析したりする手法。その代表的な手法として時系列分析や相関関係分析，クラスター分析，グループごとのクラス分類などがあり，これらの分析で販売予測や販売戦略の立案，リスク・マネジメントが可能になる。

data on file 保管文書
▸The company has a huge amount of *data on file*. 同社の保管文書は厖大だ。

data processing データ処理，情報処理
　automatic data processing 自動データ処理，自動データ処理法《略 ADP》
　centralized data processing 集中データ処理《略 CDP》
　data processing equipment データ処理機器
　data processing industry 情報処理産業
　decentralized data processing 分散データ処理，分散処理《略 DDP》
　distributed data processing 分散型データ処理，分散処理《略 DDP》
　electronic data processing 電子[電子式]データ処理，電子[電子式]情報処理《略 EDP》
　industrial data processing 工業用データ処理《略 IDP》
　integrated data processing 集中データ処理，集中情報処理《略 IDP》
　online data processing オンライン・データ処理
　remote-access data processing 遠隔アクセス・データ処理

data processing capability データ処理能力
▸Thanks to the Cell's high *data-processing capability*, the volumes of information exchanged between devices will also increase by a large margin. セル (超小型演算処理装置) の高いデータ処理能力で，機器間でやりとりする情報量も大幅に向上する。

data processing method 情報処理方式，データ処理方式
▸Each of the three banks has a different *data processing method*. 3行[3つの銀行]の情報処理方式は，それぞれ異なる。

data processing system データ処理システム
▸The firm is engaged in the design, manufacture and marketing of *data processing systems* and network data communications systems. 同社は，データ処理システムとデータ・ネットワーク通信システムの設計・製造と販売に携わっている。

data telecommunications service データ通信サービス，データ通信事業
▸Japan Telecom earns 30 percent of its sales from providing business clients with *data telecommunications services*. 日本テレコムは，企業向けデータ通信事業が売上の30％を占めている。

data transfer データ伝送，データ転送
　data transfer rate データ転送速度，データ転送率
　data transfer velocity データ伝送速度

data transmission データ伝送，データ転送，データ通信
　data transmission capacity データ伝送容量
　data transmission service データ通信サービス，データ伝送サービス
　data transmission system データ伝送方式，データ伝送システム
　data transmission technology データ伝送技

術, データ通信技術
▶Increased business volume has outstripped the bank's present *data transmission capacity*. 取引量の拡大に伴って, 同行の現在のデータ伝送容量では不十分になっている.

database 名 データベース, 基礎資料, 基本資料, 情報集積体, 情報庫 (＝data base)
  database administrator データベース管理者
  database design データベース設計
  database making データベース化
  database management system データベース管理システム《略 DBMS》
  database marketing データベース・マーケティング (顧客の性別や生年月日, 住所, 家族構成, 購買履歴などをデータベースに蓄積し, これを分析して顧客の個々のニーズに合わせた商品供給をすること)
  database producer データベース・プロデューサー (データベースのコンテンツ作成企業)
  database protection データベース保護
  database service データベース・サービス

datacop 名 データコップ (＝cybercop: ハッカーなどの不法侵入を防止する企業の専門部門や政府機関)

date 名 日時, 日付 (⇒closing date, due date)
  accounting date 決算日
  acquisition date 取得日
  base date 基準日
  consumer expiration date 有効期限
  date and year first above written 冒頭に記載した日付, 冒頭記載の年月日, 頭書の年月日
  date of conversion 転換日, 転換時
  date of declaration 配当宣言日
  date of expiration 満了日 (契約期間が円満に終了した場合)
  date of issue 発行日, 提出日, 小切手の振出日, 作成日 (＝date of issuance)
  date of maturity 満期日, 支払い期日, 支払い日
  date of shipment 船積み日, 船積み日付, 出荷期日, 出荷日付, 発送日, 船会社への貨物の引渡し日
  date of the financial statements 財務諸表日
  effective date 発効日, 施行日, 実施年月日, 取引開始日
  expiration date 行使期限, 有効期限, 満期日
  interest payment date 利息支払い日
  issue date 発行日
  offering date 募集取扱い日, 応募期日, 応募日, 申込み期日, 割当日
  report date 決算日
  settlement date 決済日

  trade [transaction] date 取引日
  valuation date 評価日

date hereof 本契約の締結日, 本契約日, 契約の日, …の日付 (＝the date of this agreement)
▶This guarantee shall be effective and valid for a period of two years from the *date hereof*. 本保証は, 本保証書の日付から2年間有効とする.

date of payment 支払い日, 決済日, 支払い期日, 払込み期日, 期日, 配当支払い日 (＝due date)
▶A Japanese plastics maker in China did not receive payments for its products from a major Chinese electrical appliance maker after the *date of payment*. 中国に進出した日本のあるプラスチック・メーカーは, 中国の大手家電メーカーから, 期日を過ぎても納品の代金支払いがなかった.

date of record 配当基準日, 名義書換え停止日 (＝record date: [配当基準日] は, 各事業年度に配当を受け取る権利のある株主を決める日のこと. 株価は, 一般に配当基準日を過ぎると配当の分だけ価値が下がって安くなる)

Davos Conference [meeting] ダボス会議 (世界経済フォーラム年次総会の通称; ⇒World Economic Forum)

day 名 日, 1日, 期日, 期限, デイ
  account day 決算日, 勘定日
  banking day 銀行の営業日
  business day 営業日, 取引日, 業務日 (＝working day)
  calendar day 暦日
  closing day 払込み日
  current days 休日・祭日込みの連続日数 (＝running days)
  day job 正規の仕事
  day order 当日注文
  day service 日帰り介護, デイサービス
  day trade デイ・トレード (＝day trading: インターネットでの株や債券などの取引)
  days of grace 猶予期間, 据え置き期間 (＝grace period)
  prompt day 競売の受渡し日, 受渡し最終日
  settlement day 決済日, 勘定日, 決算日, 受渡し日, 期日

day care 〈就学前児童の〉保育, 〈高齢者や障害者の〉介護, 養護, デイケア
  corporate day-care 企業内保育
  corporate day-care center 企業内保育所 [託児所], コーポレート・デイケア・センター
▶*Day care* needs include care of babies and infants, extended nursery service hours and

temporary nursing services. 保育のニーズには、乳幼児保育や延長保育、一時保育などが含まれる。

day-care center 保育所
▸Those entitled to entrust their children to *day-care centers* are limited to parents who regularly work full-time during daytime. 保育所に子どもを預けることができるのは、両親が昼間フルタイムで労働することを常態としている場合に限られる。

day trader デイ・トレーダー
▸The stock market is now luring not only individual investors such as *day traders*, but also people who abandoned the equity market after the economic bubble burst. 株式市場 [株式投資] は現在, デイ・トレーダーなどのようなセミプロの個人投資家だけでなく, バブル崩壊以降, 株式市場から遠ざかっていた一般の人たちをも引き付けている。

days sales outstanding 売上債権回転日数, 売上債権回収期間, 平均売掛債権滞留日数 《略 DSO》
▸*Days sales outstanding* in our core business are defined as average accounts receivable divided by average daily revenues in our core business. 当社の主力事業の平均売上債権回転日数 [平均売掛債権滞留日数] は、売掛金の平均額を主力事業の1日当たり平均収益で割ることによって得られます。

daylight saving time system サマータイム制
▸*Daylight saving time system* is applied in about 70 countries. サマータイム制は、約70か国で導入されている。

DDP 仕向け地持込み渡し (関税込み [済み]) 条件 (**delivered duty paid** の略)

DDU 仕向け地持込み渡し (関税抜き) 条件 (**delivered duty unpaid** の略)

de facto 事実上の, 実質的な, 事実上存在する, 現存する, ディファクト [デファクト]
　de facto corporation 事実上の会社
　de facto dismissal 事実上の解雇
　de facto merger 事実上の合併
　de facto standard 事実上の標準, 事実上の国際基準, 事実上の世界標準, デファクト・スタンダード
▸The investment fund has a *de facto* majority of shareholder voting rights. この投資ファンドが、実質的に株主議決権の過半数を握っている。

de jure 正当な, 法律上の, 法に適った, 適法な, デジュアリー
　de jure corporation 法律上の会社, 適法法人

de jure officer 適法役員, 法律上の役員, 法律上の公務員
de jure standard 法による基準, 法律上の基準, 公的基準, デジュアリー・スタンダード

d/e ratio 負債・自己資本比率 (**debt-equity ratio** の略)

deal 名 取引, 商売, 売買, 政策, 計画, 協定, 協約, 労使協約, 取決め, 契約, 協議, 協議書, 密約, 事件, 案件, 物, 一勝負, 取扱い, ディール (⇒share swap deal, stock swap deal)
　a big deal 一大事, 重大事件
　agree a deal 取決めをまとめる
　blockbuster deal 大型債
　bullet deal 満期一括償還債
　cash deal 現金取引
　cold deal 人気のない銘柄
　compensation deal 補償取引
　conclude a secret deal 裏取引を結ぶ
　do a deal with …と取引する
　exchange deal 為替取引
　finalize a deal for …の最終調整をする, …の最終協議をする, 最終調整に入る
　financial deal 金融取引
　fund deal 資金取引
　off-the-book deal 簿外取引
　package deal 一括取引, 一括購入, パッケージ・ディール
　seal a deal 契約を結ぶ, 取引契約に調印する
　secret deal 裏取引
　stock deal 株取引, 株式の売買
　strike a deal 取引をする, 売買する
　strike a deal with …と取引する, …と合意する
　structured deal 仕組み取引, 仕組み債
　swap deal スワップ取引
　terminate business deals with …との取引を打ち切る
　trust deal 信託契約
▸In May 2007, the ban on foreign firms taking over Japanese companies with stock swap *deals* was lifted. 2007年5月から, 株式交換取引での外資 [外資系企業, 外国企業] による日本企業買収が解禁となった。
▸In the 21-day tender offer, a surprisingly large number of individual shareholders accepted the *deal*. 21日間の株式公開買付け (TOB) で, 当初の予想を上回って多くの個人株主がTOBに応募した。
▸NYSE Group struck a *deal* to buy European bourse operator Euronext for $9.96 billion. (ニューヨーク証券取引所を運営する) NYSEグループは、欧州 (パリやオランダなど) の証券取引所を

運営する「ユーロネクスト」を99億6,000万ドルで買収する取引をした。
▸The company collapsed after its senior management's off-the-book *deals* came to light.　同社は，経営者の簿外取引が発覚してから倒産した。

deal a blow to　…に打撃を与える
▸Appraisal losses on securities holdings *dealt a blow to* the firm's earnings.　保有証券の含み損[評価損]が，同社の収益に打撃を与えた。

dealer 名　販売店，販売業者，メーカー特約店，〈有価証券取引で〉自己の勘定とリスク負担で株式や債券の売買を行う業者，ディーラー
　automobile dealer　自動車販売店，自動車販売会社，自動車ディーラー　(=vehicle dealer)
　bond dealer　債券ディーラー
　dealer aids　ディーラー援助，販売店援助　(=dealer helps)
　dealer contact　ディーラーとの接触
　dealer control　販売店管理，ディーラー管理
　dealer demand　販売店需要，販売業者需要，ディーラー需要
　dealer helps　販売店援助，ディーラー援助　(=dealer aids)
　dealer incentive　販売店刺激，販売店誘因
　dealer operation　販売店経営
　dealer promotion　販売店促進，販売店促進策　(=dealer helps)
　dealer support　ディーラー支援，販売店支援
　exchange dealer　為替ディーラー
　fixed income dealer　債券ディーラー
　National Association of Securities Dealers　全米証券業協会
　primary dealer　プライマリー・ディーラー，米国の公認政府証券ディーラー，政府公認ディーラー
　securities dealer　証券ディーラー

dealership 名　販売店，ディーラー，販売権
▸The firm had secretly repaired such defective parts through *dealerships*.　同社は，販売店を通じてこれらの欠陥部品をひそかに改修していた。

dealing 名　売買取引，取引，売買，自己売買，ディーリング
　after-hours dealing　時間外取引
　dealing cost　取引費用
　dealing size　取引単位
　exchange dealing　為替取引
　foreign exchange dealing　外国為替取引
　forward dealing　先物取引，先物為替取引
　insider dealing　インサイダー取引
　outside dealing　場外取引
　spot dealing　直物取引，直物為替取引
　stock option dealing　株式オプション取引
▸We are honest and highly ethical in all our business *dealings*.　私たちは，あらゆる事業取引で誠実かつ高い企業倫理に基づいて行動しています。

death from overwork　過労死

debacle 名　総崩れ，崩壊，〈市場の〉暴落，完敗，大失敗　(=fiasco)
▸Swiss banking giant UBS plunged to its full-year net loss after the U.S. subprime *debacle*.　スイスの金融大手UBSは，米国のサブプライム・ローン（低所得者向け住宅融資）問題の影響を受け，通期決算で税引き後赤字に転落した。

debenture 名　社債，〈米国の〉無担保債券，〈英国の〉不動産担保付き債券　(=debenture bond)
　bank debenture　金融債，銀行債，銀行債券　(金融機関が資金調達のために発行する債券)
　capital debenture　劣後債
　convertible debenture　転換社債
　corporate debenture　社債　(=corporate bond)
　debenture bond　社債，無担保社債，無担保債　(=debenture)
　debenture interest　社債利息，社債利子
　debenture stock　社債，担保付き社債　(=debenture bond)
　debentures issued　社債発行高
　profit debenture　収益社債
　unsecured corporate debenture　無担保社債
▸During the first half of the 2009, we completed a public offering in Canada of $150 million of *debentures*, due 2019.　2009年上半期に，当社はカナダ国内で満期2019年の社債1億5,000万ドルの公募発行を完了しました。

debit 名　借方，負債，引落し，デビット　(=debtor:「借方」は，勘定の左側)
　debit and credit　借方と貸方，借方・貸方
　debit balance　借方残高，貸付け残高，差引融資残高
　debit card　銀行口座即時決済，デビット・カード　(金融機関が発行するキャッシュ・カードを利用して，買い物などの支払いができる即時決済方法)
　debit equity ratio　負債持ち分比率，他人資本比率
　debit note　借方票，借方伝票，債務覚書，代金請求書，デビット・ノート　(=debit memo, debit slip, debit ticket)
　direct debit　自動引落し，直接引落し，口座引落し　(⇒**direct debit system**)
　Net-debit service　ネット決済サービス，インターネット即時決済サービス

online debit service インターネット即時決済サービス, オンライン即時決済サービス
▸The life insurer introduced a system that allows customers to pay their first insurance premiums by direct *debit* from their bank accounts. 同保険会社は, 顧客の銀行口座からの自動引落しで（契約時の）初回保険料を顧客が支払うことができるシステムを導入した。

debrief 動 〈任務や事情などの〉報告を求める, 事情聴取する

debriefing 名 任務報告, 事情聴取

debt 名 債務, 負債, 借入れ, 借金, 債権, 借入金, 借入債務, 債務証券, 債券, 金銭債務, 金銭債務訴訟, 金融債務, デット （⇒**bad debt, cash requirements, corporate debt securities, interest-bearing, long term debt, refinance**）
bank debt 銀行借入れ
corporate debt 法人債務, 企業債務
debt and equity securities 負債証券[債務証券]と持ち分証券
debt-asset ratio 負債・資産比率 （総負債の総資産に対する比率）
debt assumption 債務履行引受け, 債務の肩代わり, 債務引受契約, 債務引受契約に基づく債務譲渡, デット・アサンプション
debt due within one year 1年以内に返済予定の債務
debt equity ratio 負債・資本比率, 負債対資本比率, 負債比率, 外部負債比率, 負債倍率, デット・エクイティ・レシオ《略 DER》（＝debt-to-equity ratio）
debt factoring 債権買取り
debt-for-bond swap 債務の債券化, デット・ボンド・スワップ （＝debt-bond swap）
debt issued with stock purchase warrant 新株引受権付き社債
debt load 債務負担 （＝debt burden）
debt maturing within one year 1年以内に償還期限が到来する負債
debt reduction 債務削減, 債務減らし
debt rollover 債務返済の繰延べ （rollover＝支払い繰延べ, 借換え）
debt service 元利払い, 債務返済, 未払い金, 債務元利返済額
debt-swap arrangements 債務の株式化
debt-to-equity analysis 負債比率の分析
debt-to-equity ratio 負債比率, 負債資本比率 （＝debt equity ratio, debt ratio）
excess of debt 債務超過
financial debt 金融債務
issue debt 債券を発行する, 負債で資金を調達する
large debts 大口債権
massive debts 巨額の債務, 過剰債務
meet one's debt obligations 債務を履行する, 債務を返済する
operating debt 買掛金
pay down debt 債務を返済する （＝repay debt）
reduce debt 債務を削減する （＝trim down debt）
refinance existing debt 既存債務を借り換える
replace maturing debt 満期を迎える[満期が来た]債務を借り換える
restructuring of debt 債務の再編
retirement of debt 債務の返済
service debt 債務を履行する, 債務を返済する
subordinated debt 劣後債務, 劣後債
unconsolidated debt 単独ベースでの借入金, 非連結子会社の負債
▸From time to time, we guarantee the *debt* of certain unconsolidated joint ventures. 当社は, （当社の財務諸表に）連結されていない特定の合弁会社の負債に対して保証を行う場合があります。

debt burden 債務負担, 債務超過 （⇒**debt load**）
▸It is difficult for the company to survive on its own with its heavy *debt* burden of ¥500 billion. 同社の場合は, 5,000億円の大幅な債務超過のため, 自力での存続は難しい。

debt equity swap 債務の株式化, 債権の株式化, デット・エクイティ・スワップ《略 DES》（＝debt-equity swap, debt-for-equity swap）
▸As far as the *debt equity swap* is concerned, its main banks' holdings of outstanding shares may increase further than the 5 percent limit stipulated by the Antimonopoly Law. 債務の株式化に関するかぎり, 主力取引銀行の発行済み株式の持ち株比率が, 独占禁止法で定める5％の上限を上回る可能性がある。

debt-for-equity swap 〈貸し手にとっての〉債権株式化, 〈借り手にとっての〉債務株式化, デット・エクイティ・スワップ （＝debt equity swap）
　債務の株式化とは➡金融機関に融資（借入金）を出資に振り替えてもらい, 株券を渡して増資すること。つまり, 負債を株に変えて増資すること。こうすると, 融資を受けた企業はその借入金を返す必要もなく, また利子を払う必要もない。企業にとっては負債が減る分, 資本金などの自己資本が増え, 金融機関にとっては債権の株式化によって企業が再建を果たせば配当を受けられるし, 株価が値上がりすれば

株を売却して利益が得られるメリットがある。債務の株式化は，貸し手（金融機関）にとっては債権の株式化を意味する。
▶The bank is considering providing financial aid to the heavily indebted automaker, such as waiving debts and conducting a *debt-for-equity swap*. 同行は，債権放棄や債務（銀行にとっては債権）の株式化などで，巨額の債務を抱えたこの自動車メーカーへの金融支援を行うことを検討している。

debt instrument 債務証券, 債務証書, 債券 （＝debt, debt security）
▶One way for a company to accomplish long-term financing is through the issuance of long-term *debt instruments* in the form of bonds. 会社の長期資金調達方法のひとつは，社債の形で長期債務証券を発行して行われる。

debt load 債務負担 （＝dept burden）
▶In a move to reduce its *debt load*, the company issued 20 million common shares in March 2009. 債務負担の軽減策として，同社は2009年3月に普通株式2,000万株を発行しました。

debt outstanding 負債残高, 借入残高, 未払い負債額, 未償還債務, 未償還負債
▶The growth of our financial services was the primary reason for the increase in total *debt outstanding* and for most of our financing needs. 当社の金融サービスの成長が，主に当社の未償還債務総額の増加と資金需要の増加をもたらしました。

debt pressure 債務圧力
▶If consumer prices rose mildly over the course of a few years, it would result in a decline in interest rates in real terms and reduced *debt pressure*. 消費者物価が数年にわたって緩やかに上昇したら，実質金利の低下と債務圧力の低減につながるものと思われる。

debt rating 債券格付け, 社債の格付け, 債務証書, 債務契約書 （＝bond rating）
▶Fitch Ratings cut General Motors Corp.'s *debt ratings* to "junk." 欧州系格付け会社のフィッチ・レーティングスは，米ゼネラル・モーターズ（GM）の社債格付けを「投資不適格」に引き下げた。
▶Moody's downgraded GM's long-term *debt rating*. 格付け会社のムーディーズは，GMの長期格付けを引き下げた。

debt ratio 負債比率, 債務比率 （＝debt-to-equity ratio）
▶Our goal is a 30 percent *debt ratio* for our core business. 当社の中核事業の負債比率を30％にするのが，当社の目標です。

debt repayment 債務返済, 借金返済
▶We spent the additional fund collected through the capital increase on *debt repayment*. 当社は，増資で集めた追加資金を債務返済に充てました。

debt-ridden 形 赤字に悩む, 借金に悩む, 負債に苦しむ, 経営再建中の
▶A number of *debt-ridden* people have killed themselves, fled at night or committed crimes. 自殺や夜逃げしたり，犯罪に走ったりする債務者も出ている。

debt-saddled 形 借金を背負っている, 負債［債務, 赤字］を抱えた, 経営再建中の
▶We are attempting to improve the management of our *debt-saddled* subsidiary. 当社は現在，赤字を抱える子会社の経営改善に取り組んでいます。

debt security 債務証券, 債券, 債務証書 （＝debt, debt instrument)
　債務証券について➡債務証券は，一般に債務などの有価証券を指す。一定の額面金額（par value）と満期日（maturity date）があり，利払いがある利付き証券（interest-bearing securities）と利払いはないが割引方式で発行される割引証券（discount securities）がある。利払いがある利付き証券のうち，期間が長いものは利付き債（coupon bond）と呼ばれている。また，利払いがなく割引方式で発行される割引証券の場合は，券面に確定利息（fixed interest rate）がなく，額面（par value）より低い割引価格で発行され，満期日には額面価格で返済される。この割引証券は，米国財務省短期証券（Treasury bill）やコマーシャル・ペーパー（CP）がその代表格で，発行から償還（redemption）までの期間の利払いは一切なく，発行価格と額面価格との差額（償還差益）が利息相当分となる。米国では，コマーシャル・ペーパーなどのような短期の債務をpaper, bill, 中期債券（満期までの期間が1年超―10年程度の中期債）をnote, 長期債券（満期までの期間が10年以上の長期債）をbondなどと，期間によって表現を使い分けている。
▶We sold ¥31 billion of *debt securities* with a maturity of 50 years. 当社は，満期50年の債券［債務証券］310億円を発行しました［当社は，満期50年の債券を発行して，310億円を調達しました］。

debt servicing 債務返済, 利息払い （＝debt paying, debt service）
　debt servicing capacity 債務返済能力 （＝debt-paying ability）
　debt-servicing costs [expenses] 債務返済費用, 国債費 （＝debt-servicing expenditures）
▶The rise in *debt-servicing* costs is due to the

massive issuance of government bonds to prop up the economy. 国債費が増えたのは，景気を支えるため国債を大量に発行したためだ．

debt waiver 債権放棄，債務免除 （=debt forgiveness, debt relief, waiver of debt; ⇒**waiver**)
▶The remaining ¥20 billion of debt will be repaid through *debt waivers* by the firm's six main banks and three regional banks. 残りの負債200億円は，同社の主力取引銀行6行と地銀3行による債権放棄で返済する．

debtor 名 債務者，融資先，借方，借主，債務国《略 Dr.》
　debtor balance 借方残高
　debtor bank 債務行，破綻銀行
　debtor country 債務国 （=indebted country)
　debtor in possession 継承破産人，管理処分権保持債務者《略 DIP》
▶At least 70 businesses of Shinginko Tokyo *debtors* went bankrupt since 2005. 新銀行東京の融資先のうち，少なくとも70社が（同行開業の）2005年から経営破綻した．

debtor firm [company] 融資先企業，融資先，債務者
▶The state-backed Industrial Revitalization Corporation of Japan buys bad loans from banks and imposes strict turnaround plans on *debtor firms*. 政府系の産業再生機構は，銀行［金融機関］から不良債権を買い取り，融資先企業には厳しい企業再建計画を強制する．

debtor in possession (DIP) finance 事業再生融資，DIPファイナンス，デッター・イン・ポゼション融資 （=DIP financing, DIP plan: 不動産担保がなくても事業の継続可能性などを考慮して新規融資する仕組み）
▶A *debtor in possession (DIP) finance* formula was introduced by the Development Bank of Japan to help failed companies that still have hope for rehabilitation. 経営破綻した企業のうちまだ再建の希望が持てる企業を支援するため，日本政策投資銀行がDIPファイナンス方式を採用した．

debut 動 発売する，新規上場する，上場する，初登場する，デビューする
▶GCA Co., a mergers and acquisitions advisory company, *debuted* on the TSE's Mothers market. M&A（企業の合併・買収）助言会社のGCAが，東証マザーズに上場した．

debut 名 発売，新規上場，上場，初登場，デビュー （=initial public offering; ⇒**chipmaker**)
▶The firm surged 25.5 percent on its market *debut* on the Tokyo Stock Exchange's Mothers. 同社の株価は，東京証券取引所マザーズに上場して公開価格を25.5％上回った．

decentralization 名 分権化，非中央集権化，地方分権，地方分散，ディセントラリゼーション
　decentralization and self-governance 地方分権と自治
　decentralization and self-management 分権化と自主管理
　decentralization of management 経営の分散化，分散管理
　functional decentralization 機能的分権制
▶Reform of a social system leads to the promotion of *decentralization* and self-governance. 社会システムの改革は，地方分権と自治を促進する．

decentralize 動 分散する，分散化する，一極集中を排除する，多極分散する，分権する
　decentralized computer network 分散型コンピュータ・ネットワーク
　decentralized management 分権管理
　decentralized organization 分権組織，分権的管理組織
▶In case of transnational companies, decision making is *decentralized* and coordinated across borders, linking functions for global leverage and competitive advantage. トランスナショナル（超国籍）企業の場合，意思決定は分散・分権化され，国境を越えて調整されると同時に，諸機能を連結して地球規模のレバレッジ効果と競争上の優位性を追求しています．

decide 動 決める，決定する，解決する，判断する，決議する，判定する，判決する，判決［審判］を下す，裁決する
▶Stock buyback limits are to be *decided* at general shareholders meetings. 自社株の取得枠は，株主総会で決められることになっている．

decile 名形 十分位数(の)，デシル(の)

decision 名 決定，意思決定，決断，判断，決議，判定，判決，裁決
　business decision 経営判断，企業の意思決定，事業決定
　decision of a general meeting of stockholders 株主総会決議
　decision room デシジョン・ルーム（インテリジェント化した会議室・重役室）
　decision support system 意思決定支援システム《略 DSS》
　investment decision 投資決定，投資判断 （⇒ **full powers and authority**)
　majority decision 多数決 （=decision by a

majority)
make or buy decision 自製か購入かの決定［意思決定，選択］，自製・購入選択
operating decision 業務上の意思決定 （＝operation decision)
pricing decision 価格決定，価格設定
rating decision 格付け判断，格付けの意思決定
strategic decision 戦略的意思決定
▶*Decisions* regarding small contributions are made by each local management. 少額の寄付についての決定は，各国の経営陣が行っています。
▶Oji turned to Hokuetsu's shareholders for their *decision* on whether to integrate with Oji or remain independent. 王子製紙は，北越製紙の株主に対して，王子と経営統合するか独立路線を堅持するかの判断を仰いだ。
▶We are working with employees and the unions to increase their involvement and input in planning and *decisions*. 私ども経営陣は，従業員と組合と一緒に，企画立案と意思決定に参加して意見を述べる機会を増やす努力をしています。

decision making 意思決定，政策決定，経営判断 （＝decision-making)
bottom-up decision making 参加的意思決定，下からの意思決定
decision-making authority 意思決定権，決定権
decision-making process 意思決定過程，意思決定プロセス，政策決定の過程
decision-making skill 意思決定能力
investment decision-making 投資の意思決定
one man decision-making style ワンマン体制
top-down decision making トップ・ダウン型意思決定
unprogramed [unprogrammed] decision making 非定型的意思決定
▶Outside directors are appointed to enhance transparency in *decision-making* as well as strengthen oversight of directors who have operational responsibilities. 社外取締役任用の目的は，意思決定の透明性向上と業務執行を担う取締役の監督強化です。

decision-making forum 意思決定の場
▶These annual general meetings are the key *decision-making forums* for joint-stock corporations. これらの年次株主総会は，株式会社にとって最も重要な意思決定の場である。

declaration 名 宣言，申告，宣告，公表，決議
declaration date 配当宣言日 （＝date of declaration)
declaration of bankruptcy 破産宣告
declaration of default デフォルト宣言
declaration of dividend 配当宣言，配当決議 （＝dividend announcement, dividend declaration)

declare 動 〈配当支払いなどを〉宣言する，申告する，計上する，公表する，発表する （⇒accounting mistake, bankrupt, during the year)
be declared bankrupt 破産宣告を受ける
declare a cash dividend 現金配当を宣言する
declared capital 公示資本，表示資本
declared dividend 宣言配当金，公表配当金，配当宣言
declared income 申告所得，所得申告
declared profit 計上利益，公表利益
dividend declared 宣言配当金［配当額］，配当金，配当決議
dividends declared per common share 普通株式1株当たり配当
preferred dividends declared 優先株式の配当宣言額
▶Dividends may be *declared* by the board of directors out of the surplus or net profits of the company. 配当金は，会社の剰余金または純利益から取締役会が宣言することができる。
▶The JAL Group is expected to *declare* after-tax losses of ¥47 billion in the current business year. 日本航空は，今期は470億円の税引き後損失を計上する見通しだ。
▶The university's affiliates, including the foundation, failed to *declare* about ¥6.5 billion in income. 同大の関連会社は，財団を含めて，所得約65億円を申告しなかった。

decline 動 減少する，低下する，下落する，落ち込む，悪化する，低迷する，縮小する，マイナスになる
declining balance 定率法
declining birthrate and graying society 少子高齢化 （＝aging society and declining birthrate, declining birthrate and graying of the population)
declining business performance 業績悪化，業績低迷，業績不振
▶The *declining* business performance of publishers is related to their complicated revenue system. 出版業界の業績不振は，その複雑な収入体系と関連がある。

decline 名 減少，低下，下落，落込み，悪化，低迷，縮小
asset price decline 資産価格の下落
bond yield decline 債券利回りの下落
decline in capital expenditure 設備投資の減少

decode　　　　　　　　　　　　　　　　160　　　　　　　　　　　　　　　　deduction

decline in deficits 赤字削減
decline in inventories 在庫の減少
decline in losses 赤字縮小
earnings decline 利益の減少, 減益, 収益減 (＝profit decline)
interest rate decline 金利の低下
profit decline 利益の減少, 減益
share price decline 株価の下落
▶Boeing Co. posted a 31 percent *decline* in third quarter profits. ボーイングの第3四半期（7－9月期）の利益は，前年同期比で31％減少した。

decode 動 〈コードを〉復号する，解読する
decoding of genes 遺伝子の解読
deconstruction 名 デコンストラクション（ビジネス・モデルを従来とは異なる視点でとらえ直して，新しいモデルを作り出すこと）
deconstructor [deconstructer] 名 デコンストラクター（これまでとは異なる競争ルールを持ち込んで，既存の業界秩序を破壊してしまう企業）
decontrol 名 規制撤廃，制限解除，統制解除，統制撤廃，自由化
decoupling 名 連動しないこと，非連動，非連動性，脱同調化，ディカップリング
　decoupling theory 脱同調化理論，ディカップリング［デカップリング］論（世界景気は米国の景気と乖離して推移する，つまり米国の景気減速は中国やインドなど新興市場国の発展が続くので世界的な景気減速にはつながらない，という考え方。⇒**emerging**）

decrease 動 引き下げる，軽減する，減らす，減少する，減る，縮小する，低下する，下落する
　decreased margin 利益率の低下
　decreased profitability 収益性の低下
　decreased sales 売上高の減少, 売上の減少
　decreasing birth rate 少子化
▶Earnings *decreased* for the third quarter. 第3四半期の利益は，減少しました。

decrease 名 減少，縮小，低下，下落
　arbitrary increase or decrease method 任意増減算出法
　capital decrease 減資 (＝capital reduction, reduction of capital)
　decrease in accounts receivable (net) 売掛金の減少（純額），受取債権の減少（減額）
　decrease in accrued expenses 未払い費用の減少
　decrease in dividends 減配
　decrease in other current assets その他の流動資産の減少
　decrease in other current liabilities その他の流動負債の減少
　(decrease) increase in cash and short-term investments and borrowings 現金・預金，短期投資および短期借入金の増加（減少）
　decrease of capital 減資 (＝capital decrease, capital reduction, reduction of capital)
　net decrease in cash and cash equivalents 現金および現金等価物の純減少
　rating decrease 格下げ
▶The *decrease* in revenues in 2008 was mainly due to the reduction of revenues associated with the sale of some European businesses. 2008年度に売上高が減少したのは，主に欧州事業の一部売却に伴って売上高が減少したためです。

decruit 動 〈高齢者などを〉他社に配置換えする，格下げする
dedication 名 献身，専念，専心，除幕式，献呈，献辞
▶The many thousands of employees in our family of companies once again demonstrated their *dedication* and professionalism in support of various corporate goals and activities. 当社のさまざまな企業目標と活動を支えたのは，当期も当社のファミリー企業に勤務している十数万人の従業員の献身と職業意識です。

deduct 動 差し引く，控除する，引き落とす
▶Company employees' pension premiums are automatically *deducted* from their monthly salaries. サラリーマンの厚生年金保険料は，月給から天引きされる［自動的に差し引かれる］。

deductible 形 控除可能な，損金算入できる，経費として認められる，費用として控除される
　deductible amount 減算額
　deductible expenses 控除可能費用，損金，課税控除費目
　deductible for tax purposes 税務上損金となる
　deductible from taxable income 課税所得から控除できる
　dividends deductible as necessary expenses 配当損金算入
　tax deductible 損金算入できる，経費として認められる，損金算入項目
▶These expenses are *deductible* for tax purposes in year 5 when the liability is expected to be paid. これらの費用は，負債を支払う予定の第5事業年度に税務上，損金となります。

deduction 名 差引，控除，控除項目，差引額，控除額，減少額，減額，損金，損金算入,〈送り状価格の〉引下げ，演繹（えんえき）
　automatic deduction 自動引落し (＝direct

debit)
deduction at source 源泉徴収, 源泉徴収課税
deduction of foreign tax 外国税額控除 (= foreign tax credit)
direct payroll deduction 給与天引き方式
dividends paid deduction 支払い配当金の控除
insurance deduction 保険料控除
profits before tax deduction 税引き前利益
tax deduction 税額控除, 税控除, 減税, 税引き (=tax credit)
▸In the United States, a special *deduction* system has been implemented that allows investors to carry over capital losses from stock transactions in their current tax return to future years. 米国では, 税務申告上, 株式売買による譲渡損失を翌年以降に繰り越すことができる特別控除制度が実施されている。
▸Many of regular premium payments are made with automatic *deductions* from customers' bank accounts. 定期的な保険料支払いの多くは, 顧客の銀行口座からの自動引落しで行われている。

deed 名 行為, 行動, 実行, 事実, 実際, 功績, 書面, 証書, 捺印(なついん)証書, 譲渡証書, 不動産権利証書
act and deed 行為, 後日の証拠, 証拠物
blank deed 要項記入式証書
contract by deed 書面契約
deed absolute 無条件譲渡証書
deed assignment 財産譲渡証書, 財産譲渡
deed of arrangement 債務整理証書
deed of association 会社定款, 有限責任会社設立款
deed of contract 契約書
deed of partnership 組合規約書, パートナーシップ規約書[規約書] (=partnership deed)
deed of release 権利放棄証書 (=release deed)
deed of sale 売約証書
deed of settlement 会社設立証書
deed of transfer 譲渡証書, 財産譲渡証書, 株式売買[株式譲渡]証書, 名義書換え証書 (=deed of conveyance, transfer deed)
deed of trust 〈担保のための〉信託証書 (=trust deed)
deed poll 単独捺印証書, 平型捺印証書
escrow deed 条件付き譲渡証書, 条件付き捺印証書, 未完証書
estoppel by deed 捺印証書による禁反言
in deed and not in name 名目上でなく実際に
in deed as well as in name 名目だけでなく実際に, 名実ともに

inspectorship deed 清算監査証書, 財産監査証書 (=deed of inspectorship)
loan on deeds 証書貸付け
mortgage deed 抵当証券
notarial deed 公正証書
original deed 証書原本, 証書
quit claim deed 権利放棄証書
title deed 不動産権利証書, 権利証, 捺印証書 (=deed of title)

default 名 債務不履行, 貸倒れ, 支払い停止, 滞納, デフォルト
default premium 債務不履行プレミアム (約定利回りと期待利回りとの差)
default risk 債務不履行リスク, 不履行リスク, デフォルト・リスク
▸Subprime lenders are struggling because of rising delinquencies and *defaults*. サブプライム・ローンの融資行は, 返済遅延や債務不履行[焦げ付き]の増加で苦戦している。

defaulter 名 約束[義務, 契約, 債務]不履行者

defect 名 瑕疵(かし), 欠陥, 欠損, 不良, 〈法などの〉不備, 未整備, 欠点, 弱点, 短所, 過失, ディフェクト
defect rate 不良率
defects in the law 法の不備
defects in the rules governing mergers and acquisitions M&A (企業の合併・買収)に関するルールの不備
latent defect 隠れた欠陥, 隠れた瑕疵
production defect 製造上の欠陥
structural defect 構造上の欠陥
zero defects movement 無欠陥運動, 無欠点運動, ZD運動, ゼロ・ディフェクト運動
▸Our program provides a method for each employee in the company to examine his or her job, apply a criterion of zero *defects* and measure the results. 当社の従業員を対象としたこの制度は, 従業員がそれぞれ自分の仕事を検討し, 欠陥ゼロの基準を適用して, 仕事の成果を評価する仕組みになっています。

defective vehicle 欠陥車
▸Former managers of the company caused losses by covering up recalls of *defective vehicles* and customer complaints. 同社の旧経営陣は, 欠陥車のリコール(回収・無償修理)や顧客からの苦情を隠蔽して(同社に)損害を与えた。

defend 動 守る, 防ぐ, 防衛する, 防衛策を取る, 保護する, 擁護する, 弁護する
▸ABC Corporation, at its expense, shall *defend* any action, suit or proceeding brought against

Licensee which alleges that any Software infringes any U.S. copyright, and ABC Corporation shall pay damages finally awarded against Licensee. 本ソフトウエアが米国の著作権の侵害にあたるとしてライセンシーを相手取って訴え、訴訟が起こされるか法的手続きが取られた場合、ABCコーポレーションは自己負担でこれに抗弁するものとし、最終的にライセンシーに損害賠償金の裁定が下った場合にはABCコーポレーションがこれを支払うものとする。

▶Last year, more than 400 listed companies introduced measures to *defend* themselves against possible takeover bids. 昨年は、400社を超える上場企業が株式公開買付けによる買収防衛策を導入した。

defense [defence] 名 防衛、防衛策、防衛力、防御、保護、擁護、弁護、抗弁 (⇒ **poison-pill defense [defence]**)

 crown jewels defense クラウン・ジュエル防衛、重要資産売却作戦

 defense and space electronics 防衛・宇宙関連電子機器

 defense measure 防衛策 (＝defensive measure)

 defense strategy 防衛戦略、防衛策

 dollar defense ドル防衛 (＝defense of the dollar)

 Pac-Man defense パックマン防衛 (敵対的買収を仕掛けられた側が逆に買収を仕掛ける防衛策)

 takeover defense 買収防衛手段、防衛策、乗っ取り防衛手段、買収防衛策

▶It is necessary to place more emphasis on the dividend policy as part of *defense* against a takeover. 買収防衛策の一環として、配当政策をさらに重視する必要がある。

defensive measure 防衛策 (＝defense measure)

▶Companies are allowed to take various *defensive measures* from hostile takeover by the new corporate law. 新会社法で、企業は多彩な敵対的買収防衛策をとれるようになった。

defer 動 繰り延べる、延期する、引き伸ばす、据え置く、後回しにする

deferment 名 延期、繰延べ、据え置き

deferred 形 繰延べの、据え置きの、据え置き型の、未払いの、延期された

▶*Deferred* gains and losses are recognized when the future sales or purchases are recognized or immediately if the commitment is canceled. 繰延べ利益と損失は、将来の販売もしくは購入を認識した時点で、または契約を解除した場合には即時に認識します。

deferred income taxes 繰延べ法人所得税、繰延べ税額、繰延べ税金

▶*Deferred income taxes* arise from difference in basis for tax and financial-reporting purposes. 繰延べ法人所得税は、税務上と財務会計上の認識基準の差異から生じます。

deferred tax 繰延べ税金 (＝deferred income tax)

▶Using our former accounting method, we held *deferred tax* assets and liabilities at their original values even when tax rates changed. 当社の従来の会計処理方法では、税率が変更された場合でも、繰延べ税金資産および負債は、当初の価額で計上していました。

deficiency 名 不足、欠損、債務超過、不足額、損失金、欠如、欠乏、欠陥、欠点、弱点、不備

 capital deficiency 資本不足、資金不足

 deficiency account 欠損金勘定、欠損金計算書

 deficiency in assets 債務超過

 deficiency in technique 技術の不備

 deficiency of net assets 欠損金

 deficiency payment 不足額の支払い、不足払い、赤字補塡

 demand deficiency 需要不足

 excess or deficiency 過不足

 fiscal deficiency 財政赤字

 fund deficiency 資金不足

 money deficiency 通貨不足

 premium deficiencies 保険料の欠損額

 supply deficiency 供給不足

deficit 名 欠損、損失、欠損金、損失金、営業損失、赤字、不足、不足額、債務超過 (⇒ **current account deficit, operating deficit, trade deficit**)

 accumulated deficit 累積赤字

 capital deficit 債務超過、資本不足 (＝net capital deficiency)

 consolidated deficit 連結赤字

 deficit at the beginning of a period 前期繰延べ欠損金

 deficit-ridden 赤字に悩む

 financial deficit 経営赤字

 fiscal deficit 財政赤字

 government deficit 財政赤字

 net deficit 税引き後赤字

 operate at a deficit 赤字経営をする

 projected deficit 赤字見通し

 twin deficits 双子の赤字 (財政赤字と貿易赤字)

 unappropriated deficit 未処理欠損金

▶The company expects to post a capital *deficit* of ¥8 billion for the year ending this March. 同社は，今年3月期決算で，80億円の債務超過に陥る見通しだ。

▶The U.S. trade *deficit* dropped to $711.6 billion in 2007. 2007年の米国の貿易赤字は，7,116億ドルに減少した。

deficit settlement of accounts 赤字決算

▶Though the seven banking groups increased their capital, the effects of the capital increase were offset by the *deficit settlement of accounts*. 銀行・金融グループ7行は，資本増資を実施したが，赤字決算でその増資効果は吹き飛んでしまった。

define 動 明らかにする，明確にする，定義する，示す，規定する

▶Corporate value is *defined* as "the total of profits one company will earn in future." 企業価値は，「ある会社が将来稼ぐ利益の合計」と定義される。

▶Invoices shall be mailed upon delivery of the Product, as *defined* in Article VIII hereof. 請求書は，本契約第8条に定めるとおり，本商品の引渡しが行われたときに郵送するものとする。

defined benefit plan 確定給付年金制度，確定給付制度，給付建て年金制度，給付建て制度 （＝defined benefit pension plan, defined benefit scheme：退職後の年金給付額またはその決定方法があらかじめ明示してある年金制度）

▶We sponsor non-contributory *defined benefit plans* covering the majority of our employees. 当社は，従業員の大多数を対象とする非拠出型確定給付年金制度を設けています。

defined-contribution annuity scheme 確定拠出年金制度

▶Under the *defined-contribution annuity scheme*, workers who will receive pension payouts in the future decide how the pension fund is invested. 確定拠出年金制度では，将来年金の支払いを受ける従業員が年金積立金の運用方法を決める。

defined-contribution corporate pension plan 確定拠出型企業年金制度

▶This *defined-contribution corporate pension plan* is considered to be a Japanese version of the 401(k) scheme used in the United States. この確定拠出型企業年金制度は，米国で採用している401k制度の日本版と考えられる。

defined-contribution pension plan 確定拠出型［確定拠出］年金制度，確定拠出型年金，確定拠出制度，定額拠出年金制度，拠出建て年金制度 （＝defined-contribution annuity scheme, defined contribution pension scheme, defined contribution plan：「確定拠出年金」は，掛金の運用方法を株式や投資信託，預貯金などの金融商品から加入者自身が決める企業年金の一種）

▶The pension assets of the *defined-contribution pension plans* are basically required to be managed until subscribers turn 60. 確定拠出年金の年金資産は，原則として加入者が60歳になるまで運用を続ける必要がある。

deflation 名 通貨収縮，物価下落，デフレ，デフレーション

  asset deflation 資産デフレ，資産価値の下落
  chronic deflation 慢性的デフレ
  currency deflation 通貨収縮 （＝monetary deflation）
  debt deflation デフレの悪循環
  deflation-battered economy デフレ不況に沈んだ経済
  deflation-led recession デフレ不況 （＝deflationary doldrums, deflationary recession）
  deflation policy デフレ政策 （＝deflationary policy）
  income deflation 所得収縮
  price deflation 物価引下げ，物価デフレーション （＝deflation of prices）

▶Amid *deflation*, it is difficult for companies to pass on rising prices to consumers. デフレの中では，企業が原材料価格の上昇分を消費者に［製品価格に］転嫁するのは難しい。

deflationary 形 通貨収縮の，物価下落の，デフレの

  deflationary crisis デフレ危機，デフレ不況
  deflationary drop in the price level 物価水準の下落傾向，価格水準が下落してデフレを招くこと
  deflationary effect デフレ効果
  deflationary environment デフレ環境
  deflationary expectation デフレ期待
  deflationary gap デフレ・ギャップ
  deflationary impact デフレ効果，デフレ圧力
  deflationary recession デフレ不況
  deflationary trap デフレの罠
  the worst of the deflationary process デフレの最悪期

deflationary doldrums デフレ不況

▶The money supply for January recorded the lowest growth since December 2000, making it difficult for the economy to pull itself out of its *deflationary doldrums*　1月のマネー・サプライが2000年12月以来最低の伸びにとどまり，日本経済がデフレ不況から脱却するのが難しくなっている。

deflationary forces　デフレ要因，デフレの影響力，デフレ圧力，デフレ
▸Even blue-chip companies have been forced to drastically cut their workforces due to price-cutting competition driven by *deflationary forces*.　優良企業でも，デフレによる値下げ競争の影響で，大幅な人員削減を迫られている。

deflationary pressure　デフレ圧力，デフレ不況，デフレ
▸Businesses are cutting back on hiring to counter *deflationary pressures* induced by an influx of cheap imports from countries such as China.　企業は現在，中国などからの安価な輸入品の流入に伴うデフレ圧力に対応するため，雇用を抑制している。
▸The cuts in fiscal spending accelerated *deflationary pressure*.　歳出削減が，デフレ不況を加速させた。

deflationary spiral　デフレの悪循環，デフレ的悪循環，デフレ・スパイラル
▸The economy may fall into a *deflationary spiral* again.　経済は，再びデフレの悪循環に陥る可能性がある。

deflationary trend　デフレ傾向，物価下落の傾向，価格下落の傾向
▸A *deflationary trend* emerged with the collapse of the bubble economy.　デフレ傾向は，バブル崩壊とともに現れた。
▸The United States was able to get out of a *deflationary trend* relatively quickly.　米国は，デフレ傾向から比較的早く抜け出すことができた。

deflator 名　価格修正因子，デフレーター
▸The *deflator* indicates the overall trend in prices.　デフレーターは，物価の総合的な動向を示す。

deforestation 名　森林伐採
▸The *deforestation* of the Amazon has surged in recent months.　アマゾン流域の森林伐採が，ここ数か月で急増している。

defray 動　支払う，支出する，負担する
▸The estimated costs of ¥600 million will be *defrayed* by medical device manufacturers and financial institutions.　6億円の見積り費用は，医療機器メーカーと金融機関が負担することになっている。

deindustrialization 名　脱工業化，産業空洞化
Delaware Corporation Law　デラウエアー般会社法

delay 動　遅らせる，延ばす，延期する，遅れる，手間取る
　delayed delivery service　代行受信サービス
　delayed effect　遅延効果
　delayed interest　遅延利息，遅延金利
　delayed payment　支払いの遅延，支払いの遅れ
　delayed rate setting　金利条件設定繰延べ方式，条件設定遅延方式
　delayed settlement　特約日決済
　delayed time processing　ディレイド・タイム処理，リモート・バッチ処理
▸Most companies producing materials and parts in China either have been unable to collect bills or have received *delayed* payments.　中国に進出している部品や素材メーカーの大半が，踏み倒しや支払いの遅延の被害を受けている。

delay 名　遅延，遅滞，遅れ，延期，〈商品の〉延着，猶予
　delay and extension of time　遅延および期日延長
　delay in economic improvement　景気回復の遅れ（＝delay in economic recovery）
　delay in payment　支払い遅延，支払いの遅れ（＝delayed payment）
　delay of performance　履行遅延
　delay or omission　遅滞または不作為
▸If such *delay* shall exceed two months, either party may give written notice of termination of this agreement.　このような遅延が2か月を超える場合，いずれの当事者も，書面で本契約を解除する通告を出すことができる。
▸There is a *delay* in economic improvement among small and medium companies, as well as nonmanufacturing corporations.　中小企業や非製造業に，景気回復の遅れが見られる。

degear 動　確定利付き負債を減らして払い込み資本に代える

dehire 動　解雇する
delayering 名　階層削減
delegate 動　委任する，委託する，権限を委譲する，代理人[代表者]を任命する，代表として派遣する（⇒authority）
▸Neither party shall *delegate* its obligations under this agreement without the other party's prior written consent.　当事者はいずれも，相手方[他方当事者]の事前の同意書なしで，本契約上の当事者の義務の履行を委任してはならない。

delegation 名　権限の委任[委譲]，義務履行の委託，債務の転付，代理権の授与，下請け，代表団
　delegation of obligations　義務履行の委任[委

託], 債務の転付
delegation of performance 義務履行の委任［委託］
delegation of powers 権限の委任［委譲］, 授権
▶In the event of *delegation*, the delegating party shall remain liable to the other party. 下請けに出す場合, 下請けに出す当事者が, 引き続き相方に対して責任を負うものとする。

delinquency 名 支払い遅延, 返済遅延, 延滞, 不履行の債務
▶The percentage of credit card *delinquencies* fell sharply in the first quarter of this year. 今年第1四半期のクレジット・カードの返済遅延率は, 急減した。

delinquent balances 不良債権残高, 回収遅延残高
▶Our credit approval and monitoring have kept our percentage of *delinquent balances* and write-offs below industry norms. 与信承認条件や検査を厳しくしているため, 当社の不良債権残高と償却額は業界水準以下を保っています。

delist 動 上場を廃止する, 上場を停止する
▶Mitsubishi UFJ Securities was *delisted* from the First Section of the Tokyo Stock Exchange. 三菱UFJ証券は, 東証一部から上場廃止になった。

delisting 上場廃止, 上場停止
▶After *delisting*, shareholders cannot sell their shares on the market, but they can do so through securities houses if there are buyers. 上場廃止後は, 株主は手持ちの株を市場で売却することはできないが, 買い手がいれば証券会社を通じて売却することはできる。

deliver 動 届ける, 配達する, 引き渡す, 渡す, 交付する, 送達する, 納入する, 提供する, 達成する, 実行する,〈判定や評決などを〉行う,〈判定を〉下す,〈原油などを〉産出する
▶Both markets *delivered* positive organic growth. 両市場は, プラスの有機的成長率を達成しました。
▶The convenience stores *deliver* bento boxed meals, prepared food packages and desserts to the home of customers who register for the home delivery service. このコンビニでは, 弁当や惣菜, デザートなどを, コンビニの登録済み宅配サービス会員の自宅まで配達している。

delivery 名 配達, 送達, 配送, 出荷, 納品, 納入, 完納, 引渡し, 受渡し, 交付, 意見の発表, 陳述 （⇒ **carrier, orders on hand**）
buy for future delivery 先渡しで買う
cash on delivery sale 代金[現金]引換販売 （=COD sale, collect on delivery sale, sale for cash on delivery）
collect on delivery 代金引換渡し
delivery expense 配達費, 配送費
delivery of shares 株式の受渡し, 株式交付
delivery system 配送システム, 配達システム
delivery time 納期
export delivery 輸出出荷
orders on hand 手持ち受注分
physical delivery 現物受渡し, 現渡し, 現引き
▶After the restructuring, the group aims to strengthen its profit-making capability by establishing joint frameworks in product *delivery* and development. 再編後, 同グループは商品の配送と商品の開発を共同化して, グループ全体の収益力を強化する計画だ。
▶At *delivery*, the balance sheet will be adjusted for the stock split. 株式の交付時に, 貸借対照表は株式分割による調整を行います。
▶Most of the current orders on hand are scheduled for *delivery* in 2009. 現在の受注残高の大半は, 2009年度に納入することになっています。

delivery interval 納入期間
▶The current orders on hand have shorter *delivery intervals* compared with prior years. 現在の手持ちの受注分[受注残高]は, 過年度[過去数年]に比べて納入期間が短くなっています。

delphi [Delphi] method デルファイ法 （技術予測の手法の一つで, delphi techniqueともいう）

delta 名 デルタ （オプション価格の変化を示す指標）

demand 動 要求する, 請求する, 求める, 要する, 必要とする
▶The former head of the Murakami Fund was often dubbed a shareholder who *demands* a lot. 村上ファンドの元代表は, 「もの言う株主」とよく呼ばれた。

demand 需要, 要求, 請求, 催促, 申立て書, デマンド （⇒**consumer demand**）
actual demand 実需
aggregated demand 総需要
capital demand 資金需要, 資本需要 （=demand for capital）
credit demand 信用需要, 資金需要
demand bus 呼出しバス, デマンド・バス
demand creation 需要創造, 需要創出
demand draft 一覧払い為替手形, 一覧払い手形, 送金小切手
demand for funds 資金需要 （=demand for capital）

demand for loans 借入需要, 資金需要
demand forecast 需要予測 (=demand forecasting)
demand note 一覧払い約束手形
demand prospects 需要見通し
demand-pull inflation 需要超過によるインフレ, 需要インフレ, デマンドプル・インフレ
derived demand 派生需要
domestic demand 国内需要, 内需
external demand 海外需要, 外需 (=foreign demand, overseas demand)
imaginary demand 仮需要, 仮需
institutional demand 機関投資家の需要
investor demand 投資家の需要
latent demand 潜在需要 (=potential demand)
loan demand 借入需要, 資金需要 (=demand for loans)
payable on demand 一覧払い
rising demand 需要の増加
slowing demand 需要の低下, 需要の落込み
sluggish demand 需要低迷, 需要不振 (=slack demand, slow demand)
supply and demand outlook 需給見通し
▶Customer *demand* for the products and services of our core business continues to grow despite weak economic conditions worldwide. 世界的な景気低迷にもかかわらず, 当社の主力事業の製品とサービスに対する顧客の需要は, 引き続き伸びています.
▶The biggest factor behind the rise in oil prices is a sharp increase in *demand* from China. 原油価格高騰の最大の要因は, 中国の原油需要急増だ.

demand deposit 要求払い預金, 当座預金
▶Ordinary deposits usually bear interest while *demand* deposits carry no interest. 普通預金には通常, 利子が付くのに対して, 要求払い預金[当座預金]には利子が付かない.

demand for arbitration 仲裁の請求, 仲裁申立て書
▶The party initiating arbitration shall appoint its arbitrator in its *demand* for arbitration. 仲裁を申し立てた当事者が, 仲裁申立て書でその仲裁人を指名するものとする.

demand for loans 借入需要, 資金需要
▶Private-sector *demand for loans* is weak due to the sluggish economy. 景気低迷で, 企業の資金需要[借入需要]は弱くなっている.

demand-led economic recovery 需要主導型の景気回復, 需要主導の景気回復

▶Japan was urged to continue efforts to promote structural reforms to bring the economy back on track for a domestic *demand-led economic recovery*. 日本は, 日本経済を内需主導の景気回復軌道に戻すため, 構造改革を進める努力を引き続き行うよう求められた.

demand side 需要サイド, 需要側, デマンド・サイド
demand side management 需要管理, デマンド・サイド・マネジメント
demand side policy 需要サイドの政策
▶Businesses have enjoyed a brief respite, but prospects may not be bright if only *demand side* policies are pursued. 産業界は一息ついたようだが, 需要サイドの政策の追求だけでは, 将来の明るい展望は開けないかもしれない.

demarcation [demarkation] 名 境界, 限界, 境界設定[画定], 限界設定, 区分, 区別, 分離, 管轄
demarcation dispute 縄張り紛争
demarcation line 境界線, 限界線 (=line of demarcation)
military demarcation line 軍事境界線

demarketing 名 抑制的マーケティング, ディマーケティング (品薄の商品の需要を抑制するマーケティング活動)

demerge 動 〈事業を〉分離する, 〈子会社を本体から〉切り離す

demerger 名 会社分割, 会社からの独立

demerit system 減点主義

demise 名 死亡, 消滅, 遺譲, 権利譲渡, 権利設定

demographic 形 人口動態に関する, 人口統計学の, 人口統計上の
age-specific demographic structure 年齢別人口構成
demographic analysis 人口動態調査[分析]
demographic data 人口統計データ
demographic revolution 人口革命, 人口の急激な変化 (=demographic transition)
demographic shifts 人口構成の変化, 人口の年齢構成の変化 (=demographic change)
demographic statistics 人口動態統計, 人口統計
demographic trend 人口動態
pyramid-shaped demographic structure ピラミッド型の人口構成
▶The conventional *demographic* structure of Japan was pyramid-shaped. 従来の日本の人口構成は, ピラミッド型だった.

demographic change 〈少子化, 高齢化などの〉人口動態変化, 人口統計の変化, 人口構成の変化

▶*Demographic changes* in China, in particular the decline in the number of young people in farming villages, are affecting the labor supply.　特に農村での若年層の減少という中国の人口構成の変化が，中国の労働力供給[労働需給]に影響を及ぼしている。

demographic structure 人口構造，人口構成
▶Japan's *demographic structure* is changing drastically.　日本の人口構造の変動は急激だ。

demographics 名 人口動態，人口統計，人口統計資料，人口の年齢構成，年齢構成，人口構成，特定の読者層
　changing demographics 人口動態
　specific demographics 特定の読者層，特定の年齢層
▶Many free magazines aim for specific *demographics*, which has piqued the interest of advertisers.　無料の情報誌は特定の読者層を狙ったものが多く，広告主の関心も高まっている。

demonstration 名 展示，展覧，表示，実演，実演販売，実演宣伝，実物宣伝，実証，証明，論証，デモ，示威運動，デモンストレーション
　demonstration effect デモンストレーション効果
　demonstration parade デモ行進
　demonstration sales 実演販売，デモンストレーション・セールス
　on-site demonstration 現地実地試験
　sales demonstration 販売実演
▶The two companies began conducting a *demonstration* in Nagoya.　両社は，名古屋市内で実証実験を開始した。

demonetize 動 〈通貨の〉通用を廃止する
demutualization 非相互会社化（相互会社＝mutual company）
demutualize 動 非相互会社化する
▶Mitsui Life Insurance Co. *demutualized* and became a joint stock company in April 2004.　三井生命保険は，2004年4月から非相互会社化して株式会社になった[2004年4月から会社形態を相互会社から株式会社に転換した]。

denominated 形 …建て，…表示の（⇒**capital outflow**）
　dollar-denominated deposits ドル建て預金
　foreign currency-denominated bonds 外貨建て債券
　foreign-currency-denominated securities 外貨建て債
　in dollar-denominated terms ドル建てで，ドル表示で

　yen-denominated bonds 円建て債，円債
　yen-denominated loan 円借款
　yen-denominated profits 円建て利益
　yuan-denominated bond 人民元建て債券
▶The greater part of the consolidated revenues and assets of the Company is *denominated* in U.S. dollars.　当社の連結売上高と連結資産の大半は，米ドル建てとなっています。

department 名 部門，部，課，局，省，売り場
　accounting department 経理部
　department administration 部門管理
　department cost 部門費（＝department charge, department expense, departmental cost）
　Department of Commerce 米商務省
　Department of Justice 米司法省
　financial department 財務部
　legal department 法務部
　manufacturing department 製造部門（＝production department）
　operating department 事業部門
　producing department cost 製造部門費
　purchasing department 購買部門
　sales department 営業部門，販売部門
　shipping department 配送部
　treasury department 財務部門
▶The merger of their parts and material *departments* is also on the negotiation table.　交渉では，両社の部品と資材調達部門の統合も検討されている。

dependent 形 頼っている，依存している，…なしでは済まされない，従属の，名 扶養家族，被扶養者
　allowance for dependents 扶養控除
　dependent company 従属会社，子会社
　dependent development 従属的発展
　dependent project 相互依存的プロジェクト
　dependent variable 従属変数
▶GM pays for health care for 750,000 U.S. hourly employees, retirees and their *dependents*.　米ゼネラル・モーターズ(GM)は，米国の時間給制従業員，退職者とその扶養家族75万人の医療費を負担している。

deplete 動 使い果たす，激減させる，消耗させる，枯渇させる
depletion 名 枯渇，消耗，減耗償却（⇒**ozone depletion**）
deposit 名 預金，預金額，積立金，保証金，敷金，内金，手付け金，預託，堆積物，鉱床，埋蔵量
　bank deposit 銀行預金

business deposit 営業預金
deposit at bank 銀行預金 (=deposit money in a bank)
deposit for bond redemption 社債償還引当預金
deposit from employees 従業員預り金
deposit in current account 当座預金
deposit in trust 信託預金
deposit modifier たいせき物改質剤
deposit obligations 預金債務, 預金残高
deposit paid on construction work 工事前渡金
deposit paid to trade creditor 仕入先前払い代金
deposit received 預り金, 保証金 (=deposited money, money in custody)
fixed deposit 定期預金
promising deposits of natural gas 有望な天然ガスの埋蔵量
quick deposit 当座預金
rich deposits of uranium 埋蔵量の豊富なウランの鉱床
sea-floor hydrothermal deposits 海底熱水鉱床
time deposit 定期預金
▶Ordinary bank deposits for individuals and current *deposits* for businesses was fully guaranteed until March 31, 2003. 個人の普通預金と企業の当座預金は, 2003年3月31日まで全額保証されていた。
▶The basic marine development plan sets a goal of commercially utilizing methane hydrate and sea-floor hydrothermal *deposits* within about 10 years. 海洋開発基本計画は, メタンハイドレートと海底熱水鉱床の商業化について今後10年程度を目標に置いている。
▶The ratio of cash and *deposits* in total household assets declined 0.7 percentage point to 54.5 percent from a year earlier. 家計の金融資産総額に占める現金・預金の割合は, 前年比で0.7ポイント(0.7％)減少して54.5％となった。

Deposit Insurance Corporation 預金保険機構
▶Financial institutions pay insurance premiums to the *Deposit Insurance Corporation* according to the amount of deposits they hold. 金融機関は, 保有する預金量に応じて預金保険機構に保険料を納付している。

depository 名 供託所, 受託所, 保管所, 倉庫, 保管人, 受託者
depreciable 形 減価償却の対象となる, 減価却できる, 償却可能な, 償却性の
▶The increase in operating expenses was primarily due to depreciation expenses caused by higher average *depreciable* plant. 営業費用増加の主な要因は減価償却費で, 減価償却の対象となる有形固定資産の平均残高の拡大により, 減価償却費は増加しました。
depreciate 動 低下する, 下落する, 価値が下がる, 〈通貨を〉切り下げる, 減価償却する, 償却する, 減価する, 減価して見積もる
depreciated asset 資産価値の下落
depreciate the currency 通貨を切り下げる
▶All other plant and equipment is *depreciated* on a straight-line basis. その他のすべての工場・設備は, 定額法で償却しています。
▶The bridge *depreciates* to zero value after 40 years in terms of tax laws. この橋の耐用年数は, 税法上は40年にすぎない。
depreciation 名 減価償却, 減価償却費, 償却, 償却費, 減価, 価値低下, 平価切下げ (米国では一般に有形固定資産(property, plant and equipment)の減価償却にdepreciationを使い, 無形固定資産(intangible assets)の償却にはamortizationを使っている)
accelerated depreciation 加速償却法
competitive depreciation 〈為替平価の〉切下げ競争, 競争的平価切下げ
depreciation allowance 減価償却引当金
depreciation of the currency 通貨安
depreciation of the real exchange rate 実質為替レートの下落
dollar depreciation ドル切下げ, ドル安, ドルの下落 (=depreciation of the dollar)
machinery depreciation 機械減価
market value depreciation 市場価格の低下
tax depreciation 税務上の減価償却
yen depreciation against the dollar 円安ドル高
▶Cost of revenues, *depreciation*, and amortization are translated at the actual rates in effect when the related assets were manufactured or acquired. 売上原価と減価償却費および償却費は, 当該資産の製造日または取得日の実際の実効為替レートで換算してあります。
▶Falling stock prices and the *depreciation* of the U.S. dollar increased uncertainty over the global economy. 米国の株安やドル安で, 世界経済の不透明感が強まっている。
depreciation cost 減価償却費 (=depreciation charge, depreciation expense: 減価償却

総額のうち減価償却手続きで費用化された部分）
▸Companies will be allowed to fully write off *depreciation costs* as tax-exempt expenses. 企業は今後，減価償却費を非課税費用［損金］として全額処理できるようになる［減価償却費を100％損金算入できるようになる］．

depreciation of the yen 円安
▸The *depreciation of the yen* also has boosted profits for exporting companies. 円安も，輸出企業の利益を押し上げた．

depress 動 …の力を弱める，抑制する，低下させる，〈価値を〉下落させる
  depress economic activity 景気を低迷［沈滞さ せる］，経済活動を沈滞させる
  depress import growth 輸入の伸びを鈍化させる
  depress spending 消費低迷をもたらす
  depress the bond market 債券相場を下落させる，債券相場に冷や水を浴びせる

depressed 形 抑圧された，不景気の，不振の，下落した
  depressed cartel 不況カルテル
  depressed consumer confidence 消費者マインドの冷え込み
  depressed economy 景気低迷
  depressed industry 不況産業
  depressed inflation 抑圧されたインフレ，抑圧性インフレ
  depressed market 沈滞市況，沈滞した市況
  depressed prices 物価の下落，価格低迷
  depressed sales 販売の定価，販売低迷，販売不振

depression 名 不況，不況期，不景気，大恐慌，うつ病
  depression cartel 不況カルテル
  economic depression 不況，不景気
  structural depression 構造不況
  the Depression 大恐慌，世界大恐慌
▸Amid the recent wave of corporate restructuring, many middle-aged and older workers suffer from *depression*. 最近の企業リストラのあおりで，中高年労働者の多くはうつ病になっている．

deputy 名 代理

deregulate 動 規制を緩和する，規制を撤廃する，自由化する，市場開放する
▸Bank sales of insurance products were *deregulated* in April 2001. 保険商品の銀行窓口での販売は，2001年4月に自由化された．

deregulation 名 規制緩和，規制撤廃，自由化，市場開放
  deregulation of the power industry 電力自由化
  financial deregulation 金融の規制緩和（＝deregulation of finance）
  increasing competition due to deregulation 規制緩和による競争の激化
  interest rate deregulation 金利の自由化
▸With the increasing *deregulation* of the civil aviation industry, the world's airlines are exposed to an unprecedented scale of competition. 民間航空産業の規制緩和［空の規制緩和］が進むなか，世界の航空会社はかつてない大競争にさらされている．

derivative 名 派生商品，金融派生商品，派生物，派生物質，デリバティブ（＝derivative product, derivative financial instrument: 相場の変動を予測して行う先物取引など，特殊な取引を組み合わせた金融派生商品）
  blood derivative 血液製剤
  commodity derivatives 市況商品の派生商品
  credit derivatives 信用派生商品
  derivative action 派生訴訟，株主代表訴訟（＝derivative lawsuit, derivative suit, representative suit）
  derivative instruments 派生商品
  equity derivatives 株式派生商品
  exchange-traded derivatives 上場派生商品
  financial derivatives 金融派生商品
  interest rate derivatives 金利派生商品
  mortgage derivatives モーゲージ派生商品
  OTC derivatives 店頭派生商品
  weather derivatives 天候デリバティブ

derivative financial instruments 金融派生商品，デリバティブ
▸In the normal course of business, we use various financial instruments, including *derivative financial instruments*. 通常業務で，当社は各種の金融商品を利用しており，これには金融派生商品も含まれています．

derivative investment デリバティブ投資，金融派生商品取引
▸These losses were created by high-risk *derivative investments*. この損失は，リスクの高いデリバティブ（金融派生商品）取引で生じたものだ．

derivative product 派生商品，金融派生商品，デリバティブ（＝derivative, derivative instrument, financial derivative instrument）
▸U.S. and European banks have advanced into diverse fields, including securities business, by polishing up their financial tools for utilizing *derivative products*. 欧米の銀行は，デリバティ

ブ (金融派生商品) を活用するための金融技術を磨いて、証券業務などさまざまな分野に進出してきた。

derivative transaction 派生商品取引, デリバティブ取引
▸Takefuji Corp. may lose as much as ¥30 billion on *derivative transactions* arranged by Merrill Lynch & Co. 消費者金融の武富士は、メリルリンチがアレンジした派生商品取引で、300億円もの損失を出すおそれがある。

design 名 設計, 意匠, デザイン
  basic design 基本設計
  code design コード設計
  design automation 設計自動化, デザイン・オートメーション《略 DA》
  design engineering center 設計技術センター
  design patent 意匠特許
  design right 意匠権
  detail design 詳細設計
  file design ファイル設計
  graphic design グラフィック・デザイン
  industrial design 工業デザイン, 工業意匠, インダストリアル・デザイン
  industrial new design 実用新案
  input design 入力設計
  job design 職務設計
  operation design 作業設計
  output design 出力設計
  package design 包装デザイン, 包装意匠
  process design プロセス設計
  product design 製品のデザイン, 製品設計, 製品計画
  program design プログラム設計
  research design 調査設計
  systems design システム設計
▸These days, product *design* and planning, as well as the design of molds and other necessary tools, is done with three-dimensional computer-aided design (CAD). 今は、製品のデザイン・設計と鋳型その他の必要な工具類の設計は、三次元のCAD (コンピュータ支援設計) で行うようになった。

designation 名 表示, 記号, 指定, 指名
▸The *designation* of "SEK" is used for Swedish kronor and millions of Swedish kronor are shown as "SEK M."「SEK」の記号は、スウェーデン・クローナの表示に用いられ、百万スウェーデン・クローナは「SEK M.」で示してあります。

designer and character brand DCブランド

deskill 動 単純作業化する

desktop 形 卓上の, 卓上型, 机上型の, デスクトップ型の, 名 デスクトップ型コンピュータ, コンピュータの画面, 画面の背景
  desktop computer 卓上型コンピュータ, デスクトップ型コンピュータ
  desktop conference 卓上会議, テレビ会議《略 DTC》
  desktop management デスクトップ管理
  desktop planning デスクトップ・プランニング《略 DTP》
  desktop presentation デスクトップ・プレゼンテーション
  desktop publishing 卓上出版
  desktop videoconferencing package デスクトップ型テレビ会議装置

destination 名 仕向け地, 仕向け先, 届け先, 宛先, 最終目的, 目的, 目的地
  destination address 終点アドレス, 行き先アドレス
  destination freight 仕向け地払い運賃
  destination shopper デスティネーション・ショッパー (買う物をはっきり決めて買い物に行く人)
  final destination 最終目的地, 最終仕向け地
  FOB destination 着荷地渡し
  investment destination 投資先
  probable destination 予定仕向け地
  the port of destination 仕向け港, 目的港
▸Sales by *destination* for 2008 were $3,300 million, $1,800 million, and $440 million for the U.S., Canada and Other respectively. 2008年度の仕向け地別売上高は、米国が33億ドル、カナダが18億ドルで、その他は4億4,000万ドルでした。

deteriorate 動 悪化する, 低下する, 停滞する, 退化する, 老朽化する
  deteriorated earnings 業績の悪化
  deteriorated profitability 収益性の悪化
  deteriorating credit quality 信用の質の悪化, 信用度の悪化, 信用力の低下

deterioration 名 悪化, 低下, 減少, 停滞, 品質低下, 退化, 劣化, 老朽化
  deterioration in asset quality 資産の質の悪化
  deterioration in balance sheets 財務体質の悪化
  deterioration in financial health 財務体質の悪化
  deterioration in the business situation 経営悪化, 景況の悪化
  deterioration of corporate performance 企

業業績の悪化
earnings deterioration 収益の悪化, 業績の悪化
profit deterioration 減益, 利益の減少
▸An increasing number of loans turn out to be nonperforming due to a *deterioration* in the business situation of the borrowers. 融資先の経営悪化で, 不良債権化する貸出が増えている。

determination 名 決定, 決断, 決断力, 決心, 決意, 確定, 限定, 判断, 解決, 測定, 算定, 計算, 判決, 裁決, 終決, 〈財産権の〉消滅［終了］
determination of net income 純利益の算定
determination of the actuarial present values 保険数理上の現在価値の測定
determination of the reportable segment 報告すべきセグメントの決定
vesting percentage applicable at the date of determination 測定日に適用可能な給付額の割合

determine 動 決定する, 決断する, 決める, 決意する, 確定する, 定める, …に制限を設ける, 左右する, 強い影響を与える, 判断する, 〈問題などを〉解決する, 測定する, 算定する
▸The board of directors *determines* dividend payments based on such considerations as earnings from operations, capital requirements, and the corporation's financial condition. 配当の支払い額は, 営業利益, 資金需要や当社の財務状況などを検討した上で, 取締役会が決定しています。

devaluation 名 通貨切下げ, 通貨安, 通貨下落, 価値の低下, 評価切下げ, 低評価, 切下げ
asset devaluation 資産の評価切下げ
currency devaluation 通貨切下げ, 通貨安
devaluation of exchange rates 為替相場の切下げ, 為替レートの切下げ
devaluation risk 通貨安のリスク, 通貨切下げのリスク
dollar devaluation ドル安, ドル切下げ
gradual devaluation of the yen 円のじり安
social devaluation 社会での低評価
▸The *devaluation* of our investments in Thailand is certainly a negative consequence. 当社がタイに投資した分の価値が低下したことは, 確かにマイナス要因です。
▸The *devaluation* will enhance our competitiveness as virtually 100 percent of our products is exported. 当社の製品は100%輸出しているので, 通貨下落で当社の競争力は増すと思われます。

develop 動 開発する, 整備する, 改善する, 改良する, 発展させる, 育成する, 〈土地などを〉造成する, 展開する, 現像する

▸General Motors Corp. and Ford Motor Co. were late in *developing* low fuel consumption cars as the price of crude oil rose. ゼネラル・モーターズ (GM) やフォード・モーターは, 原油高のなかで, 低燃費車の開発が遅れた。

developer 名 開発業者, 開発会社, 不動産開発業者, 宅地造成業者, 宅地開発業者, デベロッパー
▸Real estate *developer* Mitsui Fudosan will acquire a 33.16 percent stake in Imperial Hotel for ¥86 billion. 不動産開発会社の三井不動産は, 帝国ホテルの株式の33.16%を860億円で取得する。

development 名 開発, 整備, 教育, 育成, 発展, 進歩, 進展, 展開, 推移, 動き, 情勢, 動向, 新事態, 製品 (⇒joint development, product development, research and development)
business development 事業拡大, 事業展開, 業務展開, 事業開発, ビジネス開発, ビジネスの展開
career development 社員の経歴［職歴］開発, キャリア開発
currency developments 為替動向, 為替相場の動き
development aid 開発援助
development-and-import formula [scheme] 開発輸入方式, 開発輸入
development capital 開発資金 (=funds for development)
development environment 開発環境
development from above 上からの開発, 政府主導の開発
development from below 下からの開発, 民間主導の開発
development information resources 開発情報資源
development loan 開発融資, 開発借款
development potential 開発可能性, 発展の可能性
development project 開発計画, 開発事業, 開発プロジェクト
development state enterprise 開発段階企業
development tool 開発支援ツール, 構築支援ツール
economic development 経済開発, 経済発展, 経済成長, 景気動向
energy and water development エネルギー・水資源開発
executive development 経営者教育, 経営者開発
human resources development 人的資源開発, 人材開発, 人材育成 (=development of human resources, manpower development)

industrial development 産業開発, 産業振興, 産業[工業]の発展, 工業化
infrastructure development インフラ開発, インフラ整備
interest rate developments 金利動向
Job Development Act 米国の雇用促進法
Job Development Credit 米国の雇用促進投資控除, 雇用促進税額控除
management development 経営教育, 経営者教育, 経営幹部の育成 （＝executive development)
manpower development マンパワー開発, 人的資源開発 （＝human resources development)
market development 市場開発, 市場整備, 市場の発展
national development 国土開発
new product development 新製品開発
ocean development 海洋開発
official development aid 政府開発援助
organization [organizational] development 組織開発
overseas development assistance 海外経済協力
personnel development 人員開発
professional development 職業専門家としての能力開発
property development 不動産開発
regional development 地域開発
residential plot development 宅地開発 （＝residential development)
self-development 自己啓発
skills development スキル開発
software development support ソフトウエア開発支援
sustainable development 持続可能な開発, 持続可能な発展
system development planning システム開発設計
technical [technology] development 技術開発
▸Our laboratories engage in basic research as well as product and service *development*. 当社の研究所では, 基礎研究のほかに, 製品やサービスの開発に当たっています。
▸There is a possibility that liquidity demand will increase further depending on financial market *developments*. 金融市場の今後の展開次第では, 資金需要が拡大する可能性もある。

device 名 装置, 周辺機器, 電気部品, 素子, 道具, 手段, 方策, 措置, 工夫, 考案, 操作, 計画, 図案, 模様, 意匠, デバイス

accounting device 会計上の操作
anti-inflationary device インフレ抑制の手段
device name 装置名, デバイス名, デバイス・ファイル名
devices such as personal computers and mobile phones パソコンや携帯電話などの機器
digital home electronic devices デジタル家電
electronic device 電子装置, 電子機器
financing device 財務手段
input device 入力装置
labor-saving device 省力装置
legal device 法的手段
magnetic memory device 磁気記憶装置
monetary control device 金融調節手段
motivating device 動機づけの手段, 動機づけの方策
off-balance-sheet devices オフ・バランスシート商品, オフ・バランスシート項目
output device 出力装置
peripheral device 周辺装置, 周辺機器
pointing device 画像位置指示装置
portable device 移動端末 （⇒One Seg)
protective device 保護装置
silicon on insulator device SOI素子
super lattice device 超格子素子
the volumes of information exchanged between devices 機器間でやりとりする情報の量
▸Charge coupled *devices* are used as "eyes" in digital cameras. 電荷結合素子は, デジタル・カメラの「目」として使われている。

DI 景気動向指数 （diffusion index の略)
business conditions DI 業況判断DI
coincident DI 一致指数DI
DI index 業況判断指数, 景気動向指数, DI指数 （⇒diffusion index)
DI reading DIの数値
leading DI 先行指数DI
manufacturing DI 製造業の業況判断DI
overall financial conditions DI 資金繰り判断DI
price DI 価格判断DI
sentiment DI 業況判断DI
▸*DI* consists of the leading index, coincident index and lagging index. 景気動向指数は, 先行指数と一致指数, 遅行指数から成る。

diet aid ダイエット食品 （＝weight-reducing food supplement)

difference 名 差, 差異, 違い, 格差, 差額, 不足分 （⇒temporary differences, timing differences)

common difference 公差
difference of discrepancy 相違または矛盾
discount difference 割引差額
exchange differences 為替相場の開き, 為替差額
international difference 国際格差
major differences 主要な対立点
negative difference マイナス差額, 差額がマイナスであること
positive difference プラス差額, 差額がプラスであること
trading difference 〈株式の〉取引差額
▸Deferred taxes arise because of *differences* in the book and tax bases of certain assets and liabilities. 繰延べ税金は, ある種の資産や負債について帳簿上と税務上とで差異があることから生じます。
▸The *difference* was funded by increasing notes payable by 200 million, principally through the sale of commercial paper. 資金の不足分は, 主にコマーシャル・ペーパーを発行して, 手形借入金を2億ドル増やして補填しました。

differentiate 動 差別化する, 特殊化する, 識別する, 区別する, 見分ける, 〈細胞などが〉分化する
▸In the DRAM industry, prices are the single most significant *differentiating* factor. DRAM(記憶保持動作が必要な随時書込み読出しメモリ)業界では, 価格がまさに最も重要な差別化の要因になっている。

differentiation 名 差別化, 差別, 区別, 識別, 分化
product differentiation 製品差別化, 製品の差別化
strategic differentiation 戦略的差別化
▸Quality no longer secures strategic *differentiation*, but is an operational necessity. 製品とサービスの質はもはや戦略的差別化を保証するものではなく, 業務運営の必須条件となっています。

difficulties 名 困難, 問題, 苦境, 難局, 危機, 低迷
balance of payments difficulties 国際収支の悪化
financial difficulties 財政的困難, 経営危機, 資金繰りが困難な状況
in-house difficulties 社内問題
serious difficulties 深刻な経営難
▸Earnings of the firm were impacted by *difficulties* in North American real estate markets. 同社の利益は, 北米の不動産市場の低迷による影響を受けました。

diffusion index 景気動向指数, 業況判断指数《略 DI》(「業況判断指数」は, 日本銀行が景気の実態を把握するため3か月ごとに行う企業短期経済観測調査で, 企業の景況感を示す指数)
diffusion index for employment conditions 雇用人員DI
diffusion index of leading indicators 景気先行指数DI, 景気先行指数(DI)
diffusion index of retail prices 販売価格判断DI
▸A *diffusion* index is calculated by subtracting the percentage of companies that believe business conditions are bad from companies that see them as improving. 業況判断指数(DI)は, 業況が回復していると見ている企業の割合(%)から, 業況が悪いと思っている企業の割合を差し引いて算定する。
▸The *diffusion* indexes of the coincident, leading and lagging indicators compare the current levels of various economic indicators with their levels three months earlier. 一致指数や先行指数, 遅行指数などの景気動向指数は, 各種経済指標の現状を3か月前の状況と比較したものだ。

diffusion index of business sentiment [confidence] 業況判断指数《略 DI》
▸The *diffusion index of business sentiment* among large manufacturers rose four points to 26, compared with the previous survey for the three months to June. 大企業・製造業の業況判断指数(DI)は, 前回の4-6月調査に比べて4ポイント上昇の26となった。

digital 形 数字表示式の, 計数型, デジタル方式の, 電子的手段による, データを電子化した, 電算化した, デジタル (⇒**capacity**)
digital appliances デジタル家電, ネット家電
digital broadcasting service デジタル放送, デジタル放送サービス
digital communication [communications] デジタル通信
digital consumer electronics デジタル家電
digital content デジタル著作物, デジタル・コンテンツ
digital currency 電子通貨, 電子マネー (= digital money, electronic money)
digital display デジタル表示
digital divide 情報格差, 情報化が生む経済格差, インターネットを使える人と使えない人との格差
digital economy デジタル経済 (=e-economy, new economy)
digital home appliances 情報家電, デジタル家

電 (=computerized appliances)

digital image processing デジタル画像処理

digital information デジタル情報

digital opportunity 情報化がもたらす機会, デジタル・オポチュニティ

digital rights デジタル著作権, デジタル化権 (=digitalization [digitization] rights)

digital rights management デジタル著作権管理《略 DRM》

Digital Signature Act 電子署名法

digital subscriber line デジタル加入者回線, デジタル加入者線《略 DSL》

digital terrestrial broadcasting 地上デジタル放送

digital versatile [video] disk デジタル多用途［ビデオ］ディスク《略 DVD》

digital watermarking 電子透かし技術, 電子透かし (=electronic watermarking)

digital electric appliances デジタル家電
▸The recent high growth is attributed to growing capital spending for *digital electric appliances* and the rise in exports to Asian countries. 最近の高成長の要因は, デジタル家電の設備投資拡大とアジア向け輸出の伸びにある。

digital household appliances デジタル家電
▸The sales of *digital household appliances* are brisk. デジタル家電の販売が, 好調だ。

digital photography デジタル写真技術
▸Eastman Kodak Co., the leading maker of photographic film, filed a suit against Sony alleging that Sony infringed 10 of Kodak's patents related to *digital photography*. 米写真フイルムの大手イーストマン・コダックは, ソニーがデジタル写真技術に関するコダックの10件の特許を侵害したとして, ソニーを提訴した。

digital technology デジタル技術, デジタル通信技術
▸*Digital technology* is the foundation of new telecommunications services of information age. デジタル技術は, 情報化社会の新通信サービスの基盤となっている。

digitalization 名 デジタル化, 情報のデジタル暗号化, アナログ情報のデジタル情報への変換, 信号化, 数字化 (=digitization)

digitalization right デジタル化権

full digitalization 完全デジタル化

the digitalization of the telephone network 電話網のデジタル化

▸As investment for *digitalization* is costly, we need to establish a more profitable management system, including joint investment in digital-related facilities and content with the group. デジタル化の投資負担は軽くないので, 当社は, 同グループとのデジタル関連施設への共同投資やコンテンツ［情報内容］の共有など, 収益力の高い経営システムを確立する必要がある。

dilute 動 薄める, 弱める,〈価値などを〉損なう, 希薄化する, 希釈化する, 減少する, 減額する

dilute the value of the existing shares 既存の株の価値を損なう

diluted earnings per share of common stock 希薄後普通株式1株当たり純利益

fully diluted earnings per common share 完全希薄化による普通株式1株当たり利益, 完全希薄化後普通株式1株当たり利益, 潜在株式調整後1株当たり利益

primary and fully diluted earnings per share 単純希薄化と完全希薄化による1株当たり利益

▸Hokuetsu will issue equity warrants to all existing shareholders to *dilute* Oji's voting rights and make it difficult for Oji to take control of the company. 北越製紙は, 既存の全株主に新株予約権を発行して王子製紙の議決権を減らし, 王子が北越の経営権を握るのを阻止する方針だ。

dilution 名〈株式などの〉希薄化, 希釈化, 減額, 減少, 落ち込み, 1株当たりの価値が低くなる［薄まる］こと (「希薄化・希釈化」とは, 時価発行増資や転換社債の転換, ワラント債の権利行使などによる発行済み株式総数の増加で, 1株当たり利益 (earnings per share) の減少や資産価値の目減りを招くことをいう。⇒per-share value)

dilution from new share issues 新株発行による希薄化, 増資による希薄化

dilution from the conversion of convertible bonds 転換社債の転換による希薄化

earnings dilution 利益の希薄化, 利益の落ち込み, 減益 (=dilution of earnings)

losses from dilution 減額による損失 (=dilution losses)

▸The *dilution* in earnings per share from new issuances was not material. 新株発行による1株当たり利益［純利益］の希薄化は, 重要視するほどではありません。

diminish 動 減少させる, 減らす, 縮小する, 減少する, 低下する, 低減する, 逓減する

diminished access to capital 資金調達力の低下

diminished losses 赤字解消

diminished production 生産縮小

DIP 継承破産人 (debtor in possessionの略)

DIP finance [financing] 事業再生融資, DIP ファイナンス, デッター・イン・ポゼション融資 (DIP=debtor in possession; 不動産担保がなくても事業の継続可能性などを考慮して新規融資する仕組み)

DIP finance formula DIPファイナンス方式 (=DIP formula; ⇒**debtor in possession (DIP) finance**)

DIP plan 事業再生融資制度, DIPファイナンス

direct debit system 自動引落しシステム
▶Under the *direct debit system*, the life insurer's sales employees will scan data on new customers' bank cards using portable terminals when they sign insurance policies. この口座引落しシステムでは, 顧客が保険契約をする際, 生命保険会社[同生保]の営業職員が決済の携帯端末を使って新規顧客のキャッシュ・カードのデータを読み取る。

direct disbursement system 直接支払い制 (=direct payment system)
▶In the United States and Europe, *direct disbursement systems* are a main pillar of agricultural policy and are used to grant sizable amounts of subsidies every year. 欧米では, 直接支払い制は農政の柱で, 毎年巨額の補助金を出すのに利用されている。

direct investment 直接投資 (⇒**foreign direct investment**)
　direct overseas investment 海外直接投資
　external direct investment 対外直接投資
　inward direct investment 対内直接投資
　vertical direct investment 垂直的直接投資
▶An increase in *direct investment* returns and stock dividends from Japanese investments abroad pushed the income account surplus up to a record for the fourth straight year. 直接投資の収益増と日本の海外への投資による株式の配当で, 所得収支の黒字は4年連続で最高額を更新した。

director 名 取締役, 理事, 役員, 局長 (⇒**board of directors, independent director, officer**)
　取締役とは➡取締役会のメンバーで, 業務執行についての意思決定をするのが取締役であるが, 日本と違って英米法では必ずしも会社の役員ではない。社内取締役(inside director)と社外取締役(outside director)を含めて, 取締役(director)は株主が選任し, 会社役員(corporate officer)は取締役が選任することになっている。
　acting director 仮取締役, 取締役代行, 代行取締役
　advisory director 相談役, 顧問重役
　alternative director 代理取締役, 取締役代行, 予備取締役 (=alternate director)
　board director 取締役, 委員会などの理事 (=board member)
　board of directors 取締役会, 役員会, 重役会, 理事会
　changes in directors 役員の異動
　company director 会社役員, 役員
　deputy managing director イギリスの副社長, 業務取締役代行
　director of finance 財務担当取締役
　directors and auditors' bonus 役員賞与, 役員賞与金
　directors' emoluments 取締役報酬
　directors' remuneration 役員報酬
　directors' report 取締役の報告, 取締役報告書
　disclosure of individual directors' remuneration 役員報酬の個別開示
　divisional director 部門役員, 部門担当役員
　executive director 業務執行取締役, 執行取締役, 専務・常務取締役
　full time director 常勤取締役
　inside director 社内取締役, 内部取締役, 内部重役
　loan to director 取締役貸付け金
　loans repayable to stockholders, directors or employees 株主・役員・従業員借入金
　managing director 英国企業の社長, 業務執行取締役, 専務取締役, 常務取締役《略 MD》
　meeting of board of directors 取締役会会議, 取締役会 (=board of directors' meeting)
　new director 新任取締役, 後任取締役
　outside director 社外取締役, 外部取締役
　president and representative director 代表取締役社長
　provisional director 一時取締役
　representative director 代表取締役
　senior managing director 専務取締役, 専務
▶Livedoor asked the Tokyo District Court to select a provisional *director*. ライブドアは, 東京地裁に一時取締役の選任を要請した。
▶The minimum number of *directors* for a stock company has been reduced from three to one under the new Corporate Law. (2006年5月1日に施行された)新会社法では, 株式会社の最低取締役数が3人から1人に減った。

dirigism 名 統制経済政策

dirty 形 政府の介入を受ける, 故障のある
　dirty bill of lading 故障船荷証券, 故障付き船荷証券 (=dirty B/L)
　dirty cargo 粗悪貨物

dirty float 汚い変動相場制, ダーティ・フロート (＝dirty floating rate system：通貨当局が特定の意図で市場に介入して相場操作をすること)
dirty linen 内輪のこと, 内輪の恥
dirty money 不正資金, 不正な金, 汚い金
dirty pool 卑劣な行為, 汚いやり方
dirty receipt 故障付き本船受取書
dirty tricks 卑劣な行為, 卑劣な企み, 不正活動, 中傷活動
dirty work 汚れる仕事, いやな仕事, 下働き
disappointing 形 期待外れの, …の期待を裏切る, 予想を裏切った
　disappointing GDP growth rate 期待外れのGDP成長率
　disappointing news 悪材料
　disappointing performance 期待外れの業績, 予想を裏切る業績
　disappointing results 期待外れの業績, 期待を裏切る業績, 予想を裏切る業績（＝disappointing performance）
▶This difficult global business environment impacted our business and caused *disappointing* second quarter results. この困難な世界のビジネス環境による当社業務への影響で, 第2四半期の業績は不満足な結果となりました。
disadvantage 名 不利, 不都合, 不便な点, 不利な立場, 遅れ, 劣位, 弱点, 不備, 欠陥, 損害, 損失, マイナス
▶GM's current $1,500 per worker health care expense puts the company at a significant *disadvantage* versus foreign-based competitors. GMにとって, 現在同社が負担している従業員［労働者］1人当たり1,500ドルの医療費が, 海外のライバルとの競争上, 大きなマイナスになっている。
disburse 動 支払う, 支出する
disbursement 名 〈現金・小切手などによる〉支払い, 支出, 拠出, 出資, 資金交付, 立替え, 支出額, 支払い金, 立替え金, 貸出［貸金］の実行［実施］, 実施額
　cash disbursement 現金支出
　delayed disbursement 支払いの遅延
　disbursement account 立替え勘定
　disbursement of funds 貸出の実行
　disbursement schedule 支払い一覧表
　excess disbursement 支払い超過
　extraordinary disbursement 臨時支出
　fiscal disbursement 財政出動
　government disbursement 政府支出
　initial disbursement 第一次実行, 第一実施額
　loan disbursement 貸出の実行
　net disbursement 純支出額, 支出純額
▶Measures to stimulate the economy have been implemented through fiscal *disbursement*. 財政出動で, 景気刺激策が実施された。
▶The U.S. Congress approved the *disbursement* of $18 billion to the IMF. 米国は, 国際通貨基金(IMF)に対する180億ドルの拠出を認めた。
discarded home electronics products 廃家電
discharge 動 陸揚げする, 荷揚げする, 〈荷物を〉降ろす, 解放する, 解散させる, 債務を免除する, 〈負債を〉弁済する
discharge 名 発射, 解雇, 免職, 解任, 遂行, 履行, 流出, 排出, 退院, 除隊, 〈借金の〉返済, 免責
　application of discharge 免責の申し立て
　disciplinary discharge [dismissal] 懲戒免職
　discharge allowance 解雇手当
　discharge by agreement 合意による契約の解除, 合意による契約の消滅
　discharge in bankruptcy 破産免責, 破産者の債務免除
　discharge of contract 契約の解除［解消, 消滅］
　discharge of nuclear waste 核廃棄物の流出
　discharge of waste water 廃液の排出
　discharge warning 解雇予告
　medical discharge 退院
　option of discharge 陸揚げ港選択権
　port of discharge 荷揚げ港, 陸揚げ港, 荷降ろし［荷卸し］港
　temporary discharge 仮陸揚げ
　wholesale discharge 大量解雇
disclose 動 開示する, 公開する, 公表する, 発表する, 明示する（⇒salary）
▶The Tokyo Stock Exchange obliges listed companies to *disclose* information that concerns investors. 東京証券取引所は, 投資家の利害にかかわる情報の開示を上場企業に義務付けている。
disclosure 名 企業内容の開示, 企業経営内容の公開, 企業情報の開示, 情報開示, 情報の公開, 事実の開示, 発明の開示, 開示, 公開, 公開性, 公表, 表示, 内容の特定, 告知, ディスクロージャー
　adequacy of disclosure 開示の適切性
　corporate disclosure 企業の情報開示, 企業による情報開示
　data disclosure 資料開示, 情報開示, データの開示
　disclosure of accounting policies 会計方針の開示
　disclosure of financial statements 財務諸表［財務書類］の開示, 企業財務の公開

disclosure of individual directors' remuneration 役員報酬の個別開示
disclosure of knowhow ノウハウの開示
Disclosure of Official Information Law 情報公開法
disclosure requirements 開示要件, 開示情報基準, 開示規定
disclosure system 企業内容開示制度, 開示制度, ディスクロージャー制度
fair disclosure 公正表示
financial disclosure 財務内容の開示
full disclosure 完全開示, 十分な開示, 完全表示, 完全公開性
global standard information disclosure 世界標準の情報開示
informative disclosure 情報開示
risk disclosure リスク開示
▸A proposal by our shareholders seeking *disclosure* of individual directors' remuneration gained 35 percent support. 役員報酬の個別開示を求めて6月に[6月の株主総会で]出された株主提案に対して, 35％の支持が得られた。

discontinued operation [business] 非継続事業, 中止事業, 廃止事業, 事業廃止部門

discount 動 割り引く, 割引する, 割り引いて売る[買う], 織り込む, 調整する
　be discounted back to present value 現在価値に引き直す
　be discounted to reflect real values over time 長期的な実質価値を反映するよう調整する
　discount a rate [interest rate] cut 利下げを織り込む
　discount utility charges 公共料金を割り引く
　discounted issue 割引発行
▸The stock price has already *discounted* recovery prospects. 株価は, すでに業績回復[業績回復の見通し]を織り込んでいる。

discount 名 割引, 割引率, 割引額, 割引, ディスカウント
　bank discount 銀行の手形割引, 銀行割引料 (＝banker's discount: 手形金額×日数×利率)
　be issued at a discount of …割り引いて発行される
　be sold on a discount basis 割引発行される (＝be issued on a discount basis)
　bond discounts 社債発行差金, 社債発行割引差金, 社債割引料 (社債の発行価額[売買価格]と額面金額[額面価格]との差額)
　cash discount 現金割引
　discount consumer-electronics giant 大手量販店 (⇒electronic manufacturer)
　discount house 手形割引業者, 割引業者
　discount market 手形割引市場, 割引市場, 手形市場
　discount on capital stock 株式払込み剰余金
　discount on debenture 社債の発行差額, 社債発行差金
　discount price 割引価格, 低価格, 格安
　discount store ディスカウント店, ディスカウント・ストア
　discount ticket shop 金券ショップ
　discounts on bonds payable 社債発行差金, 社債発行割引差金, 社債発行割引料 (＝bond discount)
　line of discount 割引限度
　official discount rate 公定歩合
　original issue discount 発行差金
　purchase discount 仕入割引
　quantity discount 数量割引
　seasonal discount 季節割引
▸The mileage points can be used to get preferential interest rates on loans and *discounts* on various bank service fees. このマイレージ・ポイントは, ローン金利の優遇や各種銀行手数料の割引などに利用することができる。
▸We announced a *discount* plan for new services in October 2008. 当社は, 2008年10月に新サービスの割引制度を発表しました。

discount cash flow キャッシュ・フロー割引, 割引現在価値, ディスカウント・キャッシュ・フロー《略 DCF》
　discount [discounted] cash flow method キャッシュ・フロー割引法, 割引現在価値法, 現在割引価値方式, ディスカウント・キャッシュ・フロー方式, DCF方式 (＝discount cash flow system, discounted cash flow formula [technique]: 貸倒れ引当金の必要額の算定方法として, 融資先企業の将来の予想収益などを考慮して債権の現在価値を割り出す方式)

discount period 割引期間, 割引対象期間
▸The company sold the machine under the terms and conditions of full payment within 90 days if not paid within the *discount period*. 同社は, 支払いが割引対象期間を過ぎた場合には90日以内に全額支払う条件で, この機械を販売した。

discount plan 割引制度
▸We expect the effects on revenues of this *discount plan* and 2008 price increases to offset each other. この割引制度と2008年度の値上げの収益への影響は, 相殺されると考えています。

discount rate 公定歩合（official discount rate）, 割引率
▸*Discount rate* was kept at 1.25 percent. 公定歩合は, 1.25％に据え置かれた。
▸The weighted average *discount rate* was used in determining the accumulated and accrued plan benefits. 累積年金給付債務額の算定には, 加重平均割引率が用いられています。

discount sales [sale] 割引販売, 割引売出し, 値下げセール, ディスカウント・セール（=discount selling）
▸Major retail store operators Aeon Co. and Seven and i Holdings Co. started special *discount sales* of foods imported from the United States. 流通大手のイオンとセブン＆アイ・ホールディングスは, 米国から輸入した食料品の特別値下げセールをスタートした。

discrepancy 名 相違, 差異, 差, ずれ, 食い違い, 不一致, 矛盾, 不均衡, ミスマッチ, 書類の不備
　cash discrepancies 現金過不足
　interest [interest rate] discrepancy 金利差
　price discrepancies 価格差
　statistical discrepancy 統計上の不一致

discretionary 形 任意の, 随意の, 自由裁量の, 一任された, 一任勘定の
　discretionary account 売買一任勘定, 一任勘定
　discretionary fund management 一任勘定の投資運用
　discretionary hour 自由裁量時間
　discretionary income 裁量所得, 自由裁量所得, 純可処分所得
　discretionary order 売買一任注文
　discretionary spending 随意支出
　discretionary trust 一任信託, 裁量信託
　discretionary work 裁量労働, みなし労働

discretionary contract 随意契約
▸Sixty four percent of *discretionary contracts* signed by central government ministries, agencies and other government entities were inappropriate. 中央省庁や国の機関が結んだ随意契約の64％は, 不適切だった。

discretionary power 裁量権
▸The government is considered to have a wide range of *discretionary powers*. 行政には広範囲の裁量権がある, とされている。

discretionary working system 裁量労働制（=discretionary working-hour system）
▸Under the *discretionary working system*, employees are authorized to determine their own working hours. 裁量労働制では, 従業員各自の労働時間を決めることができる。

discrimination 名 差別, 差別待遇, 区別, 識別, 識別力, 鑑識眼, 優遇, えこひいき
　card discrimination code カード識別コード
　job discrimination against women 女性に対する仕事上の差別
　pay discrimination in jobs 仕事での給与差別
　price discrimination 価格差別
　sex discrimination 性差別

diseconomy 名 不経済, デメリット
　diseconomies of scale 規模の不経済, 規模の不経済性, スケール・デメリット
　external diseconomies 外部不経済
　internal diseconomies 内部不経済

disembark 動 〈乗客・積荷を〉降ろす, 陸揚げする

disequilibrium 不均衡, 不安定

dishoard 動 流通させる, 解放する

dishonor [dishonour] 動 〈手形の〉支払い[引受け]を拒絶する, 不渡りにする, 名 〈手形の〉不渡り, 引受拒否, 支払い拒絶
　dishonor of bill 不渡り手形, 手形不渡り（=dishonored bill）
　dishonored check 不渡り小切手
　dishonored note 不渡り手形
　notice of dishonor 不渡り通知

disincentive 名 阻害要因, 抑制因子

disintegration 名 解体, 分解, 分裂, 崩壊

disinvestment 名 解約, 投資見送り, 投資引上げ, 資本の引上げ, 負の投資, マイナスの投資

dismiss 動 解雇する, 解任する, 罷免する, 追放する, 解散させる, 却下する, 棄却する
▸During an extraordinary shareholders meeting, shareholders of the company voted to *dismiss* three directors, including the president. 臨時株主総会で, 同社の株主は社長を含む取締役3人の解任案を可決した。

dismissal 名 解雇, 解任, 免職, 罷免, 追放, 解散, 却下, 棄却
▸As the firm's social responsibility, all employees who drive under the influence of alcohol on or off duty, will be asked to resign or will face *dismissal*. 同社の社会的責任として, 公私を問わず飲酒運転をした社員はすべて諭旨退職か解雇となる。

disparity 名 格差, 開き, 差, 相違, 差異, 不一致, 不均衡, 不釣り合い, 不平等（⇒gap, stock price disparity）
　disparities between public and private sector pensions 年金の官民格差

disparities between winners and losers 勝ち組と負け組の格差
disparity in technology 技術格差
economic disparity 経済格差
income disparity 所得格差（＝income divide, income gap）
public-private disparities 官民格差
societal disparities among individuals and regions 個人や地域間の社会的格差
wage disparity 賃金格差
▸Another key issue is to cut the wage *disparity* between permanent employees and part-timers and temporary employees. もう一つの重要課題は, 正社員とパートや派遣社員など非正社員との賃金格差是正だ。
▸Pay hikes are necessary to correct widening economic *disparities* among workers. 賃上げは, 広がる労働者間の経済格差を是正するためにも必要だ。
▸Societal *disparities* among individuals and regions are widening. 個人や地域間の社会的格差が, 拡大している。
▸The *disparity* between winners and losers is widening. 勝ち組と負け組の格差は, 拡大している。

dispatch 動 派遣する,〈文書などを〉発送する
▸Mitsui Fudosan will *dispatch* its executives to Imperial Hotel Ltd. 三井不動産は, 帝国ホテルに役員を派遣することになる。

dispatch 名 発送, 派遣, 迅速, 速達便, 特報, 公文書, 運送業者, 運送店（＝despatch）
dispatch of engineers 技術者派遣
dispatch staff 派遣社員（＝dispatch worker）
▸Canon Inc. will directly hire about 3,500 *dispatch* staff as regulars. キヤノンが, 3,500人の派遣社員を正社員として直接雇用する方針だ。

dispense 動 免除する
display 名 陳列, 展示, 表示, 画面表示, 表示装置, 表示端末装置, ディスプレー（⇒liquid crystal display panel）
be on display at …に陳列されている
counter display カウンター・ディスプレー
display design 展示デザイン
display of goods 商品陳列
display volume 陳列量
electrochromatic display カラー・ディスプレー
floor display フロア・ディスプレー
in-store display 店内ディスプレー, 店内陳列
liquid crystal display 液晶ディスプレー
merchandise display 商品ディスプレー, 商品陳列
plasma display プラズマ・ディスプレー
reversal display 逆転表示
screen display 画面表示
store display 店装
window display ウィンドウ・ディスプレー
▸The invention of the blue light-emitting diode (LED) has contributed to the commercialization of various types of displays, including cell phone *display* panels and large outdoor display screens. 青色発光ダイオード（LED）の発明は, 携帯電話の表示装置や野外の大型ディスプレー・スクリーンなど, 各種表示装置の商品化に貢献している。

display unit 表示装置, ディスプレー装置, 指示器
graphic display unit 図形表示装置
visual display unit 表示端末装置, ディスプレー装置《略 VDU》

disposable 形 自由になる, 利用できる, 使用できる, 使い捨ての
disposal 名 処分, 処理, 売却, 除却（⇒bad loan）
asset disposal 資産の処分, 資産売却
disposal of bad loans 不良債権の処理（＝disposal of nonperforming loans）
disposal of fixed assets 固定資産の除却
disposal of non-core assets 非中核的事業資産の売却
disposal of property, plant and equipment 有形固定資産の売却
disposal of shares 株式の売却
gain on disposal of equipment 設備処分益
disposal of facilities 設備の処分, 設備の廃棄
▸Companies are trying to improve their business foundations or structure through mergers, acquisitions, the establishment of joint ventures, the *disposal of facilities* and the sale of business rights and assets. 企業は, 企業の合併や買収, 合弁会社の設立, 設備廃棄あるいは営業権や資産の売却などによって, 事業の基盤や構造の整備に努めている。

disposal of nonperforming loans 不良債権の処理
▸With the promotion of the *disposal of nonperforming loans*, corporate failures and joblessness will increase in the short time. 不良債権処理を促進すれば, 短期的には企業倒産と失業が増える。

disposition 名 処分, 処理, 処置, 売却, 譲渡, 取

扱い, 配置, 配列, 使途, 自由裁量権
asset disposition 資産処分, 資産譲渡
capital disposition 資本支出
disposition of shares 株式の処分
source and disposition of funds 資金の源泉と使途, 資金運用表
▶The ultimate *disposition* of these matters will not have a material adverse effect on the consolidated financial position of the Company. これらの案件の最終処分で, 当社の連結財政状態に重大な悪影響が出るようなことはありません。

dispute 名 紛争, 争い, 意見の相違, 論争
act of dispute 争議行為
all disputes under this agreement 本契約に基づくすべての紛争
dispute resolution [settlement] 紛争解決, 紛争処理
dispute settlement procedures 紛争処理手続き
disputes, controversies or differences 紛争, 論争または意見の相違
industrial dispute 労働争議, 労使争議 (= industrial strife, trade dispute)
labor dispute 労働争議
matter of dispute 係争中の問題
patent dispute 特許紛争 (⇒**cross licensing agreement**)
tax dispute 税の異議申立て
trade dispute 貿易摩擦, 通商摩擦, 貿易紛争 (= trade conflict, trade friction)
▶Business *disputes* with Chinese firms, including breach of contract, accounted for 35 percent of damages suffered by Taiwan firms. 契約違反など中国企業とのビジネス上の紛争は, 台湾企業が受けた被害全体の35%を占めている。

dissolution 名 解散, 契約の解除, 解消, 取消し, 解体, 廃棄
dissolution and liquidation 解散と清算
dissolution of contract 契約の解除
dissolution of corporation 会社の解散
joint venture dissolution agreement 合弁事業解消契約

dissolve 動 解散する, 契約を解除する, 解消する, 取り消す, 解体する, 廃棄する (⇒**investment fund**)
▶Misuzu Audit Corp. was *dissolved* after several accounting scandals. 会計不祥事[監査不祥事]を受けて, みすず監査法人(旧中央青山監査法人)が解散した。

distressed 形 経営不振の, 経営難の, 経営難に陥っている, 業績悪化の, 窮地の, 困窮している, 苦しんでいる
distressed area 不況地域, 疲弊地域, 貧民地区, 被災地
distressed bank 経営不振の銀行, 経営難に陥っている銀行
distressed company 経営不振企業, 業績悪化企業
distressed loan 貸倒れ

distribute 動 分配する, 分売する, 販売する, 供給する, 配給する, 配送する, 配布する, 流通させる, 配信する
distributed artificial intelligence 分散人工知能《略 DAI》
distributed cost 配賦原価, 原価の配賦
distributed earnings 分配利益, 利益の分配
distributed processing 分散処理
▶Songs *distributed* by the five companies account for about 60 percent of the J-pop market. この5社が配信する曲は, 邦楽市場の約6割を占めている。
▶The firm is suspected to have *distributed* dividends illegally. 同社は, 違法配当の疑いが持たれている。

distribution 名 流通, 配分, 配賦, 有価証券の分売, 分配, 配当, 配給, 配布, 交付, 分布, 配信, 分類, 区分, ディストリビューション
accounting distribution 会計上の配分
chain of distribution 流通の連鎖
cost distribution 原価配分, コスト配分
distribution cost 流通費, 流通経費, 流通原価, 流通コスト, 販売費, 配給費, 配送費物流費, 物流コスト (= distribution expense)
distribution channel 流通経路, 流通チャネル, 配給経路 (= channel of distribution)
distribution expense 販売費, 配給費, 物流費, 流通費, 配送費 (= distribution cost)
distribution group 流通グループ
distribution information system 流通情報システム
distribution level 流通段階
distribution network 販売網
distribution of cost 原価配分
distribution of goods [merchandise] 商品流通
distribution of net profit 純利益処分
distribution of profits 利益分配
distribution overhead 間接販売費, 間接営業費
distribution policy 流通政策, 流通方針, 販売チャネル政策
distribution productivity 物流生産性, 流通生

産性
Distribution Replenishment Planning 流通主要量計画《略 DRP》
distribution service 配送サービス
distribution statement 分売届出書
distribution strategy 流通戦略
distribution structure 流通機構, 流通構造 (=distribution system)
distribution warehouse 流通倉庫
exchange distribution 取引所分売
film distribution 映画の配給
free share distribution 株式の無償交付
function of distribution 流通機能
funding distribution 資金調達源の分布
global distribution 国際販売
music distribution 音楽配信
network distribution ネット配信, ネットワーク配信
news distribution ニュース配信
online music distribution business インターネット音楽配信ビジネス
percentage distribution 構成比率
physical distribution 物的流通, 物流
physical distribution cost 物流コスト
physical distribution management 物的流通管理, 物流管理《略 PDM》
physical distribution value added network 物流VAN
product distribution 物流網
required distribution 配当必要額
revenue distribution 収益分布
systematization of distribution 流通システム化
unit distribution 単位分布
wealth distribution 富の配分

▶Nippon Express has expertise in the *distribution* of goods such as how to handle customs clearance and stock control. 日本通運は, 通関業務や在庫管理業務など物流のノウハウを持っている。

▶The company fares well in the domestic market in terms of sales and *distribution*. 同社は, 営業や物流面では, 国内市場に強みを持つ。

▶This product will be sold through retail computer *distribution* chains. この製品は, コンピュータの小売販売チェーン店を通じて販売されます。

distribution and marketing support company 物流・販売支援会社

▶The Toyota group has a research and development company in Thailand, as well as a *distribution and marketing support company* in Singapore. トヨタ・グループの場合, タイには研究開発会社, シンガポールには物流・販売支援会社がある。

distribution center 流通センター, 物流センター, 配送センター, 集配センター, 集散地 (=distribution faculty)

▶Nike Inc. plans to close two *distribution centers* in Oregon and Tennessee to save $200 million over 20 years. ナイキ(世界最大手のスポーツ・シューズのメーカー)が, 20年間で2億ドル削減するため, 米オレゴン州とテネシー州の流通センター2か所の閉鎖を計画している。

distribution industry 流通産業, 流通業, 流通業界

▶An improvement in employment conditions for part-time employees is becoming a major topic to be placed on the agenda in the *distribution industry*. 流通業界では, パート社員[パート従業員]の待遇改善が, 交渉[協議事項]の主な議題になってきた。

distribution network 物流網, 流通網, 流通ネットワーク, 販売網

▶Bic Camera and Edion will form a capital tie-up and cooperate in jointly procuring products and using *distribution networks*. ビックカメラとエディオンは, 資本提携して, 共同仕入れや物流網の共同利用などの面で協力する方針だ。

distribution sector 流通業界, 流通部門

▶Since 2000, the *distribution sector* has seen a series of large-scale collapses, including those of Sogo department store and Mycal Corp. 2000年来, 流通業界では, そごう, マイカルなど大型経営破綻が相次いだ。

distribution system 流通システム, 流通機構, 物流システム, 販売システム

▶One of the important characteristics of the *distribution system* of medicine in Japan is that the retail sector has been dominated by small mama and papa stores until recently and that small stores still have a large share. 日本の医薬品流通システムの重要な特性の一つは, 最近まで小売部門は家族経営の小型店が支配してきたこと, それに小型店のシェアはいまでも大きいということだ。

distributor 名 販売店, 販売代理店, 代理店, 輸入代理店, 総輸入元, 流通業者, 流通業, 配給業者, 問屋, 卸売り業者, 取次店, 配達人, ディストリビュータ

distributor network 販売網
distributor's brand 流通業者ブランド, 商業者商標

distributor's controlling 流通業者支配, 流通業者の統制力
exclusive distributor 独占販売業者
oil distributor 石油元売り
systematization of distributors 販売店系列化
▸France's Competition Commission has ordered Sony, Matsushita and Philips to pay fines for allegedly concluding price-fixing agreements on retail goods with their local *distributors*. フランスの競争評議会は, 国内販売店と小売電気製品の価格維持協定を結んだとして, ソニー, 松下電器産業とフィリップスに罰金の支払いを命じた.
▸Nippon Oil Corp. is the nation's largest oil *distributor*. 新日本石油は, 国内最大手の石油元売りだ.
▸Of the revenues generated through books sold on a commission basis, a percentage goes to the *distributor*. 書籍の委託販売で得た収入のうち, 一定の割合は取次店に支払われる.
▸Supplier shall deliver Products purchased by *Distributor* to *Distributor* at the port of Yokohama, Japan. 供給者は, 販売店が購入する本製品を, 横浜港(日本)で販売店に引き渡さなければならない.

diversification 名 多様化, 多角化, 経営多角化, 分散, 分散化, 分散投資 (⇒business diversification)
  asset diversification 資産の分散, 資産分散化
  conglomerate diversification コングロマリット的多角化
  diversification of business lines 事業分野の多角化, 業務の多様化
  diversification of product line 製品ラインの多様化
  diversification of shares 株式の多様化
  diversification of the portfolio ポートフォリオの分散, ポートフォリオの分散投資
  diversification of the product mix 製品構成の多様化, 商品構成の多様化
  diversification strategy 多角化戦略, 事業多角化戦略, 経営多角化戦略, 多様化戦略
  export diversification 輸出多様化
  horizontal diversification 水平的多角化, 水平的多様化
  international diversification 国際分散投資
  portfolio diversification ポートフォリオの分散投資
  product diversification 製品の多角化, 製品多様化
  temporal diversification 期間の分散

vertical diversification 垂直的多角化, 垂直的多様化
▸Business *diversification* at major supermarkets during the bubble years negatively impacted their corporate management. バブル期に大手スーパーが進めた事業の多角化が, 大手スーパーの企業経営に悪影響を及ぼした.

diversify 動 多様化する, 多角化する, 〈資産など を〉分散する, 分散投資する, 拡大する
  diversified assets 分散化した資産, 分散化された資産, 資産の分散化
  diversified business 経営多角化, 事業の多角化, 多角的事業
  diversified company [enterprise, firm] 多角化企業, 多角経営企業, 複合企業
  diversified investment 分散投資, 分散型投資, 投資の分散化
  diversified management 多角経営, 経営の多角化 (=diversified management operation)
  diversified portfolio 分散投資されたポートフォリオ, リスク分散型ポートフォリオ
  diversify customer base 顧客基盤を多様化する, 顧客基盤の多様化, 顧客基盤を拡大する
  diversify funding activities 資金調達の多様化を進める
  diversify into new areas 新規分野への多角化を推進する
  diversify investment risks 投資リスクを分散する
  diversify the sources of financing 資金調達源の多角化を進める, 資金調達源を拡大する (⇒ **financial base**)
▸These losses represent a tiny portion of most pension funds' well-*diversified* assets. これらの損害額は, 大半の年金基金の十分に分散化された資産のごく一部にすぎない.
▸This *diversified* holding company has interests in several smaller high technology companies. 経営の多角化を推進しているこの持ち株会社は, 中堅ハイテク企業数社の株式を所有している.

diversion 名 流用, 転用, 転換, 配置転換, 〈鉄道貨物の〉到着地変更, 迂回路, 回り道, 気晴らし, 娯楽, 牽制行動, 牽制作戦, 陽動作戦(diversionary tactics), 陽動
  farmland diversion 農地転用
  trade creation and diversion effect 貿易創出・転換効果
  trade diversion 貿易転換

diversity 名 多様性, 多角化, 分散
  business diversity 事業の多角化, 事業の多様性

diversity of activities 事業の多角化
diversity of citizenship 州籍相違
economic diversity 経済の多様性
▶We value and encourage *diversity* in our workforce. 当社は、社員の多様性を尊重し、これを促進しています。
divert 動 流用する、転用する、転換する
divest 動 〈資産などを〉整理する、売却する、手放す、取り除く、放棄する
　divest oneself of …を放棄する、…の権利などを剥奪する、…の事業を整理[売却]する
　divest unprofitable operation 不採算部門を整理する
▶We *divested* some of our nonstrategic businesses during the second quarter. 当社は、第2四半期に当社の非戦略的事業部門を売却[整理]しました。
divestiture 名 企業分割、〈資産の〉分割、〈事業や不採算店舗などの〉整理[売却]、再編成、〈権利などの〉剥奪
　corporate divestiture 企業分割、分社化、企業再編成 (=corporate separation)
　divestiture of subsidiaries 子会社再編成、子会社の再編
　mergers, acquisitions and divestitures 企業の合併、買収と分割
▶The support for reconstruction of business was provided in the form of special measures under the Commercial Code to make corporate *divestiture* easier. 事業再構築のための支援は、分社化を円滑にするなど商法の特別措置の形で行われた。
▶These gains were partially offset by a decline in other revenues attributable to the *divestiture* of the non-strategic businesses of the firm. この増加分は、同社の非戦略的事業部門の売却[整理]に伴うその他の売上高の減少により、一部相殺されています。
dividend 名 配当、利益配当、配当金、分配金 (米国では、一般に会社が四半期ごとに配当を支払う。生命保険の配当金は、主に保険料の運用収益が契約時の想定を上回った場合に、その差額が契約者に支払われる。⇒**cash dividend, quarterly dividend, stock dividend**)
　accrued dividend 未払い配当金、経過配当
　accumulated dividend 累積配当
　bond dividend 社債配当
　capital dividend 資本配当、タコ配当 (=bonus dividend)
　cash dividend 現金配当
　common stock dividend 普通株式配当金
　cum dividend 配当付き (=with dividend)
　dividend declaration 配当宣言、配当決議 (=declaration of dividend, dividend announcement)
　dividend distribution 配当支払い
　dividend earned 受取配当金
　dividend in arrears 繰越し配当金、延滞配当金、未払い優先配当金、累積未払い配当金
　dividend in kind 現物配当
　dividend income 配当所得
　dividend of earnings 利益配当
　dividend paid 支払い配当金
　dividend payout 配当性向、配当支払い、配当金の支払い、配当支払い率 (=dividend payout ratio, payout ratio; ⇒**share buyback**)
　dividend policy 配当政策、配当方針
　dividend preference 配当優先権
　dividend reinvestment 配当金再投資、株主配当再投資
　dividend requirements 配当支払い
　dividend revenue 受取配当金 (=dividend income)
　dividend to policyholders 契約者配当金
　dividend yield 配当利回り (1株の株価に対する年間配当金の割合。配当利回り=配当金÷1株の株価)
　dividends from associated company 関連会社からの配当金
　dividends on stocks 株式配当
　dividends payable 未払い配当金、未払い配当 (=dividend payable unclaimed)
　dividends per common share 普通株式1株当たり配当金
　dividends receivable 未収配当金
　dividends to shareholders 株主配当金
　ex dividend 配当落ち (=without dividend)
　final dividend 期末配当、決算配当、最終配当
　high dividend 高配当
　imputed dividend 見なし配当
　increased dividend 増配
　interim dividend 中間配当 (=midterm dividend, regular interim dividend)
　no dividend 無配
　non-dividend-paying stock 無配株
　ordinary dividend 普通配当
　pay dividends 配当金を支払う
　projected dividend 予想配当 (⇒**dividend per share**)
　reduce dividend payment 減配する

reduced dividend 減配
regular dividend 普通配当, 通常配当, 定時配当
regular year-end dividend 年度末配当, 期末配当
special year-end dividend 特別年度末配当, 特別期末配当
unclaimed dividend 未請求配当金
unusual dividend 特別配当, 異常配当
with dividend 配当付き
without dividend 配当落ち
year-end dividend 期末配当
▸The firm paid *dividends* although it had no profit available for *dividend* payment. 同社は, 配当の支払いに充てる利益が出ていないのに配当金を支払っていた。

dividend income 受取配当金, 配当金収入, 配当所得
▸A life insurer's core operating profit consists mainly of income related to insurance and investment operations, including interest and *dividend income*. 生命保険会社の基礎利益(生保の本業のもうけに当たる)の内訳は, 主に受取利息や配当金収入など保険・投資事業の関連収益だ。

dividend increase 増配, 配当の引上げ
▸This investment fund proposed a large *dividend increase* at the J-Power shareholders meeting. この投資ファンドは, Jパワーの株主総会で大幅な増配を提案した。

dividend payment 配当支払い, 配当金の支払い, 配当支払い額, 支払い配当金 (⇒dividend)
dividend payment on equity 株式配当
raising of dividend payments 増配
▸Dai-ichi Mutual Life will raise *dividend payments* by a total of about ¥4 billion for about 4.8 million policies. 第一生命保険は, 約480万件の保険契約を対象に総額で約40億円増配する。
▸JAL will resume *dividend payments* by fiscal 2010. 日本航空は, 2010年度までに復配する方針だ。

dividend per share 1株当たり配当, 1株当たり配当金, 1株当たり配当額《略 DPS》
▸We increased the projected *dividend per share* to ¥10 for fiscal 2009 from the ¥8 paid the previous year. 当社は, 2009年度の1株当たり予想配当を前期［前年度］の8円から10円に引き上げました。

dividend policy 配当方針, 配当政策
▸U.S.-based fund Steel Partners is happy at changes in Yushiro Chemical Industry Co.'s *dividend policy* taken to fend off the hostile takeover bid. 米系投資ファンドのスティール・パートナーズは, ユシロ化学工業が敵対的株式公開買付(TOB)の防衛策として行った配当方針の変更に満足している。

dividend ratio [rate] 配当率 (配当率=年間配当額÷資本金)
▸Each company is allowed to have its board of directors determine the *dividend ratio* once such a rule is written into its articles of incorporation. 企業の配当率は, その規則を定款で定めれば, 取締役会で決めることができる。
▸The *dividend rate* on the series 3 preferred shares is calculated each quarter. シリーズ3優先株式の配当率は, 四半期ごとに計算されます。

dividend reinvestment and stock purchase plan 株主配当再投資・株式購入制度 (=shareholder dividend reinvestment and stock purchase plan)
▸The *Dividend Reinvestment and Stock Purchase Plan* provides owners of common stock a convenient way to purchase additional shares. 株主配当再投資・株式購入制度は, 普通株式の株主が株式の追加購入をされるのに便利な方法です。

dividend yield 配当利回り (1株の株価に対する配当金の割合。配当利回り(%)=(1株当たり配当金÷株価)×100)
▸The *dividend yield* on the firm's shares is expected to climb to 2.1 percent this business year, based on the current stock price of ¥1,140. 今年度の同社の株式配当利回りは, 現在の株価1,140円ベースで, 2.1%に上昇する見込みだ。

dividends on preferred shares 優先株式に対する配当金
▸Earnings per common share were calculated after *dividends on preferred shares*. 普通株式1株当たり純利益は, 優先株式配当額を控除したうえで計算されています。

division 事業部, 事業部門, 部門, 部［課］, 分野, 分割, 分配, 不一致, 分裂 (⇒company system, deteriorate)
branch division 支部, 支局
business devision 事業部門, 事業分野 (⇒reorganize)
cosmetics division 化粧品事業部門
division capital 事業部資本
division of profit or loss 損益の配分
division of profits 利益分配
division of profits 利益分配
division system 事業部制
functional division 機能的分割, 職能別部門

independent division 独立事業部門
international division 国際事業部, 国際事業部門
operational administration division 業務本部
sales division 販売部門, 営業部門
unprofitable divisions 不採算部門
▸The company expects to recover by the end of fiscal 2009 on the back of proceeds from the sale of its cosmetic *division*. 化粧事業部門の売却益で, 同社は2009年度末までに利益を回復するとしている。
▸The firm downsized its semiconductor and home appliances *divisions* drastically. 同社は, 半導体と家電の事業部を大幅に縮小した。

division of businesses 企業分割
▸Forcible *division of businesses* should be considered a last resort. 企業の強制分割は, 最後の手段と考えるべきだ。

division of labor 分業
  horizontal division of labor 水平的分業
  international division of labor 国際分業
  regional division of labor 地域的分業
  vertical division of labor 垂直的分業

divisional 形 部門の, 事業部の, 分割上の, 区分上の
  divisional management 部門管理, 部門管理者, 部門経営層
  divisional performance 事業部業績
  divisional profit 事業部利益, 事業別利益 (＝departmental profit)
  divisional reporting 事業部別報告書, 事業別報告
  divisional return on investment 事業部資本利益率
  divisional organization 事業部制組織 (＝divisionalized organization)
  divisional sales 部門売上
  divisional system 事業部制 (事業部は, 製品・地域・顧客別に編成された利益責任制を持つ経営単位のこと)

dlrs ドル (dollarsの略)

do business 営業活動を行う, 営業する, 事業を行う, 事業を展開する, ビジネス活動をする, 取引する (＝operate)
▸We *do business* in some 150 countries. 当社は, 約150か国で事業を展開しています。

document 名 書類, 文書, 書式, 説明書, 仕様書, 明細書, 証書, 証拠書類, 帳票, ドキュメント (複数形には「船積み書類」の意味もある)
  aircraft documents 空輸用書類

attached document 添付書類
business documents ビジネス文書
commercial document 商業書類
delivery of document 書類の引渡し
document information 文献情報
document management system 文書管理システム
document of title 権原証券
document retrieval 文書検索
documents against acceptance 手形引受書類渡し, 引受渡し《略 D/A》
documents against payment 手形支払い書類渡し, 支払い渡し《略 D/P》
export document 輸出書類
financial document 金融書類
founding documents 設立文書
issue of document 書面の交付
legal document 法律文書
marine document 船用書類
negotiable document 譲渡可能書類, 流通書類
notarial document 公正証書
operative documents 営業書類
original document 正本, 原本
originating document 原始書類
payment against documents 書類引換え払い
shipping documents 船積み書類
title document 権利証書, 権原証書, 権原証券
transport documents 運送書類
trust document 信託証書
▸The financial statements and a score of related *documents* show that the company has a negative net worth. 財務書類と約20の関連資料は, 同社が債務超過であることを示している。

documentation 名 文書, 書類, 契約書, 契約文書, 契約書作成, 収集資料, 文書の利用, 文書の提供, 文書作成, 文書化, 文書管理, 情報管理, 文献調査, 考証, 証拠書類, 証拠書類提出, ドキュメンテーション
  bilateral documentation 相対取引の契約書
  documentation bank 契約文書作成行
  documentation costs 契約文書作成費用, 契約書類作成費
  multilateral documentation 標準取引の契約書
  obligatory documentation 義務的証拠書類提出
  program documentation プログラム文書化
  shelf documentation 一括契約書
  standard documentation 標準契約書類
  supporting documentation 証憑(しょうひょう)書類
  swap documentation スワップ契約

systems documentation システム・ドキュメンテーション

terms and documentation 取引条件と契約書

▶You may not copy any *documentation*. 文書のコピー［複製］は，一切禁止する。

Doha Round of multilateral trade talks 世界貿易機関（WTO）の新ラウンド［新多角的貿易交渉］

doing business 営業活動を行うこと，事業を行うこと，事業展開，営業行為，商行為，ビジネス活動

doing business as 通称名《略 d.b.a.》

doldrums 名 沈滞，低迷，不振，不況，不景気，中だるみ（⇒**wage growth**）

　be out of the doldrums 底を脱する

　in the doldrums 不景気で，不振の，厳しい状況の，意気消沈して

▶It is difficult to raise the consumption tax at a time when the economy is in the *doldrums*. 厳しい経済状況下で，消費税を引き上げるのは難しい。

dollar 名 ドル，ドル相場

　constant dollar basis 恒常ドル基準，恒常ドル・ベース，実質ベース

　dollar-denominated terms [basis] ドル建て，ドル表示（＝dollar terms）

　dollar terms 金額ベース

　dollar unit method 金額後出し先入れ法（＝dollar value LIFO）

　dollar value LIFO 金額後入れ先出し法，ドル価値後入れ先出し法，ドル価値法（＝dollar value method）

　dollar value method ドル価値法（＝dollar value LIFO）

　Dollars in millions 単位：百万ドル

　Dollars in millions per share amounts 単位：1株当たりの金額を除いて百万ドル

　higher dollar ドル高

　nominal dollar basis 名目貨幣基準，名目ドル基準

　strong dollar against other currencies ドル全面高

　the dollar's depreciation ドル安（＝lower dollar, the weak dollar）

▶The weaker *dollar* affected the net earnings. ドル安が，純利益に影響を及ぼしました。

domain 名 分野，範囲，領土，領域，企業の本業，事業領域，事業活動領域，企業の生存領域，ドメイン

　domain address ドメイン・アドレス（ネットワーク上のコンピュータの識別符号）

　domain business ドメイン・ビジネス（ドメイン取得手続きやドメイン名を得るなどのサービスを有料で行うビジネス）

　domain identity 事業領域の明確化

　domain name ドメイン名（インターネットに接続する組織などの名称）

domestic 形 国内の，内国の，自国の，国産の，家庭の，家庭内の

　consolidation of domestic operations 国内事業の統合

　domestic and international equities 国内株と外国株

　domestic branch network 国内支店網

　domestic building market 国内建設市場

　domestic business 国内事業

　domestic carrier 国内線航空会社

　domestic consumption 国内消費

　domestic corporation 内国法人，内国会社，州内法人，州内会社

　domestic downturn 内需の落込み

　domestic electronic control デジタル住宅

　domestic exchange 内国為替

　domestic figures 国内経済指標

　domestic industry 国内産業，家内工業

　domestic lead manager 国内主幹事

　domestic offices 国内営業店

　domestic orders 国内受注

　domestic player 国内投資家

　domestic price 国内価格

　domestic prices 国内物価

　domestic producers [manufacturers] 国内メーカー

　domestic spending 国内消費

　domestic wholesale prices 国内卸売り物価

　domestic work 家庭内労働

　gross domestic savings 国内総貯蓄

　net domestic product 国内純生産

domestic currency 国内通貨，自国通貨

　domestic currency bonds 自国通貨建て債務

　domestic currency obligation 自国通貨建て債務

domestic demand 国内需要，内需

　domestic-demand-led growth 内需型成長

　domestic demand products 国内需要財

　growth in domestic demand 内需の伸び

　increased domestic demand 内需の拡大，内需の増加［増大，伸び］

　insufficient demand 内需の不足（＝insufficiency of domestic demand）

　slowing of domestic demand 内需の減少，内需の落込み

　sluggish domestic demand 内需の低迷，国内

需要の低迷
strong domestic demand 内需好調
weak [weakened] domestic brand 内需の低迷, 国内需要の低迷
▶Expansion of *domestic demand* as a driving force to push up prices is not strong. 物価を押し上げる原動力としての内需拡大は, 強くない。

domestic economy 国内経済, 国内景気
▶The *domestic economy* has yet to show any promising signs even after the passing of the so-called lost decade. 国内経済[日本経済]は, いわゆる「失われた十年」が過ぎても, まだ明るい展望が開けないでいる。

domestic market 国内市場, 地元市場
fast-growing domestic market 急成長の国内市場, 急速に成長する国内市場
large-scale domestic market 大型の国内市場, 国内の大規模市場
open the domestic market 国内市場を開放する
▶The *domestic market* for Linux will exceed ¥12 billion by 2007. リナックスの国内市場規模は, 2007年には120億円を超えるだろう。

dominant 形 支配的な, 優勢な, 有力な, 最有力の, 最大の, 圧倒的な, 顕著な, 目立つ, 主要な, 中心的な
dominant company [firm] 支配的企業
dominant driving force 大きな原動力
dominant factor 支配的要因
dominant force 優勢な力, 最有力者
dominant gene 優勢遺伝子
dominant growth rate 支配的成長率, 際立った伸び率
dominant market share 圧倒的な市場シェア, 圧倒的なシェア
dominant patent 基本特許
dominant party 第一党, 多数党
dominant position 支配的な地位
dominant theme 最大のテーマ
dominant voice 圧倒的な発言権

donate 動 寄付する, 寄贈する
donation 名 贈与, 寄付, 寄贈, 献金, 提供, 受贈, 寄付金, 寄贈品, 受贈金, ドネーション
cash donations 寄付金
charitable donations 慈善寄付
corporate donations 企業献金, 政治献金
donation tax 贈与税
donations expense 寄付金
large donations 多額の寄付金
political donations 政治献金

under-the-table donations ヤミ献金
▶The Political Funds Control Law bars businesses and organizations from making *donations* to an individual politician. 政治資金規正法では, 政治家個人への企業・団体による献金が禁止されている。

donationware 名 ドネーションウェア（利用者に寄付を求めるシェアウェア）

door-to-door 形 戸別の, 戸別訪問の, 戸別配達の, 宅配の （＝house-to-house; ⇒channel）
door-to-door retailing 訪問販売小売業
door-to-door sales 訪問販売 （＝door-to-door distribution, door-to-door selling）
door-to-door salesman 訪問販売員
door-to-door seller 訪問販売業者
▶The Consumer Contract Law and other concerned laws are intended to crack down on coercive *door-to-door* sales. 消費者契約法などの関連法の狙いは, 強引な訪問販売などを厳重に取り締まることにある。

dormant 形 休眠中の, 休止中の, 休止状態の, 活動停止中の, 潜在的な, 潜伏中の, 未開発の
dormant account 休眠口座, 休眠口座, 休止口座 （＝sleeping account）
dormant balance 不活動残高
dormant company 休眠会社
dormant contract 上場休止契約
dormant partner 匿名社員, 匿名組合員 （＝sleeping partner）

dot-com 名 ネット［インターネット］関連企業, ドットコム （＝.com）
dot-com bubble ドットコム・バブル （＝IT bubble）
dot-com business IT関連ビジネス
dot-com company インターネット関連企業, ネット関連企業, ドットコム企業, ドットコム会社 （＝.com company）
dot-com industry ドットコム産業
dot-com issues ドットコム銘柄
▶After the bursting of the dot-com *bubble*, *dot coms*, particularly B2C companies, have had difficulties in raising funds. ドットコム・バブルの崩壊後, ドットコム（ネット関連企業）, 特に企業対消費者間の取引をしている企業は, 資金調達難に陥っている。

dot name ドット・ネーム, 個人専用ドメイン名 （＝.name: ドメイン名を運営するグローバル・ネーム・レジストリー社に年間使用料を支払って登録すると, 「自分の名前.name」というドメインを設定でき, 個人のホームページや電子メールのアドレスと

double / down payment

して使用できる)

double 動 2倍になる, 倍増する, 倍加する
▸Honda Motor Co. plans to *double* its production capacity in India by next year. 本田は, 来年までにインドでの生産能力を倍増する計画だ.
▸The sales of digital cameras *doubled* those of the previous year, assisted by rapid expansion of markets in the nation and abroad. デジタル・カメラの販売台数は, 国内外の急速な市場拡大に支えられて, 前年の2倍に増えた.

double 形 二重の, 二桁(けた)の, 2倍の, 複式の
- double auction 二重競売
- double auction market 競争売買市場
- double blow 二重の打撃
- double booking 二重予約, ダブル・ブッキング
- double chop ダブル・チョップ (メーカー名と流通業者名を併記したブランドで, コントロール・ブランドともいう)
- double counting 二重計上
- double cost averaging ドル平均法, ドル・コスト平均法
- double damages 二重賠償
- double distribution 二重配賦
- double entry bookkeeping 複式簿記
- double pricing 二重価格表示
- double sampling 二重抽出法, 重複抽出法
- double standard 二重基準
- double taxation relief 二重課税の回避
- double transfer 二重振込み, 二重送金
- double truck 見開き広告 (=double-page spread)

double-digit 形 二桁(けた)の, 二桁台の (⇒ durable product)
- double-digit gain 二桁の伸び (=double-digit growth, double-digit increase)
- double-digit growth 二桁成長, 10%を超える伸び
- double-digit inflation 二桁インフレ, 二桁の物価上昇, 10%を超えるインフレ

▸China has emerged as the world's seventh-largest economic power with year-on-year growth rates approaching *double digits*. 中国は, 前年比で[年率で]二桁近い経済成長率で世界第七位の経済大国になった.

double dip 二重払い, 二重取り, 二重の収入, 〈一定期間内の〉二度の下降[下落]

double dip recession 景気の二番底, 景気の底割れ
- enter into a double dip recession 景気が二番底に突入する
- sink into a double dip recession 景気が底割れする
▸I don't see very much chance at all for the so-called *double dip recession*. 景気がいわゆる「二番底」に向かうことは, まずないと思う.
▸The economy could sink into a *double dip recession*. 景気が底割れする可能性がある.

double withdrawal 二重引落し
▸The bank made 30,000 *double withdrawals* for transfers from customer accounts. 同行は, 顧客の口座振替えで3万件の二重引落しをした.

dovetailing 名 統合化, 適合[調和]すること
▸Professional users are calling for the *dovetailing* of different services to form comprehensive information and telecommunications solutions. 専門事務に携わっているユーザーは, 情報通信の包括的なソリューション[問題解決策]として, 各種サービスの統合化を求めている.

Dow 名 ダウ
- Dow Chemical ダウ・ケミカル (世界第2位の総合化学会社)
- New York Dow ダウ平均, ニューヨーク・ダウ (=NY Dow)
- the Dow ダウ平均株価(工業株30種), ダウ工業株平均 (=Dow Jones industrial average, Dow Jones industrials)
▸The *Dow* fell 370.03, or 2.93 percent, to 12,265. ダウ平均株価(工業株30種)は, 前日比370.03ドル安(2.93%減)の1万2,265ドルに続落した.

Dow Jones ダウ・ジョーンズ工業株平均, ダウ工業株平均, ダウ・ジョーンズ社
- Dow Jones average [Average] ダウ・ジョーンズ平均, ダウ・ジョーンズ平均株価, 株式ダウ価平均, ダウ平均
- Dow Jones Composite ダウ・ジョーンズ総合65種平均株価
- Dow Jones Index ダウ・ジョーンズ指数
- Dow Jones industrial average [Industrial Average] ダウ工業株平均, ダウ工業株30種平均, ダウ(工業株30種)平均, ダウ平均 《略 DJIA》 (=Dow Jones industrials)
- Dow Jones industrials ダウ平均株価(工業株30種) (=Dow Jones industrial average; ⇒contraction, Wall Street)
▸The *Dow Jones* plunged 370 points after an economic report that the service sector shrank in January. 1月のサービス業の業況は悪化したとの経済報告を受けて, ダウ工業株平均は370ドル急落した.

down payment 頭金, 手付け金, 前渡し金, 自

己投下資本
downfall 名 急落, 没落, 凋落, 失脚
▸The *downfall* of the firm could trigger disturbances throughout the financial market. 同社の凋落（ちょうらく）は, 金融市場全体の混乱を招く可能性がある.

downgrade 動 格下げする, 格付けを引き下げる, 下方修正する, 名 格下げ（⇒**upgrade**）
  rating downgrade 格下げ, 下方修正, 引下げ（=downgrading）
  review for possible downgrade 格下げの方向で検討する
  under review for possible downgrade 格下げの方向で検討中, 格下げの方向で格付けを見直し中
▸The *downgrade* could further hamper GM's access to funding. 今回の格下げで, GMの資金調達はさらに厳しくなる可能性がある.
▸The stock market decline can trigger *downgrades* by credit rating agencies. 株安をきっかけとして, 格付け機関による評価が引き下げられる可能性がある.

Downing Street 英国政府, 英国首相, ダウニング・ストリート（この通りの10番地が英首相公邸, 11番地が大蔵大臣公邸）

download 動 情報を転送する, 受信する, 取り込む, 複写する, ダウンロードする（⇒**upload**）

downmarket [down-market] 形 低所得消費者の, 大衆向けの, 低級の, 安物の, 下げ相場の（=downscale）

downmarketing 名 低所得者層向け広告戦略, ダウンマーケティング

downscale 形 低所得の, 大衆向けの, 低価格の, 低価格・低品質の, 廉価な, 安価な, ダウンスケール, 動 規模を縮小する, 値下げする, 安くする

downside 名 〈株価などの〉下降傾向, 下落傾向, 下落, 下降気味, 業績悪化, 現役, 不利, 不利益, 不利な点, デメリット, 悪い面, 否定的な側面（⇒**global market, upside**）
  downside potential 下落する可能性
  downside risk 下落する危険性, 下振れリスク, 下値（したね）リスク, 下値の余地, 業績悪化のリスク, 減益要因, 可能損失額, ダウンサイド・リスク
  downside risks to the economy 景気の下振れリスク, 景気が悪化するリスク
  downside support line 下値支持線（=downside support）
▸The *downside* risks to Japan's economy will increase because concerns over a U.S. slowdown are growing. 米国の景気減速に対する懸念が高まっているため, 日本の景気[日本経済]が今後悪化するリスクは増大している.

downsize 動 〈規模を〉縮小する, 削減する, 人員削減する, 〈経営を〉合理化する, リストラする, 小型化する, 軽量化する
▸Kanebo's fashion business will be *downsized* drastically. カネボウのファッション事業は, 大幅に縮小する.
▸We will either *downsize* or sell our unprofitable sections by the end of fiscal 2009. 当社は, 2009年度末までに, 不採算部門を縮小や売却する方針です.

downsizing 名 削減, 人員削減, 減額, 小型化, 軽量化, 規模縮小, 規模の縮小化, 合理化, 経営合理化, リストラ, 脱大型コンピュータ現象, ダウンサイジング
▸Struggling Victor Co. of Japan will implement a major workforce-*downsizing* program. 経営再建中の日本ビクターは, 大幅な人員削減プログラムを実施する.
  downsizing target 合理化の目標, 合理化計画の目標, 人員削減計画の目標
▸Half of the *downsizing target* planned for the year 2009 has already been met, with no redundancies being required. 人員過剰による解雇に踏み切るまでもなく, 2009年までに予定している合理化[人員削減]計画の目標の半分はすでに達成しました.

downstream 名 川下部門, 下流部門, 石油精製・販売部門, 親会社から子会社への販売, 下り, ダウンストリーム（「ダウンストリーム（下り）」は, 回線の信号の流れが電話局から利用者の方向のこと. ⇒**upstream**）
  downstream end 川下分野
  downstream industry 川下産業
  downstream investors 中小の機関投資家
  downstream market 川下部門
  downstream merger 逆吸収合併, ダウンストリーム合併（子会社による親会社の吸収合併）

downtime 名 故障時間, 機械停止時間, 使用不能時間

downtown 名 都心部, 中心街, 繁華街, 商業地区, ビジネス街, 賑やかな盛り場, ダウンタウン

downturn 名 低迷, 悪化, 下落, 下降, 下降局面, 落込み, 景気の落込み, 冷え込み, 不況, 後退, 景気後退, 衰退, 不振（⇒**upturn**）
  business downturn 不景気, 景気後退
  cyclical downturn 景気後退, 景気の悪化, 景気低迷
  downturn in demand 需要の冷え込み, 需要の

落込み
economic downturn 景気後退, 景気の悪化, 景気低迷, 景気沈滞, 景気の下降局面
market downturn 市場低迷, 市場の悪化, 市場[相場]の下落, 市場の下げ
▸The *downturn* was due mostly to the firm's failure to come out with any best-selling works. 業績不振の主因は, ベストセラーが出なくなったことにある。

downward 形 下向きの, 下方への, 減少の, 落ち目の, 下落する, 下降する, 低下する, 低落する, 衰退する, 副 下向きに, 減少へ, 低下して, 衰退して, 落ち目に, (上から)下まですべてにわたって (⇒consumer demand, upward)
downward movement of prices 物価下落[低落]の動き
downward pressure 低下圧力, 引下げ圧力
downward revision 下方修正
downward risk 損失リスク
downward sloping demand 右下がりの需要
downward trend 下落傾向, 下落基調, 下降傾向, 下降トレンド, 低下局面
from the president downward 社長をはじめ全社員
slight [modest] downward revision 小幅な下方修正
▸*Downward* revision of banks' business performance seems to be inevitable. 銀行の業績の下方修正は, 避けられない状況だ。

dowries 名 民営化支度金,〈新婦の〉持参金
DPS 1株当たり配当金 (**dividend per share**の略)
draft 名 為替手形, 手形, 小切手 (⇒come up with, current deposit)
arrival draft 着荷後一覧払い
banker's draft 銀行振出手形, 銀行為替手形, 銀行手形, 送金小切手 (=bank draft)
clean bill of draft 普通為替手形
demand draft 要求払い手形, 送金小切手《略 D/D》
documentary draft 荷為替手形
dollar draft ドル建て払い手形
draft declaration 宣言案
draft legislation 法案
draft legislation regarding possible military attacks on the nation 有事関連法案, 有事法案
draft resolution 決議草案
draw a draft at 30 day's sight on you 貴社宛に一覧後30日払い手形を振り出す
draw a draft for the invoice amount 送り状金額に対して手形を振り出す
named draft 記名式手形
negotiable draft 為替手形, 流通可能手形
no-draft export 無為替輸出
sight draft 一覧払い手形
time draft 定期払い手形
unpaid draft 不渡り手形
▸Such letter of credit shall be transferable and having the clause of definite undertaking by the issuing bank for unconditional payment against a *draft* at sight. この信用状は, 譲渡可能で, 一覧払い手形に対する無条件支払いに関して発行銀行が明確に約束した文言が入っているものとする。

drafting work 起草作業
▸The *drafting work* was undertaken with scholars, judges, public prosecutors and lawyers. 起草作業は, 学者, 裁判官, 検事や弁護士らで進められた。

drag 名 〈景気などの〉押し下げ効果, 押し下げ要因, 減速効果, マイナス要因, 阻害要因, 邪魔物, 足かせ
drag from inventory adjustment 在庫調整による景気押し下げ効果
drag on GDP growth 経済成長率を押し下げる要因, 成長率を押し下げる要因
drag on the economy 景気押し下げ効果, 景気減速要因, 成長率の押し下げ要因, 経済成長の足を引っ張る要因
fiscal drag 財政面からの景気押し下げ効果

draw 動 引き出す, 得る, おろす,〈利子を〉生む,〈小切手・手形を〉振り出す, 実行する,〈文書などを〉起草する, 起案する, 立案する
a draft drawn at 60 days after sight 一覧後60日払い手形
draw a check for $50 on the bank 銀行に50ドルの小切手を振り出す
draw a draft at 60 d/s under a confirmed credit to be opened in our favor for the corresponding value of an order 注文相当金額に対して当社を受益者とした確認信用状に基づいて一覧後60日払いの為替手形を振り出す
draw down existing stocks 在庫を取り崩す
draw (down) funds 資金を引き出す
draw on the loan 資金を引き出す
draw out excessive liquidity 過剰流動性を吸収する
draw (out) money from the bank account 銀行口座から金を引き出す
draw up a will 遺言書を作成する

draw up a blueprint for …の綿密な計画を立てる
draw up an agreement [contract] 契約書を作成する
drawing 名 図面, 製図, デッサン, 金銭の引出し, 手形の振出し, 貸付け実行, くじ引き, 抽選, 抽選会
　be on the drawing board 立案中
　drawing account 引出金勘定
　drawing board 製図板, 画板
　drawing of bill 手形の振出し
　machine drawing 機械製図, 機械図
　notice of drawing 借入通知書
　outline drawing 概略図, 外形図
　redemption by drawing 抽選償還
　shop drawing 工作図, 工場製作図
　Special Drawing Rights 対外決済に用いられるIMF（国際通貨基金）の特別引出権
　technical drawing 技術用製図
　working drawing 工作図, 設計図
drawdown 名 削減, 縮小, 低下, 減少, ローンによる資金の調達, 資金引出し, 資金引出し実行, 借用, 貸出の実行
　drawdown date 融資実行日, 貸出実行日
　drawdown period 資金引出可能期間, 資金引出期間
　drawdown swap アキュミュレーション・スワップ（＝accumulation swap：元本が徐々に増額する借入れなどに利用される）
　drawdowns of the export credits 輸出信用の資金引出し
drawee 名 手形名宛人
　drawee bank 名宛銀行
　drawee of a bill 手形名宛人
drawer 名 手形振出人, 振出人, 引出し
　cash drawer 現金引出し
　check drawer 小切手振出人
　Refer to Drawer 振出人に問い合わせのこと, 振出人回し（資金不足で不渡り返還する場合の文言）
dress up 粉飾する（＝window-dress）
▶In WorldCom's accounting fraud, it *dressed up* fees payable to other telecoms not as expenses, but as capital investments. 米通信大手ワールドコムの会計操作では, 他の通信会社に支払う回線使用料を経費に計上せず, 資本投資[設備投資]に計上していた。
drilling 名 掘削, 掘り
　directional drilling 傾斜掘り
　drilling platform 掘削プラットフォーム
　drilling rig 掘削装置, 掘削リグ

fixed drilling apparatus 固定式掘削装置
horizontal drilling 水平掘り
intangible drilling costs 無形掘削費
offshore drilling 沖合掘削, 海底油田掘削
oil drilling rig 油井掘削装置, 油井掘削リグ
sub-sea drilling 海底掘削
drive 動 …の原動力になる, …の牽引力となる, …を動かす, …をもたらす, …を喚起する
　be driven by …を原動力とする, …が追い風になる, …が大きな意味を持つ
　drive customer demand 消費者需要を喚起する
　drive growth 成長をもたらす, 成長の原動力となる
　drive the markets 相場を動かす
▶The U.S. and other overseas economies have *driven* Japan's recovery. 米国などの海外経済が, 日本の景気回復を牽引してきた。
▶These revenue increases were *driven* primarily by the year-over-year growth in the number of network access services. これらの収益の伸びは, 主にネットワーク・アクセス・サービスの利用件数が前年比で増加したことによるものです。
drive 名 政策, 主導, 動因, キャンペーン, 取組み, 組織的運動, 募金運動, 駆動装置, 装置, 気力, 決意, 意欲, 指向, 原動力, 推進力, 駆動力, ドライブ（⇒**competitive product, export drive**）
　austerity drive 緊縮政策
　disk drive ディスク装置, ディスク駆動機構, ディスク・ドライブ
　drive to promote a new product 新製品の販促キャンペーン
　efficiency drive 効率向上, 効率性の向上
　magnetic tape drive 磁気テープ駆動装置
　nationwide drive 全国運動, 全国キャンペーン
　technological drive 技術志向
▶To further improve our competitiveness, we have continued our *drive* to cut costs and expenses. 当社の競争力をさらに高めるため, 当社は継続してコストと費用の削減に全力を挙げて取り組んでいます。
drive under the influence of alcohol 飲酒運転する
▶Kirin Brewery Co. has made it a rule to dismiss any employee found *driving under the influence of alcohol*. キリンビールでは, 飲酒運転が判明した社員は解雇することにしている。
drive-through store 自動車乗り入れ[自動車通り抜け]式の店, ドライブ・スルー店
driven 形 …志向の, …主導の, …主導型の, 優先の, …中心の, …に徹する（＝-led, led by; ⇒

export-driven growth, market-driven)
business relationship driven 取引関係優先の
export-driven 輸出主導の, 輸出主導型, 輸出頼みの
futures-driven 先物取引中心の
order-driven 注文主導型の
profit-driven 利益志向の, 利益志向の強い, 利益追求型の (=profit-oriented)
retail-driven 個人投資家主導の
scale-driven 数量効果が大きい
swap-driven スワップ主導型の
▶The company's single-minded profit-*driven* corporate culture has been exposed. もっぱら利益追求の同社の企業体質が, 浮き彫りになった。
▶The Corporation made steady progress on its strategy of transforming itself into a more market-*driven* and efficient company. 当社は, 一段と市場志向の強い効率的な会社に変革する経営戦略を着実に推進した。

driver 名 原動力, 推進力, 牽引役, 主因 (=cause, driving force; ⇒**profit driver**)
growth driver 成長の原動力
key drivers 重要な原動力[推進力], 主要な原動力, 主因
main drivers 主因 (=key drivers)
▶The growth *driver* for our industry is quite simply increasing global competition. 当業界にとって, 成長の原動力[推進力]はまさにグローバル競争の激化です。

driving force 原動力, 推進力, 牽引役, 牽引車, 主因 (=driver; ⇒**housing investment**)
▶Corporate capital investment has been a *driving force* for the economic upturn. 企業の設備投資が, 景気回復の牽引役となっている。
▶Housing investment, a *driving force* for the U.S. economy until recently, has shown signs of a slowdown. 最近まで米景気を牽引してきた住宅投資に, 減速感が見られる。

DRM デジタル著作権管理 (digital rights managementの略)

drop 名 減少, 低下, 下落, 落ち込み, 低迷, 悪化, 動 減少する, 低下する, 下落する, 落ち込む (=decrease)
drop below …を割り込む
drop in asset quality 資産内容の悪化
drop in demand 需要の減少, 需要の落ち込み, 需要の減退
drop in earnings 減益 (=drop in income, drop in profits)
drop in machinery orders 機械受注の減少
drop in output 生産低下, 生産の落ち込み
drop sharply 急減する, 急速に減少する, 急落する
drop significantly 大幅に減少する, 大幅に悪化する
▶Sony Corp. saw a large *drop* in profits. ソニーは, 大幅減益となった。

drop-off service 取次ぎサービス
drop-ship 動 生産者直送で送る
drop shipment 生産者直送, 産地直送
drug business 医薬事業
▶Fujifilm will expand fully into its *drug business*. 富士フイルムは, 医薬事業に本格参入する方針だ。

dual 形 二重の, 両用の, 二元的な
dual banking system 二重銀行制度
dual corporate tax system 外形標準課税 (=local corporate tax formula based on the size of business)
dual economy 二重構造, 先進部門と後進部門の並存
dual income family 共働きの家庭
dual nature of investment 投資の二重性
dual responsibility 二重責任 (財務諸表・財務書類の作成については経営者, 監査報告書の作成については監査人がそれぞれ責任を負うこと)
dual taxation 二重課税
dual technology 両用技術
dual use packaging 二重用途包装
dual use technology 民生・軍事両用技術, 民用・軍用科学技術

dual exchange rate 二重為替相場, 二重相場, 二重相場制
▶In January 2002, the Argentine abandoned the peso's one-to-one peg to the U.S. dollar, replacing it with a *dual exchange rate*. 2002年1月に, アルゼンチンは1ドル=1ペソの固定相場制を廃止して, 代わりに二重相場制を導入した。

dual-list 動 重複上場する (⇒**delist, list**)
▶Six NYSE-listed blue-chip companies agreed to *dual-list* on Nasdaq and NYSE. ニューヨーク証券取引所に上場している優良企業6社が, ナスダック(米店頭株式市場)とNYSEへの重複上場に合意した。

dubious capital increase 架空増資
▶The former company president was indicted on fraud charges regarding a *dubious capital increase* in the firm. この元社長が, 架空増資に関する詐欺罪で起訴された。

due 名 料金, 組合費, 会員費, 会費, 使用料, 賦課金, 負担金
annual dues 年会費

due | **durable product**

club dues　クラブ会費
harbor dues　入港税
membership dues　会費, 会員負担金

due 形　正当な, 正式の, 適切な, 適正な, 適法の, 合法の, 十分な, 相当な, 合理的な, 履行義務のある, 支払い義務のある, 支払い期日のきた, 満期の過ぎた, 当然支払われるべき, 予定されている（⇒ entertainment expense）
　account due　未収金
　amount due　満期支払い高
　amounts due　債務金額
　amounts due from subsidiaries　子会社への預け金
　become due　支払い期日のきた, 支払わなければならなくなる
　collateral payment due date　担保の支払い日
　due and deferred premiums　未収保険金
　due diligence　相当の注意, 正当な努力, 事前精査, 監査手続き（契約締結前, 契約交渉中または契約締結後クロージング前に監査法人や法律事務所によって行われる財務面と法的の監査手続き）, 財務調査, デュー・ディリジェンス（＝due diligence investigation）
　due diligence investigation　事業買収前のデュー・ディリジェンス調査, 事前精査, 資産査定
　past due bill　不渡り手形
　past due loan　延滞ローン
　premium due　未払い保険料
　the date on which it is due　支払い期日
　when due　期日に, 支払い期日に, 満期が過ぎたとき
▶On June 2, 2008, we sold U.S. $200 million of 9.25% Notes *Due* June 2013.　2008年6月1日, 当社は2013年満期の利率9.25％ノート2億米ドルを発行しました。

due date　支払い期日, 返済期日, 満期日, 満期, 社債の償還日, 履行期日, 期日, 納期（＝date of payment）
▶Any unpaid amount shall bear interest from due date until paid.　未払い金額については, 支払い期日から支払われる日まで利息が付くものとする。

dull 形　活気がない, 不活発な, 沈滞した, 沈滞気味の, 不振の, 振るわない, 低迷する, 鈍い, さえない, 切れ味が悪い, 不透明な, だれ気味の
　dull market　活気のない[不活発な]市場, 景気の悪い市場, 閑散な市況, 沈滞市況, 市場低迷
　dull tone　低迷
　dull trade　不活発な商況

dummy company　トンネル会社, 架空の会社, ダミー会社
▶The secret funds were pooled in the bank accounts of *dummy companies*.　裏金は, ダミー会社の銀行口座に蓄えられていた。

dump 動　不当廉売する, 乱売する, ダンピングする
▶Cold-rolled steel products imported from Japan and other countries are being *dumped* on the U.S. market.　日本などから輸入している冷延鋼鈑が, 米市場でダンピングされている。

dumping 名　不当廉売, 投げ売り, たたき売り, 乱売,〈ゴミなどの〉投げ捨て, 廃棄物の投棄, ダンピング
　antidumping　反ダンピング, ダンピング防止
　commercial dumping　商業ダンピング
　dumping penalty margin　ダンピング率（＝dumping margin）
　exchange dumping　為替ダンピング
▶The Byrd Amendment requires antidumping and countervailing duties collected by customs authorities to be turned over to U.S. companies claiming damages for what they deem as *dumping* by overseas manufacturers.　バード法では, 税関当局が徴収したダンピング関税と相殺関税は, 海外メーカーによるダンピング（不当廉売）と認定されたものに対して損害賠償を請求した米国企業に分配しなければならない。

duplicate 名　副本, 写し, 謄本, 複写, 複製の, 形 同文の, 複製の, 控えの, 写しの, 現物どおりの, まったく同様の, 対の, 重複の
　duplicate bill　手形副本
　duplicate bill of lading　船荷証券副本
　duplicate copy　副本, 複製品
　duplicate invoice　副本送り状, 送り状副本
　duplicate receipt　領収書の控え
　duplicate sample　控え見本
　duplicate taxation　二重課税
　execute ... in duplicate originals　…の原本を2部作成する, …の原本を同文2通作成する
　make out in duplicate　正副2通作成する
▶This letter is addressed to you in *duplicate original*.　貴社宛に本レターを2部送付します。

durable product　耐久財, 耐久消費財（＝durable goods）
▶Spending on educational and entertainment *durable products*, such as flat-screen televisions, digital cameras and DVD recorders, has posted double-digit increases year-on-year since December.　薄型テレビやデジタル・カメラ, DVDレコーダーなどの教養娯楽用耐久財への消費

支出は, 昨年12月以降, 前年同月比で二桁の伸びを示している。

durable years 耐用年数
durables 名 耐久財
during the fiscal year ended March 31 3月期決算
▸Income before extraordinary items posted approximately 450.5 billion yen *during the fiscal year ended March 31*, 2009. 2009年3月期決算で, 経常利益［異常項目控除前利益］は約4,505億円となった。

during the period 期中, 当期に, 同期に
▸Earnings per common share are based on the weighted average number of shares outstanding *during the period*. 普通株式1株当たり純利益は, 期中の発行済み株式数の加重平均に基づいて計算されています。
▸The Corporation invested some $450 million in its subsidiary and associated companies *during the period*. 当社は, 同期［当期］に子会社と関連会社に4億5,000万ドル余りを投資しました。

during the year 当期, 今年度, 今期, 年間の
▸An increased quarterly dividend was declared twice *during the year*. 今年度は, 四半期増配を2回宣言しました。

duty 名 義務, 責任, 任務, 職務, 職責, 勤務, 関税, 税 (「関税」「税」の場合は, 一般に複数形が用いられることが多い; ⇒**dumping**)
　antidumping duties 反ダンピング関税, ダンピング防止関税, ダンピング関税
　compensation duties 相殺関税 (＝compensating duties, countervailing duties)
　customs duties 関税
　differential duties 差別関税
　discriminating duties 差別関税
　division of duties 職務分担, 職務の分担
　excise duty 消費税
　export duties 輸出関税 (＝export tariff)
　fiduciary duty 注意義務 (＝duty of care)
　import duties 輸入関税 (＝import tariff)
　off duty 非番, 勤務外, 勤務時間外
　night duty allowance 夜勤手当
　on duty 当番, 勤務中, 勤務時間中
　preferential duties 特恵関税 (＝preferential tariff treatment)
　protective duties 保護関税 (＝protective tariff)
　reciprocal duties 互恵関税
　retaliatory duties 報復関税
　safeguarding duties 産業保護税
　segregation of duties 職務分離, 職務の分離
　stamp duty 印紙税
▸Itoham Foods Inc. admitted its involvement in a meat importer's evasion of about ¥940 million in customs *duties* on pork imported from Europe. 大手食肉加工メーカーの伊藤ハムが, 食肉輸入業者がヨーロッパから輸入した豚肉にかかる関税約9億4,000万円を脱税した事件に関与していたことを認めた。
▸Patents obtained as a result of *duties* performed by a corporate employee belong to the employee. 企業の従業員が企業の職務の一環として得た特許権は, その従業員に帰属する。

duty-free 形 無関税の, 免税の, 無税の, 副 関税なしで, 免税で, 無税で
　duty-free allowance 免税限度
　duty-free entry 無税参入
　duty-free imports 免税輸入品
　duty-free items [goods] 免税品, 無税品
　duty-free shop 免税店

dynamics 名 力学, 動力学, 原動力, 動機となる力, 力, 動態, 動態学, 動学, 動向, ダイナミクス
　competitive dynamics 競争環境
　dynamics of the industry 業界動向, 業界動態
　economic dynamics 経済動学
　group dynamics 集団力学, グループ・ダイナミクス
　industrial dynamics 企業動態学, 産業動態, インダストリアル・ダイナミクス《略 **ID**》
　macro dynamics 巨視的動学, マクロ・ダイナミクス
　social dynamics 社会動学, ソーシャル・ダイナミクス
　systems dynamics システム・ダイナミクス

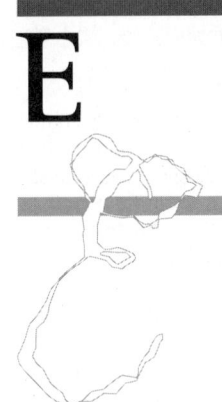

E

e

e- 電子の, 電子工学の, コンピュータ化された, 電子式, e…, イー… (＝electronic)
e-auction eオークション
e-banking ネット専業銀行, eバンキング
e-broker ネット専業証券会社, ネット証券, オンライン証券 (＝online broker, online brokerage)
e-cash 電子マネー, 電子通貨, イー・キャッシュ (＝cybercash, digital cash, e-money, electronic money)
e-economy eエコノミー (＝digital economy, electronic economy, IT economy, new economy: 情報技術(IT)による新しい経済活動のこと)
e-CRM イー・シーアールエム (**e-customer relationship management**の略。電子メールやウェブを通じて, 顧客の好みや属性, 取引履歴などに応じたコミュニケーションを実施し, 強化すること)
e-Debit 電子デビット, eデビット, Eデビット (インターネットでのデビット・カードによる即時決済)
e-government 電子政府
e-learning 電子学習, Eラーニング, eラーニング (＝distance learning, electronic learning, Web-based learning)
e-market eマーケット (＝e-marketplace)
e-marketplace 電子市場, 電子取引市場, 電子商取引市場, 仮想市場 (＝e-market, eMarketplace, electronic marketplace: 市場運営型ビジネス)
e-marketing eマーケティング
e-politics Eポリティクス (インターネットを使った政治)
e-procurement 電子調達, eプロキュアメント
e-tailing 電子商取引
e-trading 電子取引, 電子商取引, 電子売買, コンピュータ取引, 電子トレーディング, システム売買 (＝electronic trading)
e venture eベンチャー
e-bidding 名 電子入札 (＝electronic bidding, Net bidding, Net-based bidding)
▸Under the *e-bidding* system, the whole procedure—from inviting tenders to giving notification of the rules—will be conducted over the Internet. 電子入札制度では, 入札に関する事前説明から結果の通知まで, 手続きはすべてインターネット上で行われる。
e-book 名 電子書籍 (＝electronic book)
▸Matsushita, Kadokawa and TBS set up a joint firm to sell *e-books*. 松下電器と角川, TBSが, 電子書籍を販売する合弁会社を設立した。
e-business 名 eビジネス, Eビジネス (＝cyberbusiness, eBusiness, e-commerce, EC, electronic business, Internet business, IT business, Net business, online business: インターネットやパソコン通信サービスを利用して行われるビジネスのことで, インターネット上で販売, 購入から決済がすべてできるビジネスを指す)
e-business consulting services eビジネス・コンサルティング・サービス
e-business coordinator eビジネスのコーディネーター
e-business economy eビジネス経済, 電子ビジネス経済
e-business network service 電子ビジネス・ネットワーク・サービス

e-business service eビジネス・サービス
e-business opportunity eビジネスの機会
e-business solution eビジネス・ソリューション, eコマース・ソリューション
e-business strategy eビジネス戦略
▶Many companies use the Internet to create *e-business* opportunities and to strengthen existing businesses. 企業の多くは，eビジネスの機会創出と従来の事業の強化にインターネットを活用している。

e-commerce 名 電子商取引，電子決済，Eコマース (＝e-business, E-commerce, EC, electronic commerce: インターネットやパソコン通信サービスを利用した商取引)
　e-commerce industry 電子商取引業界
　e-commerce product 電子商取引製品，電子取引の商品
　e-commerce service eコマース・サービス
▶Popular *e-commerce* products are commodities such as game and music software, as well as financial commodities. 電子商取引の主力商品は，ゲームや音楽のソフトなどの商品や金融商品だ。

e-mail 名 電子メール，Eメール，eメール，メール, 動 電子メールを[で]送る (＝E-mail, email)
　attacks through e-mails 電子メールでの攻撃
　e-mail address メール・アドレス，Eメール・アドレス
　e-mail advertisement メール広告
　e-mail alert eメールによる通知，通知メール
　e-mail infected with virus ウイルスに感染したメール，ウイルス入りメール
　e-mail message 電子メールの文面，電子メールの通信文
　e-mail notification eメールによる通知
　e-mail service provider 電子メール・サービス会社
　receiver of the e-mail メールの受取人，メール受信者
　send e-mail eメールを送る
　sender of the e-mail メールの送り主，メール発信者
　suspicious e-mail 不審な電子メール
▶Attacks through *e-mails* that slowed the computer systems' functions occurred more than 100 times a day. コンピュータ・システムの機能を鈍くする電子メールでの攻撃が，1日に100回を超えた。
▶Company management can notify shareholders of annual shareholders meetings by *e-mail*. 企業経営者は，電子メールで，株主に年次株主総会の招集通知をすることができる。
▶Please give me your *e-mail* address. どうぞあなたのメール・アドレスを教えてください。

e-passport 名 eパスポート
▶The *e-passport* system simplifies immigration procedures through biometric identification specifically by scanning passport holders' irises. eパスポート・システムは，とくに旅券所持者の瞳の虹彩(こうさい)を読み取って生体認証することにより，入国手続きを簡素化するものだ。

e-tax 名 国税電子申告・納税システム
▶We can file a tax return by using the national electronic tax declaration and payment system called *e-tax*. イー・タックス(e-tax)と呼ばれる国税電子申告・納税システムを利用して，税務申告書を提出する[所得税の確定申告を行う]ことができる。

EAP 従業員支援制度，従業員支援プログラム (**Employee Assistance Program**の略。アルコール依存症や薬物乱用の従業員を，精神保健のため外部の専門機関と契約して更生させる制度)

early adopter 早期採用者

early corrective measures 早期是正措置 (＝prompt corrective action measures)
▶The government introduced the *early corrective measures* to force insurers to improve their management techniques. 早期是正措置は，生保に経営[経営手法]の改善を求める措置として政府が導入した。

early retirement 早期退職，希望退職，期限前返済
▶Ford may offer *early retirement* packages to its production workers. フォードは，生産労働者を対象に希望退職[早期退職]プランを導入する可能性がある。

early retirement and buyout packages 早期退職優遇制度
▶Ford Motor Co. will offer *early retirement and buyout packages* to all hourly workers. 米フォード・モーターは，すべての工場従業員[時間給労働者]を対象とする早期退職優遇制度を導入する。

early retirement program 早期退職制度
▶This third straight year of red ink is due to slumps in mobile phone sales and swelling costs for *early retirement programs*. この3年連続赤字の要因は，携帯電話の販売低迷と早期退職[希望退職]制度の費用増大だ。

earmark 動 予算を組む; 〈…の目的に資金などを〉当てる，計上する，指定する，…を区別する (⇒field)

▶We *earmarked* $1 million to promote the study of the emerging environmental field of industrial ecology.　産業エコロジーの新環境分野の研究を促進するため，当社は100万ドルの予算を計上しました。

earn 動　稼ぐ，稼得する，利益を上げる，報酬などを得る，獲得する，生む，もたらす，計上する（⇒define）
　amount *earned* for equity　普通株主持ち分
　earn a profit　利益を上げる
　earn interest　利息が付く
　earned income　給与所得，勤労所得
　earned premium　計上保険料
　earned surplus　利益剰余金（＝earned surplus reserve, retained earnings）
　income in the period earned　稼得した期間の利益
　interest earned on collateral　担保で付いた利子，担保から発生した利子
　net premiums earned　正味経過保険料
　pay-as-you-earn　源泉課税
　premium earned　既経過保険料
　save-as-you-earn　天引き積立て
▶Corporate value is defined as "the total of profits one company will *earn* in future."　企業価値は，「ある会社が将来稼ぐ利益の合計」と定義される。
▶Hewlett-Packard *earned* $1.55 billion, or 55 cents per share, for the first quarter ended Jan. 31.　ヒューレット・パッカードは，第1四半期（1－3月期）に15億5,000万ドル（1株当たり55セント）の利益を上げた。
▶The firm *earned* $733.4 million, or $2.36 per share, for the three months ended in September.　同社の第3四半期［7－9月期］の利益は，7億3,340万ドル（1株当たり2.36ドル）でした。

earner 名　稼ぎ手，稼得者，利益を生み出すもの，儲かる仕事
　income earner　所得稼得者
　two-earner family　共稼ぎ世帯
　wage earner　賃金労働者，勤労者，給料生活者

earning 名　利益，収益（＝income; ⇒earnings）
　earning capacity　収益力（＝earning power）
　earning rate　収益率
　expected earning　期待収益
　life-long earning　生涯賃金
　operating earning rate　営業利益率
　revenue-earning activity　収益稼得活動
earning assets　収益性資産，収益資産

▶Both companies contributed to the growth in these revenues by expanding their portfolios of *earning assets*.　両社は，保有収益資産の拡大によってこれらの増収に貢献しました。

earning power　収益力，収益性（＝earning capacity, earnings power, profitability; ⇒**instability**）
▶An increase in operating profits is said to illustrate the good business results of a company's core business and *earning power*.　営業利益の伸びは，企業の本業の好調さと収益力の高さを示すとされている。

earnings 名　収益，利益，純利益，利潤，所得，収入，投資利益，業績，決算（＝gains, profits, returns; ⇒**consolidated earnings, corporate earnings, improvement, retained earnings**）
　adjusted earnings　調整後利益
　after-tax earnings　税引き後利益
　current earnings　当期純利益（＝current income, current net income）
　earnings after taxes　税引き後利益《略 EAT》
　earnings before income taxes　税引き前利益
　earnings before tax　税引き前利益
　earnings decline　収益の減少，減益
　earnings estimate　業績予想，収益予想，利益予想（＝earnings forecast, earnings projection）
　earnings from continuing operations　継続的営業活動による利益
　earnings from operations　営業利益
　earnings gain　収益の伸び，収益の増加，増益（＝earnings growth）
　earnings goal　収益目標，業績目標（＝earnings target）
　earnings manipulation　利益の不正操作
　earnings performance　利益実績，業績
　earnings statement　損益計算書
　earnings structure　収益構造
　earnings yield　収益率，利益率，株式利回り，益回り（1株当たり利益を株価で割った数字で，株式投資から期待される報酬を示す）
　equity in earnings of unconsolidated subsidiaries　非連結子会社の持ち分利益
　equity earnings　投資損益
　increases in earnings and profit　増収増益
　interim earnings　中間利益，中間期の利益
　net interest earnings　投資収益
　parent basis earnings　単独ベースの収益
　robust earnings　業績好調
　sales and earnings gains　増収増益
　stagnant earnings　収益の悪化，業績の低迷

statement of earnings 損益計算書
statement of retained earnings 利益剰余金計算書
strong earnings 高収益，高水準の収益
▶The effects of accounting changes on future *earnings* may be quite small once we bring the balance sheet up to date. 将来の利益に対する会計処理変更の影響は，貸借対照表をいったん現状に即したものに修正してしまうと，ごく僅かになる可能性があります。

earnings forecast 業績予想，業績見通し，収益予想，利益予想（＝earnings estimate, earnings projection, profit forecast）
　full-year earnings forecast 通期の業績予想，通期の業績見通し，通期の収益予想（＝full-year earnings projection, full-year forecast）
　group earnings forecast 連結業績予想
▶For the year to March 31, 2009, the company left unchanged its group *earnings forecast* made last November. 2009年3月期決算の見通しは，同社が昨年11月に発表した連結業績予想を据え置いた。

earnings growth 収益の伸び［増加］，利益の伸び，収益率の伸び，増益（＝earnings gain）
▶Our corporate goal is to achieve at least 10 percent *earnings growth* each year. 毎年少なくとも10％の増益を達成することが，当社の企業目標です。

earnings per common share 普通株式1株当たり利益［純利益］，1株当たり利益（＝earnings per share）
　earnings per common share について ➡ *earnings per common share*（普通株式1株当たり利益，普通株式1株当たり純利益，1株当たり利益）は，earnings per share（EPS）と同義語で，会社の収益性を分析するうえで重要な指標とされ，当期純利益（net earnings, net income）を外部発行済み普通株式数（common shares outstanding, common stock outstanding）で割って算出する。米国の公開会社は，損益計算書（income statement）に1株当たり利益を表示することになっている。1株当たり利益（EPS）＝当期純利益÷普通株式数
　earnings [loss] per common share 普通株式1株当たり純利益［損失］
　earnings per common share—assuming full dilution 普通株式1株当たり利益—完全希薄化［希釈化，希釈効果］を考慮した場合，完全希薄化後普通株式1株当たり利益
▶*Earnings per common share* for the second quarter were $0.72, compared with $0.92 in the same period last year. 第2四半期の普通株式1株当たり純利益は，前年同期の0.92ドルに対して，0.72ドルでした。

earnings per share 1株当たり利益，1株当たり純利益［当期純利益］，普通株式1株当たり純利益《略 EPS》（＝earnings per common share: 1株当たり利益(EPS)＝当期純利益÷普通株式数）
▶*Earnings per share* for the first nine months of 2008 were based on 308.4 million average common shares outstanding. 2008年1－9月期の1株当たり純利益は，発行済み普通株式の平均株式数3億840万株に基づいて計算されています。

earnings projection 業績予想，収益予想，業績見通し（＝earnings forecast）
▶In the revised group *earnings projection* for fiscal 2009 through next March, the firm projects a pretax profit of ¥160 billion. 2010年3月期［2009年度］の連結業績見通しの修正で，同社は1,600億円の税引き前利益を予想している。

earnings report 業績報告，業績報告書，決算，決算報告，収益報告，損益計算書，財務計算書
　consolidated earnings report 連結決算報告［報告書］，連結業績報告書
　consolidated earnings report for the April-September period 3月期決算企業の9月連結中間決算，4－9月期の連結決算
　earnings report for the first half of fiscal 2009 2009年度上半期［1－6月期］決算，3月期決算企業の9月中間決算
　interim [midterm] earnings report 中間決算，中間決算報告［報告書］
　quarterly earnings report 四半期報告，四半期報告書
▶The firm released its *earnings report* for the first half of fiscal 2009. 同社が，2009年9月中間［2009年度上半期］決算を発表した。

earnings results 業績，決算
▶Managers had previously backed wage increases at companies with strong *earnings results*. 経営側は以前，業績のよい企業の賃上げを後押ししていた。
▶The company said it would correct its *earnings results* for the past five fiscal years. 同社は，過去5年度分の決算訂正を発表した。

earn-out 名 アーンアウト契約
EASDAQ 欧州店頭株式市場（European Association of Securities Dealers Automated Quotationsの略）
ease 名 金利減免，低金利化，利下げ，動 …の金利を下げる

easement 名 地役権
easy monetary policy 金融緩和政策, 金融緩和策 (=easy money policy, easy money step; ⇒ultra-easy [ultra-loose] monetary policy)
easy money policy 金融緩和政策, 金融緩和策, 金融緩和 (=easy monetary policy, easy money step)
▸The Bank of Japan should maintain its *easy money policy* until there is no doubt that deflation has ended. デフレが確実に終息するまで, 日銀は金融緩和を続けるべきだ。
EBC 欧州ビジネス協会 (European Business Councilの略)
EBITA 支払い利息・税金・営業権償却費控除前利益 (earnings before interest, taxes and amortization of goodwillの略)
▸Through the innovations and contributions of our people, the Corporation's organic growth increased by 11% in 2008 while *EBITA* grew by 26.5 percent. 当社の従業員の技術革新と貢献によって, 2008年の当社の有機的成長率は11%上昇し, EBITA (支払い利息・税金・営業権償却費控除前利益) も26.5%増加しました。
EBRD 欧州開発銀行, 欧州復興開発銀行 (European Bank for Reconstruction and Developmentの略)
EC 電子商取引, eコマース, エレクトロニック・コマース (electronic commerceの略)
  b to c EC 企業対消費者の取引[電子商取引], 企業と一般顧客との取引 (=B2C: business to consumerの略)
  business to business EC 企業対企業の取引[電子商取引], 企業間の取引 (=b to b EC, B2B)
  business to employee EC 企業対従業員の取引[電子商取引] (=b to e EC, B2E)
  EC site ECサイト (=online shop, virtual shop, Web shop)
  m to m EC マーケット同士の取引 (=M2M: market to market ECの略)
▸With *EC*, we can do online shopping or online banking on a network such as the Internet. 電子商取引だと, インターネットなどのネットワーク上でオンライン・ショッピングやオンライン・バンキングなどを行うことができる。
EC 欧州委員会 (European Commissionの略)
EC 経営委員会, 執行委員会 (executive committeeの略)
EC green paper ECグリーン・ペーパー
ECB 欧州中央銀行 (European Central Bankの略)
▸The *ECB* sets monetary policy for the 15 nations that use the euro currency. 欧州中央銀行(ECB)は, ユーロ通貨を使用しているユーロ圏15か国の金融政策を決める。
▸The European Central Bank (*ECB*) raised its key interest rate by a quarter of a percentage point to 2.25 percent. 欧州中央銀行(ECB)は, 主要政策金利を0.25%引き上げて年2.25%とした。
echelon 名 段階, レベル
ECN 電子証券取引ネットワーク (Electronic Communications Networkの略)
eco management 環境経営
ecocentric management 環境中心経営, 環境経営
ecocide 名 環境破壊, 環境の大量破壊
eco-conscious 形 環境を意識した, 環境問題を意識した
ecodevelopment 名 環境維持開発 (=sustainable development)
eco-factory 名 エコ・ファクトリー (地球環境問題を考慮した生産工場)
ecohouse 名 環境共生住宅, エコハウス
ecolabeling [ecolabelling] 名 環境保全ラベル, エコ表示 (=environmental labeling, green labeling)
ecological 形 生態の, 生態系の, 生態学の, 環境問題に関心のある, 環境にやさしい
  ecological accounting 生態会計
  ecological balance 生態学的均衡, 生態学的バランス
  ecological map 生態学的環境評価地図
  ecological marketing エコ・マーケティング
  ecological niche 生態的地位
  ecological pyramid 生態的ピラミッド
ecologically-friendly 環境にやさしい (=eco-friendly, environment-friendly)
ecology 名 生態, 生態系, 生態環境, 自然環境, 環境問題, 環境保護, 生態学, エコロジー
  cultural ecology 文化生態学
  ecology business エコロジー・ビジネス (=ecobusiness)
  human ecology 人間生態学
eco-management and audit scheme エコ管理監査要員
ecomaterial 形 環境にやさしい材料, 地球にやさしい材料
econobox 名 経済車, 低燃費の小型車
econometric analysis 計量経済分析
econometric model 計量モデル, 計量経済モデル, 計量経済学モデル, エコノメトリック・モデル

economic 形 経済の, 経済上の, 財政上の, 家計の, 経済学の, 実用上の, 実用的な, 実利的な, 有利な, 儲かる, 値段の安い
economic advance 経済発展
economic affairs 経済情勢, 経済事情
economic agent 経済主体, 経済行為者
Economic and Monetary Union EU経済通貨統合, 経済通貨同盟《略 EMU》
economic and price statistics 景気・インフレ指標
economic animals 経済的動物, エコノミック・アニマル
economic assistance 経済援助, 経済協力 (= economic aid)
economic bubble 経済のバブル, バブル
economic change 経済変動, 経済の変化
economic climate 経済環境, 経済情勢, 景況, 景気
economic collapse 経済崩壊
economic contraction 景気収縮, 経済的収縮, マイナス成長, 不況, 景気後退
economic convergence 経済格差の縮小
economic cooperation 経済協力
economic crime 経済犯罪 (贈収賄や横領)
economic crisis 経済危機
economic data 景気指標
economic development 経済開発, 経済発展, 経済成長, 景気動向, 経済動向, 経済情勢
economic development zone 経済開発区
economic divergence 経済格差の拡大
economic effect 経済効果
Economic Espionage Act 米国の経済スパイ法(外国政府やその関連機関の利益のために秘密を盗む経済スパイ条項と, 商業上の秘密を無断で州外, 国外に持ち出す商業秘密窃盗条項がある)
economic growth rate 経済成長率
economic hazards 経済の混乱
economic health 経済状況
economic improvement 景気回復 (= economic recovery)
economic indicator 景気指標, 経済指標
economic instability 経済不安, 経済的不安定性
economic institution 経済制度, 経済体質
economic integration 経済統合 (= economic merger)
economic loss 経済損失
economic lot size 経済的ロット・サイズ
economic management 経済運営, 経済政策
economic manufacturing quantity 経済的生産数量, 最適生産量《略 EMQ》

economic mismanagement 経済失政
economic muscle 経済力
economic opportunity 経済的機会
economic outlook 経済見通し, 景気見通し, 景気の先行き, 経済展望
economic overheating 景気過熱
economic partnership talks 経済連携協議, 経済パートナーシップ協議
economic picture 経済情勢, 経済状況 (= economic scene, economic situation)
economic plight 経済苦境
economic policy 経済政策
economic power 経済大国(economic giant), 経済力
economic prediction 経済予測, 景気予測
economic progress 経済発展, 経済の進歩
economic prosperity 経済繁栄
economic reform 経済改革
economic relations 経済関係, 経済交流
Economic Report of the President 米大統領経済報告書, 経済教書
economic research 経済調査, 経済研究, 経済調査研究
economic results 景気指標 (= economic reports)
economic sanctions 経済制裁
economic scene 経済情勢, 経済状況, 経済界
economic setbacks 景気後退 (= business setbacks)
economic slump 景気低迷, 景気悪化, 不況, 不景気
economic stability 経済安定, 経済的安定性
economic stabilization policy 経済安定政策, 経済安定化政策
economic stagnation 景気沈滞, 経済停滞
economic statement 経済声明
economic summit 経済サミット
economic union 経済統合, 経済同盟
economic upturn 景気回復 (= economic upswing)
economic value 経済価値, 使用価値
economic value added 経済付加価値《略 EVA》
economic welfare 経済的福祉, 経済的厚生 (= economic well-being)
economic woes 経済的苦悩, 経済難
economic zone 経済圏, 経済ブロック, 経済水域

economic activity 経済活動, 経済動向, 経済情勢, 景気 (⇒cartel)
▶Operations whose principal *economic activities* are undertaken in currencies other than the U.S.

dollar are classified as either integrated or self-sustaining.　主な経済活動が米ドル以外の通貨で行われている事業は、一体化した事業か自立した事業に分類されています。

economic and social instabilities　経済・社会不安
▶In Argentina and Turkey, *economic and social instabilities* are deepening.　アルゼンチンとトルコでは、経済・社会不安が深刻化している。

economic assessment　景気判断、景気の基調判断（＝assessment of the economy）
▶The Bank of Japan downgraded its economic assessment for the second straight month.　日本銀行は、景気の基調判断を2か月連続で下方修正した。

economic conditions　経済状態、経済状況、経済情勢、景気（⇒demand）
▶Global *economic conditions* improved last year, but growth was still sluggish.　世界の景気は昨年好転したが、経済の成長率はまだ低い。

economic environment　経済環境、景気
▶Major changes are taking place in the *economic environment*.　経済環境に、大きな変化が生じている。

economic expansion　景気拡大、景気回復、経済成長、経済拡張（＝business expansion; ⇒ rate of economic expansion）
▶The *economic expansion* is likely to continue for the foreseeable future.　景気拡大は、当分の間続きそうだ。

economic fundamentals　経済のファンダメンタルズ、経済の基礎的条件（＝fundamentals of the economy）
▶Exchange rates should reflect *economic fundamentals*.　為替レートは、経済のファンダメンタルズ[経済の基礎的条件]を反映しなければならない。

economic globalization　経済のグローバル化
▶An age of *economic globalization* is characterized by intense competition in the pursuit of maximum profit.　経済のグローバル化時代の特徴は、利益の極大化を求めて繰り広げられる熾烈（しれつ）な競争である。

economic growth　経済成長、景気浮揚、経済成長率（⇒crude oil, lawsuit, newcomer, revise）
▶Major developing nations are witnessing a remarkable increase in their greenhouse gas emissions as a result of their rapid *economic growth*.　主要途上国では、急激な経済成長に伴って温室効果ガス排出量の増加が著しい。

economic law　経済法則
▶Here we face *economic law* at work.　ここで機能しているのは、経済法則である。

economic mechanism　経済メカニズム
▶Traditional *economic mechanisms* in industrial nations are going through changes.　先進国のこれまでの経済メカニズムは、変化している。

economic partnership　経済連携
▶The number of bilateral or regional *economic partnerships* has been on the rise since the early 1990s.　90年代の初めから、2国間や地域的な経済連携の数は増えている。

economic partnership agreement　経済連携協定《略 EPA》
▶Japan signed its first *economic partnership agreement* (EPA) with Singapore in 2002.　日本は、2002年にシンガポールと最初の経済連携協定を結んだ。

economic performance　景気動向
▶The index of lagging indicators is designed to measure *economic performance* in the recent past.　遅行指数は、直近の過去の景気動向を示す指標だ。

economic recovery　景気回復（＝business recovery, economic improvement, economic rebound, economic revival, economic turnaround, economic upturn: 景気回復・拡大[好況]期には、消費が旺盛で企業の業績が伸び、雇用増や従業員の賃上げに結びつく。⇒recession）
economic recovery budget　景気浮揚型予算
economic recovery package　景気テコ入れ策、景気対策、景気回復策
economic recovery policy　景気テコ入れ政策（＝economic recovery program）
▶The *economic recovery* is slowing down.　景気回復の足取りが、鈍くなってきた。
▶The *economic recovery* likely will cause interest rates to rise.　景気回復で、金利が上昇しそうだ。

economic report　経済報告、経済報告書、経済白書、経済教書
monthly economic report　月例経済報告
Economic Report of the President　経済報告、米大統領経済報告
economic reports　景気指標（＝economic results）
▶In its monthly *economic report* for August, the government said the economy "remains essentially flat."　8月の月例経済報告で政府は、景気は「おおむね横ばいである」とした。

economic revival 景気回復
▸Since the collapse of the bubble economy in the early 1990s, this country has experienced several phases of *economic revival*. 1990年代はじめのバブル崩壊以降、日本は何度か景気回復局面を迎えた。

economic slowdown 景気減速
▸The Fed has to maintain guard against an *economic slowdown* and inflationary pressure. 米連邦準備制度理事会(FRB)は、今後とも景気減速とインフレ圧力を警戒する必要がある。

economic stimulus 景気刺激, 経済刺激, 景気対策, 経済対策
　economic stimulus measures 景気刺激策, 景気刺激対策, 景気対策
　economic stimulus package 景気刺激策 (= economic stimulus measures)
▸The U.S. president urged Congress to approve an *economic stimulus* package as early as possible. 米大統領は、議会に景気刺激策の法案を早期に可決するよう求めた。

economic trends 景気動向, 経済情勢
▸The U.S. Federal Reserve Board will change the pace of raising rates, depending on *economic trends*. 米連邦準備制度理事会(FRB)は、経済情勢次第で利上げのペースを変える方針だ。

economic upswing 景気回復, 景気上昇, 景気の上向き
▸The export-led economic growth could falter if the U.S. *economic upswing* slows down or if there is a rapid surge in the value of the yen. 輸出主導の経済成長は、米国の景気回復にブレーキがかかったり、急激な円高が進んだりすれば、大きくつまずく可能性がある。

economic value added 経済的付加価値, 経済付加価値《略 EVA》
▸We look at customer and employee satisfaction, our stock price and *economic value added* (EVA) in measuring our success. 当社の成功の度合いを測る物差しとして、当社は顧客と従業員の満足度、当社の株価と経済的付加価値(EVA)を見ます。

economies 名 経済, 経済性, 経済地域, 経済群, 経済国, 国, 諸国, エコノミー (⇒emerging economies)
　ASEAN economies アセアン諸国, ASEAN諸国
　economies of network 連結の経済性 (複数の企業や組織間で形成されるネットワークから生み出される経済性のこと)
　economies of scale 規模の経済, 規模の経済性, 規模の拡大, 規模の利益, スケール・メリット, 数量効果, エコノミー・オブ・スケール (= economy of scale, scale merit: 少品種大量生産の経済効率を意味する)
　economies of scope 範囲の経済, 範囲の経済性, エコノミー・オブ・スコープ (= economy of scope: 複数の製品を生産したほうが、単一の製品を生産する場合よりも生産コストが安くなる現象のことで、製品多様化・経営多角化の経済性を指す)
　economies of shotage 不足の経済
　economies of speed スピードの経済, スピードの経済性, エコノミー・オブ・スピード (= economy of speed)
　Group of Seven major economies 先進7か国 (G7), 主要7か国
　highly developed economies 先進工業国
　industrialized economies 工業国, 工業先進国
　low income economies 低所得国
　new economies 新興国
　open market economies 自由市場経済, 市場経済
▸Mergers and acquisitions to pursue *economies of scale* will be carried out worldwide. 規模の経済[規模の拡大]を追求するためのM&A(企業の合併・買収)は今後、国際的規模で実施される見込みだ。

economize 動 節約する, 最大限有効に使う

economy 名 経済, 経済性, 景気, 節約, 経済機構, 経済組織, 経済国, 社会, エコノミー (⇒ economies, global economy, world economy)
　agricultural economy 農業経済, 農業社会
　ailing economy 病める経済
　behavior of the economy 景気動向, 景気の先行き
　black economy 地下経済, 闇経済
　booming economy 好景気, 過熱気味の景気
　bottoming out of the economy 景気や物価の底入れ
　bubble economy バブル経済, バブル景気, バブル
　capitalist economy 資本主義経済
　controlled economy 統制経済
　decelerated economy 減速経済
　digital economy デジタル経済, デジタル・エコノミー (= e-economy, new economy)
　discourage the economy 景気の足を引っ張る
　e-business economy 電子ビジネス経済
　e-economy eエコノミー (= digital economy, new economy)
　free economy 自由経済

heating up of the economy 景気の過熱
IT economy IT経済, ITエコノミー
market economy 市場経済, 市場型経済
mixed economy 混合経済
national economy 国民経済, 日本経済
new economy 新しい経済, ニュー・エコノミー (=digital economy, e-economy, IT economy, new economy)
old economy オールド・エコノミー (=t-economy, traditional economy)
open economy 開放経済
outlook of the economy 景気見通し
picture of economy 景気の状況, 経済情勢 [状況]
planned economy 計画経済
real economy 実体経済
regional economy 地域経済
revitalizing the economy 経済再生
slowdown of the economy 景気減速, 不況
slowing economy 景気鈍化
socialist market economy 社会主義市場経済
strengthening economy 景気の好転
t-economy tエコノミー (=old economy, traditional economy)
throwaway economy 使い捨て経済
upturn in the economy 景気回復
weak economy 景気低迷
▶The domestic *economy* seems to remain strong. 国内景気は, 引き続き底堅いようだ [底堅く推移しているようだ].

ecoright 名 排出権 (=eco right)
eco-station 名 代替燃料供給所
ecosystem 名 生態系
▶The ministry is planning to draw up guidelines to evaluate the possible effect that medicines can have on aquatic creatures and *ecosystems*. 同省では, 医薬品が潜在的に水生生物や生態系に与える影響を評価するための指針作りを計画している。

ecotop 名 生態環境
ecotourism 名 エコツーリズム (自然景観や動植物を対象に行われる観光)
ECR 効率的な消費者対応, 効率的消費者対応 (efficient consumer responseの略)
edge 名 先端, 優位, 優位性, 優勢, 強み, 瀬戸際, 限界, 効果, 刃, 稜線, エッジ
competitive edge 競争上の優位(性), 競争力
cutting edge 鋭利な刃, 最前線, 最先端, 先頭, 主導的地位, 最新式 (=leading edge)
decisive edge 決定的優位
gain a competitive edge in the international market 国際市場で競争力をつける
gain an edge on …に対して優位を勝ち取る
have an edge 優る, 優勢である, 優位に立つ
have the edge on [over] …より少し優れている, …より少し強みがある
leading edge 主導的地位, 最先端, 最前部, 最前線, 先頭, 最新式, トップ (=cutting edge)
take the edge off 弱める, そぐ, 鈍らせる
technological edge 技術的優位, 技術的優位性
▶Rice appears to have an *edge* because of her proximity to Bush. ブッシュ大統領の信頼を得ていることから, ライス大統領補佐官が優位に立っているようだ。

EDI 電子データ交換, ビジネス文書交換 (electronic data interchangeの略)
EDP 電子データ処理, 電子情報処理 (electronic data processingの略)
EDR 欧州預託証券 (European Depository Receiptの略)
education 名 教育, 教養, 学識
adult education 成人教育
consumer education 消費者教育
life-long education 生涯教育
professional education 専門教育
▶The Corporation's wide-ranging support of *education* includes direct funding and countless hours by its volunteers in schools. 当社の広範な教育助成には, 直接助成金や各種学校での社員の活発なボランティア活動なども含まれています。

EEZ 排他的経済水域 (exclusive economic zoneの略。⇒fishing fee)
▶In terms of the combined areas of its territorial waters, exclusive economic zone (*EEZ*) and continental shelf, Japan ranks sixth in the world. 領海と排他的経済水域(EEZ), 大陸棚を合わせた面積では, 日本は世界で6番目だ。

effect 動 行う, 実施する, 成し遂げる, 手配する, 保険を付ける
effect a two-for-one stock split 1対2の株式分割を行う
effect an insurance 保険を付ける
effect payment 支払いを行う, 納付する
▶The two-for-one stock splits were *effected* in the forms of 100 percent stock dividends. これらの1対2の株式分割は, 100%株式配当形式で実施しました。

effect 名 影響, 影響額, 発効, 効力, 効果, 施行, 趣旨, 意味 (⇒adverse effect, favorable, negative effect, ripple effect, synergy effect)
boomerang effect ブーメラン効果

cumulative effect 累積影響額, 影響累計額, 累積効果
currency effects 為替の影響
dilutive effect 希薄化効果
effect of accounting change 会計処理変更の影響
effect of exchange rate changes on cash 現金預金に対する為替レート［為替相場］変動の影響［影響額］, 為替変動による現金への影響
expansionary effect 景気刺激効果
external economy effect 外部経済効果
halo effect ハロー効果, 後光効果, 光背効果
knock-on effect 連鎖反応, 連鎖効果, ドミノ効果（＝domino effect）
leverage effect 他人資本効果, テコの効果, 梃率（ていりつ）効果, レバレッジ効果
net of income tax effect 税効果後
seasonal effects 季節調整
size effect 規模効果
tax effects of timing differences 期間差異の税効果
▶A merger between life insurance companies will have little *effect*, because there is no synergy *effect*. 生命保険同士が合併しても, 相互補完関係が生まれないため, 効果は薄い。
▶Apart from these cumulative *effects* on prior years of the accounting change, our change in accounting had no material effect on net income in 2008. この会計処理の変更による過年度への累積的影響を別にすれば, 当社の会計処理の変更によって, 2008年度の純利益に重大な影響はありませんでした。
▶It would take some time for negative *effects* of the yen's appreciation to become visible. 円高のマイナス影響［悪影響］が出るまでには, 時間がかかるだろう。
effective 形 有効な, 効果的な, 効率的な, 実施されている, 実施中の, 効力をもつ, 事実上の, 実際の, 実動の
annual effective tax rate 年間実効税率
cost-effective コスト効率がよい, 費用効率がよい, 費用効果が高い
effective demand 有効需要
effective exchange rate 実効為替相場, 実効為替レート
effective income tax rate 実効所得税率, 実効税率, 実効法人税率（＝effective tax rate）
effective interest rate 実効利率, 実効金利, 実質利率（＝effective interest, effective rate of interest）
effective management 効率経営
real effective exchange rate 実質実効為替レート（＝real effective FX rate）
▶On June 30, 2008, the Corporation concluded the sale of some of its European assets *effective* February 2008 to the firm. 2008年6月30日に当社は, 当社の欧州事業資産の一部を2008年2月付けで同社に売却する手続きを完了しました。
effective book value 実質簿価
▶Bad loans should be bought at market value rather than at *effective* book value. 不良債権は, 実質簿価でなく時価で買い取るべきだ。
effective tax rate 実効税率, 法定実効税率, 税負担率（税金費用の税引き前利益当期利益に対する割合）
▶The 2008 provision for income taxes was $128 million (*effective tax rate* of 29 percent). 2008年度の納税引当金［法人税等引当金］は, 1億2,800万ドル（実効税率29％）でした。
effectiveness 名 有効性, 効率, 効果, 効力, 薬効, 成果
advertising effectiveness 広告効果
cost effectiveness 費用効果, コスト効果, 原価効率, 費用有効度
leveraged effectiveness レバレッジ効果
managerial effectiveness 経営効果, 経営手腕
operating effectiveness 事業の効率性（＝operating efficiency）運用上の有効性
▶Our aim is to offer doctors as well as patients using our pharmaceutical products a maximum of therapeutical *effectiveness* and safety. 当社の目的は, 医師や当社の医薬品を使用する患者に最大限の治療効果と安全性を提供することにあります。
▶Our global operations team is responsible for the *effectiveness* of our operations worldwide. 当社のグローバル運営チームは, ワールドワイドな効率的運営に対して責任を負っています。
efficiency 名 効率, 効率化, 効率性, 能率, 生産性, 有効性（⇒bottom line, brand image, competitiveness, heat wave, large, priority, return, ROE, thermal efficiency）
audit efficiency 監査の効率性
capital efficiency 資本効率
commercial efficiency 営業効率, 営業上の能率
cost efficiency 原価能率, 費用効率, コスト効率
distribution efficiency 流通効率
efficiency gain 生産性の伸び, 生産性の上昇, 生産性の改善
labor efficiency 作業効率
market efficiency 市場の効率性

operating efficiency 営業効率, 事業効率
operational efficiency 経営効率
plant efficiency 工場の効率性
production efficiency 生産効率
▸The automaker aims to boost the *efficiency* of development and personnel costs by focusing on the production of midsize and small cars. この自動車メーカーは，中小型車の生産に的を絞りこむことで，開発資金と開発要員費の効率化を目指している。

efficient 形 効率的な, 効率のよい, 能率的な, 有能な, 有効な
cost-efficient 費用効率がよい, 費用効率[コスト効率]が高い, コスト効率がよい, 低コストの (=cost-effective)
cost-efficient source of financing 低コストの資金調達源
efficient management 効率的経営, 経営の効率化
fuel-efficient 燃費効率のよい, 低燃費の
labor-efficient 労働効率の高い
more efficient running 運営の効率化
▸Higher gasoline prices have led to brisk sales of fuel-*efficient* cars in North America. ガソリン高騰で，北米での低燃費車の販売は好調だった。
▸We have continued our drive to streamline operations and make ourselves as *efficient* as possible. 当社は，継続して業務運営を簡素化して，できるかぎり効率的な企業になるよう全力を挙げて取り組んでいます。

efficient market 効率的市場
semi-strong efficient market 準強度の効率的市場
strong efficient market 強度の効率的市場
weak efficient market 弱度の効率的市場

effort 名 努力, 試み, 尽力, 取組み, 動き, 活動, 作業, 仕事, 運動, キャンペーン, 募集, 対策, 政策, 策, 努力の成果, 労作, 力作, 立派な演説 (⇒co-ordination, cost cut)
best efforts 最大限の努力, 最大努力, 最善の努力, 委託募集
best-efforts issue 売出発行
best-efforts selling 委託販売
collective effort 総力
cooperative efforts 協力関係
cost reduction efforts コスト削減努力, コスト削減策
expense reduction efforts 経費削減努力
gap-closing efforts 赤字削減努力
joint effort 提携関係
reorganization efforts 再編の動き
restructuring efforts 経営再建策
sales effort 販売努力
sales promotion efforts 販売促進努力, 販促努力, 営業努力
self-help efforts 自助努力
steady efforts 地道な努力, 取組み (⇒**contribute**)
streamlining efforts リストラ努力, リストラ策, 合理化措置, 合理化への取組み
▸GM has been intensifying *efforts* to reduce costs and improve quality. GMは，コスト削減策と品質改善策を強化している。
▸Our *efforts* to introduce products that meet the needs of our customers led to increased profits in all regions. 顧客のニーズにマッチした製品を導入するという当社の努力が，全地域での増益につながりました。

EFT 電子決済 (electronic funds transferの略)
EFTA 欧州自由貿易地域 (European Free Trade Areaの略)
EIA 経済統合協定 (economic integration agreementの略)
EIA 米エネルギー省エネルギー情報局 (Energy Information Administrationの略)
▸The U.S. Energy Department's *EIA* reported that oil stocks fell by 3.1 million barrels from a week earlier. 米エネルギ省のエネルギー情報局(EIA)は，原油在庫が前週より310万バレル減少したことを発表した。

elect 動 選出する, 選任する, 選ぶ, 選択する, 決める
▸Directors are *elected* by a plurality of votes cast. 取締役は，賛成多数[投票総数の過半数]で選任されます。

election 名 選出, 選任, 選挙, 投票, 選択, 選択権
election of directors 取締役の選任
election of officers 役員の選任
▸Each of the 12 nominees named in the proxy statement who stood for *election* as a director received a plurality of the votes cast. 委任状に取締役選任候補者として記載されていた12名は，それぞれ投票総数の過半数[大多数]の支持を得ました。

electric 形 電気の, 電力の, 発電の (=electrical)
electric and gas utilities industry 電気・ガス業界, 公益事業
electric appliance and material control law 電気用品取締法

electric appliance maker 電機メーカー
electric capacity 発電容量
electric car [vehicle] 電気自動車
electric enterprise law 電気事業法
electric machinery industry 電機業界
electric supply system 電力供給体制, 電力供給システム
electric utility 電気事業
▶*Electric* appliance makers enjoy robust sales of flat-screen television sets and other digital home appliances. 電機メーカーは, 薄型テレビなどデジタル家電の販売が好調だ。

electric power 電力, 電源
　electric power capacity 発電能力
　electric power cost 電力原価
　electric power development 電源開発
　electric power equipment 電力機器
　electric power generation 発電
　electric power generating cost 発電原価
　electric power generation with refuse incineration ごみ焼却発電, ごみ発電
　electric power purchased 購入電力
　electric-power retail market 電力小売市場
　electric power sold 販売電力量
　electric power system 電力系統
electric power company 電力会社
▶Electric Power Development Co., known as J-Power, is a wholesaler that sells the electricity it generates to other *electric power companies*. 電源開発(Jパワー)は, 発電した電気を他の電力各社に販売する卸企業だ。
electric power industry 電力業界, 電気事業
▶The liberalization of the *electric power industry* furthered the trend of surplus electricity being sold to power companies by major manufacturers that generate their own power supplies. 電力事業の自由化で, 自家発電している大手メーカーがその余剰電気を電力会社に売る動きが加速した。

electrical 形 電気の, 電力の, 電機 (=electric)
　electrical and electronics 電機・電子
　electrical appliance maker 家電メーカー, 電機メーカー
　electrical appliances 電気器具
　Electrical Appliances and Materials Safety Law 電気用品安全法, 電安法
　electrical distribution 送配電網
　electrical energy 電気エネルギー
　electrical impulse 電子インパルス

electrical machinery and apparatus 電気機械器具, 電機機器
electrical machinery maker 電機メーカー
electrical machinery sector 電機業界
electrical utilities 電力会社
▶In the *electrical* machinery sector, the sales of digital home appliances such as slim televisions are brisk. 電機業界では, 薄型テレビなどデジタル家電の販売が好調だ。

electricity 名 電気, 電力
　electricity consumption 電力消費 (=power consumption)
　electricity demand 電力需要 (=power demand)
　Electricity Business Act 電気事業法
　electricity generated 発電電力量
　electricity sector 電力業界
　electricity shortage 電力不足 (=power shortage)
　electricity sold 販売電力, 販売電力量
　electricity trading 電力取引, 電気の売買
　electricity trading market 電力取引市場
　electricity usage 電力使用量
　surplus electricity 余剰電気 (⇒electric power)
▶The company sells *electricity* wholesale to regional electric power companies, and does not supply *electricity* directly to households. 同社は, 電気を卸売りの形で地域の電力会社に売る売電事業を行っており, 家庭に電気を直接送る事業はしていない。
electricity industry 電力業界
▶The *electricity industry* is one of more than 20 government-designated sectors, including the weapons, aviation and nuclear power industries. 電力業界は, 武器や航空機, 原子力産業などを含めて, 国が指定する二十業種の一つだ。
electricity supply 電力供給 (=power supply, supply of electricity)
▶A stable *electricity supply* is indispensable for supporting sound economic activities and people's daily lives. 電力の安定供給は, 健全な経済活動と日常の国民生活を支えるための必須条件である。
electricity wholesaler 電力卸売り業者
▶The TCI has become the biggest shareholder in Japan's largest *electricity wholesaler*, Electric Power Development Co. 英投資ファンドのTCIが, 電力卸国内最大手の電源開発(Jパワー)の筆頭株主になった。

electron 名 電子, エレクトロン
  electron beam recorder 電子ビーム録画
  electron optics 電子光学
  electron technology 電子技術, 電子工学 (= electronics)

electronic 形 電子の, 電子工学の, コンピュータ化された, エレクトロニック
  electronic application 電子出願
  electronic authentication 電子認証
  electronic bank transfer コンピュータ利用[コンピュータ・システム]による銀行振込み
  electronic calculator 電卓 (=pocket calculator)
  electronic cash 電子キャッシュ, 電子マネー (=electronic money)
  electronic certification 電子認証
  electronic communication business 電気通信事業
  electronic conference 電子会議, 遠隔会議, 電信会議, テレコンファレンス (=teleconference, television conference, video conferencing)
  electronic data processing system 電子データ処理システム, 電子情報処理システム, 電子情報処理方式
  electronic equipment 電子機器, 電子設備
  electronic gadgets 電子機器
  electronic goods 電子製品, エレクトロニクス製品
  electronic information 電子情報
  electronic market 電子市場 (=e-market, electronic marketplace, Internet exchange)
  electronic settlement 〈ネット・ショッピングなどの〉電子決済 (⇒**Net shopping, online shopper**)
  electronic toll collection system ノンストップ自動車料金支払いシステム《略 ETC》
  electronic trading 電子取引, 電子商取引, 電子売買, コンピュータ取引, 電子トレーディング, システム売買 (=**e-commerce, e-trading**)
  electronic voting 電子投票
  ▶*Electronic* bank transfers from shinkin credit unions across the nation to other financial institutions were halted for almost 24 hours. 全国の信用金庫から他の金融機関へのコンピュータ・システムによる銀行振込みが, 約24時間停止した。

electronic brokerage 電子ブローキング
  ▶We resorted to *electronic brokerage* in which currency is directly purchased online. われわれは, オンライン(コンピュータ端末)で直接, 通貨買いを注文する電子ブローキングの手段を使った。

electronic commerce 電子商取引, 電子市場, エレクトロニック・コマース《略 EC》(=e-commerce, E-commerce, EC)
  ▶The United States is taking the world lead in the field of *electronic commerce*. 米国は, 電子商取引の分野では世界をリードしている。

electronic component 電子部品, エレクトロニクス部品
  ▶The Company manufactures a wide range of highly regarded *electronic components*, including optical devices, magnetic devices and motors. 当社は, 光学デバイス, 磁気デバイス, モーターなど幅広い分野で高い評価を得ている電子部品を製造しています。

electronic equipment maker 電機メーカー
  ▶The nation's two major *electronic equipment makers* announced plans to shed as many as 20,000 workers. 国内の二大電機メーカーが, 2万人規模の人員削減計画を発表した。

electronic manufacturer 電機メーカー
  ▶Discount consumer-electronics giants and leading *electronic manufacturers* are entering the used PC market. 大手量販店や大手電機メーカーなどが, パソコンの中古市場に参入している。

electronic marketplace 電子商取引市場, 電子市場, インターネット上の電子市場《略 EM》(=e-marketplace, electronic market, Internet exchange)
  ▶*Electronic marketplace* allows users to make purchases and enables corporations to collect extremely detailed marketing data. インターネット上の電子市場では, ユーザーはさまざまな買い物ができるし, 企業はきめ細かなマーケティング・データの収集も可能だ。

electronic money 電子マネー, 電子貨幣, エレクトロニック・マネー (=cybermoney, digital cash, digital money, electronic cash)
  ▶To use cell phones with *electronic money* functions, users need to precharge them with money. 電子マネー機能付き携帯電話を使う場合, ユーザーは事前に携帯電話に入金しておく必要がある。

electronic money business 電子マネー事業
  ▶Aeon Co. and Lawson Inc. are also discussing a possible alliance in the *electronic money business*. イオンとローソンは, 電子マネー事業での提携の可能性も検討している。

electronic payment 電子決済 （=electronic settlement）

電子決済の四つの手段:

Net banking	ネット・バンキング（銀行のホームページ画面を通して自分の口座から振込みを依頼）
online payment	オンライン決済（クレジット・カード、Eデビット、電子マネーでの支払い）
payment by prepaid card	プリペイド決済（プリペイド・カードでの支払い）
provider payment	プロバイダー決済（インターネット接続プロバイダーがクレジット・カード決済を代行）

▶Electronic money has high-growth potential, and the Company is researching a new *electronic payment* system. 電子マネーの分野は今後さらなる進展が考えられるため、当社の新たな電子決済システムの研究に取り組んでいます。

electronic point of sale イーポス《略 EPOS》

electronic voting system 電子投票制度、電子投・開票方式
▶The new *electronic voting system* has achieved the initial targets of cutting the vote-counting time and avoiding invalid votes. この新しい電子投・開票方式は、開票時間の短縮と無効票の解消という初期の狙いを達成した。

electronics 名 電子機器、電子技術、電子工学、エレクトロニクス
  consumer electronics 家電製品、家電
  consumer electronics products 家電製品
  electronics company 電子メーカー、家電メーカー、電機企業 （=electronics firm）
  electronics components 電子部品 （=electronics parts）
  electronics equipment manufacturer 半導体製造装置メーカー
  electronics industry 電子業界、家電業界、エレクトロニクス産業
  electronics manufacturer 家電メーカー （=electronics maker）
  electronics manufacturing service 製造工場請負工場《略 EMS》（電機や通信機器メーカーから商品の製造を請け負う専門企業）
  giant microelectronics ジャイアント・マイクロエレクトロニクス
  industrial electronics 産業用エレクトロニクス製品、産業用電子機器
  major consumer electronics manufacturer 大手家電メーカー
  mesoscopic electronics メソスコピック・エレクトロニクス
  microelectronics マイクロエレクトロニクス
  nanoelectronics ナノエレクトロニクス
  optoelectronics 光電子光学、オプトエレクトロニクス
  power electronics パワー・エレクトロニクス
  producer of electronics parts 電子部品メーカー
  quantum electronics 量子エレクトロニクス
  vacuum microelectronics 真空マイクロエレクトロニクス

▶Through the spinoff of domestic sales operations, the struggling *electronics* maker will downsize administrative and accounting operations as well as consolidate sales offices. 国内営業部門の分社化で、この経営不振の家電メーカーは、営業拠点の統廃合のほか、管理部門や経理部門を縮小する方針だ。

element 名 要素、要因、因子、構成要素、構成部品、部材、成分、項目、素子、エレメント
  cost elements 原価要素
  earnings momentum element 利益のモメンタム要因
  Finite Element Method 有限要素法
  Hall element ホール素子
  Josephson junction element ジョセフソン素子
  network element 通信網構成要素
  nonoperating elements 営業外項目
  surface acoustic wave element 表面弾性波素子

▶Our quality and total cycle-time reduction initiatives remain the key *elements* in achieving superior financial results. 当社の品質に対する方針と全サイクル・タイム（工程期間）短縮の方針は、今でも当社の優れた業績を達成するための中核的要素になっています。

eligible 形 有資格の、適格の、受給資格がある
  eligible charges 給付額、給付対象費用
  eligible employee 有資格従業員、受給資格のある従業員、年金加入資格のある従業員 （⇒ RONA）
  eligible receivables 適格債権
  eligible subscriber 受給資格のある加入者
  fully eligible active plan participants 受給資格取得済み在職制度加入者

▶About 1.24 million *eligible* subscribers to corporate pension plans aged 60 and over had not filed payout requests as of the end of fiscal

2006. 2006年度末の時点で，受給資格のある60歳以上の企業年金加入者の約124万人が，年金支払いの請求手続きを取っていない。
▸The employees stock purchase plan enables employees who are not participants in a stock option plan to purchase the Corporation's capital stock through payroll deductions of up to 10 % of *eligible* compensation. 従業員株式購入制度によると，株式購入選択権制度に加入していない従業員は，俸給の10%を超えない範囲で給与を積み立てて，当社株式を購入することができます。

elint [Elint] 名 電子情報，電子モニターによる情報収集活動 （electronic intelligenceの略）

EM 電子市場，電子取引市場 （electronic marketplaceの略）

embargo 名 抑留，出港禁止，入港禁止，通商停止，禁輸，禁止

embryonic stem cells ES細胞，胚性幹(ES)細胞，万能細胞 （＝embryonic stem cells, ES cells）
▸An Education, Science and Technology Ministry panel approved the nation's first project to produce human *embryonic stem cells* in vitro. 文部科学省の専門委員会は，人間のES細胞を体外で作製する国内初の計画を承認した。

emergency 名 緊急，有事，緊急事態，非常事態，突発事故
　emergency duty 緊急関税 （＝emergency tariff）
　emergency evacuation 緊急退去，緊急避難，緊急の撤退
　emergency fund つなぎ資金
　emergency funding rate 緊急貸出金利
　emergency legislation 有事法制
　emergency loan 緊急融資，つなぎ融資
　emergency measures 緊急措置
　emergency "safeguard" import restriction 緊急輸入制限(セーフガード)
　emergency shareholders meeting 緊急株主総会，臨時株主総会
　emergency tariffs 緊急関税
　financial emergency 財政危機
▸Indonesia's government declared a state of *emergency* after an earthquake killed more than 5,000 people. インドネシア政府は，地震の死者が5,000人を超えてから，非常事態を宣言した。

emergency import restrictions 緊急輸入制限，緊急輸入制限措置 （＝emergency import limits, safeguards）
▸The United States defended *emergency import restrictions* taken to protect domestic steelmakers. 米国は，鉄鋼産業を保護するために取った緊急輸入制限措置を正当化[弁護]した。

emerging 形 新興の，新生の，最新の，先端的な
　emerging industry 先端産業，先端業界
　Emerging Issues Task Force 緊急問題専門委員会
　emerging technology 先端技術，新技術
　newly emerging competitors 新規参入者
　newly emerging technologies 新技術，最新技術
▸The so-called decoupling theory holds that the effects of a U.S. slowdown can be offset by growth in *emerging nations*. いわゆるディカップリング論では，米経済の減速は新興国の成長が補う，と考えられている。

emerging company 新興企業，成長企業，新興のベンチャー企業
▸The firm received a lot of attention from investors as an *emerging* company. 同社は，新興のベンチャー企業として投資家から大いに注目された。

emerging economies 新興経済国，新興経済地域，振興経済群，新興国 （＝emerging countries, emerging nations）
▸The effects of an economic slowdown in industrialized countries stemming from the U.S. subprime woes could spread in the *emerging economies*. 米国のサブプライム(低所得者向け住宅融資)問題に起因する先進国の景気減速の影響は，新興国にも拡大する可能性がある。

emerging Internet company 新興ネット企業
▸This is the first attempt by television broadcasters to take the initiative to fuse communications and broadcasting to counter the threat from *emerging Internet companies*. これは，新興ネット企業に対抗してテレビ放送局が主導権を握り，通信と放送の融合を図る初の試みだ。

emerging market 新興市場，急成長市場，新興成長市場，エマージング・マーケット
▸The key for Toyota to overtake GM lies in the company's efforts to bolster sales at home and in *emerging markets* such as China and India. トヨタがGMを追い越すカギは，国内と中国やインドなどの新興市場でトヨタがどれくらい販売を伸ばせるかにある。

emerging technology 新技術，最新技術
▸Strategic alliances with and investments in other high-tech firms bolster our position in *emerging technologies* and developing markets.

他のハイテク企業との戦略的提携とハイテク企業への投資により、新技術と急成長市場における当社の地位は向上しています。

emission 排気, 排出, 放出, 排ガス, 排気ガス, 放出量, 放出物, 排出物 (⇒**cap**)
  carbon dioxide emissions 二酸化炭素排出量
  emission control 排ガス規制, 排気ガス規制
  emission credits 排出枠, 排出権 (＝emission permits, emission rights)
  emission filter 排ガス浄化装置
  emission [control] standard 排ガス[排気ガス]規制基準
  emission permits 排出権
  emission rights 排出権
  emission trading 排出量取引
  emission trading system 排出量取引制度
  emissions from diesel-powered vehicles ディーゼル車の排ガス
  emissions of carbon dioxide 二酸化炭素の排出量
  gas emission regulations 排ガス規制
  greenhouse gas emissions 温室効果ガス排出量
  toxic air emissions 毒性ガスの放出量
  toxic emissions 有毒排気物
  trade in CO2 emission credits 二酸化炭素の排出量[排出権]取引
  ▸Gas *emission* regulations for motorcycles apply to all motorcycle models. オートバイに対する排ガス規制は、オートバイの全車種に適用されている。

emission quota trading 排出量取引, 排出権取引
  ▸The EU began *emission quota trading* in 2005, mainly covering companies inside the regional bloc. 欧州連合（EU）は、主に域内企業を対象に2005年から排出量取引を開始した。

emission quotas 排出枠, 排出量
  ▸Tokyo urgently needs to buy *emission quotas* from countries with surpluses if it is to meet its obligations under the Kyoto Protocol. 京都議定書に基づく義務を達成するには、日本は排出枠に余裕のある国から排出量を購入する必要がある。

emission standards 排ガス基準
  emission control standard 排ガス規制基準, 排気ガス規制基準
  vehicle emission standards 自動車排出ガス基準, 自動車排ガス基準

emissions of greenhouse gases 温室効果ガスの排出量
  ▸The Kyoto Protocol requires industrial nations to reduce *emissions of greenhouse gases*, including carbon dioxide. 京都議定書は、先進各国に二酸化炭素など温室効果ガスの排出量削減を義務付けている。

employability 名 雇用適性, 雇用されうる能力, エンプロイアビリティ

employable 形名 雇用できる(人), 雇用条件にかなう

employed 形 使用した, 利用した, 投下した, 被雇用者の
  capital employed 投下資本, 使用資本
  employed director 雇用重役, 雇われ重役
  employed executive 雇われ経営者, 雇われ重役
  employed laborer 雇用労働者 (＝employed worker)
  employed management 雇用経営者, 雇われ経営者 (＝employed manager)
  employed person 就業者, 被雇用者
  net capital employed 純資本使用
  nonemployed [non-employed] worker 被雇用労働者
  return on capital employed 資本利益率, 使用資本利益率, 使用総資本利益率《略 ROCE》
  self-employed individual 自営業者 (＝self-employed person)
  turnover of total capital employed 使用総資本回転率

employee 名 従業員, 社員, 職員, 雇い人, 使用人 (⇒**career-average pay**)
  active employees 在籍従業員, 現従業員 (⇒**accumulated liability**)
  career employee 常雇い従業員
  company employee 会社員
  Employee Assistance Program 従業員支援制度, 従業員支援プログラム《略 EAP》
  employee discount 社員向け値引き, 社員値引き (＝employee pricing discount)
  employee house organ 社内報 (＝employee magazine)
  employee manual 従業員便覧
  employee on loan 出向社員
  employee ownership scheme 従業員持ち株制度
  employee rating 人事考課 (＝merit rating)
  Employee Retirement Income Security Act 1974年に制定された米国の従業員退職所得保障法, 1974年退職者年金保障法, 企業年金法, エリサ法《略 ERISA》
  employee satisfaction 従業員満足, 従業員の満足, 企業内組織の満足《略 ES》
  employee savings plan 従業員貯蓄制度, 従業員

貯蓄計画 (=employees' savings plan)
employee separations 従業員の退職
employee welfare fund 従業員福利厚生基金 (=employee benefit fund)
employees' income 雇用者所得 (=income of employed persons)
full time employee 正社員
hourly employee 時間給制の従業員
inactive employee 休職従業員
junior employee 準社員
managerial employee 管理職, 管理職従業員 (=management employee)
new employees 新規採用の人員
occupational employee 非管理職従業員
paid employee 遊休従業員
part time employee パート社員, パートタイマー, パートタイム労働者
permanent employee 正社員, 常用雇用, 常用労働者 (=full time employee, regular employee)
public employee 公務員 (=government employee)
rank-and-file employee 一般社員, 一般職員
regular employee 正社員 (=full time employee)
retired employee 退職従業員
salaried employee 月給制の従業員, 定額給従業員, サラリーマン
temporary employee 臨時従業員, 派遣社員

▸Benefits for occupational *employees* are not directly pay-related. 非管理職従業員への給付は, 給与と直接的な関係はありません。

▸The efforts of our *employees* are the basis for the success we will achieve in the years to come. 当社従業員の努力こそ, 今後の当社発展を支える礎です。

employee benefit 従業員給付

employee benefit fund 従業員給付基金, 従業員福利厚生基金
employee benefit plan 従業員給付制度, 従業員福利厚生制度, 従業員給付基金

▸It is the company's practice to fund amounts for pensions sufficient to meet the minimum requirements set forth in applicable *employee benefit* and tax laws. 適用される従業員の給付に関する法令と税法に規定されている最小限の要求を十分に満たす額を, 年金基金に積み立てるのが当社の慣行です。

employee stock compensation 従業員株式報酬制度

▸If not for expenses to cover *employee stock compensation*, the firm would have earned $2.62 per share in the third quarter. 従業員株式報酬制度の費用がなければ, 同社の第3四半期の1株当たり利益は2.62ドルでした。

employee director 社内取締役

▸*Employee directors* receive no additional compensation for service on the Board of Directors or its committees. 社内取締役には, 取締役会の取締役またはその付属委員会の委員としての役務に対して, 追加報酬は支払われません。

employee pension 従業員年金

employee pension fund 従業員年金基金, 厚生年金基金
employee pension insurance system 厚生年金
employee pension plan 従業員年金制度
employee plan issuances 従業員持ち株制度への発行
employees' pension insurance 厚生年金保険

▸The *Employees Pension* Fund is one of many corporate pension plans. 厚生年金基金は, 多くの企業年金制度の一つだ。

employee stock option plan 従業員株式購入選択権制度, 従業員株式買取り権制度, 従業員ストック・オプション制度《略 ESOP》

▸Under the Company's *employee stock option plans*, shares of common stock have been made available for grant to key employees. 当社の従業員株式購入選択権制度では, 幹部社員に普通株式を購入する権利を付与しています。

employee stock ownership plan 米国の従業員持ち株制度, 従業員株式保有制度《略 ESOP》 (=employee stock ownership trust)

▸The company's *employee stock ownership plan* will be used to finance part of the buyout deal. この買収取引の一部の資金調達には, 同社の従業員持ち株制度が利用される。

employee stock purchase plan 従業員株式購入制度, 従業員持ち株制度《略 ESPP》 (=employees' stock purchase plan)

▸The *employees stock purchase plan* enables employees who are not participants in a stock option plan to purchase the Corporation's capital stock through payroll deductions of up to 10 % of eligible compensation. 従業員株式購入制度によると, 株式購入選択権制度に加入していない従業員は, 俸給の10%を超えない範囲で給与を積み立てて, 当社株式を購入することができます。

employer 名 雇用主, 雇用者, 雇い主, 使用者, 事業主, 企業

employer-employee relations 雇用者と従業員の関係, 雇用者・従業員関係
employer interference 雇用者介入
employer's liability 雇用者責任, 使用者責任 (=employer's liability to third party)
employers' association 使用者団体, 雇い主組合
employers' contributions to social security schemes 社会保険雇い主負担
employers' income 雇用者所得
employers' organization 経営者団体
management employer 雇い主
multi-employer bargaining 団体交渉, 統一交渉
multiple employer 複合事業主
single employer 単一事業主
survey of empolyers 事業所調査
▶The *employers*' organization expressed a positive attitude toward giving pay hike in a report released last December. 経営者団体は, 昨年12月に公表した報告書で, 賃上げ容認の姿勢を表明した。
▶U.S. *employers* slashed 63,000 jobs in February 2008 from the previous month. 米国の2008年2月の就業者数は, 前月に比べて63,000人減った。

employment 名 雇用, 使用, 利用, 就労, 勤め, 職
  continuous employment system 継続雇用性
  decline in employment 雇用の低迷, 雇用の悪化
  employment adjustment 雇用調整
  employment bureau 職業安定所, 職業紹介所
  employment contract 雇用契約
  employment cost 人件費
  employment data 雇用統計 (=employment figures)
  employment environment 雇用環境
  employment examination for national government service 国家公務員採用試験
  employment insurance program 雇用保険制度 (=employment insurance system)
  employment plan 雇用計画, 採用計画
  employment promotion 雇用促進
  Employment Service 英国の雇用サービス庁
  employment service act 職業紹介事業法
  employment system 雇用制度
  Equal Employment Opportunity Act 米国の雇用機会均等法, 平等雇用機会法 (⇒**employment inequality**)
  fictitious employment of part-time workers アルバイトのカラ雇用
  full employment 完全雇用
  increased employment 雇用の伸び, 雇用の拡大, 雇用の増大
  lifetime employment 終身雇用
  manufacturing employment 製造業の雇用
  over-employment 過剰就業, 人員過剰
  temporary employment 一時雇用
▶*Employment* has soared on the strength of strong performance by industries such as the information technology, communications, medical, welfare and services sectors. IT (情報技術), 通信業, 医療・福祉・サービス業など各種産業の好調な業績に伴って, 雇用も急増している。

employment conditions 雇用情勢, 雇用環境
▶Under the current severe *employment conditions*, it is imperative to allow the private sector to fully enter the job placement field. 現在の厳しい雇用情勢のなかで, 職業紹介事業の民間への全面開放は緊急課題だ。

employment inequality 雇用の不平等
▶The Equal Employment Opportunity Law, which was enforced in 1986, prohibits *employment inequality* based upon gender. 1986年に施行された雇用機会均等法は, 男女差による雇用の不均等を禁止している。

employment insurance 雇用保険
▶The number of companies subscribing to the *employment insurance* system has been steadily increasing. 雇用保険制度に加入している事業所数は, 着実に増えている。

employment measures 雇用対策
▶The *employment measures* currently in place are limited to flexible utilization of existing laws and systems. 現在採られている雇用対策は, 現行の法律や制度の弾力的な活用の範囲にとどまっている。

employment opportunity 雇用機会, 就労機会
▶We must pour our energies into nurturing new industries that promise expanded *employment opportunities*. われわれは, 雇用機会の拡大につながる新規産業の育成に総力を注ぐ[総力を挙げる]必要がある。

employment situation 雇用情勢, 雇用状況, 雇用環境
▶There is no telling how much further the *employment situation* will continue to deteriorate. 雇用環境が今後どこまで悪化するかは, 先が読めない。

empower 動 権限を付与する, 権限を委譲する
empowerment 名 権限の付与

EMS 受託製造会社, 製造工程請負工場 (electronics manufacturing serviceの略)
▸Companies specializing in electronics manufacturing service (*EMS*) produce other firms' products at reasonable prices on their behalf by taking advantage of large-scale production facilities. 受託製造専門会社(EMS)は, 大規模な生産設備を利用して, 他社製品を安価で製造している。

EMS 携帯メール (enhanced message [messaging] service の略)

EMS 欧州通貨制度 (European Monetary System の略)

EMS 国際ビジネス郵便 (express mail service の略)

EMU 欧州経済通貨同盟, EU経済通貨統合 (Economic and Monetary Unionの略)

encash 動 現金化する, 現金で受け取る (⇒ settlement)

enclosure 名 囲い込み

encrypt 動 暗号化する
▸Data encrypted in IC chips are said to be impossible to counterfeit. ICチップの暗号化されたデータは, 偽造が不可能と言われている。

encryption 名 暗号, 暗号化, 暗号方式, 秘話化
　data encryption standard データ暗号化規格, 情報暗号化基準《略 DES》
　encryption technology 暗号化技術, 暗号技術
　digital encryption standard デジタル情報暗号化基準
　voice encryption 音声暗号化, 音声秘話化
▸Since electronic money requires safeguards against unauthorized use and counterfeiting, *encryption* technology and IC cards represent essential technologies. 電子マネーには不正使用や変造を防ぐ必要があるため, 暗号化技術やICカードがその代表的な技術とされている。

encumbered 形 債務を負った
encumbrance 名 負担
end 名 期末, 年度末, 終了, 目的, 動 終了する
　balance at end of (the) year 期末残高
　end user 最終使用者, 最終利用者, 一般使用者, 最終投資家, 端末利用者, 最終ユーザー, エンド・ユーザー
　ending balance 期末残高 (=balance at end of the year)
　ending inventory 期末棚卸し, 期末棚卸し高, 棚卸し資産期末有り高[期末保有高], 期末在庫 (=closing stock)
　front end 短期物, 前段階
　in the year just ended 前期
　short end 短期債
　year ended December 31, 2009 2009年12月31日終了事業年度, 12月期決算企業の2009年度
▸The company suffered ¥61 billion in consolidated after-tax losses at the *end* of fiscal 2008. 同社は, 2009年3月期[2008年度]に, 610億円の連結税引き後赤字に陥った。
▸The *end-of-year* account settlements of Japanese companies are generally announced in May or June. 一般に日本企業は, 5, 6月に3月期決算の発表を行う。

end-product 名 最終製品, 最終産物
endorse 動 裏書きする, 裏書譲渡する, 保証する
endorsement 名 裏書, 裏書条項, 支持, 承認, エンドースメント
endorser 名 裏書人, 裏書譲渡人
endow 動 基金を寄付する, 〈生命保険が〉支払い満期になる
endowment 名 贈与, 遺贈, 財産分与, 基本財産, 寄付金
energy 名 エネルギー, 精力, 活動力, 熱意
　a major energy 主力エネルギー
　alternative energy sources 代替エネルギー源
　atomic energy 原子エネルギー, 原子力
　energy conservation 省エネルギー, 省エネ, エネルギー節約
　energy consumption エネルギー消費
　energy crunch エネルギー危機 (=energy crisis)
　energy demand エネルギー需要
　energy-efficient thermal power generator 省エネ型火力発電所
　energy industry エネルギー産業
　energy-intensive industries エネルギー集約型産業
　energy park エネルギー資源共同利用地
　Energy Policy and Conservative Act 燃費[燃料]規制法
　energy position エネルギー保有状況, エネルギー・ポジション
　energy prices エネルギー価格
　energy stockpiling エネルギー備蓄
　energy security エネルギー安全保障
　energy structure エネルギー資源構造
　geothermal energy 地熱エネルギー
　human energy 人的エネルギー
　hydrogen energy 水素エネルギー
　International Atomic Energy Agency 国際原子力機関《略 IAEA》
　International Energy Agency 国際エネルギー

機関《略 IEA》
New National Energy Strategy 新国家エネルギー戦略 (⇒energy resources)
new sources of energy 新エネルギー, 新エネルギー源
non-oil energy sources 脱石油エネルギー
nuclear energy 核エネルギー, 原子力
ocean thermal energy 海洋熱エネルギー
primary energy source 一次エネルギー源
renewable energy 再生可能エネルギー, 自然エネルギー
renewable energy sources 恒久的エネルギー源
secondary energy 二次エネルギー
solar energy 太陽エネルギー, 太陽光
solar energy power generation system 太陽光発電システム
wind energy 風力エネルギー (=wind machine energy)
▸The three most wind-riched states of the United States have enough harnessable wind *energy* to satisfy national electricity needs. 米国で最も風力が豊かな3州(ノースダコタ, カンザスとテキサスの3州)には, 合わせて全米の電力需要を満たすだけの利用可能な風力エネルギーがある。

energy efficiency エネルギー効率
▸Japan's further *energy efficiencies* must be sought through a review of the energy-saving standards of home appliances and other products, as well as the development of energy-saving technologies. 日本のエネルギー効率改善は, 家電製品などの省エネ基準の見直しや省エネ技術の開発などにより行わなければならない。

energy resource development エネルギー資源開発
▸Sakharin-1 project is an international program for *energy resource development* off Russia's Sakharin Island. 「サハリン1」プロジェクトは, ロシア・サハリン島沖で行われているエネルギー資源開発の国際プログラムだ。

energy saving エネルギー節約, 省エネルギー, 省エネ (⇒campaign)
energy-saving air-conditioner 省エネ冷暖房装置
energy saving equipment 省エネ設備
energy savings program 省エネ計画
▸Heavy trucks and buses that weigh more than 2.5 tons are not subject to an *energy-saving* standard. 総重量2.5トン超の大型トラックやバスは現在, 省エネ基準の対象外となっている。

energy saving measures 省エネ策
▸Oil consuming countries must promote *energy saving measures* so that oil demand can be held back. 石油消費国は, 省エネ策を推進して石油需要を抑えなければならない。

energy saving technology 省エネ技術
▸The two firms plan to develop *energy saving technology* to prepare for the expected introduction of stricter global environmental regulations. 両社は, 予想される世界的な環境規制の強化に備えて, 省エネ技術の開発[共同開発]を計画している。

energy supply エネルギー供給
energy supply and demand エネルギー需給
energy supply source エネルギー供給源, エネルギー供給基地
▸China regards gas fields in the East China Sea as a key *energy supply* source for the eastern coastal areas, including Shanghai. 中国は, 東シナ海のガス田を, 上海など中国東南部沿岸地域の重要なエネルギー供給基地と位置付けている。

engagement 名 約束, 確約, 合意, 取決め, 契約, 協約, 誓約, 債務, 負債, 関与, 従事, 介入, 仕事, 用事, 用務, 業務, 雇用, 雇用期間, 交戦, 戦闘, 〈機械や部品の〉かみ合わせ
audit engagement 監査契約
be chary of forward engagement 先物契約を控える
be under an engagement 約束[契約]がある, 契約してある
break off an engagement 解約する, 破談にする
business engagement 仕事の取決め
cargo engagement 船荷契約
consulting engagements コンサルティング業務
engagement sheet 船腹予約書
engagement strategy 監査戦略
international engagement 国際取決め, 国際協約, 国際関係
letter of engagement 契約書 (=engagement letter)
make an engagement 約束する, 契約する
meet one's engagement 債務を果たす
normal engagement 通常の契約, 通常の契約履行
offer without engagement 不確定売りオファー
previous [prior] engagement 先約
recurring engagement 継続監査
without engagement 確約なしで, 確約せずに

engine 名 原動力, 牽引力, 検索エンジン(search engine), エンジン

database engine データベース・エンジン
direct-injection engine 直噴型エンジン
engine displacement エンジンの排気量
engine of growth 成長の原動力
engine of the regional economy 地域経済の牽引力
graphic engine グラフィック・エンジン
search engine 検索エンジン, サーチ・エンジン
the engine that boosts personal consumption 個人消費を押し上げる原動力
▸Capital investment, which was the *engine* for the overall economy, has lost much of its momentum. 景気全体を引っ張ってきた設備投資に, 一時の勢いがなくなっている.
▸Innovation is the *engine* that will keep us vital and growing. 革新性は, 活力と成長の原動力だ.

engineer 動 設計[建設]する, 巧みに処理[管理, 運営, 計画]する, 仕組む, 誘導する
engineered capacity 理想的生産能力 (=ideal capacity)
engineered food 加工保存食品, 加工補充食品
engineered security 仕組み証券
genetically engineered food 遺伝子組換え食品
▸Struggling Victor Co. of Japan will eliminate 1,150 jobs to *engineer* its rehabilitation. 経営不振の日本ビクターは, 再建計画を進めるため, 1,150人を削減する.

engineering 名 工学, 工学技術, 技術, 設計, 工事, 開発, 手法, エンジニアリング (⇒re-engineering, reverse)
aerospace engineering 航空宇宙工学
agricultural engineering 農業工学
automotive engineering 自動車工学
biomedical engineering 生医学工学
chemical engineering 化学工学
civil engineering project 土木工事
computer-aided engineering コンピュータ援用エンジニアリング
concurrent engineering コンカレント・エンジニアリング《略 CE》(=simultaneous engineering)
electrical engineering 電気工学
electronic engineering 電子工学
engineering and construction company エンジニアリング・建設会社, 設計・建設会社
engineering estimates 工学的見積り, 工学的見積り額
engineering change 設計変更
engineering expense 技術費
engineering goods 工学財
engineering industry エンジニアリング産業
engineering machinery maker 工学機器メーカー
engineering phase 〈商品設計の〉技術段階
engineering, procurement and construction 設計・調達と建設《略 EPC》
engineering product 工学品
engineering production 工学品生産
engineering program 開発体制
engineering staff 技術陣
engineering team 技術陣, 研究開発チーム
engineering workers 金属労組
environmental engineering 環境工学
financial engineering 財テク, 金融手法, 金融エンジニアリング
fiscal engineering 大型金融操作
forward engineering フォワード・エンジニアリング
fuzzy engineering あいまい工学, ファジー・エンジニアリング
genetic engineering 遺伝子工学
human engineering 人間工学, 人間管理
industrial engineering 経営工学, 産業工学, 工学技術, インダストリアル・エンジニアリング《略 IE》
macro-engineering [macroengineering] マクロ工学技術, マクロエンジニアリング
management engineering 経営工学, 管理工学
marine engineering 海洋工学
mechanical engineering 機械工学
petroleum engineering 石油工学
product engineering 製品エンジニアリング
production engineering 生産工学
requirement engineering 要求工学, 要求分析工学
sales engineering 販売工学, セールス・エンジニアリング《略 SE》
software engineering ソフトウエア工学, ソフトウエア技術
structural engineering 構造工学
systems engineering 組織工学, システム工学
traffic engineering standard 接続基準
transportation engineering 輸送工業
value engineering 価値工学《略 VE》
virtual engineering 仮想エンジニアリング
welding engineering 溶接工学
▸Of the total, civil *engineering* projects mainly ordered by the water department of the city accounted for about ¥23 billion. 発注総額のうち, 同市水道局が主に発注した土木工事費は約230

億円に上っている。
▶Using *engineering* estimates of total cleanup costs, we estimate our potential liability for all currently and previously owned properties.　総浄化費用の工学的見積り額を基準に，当社は，現在と過去の所有地すべてについて当社の潜在的債務額を見積もっています。

enhance 動　増す，増やす，高める，強化する，向上させる，容易にする，改善する
　enhance cash flow significantly　キャッシュ・フローを大幅に改善する
　enhance competitiveness　競争力を高める，競争力を強化する
　enhance earnings　業績を伸ばす，業績を向上させる，業績を改善する
　enhance financial health　財務の健全性を高める，財務内容［財務体質］を改善する
　enhance quality　品質を向上させる，品質を改善する
　enhanced earnings　業績向上
　enhanced messaging [message] service　携帯メール《略 EMS》
　enhanced returns　利益率の改善，収益向上
　enhanced service　サービスの高度化，高度サービス，サービスの拡張
▶The restructuring will *enhance* the Corporation's ability to compete more effectively in global markets.　この事業再編により，当社のグローバル市場での競争力は一段と高まるものと思われます。
▶The three companies aim to cut the cost of manufacturing steel products and *enhance* their products' quality by sharing some of their patents.　この3社は，特許の一部を相互利用することによって鉄鋼製品の製造コストを下げるとともに，鉄鋼製品の品質向上も目指している。

enhancement 名　増加，増大，増進，向上，改善，上昇，騰貴，強化，整備，補強，拡張，改良
　computer enhancement　コンピュータ処理による画質向上
　credit enhancement　信用補填，信用補完，信用補強
　enhancement of info-communications functions　情報通信機能の高度化
　image enhancement　画像強調
　margin enhancement　利益率の上昇
　portfolio enhancement　ポートフォリオの強化
　provide credit enhancement　信用補完を提供する，信用リスクをカバーする
　quality enhancement　品質向上
　service enhancement　サービス強化，サービス向上
▶The *enhancement* of the major banks' revenue bases is essential for the final disposal of bad loans.　不良債権の最終処理には，大手銀行の収益基盤の強化が欠かせない。

entail 動　必要とする，…を伴う，…をもたらす，…を課す，…を負わせる
▶Both companies expect the integration to *entail* about 5,000 job cuts.　両社は，この統合により約5,000人の人員削減を見込んでいる。

enter 動　記入する，記載する，市場などに参入する，〈団体などに〉加入する，加盟する，入会する，参加する，参加登録する，入る，提起する，提出する，申請する，申し出る，申し込む，〈正式に〉記録にのせる，〈判決などを〉正式に登録する，契約を結ぶ，コンピュータに〈データなどを〉入力する，立ち上げる，…にログインする，土地に立ち入る，占取する
　enter a protest　異議を申し立てる
　enter an action against　…に対する訴状を提出する，…を告訴する
　enter data incorrectly　データを誤って入力する
　enter in an account book　記帳する
　enter into an agreement　契約を結ぶ，契約を締結する（＝enter into a contract, make a contract, make and enter into an agreement）
　enter new markets abroad　海外の新市場に進出する
　enter the bond market　債券を発行する
　enter wrongly　誤記入する
▶Of the ¥28 billion to be raised by selling new shares, ¥10 billion will be invested in eMobile Ltd. which is preparing to *enter* the the mobile phone business in Japan.　新株発行で調達する280億円のうち100億円は，日本での携帯電話事業への新規参入を目指しているイー・モバイル（イー・アクセスの子会社）に出資する。
▶You may have *entered* the wrong number.　間違った番号を入力した可能性もあります。

enter into force　効力を生じる，発効する
▶The agreement shall not *enter into force* until signed.　この契約は，署名するまで効力を生じない。

enter the market　市場に参入する，市場に進出する，市場に加わる，市場を利用する
▶Since the deregulation of the civil aviation industry, two airlines *entered the market* on domestic trunk routes.　空の規制緩和［航空自由化］以来，航空会社2社が国内幹線に参入した。

enterprise 名　事業，大事業，事業体，企業，会

社, 起業家マインド, 進取の気性, 企画, 企て
accounting for business enterprises 企業会計 (＝enterprise accounting)
business enterprise 経営事業体, 営利企業, 企業
closely held enterprise 非公開会社
commercial enterprise 営利企業, 商企業
corporate enterprise 法人企業
enterprise fund 事業基金
enterprise resource planning 統合業務システム, 統合基幹業務システム, 統合基幹業績システム, 企業資源管理, 企業資源計画, エンタープライズ・リソース・プランニング《略 ERP》(企業内のあらゆる経営資源を統合的に管理すること)
enterprise tax 事業税
enterprise value 企業価値
issuing enterprise 発行体, 発行企業
manufacturing enterprise 製造業
multinational enterprise 多国籍企業
municipal enterprise 公営事業, 地方公営企業
national enterprise 国有企業, 国営企業 (＝state-run enterprise)
private enterprise 私企業, 民間企業, 一般法人
private enterprises annuity 企業年金
public enterprise 株式公開会社, 公共企業体, 公企業
small and medium enterprises 中小企業
state-owned enterprise 国有企業 (＝national enterprise)
state-run enterprise 国営企業
▶There has been no end to the declining number of small and midsize *enterprises*. 中小企業の減少に, 歯止めがかからない。

entertainment 名 接待, 歓待, 供応, もてなし, 交際
　entertainment and social expenses 接待・交際費
　entertainment expense 交際費 (＝entertainment and social expenses)
▶These *entertainment* expenses were not reckoned as due expenses. これらの交際費は, 税務当局に正当な経費と認定されなかった。

entire business year 通期, 事業年度全体 (＝entire fiscal year)
▶For the *entire business year* to Feb.28, the firm expects a net profit of ¥1.8 billion and a pretax profit of ¥3.9 billion on sales of ¥136.2 billion. 2月28日までの通期で[2月期決算で], 同社は, 1,362億円の売上高に対して18億円の税引き後利益と39億円の経常利益を予想している。

entity 名 事業体, 企業体, 組織体, 統一体, 法的存在者, 法主体, 事業単位, 単位
　accounting entity 会計実体
　affiliated entities 関係会社, 関連会社, 系列会社
　borrowing entity 発行体
　business entity 企業体, 事業体, 企業, 企業実体
　closely held entity 非公開会社
　corporate entity 企業, 企業体, 法人格
　economic entity 経済実体
　entity equity 企業持ち分, 主体持ち分
　entity's legal power 企業の法的権限
　legal entity 法人, 法的実体, 法的存在
　new entity 新組織, 新会社
　nonfinancial entity 非金融会社, 非金融事業会社
　surviving entity 存続会社, 更正会社
　tax-exempt entity 非課税組織
▶If found guilty as a corporate *entity*, Livedoor will be required to reduce its equity stake in Livedoor Securities Co. to less than 20 percent under the Securities Exchange Law. 法人として有罪が確定した場合, ライブドアは証券取引法に基づいてライブドア証券に対する同社の出資比率を20％未満に引き下げなければならない。
▶The new *entity* created by the merger can be expected to streamline management. 合併で生まれる新組織は, 経営の効率化を期待できる。
▶We forged this new *entity* out of three operating companies. 当社は, 三つの事業会社を統合してこの新会社を設立しました。

entrance 名 入社, 入会, 入場, 登場, 参入, 進出
　entrance examination 入社試験
　entrance fee 入場料, 入会金
　entrance greeter 受付案内
　entrance into the Chinese market 中国市場への進出, 中国市場への参入
　entrance money 入会金, 加盟手数料
　hold an entrance ceremony 入社式を行う

entrant 名 参加者, 新規参入者, 新規参入企業, 新規参入組, 新入社員, 新入生, 新加入者, 新入会員
　new entrant 新規参入者, 新規参入企業, 新規参入組
　new entrant to the power industry 電力業界への新規参入組

entrepreneur 名 企業家, 起業家, 経営者, 事業家, 興行主
▶Microsoft Corp., the world's largest software maker, was cofounded by Bill Gates and another young *entrepreneur* in 1975. ソフトウエア世界最大手の米マイクロソフトは, ビル・ゲイ

ツらの若手起業家が1975年に共同設立した。
▸This IT *entrepreneur* aimed to push up the aggregate market value of his company shares to the highest level in the world. このIT企業家は，自社株の時価総額世界一を目指した。

entrepreneurial 形 企業家の，起業家の，経営者の，起業家精神が旺盛な，企業家
 entrepreneurial activity 起業家活動
 entrepreneurial skills 経営技術，起業のノウハウ
 entrepreneurial spirit 企業化精神，起業家精神（＝entrepreneurialism, entrepreneurship）
 highly entrepreneurial 起業家精神が旺盛な
▸The new company benefits from the management skills, *entrepreneurial* spirit, market penetration and technology contributed by the smaller component companies. 新会社は，併合した中堅企業のもつ経営技術［経営のノウハウ］，企業家精神，市場浸透力，技術力を存分に活かしています［技術力のメリットを受けています］。

entrepreneurship 名 起業，企業家精神，起業家精神
▸It is important to encourage *entrepreneurship* through various means including assisting corporate ventures. ベンチャー支援などの起業促進が重要だ。

entrust 動 委任する，委託する，委ねる，任せる

entry 名 記入，記帳，記録，登録，登記，記載，記載事項，参加，参入，入会，入場，入国，参加者，出品物，土地への立入り，通関手続き，通関申告，入力
 barriers to entry 参入障壁（＝entry problems）
 China's entry into the WTO 中国の世界貿易機関（WTO）への加盟
 data entry データ入力
 double entry 複式記入
 entry age cost method 加入年齢方式
 entry barriers 参入障壁
 entry cost method 加入年齢方式（＝entry age cost method）
 entry costs 参入コスト（＝costs of entry）
 entry-exit registration system 出入国登録制度
 entry into Japan 日本への進出，日本市場への参入
 entry machine 初心者用パソコン，安価なモデル
 entry market 参入市場
 entry strategy 市場参入戦略
 entry visa 入国査証，入国ビザ
 free entry 自由参入
 import entry 輸入手続き
 make an entry 記入する，記帳する
 market entry 市場参入
 order entry 受注，注文処理
 original entry 原始記入
▸Wal-Mart's *entry* into Japan will accelerate the reorganization of the industry. ウォルマートの日本市場参入で，業界再編が加速するものと思われる。

environment 名 環境，情勢，動向，局面，展開（⇒business environment, economic environment）
 competitive environment 競争環境
 credit environment 信用情勢
 deflationary environment デフレ環境
 developing environments 発展途上国，開発途上国
 environment-conscious materials エコマテリアル
 environment-friendly 環境にやさしい，環境にほとんど害を与えない（＝eco-friendly, ecologically-friendly, ecologically sound）
 external environment 外部環境，外部要因，事業環境
 falling interest rate environment 金利低下局面，金利低下環境
 financial environment 金融情勢
 global environment 地球環境
 interest rate environment 金利情勢，金利動向
 investment environment 投資環境
 issuing environment 起債環境
 market environment 市場環境，相場
 operating environment 営業環境，事業環境
 organizational environment 組織環境
 political environment 政局
 regulatory environment 規制環境
 rising rate environment 金利上昇局面
 technical environment 市場の内部環境
▸The number of jobs in *environment*-focused businesses will increase by 45 percent to 2.6 million by 2015 from the 2005 level. 環境ビジネスの雇用規模は，2015年までに2005年の水準に比べて45％増の260万人に達する見込みだ。

environmental 名 環境の，周囲の，環境保護に関する，環境にやさしい，環境を害さない
 environmental assessment 環境影響評価，環境影響事前評価，環境アセスメント
 environmental conservation 環境保全（＝environmental protection）
 environmental degradation 環境悪化
 environmental disruption 環境破壊
 environmental effect 環境への影響

environmental group 環境保護団体, 環境団体
environmental hazard 公害
environmental impact assessment 環境影響評価《略 EIA》
environmental pollution 環境汚染, 公害 (= environmental contamination)
environmental responsibility 環境責任
Environmental Science Services Administration 米環境科学局《略 ESSA》

environmental protection 環境保護
Environmental Protection Agency 米環境保護局《略 EPA》
environmental protection standards 環境保護基準
▸Calls for *environmental protection*, safer products and corporate cooperation with the local community will continue to grow. 環境保護や製品の安全性, 地域社会との共生への要請は, 今後も強まるものと思われます。

environmental protection law 環境保護法
▸Like other manufacturers, we use, dispose of and clean up substances that are regulated under *environmental protection laws*. 他の製造業者と同じように, 当社も環境保護法で規制されている物質を使用し, その処分や浄化を行っています。

EPA 経済連携協定 (economic partnership agreementの略)
▸*EPAs* are better known, in general, as free trade agreements. EPAは, 一般的には, 自由貿易協定としてよく知られている。
EPA 米環境保護局 (Environmental Protection Agencyの略)
EPS 1株当たり利益, 1株当たり純利益 (⇒earnings per share)
equal 形 同じ, 等しい, 対等の, 平等な, 公平な, 互角の, 公平な, …に匹敵する, イコール
　Equal Credit Opportunity Act 信用機会均等法, 消費者信用機会均等法
　equal employment opportunity 雇用機会均等, 平等雇用機会
　Equal Employment Opportunity Commission 雇用機会均等委員会, 平等雇用機会委員会《略 EEOC》
　equal monthly payments with interest 元利均等返済
　equal opportunity 機会均等
　equal partner 対等提携, イコール・パートナー
　Equal Pay Act 賃金平等法
　equal pay for equal work 同一労働同一賃金
　equal value principle 等価交換原則
　have equal share 均等に出資する
　make equal payments 均等払いにする
equally owned by …が折半出資している, …が共同所有している

equilibrium 名 均衡, 平衡, 均衡レート
　balance of payments equilibrium 国際収支均衡, 経常収支の均衡
　consumption equilibrium 消費均衡
　equilibrium for bond yields 債券利回りの均衡水準
　equilibrium (economic) growth 均衡経済成長
　equilibrium of industry 産業の均衡
　equilibrium of the firm 企業の均衡
　equilibrium of trade 貿易の均衡
　fundamental equilibrium exchange rate ファンダメンタルズ均衡為替レート
　fundamental equilibrium level ファンダメンタルズ面の均衡水準
　general equilibrium model 一般均衡モデル
　market equilibrium 市場均衡
　neutral equilibrium 中立的均衡
　price equilibrium 価格均衡
　underemployment equilibrium 不完全雇用均衡

equipment 名 設備, 施設, 機器, 装置, 用品, 製品, 資産, エクイップメント (⇒ first-half net profit, property, plant and equipment)
　acquisition of equipment 設備購入
　add-on equipment 追加機器, 付属機器, 付属設備, アタッチメント
　audiovisual equipment AV機器
　business equipment 事務機器
　disposal of equipment 設備処分
　equipment and facilities 施設および装置, 施設・装置
　equipment investment 設備投資
　equipment purchase agreement 装置購入契約
　equipment replacement 設備更新
　equipment sales 機器販売
　gain on sale of equipment 動産売却益
　high technology medical equipment ハイテク医療機器
　idle equipment 遊休設備 (=surplus equipment)
　input-output equipment 入出力装置
　lease equipment リース資産
　loss on sale of equipment 設備売却損
　OA equipment OA機器
　obsolete equipment 老朽設備

premises and equipment, net 動産・不動産純額
semiconductor production equipment 半導体製造装置
surplus equipment 遊休設備 (=idle equipment)
telecommunications equipment 電気通信機器

▶Other capital expenditures are for *equipment* and facilities used in leasing operations, manufacturing, and research and development. その他の資本的支出は，リース業務，製造部門と研究開発に使用する施設および装置向けでした。

equity 图 株式，持ち分，持ち分権，自己持ち分，自己資本，純資産，純資産価値，正味価額，証券，エクイティ (⇒capital raising, consumer loan, partnership interest)
at equity 実価による，持ち分価格[価額]で
corporate equity 企業持ち分
cross equity holdings 株式の持ち合い
debt and equity securities 債券と持ち分証券，債券と株式
equity analyst 証券アナリスト
equity holding 株式保有，株式所有，保有株式，持ち株，出資比率，合弁 (=shareholding, stock holding, stockholding)
equity holding losses 株式含み損，保有株式の含み損
equity in earnings of unconsolidated subsidiaries and affiliated companies 非連結子会社および関連会社持ち分利益
equity in net earnings 持ち分利益，純利益に占める持ち分
equity method 持ち分法，実価法 (=equity method of accounting)
equity option 株式オプション
equity ownership 株式所有，株主所有権，自己資本，持ち株比率
equity participation 資本参加，出資，株式投資 (=capital participation)
equity partner 資本参加者，出資者
equity position 持ち株比率，出資比率
equity stake rate 持ち分比率，出資比率
equity trading business 株の取引業務，株式取引業務 (⇒equity market)
float new shares under a third party equity issue 第三者割当て増資で新株を発行する (⇒float)
new equity raising 新株発行
on the equity basis 持ち分法で

owners' equity 所有者持ち分
partners' equity パートナーの持ち分
proprietor's equity 事業主の持ち分
raise equity 増資する
stock equity 株式持ち分
straight equity 普通株，普通株式

▶Citigroup had already acquired about 68 percent *equity* in Nikko in October 2007. シティグループは，2007年10月の時点で，日興の株式の約68％をすでに取得していた。

▶The accounting changes reduced our *equity* in 2008. 会計処理の変更に伴い，当社の自己資本は，2008年度は減少しました。

equity capital 自己資本，株主資本，持ち分資本，株主の出資資本，株主持ち分，払込み資本，株式資本

企業の資本について ➡ 企業の資本は，銀行からの借入金などの他人資本と，株主からの拠出資本や利益の蓄積である利益剰余金などの自己資本とに区分される。自己資本には，要するに資本金，資本剰余金（企業の純資産額のうち資本金の額を超える部分）と利益剰余金などが含まれる。

equity capital to total assets 自己資本比率，株主資本比率
equity capital to total debt ratio 負債比率

▶Banks have been allowed to count the taxes they pay in writing off their nonperforming loans as part of their *equity capital*. 銀行はこれまで，不良債権処理の際に納める税金を自己資本の一部と見なすことができた。

equity earnings 持ち分利益，関係会社利益持ち分

▶The increase in the equity in net income of associated companies in the first quarter 2009 over 2008 is due mainly to increased *equity earnings*, of the ABC PLC. 2009年第1四半期の関連会社持ち分利益が前年同期を上回ったのは，主にABCピーエルシーの持ち分利益が増加したからです。

equity financing エクイティ・ファイナンス，新株発行による資金調達，自己資本金融，株式金融増資，自己資本の調達 (=equity finance: 社債発行や借入金によって資本を調達する方法はdebt financingという)

▶We raised $50 billion through *equity financing* deals in 2008. 当社は，エクイティ・ファイナンス（新株発行による資金調達）の取引で，2008年度は500億ドルの資金を調達しました。

equity in net assets of subsidiaries 子会社純資産持ち分

equity in net assets
▶The *equity in net assets* of non-U.S. *subsidiaries* amounted to $4.2 billion at December 31, 2008.　非米国子会社の純資産持ち分は，2008年12月31日現在で42億ドルでした。

equity in net income [earnings] of an associated company　関連会社持ち分利益，関連会社の純利益に占める持ち分
▶The *equity in net income of associated companies* in the first quarter of 2009 was $55 million, compared with $30 million in the first quarter of 2008.　2009年第1四半期の関連会社持ち分利益は，前年同期の3,000万ドルに対して，5,500万ドルでした。

equity interest　持ち分権，株式持ち分（⇒opportunity）
▶We acquired a 20% *equity interest* in the company for cash.　当社は，現金で同社の20%の株式持ち分を取得しました。

equity investment　株式投資，直接投資，出資（＝stock investment; ⇒income from equity investments）
▶*Equity investments* were a net source of cash in 2008.　2008年度は，基本的に株式投資が現金流入をもたらしました。

equity market　株式市場，証券市場，エクイティ市場
▶The suspension of its after-hours equity trading business reflects poor demand in Japan's *equity market*.　同社の株の時間外取引業務の停止は，日本の株式市場の需要低迷を反映している。

equity procurement　資本の自力調達
▶The banks boosted their capital bases with public funds and *equity procurement*.　銀行各行は，公的資金や自力調達で資本基盤を強化した。

equity purchase　株式取得，株式投資
▶Mazda Motor Corp. made its New Zealand marketing subsidiary a wholly owned subsidiary through an *equity purchase*.　マツダは，ニュージーランドの販売子会社を，株式取得により完全子会社化した。

equity securities　持ち分証券，持ち分有価証券
▶We must change the way we report and account for investments in *equity securities* in 2009.　2009年度に，当社は持ち分証券への投資に関する報告と会計処理方法を変更しなければなりません。

equity stake　持ち分，株式持ち分，出資比率（＝equity stake rate）
▶Capital gains from the sale of firm's *equity stake* will amount to about ¥50 billion.　同社の保有株式売却益は，約500億円になる見通しだ。

equity swap contract　株式交換契約
▶Citigroup Inc. and Nikko Cordial Corp. have altered their *equity swap contract* following the plunge in the stock price of Citigroup in New York.　米金融大手のシティグループと傘下の日興コーディアルグループは，ニューヨーク市場でシティグループの株価が下落したのを受けて，両社の株式交換契約の内容を変更した。

equity tie-up　資本提携
▶Three major steelmakers reached a final agreement to form an *equity tie-up*.　鉄鋼大手の3社が，資本提携を結ぶことで最終合意した。

equivalent 名　同等物，等価物，相当額，相当分，換算，換算額，同意語（⇒cash equivalents）
annual equivalent　年換算
cash and equivalents　現金および現金等価物，現金預金およびその等価物
cash equivalent value　現金等価額（＝cash equivalent amount）
certainty equivalent　確実性等価，確実性等価額
certainty equivalent return　確実性等価収益率
common equivalent shares　普通株式相当証券
common stock equivalents　準普通株式，普通株式等価物
interest equivalents　利息相当分
profit equivalent　利益同等物
▶Net earnings in 2008 were $1.56 billion, or $2.65 per fully diluted common and common *equivalent* shares.　2008年度の純利益は，15億6,000万ドル(完全希薄化後の普通株式および普通株式相当証券1株当たり2.65ドル)でした。

equivalent to　…に相当する，…に当たる，…と同じ［同価値，同量］
▶The company is scheduled to issue new shares *equivalent to* about 35 percent of of its outstanding equities for ¥1,138 per share in an effort to generate ¥30 billion.　同社は，発行済み株式数の約35％に当たる新株を1株当たり1,138円で発行して，300億円を調達する予定だ。
▶The foreign funds purchased the convertible bonds at prices *equivalent to* ¥25 per share.　海外ファンドは，1株25円で転換社債を引き受けた。

ergonomics 名　人間工学，人間環境工学，人にやさしい技術，エルゴノミクス

ERISA　エリサ法（Employee Retirement Income Security Actの略）

ERP　統合業務システム，統合基幹業務システム，統合基幹業績システム，企業資源管理，企業資源計画（経営の効率化を図るため，受注・生産管理，物流

管理，販売管理，在庫管理など企業の基幹情報処理業務を統合的に管理する情報システム；enterprize resource planning)
ERP package 統合業務パッケージ，ERPパッケージ
ERP software ERPソフト
error 名 誤謬（ごびゅう），誤記，誤差，誤り，ミス，過誤，エラー
　accounting error 経理ミス，会計上の誤謬（＝accounting mistake)
　calculation error 計算上の誤謬（＝error of calculation)
　clerical error 事務上の誤り，事務的な誤り，記帳上の誤謬
　compensating error 相殺誤差
　correction of error 誤謬の訂正，エラーの訂正
　detection of error 誤謬の発見
　error of mistake in writing 誤記上の誤謬，誤記による誤謬
　error on posting 転記上の誤謬，転記上の誤り
　errors and omissions 誤差脱漏，誤記・脱漏，過誤脱漏
　standard error 標準誤差
▶Mizuho Securities Co.'s erroneous sell order *error* was made when its staffer entered data incorrectly. みずほ証券の誤発注［発注ミス］は，同社の担当者がデータを誤って入力した際に生じた。
▶The firm failed to report a total of about ¥5 billion including simple accounting *errors*. 同社は，単純な経理ミスを含めて総額で約50億円を申告しなかった。
ES 従業員満足，従業員の満足，企業内組織の満足（employee satisfactionの略）
ES cells 胚性幹細胞，ES細胞，万能細胞（embryonic stem cellsの略）
▶*ES cells* have the potential to grow into any type of human cell or tissue in the body. ES細胞は，どんな種類の人間の細胞や人体の組織にも育つ可能性がある。
escrow 名 条件付き捺印証書，第三者寄託金，エスクロー
　escrow account エスクロー勘定，エスクロー口座
　escrow agent エスクロー代理人，条件付き証書受託者
　escrow agreement エスクロー契約
　escrow bond 条件付き譲渡証書
　escrow fund エスクロー資金，預託資金
　escrow L/C [credit] エスクロー信用状，寄託信用状
　money held in escrow 第三者の手で保管されている金
ESOP 従業員株式購入選択権制度（employee stock option planの略）
ESOP 従業員持ち株制度（＝employee stock ownership trust: **employee stock ownership plan**の略）
▶We issued 14 million new shares of common stock in connection with the establishment of an *ESOP* feature for the non-management savings plan. 当社は，非管理職貯蓄制度の一環として従業員持ち株制度(ESOP)を設けたことに関連して，普通株式新株1,400万株を発行しました。
ESOP debt guarantee reduction ESOP基金債務保証額の減少
establish 動 設立する，設置する，創設する，創立する，樹立する，形成する，確立する，制定する，定める，規定する，〈引当金や担保権を〉設定する，設ける，認定する，関係を築く，〈制度などを〉導入する，立証する
▶A pre-tax provision of $200 million ($0.57 per common share, after tax) was *established* to cover the estimated costs of this restructuring program. この事業再編計画の推定費用を補填するため，税引き前で2億ドル(税引き後で，普通株式1株当たり0.57ドル)の引当金を設定しました。
▶Each of these major subsidiaries has also *established* an audit committee that reports to their respective directors. これらの主要子会社各社も，それぞれの取締役会傘下の監査委員会を設置しています。
▶In recent years, there has been a rise in the number of women and aged people who want to *establish* enterprises. 最近では，女性と高齢者の開業希望者が増えている。
establishment 名 設立，設置，創設，創立，樹立，形成，確立，制定，規定，設定，認定，導入，立証，組織，施設，公共施設，機関，会社，商店，店，事業所，既成社会，制度，体制，体制側，上層部，支配層，支配機構，常置人員，エスタブリッシュメント
　additional establishment 追加設定
　branch establishment 支店
　business establishment 事業所
　commercial establishment 商社，商会
　establishment of a new company 新会社の設立
　establishment of a law 法律の制定
　establishment of diplomatic relations 外交関係の樹立

establishment survey 事業所調査
government establishments abroad 在外公館
industrial establishment 工場
initial establishment 当初設定
manufacturing establishment 生産会社
old establishment 老舗(しにせ)
permanent establishment 恒久的施設
service establishment 加盟店
the Establishment of the company 会社の上層部

estate 名 財産, 不動産, 地所, 私有地
　estate agent [house] 不動産仲介業者, 不動産業者
　estate car ステーション・ワゴン (=station wagon)
　estate surveyor 不動産鑑定士
　freehold estate 自由保有権, 自由保有物権
　income-producing real estate 稼動不動産
　leasehold estate 不動産賃借物権
　legal estate 不動産権
　personal estate 動産
　real estate 不動産
　trust estate 信託財産

estimate 動 見積もる, 推定する, 推計する, 予想する, 予測する, 概算する, 試算する, 評価する
▶We used our experience over the past five years to *estimate* future separations. 将来の休職を予測するにあたって, 当社は過去5年間の当社の経験値を使用しました。

estimate 名 見積り, 推定, 推計, 予想, 予測, 概算, 試算, 推定値, 推定量, 評価, 判断, 見積り書, 概算書
　accounting estimate 会計見積り, 会計上の見積り
　accounting estimate change 会計上の見積りの変更
　best estimates and judgments 最善[最良]の見積りと判断
　collateral value estimates 担保評価額
　earlier reported estimate 速報値
　estimates 見積り金額
　excess over estimate 見積り超過額
　full-year parent recurring profit estimate 通期の単独経常利益予想
　market consensus estimate 市場のコンセンサス予想
　market estimates 市場予想
　original [initial] estimate 当初予想, 当初見積り, 当初の見積り額
　preliminary estimate 暫定推定値
　profit estimate 利益予想, 損益予想, 業績予想 (=profit forecast)
　sales estimates 販売予測, 売上予測, 予想売上高 (=estimates of sales)
　street estimates 市場予測

▶Capital expenditures for 2009 are now expected to reach approximately $2,750 million from the original *estimate* of $2,200 million. 2009年度の資本的支出は現在, 当初の見積り額22億ドルに対して約27億5,000万ドルに達する見込みです。

▶The firm revised upward its earnings *estimates* for fiscal 2009 to next March. 同社は, 2010年3月期[2009年度]の業績予想を上方修正した。

estimated 形 見積りの, 推定の, 概算の
　estimated future credit losses 回収不能見込み額, 貸倒れ見積り高
　estimated liability 見積り債務, 見積り負債, 引当金
　estimated loss from bad debt 予想貸倒れ損失
　estimated revenue 見積り収益, 見積り歳入
　estimated useful life 見積り耐用年数 (=expected useful life)
　estimated value 見積り額, 評価額

▶The *estimated* lives of machinery and equipment are 2-12 years. 機械・設備の見積り耐用年数は, 2-12年となっています。

estimated cost 見積り費用, 見積り原価, 予定原価, 費用見積り (=cost estimate), 原価見積り, 推定費用 (=estimate cost)

▶The *estimated costs* of specific plans to close offices, consolidate facilities and relocate employees in the provisions for business restructuring. 事業再編成引当金には, 事業所閉鎖や施設統合, 従業員再配置など特定の計画の費用見積りが含まれています。

estimated future postemployment benefits 予測される将来の雇用後給付, 将来の見積り雇用後給付

▶This new standard requires us to accrue *estimated future postemployment benefits*, including separation payments. この新基準は, 休職手当の支払いを含めて, 予測される将来の雇用後給付を計上するよう要求しています。

estimated future retiree benefits 将来の見積り退職後給付, 予測される将来の退職後給付

▶This accounting standard requires us to accrue *estimated future retiree benefits* during the years employees are working and accumulating these benefits. この会計基準は, 従業員の受給権が発生する在職期間にわたって将来の見積り退職後

給付を費用計上するよう要求しています。
ETF 電子資金取引, 電子資金振替え, 電子決済 (**electronic transfer of funds**の略)
ETF 上場投資信託, 株価指数連動型上場投資信託 (**exchange-traded fund, index mutual fund**: 株式と同じように市場で売買する投信で, 金や銀など商品の相場に連動して値動きする)
ethical 形 倫理の, 倫理的, 道徳上の, 道義にかなった, 道徳的な, 名 一般薬, 認可薬品, 医療用薬品, エシカル・ドラッグ
　ethical business conduct 倫理的業務活動 (⇒ **internal accounting control**)
　ethical code 倫理綱領, 道徳律
　ethical drug 処方箋薬, 要指示薬, エシカル・ドラッグ
　ethical investment 倫理的投資 (= socially responsible investment)
　ethical standard 倫理基準, 倫理的基準, 倫理の規範
▶It is essential to conduct business affairs in accordance with the highest *ethical* standards as set forth in our Code of Conduct. 業務は, 当社の「行動規範」に定める最高の倫理基準に従って行うことが絶対必要です。
ethics 名 倫理, 道徳, 倫理体系, 倫理綱領, 行動の規範
　advertising ethics 広告倫理
　business ethics 商道徳
　charter of ethics 企業行動憲章
　code of ethics 倫理綱領 (= business conduct code, code of conduct)
　corporate ethics 企業倫理 (= business ethics)
　ethics charter 企業行動憲章 (= charter of ethics, corporate ethics charter, ethics code)
　ethics committee 倫理委員会
　ethics standards 倫理規程
　managing ethics 経営倫理
　professional ethics 職業倫理
▶A Harvard University *ethics* committee has given a conditional green light to a research team to grow human embryonic stem cells. ハーバード大学倫理委員会は, ヒトES細胞(ヒト胚性幹細胞)の作製をすでに承認している。
EU 欧州連合 (**European Union**の略)
　an expanded, 27-nation EU 27か国体制の拡大EU
　the enlargement of the EU 欧州連合(EU)の拡大
　the rotating presidency of the EU 輪番制の欧州連合(EU)議長国
　the EU's Constitution EU憲法
▶The economy of the 27-nation *EU* chalked up growth of 2.9 percent in 2007 after 3 percent in 2006. 2007年のEU27国全体の経済成長率は, 前年の3%に対して2.9%だった。
EU constitution EU憲法 (= EU charter: 拡大EUの基本理念をうたった前文と448条の条文からなる。任期2年半の常任議長(EU大統領)と共通外交・安保政策推進のためのEU外相を新設する。2006年11月の発効を目標としていたが, 発効には全加盟国批准が条件となっている)
Euribor 欧州銀行間取引金利, ユーリボー (**Euro Interbank Offered Rate** の略)
euro 名 ユーロ (= Euro: 欧州連合(EU)の単一通貨で, 2002年1月1日からユーロ紙幣や硬貨が市中に流通。2002年7月1日から, EMU(欧州経済通貨同盟)加盟各国の通貨 はユーロだけに統一された)
　euro banknotes ユーロ紙幣 (= euro notes)
　euro coins ユーロ硬貨
▶This announcement can be presumed to strengthen the *euro* and depress the dollar. この発表には, ユーロを上昇させ, ドルを下落させる意図があるものと推定できる。
euro zone ユーロ圏, 欧州圏 (⇒**eurozone**)
euro zone countries ユーロ圏諸国, ユーロ圏各国, ユーロ圏
▶Not only the United States but also the 15 *euro zone countries* revised downward their economic growth predictions for this year. 米国もユーロ圏15か国も, 今年の経済成長率の見通しを下方修正した。
Eurobond 名 ユーロ債, ユーロボンド
eurocurrency 名 ユーロカレンシー, ユーロマネー
euro-dollars 名 ユーロダラー (米国外の金融機関に預けられた米ドル建て預金)
euronotes 名 ユーロノート (ユーロ市場で発行される米ドルまたはユーロ建ての短期無担保約束手形)
European Central Bank 欧州中央銀行, 欧州中銀《略 **ECB**》
▶The *European Central Bank* left its benchmark rate unchanged at 4 percent. 欧州中央銀行(ECB)は, (ユーロ圏15か国の短期金利の誘導目標となる)政策金利を年4%のまま据え置いた。
European Commission 欧州委員会(欧州連合(EU)の行政執行機関)
European Court of First Instance 欧州第1審裁判所

European System of Central Banks
欧州中央銀行制度
European Union 欧州連合《略 EU》
EU関連語句

Amsterdam Treaty	アムステルダム条約
Committee of Permanent Representatives	常駐代表委員会
European Commission	欧州委員会
European Council	欧州理事会
European Parliament	欧州議会
European Union's head office	欧州連合(EU)本部, 欧州連合(EU)欧州委員会
Presidency	議長国
Treaty of Maastricht	マーストリヒト条約

▸The economic growth of the newcomers to the *European Union* is higher than the average of the previous membership. EU新加盟国の経済成長は，旧加盟国の平均より高い。

Eurostat data agency 欧州連合(EU)の統計局
▸*Eurostat data agency* said the eurozone economy slowed to 0.4 percent in the final three months of 2007. 欧州連合(EU)統計局の発表によると，ユーロ圏の2007年10-12月期の経済成長率は0.4%に鈍化した。

eurozone 名 ユーロ圏
▸*Eurozone* economic growth dipped to 2.7 percent in 2007. ユーロ圏の2007年の経済成長率は，前年比で2.7%に減少した。

EVA 経済的付加価値，経済付加価値(economic value addedの略。企業価値評価指標で，1年間に増えた株主の価値のこと。営業利益から資本コスト(税金，配当金や金利など)を差し引いた残余利益。米国のスターン・スチュワート社が提唱したもので，同社の登録商標)
▸*EVA* involves the measurement of economic returns on invested capital to ensure that we are earning more than the cost of capital. 経済的付加価値(EVA)で，投下資本に対する経済的見返りを測定して，当社が資本コストを上回る利益を上げていることを確かめることができます。

evade 動 ごまかして避ける，逃れる，免れる
▸The Tokyo Regional Taxation Bureau has filed a complaint with prosecutors against a pork import broker on suspicion of *evading* about ¥140 million in corporate tax for three years. 東京国税局は，3年間に法人税約1億4,000万円を免れていたとして，豚肉の輸入仲介業者を検察当局に告発した。

evaluate 動 評価する，判断する，検討する，見極める，…の数値を求める
evaluate a business [company] 企業評価を行う
evaluate inventories 在庫評価を行う
evaluate issuer management 発行体の経営能力を評価する
evaluate the credit risk 信用リスク[与信リスク]を評価する，クレジット・リスクを評価する
evaluated participation 社会関係参与評価《略 EP》

evaluation 名 評価，分析，診断，判定
asset evaluation 資産評価
cost benefit evaluation 費用便益評価
credit risk evaluation 信用リスク評価，信用分析
evaluation of asset values 資産価値の評価
evaluation of collateral 担保評価
evaluation of internal control system 内部統制組織の評価
evaluation of performance 業績評価 (= performance evaluation)
market evaluation 市場の評価
stock evaluation losses 株式の評価損
wage on job evaluation 職能給
▸The firm is suspected of understating its affiliates' stock *evaluation* losses in its financial paper. 同社は，有価証券報告書で子会社の株式の評価損を過小計上していた疑いがある。

even 形 同等の，対等の，互角の，公平な，動 同等にする，平衡させる，安定する，安定させる
break even 利益も損失もない
even bargain 損得なしの公平な取引，公平な取引
even growth 均等成長
even keel policy イーブン・キール政策
even lot 単位株
even number 偶数
of even date 同一日付の
on even ground 対等で，対等の立場で

event 名 動き，動向，事象，事態，発生事項，出来事，事件，成り行き，結果，事由，事柄，事項，行事，催事，イベント
crown event 冠イベント
economic events 経済の動き，経済動向，景気動向，経済事象
event-driven fund イベント・ドリブン型ファンド (国際会議や要人の来日などの重要なイベントに合わせて株価変動の予測を立て，株式を売買する手法)
event management 催事管理，イベント管理
event planner イベント・プランナー (催事の企

画, 演出, 運営などを専門に手がける者・会社)
event risk イベント・リスク
extraordinary event 異常事象
future events 将来発生する事態
internal events 内部取引事象
liquidation event 清算事由
reportable event 要報告事項
subsequent event 後発事象
termination event 解約事由
▶A favorable cycle of *events* has begun to emerge, with strong performances leading to an increase in jobs and higher wage, resulting in boosts in consumption. 好業績が雇用改善や賃金の上昇につながり,その結果消費も上向くなど,景気動向に好循環が見えてきた。

events of default 債務不履行事由,不履行事由,不履行事態,契約違反行為,デフォルト事由
▶*Events of default* shall include the failure by a party to perform a material obligation under this agreement. 不履行事由には,当事者による本契約上の重大な義務の不履行が含まれる。

evidence 名 証拠, 証拠資料, 証拠物件 (evidential matter), 証言, 指標, 兆候, 兆し
analytical evidence 分析的証拠
conclusive evidence 決定的証拠
documentary evidence 文書の証拠
evidence of a pick-up in economic activity 景気回復の兆候, 景気が上向いていることを示す指標
evidence to the contrary 反証
physical evidence 物的証拠
supporting evidence 裏づけ資料
▶In the absence of *evidence* to the contrary, the date of marine bill of lading shall be proof of the date of shipment. 反証がない場合には,海上船荷証券の日付けが引渡しの日の証拠となるものとする。

ex 前 …渡し (out of), …からの, …落ち (without), …落ちの
ex-all 全権利落ち
ex ante 事前の, 事前的な
ex ante analysis 事前分析
ex bond 保税倉庫渡し
ex-bonded warehouse 保税倉庫渡し
ex bonds ポンカス債 (=securities on an ex basis)
ex capitalization [ex cap.] 無償交付落ち, 無償増資新株権利落ちで
ex contractu 契約から, 契約上の
ex coupon [ex cp.] 利落ち

ex-coupon price of bond 債券の裸相場
ex customs compound 通関渡し条件
ex date 権利落ち日, 配当権利落ち日
ex delicto 不法行為上の
ex dividend [ex div.] 配当落ち, 配当権利落ち (期日が過ぎて配当の支払いを受ける権利がなくなること。配当付き=cum dividend)
ex-dividend date 配当落ち日, 配当支払い日
ex dock [pier, wharf] 埠頭渡し, 指定輸入港埠頭渡し条件
ex dock-duty paid 埠頭渡し関税込み, 現地渡し
ex facto 事実に従って, 行為に基づき, 事実上
ex factory 工場渡し
ex-factory price 工場出荷価格
ex gratia 好意から, 好意からの, 任意の
ex-gratia payment 好意からの支払い, 見舞金, 任意給付
ex interest [ex int.] 利落ち, 利落ちで
ex lighter 輸入港艀(はしけ)渡し条件
ex mill 製粉工場渡し条件
ex mine 鉱山渡し
ex new [ex n.] 新株落ち, 新株落ちで, 新株落ちの
ex nihilo ゼロから, 無から
ex notes ポンカス債
ex officio 職務上の, 職権上の (=by virtue of office, by virtue of official position)
ex point of origin 現地渡し
ex post 事後の, 事後的な
ex post facto 事後の, 遡及的な, 過去にさかのぼって (=after the fact)
ex quay 埠頭渡し, 埠頭渡しで, 埠頭渡しの, 埠頭渡し条件
ex-quay port of arrival 着地払い運賃
ex-quay shed 上屋(うわや)渡し
ex rail 鉄道[線路]渡し
ex rel. …に関する(事件), …から受けた通知により (ラテン語 ex relatione の略)
ex right [xr] 権利落ち, 権利落ちの, 新株引受権の付かない
ex rights price 権利落ち株価
ex ship 着船渡し, 着船渡し条件
ex store 店頭渡し
ex terms 現場渡し条件
ex warehouse 倉庫渡し (=ex godown)
ex works 工場渡し《略 EXW》
ex-works price 工場渡し値段

examination 名 監査, 検査, 検証, 調査
bank examination 銀行監査
examination by reference 照査

examination of financial statements 財務書類監査, 財務諸表の監査
  interim examination date 中間監査日
  scope of examination 監査の範囲
  ▸Our *examinations* included such tests of the accounting records and such other auditing procedures as we considered necessary in the circumstances. 私どもの監査には, 状況に応じて私どもが必要とみなした会計記録[会計報告書・財務諸表]の試査やその他の監査手続きも含まれています。

examine 動 監査する, 検査する, 検証する, 調査する
  ▸Independent accountants are retained to *examine* the Corporation's financial statements. 社外の独立した会計監査人[公認会計士]が, 当社の財務書類を監査しています。

exceed 動 …の限度を超える, 他よりすぐれる

excess 名形 超過, 超過額, 過剰, 余剰, 過度
  capital in excess of par value 株式払込み剰余金, 払込み剰余金, 資本剰余金, 株式発行差金
  capital in excess of stated value 株式払込み剰余金, 払込み剰余金, 額面超過金
  excess earning power 超過収益力
  excess funds 余剰資金
  excess liabilities 債務超過, 債務超過額 (＝excess of debts, excess of liabilities over assets, excessive liabilities, liabilities in excess of assets)
  excess of assets over projected benefit obligation 資産の予測給付債務超過額
  excess production capacity 過剰生産設備
  ▸*Excess* volatility in exchange rates is undesirable for global economic growth. 為替相場の過度の変動は, 世界の経済成長にとって望ましくない。

excess capacity 超過設備, 過剰設備, 設備過剰 (＝excess facilities)
  ▸The automobile industry suffers from an *excess capacity* equivalent to the entire capacity of a major maker. 自動車業界では, 大手メーカー1社の総生産能力に相当する過剰設備を抱えている。

excess consumption 過剰消費
  ▸The U.S. current account deficit has passed the annual $800 billion mark, reflecting *excess consumption*. 米国の経常赤字は, 過剰消費を反映して, 年間8,000億ドルの大台を超えた。

excess liquidity 過剰流動性, 余剰資金
  ▸Japanese firms are awash with *excess liquidity* after a decade of post-bubble economic restructuring efforts. 日本企業は, 10年に及ぶバブル崩壊後のリストラ策[リストラ努力]で, 余剰資金が豊富だ。

excess of liabilities over assets 債務超過, 債務超過額 (＝excess liabilities)
  ▸The company likely will face an *excess of liabilities over assets* for fiscal 2009. 同社は, 2009年度は債務超過に陥る見通しだ。

excess quotas for greenhouse gas emissions 温室効果ガスの削減分, 温室効果ガスの排出権
  ▸The *excess quotas for* carbon dioxide and other greenhouse gas emissions will be distributed to companies in accordance with the amount of funds each firm provided. 二酸化炭素などの温室効果ガスの排出権[二酸化炭素など温室効果ガス排出量の削減分]は, 各企業の基金への出資額に応じて分配される。

excessive 形 過度の, 極端な, 法外な, 不当な, 多すぎる, 過多の, 過剰な, 割高な
  excessive debt 過剰債務, 債務の過多
  excessive demands 不当な要求, 要求の行き過ぎ
  excessive dividends 過剰な配当金
  excessive inventories 過剰在庫
  excessive lending 過剰融資
  excessive profit 暴利
  excessive service 過剰サービス, サービス過剰

excessive competition 過当競争
  ▸We cannot ignore the possible negative impacts of the regulatory reforms, which may prompt *excessive competition* and weaken existing industries. 過当競争や既存産業の衰退を招く恐れがある規制改革の負の側面を, われわれは無視することができない。

excessive funding 過剰融資
  ▸The investigation committee questioned the bank's *excessive funding* of a golf course developer. 調査委員会は, ゴルフ場経営会社への同行の過剰融資を問題視した。

excessive liabilities 過剰債務
  ▸A large number of companies are burdened with massive amounts of *excessive liabilities* in sectors such as construction and wholesale. 建設や卸売りなどの分野では, 巨額の過剰債務を抱えている企業が多い。

exchange 動 交換する, 取り替える, 両替する, やり取りする, 〈契約などを〉取り交わす, 〈契約書に〉サインする
  ▸We had a $200 million gain when we *exchanged* our remaining 70% interest in the company for about 3% ownership of a leading

software development company. 当社は，同社の70%残存持ち分を大手のソフトウエア開発会社に対する3％持ち分と交換して，2億ドルの利益を上げました。
▶We plan to *exchange* one share of the firm for our 1.4 shares, making it a whole subsidiary of us. 当社は，同社株1株に自社株1.4株を割り当てる株式交換を実施して，同社を当社の完全子会社化する方針です。

exchange 名 交換，両替，為替，為替相場，〈証券や商品の〉取引所，取引，交易，交流（⇒stock exchange）
　economic exchange 経済交流
　exchange contract 為替予約
　exchange gain 為替差益（＝currency exchange gain, exchange profit）
　exchange gain from yen appreciation 円高差益
　exchange gain (loss) 為替差益(損失)
　exchange gain or [and] loss 為替差損益，為替換算差損益（＝exchange gains/losses, exchange gains and losses）
　exchange loss 為替差損
▶Income and expense items are translated at average rates of *exchange* prevailing during the year. 収益と費用項目は，期中の実勢平均為替レートで換算されています。
▶These interest rate swap agreements generally involve the *exchange* of fixed or floating interest payments without the exchange of the underlying principal amounts. これらの金利スワップ契約では，原則として元本の交換は行わず，固定金利または変動金利による支払い利息を交換する。

exchange fluctuations 為替変動，為替相場の変動，為替の騰落，為替の乱高下（＝currency swings, exchange rate movements, exchange rate moves）
▶The yen'a stable rate against the dollar serves as a stabilizing factor for importers, exporters and others doing business susceptible to *exchange fluctuations*. 円の対ドル為替相場が安定していることは，輸出入業者など為替変動に左右されやすい仕事をしている者にとって，安定要因となる。

exchange market 為替市場，取引市場
▶It is necessary to keep a watch on large fluctuations on the *exchange market* and changes in stock prices. 為替市場の乱高下や株価の動きを警戒する必要がある。

exchange of shares 株式交換

▶We computed these combined amounts assuming the merger was already completed using a one-for-one *exchange of shares*. これらの合算数値は，1対1の株式交換方式を用いて合併がすでに完了しているものとして計算しました。

exchange rate 為替相場，外国為替相場，為替レート，交換レート，交換比率，換算レート（＝currency exchange rate, rate of exchange）
　at average *exchange rates* prevailing during the year 期中の実勢平均為替レートで
　at exchange rates in effect at the balance sheet date 貸借対照表日現在の実効為替レートで，貸借対照表日現在の為替レートで
　current exchange rate 実勢為替相場，実勢為替レート，現在外貨交換レート
　exchange rate policy 為替政策
　exchange rate system 為替制度
　yen-dollar exchange rate 円ドル相場，円・ドル相場，円・ドルレート，円の対ドルレート，円とドルの為替レート
▶We forecast an *exchange rate* of ¥120 to the dollar for the current fiscal year. 当社は，今年度の為替レートを1ドル＝120円と想定しています。

exchange-traded fund 上場投資信託，株価指数連動型上場投資信託《略 ETF》
▶The *exchange-traded funds* (ETFs) are investment products similar to index mutual funds but that trade on stock exchanges like stocks. 上場投資信託(ETF)は，インデックス・ミューチュアル・ファンド(株価指数と連動するように設計された株式ポートフォリオを運用対象とする投資信託)に似ているが，株式と同じように証券取引所で売買される投資商品である。

excise 名 消費税，物品税，動 …に消費税を課す
　commodity excise 物品税
　excise duties 消費税
　excise license 間接税免許
　excise tax 物品税，国内消費税
　Federal Excise Tax 連邦物品税
　general excise tax 一般消費税

exclusive 形 独占的，排他的，専属の，専有の
　exclusive agency 独占的代理権，一手販売代理店，専属代理店，専属特約店
　exclusive dealing 排他的取引
　exclusive distributor 一手販売店，総代理店，独占的販売店，独占的代理店
　exclusive interview 単独会見，単独インタビュー
　exclusive license 独占的実施許諾，独占的実施権，独占的使用権，独占的[排他的]ライセンス
▶Subject to the terms and conditions herein

provided, Company hereby appoints Distributor as its *exclusive* distributor.　本契約に定める条件に従って，会社は，本契約により代理店を会社の一手販売店［総代理店］に指名する．

exclusive economic zone　排他的経済水域　《略 EZZ》(国連海洋法条約により，沿岸国は200カイリ（約370キロメートル）まで排他的経済水域を設定することができ，この水域で沿岸国は海洋，海底とその下で天然資源の開発，探査，管理や経済活動に関して主権的権利を持つとされる．⇒EEZ)

▶Chinese development of the Chunxiao natural gas field could lead to violation of the *exclusive economic zone* (EEZ) claimed by Japan in the East China.　中国の春暁天然ガス田開発は，日本が主張する東シナ海の排他的経済水域（EEZ）の侵犯になる可能性がある．

execute 動　執行する，実行する，実施する，遂行する，履行する，達成する，完成する，〈契約書などを〉作成する，署名する，調印する

execute a trade　取引きを執行する

execute a stock [share] split　株式分割を実施する

execute an obligation created by the contract　契約で生じた義務を履行する

▶We will continue to *execute* our strategy.　私どもは，今後とも当社の経営戦略を推進していく所存です．

execution 名　執行（証券会社などが取引を実行すること），実行，実施，履行，施行，達成，成立，業務，署名，作成，調印，締結

daily execution　日常業務

execution date of this agreement　本契約締結日

execution of loan　ローンの実行

execution of stock warrants　ワラント［株式ワラント，新株引受権］の権利行使

execution time　〈プログラムの〉実行時間（＝running time)

order execution　注文執行，注文処理（＝execution of order)

skill in trade execution　取引執行力

term of execution　履行期限

▶The responsibilities of the Executive Committee include the delegation of certain authority for *execution* of bids, proposals and contracts.　経営委員会の権限としては，入札，提議や契約などの履行に関する権限の委譲も含まれています．

executive 名　経営者，管理職，重役，会社役員，役職員，執行役員，執行部，執行機関，エグゼクティブ

account executive　広告会社の営業責任者，証券会社のセールスマン　《略 AE》

business executive　企業経営者

Chief Executive　米大統領

chief executive　企業などのトップ

chief executive officer　最高業務執行役員，最高経営責任者　《略 CEO》

company executives　会社経営者，経営者（＝corporate executives)

current executives　現経営陣，現役員，現執行役

departmental executives　部門別業務執行役員

executive changes　役員の交代

executive committee　執行委員会，業務執行委員会，経営委員会　(⇒management executive committee)

executive counselor　取締役相談役

executive director　執行取締役，業務執行取締役，専務［常務］取締役

executive office　業務執行室

executive organization　管理組織

financial executive　財務担当役員，財務管理者，財務担当経営者，財務部門の幹部

former executives　旧経営陣

managing executive　業務執行役員，経営業務執行役員，事務局長

middle management executive　中間管理者，中間管理職にある人，中堅幹部

rebel executive　造反役員

senior executive　上級役員，上級管理者，経営者

top executive　最高経営者，最高執行者，最高経営幹部，経営首脳，経営者

▶Ford Motor Co. named Annes Stevens as its No.2 *executive* for the Americas.　フォード・モーターは，アン・スティーブンス氏を米州部門のナンバー2（創業102年で初の女性上級副社長）に指名した．

executive committee　経営委員会

▶Acting as the Nominating Committee of the Board, the *Executive Committee* recommends qualified candidates for election as officers and directors of the Company.　取締役会付属の指名委員会として機能する経営委員会は，当社の役員，取締役として適格な選任候補者を推薦します．

executive compensation　業務執行役員報酬，役員報酬

▶*Executive compensation* is directly related to performance.　役員報酬は，業績と直接連動しています．

executive compensation committee　役員報酬委員会，経営幹部報酬委員会

▶Members of the *executive compensation committee* are directors who are not officers or employees of the Company or its subsidiaries. 役員報酬委員会の委員は，当社もしくは子会社の役員または従業員でない取締役で構成されています。

executive remuneration packages 執行役員の報酬
▶The company will cut *executive remuneration packages* by 25-50 percent from fiscal 2008. 同社では，2008年度から執行役員の報酬を25-50%カットする。

exempt 動 免除する，名 免除されたもの［人，機関］，免税者，形 免除された，適用除外の，適用対象とはならない
　exempt company 適用除外会社
　exempt from …を免除された，…の適用除外になる，…の適用対象とはならない
　exempt income 非課税所得
　exempt securities 適用除外証券，免税証券
　exempt stock exchange 登録免除取引所
　tax-exempt bond 免税債，非課税債券

exemption 名 免除，適用除外，例外，免責，免税，控除，課税控除，控除額
　apply for exemption 課税控除を申請する
　basic exemption 基礎控除
　duty exemption 関税免除
　exemption clauses 免責条項，免責約款
　exemption for dependents 扶養控除
　exemption for spouse 配偶者控除
　exemption of cartel カルテルの適用対象外，カルテルの適用除外
　exemption of debt 債務免除（＝債務免除）
　exemption regime 適用除外基準
　full exemption 完全免除，完全免除方式，全額免除
　personal exemption 人的控除
　private offering exemption 私募免除
　tax exemption 免税（＝exemption from tax）
　transaction exemption 取引例外
▶The *exemption* will apply to buildings and warehouses valued at ¥1 billion or more and factories valued at ¥1.5 billion or more. この免責が適用されるのは，評価額が10億円以上のビル・倉庫と15億円以上の工場である。

exercisable 形 権利の行使可能な，行使できる
▶At December 31, 2008, all of these unexercised SARs were *exercisable*. 2008年12月31日現在，この未行使の株式評価受益権（SAR）はすべて行使可能です。
▶The options are *exercisable* during a period not to exceed ten years. このオプションの行使可能期間は，10年を超えない期間となっています。

exercise 動 〈オプション取引などで〉権利を行使する，実行する，〈指導力などを〉発揮する，〈影響・圧力などを〉及ぼす
▶During 2008, 167,747 stock appreciation rights (SARs) were *exercised*. 2008年度は，167,747株分の株式評価受益権（SAR）が行使されました。

exercise 名 権利の行使，行使，実行，努力，策
　cost-cutting exercise コスト削減策
　exercise price 行使価格，権利行使価格
　refinancing exercise 借換え債の発行
　substitutional exercise of voting right 議決権の代理行使
▶The Corporation will provide the shares available upon *exercise* of options either by issuance or by purchase on the open market. 当社は，選択権の行使に必要な株式を，新規発行または公開市場で購入して提供します。

exhaust 動 使い果たす，底をつく，消耗する，疲弊させる，涸渇させる，排出する，名 排出，排気ガス
　exhaust emission standards 排ガス規制
　exhaust gas [fumes] 排気ガス，排ガス
　exhaust gas controls 排ガス規制
　exhaust heat 排熱
　exhaust pipe 排気管（＝tailpipe）
　exhaust price 証拠金残額消耗価格
　exhaust system 排気装置
　stock exhaust 品切れ
▶Most land in cities is covered with blacktop streets and concrete buildings, with the result that there is little scope for *exhaust* heat to dissipate. 都市部の大半の地面は，アスファルトの舗装道路やコンクリートのビルに覆われているため，排熱が消失する余地がない。

exhibit 動 陳列する，出品する

exhibition 名 公開，一般公開，展示，表示，陳列，展覧，実演，展覧会，展示会，出品物，展示品，公開競技，講演会，奨学金，奨学資金，エキシビション
　art exhibition 美術展
　competitive exhibition 品評会，共進会
　exhibition game 模範競技，模範演技，エキシビション・ゲーム
　exhibition sales 展示販売，展示販売商法
　international exhibition 国際展示会，万国博覧会

exhibitor 名 出展者，出品者

exit 名 撤退，退出，退場，退去，退陣，出国，出口，〈プログラムの〉終了，動 撤退する，退場する，退

陣する
- **emergency exit** 非常口
- **exit barrier** 撤退障壁, 流出障壁 （=barriers to exit）
- **exit bond** 卒業債, エグジット・ボンド
- **exit fees** 脱退手数料
- **exit/divest** 撤退/投資撤退
- **exit interview** 退職者面接
- **exit the market** 市場から撤退する
- **exit velocity** 流出速度
- **exit poll** 出口調査
- **exit value** 売却価額
- **exit visa** 出国ビザ
- **orderly exit** 秩序ある撤退
- **port of exit** 輸出港

▶After the firm's *exit*, the number of foreign companies listed on the TSE's Foreign Section dropped to 36. 同社が撤退[上場廃止]した結果, 東証外国部に上場している企業は, 36社に減少した。

Exon-Florio provision of the 1988 trade law
1988年通商法のエクソン・フロリオ条項（米国の安全保障を損なう企業買収の禁止）
▶In the United States, the *Exon-Florio provision of the 1988 trade law* can prevent takeover bids that are deemed a threat to national security. 米国では, 1988年通商法のエクソン・フロリオ条項で, 国家の安全保障上, 脅威と考えられる企業買収を阻止することができる。

exorbitant 形 法外な, 過度の, 過大な
- **exorbitant demand** 不当要求, 途方もない要求
- **exorbitant price** 法外な値段, とんでもない値段, 不当価格
- **exorbitant taxes** 法外な課税

expand 動 拡大する, 拡張する, 拡充する, 増設する, 増やす （⇒capital-intensive industry）
- **expand capacity** 設備を拡張する
- **expand economies of scale** スケール・メリットを追求する
- **expanded board** 増設ボード
- **expanded economy** 景気拡大
- **expanded lead managers** 拡大主幹事
- **expanded memory specification** 拡張メモリ仕様, イーエムエス《略 EMS》
- **expanded reproduction** 拡大再生産
- **expanded voting rights** 投票権拡大

▶The two firms signed a $50 million contract to *expand* overseas telecommunications capabilities. 両社は, 国際通信機能を拡張するための5,000万ドルの契約に調印した。

expansion 名 拡大, 拡張, 設備拡張, 景気拡大, 成長, 上昇, 多角化
- **business expansion** 事業拡大, 事業拡張, 業容拡大
- **capital expansion** 増資, 資本増強 （=capital increase, increase of capital）
- **credit expansion** 信用拡大, 信用拡張, 信用膨張, 貸出の伸び
- **economic expansion** 景気回復, 景気拡大, 景気上昇, 経済成長
- **expansion of domestic demand** 内需拡大
- **expansion period** 景気拡大局面
- **factory expansion** 工場拡張
- **market expansion** 市場拡大
- **organizational expansion** 組織拡大, 企業組織の拡大
- **output expansion** 生産の増加, 生産の伸び, 生産拡大
- **quantitative expansion** 量的拡大
- **sustained economic expansion** 持続的な経済成長, 経済の持続的な成長
- **Trade Expansion Act** 通商拡大法

▶Toyota's growth is supported by the *expansion* of sales overseas. トヨタの成長を支えるのは, 海外での販売拡大だ。

expat 名 海外駐在員, 海外移住者, 国籍離脱者 （=expatriate）

expatriate 動 国外に追放する, 名 海外駐在員, 海外移住者, 国籍離脱者

expect 動 期待する, 見込む, 予想する, 見積もる, 推定する
- **expected earnings** 期待収益
- **expected income** 期待利益, 期待収益, 期待所得
- **expected life** 見積り耐用年数, 予想耐用年数 （=expectation of life, expected useful life）
- **expected loss** 予想損失, 損失の予想, 見込まれる損失, 赤字見通し
- **expected long-term rate of return on plan assets** 年金資産[制度資産]の長期期待収益率, 期待長期資産収益率, 制度資産の予想長期収益率
- **expected realizable profit** 期待実現可能利益
- **expected return on plan assets** 年金資産[年金制度資産]の予想運用利益率, 期待運用収益率

▶We *expect* continuing growth in this segment's revenues, earnings and assets in 2009. 当社は, 2009年度も引き続き当事業部門の収益, 利益と資産の増加を見込んでいます。

expectancy 名 期待, 見込み, 予想, 予測数量, 期待利益（expectation interest）, 履行利益, 将来財産権
- **expectancy table** 予想表

expectancy theory of motivation モチベーションの期待理論
life expectancy 平均寿命, 平均余命 (=expectancy of life, expectation of life)
expectation 名 期待, 予想, 見通し, 見積り, 推定, 期待値 (⇒**total sales**)
　expectation of life 見積り耐用年数, 期待耐用年数 (=expected life)
　expectations for the year as a whole 通期予想, 通期見通し, 年間予想
　▶Contrary to prevailing market *expectations*, the central bank decided not to further ease monetary policy. 市場の大方の期待を裏切って［期待に反して］, 日銀は追加的な金融緩和策を見送った.
expected long-term rate of return 予想長期収益率
　▶The *expected long-term rate of return* on plan assets is used in the calculation of net periodic pension cost. 年金資産の予想長期収益率は, 期間年金費用純額の計算に使われる.
expected net profit 予想純利益, 予想される［見込まれる］純利益
　▶Decline in the *expected net profit* is attributable mainly to the possible unfavorable effects of the yen's rise against the dollar. 予想される純利益減少の主な要因は, 円高・ドル安の不利な影響である.
expected useful life 見積り耐用年数 (=estimated useful life, expected life)
　▶Depreciation is generally computed using the straight-line method, based on the *expected useful lives* of the assets. 原価償却は, 原則として資産の見積り耐用年数に基づいて, 定額法で計算されています.
expedite 動 促進する, 進捗させる
expenditure 名 支出, 経費, 費消, 消費量, 支払い義務額 (⇒**capital expenditure**)
　consolidated income and expenditure account 連結損益計算書
　current expenditure 当期支出, 当期支払い, 当期費用, 経常的支出
　expenditures for plant and equipment 有形固定資産購入
　expenditures for real estate, plants and equipment 不動産, 工場および設備の取得額
　expenditures for special tools 特殊工具の取得額
　fixed asset expenditures 固定資産支出額
　miscellaneous expenditure 雑費
　progress expenditure 製作費
　real expenditure 実質的経費
　▶Fixed asset *expenditures* required to support current and long-term growth increased to $3 billion from $2.1 billion in 2007. 現在の成長と長期的成長を維持するために必要な固定資産支出額は, 2007年度の21億ドルから当年度は30億ドル増加しました.
expense 動 費用処理する, 費用に計上する, 費用として計上する (⇒**cost**)
　amounts expensed as pension costs 年金原価として費用処理した額
　be expensed as written off 貸倒れ損失として費用処理する
　▶Previously, we *expensed* life insurance benefits as plans were funded. これまで当社は, 生命保険給付については, 制度に拠出が行われた時点で費用として計上していました.
expense 名 費用, 経費, 支出 (→**operating expense**)
　business expenses 営業経費, 営業費, 事業費用
　central corporate expense 本社費用
　compensation expense 報償費用
　corporate expense 本部費, 本部経費
　current expenses 経常費
　debt expense 貸倒れ損失, 社債発行費
　deferred expense 営業費用
　direct expense 直接経費
　distribution expense 販売経費, 販売費, 配電費
　estimated expense 見積り費用
　expense arising from outside manufacture 外注加工費
　expense on bonds 社債発行費
　expense paid 支払い経費, 支払い済み費用
　expenses paid in advance 未経過費用
　experimental and research expense 試験研究費
　factory expense 製造間接費
　financial expense 財務費用, 金融費用, 財務費（資金調達, 資金の管理に伴う費用）
　loss adjustment expense 損害査定費
　necessary expenses 必要経費
　nonrecurrent expense 経常外費用
　normal expense 正常費用
　occupancy expense 賃借料
　operations expenses 業務経費
　secret service expense 機密費
　standing expense 経常費
　▶In the former accounting method, we booked *expenses* for separations when we identified

them. 従来の会計処理方法では、休職に関する費用は休職を確認した時点で記帳していました。

experience 動 経験する、体験する、味わう、…になる、…を示す、…に見舞われる、〈問題などを〉抱える、…の実績がある
  experience payment default 貸倒れになる
  experience strong growth rate 力強い伸び率を示す
  experience weak demand 需要が低迷する、需要低迷に見舞われる
  ▸In the second quarter, all of our geographic markets *experienced* growth. 第2四半期は、当社の全地域市場で業績が拡大しました。
  ▸The uncertainties *experienced* in world economies will continue to pressure our industry. 世界経済が抱える不安定要因は、今後も当業界を圧迫すると思われます。

experience 名 経験、体験、習得、実績、状況、経緯、動向
  business experience ビジネス経験、企業経営の経験（⇒**serve on, a committee**）
  experience adjustment 実績による修正
  experience-based pricing 経験に基づく価格設定、実績に基づく価格設定
  experience gains and losses 経験的利得および損失
  loss experience 貸倒れ損失実績、損失経験
  management experience 経営の経験
  operational experience 業務実績
  purchase experience 購入経験、購入実績
  write off experience 償却実績

expertise 名 専門知識、専門技術、専門家の報告書、ノウハウ（＝knowhow）
  advanced expertise 先端的ノウハウ、高度な専門知識・技術
  financial expertise 金融ノウハウ
  manufacturing expertise 生産技術、生産のノウハウ
  product expertise 製品のノウハウ、製品知識、番組などの制作のノウハウ
  technical expertise 技術ノウハウ、技術的専門意見、専門技術
  technological expertise 技術的専門知識、技術ノウハウ
  ▸By utilizing Imperial Hotel's brand and hotel management *expertise*, Mitsui Fudosan and the Imperial Hotel will cooperate in the hotel and resort facilities business. 帝国ホテルのブランドとホテル運営のノウハウを生かして、三井不動産と帝国ホテルは今後、ホテル・リゾート施設事業で連携する。

expiration 名 〈契約期間の〉満了、満期、失効、終了、消滅
  expiration date 消費期限（date of expiry, expiry date）、有効期限
  ▸Upon *expiration* or termination of this contract, Distributor will immediately cease all display, advertising and use of all of Supplier's names, trademarks and logos. 本契約の満了または終了と同時に、「販売店」は直ちに「供給者」のすべての名称、商標とロゴの陳列、宣伝および使用を一切止めることにする。

expire 動 満期になる、満期を迎える、終了する、〈満期になって〉失効する、期限が切れる、消滅する
  expire or terminate 〈契約などが〉満了または終了する
  expired card 期限切れカード
  expired contract 満期契約、期間経過契約
  expired cost 費消原価
  expired deal 満期となった案件
  expired utility 経過効用、費消効用
  ▸The warrants *expire* on December 31, 2009. このワラントは、2009年12月31日に消滅する。
  ▸This agreement *expires* next month. この契約の期限は、来月切れる。

exploit 動 〈鉱山・天然資源などを〉開発する、活用する、利用する、宣伝する、搾取する（⇒**factor**）

exploration 名 探査、探鉱、探検、踏査、調査、研究、開発、診察、触診
  oil exploration 石油探査
  seismic exploration 地震探鉱、地震探査
  space exploration 宇宙開発、宇宙探検

exponential 形 指数の、指数関数的な

export 名 輸出、輸出品、輸出製品、供給
  approval of export license 輸出承認
  bounty for export 輸出助成金、輸出奨励金
  capital export 資本輸出、資本供給
  capital goods export 資本財の輸出
  collateral export 見返り輸出
  commodity export 商品輸出
  deferred payment export 延払い輸出
  documentary export bill 輸出荷為替
  Export Administration Act 米国の輸出管理法
  export base 輸出拠点
  export competitiveness 輸出競争力
  export subsidy 輸出助成金
  export surcharge 輸出課徴金
  foreign export earnings 外貨獲得
  growth in exports 輸出の伸び
  illegal export 迂回輸出

increase in exports 輸出の増加, 輸出の伸び
industrial exports 製品輸出, 工業製品輸出
invisible export 貿易外輸出
knockdown export ノックダウン輸出
manufactured exports 製品輸出, 工業製品輸出
plant export プラント輸出
service export サービス輸出
technology export 技術輸出
voluntary export restraint 輸出自主規制 （= voluntary export restriction）

▶The strong performance of major companies has been achieved because of increases in *exports* to the United States and China. 大企業が好業績を上げているのは, 米国と中国向けの輸出が伸びたからだ。

Export Administration Regulations
輸出管理規則

▶The export of products made using such confidential information is prohibited by the U.S. Department of Commerce's *Export Administration Regulations*. この秘密情報を用いて製造した製品の輸出は, 米国商務省の輸出管理規則により禁止されている。

export drive 輸出ドライブ, 輸出攻勢, 輸出競争力, 輸出拡大圧力

▶The rapid surge in the yen's value could deal a blow to Japan's *export drive* and export-related businesses. 急激な円高は, 日本の輸出競争力の低下や輸出関連企業の業績悪化をもたらす可能性がある。

export-driven growth 輸出主導の成長, 輸出頼みの成長

▶It is unclear whether *export-driven* growth can continue. 輸出頼みの成長を続けられるどうか, 先行きには不透明感がある。

export license 輸出承認

▶In order to export such data or product, a validated *export license* must be obtained. 当該データまたは製品を輸出するには, 輸出承認の許可を得なければならない。

export market 輸出市場

▶In Asia, one of Japan's main *export markets*, Thailand and Malaysia are considering raising their tariffs. 日本の主力輸出市場であるアジアでは, タイやマレーシアが関税の引上げを検討している。

export-oriented companies 輸出企業

▶*Export-oriented companies* will be hit hard if the yen accelerates its rise. 円高が加速すると, 輸出企業は大きな打撃を受ける。

expose 動 〈危険に〉さらす, 暴露する, 公然と売り出す, 陳列する, 展示する, 摘発する, すっぱ抜く, 経験させる
be exposed to credit risk 信用リスクを負う, 与信リスクを負う, 信用リスクにさらされる
be exposed to interest rate risk 金利リスクにさらされる
be exposed to losses 損失を被る
expose goods for sale 販売商品を陳列する, 販売品を展示する

exposure 名 リスク危険度, 投資, 融資, リスク資産総額, 融資総額, 与信残高, 債権額, エクスポージャー
currency exposure 為替リスク, 通貨リスク
economic exposure 経済リスク (=economic risk)
exposure limit 与信枠
exposure threshold リスク限度額
exposure to changes in interest rates 金利変動リスク
exposure to credit risk 信用リスク
exposure to interest rates 金利変動リスク
exposure to losses 損失負担, 損失リスク
financial exposure 資金負担, 金融リスク
hedge the exposure リスクをヘッジする
interest exposure 金利リスク, 金利変動リスク, 金利エクスポージャー
problem exposures 不良債権
reduce exposure to the risk of loss 損失リスクを減らす, 損失リスクを軽減する

▶We control our *exposure* to credit risk through credit approvals, credit limits and monitoring procedures. 当社は, 信用供与承認, 信用限度と監視手続きを通して信用リスクを管理しています。

▶We make interest rate swap contracts to manage our *exposure* to changes in interest rates and lower our overall financing costs. 当社は, 金利変動リスクに対処する目的と資金調達コストを低減する目的で, 金利スワップ契約を結んでいます。

express 形 急行の, 至急の, 急送の, 高速の, 速達の, 明示された, 明確な, 明白な
expropriate 動 収用する
extend 動 延ばす, 延長する, 拡大する, 拡張する, 提供する, 差し伸べる, 与える, 供与する
extend a marketing period 販売期間を延長する
extend credit 信用を供与する
extend funds 資金を拠出する
extended coverage 拡張担保
extended fund facility 拡大信用供与

▶Ford *extended* through Sept. 6 its incentive program reducing customer prices to employee-discount levels. フォードは，小売価格[顧客販売価格]を社員向け値引きの水準にまで引き下げる販売促進策を，9月6日まで延期した。

extension 名 拡大, 拡張, 延長, 機能拡張, 拡張工事, 期間延長, 付属電話機, 内線, 範囲, 程度
  double extension 二重計算
  extension of coverage 担保範囲の拡張
  extension of credit 信用供与, 信用の拡大
  extension of employment 雇用延長
  extension risk 期間延長リスク
  reserve for business extension 事業拡張積立金
external 形 外部の, 対外的な, 国外の
  external assets 対外資産, 対外資産残高
  external audit 外部監査
  external balance 対外均衡, 国際均衡
  external bond 外債
  external debt 対外債務
  external deficit 国際収支の赤字
  external demand 海外需要, 外需, 純輸出
  external diseconomies 外部不経済
  external economies 外部経済
  external financing 外部調達資金, 外部資金の調達, 外部金融 (=external funding)
  external fund 外部資金
  external growth 外部的成長, 外部的成長率
  external labor market 外部労働市場
  external reserves 対外準備, 外貨準備
  external surplus 国際収支の黒字
▶We expect to meet our cash requirements in 2009 from operations and *external* financing. 当社は，業務活動によってもたらされる資金と外部資金調達で，2009年度の必要資金を確保する方針です。
externalize 動 外部化する
extinguish 動 無効化する, 失効させる, 〈負債を〉償却する
extort 動 強要する, 強請する, 要求する
extraordinary 形 特別の, 臨時の, 異常な
  extraordinary board of directors meeting 臨時取締役会
  extraordinary credit 特別控除, 異常利益
  extraordinary expenses 臨時費用, 臨時費, 特別損失

  extraordinary gain 特別利益, 異常利得
  extraordinary income and charge 異常損益
extraordinary income 特別利益, 臨時利益
▶Sale of buildings to a subsidiary of the firm in which we hold a 25 percent interest, resulted in *extraordinary income* of $5 million. 当社が25％の株式を所有する同社の子会社に建物を売却したのに伴い，500万ドルの特別利益が生じました。
extraordinary item 特別(損益)項目, 異常(損益)項目, 臨時(損益)項目, 非経常(的)項目 (⇒ **income before extraordinary items, tax benefit**)
  after the extraordinary item 異常損益控除後
  before an extraordinary item 異常損益項目控除前利益, 異常項目控除前
▶For the nine months, net income applicable to common shares from continuing operations and before the *extraordinary item* was $115 million. 継続事業による1－9月期の普通株式に帰属する純利益は，異常損益項目控除前で1億1,500万ドルでした。
extraordinary loss 特別損失, 異常損失, 経常外損失 (=special loss)
▶The company will likely book a total *extraordinary loss* of $170 million for the potential U.S. plant closure. 同社は，予想される米国工場の閉鎖で，総額1億7,000万ドルの特別損失を計上する見込みだ。
extraordinary profit 特別利益 (保有株式の売却やメーカーの工場売却による利益)
▶The leading banks' loan loss charges were returned as *extraordinary profit*. 大手銀行の貸倒れ引当金は，特別利益として戻ってきた。
extraordinary shareholders meeting 臨時株主総会 (=extraordinary general meeting, extraordinary meeting of shareholders, special meeting of shareholders, special meeting of stockholders: 原則として年1回開く定時株主総会とは別に，定款変更など株主総会決議が必要な重要事項の決定を行うときに開く)
▶The company will hold an *extraordinary shareholders meeting* in June to choose new directors. 同社は，6月に臨時株主総会を開いて，後任取締役[新任取締役]を決める。
extrapolate 動 〈未知のことを〉推定[推測]する, 〈既知の事実を〉推定に用いる

F f

401(k) 米内国歳入庁コード401(k), 米国の企業年金（給与所得者の退職基金積立制度の一つで, 積立金は天引き貯蓄され, 税法上の所得控除が受けられる）

401(k)-style pension scheme 確定拠出型年金制度, 日本版401k（米国の企業年金「401(k)プラン」を参考にして作られた年金制度で, 加入者の運用次第で老後の受給額が変動する仕組みになっている）
▶The firm introduced a *401(k)-style pension scheme* for about 10,000 office workers. 同社は, 約1万人の内勤職員を対象に確定拠出型年金制度(日本版401k)を導入した。

FA 工場の自動化, ファクトリー・オートメーション（factory automationの略）

fab 名 工場, マイクロチップ製造工場, 工程, 拠点, 形 素晴らしい(fabulous), 卓越した, 第一級の
new fab 新工場
production fab 生産工場, 生産拠点

fabless 名 工場を持たない企業, ファブレス, 形 工場なしの, 製造設備を持たない

fabric 名 織物, 布地, 基本, 基礎, 基盤, 基本構造, 構造, 構成, 機構, 仕組み, 組織, 組立て方, 建築物
be woven into the fabric of …の一部になる
fabric softener 柔軟仕上げ剤（=fabric conditioner）
social fabric 社会構造, 社会組織（=the fabric of society）
▶We will bring about the changes we need to be successful in the global marketplace by making diversity an integral part of the *fabric* of our business. 当社は, 多様性を当社のビジネス基盤の不可欠な一部として, グローバル市場で成功を収めるのに必要な変革をもたらす方針です。

fabricate 動 組み立てる, 製作する, 製造する, 生産する, 加工する, 捏造する, 偽造する, でっち上げる, 改竄する
fabricated earnings 架空収益
fabricated expenses 架空経費
fabricated metal products 加工金属製品
fabricated parts 組立部品（=fabricating parts）
fabricated results 粉飾決算, 業績改竄
fabricating cost 製造原価
fabricating industry 組立産業
fabricating materials 組立材料, 加工材料
▶A Tokyo Electric Power Co. nuclear power station *fabricated* inspection data. 東京電力の原子力発電所が, 点検データを改竄した。
▶The president of the company ordered *fabricated* results. 同社の社長が, 粉飾決算を指示した。

fabrication 名 組立て, 製作, 製造, 生産, 加工, 工程, 構成, 捏造, 偽造, でっち上げ, 改竄, 偽造文書
fabrication capability 製造[製作]技術, 加工技術
fabrication plant 組立工場

face 名 額面, 券面, 表面, 表面記載事項, 文面, 文言, フェース（⇒fall）
face amount 額面金額, 額面価額, 額面, 券面額（=face value）
face-to-face communication 対面コミュニケーション
face-to-face group 面接集団, 対面集団

face-to-face selling 対面販売
face value 額面価格［価額］, 額面, 券面額（= face amount）
face value of bonds 社債額面
issue at face value 額面で発効する
non-face to face transaction 非対面販売
repay at face value at maturity 満期に額面で償還する
unless otherwise stated on the face of hereof 本契約書の文面上, 特段［別段］の記載がないかぎり
▸As of December 31, 2008, the outstanding zero coupon notes due 2023 had a *face* value at maturity of $140 million. 2008年12月31日現在, 2023年満期ゼロ・クーポン債の満期時の額面総額は, 1億4,000万ドルです。
▸There will be no warranties which extend beyond the description on the *face* hereof. 本書の表面に記載したこと以外の保証はないものとする［ここに記載した事項以外に, 保証はしないものとする］。

facilitate 動 助長する, 促進する, 進める, 容易にする, 楽にする
▸To *facilitate* this, reforms are necessary concerning preferential treatment in depreciation-related taxes, laws concerning bankruptcy, the division of companies and debt-equity swaps. これを進めるには, 償却関連税制の優遇措置や, 倒産・会社分割・債務の株式化に関連する法制などの改革が必要である。

facility 名 融資, 融資枠, 信用供与, 信用枠, 与信枠, 便宜, 什器（じゅうき）, 設備, 施設, 工場, 制度, ファシリティ（⇒**credit facilities**）
borrowing facilities 信用枠
credit facility 信用供与, 信用供与制度, 金融制度, クレジット・ファシリティ
excess facilities 過剰設備（= excess capacity, surplus facilities, unwanted facilities）
facilities and equipment 設備
facility fee 与信枠設定費用, ファシリティ・フィー
facility management 設備の管理・運用, コンピュータの他社管理, ファシリティ・マネジメント
factory facilities 工場設備
guarantee facility 債務保証
idle facility 遊休施設
loan facility 貸付け, 融資枠
manufacturing facilities 生産拠点, 生産設備（= production facilities）
new facilities 新規融資

production facility 生産設備
storage facilities 貯蔵設備
transmission facilities 送電設備, 変電設備
▸At December 31, 2008, the Company's total domestic and foreign credit *facilities* aggregated $2.5 billion. 2008年12月31日現在, 当社の国内および国外与信枠の総額は, 25億ドルとなっています。
▸The *facility* will be upsized. 融資枠は, 拡大される見込みだ。
▸The segment's fixed costs and production *facility* capacity increased when compared to 2007. 2007年度に比べて, 固定費や生産設備の能力は増大しました。
▸We use accelerated depreciation methods for factory facilities and digital equipment used in the telecommunication network. 工場設備と電気通信ネットワークに使用されているデジタル機器については, 当社は加速償却法で償却しています。

fact 名 事実, 真実, 実際, 実情, 真相, 現実, 申立て, 申し立てられた事実, 事項, 犯行, ファクト
after the fact control 事後管理
before the fact control 事前管理
fact database ファクト・データベース
fact-finding mission 実情調査団, 現地調査団
fact-finding survey 実態調査, 実情調査, 現地調査（= fact-finding investigation）
fact sheet ファクト・シート（事実を図表化したデータ表）
facts and figures 詳細なデータ, 正確な情報

factor 名 要素, 要因, 因子, 材料, 原動力, 金融業者, 金融機関, ファクタリング業者, 債権買取り業者, …率, 係数, 指数, ファクター（⇒**negative factor**）
buying factors 買い材料
competitive factor 競争要因
contributing factor 貢献要因
cost factor コスト要因, 原価要素
dilution factor 希薄化率
factor cost 生産要素費用, 要素費用
factor input 要素投入
factor price 要素価格
favorable factor 好材料
internal factor 内部要因
load factor 負荷率, ロード・ファクター
market factor 市場要因, 市場因子, 市場要素
multiple factors 複合的な要因
negative factor マイナス要因, 悪材料, 売り材料
one-off factor 一時的な要因
positive factor プラス要因, 好材料, 買い材料

productive factor 生産要素 （＝production factor）
production factor 生産要素
seasonal factor 季節要因
temporary factor 一時的要因
▸It will not be easy to rehabilitate the company, which has been driven into the red by multiple *factors*. 同社は，複合的な要因による赤字転落なので，再建は容易ではない。
▸Other competitive *factors* in the market for the products are service, delivery, technological capability, and product quality and performance. 市場での製品の競争要因としては，サービスや納入，技術活用能力，品質，性能なども挙げられます。
▸Speculators exploited these buying *factors*, pushing oil prices up further. 投機筋がこれらの買い材料に反応して［投機筋がこれらの買い材料を利用して］，原油価格の高騰［原油高］を増幅している。
factoring 名 債権買取り，債権取立て，売上債権の買取り業務，売却，ファクタリング
debt factoring 債権買取り
factoring company 債権買取り会社，ファクタリング会社
factoring with recourse 遡求権付き売却
factory 名 工場，生産設備，製造業，メーカー，在外［海外］代理店
assembly factory 組立工場
ex factory 工場渡し
factory backlog 製造業受注残高
factory burden 製造間接費，工場間接費 （＝factory expense, factory overhead, manufacturing overhead）
factory capacity 工場の生産能力，生産設備能力
factory closing 工場閉鎖 （＝factory closure）
factory cost 製造原価，製造コスト，工場原価 （＝manufacturing cost）
factory demand 製造業新規受注高
factory expense 製造間接費，製造経費，工場経費 （＝factory burden, manufacturing expense）
factory furniture 工場備品，工場の什器（じゅうき）備品 （＝factory fitting, factory furnitures and fixtures）
factory-gate price 工場渡し価格 （＝factory price）
factory hand 職工，工員
factory industry 工場制工業
factory management 工場管理

factory overhead cost 製造間接費 （＝factory overhead, factory overhead expense, manufacturing overhead）
factory orders 製造業受注，製造業受注高，，製造業新規受注高
factory output 製造業生産高
factory owner 工場主
factory personnel 工場労働者，工員，ブルー・カラー
factory price 工場渡し価格 （＝factory-gate price）
factory sector 製造業部門
factory shipment 工場出荷
factory shop 工場直販店 （＝factory outlet, factory-owned outlet）
factory site 工場敷地
factory space 工業用不動産
factory stockpiles 製造業在庫 （＝factory inventories）
factory supplies 工場消耗品，補助材料
factory test 工場試験
factory worker 工場労働者 （＝blue-collar worker）
obsolete factories 老朽化した生産設備
unmanned factory 無人工場
▸Toyota is considering building a *factory* to make engines for compact cars in Miyagi Prefecture. トヨタは，宮城県内に小型車のエンジン生産工場を新設する計画を検討している。
fail 動 経営破綻する，破綻する，倒産する，破産する，失敗する，…を怠る （＝collapse）
failed bank 経営破綻銀行，破綻銀行
failed borrower 融資先企業の経営破綻，経営破綻した融資先
failed company 経営破綻した企業，破綻企業
failed nonlife insurer 破綻損保
▸We *failed* to acquire a majority stake in the company in our tender offer. 当社は，TOB（株式公開買付け）で同社株の過半数株式を取得できませんでした。
fail safe 安全機能，安全装置，絶対安全性，障害時の安全性，フェール・セーフ
fail-safe system 障害時安全システム
fail soft 障害時の運転可能性，フェール・ソフト
fail-soft system 障害時運転可能システム
fail to …できない，…しない，…することを怠る
▸The facility has *failed to* pay about ¥56 million in local taxes over the last two years. 同施設は，過去2年間の地方税約5,600万円を滞納している。
▸The firm *failed to* recall about 160,000 vehicles

of 17 models. 同社は，乗用車など17車種約16万台のリコール（回収，無償交換）を怠っていた．

failure 名 経営破綻，破綻，倒産，破産，〈債務などの〉不履行，失敗，〈機械などの〉機能停止，故障，障害（=collapse）
　bank failure 銀行破綻（=bank's collapse; ⇒ ceiling, protect）
　business failure 企業倒産（=bankruptcy, insolvency）
　corporate failure 企業倒産，経営破綻（= corporate bankruptcy）
　financial failures 金融破綻
　system failure システムの故障，システムのトラブル，システム障害
　▸One insurance company's *failure* has a great impact on banks that are closely linked to the insurer by means of cross-shareholding. 生保の破綻は，株式の密接な持ち合い関係にある銀行に重大な影響を及ぼします．

fair 名 見本市，展示会，博覧会，定期市，慈善市，市，バザー，共進会，品評会，フェア
　agricultural fair 農産物共進会
　church fair 教会バザー
　county fair 郡共進会，郡農産物共進会
　floating fair 巡航見本市
　international trade fair 国際見本市
　job fair 会社説明会（=career fair）
　state fair 州共進会，州農産物共進会
　summer fair 夏の市
　trade fair 見本市
　world's fair 万国博覧会，国際見本市

fair 形 公正な，公平な，平等な，差別をしない，妥当な，適正な，正しい，美しい，魅力的な，汚れのない，フェア
　fair average quality 標準品《略 FAQ》
　fair competition 公正競争
　fair copy 清書
　Fair Credit Reporting Act 公正信用報告法，公正消費者信用報告法
　fair employment 公正雇用，公平雇用
　Fair Employment Practices Committee 米公正雇用慣行委員会《略 FEPC》
　fair labor practice 公正労働行為
　fair play 公正な取扱い，公明正大な処置，平等な行動，フェア・プレー
　fair presentation 適正表示，公正表示
　fair price 適正価格
　fair shake 公正な扱い，平等な扱い，公平な処置
　fair trade 公正取引，適正取引
　fair trade price 公正取引価格，適正取引価格
　fair trial 公正な裁判
　fair use 公正使用
　Rules of Fair Practice 公正慣習規則

fair competition 公正競争，公正な競争
　▸*Fair competition* is functioning in the nation's telecommunications industry. 国内通信業界では，公正な競争が機能している．

Fair Labor Standards Act 〈米国の〉公正労働基準法《略 FLSA》
　▸All goods were produced in compliance with the applicable requirements of the *Fair Labor Standards Act*. 商品は，すべて公正労働基準法（FLSA）の適用要件に従って生産されたものです．

fair market value 公正市場価格，適正市場価格，公正市場価値，公正価値，公正価，時価
　▸This realty had a *fair market value* of $500,000 at the date of the grant. この不動産の贈与時の時価は，50万ドルであった．

Fair Trade Commission 〈日本の〉公正取引委員会《略 FTC》
　▸The *Fair Trade Commission* plans to punish five manufacturers in Japan, Britain, France and Italy as these firms formed an international cartel. 公正取引委員会は，国際カルテルを結んでいたとして，日英仏伊のメーカー5社を処分する方針だ．

fair value 公正価額，公正価格，公正価値，公正な評価額，適正価額，時価
　▸The *fair value* of our pension plan assets is greater than our projected pension obligations. 当社の年金制度資産の公正価額は，予想年金債務額を上回っています．

fake 形 偽の，偽造の，改竄した，偽物の，いかさまの，狂言の，動 偽造する，模造する，変造する，改竄する，捏造する，複写する，模写する
　fake business trip カラ出張
　fake credit card 偽造クレジット・カード（= counterfeit credit card）
　fake product コピー製品，偽ブランド製品（= pirated product）
　fake transaction 偽装売買，偽装取引
　faked quake-resistance data 改竄した耐震強度データ，耐震強度データの改竄
　▸The practice of *fake* overtime payments had been widespread in the labor bureaus. 労働局では，カラ残業代［実態に合わない超過勤務手当］を支給する行為が横行していた．

fall 動 下落する，低下する，減少する，崩壊する，失墜する，手形の期限が来る
　fall across the board 全面安となる

fall below …を割り込む, …を割る
fall short of …を下回る
falling backlog 受注残高の減少
falling company 経営不振の会社, 経営不振企業
falling demand 需要の低下, 需要の減少
falling interest rates 金利の低下
falling market 下げ相場
falling prices 物価の下落
falling stock market 株価の下落

▶Mizuho's first-half profit *fell* 17 percent as credit costs increased and on losses related to investments in U.S. home loans to riskier borrowers. みずほの上半期利益は, 与信コストの増加とリスクの高い融資先への米国の住宅ローン投資に関連する損失で, 17％減少した。

▶The prices of these companies' stock have declined to *fall* below the face value. これらの企業の株価は, 額面を下回っている。

fall 名 下落, 低下, 減少, 崩壊, 失墜 (⇒**free fall**)
fall in rates [interest rates] 金利の低下
fall in the jobless rate 失業率の低下, 雇用の増加
fall in the value of the dollar ドル安
free fall of the stock market 株式市場の暴落, 株式市場の急落

▶The increase in employment was modest compared with the *fall* in the jobless rate. 雇用[就業者]の増加は, 失業率の減少と比べて緩やかな伸びにとどまった。

fall-back position 代替策

▶As a *fall-back position*, the government plans to privatize public corporations if it cannot abolish them. 代替策として, 特殊法人を廃止できない場合には, 政府は特殊法人の民営化を計画している。

fall flat 失敗する, 大失敗する, 成立しない, 期待にこたえられない

▶Don Quijote's Origin Toshu bid *fell flat*. ドン・キホーテがオリジン東秀に対して行ったTOB（株式公開買付け）は, 不成立に終わった。

false 形 不正な, 不法な, 不正確な, 虚偽の, 偽造の, 偽の, 人造の

false consolidated financial statements 虚偽の連結財務書類, ウソの連結財務書類

▶These four accountants worked with the firm's former executives to produce *false consolidated financial statements*. これら4人の会計士は, 同社の旧経営陣と共謀してウソの連結財務書類を作成した。

falsify 動 偽造する, 偽装する, 改竄する, 捏造する, 変造する, 詐称する, 虚偽記載する
falsified financial documents 虚偽の財務書類
falsified financial report 有価証券報告書の虚偽記載, 財務報告書の虚偽記載
falsified stock dealing 株式の偽装売買, 偽装株式取引
falsified stock option dealing 株式オプションの偽装売買, 偽装株式オプション
falsified transaction 不正取引, 仮装売買, 偽装売買, 偽装取引 (＝fake transaction, falsified trading)

▶Four certified public accountants conspired with the firm's former executives to *falsify* accounting reports. 公認会計士4人が, 同社の旧経営陣と共謀して会計報告書[有価証券報告書]に虚偽の記載をした。

family 名 一連の製品, 製品ファミリー, 製品群, 家族, 家庭, 同族, 一族, 世帯, 集団, ファミリー
corporate family グループ企業
Family and Medical Leave Act 米育児介護休業法《略 FMLA》
family buying behavior 家族購買行動
family characteristics 家族特性
family company 同族会社, 同族企業 (＝family corporation, family-owned business: 3人以下の株主が資本金の50％以上を占めている会社)
family computer communication ファミコン通信
family feud お家騒動, 内紛
family income 家族所得, 家庭所得, 家族収入, 世帯所得
family life cycle 家族ライフ・サイクル, 家族周期
family owned company 同族会社, 同族経営企業 (＝family company)
family owners 創業者一族
family ownership of business 同族会社, 自営業
full-time farm family 専業農家 (＝full-time farmer)
high-income family 高所得世帯
middle-income family 中間所得世帯
nuclear family 核家族
product family 製品群, 製品ファミリー (＝family of products)
two-earner family 共稼ぎ世帯

Fannie Mae 米連邦住宅抵当金庫, ファニー・メイ (**Federal National Mortgage Association**の通称)

FAQ よく聞かれる質問事項とその答え (Frequently Asked Questions/Frequently Answered Questionsの略)
　buyer FAQ 買い手用FAQ
　customer FAQ 顧客用FAQ
　investor FAQ 投資家用FAQ
　seller FAQ 売り手用FAQ
▸Visit *FAQ*. There you can find answers to most frequently asked questions. FAQをご参照ください。お問い合わせの多い質問に対する答えが，掲載されています。

fare 名 運賃，料金，乗客，作品，出し物
　fare increase 運賃値上げ
　joint fare 乗り継ぎ運賃
　private railway fares 私鉄運賃
　time-of-day fare 時間帯別運賃
▸Japan Airlines System Corp. and All Nippon Airways Co. have decided to raise *fares* on international flights by an average of 5 percent. 日本航空システムと全日本空輸は，国際線の旅客運賃の平均5％値上げを決めた。

Farm Credit Administration 米農業信用局《略 FCA》

farm out 下請に出す，仕事を請け負わせる，仕事をまかせる，丸投げする
▸A growing number of major general construction companies are increasingly hesitant about *farming out* their projects to subcontractors. 大手ゼネコンの間で，工事の下請業者への丸投げ（一括下請け）を自粛する動きが次第に広まっている。

FARs 米連邦調達規則 (Federal Acquisition Regulationsの略)

FASB 米国の財務会計基準審議会 (Financial Accounting Standards Boardの略)
▸The Company adopted the provisions of the *FASB*'s Statement of Financial Accounting Standards (SFAS) No. 106 in 2008. 2008年度から当社は，財務会計基準審議会（FASB）の財務会計基準書第106号を採用しました。

fast breeder reactor 高速増殖炉《略 FBR》 (=fast breeder, fast breeder nuclear reactor)
▸A *fast breeder reactor* burns plutonium and uranium, producing more plutonium than it consumes. 高速増殖炉は，プルトニウムとウランを燃やして，使った以上のプルトニウムを作り出す。

fast food 即席簡易食品，ファースト・フード (fast service foodの略)
　fast food industry 外食産業，ファースト・フード産業
　fast food outlet ファースト・フード店，ファースト・フード販売店
　fast food providers 外食業界，ファースト・フード業界

fast-growing segment 急成長分野，急成長産業部門
▸We are aiming at some of the *fast-growing segments*. 当社は，急成長産業部門の一部に狙いを定めています。

fast track 出世街道，出世コース，最短コース，突貫工事

fast-track 形 出世コースに乗った，出世コースの，出世が早い
　fast-track bill 無修正・一括審議法案，ファースト・トラック法案 (=trade promotion authority bill: 米大統領の通商交渉権限を強化する法案)
　fast-track bureaucrat キャリア官僚
▸It is the first time a *fast-track* bureaucrat has been accused of insider trading. キャリア官僚がインサイダー取引で告発されたのは，これが初めてだ。

fault 名 過失，過誤，欠陥，瑕疵（かし），欠点，不完全，故障，障害，フォールト
　fault check 故障検査
　fault clearance 故障修復，故障処理，障害時対策，障害時対応
　fault diagnosis 故障診断
　fault or negligence 過失
　fault recovery 故障回復，故障処理，故障修理，障害処理，障害時対応
　fault tolerant computer 無停止型コンピュータ
▸All materials and equipment furnished by and workmanship performed by the Contractor shall be of first quality for the grades specified and free from defects or *faults*. 工事請負業者［工事請負人，契約者］が供給するすべての資材［材料］，設備と施工の仕上がりは，規定の等級に関して最高品質のもので，瑕疵（かし）・欠陥もないものとする。
▸Maintenance of telecommunication equipments and *fault* clearance are covered by the monthly charge of this service. 通信機器の保守と故障修理［障害時対応］は，本サービスの月額料金に含まれています。

favorable 形 有利な，好都合な，好ましい，良好な，好調な，明るい，追い風になる (⇒maturity)
　favorable balance of payments 国際収支の黒字
　favorable balance of trade 輸出超過
　favorable economic and political environ-

ments 良好な政治・経済環境
favorable exports 好調な輸出, 輸出好調
favorable factor 好材料
favorable inflation outlook 明るいインフレ見通し
on favorable terms 有利な条件で
▶China is reviewing its policy of giving *favorable* treatment to foreign companies. 中国は, 外資優遇策を見直している。

FDA 米食品医薬品局 (**Food and Drug Administration**の略)
FDI 外国からの直接投資, 対内直接投資, 対外直接投資 (**foreign direct investment**の略)
FDIC 米連邦預金保険公社 (**Federal Deposit Insurance Corporation**の略)
fear 名 懸念, 不安, 警戒感, 恐れ, 疑惑
　credit fear 信用不安 (＝credit crisis, credit crunch)
　deflation fears デフレ懸念 (＝deflationary concerns, deflationary fears, fears of deflation)
　fear of unemployment 雇用不安
　fears over economic growth 景気の先行きへの懸念
　inflation fears インフレ懸念 (＝fear of inflation, inflationary fears)
　prepayment fears 期限前償還に対する懸念, 期限前償還懸念
　recession fears 景気後退の恐れ
▶The U.S. dollar temporarily dropped to the upper ¥95 level over credit *fears*. 米ドルは, 信用不安で一時, 1ドル＝95円後半台まで[後半の水準まで]下落した。

feasibility 名 実行可能性, 実現可能性, 企業化可能性, 採算性, フィージビリティ
　economic feasibility 経済的実行可能性
　feasibility study 実行[実現]可能性調査, 実行[実現]可能性研究, 企業化[事業化]可能性調査, 企業化[事業化]調査, 予備調査, 準備調査, 採算性調査, フィージビリティ・スタディ
　financial feasibility 財務上の実現可能性, 経済的実行可能性
　technological feasibility 技術的実現可能性
▶For contracts involving certain technologies, profits and revenues are deferred until technological *feasibility* is established. 一定の技術を伴う契約(請負契約)については, 技術の実現可能性が確立されるまで, 収益と利益は繰り延べられます。

featherbedding 名 〈雇用者に対する労働組合の〉水増し雇用要求, 不要人員採用要求, 不当人員要求, 生産制限要求 (これらは, 米連邦労働関係法で不当労働行為として禁止されている)

feature 動 特集する, 記事にする, 大きく取り上げる, 呼び物にする, 目玉商品にする, …を特色[特徴]にする, 主演させる, 主役を演じる, 重要な役割を演じる
▶The nation's criminal justice system has long *featured* only judges, prosecutors and lawyers. 日本の刑事司法制度は, 長いこと裁判官, 検察官と弁護士だけで構成してきた。
▶This mobile phone navigation system *features* three-dimensional directions, such as going up and down stairs. この携帯電話用ナビゲーション・システムは, 階段の上り下りなど立体的な道案内をできるのが特徴だ。

feature 名 特徴, 特色, 特性, 製品特性, 機能, 形状, 条項, 措置, 条項, 特集記事, 特別番組, 呼び物, 目玉商品, 長編映画
　added features 機能の充実
　feature story 特集記事, 特別記事
　product feature 製品特性
　protective features 保護措置
　security features 担保条項
　added features 機能の充実, 付加機能
　common features 共通点
　demand features 要求払い条項
　feature article 特集記事
　feature film 長編映画
　feature program 特集番組
▶Mobile phone subscribers are the most demanding of customers for improved service quality and *features*. 携帯電話の加入者は, サービスの質と機能の改善の面で最も要求の厳しい顧客だ。

Fed 名 米連邦準備制度理事会, FRB (＝Federal Reserve: Federal Reserve Boardの略称。米連邦準備銀行(Federal Reserve Bank)や米連邦準備制度(Federal Reserve System), 米連邦公開市場委員会(Federal Open Market Committee)を意味するときもある)
　Fed Chairman [chairman] 米連邦準備制度理事会(FRB)議長, FRB議長 (＝Fed chief, Federal Reserve Board Chairman)
　Fed [fed] funds フェデラル・ファンド《略 FF》 (＝federal [Federal] funds)
　Fed funds rate フェデラル・ファンド(FF)金利
　Fed funds target FF金利誘導目標
　Fed interest rate 米連邦金利
　Fed Wire フェド・ワイヤー (米連邦準備制度の

電子資金振替システム）
Federal 形 連邦の, 米連邦の
Federal Agricultural Mortgage Corporation 米連邦農業抵当公社, ファーマー・マック（通称）（＝Farmer Mac）
federal budget deficit 米財政赤字
Federal Deposit Insurance Corporation 米連邦預金保険公社《略 FDIC》
Federal Election Campaign Act 米連邦選挙資金規正法（米国の大統領選や連邦議員選の資金などを規制する法律）
規制の対象

hard money	ハード・マネー（連邦議会選挙の候補者への直接献金のこと）
soft money	ソフト・マネー（政党活動費や意見広告など政党への献金のこと）

Federal Emergency Management Agency 米連邦緊急事態管理庁《略 FEMA》
Federal Employers' Liability Act 連邦雇用者責任法
Federal [federal] funds rate 短期金利, FFレート, FF金利, フェデラル・ファンド金利, フェデラル・ファンド適用金利, フェデラル・ファンド・レート（＝Fed funds rate, key interest rate, key rate）

FF金利と公定歩合➡「FF金利」は短期金融市場の状況を最も敏感に反映する指標金利の一つで, 米国の民間銀行が翌日決済で相互に資金を貸し借りするときに適用する金利のこと。日銀の無担保コール翌日物金利に相当する。「公定歩合」は, FRB（米連邦準備制度理事会）が［最後の貸し手］として金融機関に貸し付けるときの金利で, 一般にFF金利より高めになる。（⇒key interest rate, key rate）

▶The *federal* funds rate, a benchmark short-term interest rate, was cut to 3.5 percent per annum and the official discount rate to 3 percent per annum. 短期金利の誘導目標であるフェデラル・ファンド(FF)金利は年3.5%, 公定歩合は年3％に引き下げられた。

Federal Home Loan Mortgage Corporation 米連邦住宅貸付抵当公社, フレディ・マック（通称）《略 FHLMC》（⇒Freddie Mac）
federal income tax 連邦所得税, 連邦法人税（⇒taxable income）
  federal income tax liability 未払い連邦所得税
  federal income tax return 連邦法人税申告書
▶The Internal Revenue Service (IRS) has examined the *federal income tax* returns for the Corporation through 2007. 米内国歳入庁(IRS)は, 2007年度までの当社の連邦法人税申告書の調査をしました。

Federal Insurance Contribution Act 米連邦保険料法, 米連邦保険拠出法《略 FICA》
Federal Open Market Committee 米連邦公開市場委員会《略 FOMC》（＝Federal Reserve Open Market Committee: 米国の金融政策の最高意思決定機関で, 短期金融政策と公開市場操作に関する方針を決定する。連邦準備制度理事会の理事7人と地区連邦準備銀行の総裁5人で構成）
Federal Reserve 米連邦準備制度理事会（＝Federal Reserve Board: 米連邦準備制度(Federal Reserve System)や連邦公開市場委員会(Federal Open Market Committee), 連邦準備銀行(Federal Reserve Bank)を意味することもある）
▶The *Federal Reserve* raised U.S. interest rates for the first time in four years. 米連邦準備制度理事会(FRB)は, 金利を4年ぶりに引き上げた。
Federal Reserve Bank 米連邦準備銀行《略 FRB》
Federal Reserve Board 米連邦準備制度理事会, 米連邦準備理事会《略 FRB》（＝Fed, Federal Reserve: 米国の連邦準備制度(FRS)の統括機関で, 正式名称はBoard of Governors of the Federal Reserve System。理事は7人で上院の承認を経て大統領が任命し, 任期は14年）
▶The U.S. *Federal Reserve Board* announced significant cuts in interest rates. 米連邦準備制度理事会(FRB)が, 大幅利下げを発表した。
Federal Reserve System 米連邦準備制度
federal statutory tax rate 連邦法定税率, 連邦法人税率（＝federal statutory rate）
Federal Trade Commission 米連邦取引委員会《略 FTC》（＝U.S. federal antitrust regulators: 米国の独占禁止法施行機関）
▶The U.S. *Federal Trade Commission* concluded there was not enough evidence that a Sony-BMG merger would violate U.S. antitrust laws. 米連邦取引委員会(FTC)は, ソニーとBMG（独複合メディア大手ベルテルスマンの音楽事業部門）の統合が米国の独占禁止法に違反することを示す十分な証拠はない, との結論を下した。
Federal Unemployment Tax Act 米連邦失業保険税法
fee 名 料金, 入会金, 入場料, 納付金, 会費, 手数料, 使用料, 報酬, 謝礼, 実施料, 対価, 所有権, 相続財産権, フィー
  after fee 手数料込みで（＝at full fees）
  application fee 出願手数料
  asset management fee 資産運用手数料
  audit fee 監査料, 監査報酬

contingent fee 成功報酬
entrance fee 入会金
fees and permits 免許料
fixed fee 固定報酬
legal fee 弁護士手数料
medical fees 医療費 (=medical costs)
redemption fee 解約手数料
underwriting fee 引受手数料

▸In Japan, the *fee* for transmitting or receiving data at a rate of 100 kilobytes per second via broadband is the world's lowest at only nine cents. 日本の場合，1秒に10万バイトの情報を送受信する料金は，たった9セントで世界一安い。

▸When music from a CD is used for a TV program, a broadcaster must pay the usage *fee* after using it. テレビ番組にCDの音楽を使う場合には，放送局がその後で使用料を支払わなければならない。

feed 動 〈機械に〉原料を送る，〈原料を〉機械に送り込む，〈作業を〉送る，供給する，名 供給，原材料，燃料

feedback 名 フィードバック，反応，反響，声，意見，帰還，自動制御機能
feedback control フィードバック機能 (結果と目標を比較評価しながら行動を目標に近づけること)
feedback from a consumer 消費者からの声，消費者からの意見
inverse feedback 抑圧帰還
regenerative feedback 再生帰還

▸The questionnaire helped the company obtain *feedback* from customers. アンケートで，同社は顧客の声を聴くことができた。

fetch 動 …で売れる，…の値を付ける，…の高値を呼ぶ

▸Shares in McDonald's Co. (Japan), a leader in the nation's fast-food industry, *fetched* an initial price of ¥4,700. ファースト・フード業界最大手の日本マクドナルドの株が，1株当たり4,700円の初値を付けた。

FHLMC 米連邦住宅貸付抵当公社 (Federal Home Loan Mortgage Corporationの略)

fiasco 名 大失敗，大失態，不首尾

▸In the United States, the subprime mortgage *fiasco* is affecting its real economy. 米国では，サブプライム・ローン(低所得者向け住宅融資)の焦げ付き問題が，実体経済に影響を及ぼしている。

fiber optic lines 光ファイバー・ケーブル (=fiber optic lines)

▸KDDI and Russia's OAO Rostelecom will together spend ¥5 billion to lay undersea *fiber optic lines* between the two countries. KDDIとロシアのOAOロステレコムが，50億円の折半投資で日露間に海底光ファイバー・ケーブルを敷設することになった。

fiber optic network 光ファイバー網，光ファイバー通信ネットワーク (⇒**cost effectiveness**)

fiber optics 光ファイバー，ファイバー光学，光学繊維，光ファイイバー技術 (=optical fiber)
fiber optics business 光ファイバー事業，光ファイバー通信事業，光ファイーによる通信サービス事業 (=fiber optics communications business)
fiber optics network 光ファイバー網，光ファイバー通信ネットワーク (=fiber network, fiber-optic cable network, fiber optic network)

▸*Fiber optics* is the route that information services, such as high-definition TV, interactive education or shopping, will take to consumers. 光ファイバーは，ハイビジョン(HDTV)，対話型テレビ教育やテレビ・ショッピングなどの情報サービスを消費者に送り届けるためのケーブルです。

fiduciary 形 受託者の，被信託人の，信託の，信用の，保証の

field 名 領域，分野，市場，実地，現場，現地，出先，天然資源の埋蔵地帯，産出地帯，フィールド (⇒**gas**)
business fields 事業分野，業種
enter a new field 新分野に参入する
field engineer サービス技術者
field office 営業所
field premises 現地事務所
field research 実地調査，現地調査，現場調査
field sales force 外務員，外交販売員 (=field salesman, field salesperson)
field study 実地調査，現地調査，実地研究，フィールド・スタディ
field test 実地検査，実地試験，フィールド・テスト
field work standard 監査実地基準
gain the field 市場を獲得する
gas field ガス田
oil field 油田
other business fields 異業種
playing field 事業環境，競争条件
regulatory field 規制分野

▸Iran's Pars South and the adjacent Qatar's North Field gas *fields* are respectively the largest and second largest natural gas reserves in the world. イランの南パルス・ガス田とこれに隣接するカター

ルのノースフィールド・ガス田の天然ガス埋蔵量は，それぞれ世界第一位と第二位である．
▸The firm has earmarked a total of ¥37 billion in the two business *fields* in fiscal 2008. 同社は，2008年度に両事業分野に計370億円投資した．
▸The strength of Japanese industry is said to come from the knowledge and technical know-how that skilled workers have cultivated in the *field*. 日本の産業の強みは，熟練工が現場で培った知識と技術ノウハウにある，と言われる．

fierce competition 熾烈な競争
▸Many regional general contractors are facing financial difficulties as a result of *fierce competition*. 地方ゼネコンの多くは，熾烈な競争で経営不振に陥っている．

FIFO 先入れ先出し法 (=FIFO cost method, FIFO method; ⇒**first-in, first-out basis [method]**, LIFO)
▸Inventories are valued at the lower of cost (calculated generally on a *FIFO* basis) or net realizable value. 棚卸し資産は，取得原価（原則として先入れ先出し法で計算）と正味実現可能価額のうち，低いほうの価額で評価されています．

fifty-fifty joint venture 折半出資の合弁会社 (=50-50 joint venture, 50% joint venture)
▸The two companies will set up a *fifty-fifty joint venture* for the Japanese version of MySpace, the world most popular social networking service. 両社は，折半出資の会社を新設して，世界で最も人気があるソーシャル・ネットワーキング・サービス(SNS)「マイスペース」の日本語版サービスを提供する．

figure 🅶 数値，数量，数字，データ，統計，指数，指標，総額，決算，実績，業績，値段，価格，売上高，計算，図，図案，図形，イラスト，人物，スタイル，プロポーション
　advanced figures　速報値
　corresponding figures　比較対応数値
　figure this quarter　当四半期の業績
　financial figures　財務実績，業績，決算 (⇒reflect)
　net figure　当期利益
　reported figures　公表データ，公表財務データ
　retail sales figures　小売上高，小売販売の実績
　second quarter figures　第2四半期の実績，第2四半期決算
　trade figures　貿易統計
　year-end figures　年度末の決算，決算
▸Figures are on consolidated basis. 数値は，連結ベースです．

▸Previously reported figures have been restated. 前期までの報告書に掲げた数値は，修正・再表示[修正して再表示]されています．
▸The *figures* this quarter include the consolidation of the company, a leading United Kingdom telecommunications firm. 当四半期の業績には，同社（英国の大手通信会社）の連結分も含まれています．

file 🅳 提出する，申請する，申し立てる，保管する，整理保管する (⇒civil, protection)
　file a damages suit against …を相手取り損害賠償を求める訴訟を起こす
　file a declaration of bankruptcy and a request for asset protection with …に破産宣告と財産保全の処分を申請する，…に破産宣告と財産保全の処分を申し立てる
　file a shelf registration statement with the U.S. Securities and Exchange Commission 米証券取引委員会(SEC)に一括登録[発行登録]届け出書を提出する (⇒**shelf registration statement**)
　file final reports on income for this year 今年度の確定申告書を提出する
　file for bankruptcy 破産を申し立てる，破産申請する，破産法を申請する，再生法を申請する (=file for insolvency)
　file for court protection from creditors 資産保全を申請する，破綻申請する，会社更生手続きを申請する (=file for protection from creditors, seek court protection from creditors)
　filed documents in a computer パソコン内の文書ファイル
▸All the *filed* documents in computers were erased by the virus. ウイルスで，パソコン内の文書ファイルがすべて消去されてしまった．
▸English conversation school chain operator Nova Corp. *filed* for court protection from creditors under the Corporate Rehabilitation Law. 英会話学校を運営するNOVAが，会社更生法の適用[会社更生法に基づく資産保全]を申請した．
▸The parent company of Tower Records, the pioneering record retailer that invented the music megastore, has *filed* for bankruptcy. 音楽の超大型チェーン店を最初に展開したレコード小売店の草分けともいえるタワー・レコーズの親会社が，破産申請した．

file 🅽 資料，記録，目録，名簿，調書，ファイル
　audit file　監査調書
　backup file　バックアップ・ファイル（オリジナル・ファイルを複製して作った予備ファイルのこと）

close a file ファイルを閉じる
configuration file 環境設定ファイル
customer information file 顧客情報ファイル
copy a file ファイルをコピーする
create a file ファイルを作成する
detail file 明細ファイル (=transaction file)
disk file ディスク・ファイル (フロッピー・ディスクやハード・ディスクに記録されたファイルのこと)
existing files 既存のファイル
file compression/depression ファイルの圧縮/解凍
file format ファイル形式
file generating ファイル作成
file maintenance ファイルの保守, ファイルの維持管理, ファイル・メンテナンス
file name ファイル名
file operation (作成・削除・更新などの)ファイル操作
file organization ファイル編成
file renewal ファイル更新 (=file update)
file server ファイル・サーバー
file transfer ファイル転送
file transmission ファイル伝送
files on the Internet インターネット上のファイル
master file 基本ファイル, マスター・ファイル
open a file ファイルを開く
recently used files 最近使ったファイル
text file テキスト・ファイル
transaction file トランザクション・ファイル (=detail file: マスター・ファイルに処理を加えて新たに発生したファイルのこと)
▶The virus infects computers when the *file* of animation footage is opened and destroys data in the computers or leaks personal information. このウイルスは, アニメ画像のファイルを開くとパソコンに感染して, パソコン内のデータを破壊したり, 個人情報を流出させたりする。

file sharing ファイル交換, ファイル・シェアリング (LAN上にあるコンピュータでファイルを共有して使うこと)
  file-sharing of music on Net service 音楽ネット交換サービス (=online music file-sharing service: インターネットで音楽データなどを無料でやり取りするサービス)
  file-sharing program ファイル交換ソフト (=file-sharing software)
  file-sharing service ファイル交換サービス (=file swapping service)
  file-sharing software ファイル交換ソフト
  online music file-sharing service 音楽ネット交換サービス
  the Winny file-sharing software ファイル交換ソフト「Winny (ウイニー)」
▶*File-sharing* software is estimated to be used by about 1.3 million people in Japan. ファイル交換ソフトは, 日本では約130万人が利用していると思われる。
▶The Tokyo District Court said in an interim ruling that an online music *file-sharing* service by MMO Japan Ltd. has violated the Copyright Law. 東京地裁は, 中間判決で, 日本エム・エム・オーがインターネットで運営している音楽ファイル交換サービスは著作権法に違反していると述べた。

filtering service 有害サイトの遮断サービス, 有害サイトの選別サービス
filtering software 遮断ソフト
finance 動 融資する, 貸し付ける, 出資する, 資金を出す, 資金を供給する, 資金を調達する, 〈赤字などを〉埋め合わせる, 補填する, …の資金に充てる
  ability to finance 資金調達力
  amount financed 融資金額, 貸出額, 元金
  be financed by debt 借入れで調達する, 負債による資金調達を行う
  be financed by equity 株式で調達する
  be fully financed by …が100%出資する
  finance capital needs 資金需要を賄う
  finance government deficits 財政赤字の穴埋めをする, 財政赤字を補填する
  finance mergers or acquisitions 合併や買収の資金調達をする
  finance stock buybacks 自社株買戻しの資金を調達する
  finance jointly 共同出資する (=jointly finance)
▶This capital tie-up is aimed at partially *financing* the firm's project to build a new production facility for high-quality printing paper. この資本提携の目的は, 上質印刷用紙の新生産設備を建設する同社プロジェクトの資金調達の一部にすることにある。
▶We raised ¥100 billion from the bond issue to *finance* our restructuring in 2008. 2008年度に当社は, 社債発行で1,000億円を調達してリストラ資金に充てました。

finance 名 金融, 財務, 財務内容, 財政, 財力, 財源, 資金, 資金調達, 融資, ファイナンス
  asset finance 資産金融, アセット・ファイナンス
  bridging finance つなぎ融資 (=bridge fi-

nancing)
business finance 企業財務, 経営財務
capital finance 資本調達
co-finance 共同融資
corporate finance 企業金融, 企業財務, 企業の資金調達, 法人金融, コーポレート・ファイナンス
debt finance デット・ファイナンス, 負債金融, 負債による資金調達
equity finance エクイティ・ファイナンス, 株式発行による資金調達
external finance 外部資金
finance committee 財務委員会
finance income 金融収益
internal finance 内部資金
inventory finance 在庫金融
lease finance リース金融
loan finance 融資
self-finance 自己金融
sales finance 販売金融
surplus finance 黒字財政

▸*Financial* institutions extend loans to specified projects of companies by project finance. 金融機関は, プロジェクト金融で, 企業の特定の事業に融資している.

▸The two banks will tie up in online *finance*. 両行は, オンライン金融で提携する.

finance charge 財務費用, 金融費用, 融資手数料, ファイナンス・チャージ

▸Any payment not made when due will incur a *finance charge*. 支払い期日までに支払いが履行されない場合には, 金融費用が発生する.

finance receivables 貸出残高, 貸出債権, 金融債権, 金融売掛債権, 債権

▸We invested in additional *finance receivables*. 当社は, 金融売掛債権に追加的投資を行いました.

finance subsidiary 金融子会社, 金融事業を営む子会社

▸The *finance subsidiaries* of the Corporation, which in the past were accounted for by the equity method, are now fully consolidated. 前期[前年度]まで持ち分法で会計処理していた当社の金融事業を営む子会社[金融子会社]は, 当期[当年度]からすべて連結の範囲に含めてあります.

financial 形 金融の, 財務の, 財務上の, 金銭的, 金銭面での
 financial adviser [advisor] 財務顧問
 Financial Accounting Standards Board 財務会計基準審議会《略 FASB》
 financial accounts 英国の財務諸表, 財務書類, 財務勘定, 財務報告書

financial activity 資金調達活動, 財務活動
financial aid package 金融支援策, 財政援助策 (=financial assistance package, financial rescue package)
financial asset 金融資産, 貨幣性資産
financial assets and liabilities 貨幣性資産と貨幣性負債
financial burden 財務負担, 財政負担, 金融負担
financial comments 財務書類注記, 財務諸表注記 (=notes to financial statements)
financial community 金融業界, 金融界, 金融証券業界
financial comparison 財務比較
financial cost 金融費用, 財務費用, 財務コスト, 資金コスト
financial costs of goods manufactured 製品原価
financial crisis 金融危機, 金融パニック, 金融恐慌, 経営危機, 経営難, 経営破綻(はたん) (=financial difficulties)
financial flexibility 財務弾力性, 財務上の柔軟性, 不測の事態が生じたときの資金調達能力
financial gearing 財務レバレッジ, 負債比率, ギアリング (=financial leverage, gearing, trading on the equity)
financial goods 金融商品 (=financial instruments, financial products)
financial misconduct 不正会計処理, 粉飾決算
financial performance 財務実績, 財務業績, 財務面での実績, 業績, 財務状態, 財務状況, 財政状況
financial product 金融商品 (=financial goods, financial instrument)
financial ratio 財務比率, 財務指標
financial revenue and expense 財務損益
financial situation 財務状態, 財政状態, 財務状況, 財務体質 (=financial condition, financial position, financial standing)
financial solvency 財務流動性
financial soundness 財務上の健全性, 財政の健全性, 経営の健全性 (=financial health)
financial status 財政状態, 財務状況, 財務内容, 金融機関の体力 (=financial position, financial standing)
financial straits 財政難, 財政困難, 財務危機, 財政逼迫, 財政的苦境, 困難な資金繰り, 金に困ること, 財務力の低下, 金融機関の体力の低下 (=financial difficulties)
financial stringency 金融逼迫 (=financial pressure, monetary stringency)

financial stress 経営難, 信用逼迫
financial window-dressing 会計操作
financial year 会計年度, 事業年度, 営業年度, 会計期間 （＝business year, fiscal year）
▶The growth of our *financial* services and leasing business was the primary reason for the increase in total debt outstanding and for most of our financing needs. 当社の金融サービスおよびリース事業の成長が, 当社の負債総額の増加と資金需要の大半の主な要因です。

financial assistance 金融支援, 資金援助 （＝financial aid, financial backing, financial support）
▶The company and the six main banks are expected to reach a basic agreement in early November about the scope of the *financial assistance* and asset sales. 同社と主力取引銀行6行は, 11月初めに金融支援の枠組みと資産売却について基本合意に達する見込みだ。

financial base 財務基盤, 経営基盤 （＝financial footing, financial foundation; ⇒**management buyout**）
▶Mitsui Life Insurance Co. became a joint stock company from a mutual company in a bid to reinforce its *financial base* by diversifying funding resources. 三井生命保険は, 資金調達源を拡大して財務基盤を強化するため, 相互会社から株式会社に転換した。

financial business 金融業務, 金融事業
▶The company sold all of its *financial businesses* to an investment firm for about ¥20 billion. 同社は, 同社の全金融事業を約200億円で投資会社に売却した。

financial condition 財政状態, 財政状況, 財務状態, 財務状況, 財務内容, 財務基盤, 金融情勢 （＝financial position, financial state）
▶Our *financial condition* gives us easy access to financing when we need it. 当社の財政状態からすると, 当社は資金需要時にたやすく資金を調達することができます。

financial data 財務データ, 財務情報, 財務資料
▶We included some of these combined amounts at the bottom of the ten-year summary of selected *financial data*. 過去10年間の要約主要財務データの最後に, 合算した数値の一部が掲げられています。

financial difficulties 財務悪化, 財政の困難, 財政難, 財政逼迫, 経営危機, 経営難, 経営不振 （＝financial disarray, financial distress, financial straits; ⇒**about-face**）

▶The Company will reduce its capital by 99.7 percent to ¥100 million to make shareholders accountable for its *financial difficulties*. 当社は, 経営不振の株主責任を明確にするため, 99.7%の減資を実施して資本金を1億円とする。

financial engineering technology 金融技術
▶Citigroup will link its *financial engineering technology* and worldwide network with Nikko's domestic sales network. 米シティグループは, 同社の金融技術や世界の顧客網と日興の国内営業基盤［販売網］を結び付ける方針だ。

financial figures 業績, 決算
▶The firm's earnings from May are reflected in our *financial figures* for the April-September period. 同社の5月以降の収益は, 当社の4－9月期の業績［決算］に組み入れてあります。

financial futures 金融先物, 金融先物取引
financial futures instrument 金融先物商品
financial futures transaction 金融先物取引
▶Under the *Financial Futures* Law, dealers are not allowed to market low-margin foreign exchange products either by directly or by phone. 金融先物取引法では, ディーラーは少ない証拠金での外国為替商品の直接販売または電話での販売は禁止されている。

financial group 金融グループ, 融資団
▶Today, *financial groups* have come to operate diverse businesses under their umbrella, such as banks, securities firms and insurance companies. 今は, 金融グループが, 銀行や証券会社, 保険会社を傘下に収めて多様な事業を展開するようになってきた。

financial health 財務［財務上］の健全性, 財務内容, 財務状況, 財務体質, 経営の健全度［健全性］ （＝financial soundness）
▶The planned capital increase is designed to strengthen the financial group's *financial health*. 増資計画の目的は, 同フィナンシャル・グループの経営［財務］の健全性強化にある。

financial hemorrhaging 金融上の損失, 損失 （＝financial loss）
▶With a view to stemming the airlines' *financial hemorrhaging*, the Construction and Transport Ministry asked the Development Bank of Japan to provide emergency loans to the two carriers. 航空会社の損失を阻止するため, 国土交通省は, 日本政策投資銀行に対して両航空会社への緊急融資を要請した。

financial information 金融情報, 財務情報

financial institution　金融機関
▸Swelling losses for U.S. *financial institutions* have pushed down stock prices on the New York market.　米金融機関の損失拡大で、ニューヨーク市場の株価が下落している。

▸The financial statements and other *financial information* included in this annual report were prepared in conformity with generally accepted accounting principles.　この年次報告書に記載されている財務書類とその他の財務情報は、一般に公正妥当と認められた会計原則に従って作成されています。

financial instrument　金融商品, 金融資産, 金融手段, 金融証券 (＝financial goods, financial product)
▸These *financial instruments* include commitments to extend credit, letters of credit, guarantees of debt, interest rate swaps and cap agreements, and foreign currency exchange contracts.　これらの金融商品には、信用供与契約、信用状、債務保証、金利スワップおよび金利キャップ契約と外国為替予約が含まれています。

financial market　金融市場 (⇒**downfall, instability**)
▸Central banks in the United States and Europe have provided funds to *financial markets* to try to stabilize markets.　欧米の中央銀行は、これまで金融市場に資金を供給して、市場安定化に努めてきた。

financial position　財政状態, 財務状態, 財務状況, 財務体質, 資金繰り (＝financial condition, financial situation, financial standing; ⇒ **closing balance sheet**)
▸The financial statements referred to above present fairly the *financial position* of the company in conformity with generally accepted accounting principles.　上記の財務書類は、同社の財政状態を、一般に認められた会計原則に準拠して適正に表示しています。

financial pressure　財政難, 金融面の圧迫, 経営の圧迫
▸Daiei's business diversification led to rising debts that placed *financial pressure* on the company.　ダイエーの事業多角化は、借入金の増大につながり、それが会社の経営を圧迫する結果となった。

financial records　財務記録
▸*Financial records* are adequate and can be relied upon.　財務記録は、適切で信頼性がある。

financial reporting　財務報告, 財務会計, 財務報告会計
▸The goal of *financial reporting* is to give investors the information they need to understand how we are doing over time and in comparison with other companies.　財務報告の目標は、当社が現在にいたるまで、また他社との比較でどのような経営をしているかを投資家に理解してもらうために必要な情報を、投資家に提供することにあります。

financial results　財務成績, 財務実績, 業績, 金融収支, 決算 (⇒**goods**)
▸Livedoor Co. dressed up the *financial results* of Livedoor Marketing Co. by posting bogus sales in 2004.　ライブドアは、2004年に架空の売上を計上して、ライブドアマーケティングの決算[業績、財務実績]を粉飾した。

financial revitalization program　金融再生プログラム (＝financial revitalization plan, financial revival program)
▸The bank became the first financial institution to receive special government assistance under a *financial revitalization program*.　同社は、金融再生プログラムに基づき政府の特別支援を受ける金融機関の第一号となった。

financial sanctions　金融制裁
▸Pyongyang's accounts with Banco Delta Asia in Macao were frozen under U.S. *financial sanctions*.　マカオの銀行「バンコ・デルタ・アジア」にある北朝鮮の口座が、米国の金融制裁を受けて凍結された。

financial services　金融事業, 金融サービス, 金融サービス業務
▸*Financial services* account for about 60 percent of the company's overall sales.　金融事業は、同社の売上全体の6割を占めている。

▸Our *financial services* businesses are growing because we are investing in new assets.　当社の金融サービス業務は、新資産への投資で拡大しています。

financial services business　金融サービス事業
▸We are investing in finance receivables, particularly credit card receivables, to increase revenues and earnings from our *financial services* businesses.　当社は、金融サービス事業による収益と利益を増やすため、金融債権、とくにクレジット・カード債権に投資を行っています。

Financial Stability Forum　金融安定化フォーラム《略 **FSF**》(G7主要先進国と発展途上国、国際通貨基金、世界銀行、国際証券監督者機構の各代表で構成される)

▸An interim report of the *Financial Stability Forum* called for measures such as a review of evaluation system of securitized products.　金融安定化フォーラムの中間報告は，証券化商品の評価方法見直しなどの措置を求めた。

financial statement　財務報告書，財務報告，有価証券報告書《略 F/S》(financial statementは，financial statements（財務書類・財務諸表）の形容詞として使われることもある）

　falsification of financial statements　有価証券報告書の虚偽記載
　financial statement date　決算日
　semiannual financial statement　半期（財務）報告書

▸Certain *financial statement* amounts are translated at historic exchange rates.　一部の財務書類の数値は，取引日の為替レートで換算されています。

financial statements　財務諸表，財務書類，企業財務情報，決算書，経営分析，有価証券報告書（⇒**accompanying notes to financial statements, consolidated financial statements**）

　財務書類について⇒通常，財務書類にはbalance sheet（貸借対照表），income statement（損益計算書）とcash flow statement（キャッシュ・フロー計算書）のほか，statement of stockholders' equity（株主持ち分計算書）やstatement of changes in financial position（財政状態変動表）などが含まれる。米国企業の年次報告書や四半期報告書その他で公表される財務書類は，だいたい連結財務書類で，一般に貸借対照表(balance sheet)，損益および剰余金計算書(statement of income and retained earnings)，財政状態変動表(statement of changes in financial position)，会計処理方針の説明(disclosure of accounting policies)と財務書類注記(notes to financial statements)で構成されている。ただし，会計処理方針の説明は財務書類注記［財務諸表注記］に盛り込まれることもある。このほか，期中に増資(capital increase)や株式の償還(redemption)，自社株取引(treasury stock transaction)などの資本勘定(capital accounts)に変動が生じた場合には，資本勘定計算書(capital statement)が利用される。なお，貸借対照表は財政状態（資産内容）を，損益および剰余金計算書は経営成績（営業実績）を，また財政状態変動表は資金投下と資金調達（資金繰り）を示す。

　interim financial statements　中間財務諸表，中間財務書類（＝interim report, interim statements）

international financial statements　国際財務諸表
summarized financial statements　要約財務書類，財務書類要約

▸Companies listed on Japan's stock markets are required to release *financial statements* every quarter starting in fiscal 2007.　日本の株式市場に上場している企業は，2007年度から財務諸表の四半期開示を義務付けられている。

financial strength　資金力，財力，財務力，財務体質，財務内容，財務面での健全性，財政的強み，支払い能力，金融機関の体力

▸The company's *financial strength* has deteriorated since a series of scandals including the mislabeling of beef by its subsidiary.　同社の財務体質は，子会社による牛肉の偽装表示など一連の事件以来，悪化している。

financial structure　財務構成，資本構成，金融組織

　財務構成と資本構成について⇒「財務構成」（資金調達の状態）は資本をどの源泉から調達したかを示すもので，資本構成(capital structure)に短期債務(short term debt)や買掛金(account payable)などを加えたもの。これに対して「資本構成」は，資本総額に占める他人資本（負債）と自己資本の構成割合をいう。

financial support　金融支援，資金負担（＝financial aid, financial assistance, financial rescue）

▸*Financial support* is the prerequisite for the two firms' funding of the issuance of new shares.　金融支援は，両社の増資引受けの前提条件となっている。

financial system　金融制度，金融システム
▸Uncertainty remains regarding Japan's *financial system*.　日本の金融システムには，不安が残る。

financial system crisis　金融危機，金融システム危機

▸Before the new law's enactment, an injection of public funds into a single financial institution was allowed only when there were fears of a *financial system crisis*.　新法の制定前は，金融危機の恐れがある場合に限って，個別の金融機関に公的資金を注入することができた。

financial unrest　金融不安（＝financial uncertainty）

▸Nonperforming loans are a source of financial unrest.　不良債権が，金融不安の発生源になっている。

financially troubled　経営危機に直面してい

る, 経営が悪化した, 経営難の, 経営不振の, 財政が逼迫した, 財政難の, 財政難に陥っている
▶*Financially troubled* Shinginko Tokyo plans to slash its deposits to ¥20 billion by fiscal 2011. 経営難の新銀行東京が, 2011年度までに預金量を200億円に圧縮する計画だ。

financier 名 財政家, 財務官, 金融業者
financing 名 資金調達, 資本調達, 金融, 融資, 借入れ, ローン, 財務, 資金 (⇒**bank loan**, **debt instrument**, **debt outstanding**, **exposure**, **external**)
 bridge financing つなぎ融資
 debt financing 他人資本調達, 負債による資金調達, 借入金融, 負債金融 (=debt finance: 社債の発行や約束手形の振出し, 短期・長期の借入金などで資金を調達する方法。これに対して, 株式発行による資金調達方法をequity finance, equity financingという)
 direct financing via stock markets 株式市場を通じて資金を調達する直接金融
 external bond financing 外債発行による資金調達
 financing act 出資法
 financing activities and capitalization 資金調達活動と資本化
 financing agreement 借入契約, 融資契約, 金融協定
 financing bill 政府短期証券
 financing cost 資金調達コスト, 金融費用, 金融コスト
 financing demand 借入需要, 資金需要 (=financing requirements)
 financing operations 融資活動, 金融活動, 金融事業, 財務活動, 財務
 foreign trade financing 外国貿易金融 (輸出入必要資金の融通)
 gross financing needs 総調達額
 interim financing つなぎ融資
 joint financing 協調融資 (=cooperative financing)
 left-hand financing 資産担保資金調達
 product financing arrangements 製品金融の取決め
 receivables financing 債権融資
 straight financing 直接融資
 tax-exempt financing 免税債での資金調達
 up-coming financing 当面の資金調達
▶Our long-term *financing* was accomplished through the issuance of long-term debt instruments. 当社の長期資金調達は, 長期債務証券を発行して行われた。
▶We sometimes guarantee the *financing* for product purchases by customers outside the U.S. 当社は, 米国外の顧客が製品を購入する際の資金調達に対して保証を行う場合があります。

financing activities 財務活動, 金融活動, 資金調達活動, 資金調達と返済に関する活動
▶Cash used for *financing activities* resulted from a dividend payment and the repayment of debt. 財務活動に使用した現金は, 支払い配当金と債務返済によるものです。

financing commitment 資金調達契約
▶The Company's financial instruments include foreign currency contracts and other *financing commitments*. 当社の金融手段としては, 外貨取引契約やその他の資金調達契約もあります。

financing requirements 資金調達必要額
▶*Financing requirements* for 2008 include the purchase for cancellation of a portion of another series of preferred shares for a total amount of $40 million. 2008年度の資金調達必要額には, 他の優先株式シリーズの一部4,000万ドルを消却するための購入資金も含まれています。

fine 名 罰金, 違約金, 制裁金, 課徴金, 手数料, 許可料
▶American International Group agreed to pay a $10 million civil *fine* to settle the SEC's allegations that it fraudulently helped another company falsify its earnings report and hide losses. 米保険大手のAIG (アメリカン・インターナショナル・グループ) は, 同社が他社の業績報告書改竄と損失隠しに不正に手を貸したとする米証券取引委員会(SEC)の告発を受け, この問題を解決するために民事制裁金1,000万ドルを支払うことに同意した。

finished company 企業としての役割を終えた企業

finished goods 製品, 完成品, 完成財, 加工品 (=finished product; ⇒**manufacturing overhead**)

finished product 製品, 最終製品, 完成品, 完成財, 加工品 (=end product, finished goods)
▶Costs incurred subsequent to establishment of technological feasibility to produce the *finished product* of software are generally capitalized. ソフトウエアの完成品を制作するための技術的可能性が明らかになった後に発生した原価は, 原則として資産に計上されています。

fire 動 解雇する

firewall [**fire wall**] 名 防禦壁, 業務隔壁, 情報隔壁, 情報漏洩防止システム, 〈ネット上の〉セ

キュリティ・システム, 不正侵入防止機能［防止装置］, ファイアウォール（「情報隔壁」は, 同グループの銀行と証券会社が顧客情報を共有することを禁止することをいう）
▶The Financial Services Agency mooted a policy of relaxing constraints on a *firewall* between banking and securities institutions.　金融庁は, 銀行と証券会社間のファイアウォール（業務隔壁）規制を緩和する方針を打ち出した。

firm 名　会社, 企業, 法人, 商社, 商会, ファーム
　audit firm　監査人
　business firm　営利企業
　consulting firm　コンサルタント事務所
　controlled firm　傘下企業　（＝subordinated firm）
　CPA firm　監査法人
　diversified firm　多角的企業, 多角化企業
　dominant firm　支配的企業, 優越企業
　foreign-affiliated firm　外資系企業, 外資
　law firm　法律事務所
　multi-industry firm　他業種企業　（＝multi-market firm）
　target firm　目標会社
▶Thus far restructuring in the domestic pharmaceutical industry has been limited to takeovers by foreign *firms*.　これまでのところ国内製薬業界の再編は, 外資による買収に限られている。

first half　上半期, 上期, 前半　（＝first six months: 下半期はlatter half, second halfという）
▶After declining in the *first half* of the year, net earnings increased during the third quarter.　純利益は, 当年度上半期に落ち込んだ後, 第3四半期に増益基調に転じました。

first-half account settlement　上半期決算, 中間決算　（＝first-half results）
▶The company was in the black for its *first-half account settlement* in June.　同社は, 6月中間決算は黒字でした。

first-half loss　上半期損失, 上期の損失［赤字］
▶The Company's *first-half loss* narrowed 85 percent mainly due to the weaker yen.　当社の上半期損失は, 主に円安で85％縮小しました。

first-half net profit　上半期の税引き後利益［純利益], 上期の税引き後利益［純利益］
▶Precision equipment maker Nikon Corp. posted a 20 percent rise in *first half net profit*, helped by healthy sales of digital cameras and production equipment for crystal displays.　精密機器メーカー, ニコンの上半期の税引き後利益は, デジタル・カメラと液晶ディスプレー製造装置の好調な販売に支えられて, 20％増加した。

first half of fiscal 2009　2009年上半期, 2009年度上期
▶The firm set new highs in both group net profit and operating revenues in the *first half of fiscal 2009*.　同社の2009年上半期決算は, 連結税引き後利益も売上高も過去最高となった。

first-in, first-out basis [method]　先入れ先出し法《略 FIFO》
▶Inventories are valued at the lower of average cost (which approximates computation on a *first-in, first-out basis*) or market, less progress payments on long-term contracts.　棚卸し資産は, 平均法による原価（先入れ先出し法に基づく原価とほぼ同額）または市場価格のいずれか低いほうの価額で評価し, 長期請負契約に関する前受金を控除して表示されています。

first quarter　第1四半期
▶In the *first quarter* of 2009, both revenue and profits increased.　2009年第1四半期は, 増収増益となりました。

first-quarter consolidated net income　第1四半期の連結純利益
▶The Company's *first-quarter consolidated net income* was $310 million.　当社の第1四半期の連結純利益は, 3億1,000万ドルでした。

first quarter earnings per share　第1四半期の1株当たり利益, 第1四半期の普通株式1株当たり純利益
▶*First quarter earnings per share* were based on 320 million average common shares outstanding.　第1四半期の普通株式1株当たり純利益は, 発行済み普通株式の平均株式数3億2,000万株に基づいて計算されています。

first quarter ended March 31　3月31日終了の第1四半期, 1－3月期
▶Hewlett-Packard earned $1.55 billion, or 55 cents per share, for the *first quarter ended March. 31*.　ヒューレット・パッカードは, 第1四半期（1－3月期）に15億5,000万ドル（1株当たり55セント）の利益を上げた。

first quarter profit　第1四半期の利益, 第1四半期の黒字
▶The Company's *first quarter profit* was slightly higher than for the same period last year.　当社の第1四半期利益は, 前年同期よりいくぶん増加しました。

first quarter results　第1四半期の業績
▶*First quarter results* were consistent with expectations.　第1四半期の業績は, 当初の予想に沿

うものでした。

First Section of the Tokyo Stock Exchange 東京証券取引所一部, 東証一部 (= Tokyo's first exchange)

first six months 上半期, 上期 (3月期決算企業の場合は4-9月期で, 12月期決算企業の場合は1-6月期を指す)
▸During the *first six months* of 2008, the Corporation issued $550 million of debentures in Canada. 2008年上半期に, 当社はカナダで5億5,000万ドルの無担保社債を発行しました。
▸For the *first six months*, consolidated net income was $495 million. 上半期の連結純利益は, 4億9,500万ドルでした。

first-to-file principle 先願主義, 最先出願者特許主義 (= first-to-file principle)
▸The *first-to-file principle* allows a patent to the first filer of a patent application rather than to the inventor of the subject of the patent. 特許の「先願主義」では, 特許対象の(最初の)発明者ではなく, 最初の特許出願者に特許が認められる。

first-to-invent principle 先発明主義, 最先発明者特許主義 (米国などでは, 日本と違って出願日を問題にしないで, 最初の真正な発明者に特許権を与える「先発明主義」を採用している)
▸In case of the *first-to-invent principle*, companies are forced to consume time and money proving first invention in patent disputes. 先発明主義の場合, 企業は特許紛争で先に発明したことを証明するのにどうしても時間と金がかかることになる。

fiscal 形 財政の, 財政上の, 国庫の, 国庫収入の, 会計の, 会計上の, フィスカル
　fiscal action 財政措置
　fiscal agent 財務代理機関(銀行や信託会社など), 財務代理人
　fiscal and economic policies 経済財政政策
　fiscal and tax stimulus measures 財政・税制面からの景気刺激策
　fiscal consolidation 財政引締め
　fiscal deficits 財政赤字, 財政不足, 財政不足額
　fiscal drag 財政による景気抑制[減速]効果, 財政面からの景気押し下げ効果, 財政的歯止め, フィスカル・ドラッグ
　fiscal engineer [engineering] 大型金融操作
　fiscal expenditure 財政支出
　fiscal investment and loan program 財政投融資計画, 財政投融資, 財投《略 FLP》
　fiscal management 財政運営
　fiscal package 財政刺激策, 財政面からの景気対策, 財政出動
　fiscal performance 財政収支
　fiscal period 会計期間
　fiscal plan [planning] 財政計画
　fiscal plight 財政難
　fiscal policy 財政政策
　fiscal resources 財源
　fiscal retrenchment package 財政緊縮策
　fiscal spending 財政支出, 歳出 (⇒**deflationary pressure**)
　fiscal stimulus measures [package] 財政刺激策, 財政面からの景気刺激策, 財政出動
　fiscal structural reform 財政構造改革
　fiscal stamp 収入印紙
　fiscal structure 財政体質
　fiscal surplus 財政黒字
　fiscal tightening 財政引締め, 財政緊縮
　the fiscal first half to Sept. 30 9月中間決算, 4-9月期
　the fiscal half year 中間決算

fiscal condition 財政状況
▸*Fiscal condition* will deteriorate further. 財政状況は, これから一段と悪化する。

fiscal crisis 財政危機
▸Most local governments face serious *fiscal crises*. 地方自治体の大半が, 深刻な財政危機に直面している。

fiscal first half 今年度上半期, 上半期, 上期
▸Life insurers customarily do not release financial results for the *fiscal first-half*. 生命保険会社は, 慣例として上半期の決算を公表していない。

fiscal measures 財政政策, 財政措置, 財政出動
▸Various pump-priming measures, including *fiscal measures*, have been taken since last year. 財政出動も含めて, 昨年来, さまざまな景気浮揚策が取られてきた。

fiscal reconstruction 財政再建, 財政の立て直し (= fiscal rehabilitation, fiscal restructuring)
▸Without an economic recovery and the resultant recovery of tax revenues, *fiscal reconstruction* will be made difficult. 景気回復[経済の再生]とそれによる税収の回復がなければ, 今後の財政再建もおぼつかない。

fiscal reform 財政改革
▸Priority should be given to public spending, to establish a firm foundation for economic recovery and the subsequent job of tackling *fiscal reform*. 景気を回復し[経済を立て直し], 財政改革に取り組むための強固な基盤を確立するに

は，公共支出を優先的に考えなければならない。

fiscal situation 財政事情，財政状況
▸Japan's *fiscal situation* is the most critical among the industrialized nations. 日本の財政事情は，先進国のなかでも最悪だ。

fiscal stimulus package 財政的な景気刺激策
▸Bush met with Republican and Democratic leaders of Congress to discuss a *fiscal stimulus package*. ブッシュ大統領は，共和・民主両党の議会指導者と会談して財政的な景気刺激策を検討した。

fiscal year 会計年度，事業年度，営業年度，年度，会計期間《略 **FY**》(=business year, financial year, fiscal period; ⇒**current fiscal year**)
 the entire fiscal year 通期，事業年度全体
 the first half of the fiscal year 年度前半，今年度前半，上半期，上期
 the fiscal year ended March 31 3月31日終了事業年度，3月期決算
 the fiscal year ending December 2009 2009年12月期，2009年12月期決算，2009年12月終了事業年度
 the full fiscal year 通期 (=full business year)
 the full fiscal year ending March 31 3月31日終了の通期，3月期決算 (⇒**forecast**)
 the last fiscal year 前年度，前期
 the latter half of this fiscal year 今年度後半，今年度下半期
 this fiscal year 今年度，今期
▸We include the accounts of operations located outside the U.S. on the basis of their *fiscal years*, ended either November 30 or December 31. 米国以外の関係会社の財務書類は，11月30日または12月31日終了する各社の会計年度に基づいて連結されています[連結財務書類に組み入れてあります]。

fiscal year end 決算日，決算期末
▸The Corporation's *fiscal year end* is December 31. 当社の決算日は，12月31日です。

fiscal year through March 3月期決算
▸We now expect group net profit of ¥80 billion for the *fiscal year through March* 2010. 当社は現在，2010年3月期決算で800億円の連結税引き後利益を見込んでいます。

fishing fee 入漁料
▸Fishermen catching tuna in the exclusive economic zone of foreign countries are required to pay *fishing fees*. マグロ漁船が他国の200カイリ排他的経済水域(EEZ)内で操業する場合，マグロ漁船は入漁料を支払わなければならない。

fit 動 適合する，ぴったり合う，うまくはまる，一致する，調和する，適応する，順応する，合わせる，適したものにする，適応させる，資格を持たせる，準備させる
 fit customer needs 顧客のニーズに合う
 fit in 適合させる，はめ込む，…に適応する
 fit in with …と一致する，…と適合[調和]する，…に合う
 fit into …に適合する，…にぴったり合う，…と調和する
 fit oneself for …に適したものにする，…に耐えられる力をつける
 fit out [up] 手を加える，装備する，装備を整える，備え付ける

fit 名 適合，適合度，適合性，出来具合，順応，対応，受験準備(preparation)
 a perfect fit 完全な適合，完全な対応
 goodness of fit of distributions 分布の適合度
 test for [of] goodness of fit 適合度検定

fitness for any particular purpose 特定目的適合性，特定目的への適合性
▸Seller warrants the *fitness for any particular purpose* of the goods. 売り主は，商品の特定目的適合性を保証する。

fittings 名 家具，造作，調度，建具類，取付け品，備品，付属品，付属器具，部品，継手(つぎて)
 fixtures and fittings 付帯設備
 gas fittings ガス器具
 pipe fittings 管継手

five-day week 週休2日制，週5日制 (=five-day working week system, five-day workweek)

fix 動 固定する，設定する，決める，特定する，定める，取り決める，修理する，直す，〈問題などを〉改善する，立て直す，解決する，不正操作する，〈賄賂を使って〉買収する，抱き込む，八百長をする，いかさまをする，〈食事などを〉用意する[作る]，名 窮地，苦境，苦しい立場，買収，八百長，不正，いかさま，〈一時的な〉解決策，理解，〈航空機などの〉位置，位置確認，位置決定，プログラムの修正，〈機械などの〉調子
 be in a fix 苦境に陥っている
 be in a good fix 調子がいい[良い]
 fix a price 値段を決める，価格を設定する
 fix a software bug ソフトのバグを直す
 fix the economy 経済を立て直す
 fix up a meeting 会議の手はずを整える
 get a fix on …を理解する
 look for a quick fix その場しのぎの手段を探す
▸Unless otherwise expressly agreed by the

parties hereto in writing, the prices stated in this agreement are *fixed* during the term of this agreement. 本契約当事者の書面による別段の明確な合意がないかぎり，本契約書に記載した価格は，本契約期間中，固定価格とする．

fixed 形 固定した，固定式の，固定型，確定した，変動しない，一定の，安定した

  fixed commission 固定手数料

  fixed cost 固定費，固定的費用，固定原価 （＝fixed expense）

  fixed date 確定日，約定期日，指定期日

  fixed debt 固定借入金

  fixed employee stock option plan 固定型従業員ストック・オプション制度

  fixed exchange rate 固定為替相場，固定為替レート，固定相場

  fixed expenditure 固定費，固定的費用 （＝fixed cost, fixed expense）

  fixed interest 固定金利，確定利子 （＝fixed interest rate）

  fixed liability 固定負債，長期負債

  fixed loan 固定貸付け金，長期貸付け金，長期借入金

  fixed overhead cost 固定間接費 （＝fixed production overhead cost）

  fixed percentage method 定率法 （＝declining balance method, fixed percentage on reducing balance method, fixed rate method）

  fixed rate debt 固定利付き債

fixed asset 固定資産 （＝capital asset, fixed capital, long-lived asset: 会社の営業活動のために長期的に使用される資産で，これには支店網や建物，営業用備品，土地，機械，工場設備などが含まれる）

  fixed asset investment 固定資産投資，長期投資

  fixed assets to net worth 固定比率 （＝固定資産÷純資産）

▶All *fixed assets* are depreciated on the straight line basis. 有形固定資産は，すべて定額法で償却されています．

fixed asset expenditures 固定資産支出額

▶The semiconductor products segment continues to comprise the largest portion of *fixed asset expenditures*. 半導体事業部門が，引き続き固定資産支出額のうち最大の比率を占めています．

fixed asset investment 固定資産投資

▶*Fixed asset investment* soared nearly 30 percent from a year ago during the July-September quarter. 7－9月期の固定資産投資は，前年同期比で3割近く増加した．

fixed collateral 根(ね)抵当，根抵当権

▶The bank had already secured it as *fixed collateral*. 同行は，それには根抵当権をすでに設定していた．

fixed deposit 定期預金，定期性預金

▶Expecting the natural attrition of *fixed deposits*, the bank will reduce the deposits to ¥197.4 billion by fiscal 2009. 定期預金の自然減を見込んで，同行は預金量を2009年度は1,974億円まで減額する．

fixed income 債券，確定利付き証券，確定報酬，固定収入

  fixed income market 債券市場

  fixed income security 確定利付き証券，固定金利の証券，債券 （＝fixed income investment:「確定利付き証券」は，利率や配当率が証券の発行時から償還時まで一定で変わらない証券のこと）

fixed overhead 固定製造間接費，固定間接費 （＝fixed factory burden, fixed factory overhead）

▶*Fixed overhead* is absorbed as a cost of product. 固定間接費は，製品原価の一部として配賦されて[含まれて]います．

flack 名 広報，宣伝，広報担当者

flag 動 低迷する，活力がなくなる，衰える，しおれる，薄れる

  flagging demand 低迷する需要，需要低迷，需要の軟調

  flagging economy 低迷する経済，景気[経済]の低迷

flag 名 旗，国旗，〈タクシーの〉空車標識

  flag carrier 一国の代表的な航空[船]会社，国営または半官半民の航空会社，フラッグ・キャリア[キャリヤー]

  Flag Day （米国の）国旗制定記念日（1777年6月14日に星条旗を米国の国旗として制定）

  flag of convenience 便宜置籍国の旗[国旗]

  flag of [on] convenience ship [vessel] 便宜置籍船

  flag stop 信号停車駅

  house flag 社旗

  show the flag 立場を表明する，外国の港を正式に訪問する

flagship 名 主力商品，主力製品，目玉商品，最重要製品，目玉，最も代表的なもの，最も重要なもの，旗艦，最高級船，最大の船[航空機]，最上位機種，主力機種

  flagship carrier 代表的な航空会社

  flagship film camera フイルム・カメラの最上位機種

  flagship operation 主力事業

  flagship product 主力製品，主力商品，目玉商品

flagship store 旗艦店, 母店, 主力店, 主力店舗
▸Alitalia is the Italian *flagship* carrier. アリタリア航空は、イタリアを代表する航空会社だ。

flat 形 単一の, 一律の, 均一の, 変化がない, 横ばい［横ばい状態］の, 伸び悩みの, 平坦な
  be almost [virtually] flat ほぼ横ばい, ほぼ横ばい状態
  flat profits 利益横ばい
  flat rate 定額料金, 均一料金, 一括金利, フラット・レート
  flat tax 一律課税, 均一税
  flat yield 直接利回り
▸Business communications systems revenues were essentially *flat* in the second quarter. ビジネス通信システムの売上高は、第2四半期はほぼ横ばいでした。

flat-panel TV 薄型テレビ
▸Hitachi Ltd. has revised down expected overall sales for its *flat-panel* TV sets in fiscal 2010 by about 45 percent. 日立製作所は、2010年度の同社の薄型テレビ全体の販売予想を、約45%下方修正した。

flat-rate 形 定額料金の, 均一料金の, 一括金利の
  flat-rate formula 定額方式, 均一方式
  flat-rate freight 均一運賃, 均一料金
  flat-rate pricing scheme 定額料金制, 均一料金制
  flat-rate tariff 均一料金表

flaw 名 欠陥, 瑕疵(かし), 欠点, 不備, 弱点, 短所

fleet 名 保有全車両, 全船舶, 全航空機, 船舶隊, 船隊, 航空機隊, 輸送船団, 船団, フリート
  air fleet 航空機団
  fishing fleet 漁船団
  fleet cars 量販者
  fleet policy 自動車一括保険, 多数契約保険証券, フリート保険
  fleet rating フリート料率制度
  oil tanker fleet 保有する原油タンカー
  taxi fleet 保有タクシー, タクシー会社
  whaling fleet 捕鯨船団

flexible 形 柔軟な, 順応性のある, 融通のきく, フレキシブル
  flexible budget 弾力性予算, 変動予算
  flexible [magnetic] disk フロッピー・ディスク
  flexible exchange rate 変動為替相場, 屈伸替相場, 変動相場 (=floating exchange rate, floating rate)
  flexible hours フレックス・タイム (=flexible time, flexible working hours, flextime)
  flexible machining cell フレキシブル加工セル 《略 FMC》
  flexible manufacturing cell フレキシブル生産セル 《略 FMC》
  flexible manufacturing system フレキシブル生産システム, フレキシブル生産ライン, 多品種少量自動車生産システム 《略 FMS》 (一般に, NC工作機械, 産業用ロボット, 自動搬送システム, 自動倉庫システム, 自動保守・点検システム, コンピュータ中央管理システムで構成)
  flexible price 伸縮価格
  flexible rate 変動金利
  flexible tariff 伸縮関税
  flexible work hours 裁量労働制, 時差出勤制, 自由勤務時間制, フレックス・タイム制 (=flexible hours, flexible working hours system, flextime)
▸The *flexible* working hours system has been applied only to 11 occupations, including that of attorney and designer. 裁量労働制を導入しているのは現在、弁護士やデザイナーなど11種の職種に限られている。

flexplace [flexiplace] フレックスプレース (在宅勤務ができる自宅のオフィス空間)

flextime [flexitime] 名 時差出勤, 時差出勤制, 自由勤務時間, フレックス・タイム (=flexible time, flexible hours, flexible working hours)

flexyear 名 年間フレックス・タイム制, 年間フレックス制

flight 名 飛行, 定期航空便, 航空便, 逃避, シフト, 脱出, 逃走, 敗走, フライト
  flight attendant 客室乗務員
  flight control 航空管制
  flight controller 航空管制官
  flight deck 操縦室, 飛行甲板
  flight engineer 航空機関士
  flight information region 飛行情報区
  flight manifest 乗客名簿
  flight money 逃避資金
  flight of capital 資本逃避, 他国への資本流出
  flight of deposits 預金の預け替え
  flight path 計画飛行コース
  flight recorder フライト・レコーダー
▸A massive *flight* of deposits from less reliable financial institutions to strong ones may arise. 信頼度の低い金融機関から安全な金融機関への大がかりな預金の預け替えが、発生する可能性がある。
▸The two companies are set to sign a one-year contract to offer code-share *lights* on their winter schedules, which begin in late October

and end next March. 両社は，1年契約を結んで，10月末から来年3月まで適用される冬ダイヤから共同便を運航することになっている。

flip 動 転売する，借り換える

float 動 〈株や債券などを〉発行する，新規に発行する，株式公開する，〈会社を〉新規上場する，〈会社を〉設立する，〈通貨を〉変動相場制に移行する，変動相場制にする，変動相場制である，〈小切手を〉不渡りにする，提案する，提示する（⇒**bank debenture**, **preferred securities**）

float a loan 起債する

float an issue of stock 株式を発行する

float on the stock exchange 証券取引所に上場する

let the currency float 通貨を変動相場制にする，通貨を変動相場制に移行する

▸As part of its capital and business tie-ups with Livedoor, Fuji TV paid ¥44 billion for new shares *floated* by Livedoor under a third-party equity issue. ライブドアとの資本・業務提携の一環として，フジテレビは，第三者割当で増資でライブドアが発行した新株を［ライブドアによる第三者割当増資を］440億円で引き受けた。

▸The bank will discontinue issuing bank debentures to companies next March and *float* straight bonds instead. 同行は，企業向けの金融債発行を来年3月で停止し，それ以降は普通社債を発行する。

float 名 証券の発行，通貨の変動，変動相場制，流通量，未決済小切手，取立て中の手形・小切手類，浮動株数，小口現金，設立，フロート

added float 追加発行

free float 浮動株，浮動株式

public float 公開株

floatation 名 株式の新規発行，売出し，株式公開 （=flotation）

floating 形 流動的，流動する，変動する，流通する，浮動的な

floating asset 流動資産 （=circulating asset, current asset, near-cash asset）

floating capital 流動資本 （=circulating capital, net current assets, working capital）

floating charge 浮動担保，包括担保 （社債を発行する場合に設定する担保で，日々変動する会社の資産を包括して担保にするもの）

floating cost 変動費

floating debt 流動負債 （=current liability, floating liability）

floating exchange rate 変動為替相場，変動相場 （=flexible exchange rate）

floating deposits 流動性預金

floating interest rate 変動金利 （=floating rate）

floating liability 流動負債 （=current liability, floating debt）

floating rate 変動金利，変動利率(floating interest rate), 変動相場(floating exchange rate), 変動レート

floating rate bond 変動利付き債

floating shares 浮動株 （=floating stock, floating supply of stocks: 安定株の反対で，市場で転々と流通している株のこと）

floating system 変動相場制

▸The Company's finance subsidiary has outstanding *floating* to fixed interest rate commercial paper swaps totaling $50 million at December 31, 2008. 当社の金融子会社には，2008年12月31日現在，変動金利を固定金利に変更する総額5,000万ドルの未決済コマーシャル・ペーパー金利スワップ契約があります。

flood 動 殺到する，氾濫する，どっと押し寄せる，名 殺到，氾濫

be flooded with foreign goods 国外製品［商品］がどっと押し寄せる

be flooded with sellers 大量の売りを浴びる，売り一辺倒になる

floor 名 下限，底，底値，売り場，店内，〈証券取引所の〉立会場，議場，床，発言権，フロア

floor area 床面積

floor broker 場内仲買人，立会場ブローカー

floor manager 売り場監督

floor member 立会場会員

floor plan 平面図

floor-plan financing 在庫金融，購入資金融資，即金融

floor planning 在庫金融

floor price 底値，最低価格，下限価格

floor sample 店頭サンプル商品

floor stock 店内在庫

floor-to-time 加工時間

floor trader 取引所の場内会員，登録トレーダー，フロア・トレーダー

floor trading 立会場取引

floor walker 店内巡視員，売り場監督

flow 名 流れ，流出，移動，移転，循環，フロー （⇒**cash flow**）

capital flows 資本移動，資本の流れ，資本流出，資本流入

capital flows in 資本の流入

capital flows out 資本の流出

cash flow-through　資金の流れ
cross-border capital flows　国際的な資本移動，国際的な資金フロー
deal flow　取引量，取引の案件数
financial flow　金融の流れ，財務フロー，資金フロー，資本移動
flow line　流れ経路，流動経路
flow of funds　資金移動，資金循環，資金フロー，マネー・フロー
flow of goods and money　モノとカネの流れ
money flow　資金循環，マネー・フロー
net long-term capital flow　長期資本収支
new coverage flows　新規保険契約の収益
open capital flows　資本移動の自由化
secondary flows　流通市場の取引
speculative financial flows　投機的な資金移動
▶The international flow of goods, services and funds became freer and more globalized.　物，サービスと資金の国際的な流れは，一段と自由になり，また一段とグローバル化した。

fluctuate 動　変動する，上がり下がりする，乱高下する
▶The gain from stock options fluctuates depending on the option holder's investment judgment over the timing of purchase and changes of the stock price.　ストック・オプション（自社株購入権）の利益は，購入時期と株価変動に対するオプション保有者［オプションの買い手］の投資判断によって上下する。

fluctuation 動　変動，変化，上がり下がり，乱高下，騰落，動き（⇒exchange fluctuations）
currency fluctuations　為替変動，為替レートの変動
economic fluctuation　経済変動，景気変動
exchange fluctuation　為替変動，為替相場の変動，為替の騰落，為替の乱高下（= exchange rate fluctuation）
foreign exchange fluctuations　為替相場の変動（= exchange fluctuation）
market fluctuations　市場変動，市況の変動
price fluctuation　物価の変動，価格騰落，株価の乱高下
seasonal fluctuation　季節変動
▶Fluctuations in stock prices could adversely affect major life insurers' finances.　株価変動は，大手生保各社の財務内容にマイナス影響を与えかねない。
▶Foreign exchange fluctuations are affected not only by economic fundamentals, but also by psychological factors.　為替相場の変動は，経済のファンダメンタルズだけでなく，心理的な要因による影響をも受ける。

fluctuations in foreign exchange rate　為替相場の変動，外国為替相場の変動（= foreign exchange fluctuations, foreign exchange rate fluctuations）
▶Yen-denominated trade frees domestic companies from the risk of fluctuations in foreign exchange rate.　円建て貿易は，国内企業にとって為替変動のリスクがない。

FNMA　米連邦住宅抵当金庫（Federal National Mortgage Associationの略）

focal point　焦点
▶The focal point of the wage negotiations was on how management could maintain employment.　経営側が雇用の維持に向けてどう動くかが，今回の賃上げ交渉の焦点だった。

focus 動　焦点を合わせる，…に集中する，…に焦点を絞る
▶We are focusing our investments to take advantage of the opportunities in our industry.　当社は現在，当業界での事業機会の向上に焦点を絞った投資を展開しています。

focus 名　焦点，中心，軸，集中，集中化，傾斜，注目の的，震源地，フォーカス
cost focus strategy　コスト集中戦略
customer focus　顧客中心，顧客中心主義，顧客重視，顧客重視の姿勢，顧客志向，顧客の満足度重視，顧客の満足に力を入れる（⇒core strategy）
differentiation focus strategy　差別化集中戦略
effective management focus　経営効率の重視，焦点を絞った効率経営
focus on service quality　サービスの質の重視
focus on the bottom line　利益重視，利益を重視する姿勢［利益重視の姿勢］
global focus　グローバル志向
▶We are building a strong management team with a global focus.　当社は，グローバル志向の強力な経営陣を築き上げています。

focus on　…に焦点を当てる，…に焦点を合わせる，…に焦点を置く，…的を絞る，…を重視する，…を強調する，…を中核に据える，…を中核事業にする，…に力を注ぐ，…に注目する，…に執着する，…に結集する（⇒business structure）
▶As our strategy, we focus on those product lines vital to our future by streamlining our operations and redeploying assets.　当社の戦略として，当社は業務の効率化と資産の有効利用により，当社の将来を支える製品ラインに焦点を当てて

います。
-focused …に的を絞った, …重視の, …中心の, …関連の
　customer-focused management 顧客重視の経営
　environment-focused businesses 環境関連事業
▶The government's plan includes measures for increasing information disclosure to encourage investment in environment-*focused* businesses. 政府の計画には, 環境関連事業への投資を促す情報開示強化の仕組みも含まれている。

fold up 廃業する, 商売をやめる, 店じまいする, 破産する, 潰れる, だめになる, 中止になる, 生産を中止する
▶The company *folded up* due to the business depression. 不景気で, 同社は潰れた。

follow 動 追随する, 従う, 追求する, 継続する, 追跡する, 後からついてくる (⇒**formula**)

follow suit 追随する, 先例に従う, 前例に倣う, 人のまねをする
▶Even if the United States does decide to shift its easy money policy, Japan will not immediately be in a position to *follow suit*. たとえ米国が金融緩和政策の転換に踏み切っても, 日本が直ちに追随する環境にはないようだ。

follower 名 追随者, 模倣者, 亜流, 信奉者, フォロワー
　follower country [nation] 追随国
　follower role 追随者の役割
　market follower マーケット・フォロワー (シェアの拡大に挑戦しないで現状維持で満足する企業)
　price follower 価格追随者

FOMC 米連邦公開市場委員会 (Federal Open Market Committeeの略。⇒**overnight loan**)
▶The *FOMC* minutes hinted at the end to Fed rate hikes. 米連邦公開市場委員会 (FOMC) の議事要旨は, FRB (連邦準備制度理事会) の利上げ打ち止めを示唆した。

food 名 食品, 食糧, 食材, フード
　food additives 食品添加物
　food and beverage industry 食品・飲料業界
　Food and Drug Administration 米食品医薬品局《略 FDA》
　food company 食品会社, 食品メーカー
　food distribution center 食品流通センター, 食品集配センター
　food manufacturer 食品メーカー (=food maker)
　food processing industry 食品加工業界
　Food Recycling Law 食品リサイクル法
　Food Sanitation Law 食品衛生法
　food security 食糧安全保障
　food service industry 外食産業, 外食業界
　food stamp 食料クーポン, フード・スタンプ (=food coupon: 米政府から生活保護者と失業保険受給者に支給される)
　food supply 食料供給
　fresh food 生鮮食品, 生鮮食料品
　frozen food 冷凍食品
　GM food 遺伝子組換え食品 (=genetically modified food)
　health food 健康食品
　organic food 有機食品, 自然食品
　retort food レトルト食品

food poisoning 食中毒
▶The Chinese-made vegetables are shunned in the wake of a series of *food-poisoning* cases caused by Chinese-made frozen gyoza dumplings. 中国産野菜は, 中国製冷凍ギョーザによる一連の食中毒事件を受けて, 敬遠されている。

food safety 食の安全, 食品の安全性
▶Mad cow disease and bird flu threatened *food safety*. 狂牛病や鳥インフルエンザなどが, 食の安全を脅かした。

food self-support ratio 食料自給率 (=food-self sufficiency ratio)
▶The nation's *food self-support ratio* has dropped to 40 percent, the lowest among advanced countries. 日本の食糧自給率は, 先進国で最低の40%に落ち込んだ。

foodstuff 名 食料, 食料品, 食糧

foot 動 支払う, 負担する, …の責任を負う
▶Under the Automotive Recycling Law, the cost of disposal will be *footed* by the vehicle's owner. 自動車リサイクル法では, 処理費用は車の所有者が負担する。

footfall 名 入場者数

foothold 名 足場, 足がかり, 基盤
▶We have gained a *foothold* in many markets that are growing faster than those in the U.S. 当社は, 米国市場を上回る速度で成長を続ける多くの海外市場で, 事業基盤を確保しました。

footing 名 合計, 合算, 突合せ, 合計検算, 締切り, 入会金, 立場, 足場, 足がかり, 地歩, 地盤, 基盤, 関係, 間柄
　financial footing 財務基盤, 経営基盤 (=financial base)
　forge a solid footing 足元を固める

on an equal footing 対等の立場で
verification of footing and posting 計算突合せ
▶To establish a solid financial *footing*, we have been strengthening our shareholders' equity. 磐石な財務基盤[経営基盤]を確立するため，当社は株主資本[自己資本]を強化しています。

FOR 貨車渡し（**free on rail** の略）

force 图 力, 勢力, 影響力, 要因, 材料, 有効性, 法的効力, 拘束力, 兵力, 軍隊, 軍
 be put into force 実施される, 施行される, 効力を発生する
 bring ... into force …を実施する
 come into force 実施される, 施行される, 効力を発生する, 発効する
 competitive forces 競争原理
 driving force 原動力, 推進力
 economic force 経済力, 経済勢力
 field sales force 外交販売員, 外務員（=field salesman, field salesperson)
 fundamental force ファンダメンタルズ要因
 guiding force 推進力, 指針
 join forces with …と協力する, …と力を合わせる, …と連携する, …と提携する
 labor force 労働力
 market forces 市場の力, 市場諸力, 市場要因, 市場原理, 需給関係
 marketing force 営業担当員
 marketing forces マーケティング要因, マーケティング諸力
 negative force 懸念材料, マイナス要因
 open-market forces 市場原理
 productive force 生産力
 sales force 販売員, 販売要員, 販売力
 sales force recruitment 販売員募集
 task force 対策委員会, 対策本部, 専門調査団, 特殊任務を持つ機動部隊, タスク・フォース
 technical force テクニカル要因
 underlying forces 構造的要因
 work force 労働力, 従業員, 労働者（=workforce)
▶Foreign exchange rate should be determined by market *forces*. 為替レートは，市場要因によって決めるべきだ。
▶No company or institution is immune to the *forces* of a paradigm change. どんな企業また機関も，社会的パラダイムの変化の影響力から免（まぬが）れることはできません。
▶We have put more men and women in our customers' plants and laboratories and offices, increasing our worldwide marketing *force*. 当社は，世界各地の営業担当員を増やして，お客さまの工場や研究所や事務所にさらに多くの当社従業員を派遣しました。

forecast 動 予測する, 予想する, 予見する, 予知する
▶The firm *forecasts* ¥50 billion loss for fiscal 2009. 同社は，2009年度の業績見通しとして500億円の赤字を予想している。

forecast 图 予測, 見通し, 予知, 予見, 予想, 予報（=forecasting; ⇒**full-year earnings**, **profit forecast**)
 business forecast 景気予測, 景気見通し, 業績見通し, 業績予測, 経営予測
 cash forecast 資金予測（=forecast of cash)
 company forecasts 会社予想
 demand forecast 需要予測
 earlier forecast 当初予想
 economic forecast [forecasting] 経済予測, 経済見通し, 景気予測, 景気見通し
 financial forecast 財務予想, 財務予測, 財務見通し, 業績予想, 業績見通し
 forecast excess returns 予想超過収益率
 forecast of sales 売上高予測, 売上高の見通し, 予想売上高, 販売予測
 growth forecast 成長見通し, 伸び率見通し（=growth prospect)
 operating profit forecast 営業利益予想, 営業利益見通し
 sales forecast 売上高の見通し, 販売予測（=forecast of sales)
▶Seven & I Holdings Co. expects an additional ¥30 billion in operating profit by 2009 from earlier *forecasts*. セブン＆アイ・ホールディングスは，2009年までに前回の予想に比べて新たに300億円の営業利益を見込んでいる。
▶Sharp Corp. kept its full-year *forecasts* unchanged. シャープは，通期業績見通しを据え置いた。
▶The company revised upward its group net profit *forecast* for the year through next March to ¥101.8 billion. 同社は，来年3月期[今年度]の連結純利[税引き後利益]予想を1,018億円に上方修正した。

forecasting 图 予測, 予想, 見通し
 business forecasting 業績予測[予想], 事業予測, 企業予想, 景気予測
 profit forecasting 利益予測, 利益予想, 収益見通し
 technological forecasting 技術予測

foreclose 動 除外する, 排除する, 専有する, 抵当流れにする

foreclosure 名 抵当流れ, 質流れ, 抵当権の請戻し権喪失, 担保権実行, 担保権行使, 物的担保実行手続き
 foreclosure proceedings 担保権実行手続き
 home foreclosures 住宅の差し押さえ
 in-substance foreclosure 実質的な担保権行使
▸Home *foreclosures* and late payments on home mortgages are likely to rise for a while longer. 住宅の差し押さえや住宅ローン延滞件数の増加は, しばらく続く見通しだ。

forefront 名 第一線, 先頭, 最前部, 最前線, 最先端, 中心, 重要部分
▸Microsoft has been at the *forefront* of the IT industry since it was established in 1975. 米マイクロソフトは, 1975年の創業以来, IT（情報技術）業界をリードしてきた。

foreign 形 外国の, 海外の, 対外
 foreign aid 対外援助
 foreign asset 海外資産, 外国資産, 対外資産, 在外資産, 外貨建て資産
 foreign bill 外国為替, 外国為替手形 (=foreign bill of exchange)
 foreign bond 外債, 外国債券
 foreign borrowings 外貨建て債務, 対外借入れ
 foreign branded product 海外ブランド品
 foreign business income 海外事業所得, 外国での事業所得
 foreign capital 外資, 外国資本
 foreign cash reserves 外貨準備高, 外貨準備 (=foreign currency reserves, foreign reserves)
 foreign corporation 外国法人, 外国企業
 Foreign Corrupt Practices Act 米国の海外不正支払い防止法, 海外不正行為防止法
 foreign debt 対外債務, 外貨債務, 外貨建て負債
 foreign debt servicing 対外債務の返済, 外貨債務の返済
 foreign demand 外需, 海外需要
 foreign entity 在外事業体
 foreign financing 対外借入れ
 Foreign Labor Certification 外国人労働者雇用許可
 foreign ownership 外国人持ち株比率, 外国人保有比率, 外国資本の所有
foreign currency 外国通貨, 外貨, 為替, 為替相場
 foreign currency assets 外貨建て資産
 foreign currency bond 外貨建て債, 外貨建て債券 (=foreign currency-denominated bond)
 foreign currency-denominated assets 外貨建て資産
 foreign currency-denominated bond 外貨建て債券
 foreign currency deposit 外貨預金
 foreign currency earnings 外貨建て収益
 foreign currency exposure 為替リスク
 foreign currency fluctuation 為替相場の変動
 foreign currency loan 外貨建て借入金, 外貨ローン
 foreign currency obligations 外貨建て債務
 foreign currency product 為替商品
 foreign currency restrictions 外貨規制
 shortage of foreign currency 外貨不足
▸*Foreign currency-denominated assets* and liabilities are translated at year-end rates in the consolidated financial statements. 外貨建ての資産と負債は, 連結財務書類上, 期末レートで換算されています。

foreign currency exchange contract 外国為替契約, 外国為替予約 (=foreign exchange contract)
▸To manage our exposure to changes in currency exchange rates, we enter into *foreign currency exchange contracts*. 為替相場の変動によるリスクを管理するため, 当社は外国為替予約を締結しています。

foreign currency market 為替市場, 為替相場 (=foreign exchange market)
▸Japan's foreign reserves swelled rapidly due to large-scale government operations in *foreign currency markets* through yen selling and dollar buying in 2003 and 2004. 日本の外貨準備高は, 2003年と2004年に政府が行った円売り・ドル買いによる大規模な為替市場への介入により膨らんだ。

foreign currency reserves 外貨準備高, 外貨準備 (=foreign cash reserves, foreign exchange reserves, foreign reserves, forex reserves:「外貨準備」は, 海外への支払いに備えて国や日銀が保有している外貨建て資産の金額)
▸The *foreign currency reserves* of Japan exceeded $1 trillion for the first time. 日本の外貨準備高は, 初めて1兆ドルを突破した。

foreign currency transaction 外貨建て取引
▸The effects of *foreign currency transactions* and of remeasuring the financial position and results of operations into the functional currency are included in the statement of

earnings. 外貨建て取引と財政状態や経営成績の機能通貨による再測定の影響額は，損益計算書に記載されています。

foreign currency translation 外貨換算，外貨換算差額
- **foreign currency translation gains** 外貨換算差益
- **foreign currency translation losses** 外貨換算差損
▸*Foreign currency translation* adjustments are accumulated in a separate component of stockholders' equity. 外貨換算調整額は，株主持ち分の独立した一項目として累計されています。

foreign direct investment 外国からの直接投資，対内直接投資，対外直接投資《略 **FDI**》
▸Outstanding *foreign direct investment* in Japan accounts for only about 3 percent of the nation's gross domestic product. （日本の外資受入額を示す）対内直接投資残高は，国内総生産（GDP）の3％程度に過ぎない。

foreign exchange 外国為替，為替，外国為替取引，為替差損益，外貨 （＝forex, FX）
- **Foreign Exchange and Foreign Trade Law** 外国為替及び外国貿易法，外為法
- **foreign exchange dealer** 為替ディーラー，為替担当者
- **foreign exchange loss** 為替差損 （＝forex loss）
- **foreign exchange position** 外国為替持ち高
- **foreign exchange rate** 外国為替レート，為替レート，外国為替相場
- **foreign exchange reserves** 外貨準備高 （＝foreign reserves, forex reserves）
▸Ahead of the current vigorous stock market, there are still some hurdles such as increasing tension in Iraq and *foreign exchange* issues. 活発な株式市場の先行きには，まだイラク情勢の緊迫化や為替問題などのハードルがある。
▸Exports provide a source of *foreign exchange*. 輸出は，外貨獲得の資金源になっている。

foreign exchange contract 外国為替予約，外国為替契約 （＝foreign currency exchange contract）
▸Our *foreign exchange contracts* almost entirely hedge firmly commercial purchases and sales. 当社の外国為替契約は，ほとんどすべての確約済み購入と販売をヘッジするものです。

foreign exchange gains 為替差益
▸The increases in earnings were due mainly to the inclusion of equity in net earnings of ABC Corp. for the full year 2006 plus *foreign exchange gains*. この増益は，主にABC社の持ち分利益を通期で連結計上したことと，為替差益によるものです。

foreign exchange gains and [or] **losses** 為替差損益 （＝forex gains or losses）
▸*Foreign exchange gains and losses* on payments during the year are credited to, or charged against, income before taxes in the year they arise. 期中の決済から生じた為替差損益は，発生年度に損益として法人税等前利益に計上されています。

foreign exchange margin trading 外国為替証拠金取引 （＝FX margin trading）
▸Profits earned through *foreign exchange margin trading* are taxable as an individual's miscellaneous income. 外国為替証拠金取引で生じた利益は，個人の雑所得として課税対象になる。

foreign exchange market 外国為替市場，外為市場，為替相場
▸The Bank of Japan intervened in the *foreign exchange market* for the fifth time in five weeks. 日銀は，5週間で5回，外国為替市場に介入した。

foreign exchange trading 外国為替取引 （＝foreign exchange dealing, foreign exchange transaction）
▸*Foreign exchange trading* with low margin requirements is banned. 少ない証拠金での外国為替取引［外国為替証拠金取引］は，禁止されている。

foreign firm 外国企業，外資系企業，外資
▸Any acquisition of a Japanese steelmaker by a *foreign firm* could impact Japanese automobile manufacturers. 外国企業による日本の鉄鋼メーカーの買収は，日本の自動車メーカーに影響を及ぼす可能性がある。

foreign fund 海外ファンド，海外投資ファンド （＝foreign investment fund）
▸The *foreign funds* converted the convertible bonds into shares of the company. 海外ファンドが，その転換社債を同社の株式に転換した。

foreign investment fund 外資系投資ファンド
▸*Foreign investment funds* are inclined to prioritize a short-term profit making. 外資系投資ファンドは，短期的な利益を優先しがちだ。

foreign investor 外国投資家，海外投資家，外資
▸A *foreign investor* is required to gain prior authorization to buy a stake of 10 percent or more in a Japanese company in a government-

designated business field. 国が指定する業種の国内企業の株式を，外資が1社で10%以上取得する場合，外資はその事前承認を得なければならない。

foreign reserves 外貨準備，外貨準備高 （= foreign cash reserves, foreign currency reserves, foreign exchange reserves, forex reserves）
▸The *foreign reserves* of Japan are the world's second-largest after China. 日本の外貨準備高は，中国に次いで世界第2位だ。

foreign subsidiary 外国子会社，海外子会社，在外子会社
▸In preparing the consolidated financial statements, all items in the income statements of *foreign subsidiaries* are translated into Swedish kronor at the average exchange rates during the year. 連結財務書類の作成上，外国子会社の損益計算書の項目は，すべて年間平均換算レートでスウェーデン・クローナに換算されています。

foreign tax credit 外国税額控除
▸Should these undistributed earnings be distributed, *foreign tax credits* would reduce the additional U.S. income tax which would be payable. これらの未処分利益を仮に分配した場合，米国で追加的に生じる法人税等の金額が，外国税額控除により引き下げられます。

forensic 形 法廷の，弁論の，討論の，科学捜査の，法医学の
　forensic doctor 法医学者，監察医，検死官
　forensic evidence 法医学的証拠
　forensic expert 科学捜査官
　forensic medicine 法医学 （= legal medicine）
　forensic pathologist 犯罪病理学者
　forensic psychiatry 司法精神医学
　forensic science 科学捜査，法医学

forerunner 名 先駆，先駆者，前身，予兆，前兆，先行指標 （⇒**online shopping mall business**）
▸The core private machinery orders are considered a *forerunner* of trends in capital spending. 実質民間機械受注は，民間設備投資の先行指標とされている。

foresee 動 予想する，予見する，見込む
▸Citigroup Inc. *foresees* a sharp fall of about 60 percent in third quarter profit due to failed mortgage investments. 米大手銀行のシティグループは，サブプライム・ローン（米国の低所得者向け住宅融資）関連の担保不動産投資の失敗で，第3四半期（7-9月期）は約60％の大幅減益を見込んでいる。

foresight 先見性，先見の明，洞察力，見通し，計画性，周到な準備

▸Companies with *foresight* and insight are eager to invest in solutions that will increase their competitiveness. 先見性と洞察力を兼ね備えた企業は，自らの競争力を高める分野に積極的に先行投資します。

forex 名 為替，外国為替 （= foreign exchange）
　forex business 為替取引 （= foreign exchange transaction, forex trading）
　forex intervention 為替介入
　forex interventions 為替介入額
　forex reserves 外貨準備高，外貨準備 （= foreign currency reserves, foreign exchange reserves, foreign reserves）
▸Japan's *forex reserves* climbed to $996 billion at the end of January due to a rise in gold and bond prices. 日本の1月末の外貨準備高は，金と債券相場の上昇で9,960億ドルに増加した。

forfeit 名 罰金，追徴金，没収物，喪失，剥奪，形 没収された，喪失した，動 喪失する，…の権利を失う，没収する

forfeiting 名 買取り，買取り金融，フォーフェイティング （輸出長期延べ払い手形の非遡及的割引）

forfeiture 名 没収，失権，失効，没収物，罰金

forgive 動 〈借金・債務者を〉免除する

forgiveness 名 放棄，免除
　debt forgiveness 債権放棄，債務の免除，債務救済 （= debt relief, debt waiver, forgiveness of debt, loan forgiveness, loan write-off）
　forgiveness of liabilities 債務免除
▸The company increased the amount of debt *forgiveness* by its creditors to ¥98.9 billion from ¥90.9 billion. 同社は，取引金融機関による債務免除額を909億円から989億円に引き上げた。

forgo [forego] 動 見送る，断念する，差し控える，遠慮する，やめる
▸The Bank of Japan's policy-setting panel unanimously decided to *forgo* an increase in its key short-term interest rate. 日銀の政策決定委員会は，短期金利（無担保コール翌日物）の誘導目標引上げの見送りを，全員一致で決めた。

fork 動 〈現金・税金などを〉支払う

form 動 設立する，組織する，組成する，結成する，作り出す，築く，構築する，形成する，設定する
　form a joint venture 合弁会社を設立する
　form a portfolio ポートフォリオを構築する
　form an underwriting group 引受団を組成する
▸Seven & I Holdings Co. was *formed* on Sept. 1, 2005 as the holding company of Ito-Yokado, Seven-Eleven Japan and Denny's Japan Co. セブン＆アイ・ホールディングスは，イトーヨーカ堂，

セブン-イレブン・ジャパンとデニーズ・ジャパンの持ち株会社として, 2005年9月1日に設立された。

form 名 様式, 書式, 形式, 表現形式, 式, 形態, 様態, 形状, 外観, 外形, 構図, 構成, 種類, フォーム (⇒participant)
- **bearer form** 無記名式
- **form of business organization** 企業形態, 企業組織の形態
- **form of financial statements presentation** 財務諸表の表示様式
- **graphic form** 図表形式
- **order form** 注文書式
- **organization form** 組織形態
- **statement form** 報告式 (=narrative form, report form)
▸The 2007 and 2008 two-for-one stock splits were effected in the *form* of 100% stock dividends. 2007年度と2008年度の1対2の株式分割は, 100%株式配当形式で実施されました。

Form 10-K 様式10-K, フォーム10-K (⇒ **annual report**)
様式10-Kとは➡ 米国の有価証券報告書の一種。米国の公開会社(証券取引所上場企業や店頭公開企業など)が, SEC(米国証券取引委員会)に提出する財務報告の様式で, 株主向け年次報告書と同じく会計監査済み(audited)のものでなければならない。
▸The Annual Report on *Form 10-K* is available from the date of its filing with the Securities and Exchange Commission in the United States. 様式10-Kに基づく当社の年次報告書は, 米国の証券取引委員会(SEC)への提出日以降に入手できます。

Form 10-Q 様式10-Q, フォーム10-Q (第1四半期から第3四半期までの特定の財務情報に関する四半期報告書)
▸The *Form 10-Q* Quarterly Report filed with the Securities and Exchange Commission will be available in May. 米国証券取引委員会(SEC)に提出した様式10Qによる四半期報告書は, 5月に配布可能となります。

formation 名 形成, 策定, 決定, 設立, 創立, 創業, 構築, 構成, 統合, フォーメーション
- **cartel formation** カルテルの形成
- **formation of a company** 会社設立, 会社創業 (=company formation)
- **formation of alliances** 提携関係の構築
- **gross capital formation** 総資本形成
- **land formation** 土地造成
- **monetary capital formation** 金融資本形成
- **policy formation** 政策策定, 政策決定
- **price formation** 価格形成
- **the formation of management of a new company** 新会社の役員構成
- **W formation** W型相場, ダブル・ボトム(double bottom)型の相場

formula 名 方式, 公式, 書式, 算式, 路線, 処理方法, 解決方法, 解決策, 案, 食品の製法, 調理法, フォーミュラ
- **book building formula** 需要予測方式, ブック・ビルディング方式
- **cost compensation formula** コスト上乗せ方式
- **development-and-import formula** 開発輸入方式
- **earnings-related formula** 給与比例方式
- **flat rate formula** 定額方式
- **formula investment [investing]** フォーミュラ投資 (一定の投資計画に基づく証券・株式の投資)
- **formula plan** フォーミュラ・プラン (フォーミュラ投資を行う場合の一定の投資計画)
- **general formula** 一般的公式
- **legal formula** 法律文書の書式
- **peace formula** 和平案, 講和案
- **well-formed formula** 論理式
▸By following his predecessor's inflation-fighting *formula*, the new Fed chairman Ben Bernanke has reassured the market. 米連邦制度理事会(FRB)前議長のインフレ抑制路線を継承して, ベン・バーナンキ新議長は, 市場に安心感を与えた。

for-profit 形 営利目的の
fortune 名 富, 財産, 資産, 大金, 繁栄, 運, 運勢, 運命, 幸運, 女神
- **a child of Fortune** 運命の寵児 (=a Fortune's favorite)
- **a small fortune** 大金, 多少の財産
- **be at the top of Fortune's wheel** 幸運の絶頂にある
- **cost a fortune** 大金がかかる
- **expectant fortune** 見込み資産, 期待財産
- **family fortune** 同族資産, 同族財産
- **fortunes** 明暗, 盛衰, 浮き沈み
- **have fortune on one's side** 運に見方される
- **make a [one's] fortune** 一儲けする, 金持になる
- **seek one's fortune** 立身出世を求める
- **try one's fortune** 運試しをする

forum 名 公開討論会, 交流の場, 交流広場, 広場, 裁判所, 法廷, フォーラム

forward 名 先物, 予約取引, 先渡し取引, 先渡し契約, 繰延べ, フォワード
- **forward contract** 先渡し契約, 先物契約, 予約契約
- **forward exchange** 先物為替, 先渡し為替, 為替

先物

forward rate 先渡し金利, 先渡しレート, 先物為替相場, 先物相場, 予約相場 （＝forward exchange rate）

forward trading 先渡し取引, 先物取引 （＝forward bargain）

forward transaction 先物取引, 先物為替取引, 先物為替予約取引, 為替予約 （＝forward contract, forward dealing）

▶The exporting companies are attempting to avoid further foreign exchange losses arising from the yen's appreciation by buying *forward* contracts. 輸出企業は, 買い為替予約（買い予約）で円高による為替差損を避けようとしている。

▶We enter into foreign exchange contract, including *forward*, option and swap contracts. 当社は, 先物, オプション, スワップなどの外国為替予約を締結しています。

forward exchange contract 先物為替予約

▶The Corporation acquired a 60-day *forward exchange contract* for US $1,000,000, in anticipation of an increase in the spot rates for US dollars. 当社は, 米ドルの直物レートが上がるのを期待して100万米ドル, 60日後の先物為替予約を取得した。

forward-looking 形 将来を見越した, 将来を見据えた, 将来を見通した, 進歩的な, 前向きの, 未来志向の

▶Companies that have completed restructuring have begun making *forward-looking* investments. リストラを完了した企業が, 将来を見越した投資を始めている。

fossil fuels 化石燃料

▶Climate change is due to rising atmospheric levels of carbon dioxide, largely from burning *fossil fuels*. 気候変動の原因は, 主に化石燃料の燃焼による大気中の二酸化炭素濃度の上昇にある。

foundation 名 基盤, 基礎, 土台, 根拠, 建設, 設立, 創立, 創業, 基金, 維持基金, 奨学基金, 基本金, 財団, 事業団, 基礎化粧品, ファンデーション

business foundation 事業基盤, 経営基盤, 経営の根幹, 経営体力

financial foundation 財務基盤, 経営基盤 （＝financial base, financial footing）

foundation of management 経営基盤

incorporated foundation 財団法人

private foundation 私的財団

▶The survey found about 68 percent of M&As were aimed at strengthening the *foundations* of existing businesses. 調査の結果, M&A（企業の合併・買収）の目的は約68％が既存事業の基盤強化であった。

foundation fund 〈保険会社の〉基金（株式会社の資本金に相当）, 基本積立金

▶Life insurer's *foundation* fund is equivalent to capital for a stock company. 生命保険会社の基金は, 株式会社の資本金に相当する。

founder 創設者, 創業者, 創始者, 設立者, 発起人, 開祖

▶The *founder* of Enron Corp. ascended to the pinnacle of U.S. business only to tumble into disgrace. 米エネルギー大手エンロンの創業者は, 米ビジネス界の頂点に上り詰めた後, 失脚して名を汚すだけの結果となった。

founder chairman 創業者会長

fourth quarter 第4四半期

fourth quarter earnings 第4四半期の利益, 第4四半期の純利益

fourth quarter results 第4四半期の業績

▶Ford Motor Co. lost $45.8 billion in the *fourth quarter* amid slumping sales and huge restructuring costs. フォード・モーターの第4四半期決算は, 販売不振と多額のリストラ費用で, 458億ドルの赤字となった。

fraction 名 断片, 破片, 一部, 小部分, 少量, 端株, 分数, 分別, 留分

common [vulgar] fraction 分数, 常分数, 普通分数

decimal fraction 小数

fraction defective 不良率

ractions omitted 端数切捨て

gross investment as a fraction of GDP 総投資の対GDP比率

fractional 形 ほんの僅かの, 取るに足りないほどの, 端数の, 断片の, 小額の, 端株（はかぶ）の, 分数の

adjustment for fractional differences 四捨五入による調整

fractional banking 部分準備銀行制度

fractional bargaining 個別交渉, 部分交渉 （＝fragmented bargaining）

fractional currency 小額通貨, 小額貨幣, 補助通貨

fractional decline 微落

fractional equation 分数方程式

fractional expression 分数式

fractional figure 端数

fractional free issue [distribution] 小刻み無償交付

fractional numbers 分数
fractional order 端株注文
fractional premium 端数保険料
fractional reserve system 部分準備制度
fractional share [stock] 端株, 端数株, 単位未満株

framework 图 枠組み, 骨組み, 関係, 体系, 制度, 仕組み, 環境
  agreed framework on new trade rules 新貿易ルールの枠組み合意（＝framework agreement on new trade rules）
  economic framework 経済関係
  framework accord 枠組み合意（＝framework agreement）
  institutional framework 制度的枠組み
  new budgetary framework 新予算制度
  regulatory framework 規制の枠組み, 規制上の枠組み, 規制体系, 規制環境
  the framework for tackling unemployment 失業対策の骨格
  Third Conference of Parties to the United Nations Framework Convention on Climate Change 気候変動枠組み条約第三回締約国会議, 温暖化防止京都会議, 京都会議
▶The WTO members managed to work out the *framework* accord through negotiations. 世界貿易機関(WTO)加盟各国は, 協議を重ねて何とか枠組み合意文書をまとめ上げた。

franchise 图 事業免許, 営業免許, 営業免許権, 営業権, 独占[一手]販売権, 加盟権, 営業地域, 営業基盤, 営業網, 特許, 特権,〈スポーツなどの〉本拠地占有権, フランチャイズ, 動 営業免許を与える, 独占販売権を与える
  area franchise 地域フランチャイズ
  business franchise 営業基盤, 市場支配力
  franchise chain フランチャイズ・チェーン《略 FC》
  franchise chain system フランチャイズ制
  franchise expansion 営業網の拡大
  franchise fee フランチャイズ料
  franchise fee revenue フランチャイズ収益, 受取フランチャイズ料
  franchise operation フランチャイズ運営
  franchise protection フランチャイズ保護
  franchise rights フランチャイズ権
  franchise selling 特約販売
  franchise system フランチャイズ・システム《略 FS》
  franchise tax 事業免許税, 営業税, 特別事業税, カリフォルニア州などの法人税, 年次報告書登録税, 年次登録税
  franchise value 営業権, フランチャイズの価値
  franchised dealer フランチャイズ加盟販売店, 一手販売権付きディーラー
  franchised restaurant フランチャイズ加盟レストラン, フランチャイズ・レストラン
  franchised retail store フランチャイズ加盟小売店
  initial franchise fee フランチャイズの頭金代, フランチャイズ料頭金
  Japan Franchise Association 日本フランチャイズチェーン協会
  operating franchise 営業基盤
  restaurant franchise レストラン・チェーン
  state franchise tax 州法人税
▶The company is seeking real estate *franchises* to begin operation in May. 同社は, 5月から展開する不動産のフランチャイズ店[フランチャイズ方式の不動産業者]を募集している。

franchise agreement フランチャイズ契約, フランチャイズ契約書
▶About 20 real estate firms have signed a *franchise agreement* with the company. 約20社が, すでに同社とフランチャイズ契約を結んでいる。

franchisee 图 フランチャイズ加盟店, 一手販売権者, チェーン店, フランチャイジー
▶The company is aiming to create 100 *franchisees* in its first fiscal year. 同社は, 初年度で100店のフランチャイズ加盟店獲得を目指している。

franchising フライチャイジング（チェーン組織の店舗展開で, フランチャイザー（本部））が各加盟店に与える免許行為）

franchisor フランチャイズ本部, 本部, フランチャイズ主宰者, フランチャイザー

fraud 图 詐欺, 詐欺行為 (⇒online fraud)

fraudulent 图 詐欺の, 詐欺的な

FRB 米連邦準備銀行 (Federal Reserve Bankの略)

FRB 米連邦準備制度理事会 (Federal Reserve Boardの略)

Freddie Mac 米連邦住宅貸付抵当公社, フレディ・マック (Federal Home Loan Mortgage Corporationの通称)
▶*Freddie Mac* understated profit for 2001 and earlier periods by more than $6 billion. フレディ・マック(米連邦住宅貸付抵当公社)は, 2001年とそれ以前の利益を, 実際より60億ドル以上少なく計上していた。

free 形 自由な, 制限[制約]を受けない, 独立の, 任意の, 自主的な, 無料の, 無償の, 免除された

free balance 正味残高
free distribution 新株の無償交付（＝free share distribution），無償増資
free distribution of common shares 無償増資，普通株式の無償交付
free fall 急落，暴落，棒落ち，棒下げ
free floating exchange rate system 自由変動相場制
free issue 無償交付（＝bonus issue）
free market price 市中相場
free-marketer 自由市場主義者
free reserve 任意積立金
free share 無償株
free share distribution 株式の無償交付
free surplus 自由剰余金，処分可能剰余金，未処分剰余金
free trade agreement 自由貿易協定《略 FTA》
interest free 無利息の
risk free asset 無リスク資産，安全資産
tax free 非課税の，免税の（＝free of tax）
▸The U.S. dollar entered a *free* fall against the yen and the euro. 米ドルが，円とユーロに対して急落した。

freehold 名 自由保有権，自由保有不動産
freeze 動 凍結する，固定する，使用［製造，販売］を禁止する
freight 名 貨物，貨物列車，用船，貨物運送，貨物便，運送料
freightage 名 貨物運送，貨物運送料，積荷
fresh capital 新規資本，追加資本，増資
▸Japanese companies actively tapped the stock market to raise *fresh capital*. 日本の企業が，新規資本を調達するため株式市場で積極的に起債した。

freshness date 品質保持期限
▸An employee of Nippon Ham sold 80 kilograms of beef that was past its *freshness date*, to a restaurant. 日本ハムの社員が，品質保持期限切れの牛肉80キロをレストランに販売していた。

friction 名 対立，不和，不一致，摩擦，軋轢，抵抗
automobile trade friction 自動車摩擦（＝friction over automobile trade）
economic friction 経済摩擦
financial friction 金融摩擦
investment friction 投資摩擦
trade friction 貿易摩擦，通商摩擦
tax friction 税制摩擦

-friendly …に役に立つ，…に有利な，…にやさしい，…が使いやすい，…になじみやすい
customer-friendly market 顧客に有利な市場
eater-friendly 消費者にとって食べやすい
eco-friendly 環境にやさしい，自然環境にあった（＝environmentally friendly）
environment-friendly technology 環境にやさしい技術
friendly acquisition 友好的買収（＝friendly takeover)
investor-friendly 投資家になじみやすい
people-friendly justice system 身近な司法制度
planet-friendly 地球にやさしい
user-friendly ユーザーに使いやすい，ユーザーに分かりやすい，使いやすい，使い勝手がよい，操作が簡単な
▸Honda Motor Co. wants to develop bioethanol vehicles as a pillar of the environmentally *friendly* technologies that the company promotes, such as hybrid cars. ホンダは，ハイブリッド車など同社が推進する環境にやさしい技術の柱として，バイオエタノール車の開発を目指している。

friendly offer 友好的買収
▸White knight is a company that saves another firm threatened by a hostile takeover by making a *friendly offer*. ホワイト・ナイトは，友好的な買収により，敵対的買収の脅威にさらされている他企業を救済する企業のことだ。

friendly takeover 友好的買収（＝friendly acquisition）
▸It is difficult to materialize a triangular merger scheme unless it is a *friendly takeover*. 友好的な買収でないと，三角合併を実現するのは難しい。

friendly takeover bid 友好的株式公開買付け，友好的TOB，株式公開買付けによる友好的買収，友好的買収
▸Nishin Food Products has obtained 86.32 percent of Myojo Food's outstanding shares in a *friendly takeover bid* for about ¥32 billion. 日清食品は，友好的TOB（株式公開買付け）で明星食品の発行済み株式の86.32％を買い取ったが，買取り価格は約320億円だった。

friendly tender offer 友好的株式公開買付け，友好的TOB（＝friendly takeover bid）
▸Kirin Brewery Co. will launch a *friendly tender offer* for Mercian shares in a capital and business alliance. キリンビールは，資本・業務提携としてメルシャン株式の友好的TOB（株式公開買付け）を実施する。

fringe benefit 付加給付，付帯給付，経済的利益，給与外給付，福利厚生費，フリンジ・ベネフィット
fringe benefit plan 付加給付制度

front 名 活動の最前線, 前線, 先頭, 最前列, 冒頭部分, 表面, 第一面, 方面, 面, 分野, 協力, 提携, 運動, フロント, 形 正面の, 前方の, 表向きの, 名目上の, 第一面の
- **be on the front burner** 重要視されている, 最優先されている
- **form [show, present] a united front against** …に対して共同戦線を張る
- **front burner** 最優先事項, 最優先課題, 優先的考慮事項, 優先事項, 最大の関心事, 重大な関心事 (＝front burner issue; ⇒**back burner**)
- **front company** 幽霊会社, 名目会社, ペーパー・カンパニー, ダミー会社
- **front cover inside** 表二
- **labor front** 労働運動, 組合運動
- **front-line employees** 第一線で活躍する従業員
- **front money** 前金, 前払い金
- **front side** 書類の表, 表面 (裏面＝back side)
- **on both the fiscal and monetary fronts** 財政・金融両面で
- **on the economic front** 経済活動の面で
- **put on the front burner** 最重視する, 最優先する, 優先する
▸ As the way to make a real progress on the environmental *front*, we set aggressive goals and used quality control techniques to achieve them. 環境の面 [環境問題] で実質的に前進する手段として, 当社は積極的な目標を掲げ, その目標を達成するための品質管理手法を採用しました。

front end 店頭, 前段階, 債券の短期物, 基近物
- **front-end loading [load]** 先取り手数料
- **front end of the Treasury market** 米国債短期物

front line 最前線, 第一線
▸ The two companies' employees are competing on the *front line* of promotion and sales. 両社の社員は, 販促や販売の最前線で競いあっている。

front-load 動 前倒しする
▸ We plan to *front-load* our current restructuring plan by three years. 当社は, 現行のリストラ (人員削減) 計画を3年前倒しする方針です。

front-loading 名 前倒し, 前倒し執行

front runner [front-runner, frontrunner] トップ企業, 第一人者, 最有力候補者, 優勝候補, トップランナー
▸ Toyota is the *front-runner* among companies that turn out goods using the distinctive Japanese method of production. トヨタは, 日本独特の生産方法で製品を生産している企業のトップ企業だ。

FSF 金融安定化フォーラム (Financial Stability Forumの略。金融監督の国際協調強化のため, 1999年2月のG7で設立を決定。現在, G7各国と国際通貨基金 (IMF), 世界銀行のほかにオランダ, スイス, オーストラリア, シンガポール, 香港の各代表者が参加。⇒Financial Stability Forum)

FSF フリーソフトウエア財団 (Free Software Foundationの略)

FTA 自由貿易協定 (free trade agreementの略)

FTA 自由貿易地域, 自由貿易圏 (free trade areaの略)

FTC 日本の公正取引委員会 (⇒Fair Trade Commission)

FTC 米連邦取引委員会 (⇒Federal Trade Commission)

fuel 名 燃料, エネルギー
- **alternative fuels** 代替燃料
- **clean fuels** クリーン燃料
- **fossil fuel reserves** 化石燃料埋蔵量
- **fossil fuel tax** 炭素税
- **fuel consumption** 燃料消費
- **fuel efficiency** 燃料効率, 燃費効率, 燃費, 省エネ
- **fuel mix** 電源構成
- **fuel oil** 重油
- **fuel prices** エネルギー価格
- **jet fuel** ジェット燃料
- **mineral fuels** 鉱物燃料
- **nuclear fuel** 核燃料
- **renewable fuel** 再生可能燃料
- **synthetic fuels** 合成燃料

▸ For JAL, a price hike of jet *fuel* by $1 per barrel means a drop of ¥5.5 billion in its recurring profit on a consolidated basis a year. 日航システムの場合, ジェット燃料の価格が1バレル当たり1ドル上昇すると, 年間の連結経常利益が55億円減る。

fuel cell 燃料電池

燃料電池とは ➡ 水に電気を通して水素と酸素に分ける電気分解とは逆の原理で, 石油やガスなどから取り出した水素と, 空気中の酸素を化学反応させて電気を作る仕組み。大気汚染源の窒素酸化物や硫黄酸化物が出ないため, 究極のクリーン・エネルギーといわれる。

- **fuel-cell vehicle** 燃料電池自動車
- **molten carbonate fuel cell** 溶解炭酸塩型燃料電池

fulfill [fulfil] 動 〈義務・約束などを〉果たす, 履行する, 遂行する, 実行する, 完了する, 〈条件を〉満たす, 充足する, 〈仕事を〉終える, 〈法律や命令に〉従う
- **fulfill one's campaign promises** 選挙公約を果

fulfill one's duties 任務をまっとうする, 任務を完了する, 任務を終える
fulfill one's [the] obligations 義務を果たす, 義務を履行する
fulfill one's potential …の可能性を最大限に発揮する[実現する]
fulfill one's promise 約束を履行する, 約束を果たす
fulfill oneself in …に[…で]自分の力を十分に発揮する
fulfill the guarantee obligations 保証債務を履行する
fulfill the order of one's superior 上司の命令に従う
fulfill the terms of the agreement 契約条項を履行する, 契約の条件を満たす

fulfillment [fulfilment] 名 履行, 遂行, 実行, 実現, 成就, 達成, 完了
a sense [feeling] of fulfillment 充足感, 満足感, 充実感, 達成感
fulfillment of the capital adequacy ratio requirements 自己資本比率基準の達成
partial fulfillment of the requirements 要件[必要事項, 基準]の一部履行
punctual fulfillment of the agreement 契約の期限どおりの履行
self-fulfillment 自己実現

full 形 完全な, 全部の, 十分な, 全面的, 正式の, 正規の, 詳しい, 充実した, 総額の
full actuarial liability 年金数理上の負債総額
full amount 全額, 総額
full dilution 完全希薄化, 完全希釈化, 完全希釈効果
full disclosure 完全開示, 完全表示, 十分な開示, 完全公開性
full eligibility 完全受給権取得, 完全受給資格取得, 完全適格者
full elimination 全額消去
full fair value method 全面時価評価法
full pension 完全年金
full provision basis 完全税効果会計, 所得税の完全期間配分 (＝comprehensive tax allocation)
full turnkey 一括受注・発注方式, フルターンキー
full value insurance 全額保険

full business year 通期 (＝full fiscal year)
▶For the *full business year* ending next March, the firm expects its group net profit to climb 17.6 percent from fiscal 2008. 来年3月までの通期で, 連結純利益は2008年度比[前期比]で17.6%増加する, と同社は予想している。

full capacity 完全操業度, フル稼働
▶Pipeline systems out of Canada have been operating at *full capacity*. カナダ国外のパイプライン・システムは, フル稼働を続けています。

full consolidation 全部連結, 完全連結, 総額連結 (⇒account balance)
▶The 2008 results include the *full consolidation* of SLM's results from March 1, 2008 until March 31, 2007. 2008年度の業績には, 2007年3月1日から2007年3月31日までのSLM社の業績の完全連結分も含まれています。

full cost 全部原価, 総原価, 総括原価, フル・コスト (＝fully allocated cost, fully distributed cost)
▶One of the most significant factors causing these differences between Canadian and U.S. GAAP is the application of *full cost* accounting rules for oil and gas. カナダ会計基準と米国会計基準の間でこれらの差異が生じている最大要因の一つは, ガスおよび石油事業に対して適用される総原価計算の基準です。

full employment 完全雇用
▶While preserving *full employment*, we have reduced our total work force. 完全雇用を保持しつつ, 当社は全体の従業員数を削減してきました。

full fiscal year to March 31 3月31日までの通期, 3月期決算 (＝full fiscal year ending March 31)
▶For the *full fiscal year to March 31*, the firm expects to post a group net loss of ¥47 billion. 3月期決算で, 同社は470億円の連結税引き後赤字を見込んでいる。

full-fledged 形 本格的な, 本腰を入れた, 一人前の, れっきとした, 立派な
full-fledged recovery track 本格回復の軌道
full-fledged threat 現実的な脅威
full-fledged work on compiling the budget 本格的な予算編成作業
make a full-fledged recovery 本格的に回復する
▶The WTO is trying to implement the *full-fledged* multilateral free trade system globally. 世界貿易機関(WTO)は, 本格的な多角的自由貿易体制を世界レベルで実施しようとしている。

full powers and authority 全権能と権限
▶The Investment Committee is vested with the *full powers and authority* of the board in cases when investment decisions are required urgently. 投資委員会は, 緊急を要する投資の決

定について，取締役会の全権能と権限を付与されています。

full-scale recovery 本格回復, 本格的な回復, 全面回復, 全面的な回復 （＝full-fledged recovery, full recovery）
▸The economy is on track for a *full-scale recovery*. 景気は，本格的な回復軌道に乗っている。

full service 完全サービス
▸The new campus includes a *full-service* cafeteria, ATMs and a health center offering comprehensive occupational health and wellness programs to all employees and their families. この新事業施設には，完全サービスのカフェテリアやATM（現金自動預け払い機）のほか，従業員とその家族に総合健康管理プログラムを提供する保健センターが設置されています。

full year 通期, 通年, 1年分
  full-year consolidated net profit 通期の純利益, 通期の税引き後利益
  full-year dividend 通期配当, 年間配当
  full-year profit and revenue 通期の利益と売上高
  full-year profit forecast 通期の利益予想, 通期の利益見通し, 通期の損益予想 （＝full-year profit estimate）
  full-year results 通期決算, 通期業績
  full-year revenues 通期の売上高
  full-year sales 通期の売上高
▸The equity in net earnings of the company was consolidated for the *full year* of 2008. 同社の持ち分利益は，2008年度通期で連結計上されています。

full-year earnings 通期の収益, 通期の業績
  full-year earnings forecast 通期の業績予想, 通期の業績見通し, 通期の収益予想 （＝full-year earnings projection, full-year forecast）
  full-year earnings target 通期の収益目標, 通期の業績目標
▸Daiwa Securities Group does not give a *full-year earnings* forecast. 大和証券グループは，通期の業績見通しは行っていない。

full-year forecast 通期業績見通し, 通期予想, 通期の業績予想 （＝full-year earnings forecast, full-year earnings projection, full-year outlook）
▸Honda raised its *full-year forecast* as sales surged in Asia. 本田は，アジアでの販売急増で通期の業績予想を上方修正した。
▸Mizuho Financial Group Inc. cut its *full-year forecast* to ¥650 billion from ¥750 billion. み

ずほフィナンシャルグループ（FG）は，通期業績予想を当初の7,500億円から6,500億円に（1,000億円）下方修正した。

full-year group operating profit 通期の連結営業利益
▸The company's *full-year group operating profit* is now estimated at ¥2.2 trillion. 同社の通期連結営業利益は，現段階で2兆2,000億円になる見通しだ。

full-year net income forecast 通期の純利益予想, 通期の税引き後利益予想
▸The firm kept its *full-year net income forecast* unchanged. 同社は，通期の純利益[税引き後利益]予想を据え置いた。

full year to March 31 3月31日までの通期, 3月期, 3月期決算
▸For the *full year to March 31*, 2009, the company's group net and pretax profits are expected to amount to ¥100 billion and ¥170 billion respectively. 2009年3月期の同社の連結税引き後利益と税引き前利益は，それぞれ1,000億円と1,700億円に達する見込みだ。

fully 副 完全に, 全部, 十分に, 正確に, 詳細に, 詳しく, 少なくとも
  fully allocated cost 全部配賦原価 （＝full cost）
  fully eligible active plan participants 受給資格取得済みの在職制度加入者
  fully funded 全額出資の, 全額拠出される, 十分積み立てられている
  fully funded affiliate 全額出資子会社
  fully funded pension 全額年金積立金
  fully owned subsidiary 完全所有子会社, 全額所有子会社, 100％子会社 （＝fully funded affiliate, fully owned unit, totally held subsidiary, wholly owned company）
  fully-paid capital stock 全額払込み済み株式 （＝fully paid share）
  fully vested 十分受給権が発生している, 受給権が確定している
  fully vested employees to pension plan 年金受給権確定従業員

fully consolidated 全部連結されている, すべて連結の範囲に含めてある
▸The company's results are *fully consolidated* in our financial statements. 同社の業績は，当社の財務書類に100％連結されています。

fully diluted 完全希薄化後の, 完全希薄化
  on a fully diluted basis 完全希薄化ベースで
  primary and fully diluted earnings per share

単純希薄化と完全希薄化による1株当たり利益
▶Primary earnings per common and common equivalent share were the same as *fully diluted* for all years shown.　普通株式および普通株式相当証券の1株当たりの希薄化前利益は，表示した全事業年度について完全希薄化後利益と同じでした．

fully diluted earnings per share　完全希薄化1株当たり利益，1株当たり完全希薄化後純利益，潜在株式調整後純利益　（=fully diluted EPS）
▶*Fully diluted earnings per share* were $2.65, up 49% from $1.78 in 2007.　1株当たり完全希薄化後純利益は，2007年度の1.78ドルを49%上回って，2.65ドルとなりました．

function 動　機能する，作動する，動く，働く，職務［機能，役目］を果たす　（⇒ATM card）
▶The managerial system of NHK is considered as having ceased to *function* properly.　NHKの経営体制は機能不全に陥った，と見られている．

function 名　機能，職能，職務，任務，業務，役目，役割，働き，部門，公式の行事，関数
　broking function　証券業務
　cost function　費用関数，原価関数
　intermediary function　仲介機能
　investment function　投資業務，投資関数
　finance function　財務職能
　internal audit function　内部監査機能
　line function　ライン機能
　physical distribution function　物流機能
　R&D functions　R&D部門，研究開発部門
　self-regulatory function　自主規制機関，自主規制の機能
　wages [pay] according to function　職務給
▶Having sales and marketing, product, and research personnel working in close proximity should permit synergy and closer coordination between the *functions*.　営業・マーケティング，製品部門と研究部門の従業員が近接して仕事に取り組むことにより，部門間の相乗効果と協調関係が生まれるはずです．
▶We want to beef up the original *functions* of futures trading, such as hedging the risk of price fluctuations, and setting proper prices in the market.　相場変動リスクの回避や市場での公正な価格形成など，先物取引の本来の機能を強化したい．

functional 形　機能の，職能の，職務上の，職掌上の，部門の，関数の
　functional approach　機能研究，機能的研究，機能的アプローチ，関数論的方法
　functional authority　職能的権限
　functional budget　機能別予算，部門予算
　functional currency　機能通貨，法貨
　functional division　職能別部門
　functional layout　機能配置
　functional responsibility　職能上の責任
▶Local currencies are generally considered the *functional* currencies outside the United States.　米国外では，一般に現地通貨を機能通貨と見なしています．

fund 動　資金を調達する，積み立てる，資金を賄う，資金を提供する，拠出する，出資する，〈赤字などを〉補塡する　（⇒tax）
　amounts funded　積立額
　be fully funded　十分積み立ててある
　be funded equally by　…が折半出資する
　fund large public expenditures　巨額の財政赤字を賄う
　fund pension costs as accrued　年金費用を発生時に積みたてる
　fund through issuance of debt　債券の発行で資金を調達する
　funded debt　固定債務，長期負債，外部負債，社債発行借入金，英国の有期国債，確定公債
　funded pension plan　積立年金制度，年金基金制度，年金基金制
　funded status　基金の状態，積立状況，拠出状態
　jointly funded organization　共同出資の組織
　liability for pension expense not funded　未積立年金費用債務
　net funded debt　純借入債務
▶This joint news Web site will be operated by a jointly *funded* organization.　この共同ニュース・サイトは，共同出資の組織が運営する．

fund 名　資金，基金，積立金，ファンド　（⇒investment fund, sovereign wealth fund）
　advance of funds　資金の提供
　amortization fund　減債基金
　application of fund　資金の使途
　assumed rates of return on pension funds　予想年金基金運用収益率
　automated fund transfer account　自動振替口座
　bond fund　債券投資信託，債券ファンド
　buyout fund　買収ファンド
　capital fund　設備資金，資金，基本金，資本基金
　classified fund　機密費
　collecting and providing of funds for terrorists　テロ資金の収集・提供
　consolidated funds statement　連結資金計算書
　cost of borrowed funds　資金調達コスト

cost of funds 資金調達コスト, 資金調達原価, 資金コスト

current funds 流動資金, 当座資金, 運営資金, 一般財政

debt service fund 借入返済基金

demand for funds 資金需要

discretionary fund 売買一任勘定資金

employee's pension fund 従業員年金基金, 厚生年金基金

endowment fund 寄贈基金

equity fund 自己資金, 出資金, 株式ファンド, 投資ファンド (同業他社の平均的収益力を上回る収益力)

excess fund 余剰資金

external fund 外部資金, 外部調達資金 (＝external funding)

fund deal 資金取引 (＝fund transaction)

fund flow 資金フロー, 資金収支, 資金循環, ファンド・フロー

fund for retirement of bond 社債償還基金 (＝bond retirement fund)

fund from operations 営業活動による資金

fund in hand 手持ち資金, 手元資金, 資金有り高 (＝fund on hand)

fund management 資金運用, 資金管理, 投資運用, 投資管理, 投資顧問

fund-of-funds ファンド・オブ・ファンズ (投資信託に投資する投資信託(「投信の投信」)で, 投資家から集めた資金の運用を, 別の複数の投資信託に再委託する仕組み)

fund manager 資金運用者, 資金管理者, 資金運用[管理]担当者, 金融資産運用者, ファンド・マネージャー

fund-raising cost 資金調達コスト, 資金調達費用 (＝fund-raising expense)

funds borrowed 借入金, 借用金

funds from external sources 外部調達資金

funds from operations 営業活動による資金, 営業活動から得た資金 (＝funds provided by operations)

funds provided by operations 営業活動により得た資金, 営業活動によって供給された資金, 営業活動による資金 (＝funds provided from operations)

funds provided from net earnings 純利益により得た資金, 純利益で得た資金

funds provided from operations 営業活動から得られた資金, 営業活動による資金, 営業活動から生じた資金 (＝funds provided by operations)

income fund 収益配当型投資信託, インカム・ファンド

index mutual fund インデックス・ミューチュアル・ファンド (＝index fund: 株価指数と連動するように設計された株式ポートフォリオを運用対象とする投資信託)

internal fund 内部資金

invest in the fund ファンドに出資する

invested fund 投下資本, 投資資金

liquid fund 流動資金, 当座資金

loanable fund 貸付け資金, 貸出の原資

operating fund 運転資金, 運用資金

pension fund 年金基金, 年金資金, 年金積立金

petty fund 小口資金

plant expansion fund 工場拡張基金

redemption fund 償還基金

revolving fund 回転資金

shareholders funds 株主資本

shift of funds 資金の移動

slush fund 不正資金, 賄賂(わいろ)資金, 贈賄(ぞうわい)資金

source and application [disposition] of funds 資金の源泉と使途

sources and uses of funds 資金収支表

urgent fund 緊急資金

use of funds 資金の使用, 資金の使途

▶ *Funds* provided from net earnings, depreciation, and amortization were offset primarily by investment outflow and increased working capital requirements. 純利益と減価償却[減価償却および償却]で得た資金は, 主に投資支出額と必要運転資本の増加額で相殺されました。

fund raising 資金調達, 資本調達

▶ Japan Airlines Corp. is expected to fall short of its planned *fund-raising* target by about ¥50 billion due to lower stock price. 日本航空では, 株価の下落で, 当初計画の資金調達目標を約500億円下回る見通しだ。

fund-raising plan 資金調達計画

▶ The firm's ¥560 billion syndicated-loan from 31 banks and leasing companies is part of its *fund-raising* plan. 同社が銀行やリース会社から受ける560億円の協調融資は, 同社の資金調達計画の一環だ。

fundamental profit 基礎利益 (＝basic profit: 「基礎利益」は, 保険の販売など, 本業の保険業務による収益[利益]を意味する)

fundamentals 名 基本, 原理, 根本原理, 基礎, 基礎的条件, 基本的指標(国の成長率, インフレ率, 財政収支, 金融情勢, 為替レート, 経常・貿易収支の六つ), ファンダメンタルズ

company fundamentals 企業のファンダメンタ

ルズ
economic fundamentals 経済のファンダメンタルズ, 経済の基礎的条件, 景気のファンダメンタルズ （＝fundamentals of the economy）
financial fundamentals 財務面のファンダメンタルズ, 財務体質
▸We do not see anything in the *fundamentals* of our business that would cause us to change our strategy of investing for profitable growth. 当社の事業基盤に, 高い利益を生む成長をめざした当社の投資方針の変更を迫るような要素は, 見当たりません。

funding 图 資金調達, 調達, 調達手段, 積立て, 資金化, 資金源, 長期債化, 長期国債の借換え, 基金設立, 融資, 拠出, 資金供与, 資金提供, 出資, 事業費, 財政援助
advance funding method 事前積立方式
cost of floating rate funding 変動金利による資金調達コスト
direct funding 直接融資
employee pension funding 従業員年金基金への拠出
external funding 外部資金調達 （＝external financing）
funding capacity 資金調達能力
funding cost 資金調達コスト （＝cost of funding）
funding for redemption of corporate bonds 社債の償還資金
investment funding 投資金融
long-term funding 長期資金の調達
terminal funding 年金現価積立方式
terminal funding method 年金現価充足方式
▸During 2008, the Company experienced a significant increase in its cash requirements because of *funding* of the Profit Sharing and Pension Trust plans. 利益分配および年金信託制度への資金拠出により, 2008年度は必要資金が増加しました。

funding contributions 年金積立額
▸The cumulative difference between amounts expensed as pension costs and the *funding contributions* is reflected on the consolidated balance sheet. 年金原価として費用処理した額［年金費用］と年金積立額の間の累積差額は, 連結貸借対照表上に表示されています。

furnish 動 提供する, 供給する, 取り付ける
▸Company shall further *furnish* Licensee with the following technical information relating to the machinery of the plant free of charge. 会社は, プラントの機械類に関してさらに次の技術情報をライセンシーに無償で提供する。

further 形 一層の, 一段の, 追加の
further cost cutting 一層のコスト削減
further earnings decline 業績の一段の悪化
further payment 追加支払い
further rate cut もう一段の利下げ

furtherance 图 促進, 推進, 助成, 助長
▸Management of the corporation, in *furtherance* of the integrity and objectivity of data in the financial statements, has developed and maintains, a system of internal accounting controls. 当社の経営者は, 財務書類に含まれる［財務書類上の］データの完全性と客観性を高めるため, 会計に関する内部統制組織［内部会計統制組織］を整備［開発］し, これを維持しています。

futures 图 先物, 先物取引, 先物契約, 先物為替 （⇒commodity futures trading）
bond futures 債券先物, 債券先物取引
commodity futures 商品先物
currency futures 通貨先物, 通貨先物取引
financial futures 金融先物, 金融先物取引
financial futures market 金融先物市場
futures contract 先物契約
futures trading 先物取引
index futures 指数先物
interest rate futures 金利先物, 金利先物取引
New York Futures Exchange ニューヨーク先物取引所
option on futures 先物オプション
stock futures 株式先物
stock index futures 株価指数先物
synthetic futures 合成先物
▸These financial goods listed on the TSE include convertible bonds, government and corporate bonds, as well as stock index *futures* and options. 東証の上場金融商品には, 転換社債や国債, 社債のほか株価指数先物, 株価指数オプションなどがある。

FX 外国為替 （＝foreign exchange, forex）
FX margin trading 外国為替証拠金取引, FX取引 （FX取引では, 一定額の現金を証拠金として差し入れ, それを担保にインターネットなどで外貨を売買できる）
▸In *FX margin trading*, investors can expect high returns from a relatively small amount of capital. 外国為替証拠金取引では, 投資家は, 比較的わずかな資金でハイリターンを期待できる。

FY 会計年度, 事業年度, 営業年度, 年度 （**fiscal year**の略）

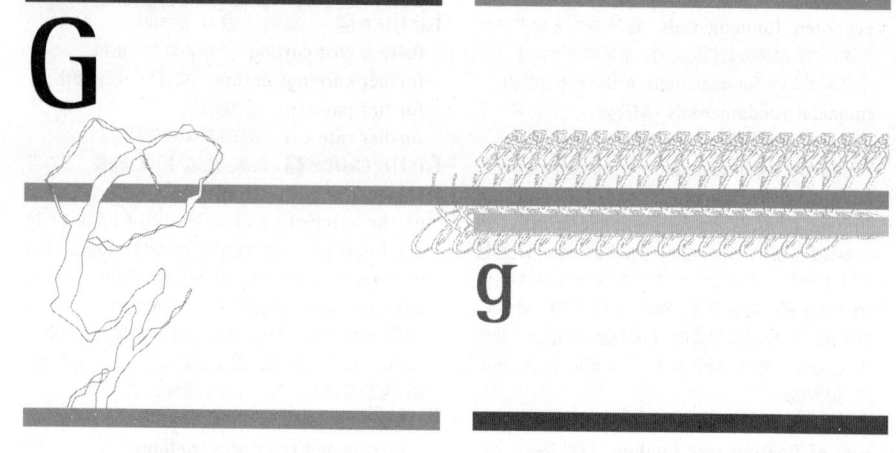

G7 先進7か国財務相・中央銀行総裁会議, 先進7か国会議, 7か国蔵相会議 （＝Group of Seven: 英・加・仏・伊・独・日・米の7か国が参加。2003年からロシアが参加して, G8（Group of Eight）となる）
G7 leaders G7首脳 （＝Leaders of the Group of Seven）
G7 nations 先進7か国, 主要7か国 （⇒**Group of Seven nations**）
G7 statement G7声明
the chair of the G7 meeting G7議長国
▸*G7 leaders failed to take concrete action for policy coordination.* G7首脳は, 具体的な政策協調策を取ることができなかった。
G8 主要8か国, 主要8か国首脳会議, 8か国蔵相会議, 中南米8か国グループ （＝Group of Eight）
G8 leaders G8首脳
G8 summit 主要8か国首脳会議, G8サミット
GAAP 一般に認められた会計原則［会計基準］, 一般に公正妥当と認められた会計原則, 一般会計原則［会計基準］, 会計基準, ジー・エイ・エイ・ピー, ギャップ （⇒**generally accepted accounting principles**）
▸*The consolidated financial statements have been prepared in accordance with German GAAP.* この連結財務書類［財務諸表］は, ドイツの一般に公正妥当と認められた会計基準［ドイツの会計基準］に従って作成されています。
GAAS 一般に認められた監査基準, 一般に公正妥当と認められた監査基準 （generally accepted auditing standardsの略。⇒**misstatement**）
gadgetry 名 便利な小型機器［機械類］, 電気器具類, 小道具類
▸*The government will introduce more IT gadgetry*

such as IC tags and GPS-related equipment to help improve relief delivery operations in large-scale natural disasters. 大規模災害時の支援物資の輸送活動を促進するため, 政府はICタグ（電子荷札）やGPS（全地球測位システム）関連機器などの情報技術（IT）機器類を本格的に導入する方針だ。
gain 動 得る, 獲得する, 入手する, 達成する,〈技術などを〉身につける,〈経験などを〉積む, 増加する, 増大する, 増進する, 増す, 向上する, 上がる, 上昇する
gain control [dominance] 支配権を得る, 経営権を得る［握る］, 主導権を得る
gain experience 経験を積む
gain market share シェア［市場シェア］を獲得する, シェアを拡大する, シェアを伸ばす, シェアを奪う
gain market share from …からシェアを奪う
gain technical information 技術情報を手に入れる, 技術情報を入手する
▸*For the April-September period, operating profit gained 12 percent from the year before.* 4－9月期（3月期決算企業の上半期）の営業利益は, 前年同期比で12％増加しました。
gain 名 利益, 利潤, 利得, 増加, 増大, 増進, 伸び, 拡大, 上昇, 向上, 差益, ゲイン （⇒**capital gain, latent gain, unrealized gain**）
contingent gain 偶発利益 （＝gain contingency）
currency gain 為替差益
earnings gain 収益の伸び
gain contingencies 偶発利益事象, 偶発利益
gain from forgiveness of debt 債務免除益
gain from appreciation of securities 有価証

券評価益
gain from operations 営業利益
gain from reduction of capital stock 減資差益 (=gain from capital reduction)
gain on bond conversion 社債転換差益
gain on disposal of equipment 設備処分益
gain on redemption of stock 株式償還益
gain on retirement of treasury stock 自己株式消却益
holding gain 保有利益
market share gains マーケット・シェアの拡大, 市場シェアの拡大
net realized and unrealized capital gains 純実現・未実現キャピタル・ゲイン
post net gains 黒字を計上する
purchasing power gain or loss 購買力損益 (=gain or loss in purchasing power)
productivity gain 生産性の向上
sales and earnings gains 増収増益
secure gains 利益を確保する
stockholding gains 保有株式の含み益
unrealized gains on [in] securities 証券含み益
unrecognized net gain 未認識純利益
▶Foreign investors who were exchanging dollars for yen to buy Japanese shares began selling their stocks because of the possible rate hike to secure their *gains*. ドルを円に換えて日本株を買っていた外国人投資家が, (米国の) 利上げ観測で, 利益を確保するために日本株を売りはじめた。
▶We had a $50 million *gain* on this sale. 当社は, この売却で5,000万ドルの利益を上げました。

gain and loss [gain or loss] 損益
▶When we dispose of assets that were depreciated using the unit method, we include the *gains or losses* in operating results. 個別償却法で償却した資産を処分する場合, その利益または損失は営業損益に含めます。

gain in revenues 売上高[収益]の伸び, 増収
▶A *gain in revenues* was recorded in 2008 despite the intense competitive environment in North America. 2007年度は, 北米市場で競争が激化した[北米市場での熾烈な競争環境]にもかかわらず, 売上高の伸びを記録しました。

gamble 動 冒険する, 賭け事をする, 名 投機売買, 賭博

game 名 事業, 計画, 職業, 仕事, 商売, 駆け引き, 計略, 策略, 試合, 狩猟, 猟, 娯楽, 遊戯, ゲーム
bargaining game 交渉ゲーム
game console ゲーム機

game plan 戦略, 方針, 予定の行動, 行動計画, 作戦計画, 慎重な計画, ゲーム・プラン
game park [reserve] 禁猟区, 鳥獣保護区
game theory ゲーム理論
management game マネジメント・ゲーム
money game マネー・ゲーム
public relations game 広告業, 宣伝業 (=advertising game)
simulation game シミュレーション・ゲーム
zero-sum game ゼロ和ゲーム, ゼロサム・ゲーム
▶Listed companies need to formulate *game* plans to continue to increase their profits. 上場企業は, 増益を続けるための戦略策定を求められている。

GAO 米会計検査院 (General Accounting Officeの略)

gap 名 格差, 隔たり, 開き, 差, 不一致, 相違点, 落差, 空白, ギャップ
demand supply gap 需給ギャップ (=gap between demand and supply)
generation gap 世代間の断絶, 世代間ギャップ
income gap 所得格差
price gap 価格の開き
technology gap 技術格差, 技術ギャップ
the gap in the market 市場参入の好機, 新製品開発の好機
trade gap 貿易赤字
wage gap 賃金格差
▶The increase in people engaged in part-time jobs and wage disparities caused by differences in corporate size and industrial sectors are cited as major reasons for the growing income *gap*. パートタイマーの増加や企業規模・業種による賃金格差が, 所得格差拡大の大きな理由に挙げられている。

garage entrepreneur ガレージ起業家 (自宅ガレージでの事業から大企業にまで発展させる実業家のこと)

garage sale 中古品販売, ガレージ・セール

garnish 動 装飾する, 差し押さえる

garnishee 動 差し押さえる, 名 差し押さえ通告を受けた人, 第三債務者

gas 名 ガソリン (=gasoline, petrol), 気体, ガス
coal gas 石炭ガス
commercial gas 業務用ガス
fuel gas 燃料ガス
gas fittings ガス器具
gas grids ガス・パイプライン網
gas-guzzler 大型車, 燃費効率の悪い車, 高燃費車
gas hydrate ガス・ハイドレート (海底資源の一つ)

gas mileage 1ガロン当たりの走行マイル数, 燃費, 燃料消費量 (=gasoline mileage)
gas sipper 低燃費車, ガソリン消費の少ない車
gas station 給油所, ガソリン・スタンド (=filling station, service station)
gas storage ガス貯蔵
industrial gas 工業用ガス, 産業用ガス
liquefied natural gas 液化天然ガス《略 LNG》
liquefied petroleum gas 液化石油ガス《略 LPG》
natural gas deliverability 天然ガスの供給能力
natural gas distribution 天然ガスの配給
natural gas field 天然ガス田
oil and gas producing company 石油・ガス採掘会社
propane gas プロパンガス
residential gas 家庭用ガス
tear gas 催涙ガス

▸China proceeds with the development of natural *gas* fields in the East China Sea. 中国は, 東シナ海で天然ガス田開発を進めている。

gas-electric hybrid car ガソリン・電気併用ハイブリッド車
▸There are now three *gas-electric hybrid car* models on the market: the Toyota Prius, the Honda Insight, and the hybrid version of of the Honda Civic. 市場には現在, トヨタのプリウス, ホンダのインサイトとホンダ・シビックのハイブリッド版と, 3種類のガソリン・電気併用ハイブリッド車が存在する。

gasoline 名 ガソリン, 揮発油 (=gas)
gasoline mileage 燃費
gasoline tax ガソリン税
high octane gasoline ハイオクタン・ガソリン
lead-free gasoline 無鉛ガソリン
leaded gasoline 有鉛ガソリン
oxygenated gasoline 高酸素含有ガソリン
premium leaded gasoline プレミアム鉛化ガソリン
reformulated gasoline 改良ガソリン
regular unleaded gasoline 無鉛レギュラー・ガソリン
unleaded gasoline 無鉛ガソリン

▸Hikes in *gasoline* prices are accelerating. ガソリン価格の上昇は, 急ピッチだ[加速している]。

gas-to-liquid (GTL) products GTL製品
gate 名 門, 出入り口, 入場者, 入場者数, 入場料, 入場料総額
gauge [gage] 動 判断する, 評価する, 測定する, 計測する, 算定する, 算出する

▸In the term-end settlement of accounts at the end of September, most companies use the daily average for a month of the share prices in *gauging* the value of latent gains or losses in their stockholdings. 9月末の期末決算で[9月中間決算で], 大半の企業は, 保有株式の含み損益を算出する際に株価の月中平均を使っている。

gauge 名 基準, 尺度, 指標, 計器, 測定用器具 (=gage; ⇒key gauge)
the most closely watched gauge of money supply 特に注目されるマネー・サプライの指標, 代表的なマネー・サプライの指標
the most widely used gauge of inflation 最も広く使用されているインフレ(物価上昇率)の基準

▸The key *gauge* of consumer prices dropped 0.2 percent from a year earlier. 消費者物価指数は, 前年度に比べて0.2%下落した。
▸The nation's most closely watched *gauge* of money supply grew 2 percent in December from a year earlier. 日本の代表的なマネー・サプライの指標が, 12月は前年同月比で2%増加した。

GCC 湾岸協力会議 (Gulf Co-operation Councilの略)
GDP 国内総生産 (gross domestic productの略)
advanced GDP figures GDP速報値
annualized nominal GDP growth 年率換算での名目GDP成長率
GDP growth rate GDP成長率
GDP revisions GDP改定値
nominal GDP 名目GDP (⇒price fluctuation)
per capita GDP 人口1人当たりのGDP
real GDP 実質GDP (国内経済がある一定の期間に生み出したモノやサービスを合計した金額から物価変動の要因を取り除いた額)
real GDP growth 実質GDP成長率

▸The annualized nominal *GDP* growth marked the first decline in five quarters. 名目GDPは, 年率換算で5四半期ぶりにマイナス成長となった[年率換算での名目GDP成長率は, 5四半期ぶりに減少した]。

gear 名 歯車, 伝動装置, 道具, ギア, 動 連動する
gearing 名 負債, 負債比率, 純負債比率, ギアリング (=financial leverage, leverage, trading on the equity)
acceptable gearing 許容範囲の負債比率
financial gearing 財務レバレッジ, ギアリング, 借入比率, 負債比率, 資金調達力比率 (企業の資本構成に占める負債の額)

gearing effect レバレッジ効果
group gearing 連結純負債比率
gearing adjustments ギアリング調整［修正］, 負債調整額, ギアリング調整額
gearing proportion 負債調整率, ギアリング調整率
gearing ratio 株主資本負債比率, 優先資本比率, ギアリング比率, ギアリング・レシオ （＝the ratio of net debt to equity）
high gearing 大きな負債
increase [boost, improve] gearing 負債比率 ［借入比率］を引き上げる
net gearing 純負債比率 （＝net gearing level）
reduce gearing 負債比率を引き下げる
▶We reduced the ratio of net debt to equity (*gearing* ratio) to 15 percent in 2008. 2008年度は, 株主資本純負債比率（ギアリング・レシオ）を15％に引き下げました。

gene 名 遺伝子
gene bank 遺伝子銀行
gene information 遺伝子情報
gene splicing 遺伝子組換え （＝gene transplantation）
gene therapy 遺伝子治療
gene therapy treatment 遺伝子治療法
▶Human *genes* are composed of 3 billion chemical units of four varieties that are linked together. 人間の遺伝子は, 4種類の化学物質（塩基）が30億つながって構成されている。

general 形 一般の, 一般的な, 全般的な, 総合的, 多岐にわたる, 概略的な, 概略の, 通常の, 総…
general administrative expense 一般管理費, 総務費, 本社費 （＝general administration cost, general and administrative expense）
general assembly 総会, 大会
general consumer goods 一般消費財
general expense 一般費, 一般経費, 間接費, 総経費 （＝general cost, general operating expense, selling and administrative expense）
general glut 全面的過剰生産
general legal services 一般法律業務
general management 総合管理, 全般管理
general market 市場全般, 市場平均
general merchandise store 総合スーパー《略 GMS》
general mortgage bond 一般担保付き社債
general obligation bond 一般財源債, 一般保証債
general office employee 一般職
general public works 一般公共事業

General Services Administration 米一般調達局, 米調達局, 米共通役務庁
general shareholders [shareholders'] meeting 株主総会 （＝general meeting, general meeting of shareholders, shareholders' general meeting, stockholders' meeting）
general staff 管理スタッフ, ゼネラル・スタッフ, 参謀, 幕僚
general syndication 一般シ団の組成
general trading company 総合商社

general contractor 総建築請負業者, 元請業者, 一般請負人, ゼネコン
▶Aoki Corp. became the first *general contractor* with debt waivers to have collapsed. 債権放棄を受けているゼネコンで経営破綻したのは, 青木建設が初めてだ。

general corporate expenses 一般本社経費, 全社共通費, 全社一般経費, 会社全体の一般的経費, 一般間接経費
▶Operating profit excludes general corporate expenses, net interest and income taxes. 営業利益に, 全社一般経費と支払い利息純額, 法人税等は含まれていません。

general corporate purposes 一般事業目的
▶The proceeds from all newly issued shares were used for *general corporate purposes*. 新規発行株式の売却代金は, すべて一般事業目的に使用しました。

general meeting 総会, 株主総会 （＝general shareholders meeting）
annual general meeting 年次総会, 年次株主総会
extraordinary general meeting 臨時株主総会 （＝extraordinary meeting of shareholders）
first general meeting 創立総会
general meeting of stockholders [shareholders] 株主総会 （＝general shareholders meeting）
regular general meeting 定例総会, 定例株主総会 （＝ordinary general meeting）
▶A majority of businesses that closed their accounts for the year to March 31 plan to hold their respective *general meetings* of shareholders next week. 3月期決算企業の大半は来週, それぞれ株主総会の開催を予定している。

generally accepted accounting principles 一般に認められた会計原則, 一般に認められた会計基準, 一般に公正妥当と認められた会計原則［会計基準］, 一般会計基準《略 GAAP》 （＝generally accepted accounting practices, gener-

ally accepted accounting standards)
▸The consolidated financial statements were prepared in accordance with Canadian *generally accepted accounting principles*.　この財務書類は，一般に認められたカナダの会計基準［カナダの一般会計基準］に従って作成しました．
　　generally accepted auditing standards　一般に認められた監査基準《略 GAAS》
▸Our examinations were made in accordance with *generally accepted auditing standards*.　私どもの監査は，一般に公正妥当と認められる監査基準に準拠して行われています．
generate 動　生み出す，生む，創造する，生成する，引き起こす，誘発する，獲得する，…を占める，計上する，発生する
　　ability to generate cash　収益力
　　generate cash　収益を上げる，キャッシュ・フローを生み出す
　　generate cash flow　現金収入を得る，キャッシュ・フローを生み出す［生成する］
　　generate foreign exchange　外貨を得る，外貨を獲得する
　　generate operating margin　営業収益を計上する
　　generate profits　利益を生み出す，利益を生む
▸Cash requirements in 2009 will be met by internally *generated* funds.　2009年度の資金必要額は，内部調達資金で賄う予定です．
▸Funds *generated* from operations increased to $115 million from $90 million in the first quarter.　事業活動に伴って発生した資金は，第1四半期の9,000万ドルから1億1,500万ドルに増加しました．
generation 名　世代，発生，生成，形成，創出，産出，生産，発電，ジェネレーション　(⇒**wage cuts**)
　　baby-boom generation　団塊の世代
　　capital generation　資本創出
　　cash generation　キャッシュ・フロー，キャッシュ生成能力
　　coal thermal power generation　石炭火力発電
　　cogeneration　コジェネレーション，電気・熱併給，熱併給発電
　　combined cycle generation　複合サイクル発電，複合発電　(＝power generation by combined cycle)
　　electric power generation　発電
　　generation capability　発電能力
　　geothermal generation　地熱発電　(＝geothermal power generation)
　　integrated gas combined cycle generation　石炭ガス化複合サイクル発電
　　internal capital generation　内部資本形成率，内部資本創出率
　　internal cash generation　内部キャッシュ・フロー，内部キャッシュ生成能力
　　magnetohydrodynamic power generation　電磁流体力学発電，MHD発電
　　new generation product　新世代の機種
　　nuclear power generation　原子力発電
　　ocean thermal energy conversion generation　海洋温度差発電
　　photovoltaic power generation　太陽光発電
　　power generation　発電
　　power generation from urban waste　ゴミ発電
　　pumped-power generation　揚水発電　(＝pumping-up hydraulic power generation)
　　revenue generation　収益確保
　　solar electric generation　太陽光発電　(＝solar energy power generation)
　　solar thermal electric generation　太陽熱発電　(＝solar thermal power generation)
　　steam power generation　火力発電
　　terrestrial heat power generation　地熱発電　(＝terrestrial geothermal power generation)
　　trip generation　発生交通量，トリップ発生
　　wave activated generation　波力発電
　　wholesale generation　卸電気事業者
　　wind generation　風力発電　(＝wind power generation)
▸Sanyo Electric Co. will invest more than ¥200 billion in its rechargeable battery and photovoltaic power *generation* businesses over the three years from fiscal 2008.　三洋電機は，充電池と太陽光発電の2事業を2008年度から3年間で2,000億円強投資する．
generator 名　…発生器，発電機
generic 形　一般の，通常の，総体的な，包括的，一般名の，商標登録による保護を受けていない，ジェネリック
　　generic product　無印商品　(＝generic brand, generics, nobrand)
　　generic rating　包括的格付け
　　generic technology　基礎技術，先導の基礎研究，ジェネリック・テクノロジー
　　generics　無印商品，商標登録されていない一般商品，ノーブランド商品　(＝generic brand, generic product, nobrand)
generic drug　後発医薬品，ジェネリック医薬品
▸A new firm to be formed from the merging of

Mitsubishi Pharma Corp. and Tanabe Seiyaku Co. will enter the *generic drug* market as an all-round producer of pharmaceuticals.　三菱ウェルファーマと田辺製薬の合併で設立される新会社は，総合医薬品メーカーとして後発医薬品［ジェネリック医薬品］市場に参入する。

genetic engineering　遺伝子工学（＝biogenetics）
▶The United States had a bitter experience with food products made by *genetic engineering*.　米国は，遺伝子組換え食品では苦い経験がある。

genetic material　遺伝子試料
▶A Japanese researcher was indicted on charges of stealing *genetic material* on Alzheimer's disease.　アルツハイマー病の遺伝子試料を持ち出した罪で，日本人研究者が起訴された。

genetically modified　遺伝子組換えの《略 GM》（＝genetically engineered）
　genetically modified food　遺伝子組換え食品（＝genetically altered food, GM food）
　genetically modified organisms　遺伝子組換え作物，遺伝子組換え農産物《略 GMOs》
　genetically modified plant　遺伝子組換え植物
　genetically modified seeds　遺伝子組換え種子
▶Strong concerns have been raised over the effects that *genetically modified* food may have on the human body and on environment.　遺伝子組換え食品の人体や環境への影響については，疑問視する見方が強い。

gentrify 動　再開発して高級化する，〈スラム街の〉住宅地の中流階級化，〈商品を〉高級市場向けに転換する

geographic market　地域市場

geographic revenues　地域別売上高
▶*Geographic revenues* from customers are based on the location of the selling organization rather than the location of the customer.　地域別顧客売上高は，顧客の所在地ではなく，販売組織の所在地に基づく売上高です。

geopolitical risks　地政学的リスク
▶The surge in oil prices reflects a massive influx of speculative funds into oil markets against the backdrop of these *geopolitical risks*.　原油価格の急騰は，これらの地政学的リスクを背景に，原油市場への投機資金の大量流入を反映している。

ghost 名　幽霊，幻，ゴースト，動　つきまとう

giant 名　巨大企業，大国
　economic giant　経済大国（＝economic power, economic superpower）
　electronic giant　電機大手，大手電機

international giant　国際的巨大企業，国際大手企業（＝international giant firm, international giant corporation）
▶The nation's four electronic *giants* reported blows to profits in the April-June quarter.　電機大手4社の4－6月期の収益は，大幅に悪化した。

gig 名　〈音楽関係の〉仕事，出演，出演契約，ライブ

gilts 名　ギルト債，英国国債
　gilt-edged credit quality　最優良の信用力
　gilt-edged security　ギルト・エッジ債，ギルト債，一流証券，優良証券
　gilt-edged stock　ギルト債，一流株，優良株

Gini coefficient　ジニ係数（＝Gini Index, Gini rate）
▶Since the 1980s, Japan has been witnessing a mild increase in its *Gini coefficient*, which is a measure of income disparities.　1980年代以降，日本は，所得格差を示す指標であるジニ係数が緩やかに上昇している。

Gini Index　ジニ係数（＝Gini coefficient, Gini ratio）
▶*Gini Index* readings are the gauges for measuring the degree of income inequality in a population.　ジニ係数は，国民の所得配分不平等の程度を測る指標だ。

Ginnie Mae　ジニー・メイ（米国の住宅抵当公庫 Government National Mortgage Association の愛称）

giveaway 名　景品，懸賞付き番組，不法取引，秘密漏洩

glitch 名　突然の故障，障害，異常，誤作動，突発事故，欠陥，トラブル
　computer glitch　コンピュータの誤作動
　glitch-free　故障を起こさない，異常のない，トラブルが生じない
　software glitch　ソフトウェアの欠陥
　system glitch　コンピュータのシステム障害
▶The Tokyo Stock Exchange was forced to suspend trading in the futures contract based on the TOPIX due to its computer system *glitch*.　東京証券取引所は，コンピュータのシステム障害で，東証株価指数（TOPIX）先物取引の取引停止に追い込まれた。

global 形　全世界の，世界の，全世界的，国際的な，世界的規模の，地球規模の，地球全体の，グローバルな，広範囲の，全体的な，全面的な，包括的，総合的な，グローバル
　global competition　国際競争，グローバルな競争（＝international competition）
　global productivity　総生産性

global sales 世界全体での売り上げ

global standard 世界標準, グローバル・スタンダード
▸One of the aims for the three banks to merge into the Mizuho Financial Group was to survive the *global* competition by exploiting the banks' combined strength.　3行がみずほフィナンシャルグループに合併する目的[狙い]の一つに, 3行の統合力を駆使して国際競争に勝ち抜くことがあった。

global company 世界企業, グローバル企業
▸To grow, we have to be a *global company*.　当社が成長するためには, グローバル企業になる必要があります。

global competitiveness 国際競争力
▸The goal of the restructuring is to reinforce our *global competitiveness*.　この事業再構築は, 当社の国際競争力の強化を目的としている。

global economy 世界経済, 世界の景気, 地球規模の経済 (＝world economy)
▸Based on our expectations for the *global economy*, we expect greater sales growth in 2009.　世界景気に対する当社の期待によれば, 2009年度は一段と大きな売上の伸びを見込んでいます。
▸The *global economy* has been deteriorating even more rapidly since the beginning of this month.　世界経済は, 今月に入って一段と急速に悪化している。
▸The United States is important for the *global economy*.　米国は, 地球規模の経済にとって重要である。

global market グローバル市場, 世界市場, 国際市場, グローバル・マーケット (＝global marketplace, international market)
▸Instability in *global markets* is increasing with rising downside risks.　下振れリスクの増大とともに, グローバル市場の不安定性は高まっている。

global positioning system 全地球測位システム, 全地球位置把握システム, 世界的位置決定システム, 世界測位衛星システム《略 GPS》(⇒ gadgetry)
▸KDDI's au mobile phones currently provide a pedestrian navigation service by using the *global positioning system*.　KDDIは現在, 携帯電話のauで, 全地球測位システムを利用して歩行者の道案内サービスを提供している。

global strategy 世界戦略, 国際戦略, グローバル戦略
▸The export base of Thai is part of Nissan's *global strategy* to include ASEAN countries in its component supply network.　タイの輸出拠点は, ASEAN（東南アジア諸国連合）諸国を日産の部品供給ネットワークに組み込む日産の世界戦略の一環だ。

global warming 地球温暖化 (＝the warming of the earth)
▸Carbon dioxide is one of the gases that contribute to *global warming*.　二酸化炭素は, 地球温暖化の原因となっているガスのひとつだ。

global warming gas 地球温暖化ガス (＝greenhouse gas)
▸The United States is the largest producer of *global warming gases*.　米国は, 地球温暖化ガスの最大の排出国だ。

globalization 名　グローバル化, 世界化, 国際化, 地球的規模化, 全世界一体化, グローバリゼーション

　　economic globalization 経済のグローバル化
　　market globalization 市場のグローバル化
▸Our strategy for the second half of 2009 is to continue the *globalization* of our business while gaining market share in North America.　北米の市場シェアを拡大する一方, 事業の国際化を引き続き推進するのが, 2009年度下期の当社の経営戦略です。

glut 名　供給過剰 (＝oversupply)
▸The United States called on Japan to reduce uneconomic excess capacity among steelmakers in a bid to cope with a *glut* on the global steel market.　世界の鉄鋼市場の供給過剰に対処するため, アメリカは日本に対して鉄鋼業界の非経済的な過剰生産設備の削減を求めた。

GM 遺伝子組換えの (⇒**genetically modified**)
　　GM labeling 遺伝子組換え食品の表示, 遺伝子組換えの表示
　　GM materials 遺伝子組換え原料[原材料]
▸*GM* labeling for the 30 food products became mandatory from the spring of 2001.　2001年の春から, 食品30品目について遺伝子組換えの表示が義務付けられている。

GNMA 米政府住宅抵当金庫 (Government National Mortgage Associationの略)

go ahead 前に進む, 進展する, 出世する, 成功する
▸The merger plan will not *go ahead* unless the bank makes unstinting efforts to cut its nonperforming loans.　同行が不良債権の削減に向けて惜しみない努力をしないかぎり, 統合計画が前に進むことはないだろう。

go bankrupt 破産する, 倒産する, 破綻する (⇒**seniority**)
▸The firm *went bankrupt* saddled with a ¥150

billion debt in April 2008. 同社は，1,500億円の負債を抱えて2008年4月に破産した。

go into default 債務不履行になる
▶Many home mortgages *went into default*. 多くの住宅ローンが債務不履行になった。

go out of business 廃業する
▶In recent years, Japan has seen a sharp increase in the number of small and midsize corporations *going out of business*. ここ数年，日本では中小企業の廃業が急増している。

go private 〈株式を〉非公開化する，非公開会社にする（⇒going private）
▶We decided to *go private* in October. 当社は，10月に株式の非公開化を決めました。

go public 株式公開する，〈株式を〉上場する，〈秘密情報を〉公開する
▶Mitsui Life Insurance Co. will postpone its plan to *go public* on the Tokyo Stock Exchange until after this summer. 三井生命保険は，東京証券取引所への上場計画を，今夏以降まで延期することになった。

goal 名 目標，目的，ゴール
　budget goal 予算目標
　business goal 企業目標
　company goal 企業目標，会社目標（＝corporate goal）
　earnings goal 収益目標，業績目標（＝earnings target）
　financial goal 財務目標
　financial sales goal 売上目標
　profit goal 利益目標
▶Our *goal* is to dramatically increase that portion of our revenues coming from international activities. 当社の目標は，当社の収益のうち国際事業により生じる部分の大幅増にあります。
▶The company again failed to meet earnings *goals* in fiscal 2008. 同社は，2008年度も収益目標を達成できなかった。

going 形 現在の，現行の，現存する，うまく行っている，順調な，手に入る（available），入手できる，運転中［稼働中］の，営業中の，儲かっている，名 状態，状況，進み具合，出発，退職，死去
　be in going order 使用できる状態にある
　going business 継続企業，持続的企業，現に事業活動をしている企業，順調な経営，儲かっている商売，営業中の会社［商売］
　going long 思惑買い，見込み買い，ロングにする
　going organization 持続的組織，継続的組織
　going price 現行価格，時価
　going rate 現行料金，現行運賃，現行レート，現行の利率，実勢金利，実勢レート，相場
　going-rate pricing 実勢価格
　going short 思惑売り，見込み売り，ショートにする
　going yield 流通利回り
　going value 経営価値

going concern 継続企業，営業している企業，企業の存続可能性，ゴーイング・コンサーン（＝ongoing concern)
▶The *going concern* rules require corporations to state in their financial statements whether they are in danger of net capital deficiency, defaults of obligations and continued operating losses. ゴーイング・コンサーン（企業の継続能力）規定は，債務超過や債務不履行，継続的な営業損失などが発生する恐れがあるかどうかを財務書類［財務諸表］に明記するよう企業に義務付けている。

going private 株式の非公開化，株式を非公開にすること，非公開会社化（一般に，上場会社が外部発行済み株式を買い戻して自社を非公開会社にすること）

going public 株式の新規公開，株式公開，機密情報の公開（＝flotation, IPO, listing: 証券取引所や店頭市場に株式を新規公開して，上場会社になること）

golden handcuffs 転職防止のための社員に対する特別優遇措置，転職防止優遇措置，ゴールデン・ハンドカフ（ストック・オプション（自社株購入権）がゴールデン・ハンドカフの手段として使われることもある）

golden handshake 会社重役の高額の退職手当［退職金契約］，退職勧奨金，ゴールデン・ハンドシェイク（米語でgolden parachuteという）

golden parachute 黄金の落下傘，会社重役の高額の退職手当［退職金契約］，幹部退職金，特別報酬，割増退職金，退職補償金（＝golden handshake: parachuteは「退職金」という意味）

golden share 黄金株，特権株（「黄金株」は，株主総会での合併などの提案に拒否権を発動できる「拒否権付き株式（種類株式）」のこと）
▶*Golden shares* give even holders of a single share the veto right to block hostile takeover bids. 黄金株では，1株の株主にも敵対的買収案を阻止するための拒否権が与えられる。

good 形 好調な，堅調な，優良の，優秀な，良好な，好材料の，強気の，十分な，かなりの，高い，大幅な，一流の，親切な
　be good to customers 顧客に親切にする
　good debt 優良貸付け，優良債権，優良貸金，回収確実な貸金

good faith 善意, 誠実, 誠意, 正直
good growth 大幅な伸び, 高い伸び率, 高成長
good liquidity 流動性が良好なこと, 流動性が高いこと
good paper 一流商業手形
good people 優秀な人材, 優秀な社員
good people company グッド・ピープル・カンパニー（従業員の幸福を最重視する会社。ヘルシー・カンパニー（healthy company）ともいう）
good results 好業績, 好決算, 業績好調
good years 業績好調時
▸While these short-term financial results are disappointing, demand for our products and services continues to be *good* worldwide.　短期の財務成績［業績］は満足が得られるものではありませんが, 当社の製品とサービスに対する需要は, 引き続き世界各地で好調です。

good news よい知らせ, 明るい材料, 好材料
▸There is *good news* about private consumption, which accounts for nearly 60 percent of GDP.　国内総生産（GDP）の約60％を占める個人消費には, 明るい材料がある。

good performance 業績好調, 好業績（＝good business performance, good results, strong performance）
▸Though the global economy continues to be uncertain, we are cautiously optimistic that 2009 will continue to be another year of *good performance*.　世界経済は依然として不確実な状況が続いていますが, 慎重に見て, 当社は2009年度も引き続き好業績を達成できるものと, 楽観的な見通しを持っています。

goods 名 物品, 商品, 製品, 財貨, 財産, 財, 貨物, 動産, 有体動産
　bonded goods 保税貨物（＝goods in bond）
　capital goods output 資本財生産
　collateral goods 担保品
　completed goods 完成品
　consigned goods 委託品
　convenience 最寄り品, 手近品（日常生活の維持に欠かせない消費財のこと）
　damaged goods 傷物
　defective goods 仕損じ品
　durable goods 耐久財
　electrical goods 電化製品
　electronic goods 電子製品
　final goods price 製品価格
　general consumer goods 一般消費財
　goods in process 仕掛（しかけ・しかかり）品（＝goods in progress, product in progress, stock in process, work in process）
　goods in stock 在庫品, 商品在高, 手持ち商品（＝goods on hand）
　goods-oriented economy ハード社会
　industrial goods 産業財
　intermediate goods 中間財
　luxury goods 贅沢品
　manufactured goods 工業製品
　partially finished goods 半製品
　primary goods 一次産品
　producer goods 生産財, 工業製品
　reserve for returned goods 返品調整引当金
　seasonal goods 季節的商品
　semifinished goods 半製品
　shopping goods 買い回り品（ファッション関連や耐久消費財などの商品）
　speciality goods 専門品（＝specialty goods）
　taxable goods 課税対象商品
▸The cost of finished *goods* and work in process comprise material, labor, and manufacturing overhead.　製品と仕掛品の原価は, 材料費と労務費と製造間接費からなっています。

goods and services 財貨とサービス, 財貨・サービス, モノとサービス, 財貨と役務, 財貨と用役（＝services and goods）
▸Current account surplus is the gauge of trade in *goods and services*.　経常収支の黒字は, モノやサービスの取引を示す指標である。

goodwill 名 営業権, のれん, 得意先, 信用, 信頼, 善意, 好意, 親善, 快諾
　営業権［のれん］とは⇒企業の超過収益力（同業種の企業の平均を上回る利益を上げることができる能力）をもたらす無形固定資産で, 具体的には企業の有能な人間資産（経営者, 従業員）, 優れた技術やノウハウ, 優良なブランド・イメージ, 店舗の立地条件, 有利な仕入れ先や得意先との関係などをいう。営業権は企業の財産であるが, これを貸借対照表に資産として計上できるのは, 有償で譲り受けた場合か, 合併で有償取得した場合に限られる。
▸*Goodwill* is amortized over its estimated life.　営業権は, 見積り有効期間にわたって償却されています。
▸We amortize *goodwill* on a straight-line basis over the periods benefited, principally in the range of 10 to 15 years.　当社は, 営業権を, 基本的に10年から15年の利益発生期間にわたって定額法で償却しています。

govern 動 支配する, 管理運営する, 監督する, …が適用される, 規定する, …の基準となる, 優先する, 決める, 採用する（⇒**internal accounting**

control)
be governed by the law of …の法律が適用される, …の法律を準拠法とする
governed market 管理市場
governing body 監督機関
▸Capital subscription in a Chinese bank is *governed* by foreign currency restrictions. 中国の銀行への出資には, 外資規制がある。
▸The laws of Japan shall *govern* as to matters involving the governance of the new company. 新会社の管理・運営に関する事項については, 日本法が適用される [日本法を準拠法とする]。

governance 名 統治, 支配, 管理, 管理法, 経営法, 統治能力, ガバナンス (⇒**corporate governance, govern**)
corporate governance reform bill 企業統治改革法案
global governance 地球的規模の統治, グローバル・ガバナンス
information governance 情報ガバナンス, 情報統治
information technology governance ITガバナンス (IT全般の統治能力のこと)
▸U.S. corporate *governance* regulations are too harsh. 米国の企業統治法 [企業改革法] は, 厳しすぎる。

government 名 政府, 政権, 政治, 行政, 行政府, 内閣, 管理, 支配, 省庁
central government 中央政府, 国
coalition government 連立政権
government-affiliated investment fund 政府系ファンド, 政府系投資ファンド (＝sovereign wealth fund; ⇒**clout**)
government agency 政府機関
government-business complex 官民協調 (＝government-business cooperation)
government fund 政府資金
government loan and investment program 財政投融資
Government National Mortgage Association 政府住宅抵当金庫《略 GNMA》(通称: ジニー・メイ)
government obligations 米政府証券, 政府債, 国債
government-owned enterprise 国営企業
government procurement 政府調達
government regulators 規制当局
government sector 政府部門, 公共部門
government-sponsored entity 政府系機関
government securities 国債, 公債
local government 地方政府, 地方自治体, 地方公共団体, 地方
government bond 国債
auction of government bonds 国債の入札, 国債入札
foreign government bond 外国国債
government bond issue 国債発行
government bond yield 国債利回り
government bonds outstanding 国債残高
▸Debt servicing expenditures are used to pay interests for previously issued *government* bonds and to redeem the bonds. 国債費は, 過去に発行した国債の利払いや国債の償還に充てられる。

GPS 全地球測位システム (⇒**global positioning system**)
▸The *GPS* system does not provide information on moving up and down. この全地球測位システム (GPS) を利用したシステムは, 上下移動に関する情報を提供できない。

grace 名 支払猶予, 恩寵, 恩赦, 優美
grace period 猶予期間, 据え置き期間, 払込み猶予期間 (＝days of grace)
gradation 名 段階的移行, 漸次的移行, 徐々の変化, 段階, 色調の濃淡, グラデーション
grade 名 格付け, 等級, 段階, グレード
high-grade corporate bond 高格付け社債
high-grade stock 優良株
investment grade 投資適格格付け (＝investment-grade, investment-grade rating)
investment grade quality 投資適格
noninvestment grade 投機的格付け (＝speculative grade)
noninvestment grade bond 投機的格付け債, 投資不適格格付け, 高利回り債
rating below investment grade 投資適格以下の格付け
speculative-grade bond 投機的格付け債券
speculative-grade issuer 投機的格付けの発行体
trade by grade 格付け取引
▸A rating below investment *grade* makes it harder and more expensive to borrow money. 投資適格以下の格付けだと, 資金の調達が難しくなるし, 資金調達コストも高くつく。

grading 名 〈商品などの〉格付け, 等級格付け
grant 動 与える, 付与する, 許諾する, 許可する, 承諾する, 認める, 譲渡する, 移転する
grant a license 実施権を許諾する, 実施権を付与する, 使用権を与える 使用許諾を与える
grant permission 許可を与える

▶Licensee shall not be permitted to sublicense the license *granted* hereunder to others. ライセンシー（実施権者）は，本契約に従って許諾された実施権を他者にサブライセンスすることはできない。

▶The exercise price of any stock option is equal to or greater than the stock price when the option is *granted*. ストック・オプションの行使価格は，オプションが付与された時の株価と同等，またはそれを上回る価格になっています。

grant 图 権利の付与，財産の移転，譲渡，譲与，実施許諾，政府の補助金，助成金，交付金，無償資金，無償給付，研究助成金，奨学金
　block grant 包括補助金
　Federal grants to States 連邦から州への交付金
　grant element 〈政府借款中の〉贈与比率
　grant-in-aid 補助金，交付金，助成金
　grant of an option オプションの付与
　grant of license 実施権の許諾，実施権の付与，使用許諾，商標使用許諾
　grant of patent license 特許実施権の許諾［付与］，特許ライセンスの付与
　land grant 土地使用権
　loan grants 借款
　operation grant 運営費補助
　percentage grant 定率補助金

▶Simultaneously with the *grant* of an option, the employee may also be granted the right to a special compensation payment. オプションの付与と同時に，従業員に対しては，特別報酬の支払いを受ける権利を付与することもあります。

grantee 图 被譲与者，被許可者，被許諾者，譲受人（⇒**grantor**）

grantor 图 譲渡人，譲与人，許諾者，ライセンス許諾者，〈特許権など知的財産権の〉使用許諾者，不動産権設定者

▶Each party, as *Grantor*, on behalf of itself and its Subsidiaries, grants to the other party, as Grantee, a worldwide and nonexclusive license under the *Grantor's* licensed products and copyrights. ライセンス許諾としての各当事者は，自社とその子会社を代表して，ライセンス許諾者の許諾製品［契約対象製品］と著作権に基づく世界を対象とした非独占的なライセンスを，被許諾者としての相手方に許諾する。

gratis 形 無料の，無償の，任意の，副 無料で，無償
　gratis dictum 任意的陳述
　gratis issue 株式分割
　gratis retirement of stocks 株の無償償却

gratuitous 形 無料の，無償の，無報酬の，正当な理由のない，根拠のない，いわれのない，不必要な
　gratuitous bailment 無償寄託
　gratuitous contract 無償契約
　gratuitous promise 無償の約束

gratuity 图 贈り物，心づけ，チップ

gray [grey] 形 灰色の，あいまいな，どっちかずの，高齢者の
　gray information 入手困難な科学技術情報，灰色方法
　gray knight 灰色の騎士（株式公開買付け（YOB）で動向が分からない参加者）
　gray market 発行前取引，闇類似市場，グレー・マーケット

grease 图 脂，グリース，動 賄賂を使う

green 形 環境の，環境保護の，環境にやさしい，環境に配慮した，許可された，準備完了の，予定通りに進んだ，グリーン
　green audit 環境監査
　green business 環境事業，環境ビジネス
　green card 米国での労働許可証，外国人永住許可証，英国での国際自動車保険証
　green consumer 緑の消費者，グリーン・コンシューマー
　green effect 温室効果
　green labeling [labelling] 緑の表示，エコ表示
　green light 正式許可，認可，ゴーサイン
　green power 金，金力，財力
　green product エコ製品，環境にやさしい製品，グリーン・プロダクト
　green revolution 緑の革命（穀物増産のための技術革新），環境革命，環境に対する関心の高まり
　green shoots 景気回復の動き，回復の兆し，成長［発展，復活］の兆し，再生の動き
　green technology 環境技術

▶The government plans to expand the nation's *green* businesses to about ¥83 trillion in 2015 from ¥59 trillion in 2005. 政府は，国内環境事業の市場規模を2005年の59兆円から2015年には約83兆円（約1.4倍）に拡大させる方針だ。

Green Belt Movement グリーン・ベルト運動

▶The *Green Belt Movement* has sought to empower women and better the environment. グリーン・ベルト運動は，女性の地位向上と環境改善を目指している。

green investment scheme グリーン投資スキーム《略 **GIS**》

▶The *green investment scheme* (GIS) obliges Russia to spend profits from the emission quota trade on environmental protection measures. (京都議定書が定める)グリーン投資スキーム(GIS)で，ロシアは排出量取引の売却益を環境対策に使うことが義務付けられている。

green productivity 環境にやさしい生産性，グリーン・プロダクティビティ
▶*Green productivity* reduces pollution and wasts, or it saves energy and resources, or it cuts down on the use of toxic materials. グリーン・プロダクティビティは，公害や廃棄物を減らすこと，ありはエネルギーや資源を減らすこと，あるいは有害物質の使用量を減らすことだ。

green tax 環境税 (＝environmental tax)
▶The Saitama prefectural government aims to introduce its own *green tax* on residents in order to preserve greenery. 緑地保全のため，埼玉県が住民課税として独自の環境税導入を目指している。

greenery on a rooftop 屋上緑化
▶The Tokyo and Hyogo prefectural governments have made it obligatory for newly constructed buildings to have *greenery on their rooftops*. 東京都と兵庫県は，新築ビルに屋上緑化を義務づけている。

greenhouse 名 温室，地球の大気，温室効果ガス
　greenhouse effect 温室効果，地球温暖化の効果
　greenhouse emissions 温室効果ガスの排出量 (＝greenhouse gas emissions)
　greenhouse gas emission trading 温室効果ガスの排出量取引
　greenhouse pollutant 温室効果の原因となる物質
　greenhouse tax 温室効果税 (＝carbon tax)
　greenhouse warming 温室効果による温暖化 (＝global warming)

greenhouse gas 温室効果ガス，地球温暖化ガス，温暖化ガス《略 **GHG**》(＝global warming gas, greenhouse effect gas)

greenhouse gas emissions 温室効果ガス排出量，温室効果ガスの排出量，地球温暖化ガスの排出量 (＝emissions of greenhouse gases, greenhouse gas discharge)
▶Major developing nations are witnessing a remarkable increase in their *greenhouse gas emissions* as a result of their rapid economic growth. 主要途上国では，急激な経済成長に伴って温室効果ガス排出量の増加が著しい。

grievance 名 苦情，不満，不服申し立て
grind 動 粉にする，粉砕する，研ぐ，磨く，無理やり詰め込む，こつこつ仕事をする

grocery store 日用雑貨・食料品店，食品スーパー
gross 形名 総体(の)，総額，総計，グロス
gross capital expenditures 資本的支出総額
▶*Gross capital expenditures* were $519 million for the first quarter of 2009. 2009年第1四半期の資本的支出総額は，5億1,900万ドルでした。

gross domestic product 国内総生産《略 **GDP**》(国内総生産(GNP)から海外からの純所得(利子・配当・利潤など)を差し引いたもの)
▶The *gross domestic product* rose 3.7 percent on an annual basis in the October-December period of 2007. 2007年10－12月期の国内総生産(GDP)の伸び率[実質成長率]は，年率換算で前期比3.7％増加した。

gross income 売上総利益，総収益，総収入，総所得，総益金
▶For 2008 as a whole, net earnings rose by about 10 percent while *gross income* increased approximately 6 percent. 2008年度全体としては，純利益は約10％伸び，総収益はおよそ6％増加しました。

gross margin 売上総利益，売上利益，粗利益，売上利益率，粗利益率 (＝gross margin percentage, gross margin ratio; ⇒**margin, pressure**)
▶The *gross margin* of 40.5 percent in 2008 was marginally down from 40.7 percent in 2007. 2008年度の40.5％の売上利益率は，前年度の40.7％を少々下回りました。

gross margin percentage 売上総利益率，粗利益率 (＝gross margin ratio, gross profit ratio, operating ratio; ⇒**cost control**)
▶The *gross margin percentage* improved since 2007 because of a smaller workforce. 売上総利率は，人員削減により2007年度以来，改善しました。

gross operating profit 業務粗利益
▶Banks have paid hardly any corporate enterprise tax though they made even larger *gross operating profits* than they did during the bubble economic era. 銀行は，バブル期より大きな業務粗利益を上げたものの，法人税をほとんど負担して[支払って]いない。

gross premium 総保険料，表定保険料，営業保険料 (「営業保険料(gross premium)」は，純保険料(net premium)＋付加保険料(loading)で算出される)
▶*Gross premium* refers to the amount that policyowners actually pay for their insurance.

総保険料とは，契約者が実際に支払う保険契約料の額のことをいう。

gross profit 売上総利益, 粗利益, 粗利, 差益 (=gross margin, gross profit margin, gross profit on sales: 売上総利益＝純売上高－売上原価)
▶This product was the prime contributor to the increase in *gross profit* in 2008.　2008年度の売上総利益の増加に，本製品がとくに大きく貢献しました。

gross profit margin 売上総利益率, 売上利益率, 売上総利, 粗利益率, 粗利率 (=gross margin)
▶*Gross profit margins* for the third quarter of 2008 were 39.8 percent of revenues, compared with 41.5 percent of revenues in the same period last year.　2008年第3四半期の売上総利益率は，前年同期の41.5％に対して39.8％でした。

groundbreaking 名 起工, 起工式 (groundbreaking ceremony), くわ入れ式, 形 起工(式)の, 革新的な, 草分けの, 新生面開拓の
▶Toyota Motor Corp. held a *groundbreaking* ceremony for its car assembly plant in St. Petersburg.　トヨタ自動車は，ロシアのサンクトペテルブルクで自動車組立工場の起工式を行った。

group 名 企業集団, 集団, 団体, 連結, 企業グループ, グループ (⇒growth prospects)
　business group 企業グループ (=corporate group)
　business groups 実業界
　consolidated group 連結企業グループ, 連結対象の会社グループ, 連結企業集団, 連結集団 (=consolidation group)
　corporate group 企業グループ, 企業集団 (=business group)
　corporate group tax system 連結納税制度 (=consolidated taxation system, group taxation system)
　financial group 金融グループ, 融資団
　group company グループ会社, グループ企業, 系列企業 (=group firm)
　group earnings forecast 連結業績予想, 連結業績見通し, 連結収益予想, 連結利益予想 (⇒**earnings forecast**)
　group financial statements 連結財務書類［財務諸表］, 企業集団財務諸表 (=group accounts)
　group firm グループ会社, グループ企業, 系列企業 (=group company; ⇒**cut**)
　group relief グループ税額控除
　group results グループの業績, グループ企業の

連結業績, 連結決算 (=consolidated results)
　group taxation system 連結納税制 (=consolidated return system, consolidated tax payment system, consolidated taxation system, corporate group tax system)
　industry group 業界団体, 経済団体, 業界
　interest group 利益団体, 利益集団, 圧力団体
　investment group 投資グループ
　manager group 幹事団, 幹事グループ, 幹事銀行団
　on a group basis 連結ベースで, 連結ベースの (=on a consolidated basis)
　underwriting group 引受団
▶The *group* will be able to raise its consolidated recurring profits to more than ¥20 billion from the current ¥4 billion or so through the reorganization.　再編により，同グループは今後，グループ全体で現在の40億円程度の経常利益を200億円以上にすることができる。

group accounts 連結財務書類, 連結財務諸表, グループ財務書類, 企業集団財務諸表 (=consolidated accounts, consolidated financial statements, group financial statements)
▶The figures of the firm's *group accounts* have not been released.　同社の連結決算の成績［数値］は，まだ発表されていない。

group after-tax profit 連結税引き後利益
▶*Group after-tax profit* in the first six months plunged 62 percent to ¥195 billion from a year earlier.　上半期の連結税引き後利益は，前年同期比62％減の1,950億円でした。

group interim report 連結中間決算報告, 連結中間決算報告書
▶The company's *group interim report* was compiled using U.S. accounting rules.　同社の連結中間決算報告書は，米国の会計基準を用いて作成された。

group net income 連結純利益, 連結税引き後利益 (=consolidated net income)
▶*Group net income* in the second quarter fell to ¥81 billion.　第2四半期の連結純利益は，810億円に減少しました。

group net loss 連結純損失, 当期連結純損失, 連結税引き後赤字 (=consolidated net loss: 企業グループ全体の税引き後損失)
▶The firm posted a *group net loss* of ¥1.5 billion for the April-September fiscal first half due to the high cost of warding off a hostile takeover bid.　9月中間決算で同社は，敵対的TOB（株式公開買付け）を回避するために多額の費用が発生した

ため，15億円の連結税引き後赤字となった．

group net profit 連結純利益，当期連結純利益，連結税引き後利益（=consolidated net profit: 企業グループ全体の税引き後利益）
▸The firm's *group net profit* plunged 72.3 percent to ¥21.2 billion in the six months through Sept. 30, 2008 from a year earlier. 2008年9月中間決算で，同社の連結税引き後利益は，前年同期比72.3％減の212億円となった．

group net sales 連結税引き後売上高，連結純売上高
▸The Company's *group net sales* are estimated at ¥22.3 trillion for the current business year. 当社の連結税引き後売上高は，今期は22兆3,000億円に達する見込みです．

Group of Seven nations 先進7か国，主要7か国，G7（=Group of Seven major economies）

group operating loss 連結営業損失，連結営業赤字（=consolidated operating loss）
▸We suffered a *group operating loss* of ¥3billion in the first half of fiscal 2008. 当社の2008年上半期の連結営業収益は，30億円の赤字でした．

group operating profit 連結営業利益，連結営業黒字（=consolidated operating profit）
▸The firm's *group operating profit* forecast for the current year was downgraded to ¥35 billion. 同社の今年度の連結営業利益見通しは，350億円に下方修正された．

group operating revenue 連結営業収益，連結営業収入，連結売上高
▸NTT Corp. incurred *group operating revenue* and profit falls in fiscal 2004 for the first time since its 1985 privatization. NTTは，2004年度の連結決算で，1985年の民営化以来初めて（前期比で）減収減益となった．

group pretax loss 連結税引き前損失，連結経常損失（=consolidated pretax loss）
▸The firm revised downward its *group pretax loss* estimate for the first half of fiscal 2009. 同社は，2009年度上半期の連結税引き前損失予想を下方修正した．

group pretax profit 連結税引き前利益，連結経常利益（=consolidated pretax profit）
▸For the April-September period, *group pretax profit* gained 11.6 percent to ¥333 billion. 4-9月期の連結税引き前利益は，前年同期比で11.6％増の3,330億円でした．

group sales 連結売上高（=consolidated revenues, consolidated sales）
▸The Company's *group sales* fell 22.3 percent to

¥672.11 billion in the March-August period due to closure of its money-losing stores. 当社の8月中間決算で［当社の3-8月期決算で］，連結売上高は，不採算店舗［赤字店舗］の閉鎖で22.3％減の6,721億1,000万円でした．

groupware 图 グループウェア

grow 増加する，増大する，拡大する，高まる，伸びる，成長する，発展する，向上する，栽培する，伸ばす
　fast-growing sector 急成長部門
　grow earnings 利益を増やす，利益を伸ばす
　grow steadily 順調に伸びる
　growing competition 競争の高まり，競争の激化
　rapidly growing market 急成長市場，急拡大市場
▸Mobile phone subscribers are the fastest *growing* segment of the telephone market. 携帯電話の加入者は，電話市場で最も急成長を遂げている部門である．
▸The combined sales of 813 nonfinancial companies in the April-September period *grew* 6.3 percent over the previous year. 金融を除く企業813社の上期（4-9月期）の売上高の合計は，前年同期比で6.3％増加した．

growth 图 成長，成長率，経済成長，伸び，伸び率，増加，増大（⇒economic growth, sustainable）
　asset growth 資産の伸び率
　balance sheet growth 資産の増加
　capex growth 設備投資の増加
　consolidated EPS growth 連結ベースのEPS伸び率
　credit growth 貸出の伸び，貸出残高の伸び
　cyclical growth 循環的成長
　dividend growth 配当の伸び，配当伸び率，増配率
　earnings growth 収益の伸び，収益伸び率
　economic growth rate 経済成長率
　growth in profits 利益の増加，増益
　growth industry 成長産業
　growth rate 成長率，伸び率
　internal growth 内部成長，内部の成長
　lower growth 伸び率の低下，成長鈍化，経済成長率の低下
　market growth 市場成長，市場の拡大
　net profit growth 純益の伸び，純益伸び率
　organic growth 内部成長
　output growth 生産の伸び
　pickup in growth 伸び率の上昇，伸び率の回復，景気の上向き，景気の勢いの回復
　profit growth 増益，利益の伸び

rapid growth　急激な増加, 急成長
real growth rate　実質成長率, 実質経済成長率（＝real growth）
slower growth　低成長, 伸びの鈍化, 伸び率［成長率］の低下, 伸び悩み, 景気低迷
solid demand growth　着実な需要の伸び
strong growth　力強い伸び, 急増, 力強い経済成長
strong profit growth　大幅増益
▶Our *growth* comes from competing successfully worldwide, offering new technology and high-quality products and services.　当社の成長は, 新技術と高品質の製品・サービスを提供して, グローバル競争に勝ち抜くことから生まれます。

growth in revenues and earnings　収益と利益［純利益］の伸び, 増収増益
▶Investments in our network, financial operations and alliances will pave the way for further *growth* in revenues and earnings.　通信ネットワークや金融業務, 他社との提携への投資によって, さらなる増収増益が可能になります。

growth opportunity　成長の機会
▶Companies move toward more global markets in search of new *growth opportunities*.　企業は, 新たな成長の機会を求めて, 一段とグローバル市場への進出を図っています。

growth prospects　成長見通し
▶The company's poor corporate image is detrimental to the long-term *growth prospects* of its corporate group.　同社の悪い企業イメージは, 同社の企業グループの長期成長見通しにはマイナス要因だ。

growth target　成長目標
▶Our financial performance met *growth targets* despite the less favorable business and economic environment.　当社の財務面での業績は, 事業および経済環境が低調だったにもかかわらず, 成長目標を達成しました。

guarantee 動　保証する, 請け合う, 確約する
　guaranteed amount　保証額
　guaranteed bond　保証付き社債
　guaranteed dividend　保証配当, 確定配当
　guaranteed payback　確定利回り
　guaranteed yield　予定利率（＝promised yield: 生命保険会社が保険契約者に約束した運用利回り）
▶We sometimes *guarantee* the debt of certain unconsolidated joint ventures.　当社は, 当社の財務書類に連結されていない一部の合弁会社の負債に対して保証を行うときもあります。

guarantee 名　保証, 保証人, 引受人, 保証額, 保証契約, 保証書, 保証状, 担保, 抵当, 担保物
　advancing guarantee　融資保証
　bank guarantee cost　銀行保証料
　basic guarantee　根（ね）保証（＝initial guarantee）
　corporate guarantee　企業保証
　debt guarantee　債務保証
　export credit guarantee　輸出信用保証
　financial guarantee　金融保証, 信用保証
　guarantee fee　保証手数料, 保証料（＝guarantee charge）
　guarantee liabilities　保証債務, 支払い保証（＝liabilities for guarantee）
　guarantee money　保証金, 差入れ保証金
　guarantee of debt　債務保証（＝debt guarantee）
　guarantees of indebtedness of others　第三者の債務に対する支払い保証
　loan guarantee　融資保証, 貸出保証, 信用保証
　maturity guarantee　満期保証
　minimum guarantee　最低保証金
　performance guarantee insurance　履行保証保険, 契約履行保証保険
　tender guarantee　入札保証
▶The Corporation did not honor the debt *guarantee* on a total of ¥50 billion.　当社は, 総額500億円の債務保証を引き受けませんでした。

guarantor 名　保証人

guideline 名　基準, 指導基準, 運用基準, 指導指針, 指標, 上限, ガイドライン
　asset guideline period　法定耐用年数
　budget guideline　予算編成方針（＝budgeting policy）
　capital guideline　自己資本比率の基準
　credit risk guideline　信用リスク基準
　management guideline　経営方針
　Tier 1 capital guideline　基本的項目基準
▶Savings plans for the majority of our employees allow employees to contribute a portion of their pretax and/or after-tax income in accordance with specified *guidelines*.　大多数の当社従業員のための貯蓄制度では, 従業員は従業員の税引き前所得または税引き後所得（あるいはその両方）の一部を, 特定の基準に従って拠出することができます。

H

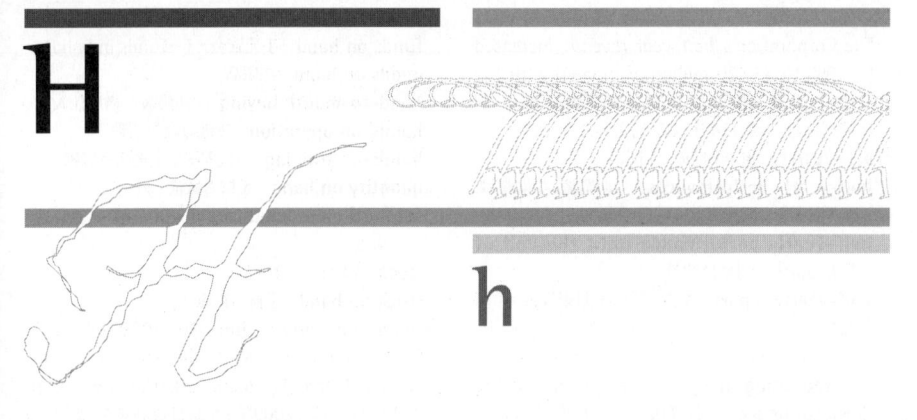

H1 losses 上半期損失, 上半期の赤字
H2 profits 下半期利益, 下半期の黒字
H2FY2009 2009年下半期
hacking 名 〈コンピュータ・システムへの〉不正アクセス, ハッキング
▶Calling computer security one of the top problems in the United States, the government is forming special units to prosecute *hacking* and copyright violation. コンピュータのセキュリティを米国の最重要問題のひとつとして, 米政府は現在, ハッキング(不正アクセス)や著作権侵害などを摘発する特別専門班を設置している。

haggle 動 値切る, 押し問答する, 言い争う, やり合う
　haggle over the budget bill 予算案をめぐってやり合う
　haggle over the price 値切る

haircut 名 超過担保, 担保掛け目, 有価証券担保貸付けの掛け目, ヘアカット (「ヘアカット」は, 保有証券のリスク度やリスク・ヘッジの有無から試算される評価損のこと)
　haircut finance 有価証券担保貸付け

half 名 中間, 半期, 半分 (⇒first half, second half)
　half-finished goods 半製品
　half-fiscal year account 中間決算
　the first half of the fiscal year 上半期, 上期 (＝the first half)
　the first half of the January to December business year 1-6月中間期決算, 今年度中間決算, 今年度上半期
　the first half of the year 上半期, 上期, 今年度上半期[上期], 今年度前半, 今年前半 (＝the first half, the former half of the year)
　the second half of the year [fiscal year] 下半期, 下期, 今年度下半期[下期], 今年度後半, 今年後半 (＝the latter half of the year, the second half)
▶The firm's 1st-*half* net profit plunged 74% from a year earlier to ¥120 billion. 同社の上半期の連結税引き後利益は, 前年同期比74％減の1,200億円となった。
▶The firm returned to the black in the first-half of this business year. 同社は, 今年度上半期に[上期に, 中間決算で]黒字に転換した。

half year 半期, 中間
　half-year earnings report 半期業績報告, 中間決算報告, 中間決算 (＝interim earnings report)
　half-year earnings report for the fiscal period up to September 9月中間決算, 上半期(4-9月期)業績, 上半期決算
　half-year financial statements 中間財務書類, 中間企業財務情報
　half-year report 半期報告書, 中間事業報告書, 中間営業報告書
　half year to Sept. 30 4-9月期, 3月期決算企業の上半期[上期], 9月中間決算
　half-year trading figures 中間決算
half-year ended Sept. 30 9月中間決算, 3月期決算企業の4-9月期
▶Loan write-off costs at the bank amounted to ¥450 billion for the *half-year ended Sept. 30*. 同行の9月中間決算の不良債権処理費用は, 4,500億円だった。
half-year revenue 半期売上高, 中間決算で

の売上高
- The Corporation's *half-year revenue* increased by 15% to $3,420 million, compared with the same period last year.　当社の半期売上高は，前年同期比15%増の34億2,000万ドルでした。

half-yearly 形　半期の，中間の
　half-yearly performances　半期業績，中間業績，半期決算，中間決算
　half-yearly performance until the end of February　2月中間決算
　half-yearly report　半期報告，半期報告書，中間報告
- *Half-yearly* performance was affected by the weakening of the U.S. dollar against the Canadian dollar.　半期業績は，カナダ・ドルに対する米ドル安の影響を受けました。

hallmark 動　保証する，…に品質保証［証明］印を押す，折り紙をつける，太鼓判を押す，名　品質保証，品質証明，優良刻印，〈金・銀の純度を示す〉検証刻印，特質，特徴
　bear the hallmark of　…を保証する，…を証明する

halo effect　後光効果，光背効果，ハロー効果（人事考課で，特定の強い印象が評価につながること）

halve 動　半減させる，50%削減する，半分に引き下げる，半分に減らす，二等分する，半額にする
- With this financial support, along with property sales, the company plans to *halve* its approximately ¥540 billion consolidated interest-bearing debts.　この金融支援と資産売却を組み合わせて，同社は約5,400億円の連結有利子負債を半減させる方針だ。

hammer 動　打撃を与える，激しく非難［攻撃］する，完全に打ち負かす，株価を下げる
　hammer (away) at　…に精を出す，激しく攻撃する，繰り返し強調する
　hammer home　〈議論などを〉叩き込む，銘記させる
　hammer out　打ち出す，まとめる，考え出す

hammer 名　〈競売人の〉木づち
　be due for the hammer　解雇される運命にある
　come [be, go] under the hammer　競売で売られる，競売に付される
　go [be] at it hammer and tongs　激しくけんか［口論，議論］する，猛烈に働く

hand 名　手元，手持ち，所有，管理，支配，技量，職工，職人，人手，担当記者，署名，参加，関与
　cash in hand　手元現金（＝cash on hand）
　change hands　持ち主［所有者］が変わる，持ち主

を変える，商品が売れる
　funds on hand　手元資金（＝funds in hand）
　goods on hand　在庫品
　hand-to-mouth buying　当用買い，当用仕入れ
　hands-on operation　実地の職業活動
　hands-on training　実地研修，実地職業訓練
　quantity on hand　手持ち数量
　set [put] one's hand to a document　書類に署名する
　stock in hand　在庫品
　stock on hand　手持ち在庫
- Orders on *hand* at June 30, 2009 were U.S. $1.80 billion from $1.71 billion of orders on hand at March 31, 2009.　2009年6月30日現在の受注残高は，2009年3月31日現在の17億1,000万米ドルに対して18億米ドルでした。
- We have hereinto set our *hands* and seals.　われわれは，この契約書に署名捺印した。

handheld 形　手で持てる，小型の，携帯用の，携帯型の
　handheld communications devices　携帯型通信機器
　handheld device　携帯型の装置，ハンディタイプの装置

handling 名　取扱い，操作，処理，荷役，運搬，ハンドリング
　ground handling　地上業務
　handling charge　取扱い手数料（＝handling expense, handling fee）
　handling customer complaint　顧客苦情処理
　handling of goods　商品の取扱い，商品荷役
　handling time　荷役時間，作業時間
　materials handling　荷役，荷役運搬，資材運搬，運搬管理，原材料取扱い，マテハン，マテリアル・ハンドリング
　physical handling　物的運搬，物の移動方法

handset 名　〈電話の〉送受話器，〈携帯電話や無線機の〉端末機，携帯電話，ハンドセット

Hang Seng Index [index]　ハンセン株価指数，ハンセン指数（香港で取引される33銘柄の価格変動を測る指標で，香港のハンセン（恒生）銀行が発表。金融，商工業，不動産，公益事業の4業種別指数に分かれている）
　Hang Seng index futures　ハンセン指数先物
　Hang Seng industry sub-index futures contracts　ハンセン業種別サブ・インデックス先物取引

harassment 名　嫌がらせ，ハラスメント（⇒ bulling in the workplace, lawsuit）
　harassment at work　職場での嫌がらせ

moral harassment 職権による人権侵害, 職場での上司による嫌がらせ
sexual harassment in the workplace 職場での性的嫌がらせ, 職場でのセクハラ
▶We have zero tolerance for sexual *harassment* or discrimination of any kind. 当社では, セクハラや差別は一切容認しない。

harbor [harbour] 名 港, 避難港, 港湾, 避難所, 隠れ場所, タンク集積所, ハーバー
  dock harbor ドック港
  harbor dues 入港税, 入港料
  harbor facility 港湾施設
  harbor master 港湾管理者, 港務官
  harbor transport business 港湾運送業, 港運業
  harbor transportation 港湾運送, 港運
  harbor works 築港工事
  safe harbor provisions 例外規定
  safe harbor rule 安全条項(規則や法律に抵触しないためのガイドライン), 避難条項安全港規則, 安全港ルール, セーフ・ハーバー・ルール(「セーフ・ハーバー・ルール」は, 会社が自社株を買い戻すときの規則を定めた米証券取引委員会 (SEC)規則10-bの通称)
  tidal harbor 潮港

hard 形 困難な, 厳しい, 硬い[堅い, 固い], 硬貨の, 現金の, 強気の, 高値安定の, ハード
  drive [strike] a hard bargain 有利な取引[取決め]を結ぶ
  hard cash 現金, 硬貨
  hard copy 印刷物, データやプログラムを紙に印刷したもの, ハード・コピー
  hard core 中核, 中核分子, 主要部分, 慢性失業者
  hard disk [disc] drive 固定磁気ディスク装置, ハードディスク装置《略 HDD》
  hard dollars サービス代金直接払い方式, ハード・ドル
  hard goods 耐久消費財, 耐久財, ハード・グッズ (=durable goods)
  hard-landing policy 強行路線
  hard line 強硬路線, 強気路線
  hard lines 不運 (=hard luck)
  hard loan 融資条件の厳しい融資, 交換可能通貨での返済を条件とする融資, ハード・ローン
  hard sell 積極販売, 説得販売, 強引な販売, 押し売り, 強引な売り込み, ハード・セル (=high-pressure selling)
  hard times 不景気

hard currency 硬貨, 交換可能通貨, 米ドルや金と交換できる通貨 (=hard money)
▶Banks reopened their *hard currency* tills. 銀行は, ハード・カレンシーの現金引出し業務を再開した。

hard landing 強行着陸, ハードランディング
▶The government is likely to maintain the *hard-landing* economic policy. 政府は, 強行着陸[ハードランディング]の経済路線を維持する見込みだ。

hardware 名 コンピュータの機械本体と周辺機器, 機械, 機器, 装置, 構成機器, 設備, 武器, ハードウエア
  hardware product ハードウエア製品
  hardware trouble ハードウエア障害
  key hardware 主要設備
▶The majority of the *hardware* and software we provide to the firm will be supplied from our Bramalea facility in Brampton, Ontario. 当社が同社に提供するハードウエアとソフトウエアの大半は, カナダ・オンタリオ州ブランプトン市にある当社の工場から供給します。

harmonize 動 調和させる, 調和・協調を図る, 平準化する
  Harmonized Commodity Description and Coding System HS商品分類
  harmonized standard industry classification 国際統一商品分類システム, HS方式の商品分類

harness 動 制御する

haul 動 運搬する, 名 輸送, 運搬, 運搬量, 運搬経路

haulage 名 運搬, 運送業, 運賃, 運搬量, 運搬経路
  haulage road 運搬坑道
  haulage volume 輸送数量
  horse haulage 馬力運搬

haven 名 避難所, 避難場所, 安息地, 安全な場所, 逃避先, 港
  investment haven 安全な投資先 (=safe haven)
  safe-haven quality 質への逃避先, 安全な投資先
  tax haven 租税回避地, 税金天国, タックス・ヘイブン
▶The funds that so abundantly seek safe *haven* in New York today can flow outward tomorrow. 安全な投資先を求めて今日ニューヨークにあふれるほど集まった資金も, 明日には外へ流出しかねない。

hazard 名 危険, 危険性, 危険物, 危険要因[要素], 阻害要因, 危険事情, 害悪, 害毒, 混乱, 障害, 偶然, 運, ハザード
  economic hazards 経済的混乱
  environmental hazards 環境汚染
  fire hazard 火事の原因
  hazard bonus 危険手当
  hazard label 危険標識ラベル
  hazard map 災害地図, 災害予測図, ハザード・

マップ
health hazard 健康上の危険
hazard pay 危険手当 （＝danger money）
investment hazards 投資の障害
moral hazard 倫理の欠如, 道徳的危険, モラル・ハザード
occupational hazard 職業上の危険
physical hazard 物的危険
political hazard 政治的危険
public hazards 公害
radiation hazards 照射による危険
traffic hazard 交通事故

head 動 …を率いる, …を統括する, 会社を経営する
▶The company's business management and planning headquarters is *headed* by its representative director. 同社の経営企画管理本部は, 代表取締役が統括している。

head 名 責任者, 最高責任者, 指導者, 経営者, 社長, 党首
department head 部門責任者, 部門担当責任者
group head グループ代表
official head 社長
per head 1人当たり
section head 部門責任者
▶The time vice president of the bank was the *head* of the department in charge of assessing the financial status of large borrowers. 同行の元副頭取は, 大口融資先の財務内容審査部門の最高責任者だった。

head office 本社, 本店, 本部, 本拠 （＝headquarters, home office）
▶The firm relocated its *head office* from Tokyo to Kyoto. 同社は, 本社を東京から京都に移転した。

headhunt [**head-hunt**] 動 〈人材を〉引き抜く, 〈人材を〉スカウトする, ヘッドハンティングする

headhunter 名 人材スカウト会社, 人材スカウト業, 人材スカウト係

headhunting 名 人材スカウト

headline 名 見出し

headquarters [**headquarter**] 名 本社, 本店, 本部, 統括本部 （＝front office, head office, main office）
administrative headquarters 管理本部
area headquarters 地域本部
regional headquarters 地域統括本部
▶In 2008, $800 million was included in selling, general and administrative expenses for manufacturing and *headquarters* consolidations. 2008年度は, 販売費および一般管理費として製造部門と本社機構の統合化のための費用8億ドルが含まれています。

health 名 健康, 健全性, 保健, 医療, ヘルス （⇒financial health）
corporate financial health 企業の財務健全性, 企業の財務体質, 企業の財務状況
corporate health 企業の健全性, 企業体質, 経営体質
credit health 信用の健全性, 信用の質
health activities ヘルスケア事業
health supplements 健康補助食品
mental health 心の健康, 心の健康管理, 精神衛生, メンタルヘルス
National Health Service 国民医療制度
retiree health benefits 退職者健康保険

health care [**healthcare**] 健康医療, 健康管理, 医療, 医療保険, ヘルスケア
health care expense 健康医療費, 医療費 （＝health care cost: 福利厚生の一環として, 米国の企業は従業員や退職者の医療保険への加入を支援している）
health care industry 医療産業 （＝health care service）
health care services 医療サービス

health care benefits 健康保険給付, 健康管理給付, 医療給付
▶Previously, we expensed *health care benefits* as claims were incurred. これまで当社は, 医療給付については請求が生じた時点に費用として計上していました。

health care cost 医療費, 医療費用 （＝health care expense）
▶GM has conducted intense discussions with the unions about how to reduce *health care costs*. GMは, 医療費負担の軽減について, 自動車労組(UAW) と精力的に交渉を進めている。

health insurance 健康保険
health insurance association 健康保険組合
health insurance card 保険証
health insurance expense 健康保険料
health insurance industry 健康保険業界
health insurance plan 健康保険制度, 健康保険 （＝health insurance system）
health insurance system 健康保険制度, 医療保険制度 （＝health insurance plan）
health insurance union 健康保険組合 （＝health insurance association, health insurance society）

healthy 形 健全な, 好調な, 順調な, 堅調な, 有益な, 相当な, かなりの

healthy balance sheet 健全な財務体質
healthy earnings 好業績
healthy increase 好調な伸び，順調な伸び，堅調な伸び（=healthy gain, healthy growth）
healthy sales 好調な販売
▸Nicon Corp. posted a 20 percent rise in its first half net profit, helped by *healthy* sales of digital cameras and production equipment for crystal displays. ニコンの上半期の税引き後利益は，デジタル・カメラと液晶ディスプレー製造装置の好調な販売に支えられて，20％増加した。

hearing 名 意見聴取，聴聞会，〈裁判所の〉審理，公判，審問，〈委員会などの〉尋問，審判
FTC hearings 公正取引委員会（FTC）の審判
open hearing 公聴会
private hearing 非公開の聴聞会
public hearing 公聴会

heat island phenomenon ヒート・アイランド現象
▸The rise in temperature due to the *heat island phenomenon* is occurring at a pace several times faster than that of global warming. ヒート・アイランド現象による気温上昇は，地球温暖化の数倍の速度で進んでいる。

heat wave 熱波，炎暑
▸*Heat waves* have become so severe that they are adversely affecting people's health and job efficiency. 熱波は厳しく，われわれの健康や仕事の能率に悪影響を与えている。

heavy 形 重い，重質の，大量の，大規模な，大型の，多額の，巨額の，重大な，活発な
heavy additional tax 重加算税
heavy and chemical industries 重化学工業
heavy chemicals 工業薬品，粗薬品（酸，アルカリ，塩酸など）
heavy crude 重質原油（=heavy crude oil）
heavy-duty truck 大型トラック
heavy equipment 重機，重電機器
heavy industries 重工業，重化学工業
heavy investment 大型設備投資，多額［巨額］の設備投資（=heavy capex）
heavy lifting 重労働，力仕事
heavy losses 巨額の損失
heavy machinery manufacturer 重機械メーカー，重機メーカー
heavy market 下落相場，軟調相場
heavy penalty tax 重加算税
heavy share 値がさ株
heavy trading 大商い，活発な取引
heavy user 大量利用者，ヘビー・ユーザー

heavy workload 過重労働
▸Such a *heavy workload* cannot continue for a long time. こうした過重労働は，長期間続くはずがない。

hedge 動 損失予防策をとる，売り［買い］つなぎして損失を防ぐ，分散投資して損失リスクを少なくする，掛けつなぎする，掛けつなぐ，リスクを回避する（⇒risk）
hedge against future cash flows 将来のキャッシュ・フローをヘッジする
hedge exchange risk 為替リスクを少なくする，為替リスクをヘッジする
hedge interest rate risk 金利リスクをヘッジする
hedge one's bond portfolio 債券ポートフォリオをヘッジする
▸Gains and losses on these forward contracts will offset losses and gains on the assets, liabilities and transactions being *hedged*. これらの先物為替予約から生じる利益と損失は，ヘッジの対象となっている資産，債務と取引から生じる損失および利益と相殺される。
▸Japanese companies can *hedge* exchange risks and improve their business image abroad through external bond financing. 日本企業は，外債発行による資金調達で，為替リスクを回避するとともに海外での企業イメージアップを図ることができる。

hedge 名 備え，損失予防手段，防護策，掛けつなぎ売買，保険つなぎ，為替リスクの防止［軽減］，ヘッジ（=hedging）
as a hedge against drops in stock prices 株価下落リスクに備えて
as a hedge against losses 損失に対するつなぎとして
hedge-buying 買いつなぎ（=buying hedge）
hedge gains and losses ヘッジ損益
hedge-selling 売りつなぎ（=selling hedge）
hedge transaction ヘッジ取引
short hedge 売りヘッジ
▸Gains and losses on *hedges* of existing assets or liabilities are marked to market on a monthly basis. 既存の資産または債務のヘッジに関する損益は毎月，評価替えされます。

hedge fund ヘッジ資金，短期投資資金，ヘッジ・ファンド（「ヘッジ・ファンド」は，投資家から集めた資金を株式や債券，通貨，原油など幅広い市場で運用し，最先端の経済学理論や数学理論，金融手法を駆使して損失の回避（ヘッジ）に努めながら収益を追求する一種の投資信託。⇒carry trade）

▶Many major finance firms as well as pension funds of nonfinancial entities have invested in the *hedge fund*. このヘッジ・ファンドには，多くの金融大手のほか，非金融事業会社の年金基金も投資している。

help 動 支援する，援助する，後押しする，助ける，支える，助長する，促進する，改善する，活性化する，…の要因となる，…に貢献する，…に寄与する
▶Solid performances by automakers have *helped* material suppliers and parts makers boost their business performances. 自動車メーカーの好業績[堅調な業績]が，素材メーカーや部品メーカーの業績向上を後押ししている。

help 名 援助，支援，助力，助け，救済手段，従業員，雇い人，解説機能，ヘルプ
　dealer helps 販売店援助
　help desk 問い合わせ窓口，顧客サービスの部署
　help function 解説機能，ヘルプ機能
　help screen 説明画面，ヘルプ画面
　help-wanted ad 求人広告
　self-help 自助，自力救済，自助努力
helping hand 救いの手，支援の手，援助の手，手助け
▶The company decided to seek a *helping hand* from the investment fund. 同社は，この投資ファンドに支援を求めることにした。

hidden 形 隠された，隠れた，簿外の
　hidden agenda 隠された動機，秘密のもくろみ，下心
　hidden assets 含み資産
　hidden gains 含み益
　hidden guarantee of obligation 簿外債務保証
　hidden inflation 隠れたインフレーション
　hidden property 含み資産
　hidden reserves 秘密積立金，含み資産
　hidden talents 隠れた才能
　hidden unemployment 隠れた失業，偽装失業
HIFO 最高価格払出し法，最高価格先出し法，最高原価先出し法，高入先出し法 （＝highest-in first-out method）

high 形 高い，高度な，高水準の，高級な，強い，大きな，最重要な，活発な
　high added value 高付加価値
　high credit standing 高い信用力，高い信用度 （＝good credit standing）
　high domestic demand 内需拡大
　high margin business 利益率が高い事業
　high-profile 脚光を浴びる，世間の注目を集める，人目を引く，注目の，著名な，明確な，鮮明な，大型の

　high profile project 大型プロジェクト
　high quality service 高品質サービス
　high return 高い運用益，高い利回り，高い収益率，高リターン，ハイリターン （⇒FX margin trading）
　high-speed Net access 高速ネット接続
　higher cost 費用の増加，コスト増，コストの上昇
　higher earnings 増益，高収益
　higher prices 値上げ，物価上昇，価格上昇
　higher profitability 高収益
　higher profits 増益，高収益
　higher turnover 売上高の増加，取引の活発化 （⇒turnover）
　higher volume 販売数量の増加
　higher yen 円高
　highest-in first-out method 最高価格払出し法，最高価格先出し法，最高原価先出し法，高入先出し法 《略 HIFO》
▶The segment was generally able to offset *higher* costs by improving yields, increasing factory utilization rates and *higher* worker productivity. 歩留まりの改善，工場稼動率の上昇や労働者の生産性向上により，当部門は全般にコストの増加分を相殺することができました。

high 名 高値，最高，最高値，最高記録，新記録 （⇒low, record-high net profit）
　a record high 過去最高
　an all time high 過去最高，史上最高値，上場来の高値，過去最多，過去最悪
　from a low of ... to a high of ... 最低…から最高…まで
　rally through the old highs 最高値を更新する
　reach a new historical high 過去最高を更新する
　set [hit] a new high 新記録を樹立する，過去最高を更新する，過去最高となる
▶The Dow Jones average reached a four-month *high* of 9,374. ダウ・ジョーンズ平均は，9,374ドルで4か月ぶりの高値を付けた。
▶We set new *highs* in both consolidated net profit and sales in 2008. 2008年度は，連結純利益[連結税引き後利益]も売上高も，過去最高を更新しました。

high-end 形 高級志向の，高級の，超高速の，高速型，高度な，最高価格帯の，高価な，フル装備の，ハイエンド
　high-end goods 高額商品，高価な商品，高級品
　high-end machine ハイエンド機種，最高価格帯のコンピュータ
　high-end workstation 超高速型ワークステー

ション
high-end user ハイエンド・ユーザー（自分でシステムを構築するユーザー）
▶China's *high-end* cosmetics market is in a full-fledged growth period. 中国の高級化粧品市場は，本格的な成長期にある。

high performance 好業績，高収益，高性能
▶The increase in sales of digital cameras was crucial to the company's *high performance*. 同社の高収益の原動力は，デジタル・カメラの販売の伸びだ。

high-priced product 高価格品，高額商品
▶Canon continues to manufacture domestically *high-priced products* that require high technology for their manufacture, such as equipment to produce semiconductors. キヤノンは，半導体製造装置など高い製造技術が要求される高価格品の国内生産を続けている。

high-tech 名 先端技術，高度技術，高度科学技術，ハイテク（＝high technology）
　high-tech bubble ハイテク関連株の狂乱バブル，ハイテク・バブル
　high-tech company ハイテク企業，ハイテク関連企業，ハイテク・メーカー（＝high-tech firm）
　high-tech gears ハイテク機器
　high-tech industrial sector ハイテク産業分野
　high-tech industry 先端産業，高度技術産業，ハイテク産業（＝high technology industry）
　high-tech issues ハイテク銘柄
　high-tech product ハイテク商品
　high-tech shares ハイテク株，ハイテク株の株価
▶Lower investment in plants and equipment in the *high-tech* industry and plunging prices of the stock of the electronics giants known as the best of blue-chip companies may further dampen overall demand. ハイテク産業の設備投資抑制や，優良企業の代表である大手電機株の急落も，需要全体の落ち込みにつながる可能性がある。

high technology 高度先端技術，高度技術，ハイテク，ハイテクノロジー（＝advanced technology, high-tech）
▶Passenger plane production integrates sophisticated machine and electronic parts, advanced materials and the latest *high technologies* to realize safe products that will endure severe conditions. 旅客機製造は，高度な機械・電子部品や最先端の材料と最新のハイテク技術を融合させて，過酷な使用条件に耐える安全な製品を実現する。

high-yield 形 高利回りの

high yield bond 高利回り債
▶These institutional investors invest in *high yield bonds* because interest rates are almost zero. これらの機関投資家は，金利がゼロに近いため，高利回り債に投資している。

highly enriched uranium 高濃縮ウラン《略 HEU》
▶*Highly enriched uranium* (HEU) can be used to make nuclear warheads if enriched to a sufficiently high level. 高濃縮ウランは，十分高レベルまで濃縮すると，核弾頭の製造に利用することができる。

hike 名 引上げ，値上げ，値上がり，上昇（⇒ price hike, wage hike）
　basic rate hike 基本料金の引上げ
　discount rate hike 公定歩合の引上げ
　fare hike 料金引上げ
　hike in the consumption tax 消費税の引上げ
　income tax hike 所得税の引上げ
　interest rate hike 利上げ，金利の引上げ（＝rate hike）
　tax hike 増税
▶A major film maker refrained for two months from shifting the raised costs caused by the *hike* in the price of polypropylene in June to product prices. ある大手のフイルム・メーカーは，6月のポリプロピレン（PP）の値上げによるコスト高［コストの上昇分］を2か月間，製品価格に転嫁しなかった。
▶In the spring wage talks, the unions of major electrical appliance makers will seek a ¥2,000 monthly wage *hike*, as it did in its request last year. 今年の春闘で，主要電機メーカー労組は，昨年要求と同じく月2,000円の賃上げを要求する。

hire 動 採用する，雇う，雇用する，賃貸しする，賃借りする，金を払う
▶Many companies stopped *hiring* new graduates when the labor market was tight. 労働需給［労働市場］が逼迫しているときは，多くの企業が新卒採用を中止した。

hire 名 賃金，給料，使用料，賃借料，社員，新入社員
　charter hire 用船料
　hire charge 賃借料
　hire plan 賦払い，分割払い，割賦
　hire purchase 分割払い［月賦］購入方式（installment plan），買取り選択権付きリース，買取り権付きリース，ハイア・パーチェス
　hire purchase lending 割賦ローン
　hire purchase transaction 買取り選択権付きリ

ース取引
hiring 名 採用, 雇用, 新入社員
historical [**historic**] 形 歴史的, 過去の, 取得時の, 取引発生日の
 historical cost 取得原価, 歴史的原価, 取得時の為替レート (＝acquisition cost, actual cost, historical buying price: 資産の取得に要した金額。実際の取引価額(historical buying price)を指す場合もある)
 historical data 過去のデータ, 過去の実績, 実数値
 historical earnings 過去の業績, 収益[売上高]の実績
 historical information 実績データ
 historical net asset value 前期基準の1株当たり純資産
 historical performance 過去の実績, 過去の運用実績
 historical price 歴史的原価 (過去の実際の取引価格)
 historical rate 取得時レート, 取引日レート, 発生時レート, 取得時の為替レート, 為替の取引発生日相場
 historical cost basis 取得原価基準, 取得原価主義, 取得原価法 (＝acquisition cost theory)
  取得原価主義について➡資産の価額を, そのために要した支出額によって評価する考え方を, 「取得原価主義」という。資産の評価原則としては, 取得原価主義のほかに, 時価主義(market value basis)と低価主義(lower of cost or market basis)がある。
 ▶The consolidated financial statements have been prepared on the *historical cost basis* in accordance with accounting principles generally accepted in Canada. 連結財務書類は, カナダで一般に公正妥当と認められた会計原則[会計基準]に従い, 取得原価基準に基づいて作成されています。
 historical summary 財務の推移(過年度の主要財務数値を比較形式で示したもの), 過去の推移, 過去の状況
 ▶The various types of accounting changes may significantly affect the trends shown in comparative financial statements and *historical summaries*. 各種の会計上の変更は, 比較財務書類に示されている傾向や過去の財務の推移に重要な影響を及ぼす可能性があります。
hit 動 打撃を与える, …に達する, 記録する, 打つ
 be hard hit ひどい目にあう, 大きな打撃を受ける
 hit a new high 新高値を付ける, 過去最高値を記録する, 過去最高値となる
 hit a new low 新安値を付ける, 最安値を更新する
 hit a record high 過去最高に達する
 hit an all-time high 過去最高に達する, 史上最高値を記録する, 最高記録に達する
 hit an all-time record high 史上最高値を付ける, 上場来の高値を付ける
 hit bottom [**the bottom**] 底入れする, 底を打つ, 最低レベルに達する, 底値に達する (＝bottom out)
 hit the market 市場に登場する
hit 名 〈ホームページなどの〉利用, アクセス, 〈検索時の〉該当項目, ヒット
▶There was no *hit* obtained in the search. 検索で, 該当項目は得られなかった。
hit product ヒット商品
▶Sony is on its way to a turnaround in its core electronics business because of *hit products* such as liquid-crystal display TVs and digital cameras. 液晶テレビやデジタル・カメラなどのヒット商品があるため, ソニーの主力のエレクトロニクス事業は, 業績が改善している。
HMO 健康維持機構 (health maintenance organization の略)
hoard 動 貯蔵する, 秘蔵[退蔵, 保蔵]する, 蓄える, ためる, 買いだめする
 hoard food 食糧を蓄える
 hoard goods 品物を買いだめする
 hoarded cash 退蔵現金
 hoarded currency [**money**] 保蔵通貨
 hoarded goods 退蔵品, 退蔵物資
 propensity to hoard 保蔵性向
hoarding [**hoard**] 名 貯蔵, 秘蔵, 蓄え, 退蔵, 死蔵, 保蔵, 買いだめ, 広告板(billboard), 掲示板
 gross hoarding 総保蔵
 hoarding demand 退蔵需要
 hoarding equipment 揚貨設備
 international hoarding 国際保蔵
 net hoarding 純保蔵
 private hoarding 民間保蔵, 民間の退蔵
hock 名 質, 入質, 借金
holder 名 保有者, 所有者, 所持人, 株主, 契約者, 会員 (＝owner)
 asset holder 資産保有者
 bank account holder 銀行口座の名義人
 bill holder 手形所持人
 bond holder 社債保有者
 card holder カード会員 (＝cardholder)
 check holder 小切手振出人

holding

debt holder 債券保有者
equity holder 持ち分証券保有者
holder in bad faith 悪意の第三者, 悪意取得者
holder in due course 善意の第三者, 善意取得者, 正当所持人
holder of record 株主名簿上の株主, 登録保有者, 登録株主
option holder オプションの買い手
policy holder 保険契約者 (＝policyholder)
security holder 証券保有者, 証券所有者

▶*Holders* of about 268.64 million shares, or 63.71 percent of all shares of Hanshin Electric Railway Co., accepted Hankyu's public tender offer. 阪神電鉄の約2億6,864万株の株主(発行済み株式の63.71%)が, 阪急の株式公開買付け(TOB)に応募した。

holding 名 所有, 保有, 保持, 占有, 所有持ち分, 保有株, 持ち株比率, 子会社, 所有財産, 保有財産
cross holding 株式持ち合い (＝mutual holding of stocks)
direct holding 直接所有, 直接保有
equity holding income 持ち分法利益
holding gains and losses 保有損益, 保有利得および損失 (＝holding gains and/or losses)
holding period return 所有期間利回り
inventory holding gain 棚卸し資産保有利得
land-holding tax 土地保有税
realized holding gain or loss 実現保有損益
reciprocal share holding 株式持ち合い
speculative holding 投機的保有

▶The U.S. investment fund will offer 25 percent of its *holding*. この米国の投資ファンドは, 保有する株式の25%を売り出す。

holding company 持ち株会社 (＝holding corporation:「持ち株会社」は, 他の会社の株式を, 投資目的でなく事業活動支配のために保有する会社)
bank holding company 銀行持ち株会社
financial holding company 金融持ち株会社
industrial holding company 製造業持ち株会社
insurance holding company 保険持ち株会社
investment holding company 投資持ち株会社
management holding company 経営持ち株会社
private industrial holding company 民間持ち株会社
public utility holding company 公益事業持ち株会社
pure holding company 純粋持ち株会社
state-owned holding company 国営持ち株会社

▶The *holding company* is expected to take an equity stake of around 10 percent in a consumer credit firm. この持ち株会社は, 消費者金融会社の株式持ち分約10%を取得する見込みだ。

▶The trust bank will establish a financial *holding company* in fiscal 2009. 同信託銀行は, 2009年度に金融持ち株会社を設立する方針だ。

▶The two firms integrated their operations under a *holding company* on Oct. 1, 2008. 2008年10月1日に, 両社は持ち株会社の下に経営統合した。

holdings 名 持ち株, 保有株, 保有高, 持ち株比率, 持ち株会社, 資産
blue-chip holdings 優良持ち株
bond holdings 債券保有高
company's holdings 会社の資産
dollar holdings ドル保有高
draft holdings 手形保有高
gold holdings 金準備
inventory holdings 在庫保有量
national holdings 国家資産
real estate holdings 保有不動産
securities holdings 保有有価証券, 保有証券 (保有する株式や債券のこと)
stock holdings 保有株式, 持ち株, 出資比率

▶*Holdings* in associated companies are reported in accordance with the equity method. 関連会社株式は, (連結財務書類上)持ち分法に従って報告されています。

hollowing-out 名 空洞化 (＝hollowing, hollowing out, hollowization)
the hollowing-out of employment opportunities 雇用空洞化
the hollowing-out of (Japanese) industry 産業空洞化 (＝deindustrialization)
the hollowing-out of tax revenue 税の空洞化
the hollowing-out of the corporation 企業の空洞化
the hollowing-out of the national pension system 国民年金の空洞化

home 名 家庭, 住宅, 発祥地, 本元, 本拠地, 本国, ホーム
home banking ホーム・バンキング
home-based worker 在宅就労者, 在宅勤務者 (＝homeworker)
home builder 住宅メーカー
home economist 家政学士, ホーム・エコノミスト
home economist in business 消費者問題担当者, ヒーブ

home loan 住宅ローン (＝home mortgage)
home network appliance system ネットワーク家電
home office 本社, 本店, 本部
home renovation 住宅リフォーム
home renovator 住宅リフォーム業者
home sales 住宅販売
home shopping ホーム・ショッピング
home trading ホーム・トレーディング (＝home trade, Net trading, online trading)

home appliance 家電, 家庭用電気器具, 白物
computerized home appliances デジタル家電
digital home appliances デジタル家電
home appliance manufacturer 家電メーカー (＝electrical appliance maker)
▶Sales of computerized *home appliances* are less brisk than they had been until a few months' ago.　デジタル家電の販売は，数か月前までの勢いがなくなっている。

home delivery 宅配便
home delivery operator 宅配業者, 宅配業
home delivery service 宅配サービス, 宅配業務, 宅配事業
▶Seven-Eleven Japan Co. is improving its *home delivery* service to encourage its use by the elderly and others who find it difficult to go to its stores.　セブン－イレブン・ジャパンは，来店が難しい高齢者などにも同店を利用してもらうため，宅配事業に力を入れている。

homogeneous 形 均質の, 同種の, 等質の, 同質の
homogeneous assets 同種資産
homogeneous market 同質市場
homogeneous oligopoly 同質寡占
homogeneous product 同質的製品, 同質的生産物
▶A *homogeneous* workforce enables companies to produce products of the same quality anywhere in the world.　労働力が均質なら，企業は世界のどこでも同じ品質の製品を生産することができる。

honorarium 名 謝礼, 謝金
horizon 名 水平線, 地平線, 視界, 視野, 限界, 範囲, 前途, 目標, 行く末, 期間, 所有期間, ホライズン (⇒**time horizon**)
horizon return 所有期間利回り
investment horizon 所有期間, 投資対象
▶Economic recovery is on the *horizon*, but the employment situation remains severe.　景気回復の兆しは見えるが，雇用情勢はまだ厳しい。

horizontal 形 水平的, 同業異種間の, 横割りの, 横の (⇒**vertical**)
horizontal acquisition 水平的買収
horizontal amalgamation 水平的合併
horizontal combination 水平的企業結合, 同業種間の企業結合
horizontal competition 水平的競争
horizontal consolidation 水平的合併, 水平的新設合併, 同業種間の合併［新設合併］
horizontal diversification 水平的多角化
horizontal influence 水平的影響
horizontal integration 水平的統合
horizontal international specialization 水平的国際分業, 水平的分業
horizontal market 水平的市場
horizontal marketing system 水平的マーケティング・システム
horizontal merger 水平的合併
horizontal organization 水平的組織
horizontal price agreement 水平的価格協定
horizontal publication 総合業界紙
horizontal specialization 水平的分業, 水平的国際分業 (＝horizontal international specialization)
horizontal trade 水平貿易

host 名 主催者, 開催国, 開催地, 議長国, 会場提供者, 〈番組の〉司会者, ホスト
host country 相手国, 進出国, 進出先, 投資先の国, 受入れ国, 営業国, 現地
▶China is the *host* of the six-way talks.　中国は，6か国協議の議長国だ。

host computer ホスト・コンピュータ, 大型汎用機, ホスト計算機, 多重アクセス・コンピュータ
▶The leaked information was part of personal data on about 2.5 million people kept on the *host computer* at the firm's head sales office for eastern Japan.　流出した情報は，同社の東日本営業本部がホスト・コンピュータで管理している約250万人分の個人データの一部である。

hostile 形 敵対的, 敵対する
hostile acquirer 敵対的買収者 (＝hostile bidder, hostile takeover bidder)
hostile bid 敵対的TOB（株式公開買付け), 敵対的買収, 敵対的買収提案 (＝hostile takeover bid)
hostile mergers and acquisitions 敵対的M&A（企業の合併・買収), 敵対的M&A
hostile tender offer 敵対的TOB（株式の公開買付け), 敵対的な株式公開買付け
▶We launched the *hostile* bid for the firm's

shares. 当社は，同社株の敵対的公開買付け(TOB)を実施しました。

hostile takeover 敵対的買収, 敵対的M&A（＝hostile acquisition, unsolicited takeover）
  hostile takeover bid 敵対的株式公開買付け, 敵対的TOB, 株式公開買付けによる敵対的買収, 敵対的買収 （＝hostile bid）
  hostile takeover bidder 敵対的買収者 （＝hostile acquirer, hostile bidder）
  ▸In order to forestall *hostile takeover* bids, companies should raise their corporate value. 敵対的TOB（株式公開買付けによる企業買収）を未然に防ぐには，企業が企業価値を高めなければならない。

hot 形 最新の，いま話題の，人気のある，飛ぶように売れる，需要の多い，ホットな
  hot check 不良小切手, 不正小切手
  hot commercial 最新のコマーシャル
  hot item 売れ筋の商品 （＝hot-selling item）
  hot issue 超人気株, 人気新銘柄, ホット・イシュー （＝hot stock）
  hot line 緊急用直通電話, 直通電話サービス, ホットライン
  hot money 投機資金, 国際短期資金
  hot number 売れ筋商品
  hot seller 売行き好調な品物
  hot shot [hotshot] 最新ニュース，ホット・ニュース

hot-desking 名 事務机共用制, ホットデスキング

hot-selling 形 売れ筋の
  ▸*Hot-selling* publication lines have been shifting away from conventional book types toward low-priced pocket-edition paperbacks. 売れ筋の出版物は，従来の本のタイプから安価な新書版に移っている。

hour 名 時間, アワー
  after hours 勤務時間後に，営業時間後に
  after-hours dealing 時間外取引
  average weekly hours 週平均労働時間 （＝hours worked）
  direct hours 直接労働時間
  idle hour 不働時間
  machine hour 機械時間
  man hour 工数, マン・アワー
  office hours 営業時間 （＝operating hours）
  statutory working hours 法定労働時間
  working hours 労働時間, 作業時間

house 名 商社, 会社, 業者, 取引所, 住宅, ハウス
  acceptance house 引受商社
  bond house 証券会社
  brokerage house 証券会社
  clearing house 決済機関, 手形交換所, 清算機関, クリアリング・ハウス
  customs house 税関
  discount house 手形割引業者, 割引業者, 割引商社
  exchange house 為替取引所, 両替所
  finance house 金融会社
  foreign currency house 両替所
  halfway house 中間施設
  house mark 基本商標, ハウス・マーク
  House of Representatives 米下院
  house organ 企業のPR誌[広報誌], 社内報, 機関誌, ハウス・オーガン
  house renovator 住宅リフォーム会社 （＝housing renovation firm）
  in-house brand 自社ブランド
  issuing house 証券発行会社
  securities house 証券会社
  swap clearing house スワップ清算機関
  trading house 証券会社, 商社

household 名 家庭, 世帯, 所帯, 家計
  household appliances 家電製品
  household product 家庭用品
  household sector 消費者, 家計部門
  household survey 家計調査
  low income households 低所得者層
  non-salaried household 一般世帯
  wage-earning households サラリーマン世帯, 勤労者世帯
  ▸The outstanding balance of financial assets held by *households* stood at ¥1,544.83 trillion as the end of December 2007. 2007年末現在の個人が持っている金融資産の残高は，1,544兆8,300億円となった。

household assets 家計金融資産, 個人の金融資産, 個人金融資産
  ▸The ratio of cash and deposits to Japan's total *household assets* came to 50.8 percent in 2007. 日本の個人が持っている金融資産全体に占める現金・預金の比率は，2007年は50.8％となった。

household outlays 1世帯当たり消費支出, 家計支出, 個人消費 （＝household spending）
  ▸The nation's *household outlays* fell 2.6 percent in June from a year earlier in real terms for the first year-on-year decline in eight months. 日本の6月の1世帯当たり消費支出額は，(物価変動の影響を除いた)実質で前年同月比2.6％減と，前年比で8か月ぶりに減少した。

household savings 家計の貯蓄, 家計貯蓄
▶The level of *household savings* used to be the highest among industrial nations. （日本の）家計貯蓄の水準は, 以前は先進国でいちばん高かった。

household spending 家計支出, 世帯の消費支出, 個人消費
▶Healthy corporate performances will improve employment and income conditions, thus leading to a rise in *household spending*. 企業業績が好調だと, 雇用情勢と所得動向が改善し, これが家計部門にも波及する[個人消費の増加にもつながる]。

housing investment 住宅投資
▶*Housing investment*, a driving force for the U.S. economy until recently, has shown signs of a slowdown. 最近まで米景気を牽引してきた住宅投資に, 減速感が見られる。

housing loan 住宅ローン (=home loan, home mortgage)
▶The additional provisions boosted the bank's credit costs related to the U.S. *housing loan* market woes in the April-September period to ¥19.8 billion. 引当金の積み増しで, 米住宅ローン市場低迷関連の同行の与信コストは, 4-9月期で198億円に増加した。

housing market 住宅市場
▶The U.S. economy has been hit by a chilled *housing market* and shrinking employment. 米経済は, 住宅市場の冷え込みと雇用の落ち込みで打撃を受けている。

housing starts 住宅着工, 住宅着工件数, 住宅着工戸数, 新設住宅着工戸数 (⇒increase)
▶Revenue growth in 2007 was primarily due to higher demand as a result of record *housing starts*. 2007年の売上高の伸びは, 住宅着工件数が過去最高に達したことに伴って, 需要が高まったことが主な要因です。

HP 分割払い購入 (**hire purchase** の略)
HR 人事部 (**human resources** の略)
hub 名 中心, 中核, 中枢, 拠点, 集線装置 (LANなど複数のケーブルを束ねる機器), ハブ
　hub airport 拠点空港, ハブ空港
　hub of commerce 商業の中心
human 形 人間の, 人間的, 人的, ヒューマン

human assessment ヒューマン・アセスメント (経営管理技法の一つで, 管理職の総合啓発訓練, マネジメント適正度診断, 昇進候補者の選択などが含まれる)
human capital 人的資本, 人的資源, 人材
human ecology 人間生態学, 人間環境, ヒューマン・エコロジー
human engineering 人間管理, 人間工学《略 HE》
human error 人災, 人為ミス
human relations 人間関係, 対人関係
human services 人的サービス, 福祉サービス
human-wave tactic [tactics] 人海戦術

human cloning コピー人間作り, ヒトのクローン
▶EU funding for embryonic human stem cell research will continue through 2013, under new rules that prevent *human cloning* and destroying embryos. ヒトのクローン作りと胚の損傷を禁止する新ルールに従って, 欧州連合 (EU) は, ヒト胚性幹細胞研究に対する資金の拠出を2013年まで継続する予定だ。

human resources 人的資源, 人材, 人事部
　human resources development 人的資源開発, 人材開発
　human resources management 人的資源管理《略 HRM》(人事労務管理のこと)
▶Outsourcing is actively utilized in Europe and the U.S. by venture businesses that lack adequate *human resources*. アウトソーシングは, 欧米では人的資源を十分に確保できないベンチャー企業によって積極的に活用されています。

hush money 口止め料
▶The company paid ¥63 million *hush money* to a construction firm. 同社は, 建築会社に6,300万円の口止め料を支払っていた。

hybrid car ハイブリッド車, ガソリン電気自動車 (=hybrid electric vehicle; ⇒lithium ion rechargeable battery)
▶Toyota will sell 300,000 gasoline-electric *hybrid cars* worldwide by the end of next year. トヨタは, 来年末までにガソリンと電気を併用するハイブリッド車を世界市場で30万台販売する方針だ。

hype 名 誇大広告

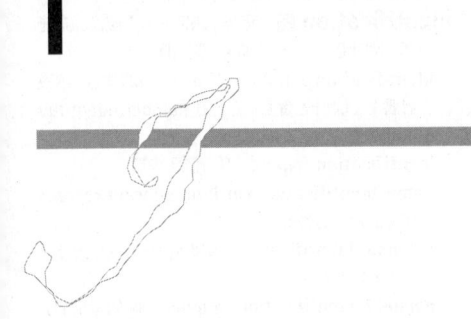

IAEA 国際原子力機関 (International Atomic Energy Agencyの略)
IAS 国際会計基準 (⇒International Accounting Standards)
▸Japanese companies listed on the London Stock Exchange will submit financial reports based on the *IAS* or the U.S. GAAP. ロンドン証券取引所に上場している日本企業は今後, 国際会計基準か米国会計基準に基づく[準拠した]財務報告書を提出することになる.
IATA 国際航空輸送協会, イアタ (International Air Transportの略)
IBBR 銀行間取り手金利, インターバンク・ビッド・レート (interbank bid rateの略)
IBOR 銀行間出し手金利, インターバンク・オファード・レート (interbank offered rateの略)
IBRD 国際復興開発銀行, 第一世銀, 世界銀行 (International Bank for Reconstruction and Developmentの略)
i/c …担当の (in chargeの略)
IC 集積回路 (integrated circuitの略)
  analog IC アナログIC
  application-specific IC 特注集積回路, 特定用途向けIC《略 ASIC》
  bipolar IC バイポーラ型IC, バイポーラIC
  custom IC 特注IC, カスタムIC, カスタム・チップ (ユーザーの注文により作られるIC)
  digital IC デジタルIC
  hybrid IC 混成集積回路, ハイブリッドIC
  IC memory 半導体記憶装置
  IC package 半導体封止剤
  large scale IC 大規模[高密度]集積回路《略 LSI》 (=large scale integration)
  linear IC リニア集積回路, リニアIC
  medium scale IC 中規模集積回路《略 MSI》 (=medium scale integration)
  monolithic IC 半導体集積回路, モノリシックIC
  MOS IC 金属酸化物半導体集積回路, MOS集積回路, モスIC, モス型IC (metal oxide semiconductor ICの略)
  opto-electronic IC 光電子集積回路《略 OEIC》
  small scale IC 小規模集積回路《略 SSI》 (=small scale integration)
  ultra large scale IC 超超[極超]大規模集積回路《略 ULSI》 (=ultra large-scale integration)
  very large scale IC 超大規模集積回路, 超LSI《略 VLSI》 (=very large scale integration)
IC ATM card ICキャッシュ・カード
▸The new *IC ATM cards* of the bank will have advanced functions such as digital money and a point system. 同行の新型ICキャッシュ・カードには, デジタル・マネーやポイント制などの先端機能が採用される.
IC card ICカード (=smart card, smart credit card: ICチップを埋め込んだカード)
  IC card applied technology ICカード応用技術
  IC card cashless account settlement system ICカード・キャッシュレス決済システム, キャッシュレス決済システム
  IC card-compatible vending machine ICカード対応の自動販売機
IC chip IC (集積回路) チップ (=silicon chip)
▸The government has decided to introduce passports containing *IC chips*. 政府は, ICチップ付き旅券の導入を決めた.
IC tag ICタグ, 電子荷札 (⇒gadgetry)

ICタグとは➡基盤上にトランジスターやダイオードなどの素子を装着して各種機能を持たせた集積回路(IC)に，無線通信用の微小なアンテナを付け，無線で情報を送受信できる電子荷札のこと。通信距離は，数ミリから数メートルまで。
▸*IC tags* are helpful for managing distribution. ICタグ(電子荷札)は，流通管理に有用だ[効果がある]。

ICA 国際商事仲裁 (**International Commercial Arbitration**の略)

ICA 国際仲裁裁判所 (**International Court of Arbitration**の略)

ICAO 国際民間航空機関, イカオ (**International Civil Aviation Organization**の略)

ICC 国際商工会議所(**International Chamber of Commerce**の略)

ICC 米州際通商委員会(**Interstate Commerce Commission**の略)

icon 絵文字, アイコン (⇒**identification**)

ID 発信者番号, 識別符号, 識別番号 (**identification**の略)
　digital ID デジタルID
　ID card 身分証明書, IDカード (=**identity card**)
　ID number ID番号, 識別番号, 納税者番号, 取引先番号 (=**identification number**)
　log-in ID ログインID (=**user ID**)
　source ID ソースID
　user ID ユーザーID

IDA 国際開発協会, 第二世界銀行 (**International Development Association**の略)

IDB 米州開発銀行 (**Inter-American Development Bank**の略)

idea 着想, 思いつき, 発想, 構想, 発案, 案, 考え, 考え方, 意見, 知識, 認識, 計画, 意図, ねらい, 思想, 概念, 観念, アイデア
　fresh idea 斬新なアイデア
　idea processing 発想支援
　new idea 新しいアイデア, 新構想, 新しい思想
　outdated idea 時代遅れの思想
　product idea 製品[商品]のアイデア
▸It is to our benefit to be able to use *ideas* that others create. 他社が生み出したアイデアを利用できるのは，当社にとっても利益になります。

identifiable asset 識別可能資産, 固有資産, セグメント固有資産, セグメント帰属資産, 総資産 (⇒**industry segment**)
▸*Identifiable assets* (excluding intersegment receivables) are the Company's assets that are identified with classes of similar products or operations in each geographic area. 固有資産(部門間受取債権を除く)は，当社資産を各地域ごとに同種の製品または事業で分類した資産です。

identification 照合, 識別, 本人確認, 身元確認, 識別番号, 発信者番号《略 **ID**》
　identification number ID番号, 識別番号, 納税者番号, 取引先番号 (=**ID number, identifier number**)
　identification papers 身分証明書類
　name-identification work on pension records 年金記録の名寄せ
　personal identification card system 社員証カード・システム
　personal identification number 個人識別番号, 銀行カードの個人暗証番号, 暗証番号, パスワード《略 **PIN**》
　the identification of a bank account holder 銀行口座名義人の本人確認
▸The use of easily recognizable icons and pictograms allows instant *identification* and selection of the required functions. 簡単に見分けがつくアイコンや図形が用いられているため，必要な機能を視覚的に識別・選択することができます。

identity 身元, 正体, 素性, 身分証明, 本質, 本人, 自分自身, 己(おのれ)自身, 自己認識, 個性, 独自性, 性格, 主体性, 同一, 同一性, 自己同一性, 一致, 帰属意識, 意識, 伝統, 類似, 類似例, 民族性, 国民性, 一体性, アイデンティティ
　brand identity 商標の存在価値, 商品の独自性, ブランド・アイデンティティ
　corporate identity コーポレート・アイデンティティ, 企業イメージ統合戦略《略 **CI**》
　cultural identity 独自の文化意識, 文化の独自性, 文化の伝統
　group identity グループ意識, 集団主義
　identity card IDカード (=**identification card**)
　identity crisis 自己喪失, 自己認識の危機, 自己同一性認識の危機, アイデンティティ・クライシス
　national identity 民族性, 国民性, 民族意識
　rate of identity 知名率
　self-identity 自己意識, 自我意識
　verify the identity of new depositors 新規預金者の身元確認をする
▸The new virus called KLEZ is said to be capable of sending e-mails under an *identity* assumed from among the names kept in a personal computer infected with the virus. KLEZと呼ばれるこの新手[新型]のコンピュータ・ウイルスは，ウイルスに感染したパソコン内の名前[アドレス]を詐称してメール[Eメール]を送ることができると

言われる。

idle 形 遊休の, 不動の, 休止の, アイドル
　idle capacity 遊休生産能力, 不動生産能力［生産設備］
　idle cash 遊休資金, 余剰資金
　idle equipment 遊休設備
　idle facility 遊休施設, 休止施設
　idle money 遊休資金, 遊び金 (=inactive money)
　idle plant 遊休設備, 遊休工場設備 (=idle plant capacity)
　idle property 遊休資産, 休止資産
　idle real estate 遊休不動産
　idle time 遊休時間, 不稼動時間, 遊び時間, 空き時間, アイドル・タイム

IE 生産工学, 産業工学, インダストリアル・エンジニアリング (industrial engineeringの略)

IEA 国際エネルギー機関 (International Energy Agencyの略)

IEC 国際電気標準会議 (International Electrotechnical Commissionの略)

IFC 国際金融公社, 第三世銀 (International Finance Corporationの略)

IFRS 国際財務報告基準 (⇒International Financial Reporting Standardsの略)

IIRF 国際IR連盟 (International Investor Relations Federationの略)

illegal 形 違法な, 不法な, 非合法な, 不正な (=illicit, unlawful)
　illegal donations ヤミ献金
　illegal dumping 不法投棄
　illegal employment 不法就労
　illegal lending 違法貸付け, ヤミ金融
　illegal moneylender 違法金融業者, ヤミ金融業者
　illegal operation 不法操作
　illegal transaction 仮装売買, 不正取引, 不正取引の売買業務 (=illegal trade)
　illegal worker 不法就労者

illegal access 不正アクセス (=hacking)
▶More than 400 cases of *illegal access* to the Internet were reported in the nation last year. 昨年は, 400件を超えるインターネットへの不正アクセスが国内で報告されている。

illegal export 不正輸出, 違法輸出 (=unlawful export)
▶The Man Gyong Bong also turned out to have played a role in *illegal exports* of missile parts from Japan. 北朝鮮の貨客船「万景峰号」が, 日本からのミサイル部品の不正輸出にかかわっていたことも判明している。

illegal trade 不正取引
▶Japan should further work to crack down on the *illegal trade* of missile-related components, drugs and counterfeit banknotes. 日本は, ミサイル関連部品の不正取引や麻薬, 偽造紙幣などの取締りを一層強化しなければならない。

illicit loan operator 違法貸金業者, ヤミ金融業者

illicit moneylender ヤミ金融業者 (=illegal money lender, unauthorized moneylender)

illiquid 形 流動性のない, 流動性に乏しい, 換金しにくい, 容易に現金に転換できない
　illiquid asset 流動性に乏しい資産, 流動性の低い資産, 流動性のない資産
　illiquid issues 流動性の低い銘柄

ILO 国際労働機関 (International Labour Organizationの略)

image 名 画像, 映像, 心像, イメージ
　brand image ブランド・イメージ, ブランドに対する全体的知覚
　corporate image 企業イメージ, コーポレート・イメージ
　global image 全地球的イメージ, グローバル・イメージ
　image advertising イメージ広告
　image building イメージ構築, イメージ作り, イメージアップ
　image character イメージ・キャラクター
　image consultant イメージ・コンサルタント
　image formation イメージ形成
　image input 画像入力 (=image scanning)
　image processing 画像処理, イメージ処理
　image reader 画像読取り装置, 画像入力装置, イメージ・リーダー (=image scanner)
　image strategy イメージ戦略
　image survey イメージ調査
　media image 媒体イメージ
　moving image 動画
　product image 製品イメージ, 商品イメージ, プロダクト・イメージ
　still image 静止画像
▶The company's poor corporate *image* is detrimental to the long-term growth prospects of its corporate group. 同社の悪い企業イメージは, 同社の企業グループの長期成長見通しにはマイナス要因だ。

imbalance 形 不均衡, 差, アンバランス
　balance of payments imbalance 国際収支の不均衡 (=payment imbalance)

basic imbalance 基礎的不均衡
inventory imbalance 過剰在庫
macro imbalances マクロ経済の不均衡
structural imbalance 構造的不均衡
supply and demand imbalances 需要と供給の不均衡, 需給不均衡 (=imbalances between supply and demand)
trade imbalance 貿易の不均衡, 貿易不均衡
workload imbalance 作業負担量[仕事量]の不均衡, 労働力の不均衡

▶The undervalued yuan has increased China's international competitiveness, adding to its trade *imbalances* with the United States and other nations. 人民元の過小評価が, 中国の国際競争力を高め, 米国などとの貿易不均衡を拡大している。

▶We prefer to move people to work and work to people as a means of addressing workload *imbalances*. 当社は, 労働力不均衡を是正する手段として, まず人員の配置転換や人員に応じた業務の再配分を行う方針です。

IMF 国際通貨基金 (⇒International Monetary Fund)

immediate 形 即座の, 即時[即刻]の, 当面の, 目下の, 目先の, 目前の, 短期的な, 現在の, 隣接した
immediate access 即時アクセス
immediate annuity 即時年金, 即時型年金
immediate earnings outlook 当面の業績見通し, 当面の収益見通し
immediate improvement 目先の業績改善
immediate processing 即時処理 (=demand processing, inline processing)
immediate recognition as an expense 費用としての即時認識
immediate settlement 即時決済

immobilize 動 流通停止にする,〈流動資本を〉固定資本化する

immovable [immoveable] 形 動かない, 動かせない, 不動の

IMO 国際海事機関 (International Maritime Organizationの略)

impact 動 影響を及ぼす, 影響[衝撃]を与える, …への効果がある

▶The realignment and streamlining of the Corporation begins to *impact* earnings. 当社の再編と効率化の利益への効果が, 見られるようになった。

impact 名 影響, 効果, 衝撃, 刺激, インパクト
before the impact of restructuring costs 再編成費用の影響額控除前

disinflationary impact インフレ抑制効果
financial impact 財務上の影響, 財務的影響
forex impact 為替による影響, 為替の影響 (=foreign exchange impact)
impact from currency fluctuation 為替変動による影響, 為替変動の影響
impact loan 使途を限定しない外貨貸付け, 外貨借款, 外貨借入れ, インパクト・ローン
impact of currency swings 為替相場の影響
impact of the declining cycle 景気後退の影響
impact on competitive position 競争力への影響, 競争力に与える影響
lasting impact 長期効果
negative impact マイナス影響, マイナス効果, 悪影響
reflationary impact 景気刺激効果

▶As the financial results show, the *impact* of our actions toward creating a leaner, more aggressive company has begun to appear. 業績が示すとおり, 当社を一段とスリムで活動的な企業にするために私どもが取った措置の効果が, 見られるようになりました。

▶Earnings per common share before the *impact* of these restructuring costs would have been $1.30. これら再編成費用の影響額控除前の普通株式1株当たり利益は, 1.30ドルとなります。

impair 動 損なう, 弱める, 減じる, 劣化する, 制約する
impaired capital 資本の欠損, 資本金の欠損
impaired risks 信用リスク

impaired asset 不良債権, 不良資産

▶Charges included in other accounts were primarily for expenses related to writing down *impaired assets* and merger-related expenses. その他の勘定科目に計上した費用は, 主に不良資産の評価減と合併関連の費用です。

impaired loans 不良債権, 劣化した貸出金, 貸出金の劣化

▶We compute present values for *impaired loans* when we determine our allowances for credit losses. 当社の貸倒れ引当金を決定するにあたって, 当社は不良債権の現在価値を計算します。

impairment 名 減損, 資本金の欠損, 損耗, 減価, 価値の下落, 劣化, 評価減
assessment of impairment 価値の下落の評価
impairment loss 減損損失, 減損処理による損失
impairment of loans 貸出金の劣化, 貸付け金の破損, 不良債権, 貸付け金の評価損
impairment of value 資産価値の損耗
indication of an asset's impairment 減損の

impasse | **import quota system**

兆候
permanent impairment in value 回復不能減価
▸The sharp downward revision stems from an *impairment* loss on plasma display production facilities. この大幅な下方修正は，プラズマ・ディスプレー生産設備の減損処理に伴う損失によるものだ．

impasse 名 袋小路，行き詰まり，行き悩み，窮地，難局，対立，不振
▸It appears to be difficult to break the long-term sales *impasse*. 長期的な売れ行き不振を打開するのは，難しそうだ［容易ではなさそうだ］．

implement 動 実施する，実行する，遂行する，施行する，適用する
▸In 2007, we *implemented* Statement of Financial Accounting Standards (SFAS) 96. 2007年度から，当社は財務会計基準書（SFAS）第96号を適用しています．

implementation 名 実施，実行，遂行，履行，施行，運用，適用，開発，構築，実現，実装，インプリメンテーション
  implementation guide 適用指針
  implementation stage 実施段階
  intranet implementation イントラネット構築
  policy implementation 政策実施，政策の遂行
  software implementation ソフトウエア開発
  system implementation システム開発，システムの開発・構築

implied 形 黙示の，間接的な
  implied authority 黙示の代理権
  implied contract 黙示契約
  implied terms 黙示条件，黙示条項
  implied waiver 黙示の権利放棄
  implied warranty 黙示の保証，黙示の担保

import 動 輸入する，〈データなどを〉転送する，移動する，取り込む，持ち込む，発生させる
  develop-and-import scheme 開発輸入方式，開発輸入
  import data from the database データベースからデータを取り込む
  import inflation インフレを発生させる，インフレを招く
  import technology 技術を輸入する，技術を導入する
  imported goods 輸入品
  imported oil 輸入原油
▸The volume of fresh vegetables *imported* from China in February fell about 40 percent from a year ago. 2月に中国から輸入した生鮮野菜の量は，1年前より［前年同月比で］約4割減少した．

import 名 輸入，輸入品，輸入製品，導入，重要性，意味，インポート
  agricultural imports 農産品の輸入
  blanket import 一元輸入
  bounty for import 輸入助成金，輸入奨励金
  capital import 資本輸入，外資導入
  consignment import 委託輸入
  declaration of import 輸入申告
  development-and-import scheme 開発輸入方式，開発輸入
  emergency import 緊急輸入
  import agency 輸入代行業者
  import agent 輸入代理店（＝import commission house）
  import bill 輸入手形
  import curbs 輸入制限
  import clearance 輸入通関
  import duty 輸入税（＝import tax）
  import entry 輸入手続き
  import license 輸入許可，輸入承認
  import quota 輸入割当て，輸入割当数量，輸入枠
  import restrictions 輸入規制，輸入制限
  import surcharge 輸入課徴金（＝import surtax）
  invisible export and import 貿易外収支
  knockdown import ノックダウン輸入，国内組立 て
  manufactured imports 製品輸入，工業製品輸入
  ordered import 企画輸入
  parallel import 並行輸入
  speculative import 思惑輸入
  steel imports 輸入鉄鋼製品，鉄鋼輸入品
  tariffs on steel imports 輸入鉄鋼製品に対する関税
  tax-free imports 免税輸入品（＝tax-exempt imports）
  technology import 技術輸入，技術導入
  visible import 商品輸入
▸All *imports* of beef, processed beef products and cattle from Canada were halted after receiving a report about the first BSE case in 10 years in the North American country. カナダで10年ぶりにBSEが発生したとの報告を受けて，カナダからの牛肉や牛肉加工品，生きた牛の輸入が全面停止された．

import quota system 輸入割当制度
▸Japan maintains an *import quota system* for nori to help protect domestic producers. 国内生産者の保護を支援するため，日本は依然，食用のりの輸入割当制度を堅持している．

impose 動 課税する，〈税金などを〉課する，〈義務などを〉負わせる，〈危険などを〉与える，〈条件などを〉設ける，売りつける，押し付ける
▶No penalty taxes were *imposed* as the company was in the red. 同社は赤字だったので，追徴課税はされなかった。

imprest 名 公用前渡し金

improve 動 改良する，改善する，改革する，促進する，推進する，強化する，高める，向上させる，拡大する，発展させる，好転させる
　improve competitive position 競争力を高める（＝improve competitiveness）
　improve market share 市場シェアを拡大する，シェアを拡大する
　improve the financial position 財務体質を改善する
　improved productivity 生産性の向上
　improved profit margins 利益率の上昇，利益率の増加
　improved quality 品質向上
　improved results 業績向上，業績改善
▶The company is to hold a news conference to unveil a set of its programs to *improve* its corporate value. 同社は，記者会見を開いて，企業価値を高めるための一連のプログラムを発表する。
▶The company will reduce its interest-bearing debts to *improve* its financial health. 財務体質を改善するため，同社は有利子負債を削減する。
▶We dedicate ourselves to *improved* customer service and strict cost controls. 当社は，顧客サービスの改善とコスト管理の徹底化を図っています。

improvement 名 改良，改善，改革，促進，推進，向上，進歩，増加，伸び，上昇，拡大，〈景気などの〉回復，好転，改良工事，改修工事，整備，付属設備，改良費
　buildings and improvements 建物および付属設備
　cost improvements コスト削減
　harbor improvement 港湾整備
　improvement cost 改良費（＝betterment expense, improvement expense）
　improvement in operating margins 営業利益率の向上
　improvement in profitability 収益性の改善，収益力の改善
　interest margin improvement 利ざや改善
　land improvement 土地改良
　land and improvements 土地および付属設備
　leasehold improvement 賃借物改良費，内装費
　margin improvement 利ざやの拡大，利ざや改善
　operating improvements 業績向上
　practice improvement 業務改善
　product improvement 製品改良
　productivity improvement 生産性向上
　quality improvement 品質改善，品質向上
　technological improvement 技術力の向上，技術の改善
　trade (balance) improvement 貿易収支の改善
　yield improvement 利回り改善，利回りの向上
▶Our business in Latin America was good mainly due to economic conditions and our product line *improvements*. ラテン・アメリカでの当社のビジネス［業績］は好調で，その主因としては経済環境と当社の製品ラインの改善が挙げられます。
▶We are aiming for a steady annual *improvement* in earnings of five percent or more. 当社は毎年，5％以上の利益増加率の安定確保を目指しています。

impute 動 帰する，帰属させる，帰属計算する，転嫁する，…の責に帰する

inactive 形 不活発な，遊休の，休眠の，動いていない

inappropriate payment 不正支出
▶The firm's *inappropriate payments* are suspected to have begun more than 15 years ago. 同社の不正支出は，15年以上も前から行われていた疑いがある。

inauguration ceremony 就任式，発会式，発足式，落成式，開業式，開通式，開会式，除幕式（＝inaugural ceremony）
▶The presidents of the group companies attended the *inauguration ceremony* at the holding company's head office. グループ企業各社の首脳が，この持ち株会社の本社で開かれた発足式に出席した。

incalculable 形 数え切れない，計算できない，予想できない，あてにならない

incentive 名 刺激，誘因，動機，励み，奨励，販売奨励金，促進策，振興，報奨，報奨金，出来高払い，利点，インセンティブ（⇒shareholders incentives）
　average incentive per vehicle 1台当たりの平均販売奨励金
　economic incentive 経済的誘因
　export incentives 輸出振興策
　financial incentives 特別手当
　foreign tax incentives 外国租税優遇措置
　incentive compensation 奨励報奨制度
　incentive payment system 奨励給（＝in-

centive system)
incentive program 報奨制度, 勤労奨励制度, 促進計画, 販売促進策
incentive stock option 奨励株式オプション
incentive stock option plan 奨励株式オプション制度, 自社株購入選択奨励制度
incentive to default デフォルトの誘因
incentive trip 報奨旅行, 報奨ツアー
incentive wage 能率給, 奨励給, 報奨金
interest incentive effect 利子刺激効果
incentive fee 成功報酬, 報奨金, インセンティブ・フィー
incentive scheme 奨励制度, 報奨制度
incentive stock option 奨励株式オプション, 奨励ストック・オプション制度《略 ISO》
refinancing incentive 借換えの利点
sales incentives 販売奨励金, 販売促進策
shareholders incentives 株主優待
tax incentives 税制上の優遇措置
▸GM has replaced zero financing with other sales *incentives*. GMは最近、ゼロ金利ローンに代わる他の販売促進策を導入した。
▸Shareholders *incentives* are designed to encourage shareholders to hold onto their stocks over the long term. 株主優待の狙いは、株主の株式の長期保有促進にある。
▸We have offered financial *incentives* to individuals retiring or resigning from the company. 当社は、早期退職を検討している社員に対して、特別退職手当を支給しています。

incentive award 奨励報酬, 報奨金
▸The stockholders approved the long-term performance plan, which provides for *incentive awards* to be made to officers and other key employees. 役員と幹部社員に奨励報酬を与える長期パフォーマンス・プランが、株主によって承認されました。

incentive compensation plan 奨励報償制度（会社が一定以上の利益を上げたとき、経営者を対象に規定の報酬以外にボーナスを支払う制度）
▸Under the Corporation's *incentive compensation plan*, its president is to receive a bonus equal to 10% of the Corporation's income before deducting income tax. 当社の奨励報償制度では、社長は、所得税控除前の当社利益の10％相当のボーナスがもらえる。

incentive plan 報奨制度, 報奨金制度（＝incentive program, incentive scheme; ⇒RONA）
company executive incentive plan 会社幹部報奨金制度
executive incentive plan 幹部報奨金制度
long-range incentive plan 長期報奨金制度
RONA incentive plan 純資産利益率（RONA）報奨金制度
savings incentive plan 貯蓄奨励プラン
▸A new long-range *incentive plan* was established to reward participating elected officers for the Company's achieving outstanding long-range performance. 特に際立った長期業績を会社が達成した場合、それに参加した選任役員に報奨を与えるために、当社は新しい長期報奨金制度を設けました。

incentivize 動 報奨金で奨励する
inception 名 開始, 開業, 初め, 発端
inception of operations 営業開始, 事業開始, 開業
inception of the pension plan 年金制度の開始, 年金制度開始年度［採用年度］
▸We have carried no allowance for doubtful accounts from the *inception* of operations in 1990. 1990年の開業時から、当社は貸倒れ引当金の設定は行っていません。

incidence 名 発生率, 影響の範囲, 負担範囲, 発病率, 患者数, 帰着
incidence of taxation 租税の帰着
incidental 形 付随的な, 付随して起こる
incidentals 名 付帯費用, 付随費用
incipient recovery 景気回復の局面, 景気持ち直しの局面
incl. …を含めて（**inclusive, including**の略）
include 動 含む, 包含する, 算入する, 組み入れる, 計上する, 処理する, 記載する, 盛り込む, 表示する, 掲載する, 収録する, 定める（⇒**income, prospectus**）
be included in income 利益として計上される, 損益として計上される
Shipping Included 送料込み
▸In the latest account settlements, banking groups gave up *including* sizable deferred tax assets in their equity capital. 今決算で、銀行グループは、巨額の繰延べ税金資産の自己資本への計上を見送った。
▸The Company provides for income taxes based on accounting income for tax purposes *included* in the financial statements. 当社は税務上、財務書類に表示する会計上の利益に基づいて法人所得税を算定しています。

include, but not limited to …を含むがこれには限定しない, …などを含む
▸The technical information provided by the

other party hereunder shall *include, but not limited to*, the following. 本契約により他方当事者が提供する技術情報は、以下等を含むものとする。
inclusion 名 包括, 包含, 算入
inclusive 形 含めて, 算入して, …込みで, 包括的な
income 名 利益, 収益, 所得, 損益 (= earnings; ⇒ corporate income, dividend income, net income, operating income)
  business income 企業利益, 企業収益, 事業所得
  capital income 資本所得, 資本的収入
  consolidated income 連結利益
  corporate income 法人所得
  disposable income 可処分所得
  earned income 給与所得, 勤労所得
  financial income 財務収益, 金融収益
  fixed income securities 確定利付き証券, 債務証券, 債券
  income accrued from domestic sources 国内源泉所得
  income attributable to ordinary activity 経常損益
  income available to common share 普通株配当可能利益
  income and profit 収益と利益
  income bond 利益社債, 収益社債, 利益債券
  income charges 営業外費用
  income deductions 利益控除項目, 収益控除項目, 営業外費用・損失
  income earned 稼得利益, 実現利益
  income earned abroad 海外収益
  income forecast 収益見通し, 収益予想 (= earnings forecast, profit forecast)
  income gain 金利・配当収入, インカム・ゲイン, 所得の伸び, 増収
  income in advance 前受収益
  income loss 減収
  interest income 受取利息
  investment income 投資利益, 投資収益, 投資所得, 投資収入
  national income 国民所得
  net income 純利益, 当期純利益
  nonoperating income 営業外損益, 営業外収益
  one-time income 一時所得
  ordinary income 経常損益
  personal income 個人所得
  premium income 収入保険料
  real income 実質所得, 実質利益
  salary income 給与所得
  stock option income ストック・オプション利益
  taxable income 課税所得, 申告所得
  wage income 賃金所得

▶ *Income* includes operating income, restructuring costs, income from equity method investments, dividends received, gain (loss) on sale of securities and interest income. 利益には, 営業利益, 事業再編成費用, 持ち分法による投資利益, 受取配当, 有価証券売却損益と受取利息などが含まれています。

▶ The firm failed to declare about ¥3 billion in *income*. 同社は, 所得約30億円を申告しなかった。

▶ We saw a decline in *income* related to investments and joint ventures in 2008. 2008年度は, 投資とジョイント・ベンチャー関連の利益が減少しました。

income account 所得勘定, 所得収支(海外子会社の収益や海外株式の配当などを示す), 損益勘定, 損益計算書

▶ The nation's *income account* in 2007 reached yet another record-high surplus of ¥16.27 trillion. 日本の2007年の所得収支は, 16兆2,700億円で最高額を更新した。

income account surplus 所得収支の黒字

▶ The *income account surplus* exceeded that of merchandise trade for the third straight year. 所得収支の黒字は, 3年連続して貿易収支の黒字を上回った。

income and employment situations 所得・雇用環境

▶ Under the severe *income and employment situations*, personal consumption has yet to show indications of a full-fledged recovery. 厳しい所得・雇用環境の下で, 個人消費に本格的な回調の気配がまだ見えない。

income before income taxes 税引き前利益, 法人税控除前, 法人税考慮前利益

▶ The tax effects of restructuring charges were magnified by the lower *income before income taxes*. 法人税考慮前利益が低水準だったため, 事業再編成費用の税効果が拡大しました。

income disparity 所得格差 (= income gap)

▶ The widening *income disparities* among young people could lead to an expansion in the gap among members of the population as a whole. 若年層の所得格差拡大は, 国民全体の格差拡大につながる可能性がある。

income from direct investments 直接投資収益

▶ *Income from direct investments* reflected profits made from overseas subsidiaries. 直接

投資収益は，海外子会社から上げた利益を反映しています。

income from equity investments 株式投資収益

▶*Income from equity investments* declined in 2008 after increasing in 2007.　2008年度の株式投資収益は，2007年度に増加した後，減少しました。

income indemnity system 所得補償制度，直接支払い制度

▶The *income indemnity system* for farmers would guarantee incomes for farm households of set sizes that are committed to continue farming.　農家に対する直接支払い制度は，継続して農業に取り組む一定規模の農家に対して所得を保証するものだ。

income gap 所得格差（＝income disparity）

▶The *income gap* between those earning a lot and those who are not is widening.　高所得者と低所得者との所得格差は，広がっている。

income statement 損益計算書《略 I/S》

（＝earnings statement, income account, profit and loss statement, statement of earnings, statement of income, statement of operations：1年の会計期間の収益と費用をすべて記載して経常利益を示し，これに特別損益項目を加減して当期純利益を表示するもの）

▶We divide the revenues and costs of our core business into three categories on our *income statement*.　当社の損益計算書では，中核事業の収益と費用を3部門に分類しています。

income statement amounts 損益計算書の金額

▶For operations outside of the U.S. that prepare financial statements in currencies other than the U.S. dollar, we translate *income statement amounts* at average exchange rates for the year.　米ドル以外の通貨建てで財務書類を作成している米国外事業については，損益計算書の金額は事業年度の平均為替レートに基づいて換算されています。

income tax 所得税，法人税，法人所得税

income tax expense 法人税額，法人所得税費用，所得税費用，税金費用　（⇒**fourth quarter results**）
income tax payments 法人税等の支払い額
income tax rate 法人税率，所得税率
income taxes 法人税等，法人所得税，税金費用，法人税，住民税および事業税　（＝taxes on income）

▶*Income taxes* are generally not provided on cumulative undistributed earnings of certain non-U.S. subsidiaries.　法人税等は，一般に米国外子会社数社の累積未分配利益については計上されません。

incoming 形 入ってくる，受け取る，後任の

incompatible 形 互換性のない，相容れない，矛盾する

incompetent 形 無能な，役に立たない，無能力の，証拠能力のない，無資格の，不適格な

incorporate 動 設立する，会社組織にする，組み込む，組み入れる，合併する，契約の一部とする

▶Neither party has an obligation under this Agreement to offer for sale products using or *incorporating* the confidential information.　いずれの当事者にも，この秘密情報を使用したまたは組み込んだ製品を販売に供する本契約上の義務はない。

incorporated 形 法人の，会社（組織）の，株式会社の，合同した，編入した

a company incorporated and existing under the laws of …の法律に基づいて［…の法律に準拠して］設立され現存する会社
incorporated association 社団法人
incorporated by reference 参照により組み込んだ，参照により組み込まれる
incorporated company 会社
incorporated foundation 財団法人

incorporation 名 会社の設立，法人格の付与，法人組織，会社，合併，編入，組込み

articles of incorporation 基本定款，会社定款，定款
certificate of incorporation 会社［法人］設立証書，会社定款，定款
incorporation by reference 参照による組込み，参照による編入
incorporation expenses 設立費用

▶The articles of *incorporation* provide for an unlimited number of first preferred shares and second preferred shares.　定款には，第一優先株式と第二優先株式の発行株式数に関する制限は設けられていません。

Incoterms 名 インコタームズ（**International Commercial Terms**の略。国際商業会議所が1936年に制定した「貿易条件の解釈に関する国際規則（International Rules for the Interpretation of Trade Terms）」の通称で，改訂された2000年版インコタームズではCIF（運賃保険料込み条件）やFOB（本船渡し条件）などを含めて13種類の貿易条件が定義されている。⇒**trade terms**）

2000年版Incotermsで定義された貿易条件:

CFR	運賃込み条件 (cost and freightの略)
CIF	運賃保険料込み条件 (cost, insurance and freightの略)
CIP	運送費保険料込み条件 (carriage and insurance paid toの略)
CPT	運送費込み条件 (carriage paid toの略)
DAF	国境持込み渡し条件 (delivered at frontierの略)
DDP	仕向地持込み渡し・関税込み条件 (delivered duty paidの略)
DDU	仕向地持込み渡し・関税抜き条件 (delivered duty unpaidの略)
DEQ	埠頭持込み渡し条件 (delivered ex quayの略)
DES	本船持込み渡し条件 (delivered ex shipの略)
EXW	工場渡し条件 (ex worksの略)
FAS	船側渡し条件 (free alongside shipの略)
FCA	運送人渡し条件 (free carrierの略)
FOB	本船渡し条件 (free on boardの略)

▶Unless otherwise expressly provided for in this agreement, the price and trade term "C.I.F." shall be interpreted in accordance with Incoterms 2000. 本契約に特に明示の規定がないかぎり[本契約で別段に明確に規定しないかぎり]，価格と貿易条件のCIFは，2000年版インコタームズに従って解釈する．

increase 動 増やす，上昇させる，引き上げる，押し上げる，拡大する，高める，伸ばす，強化する，増大する，増加する，増える，伸びる，激化する
　increase capital strength 資本基盤を強化する
　increase inhouse processing 内製比率を高める
　increase one's capital 増資する，資本金を増やす
　increase one's equity ownership 持ち株比率を引き上げる
　increase shareholders value 株主価値を高める，株主の利益を高める
▶In the first half of the year, Honda increased U.S. market share to 8.9 percent from 8.1 percent. 今年度の上半期に，ホンダは米国でのシェア（市場占有率）を8.1%から8.9%に伸ばした．
▶Our overall objective is to increase value for our shareholders. 当社は，株主の皆さまの価値[利益]を高めることを，全社的目標としています．
▶To increase our presence outside the U.S., we are hiring employees, building plants and forming joint ventures. 米国外での当社の事業基盤を強化するため，当社は従業員の雇用，工場建設や合弁会社の設立に取り組んでいます．

increase 名 増加，増大，伸び，上昇，引上げ，拡大，高まり（⇒capital increase）
　base rate increase 基準金利の引上げ
　cost increases コストの上昇
　dividend increase 増配，配当引上げ（＝increase dividend）
　general capital increase 一般増資
　increase in revenues and profits 増収増益，収益と利益の増加
　increases in income and profit 増収増益
　increase of capital stock 増資（＝increase in capital stock, increase of capital）
　increase of sales 売上増加
　inventory increase 在庫の増加
　paid-in capital increase 有償増資
　post a healthy increase 好調な伸びを示す
　price increase 価格上昇，価格の高騰，値上がり，値上がり率，インフレ率
　productivity increase 生産性の伸び
　rate increase 利上げ，料金引上げ
　rating increase 格上げ
　supply increase 供給増
　tax increase 増税
　wage increase 賃上げ，賃金引上げ，賃金の上昇，ベース・アップ
▶Concerning their corporate performance, the Japan's business leaders foresee an increase in revenues and profits. 企業の業績について，日本の企業経営者は増収，増益を見込んでいる．
▶The increase reflected the strong level of new housing starts. この伸びは，新規住宅着工件数の大幅増を反映しています．

increased 形 増加した，増大した，上昇した，増えた，…の増加，…の上昇，…の拡大
　increased competition 競争の激化
　increased demand 需要の増加，需要増，需要の伸び（＝demand growth）
　increased dividends received 受取配当金の増加
　increased earnings per share 濃縮化1株当たり利益
　increased investment 投資の拡大
　increased liquidity preference 流動性選好の高まり
　increased productivity 生産性の向上，生産性の伸び
　increased quarterly dividend 四半期増配，四半期配当の引上げ
　increased risk リスク増大
　increased sales 販売の増加，販売の伸び，売上[売上高]の伸び
　increased utilization 設備稼動率の上昇
▶An increased demand for steel sheet helped

major steelmakers, including Nippon Steel Corp., post record high recurring profits.　鋼板の需要増で，新日本製鐵など鉄鋼大手の経常利益が，過去最高を記録した。
▸There have been *increased* sales in markets overseas.　海外市場では，販売が伸びている。

increment 名　増加，増大，増進，増強，増加量，増分，増額，利益，インクリメント

incremental 形　増大する

incrementalism 名　漸進主義，段階的な金利調整
▸U.S. Fed Chairman Ben Bernanke has chosen *incrementalism* over radical change in his first meeting.　米連邦準備制度理事会(FRB)のベン・バーナンキ議長は，最初の連邦公開市場委員会(FOMC)で，急進的な変化よりも漸進主義[段階的な金利調整]を選んだ。

incubation business　ベンチャー企業育成事業，ベンチャー企業支援事業，インキュベーション・ビジネス

incubation period　潜伏期間，孵化期間
▸Mad cow disease has an *incubation* period of four to five years.　狂牛病(BSE)には，4年から5年の潜伏期間がある。

incubator　企業育成機関，企業育成施設，インキュベーター（=business incubator: 創造性に富む独自の技術や経営ノウハウを持つ研究開発型ベンチャー企業などを対象に，自治体などが研究施設，事務・視聴覚機器や資金援助などを行い，その自立化を支援する方法をいう）

incubator facility　企業育成施設，保育施設，保育的便益，育成的便益

incumbent 形　現職の，在職の，義務として課される
incumbent executives　現経営陣，現職の経営陣

incur 動　引き起こす，発生させる，招く，〈損失・損害を〉被る[受ける]，負う，負担する，引き受ける，負債に陥る
cost incurred　発生原価
incur a loss　損失を被る
incur the borrowing costs　借入[資金調達]コストを負担する
incur unseen liabilities　不測の債務を負う，不測の債務が発生する
incurred cost　発生原価，賦課原価（=cost incurred, incurred expense）
incurred expense　発生費用（=incurred cost）
losses incurred by writing off nonperforming loans　不良債権処理で生じた損失額
▸The company *incurred* ¥2.5 billion of after-tax losses in its semiannual settlement of accounts.　同社は，中間決算で税引き後損失が25億円に達した。
▸We *incurred* the following interest costs in connection with these activities.　これらの活動との関連で，次の利子費用が発生しました。

indebted 形　負債がある，借金がある，債務を抱えた
indebted company　赤字会社，債務を抱えた企業
indebted countries　債務国

indebtedness 名　負債，債務，負債額，借入金，貸付け金
guarantee of indebtedness　債務保証
indebtedness of affiliates　関係会社貸付け金
indebtedness to affiliates　関係会社借入金
net indebtedness　正味負債，純負債額，純借入比率
over-indebtedness　債務過多
▸Thanks to the inflow of funds from the successful share issue, net *indebtedness* has been markedly reduced.　成功を収めた(新規)株式発行による資金の流入により，正味負債は大幅に縮小しました。

indemnity 名　補償，損失補償，損害填補，損失補償契約，補償金，賠償，賠償金
income indemnity　所得補償
indemnity against a loss　損失に対する補償，損失補償
indemnity against liability　免責の補償
right of indemnity　求償権　(⇒right)
severance indemnity　退職給与
▸Other liabilities consist principally of *indemnity* and retirement plan reserves for non-U.S. employees.　「その他の負債」の主な内訳は，米国外の従業員に対する補償と退職給付引当金です。

indenture 名　契約書，証書，目録

independence 名　独立，独立性，自立，自主性
auditor's independence　監査人の独立性
independence and integrity　独立性と信頼性
independence of management　経営の自主性
▸We would honor the *independence* of the firm's management.　当社としては，同社の経営の自主性は尊重したいと思っております。

independent 形　独立した，自立した，独立系，個別の，自主的な
independent accountant　独立会計士，独立監査人，独立した会計監査人（一般に公認会計士をいう）
independent administrative institution　独立行政法人
independent advisory body　独立諮問機関，第

三者による諮問機関
independent auditor 独立監査人, 独立した会計監査人, 外部監査人
independent contractor 独立業務請負人, インディペンデント・コントラクター《略 IC》(個人が企業と契約して, 専門性の高いプロジェクトを請け負う人)
independent consulting firm 独立系コンサルティング会社
independent factory price 公正な工場渡し価格
independent oversight board 独立監視委員会 (⇒consulting)
independent rating agency 独立格付け機関
independent regulator 独立規制当局
independent store 独立店, 独立店舗
Independent System Operator organizations 独立系統運用機関 (送電線の運用・管理にあたる非営利組織)
independent use and disclosure of confidential information 秘密情報の自由な使用と開示
▸*Independent* accountants are retained to examine our financial statements. 独立した会計監査人が, 当社の財務書類[財務諸表]を監査しています.
▸The audit committee meets periodically with management, the internal auditors and the *independent* auditors to review the manner in which they are performing their responsibilities. 監査委員会は, 経営陣, 内部監査人, 外部監査人[独立監査人]と定期的に会合して, これら経営陣や監査人がどのようにその職責を果たしているかについて検討します.

independent director 社外取締役, 独立取締役
▸Comcast Corp., the nation's largest cable operator, called on Disney's *independent directors* to open talks on its all-stock takeover offer. 米ケーブルテレビ最大手のコムキャストは, ディズニーの社外取締役に, コムキャストが提出した全株買取り案[全株買取りによる企業買収提案]の協議開始を求めた.

in-depth 形 徹底的な, 詳細な, 綿密な, 掘り下げた, 突っ込んだ, 完全な, 均衡のとれた, 豊富な, 十分に発達した, 深層の
in-depth background 豊富な経験
in-depth discussion 突っ込んだ議論
in-depth feasibility study 綿密な事業化調査
in-depth investigation [survey] 徹底調査, 綿密な調査, 突っ込んだ調査
in-depth-report 詳細な報告, 徹底取材した報告書[記事]
in-depth studies 突っ込んだ研究, 掘り下げた研究

index 動 消費者物価指数にスライド[連動]させる, スライド[指数化]方式にする
a system of indexing benefits to consumer price movements 公的年金給付額を消費者物価の変動にスライドさせる制度[物価スライド制]
indexed bond インデックス債
indexed government bond 物価連動債
inflationary indexed bond インフレ連動証券

index 名 指数, 指標, 指針, 索引, インデックス
business index 景気指標
coincident index 一致指数
commodity index 商品指数
composite index 景気総合指数《略 CI》
consumer price index 消費者物価指数《略 CPI》
DI index 業況判断指数, 景気動向指数, DI指数 (DI=diffusion index)
diffusion index 景気動向指数
general index of retail prices 小売物価総合指数
index of industrial output 鉱工業生産指数, 工業生産指数 (=index of industrial production)
index of leading economic indicators 景気先行指標総合指数, 景気先行指数, 先行指数 (景気先行指数は, 景気の現状より約6か月先の景気の動きを示す指標)
index of output 生産指数
lagging index 遅行(ちこう)指数
leading index 先行指数
Nasdaq composite index ナスダック総合株価指数, ナスダックの総合指数
Nikkei Index 日経平均
NYSE Composite Index NYSE総合株価指数
stock price index 株価指数 (=stock index)
▸The industrial production *index* improved in May, the first month-on-month rise in three months. 鉱工業生産指数は5月に回復し, 3か月ぶりに前月比でプラスに転じた.

indicator 名 指数, 指標, 指針, インディケーター
coincident indicator 一致指数
DI of the coincident indicators 景気一致指数 (DI)
DI of the lagging indicators 景気遅行指数(DI)
DI of the leading indicators 景気先行指数(DI)
economic indicator 経済指標, 景気指標
financial indicator 財務指標
inflation indicator インフレ指標

key economic indicators 主要経済指標
labor market indicators 労働統計
lagging indicator 遅行指数
leading indicator 先行指数
monetary indicators 金融指標
numerical indicator 数値目標
performance indicator 業績指数, 業績指標
profitability indicator 収益性指標
▸Solvency margin is an *indicator* of an insurance company's financial health. ソルベンシー・マージン(支払い余力)比率は，保険会社の財務の健全性を示す指標の一つである。

indirect 形 間接の, 間接的な, 二次的な
individual 形 個人の, 個人的, 個別の, 個々の
  individual basis 個別基準
  individual brand 個別商標
  individual cost 個別原価
  individual depreciation 個別減価償却, 個別償却
  individual enterprise 個人企業
  individual financial assets 個人金融資産
  individual life insurance 個人生命保険, 個人保険
  individual meeting 個別訪問 (=face-to-face meeting: IR活動の一つで，機関投資家や証券会社に出向いて直接会社の業務内容などを説明)
  individual production 個別生産
  individual retirement account 個人年金退職金勘定, 個人退職所得勘定, 個人退職金口座制度 《略 IRA》
  individual retirement savings plan 個人退職貯蓄制度
  individual shareholder 個人株主
  individual stock options 個別株オプション
  Individual Training Accounts 個人訓練口座 《略 ITA》

individual consumption 個人消費
▸The downward revision of the fiscal 2008 growth projection was made due to a drastic slowdown in *individual consumption* and meager price increases. 2008年度の経済成長見通しの下方修正は，個人消費の大幅な減速と物価上昇率の鈍化が原因だった。

individual investor 個人投資家
▸In Germany, *individual investors*' capital gains are not normally taxed. ドイツでは，個人投資家の譲渡益については通常，非課税となっている。

induce 動 引き起こす, 誘導する, 帰納する, 誘って…させる
induced pluripotent stem cell 人工多能性幹細胞, 万能細胞, iPS細胞 (=iPS cell)

▸A Kyoto University research group led by Prof. Yamanaka has successfully produced *induced pluripotent stem cells* from the stomach and liver cells of mice. 京都大学の山中教授らの研究グループが，マウスの胃や肝臓の細胞からiPS細胞を作るのに成功した。

inducement 名 誘因, 刺激, 動機, 勧誘, 奨励
  foreign capital inducement 外資導入
  inducement coefficient 生産誘発係数
  inducement to change insurer 〈保険の〉乗換え契約勧誘
  inducement to invest [investment] 投資誘因

induction 名 導入, 誘導, 入会, 入社, 加入, 加盟, 帰納, 帰納法
  induction ceremony 入社式
  induction course 新入社員研修, 新入社員のオリエンテーション
  induction of foreign capital 外資導入

industrial 形 産業の, 工業の, 鉱工業の, 工業の発達した, 工業生産の, 産業[工業]用の, インダストリアル
  industrial accidents 労働災害, 労務災害, 業務災害 (=industrial injuries)
  industrial action 労働争議, 争議行為, 順法闘争, 抗議行動, ストライキ (=job action)
  industrial activity 産業活動
  industrial affiliations 企業系列
  industrial applicability 産業上の利用性
  industrial average 工業株平均
  industrial base 産業基盤, 工業基盤
  industrial bond 事業債, 工業債, 産業債, 企業債
  industrial boom 産業好景気, 好景気, 好況
  industrial capacity 工業生産能力, 工業設備, 工業能力
  industrial commodity industry 素材産業 (=basic material industry)
  industrial complex 工業団地, コンビナート, コングロマリット
  industrial conversion 産業転換
  industrial delivery 鉱工業製品出荷
  industrial demand 工業製品需要, 鉱工業製品需要
  industrial depression 産業不景気, 産業不況, 不況
  industrial development bond 産業開発債, 産業誘致債
  industrial disaster 産業災害
  industrial disease 職業病, 産業病 (=occupational disease)
  industrial engineer 生産管理技術

industrial equipment 産業機械, 産業設備
industrial espionage 産業スパイ, 産業スパイ行為 (=industrial spy)
industrial expansion 工業生産の拡大
industrial firm 事業法人
industrial growth 工業生産の伸び
industrial harmony 労使協調
industrial health 産業衛生, 産業衛生学, 労働衛生
industrial holding company 製造業持ち株会社
industrial land 工場用地
industrial management 産業経営, 工業経営, 工場管理
industrial migration 産業移動
industrial nations 工業国, 工業先進国, 先進国 (=industrial countries, industrialized countries)
industrial organization 産業組織, 産業団体, 業界 (⇒conflict of interest)
industrial output data 鉱工業生産指数
industrial park 工業団地, 工業用地, 工場用地 (=business park, industrial complex, industrial estate)
industrial polluter 公害産業
industrial potential 潜在工業力
industrial power 産業力, 工業力
industrial powers 先進国, 工業国, 工業大国
industrial price 工業製品価格
industrial product 工業製品, 鉱工業製品
industrial production index 鉱工業生産指数, 工業生産指数 (=industrial output index)
industrial profit 企業利潤
industrial public nuisance 産業公害 (=industrial pollution)
industrial rationalization 産業合理化
industrial relations 労使関係, 労資関係
industrial revitalization 産業活性化, 産業再生
industrial right 工業所有権 (=industrial property right)
industrial selling 資材販売, 生産財販売
industrial site 産業用地, 工業用地 (=industrial space)
industrial skills 産業技術
industrial society 産業社会, 工業社会, 工業化社会
industrial strife 労使争議, 労使紛争 (=industrial dispute)
industrial union 産業別労働組合
industrial unrest 労働争議 (=industrial strike)
industrial visits 工場視察
industrial waste 産業廃棄物, 工場廃棄物
industrial worker 工員, 産業労働者
industrial world 産業界, 工業界

industrial machinery 産業機械
▶*Industrial machinery*, such as semiconductor production equipment, plant construction and the opening of new supermarket stores have begun to pick up steam. 半導体製造装置などの産業機械や工場建設, スーパーの新規出店などに, 次第に動きが出ている。

industrial nations and territories 先進国と地域
▶The Kyoto Protocol requires 39 *industrial nations and territories* to reduce their greenhouse gas emissions. 京都議定書は, 先進39か国・地域に温室効果ガスの削減を義務付けている。

industrial output 工業生産, 工業生産高, 鉱工業生産, 鉱工業生産高 (=industrial production)
▶The nation's *industrial output* rose a seasonally adjusted 0.5 percent in May from the previous month. 日本の5月の鉱工業生産高は, 前年同月比で0.5%(季節調整値)増加した。

industrialization 名 工業化, 産業化
  export-led industrialization 輸出主導型工業化, 輸出リード型工業化
  import-substituting industrialization 輸入代替工業化
  inward-looking industrialization 内向型工業化, 内部志向工業化
  regional industrialization 地域工業化

industrialize 動 工業化する
  industrialized countries [economies, nations] 工業国, 先進国, 先進工業国, 工業先進国
  industrialized science 産業化科学
  less industrialized nation [country] 後発工業国
  newly industrialized nation 新興工業国

industry 名 産業, 工業, 産業界, 工業会, 業界, …業, 業種, メーカー
  advertising industry 広告業界, 広告産業
  aerospace industry 航空機産業
  apparel industry アパレル産業, アパレル業界 (=clothing industry)
  auto industry 自動車産業, 自動車業界
  banking industry 銀行業界
  basic material industry 素材産業
  brain industry 頭脳産業
  ceramic [ceramics] industry 窯業
  commercial industry 流通業

education industry　教育産業
emerging industry　先端産業
fashion industry　ファッション産業
financial industry　金融業界, 金融915, 金融産業 (⇒collection of debts)
food industry　食品業界
food service industry　外食産業
health industry　健康産業
heavy industries　重工業, 重化学工業
high-tech industry　ハイテク産業
housing industry　住宅産業
industry classification　業種分類
industry-government alliance　官民協力, 官民共同
industry group　業界団体, 経済団体, 業種
industry standard　産業基準, 業界標準, 業界規格, 統一基準
industry surrounding governments　行政周辺産業
information industry　情報産業
key industry　基幹産業, 基礎産業, 重要産業
knowledge industry　知識産業
leading industries　主力産業
leisure industry　レジャー産業
light industries　軽工業
materials industry　素材産業
medical industry　医療産業
nuclear power industry　原子力産業
ocean industry　海洋産業
paper industry　紙パルプ業界(pulp and paper industry), 製紙業(paper-manufacturing industry)
petrochemical industry　石油化学産業
power industry　電力業界
process industry　加工産業, 装置産業
processing industry　加工産業
refrigeration industry　低温産業
reproductive industry　再生産業
semiconductor industry　半導体産業
service industry　サービス産業 (=service-oriented industry)
steel industry　鉄鋼産業
strategic industry　戦略産業
supporting industry　すそ野産業
warehousing industry　倉庫業
▶Automobile and electric appliance *industries* show good business performance.　自動車と電機業界は, 業績好調だ。
▶Equipment sales in our telecommunications *industry* typically tend to lag economic upturns.　通信業界の機器販売は, 景気回復より遅れるのが通常です[通信機器販売は通常, 景気回復に遅行する傾向があります]。
▶Manufacturing *industries*, especially materials industries, will face tough decisions on plant and equipment investment.　製造業, とくに素材産業では, 設備投資の判断が難しくなる。
▶Nonmanufacturing *industries* posted a 23 percent increase in recurring profits.　非製造業の経常利益は, 23%増加した。
▶Our operations in the financial services and leasing *industry* involve direct financing and finance leasing programs for our products and the products of other companies.　金融サービスとリース業界での当社の事業には, 当社製品と他社製品に関する直接融資とファイナンス事業も含まれています。

industry association　業界団体 (=industry group)
▶*Industry associations* have agreed to support the elimination of tariffs on textile products.　業界団体が, 繊維製品の関税撤廃を支持することで合意した。

industry segment　事業別セグメント, 産業別セグメント, 産業セグメント, 事業区分, 事業分野, 事業部門 (=industrial segment)
▶This *industry segment* represents more than 90% of consolidated revenue, operating profit and identifiable assets.　この事業部門は, 連結総売上高[総収益]と営業利益, 識別可能資産[固有資産]の90%以上を占めています。

inelastic　形　非弾力的な(変化に対して反応が少ないこと)

inertia　名　慣性, 惰性, 不活発, 不振, 停滞
　economic inertia　景気停滞
　inertia effect　慣性効果
　inertia selling　押し付け販売

inflate　動　膨らませる, かさ上げする, 上乗せする, 〈価格などを〉つり上げる, 上昇させる, 押し上げる, 誇張する (⇒commission)
▶The banks' equity capital is *inflated* by so-called "deferred tax assets."　銀行の自己資本は, いわゆる「繰延べ税金資産」でかさ上げされている。
▶The weak yen has also *inflated* the firm's profits, which were converted into Japanese currency from dollars.　円安も, ドルから円に換算した同社の利益を押し上げた。

inflated　形　暴騰した, 〈通貨が〉著しく膨張した

inflation　名　インフレ, インフレ率, 物価上昇, 物価上昇率, 一般物価変動, 物価高騰, 通貨膨張, イ

ンフレーション (⇒consumer price index, in-flationary)
consumer inflation 消費者物価の上昇
core inflation 基礎インフレ率, コア・インフレ率
cost-push inflation 生産費の上昇によるインフレ, コスト・プッシュ・インフレ (=cost inflation)
demand-pull inflation 需要インフレ, デマンドプル・インフレ (総需要に生産量が追いつかないで起こるインフレ)
galloping inflation 急激なインフレ
general inflation 一般物価水準の上昇
hyper-inflation [hyperinflation] 超インフレ
inflation pressure インフレ圧力
inflation psychology インフレ心理
inflation rate 物価上昇率
inflation target インフレ目標
raging inflation 狂乱物価, 狂乱インフレ
stock price inflation 株価急騰
true inflation 真正インフレ
underlying inflation 基礎インフレ率
vicious inflation 悪性インフレ (=malignant inflation)

▸*Inflation* in the countries that use the euro has been at a record of 3.2 percent since the start of the year. ユーロ圏の物価上昇率は, 年初以来, 過去最高の3.2％で推移している。

inflation-adjusted 形 インフレ調整後[調整済み]の
inflation-adjusted long-term rates インフレ調整後の長期金利
inflation-adjusted rate of economic growth 実質経済成長率
inflation-adjusted real terms インフレ調整後の実質, 物価変動の影響を除いた実質

▸Gross domestic product will rise 2 percent in *inflation-adjusted* real terms and 2.2 percent in nominal terms in fiscal 2007 from the fiscal 2006 figure. 2007年度の国内総生産（GDP）の成長率は, 物価変動の影響を除いた実質で前年度比2％, 名目で2.2％になる見通しだ。

inflationary 形 インフレの, インフレを誘発する, インフレを引き起こす
anti-inflationary measures インフレ抑制策
inflationary expansion 価格景気
inflationary expectations インフレ期待
inflationary gap インフレ・ギャップ (完全雇用の達成に必要な有効需要を上回る需要があること)
inflationary hedge インフレ・ヘッジ (株・金・土地などへの投資など, インフレによる通貨価値の下落に伴う損失を防ぐために取る手段)
inflationary jitters インフレ不安, インフレ懸念, インフレ心理
inflationary pressure インフレ圧力, インフレ誘発の圧力
inflationary sentiment インフレ心理, インフレ・マインド
inflationary spiral 悪性インフレ, インフレの悪循環
inflationary target インフレ目標 (=inflation target)
inflationary trend インフレ傾向, インフレ動向

▸Many countries have been successful in controlling inflation with *inflationary* target policy. これまでに多くの国が, インフレ目標政策を導入してインフレのコントロールに成功している。

inflow 名 流入, 流入額, インフロー
asset inflow 資産流入額
capital inflow 資本流入, 資金の流入, 流入資金, 買い越し
combined inflows (outflows) 合算資金収入（支出）
foreign capital inflows 外資流入, 外国からの資金流入, 外貨の流動性
foreign inflows 外資流入, 外貨流入 (=foreign capital inflows)
import inflow 輸入拡大
net cash inflow 純資金収入額
net inflow 流入超, 入超

▸The money market is overheated by massive money *inflows* from banks on fading concerns over a financial system crisis. 金融システム不安[金融システム危機に対する懸念]の後退により, 短期金融市場は, 銀行からの巨額の資金流入で過熱感が強まっている。

influx 名 流入, 殺到, 流れ込み
an influx of complaints 苦情の殺到
influx of foreign capital 外資の流入
influx of foreign funds 海外[国外]資金の流入, 海外[国外]からの資金流入

▸Long-term interest rates have so far been held down due to an *influx* of money from abroad. 長期金利はこれまで, 海外マネーの流入で低く抑えられていた。

infomercial 名 情報コマーシャル, インフォマーシャル (商品についての詳細な情報を提供する長めのコマーシャル)

information 名 情報, 消息, 知識, ニュース, インフォメーション (⇒financial information,

management information, personal information)
background information 背景説明
benefit information 給付情報
business information 企業情報
capsule information 要約情報
corporate information 会社情報
false information 虚偽の情報
financial information 金融情報, 財務情報
individual information 個人情報
information about customers 顧客情報
information appliance 情報家電, 情報家電品（情報機器と家電品を組み合わせた製品）
information democracy 情報民主主義, 情報に関する基本的権利
information disclosure 情報開示, 情報公開
information meeting 企業説明会, 会社説明会, インフォメーション・ミーティング（証券アナリストやファンド・マネージャーなどに対して経営方針や経営理念, 業務内容などを定期的に紹介する企業説明会。⇒investor relations）
information network system 高度情報通信システム《略 INS》
information provider 情報提供者, 情報提供事業者, インフォメーション・プロバイダー《略 IP》
information resource 情報資源
information technology bubble IT（情報技術）バブル, ネット株バブル（＝IT bubble, Net bubble）
information transmitter 情報発信者, 発信者
inside information 内部情報, インサイダー情報, 未公開の重要情報, インサイド情報（＝insider information）
internal information 内部情報
investment information 投資情報
privileged information 内部情報
public information 公開情報, 情報公開, 広報
rating information 格付け情報
sales information 販売情報
update information 最新情報
▶Individual *information* on credit cards was compromised from August to May.　クレジット・カードの個人情報の流出は, 昨年8月から今年の5月にかけて発生した［クレジット・カードの個人情報は, 昨年8月から今年5月にかけて漏れた］.

information beacon　情報標識
▶An *information beacon* transmits position information such as latitude, longitude and height.　情報標識は, 緯度や経度, 高さなどの位置情報を発信する.

information flow　情報量
▶Some Internet providers restrict *information flow* through their lines.　インターネット接続業者の一部は, 自社の回線で情報量を制限している.

information technology　情報技術, 情報通信技術, 情報処理技術, 情報工学, 情報科学, インフォメーション・テクノロジー《略 IT》（＝Info technology, info-technology, infotech）

informed consent　十分な説明に基づく同意, 十分な情報提供に基づく同意, 説明を受けた上での承諾・同意, 口頭でなく文書による同意, 納得診察, インフォームド・コンセント
▶The Medical Service Law of Japan urges medical care providers to adhere to the principle of *informed consent*.　日本の医療法は, インフォームド・コンセントの原則を守るよう医療従事者に求めている.

infrastructure 名　インフラストラクチャー, インフラ,〈経済・社会・産業の〉基盤, 社会的生産基盤, 基本施設［設備］, 社会資本,〈企業［組織］の〉下部組織, 下部構造, インフラ整備
business infrastructure 営業基盤
industrial infrastructure 産業基盤, 産業インフラ
infrastructure development インフラ開発, インフラ整備
investment in public infrastructure インフラ整備投資, 社会資本投資
IT infrastructure ITインフラ
operational infrastructures 事業のインフラ
social infrastructure 社会的経済基盤, 社会資本, 社会資本整備, 社会的生産基盤, 社会のインフラ
telecommunications infrastructure 通信基盤, 通信インフラ
transport infrastructure 輸送インフラ
▶MVNOs do not need to build networks and other *infrastructure* from scratch to enter the cell phone business.　携帯電話事業に参入するのに, 仮想移動体事業者（MVNO）は通信網などのインフラを一から構築する必要がない.

infringe on [upon]　…を侵害する, …に違反する
▶Sharp has accused manufacturers in Taiwan of *infringing on* its intellectual property rights.　シャープは, 知的財産権侵害で台湾メーカーを訴えた.

infringement 名　権利の侵害, 侵犯, 契約違反
infringement of patents 特許権侵害（＝patent infringement）

infringement of privacy プライバシーの侵害
infringement of the law 法律違反, 法令違反
infringement remedy 権利侵害に対する救済
▸Seller shall not be responsible for any *infringement* of any industrial property right. 売り主は, 工業所有権の侵害については責任がないものとする.

infusion 名 注入, 投入, 投下 （＝injection）
　equity infusion 資本投下, 資本参加
　infusion of public funds 公的資金の注入, 公的資金の投入 （＝injection of public funds）
▸The *infusion* of public funds into major banks was originally meant to free banks from their need to contract total lending to maintain capital adequacy ratios. 大手銀行への公的資金注入のそもそもの狙いは, 自己資本比率を維持するために貸出総額を縮小せざるをえない事態から銀行を解き放つことにあった.

ingredient 名 要素, 要因, 構成要素, 必要な条件, 成分, 成分表示, 材料, 原材料, 原料
　expired ingredient 消費期限切れの原材料
　ingredient costs 原料コスト
　key ingredient 主要要件, 重要要件［要因］
　the mix of ingredient 成分の構成, 構成要素［材料］の組合せ
▸As we move forward, our commitment to the communities in which we work is an essential *ingredient*. 企業活動を推進するにあたって, 私たちが業務展開している地域社会に対する企業責任の遂行は, 必要不可欠の条件となっています.

inherit 動 相続する, 受け継ぐ
inheritance 名 相続, 相続権, 相続財産
in-home 形 在宅の, 在宅でできる, 自宅でできる
　in-home computer banking ホーム・バンキング （＝home banking）
　in-home buying 在宅購買 （＝home buying, in-home shopping）

in-house [inhouse] 形 社内の, 内部の, 企業内の, 組織内の, 内製の
　in-house agency 広告代理店の制作下請け子会社 （＝house agency）
　in-house chip 内製チップ, 内製半導体素子
　in-house company 社内カンパニー, 分社
　in-house database インハウス・データベース （＝online database: 電話回線で検索できるデータベースのこと）
　in-house day care 社内育児
　in-house newsletter [publication] 社内報
　in-house processing 内製, 内部処理, 内製比率
　in-house proofreading 社内校正
　in-house publishing 企業内出版
　in-house reforms 社内改革 （＝internal reforms）
　in-house staff recruitment system 社内公募制度
　in-house supplier 内製メーカー
　in-house unemployment 企業内失業, 企業内失業者
　in-house union 企業別組合

in-house college 社内大学
▸To gain promotions in the company, new employees will need to complete the required courses at the *in-house college*. 同社で昇格・昇進するには, 新入社員は, 社内大学の必修科目を修了しなければならない.

in-house investigation 社内調査, 内部調査 （＝in-house inspection, in-house probe, internal investigation）
▸Six major nonlife insurers found the nonpayment of third-sector insurance money through *in-house investigations*. 損害保険大手6社の第三分野保険の保険金不払いは, 社内調査で判明した.

in-house meeting 社内会議
▸An *in-house meeting* was held to address the problem. この問題を処理するため, 社内会議が開かれた.

in-house rule 社内規則
▸Compliance officers check whether the activities of company executives and employees are legal and comply with *in-house rules*. コンプライアンス・オフィサーは, 経営者と従業員の活動が合法的に行われているかどうか, また社内の規則に従って行われているかどうかをチェックする.

initial 形 最初の, 初めの, 初期の, 期首の, 当初の, 設立時の
　initial balance 期首残高 （＝beginning balance）
　initial capital 当初資本, 期首資本, 保険会社の基金（株式会社の資本金に相当）
　initial costs 初期費用
　initial investment 初期投資, 初期投資額, 原始投資, 原初投資
　initial public offering price 公募価格, 売出価格, 公募売出価格
▸MVNOs can enter the cell phone business at low *initial* costs. 仮想移動体通信事業者（MVNO）は, 安い初期費用で携帯電話事業に参入することができる.

initial development 初期開発

▶The company is excellent in its total production system, from the *initial development* and design through to procurement and production.　同社は，初期開発と設計から調達と生産までのトータルな生産方式が特に優れている。

initial estimate　当初予想，当初見積り，当初見積り額　（＝original estimate）
▶The firm is likely to book an operating loss of ¥60 billion in a turnabout from an *initial estimate* of ¥14 billion in profit.　同社は，当初の140億円の利益予想から一転して，600億円の営業赤字［営業損失］になる見通しだ。

initial price　初値（はつね），初回価格　（＝initial share price, initial stock price）
▶The firm's stock fetched an *initial price* of ¥2.95 million in the morning on the TSE's Mothers market for emerging companies after its Thursday debut.　同社株は，木曜日の上場後，新興企業向け市場の東証マザーズで，午前に295万円の初値を付けた。

initial projection　当初予想，当初の見通し
▶The company's operating profit from cell phone and digital camera operations is expected to be ¥20 billion lower than its *initial projection*.　同社の携帯電話事業とデジタル・カメラ事業の営業利益は，同社の当初予想を200億円下回ると予想されている。

initial public offering　株式公開，新規株式公開，新規株式公募，新規公募，上場直前の公募，第1回株式公募，株式の公開公募，上場《略 IPO》　（＝debut, initial public offer; ⇒ **public offering**)
　IPO（公開公募・新規公募）とは➡証券取引所に株式を新規公開するなどして，企業が一般投資家に株式を初めて売り出すこと。一般には，引受業務を担当する投資銀行が，発行会社から株式をまとめて買い取って一般の投資家に売り出す。すでに株式を公開している企業が一般投資家に新規発行株式を売り出す場合を，公募(public offering)あるいは募集(primary offering)という。
▶In September 2008 we sold 6,000,000 share of common stock in an *initial public offering*.　2008年9月に，当社は第1回株式公募で600万株の普通株を売り出しました。

initiative 名　独創力，独自性，自主性，率先，主導権，主導，議案提出権，発議，発案，…案，政策，構想，方針，イニシアチブ
　individual initiative　個人の自主性
　initiative spirit　企業心
　multilateral initiative　多国間交渉
　new trade initiative　新貿易構想
　policy initiatives　政府の政策
　private initiatives　民間プロジェクト
　put forward an initiative　解決案を示す
　Structural Impediments Initiative　日米構造協議
▶The Corporation is trying to restructure itself under the *initiative* of its banks.　当社は，取引銀行主導のもとに再建を目指しています。

inject 動　注入する，投入する，供給する
▶The U.S. Federal Reserve Board will *inject* $200 billion into banks.　米連邦準備制度理事会(FRB)が，金融機関に2,000億ドル（約20兆円）供給する。

injection 名　注入，投入，供給
　capital injection　資本の注入，資本の増強，増資，保険会社への基金拠出，保険会社の基金増資　（＝capital increase）
　injection of equity　増資
　injection of public funds　公的資金の注入，公的資金の投入　（⇒**financial system crisis**）
　liquidity injection　流動性の供給
▶Shinginko Tokyo asked the metropolitan government for an additional capital *injection* of ¥40 billion.　新銀行東京は，都に400億円の追加出資を要請した。
▶This life insurer sought capital *injection* of 70 billion yen from financial institutions.　この生命保険会社は，金融機関に700億円の基金拠出［基金増資］を要請した。

injunction 名　差止命令，差止請求，禁止命令
　mandatory injunction　命令的差止命令，作為命令的差止命令，作為的差止命令
　prohibitory injunction　禁止的差止命令
　provisional injunction　仮処分，暫定的差止命令　（＝preliminary injunction）
▶The Tokyo District Court issued a provisional *injunction* to stop the publication of the weekly magazines's latest issue.　東京地裁は，同週刊誌の最新号について，出版禁止の仮処分決定をした。

injury 名　損害，権利侵害，違法行為

ink an agreement　契約書［協定書］に署名する，契約を結ぶ，協定を結ぶ
▶NTT DoCoMo and Lawson have *inked a* business and capital tie-up *agreement*.　NTTドコモとローソンが，資本・業務提携契約を締結した。

innovation 名　革新，革新性，刷新，斬新，改革，変革，開発，新制度，〈新制度などの〉導入，画期的な新製品，新軸軸，新工夫，新手法，新発明，技術革新，経営革新，イノベーション　（⇒**engine**）
　business innovation　経営革新

capital-intensive innovation 資本集約的技術革新
economic innovation 経済革新, 経済的革新
export-biased innovation 輸出偏向型技術革新
innovations in the distribution industry 流通業界の革新
labor-saving innovation 労働集約的技術革新
land-using innovation 土地使用的技術革新
process innovation 生産工程の刷新・革新, 生産工程の技術革新, プロセス・イノベーション
product innovation 製品開発, 商品開発, 画期的な新製品, 製品イノベーション
resource-intensive innovation 資源集約的技術革新
technical innovation 技術革新 (=technological innovation)

▸*Constant innovation* will be essential to revitalize small and midsize enterprises and regional economies. 中小企業と地域経済の再生には, 恒常的な経営革新が不可欠である。

▸The telecommunications business faces continued technological *innovation*. 通信業界は, なお技術革新が続いている。

innovative 形 革新的な, 斬新な, 新機軸の, 画期的な, 新しい, 最新の (=innovatory)
　innovative activity 革新的活動
　innovative decision 革新的意思決定
　innovative foreign technologies 斬新な外国の科学技術
　innovative genius 革新を生み出す才能
　innovative manufacturer 革新的なメーカー
　innovative product 革新的な製品, 画期的な製品, 斬新な製品, 新製品
　innovative value-added goods 革新的な付加価値商品[製品]

▸Japanese firms face the task of developing *innovative* value-added goods and services. 日本企業は, 課題として革新的な付加価値商品とサービスの開発が求められている。

▸The company pioneered a variety of *innovative* promotions to add new accounts. 同社は, 各種の斬新な販促活動によって, 新口座[新規顧客]を増やしました。

input 名 投入, 入力, インプット
　basic input materials 原材料
　capital input 資本投入, 資本拠出
　data input データ入力
　input cost 投入価格, 投入コスト
　input device 入力装置 (=input unit)
　input-output analysis 産業関連分析, 投入産出分析, インプット・アウトプット分析
　input price 仕入れ価格, 投入物価
　labor input 労働投入量

inquire 動 質問する, 問い合わせる, 調べる, 調査する

inquiry 名 問い合わせ, 引合い, 照会, 引合書, 照会状, 調査, 審査
　confidential inquiry 信用問い合わせ, 秘密調査
　inquiry agency 信用調査機関
　inquiry and order 引合いと注文
　inquiry frequency 照会件数
　inquiry of credit data 信用照会 (=inquiry of credit profile)
　letter of inquiry 照会状, 問い合わせ状

insert 名 はさみ込み広告

in-shop 形 事業所レベルの, 事業所内の, 事業所で内製化した, 完全下請の

insider 名 インサイダー, 内部者, 関係者 (「インサイダー」は, 証券の投資判断に影響を及ぼす未公開の重要情報を知ることができる立場にいる公開会社の役員や取締役, 主要株主などをいう)

insider trading インサイダー取引, 内部者取引 (=insider dealing, insider stock trading: 内部情報(insider information)を利用して証券取引を行うこと)

▸*Insider trading* is prohibited under the Securities and Exchange Law. インサイダー取引は, 証券取引法で禁じられている。

insolvency 名 支払い不能, 債務超過, 倒産, 破綻 (=bankruptcy, business failure)
　file for insolvency proceedings with …に破綻処理手続きを申請する
　obligor insolvency 債務者の支払い不能
　practical insolvency 実質的破産

insolvent 形 支払い不能の, 返済不能の, 債務超過の, 倒産した, 破綻した, 名 支払い不能者, 破産者

▸The Corporation took over millions of yen in personal and corporate debts of the *insolvent* company. 当社は, 債務超過の同社の個人債務や法人債務数百万円の肩代わりをした。

inspection 名 検査, 帳簿の閲覧, 査察, 視察, 点検, 実査, 査閲, 監査 (=investigation)
　car inspection 車検
　certificate of inspection 検査証明書
　continuous inspections 継続的点検
　import inspection 輸入検査
　in-house inspection 社内調査, 内部調査 (⇒ in-house investigation)
　inspection right 閲覧権

inspection sales technique　点検商法
inspection tour　視察旅行
intrusive inspection　強制力を伴う査察
on-the-spot inspections　立ち入り検査
physical inspection　実査
random inspections　抜き打ち査察
regular inspection　通常検査
sampling inspection　抜き取り検査
site inspection　現場検査
special inspection　特別検査
surprise inspection　抜き打ち検査
▶We take responsibility by setting safety standards and conducting surprise *inspections*.　当社は，自己責任で安全基準を設けたり抜き打ち検査を行ったりしている．

Inst. [inst.] 名　今月　(instantの略; cf. prox. [proximo] 来月, ult. [ultimo] 先月)
the Daily Yomiuri of the 5th inst.　今月5日付け「デイリー・ヨミウリ」

instability 名　不安, 動揺, 不安定, 不安定要因, 不安定性　(⇒global market, stability)
economic instability　経済的不安, 経済的不安定
financial market instability　金融市場の動揺, 禁輸市場不安
▶Financial market *instability* sparked by the U.S. subprime mortgage crisis continues.　米国のサブプライム・ローン（低所得者向け住宅融資）問題に起因する金融市場の動揺は，まだ収まっていない．
▶The *instability* of life insurance firms and the lowered earning power of banks with massive bad loans have become the two major factors rocking the financial system.　生保各社の経営基盤の不安定と，巨額の不良債権に苦しむ銀行の収益力低下が，金融システムを揺るがしている二大要因になっている．

install 動　〈設備を〉取り付ける, 据え付ける, 設置する, インストールする, 組み込む
▶Microsoft has changed its new operating system to make it easier for users to access Eastman Kodak digital camera software and services that they have *installed* on their computers.　マイクロソフトは，同社の最新基本ソフトを変更して，ユーザーがコンピュータにインストールしたイーストマン・コダックのデジタル・カメラのソフトウエアとサービスにアクセスしやすいようにした．

installation 名　導入, 設置, 取付け, 据え付け, 〈ディスクの〉初期化［初期設定］, 敷設, 架設, 工事, 施設, 設備, 装置, インスタレーション
installation cost　据え付け費　(＝installation charge, installation expense, installation fee)
installation of computers　コンピュータの導入・設置
installation of telecommunication systems　通信システムの構築
installation time　導入期間
▶The other products segment consists of the design, *installation* and operation of business information and telecommunications system.　他の製品部門は，ビジネス情報と電気通信システムの設計，設置と運転からなっています．

installment [instalment] 名　分割払い, 割賦払い, 月賦払い, 割賦金　(＝easy payment)
consumer installment credit　消費者信用残高, 消費者信用
installment (account) payable　割賦未払い金
installment (account) receivable　割賦売掛金, 割賦未収金, 割賦債権
installment acquisition　分割購入
make payments in installments　割賦返済する
monthly installment sales　月賦販売, 月賦
redemption by yearly installment　年賦償還

installment plan　割賦制度
▶The newly introduced *installment plan* allows purchasers to pay no initial payments.　新たに導入された割賦制度では，購入者は頭金［契約金］の支払いが不要となっている．

installment sales　割賦販売, 割賦販売高, 割賦売上, 掛売上高
▶The principal items making up the deferred tax provision for 2008 included $250 million for sales-type leases and *installment sales*.　2008年の繰延べ税額を構成する主な項目には，販売型リースと割賦販売の2億5,000万ドルも含まれています．

installment receivables　割賦債権
▶The non-U.S. finance subsidiaries finance *installment receivables* in some cases.　米国外の金融子会社は，割賦債権に対する金融を行う場合もあります．

instant 形　即席の, 即時の, 即座の, 今月の（略 inst.），インスタントの，名　即時, 瞬間, 今月（⇒ Inst. [inst.]）
instant access　すぐ手に入る, すぐ利用できること
instant coupon　商品添付の景品券
instant infrastructure　即席インフラ

Institute for Supply Management　全米供給管理協会《略 ISM》(毎月発表する「サービス業景況感指数」は，景気の変わり目を知るための代表的な先行指標で，指数は50が好不況を判断する分かれ目となる．⇒ISM)

institution 名　機関, 金融機関, 組織, 法人, 企

業, 会社, 施設 （⇒financial institution）
▸As ways to fend off takeovers, it is highly likely that Japanese financial *institutions* will aim to become conglomerates.　買収への防衛策として, 日本の金融機関が複合企業化を目指す可能性が高い.

institutional investor　機関投資家
▸Mitsubishi Tokyo Financial Group Inc. will issue ¥165 billion worth of preferred securities to *institutional investors*.　三菱東京フィナンシャル・グループは, 機関投資家向けに1,650億円の優先出資証券を発行する.

in-stock 名　在庫あり
in-store 形　店内の, 店頭の, 店舗レベルの, インストア
　in-store display　店内陳列
　in-store marketing　インストア・マーケティング《略 ISM》
　in-store marking　インストア・マーキング（マーキング機器を使って品名や価格などを商品に印刷・添付すること）
　in-store merchandising　店内品揃え, インストア・マーチャンダイジング
　in-store promotion　店内プロモーション, 店頭プロモーション, 店内販売促進
　in-store space　店内売り場, 店内空間
　in-store stimuli　店内刺激

instrument 名　証券, 手形, 法律文書, 証拠文書, 器具, 器械, 機器, 方策, 方便, 手段, 商品
　bond instrument　公債
　cash instrument　現物商品
　credit instrument　信用証券（＝instrument of credit）
　derivative instrument　派生商品
　debt instrument　債務証書, 債務証券
　electronic instruments　電子機器
　equity instrument　資本証券, 持ち分証券
　financial instruments　金融手段, 金融商品
　fiscal instrument　財政手段
　hedge instrument　ヘッジ商品
　instrument of transfer　譲渡証書
　monetary instrument　金融手段
　negotiable instrument　流通証券
　short-term instrument　短期証券
　treasury instruments　財務省証券
　Uniform Negotiable Instruments Law　統一流通証券法
▸Such counterparts shall together constitute only one *instrument*.　これらの副本は, 全部合わせてひとつ［唯一］の法律文書を構成するものとする.

insurable 形　保険が付けられる, 保険に適する
　insurable contingency　保険事故
　insurable interest　被保険利益, 保険契約の目的
　insurable property　被保険物件, 保険可能な資産
　insurable risk　保険事故, 保険可能リスク, 保険体
　insurable value　保険価額
　insurable years　加入可能年数

insurance 名　保険, 保険契約, 保険金額, 保険金, 保険料, 保険条件
　accident insurance　災害保険
　annuity insurance　年金保険
　business insurance　事業保険
　casualty insurance　損害保険, 災害保険
　cargo insurance　貨物保険
　corporate employees' pension insurance plan　厚生年金保険
　corporate insurance　企業保険
　cost, insurance and freight　運賃保険料込み値段《略 CIF》
　employment insurance　雇用保険
　exchange risk insurance　為替変動保険
　financial insurance　融資保険
　government-run nursing care insurance system　介護保険制度
　group insurance　団体保険
　health insurance society　健康保険組合
　insurance agent　保険募集人, 保険代理店, 保険代理人（保険募集人＝field underwriter, life underwriter）
　insurance amount　保険金額
　insurance claims　損害保険の請求額, 未収保険金, 保険金
　insurance coverage　保険担保, 保険塡補範囲, 付保危険
　insurance dividend　保険契約者配当金
　insurance expense　未払い保険料
　insurance fund　保険資金, 保険基金, 保険金, 保険預り金
　insurance general expense　保険一般経費
　insurance policy　保険証券, 保険証書, 保険契約, 保険
　insurance premium revenue　保険料収入（＝premium revenue:「保険料収入」は, 一般企業の売上高にあたる）
　insurance revenue　保険料収入（＝insurance premium revenue）
　keyman insurance　経営者保険
　medical insurance　医療保険
　mutual insurance　相互保険

nonlife insurance 損害保険
pension insurance 年金保険
prepaid insurance 前払い保険料 (＝prepaid insurance premium)
unemployment insurance 失業保険

insurance benefits 保険給付金, 保険金
▶Japan's top six nonlife insurance companies have failed to pay *insurance benefits* to policyholders in 262,158. 日本の損害保険大手6社の保険契約者に対する保険金不払い件数は，26万2,158件に達している。

insurance contract 保険契約
▶The Insurance Business Law prohibits life insurers from lowering their promised yield rates on existing *insurance contracts* prior to their collapse. 保険業法は，生命保険会社が破綻前に既契約分の保険契約の予定利率を引き下げることを禁止している。

insurance money 保険金
▶Aioi Insurance Co. has called on Mitsubishi Motors Corp. to pay it about ¥30 million, the full amount of *insurance money* the nonlife insurer paid to a victim of a traffic accident. あいおい損害保険は，同社が交通事故の被害者に支払った保険金の全額約3,000万円の支払いを，三菱自動車に請求した。

insurance policyholder 保険契約者
▶There is a negative spread between the yield guaranteed to *insurance policyholders* and their investment returns. 今は，保険契約者に保証した利回り[予定利率]と運用利回りが逆ざや状態(運用利回りが保険契約者に保証した利回りを下回る状態)にある。

insurance premium 保険料 (＝insurable expense, insurance expense)
▶The *insurance premiums* are determined by the age and other characteristics of policyholders. この保険料は，保険加入者の年齢などの特性に応じて決められる。

insurance underwriting 保険引受け
▶The five business fields in the tie-up agreement are product development, marketing, *insurance underwriting*, damage assessment and reinsurance. 提携契約の5業務分野は，商品開発，マーケティング，保険引受け，損害査定と再保険である。

insure 動 〈加入者が…に〉保険をかける, 保険を付ける, 付保する, 〈保険業者が…について〉保険契約を結ぶ, 保険契約する, 保険を引き受ける, 保険証券を発行する, 保証する, 補償する, 請合う, 確保する

federally insured deposits 米連邦預金保険付保預金
insure a person against death …〔人〕に生命保険をかける
insure against all risks オールリスク保険をかける，全危険担保の条件で保険契約を結ぶ
insure one's life with the company 同社と生命保険契約を結ぶ
insure one's property against fire …の財産に火災保険をかける
insure one's property for $500,000 …の財産に50万ドルの保険をかける
▶User shall, at its expense, keep the Equipment *insured* against all risks until returned to Lender. ユーザーは，「機器」を貸主に返還するまで，ユーザーの費用負担で「機器」にオールリスク保険をかけなければならない。

insured 形 保険に入っている, 保険付きの
insured amount 保険金額, 保険契約金額 (＝life insurance coverage)
insured par 付保総額
insured period 加入期間
insured person 被保険者
sum insured 保険金額

insurer 名 保険会社, 保険業者, 保険者, 保証人 (＝insurance company, insurance enterprise, insurance firm)
bond insurer 債券保険会社
life insurer 生命保険会社
mutual life insurer 生命保険相互会社
property and casualty insurer 損害保険会社, 損保会社
▶The *insurer* aimed to improve profitability by being reluctant to pay insurance benefits. この保険会社は，保険金の支払いを渋って収益の向上を目指した。

intangible 形 無体の, 無形の, 実体のない, 名 無形財産

integrate 動 統合する, 一本化する, 一元化する, 一体化する, 統一する, 系列化する, 一貫生産する
be integrated into …に溶け込む
computer integrated manufacturing (system) コンピュータ統合生産, コンピュータ統合生産システム, シム《略 CIM》
▶Both insurance companies do not plan to *integrate* their information systems for the time being. 両保険会社は当面，情報システムの統合を行う計画はない。
▶By attaching IC tags to aid supplies or having transport vehicles equipped with GPS, the

government will manage aid delivery in a more *integrated* manner.　支援物資にICタグ（電子荷札）を付けたり，輸送トラックにGPS（全地球測位システム）を搭載して，政府は支援物資の輸送・配布状況を一元的に管理する方針だ。
▸Oji turned to Hokuetsu's shareholders for their decision on whether to *integrate* with Oji or remain independent.　王子製紙は，北越製紙の株主に対して，王子と経営統合するか独立路線を堅持するかの判断を仰いだ。

integrate businesses　経営統合する　（＝integrate operations）
▸An increasing number of regional banks are discussing *integrating* their *businesses*.　地域銀行［地域金融機関］の間で，経営統合［再編］の動きが加速している。

integrate operations　経営統合する　（＝integrate businesses, integrate management）
▸Within one year from the stock transfer, both companies are to *integrate operations*.　株式譲渡から1年以内に，両社は経営統合する。

integrated 形　統合された，一本化された，一元化した，一体化した，統一された，系列化された，一貫生産の，総合的，人種差別をしない
　horizontally integrated　水平統合された，水平統合，水平的統合
　integrated circuit　集積回路《略 IC》　（⇒IC）
　integrated commerce environment　統合商用環境　（インターネット上でビジネスを展開するのに必要な各種サービスとソフトウエア・ツールで，決済サービスや顧客管理，店舗管理などが含まれる）
　integrated data processing　集中データ処理，集中情報処理，総合データ処理《略 IDP》
　integrated foreign operations　一体化した海外事業
　integrated package　総合対策，統合対策，総合政策，統合政策
　integrated production site　一貫生産拠点
　integrated transport policy　総合交通政策
　vertically integrated business　垂直統合された事業
　vertically integrated marketing　販売の垂直統合，一貫販売体制

integrated management　経営統合
▸If our tender offer goes through, we will be able to make the firm a wholly owned subsidiary under an *integrated management*.　当社の株式公開買付け（TOB）が成立すれば，当社は経営統合により同社を完全子会社化することができる。

integrated operations　一体化した事業，統合［統合による］事業，経営統合，事業統合，一貫作業，一貫した体制，一貫生産体制，一貫生産拠点
▸*Integrated operations* are those whose economic activities have a direct effect on the cash flows and operations of the parent company.　一体化した事業とは，その経済活動が親会社のキャッシュ・フローと事業に直接影響を与える事業のことです。

integration 名　統合，経営統合，一本化，一元化，一体化，統一，企業の系列化，集約化，環境への適応，一体感，集積回路（integrated circuit），人種統合，人種差別撤廃　（⇒**management integration**, **operational integration**）
　backward integration　後方統合
　business integration　事業統合，経営統合　（＝integration of business, merger）
　currency integration　通貨統合
　downstream integration　下流部門の統合
　economic integration　経済統合
　financial integration　金融統合
　forward integration　前方統合
　horizontal integration　水平統合
　integration efficiency　統合効果
　integration of affiliates　関連会社の統合
　integration of distribution system　流通系列化
　integration of physical distribution　物流の統合
　management integration　経営統合　（＝operational integration）
　medium scale integration　中規模集積回路《略 MSI》　（＝medium scale integrated circuit）
　phased integration　段階的な統合
　social integration　社会の一体感
　system [systems] integration　システム統合，システム統合化
　system integration architecture　システム構築体系
　vertical integration　垂直統合
　very large scale integration　超大規模集積回路，超LSI　（＝very large scale integrated circuit）
▸The *integration* of computer systems is indispensable in unifying documentation and also for such tasks as the placing of orders with factories, product delivery and information management.　文書作成や，工場への発注，納品，情報管理などを一元化する上で，コンピュータのシステム統合は不可欠である。
▸We have submitted a business *integration*

proposal to the firm to acquire all of its ordinary shares through a takeover bid. 株式公開買付け(TOB)で同社の普通株式を全株取得するため，当社は同社に経営統合案を提出しました[経営統合を申し入れました]．

intellectual asset 知的資産
▶*Intellectual assets* include industrial expertise and brands, in addition to intellectual properties such as patents. 知的資産には，特許などの知的財産のほかに，企業のノウハウやブランドなどが含まれる．

intellectual property 知的財産，知的所有権，知的財産権 (=intellectual property right)
▶We continually assess the relationship between our company and others in our industry with regard to the protection of our *intellectual properties*. 当社の知的財産の保護に関しましては，私どもは当社と業界他社との関係を絶えず見直しております．

intellectual property dispute 知的財産権紛争
▶Toshiba Corp. has settled an *intellectual property dispute* over flash memory chips with U.S. semiconductor maker Micron Technology. 東芝は，フラッシュメモリ・チップ(電気的に一括消去・再書込みが可能なメモリ・チップ)をめぐるマイクロン・テクノロジー社(米国の半導体メーカー)との知的財産権紛争に決着をつけた．

Intellectual Property High Court 知的財産高等裁判所，知財高裁
▶The *Intellectual Property High Court* specializes in lawsuits over intellectual property, such as the infringement of patents. 知的財産高等裁判所は，特許権侵害など知的財産をめぐる訴訟を専門に手がける．

intellectual property right 知的所有権，知的財産権《略 IPR》(=intellectual property)
知的所有権に含まれるもの

copyright	著作権
database	データベース
computer program	コンピュータ・プログラム
knowhow	ノウハウ
patent	特許権
registered design	意匠権
registered trademark	商標権
software	ソフトウエア
trade secret	企業秘密，トレード・シークレット
utility model	実用新案権

intelligence 名 知能，知性，理解力，情報，情報収集，情報操作，情報機関，戦略情報，諜報，インテリジェンス
artificial intelligence 人工知能《略 AI》
human intelligence 人的情報収集《略 HUMINT》
intelligence car 知能自動車，インテリジェンス・カー
intelligence-gathering system 情報収集システム
intelligence network 情報網
intelligence service 情報サービス，諜報機関
marketing intelligence マーケティング戦略情報
▶President Bush backed the creation of an *intelligence* czar and counterterrorism center. ブッシュ米大統領は，情報機関の統括責任者とテロ対策センターの新設を支持した．

intelligent 形 知的な，知能的な，高機能の，高度の，高いレベルの知能を持つ，情報処理能力を持つ，情報処理能力が付加してある，データ処理能力を持っている，コンピュータで集中管理された，インテリジェント機能を備えた，インテリジェント
intelligent agent 情報の代理店，インテリジェント・エージェント
intelligent building 情報化ビル，高機能ビル，高度情報化建築物，高度情報化対応型ビル，インテリジェント・ビル
intelligent city 高度情報都市，インテリジェント・シティ
intelligent communications 知的通信，知能通信，高度通信
intelligent manufacturing system 知的生産システム
intelligent materials 知能材料
intelligent network 高度機能ネットワーク，インテリジェント・ネットワーク
intelligent sensor 知能センサー (=smart sensor)
intelligent transport system 高度道路交通システム，知的道路情報システム，インテリジェント交通システム《略 ITS》(自動車交通情報システムの総称)

intensify 動 強める，高める，強化する，増強する，激化する，強くなる，激化する，高まる，活発になる
intensified global competition グローバル競争の激化
intensified price competition 価格競争の激化
▶GM has been *intensifying* efforts to reduce costs and improve quality. GMは，コスト削減

策と品質改善策を強化している。

intensive 形 …集約的, …集約型, …集約性の高い, 集中的, 熾烈な, 厳しい, 徹底的な
- **capital-intensive business** 資本集約型事業
- **energy-intensive industry** エネルギー集約型産業
- **human capital-intensive company** 人材集約型企業
- **intensive agriculture** 集約農業
- **intensive care unit** 集中治療室《略 ICU》
- **intensive price competition** 熾烈な価格競争
- **intensive regulation** 厳しい規制
- **knowledge-intensive industry** 知識集約型産業
- **knowledge-intensive operations** 知識集約型事業
- **labor-intensive** 労働集約型, 労働集約的
- **labor-intensive functions** 労働集約型業務
- **labor-intensive industry** 労働集約型産業
- **labor-intensive products** 労働集約性の高い製品
- **land-intensive manufacturing** 土地集約型産業
- **materials-intensive** 原材料多消費型の, 原材料［原料］集約的な
- **R&D-intensive industry** 研究開発集約型産業
- **resource-intensive activities** 資源集約型産業
- **technology-intensive product** 技術集約性の高い製品

▶Initially, Japanese corporations starting business in China were largely such labor-*intensive* firms as textile-processing companies. 当初, 中国に進出した日本企業は, 主に繊維加工業などの労働集約型企業であった。

interactive 形 双方向の, 対話式の, 会話型, 対話処理, 対話性, 相互作用の, 相互に情報を交換できる, インタラクティブ
- **interactive function** 相互作用機能, インタラクティブ機能
- **interactive media** 対話型メディア, 双方向メディア（双方向CATVなど, 端末間からも交信できるメディア）
- **interactive processing** 対話型処理, インタラクティブ処理
- **interactive software** 対話型ソフト
- **interactive TV** 双方向テレビ, インタラクティブTV

interarea accounts receivable 地域間の売掛金

▶*Interarea accounts receivable* and the unamortized portion of service charges have been eliminated in consolidation. 各地域間の売掛金とサービス料の未償却部分は, 連結決算上, 消去されています。

interarea transfer 地域間振替え

▶*Interarea transfers* consist principally of completed machines, subassemblies and parts, and software. 地域間振替えの内訳は, 主に完成機械, 半製品・部品とソフトウエアとなっています。

interbank 形 銀行間の, インターバンク
- **interbank borrowing** 銀行間借入れ
- **interbank business** 銀行間取引（＝interbank deal）
- **interbank funding** インターバンク市場での資金調達, インターバンク調達
- **interbank lending** 銀行間貸出
- **interbank line** 銀行間資金供与枠, インターバンク資金供与枠
- **interbank market** 銀行間市場
- **interbank rate** 銀行間金利, 銀行間相場, インターバンク相場
- **interbank trading** 銀行間売買
- **interbank transaction** 銀行間取引, インターバンク取引（＝interbank dealing）
- **London interbank bid rate** ロンドン銀行間取り手金利
- **New York interbank offered rate** ニューヨーク銀行間出し手金利

intercompany 形 会社間の, 親子会社間の, 内部の
- **intercompany bondholdings** 会社間の社債の持ち合い
- **intercompany dividend** 会社間配当
- **intercompany investment** 会社間投資, 内部投資
- **intercompany loan** 会社間貸付け, 関係会社からの借入金
- **intercompany profit and loss** 内部損益, 連結未実現損益
- **intercompany sales** 会社間売上, 内部取引高

▶Revenues and expenses, including gains and losses on foreign exchange transactions other than long-term *intercompany* advances, are translated at average rates for the period. 収益と費用は, 親子［連結］会社間の長期貸付け金以外の外貨建て取引から生じる損益を含めて, 期中平均為替レートで換算されています。

intercompany profit 会社間利益, 会社相互間利益, 内部利益

▶*Intercompany profits* are eliminated in connection with preparation of the consolidated financial statements. 連結財務書類作成上, 内部

利益は消去されています。

intercompany transaction 会社間取引, 親子会社間取引, 内部取引, 関係会社間取引, 連結会社間取引（同一会社内の本支店間の取引関係）
▶All other significant *intercompany transactions* have been eliminated in the consolidated financial statements. 他の主要な内部取引は, すべて連結財務書類上, 消去されています。

intercorporate stockholding 企業間株式保有, 持ち株制度

interest 图 利息, 利子, 金利, 株, 持ち分, 利益, 権益, 利権, 利害関係, 関係者, 同業者, 業界, 企業, …側
- **actual interest** 実効金利（=actual interest rate）
- **arrear of interest** 遅延利子, 遅延利息（=delayed interest）
- **back interest** 未払い利息
- **bond interest** 社債利息, 債券利息
- **business interests** 企業利益
- **competing interests** 競業利益, 利害の対立
- **compounded interest** 複利（=compound interest, interest upon interest）
- **debenture interest** 社債利息
- **ex interest** 利落ち
- **financial interest** 財務上の利害関係, 経済的利害関係, 投資関係者
- **implicit interest** 計算上の利息（=imputed interest）
- **imputed interest** 計算利子[利息], 適用利息, 付加利子, 帰属利子, 自己資本利子（=implicit interest）
- **interest accrued** 未払い利息, 未収利息
- **interest advance** 前払い利息
- **interest and dividend income** 受取利息および配当金（=interest and dividends received）
- **interest and dividends received** 受取利息および配当
- **interest burden** 金利負担
- **interest charge** 支払い利息
- **interest charged on the loan** 返済金利
- **interest earned** 未収利息
- **interest, gain on securities sold, dividends and other** 受取利息, 有価証券売却益, 配当他
- **interest group** 利益集団
- **interest paid** 支払い利息
- **interest payable** 未払い利息
- **interest prepaid** 前払い利息
- **interest receivable** 未収利息
- **interest received** 受取利息

- **loan interest** 貸付け利子
- **majority interest** 過半数持ち分, 過半数株式（=controlling interest）
- **market interest** 市場実勢金利
- **minority interest** 少数株主持ち分, 半数未満の出資
- **negative interest** マイナスの金利, 逆金利
- **nominal interest** 表面利率, 名目金利
- **paid interest** 返済利息
- **remaining interest** 残余権（=residual interest）
- **security interest** 有価証券利息, 担保権
- **simple interest** 単利
- **stock interest** 株式持ち分
- **stockholder's interest** 株主持ち分
- **system of interest** 金利体系
- **vested interest** 既得権, 既得権益, 確定権利

▶We have a 49% *interest* in a joint venture with the company. 同社との合弁事業[合弁会社]に対して, 当社は49%の持ち分を所有しています。
▶We seek a healthy balance between business *interests* and environmental protection. 当社は, 企業利益と環境保護との健全なバランスを求めています。

interest-bearing 圏 利付きの, 有利子の, 利息条件付きの
- **interest-bearing debt** 有利子負債（=interest bearing liability:「有利子負債」は, 金利を付けて返済しなければならない債務のこと）
- **interest-bearing notes receivable** 利息条件付き受取手形
- **interest-bearing receivable** 利付き債権
- **interest-bearing security** 利付き証券

▶Other securities consist of marketable securities and *interest-bearing* bank deposits with varied maturity dates. 「その他の有価証券」の内訳は, 市場性ある有価証券と満期日が異なる利付き銀行預金です。
▶We had about ¥1 trillion of *interest-bearing* debts as of the end of December 2007. 2007年12月末時点で, 当社は約1兆円の有利子負債を抱えています。

interest cost 利息費用, 利子費用, 支払い利息（=interest charge, interest expense）
- **interest cost on accumulated postretirement benefit obligation** 累積退職後給付債務の利子費用
- **interest cost on the projected benefit obligation** 予定給付債務の利息費用[利子費用]

interest coverage ratio 利払い余力率, 利

子支払い保証倍率, インタレスト・カバレッジ比率, インタレスト・カバレッジ・レシオ（＝interest cover, interest coverage, times interest covered, times interest earned ratio: 企業の金利支払い能力を見る指標）
▸*Interest coverage ratio* is calculated as income divided by interest expense.　利払い余力率は, 利益を支払い利息で割って[除して]算出します。

interest expense　支払い利息, 利息費用, 利子費用　（＝interest charge, interest cost; ⇒**refinancing**）
▸The Company's cash payments for *interest expense* were $200 million in 2008.　当社の支払い利息（計上額）のうち現金支払い額は, 2008年度は2億ドルでした。

interest income　受取利息, 利息収益, 利息収入, 金利収入
▸Our *interest income* declined because we had less cash on hand and interest rates were lower.　利息収入は, 手元現預金が少なく, 金利が低下したために減少しました。

Interest Limitation Law　利息制限法
▸Most consumer financing firms offer loans at gray-area interest rates somewhere between the two upper limits under the *Interest Limitation Law* and the Investment Deposit and Interest Rate Law.　ほとんどの消費者金融会社は, 利息制限法と出資法の二つの上限金利間のグレーゾーン（灰色）金利で融資している。

interest on　…の利子, …の利息
　interest on borrowings　借入金利子, 借入金利息　（＝interest on loans）
　interest on debt　支払い利息
　interest on lendings　貸出金利息
　interest on loans　借入金の金利, 借入金利息, 貸付け金利息, 貸付け利子, 貸出金利　（＝interest on borrowings, interest rate on loans）
　interest on security　有価証券利息
▸During 2008, *interest on* borrowings amounted to $1,100 million.　2008年度の借入金利息は, 11億ドルに達しました。

interest payment　利払い, 金利の支払い, 利子支払い, 利息の返済, 支払い利息
▸This was considered as *interest payments* and did not reduce the principal of their loan.　これは利払いと見なされたため, 借入金の元本は減らなかった。

interest payment burden　金利負担　（＝the burden of interest payment）
▸Long-term interest rates have been edging up, threatening heavier *interest payment burdens* for people with mortgages and companies with debts.　長期金利がじりじりと上昇して, 住宅ローンを抱える家庭や借金のある企業の金利負担が増す恐れがある。

interest rate　金利, 利息, 利子率, 利率　（⇒**carry trade, interest payment burden, key interest rate, long-term interest rate**）
　compound interest rate　複利　（元本と利息に金利が付く）
　fixed interest rate　固定金利
　floating interest rate　変動金利
　implicit interest rate　包括利率
　interest rate cut　金利の引下げ, 利下げ
　interest rate hike　金利上昇, 利上げ, 金利引上げ　（＝interest rate increase）
　interest rate on loans　貸出金利　（＝interest on loans, loan interest rate）
　legal ceiling on interest rates　法定金利の上限　（＝legal cap on interest rates, legal interest rate cap, legal interest rate ceiling）
　market interest rate　市中金利, 市場金利　（＝open market rate）
　preferential interest rate for companies　企業向け融資の優遇金利
　ultralow interest rates　超低金利
　upper limit of interest rates　金利の上限, 上限金利
　zero-interest rate policy　ゼロ金利政策
▸Should the *interest rate* rise, it will become more expensive for companies to borrow money.　金利が上昇すると[金利上昇局面では], 企業の資金調達コストが重くなる。

interest rate policy　金利政策
▸The central bank of Japan ended its zero *interest rate policy* in July 2006, with its key interest rate raised to 0.25 percent.　日銀（日本の中央銀行）は, 基準金利を0.25％に引き上げて, 2006年7月にゼロ金利政策を解除した。

interest rate swap　金利スワップ　（＝interest swap: 同一通貨間で固定金利と変動金利の債権または債務を交換する取引）
　interest rate swap agreement　金利スワップ契約　（＝interest rate swap contract）
　interest rate swap bond　金利スワップ債　（＝interest swap bond）
▸We enter into *interest rate swap* agreements to manage our exposure to changes in interest rates.　金利変動リスクに対処するため, 当社は金利スワップ契約を結んでいます。

interest revenue 受取利息, 利息収益, 利息収入, 利子収入 (＝interest received)
▸The finance subsidiary's *interest revenue* is included in the Corporation's consolidated net sales. 金融子会社の受取利息は, 当社の連結売上高に含まれています。

interested parties 利害関係者 (＝interest group, interest parties, interested persons: 株主や債権者, 取引先, 顧客などをいう)
▸Joint-stock companies are obliged to announce important matters, including the issuance of new shares, stock splits and settlement of accounts, for investors and other *interested parties* by legal notifications. 株式会社は, 法定公告で新株発行や株式分割, 決算などの重要事項を投資家などの利害関係者に公表することを義務付けられている。

interface 名 接続装置, 接続技術, 〈機能の異なる装置間で情報のやりとりをするための〉規格境界面, 中間領域, 接触面, インターフェース
▸An *interface* is necessary at the customer's LAN in order to connect the router equipment. ルータを接続するために, お客さまのLAN側にインターフェースが必要になります。

interim 形 中間の, 半期の, 期中の, 中間会計期間の, 暫定的な, 一時的な, 仮の
  interim closing 中間決算, 半期決算 (＝interim earnings report, interim financial results, interim results, interim settlement of accounts)
  interim committee 暫定委員会
  interim contract [agreement] 暫定契約, 仮契約
  interim earnings report 中間決算, 中間決算報告, 中間利益報告書 (＝interim financial results, interim results, midterm earnings report)
  interim financing つなぎ資金
  interim government 暫定政府
  interim interest 中間利息
  interim net profit 中間期の純利益, 半期の純利益, 中間期の税引き後利益
  interim operating profit 中間期の営業利益, 半期の営業利益
  interim report 中間報告, 中間決算報告書, 半期報告書
  interim ruling 中間判決
  regular interim dividend 中間配当
interim dividend payout 中間配当支払い, 中間配当支払い額
▸Both *interim* and year-end *dividend payouts* are each projected at ¥3 per share. 中間配当と期末配当の支払い額は, それぞれ1株当たり3円となる見込みです。

interim financial results report 中間決算報告
▸Many companies have announced an increase in cash dividends in their *interim financial results reports*. 中間決算報告で, 配当金の引上げを発表する企業が多かった。

interim profit 中間期の利益, 半期利益, 半期決算利益
▸*Interim profit* increased 8 percent from the year before. 同社の半期決算利益は, 前年同期比で8％増加した。

interim report 中間報告, 中間決算報告, 半期報告, 半期報告書 (＝midterm report)
▸The domestic life insurance companies released *interim reports* on the results of their in-house probes. 国内の生命保険各社が, 社内調査の結果に関する中間報告を発表した。

interim settlement of accounts 中間決算
▸Neither of Mitsui Trust Holdings, Inc. and another major financial group has yet released reports on its *interim settlement of accounts*. 三井トラスト・ホールディングスなど2大金融グループは, まだ中間決算報告を発表していない。

interlocking directorate 兼任重役, 兼任役員

interlocking stockholding 株式持ち合い (＝interlocking shareholding)

intermediary 形 中間の, 仲介の, 中継の, 名 仲介業者, 仲介機関
  financial intermediary 金融仲介機関, 金融機関
  intermediary bank 仲介銀行, 受け皿銀行, 取立銀行
  intermediary dealer 中間業者 (＝go-between dealer)
  intermediary fee 仲介手数料
  intermediary function 仲介機能
  intermediary seller 中間販売業者, 仲介業者
  market intermediary 証券会社

intermediate 形 中間の, 中間に位置する, 中級の, 中級レベルの, 中期の, 名 仲介者, 中間生成物, 中期物, 〈コンパクト・カー（小型車）と大型車(full-sized car)の中間の〉中型車
  intermediate course 中級コース
  intermediate demand 中間需要
  intermediate goods 中間財

intermediate market 中間市場, 中期物
intermediate planning 中期計画, 中期経営計画
intermediate securities 中期債
intermediate sort 中間取揃え
intermediate technology 中間技術
intermediate term loan 中期ローン
West Texas Intermediate テキサス産軽質油 (⇒WTI)

intermediation 名 金融仲介, 仲介化, 金融仲介機関利用

Intermodal Surface Transportation Efficiency Act 陸上一貫輸送効率化法

intermodal transportation system 複合一貫輸送

internal 形 内部の, 社内の, 国内の
internal capital generation 内部資本形成, 留保利益
internal capital growth 内部資本形成率
internal cash 内部資金, 内部キャッシュ
internal conflict 内紛, 内紛騒動 (＝infighting)
internal data network 社内データ通信ネットワーク
internal documentation 内部文書
internal funds 内部資金, 自己資金
internal information 内部情報, 社内情報
internal investigation 社内調査, 内部調査 (＝in-house investigation)
internal profit 内部利益
internal rate of return 内部利益率, 内部収益率《略 IRR》
internal transfer profit 内部振替利益, 本支店振替利益
internal use 社内の使用, 社内の使途
internal user 内部情報利用者

internal accounting control 内部会計統制, 会計に関する内部統制
▶The *internal accounting control* process includes management's communication to employees of policies which govern ethical business conduct. 会計に関する内部統制の手順には, 経営者の従業員に対する倫理的業務活動に関する方針[倫理的業務遂行の管理方針]の通達も含まれています。

internal audit 内部監査 (＝internal auditing)
▶Outside directors chair the *internal audit* and compliance committee, the nomination committee and the compensation committee. 外部取締役は, 内部監査・法令遵守委員会, 指名委員会と報酬委員会の各委員長を務めています。

internal auditor 内部監査人 (⇒monitor)
▶Periodically, the *internal auditors* and the independent auditors meet privately with the audit committee. 定期的に, 内部監査人と外部監査人は監査委員会と非公式に会合しています。

internal control 内部統制, 社内管理, 内部チェック, 内部チェック体制 (「内部統制」は, 粉飾決算や経営者の不正・ごまかしなど, 企業の不祥事を防ぐため, 社内の管理・点検体制を整え, 絶えずチェックすることをいう。日本の上場企業は, 2008年度から内部統制に関する報告が義務付けられている。⇒**accountability**)
▶To maintain its system of *internal controls*, management carefully selects key personnel and establishes the organizational structure to provide an appropriate division of responsibility. 内部統制組織を維持するため, 経営陣は幹部要員を慎重に選定し, その責任分担を的確に行う組織機構を確立しています。

internal control system 内部統制組織, 内部統制機構 (＝system of internal controls)
▶Our *internal control system* is reviewed, evaluated and revised as necessary in light of the results of constant management oversight, internal and independent audits, changes in our business and other conditions. 当社の内部統制組織は, 経営者の不断の監視, 内部監査や外部監査, 当社の事業やその他の条件の変動などに照らして随時, 必要に応じて見直し, 評価し, 改善を重ねています。

internal growth 内部成長, 内部成長率
▶To promote the *internal growth* of ABC Inc. and the value of its shares, the proportion of earnings invested in the corporation should be permitted to grow. ABC社の内部成長を促し, 当社株式の価値を高めるためには, 収益のうち当社自体に対する投資比率を引き上げる必要があります。

internal management system 内部管理体制
▶The bank had problems with its *internal management system* and other business schemes. 同行は, 内部管理体制など業務体制に問題があった。

internal resources 内部資金, 手元資金
▶The company plans to make initial investments of about ¥200 billion from *internal resources*. 同社では, 当初の約2,000億円の投資額は内部資金[手元資金]を充てる計画だ。

Internal Revenue Code 内国歳入法, 内国歳入法典《略 IRC》(米国の連邦税法)

▶The Company's policy is to fund the maximum amount allowable based on funding limitations of the *Internal Revenue Code*.　当社は，内国歳入法の拠出限度額に基づいて許容できる最高の金額を拠出する方針です。

Internal Revenue Service 〈米国の〉内国歳入庁《略 IRS》

▶The *Internal Revenue Service* has examined and accepted income tax returns of the Company.　米内国歳入庁は，当社の所得税申告書を調査して，これを承認しました。

internalization 名 内部化，内部調達

internally generated funds 内部調達資金　(⇒generate)

international 形 国際的，国際間の，国際上の，インターナショナル

International Bar Association 国際法曹協会
international business activities 国際事業活動，国際ビジネス
international business strategy 国際事業戦略，国際企業戦略，グローバル戦略　(=global business strategy)
international consortium 国際共同事業体，国際借款団，国際融資団
International Convention for the Safety of Life at Sea 海上安全に対する国際協定
international division of manufacturing 国際分業
international double taxation 国際二重課税　(=international double tax)
International Energy Agency 国際エネルギー機関《略 IEA》
international flight 国際線
International Institute for Management Development 国際経営開発研究所
International Labor Organization 国際労働機関《略 ILO》
international lending 国際融資，対外融資
international loan 対外融資，国際貸付け
International Maritime Organization 国際海事機関《略 IMO》
International Organization for Standardization 国際標準化機構《略 IOS》　(=International Standardization Organization)
international tax convention [treaty] 国際租税条約

▶*International* businesses performed particularly well, with increased sales in Japan, other Pacific Rim countries and Europe.　国際事業部門の業績はとくに好調で，日本その他の環太平洋諸国と欧州で売上が増加しました。

International Accounting Standards

国際会計基準《略 IAS》　(⇒International Financial Reporting Standards)

　国際会計基準について➡米国の企業会計基準と並ぶ世界の2大会計基準。国際会計基準は，欧州が主導する国際会計基準審議会(IASB)が作成している。欧州各国のほかに，ロシア，オーストラリア，中南米諸国など約90か国が採用を決めている。欧州連合(EU)は，2005年から域内の上場企業に国際会計基準の決算開示を義務付け，2007年からは域内上場の外国企業にもEUの国際基準と同レベルの開示を求めている。日本の会計基準は，1999年度に連結会計とキャッシュ・フロー計算書，税効果会計，2000年度に退職給付会計や金融商品の時価会計，2005年度から減損会計が導入された。その結果，日本の会計基準は現在，国際会計基準と基本的に同等であるとの評価が得られるようなった。なお，国際会計基準審議会(IASB)が設定する国際会計基準のIASは，2005年1月1日から新しい呼び名として「国際財務報告規準(International Financial Reporting Standards)に改められた。

international activities 国際事業

▶All *international activities* provided 25 percent of consolidated revenues in 2008.　2008年度は，国際事業が連結収益の25％を占めました。

international balance of payments

国際収支　(=balance of payments, balance of international payments)

国際収支関連用語:

basic balance	基礎収支
capital balance	資本収支
current account balance	経常収支　(=**current balance**)
foreign reserves	外貨準備
goods & services balance	貿易・サービス収支
income balance	所得収支
investment balance	投資収支
invisible balance	貿易外収支
long-term capital balance	長期資本収支
overall balance	総合収支
services balance	サービス収支
short-term capital balance	短期資本収支
trade balance	貿易収支
transfer balance	移転収支

international competition 国際競争　(=global competition)

▶As a measure against drops in sales prices due to *international competition*, Canon has made efforts to emphasize the production of value-added products.　国際競争による売価低下への対抗策として，キヤノンは高付加価値製品の生産に重点を置いている。

international competitiveness　国際競争力（＝international competitive edge）
▸Asian countries such as China, with lower wages, have been closing the gap on Japan in *international competitiveness*.　中国など低賃金のアジア諸国は，日本との国際競争力のギャップを埋めてきている。

International Financial Reporting Standards　国際財務報告基準《略 IFRS》（国際財務報告規準(IFRS)は，国際会計基準審議会(IASB)が設定するIAS（国際会計基準）の新しい呼び名で，2005年1月1日に採択された。⇒**International Accounting Standards**）
▸*International Financial Reporting Standards* (IFRS) were adopted as from 1 January 2005.　国際財務報告基準(IFRS)は，2005年1月1日に採択された。
▸The Group's sales figures have been restated following the retrospective application of new *International Financial Reporting Standards*.　当グループの売上高の数値は，新国際財務報告基準(IFRS)を遡及的に適用して，再表示されています。

international market　国際市場（＝global market）
▸We will expand our presence and improve customer service and support in all markets, particularly the *international market*.　当社は，とくに国際市場を中心に，全市場で当社の事業基盤を拡大し，顧客サービスと顧客支援体制を強化・改善する方針です。

International Monetary Fund　国際通貨基金《略 IMF》
▸The *International Monetary Fund* (IMF) plans to draw up the code of sovereign wealth funds by August 2008.　国際通貨基金(IMF)は，2008年8月までに政府系投資ファンドの投資指針を策定する方針だ。

international operations　国際事業，海外事業，海外事業活動，国際業務
▸Revenues from *international operations* in 2008 decreased 16 percent from $242 million (five percent of total revenues) in 2007.　2008年度の国際事業部門の売上高は，前年度の2億4,200万ドル（総売上高の5％）から16％減少しました。

Internet　名　インターネット，ネット（＝internet, INET, Net: **internetwork**の略）

copyright on Internet　インターネット著作権
electric household appliances for Internet　ネット家電，インターネット家電
Internet auction site　ネット競売サイト，ネット・オークション・サイト
Internet banking　ネット・バンキング，インターネット・バンキング（＝Net banking）
Internet-based commerce　ネット商取引，ネット取引（＝e-business, electronic commerce, Internet commerce）
Internet bulletin board　ネット掲示板
Internet delivery business　インターネット配信ビジネス
Internet investor　ネット投資家，ネット投資会社，ネット投資機関
Internet music delivery　ネット音楽配信
Internet only bank　ネット銀行，ネット専業銀行（＝Internet bank）
Internet payment　ネット決済，インターネット決済
Internet procurement　ネット調達
Internet Protocol telephone service　インターネット・プロトコル電話サービス，IP電話サービス（＝IP telephone service, IP call service）
Internet-related firm　ネット関連企業
Internet retailer　ネット小売店，ネット販売店，ネット小売企業
Internet share transaction　株式のネット取引，インターネットでの株式取引
Internet shopping　ネット通販，インターネット・ショッピング（＝electronic commerce, Net shopping, online shopping, virtual shopping）
▸Nippon Television Network Corp. and Fuji TV have embarked on projects to distribute television programs via the *Internet*.　日本テレビ放送網やフジテレビは，テレビ番組のネット配信事業に乗り出している。

Internet bank　ネット銀行
▸The new *Internet bank* will be equally owned by the two firms with initial capital of ¥20 billion.　新ネット銀行は，当初資本が200億円で，両社が折半出資する。

Internet-based bank　ネット専業銀行（＝Internet bank, Net bank, Net-only bank, online bank）
▸Internet shopping mall Rakuten Inc. and Tokyo Tomin Bank are planning to found a joint *Internet-based bank*.　ネット・ショッピング・モールの楽天と東京都民銀行が，共同出資によるネット専

業銀行の設立を計画している。

Internet-based banking venture ネット専業銀行業務
▸An *Internet-based banking venture* between the firms will handle deposits, foreign exchange, small business and personal loans and sales of securities and other investment products. 両社のネット専業銀行業務では，預金や外国為替，中小企業や個人向け融資のほかに，有価証券その他の投資商品の販売も取り扱う。

Internet business ネット事業，インターネット事業 （=Internet-based business）

Internet deal ネット取引
▸Falsified or borrowed names are used in many *Internet deals*, leaving no tangible business records. ネット取引では，仮名や借名が使われることが多く，取引記録が書類で残らない。

Internet firm ネット企業 （=Internet company, Internet corporation）
▸Many *Internet firms*, especially B2B companies, are still growing strongly. 多くのネット企業，とりわけB2B（企業間の取引）企業は，今でも力強い成長を遂げている。

Internet jams ネット渋滞
▸About 40 percent of Internet providers restrict communication by heavy users to prevent *Internet Jams*. ネット渋滞を避けるため，インターネット接続業者の約4割がインターネットの大量利用者の通信量を制限している。

Internet search service インターネット検索サービス
▸Yahoo Inc. is the world's second-largest *Internet search service* company. 米ヤフーは，インターネット検索サービスで世界第2位の企業だ。

Internet service provider business [**service**] インターネット［ネット］接続サービス事業
▸We span off our *Internet service provider business* on July 1, 2008. 当社は，自社で運営しているインターネット接続サービス事業を，2008年7月1日付けで分社化しました。

Internet shopping mall operator インターネット上の仮想商店街運営会社，仮想商店街の運営会社 （=Net shopping mall operator, online shopping mall operator）
▸NTT DoCoMo Inc. formed a capital tie-up with *Internet shopping mall operator* Rakuten Inc. in the Internet auction business. NTTドコモが，インターネット・オークション事業で電子商取引大手の楽天［仮想商店街を運営している楽天］と資本提携した。

Internet trading インターネット取引，ネット取引，インターネット販売，ネット・トレーディング，インターネットによる売買，ネット販売 （=Net trading, online trade, online trading）
▸We are setting up the *Internet trading* of plasma display panels. 当社は現在，プラズマ・ディスプレー・パネルのインターネット販売を計画している。

Internet user インターネットの利用者，インターネット・ユーザー
▸The ratio of *Internet users* to the nation's overall population hit a new high of 66.8 percent last year. インターネット利用者の日本全国の人口に対する普及率は，66.8％と過去最高を記録した。

internship 名 就業体験，就労体験，インターンシップ
▸Temporary staffing service company Pasona Inc. has launched an agricultural *internship* program to foster future farmers. 人材派遣会社のパソナが，将来の農家［農業者］育成のため，農業インターンシップ・プログラムを開始した。

intersegment 部門間の
　intersegment sales セグメント間売上げ

intervene 動 介入する
▸Japan used ¥2.25 trillion from Nov. 27 to Dec. 26 to *intervene* in the currency market. 11月27日から12月26日に日本が実施した外国為替市場への介入の額は，2兆2,500億円に達した。

intervention 名 介入，市場介入，協調介入，仲裁，調停，干渉
　conduct yen-selling intervention 円売り介入を実施する
　currency market intervention 為替市場への介入，為替市場介入 （=foreign exchange intervention, forex intervention）
　dollar-buying intervention ドル買い介入
　excessive intervention in management by a large shareholder 大株主の過剰な経営介入
　forex intervention 為替介入
　intervention in management 経営介入，経営への口出し
　intervention rate 市場介入金利
　joint intervention 協調介入，協調市場介入 （=coordinated intervention, joint market intervention）
　the joint Japanese-U.S. intervention in the monetary market 日本と米国の為替市場への協調介入
　three-way intervention 三極の市場介入

yen-selling, dollar-buying intervention 円売り・ドル買い介入
▸Japan is ready to counter the yen's rapid rise with dollar-supporting market *intervention*. ドルの下支えを図る市場介入により，日本は急激な円高を阻止する構えだ．

interview 名 面接，面接法，面談，会見，会談，診察，インタビュー
　depth interview 深層面接，深層面接法
　exclusive interview 独占インタビュー
　group interview 集団面接法，グループ面接法
　interview survey 面接調査
　job interview 就職面接（＝interview for a job）
　press interview 記者会見
　telephone interview 電話調査

intraday 形 1日のうちの，日中の，日日の

introduce 動 導入する，発売する，売り出す，公開する，上場する，紹介する
▸The company will *introduce* an early retirement scheme in July. 同社は，7月から早期退職制度を導入する．

introduction 名 導入，発売，公開，持ち込み，紹介
　introduction of a new product 新製品の発売，新製品の市場導入，新製品の投入
　introduction of stock 株式公開
　introduction stage of PLC 製品ライフ・サイクルの市場導入期
　introduction of technology 技術の導入
▸The segment's revenue growth was achieved through higher sales volumes and the *introduction* of new products. 当部門の増収は，販売数量の増加と新製品の投入で達成しました．

intrust ＝entrust
invalidity 名 無効，就労不能
inventory 名 在庫，在庫品，棚卸し，棚卸し品，棚卸し資産，棚卸し高，棚卸し表，財産目録，目録，保有品
　carry inventory 在庫を抱える
　cuts in inventory 在庫削減，在庫削減幅
　finished goods inventory 製品在庫
　inventory adjustment 在庫調整，棚卸し修正
　inventory reduction 在庫削減，在庫圧縮，在庫整理
　inventory shortage 棚卸し減耗，棚卸し減耗費，棚卸し差損費
　inventory turnover 棚卸し資産回転率，在庫回転率
　inventory valuation 棚卸し資産評価，棚卸し評価（＝inventory pricing）
　inventory value 在庫［在庫品］評価額，棚卸し資産評価額
　liquidate inventories 在庫を削減する，在庫を取り崩す
　rebuild inventories 在庫を積み増す
　right inventory 適正在庫
▸GM is reducing its vehicle *inventory* in an attempt to bolster profits. GMは現在，収益を改善するため，在庫を圧縮している．
▸*Inventories* are valued at the lower of average cost (which approximates computation on a first-in, first-out basis) or market (i.e., net realizable value or replacement cost). 棚卸し資産は，平均法による原価（先入れ先出し法に基づく原価とほぼ同額）または市場価格（実現可能価格または再調達価格）のいずれか低いほうの価額で評価されています．

inventory cost 在庫費用，棚卸し資産原価，棚卸し資産の取得原価（＝inventoriable cost）
▸*Inventory cost* is generally determined on a first-in, first-out basis. 棚卸し資産の原価は，原則として先入れ先出し法で算定されています．

inventory level 在庫水準
▸Higher *inventory levels* are associated with our sales growth. 在庫水準が高いのは，当社の販売増による影響です．

inventory management 在庫管理（＝inventory control）
▸Improved inventory management in 2008 led to increased inventory turnover. 2008年度は，在庫管理が改善して在庫回転率が高まりました．

inventory turn 棚卸し資産回転率（＝inventory turnover）
▸*Inventory turns* decreased slightly to 5.7 in 2008 from 5.8 in 2007. 棚卸し資産の回転率は，2007年度の5.8から2008年度は5.7にわずかながら減少しました．

invest 動 投資する，出資する，投下する，投入する，運用する
　invest in a joint venture 合弁会社に投資する
　invest in real estate 不動産に投資する
　invested amount 投資額
　invested assets 運用資産
　invested capital 投下資本，拠出資本，株主資本（＝contributed capital;⇒stockholders' equity）
　invested fund 投下資本，投資資金
▸We *invest* in the future by *investing* in education. 当社は，教育に投資することにより，将来に投資しています．

investee company 被投資会社（他社に20-50％の株式を所有されている会社）

investing activities 投資活動
▶This increase in net cash used for *investing activities* is due to an increase in the purchase of marketable securities. 投資活動に使用した純キャッシュのこの増加は，市場性ある有価証券の購入量増加によるものです。

investment 名 投資, 出資, 運用, 投資額, 投資物, 投資事業, 投資資産, 投資勘定, 資金投下, 証券, インベストメント（＝investing; ⇒**capital investment, direct investment, equity investment**)
  corporate investment 企業投資, 企業の設備投資, 民間設備投資
  current investment 短期投資
  early investment 早期投資
  fixed asset investment 固定資産投資
  fixed investment 固定資本投資, 設備投資
  foreign investment 外国[海外]からの投資, 外国資本の投資, 対内投資, 対外投資
  industrial investment 産業投資, 事業投資
  investment business 投資業務, 投資事業
  investment company 投資会社, 投資信託会社（＝investment firm, management company：一般から広く資金を集めて証券類に投資する投資信託業務を行う会社）
  investment credit 投資税額控除, 投資減税（＝investment tax credit）
  investment decision 投資判断, 投資の意思決定, 投資決定
  Investment Deposit and Interest Rate Control Law 出資法（出資の受入れ，預り金及び金利等の取締りに関する法律）
  investment fund rating company 投信評価会社
  investment gains or losses 投資利得または損失
  investment-grade securities 投資適格債
  investment in associated company 関連会社に対する投資
  investment income 投資利益, 投資収益, 投資所得, 投資収入
  investment information 投資情報
  investment money 投資資金, 投資金, 出資金
  investment opportunity 投資機会, 投資対象, 運用先
  investment performance 投資実績, 運用実績, 投資成績（＝investment results）
  investment risk 投資リスク
  investment target 投資対象, 投資目標
  investment tax credit 投資税額控除（＝investment credit; ⇒**amortize**）
  investment union 投資組合
  investments in securities 投資有価証券（＝investment securities）
  labor saving investment 省力化投資
  less investment in plant and equipment 設備投資の抑制
  new investment 新規投資
  portfolio investment 証券投資, 株式・債券投資, ポートフォリオ投資
  security investment 証券投資
▶Bush emphasized he would keep the dollar strong in order to attract foreign *investment* to the United States. ブッシュ大統領は，外国資本の対米投資を促すため強いドル政策の堅持を協調した。
▶In 2008 we made a $500 million *investment* in the company. 2008年度に，当社は同社に5億ドルの投資をしました。
▶The initial *investment* in equipment for the new facility will be ¥1.55 trillion. 新工場設備に対する初期投資額は，1兆5,500億円になる見込みだ。

investment bank 投資銀行（投資銀行の主な業務は，証券引受け（underwriting），新規株式公開（IPO）とM&A（企業合併・買収）の仲介）
▶U.S. *investment bank* Goldman Sachs Group Inc. will invest ¥41 billion in the reconstruction of ailing construction firm Fujita Corp. 米投資銀行のゴールドマン・サックス・グループが，経営不振のフジタ（総合建設会社）の再建に410億円投資する。

investment capital 投資資本（投資に充当する資金）
▶The funds gained from the sale of shares will permit the firm to undertake capital expenditures without calling on further *investment capital* from its parent company. 株式売却で調達した資金によって，同社は親会社に追加投資資本[資本投資]を求めることなく，設備投資ができる状況にあります。

investment costs 投資コスト
▶Huge *investment costs*, such as those for developing environment-friendly technology, have made it difficult for an automaker to survive competition on its own. 環境にやさしい技術の開発費など，巨額の投資コストが見込まれるため，自動車メーカー1社が独力で競争に生き残るのは難しくなっている。

investment fund 投資ファンド（機関投資家

などから資金を集めて，不良債権の売買や企業買収などを行う組織)，投資信託，投資資金
- *Investment funds* do not hesitate to dissolve a company and strip its assets after acquiring the management rights of the company. 投資ファンドは，会社の経営権を取得した後，会社を解散してその資産を売り払うこともいとわない。
- The *investment fund's* investors and investments have yet to be determined. この投資ファンドの出資者と資産の運用内容は，まだ不明だ。

investment in affiliated company
[concern] 関係会社投資，関連会社投資勘定
- The *investments in affiliated companies* (20% to 50% owned) are accounted for by the equity method. 20－50％所有の関連会社投資勘定は，持ち分法により会計処理されています。

investment in home building 住宅建設投資
- *Investment in home building* in the fourth quarter was slashed by 19.1 percent on an annualized basis. 第4四半期の住宅建設投資は，年率換算で19.1％減少した。

investment in plant and equipment 設備投資
- Beset by heavy debts combined with problems of their excessive *investment in plants and equipment*, Japanese corporations are facing stiff competition from Chinese and other Asian companies. 巨額の債務や過剰設備投資の問題に苦しむ日本企業は，中国などアジアの企業から厳しい競争を仕掛けられている。

investment portfolio 投資ポートフォリオ，投資資産，投資資本構成，投資の内容
- As of December 31, 2008, the *investment portfolio* was predominantly long-term-bonds and equity investments. 2008年12月31日現在，投資ポートフォリオは主に長期債券と株式投資です。

investment profitability 投資収益性
- We will adhere to our proactive management policies that place the utmost emphasis on *investment profitability*. 当社は，今後も投資収益性を重視した攻めの経営姿勢を貫く方針です。

investment ratio 出資比率
- These five companies are working on the *investment ratios* and formation of management of the new company. この5社は現在，新会社の出資比率や役員構成などの詰めの作業を進めている。

investment seminar 投資セミナー
- *Investment seminars* targeting women are becoming increasingly popular. 女性対象の投資セミナーの人気が高まっている。

investment trust 投資信託，投信 (一般投資家から資金を集め，集めた金を専門家が株や債券などに投資して，その運用益を投資家に還元する金融商品)
- Fund-of-funds do not invest capital directly in stocks and bonds, but reinvest it in other *investment trusts* as a way to minimize risks. ファンド・オブ・ファンズは，(投資家から集めた)資金を株式や債券に直接投資せず，リスクを最小限に抑える手段として他の複数の投資信託に再投資する。

investment trust fund 投資信託基金，投資信託
- Against the backdrop of the liberalization of the financial industry, pension funds and *investment trust funds* grew sharply. 金融自由化を背景に，年金基金や投資信託基金が急成長した。

investor 图 投資家，投資者，投資会社，出資者，出資企業，資本主，投資側，投資国，〈権利などの〉授与者，インベスター (⇒institutional investor, investment fund)
accounting for investors 投資家のための会計
bloc investor 大口投資家
debt investor 債券投資家，債券保有者
equity investor 株式投資家
fixed income investor 債券投資家，確定利付き証券への投資家
institutional investor 機関投資家 (＝institutional lender)
private investor 個人投資家，民間投資家
professional investor 機関投資家 (＝institutional investor, wholesale investor)
retail investor 小口投資家，個人投資家，最終投資家 (＝small investor)
- Our overseas *investors* account for about 24 percent, which would shrink to 18.6 percent after we raise capital. 当社の外国人株主[外国人投資家]は，約24％を占め，増資後は18.6％に減少します。
- The company has received about ¥780 billion in cash and debt waivers from shareholders and *investors* in two bailouts. 同社は，2度の金融支援で，株主と出資企業から約7,800億円の資金提供と債務免除を受けている。

investor [investors] relations 投資家向け広報，投資家向け広報活動，投資家向け情報公開，財務広報，証券広報，戦略的財務広報，対投資家関係，IR活動，インベスター・リレーションズ《略IR》

(⇒IR, roadshow)
　Investor Relations (IR) とは➡株主や投資家に対して投資判断に必要な情報を提供することがインベスター・リレーションズで，一般にIR (アイアール) と呼ばれている。各企業が実践しているIR活動のツールとしては，アニュアル・レポート (年次報告書) や事業報告書，ファクト・ブック，ニューズレターなどの出版物のほか，インフォメーション・ミーティング (証券アナリストやファンド・マネージャーなどに対して経営方針や経営理念，業務内容などを定期的に紹介する企業説明会)，決算説明会に加えて，個別訪問 (機関投資家や証券会社に出向いて直接会社の業務内容などを説明) などがある。会社や工場見学などをIR活動の一つにしているところもあり，またインターネットのホームページにも一般に会社概要や事業内容，商品情報，採用情報などを掲載しているところが多い。

▶The form 10-K annual report for 2008, as filed with the U.S. SEC, is available without charge upon request to *Investor Relations* of the Corporation. 米証券取引委員会 (SEC) に提出した様式10-Kに基づく2008年度年次報告書は，当社のIR担当部署へご請求いただければ無料で提供しています。

invisible 形 目に見えない，無形の，隠れた，貿易外の，サービス産業の
　current invisible operations 経常的貿易外取引
　induced invisible trade balance 貿易付帯収支
　invisible account 貿易外収支 (=balance of [on] invisible trade)
　invisible assets 無形資産
　invisible balance 貿易外収支 (=invisible trade balance)
　invisible earnings 貿易外収益
　invisible exports and imports 貿易外輸出入，無形の輸出入，貿易外収支
　invisible industry 観光産業
　invisible trade 貿易外取引，目に見えない貿易，無形の貿易，サービス貿易
　the invisible hand of the market 市場の目に見えない手
　the service part of the invisible account 貿易外収支サービス部門

invisibles 名 貿易外収支，無形貿易収支

invoice 名 送り状，仕入書，請求書，積み荷明細書，インボイス
　commercial invoice 商業送り状，商業インボイス (輸出者が輸入者にあてて作成する積み荷の明細書で，請求書と納品書の性格を持つ。輸出入通関手続きの際，申告書類の一部として税関に提出される)
　consignment invoice 委託販売用送り状，委託販売送り状
　consular invoice 領事送り状，コンシュラー・インボイス
　customer invoice 顧客[得意先]への請求書
　customs invoice 税関送り状 (輸出者が輸入地の税関用に作成し，税関が輸入貨物に対する課税価格を決定する際の資料となる)
　gross invoice price 総送り状価格
　invoice amount 送り状価格，請求金額
　invoice back 仕切り戻し
　invoice cost 送り状価格[価額]，取得原価
　invoice discounting 債権の売却
　invoice number 送り状番号
　invoice price 送り状価格，仕切り状価格，仕切り価格，インボイス価格，請求書価格直接原価，本体価格，先物契約などの決済価格
　invoice quantity 送り状数量
　invoice value 送り状金額，送り状価格[価額]
　invoice weight 送り状重量
　last invoice cost method 最終取得原価法
　net invoice price 正味送り状価格，正味請求書価格
　official invoice 公用送り状 (税関送り状と領事送り状を指し，輸入通関のとき課税価格の決定やダンピング防止などのために使用される)
　paid invoice 支払済み請求書
　proforma [pro forma] invoice 見積り送り状，仮送り状，試算用送り状
　purchase invoice 仕入請求書
　sales invoice 売買用送り状，売買送り状 (積み荷の明細書で，計算書・請求書の性格をもつ。一般に「送り状 (commercial invoice)」というときは，この売買送り状を指す)
　sample invoice 見本用送り状
　shipping invoice 船積みインボイス (契約商品の船積み後に輸出者が作成する商業送り状)

▶We drew a draft for the *invoice* amount. 送り状金額に対して，当社は手形を振り出した。

IOE 国際経営者団体連盟 (International Organization of Employersの略)

IOS 国際標準化機構 (International Organization for Standardizationの略)

IOSCO [íosco] 証券監督者国際機構，証券規制監督者国際機構，イオスコ (International Organization of Securities Commissionsの略。世界100か国の証券監督当局や証券取引所が加盟)

IP インターネットの通信規約 (internet protocolの略)

corporate IP telephone market 企業向けIP電話市場
IP address IPアドレス
IP connection service IP接続サービス
IP phone network IP通信網
IP phone user IP電話ユーザー
IPCC 気候変動に関する政府間パネル（International Panel on Climate Changeの略）
IPO 株式公開，新規株式公開，新規株式公募，公開公募，新規公募，上場（initial public offeringの略．会社が一般投資家に株式を初めて売り出すこと．⇒initial public offering）
IPO price 公開価格，公募価格
IPO shares 新規公開株
▸An increasing number of companies want to undertake *IPOs* while stock markets remain brisk. 株式市場が活況のうちに上場したい［株式を新規公開したい］，という企業が増えている．
IPP 独立系発電事業者，独立発電事業者（independent power producerの略）
iPS cell iPS細胞（⇒induced pluripotent stem cell）
▸A Kyoto University research team's *iPS cells* have the potential to develop into almost any kind of cell, including organ and tissue cells, from human skin cells. 京大研究チームが作製したiPS細胞は，人間の皮膚の細胞から様々な臓器や組織の細胞などあらゆる細胞に変化する可能性を持っている．
IR 情報検索（information retrievalの略）
IR 投資家向け広報，投資家向け広報活動，財務広報，インベスター・リレーションズ（investor relationsの略．「IR」は，有価証券報告書や決算短信のほかに，決算説明会，工場見学などのIR活動を含めて，株主や投資家に対して投資判断に必要な情報を提供すること．⇒investor relations, roadshow）
IIRF 国際IR連盟（International Investor Relations Federationの略）
IR activities IR活動
IR campaign IRキャンペーン，IR活動，投資家説明会
IR meeting 投資家説明会，IR説明会，会社説明会，IRミーティング（＝IR session）
IR representative IR担当者
JIRA 日本IR協議会（Japan Investor Relations Associationの略）
NIRI 全米IR協会，IR全米協会（National Investor Relations Instituteの略）
irrecoverable 形 回収不能の，回復不能の，取り返せない，取戻し不能の

irredeemable 形 買戻しできない，償還されない，名 無償還公債，無償還社債
irregular 形 不規則な，難のある，傷物の
irregularity 名 不正行為，不法行為，乱脈経営，乱脈融資，不祥事，不品行，不規則性，変則，誤記（⇒accounting irregularities）
errors and irregularities 誤謬や不正
irregularities such as influence-wielding, bid-rigging and subcontracting entire public works contracts 口利きや談合，公共事業の丸投げなどの不正行為
trading irregularities 不正取引
▸Accounting *irregularities* were found at Nikko Cordial. 日興コーディアル証券で，不正会計問題が発覚した．
IRS 米内国歳庁（Internal Revenue Serviceの略）
▸The *Internal Revenue Service* has completed its field audit of the federal income tax returns of 2006 and 2007. 米内国歳庁（IRS）が，2006年度と2007年度の連邦法人税申告についての現地監査を終了しました．
ISBN 国際標準図書番号（International Standard Book Numberの略）
ISM 全米供給管理協会（⇒Institute for Supply Management）
▸The *ISM's* index of service sector activity dropped below 50, a level that indicates contraction. 全米供給管理協会（ISM）のサービス業景況感指数は，50を割り込んで不況［景気後退期］を示す水準となった．
ISO 国際標準化機構（正式名称はInternational Organization for Standardizationで，International Standards Organizationともいう）
ISO 9000 品質管理と品質保証に関するISOの国際規格
ISO 14000 環境管理システムと環境監査に関するISOの国際規格
ISO 14001 環境管理に関するISOの国際規格（ゴミ分別や節電，コピー用紙の使用枚数など，企業などが環境への負荷を減らす数値目標を設けて計画的に取り組んでいることを証明して認証を得る）
ISO 15408 情報セキュリティに関するISOの国際規格
ISO certification ISOの認定
▸Fujiya was found to have failed to meet the *ISO 9001* quality management standard at three factories. 不二家は，3工場でISOの品質管理基準「ISO 9001」を満たしていないことが判明した．

▶*ISO* 9001 is the highest quality certification of the International Organization for Standardization. ISO 9001は，国際標準化機構（ISO）の最高の品質基準である。
▶Our five manufacturing facilities are now *ISO*-certified. 当社の5か所の製造施設は現在，ISOの認定を受けています。

ISS 国際宇宙ステーション（international space stationの略）

ISSN 国際標準逐次刊行物番号（international standard serial numberの略）

issuance 名 発行，支給，配給，刊行，入札（⇒ new share issuance）
　CP issuance CP発行
　debt issuance cost 社債発行費，債券発行費
　deficit issuance 赤字国債
　issuance of capital [stock] 株式の発行
　issuance of new shares 新株発行，増資（＝ new share issuance, new share issue）
　issuance volume 発行額
　new bond issuance 起債
　quarterly issuance 四半期入札
　size of the issuance 発行規模
▶During 2008, conversions of convertible debentures resulted in the *issuance* of 968 shares of the Corporation's capital stock. 2008年度は，転換社債の転換により，968株の当社株式を発行しました。
　issuance of preferred shares 優先株式の発行
▶During the first nine months of 2008, the Corporation raised $500 million by the *issuance of preferred shares*. 2008年1-9月期に，当社は優先株式を発行して5億ドルを調達しました。

issue 動〈証券などを〉発行する，売り出す，起債する，〈手形を〉振り出す，配当を行う，発表する，公表する（⇒government bond）
　issued and outstanding 外部発行済み，発行済み，発行済み株式
　issued capital 発行済み資本，発行済み株式（＝ issued share capital）
　issued share capital 発行済み株式資本，発行済み株式資本金（＝issued capital）
▶The firm *issued* common stocks to raise capital. 同社は，資金調達のため普通株式を発行した。

issue 名 証券，株，銘柄，発行，発行債，発行部数，交付，〈手形の〉振出し，問題，問題点，争点，論点（⇒share issue limit）
　capital issue 新株発行，株式発行，資本発行，増資
　capitalization issue 資本金組入れ発行，資本組入れ株式発行
　free issue 無償交付
　issue at market price 時価発行
　issue at par 額面発行，平価発行
　issue capital 発行済み株式資本金
　issue price 発行価格
　issue to stockholders 株主割当て
　share and debenture issue expense 株式・社債発行費
　stock issue cost 新株発行費（＝stock issue expense）
▶The company's shares were included in the 225-*issue* Nikkei Stock Average. 同社の株式は，日経平均株価（225種）に組み入れられた。
▶The new *issues* of medium and long-term corporate bonds are necessary for investment in plant and equipment. 企業の設備投資には，中長期社債の新規発行が必要だ。

issued shares 発行済み株式，発行済み株式数，発行株式数（＝issued stocks: 会社の授権株式（会社が発行できる株式の上限数）のうち，すでに発行された株式の総数）
▶Market capitalization is calculated by multiplying the number of a company's *issued shares* by their market price. 株式の時価総額は，企業の発行済み株式数に株式の時価を掛けて算出される。

issuer 名 発行人，〈手形などの〉振出人

IT 情報技術（information technologyの略）
　IT bubble ITバブル，IT投資バブル，ネット株バブル（＝the bubble in IT investments）
　IT business ITビジネス（＝information technology business）
　IT copyright IT著作権
　IT economy IT経済
　IT governance ITガバナンス（企業のITパワー，IT全般の統治能力のこと）
　IT investment IT投資（＝information-technology investment, investment in IT）
　IT issues IT関連銘柄
　IT management IT経営，ITマネジメント
　IT marketing ITマーケティング（＝e-marketing, Internet marketing）
　IT recession IT不況
　IT-related plant and equipment IT関連設備
　IT revolution 情報技術革命，IT革命
　IT strategy IT戦略
▶Microsoft Corp. has used a stock option program to attract talented *IT* professionals. マイクロソフトは，有能なIT（情報技術）専門家を確保す

るためにストック・オプション制度を使っている。

item 名 項目, 品目, 種目, 細目, 事項, 商品, 用品, 品物, アイテム
  abnormal item 異常項目
  adjustment item 修正項目, 調整項目
  balance sheet item 貸借対照表項目
  base item 基本項目
  basic item 定番商品, ベーシック商品
  big item 目玉商品
  big-ticket item 高額商品, 高価な商品
  brand-named item 銘柄品, メーカー品
  corporate items 本社事項
  fungible items 汎用品
  infrequent item 突発事項
  item control 単品管理
  line item 勘定科目
  must-have item どうしても欲しい商品
  operating item 営業項目, 営業品目
  popular item 売れ筋商品, 売れ筋, 人気商品 (=hot item)
  prior period item 前期修正項目
  sensitive item 輸入要注意品目
  specified food products 指定食品
  unusual item 特別損益項目
  winter item 冬物商品

▸Among *items* shipping briskly were electronic devices, telecommunications equipment, liquid crystal display TVs and automobiles. 輸出が好調だった品目としては, 電子装置, 通信機器, 液晶テレビや自動車などがある。

▸Labeling is mandatory for only a small fraction of food products which have been defined as specified food *items*. 表示義務の対象は, 指定食品と定められたごく一部の食品だけだ。

itemize 動 個別項目化する
itemized deductions 名 個別控除, 所得控除項目
items of business 議案, 議事

▸The Proxy Statement describes the *items of business* to be voted on at the Annual Meeting. 議決権代理行使勧誘状には, 定時株主総会で票決される議案についての説明がなされている。

ITER 国際熱核融合実験炉 (International Thermonuclear Experimental Reactorの略)

▸The *ITER* project is aimed at creating "mini sun" on the Earth by creating nuclear fusion. 国際熱核融合実験炉(ITER)は, 核融合を実現して地上に「ミニ太陽」を作るのが目的だ。

ITU 国際電気通信連合 (International Telecommunication Unionの略)

J / j

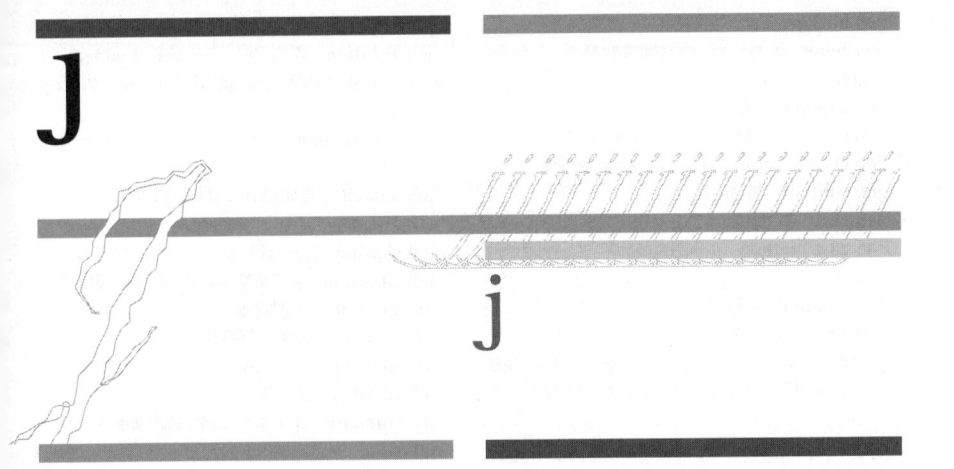

J-curve 名 Jカーブ（為替レートの変動の効果を示すグラフの形）

January-to-March quarter 1-3月期, 12月期決算企業の第1四半期, 3月期決算企業の第4四半期
▸The percentage of credit card payments that were past due date fell in the *January-to-March quarter*. クレジット・カードの支払い遅延率[期限を過ぎたクレジット・カードの返済遅延率]は、1-3月期に急減した。

Japan Aerospace Exploration Agency 宇宙航空研究開発機構

Japan Association of Corporate Executives 経済同友会

Japan Bank for International Cooperation 国際協力銀行（海外経済協力基金(OECF)と日本輸出入銀行が合併して、1999年10月から業務を開始）

Japan Business Federation 日本経済団体連合会, 日本経団連《略 JBF》

Japan Chamber of Commerce and Industry 日本商工会議所

Japan Consumers' Association 日本消費者協会

Japan External Trade Organization 日本貿易振興機構（ジェトロ）

Japan Federation of Bar Associations 日本弁護士連合会

Japan Independent Stores Association 日本商店連盟, 日商連

Japan money ジャパン・マネー（日本企業の海外投資資金・資本）

Japan-U.S. Business Conference 日米財界人会議

Japanese Agricultural Standards 日本農林規格《略 JAS》
▸Wholesalers are only allowed to put organic *Japanese Agricultural Standards* marks on fruit and vegetables that are grown without using chemical fertilizers and agricultural chemicals for a certain period of time. 卸売業者は、化学肥料や農薬を一定期間使わないで栽培した果物や野菜にだけ有機JAS（日本農林規格）マークを付けることができる。

Japanese Welfare Pension Insurance Law 厚生年金保険法

Jasdaq 名 ジャスダック（Japan Securities Dealer's Association Quotationの略。日本の新興企業向け株式店頭市場。2004年12月13日、店頭市場から証券取引所(Jasdaq Securities Exchange)に移行して取引を開始）

jeopardy 名 危険

JIT かんばん方式, ジット （⇒just-in-time)

JLL financing 日本型レバレッジド・リース(JLL)方式による資金調達

job 名 職, 職場, 職務, 任務, 業務, 雇用, 就職口, 働き口, 仕事, ジョブ
 completed job method of accounting 工事完成基準 （=completed job method）
 creation of job opportunities 雇用機会の創出
 job action 順法闘争, スローダウン(slowdown: 故意の減産・操業短縮, のろのろ戦術, 怠業), 組織的抗議行動 （=industrial action）
 job applicant 求職者
 job application 求職
 job assignment 職務割当て

job background 職務経歴
job bank 人材銀行, 国営職業斡旋所 (＝job-center)
job category 職務
job change 転職 (＝job hopping)
job classification 職務分類, 職階, 職階制
job content 職務内容
job cost 個別原価
job cost method 工事別原価計算, 工事別原価計算法
job creation 雇用創出
job depth 職務深度
job description 職務記述書, 職務分掌規定, 職務内容説明書（職位の権限と責任事項を記載したもの）
job design 職務設計
job discrimination 仕事上の差別
job diversification 職種の多様化
job enlargement 職務拡大
job enrichment 職務充実, 職務充実化
job entry ジョブ入力
job evaluation 職務評価, 職務査定
job experience 職務経験
job festival [fair] 大学構内での就職説明会
job fulfillment 仕事の充実
job hopping 転職 (＝job change)
job hunter 求職者
job hunting 求職, 求職活動, 就職活動, 仕事探し (＝job seeking)
job improvement 職務改善
job insecurity 雇用不安
job interview 就職面接, 求職面接
job knowledge 職務知識
job leaver 離職者
job loser 失職者, 失業者
job loss 失職, 失業
job lot 規格はずれ品, 不揃い商品, 大口商品, 端株, 作業ロット, 小口取引, ロット
job management ジョブ管理
job-oriented terminal 特定業務用端末装置
job performance 職務遂行, 職務能力, 仕事ぶり
job placement 就職斡旋, 就職紹介 (job introduction), 労働者派遣
job processing ジョブ処理
job rate 職務給
job rating 職務評価
job redesign 職務再設計
job-related accommodation 社宅
job request system ジョブ・リクエスト制度（社内で好きな仕事につく制度）

job requirement 職務資格
job rotation 職務配置, 職務転換, 配置転換, 計画的異動, 職務歴任制, 職場輪番制, ジョブ・ローテーション
job satisfaction 職務満足, 仕事の満足感, 仕事のやりがい
job search 求職活動, 求職, 職探し (＝job hunting)
job sharing 仕事分担, ジョブ・シェアリング
job situation 雇用情勢, 雇用状況, 雇用環境
job specialty 専門職種
job specifications 職務明細書
job splitting 作業分割
job stability 雇用安定
job standard 作業標準, 課業, 職務基準
job step ジョブの構成単位, ジョブ・ステップ
job study 作業研究, 職務研究
job tax credit 雇用促進税額控除
job title 職階
job transfer 転勤
job vacancy 求人
job work 請負仕事, 注文仕事
key job 基準職務
new jobs 新規雇用
provide jobs 雇用を創出する
skilled job 熟練労働, 熟練度の高い職
specific job order 特定製造指図書
unskilled job 単純労働, 熟練度の低い職
wage on job classification 職階給, 職階制賃金, 資格給
wage on job evaluation 職能給 (＝wage based on job evaluation)
▶Struggling Sanyo Electric Co. will speed up *job cuts*. 経営再建中の三洋電機が, 人員削減を加速する。

job cut 人員削減
▶The two banks expect the integration to entail about 4,000 *job cuts*. 両行は, この統合により約4,000人の人員削減を見込んでいる。

job development 雇用促進, 職務促進, 職業開発
Job Development Act 雇用促進法
job development credit 雇用促進税額控除, 職業開発税額控除 (＝targeted job tax credit)

job hopper 転職者
▶The number of *job hoppers* is increasing as many students are unable to learn the necessary skills needed for the workplace. 学生の多くが職場で必要な技能を学べないので, 転職者の数が増えている。

job increase 雇用の増加, 雇用の伸び (=job gains, job growth)
▸Economic recoveries no longer promise *job increases*. 景気回復は，もはや雇用の増加[雇用回復]に結びつかなくなっている。

job market 雇用市場, 労働市場, 求人市場, 雇用情勢, 雇用
▸The robust economy of the United States saw the 41st consecutive monthly expansion of its *job market* helped by the creation of 7.2 million jobs. 好調な米経済は，720万人の雇用創出に支えられて41か月連続，雇用が拡大した。

job offer 求人
　job offers 求人数, 有効求人数
　job offers to applicants ratio 有効求人倍率 (=job-offer to job-seeker ratio)
▸The ratio of *job offers* to job seekers stood at 0.48, or 48 offers for every 100 job seekers. 有効求人倍率は0.48倍で，求職者100人に対して有効求人数は48人の割合になっている。

job opening 欠員, 求人, 求職
　job openings 求人数, 新規雇用, 新規雇用数
　job openings per job seeker 有効求人倍率, 求人倍率 (=job offers to job seekers)
▸Reducing the number of hours of overtime may not only help those workers retain their jobs, but also increase *job openings*. 残業時間数の削減は，雇用の維持だけでなく，新規の雇用を増やす可能性がある。

job opportunity 雇用機会, 就労機会, 就業機会, 就業のチャンス, 求人 (=employment opportunity)
▸To expand *job opportunities*, it is becoming critically important to create policies that ensure long-term employment for part-time and contract workers. 雇用機会を拡大するには，パートや契約社員の長期雇用を可能にする施策がきわめて重要になっている。

job order 製造指図書, 指図書, 作業票
　job order costing 個別原価計算
　job order production 個別生産, 個別受注生産, 注文生産

job referral 職業紹介
▸The current support system for jobseekers from training to *job referrals* and to employment is not well designed. 訓練から職業紹介と就職にいたるまで就職困難者を支援するための現在の体制は，十分に整備されていない。

job security 雇用確保, 雇用の安定, 職務保障, 職の安全
▸The labor union has attached the highest priority to maintaining *job security* for its member workers. 組合側は，組合員の雇用安定維持を第一に考えてきた。

job seeker 求職者, 就職困難者 (=job hunter; ⇒job offer, job referral)
▸Many young people were unable to find the jobs they preferred during the glacial period of *job seekers*. 若者の多くは，就職氷河期には，希望する就職先が見つからなかった。

job training 職業訓練
　job training activities 職業訓練活動
　Job Training Partnership Act of 1982 米国の1982年職業訓練協力法
　job training program 職業訓練プログラム
　off-the-job training 職場外訓練, 職場外教育訓練
　on-the-job training 職場内訓練, 職場内教育訓練《略 OJT》
▸Unemployment benefits are paid to job seekers who are receiving *job training*. 職業訓練を受けている求職者に対して，失業手当が支給される。
▸We have actively supported *job-training* efforts for disadvantaged and handicapped persons for more than 20 years. 当社は，過去20年以上にわたって，経済的に恵まれない人たちや身体障害者のための職業訓練制度を積極的に支援してきました。

job worries 雇用不安
▸With the unemployment rate having fallen to 4.7 percent in March, *job worries* have alleviated. 3月の完全失業率が4.7％に減少して，雇用不安が軽減した。

jobcentre 名 公共職業紹介所
jobless 形 失業中の, 無職の, 失業者の, 仕事のない
　jobless claims 失業保険新規受給申請者数, 失業保険新規申請件数
　jobless figures 失業者数, 雇用統計
　jobless insurance 失業保険
　jobless recovery 雇用なき経済回復, 雇用の回復なき景気回復, ジョブレス・リカバリー

jobless rate 失業率, 完全失業率 (=unemployment rate)
▸The seasonally adjusted *jobless rate* increased by 0.3 percentage point in June to a record 4.9 percent. 6月の完全失業率（季節調整値）は，前月比0.3％[0.3ポイント]増の4.9％で，過去最高となった。

joblessness 名 失業, 失業率, 完全失業率 (=unemployment)

▶Anxiety over *joblessness* remains. 雇用不安は，解消されていない。

jobseeker 名 求職者
- **jobseeker's Agreement** 求職者協定，求職者合意制度
- **jobseeker's allowance** 求職者給付

join a company 入社する
▶Japanese graduates can't contribute to their companies unless they receive technical training after *joining a company*. 日本の大卒者は，入社後に技術研修を受けないと会社の使い物にならない。

join forces [hands] 連携する，提携する，力を合わせる，協力する，手を組む，手を結ぶ，勢力を結集する，統一会派を組む
▶The two companies agreed to *join forces* in developing next generation chip technology. 両社は，次世代半導体チップ技術の共同開発を進めることで合意した。

join the board 取締役会に加わる，取締役に就任する，取締役に選任される
▶Four new directors *joined the board* at last year's annual meeting. 昨年度の定時株主総会で，新取締役4名が取締役会に加わりました［新たに4名が取締役に選任されました］。

joint 形 共同の，合同の，連帯の，連合の，合弁の，共有の，共通の，ジョイント
- **joint adventure** 共同企業体，合弁事業
- **joint and several guarantee** 連帯保証，連帯債務，共同債務
- **joint and several liability** 連帯責任，連帯債務（＝joint and separate liability）
- **joint business** 共同事業
- **joint capacity cost** 共通固定費
- **joint capital** 合併資本，共同資本
- **joint company** 共同運営会社，合弁会社（＝joint concern）
- **joint consultation system** 労使協議制
- **joint delivery** 共同配送
- **joint effort** 提携関係
- **joint financing** 協調融資（＝joint finance）
- **joint fixed cost** 共通固定費
- **joint holding company [firm]** 共同持ち株会社
- **joint implementation** 共同実施
- **joint intervention** 協調介入，協調市場介入（＝coordinated intervention, joint market intervention）
- **joint investment** 共同投資，合弁
- **joint leadership** 共同指導，ジョイント・リーダーシップ
- **joint liability** 共同債務，連帯責任
- **joint management association** 管理組合
- **joint market intervention** 協調介入，協調市場介入
- **joint product** 連産品，結合生産物（＝co-product: 同一の工程で同一の原料から同時に生産される製品）
- **joint research** 共同研究
- **joint shareholder** 共同株主
- **joint signature** 連署
- **joint sponsorship** 共同主催，共催
- **joint stock** 共同資本，共同出資，株式組織
- **joint stock association** 株式社団，株式会社
- **joint strike** 統一スト
- **joint subsidiary** 共同子会社
- **joint undertaking** 共同事業

joint development 共同開発
▶Aeon's proposal for business tie-up with Lawson includes the *joint development* of private brand products. イオンのローソンとの業務提携案には，自主開発（プライベート・ブランド）商品の共同開発が含まれている。

joint holding company 共同持ち株会社
（＝joint holding firm）
▶Rakuten has proposed integrating the firms' management under a *joint holding company*. 楽天は，共同持ち株会社の設立による［共同持ち株会社方式での］両社の経営統合を提案した。
▶Supermarket chain operator Ito-Yokado Co. and two group companies established a *joint holding company* on Sept. 1, 2005 through share swaps. 大手スーパーのイトーヨーカ堂とグループ企業2社が，株式交換により2005年9月1日に共同持ち株会社を設立した。

joint product development 製品［商品］の共同開発
▶Isetan and Tokyu have reached a basic partnership agreement, including *joint product development* and the integration of sales information systems. 伊勢丹と東急百貨店が，商品の共同開発や販売情報システムの統合などを含めて，提携の基本合意に達した。

joint production 共同生産
▶Toyota showed GM its advanced production system through *joint production*. トヨタは，共同生産を通じてGMにトヨタの優れた生産システムを証明した。

joint stock company 株式会社(joint stock corporation, stock company), 公開会社, 上場会社(publicly limited company)

▶These annual general meetings are the key decision-making forums for *joint-stock companies*. これらの年次株主総会は，株式会社にとって最も重要な意思決定の場である。

joint venture 合弁会社，合弁事業，合弁，共同企業，共同企業体，共同事業，共同事業体，共同出資会社，共同出資事業，ジョイント・ベンチャー《略 JV》(= corporate joint venture, joint business, joint venture company)

fifty-fifty joint venture 折半出資の合弁会社 (= 50-50 joint venture, 50% joint venture)

joint venture plant 合弁工場

joint venture statement 共同出資事業計算書

joint venture tender 合弁株式公開買付け (2社以上の会社が，資本を持ち寄って他社を乗っ取ること)

▶All Nippon Airways Co. is to form a *joint venture* with InterContinental Hotels Group PLC. 全日本空輸が，インターコンチネンタル・ホテルズ・グループ (世界最大手の英国系ホテル・チェーン)と共同出資会社を設立する。

▶Softbank and News Corp. will set up a fifty-fifty *joint venture*. ソフトバンクとニューズ・コーポレーション (米メディア・娯楽大手)が，折半出資の会社を新設する。

▶Sony Corp. and Sharp Corp. will set up a *joint venture* to produce and sell liquid crystal displays for TVs. ソニーとシャープは，液晶テレビ用パネルを共同で生産・販売する合弁会社を設立する。

joint venture company 合弁会社

▶The firm will have an initial ownership of forty percent of the voting shares of the *joint venture company*. 同社の当初の出資比率は，合弁会社の議決権付き株式の40％とする方針だ。

joint venture plant 合弁工場

▶Toyota plans to build a *joint venture plant* in Guangzhou, China. トヨタは，中国の広州に合弁工場の建設を計画している。

jointly develop 共同開発する

▶Sumitomo Mitsui Banking Corp. has *jointly developed* with American International Group Inc. a foreign bond investment product targeting retired baby boomers. 三井住友銀行が，団塊の世代の定年退職者をターゲットにした外債の金融商品を，米保険最大手のAIGグループと共同開発した。

jointly own 共同所有する，共同出資する (= equally own)

▶GM and Toyota are each set to invest tens of billions of yen in a plant they *jointly own* in California. GMとトヨタはそれぞれ，両社が共同出資する米カリフォルニア州の工場に数百億円を(追加)投資する方針だ。

jointly set up a new company 共同出資で新会社を設立する

▶The two companies *jointly set up a new company*. 両社は，共同出資で新会社を設立した。

journal 图 専門誌，雑誌，新聞，会報，機関誌，定期刊行物，日誌，日記，日録，仕訳帳，議事録，国会議事録，ジャーナル

financial journal 金融紙

journal entry 仕訳

journal slip 仕訳伝票

medical journal 医学雑誌，医学誌，医学専門誌

sales journal 売上仕訳帳

scientific journal 科学雑誌，科学誌，科学専門誌

transaction journal 取引記録

judgment [judgement] 图 判断，判断力，見識，分別，意見，見解，判決，裁決，審判

accounting judgment 会計上の判断

fine judgment 難しい判断

judgment creditor 判決による債権者，判決債権者

judgment debtor 判決による債務者，判決債務者

management judgment 経営者の判断

matter of judgment 判断事項

professional judgment 職業上の判断

rating judgment 格付け判断

seasoned judgment 適切な判断

▶Estimates included in the financial statements were based on *judgments* of qualified personnel. 財務書類に記載した見積り額は，有資格者の判断に基づいています。

July-September quarter 7-9月期，12月期決算企業の第3四半期

▶The security firm expects to book about ¥73 billion in losses related to its residential mortgage-backed securities business in the *July-September quarter*. 同証券会社は，7-9月期に住宅融資証券事業の関連損失として730億円を計上する見通しだ。

juncture 图 事態，危急の事態，時期，重大時期，時点，危機

▶The central bank's quantitative easing policy is also at a critical sink-or-swim *juncture*. 日銀の量的緩和策も，今は剣が峰に立たされている。

junior 形 下級の，下位の，後順位の，劣後の，小規模の，ジュニア (⇒senior)

Junior Chamber of Commerce 青年会議所《略 JCC》

junior claim 劣後請求権

junior common stock 劣後普通株式
junior creditor 下位債権者, 後順位債権者, 劣後債権者
junior debt 劣後債務
junior department store 小規模デパート, ジュニア・デパート
junior partner 少数株主
junior securities 下位証券, 劣後債券
junior security interest 後順位担保権, 劣後担保権

junk 名 投資不適格, ジャンク債, ジャンク
　junk bond [issue] ジャンク債, くず債券, 格付けの低い債券, 高利回り債
　junk food 高カロリー・低栄養価のスナック食品, ジャンク・フード
　junk issuer ジャンク債発行体
　junk mail ジャンク・メール（インターネット経由などで送られてくる商品の宣伝など, 不要なEメール）
　junk shop 古物商
　junk status [territory] 投資不適格のレベル, 投機的レベル
▸Standard & Poor's cut its ratings on General Motors Corp. deeper into *junk* status. 米格付け会社のスタンダード・アンド・プアーズは, ゼネラル・モーターズ（GM）の格付け（長期債務格付け）を, 投資不適格のレベルに（投資不適格レベルのダブルBからダブルBマイナスに）さらに1段階引き下げた。

junk territory 投資不適格レベル（＝junk status）
▸Two influential rating firms lowered Ford Motor Co.'s credit ratings a notch deeper into *junk territory*. 大手［有力な］格付け機関2社が, 米フォードの信用格付けを「投資不適格レベル」にさらに1段階引き下げた。

jurisdiction 名 裁判管轄, 裁判管轄権, 裁判権, 管轄権, 管轄区域, 法域権限, 司法権, 司法行政, 司法権, 行政権や徴税権などを行使できる国家や地方自治体
　competent jurisdiction 正当な管轄権
　court of competent jurisdiction 正当な管轄権のある裁判所, 管轄裁判所
　exclusive jurisdiction 専属的裁判管轄, 専属管轄
　nonexclusive jurisdiction 非専属的裁判管轄権
　personal jurisdiction 対人管轄権
　subject matter jurisdiction 事物管轄権
▸Each party hereby agrees that the Tokyo District Court shall have exclusive *jurisdiction* for the first instance over any lawsuit in connection with this agreement. 本契約に関する訴訟はすべて東京地方裁判所を第一審の専属管轄とすることに, 各当事者は本契約により同意する。

just-in-time かんばん［カンバン］方式, ジャストインタイム, ジット《略 JIT》（＝JIT, JIT system, just-in-time system, "Kanban" system: トヨタ自動車の生産管理方式で, 部品の在庫ゼロ状態をめざして, 必要なときに必要な量だけ部品を納入させる方式）
　just-in-time employee 契約社員, かんばん方式社員
　just-in-time inventory management ジャストインタイムの在庫管理方式, かんばん方式
　just-in-time marketing ジャストインタイム・マーケティング
　just-in-time physical distribution ジャストインタイム物流
　just-in-time production system ジャストインタイムの生産方式, かんばん方式
　just-in-time system かんばん方式, ジャストインタイム方式, ジャストインタイム・システム（＝just-in-time method）
▸Car manufacturers are indicating they may emulate Toyota's *just-in-time* system. 自動車メーカー各社は, 必要なときに必要な量だけつくるトヨタの「かんばん方式」を見習う姿勢を強めている。

JV 共同事業体, 共同企業体, ジョイント・ベンチャー（⇒joint venture）

K k

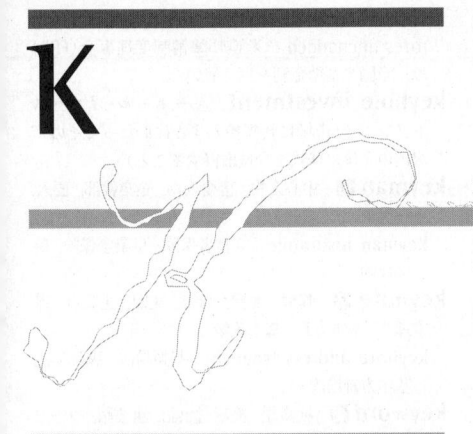

kangaroo bonds カンガルー債 (米国で発行される豪ドル建て債券)
kangaroo system トラックと鉄道による複合一貫輸送, カンガルー方式
KB キロバイト (=K, Kbyte: kilo-byteの略。1キロバイト=1024バイト)
KBM 知識ベース・マシーン (knowledge-based machineの略)
KDD データベースによる知識発見 (=data mining: knowledge discovery in databaseの略)
KE 知識エンジニア, ナレッジ・エンジニア (knowledge engineerの略)
keel 名 入港, 停泊
keen 形 〈競争が〉激しい, 〈価格が〉他に負けない
keep 動 維持する, 保持する, 据え置く, 続ける, 保存する, 保管する, 管理する, 経営する, 在庫として持つ, 常備する, 書き記す, 記入する, 〈規則などを〉守る
  keep hold of market share シェア[市場シェア]を維持する
  keep short rates on hold 短期金利を据え置く, 短期金利を低水準で維持する
  keep the book 帳簿に記入する, 帳簿をつける
  keep the company alive 会社を存続させる, 生き残りをかける
  keep the Federal funds rate unchanged フェデラル・ファンド金利を据え置く
  ▶Discount rate was *kept* at 1.25 percent. 公定歩合は, 1.25%に据え置かれた。
keep-harmless clause 損失補填規定 (=indemnity clause)
keep up with …について行く, …に遅れないようにする, …に追いつく, …に対応する, …に適応する, …と歩調を合わせる, …に屈しない
  ▶The current system of national government employees and its operation have not *kept up with* the changing times. 現在の国家公務員制度とその運用は, 時代の変化に対応しきれなくなっている。
Keogh 名 自営業者退職年金制度, 個人年金積立奨励制度, キオ・プラン[ケオ・プラン] (=individual retirement account, qualified pension plan, Keogh plan)
  Keogh account キオ口座
  Keogh plan キオ・プラン
kernel 名 カーネル (パソコン用基本ソフト(OS)の中核となるプログラム)
key 形 重要な, 主要な, 枢要な, 最大の, 基幹の, 中心の, 中核の, 基軸の, キー
  key account 主要得意先, 主要顧客, 上得意先
  key areas 中核業務, 主要部門, 主要セクター
  key buying influence 主要な購買影響者《略 KBI》
  key currency 基軸通貨, 国際通貨, キー・カレンシー
  key determinant 最大の要因, 主要要因
  key economic data 主要景気指標 (=key economic indicators, key economic series)
  key hardware 主要設備
  key industry 基幹産業, 主要産業
  key item 主要品目, 主要商品
  key job 基準職務
  key money 基軸通貨(key currency), 保証金, 手付け金, 礼金, 権利金
  key Nikkei Index 日経平均株価(225種)
  key official [officer] 幹部

key resistance 主要な抵抗線
key technology 基盤技術
key tenant 核テナント, 核店舗, キー・テナント
key-capture software キーキャプチャー・ソフト（打ったキーを自動的に記録するソフト）
▸This *key-capture software* can be obtained easily on the Internet, and managers use it to monitor employees. このキーキャプチャー・ソフトは, ネット上で容易に手に入り, 経営者は社員の監視に使っている。
key gauge 指数, 指標, 重要［主要］な基準［尺度］（⇒**gauge**）
▸A *key gauge* of the current state of the nation's economy stayed below the boom-or-bust line of 50 percent in October for the third straight month. 国内景気の現状を示す主要基準（景気一致指数）が, 10月は景気判断の分かれ目となる50％を3か月連続下回った。
▸The *key gauge* of the nation's money supply rose 2.1 percent in January 2008 from a year earlier. 日本の2008年1月のマネー・サプライ（通貨供給量）の指標は, 前年同月比で2.1％増加した。
key interest rate 政策金利, 主要政策金利, 基準金利, 指標金利, 金利の誘導目標, FF金利（＝benchmark rate, key rate; ⇒**Bank of England, interest rate policy**）
▸The Bank of Japan left its *key interest rate* unchanged at 0.5 percent. 日銀は, 政策金利を0.5％に据え置いた。
▸The European Central Bank raised its *key interest rate* by a quarter of a percentage point to 3.5 percent. 欧州中央銀行（ECB）は, 主要政策金利を0.25％引き上げて年3.5％とした。
▸The U.S. Federal Reserve Board slashed a *key interest rate* by three-quarters of a point. 米連邦準備制度理事会（FRB）は, フェデラル・ファンド（FF）金利を（現行の3％から）0.75％引き下げた。
key rate 政策金利, 基準金利, 指標金利（＝key interest rate: 米国の場合, a key rate (a key interest rate)はフェデラル・ファンド（FF）金利を指し, key rates（複数形）は公定歩合（official discount rate）とフェデラル・ファンド（FF）金利の誘導目標の二つを指す。なお, 日銀の「公定歩合」は2006年8月11日から「基準割引率および基準貸付利率」に変更された。⇒**key interest rate, official discount rate**）
▸The U.S. Federal Reserve Board held a *key rate* steady at 5.25 percent. 米連邦準備制度理事会（FRB）は, フェデラル・ファンド（FF）金利の誘導目標を年5.25％に据え置いた。
▸The U.S. Federal Reserve Board left U.S. *key rates* unchanged. 米連邦準備制度理事会（FRB）は, 米国の基準金利を据え置いた。
keyhole investment キーホール・インベストメント（市場に新規参入するにあたってその市場内の企業の株式を少量取得すること）
keyman 图 中心人物, 重要人物, 企業幹部, 要人, キーマン
　keyman insurance 経営者保険, 事業家保険, 幹部保険
keynote 图 基調, 要旨, 骨子, 主眼, 主眼点, 基本理念, 基本方針, 基本政策
　keynote address [speech] 基調講演, 基調演説, 基本方針演説
keyword 图 検索語, 検索対象語, 重要語, キーワード
　keyword search advertisement [advertising] キーワード・サーチ広告（検索エンジンで関連用語を検索したときに現れる広告）
kickback 图 不当な手数料, 割戻し金, バック・リベート, 裏金, 賄賂（わいろ）, リベート
▸The firm paid *kickbacks* to five of the Japanese companies. 同社は, 日本企業5社にリベートを支払った。
kickback of duty 戻し関税
killer bees キラー・ビーズ（敵対的買収を防ぐための専門家集団）
kilobits per second キロビット毎秒, キロビット／秒《略 Kbps》
kind 图 物品, 品物, 現物, 本質, 種類
　dividends-in-kind 現物配当
　tax payment in kind 物納
　wage in kind 現物給与
▸Payment was made in *kind*. 支払いは, 物品で行われた。
kit 图 道具一式, 用具ひと揃い, セット, 組立部品一式, キット
　campaign kit キャンペーン・キット
　cosmetic kit 化粧道具箱, 化粧品セット（＝makeup kit）
　demonstration kit デモンストレーション・キット
　golfing kit ゴルフ用具一式
　meal kits キット食品
　promotional kit プロモーション用具
　selling kit 販売セット
　trial kit 試供品セット
▸Meal *kits*, which are prepared packages of vegetables, meat and seasoning, are attracting working wives and singles, because with just a

little bit of cooking the *kits* can become freshly made dishes. 野菜や肉類，調味料をパックしたキット食品は，ひと手間かけるだけで作りたての料理ができるので，共働きの主婦や単身者を引きつけている。

kite 名 空手形，融通手形
kiting 名 株価のつり上げ
KM 知識管理，ナレッジ・マネジメント（**knowledge management** の略）
knock-on effect 連鎖反応，連鎖効果，ドミノ効果
know your customer 顧客熟知
know-your-customer rule 顧客熟知の原則，顧客熟知規則
knockdown 形 格安の，廉価な，特価の，最低の，組立方式の，現地組立方式の，ノックダウン方式の，ノックダウン
  knockdown bid 最低の付け値
  knockdown export 現地組立輸出，ノックダウン輸出
  knockdown import 国内組立輸入
  knockdown price 最低価格，最安値，格安値
  knockdown system 現地組立方式，ノックダウン方式（＝knockdown plan）
knowhow [**know-how**] 名 ノウハウ，技術情報，技術知識，専門知識，専門技術，製造技術，技術秘密，技術秘訣，手法，秘伝，奥義，秘訣，コツ（＝expertise）
  business knowhow 経営手法，商売の秘訣，商売のコツ
  computer knowhow コンピュータ技術
  confidential knowhow 秘密ノウハウ
  conveyance of knowhow ノウハウの供与
  industrial knowhow 産業技術
  knowhow fee ノウハウ料
  knowhow license agreement ノウハウ・ライセンス契約
  knowhow licensing agreement ノウハウ使用許諾契約
  knowhow transfer ノウハウ譲渡，ノウハウの移転
  management knowhow 経営のノウハウ，経営の専門知識
  technical knowhow 技術専門知識，技術的専門知識，技術ノウハウ
  transfer of knowhow and technical assistance ノウハウの移転と技術援助
▶ We will organize and lead teams of experts from other companies to provide technical *knowhow* for the global environment problems. 当社は，他社の技術専門家チームを組織・指揮して，地球規模の環境問題に関するノウハウを提供することになっています。

knowledge 名 知識，知的資産，認識，理解，承知，精通，熟知，情報，知りうる範囲，ナレッジ
  common knowledge 周知の事実
  corporate knowledge 企業知識，企業情報
  exclusive knowledge 専門知識
  explicit knowledge 形式知
  industry knowledge 業界知識
  knowledge acquisition 知識獲得
  knowledge base system 知識ベース・システム（＝expert system, knowledge-based system）
  knowledge-based facility 知識ベース機能
  knowledge-based society 知識中心社会
  knowledge discovery in database データベースによる知識発見《略 KDD》（＝data mining）
  knowledge engineer 知識エンジニア，ナレッジ・エンジニア《略 KE》（人工知能を応用したシステムの分析設計を行うソフトウエア・エンジニア）
  knowledge engineering 知識工学
  knowledge factory 知識工場，情報工場，ナレッジ・ファクトリー
  knowledge industry 知識産業，情報産業
  knowledge intensive [**knowledge-intensive**] **industry** 知識集約型産業
  knowledge management 知識管理，知的資産管理，知識経営，ナレッジ経営，ナレッジ・マネジメント《略 KM》（業務の知識や知恵，経営資源としての知識を，データベース化して共有・活用して新たに創造すること）
  knowledge market ナレッジ・マーケット
  knowledge network 知識ネットワーク
  knowledge representation 知識表現
  knowledge system 知識システム，知識ベース，人工知能システム，エキスパート・システム（常識，経験則，事実，対処法などをデータベース化したもの）
  knowledge worker 知的労働者，知識労働者，ナレッジ・ワーカー
  prior knowledge 予備知識
  public knowledge 公知
  tacit knowledge 暗黙知
  very large knowledge base 大規模知識ベース
▶ ABC shall forthwith upon coming to its *knowledge* notify the licensor of any infringement or threatened infringement or counterfeit of the Trademarks. 本商標が侵害されたり，侵害されそ

うになったり，偽物が作られたりしていることをABCが知った場合，ABCは直ちにこれをライセンサーに知らせるものとする。

knowledgeable sources 消息筋 （＝informed sources）

known 形 既知の, 周知の, 公知の
  known loss 既知の損害
  known misstatement 既知の虚偽表示
  known programing [programming] 公知のプログラミング
  less-known issuer 知名度の低い発行体
  less-known name 無名の銘柄
▸Distributor agrees to notify Supplier of any *known* or suspected infringement of Supplier's intellectual property rights that comes to Distributor's attention. 販売店の注意に止まって供給者の知的所有権[知的財産権]の侵害を知るかその恐れがある場合，販売店はこのことを供給者に通告することに同意する。

krona 名 クローナ
  Euro-krona market ユーロ・クローナ債市場
  Swedish krona スウェーデン・クローナ

krone 名 クローネ
  Danish krone デンマーク・クローネ
  Norwegian krone ノルウェー・クローネ

Kyoto pact 京都議定書 （＝Kyoto Protocol）
▸There may be little progress in reducing greenhouse gas emissions even after the *Kyoto pact* takes effect. 京都議定書が発効しても，温室効果ガス排出量削減の実効性は乏しい。

Kyoto Protocol 京都議定書 （＝the Kyoto pact, the global climate pact）
▸The *Kyoto Protocol* requires Japan to cut greenhouse gas emissions by 6 percent from the 1990 level by 2012. 京都議定書は，日本に対して2012年までに1990年比で6％の温室効果ガス排出量削減を義務付けている。

L

label 名 ラベル, レッテル, 表示, 商標, ブランド, 荷札, レコード会社, レーベル
  bogus date label 日付偽装表示, 日付偽装
  country-of-origin label 原産地表示
  descriptive label 記述的ラベル, 記述的表示, 追加表示 (=descriptive labeling)
  grade label 等級ラベル
  informative label 説明ラベル, 説明表示 (=descriptive label)
  Label Clause レッテル約款
  luggage label 荷札 (=baggage tag)
  "Made in the EU" label 「EU製」の表示
  performance label 性能表示
  private label 商業者ラベル, 自家商標 (=private brand)
  private label merchandise [product] プライベート・ブランド商品
  store label 商店レッテル
labeling 名 表示, 分類, ラベル表示, ラベルの貼付, ラベリング (=label)
  best before date labeling 賞味期限の表示
  descriptive labeling 記述的ラベル表示, 種類別標札貼付, 品質表示(商品の特性や用途, 使用法などを文字や絵で表示する方法)
  false labeling of beef products 牛肉の偽装表示, 牛肉偽装
  false labeling of food 食品の偽装表示, 食品偽装
  food labeling 食品表示
  grade labeling 等級ラベル表示
  informative labeling 説明ラベル表示 (=descriptive labeling)
  ingredient labeling 成分表示
  mandatory labeling 義務表示
  mislabeling 偽装表示, 不当表示, 不正表示
  mislabeling fraud 偽装工作
  ▶Japan requires *labeling* of 30 genetically modified food items from 2001. 日本は, 2001年から遺伝子組換え食品30品目について表示を義務付けている。
labor [labour] 名 労働, 労務, 労働力, 労働者, 労働者側, 仕事
  cheap labor 低賃金労働, 低賃金の労働力
  contract labor arrangements 委託生産方式
  direct labor 直接労働, 直接作業, 直接労務費, 直接工
  division of labor 分業
  employed labor force 雇用者数
  indirect labor 間接労働, 間接作業, 間接労務費, 間接工
  international division of labor 国際分業
  labor adjustment 雇用調整
  labor and capital 労資
  labor and industry 労使
  labor and management 労使
  labor and overhead 労務費および間接費
  labor- and land-intensive industries 労働集約型・土地集約型産業
  labor availability 労働需給
  labor bank 労働金庫
  labor-capital reconciliation 労使協調
  labor certification 労働証明書
  labor contract 労働契約 (=labor commitment)
  Labor Day 労働者の日, 労働記念日(米国・カナ

ダは9月の第一月曜日，英国は5月1日）
labor demand 労働力需要，労働需要
labor dispute 労働争議，労使紛争 （＝industrial dispute）
labor earnings 勤労所得
labor efficiency 作業効率，作業能率
labor equipment ratio 労働装備率
labor exchange 英国の職業安定所，職業紹介所
labor federation 労働団体
labor-hearing system 労働審判制度（解雇や職場での嫌がらせなど労働者と会社間の紛争を迅速に解決するため，労使双方の幹部やOBが，審判員として裁判官と対等の立場で審理に加わる制度）
labor hoarding 労働保蔵
labor input 労働投入量
labor-intensive 労働集約的な，労働集約型の
labor management 労務管理
labor mobility 労働移動性，労働力の移動性，労働流動性，転職
labor organization 労働組織，労働団体，労働機関
labor piracy 従業員の引き抜き
labor productivity index 労働生産性指数
labor reductions 人員削減
labor relations 労使関係，労働関係
labor share 労働分配率
labor shortage 労働力不足，労働者不足，人手不足
Labor Standards Bureau 労働基準局
labor standards inspection office 労働基準監督署
Labor Standards Law 労働基準法
labor strife 労働争議 （＝labor trouble）
labor supply 労働力供給，労働需給
labor turnover 離職率，労働回転率，労働力の移動
labor unrest 労働争議，労働不安
labor using industry 労働使用的産業
low-cost labor 低賃金の労働力，低コストの労働力
skilled labor 熟練労働，熟練労働者
spring labor offensive 春闘 （＝spring wage talks）
surplus labor 余剰労働力，剰余労働
tight labor conditions 労働需給の逼迫，労働力需給の逼迫
unit labor cost 単位労働コスト
unskilled labor 未熟練労働力，不熟練労働
labor agreement 労使協約，労働協約 （＝collective agreement, collective bargaining agreement, labor collective agreement, labor contract, trade agreement）
▶Our management and union bargainers negotiated innovative *labor agreements* with provisions for employees' career security and well-being as well as higher wages. 当社の経営陣と組合の交渉担当者が，従業員の雇用確保，福利厚生と賃上げに関する規定を盛り込んだ革新的な労使協約について協議しました。

labor cost 人件費，労務費，労働コスト，労務コスト
▶In China, the number of migrant workers has decreased, resulting in increases in *labor costs* at a record high pace. 中国では，出稼ぎ労働者の数が減少し，人件費はこれまでにないペースで上昇している。
▶*Labor costs*, often cited as a major weakness of Japanese companies, have been falling. 日本企業の大きな弱点とされる人件費は最近，減少している。

labor cost per hour 1時間当たりの労働コスト
▶*Labor cost* per hour in the new EU member countries is only one-fifth of the average in the old member nations. EU新加盟国の1時間当たりの労働コストは，旧加盟国平均の5分の1にすぎない。

labor distribution rate 労働分配率 （企業の利益がどれだけ労働者に還元されているかを示す指標で，企業が生産活動で生み出した付加価値に占める人件費の割合を指す）
▶Pay hikes are necessary because *labor distribution rate* has been falling for many years. 労働分配率が以前から下がり続けているため，賃上げが必要だ。

labor force 労働力，労働人口，労働力人口 （＝work force）
employed labor force 雇用者数
labor force participation rate [ratio] 労働力率，就業率
labor force population 生産年齢人口
labor force quality 労働力の質 （＝quality of the labor force）
labor force training 職業訓練
limited labor force 労働力不足
potential labor force 潜在的労働力
▶An inexpensive, educated *labor force* in new EU member countries is also attractive to companies in and out of the EU. EU新加盟国の安価で教育水準の高い労働力も，EU内外の企業にとって魅力的だ。

labor-management 形 労使の, 労使間の
　labor-management accords 労使協約
　labor-management cooperation 労使協調
　labor-management dispute 労使紛争, 労使対決
　labor-management harmony 労使協調
　labor-management relations 労使関係 (＝labor relations)
　Labor-Management Relations Act of 1947 米国の1947年労使関係法 (通称でTaft-Hartley Act (タフト・ハートレー法)という)
　Labor-Management Reporting and Disclosure Act 米国の労働組合運営報告開示法 (通称でLandrum-Griffin Act (ランドラム・グリフィン法)という)
　labor-management talks 労使交渉
▸The company's *labor-management* relations are amicable at present. 同社の労使関係は, 今のところ良好だ.

labor-management negotiation 労使交渉 (＝labor-management talks)
▸The *labor-management negotiations* are expected to heat up toward March 12, when answers from companies are concentrated. 労使交渉は, 会社側の回答が集中する3月12日頃が山場と見られる.

labor market 労働市場, 労働需給
　labor market conditions 労働需給 (＝labor market situation, supply and demand on the labor market)
　labor market data 雇用統計 (＝labor market statistics)
　labor market environment 雇用情勢 (＝labor market conditions, labor market situation)
　labor market situation 雇用情勢 (＝labor market conditions, labor market environment)
▸In the business world, there can be said to be a liquidation of *labor markets*. 産業界では, 労働市場の流動化が起きているといえる.

labor offensive 労働攻勢
▸In this spring's *labor offensive*, many companies could not afford to raise the basic wages of their employees. 今年の春闘で, 多くの企業は社員のベアを引き上げられなかった.

labor productivity 労働生産性 (＝worker productivity)
▸U.S. *labor productivity* slowed sharply in the final three months of 2008. 2008年10−12月期の米国の労働生産性は, 大幅に低下した.

labor saving 省力, 省力化, 労働節約 (＝laborsaving)
　investment for labor saving 省力投資, 省力化投資 (＝labor saving investment)
　labor saving equipment 省力機器
　labor saving industry 省力産業
　labor saving machinery industry 省力産業, 省力機械工業

labor union 労働組合, 労組, 労働団体 (＝trade union; ⇒**AFL-CIO**)
米国の主要労組

AFSCME	米国州・郡・市職員連盟 (American Federation of State, County, and Municipal Employeesの略)
IAM	国際機械工・航空宇宙労働者組合 (International Association of Machinists and Aerospace Workersの略)
IBEW	国際電気工組合 (International Brotherhood of Electrical Workersの略)
IBT	全米トラック運転手組合 (＝Teamsters, Teamster's Union: International Brotherhood of Teamstersの略)
UAW	全米自動車労組 (United Automobile Workersの略)
USWA	アメリカ鉄鋼労働者合同組合 (United Steelworkers of Americaの略)

▸Most major *labor unions* of automobile and electrical appliance makers have already submitted their demands. 鉄鋼や自動車, 電機などの大手労組の要求が, ほぼ出そろった.

lackluster 形 活気がない, 活気が乏しい, 不活発な, 不振の, 停滞した, 動きが鈍い, 足どりが鈍い, 伸び悩みの (＝sluggish)
　lackluster consumption 消費の低迷
　lackluster economy 景気停滞
　lackluster sales 販売不振, 販売低迷
　lackluster trading 薄商い
▸One major factor behind *lackluster* consumption and price increases is the slow increase in wages. 消費の低迷や物価上昇率の伸び悩みの背景にある大きな要因の一つは, 賃金上昇の鈍さだ.

laden 形 貨物を積載した
lag 動 出遅れる, 遅行する, 予定通り進行しない, …に追いつかない, …についていけない, 下回る
　lag behind …から取り残される, …より遅れる, …を下回る
　lagging indicator 遅行指標 (＝lagging index)
▸Sales and profits for the handheld PlayStation Portable have also been *lagging*. 携帯型ゲーム機「プレイステーション・ポータブル(PSP)」の売上高と利益も, 業績予想を下回っている.

laggard 形名 遅れがちな(人[もの]), 出遅れ株
lagging index 遅行(ちこう)指数 (＝lagging

indicator: 現状の景気の動きに遅れて動く(半年から1年遅れる)経済指標)
▶The *lagging index* was 40 percent, compared with 16.7 percent the previous month. (景気の動きに半年から1年遅れる)遅行指数は，前月の16.7%に対して40%となった。

LAN 狭域通信網，域内通信網，企業内通信網，構内通信網，ローカル・エリア・ネットワーク，ラン (**local area network**の略．⇒**base station**)
▶Wireless *LANs'* reliance on radio waves may allow third parties to hack into them. 無線LAN(構内情報通信網)は電波に頼っているため，第三者に電波を盗用される[第三者が電波に不正アクセスする]恐れがある。

land 動 獲得する，手に入れる，得る，引き上げる，陸揚げする，着陸させる，打撃を加える，着陸する，接岸する
▶A consultancy company *landed* exclusive government contracts to dispose of chemical weapons abandoned in China. 中国に遺棄された化学兵器の処理事業を，コンサルタント会社1社が国から独占受注していた。

land 名 土地，用地，農地，農耕地，陸，陸地，地帯，場所，所有地，国土，ランド
  agricultural land 農地
  commercial land 商業地
  development land 開発用地
  land, building and equipment 土地，建物および設備
  land, building and fixtures 土地，建物および設備
  land cost 用地費
  land holding tax 地価税 (=**land price tax**)
  land improvements 土地改良，土地付属施設
  land taxation system 土地税制
  leasehold land 賃借地
  loans secured on land 不動産担保ローン
  loss on land sales 土地売却損
  oil lands 石油産出地帯
  posted prices of land 地価公示価格
  residential land 住宅地
▶We lease *land*, buildings and equipment through contracts. 当社は，契約により土地，建物と設備を賃借りしています。

land deal 土地取引
▶Japan's maximum rate of inheritance tax at 70 percent is another factor hampering *land deals*. 日本の相続税の最高税率が70%であることも，土地取引を阻害している要因の一つである。

land price 地価，土地価格

land price spiral 地価高騰
land price tax 地価税 (=**land value tax**)
▶Additional nonperforming loans are created due to falling *land prices*. 地価の下落で，不良債権が新規に発生している。
▶There was a trend toward *land prices* rising for the year to July. 今年7月1日時点の地価は，上昇傾向にある。

land shark 地上げ屋 (=**land speculator**)
▶*Land sharks* are back on the scene. 地上げ屋が復活している。

land sharking 地上げ，地上げ行為
▶The firm's rapid growth was a result of the *land-sharking* operations by a real estate company president. 同社の急成長は，不動産会社の社長が地上げを進めたことによるものだった。

land tax system 土地税制 (=**land-related tax**)
▶Measures to stop property values from falling, including a review of *land tax system*, are also important. 土地税制の見直しなど，資産価格の下落を食い止める施策も重要だ。

landmark 名 画期的な出来事[事件，発見]，目印，陸標，境界線，歴史的建造物，ランドマーク
  landmark court decision 画期的な判決
  landmark study 画期的な研究
  landmarks in history 歴史上の大事件

lapse 名 〈権利・特権の〉消滅，失効，減少，下降，動 失効する，消滅する，〈期限が〉切れる，〈権利などを〉失う

large 形 大規模の，巨大な，巨額の，大型の，大量の，大手の，広範囲の，主要な，重要な，大幅な，全般的な
  large acquisition 大型買収
  large capitalization [capital] stock 大型株
  large company [firm] 大手企業，大企業
  large customers 大口顧客
  large deficit 巨額の赤字，大幅赤字
  large equity holder 大株主 (=**large shareholder**)
  large gains in productivity 生産性の大幅の伸び，生産性の大幅上昇，大幅な生産性向上 (=**large productivity gains**)
  large-lot savings 大口預金
  large merger 大型合併
  large order [lot-order] 大口注文，大量注文
  large-scale en bloc casting technology 大型一体鋳造技術
  Large Scale Retail Law 大規模小売店舗法，大店法

large shareholder 大株主, 大口株主 (=large stockholder, major shareholder)
report on large stockholders [shareholders] 大量保有報告書
▸Banks made *larger* gross operating profits than they did during the bubble economic era. 銀行は，バブル期よりも大きな業務粗利益を上げた。
▸We achieved both growth and efficiency, while maintaining a *large* profit. 当社は，成長と効率を両立させる一方，高水準の利益を維持した。

largest shareholder 筆頭株主, 大株主
▸Marubeni Corp. is the *largest shareholder* in Daiei Inc. 丸紅は，ダイエーの筆頭株主だ。

laser 名 レーザー
　laser beam machining レーザー加工
　laser device レーザー発光素子 (⇒**optical fiber**)
　laser nuclear fusion レーザー核融合
　laser processing レーザー加工
　laser surgery レーザー光線手術
▸The HD DVD and Blu-ray technologies use blue *lasers*, which have shorter wavelengths than conventional red lasers. HD（高品位）DVD技術とブルーレイ・ディスク(BD)技術は，従来の赤色レーザーより波長が短い青色レーザーを使う。

last half 下半期, 下期 (⇒**first half, latter half**)
▸The pressures on gross margins and earnings affected the *last half* of 2008. 売上利益率と利益の低下が，2008年下半期[下期]の業績に影響を及ぼしました。

last-in, first-out 後入れ先出し, 後入れ先出し法《略 **LIFO**》(⇒**FIFO**)

latecomer 名 後発, 後発組, 後発企業, 後から加わった者, 最近参入した企業, 新入り, 新規参入者 (⇒**newcomer**)
▸Google, a *latecomer* founded in 1998, rapidly went from strength to strength through its online advertisement business linked with Net search services. 1998年創業の後発組のグーグルは，ネット検索サービスと連動したオンライン広告で急成長した。

latent 形 潜在的な, 表面に出ない, 隠れた, 含みを持つ（企業保有資産の現在価値[市場価値]が帳簿上の価格を上回っている場合に「含みを持つ」という）
　latent asset 含み資産（企業保有資産の現在価値[市場価値]が，帳簿上の表示価格より大きい場合の差額）
　latent debts 隠れ借金

latent gains or losses 含み損益, 評価損益 (=latent profits or losses)
latent profits and losses 含み損益 (=appraisal profits and losses, latent gains and losses, unrealized profits and losses)
latent stock gains 株式含み益, 株の含み益, 株式評価益 (=latent profits in stocks)
latent value 含み益 (=latent gain, latent profit)
▸We must charge off *latent* losses on our real estate holdings. 当社は，保有不動産の含み損の処理に迫られています。

latent defect 隠れた欠陥, 隠れた瑕疵（かし）
▸The manufacturer shall be liable for the *latent defects* of the products. 本製品の隠れた欠陥[瑕疵]については，製造業者が責任を負うものとする。

latent gain 含み益, 評価益 (=appraisal gain, latent profit, unrealized gain)
▸Increases in *latent gains* from these banks' stockholdings are considered far smaller than latent losses in their bond holdings. これらの銀行が保有する株式の含み益の増加分は，保有債券の含み損よりはるかに小さいと見られる。

latent loss 含み損, 評価損 (=appraisal loss, unrealized loss: 保有する株式や債券などの有価証券や不動産の取得原価[購入価格]を時価評価額で差し引いて出た損失のこと)
▸The Corporation had a total ¥30 billion in *latent losses* for its stockholdings as of December 31, 2007. 2007年12月31日現在，当社は計300億円の株式含み損を抱えています。

latent profit 含み益, 評価益 (=appraisal profit, latent gain, unrealized profit, valuation profit: 保有する株式や債券などの有価証券や不動産の取得原価[購入価格]を時価評価額で差し引いて出た利益のこと)
▸*Latent profits* in real estate, stocks or other assets are posted after assessing the assets at market value. 不動産や株などの資産の含み益は，時価で資産を評価した後計上される。

latest 形 最新の, 最先端の, 今回の, 今年度の, 最終の
　the latest discount rate cut 今回の公定歩合引下げ
　the latest information 最新情報
　the latest installment 最新作
　the latest production technology 最先端生産技術
　the latest purchase cost 最終仕入原価, 最終取得原価

▶The *latest* change in tone of the economic upturn is a temporary phenomenon. 今回の景気回復の変調は、一時的な現象である。

latter half 下半期、下期、後半 （＝the latter half of the year, the latter half year, the second half of the year; ⇒**first half**）
▶In the *latter half* of 2008, we raised our prices and fees. 2008年度下期に、当社は製品価格と料金を引き上げました。

launch 動 開始する、着手する、発売する、売り出す、市場に出す、導入する、投入する、上場する、〈コンピュータ・プログラムを〉立ち上げる [起動する]、〈ロケットなどを〉打ち上げる [発射する]、〈船を〉進水させる
　launch a campaign キャンペーンを実施する、キャンペーンを行う、キャンペーンを開始する
　launch a hostile takeover bid 敵対的な株式公開買付けを実施する、敵対的買収を仕掛ける
　launch a new product 新製品を発売する
　launch a Web site ウェブ・サイトを開設する
　launch cell phone services 携帯電話サービスを開始する
　launch funds ファンドを設定する
　launch futures on stocks 株式先物を上場する
▶The firm plans to *launch* a tender offer from Nov. 16 to Dec. 14. 同社は、11月16日から12月14日までTOB（株式公開買付け）を実施する予定だ。
▶Under the new Corporate Law, anyone is allowed to *launch* a publicly traded company even with ¥1. 新会社法では、（資本金）1円でも公開企業を設立することができる。
▶Yomiuri, Nikkei and Asahi agreed to *launch* a joint Web site. 読売、日経と朝日が、共同サイト [共同ニュース・サイト] を開設することで合意した。

launch 名 発表、起債発表、開始、着手、新製品の発売、上市、導入、実施、ローンチ （＝launching）
▶We have evolved into the country's top retailer since the *launch* of our first outlet in 1990. 当社は、1990年に1号店を開いて以来、国内トップの小売り業に成長しました。

launching 名 開始、着手、導入、販売開始、発売、発表、〈債券などの〉発行、上場、〈ホームページなどの〉開設、実施

launder 動 不正資金を洗浄する、不正資金の出所を隠し、合法的に偽装する、マネー・ロンダリングをする
　launder money through a foreign private bank account 海外のプライベート・バンクの銀行口座を通じて資金を洗浄する
　laundered funds 洗浄資金、洗浄された資金、資金の洗浄
▶Money was *laundered* through a foreign private bank account. 資金は、海外のプライベート・バンクの銀行口座を通じて洗浄された。

laundering 名 不正資金の洗浄、不正資金の出所偽装工作、犯罪資金の洗濯、マネー・ロンダリング （＝money laundering; ⇒**money laundering**）
▶The *laundering* of illegally earned profits is prohibited by the Investment Law. 違法収益の洗浄 [出所偽装工作] は、投資法で禁止されている。

laundry 名 資金洗浄
layaway 名 留め置き商品
law 名 法律、法、コモン・ロー、規範、法則
　Air Pollution Control Law 大気汚染防止法
　Amended Usury Law 改正出資法
　applicable law 適用法、準拠法 （＝governing law）
　blue sky law 不正証券取引禁止法、ブルー・スカイ法
　by-laws 付属定款、通常定款、準則、付則 （＝by-laws, byelaws）
　Commercial Law 商法
　company law 会社法
　Export and Import Transaction Law 輸出入取引法
　federal procurement law 連邦調達法
　financial services law 金融サービス法
　governing law 準拠法、適用法 （＝applicable law）
　Labor Standards Law 労働基準法
　law firm 法律事務所
　law school 法科大学院、ロースクール
　model investment law モデル投資法
　product liability law 製造物責任法
　small loan law 小口金融法
　state law 州法
　statutory law 制定法

lawsuit 名 訴訟 （＝suit）
　file a lawsuit against …を相手取って提訴する、訴訟を起こす、…を提訴する、告訴する
　file a lawsuit against A with B Aを相手取ってBに提訴する、Aを相手取ってBに訴訟を起こす
　file a lawsuit with the Tokyo District Court 東京地裁に提訴する
　withdraw [drop] a lawsuit against …に対する訴訟を取り下げる
▶The president and chief executive officer of Toyota Motor North America was accused in a sexual harassment *lawsuit*. 北米トヨタ自動車の社長兼最高経営責任者が、セクハラ（性的嫌がらせ）

で提訴された。

lay judge system 裁判員制度, 一般人による裁判員制度
▸The *lay judge system* obliges members of the public to take part in the judicial process. 裁判員制度は、国民に司法への参加を義務付けるものだ。

lay off 解雇する, 削減する, 低減する, 雇用調整する, 解消する, 回避する, レイオフを進める
　lay off employees 従業員を解雇する, 従業員のレイオフを進める
　lay off financial risk 金融リスクを低減する, 金融リスクをヘッジする
　lay off risk リスクを軽減する, リスクを回避する
▸We have not *laid off* anyone in over 50 years anywhere in the world. 当社は、過去50年以上にわたって、世界のいずれの地域でも1人として解雇したことはありません。

layoff 图 解雇, 削減, 低減, 人員削減, 一時解雇, 一時解休, 雇用調整, 休養期間, 休暇, レイオフ (＝lay-off, redundancy)
　large scale layoffs 最規模な雇用調整
　temporary layoff 一時解雇, 一時解休
▸The *layoffs* will account for about 7 percent of its global workforce of 150,000. 今回の人員削減は、全世界の従業員15万人の約7％に当たる。

LBO 借入資金による企業買収, 企業担保借入買取り（買取相手先企業の資産や将来のキャッシュ・フローなどを担保にして、金融機関から買収資金を借り入れる方式のことをいう。⇒**leveraged buyout [buy-out]**）
　LBO company 借入比率の高い企業, 負債比率が高い企業, LBO企業（＝highly leveraged company）
　LBO finance LBOファイナンス
　reverse LBO 逆LBO, LBO株の公開, リバースLBO
▸New York-based Citigroup has advised on about one-third of the about $61 billion of leveraged buyouts (*LBO*) worldwide this year. シティグループ（ニューヨーク）は、今年の世界のLBO取引高約610億ドルのうち、約3分の1について専門の助言を行った。

L/C 信用状, エルシー（**letter of credit**の略。複数形は**L/C's, L/Cs**; ⇒**letter of credit**）
　L/C advising bank 信用状通知銀行, 信用状取次銀行
　L/C applicant 信用状発行依頼人
　L/C beneficiary 信用状受益者
　L/C confirming bank 信用状確認銀行
　L/C establishing bank 信用状発行銀行, 信用状開設銀行（＝**L/C issuing bank, L/C opening bank**）
　L/C margin money 信用状開設保証金
　L/C notifying bank 信用状通知銀行（＝**L/C advising bank, L/C transmitting bank**）

LCA ライフ・サイクル・アセスメント（**life cycle assessment**の略。製品の設計・製造段階から廃棄・リサイクルに至るまでの各段階で環境に与える影響を、二酸化炭素の排出量やエネルギー使用量などに換算して評価する手法）

LCD 液晶表示装置, 液晶ディスプレー（**liquid crystal display**の略）
　LCD TV 液晶テレビ

LDC 発展途上国（**less-developed country**の略）

lead manager 主幹事, 引受主幹事, 幹事銀行, 幹事行
　co-lead manager 共同主幹事（＝**joint lead manager**）
　domestic lead manager 国内主幹事
　expanded lead manager 拡大主幹事
　international lead manager 国際主幹事

lead time 先行期間, 準備期間, 生産準備期間, 企画段階から生産開始までの所要時間, 発注から納品までの期間, 調達期間, 入荷期間, 納期, リード・タイム

leader 图 経営者, 経営陣, 首脳, 首脳陣, 指導者, 指導部, 党首, 院内総務(米議会), 最大手, おとり商品, 目玉商品, 特売品, 主力株, 一流株, 社説, 〈新聞の〉トップ見出し, リーダー
　business leaders 実業界の指導者, 財界の指導者, 財界首脳, 経済界の首脳, 企業経営者, 企業のトップ
　deputy leader ナンバー2
　floor leader 米議会の院内総務（各党の議員総会で選出される上下両院各1名の院内総務で、党の院内活動を統括）
　House Majority leader 下院院内総務
　industrial nations' leaders 先進国首脳, 先進各国の首脳, 主要国首脳（＝**leaders of industrial nations**）
　industry leader 業界リーダー, 業界最大手
　leader merchandising おとり商品政策, おとり商品戦略
　leader of the business community 財界リーダー
　leader price 指導価格
　leader pricing おとり価格設定
　leaders at the company 同社[当社]の経営陣
　loss leader おとり商品, 特価品, 目玉商品, おとり政策
　market leader 主導株, 先導株, マーケット・リ

ーダー
  political leaders　政府指導者, 政府高官
  price leader　価格先導者, 価格指導者, 目玉商品, プライス・リーダー
  Senate leaders　上院指導部
  ▸We are the world's networking *leader*, providing communications services and products to businesses, consumers and telecommunications services providers.　当社はネットワーキングに関して世界のリーダーであり, 通信サービスと通信関連製品を企業, 消費者と電気通信サービス事業者に提供しています。

leadership 名　指導, 指揮, 指導力, 統率力, 指導性, 指導者の資質, リーダー性, 体制, 政権, 同業他社に対する優位性, 優位な立場, リーダーシップ
  business leadership　ビジネス・リーダーシップ
  industry leadership　業界のリーダー
  leadership position　主導的地位 (＝leading position)
  leadership role　指導者の役割, 指導的役割
  new leadership　新体制
  price leadership　価格先導制, 価格指導力, 価格指導性 (「価格先導制」は, 指導的企業が発表した価格を, 他社が受け入れること)
  under the leadership of　…の指導の下で, …の体制で
  union leadership　組合指導者
  ▸Under the new *leadership*, the top three posts – chairman, president and senior managing director – have been filled by people from departments that have had no links to the president post before.　新体制では, 会長, 社長と専務の経営トップ3人は, これまで社長ポストと縁のなかった部門の出身者で占められている。
  ▸We continue to maintain our technology *leadership* through a combination of internal investments and selected partnerships with others.　当社は, 社内投資に力を入れる一方, 優れた外部企業との協力関係を通して技術面でのリーダーシップを堅持しています。

leading 形　主要な, 最重要な, 一流の, 大手の, 有力な, 主力の, 首位の, 主導的
  leading commodity　主力商品
  leading indicator　先行指標, 先行指数
  leading industries　主力産業
  leading stocks　花形株

leading company　主要企業, 大手企業, 先導企業, 有力企業 (＝leading firm)
  ▸More than 70 percent of *leading companies* are worried about becoming the target of a hostile takeover.　主要企業の70％以上が, 敵対的買収の対象になる[敵対的買収を仕掛けられる]のを懸念している。

leading edge　主導的地位, 最先端, 最前部, 最前線, 先頭, 最新式, 最新型, 最新鋭, トップ (＝cutting edge, sophisticated, state-of-the-art, top of the line)
  leading-edge area　最先端分野
  leading-edge technology　先端技術, 最先端技術, 最新技術
  leading edges of innovation　技術革新の最先端

leading index　先行指数, 景気先行指数, 景気先行指標総合指数 (＝leading indicator, the index of leading economic indicators：)
  ▸The *leading index* comprises such indicators as job offers, new orders for machinery and housing starts, which are considered indicative of how the economy will perform for the next three to six months.　先行指数は, 3か月から6か月先の景気の動きを示すものと考えられる有効求人数や新規機械受注, 新規住宅着工件数などの指標から成る。

leading position　主導的地位
  ▸The company holds a *leading position* in global markets in the area of multimedia application development.　同社は, マルチメディア・アプリケーション開発の分野では, グローバル市場で主導的地位を堅持している。

leakage of client information　顧客情報の漏洩, 顧客情報の流出

leaked personal information　流出した個人情報, 個人情報の流出
  ▸As the result of an in-house investigation, it is highly likely that the *leaked personal information* has been taken from the firm directly.　内部調査の結果, 流出した個人情報は社内から直接持ち出された可能性が高い。

lean 形　脂肪の少ない, 赤身の, 筋肉質の, 乏しい, やせた, 不毛な, 困難な, 貧弱な, 消費の少ない, 採算がとれる
  lean beef　赤身の牛肉
  lean crop　不作, 凶作
  lean diet　栄養のない食事
  lean years　困難な時期, 不漁年, 不景気の時代
  leaner inventories　在庫水準の低下
  leaner management　経営の合理化

leap 動　跳ね上がる, 急上昇する, 急増する, 急拡大する, 躍進する, 昇進する
  ▸Intel's profit *leaped* 43 percent in the third quarter.　インテルの第3四半期の利益は, 43％急

増した。

lease 動 賃貸しする, 賃借りする, 貸し出す, 借り上げる, リースする
- **leased asset** リース資産, 賃貸資産 (=leased property)
- **leased equipment** リース資産 (=lease equipment)
- **leased facility** 専用設備
- **leased goods** リース物件, 賃貸借物件, 賃借物件, 貸与物件 (=leased object)
- **leased machine** リース機械
- **leased property** リース資産, リース物件
- ▶We *lease* airplanes, energy-producing facilities and transportation equipment under leveraged leases. 当社は, レバレッジド・リースで航空機, エネルギー生産施設と輸送設備をリースしています。

lease 名 賃貸借, 賃貸借契約(書), 借地［借家］契約, 鉱物資源の開発契約, リース取引, リース契約, リース (⇒**capital lease, leveraged lease, noncancelable, operating lease, sales-type lease**)
- **cancellable lease** 解約可能リース契約, 中途解約可能リース
- **equipment held for lease** リース用資産
- **equipment lease** 設備機器リース, 設備リース
- **financial lease** 金融性リース, 融資リース, ファイナンス・リース, ファイナンシャル・リース (=finance lease)
- **financial lease financing** ファイナンス・リースによる資金調達
- **lease agreement** 賃貸借契約, リース契約 (=lease contract)
- **lease commitment** 賃貸借契約, リース契約, リース契約債務 (=leasing commitment)
- **lease financing** リース金融
- **lease liability** リース債務 (=lease obligation)
- **lease of employees** 出向
- **lease terms** リース条件, 賃貸借条件, リース期間
- **renewal or extension of lease** リースの更新または延長
- ▶For *leases* which qualify as sales-type leases, the sales revenue is recorded at the inception of the lease. 販売型リースと定義されるリースについては, リース開始時に売上収益が計上されます。

lease obligation リース債務, リース契約
- ▶At December 31, 2008, future minimum *lease obligation*, net of minimum sublease rentals, for the next five years and beyond are as follows. 2008年12月31日現在, 今後5年間とその後の最低転貸し料収入控除後の将来最低リース債務は, 次のとおりです。

lease payments リース支払い額, リース料の支払い, リース料
- ▶The table below shows our future minimum *lease payments* due under noncancelable leases at December 31, 2008. 次表は, 2008年12月31日現在の解約不能リースの将来における当社の最低支払い額を示しています。

lease receivable リース債権
- ▶*Lease* and loan *receivables* were sold to the company. リース債権やローン債権が, 同社に売却された。

leaseback 名 リースバック, リースによる借戻し, 設備貸与 (保有資産を売却して, 売却先から賃借すること)

leasehold 名 借地, 借地権, 賃借資産, 賃借不動産, 土地賃借権, 定期賃借権, リース物件
- **leasehold improvement** 賃借資産付属施設, 借地［借家］の改良, 賃借物件改良
- **leasehold interest** 利用権
- **leasehold land** 賃借地, 借地
- **leasehold property** 定期借用資産
- **leasehold value** 借地価値

leasing 名 賃貸借, リース
- **leasing income** リース料収入, リース収益
- **leasing right** リース権, 持ち分権
- ▶Capital requirements due to the growth of our financial services and *leasing* business will continue to grow in 2009. 当社の金融サービスとリース事業の拡大により, 資金需要は2009年度も引き続き伸びるものと思われます。

leave 名 休暇, 欠勤, 休暇期間, 休暇許可, 許可
- **annual paid holiday** 年次有給休暇 (=annual leave with pay)
- **childcare leave** 保育休暇, 育児休暇
- **childcare leave system** 育児休業制度
- **family leave** 家族休暇, 家族看護休暇, 家族介護休暇 (=family-care leave)
- **mass leave** 一斉休暇
- **maternity leave** 出産休暇, 育児休暇, 育児休業
- **paid leave** 有給休暇
- **parental leave** 育児休業
- **paternity leave** 男性の育児休業, 男性のための産休
- **sick leave** 病気休暇, 療養休暇
- **special leave of absence** 特別休職, 特別休暇
- **take French leave** 無断欠勤する

▸The firm allows employees to set aside annual paid *leaves*, which lose effect after two years under the law.　同社では，法律上は2年で失効する年次有給休暇の積立てを，従業員に認めている。

LED　発光ダイオード　（⇒**light-emitting diode**）
　blue LEDs　青色発光ダイオード
　green LEDs　緑色発光ダイオード
　red LEDs　赤色発光ダイオード

-led　…主導の，…主導型，…先行型，…の指導による，…による，…中心の　（＝**-driven, led by, -oriented**）
　deflation-led economic slowdown　デフレ不況
　demand-led recovery　需要主導型の回復，需要主導型の業績［景気］回復
　export-led economic recovery　輸出主導型の景気回復，輸出頼みの景気回復
　export-led economies　輸出主導型経済
　export-led growth　輸出先行型成長，輸出主導型成長，輸出リード型成長
　export-led industrialization　輸出主導型工業化，輸出リード型工業化

▸The shift toward a domestic demand-*led* economy will be needed in Japan.　これからの日本は，内需主導型経済への転換が必要だ。

ledger 名　元帳，台帳，原簿
　cost ledger　原価元帳
　customers' ledger　得意先元帳，売上元帳
　land ledger　土地台帳
　ledger balance　元帳残高
　plant ledger　固定資産台帳

legacy 名　遺産，遺贈財産，名残，過去，後遺症
　negative legacy　負の遺産
　nonperforming loans and other negative legacies of the bubble economy　不良債権その他バブル期の負の遺産

legal 形　法律の，法律上の，法定の，法的な，合法的な，適法の，司法の場での，リーガル
　legal battle　法廷闘争
　legal capital　法定資本，法定資本金
　legal ceiling　法定金利の上限　（＝**legal cap, legal interest rate ceiling**）
　legal contract　適法契約
　legal entity　法人，法的主体，法的実体
　legal fee　弁護士費用
　legal holiday　祝祭日，法定休日，国民休日，公休日
　legal interest rate　法定金利
　legal obligation　法的義務
　legal opinion　法律意見書，リーガル・オピニオン
　legal proceedings　訴訟手続き
　legal reserves　法定準備金　（＝**legal capital reserves, legally required reserves**）

legal action　法的措置，法的手続き，法律上の訴え，訴訟

▸There is a contractual clause stipulating that Japanese PC makers will take no *legal action* even if Microsoft Corp.'s technologies are deemed to violate their patents.　マイクロソフト社の技術が日本のパソコン・メーカーの特許侵害にあたるとしても，日本のパソコン・メーカーは法的措置を一切取らない［訴訟を起こさない］，と定めた契約条項がある。

legal notification　法定公告

▸*Legal notifications* are advertisements with immense public importance.　法定公告は，公共的性格が非常に強い広告だ。

legal representative　法務担当者

▸The project team consists of lawyers and *legal representatives* of various firms.　プロジェクト・チームは，弁護士や各種企業の法務担当者で構成される。

legality 名　合法性，適法性

▸The *legality* of the strike is sure to be discussed in the days ahead.　今後，ストの合法性が議論されることになろう。

legislation 名　法律，制定法，立法

▸There is no *legislation* in Japan that regulates the creation of computer viruses.　日本には，コンピュータ・ウイルスを規制する法律がない。

lemon 名　欠陥車，欠陥商品，不良品，健全性に劣るもの
　lemon law　欠陥車補償法

lend 動　貸す，貸し付ける，融資をする

lender 名　貸し手，貸主，金融機関，銀行，融資行，融資者，資金の出し手，貸金業者

▸Ford's increase in a revolving credit facility is due to overwhelming support by *lenders*.　米フォードの回転融資枠引上げは，金融機関の強力な支援によるものだ。

▸The company has been refused additional credit by its *lenders*.　同社は，融資行から新規融資を拒否された。

lending 名　貸出，貸付け，融資，貸借
　bank lending　銀行貸出，銀行融資
　commercial lending　商業貸出，商業貸付け，民間融資
　consumer lending　消費者金融，消費者ローン
　corporate lending　企業向け貸出，企業向け貸付け，企業向け融資

direct lending 直接融資
excessive lending 過剰融資
lending balance 貸出残高
lending interest rate 貸出金利（＝lending rate)
lending period 融資期間, 貸出期間, 貸付け期間
lending right 貸与権
lending standards 与信基準
net lending 資金過不足, 貯蓄差額投資
new lending 新規貸出
restricted lending 貸し渋り

▸The bank's rate of nonperforming loans against overall *lendings* stood at 2.07 percent as of March 31, compared to 3.33 percent a year ago. 同行の貸出全体に占める3月31日現在の不良債権の比率は, 1年前の3.33％に対して2.07％となった。

lending rate 貸出金利（＝lending interest rate)
emergency lending rate 緊急貸出金利
general lending rate 一般貸出金利
minimum lending rate 最低貸出金利
prime lending rate 一流企業向け最優遇貸出金利, 一流企業に対する短期貸付け金利, プライム・レート（＝prime rate)
short-term prime lending rate 短期プライム・レート

▸Under the Interest Limitation Law, the upper limit of *lending rates* is set at between 15 to 20 percent per annum. 利息制限法では, 貸出金利の上限は年15−20％に定められている。

lending service 融資業務
▸Rakuten Inc. plans to start the corporate *lending service* with the companies that own the about 44,000 online stores at Rakuten Ichiba. 楽天は, 楽天市場にオンライン・ストアを出店している約44,000の出店企業から, 法人向け融資業務を開始する計画だ。

length of service 勤続年数, 在任期間
▸The pension benefits are based on *length of service* and rate of compensation. 年金給付額は, 勤続年数と報酬額に基づいて決定されます。

lessee 名 賃借人, 借地人, 借家人, 借主

lesser of two evils 次善の策
▸Since shares could become wastepaper after a bankruptcy, the reconstruction program may be seen as the *lesser of two evils*. 経営破綻後は株式が紙くずになる可能性があるので, 再建計画は次善の策かもしれない。

lessor 名 賃貸人, 貸主, 地主, 家主
letter 名 書簡, 書状, 文書, 証書, 証明書, 免許状, 意見書, 報告書, 確認書, 手紙, レター

collections letter 督促状
dividend procedure letter 配当手続き書
investment letter 投資確認書
letter agreement レター形式の契約書
letter for underwriter 証券引受人への書簡
letter of advice 通知書, 通知状, 手形通知状, 証明書
letter of allotment 株式割当て通知書
letter of attorney 委任状, 弁護士の書簡
letter of comfort 財務内容に関する意見書, 調査報告書, 念書, コンフォート・レター（＝comfort letter)
letter of inquiry 照会状, 引合状
letter of intent 予備的合意書, 仮合意書, 仮契約書, 趣意書, 基本合意書, レター・オブ・インテント
letter of procuration 株主総会などの代理委任状
letter of proxy 委任状
letter of understanding 合意書, 基本合意書（＝letter of intent)
letter of withdrawal 辞退書
letter ruling 書面回答
opinion letter 意見書
transmittal letter 送り状

letter of credit 信用状《略 L/C》（⇒L/C)
信用状について➡信用状は銀行が取引先(貿易取引の場合は輸入者)の依頼に応じてその信用を補強するために発行する証書で, 主に売買商品の代金決済に用いられる。貿易取引の商品代金の決済に用いられる信用状を商業信用状(commercial letter of credit)という。一般に, 発行銀行が手形の引受け, 支払いを保証・確約する取消し不能信用状(irrevocable L/C)となっている)

acceptance letter of credit 引受信用状
bank letter of credit 銀行信用状
commercial letter of credit 商業送り状
documentary letter of credit 荷為替信用状
export letter of credit 輸出信用状
irrevocable letter of credit 取消不能信用状
negotiation letter of credit 買取銀行[手形買取銀行]無指定信用状（＝general L/C, open L/C)
revolving letter of credit 回転信用状
usance letter of credit 期限付き信用状, ユーザンス信用状

▸*Letters of credit* are purchased guarantees that ensure our performance or payment to third parties in accordance with specified terms and conditions. 信用状とは，特定の条件に従って当社の第三者に対する義務の履行または支払いを確実なものにするために買い取った保証です。

level 名 水準，標準，程度，数値，高さ，段階，面，観点，幅，水位，レベル

  at the net level 当期利益で，当期損益レベルで
  at the operating level 営業利益で
  be at near record low levels 過去最低に近い水準にある
  borrowing level 資金調達コストの水準
  cabinet level 閣僚級
  consumption level 消費水準
  current level of earnings 現在の収益水準
  debt level 負債［債務］水準
  emission level 排ガス・レベル，排出レベル，排出量
  historical level of loss 過去の損失率
  interest rate level 金利水準
  inventory level 在庫水準
  level playing field 共通の土俵，平等の競争条件
  middle management level 中間管理層
  new levels of sophistication 一段と高い水準
  net level 当期利益ベース
  performance level 業績水準
  permissible level 許容水準
  price level 物価水準
  remain at about the same level ほぼ同水準にとどまる
  remain at high levels 高水準で推移する
  saturation level 普及率，飽和水準
  savings level 貯蓄率
  share price level 株価水準（＝stock market level）
  stay at a high level 高水準で推移する，高水準を維持する
  volume level 操業度
  ▸The current stock market *level* is based more on fear than on the economic fundamentals. 現在の株価水準は，経済の基礎的条件というより，不安によるものだ。

level off 横ばい状態になる，成長が止まる，伸び悩む，水平になる，水平飛行をする，平均化する
  ▸Corporate profits have remained high although they are *leveling off*. 企業収益は，伸び悩んでいるものの，高い水準で推移している。

leveling off 横ばい状態，踊り場（＝leveling out）

leverage 動 借入金で投機をする，…を利用する，生かす，借入金で〈企業などを〉買い取る
  ▸We believe there is an opportunity to *leverage* the strength of the balance sheet to deal with the demands of the business in the future. 財務内容の強みを生かして，将来，事業のニーズに対応する機会はあると思います。

leverage 名 借入れ，借入比率，借入余力，負債，負債比率，借入資本，財務レバレッジ，テコ，テコの作用，手段，影響力，力，有利な立場，レバレッジ（「レバレッジ」は投資額に対する借入金の割合で，「財務レバレッジ」は資本金に対する負債の割合(debt-to-equity ratio: 負債自己資本比率，外部負債比率)の高さを示す）

  capital leverage 財務レバレッジ，資本レバレッジ
  debt leverage 債務レバレッジ，債務テコ入れ，デット・レバレッジ（金融機関からの借入れで企業買収資金の一部をまかなうとき，自己資金にもたらされる収益を拡大するために用いられる方法）
  economic leverage 経済的影響力
  financial leverage 財務レバレッジ，借入比率，負債比率，ギアリング，ファイナンシャル・レバレッジ（＝gearing, financial gearing, trading on the equity）
  leverage effect 梃率（ていりつ）効果，テコの効果，レバレッジ効果，他人資本効果
  leverage position 財務状況
  leverage ratio 負債比率，レバレッジ・レシオ，レバレッジ比率（＝leverage test）
  risk-adjusted leverage リスク調整後の負債比率
  ▸Banks could use their *leverage* on borrowers to engage in unfair life insurance sales practices. 銀行が融資先への有利な立場を利用して，不公正な生保販売を行う可能性がある。

leveraged 形 借入金による，借入金を利用した，借入資金による
  conservative-leveraged company 負債比率が低い企業
  high-leveraged acquisition 多額の借入れによる企業買収
  highly leveraged company 負債比率が高い企業
  highly leveraged transaction 負債比率が高い取引，ハイ・レバレッジ取引
  leveraged effectiveness レバレッジ効果，他人資本効果（＝leverage effect）
  leveraged finance レバレッジ金融
  leveraged recapitalization 借入資金による資本の組換え，レバレッジド・キャピタライゼーション

leveraged buyout [buy-out] 借入資金による企業買収，企業担保借入買取り，レバレッジ

ド・バイアウト《略 **LBO**》（＝leverage buyout [buy-out]）: 買収先の会社（ターゲット企業）の資産や収益力を担保にして金融機関から買収資金を借り入れ，ターゲット企業を買収すること。⇒**LBO**）

leveraged lease レバレッジド・リース
▸These *leveraged leases* have original terms ranging from 10 to 30 years and expire in various years from 2008 through 2033. これらのレバレッジド・リースは，当初の期間が10年から30年で，2008年から2033年までの各年度に満期となります。

levy 動 賦課する，徴収する，取り立てる，差し押さえる

liability 名 責任，義務，負担，負担額，債務，負債，借金，賠償責任（⇒**contingent, current liabilities**）
- **accrued liabilities** 未払い費用，未払い負債，見越し負債
- **amount of liabilities** 負債金額
- **actuarial liability** 保険数理上の債務
- **auditor's liability** 監査人の責任
- **capital liability** 資本負債
- **external liabilities** 対外債務，外部負債
- **financial liabilities** 金融負債
- **fixed liability** 固定負債
- **hidden liability** 簿外債務
- **income tax liability** 未払い所得税，未払い法人税
- **insurance liabilities** 保険契約準備金
- **interest liability** 未払い利息
- **internal liability** 内部負債
- **joint and several liability** 連帯責任
- **liabilities and capital** 負債および資本（他人資本と自己資本）
- **liabilities and stockholders' equity** 負債および株主持ち分，負債および資本
- **liabilities assumed** 引継負債
- **liabilities exceeding assets** 債務超過（＝excess liabilities, excess of liabilities over assets, liabilities in excess of assets）
- **liabilities for [on] guarantee** 保証債務
- **liability exposure** 債務負担
- **liability for damages** 損害賠償責任
- **liability for guarantee** 保証債務，債務保証（＝liability on guaranty）
- **liability for service guarantees** 品質保証引当金
- **liability ratio** 負債比率
- **limited liability company** 有限会社，有限責任会社《略 **LLC**》（＝limited company）
- **long term liabilities** 長期負債，長期債務，固定負債（＝long term debts, long term obligations）
- **net liabilities** 正味負債，債務超過額
- **noncurrent liabilities** 非流動負債
- **off-the-book liabilities** 簿外債務（＝off-the-book debts）
- **past service liability** 過去勤務債務
- **product liability** 製造物責任《略 **PL**》
- **tax liability** 租税債務
- **total liabilities and net worth** 総資本
- **total liabilities and stockholders' equity** 負債および資本の部合計

▸Existing limited *liability* companies are allowed to remain intact or change themselves into stock companies under the new Corporate Law. 新会社法では，既存の有限会社はそのまま存続するか，株式会社に（商号を）変更することができる。
▸The firm's *liabilities* actually exceeded its assets. 同社は，実際は債務超過だった。
▸This charge reflects $12,000 million of *liabilities* less $2,000 million of plan assets. この金額［費用］は，120億ドルの債務額から20億ドルの制度資産を差し引いたものです。

liability method 負債法，債務法，負債方式，債務方式
▸Under United States GAAP, companies are required to adopt the *liability method* for income taxes. 米国の会計基準によれば，企業は，法人所得税の会計処理に債務法［負債法］を採用しなければならない。

liaison office 連絡事務所，駐在員事務所

liberalization 名 自由化，規制緩和，開放，国際化（＝deregulation）
- **capital liberalization** 資本自由化
- **exchange liberalization** 為替自由化
- **full liberalization** 全面開放，完全自由化
- **liberalization of brokerage commissions** 委託手数料の自由化
- **liberalization of brokerage commissions on commodity futures** 商品先物取引の委託手数料の自由化
- **liberalization of commissions** 売買手数料の自由化，手数料の自由化
- **liberalization of interest rates** 金利の自由化
- **liberalization of mail services** 郵便事業の自由化，郵便事業の開放
- **liberalization of power-supply business** 電力自由化
- **liberalization of the electricity market** 電力

市場の自由化，電力自由化，電力市場の規制緩和（＝power liberalization）
liberalization of the financial industry 金融自由化，金融の規制緩和（＝financial deregulation, financial liberalization）
liberalization of the Yen 円の国際化
market liberalization 市場の自由化，市場開放，市場の規制緩和
partial liberalization 部分開放，一部開放
price liberalization 価格自由化
total liberalization of brokerage commissions 委託手数料の完全自由化
▶It was the *liberalization* of commissions that triggered a fierce battle for survival and a stormy realignment in the British securities industry. 英国の証券業界の生き残りをかけた熾烈な戦いと業界再編に火をつけたのは，手数料の自由化である．

liberalization of the labor market 労働市場の開放
▶*Liberalization of the labor market*, including accepting nurses and caregivers, is a tough new issue. 看護師や介護士の受入れなど労働市場の開放は，新たな難問だ．

liberalize 動 自由化する，規制緩和する，開放する，解禁する，撤廃する
liberalized capital transaction 資本自由化
liberalized foreign investments 外資自由化
liberalized investment barriers 投資障壁の撤廃
liberalized regulatory framework 規制撤廃，規制緩和
liberalized trade 貿易自由化
▶Brokerage fees on stock and other transactions are fully *liberalized*. 株式その他の取引の売買手数料は，完全に自由化されている．

LIBOR ロンドンの銀行間取引金利，ロンドン銀行間オファー・レート，ライボー（**London interbank offered rate**の略）
▶Floating rate payments are based on rates tied to prime, *LIBOR* or U.S. Treasury bills. 変動金利の支払い利率は，プライム・レート，ロンドン銀行間取引金利または米財務省短期証券の利回りに基づいて決定されます．

license 動 免許［認可，許可，特許］を与える，許諾する，実施許諾する，使用許諾する，許可する，ライセンス供与する
licensed invention 実施許諾発明
licensed manufacture 許諾製造
licensed patent 実施許諾特許，許諾特許，許諾対象特許
licensed software 使用許諾ソフトウエア，許諾対象ソフトウエア
▶With regard to our intellectual properties, we will continue to *license* our patents. 当社の知的財産権については，当社は今後とも特許のライセンス供与をする方針です．

license [licence] 名 営業免許権，許可，認可，免許，特許，許諾，実施許諾，〈商標やソフトウエアなどの〉使用許諾，実施権，使用権，鉱業権，不動産の立入り権，許可書，免許状，ライセンス
business licenses and fees 事業免許料
compulsory license 強制実施
concurrent license 同時ライセンス
export license 輸出承認
investment license 投資認可
license contract expense ライセンス契約費用
license expense 免許料
license of business 営業免許
license production ライセンス生産
license registration 免許登録
license territory 実施許諾地域，使用許諾地域
permits and licenses 許認可費用
registration and license tax 登録免許税
software product license ソフトウエア使用許諾契約（＝software license agreement）
source license ソース・ライセンス（プログラムのソースを含めた形でのソフトウエアの提供）
▶The banking *license* of the Tokyo branch of Credit Suisse Financial Products was revoked in 1999. クレディ・スイス・ファイナンシャル・プロダクツ銀行の東京支店が，1999年に銀行免許を取り消された．

license agreement 実施権許諾契約，特許権実施契約，実施許諾契約，技術援助契約，ライセンス契約（特許やノウハウ，商標などの権利者が，一定の条件のもとに権利者以外の者にその使用・利用を許す場合の契約）
cross license agreement 交互実施許諾契約，クロス・ライセンス契約（⇒cross licensing）
design license agreement 意匠ライセンス契約
knowhow license agreement ノウハウ・ライセンス契約
software license agreement ソフトウエア使用許諾契約，使用許諾契約，ソフトウエア・ライセンス契約
trademark license agreement 商標ライセンス契約

license fee 免許料，免許手数料，特許権使用料，実施料，ライセンス料（＝licensing fee）

▶Revenue is recognized from software when the program is shipped or as monthly *license fees* accrue. 収益は，ソフトウエアについてはプログラムの出荷時に，または毎月の特許権使用料の発生時に計上しています。

licensed product 実施許諾製品，〈商標やソフトウエアの〉使用許諾製品，契約対象製品，ライセンス製品

▶The licensee may export the *licensed products* manufactured under the license to any other countries. ライセンシーは，この実施権に基づいて製造した実施許諾製品を他のいかなる国にも輸出することができるものとする。

licensee 名 〈特許権などの〉実施権者，〈商標権などの〉使用権者，被許諾者，被実施権者，許可［認可，免許］を受けた者，免許保有者，免許権保持者，〈土地・建物への〉立入り権者，ライセンシー

▶*Licensee* shall not change the manner of use of Trademarks or combine Trademarks with any other letters, names, trademarks, marks or other indications ライセンシーは，本商標の使用方法を変更せず，本商標に他の文字，名称，商標，標章や他の表示を結合することも一切しないものとする。

licenser [licensor] 名 実施権許諾者，使用権許諾者，技術実施許諾者，ライセンス許諾者，許可者，認可者，ライセンサー

▶*Licensor* owns or controls the rights in and to the licensed property. ライセンサーは，ライセンス対象の財産の権利を所有あるいは支配している。

licensing 名 実施許諾，使用許諾，認可，免許，許認可，ライセンス供与，ライセンス契約，資格認可，ライセンシング

 cross licensing クロス・ライセンス，交互実施許諾，特許権交換，特許技術の交換，相互特許使用権（＝cross license）

 cross licensing 交互実施許諾，特許権交換，特許技術の交換，相互特許使用権，クロス・ライセンス（＝cross license）

 director of patent licensing 特許許諾担当取締役

 licensing agreement ライセンス契約，ライセンス供与契約，使用許諾契約

 licensing business 商品化権許諾業，ライセンス・ビジネス

 licensing fee 実施料，ライセンス料（＝license fee）

 licensing of technology 技術供与

 licensing practice 特許認可手続き，ライセンス契約の手続き

 licensing right 実施権，使用許諾権

 licensing rules ライセンス規約，使用許可規約

 licensing system 免許制

 patent licensing 特許実施権，特許実施許諾，特許許諾，特許のライセンス供与

 technology licensing arrangements 技術のライセンス契約

▶We made some adjustments to our *licensing* practices. 当社は，当社の特許認可手続きを一部変更しました。

lien 名 先取特権，留置権，物的担保，担保権，リーエン

 equitable lien 先取特権，優先弁済権

 junior lien bond 後順位先取特権付き社債

 lien creditor リーエン債権者

 liens on assets 資産に対する担保権，資産に対する先取特権

 possessory lien 留置権，占有リーエン，コモン・ロー上のリーエン（＝common law lien）

▶The Shares are free and clear of any *liens*, charges or other encumbrances. 本株式は，先取特権，担保権その他の制限［負担，障害］の対象に一切なっていない。

life 名 生活，暮らし，生命，寿命，期間，活動，活動期間，存続，存続期間，耐用期間，耐用年数，年数，継続期間，ライフ

 actual life 実際耐用年数

 asset life 資産の耐用年数

 average life 平均期間，平均残存期間，平均償還期間

 composite life 総合耐用年数（＝composite useful life）

 contractual life 契約期間

 economic life 経済的耐用年数，経済寿命（＝economic age），経済生活

 expectation of life 見積り耐用年数（＝expected life）

 legal life 法定有効期間

 life annuity 生涯年金，終身年金，生命年金

 life period 耐用年数

 life span 存続期間

 life to call 据え置き期間

 mean expectation life 平均余命

 option life オプション行使期間

 physical life 物理的耐用年数

 probable life 予想耐用年数

 product life 製品寿命，製品サイクル（＝product cycle）

 productive life 生産年数

 remaining life 残存期間，残存年数，残存耐用

年数
　remaining life of the issue　社債の残存期間
　remaining useful life　残存耐用年数　(＝residual service life)
　service life　耐用年数
　total economic life　通算経済的耐用年数
▶Amounts receivable or payable and gains or losses realized under swap agreements are recognized as yield adjustments over the *life* of the related debt.　スワップ契約に基づいて実現した受取金や支払い金と利益および損失は，当該債務が存続する間，利回り調整として認識されます。

life cycle　製品のライフサイクル(product life cycle), 生活循環, 寿命, ライフサイクル
　life cycle costs　ライフサイクル・コスト　(プロジェクトの全期間にわたって発生する費用)
　product life cycle　商品[製品]ライフサイクル, 製品サイクル
▶We are committed to reducing the environmental impact at every stage of a product's *life cycle*, from design, to manufacture, to use, and to disposal.　当社は，設計から製造，使用と廃棄にいたるまで，製品のライフサイクルの各段階での環境への影響軽減に全力を挙げています。

life insurance　生命保険
　life insurance benefits　生命保険給付
　life insurance benefits for retirees　退職者に対する生命保険給付
　life insurance coverage　保険金額, 保険契約金額, 生命保険給付　(⇒**coverage**)
　life insurance deduction　生命保険料控除
　life insurance in force　生命保険の保有契約高
　life insurance industry　生命保険業界, 生保業界
　life insurance premium　生命保険料
　life insurance product　生命保険商品, 生保商品
▶*Life insurance* benefits for retirees are expensed as funded, during the post-employment period.　退職者への生命保険給付は，退職後の期間中に基金が積み立てられた時点で費用として計上されます。

life insurer　生命保険会社　(＝life insurance company, life insurance firm)
▶The top 10 *life insurers* in the nation reported a total of ¥1.46 trillion in valuation losses on their securities holdings.　国内生保の上位[主要]10社の保有有価証券[保有株式]の減損処理額は，10社合計で1兆4,600億円に達した。

life support　生命維持装置
▶No currency can be considered strong if it is propped up by *life support* such as intervention.　市場介入というような生命維持装置で支えられてい

る通貨は，強い通貨とはいえない。

lifeline 名　生命線, 命綱, 生活物資補給路, ライフライン
▶Quality management is our *lifeline*.　品質管理は，当社の命綱だ。

lifestyle 名　生活様式, 生き方, 暮らしぶり, ライフスタイル
▶Along with the regionalization of pop industries, new standardized patterns of consumption and *lifestyle* are emerging in East Asia.　文化産業の地域化とともに，均質の新しい消費パターンとライフスタイルが東アジアに生まれている。

Lifestyles Of Health And Sustainability　健康と環境重視の生活様式, ロハス　(健康と環境を重視し，持続可能な社会のあり方を求める生活様式のこと)

lifetime employment　終身雇用
▶Efforts by the corporate sector to set great value on employees through the lifetime employment system has served to accumulate good human resources.　終身雇用制で従業員を大事にする企業の姿勢が，優れた人的資源の蓄積に役立っている。

LIFO　後入れ先出し法　(＝LIFO cost method, LIFO method: last-in, first-outの略; ⇒**FIFO**)
▶We changed our inventory cost flow method to the FIFO cost method from the *LIFO* cost method on January 1, 2007.　2007年1月1日から当社は，当社の棚卸し資産原価算定の方法を，後入れ先出し法から先入れ先出し法に変更しました。

light-emitting diode　発光ダイオード《略**LED**》(電流を光に変換する半導体で，携帯電話の表示装置や大型スクリーンなどに使われる)
▶Shuji Nakamura invented the blue light-emitting diode (LED) while working at Nichia Corp.　中村修二氏は，日亜化学工業に勤務中，青色発光ダイオードを発明した。

lighting technology　発光技術　(⇒**high-profile**)

like-for-like 形　既存店ベースの, 同一条件の, 同種の, 同等の
　like-for-like growth in sales　既存店ベースの販売の伸び, 既存店ベースの売上高の伸び
　like-for-like replacement　同種交換, 同等交換
　like-for-like volume growth　既存店ベースの販売数量の伸び
　measure on a like-for-like basis　同一条件で測定する
　on a like-for-like basis　既存店ベースで, 同一条件で, 同一条件の下で

sales volume on a like-for-like basis 既存店ベースの売上高
▶The sales volume on a *like-for-like* basis fell by three percent. 既存店ベースの売上高は，3％減少した。

likely 形 有望な，見込みのある，有力な，有力とされる，予想される，必死である
  be likely to …する見通しだ，…する見込みだ，…する模様だ，…しそうだ，…の可能性が大きい［高い］，…する公算が大きい
  likely debt burden 予想される債務負担額
  likely fare hike 予想される運賃の値上げ
  the most likely explanation 最も納得のいく説明
  the most likely scenario 特に可能性が高いシナリオ
▶The firm is *likely* to price the professional baseball club between ¥20 billion and ¥25 billion. 同社は，プロ野球球団の売却額について200億円から250億円程度を提示している模様だ。

limit 名 限度，極度，限界，制限，限度額，リミット
  borrower limit 与信限度
  credit limit 信用限度，与信限度，信用貸出限度
  daily price limit 値幅制限（＝price limit）
  lending limit 貸出限度
  lower limit 値幅制限の下限
  manager's discretionary limit 支店長の専決限度
  order without limit 成り行き注文
  policyholder limits 保険契約者に対する与信限度
  price limit 値幅制限，ストップ値段
  stock-buying limit 株式買入れ枠
  stop limit ストップ・リミット
  stop limit order 指し値注文
  trading limit 取引制限
▶In technology, there are no *limits* in sight for improvements in performance, function and value. テクノロジーの面では，性能，機能と価値の向上に限界はなさそうである。
▶There are legally two different upper *limits* for lending interest rates. 貸出金利の上限が法律上，二つある。

limited liability company 有限会社
▶Existing *limited liability companies* are allowed to remain intact or change themselves into stock companies under the new Corporate Law. 新会社法では，既存の有限会社はそのまま存続するか，株式会社に（商号を）変更することができる。

limited liability partnership 有限責任事業組合，有限責任パートナーシップ《略 **LLP**》
▶*Limited liability partnership* (LLP) is a new form of business entity that is not a joint stock company or business union. 有限責任事業組合（LLP）は，株式会社でもなく，事業組合でもない新しい事業体だ。

line 名 〈商品の〉種類，機種，事業部門，組立工程，路線，方針，〈損益計算書の〉経常利益［当期純利益］，電話線，伝送路，回線，ライン （⇒**bottom line**, **business line**, **monoline**, **product line**）
  above the line 経常収支，経常支出，範囲内
  above the line profit 経常利益
  assembly line 組立ライン，流れ作業，アセンブリ・ライン
  bank line 銀行与信枠
  below the line 異常損益項目，範囲外
  full line 全機種，全製品，全品種，フルライン
  line and staff organization ライン・アンド・スタッフ組織，ライン・スタッフ組織，直系参謀組織
  line authority ライン権限，管理者の権限
  line-by-line analysis 事業分野別分析
  line control ライン統制
  line department ライン部門（総務，人事，経理，調査，企画などのスタッフ部門に対して，製造業の生産部門・販売部門，販売業の仕入れ部門・販売部門など直接売上げにかかわる部門をライン部門という）
  line function ライン機能
  line item 勘定科目
  line management ライン部門管理
  line manager 製造・販売部門の意思決定者，ライン・マネジャー
  line organization ライン組織，直系組織，直線式組織，軍隊組織
  line production ライン生産，流れ作業生産，流れ作業，直線生産
  line robbing 品揃えの拡大，ラインロビング
  merchandise line 商品構成
  net errors and omissions line 純誤差脱漏項目
  net sales by product line 製品別売上構成
  price line 価格線
  product line control 製品別管理
  production line 生産ライン
  straight line depreciation 定額償却，定額法
  top line 売上高
▶Extraordinary losses have also battered the company's bottom *line*. 特別損失も，同社の業績を直撃した。

line of business 事業の種類，業種，事業部門，

事業分野, 事業ライン, 営業品目, 営業項目, 営業科目 （＝business line）
line of business information 事業の種類別情報, 事業分野別情報, 業種別情報
line of business reporting 事業の種類別報告, 事業分野別報告, 業種別報告
▸This realignment decentralizes the Corporation into a series of largely autonomous *lines of business*. この再編成により, 当社の組織は, 自主性の高い一連の事業部門に分散されています。

line of credit 信用限度, 信用供与限度, 信用供与枠, 与信限度枠, 融資限度, 貸出限度額, 借入限度額, 借入枠, 借入枠中未借入額, クレジット・ライン （＝credit line）
▸Leverage was increased through a *line of credit*. 与信限度枠を使って, レバレッジを引き上げた。

line of products 製品ライン, 商品ライン, 商品群, 製品系列, 製品種目, 製品品目, 製品構成, プロダクト・ライン （＝product line）
▸Operations involve the design, manufacture and sale of a diversified *line of products*. 当社の事業には, 各種製品品目の設計, 製造と販売が含まれています。

lineup 名 顔ぶれ, 陣容, 編成, 布陣, 品ぞろえ, 商品構成, 機種構成, 車種構成, 製品一覧表, テレビ番組編成予定表, ラインアップ
▸Existing convenience stores had too narrow product *lineups*. 既存のコンビニは, 商品数を絞り込みすぎた。
▸Shop 99 has two to four times more variety in its product *lineup* compared with other convenience stores. ショップ99は, 品ぞろえが他のコンビニよりも2-4倍多い。

link 動 連結する, 関連付ける, 連動させる, リンクする, 名 関係, 結合, 連環, 連動, 輪, 結合させるもの, リンク
　bond-linked to stock price index 株価指数連動債
　link index 連環指数
　link structure 連環構造
　link system 輸出入リンク制
　Nikkei-linked bond 日経平均リンク債
　personal link-up 人的結合
　synergistic links 相互補完の関係
　trade and capital links 貿易・投資関係
　yen-linked bond 円リンク債
linkage 名 連関, リンケージ
lion's share 最大の比率, 最大のシェア, 最大の部分, 大きい取り分, 大部分, 一番おいしいところ
▸The *lion's share* of these contributions goes to educational institutions, but we also support health, cultural activities and the like. この寄付金の大部分は, 教育団体に割り当てられますが, 当社は保健衛生や文化活動などにも援助を行っています。

liquefaction 名 液化, 液状化現象
▸With Japanese technology, coal *liquefaction* will prove commercially if crude oil prices stay above $30 a barrel. 原油の価格が1バレル＝30ドル以上なら, 日本の技術で石炭の液化は採算が取れる。

liquefied natural gas 液化天然ガス《略 LNG》
▸Transporting natural gas in solid form is much cheaper than moving *liquefied natural gas*. 天然ガスを固形化して輸送するほう（天然ガス・ハイドレート輸送）が, 液化天然ガス（LNG）を運ぶよりずっとコストが安い。

liquid 形 流動性がある, 流動性の高い
　liquid asset 流動資産, 流動性の高い資産, 当座資産
　liquid asset ratio 当座資産比率, 当座資産構成比率
　liquid capital 流動資本
　liquid fund 流動資金, 当座資金
　maintain liquid capital 流動資本を維持する
　net liquid assets 純流動資産
　short-term liquid investments 流動性のある短期投資
▸Temporary cash investments are highly *liquid* and have original maturities generally of three months or less. 短期投資は, 非常に流動性が高く, 原則として3か月以内に当初の期限が到来するものです。
▸The company considers all highly *liquid* investments purchased with an original maturity of three months or less to be cash equivalents. 当社は, 取得日から満期日までの当初期間が3か月以内の流動性が高い投資を現預金等価物としています。

liquid crystal display panel 液晶ディスプレー・パネル, 液晶パネル
▸Hitachi, Ltd. and Matsushita Electric Industrial Co. are considering jointly manufacturing large *liquid crystal display panels* for flat-screen televisions. 日立製作所と松下電器産業は, 薄型テレビ用の大型液晶パネルの共同生産を検討している。

liquid crystal screen TV 液晶テレビ （＝liquid crystal display television）
▸The firm did not announce the sales plan for *liquid crystal screen TV* sets for 2009. 同社は,

2009年の液晶テレビの販売計画を公表しなかった。

liquid investment 流動性の高い投資
▶All highly *liquid investments* with a maturity of three months or less at date of purchase are considered to be cash equivalents. 購入日から3か月以内で満期となる非常に流動性の高い投資は、現金等価物として扱っています。

liquidate 動 〈借金や負債を〉弁済する、決済する、清算する、処分する、処理する、〈証券や資産などを〉売却する、現金化する、〈在庫を〉削減する、〈会社などを〉整理する、解散する、破産する
▶The prospects for *liquidating* nonperforming loans are dim. 不良債権処理の見通しは、はっきりしない。

liquidation 名 流動性、流動化、決済、清算、処分、処理、整理、解散、破産、売却、現金化、換金(「流動化」は、保有資産の支配権を第三者に移転して資金調達すること)
　automatic liquidation 自動決済
　go into liquidation 破産する、清算を開始する、清算する、解散する
　insolvent liquidation 支払い不能による清算
　liquidation of bad debts 不良債権の処理
　liquidation of inventories 在庫削減、在庫整理、在庫取り崩し (=inventory liquidation)
　liquidation of securities holdings 保有有価証券の売却
　liquidation of the assets 資産の売却 (=asset liquidation)
　profit and loss from liquidation 清算損益 (=liquidation profit and loss)
▶The Tokyo Stock Exchange (TSE) will move the company's stock to TSE's *liquidation* post from the monitoring post. 東京証券取引所(東証)は、同社株を監理ポストから整理ポストに移す。

liquidity 名 流動性、流動性、流動資産の換金性、流動資産の換金能力、流動性の高さ、資金繰り、資金 (⇒broadly defined liquidity, excess liquidity, tax authorities)
　流動性とは➡流動性は、一般に株式や債券などの流通性のことで、marketability (市場性: 市場で容易に売買できること)とほぼ同じ意味を持つ。このほかに、自己資産を現金化する能力を意味する場合もある。
　ample liquidity 高い流動性、流動性の高さ、豊富な資金、大量の資金、潤沢な資金
　corporate liquidity 企業の手元流動性
　excess liquidity 過剰流動性、余剰資金
　internal sources of liquidity 内部流動性 (=internal liquidity)
　liquidity allocation 資金供給
　liquidity and capital resources 流動性と資本の源泉
　liquidity at hand 手元流動性
　liquidity demand 流動性需要、資金需要
　liquidity of investments in corporate securities 投資有価証券の流動性
　liquidity preference 流動性選好
　liquidity trap 流動性のわな
　outside sources of liquidity 外部流動性 (=external liquidity)
　tightened liquidity 資金繰りの悪化

list 動 上場する、上場される、表示する、表記する、記載する、掲載する、記録する、計上する、名を挙げる、指定する
　listed investment 上場証券に対する投資
　listed securities 上場有価証券、上場株式
　listed share 上場株式、上場株 (=listed stock)
▶The company *listed* its shares on the New York Stock Exchange in fiscal 2007 to expedite fund procurement in the U.S. markets. 米市場で機動的に資本調達するため、同社は2007年度に米ニューヨーク証券取引所に株式を上場した。

list 名 表、名簿、一覧表、目録、明細書、リスト
　foreign buyers list 海外商社名簿
　list of weight and measurement 重量・容積証明書
　list price 定価、表示価格 (=sticker price)
　list supplier リスト業者、DM用名簿供給者
　operation list 作業手順書
　packing list 包装明細書
　price list 価格表
　stockholder list 株主名簿 (=list of stockholders)
　watch list 監理ポスト
▶In the online survey of corporate brands, the firm did not make the *list* in 2008. インターネットでの企業ブランド意識調査で、同社は2008年に名前が挙がらなかった。
▶The Tokyo Stock Exchange placed shares in the company on a *watch list* to warn investors the firm may fall under the category of "delisted." 東京証券取引所は、同社株を「上場廃止」の可能性があることを投資家に警告する「監理ポスト」に置いた[移した]。

list of shareholders 株主名簿 (=list of stockholders, shareholders list)
▶Oji Paper is considering asking the Tokyo District Court to allow it to examine the *list of shareholders* in Hokuetsu Paper. 王子製紙は、

東京地裁に対して北越製紙の株主名簿の閲覧を求めること[閲覧を求める仮処分申請]を検討している。

listed company 上場会社, 上場企業, 公開会社, 公開企業 (＝listed corporation, listed firm; ⇒row)
▸*Listed companies* have recently become afraid of being the target of hostile takeover bid. 上場企業は最近, 敵対的買収の標的になるのを恐れるようになった。
▸There are about 1 million stock companies nationwide, and about 4,000 of them are *listed companies*. 国内には株式会社が約100万社あり, そのうち4,000社前後が株式を上場している公開会社だ。

listing 名 上場, 不動産仲介, 不動産仲介契約, 名簿, 表, 表の作成
　backdoor listing 裏口上場 (非上場企業が上場企業を買収して上場を果たすこと)
　eligibility criteria for listing 上場基準
　exchange listing procedures 証券取引所上場手続き
　listing fee 上場手数料
　listing particulars 上場目論見書, 上場明細書, 上場開示項目 (⇒prospectus)
　listing requirement 上場基準, 上場審査基準, 上場要件 (＝initial listing requirements, listing rule)
　multiple listing 同時上場
　new listing 新規上場
　official listing 公的相場表
　preliminary application for listing 上場の仮申請
　public listing 上場
　stock exchange listing 上場証券取引所, 証券取引所への上場
　stock listings 株式上場証券取引所
▸Mitsui Life Insurance Co. intends to postpone its planned TSE *listing*. 三井生命保険は, 計画していた東証(東京証券取引所)への上場を延期する予定だ。

lithium ion rechargeable battery リチウムイオン充電池
▸*Lithium ion rechargeable batteries* are used for personal computers, cell phones and hybrid electric vehicles. リチウムイオン充電池は, パソコンや携帯電話, ハイブリッド車(ガソリン電気自動車)などに用いられている。

litigate 動 訴訟を起こす, 起訴する
livestock 名 家畜
　livestock industry 畜産業界

LLC 有限責任会社, 〈日本の〉合同会社 (⇒**limited liability company**)
　LLCについて➡アメリカのLLCは, ベンチャー企業などが資金調達をしやすくするために考え出された制度で, 構成員間の関係を自由な合意で決めることができる組合(パートナーシップ)に対し, 企業の法人格と構成員の有限責任を与えたものである。LLCでは, 損益が直接, 構成員(出資者)に配分される。また, LLCには法人所得税が課税されない。(2003年12月8日付読売新聞「けいざい講座」から一部引用)

LLP 有限責任パートナーシップ, 有限責任事業組合, 有限責任組合 (⇒**limited liability partnership**)

LNG 液化天然ガス (**liquefied natural gas**の略)
▸*LNG* is more cost-efficient than NGH when transported in large quantities over a long distance. 液化天然ガス(LNG)は, 長距離を大量に運ぶ場合には天然ガス・ハイドレート(NGH)より費用[コスト]効率が高い。

load 名 積荷, 積載量, 分担量, 仕事量, 付加料, 販売手数料, 動 …に荷を積む, 載せる, 詰め込む, 〈データを主記憶に〉読み込む, ロードする

loan 動 融資する, 貸し出す, 貸し付ける
▸The bank *loaned* the company a total of ¥5 billion in 25 separate transactions. 同行は, 同社に25回, 総額で50億円を融資した。

loan 名 貸付け, 貸出, 融資, 借入れ, 債権, 貸出債権, 債務, 借款, 債券発行, 貸付け金, 借入金, ローン
　accounting for impairment of loans 貸出金劣化の会計処理
　accounting for loan losses 貸倒れ損失の会計
　arrears on loan repayments 延滞債権
　balance of loans 融資残高
　construction loan 建設借入金, 建設ローン
　dead loan 焦げ付き貸金
　debt loan 借入金
　fees on loans 貸出金手数料
　housing loan 住宅金融, 住宅ローン
　interest on loans 貸付け金利息
　loan capital 借入資本 (＝long-term loan)
　loan credits 債権 (＝loan claims; ⇒**purchasing**)
　loan disposal costs 債権処理費用, 不良債権処理費用 (＝credit costs)
　loan from officer 役員借入金 (＝loan payable from officer)
　loan funds 貸出資金, 貸付け資金, 融資資金, 借款

loan guarantee 債務保証, 融資補償, 融資の信用保証, 貸出保証

loan interest rate 貸出金利 (=interest rate on loans, lending rate)

loan origination fees 貸付け手数料, 貸出金実行手数料

loan payable from officer 役員借入金 (= loan from officer)

loan recipient 融資先, 融資先企業

loan redemption 借入金償還

loan sharking 高利貸し業, ヤミ金融, ヤミ金融業

loan to affiliated companies 関係会社貸付け金 (=loan to affiliates)

loan to director 取締役貸付け金

loan to officer 役員貸付け金

loans and discounts 貸出金

loans payable 借入金

loans receivable 貸付け金

loans secured by real estate 不動産担保[抵当]貸付け金

loans secured by stock and bonds 有価証券担保貸付け金

loans to stockholders 株主貸付け金

make a loan 融資する, 貸し出す, 融資を実行する, 貸し付ける

outstanding loan 融資残高

receive loans from …から融資を受ける

repay the loan ローンを返済する, 借入金を返済する

securitizing of loans 債権の証券化, 融資の証券化

sound loan 正常債権, 健全債権

troubled loan 不良債権

▸The company plans to use the *loans* mainly to finance its planned capital investment. 同社は, この借入金を使って, 主に予定している設備投資に充てる計画だ。

▸We must change our accounting for the *loans* we make to customers by 2009. 当社は, 2009年までに, 顧客に対して行っている融資の会計処理方法を変更しなければなりません。

loan assessment 債権の査定

▸The bank conducted lenient *loan assessments* on borrowers, even those experiencing serious financial trouble. 同行は, 借り手企業に対する債権の査定では, 経営内容が危機的状況にある企業でも, 甘い査定をしていた。

loan assets 貸出資産

▸A U.S.-style formula for calculating loan-loss reserves assesses *loan assets* more strictly. 貸出資産の評価については, 米国流の貸倒れ引当金の算定方式のほうが厳しい。

loan collection 債権回収

▸The financial institutions were asked to temporarily halt *loan collection*. 金融機関は, 債権回収の一時停止を求められた。

loan facility 貸付け, 融資枠, 融資金

▸This yen *loan facility* is for general corporate purposes. この円融資枠は, 一般事業目的に使用される。

loan forgiveness 債権放棄, 債務免除 (= debt forgiveness, debt waiver, loan waiver, loan write-off)

▸The three banks abandoned their initial plan to grant *loan forgiveness* to part of their claims on ¥1.6 trillion in loans to the company. 3行は, 1兆6,000億円の同社向け債権請求の一部について債権を放棄する当初案を断念した。

loan loss 貸倒れ, 貸倒れ損失, 不良債権, 不良貸付け

declare a loan loss 貸倒れ損失を計上する

loan loss provisioning 貸倒れ引当金繰入れ額, 貸倒れ引当金 (=loan loss provisioning charge)

loan loss ratio 貸倒れ実績率

loan losses 貸倒れ損失額

loan loss charge 貸倒れ損失額, 貸倒れ引当金, 不良債権額, 不良債権処理額, 不良債権処理損 (=bad debt clean-up charge, loan loss cost)

▸We expect group *loan-loss charges* of ¥900 billion for fiscal 2009. 当行は, 2009年度は連結で9,000億円の不良債権額を見込んでいます。

loan loss provisions 貸倒れ引当金 (=loan loss reserves)

bolster [hike, increase] loan loss provisions 貸倒れ引当金を積み増す

loan loss provisions of doubtful debts 不良債権に対する貸倒れ引当金

▸Consolidated pretax profit declined 38 percent due to increased *loan-loss provisions* for clients facing declining earnings. 連結税引き前利益は, 収益が低下している取引先[融資先]に対する貸倒れ引当金を積み増したため, 38%減少しました。

loan loss reserves 貸倒れ引当金, 貸倒れ準備金 (=loan loss provisions, reserves for bad loans, reserves for loan losses, reserves for possible loan losses:「貸倒れ引当金」は, 融資などの債権から担保などを差し引いた金額に対して, 貸出先企業が倒産して回収できない確率を考慮して積み立てる。経営状況が悪い企業向けの債権ほど, 引当率

increase loan loss reserves 貸倒れ引当金を積み増す, 貸倒れ引当金を強化する
reduce the loan loss reserves 貸倒れ引当金を減らす
set aside loan loss reserves 貸倒れ引当金を積み立てる
▶The effective book value is calculated by subtracting amassed *loan loss reserves* from the original amount of money that was lent. 実質簿価は, 債権の元々の額(貸し付けた元々の金額:簿価)から, (銀行が)積み立てた貸倒れ引当金を差し引いて算定する。

loan recipient 融資先, 融資先企業
▶Currently, loan loss reserves are calculated on the basis of the probability of *loan recipients* going bankrupt. 現在, 貸倒れ引当金は融資先企業の(過去の)倒産確率に基づいて算定している。

loan reserves 債権に対する引当金
▶Regular FSA inspections are conducted after banks close their accounts in March, and focus on whether their *loan reserves* are adequate. 金融庁の通常検査は3月の銀行の決算後に行われ, 主に債権に対する引当金が十分かどうかなどを点検する。

loan shark 高利貸し, サラ金, サラ金業者, ヤミ金融業者
▶Most of the people who have used *loan sharks* have borrowed sums from various consumer loan firms that they are unable to repay. ヤミ金融の利用者の大半は, 複数の消費者金融会社から利用者の返済能力を超える金額を借り入れている。

loan values 債権の現在価値, 借入限度額
▶*Loan values* are calculated based on projections of how profitable a borrower is likely to be in the future. 債権の現在価値は, 融資先企業の予想収益に基づいて算定されています。

loan waiver 債権放棄, 債務免除 (＝debt forgiveness, debt waiver, loan forgiveness, loan write-off)
▶The major banks managed to write off ¥5.11 trillion worth of bad loans using financial assistance and legal procedures such as *loan waivers* for large-lot borrowers as well as by selling bad loans to the Resolution and Collection Corporation. 大口融資先への債権放棄などの金融支援や法的整理, 整理回収機構(RCC)への不良債権売却などで, 大手行は最終的に5兆1,100億円の不良債権を処理した。

lobby 圧力団体, ロビー団体, 院外団, 陳情団, ロビー
business lobby 財界の圧力団体, 財界ロビー
lobby group 圧力団体, 政治的圧力団体, ロビー団体, ロビー活動団体 (＝lobbying group)
lobbying ロビー活動, 院外活動, 議会工作, 陳情運動, 請願運動, ロビーイング
Administration lobbying 議会工作
gun lobbying 銃砲規制反対派
lobbying campaign ロビー活動 (＝lobbying effort)
lobbying group ロビー活動団体, 圧力団体 (＝lobby group)
political lobbying group 政治的圧力団体

local 地元の, 土地の, 現地の, 地方の, 市内の, 同一区内の, ローカル
local area network 狭域通信網, 域内情報通信網, 企業内情報通信網《略 LAN》
local authority 地方自治体
Local Autonomy Law 地方自治体法 (⇒ agent)
local call 市内通話, 市内通信サービス
local content 現地調達, 現地調達率, ローカル・コンテント
Local Content Act 自動車部品国内調達法, 現地調達率規制[条項], ローカル・コンテント法
local government 地方政府, 地方自治体, 地方公共団体, 地方
local manufacture 現地生産
local partner 現地パートナー
local telecommunications facilities 地域通信設備

local assembly capacity 現地生産能力 (＝local output capacity)
▶Toyota will strengthen its *local assembly capacity* not only in North America but also in China, Europe, India and Russia. トヨタは, 北米に加えて, 中国や欧州, インド, ロシアでの現地生産能力を強化する方針だ。

local businesses 地元企業, 地場産業, 国内企業, 国内業界
▶The priority of some Chinese provincial governments is to help *local businesses* expand. 中国の一部の地方政府は, 地元企業の新興を優先している。

local currency 現地通貨, 現地通貨建て, 国内通貨, 国内通貨建て, 自国通貨
▶Non-U.S. subsidiaries which operate in a *local currency* environment account for approximately 90% of the Company's non-U.S. revenue. 現地通貨を用いる経済環境で営業活

動を営む米国外子会社は，当社の米国外収益の約90%を占めています[約90%を稼得しています]．

local procurement 現地調達
▸The Russian government plans to require Toyota to increase *local procurement* of components. ロシア政府は，部品の現地調達拡大をトヨタに義務付ける方針だ．

local production 現地生産，国内生産（＝local assembly, local output）
▸The company may experience difficulties in setting up a global parts supply and distribution networks as it expands *local productions*. 世界各地での現地生産が拡大するにつれ，同社は，グローバルな部品メーカーの供給体制や物流網の確立が難しくなる可能性もある．

local production system 現地生産体制，現地生産方式，現地生産システム
▸The firm strengthened its *local production system* by putting factories into operation in such places as France, Russia, and Guangzhou, China. 同社は，フランスやロシア，広州(中国)などで工場を稼動させ，現地生産体制を強化した．

localization 名 ローカリゼーション(国や地域に応じてソフトウエアやハードウエアの仕様を変更すること)，地域的集中，地域特化，局地化，局部限定

localization economies 地域特化の経済

localization of industry 産業の地域的集中

personnel localization 人材の現地採用
▸The partners we need are not telecom carriers, but companies that can support the *localizations* and content suppliers. 当社が求めているパートナーは，通信事業者ではなく，ロカリゼーションのサポートをしてくれる企業とコンテンツ・サプライヤーです．

localize 動 一地域に制限する，ローカライズする

locate 動 設ける，置く，開設する，開業する

be located at …に位置する，…にある，…に置いてある

locate production sites in China 中国に生産拠点を置く
▸We include the accounts of operations *located* outside the U.S. on the basis of their fiscal year. 米国外子会社[関係会社]の財務書類は，各子会社の事業年度[会計年度]に基づいて連結されています．
▸We *located* a new branch in New York. 当社は，ニューヨークに支店を開設しました．

location 名 立地，立地条件，場所，位置，配置，所在地，拠点，用地，敷地，データの記憶場所，野外撮影場，ロケーション

degree of location 集積度

fixed location 固定ロケーション（商品を置く場所の固定化）

free location フリー・ロケーション（商品を置く場所の自由化）

geographical location 地理的位置

industrial location 産業立地，工業立地，産業配置（＝location of industry）

location decision 立地決定

location factor 立地要因（＝location force）

manufacturing location 工業立地

offshore locations 海外拠点

one hundred percent location 最適店舗立地

plant location 工場所在地，工場立地，工場用地

prime location 一等地

store location 店舗立地，商業立地

strategic location 地理的条件，地理的に有利な条件（＝strategic geographic location）
▸Revenues from customers (based on the *location* of the selling organization rather than the *location* of the customer) increased in Canada and the United States. 地域別顧客売上高(顧客の所在地ではなく，販売組織の所在地に基づく売上高)は，カナダと米国で増加しました．
▸Toyota is considering Miyagi Prefecture as a possible *location* for its compact car engine plant. トヨタは，小型車のエンジン工場の有力な建設地として，宮城県を検討している．

lock 動 締める，閉じる，〈資本を〉固定させる

lock in 利益や価格を確定する，コストを固定する，確保する
▸Investors sold shares across the board to *lock in* profits. 利益を確定するため，投資家が全銘柄にわたって株を売り進めた．

lockstep 名 型にはまったやり方，がんじがらめの配列，(前の人と間隔を詰めて歩調を合わせる)密接行進法
▸The adverse effects of the national public servant system include the seniority system, *lockstep* mentality, a vertically compartmentalized administrative structure, rigidity and ineffectiveness. 国家公務員制度の弊害として，年功序列，横並び(型にはまった物の考え方)，縦割りの行政機構，硬直性や非効率などが挙げられる．

lodge 動 預ける，〈申告書などを〉提出する，〈苦情などを〉申し立てる

lodgement [lodgment] 名 〈抗議などの〉申し入れ，〈担保などの〉供託

loft business ロフト・ビジネス（不用倉庫を活用するビジネス）

log 名 航海日誌，航空日誌，業務日誌，〈コンピュ

―ターの〉ログ

logistics 名　後方業務, 後方支援技術, 物流管理, トータル物流管理, 効率的物流システム, 事業の詳細な計画・実行, ロジスティクス（＝business logistics）

logo 名　標識, 意匠, 商標文字, ロゴ

Lohas　ロハス, 健康と環境に配慮したライフスタイル（Lifestyles Of Health And Sustainabilityの略）

lombard 動　金を融通する, 金を貸す

Lombard 名　銀行, 銀行家, 金貸し, 質屋
　floating Lombard rate　変動ロンバード金利
　Lombard borrowing　ロンバード借入れ
　Lombard credit　ロンバード貸付け
　Lombard lending　ロンバード貸出
　Lombard loan　ロンバード貸付け, 有価証券担保融資
　Lombard rate　ロンバード金利, 有価証券担保貸付け金利, 証券担保利率, ロンバード・レート
　Lombard rate hike　ロンバード金利の引上げ

Lombard Street　英ロンドンのロンバード街, ロンドンの金融街, ロンドンの金融界, ロンドンの金融市場, ロンドンの株式界

long 形　長い, 長期の, 買い待ちの, 強気の, 見込み薄の, 危険な

long-dated 形　長期の

long term　長期
　long-term accounts payable　長期未払い金
　long-term bond　長期債, 長期社債
　long-term borrowing　長期借入金
　long-term capital balance　長期資本収支（＝long-term balance of capital account）
　long-term deposit　長期性預金
　long-term loans　長期貸付け金, 長期融資, 長期借入金

long-term contract　長期契約, 長期請負契約, 長期工事契約
▸The Corporation uses the percentage of completion method to recognize revenues and costs associated with most *long-term* contracts.　当社では, 進行基準を用いて大半の長期請負契約に関する収益と費用を認識しています。

long-term debt　長期債務, 長期負債, 長期借入金, 長期借入債務, 固定負債（＝long term borrowings, long term obligation）
▸About $830 million of *long-term debt* matures during the year.　長期債務のうち約8億3,000万ドルは, 今年度に満期が到来します[満期を迎えます]。
▸The Company's *long-term* debt is rather small.　当社の長期借入金は, どちらかというと少ないほうです。

long-term debt rating　長期格付け
▸General Motor's *long term debt rating* was slashed one level to Caa1 by Moody's Investors Service.　ゼネラル・モーターズ（GM）の長期債格付けを, 米格付け会社のムーディーズ・インベスターズ・サービスが1段階下のCaa1に引き下げた。

long-term debt-to-total capital　長期負債対総資本比率
▸*Long-term debt-to-total capital* is used to gauge a company's financial strength.　長期負債対総資本比率は, 企業の財務力測定に用いられます。

long-term finance receivables　長期金融債権, 長期金融売掛債権
▸*Long-term finance receivables* of $300 million in 2008 are included in other assets.　2008年度の3億ドルの長期金融債権は, その他の資産に含まれています。

long-term financing　長期資金調達
▸Our *long-term financing* was accomplished through the issuance of long-term debt instruments.　当社の長期資金調達は, 長期債務証券を発行して行われた。

long-term incentive program　長期奨励報酬制度, 長期勤労奨励制度
▸In our *Long Term* Incentive *Program*, we grant stock options, stock appreciation rights (SARs) and other awards.　当社の長期勤労奨励制度には, ストック・オプションや株式評価受益権（SAR）などの奨励制度があります。

long-term interest rate　長期金利
　　長期金利とは➡ 期間1年以上の金利で, 新規発行された10年物国債（長期国債）の流通利回りを指標に使う。国債価格が上がれば長期金利が下がる関係にある。企業向け貸出や住宅ローン金利にも影響する。景気が悪いと経済活動が停滞し, 長期金利も下がる。
▸The rise in *long-term interest rates* may apply the brakes on the recovery.　長期金利の上昇は, 景気回復にブレーキをかけかねない。

long-term monetary assets　長期貨幣性資産
▸*Long-term monetary assets* and liabilities are translated at the exchange rates in effect at the balance sheet date.　長期貨幣性資産および負債は, 貸借対照表日[決算日]現在の実効為替レートで換算されています。

long-term planning　長期経営計画, 長期計画（＝long-range planning）

▸Our *long-term planning* will give us a strong global position in the expanding wireless market.　当社の長期計画によって，当社は拡大する無線通信市場で世界的に強力な事業基盤を確立する方針です。

long-term receivable　長期受取債権, 長期債権, 長期受取勘定
▸The Corporation's financial instruments include accounts receivable, short-term investments, *long-term receivables*, accounts payable, notes payable and long-term debt.　当社の金融手段［金融資産］としては，売掛金，短期投資，長期受取勘定，買掛金，短期借入金や短期債務などがあります。

longs 名　長期債券, 強気筋

lose 動　赤字を出す, 損失を被る, 失う,〈競争などに〉負ける, 下落する
▸GM, the world's largest automaker, *lost* $1.6 billion in the third quarter, or $2.89 per share.　自動車世界最大手のGMの第3四半期(7－9月期)決算は，16億ドル(1株当たり2.89ドル)の赤字となった。

loser 名　負け組, 負け組企業, 失敗企業, 敗者, 値下がり銘柄, 値下がり株　(⇒winner)
▸Even within the same electrical machinery sector, the difference between winners and *losers* has become more apparent.　同じ電機業界でも，勝ち組と負け組の差が鮮明になっている。
▸What distinguishes the winners from the *losers* is the ability to anticipate and influence these kinds of changes—to be leaders, not victims, of change.　勝者と敗者を決める大きな要因は，この種の変化を予期し，それに流動的に対応する能力，つまり変化の波に流されずに変化を制する能力です。

loss 名　損失, 欠損, 欠損金, 赤字, 赤字額, 損害, 損害額, 減損, 減少, ロス
　accounting loss　会計上の損失
　annual profit and loss　年次損益
　book loss　評価損, 含み損
　conditional loss　機会損失
　contingent loss　偶発損失
　credit loss　信用損失, 貸倒れ
　default loss　デフォルト損
　embedded losses　含み損
　expected losses　予想損失, 損失の予想額
　financial loss　財務会計上の損失, 財務上［会計上］の損失, 金融上の損失, 損失
　historical loss experience　過去の損失実績
　holding gain or loss　保有損益
　huge losses　巨額の損失
　interim losses　中間期の損失, 半期損失, 半期決算損失
　loss carryover [carry-over]　欠損金の繰越し (＝carryover of deficit)
　loss contingencies　偶発損失事象, 偶発［偶発的］損失
　loss from prior period adjustment　前期損益修正損
　loss from valuation of securities　有価証券評価損　(＝loss from securities revaluation, loss from write-down of securities)
　loss of operating earnings　営業利益の減少, 営業減益
　loss on bad debt　貸倒れ損
　loss on bond conversion　社債転換差損
　loss on disposal of property　動産・不動産処分損
　loss on foreign exchange　外国為替差損
　loss on impairment　減損損失
　loss on retirement of fixed assets　固定資産除却損
　loss or gain on retirement of fixed assets　固定資産除却損益
　loss on sale of real estate　不動産売却損
　loss per share　1株当たり純損失, 1株当たり損失
　loss projections　損失予想額, 予想損失額
　losses from bad loan disposals　不良債権処理損失額, 不良債権処理による損失額, 不良債権処理に伴う損失額
　losses in stock transactions　株式売買の損失
　normal loss　正常な減損
　periodic loss　期間損失
　potential loss　潜在的損失, 予想損失
　reduced losses　赤字縮小, 赤字幅の縮小, 損失幅の縮小　(＝lower losses, smaller losses, reduction in losses)
　special losses　特別損失
　tax loss　税務上の欠損金
▸The bank recorded *losses* in the accounting period ending March 31 due to bad loan write-offs.　同行は，不良債権処理のため，3月期決算［3月31日終了の会計年度］で赤字になった。
▸GM is suffering major *losses*.　GMは，巨額の赤字に苦しんでいる。
▸We incurred a *loss* of $60 million in connection with the sale of U.S. oil and gas interests.　当社は，米国の石油・ガス利権の売却に関連して6,000万ドルの損失を被りました。

loss carryback [carry back]　欠損金の繰

戻し
▶No financial recognition is allowed for net deferred tax assets in excess of the amount that could be recovered as income tax refunds through existing *loss carryback* or carryforward provisions.　現行の欠損金の繰戻しまたは繰延べの規定(財務会計基準書(SFAS)第96号の規定)により，還付税金として取り戻すことができる金額を超えて繰延べ税金資産純額を会計上，計上することは認められていません。

loss carryforward [carry forward]　欠損金の繰越し，損失の繰延べ，繰越し欠損金
▶As December 31, 2008, certain non-U.S. subsidiaries had *loss carryforwards* for income tax reporting purposes of $39.7 million, with expiration dates starting in 2009.　2008年12月31日現在，一部の非米国籍子会社の繰越し欠損金は税務上3,970万ドルで，その繰越し期限は2009年以降到来します。

loss leader　目玉商品，特売品　(客寄せのため損を覚悟で売る商品)

loss-making [lossmaking] 形　赤字続きの，赤字の，採算が合わない
　loss-making area　不採算部門　(=lossmaking)
　loss-making business results　赤字決算
　loss-making outlet　赤字店舗　(=money-losing outlet)
▶The company window-dressed its *loss-making* business results for the business year to the end of September 2008.　同社は，2008年9月期の赤字決算を粉飾していた。

loss-sharing system　ロス・シェアリング方式，損失分担方式
▶The Financial Services Agency applied a *loss-sharing system* when it sold the bank.　同行の営業譲渡の際，金融庁はロス・シェアリング方式(国と譲渡先が損失を分担する方式)を適用した。

lost decade　失われた10年　(1990年代初め頃から続いた日本の景気後退[景気停滞]の10年)
▶The domestic economy has yet to show any promising signs even after the passing of the so-called *lost decade*.　日本経済は，いわゆる「失われた10年」を過ぎてもまだ明るい展望が開けないでいる。

lot 名　取引数量，最低取引単位，区画，地所，敷地，分け前，動　区分する，割り当てる

low 名　安値，底値，最低，底，最安値，最低値，最低記録
　a closing low　終値での最安値
　a new low　新安値，最安値の更新

　an all time low　過去最低，史上最安値，上場来の安値，過去最良
　an intraday low　取引時間中の安値，ざら場の安値
　all time lows　過去最低の水準　(=historic lows)
　fall to new lows　史上最安値を更新する　(=set new all-time lows)
▶Tokyo stocks tumbled to a 15-month closing *low* as uncertainties continued to grow about the outlook for the Japanese and U.S. economies.　東京株[東京株式市場の株価]は，日米経済の先行き不透明感の高まりを受け，終値で1年3か月ぶりの最安値となった。

low cost　低コスト，低費用，低原価
　low cost labor　低コスト労働力，低賃金の労働力
　low cost loan　低金利ローン，低費用融資，低利融資
▶The company has been building new factories at breakneck speed in *low-cost* countries such as China, Brazil, Hungary and Mexico.　同社は，中国やブラジル，ハンガリー，メキシコなどの低コスト国で，猛スピードで新工場を建設している。

low-interest loans　低利融資
▶The bank will provide the ailing automaker with *low-interest loans* in a bid to help manage its cash flow and conduct its corporate restructuring.　同行は，経営再建中のこの自動車メーカーの資金繰りやリストラを支援するため，低利融資を実施する方向だ。

lower 動　引き下げる，低減する，下げる，下落する，低下する，下がる，減少する
▶The company *lowered* its half-year net profit forecast.　同社は，半期純利益予想を引き下げた。

lower 形　低いほうの，下部の，下級の，下等の，下層の
　lower aggregate cost or market　総額低価法
　lower of average cost or market　平均原価または時価のいずれか低いほう(の金額)，平均原価時価低価法
　lower of cost and net realizable value　(資産の)取得原価と正味実現可能価額のうち低いほうの価額
　lower of cost or market value　原価時価比較低価
　lower realizable value or replacement price rule　実現可能価額取替原価比較低価法
　lower revenues　売上高の減少，収益の減少，減収
▶Our earnings per share were affected both by *lower* revenues and reduced gross margins.　当

社の1株当たり利益は，売上高の減少と売上利益率の低下の影響を受けました。

lower gross margins 売上利益率の低下，粗利益率の低下（＝reduced gross margins）
▸Price competition has been a contributing factor to the segment's *lower gross margins*. 当部門の粗利益率の低下をもたらした要因の一つは，価格競争だ。

lower of cost or market 低価法，低価基準《略 LCM》（＝cost or market, whichever is lower basis [method]）
　lower of cost (first-in, first-out) or market 先入れ先出し法に基づく低価法
　lower of cost or market basis [method] 低価法，低価基準，低価主義，(資産の取得)原価または時価のいずれか低い金額，原価時価比較低価法《略 LCM》
▸Inventories are stated at the *lower of cost or market*. 棚卸し資産は，低価法で計上しています。

loyalty 名 忠実性，忠実度，忠誠心，信頼度，ロイヤルティ
　brand loyalty ブランド・ロイヤルティ，商標忠実性
　consumer loyalty 消費者のロイヤルティ，消費者の忠実性
　customer loyalty 顧客ロイヤルティ，顧客の忠誠度，顧客の忠誠心
　store loyalty 店舗ロイヤルティ，ストア・ロイヤルティ

LP 有限責任組合，合資会社（**limited partnership** の略）

LTV 不動産価格に占める負債比率（**loan to value** の略）

lucrative 形 利益が得られる，儲かる，大変金になる，利益の大きい，有利な（＝profitable; ⇒ **cash deposits**）
　lucrative business 儲かる商売，有利な事業
　lucrative company 有力企業
　lucrative investment 有利な投資
　lucrative upstream division 利益の大きい原油採掘[原油生産]部門
▸Helping firms go public is a *lucrative* business for securities firms. 企業の上場を手伝う業務は，証券会社の収益源だ。

lure 動 勧誘する，誘い込む，取り込む
　lure customers 顧客を勧誘する，顧客を取り込む
　lure foreign companies 外資を導入する，外国企業を誘致する
▸Loan sharks *lure* borrowers through billboards and ads that bear only mobile phone numbers. ヤミ金融業者は，携帯電話の番号しか載せていない看板や広告で客を集めている。
▸The state of Development and Reform Commission of China will shift its policy of *luring* foreign companies from quantity to quality. 中国の(経済政策を統括する)国家発展改革委員会は，外資導入の方針を量から質に転換する方向だ。

luxury 名 贅沢品，奢侈品
luxury brand 高級ブランド
▸An increasing number of foreign *luxury brands* are moving into Ginza. 海外高級ブランドが銀座に続々出店[進出]している。

M / m

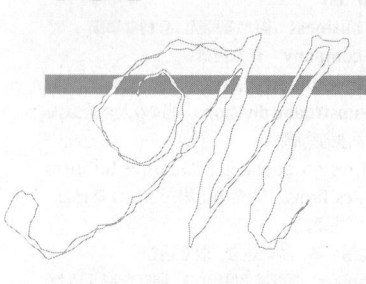

M 通貨供給量, マネー・サプライ (**money supply** の略)

M1 マネー・サプライM1, エム・ワン (=M one: M1＝預金通貨＋現金通貨)
▸The balance of *M1*, or cash in circulation plus deposit money, climbed 32.6 percent to ¥331.9 trillion. 現金通貨(個人や企業が保有する現金)に預金通貨(普通預金や当座預金など)を加えたM1の残高は, 32.6％増の331兆9,000億円となった。

M2 マネー・サプライM2, エム・ツー (=M two: M2＝預金通貨＋現金通貨＋定期性預金が中心の準通貨)
▸*M2* consists of cash in circulation, demand deposits and quasi money. M2は, 現金通貨と要求払い預金(現金通貨: deposit money)と準通貨から成る。

M3 マネー・サプライM3, エム・スリー (=M three: M2に譲渡性預金(CD)と郵便局, 農協, 信用金庫などの預貯金や信用元本などを加えたもの)

M&A 企業の吸収合併, 合併・買収, 企業取得と合併 (**merger and acquisition** [**mergers and acquisitions**]の略)
  M&A advisory firm M&A (企業の合併・買収)助言会社
  M&A bid 企業の合併・買収提案, M&Aの提案
  M&A deal M&A取引, M&A案件 (=M&A transaction)
  M&A information 企業の合併・買収情報, M&A情報
  strategic M&A 戦略的M&A (事業の再構築を目的とするM&A)
▸The recent *M&A* is a strategy with an eye on Asia, which has a great potential for sales growth. 今回のM&Aは, 販売が伸びる可能性が大きいアジアを視野に入れた戦略です。

ma-and-pa store 小売零細店, 零細小売店 (=mamma and papa store)

machine 名 コンピュータ, 機械, 機器, ミシン, 自動車, マシン
  automatic teller machine 現金自動預け払い機《略 ATM》
  automatic vending machine 自動販売機
  billing machine 請求書作成機
  business machine 事務機械, 事務機器
  idle machine 遊休機械
  leased machine リース機械
  machine hour 機械時間, 機械運転時間, 機械1台1時間当たり
  machine hour rate 機械時間率, 機械率
  machine readable form 機械読取り可能な形
  machine time 機械作動時間
  machine tool 工作機械
  quotation machine 相場表示機
  time keeping machine タイム・レコーダー
▸This listing must include a description of when, where, and how information is collected on production volume, labor hours, *machine* hours, etc. このリストには, 製造量や労働時間, 機械時間などに関して, その情報収集の日時や場所, 方法を記載するものとする。

machinery 名 機械, 機械装置, 機器, 機構, 組織
  electrical machinery 電機
  electronic machinery industry 電機業界
  industrial machinery 産業機械, 産業用機械
  machinery and equipments 機械設備, 機械・設備, 機械装置, 機械および装置

office machinery オフィス機器, 事務機器
transport machinery 輸送機器
transportation machinery 輸送機器, 輸送用機械
▶We depreciate our *machinery* using an accelerated method of depreciation for income tax reporting. 当社は，税務会計上[税務上]は加速償却法を使用して機械の減価償却を行っている。

machinery orders 機械受注, 機械受注額
　core private machinery orders 実質民間機械受注, 実質機械受注(船舶・電力を除く民間需要) (=core private-sector machinery orders)
　private machinery orders 民間機械受注
　public machinery orders 官公機械受注, 機械受注のうち公共部門の需要
▶Core *machinery orders* in December 2007 dropped a seasonally adjusted 3.2 percent from the previous month to ¥1.02 trillion. 2007年12月の実質民間機械受注額(季節調整値)は，前月比3.2%減の1兆200億円となった。
▶*Machinery orders* for the April-June quarter are expected to fall 3.2 percent. 4－6月期の機械受注は，3.2%減少する見通しだ。

machining 加工, 機械加工, マシニング
　electrical discharge machining 放電加工
　electron beam machining 電子ビーム加工
　ion beam machining イオン・ビーム加工
　laser beam machining レーザー加工
　machining center マシニング・センター
　micro machining 微細工加工, マイクロマシニング
　ultraprecision [ultra precision] machining 超精密加工
　ultra sonic machining 超音波加工
　water-jet machining ウォータージェット加工

magazine 雑誌, 定期刊行物, 情報番組, 倉庫, 貯蔵所, 弾薬庫, マガジン
　internal magazine 社内報
　international magazine 国際誌
　magazine advertising 雑誌広告
　magazine for public relations ピーアール誌, PR誌
　mass magazine 一般大衆向け雑誌, 大衆雑誌
　monthly magazine 月刊誌
　news magazine program [programme] ニュース情報番組
　quality magazine 高級誌, クオリティ・マガジン
　weekly magazine 週刊誌

magnet store 核店舗
magnetic information 磁気情報
▶The *magnetic information* on a cash card can be read easily with a machine, and is used for forging cards. キャッシュ・カード上の磁気情報は，機器で簡単に読み取られて，カードの偽造に使われている。

Magnuson-Moss FTC Improvement Act マグヌソン・モス連邦取引委員会修正法
Magnuson-Moss Warranty Act マグヌソン・モス保証法
maiden 形 初の, 初めての, 初回の, 初舞台の, 未婚の, 未使用の
mail 名 郵便, 郵便制度, 郵送係, メール, 動 郵送する, 投函する
　air mail 航空便
　certified [certificate] mail 配達証明付き郵便, 配達証明郵便
　content-certified mail 内容証明郵便
　delivery-certified mail 配達証明郵便
　direct mail ダイレクト・メール《略 DM》
　electronic mail [e-mail] 電子メール, 電子郵便
　express mail 速達郵便
　International Express Mail Service 国際エクスプレス・メール《略 EMS》
　international mail service 国際郵便
　junk mail 屑(くず)メール (=spam, spam mail)
　lower priority mail 指定外郵便
　mail bomb 郵便爆弾, メール爆弾 (超多量のメールを送ってシステムに支障をきたすこと)
　mail charge 郵便料金
　mail order 通信販売(mail selling, mail order selling), 通信販売の注文
　mail survey 郵送調査法, メール・サーベイ
　mail transfer 郵便料金, 郵便振替料金
　premium postal services 至急郵便
　registered mail 書留郵便, 書留
　spam mail 迷惑メール, スパム・メール (=junk mail, spam)
　standard mail 普通郵便
　surface mail 船便, 船舶[陸上]輸送郵便物
　voice mail ボイス・メール
mailer 名 差出人, 郵便利用者, 郵送係
mailing list 郵送先名簿, メーリング・リスト
main 形 主な, 主要な, 主力の, 最も重要な, 最大の, メイン
　main business 主力事業, 本業, 主要事業部門
　main chance 金もうけの絶好の機会, 自分の利益
　main competitor 最大の競争相手
　main determinant 最大の要因
　main economies 主要国

main exports 主要輸出品
main financing banks 主力取引銀行, 主力行
main investor 最大の投資家
main memory 主記憶装置 (＝main storage)
main order 主指図書 (＝main production order)
main store 本店, 母店 (＝parent store)
Main Street 国内産業, 米小都市の大通り (＝英国のHigh Street)
main taker 最大の需要筋
▸Companies must be generating operating profits from their *main* businesses to seek debt waivers from the creditor banks.　取引銀行に債権放棄を求めるには，企業はその主要な事業部門で営業利益を上げていなければならない。

main bank 主要取引銀行, 主取引銀行, 主力行, メインバンク (＝main financing bank)
▸The firm's *main bank* will swap ¥20 billion in debt into stock.　同社の主力取引銀行は，200億円分の債権の株式化を行う[200億円分の債権を株式に切り替える]。

main business 主力事業, 中核事業, 本業 (＝core business, main operation, mainstay business)
▸Operating profit from *main businesses* increased 6 percent to ¥950 billion.　本業[主力事業]による営業利益は，6%増の9,500億円となった。

mainframe 名 汎用の大型コンピュータ, メインフレーム (＝mainframe computer)

mainline products 主力製品, 主力商品 (＝mainstay products)
▸Orders for our *mainline products* shrank by half on a year-on-year basis.　主力商品の受注が，前年同期比で半減した。

mainline telecommunications equipment 通信機器本体

mainstay 名 主力, 主力商品, 支え, 支柱, 大黒柱, 頼みの網, 拠り所
mainstay issues 主力銘柄
mainstay products 主力製品, 主力商品
▸Nipponkoa's net premium revenues dropped to 0.9 percent due to declines in its *mainstay* automobile insurance policies.　日本興亜損保の正味収入保険料は，主力の自動車保険[自動車保険契約]の減少で，0.9%減少した。

mainstream 名 主流, 本流, 主潮 (「非主流」は nonmainstream)
▸The *mainstream* in the financial services sector used to be banks and securities companies operating as "financial specialty stores" on their own.　これまで金融サービス部門の主流といえば，「専門店」としてそれぞれ独立して運営してきた銀行や証券会社だった。

maintain 動 維持する, 持続する, 保つ, 守る, 保守する, 保全する, 整備する, 据え置く
maintain a market 市場を形成する
maintain a steady hand 金融政策を据え置く
maintain customers 顧客をつなぎ止める
maintain diversification 多角化を進める
maintain one's financial health [strength] 財務の健全性を維持する, 健全な財務体質を維持する
maintain staff 事務所を構える
maintained mark-on 実現値入れ額 (純売上高と総売上原価との差)
maintained markup 実現値入れ率 (実際販売価格と商品原価との差)
maintained price 維持価格
▸Moody's Investors Service cut Japan's yen-denominated debt rating by one notch to Aa3 from Aa2 and *maintained* a negative outlook.　米国の格付け会社ムーディーズは，日本の円建て国債の格付けを「Aa2」から「Aa3」に一段階引き下げ，「ネガティブ（弱含み）」の見通しを据え置いた。

maintenance 名 維持, 保守, 保全, 整備, 維持管理, 修理点検, メンテナンス
area maintenance 地域保全
income maintenance policy 所得維持政策, 利益維持政策
maintenance and inspection 保守・点検
maintenance and repairs 維持修繕費
maintenance charge 維持費, 保守費, メンテナンス費 (＝maintenance cost, maintenance expense)
maintenance reserve 維持費引当金
master maintenance マスター更新
mechanical maintenance consumables 機械消耗品
preventive maintenance 定期保守, 予防的保守
repairs and maintenance 修繕維持, 修繕維持費
resale price maintenance 再販価格維持, 再販売価格維持《略 RPM》

major 形 主要な, 重大な, 大手の, 大口の, 大規模な, 大きいほうの, 大部分の, 過半数の, 多数の, メジャー
major banking groups 大手銀行グループ, 大手銀行・金融グループ
major bottom 大底
major business segment 主要事業分野

major contract 大口契約, 主要契約
major currency 主要通貨
major customer 大口顧客, 主要得意先
major electronics manufacturer 大手家電メーカー
major equipment 主要設備
major importer 輸入大国, 主要輸入国
major investments 大型投資, 大規模投資
major leagues 先進工業国
major player 大手企業, 大手, 大口の買い手
major powers 主要国
major retail center 主要ショッピング・センター, 一流小売センター
major service 主要サービス
major user 大口ユーザー
the world's major companies 世界の大企業, 世界の大手企業, 世界の主要企業
▸Despite stiff price competition, expansion abroad and into new customer segments, improved global economic conditions and *major contract* wins raised sales in 2008. 厳しい価格競争にさらされながらも, 国外事業の拡大や新規顧客への食いこみ, 世界景気の好転と大口契約の獲得などで, 2008年度の売上高は増加しました。

major shareholder 大株主, 大口株主, 主要株主 (=large shareholder, major stockholder; ⇒**listing requirement**)
▸According to a listing requirement, *major shareholders* are prohibited from owing more than an 80 percent stake in a company. 上場基準によると, 大株主は80％を超える会社株式の所有は禁じられている。

majority 名 過半数, 大多数, 多数, 大半, 大部分
early majority 初期追随者 (イノベーションの普及過程で初期採用者 (early adopters) の後に続く者)
late majority 後期追随者 (イノベーションの普及過程で初期追随者 (early majority) の後に続く者)
majority control 過半数支配, 過半数所有支配
majority decision 多数決
majority interest 過半数持ち分, 多数株主持ち分 (=consolidated equity: 連結持ち分, 親会社持ち分)
majority leader 院内総務
majority owned company 過半数所有会社, 過半数子会社 (=majority owned subsidiary: 社外議決権株式の50％超を他の会社に所有されている会社・子会社)
majority owner 過半数株主
majority rule 多数決

majority share 過半数の株式 (=majority stake)
majority shareholder [stockholder] 過半数株主, 支配株主
majority vote 多数投票
simple majority 単独過半数
▸According to the NYSE's new rules, corporate boards must be composed of a *majority* of independent directors. ニューヨーク証券取引所 (NYSE) の新上場基準によると, 企業 (上場企業) の取締役の過半数は社外取締役にしなければならない。

majority owned subsidiary 過半数所有子会社 (50％を超える議決権株式を所有する子会社)
▸The consolidated financial statements include the accounts of the Company and those *majority owned subsidiaries* where the Company has control. 連結財務書類 [連結財務諸表] には, 当社と当社の支配下にある過半数所有子会社の財務書類が含まれています。

majority stake 過半数株式
▸Aeon Co. has acquired a *majority stake* in Diamond City Co. through a public tender offer. イオンは, 株式公開買付け (TOB) でダイヤモンドシティ (ショッピングセンター開発会社) の過半数株式を取得した。

majors 名 国際石油資本 (メジャー), 大手メーカー, 業界最大手 (=major oil companies, oil majors)
▸International chemical and oil *majors* are building huge chemical plants one after another in China. 中国では, 欧米の大手化学メーカーや国際石油資本 (メジャー) の大規模化学プラントの建設ラッシュを迎えている。

make up for …を補填する, …の穴埋めをする, …を埋め合わせる, 帳消しにする
▸Some banks have been forced to liquidate their legal reserves due to the need to dispose of huge amounts of bad loans and *make up for* latent stock price losses. 巨額の不良債権の処理と株式含み損の補填に迫られ, 一部の銀行は法定準備金の取崩しに追い込まれている。

makeover 名 イメージ・チェンジ, 模様替え, お色直し, 改良, 改造, 改装, 改築, 改善, 練り直し, 変身
▸The firm's *makeover* could backfire badly. 同社のイメージ・チェンジは, 大いに裏目に出る可能性がある。

maker 名 製造業者, 制作会社, 製作者, 器具, 機器, メーカー (=manufacturer, producer; ⇒

為, 背任行為, 汚職 (=malpractice)

malfunction 名 機能障害, 機能不全, 故障, 誤作動 (⇒computer malfunction)
▸The computer *malfunction* was due to a glitch in the software. コンピュータのシステム障害[コンピュータの障害・誤作動]は, ソフトの不具合が原因だった。

mall 名 商店街, ショッピング・センター, モール (⇒shopping)
　electronic mall 電子モール (=online mall, virtual mall)
　Internet shopping mall インターネット上の仮想商店街
　online mall オンライン・モール (=virtual mall, virtual shopping mall)
　virtual mall 仮想商店街, 仮想モール, バーチャル・モール (=virtual shopping mall)

manage 動 管理する, 経営する, 統括する, 統率する, 監督する, 幹事を務める, 運用する, 運営する, 運用管理する, うまく処理する, 対処する, 取り扱う, 使いこなす, 〈困難などを〉乗り切る, 切り抜ける
　manage liquidity 流動性を抑える
　manage the business 事業を統括する
　manage the portfolio ポートフォリオを運用する
　manage the risk exposure リスクを管理する
　manage the syndication シンジケート団を取り仕切る
▸Investors are buying into the potential of a company, not to *manage* it. 投資家は, 企業の経営権ではなく, 企業の将来性を買っている。
▸We will stay the course, *managing* expenses tightly and pursuing new market opportunities. 私どもは, 当社の経営路線に基づき, 支出管理を強化するとともに, 新たな市場機会を追求していく方針です。

management 名 経営, 管理, 運用, 運営, 取扱い, 業務執行, 経営管理, 経営陣, 経営側, 経営者側, マネジメント (⇒corporate management)
　balance sheet management 財務管理, バランス・シート管理
　business management 企業経営, 企業管理, 経営管理, 業務管理, 経営
　bond management 債券運用, 債券管理
　cash flow management キャッシュ・フロー経営 (=cash-flow management: 現金の流れを最大化することを指針として経営の舵取りをする経営手法。流動資産が大きく, 在庫(棚卸し資産)や債権(売掛金や受取手形など)の期間が短けれ

---

makeup 名

electric)
　car maker 自動車メーカー, 乗用車メーカー (=auto maker, car producer)
　computer makers コンピュータ業界
　covenant maker 協約締結者
　decision maker 意思決定者, 政策担当者
　film maker 映画製作者
　ice maker 製氷機
　lawmaker 国会議員, 立法者
　maker's credit 延べ払い輸入, メーカー系クレジット
　maker's credit company メーカー系クレジット会社
　market maker 市場開拓者, 証券業者, マーケット・メーカー(証券のディーラー), 値付け業者
　monetary policy makers 金融当局
　pace maker [pacemaker] 先導者, 主導者, 心臓ペースメーカー, ペースメーカー
　policy maker [policymaker] 政策立案者, 政策担当者, 政府高官
　policy makers 政策当局
　price maker 価格決定者, 価格形成者, プライス・メーカー

makeup 名 組織, 構造, 構成, 組立て, 陣容, 〈新聞の〉割付け, 化粧, 化粧品
　makeup kit 化粧品セット
　makeup time やり直し時間
　makeup wages 補充賃金, 補足賃金 (=make-up pay)
　makeup-work 補充作業
▸The *makeup* of government bond issuance for this fiscal year is vulnerable to rises in long-term interest rates. 今年度の国債発行の構成は, 長期金利上昇の影響を受けやすい。

making 名 製造, 制作, 形成, 決定, 成功, 発展, 成長の原因[要因], メーキング
　decision making 意思決定, 政策決定
　iron making 製鉄
　market making 値付け業務, マーケット・メーキング
　nonprofit making corporation 非営利法人
　policy making 政策決定, 政策立案 (=policymaking)
　profit making 利潤追求, 利潤創出, 利益獲得, 営利
　rate making 料金算定, 料金決定, 利率決定
　top-down decision making トップ・ダウン型の意思決定
　wage making 賃金形成, 賃金決定

malfeasance 名 不正行為, 違法行為, 不法行

ば，キャッシュ・フローは増大する）
cash management 現金預金管理，現金管理，資金管理，キャッシュ・マネジメント
corporate management 企業経営
credit management 与信管理，信用管理
current asset management 流動資産管理
demand side management 需要管理，デマンド・サイド・マネジメント
effective management 効率経営，効率的な経営，効果的な経営
expanded management fee 拡大幹事手数料
financial management 財務管理，財テク（資金の運用と調達についての検討）
financial market 金融市場（「金融市場」は，資金の供給者である貸し手と資金の需要者である借り手との間で資金取引が行われる場）
financial risk management 金融リスク管理，金融リスク・マネジメント
fiscal management 財政運営
fund management 資金運用，資金管理，投資運用，投資管理，投資顧問
fund management operation 資金運用
investment management 投資管理，投資運用，投資顧問
management advisory services 経営助言サービス，経営者への提案業務《略 MAS》（＝management services）
management change 経営刷新，経営陣の交替
management competency 経営者の資質
management control 経営者支配，経営支配，経営支配権，経営管理，経営統制
management crisis 経営危機
management decision 経営者の意思決定，経営意思決定，経営判断（＝managerial decision）
management efficiency 経営効率，事業効率
management expense 管理費，運用経費，経費費用（＝management charge）
management fees 経営報酬，役員報酬，運用報酬，幹事手数料，管理手数料
management information 経営情報
management of affairs 事務管理
management of funds 資金繰り，資金管理，資金運用（＝fund management）
management of idle money 余資運用
management report 経営報告，経営報告書，経営管理報告書，経営者の報告，経営者の報告書
management restructuring plan 経営健全化計画
management system 経営システム，経営体制，管理システム，管理方式，マネジメント・システム

management's illegal acts 経営者の違反行為
portfolio management 最適資産管理，資産管理，資産運用，資金運用，ポートフォリオ管理，ポートフォリオ運用，ポートフォリオ・マネジメント
profit management 利益管理
purchasing management 購買管理
risk management 危険管理，危機管理，リスク管理，リスク・マネジメント
stock management 株の運用，株式運用
systems management システム管理《略 SM》
value-oriented management 価値重視の経営
working capital management 運転資本管理
▶Rakuten has proposed integrating the firms' *management* under a joint holding company. 楽天は，共同持ち株会社の設立による［共同持ち株会社方式での］両社の経営統合を提案した。
▶The financial statements have been prepared by *management* in conformity with U.S. GAAP (generally accepted accounting principles). 財務書類［財務諸表］は，米国会計基準（米国で一般に公正妥当と認められた会計基準［会計原則］）に従って，経営者が作成しました。

management and labor 労使，労働側と経営側，労働者側と経営者側（＝labor and management）
▶*Management and labor* compromised and postponed a strike. 労使双方が歩み寄り，ストを延期した。

management buyout [buy-out] 経営者による自社買収，経営陣による自社株の公開買付け，経営者による営業権取得，経営陣による企業買収，マネジメント・バイアウト《略 MBO》（「MBO」とは，企業の経営者が，一般株主や親会社などから自社株を買い取って，企業や事業部門の経営権を買い取ることをいう。⇒MBO）
▶The management has decided to implement *management buyout* to enhance the financial base. 経営陣は，経営基盤を強化するため，経営陣による企業買収（MBO）の実施を決めた。

management employees 管理職
▶Benefits for *management employees* are principally based on career-average pay. 管理職に対する給付は，基本的に職歴平均給方式に基づいています。

management environment 経営環境
▶*Management environments* are much better than before. 経営環境は，以前よりはるかに良くなっている。

management executive committee 経営執行委員会

▶The *Management Executive Committee* leads the development and implementation of our mission, values and strategic intent.　経営執行委員会は，当社の使命，価値観，戦略的意図の策定と実施の先頭に立っています．

management integration　経営統合（＝business integration, management merger, operational integration）
▶Konaka Co. emphasized the advantages of the *management integration* with menswear chain Futata Co.　コナカは，紳士服チェーンのフタタとの経営統合による（経営）メリットを強調した．

management offering　経営陣に対する株式発行［株式の売出し］
▶We sold approximately 850,000 shares of common stock in a *management offering*.　当社は，経営陣に対する株式発行で約85万株の普通株式を売り出しました．

management plan　経営計画（＝management planning）
▶Shinginko Tokyo has changed its *management plan* three times in the three years since its establishment.　新銀行東京は，開業から3年で経営計画を3回変更した．

management reconstruction program　経営再建計画，再建計画
▶The bank announced the *management reconstruction program* aiming at restoring profitability by the end of fiscal 2011.　同行は，2011年度末までの黒字化を目指す経営再建計画を発表した．

management renewal　経営刷新，経営陣の刷新
▶Constant *management renewal* is essential to success.　絶えざる経営刷新［経営陣の刷新］は，企業の発展に不可欠である．

management resources　経営資源
▶We must concentrate manpower, money and other *management resources* on profit-making sources.　人材や資金などの経営資源を，収益源に集中させる［投入する］必要がある．

management right　経営権
▶Stock trades involving the transfer of *management rights* has been undertaken, in principle, through a takeover bid.　経営権の移動を伴う株取引は，原則として株式公開買付け（TOB）で行われてきた．

management strategy　経営戦略
　long-term management strategy　長期経営戦略

　midterm management strategy　中期経営戦略
▶Foreign companies doing business in China may have to revise their *management strategies* if labor costs continue to climb there.　中国で人件費の上昇が続けば，中国進出の外国企業は，経営戦略の見直しを迫られるかもしれない．

management structure　経営組織，経営機構，経営形態
▶We announced a new *management structure* in February as a further initiative to align ourselves to compete more effectively in the global marketplace.　当社は2月に，グローバル市場で一段と効果的に競争する体制を整えるためのさらなる施策として，経営機構［経営組織］の改革を発表しました．

management style　経営手法，経営姿勢，経営スタイル，経営方式
▶The U.S. business *management style* is characterized by greater transparency and accountability of business management, symbolized by outside directors, corporate executive officers, independent auditors and compliance officers.　米国型企業経営の特色は，社外重役や業務執行役員，独立監査人（外部監査），コンプライアンス・オフィサー（法令・規則遵守担当役員）などに象徴されるように，経営の透明性や説明責任にある．

management system　経営体制，経営システム，管理システム，経営者組織，マネジメント・システム
▶In a move to reform its board of directors into a U.S.-style system of corporate governance, the company introduced a committee-based *management system* along with the revised Commercial Code.　取締役会を米国流の会社管理・運営方式に改革する動きとして，同社は，商法改正に伴って委員会ベースの経営システムを導入した．

management team　経営陣，マネジメント・チーム（＝management profiles）
　current management team　現経営陣
　new management team　新経営陣
▶Marubeni initially planned to maintain Daiei's current *management team* until next May.　丸紅は当初，来年5月までダイエーの現経営陣の続行を予定していた．

manager 名　経営者，管理者，幹部，幹部社員，部長，理事，〈銀行の〉支店長，幹事（引受会社），投資顧問，支配人，責任者，管財人，マネージャー（⇒ **corporate manager**, **lead manager**）
　asset manager　投資顧問業，アセット・マネージャー

bank manager 銀行支店長
bond manager 債券運用者, 債券管理者, 債券運用担当者, 債券管理担当者, ボンド・マネージャー
company managers 会社経営者, 会社の経営陣, 会社幹部, 企業経営者
Branch Manager Meeting 日銀支店長会議
co-lead manager 共同主幹事 (＝joint lead-manager)
customer relations manager 顧客関係担当者
department manager 部門責任者
division manager 部長
executive manager 執行役員
front-line [first-line] manager 第一線の部長 [課長]
fund manager 資金運用者, 資金管理者, 資金運用担当者, 資金管理担当者, 金融資産運用者, ファンド・マネージャー
general manager 総支配人, 全般的管理者, 事業本部長, 部長, ゼネラル・マネージャー
general sales manager 営業部長
investment manager 投資顧問, 投資運用会社, 運用会社, 投資マネージャー
managers 経営陣, 経営側, 会社側
operating manager 経営幹部
personnel manager 人事担当重役
portfolio manager 資産管理者, 資産運用者, ポートフォリオ運用者, ポートフォリオ・マネージャー
professional manager 専門経営者
sales manager 販売部長, 営業部長, 営業担当責任者
section manager 課長
sole manager 単独主幹事
store manager 店長
syndicate manager シンジケート団幹事, シ団幹事
▶We have reduced our *managers* by 3,000. 当社は, 管理職を3,000人削減しました。
▶While stock prices shifted upward, the sentiments of corporate *managers* have shown signs of improvement lately. 株価が上昇に転じる一方, 最近は企業経営者の景況感も改善の兆しを見せている。

managerial 形 経営[管理, 操作, 処理]の, 経営上の, 経営者の
managerial abilities 経営力, 管理者能力
managerial control 経営統制, 管理的統制, 経営権
managerial decision 経営の意思決定, 経営判断 (＝management decision)

managerial efforts 経営努力
managerial employee 管理職
managerial functions 経営者の職能
managerial philosophy 経営理念
managerial policy 経営方針
managerial position 管理職 (＝management position)
managerial problems 経営上の問題
managerial resources 経営資源
managerial system 経営体制
▶It is a wise *managerial* decision to give up the profits accrued from the erroneous sell order. 売り注文のミス[誤発注]で得た利益を返上するのは, 賢明な経営判断だ。

mandate 動 義務付ける, 強制する, 命じる, 権限を与える, …の統治を委任する, マンデートを獲得する
federally-mandated services 米連邦から委託されたサービス
mandated group マンデートを獲得したグループ
original mandated amount 調達予定額
▶WTO-*mandated* talks start in Geneva this week. 世界貿易機関(WTO)が義務付けている話し合いは, ジュネーブで今週スタートする。

mandate 名 権限, 権能, 要求, 命令, 指令, 委託, 委任, 委任契約, 委任統治, 植民地, 選挙民の信任, 〈手形や小切手の〉支払い委託, 無償のサービス契約, 〈社債発行者からの主幹事に対する〉引受業務の依頼[委任], マンデート
bank mandate 銀行委任書
competition for the mandate マンデート獲得競争, マンデート争奪戦, 主幹事争い
financing mandate 資金調達のマンデート
have a mandate to …する権限がある
mandate letter 委任状, マンデート・レター (＝letter of mandate)
seek a mandate for …への支持を求める

mandatory 形 命令の, 委任の, 委任された, 強制的な, 義務的な
mandatory clause 必須条項, 強行規定
mandatory control 法的規制
mandatory convertible instruments [securities] 強制転換社債
mandatory credit line 法廷信用枠 (＝mandatory line of credit)
mandatory redemption 強制償還
mandatory requirements 強制要件
mandatory retirement age 定年
mandatory spending 義務的経費

manipulate 動 操作する, 操縦する, 巧みに操る
▶Participants in the market process information transmitted globally in real time, *manipulate* it in some cases and try to win profit by moving large amounts of money in this information war zone. 市場参加者は, リアルタイムでグローバルに伝達される情報を処理し, 場合によってはそれを操作しながら, この情報戦争の戦場で巨額の資金を動かして利益を得ようとしている。

manipulation 名 操作, 不正操作, 市場操作, 相場操縦
  accounting manipulation 会計操作 (=accounting fraud)
  earnings manipulation 利益の不正操作
  financial manipulation 経理操作
  income manipulation 利益操作
  manipulation of accounts 粉飾 (=equation manipulation)
  stock price manipulation 株価操縦, 株価操作 (=stock manipulation)
▶Market *manipulation* has been occurring in connection with new share issues. 増資に絡んで, 株価操作が行われている。
▶The accounting *manipulations* went unnoticed by the company's auditors and the board of directors. 会計操作は, 同社の監査役や取締役会が見過ごしていた。

manpower 名 労働力, 労力, 人的資源, 人材, 人手, 労働人員, 人員, 従業員, 従業員数, マンパワー
  lack of manpower 人材不足, 人手不足, 労働力不足 (=manpower shortage)
  Manpower Development and Training Act 人的資源開発訓練法
  manpower management 労働力管理, 労務管理
  manpower planning 人員計画, 要員計画, マンパワー・プランニング
▶Added value per employee indicates the degree of excessive manpower. 従業員1人当たりの付加価値額は, 余剰人員の度合いを示す。

manual 名 手引書, 入門書, 参考書, 案内, 便覧, 作業手順書, 仕様説明書, 取扱い説明書, 解説書, 業務規定, マニュアル (⇒on-the-spot inspection)
  instruction manual 取扱い説明書
  listed company manual 上場企業便覧
  operating manual 業務マニュアル, 業務便覧, 操作マニュアル, 使用マニュアル
  operation manual 操作マニュアル, オペレーション・マニュアル
  operations manual 作業マニュアル
  procedures manual 手続きマニュアル, 業務マニュアル
  reference manual リファレンス・マニュアル (ソフトの機能の解説書)
  setup manual セットアップ・マニュアル (ソフトをセットアップするための説明書)
  system [organization] manual 組織便覧
  system overall manual システム概要説明書
  user's manual ユーザー・マニュアル
▶Licensor shall provide Licensee with an operating *manual* concerning the proprietary information. ライセンサーは, ライセンシーに専有情報に関する使用マニュアルを提供する。

manufacture 動 製造する, 生産する, 製作する, 名 製造, 生産, 製作, 製品
  jointly manufacture 共同生産する (⇒liquid crystal display panel)
  manufactured goods 工業製品, 工業品, 加工品, 生産品, 製品 (=manufactured product)
  manufactured imports 製品輸入, 工業製品の輸入
  manufactured material 自製材料
  manufactured product 工業製品
▶Toyota *manufactured* 9,497,754 units across the world in 2007, up 5.3 percent on the previous year. トヨタは, 2007年の世界全体の生産台数が前年比5.3%増の949万7,754台となった。

manufacturer 名 製造業者, 製造者, 製作者, メーカー, 工場主 (=maker, producer)
  domestic manufacturers 国内メーカー
  major electric appliance manufacturers 大手電機
  manufacturer-retailer alliance 製販同盟
  manufacturers' new and unfilled orders 製造業の新規受注高と受注残高
  PC manufacturer パソコン・メーカー
  post-manufacturer inventories 流通在庫
  steel manufacturers 鉄鋼業界
▶Major electric appliance *manufacturers* and 10 telecommunication companies turned profits for the year ended March 31. 3月期決算では, 大手電機と情報通信10社が, 黒字に転換した。
▶PC *manufacturers* are trying hard to stimulate consumer demand this autumn and winter by marketing new products with particular emphasis on audiovisual functions. パソコン・メーカー各社は, AV (音響・映像) 機能を重視した新製品を販売して, 秋冬の消費需要の喚起に懸命だ。

manufacturing 名 製造, 生産, 加工, 製作, マニュファクチュアリング

computer-aided manufacturing コンピュータ支援［援用］製造
computer integrated manufacturing コンピュータ統合生産(システム)《略 CIM》
economic manufacturing quantity 経済的生産数量, 最適生産量
intelligent manufacturing system 知的生産システム
local manufacturing 現地生産
manufacturing burden 製造間接費 (=factory burden, factory overhead, manufacturing overhead)
manufacturing capacity 生産能力, 製造能力
manufacturing expense 製造経費, 製造間接費
manufacturing facilities 製造施設
manufacturing indirect cost 製造間接費 (=factory overhead, manufacturing overhead cost)
manufacturing industry 製造業
telecommunications equipment manufacturing 通信機器の製造, 通信機器製造事業
virtual manufacturing 仮想生産, バーチャル・マニュファクチュアリング
▶Under a technology transfer and supply agreement, local manufacturing of this integrated services network will be phased in, beginning with system assembly and test and moving rapidly to full *manufacturing*, using locally available materials and components. 技術移転・納入契約に基づき，この統合サービス・ネットワークの現地生産は，当初はシステムの組立てと検査作業から段階的に開始し，その後現地調達可能な資材と部品を使用して完全現地生産に早急に移行することになっている。
▶We have closed some of our *manufacturing* facilities worldwide. 当社は，当社の世界の製造施設を一部閉鎖しました。

manufacturing cost 製造原価, 製造コスト, 生産コスト (=cost of goods manufactured, output cost, production cost)
▶Our global product organizations helped to improve our margins through product redesign to lower *manufacturing costs*. 当社のグローバル製品事業部門は，製造コスト低減のための製品再設計により，当社の利益率改善に寄与しました。

manufacturing cycle time 製造所要時間
▶We have reduced our *manufacturing cycle time* and improved the quality of our products. 当社は，製造所要時間の削減と当社製品の品質改善［向上］に取り組んでいます。

manufacturing operations 製造事業, 製造部門, 生産子会社［関連会社］
▶*Manufacturing* and distribution *operations* in any one foreign country do not account for more than 10% of consolidated net sales or total assets. 国外で，製造および販売事業が連結純売上高または総資産の10％を超える国はありません。

manufacturing overhead 製造間接費
(=factory burden, factory overhead, manufacturing overhead cost)
▶The cost of finished goods and work in process comprise material, labor, and *manufacturing overhead*. 製品と仕掛品の原価は，材料費と労務費と製造間接費から成っています。

manufacturing process 製造工程
▶We are pursuing ambitious efforts to decrease toxic air emissions and *manufacturing process* waste. 当社は，毒性ガス放出の削減や製造工程での産業廃棄物の削減に意欲的に取り組んでいます。

manufacturing system 生産システム
▶Matsushita Electric Industrial Co. has taken the Japanese-style *manufacturing system*. 松下電器産業は，日本流の生産システムを取り入れている。

map out 詳細な計画を立てる, 綿密に計画する, 計画する, まとめる, 策定する, 詳細に示す
map out monetary policy 金融政策を決める
map out the basic plan 基本計画をまとめる, 基本計画を立てる
▶Toyota has *mapped out* plans to add 10 new automobile assembly plants worldwide by the end of 2010. トヨタは，2010年末までに世界各地の10か所に自動車組立て工場を新設する計画をまとめた。

margin 名 売上総利益, 利益率, 利ざや, 証拠金, 委託証拠金, 委託保証金, 担保金, 手付け金, マージン (⇒after-tax margin, gross margin, gross profit margin)
additional margin 追加証拠金
gross margin ratio 売上総利益率, 粗利益率 (=gross margin percentage)
margin requirement 証拠金, 証拠金所要額, 証拠金規定額, 証拠金率
margin trading 信用取引, 証拠金取引 (=margin transaction; ⇒FX margin trading)
narrow margin 薄利
narrow profit margins 利ざやが薄いこと
net margin 純販売利益, 純売買差益, 純利益
net profit margin 売上高利益率
operating income margin 営業利益率 (=

operating margin)
product margins 製品利益率
profit margin 利益率, 利ざや
profit margin on sales 売上高利益率
▸We improved our gross and net *margins* on sales with net earnings increasing to 10 percent and earnings per share increasing 12 percent. 当社の純販売益率と販売利益率も改善し, 純利益は10％増加, 1株当たりの利益は12％増加しました。

margin improvement 利益率改善
▸In managing the business, we achieved 14 percent growth in earnings per common share through *margin improvement* and prudent expense controls. 業務運営の面では, 利益率の改善と支出抑制の徹底により, 普通株式1株当たり純利益は14％増加しました。

margin percentage 利益率
▸The continuing shift in revenue mix to other services from higher-margin rentals led to a decline in the *margin percentage* in 2008. 高利益率のレンタル事業からその他のサービスへの売上構成の変化が続いたため, 2008年度は利益率が低下しました。

margin requirement 証拠金, 証拠金率
▸The Diet enacted laws to impose restrictions on foreign exchange trading with low *margin requirements*. 少ない証拠金での外国為替取引［外国為替証拠金取引］を規制する法律が, 国会で成立した。

margin trading 信用取引 (＝margin transaction)
▸The funds were procured through *margin trading*, which enables investors to trade amounts nearly three times larger in value than in money they actually hold, by offering cash and stocks as collateral to securities companies. その資金は, 投資家が証券会社に現金や株を担保として差し入れて, 手持ち資金の3倍近い額の株を売買できる「信用取引」で調達した。

marginal 形 限界の, 限界収益点の, 下限に近い, 欄外の
　marginal benefit 限界便益
　marginal capital market 小規模な資本市場
　marginal demand 限界需要
　marginal income 限界利益
　marginal propensity to expend 限界支出性向
　marginal revenue 限界収入
marginal increase 小幅の伸び, 微増
▸Business communications systems and terminals revenues showed only a *marginal increase* in 2008 to $1.31 billion (24 percent of total revenues) from $1.30 billion in 2007. ビジネス通信システムと端末装置の2008年度の売上高は, 前年度の13億ドルに対して13.1億ドル（総売上高の24％）で, ほんの微増にとどまりました。

mark 名 水準, 標準, …台, …の大台, 記号, 符号, 標識, 標的, 目標, 成績, 評価, マーク
　abandonment of mark 登録商標の放棄
　care mark 注意マーク
　case mark 荷印, ケース・マーク
　counter mark 副マーク (荷送人の輸出商, メーカーを示す記号)
　country of origin mark 原産地国マーク
　main mark 主マーク (荷受人を示す記号)
　mark reader マーク読取り装置
　mark scanning マーク読取り (＝mark sensing)
　mark sheet 輸入報告書
　national origin mark 国別製造元表示, 原産地国マーク
　port mark 仕向港マーク (仕向地または仕向港を示す)
　quality mark 品質マーク
　service mark サービス・マーク, サービス業者のサービス識別標章
　shipping mark 荷印 (貿易貨物の外装に刷り込む記号)
　symbol mark シンボル・マーク
▸Toyota's midterm account settlement will certainly exceed, for the first time, the ¥10 trillion *mark* for the midterm business results. トヨタの中間決算では, 中間期の業績で初めて10兆円台を突破するのは確実となっている。

mark to market 動 評価替えする, 時価で評価する, 値洗いする (⇒**hedge**)
　mark to market securities inventories 商品有価証券を時価で評価する
　mark to market the positions ポジションの値洗いをする
　marked-to-market value 時価評価額, 値洗い後の価格

mark-to-market 名 評価替え, 値洗い (＝mark to the market: 手持ち証券などの価値を現在市場価値に評価し直すこと)
　mark-to-market accounting practices 時価による会計処理, 時価会計, 時価主義会計
　mark-to-market accounting standard 時価会計基準
　mark-to-market appraisal 時価評価, 時価による評価

mark-to-market basis 値洗い基準
mark-to-market method 時価法, 市場連動法
mark-to-market value 時価評価額, 値洗い後の価格
total mark-to-market value of stocks 株式の時価総額

▸Since the introduction of the *mark-to-market* accounting system, corporations have been required to report their estimate of losses if the value of their shareholdings has dropped more than 50 percent from their purchasing prices. 時価会計制度の導入以来, 保有株式の価格が取得価格より5割以上下落した場合, 企業は評価損の計上を義務付けられている。

markdown 名 値下げ, 価格の引下げ, 値下げ幅, 評価下げ, 店頭取引ブローカーの手数料, マークダウン (値上げ=markup)
 markdown cancellation 値下げの取消し, 値下げ訂正
 markdown money 値下げ補償金
 markdown planning 値下げ計画
 markdown ratio 値下げ率

▸At the stores of Aeon and Ito-Yokado, foods imported from the United States are being sold at a 20 percent to 30 percent *markdown*. イオンとイトーヨーカ堂の店舗では, 米国から輸入した食料品が, 2割-3割値下げして販売されている。

market 動 販売する, 売り出す, 市場に出す

▸Honda Motor Co. would be the first to *market* vehicles that run on bioethanol alone. バイオエタノールだけで走る車を販売するのは, ホンダが初めてだ。

market 名 市場, 市中, 相場, 市況, 売買, 販路, マーケット (⇒opportunity)
 active market 活況市場
 aftermarket 販売後市場, 有価証券の流通市場, 補修部品市場, 関連ハードウエア／ソフトウエア／周辺装置の市場, アフター・マーケット (=after market, aftermath market)
 appear on the market 上場する
 bear market 弱気市場, 下げ相場, 売り相場
 bull market 強気市場, 上げ相場, 買い相場
 capture the market シェアを獲得する
 corner the market 市場を買い占める
 credit market 金融市場, 信用市場, 発行市場
 enter the market 市場に参入する, 市場に進出する, 市場を利用する, 市場に加わる
 European-style single market 欧州型単一市場
 exchange market 為替市場
 issue market 発行市場 (=investment market)
 M&A market M&A市場
 make a market マーケット・メークを行う, 市場を形成する, 値付け業務を行う, マーケット・メーキング (=market making)
 make inroads in the market 市場に参入する
 market abuse 相場操縦
 market crash 暴落
 market development 市場開発, 市場開拓, 営業開発
 market downfall 市場急落
 market interest rate 市中金利 (=open market rate)
 market leader 商品購入決定者, 商品購入影響者, 消費者, 主導株, 先導株, マーケット・リーダー
 market liquidity 市場流動性, 金融商品市場で株式や債券などを売買するための豊富な資金
 market maker 市場開拓者, 市場を形成する消費者, 証券業者, 証券ディーラー, 値付け業者, マーケット・メーカー (「値付け業者」は, 株や債券などの流通市場で価格形成を行う証券業者のこと)
 market method 時価法
 market penetration 市場浸透, 市場浸透力
 market quotes 市場相場価額
 market testing system 市場化テスト (官民競争入札)
 market trial 市場実験
 primary market for securities 証券の発行市場
 put ... on the market …を売りに出す, …を発売する, …を市販する
 secondary market 流通市場
 security market 証券市場
 sensitive market 不安市況, 不安定市場
 shares on the market 流通している株式
 stock and bond markets 株式・債券市場
 strong market 強気市場, 強気市況
 tap the market 市場に登場する, 市場で調達する
 time the market 市場の好機を選ぶ, 市場のタイミングをとらえる, 市場のタイミングを判断する, 市場のタイミングに合わせる, 市場のタイミングを図る
 trading market 流通市場, トレーディング・マーケット
 weak market 軟弱市況, 軟調市況 (=soft market)

▸Bandai badly needs to enter new fields due to the shrinking toy *market*. バンダイは, 玩具市場の縮小で, 新分野への参入[展開]が急務となっている。

- ▸*Markets* for telecommunication services are extremely competitive.　電気通信サービス市場は，極めて激しい競争にさらされています。

market capitalization　株式の時価総額　（＝market cap., market capitalization value: 株式の外部発行済み株式総数に株式の時価を掛けた額）
- ▸The fall in the stock price lowers the company's *market capitalization*.　株価の下落で，同社の時価総額は目減りしている。
- ▸The group implemented its creative financial strategy to seek an explosive growth by bloating its *market capitalization*.　同グループは，時価総額を膨らませて急成長を求める独創的な財務戦略を実行した。

market conditions　市場の状態，市場環境，市場の状況，市況
- ▸Despite sluggish *market conditions* in Japan, the market share of Toyota brand vehicles rose to 46.1 percent.　日本国内の市況低迷にもかかわらず，トヨタ・ブランド車の市場シェアは，46.1％に増加した。
- ▸Such *market conditions*, along with a slow-growing economy, make the ongoing need for active cost controls even more urgent.　この市場環境と景気低迷で，継続的に積極的なコスト管理を進める必要性は，一段と緊急性を増しています。

market demand　市場の需要
- ▸Because of the strong *market demand*, the available quantity of some products has been allocated between customers from time to time.　市場需要が大幅に伸びているため，調達可能な一部の製品は，お客さまの間で割当て配分している状況です。

market-driven 形　市場原理に基づく，市場志向の，市場優先の　（＝market-based, market-oriented）
- ▸*Market-driven* quality means understanding quality as our customers see it.　市場志向の品質とは，お客さまの立場に立って品質を追求することを意味します。

market economy　市場経済
- ▸About 16 years have passed since China introduced a *market economy*.　中国が市場経済を導入して，ほぼ16年になる。

market environment　市場環境
- ▸Even with the demands of a difficult *market environment*, we have continued to invest in our people.　厳しい市場環境のもとで需要が鈍化しているものの，当社は引き続き人材開発に投資し

ています。

market growth　市場の拡大，市場の伸び，市場の成長　（＝market expansion）
- ▸*Market growth* is expected in Asian regions.　アジア地域では，将来の市場の成長が見込める。

market manipulation　市場操作，株価操作，相場操縦
- ▸Penalties against insider trading and *market manipulation* have been strengthened.　インサイダー取引や相場操縦などに対する罰則が，強化された。

market player　市場関係者，市場参加者，市場筋，マーケット・プレーヤー　（＝market participant; ⇒**participant**）
- ▸The annualized GDP growth rate in the third quarter of the year was much lower than the prediction by many *market players*.　今年第3四半期(7～9月期)の年率換算でのGDP（国内総生産）成長率は，市場関係者の大方の予想を大幅に下回った。

market price　市場価格，市価，時価，売価，相場，実勢価格　（＝market value）
- ▸Net capital expenditures for the network, at *market price*, were $2.5 billion in 2008.　通信ネットワークの資本的支出純額は，市場価額で2008年度は25億ドルでした。
- ▸The offered price was set at levels below *market prices*.　買付け価格[提示価格]は，時価を下回る水準に設定された。

market principles　市場原理
- ▸*Market principles* and competition have been emphasized in recent years.　最近は，市場原理と競争が重視されてきました。

market rate　市場金利，市場相場，市場レート，銀行間相場
　money market rate　市中金利，短期市場金利
　open market rate　短期市場金利
　prevailing market rate　市場実勢金利
　short-term money market rate　短期市場金利
- ▸Banks' fund-raising costs have increased, reflecting the rise in *market rates* after the Bank of Japan abandoned its zero-interest policy.　日銀のゼロ金利政策解除に伴って市場金利が上昇したのを反映して，銀行の資金調達コストが増大した。

market-related asset value method　市場関連資産価格方式
- ▸The Corporation uses a three-year, *market-related* asset value method of amortizing asset-related gains and losses.　当社は，資産関連損益

を償却するため，3年間の市場関連資産価格方式を採用しています。

market risk　市場リスク
▸These financial instruments are subject to market risks resulting from exchange rate movements.　これらの金融手段[金融商品]は，為替の変動による市場リスクにさらされています。

market share　市場占拠率，市場占有率，市場シェア，マーケット・シェア，シェア（＝share）
▸GM has been suffering from declining U.S. *market share*, rising costs for materials like steel and a drop in sales of sport utility vehicles.　米ゼネラル・モーターズは，米国内シェアの低下や鉄鋼など原材料コストの上昇，スポーツ用多目的車（SUV）の販売減に見舞われている。

market turmoil　市場の混乱，市場の動揺（⇒turmoil）
▸The financial *market turmoil* is caused by the U.S. subprime loan crisis.　金融市場の混乱は，米国のサブプライム・ローン（低所得者向け住宅融資）問題によるものだ。

market valuation　時価総額
▸At current prices, the company's *market valuation* is more than $1.5 billion.　現在の株価で，同社の時価総額は15億ドルを超えている。

market value　市場価値，市場価格，市価，時価，時価評価額（＝market price）
　current market value　市場の実勢価格，現在の市場価格，現在の市場価値，現行の市場価格，時価（＝current market price）
　estimated market value　見積り市場価値
　market value basis　時価主義，時価基準（＝market price basis）
　market value method　市場価額法，市価法，時価法（＝market price method）
　market value per share　1株当たり市場価値，株価
　open market value　公開市場価値
　present market value　時価（＝current market value）
　secondary-market value　流通市場価格
▸Because of declines in the firm's *market value*, we wrote down this investment by $70 million in 2008.　同社の株価が下落したため，当社はこの投資について2008年度に7,000万ドルの評価減を計上しました。
▸In financial institutions, an accounting system to evaluate assets based on *market values* was introduced in April 2004.　金融機関の場合は，時価会計制度（時価に基づいて資産を評価する制度）

が，2004年4月から導入された。

marketable 形　市場性ある，売買可能な
　investment in marketable securities　有価証券投資，市場性証券への投資
　marketable assets　市場性資産
　marketable commodity　市場性ある商品
　marketable debt security　市場性ある債務証券，市場性ある債券
　marketable equity securities　市場性ある持分証券[有価証券]，市場性ある株式
　marketable investment securities　市場性ある投資有価証券
　marketable issue　市場性証券
　marketable nonequity security　市場性ある債券（＝marketable debt security）
　marketable product　商品
　marketable securities　市場性ある有価証券，市場性有価証券，市場性証券，有価証券
　marketable securities, at cost, which approximates market　市場性ある有価証券—原価評価で時価とほぼ等しい
　non-marketable securities　市場性のない有価証券，非市場性証券
▸Corporate assets primarily include cash, *marketable* securities, equity investments and the administrative headquarters of the Company.　全社一般資産の主な内訳は，現預金，市場性有価証券，株式投資と当社の管理本部資産です。

marketeer 名　マーケティング専門家，市場商人
marketer 名　販売促進員，市場参加者
marketing 名　市場取引，市販，販売，売買，流通，配給，分配，公開，マーケティング（「マーケティング」は，優れた製品を適正な価格で，最適な販売チャネルを通じて消費者に提供するための活動のこと）
　area marketing　エリア・マーケティング（特定地域を対象とし，その市場特性の差異を考慮して展開する地域密着型のマーケティング活動のこと）
　culture marketing　カルチャー・マーケティング
　database marketing　データベース・マーケティング（顧客の性別や生年月日，住所，家族構成，購買履歴などをデータベースに蓄積し，これを分析して顧客の個々のニーズに合わせた商品供給をすること。one-to-one marketingやRFM分析（RFM analysis）などは，その代表例）
　ecological marketing　生態的マーケティング，エコロジー・マーケティング
　global marketing　世界的マーケティング，地球規模のマーケティング，グローバル・マーケティ

ング

industrial marketing 生産財マーケティング（最終消費者を販売対象としない工業製品や原料など，対企業向けのマーケティング活動のこと。その特徴として，需要者が少数で，合理的購買意思決定をすること，それに契約が多額で長期的に安定したものが多いことなどが挙げられる）
international marketing 国際マーケティング（＝global marketing）
internet [Internet] marketing インターネット・マーケティング
managerial marketing 経営者的マーケティング，マネジリアル・マーケティング
marketing activity マーケティング活動
marketing agency マーケティング・エージェンシー（市場調査や商品計画，販売促進などを専門とする広告会社）
marketing agreement 販売協定，マーケティング協定
marketing allocation マーケティング活動配分
marketing communication マーケティング・コミュニケーション
marketing control マーケティング統制
marketing cost 流通費，マーケティング費用，マーケティング原価，マーケティング・コスト
marketing decision support system マーケティング意思決定支援システム
marketing efficiency マーケティング効率
marketing effort マーケティング努力
marketing environment マーケティング環境
marketing executive マーケティング担当役員（＝marketing director）
marketing expense 販売費，営業費，マーケティング費用，マーケティング・コスト（＝marketing cost, selling expense: 広告宣伝費（advertising expense）や販売促進費（sales promotion cost），販売手数料（sales commission），販売員給料（payroll），運賃（freight-out）などが含まれる）
marketing financing 販売金融，マーケティング金融
marketing function マーケティング機能，マーケティング職能
marketing goal マーケティング目標
marketing information マーケティング情報
marketing management マーケティング管理
marketing map 経済市場地図，マーケティング・マップ
marketing mix マーケティング・ミックス（マーケティング目標達成のためのマーケティング手段の組合せ）
marketing operation マーケティング運営，マーケティング活動，マーケティング操作
marketing organization マーケティング組織
marketing orientation マーケティング志向
marketing planning マーケティング計画策定，マーケティング計画
marketing strategy マーケティング戦略
marketing system マーケティング・システム
micro marketing ミクロ・マーケティング（個別企業，企業経営者の立場からマーケティングを分析し，研究するもの）
marketing opportunity マーケティング機会（＝market opportunity）
marketing policy マーケティング政策，マーケティング方針
marketing profitability マーケティング収益性
marketing stimuli マーケティング刺激
mass marketing マス・マーケティング
occasional marketing オケージョナル・マーケティング（消費者の生活の場面・内容に即応した販売活動による売上確保の方法）
one-to-one marketing ワン・トゥ・ワン・マーケティング（インターネットを利用して，各顧客のニーズに応じた商品を提供して販売促進を図るマーケティング手法）
orderly marketing 秩序あるマーケティング活動，オーダリー・マーケティング
niche marketing すき間市場販売戦略，ニッチ・マーケティング（未開発のすき間市場・ニッチ市場への適応をめざすマーケティング）
permission marketing パミッション・マーケティング（＝opt-in mail: ダイレクト・メールを受け取ることにあらかじめ同意した顧客に対して，その顧客情報，例えば顧客の趣味や興味領域に応じてダイレクト・メールで製品情報や買い物情報などを送る手法）
relationship marketing リレーションシップ・マーケティング（顧客との関係性を前提にしたマーケティング。顧客の離反因子や見込み客の発見など，データ・マイニング技術を駆使した分析で，顧客戦略の策定を支援するもの）
retail marketing 小売業のマーケティング
social marketing ソーシャル・マーケティング（企業の社会的責任（商品の安全性への配慮，環境保全や地域社会への貢献）を果たすために行う企業の市場活動）
strategic marketing 戦略的マーケティング
target marketing 標的マーケティング，目標マーケティング，ターゲット・マーケティング

telemarketing テレマーケティング（=telephone shopping, teleshopping: 電話での商品販売法，または電話での各種調査や案内，コールセンター構築のサポートなどを行う会社のこともいう）

test marketing テスト・マーケティング，試験販売（新製品の本格的な市場導入前に，選定した特定の地域で新製品のためのマーケティング・プログラムをすべてテストすること）

total marketing トータル・マーケティング（全社的な視点に立ってマーケティング活動を統合的に管理（計画・組織・実施・統制）すること）

transportation marketing 運輸マーケティング

viral marketing バイラル・マーケティング（利用者の口コミによる販売促進手段のこと）

Web marketing ウェブ・マーケティング（=Internet marketing）

▸Brewers are stepping up *marketing* of more flavored high-quality beer called premium beer. ビール会社各社は，味わいを強調したプレミアム・ビールと呼ばれる高級ビールの販売を強化している。

▸Since early 2005, the number of men and women on the front line around the world, principally in *marketing* and programming, has increased by more than 10,000. 2005年初め以降，世界の第一線で仕事をしている主に営業とプログラミング関連部門の男女従業員の数は，1万人以上増加しました。

marketing and sales expenses マーケティングおよび販売費，マーケティング・販売費

▸*Marketing sales expenses* for new services rose in 2008. 2008年度は，新サービスのマーケティングおよび販売費が増加しました。

marketing research マーケティング調査，市場調査，マーケティング研究，マーケティング・リサーチ

- **marketing [market] research agency** 市場調査代理店，市場調査機関
- **marketing research firm [company]** 市場調査会社
- **marketing research procedure** 市場調査手順，マーケティング・リサーチ手続き

marketmaker 名 マーケットメーカー（価格形成が可能な，自己勘定で売買を行う証券業者）

marketplace 名 市場，商業界

markup 名 値上げ，値入れ，値入れ額，値入れ率（商品の原価と売価の差），マークアップ
- **initial markup** 初回値入れ率
- **maintained markup** 実現値入れ額，実現値入れ率

markup cancellation 値入取消し，値入訂正
markup goal 値入れ率目標
markup planning 値入れ率計画
markup pricing 値入れ法
markup reduction planning 値下げ計画

mask work マスクワーク（半導体チップの表面に印刷される回路パターン）
- **a semiconductor chip product in which the mask work is embodied** マスクワークを具現した半導体チップ製品
- **commercially exploited mask works** マスクワークの商業的利用，商業的に利用されたマスクワーク
- **each layer of the mask work** マスクワークの各層
- **mask work design** マスクワーク・デザイン
- **mask work right** マスクワーク権（知的所有権・知的財産権の一つで，日本法の半導体集積回路の「回路配置利用権」に相当）

▸Seller assigns to Buyer all rights, titles and interests in and to all trademarks, copyrights and *mask work* rights in any material created for Buyer under this contract. 売り主は，この契約に基づいて買い主のために創造・開発した素材のあらゆる商標，著作権，マスクワーク権の権利，権原と権益を買い主にすべて譲渡する。

mass 名 集団，大衆，群衆，大量，大部分，大半，多数，質量，マス
- **critical mass** 最低限の経済規模，限界量，限界質量，臨界量，臨界質量
- **statistical mass** 統計集団
- **working mass** 勤労大衆

mass 形 大量の，大衆の，集団の，多数の，マス
- **mass communication** マスコミ，大衆伝達
- **mass communication media** 報道機関
- **mass culture** 大衆文化
- **mass customization** 大量特注生産
- **mass discounter** ディスカウント・ストア
- **mass display** 大量陳列
- **mass distribution** 大量販売，大量流通
- **mass market** 大量消費市場，大衆消費市場，大量販売市場，大量市場
- **mass marketing strategy** マス・マーケティング戦略
- **mass media** マスコミ，大衆媒体，マスメディア
- **mass media vehicle** マスメディア伝達
- **mass merchandiser** 量販店，量販業者，ディスカウント・ショップ
- **mass merchandising** マス・マーチャンダイジング

mass outbreak of food poisoning 食中毒の集団発生
mass production 大量生産, 量産, マスプロ
mass protest rally 抗議大集会
mass retailer 量販小売業
mass transit system 大量輸送システム
mass transportation 大量輸送, 大量運輸
▶The age of *mass* manufacturing, *mass* marketing, and *mass* media brought together capital and labor in vast pyramidal corporations, tying workers to the machine and the tube. 大量生産, 大量販売とマスメディアの時代は, 資本と労働を大規模なピラミッド構造の企業にもたらし, 労働者を機械（コンピュータ）とブラウン管（テレビ）に縛りつけた.

mass-consumption society 大量消費社会
▶Daiei grew rapidly as a dynamo of the *mass-consumption society* by offering discount goods made possible through mass purchasing. ダイエーは, 大量仕入れで可能になった格安商品を提供して［値引き販売をして］, 大量消費社会の担い手として急成長した.

mass-produce 動 量産する, 大量生産する
mass production 大量生産, 量産, マスプロ
▶Elpida aims to start *mass production* at its new plant. エルピーダは, 新工場での量産化をめざしている.

massive 形 巨額の, 多額の, 巨大な, 大量の, 多量の, 多大の, 大規模な, 大がかりな, 大幅な, スケールの大きい, 大きい, 大型の, 旺盛な, 充実した
massive debt loads 巨額の債務負担, 巨額の債務
massive demand 旺盛な需要
massive dollar buying 大量のドル買い
massive financial assistance 巨額の金融支援, 巨額の財政援助
massive flight of capital 大量の資金移動
massive increase in government spending 大型の財政出動
massive investment 大規模投資, 大がかりな投資, 巨額の投資
massive loss 巨額の損失, 大幅損失, 大幅赤字
massive outflows of capital and technology 資本と技術の大量流出
▶Loan disposal costs are likely to result in *massive* losses. 債権処理費用で, 大幅な赤字に陥る見通しだ.
▶The *massive* gains in stockholdings' latent value will raise the banks' net worth ratios markedly. 保有株の含み益の大幅増加で, 銀行の自己資本比率も大きく向上する見込みだ.

massive debts 巨額の債務, 過剰債務
▶The bank has also lent money to many start-up firms laden with *massive debts*. 同行は, 多くの過剰債務の新興企業［ベンチャー企業］にも融資している.

massive intervention 巨額の介入
▶The yen rose only slightly against the dollar during the business year thanks to the Japanese government's *massive intervention*. 日本政府の巨額介入があって, 期中の対ドル相場は小幅な円高にとどまった.

massive issuance 大量発行
▶The rise in debt-servicing costs is due to the *massive issuance* of government bonds to prop up the economy. 国債費が増えたのは, 景気を支えるため国債を大量に発行したためだ.

massive selling 大量の売り
▶At this point, only massive dollar buying could balance the *massive selling*. この時点で, 大量のドル売りには大量のドル買いで対抗するしかない.

master 形 主要な, 中心の, 最重要な, 元になる, 基本の, 標準的な, 優れた, 一流の, 名人の, マスター
master budget 総合予算
master contract 基本契約, 包括契約
master craftsman 一流の職人
master file 基本ファイル, マスター・ファイル
master plan 基本計画, 総合計画, マスター・プラン
master policy 一括保険証券, 団体保険の親証券
master production schedule 基準生産計画《略 MPS》
▶The firm's business strategy *master* plan sets outs the planned direction for the three years from fiscal 2008. 同社のビジネス戦略の基本計画は, 2008年度から3年間の事業方針を示している.

master agreement 標準契約, 標準契約書, マスター契約, マスター契約書, 基本契約
master resale agreement 包括レポ契約書
rate and currency swap master agreement 金利スワップ・通貨スワップ標準契約書
umbrella master agreement 包括標準契約書

Master of Business Administration 経営管理学修士, 経営学修士《略 MBA》

mastermind 名 首謀者, 指導者, 主導者, 黒幕, 計画立案者, 立案者, 傑出した知性［知能］, 優れた知性［知能］の持ち主, 動 陰で指揮する, 首謀者として指揮する
▶He was the *mastermind* behind a string of violations of the Securities and Exchange Law

by the Internet service firm. 氏は，このインターネット・サービス会社による一連の証券取引法違反行為を主導していた。

match 動 支払う，…と一致する，…と調和する，…に見合う
▶We *match* a percentage of the employee contributions up to certain limits. 当社[会社]は，従業員拠出金の一定の割合を，一定限度まで負担[資金援助]しています。

matching 名 突合せ，照合，対応，費用・収益の対応，調整，整合，決定，マッチング
 automated trading and order-matching system 自動取引・注文執行システム
 matching costs and revenues 費用と収益の対応，費用収益対応
 matching gift 同額拠出制度，マッチング・ギフト(社員が社会福祉などに寄付した場合，会社側もそれと同額の寄付をする制度)
 matching grant 同額拠出[対応拠出]条件付き交付金
 matching rate 照会適合率，マッチング率
 matching system マッチング方式(研修医の研修先の決定方法)
 transaction matching instruction 取引照合指図
▶*Matching* of your request with sellers in our database is based on the products or services, budget, location, and other factors you specified on your request. 貴社の見積り依頼書と当社のデータベース内の売り手とのマッチングは，製品，サービス，予算，所在地，その他貴社が見積もり依頼書で指定した要件に基づいて行います。
▶Several hospitals fear the *matching* system could result in interns concentrating only on well-known hospitals. このマッチング方式で，研修医が有名病院だけに集中する結果になる可能性があると懸念する病院もある。
▶We believe FIFO more clearly reflects income by providing a better *matching* of current cost and current revenue. 当社は，先入れ先出し法のほうが，当期収益と当期費用の適切な対応によってより明確に利益を反映すると思っています。

material 名 材料，材質，原料，資料，素材，物質，構成物質，服地，マテリアル
 advanced composite materials 先進複合材料《略 ACM》
 advanced materials 新素材
 biocompatible metal materials 生体用金属材料
 biomechanical materials 生体材料
 building materials 建築材料，建材
 composite materials 複合材料
 crude materials 原材料
 documentary material 証拠書類
 eco materials エコマテリアル
 electronic materials 電子材料
 foreign materials 輸入資材
 hazardous materials 有害物質
 housing materials 建築資材
 industrial material prices 工業製品価格
 industrial materials 工業原料，工業製品
 input materials 投入原材料
 intelligent materials インテリジェント材料
 material cost 材料費，材料主費
 material procurement 原材料の調達 (＝procurement of materials)
 materials and services 資材と用役
 materials and supplies 原材料および貯蔵品，材料および貯蔵品，資材，原材料
 materials handling 荷役，荷役運搬，資材運搬，運搬管理，マテハン，マテリアル・ハンドリング
 materials in process 仕掛け材料費，原材料仕掛け品
 materials inventory 材料棚卸し高
 materials management 資材管理 (＝materials control)
 materials specification 材料仕様書，材料明細書
 organic-inorganic hybrid materials 有機・無機ハイブリッド材料
 presentation materials プレゼンテーション用資料
 promotional materials 販促資料 (＝sales materials)
 raw materials 原材料
 related materials 関連資料
▶Rising prices for raw *materials*, such as steel, and crude oil could have an adverse impact. 鉄鋼などの素材や原油価格の高騰が，マイナス材料だ。

material 形 重要な，大きな影響力のある，物的，物質的な，有形の
 material adverse change 重大な事態の変化
 material breach 重大な違反，重大違反 (＝material violation)
 material circumstances 重要事項
 material difference 重要な差異
 material effect 重大な影響，大きな影響
 material fact 重要な事実，重要事実
 material misrepresentation 重大な不実表示
 material property 有形財産

material respect 重要な点, 重要事項
- The impact of this accounting change was not *material*. この会計処理方法の変更による影響は, 重要なものではありません。
- We have no present plans to sell *material* interests in subsidiaries. 当社は現在, 重要な子会社持ち分を売却する予定はありません。

material procurement 原材料の調達
- We intend to reinforce the company's business through the relationship with the company in such areas as *material procurement* and trading of paper-pulp products. 当社は, 原材料の調達や紙パルプ製品の取引などの面での同社との関係により, 同社事業のテコ入れを目指している。

matter 問題, 主題, 対象, 内容, 事項, 議題, 事態, 事柄, 主要事実, 重要
- **all matters relating hereto** 本契約に関連する一切の事項
- **commercial matters** 商業上の問題
- **key corporate matters** 重要な経営事項
- **subject matter** 本件, 契約の主題・内容, 目的物, 目的事項, 対象物, 対象事項, 裁判での係争物, 訴訟物
- **subject matter of insurance** 保険の目的, 保険の対象
- Environmental and other *matters* are subject to many uncertainties, and outcomes are not predictable with assurance. 環境その他の問題は, 多くの不確定要素の影響を受けるため, その帰結を確実に予測するのは不可能です。
- This agreement sets forth the entire agreement and understandings between the parties as to the subject *matter* of this agreement. 本契約は, この契約の主題に関する当事者間の完全合意と了解事項を定めるものである。

mature 満期になる, 期日が到来する, 支払い期日になる
- **matured bond** 満期後社債
- **matured bonds unredeemed** 期日到来未償還社債
- **matured liability** 支払い期日到来負債, 期日到来債務
- **matured note** 満期手形
- **maturing debt** 満期が到来した債務, 満期償還額
- **refinance maturing debt issues** 満期を迎えた債務を借り換える
- **repayment [payment] of maturing CP** 満期が来た [満期が到来した, 満期を迎える] CPの償還
- About $830 million of long-term debt *matures* during the year. 長期債務のうち約8億3,000万ドルは, 今年度に満期が到来します [満期を迎えます]。
- Government bonds to be refunded as they *mature* are worth about ¥110 trillion this fiscal year. 今年度は, 償還期限が来て借り換える国債が約110兆円もある。

maturity 満期, 支払い期限, 支払い期日, 支払い日, 弁済期限, 償還期限, 期限, 一括返済
- **cancellation before maturity** 中途解約
- **current maturity** 残存期間
- **debt maturity** 債務支払い日, 債務の償還期限
- **final maturity** 償還期日, 最終満期
- **full repayment before maturity** 早期完済
- **maturity date** 満期日, 満期, 支払い期日, 償還日
- **maturity value** 元利合計, 満期日の価額, 満期償還価額, 満期価値
- **original maturity** 当初満期
- **redemption of maturity** 満期償還
- **residual maturity** 残余期間
- We took advantage of favorable levels of interest rates to extend debt *maturities* by refinancing a substantial amount of long-term debt. 当社は, 有利な金利水準を利用して, 長期負債の相当額を借り替えることにより債務の償還期限を延長しました。

maximization 最大化, 極大化
- **maximization of shareholder values** 株主価値の最大化
- **output maximization** 産出量最大化, 産出量極大化
- **profit maximization** 利益[利潤]極大化, 利益の最大化
- **utility maximization** 効用極大化

maximum 最高, 最大, 最大量, 最大数, 上限, 最高の, 最大の, 最大限の
- **maximum commission fees** 手数料の上限
- **maximum limits** 発行枠, 発行限度, 最高限度, 最高限度額
- **maximum loss** 最大損失
- **maximum pension provision** 最高年金計上額
- **maximum stock** 最高在庫, 最高在庫量
- **maximum sustainable yield** 最大持続生産量《略 MSY》
- Our *maximum* potential loss may exceed the amount recognized in our balance sheet. 当社の最大予想損失額は, 貸借対照表上で認識された額を上回る可能性があります。

maximum lending rate 貸出金利の上限 (＝highest lending rate)
- All four of Japan's major consumer loan firms will lower their *maximum lending rates* to

below 20 percent. 国内消費者金融大手の4社すべてが，貸出金利の上限を20％以下（現行の出資法の上限金利は年29.2％）に引き下げる。

may 動 …することができる，…する権利がある（＝can：契約書や法律文書でmayが使われる場合は，「権利，許可」を表す）

▸This Agreement *may* be amended only by a written instrument signed by duly authorized representatives of both parties. 本契約書は，両当事者の正当な権限をもつ代表が署名した書面［文書］によってだけ修正することができる。

may not …してはならない，…することはできない，…する権利はない

契約書や法律文書でmay notが使われる場合は，基本的にshall notと同じく「禁止」を表し，「…してはならない」の意味になる。ただし，may notには「…することができない，…する権利はない」の意味もある

▸This Agreement may not be assigned to a third party without the prior written consent of both parties. 本契約は，両当事者の書面による事前の合意［両当事者の事前の承諾書］なしで第三者に譲渡することはできない［譲渡してはならない］。

MBA 経営管理学修士，経営学修士号（**Master of Business Administration**の略。ビジネス・スクール（経営学大学院）の修士課程修了者に与えられる学位。実務家養成のため，会計・法務などのカリキュラムを実践的に学ぶのが特徴）

MBA 米抵当銀行協会，モーゲージ・バンカーズ協会（**Mortgage Bankers Association**の略）

MBI マネジメント・バイイン（**management buyin**の略。買収者がターゲット会社の経営者ではなく，企業投資ファンドなどの部外者で，買収後は一般に取締役会に投資ファンドの代表者を派遣して会社の経営に深く関与する場合をMBIという）

MBO 経営者による自社買収，経営者による営業権取得，マネジメント・バイアウト（⇒management buy-out [buyout]）

MBOとは➡企業の経営者が，一般株主や親会社などから自社株を買い取って，企業や事業部門の経営権を買い取ること。一般に，敵対的買収の防衛や子会社が独立する際に用いられるM&A（企業の合併・買収）の手法。上場企業の場合は，経営陣が買収を実施する会社を別に設立し，自社の資産を担保にして投資会社や金融機関から融資を受け，その資金でTOB（株式公開買付け）を行い，一般株主から株式を広く買い集めることが多い。最近は，非上場にすることを目的に実施する例が目立っている。その背景には，敵対的買収への防衛策のほかに，株式持ち合いが崩れて年金基金のような「物言う株主」が増えてきたことなどの要因があるといわれる。親会社から自社株を買って子会社が独立する際の利点としては，社内体制が変わらないことや，親会社との関係が比較的良好に保たれる点が挙げられる。

MBS 抵当証券担保付き証券，モーゲージ担保証券（＝**mortgage-backed certificate**の略。モーゲージ（不動産担保付きローン債権）を裏付けとして発行される証券の総称）

measure [measures] 名 対策，措置，対応，政策，施策，方策，策，手段，比率，指標，尺度，基準測定値，測度（⇒**negative spread**）

additional antideflationary measures 追加デフレ策
administrative measures 行政措置
antideflationary measures デフレ対策，デフレからの脱却策
antiinflationary measures インフレ対策，インフレ抑制策，インフレ措置
broad measure of money supply 広義のマネー・サプライ指標
catch-up measures 後手後手の対応
common measures 共同対策
counter measures 対抗措置，対抗手段，対策
debt measures 債務比率
deficit reduction measures 赤字削減策
economic stimulus measures 景気刺激策
effective measures 効果的な対策
emergency measures 緊急対策，緊急措置
fiscal measures 財政政策，財政措置
inflation measures インフレ指標
internal measures 社内対策
lasting measure 恒久的措置
liberalization measures 自由化措置，規制緩和措置
measure of risk aversion リスク回避度
monetary measures 金融政策，金融措置
narrow measure of money supply 狭義のマネー・サプライ指標
package of measures 対策
political measures 政策手段，政策の手
preventive measures 予防策，予防の対策，防止策，対策
protectionist measures 保護貿易政策，貿易保護手段
protective measures 保護措置，対応策
punitive measures 制裁措置，報復措置
reflationary measures 通貨調節策，リフレ政策
restructuring measures リストラ策
retaliatory measures 報復措置
safeguard measures 緊急輸入制限措置

special tax relief measures 特別減税措置, 税金の特別減免措置
temporary measure 時限措置
workable measures 実行可能な施策
▶The firm is under pressure to introduce job cuts and other restructuring *measures*.　同社は, 人員削減などのリストラ策の導入に迫られている。

measurement 名　測定, 計算, 算定, 計量, 測定値, 指標, 尺度　(⇒projected benefit obligation)
cost measurement 原価計算
financial measurement 財務指標
list of weight and measurement 重量・容積証明書
measurements 測定値, 寸法, 長さ, 大きさ, サイズ
performance measurement 業績測定, 性能測定

MEBO 経営陣と従業員による企業買収　(management employee buy-out [buyout]の略)

mecenat 名　文化活動への貢献・寄与, 芸術・科学支援活動, 文化支援, 文化支援事業, メセナ
▶The company carries out four main activities as the basis for its social service: philanthropy, volunteer programs, *mecenat*—patronage of the arts and sciences, and regional environmental protection.　同社では, 社会貢献の柱として寄付活動, ボランティア活動, メセナ(芸術・科学支援活動)と地域環境保護の四つの活動を実施している。

media 名　媒体, 商品, マスコミ, 報道機関, メディア
advertising media 広告媒体, 広告メディア
mass communication media マスコミ・メディア, マスコミ媒体, 報道機関
mass media マス・メディア
media advertising 媒体広告
media effect 媒体効果
media mix 媒体ミックス, 広告媒体の組合せ, メディア・ミックス
media planning 媒体計画
media selection 媒体選択
media storm メディア旋風
media strategy メディア戦略
news media ニュース報道, 報道機関, マスコミ
print media 印刷媒体
savings media 貯蓄商品

median 名　中央値, 中位数, メディアン, 形　中央の, 中間の, 中位の
median family メディアン世帯
median income 中位の収入
median strip 〈統計での〉中央値[中位数], 中央分離帯
national median 全国中央値

mediate 動　調停する, 仲裁する, 和解させる, 取り次ぐ

Medicaid メディケイド(米国の低所得者や身体障害者のための医療扶助で, 州と連邦政府が共同で行う; ⇒medicare)

medical expenses 医療費
▶The burden of *medical expenses* for current and retired employees, made obligatory through labor management accords, hangs heavy on GM.　労使協約で課せられた社員と退職者に対する医療費の負担が, GMに重くのしかかっている。

medical services 医療サービス　(⇒informed consent)
▶A reorganization of *medical services* for the elderly already has been postponed to fiscal 2008.　高齢者医療サービスの再編は, すでに2008年度まで先送りされている。

Medicare 名　高齢者医療保障制度, 高齢者医療保険, メディケア
▶Bush is seeking $78 billion savings in the government's health care programs—*Medicare* for the elderly and Medicaid for the poor—over the next five years.　ブッシュ米大統領は, 公的医療保険制度(高齢者のための「メディケア」と低所得者層のための「メディケイド」)の支出削減として, 今後5年で780億ドルの削減を求めている。

medium 名　媒介, 手段, 報道機関, 中期国債

meet 動　〈需要や要求などを〉満たす, 〈目標などを〉達成する, うまく処理する, 対応する, 履行する, 〈費用などを〉支払う, 〈期待などに〉添う
meet a criteria 基準を満たす, 基準をクリアーする, 基準に適合する
meet customer needs 顧客のニーズに対応する, 顧客のニーズを満たす
meet expenses 費用を支払う, 費用を賄う
meet increasing demand 需要増[需要の増加]に対応する
meet one's obligations 債務を履行する, 債務を返済する
meet requirements 必要条件[要件]を満たす, 要求に応じる, 基準を満たす
▶External funds required to *meet* the additional cash requirements in 2009 will be obtained by offering debt securities in the market.　2009年度内に発生する追加資金必要額を賄うための外部調達資金は, 市場で債券を募集発行して調達する予定

meeting 名 会議, 会, 総会, 大会, 理事会, 場, ミーティング (⇒**general meeting, shareholders meeting**)
  closed meeting 非公開協議
  creditors' meeting 債権者会議, 債権者集会 (⇒**bankruptcy procedures**)
  due diligence meeting 新証券発行説明会
  extraordinary meeting 臨時総会 (米国では **special meeting**という)
  inaugural meeting 創立総会
  managing directors' meeting 常務会
  meeting of representatives of policyholders 保険会社の総代会 (=meeting of policyholder representatives, policyholders' representative meeting: 株式会社の株主総会にあたる)
  one-on-one meeting 投資家との個別ミーティング (=one-to-one meeting)
  ordinary council meeting 定例理事会 (=regular council meeting)
  stockholders [shareholders] meeting 株主総会 (=shareholders' meeting, stockholders' meeting)
▸This issue was settled at the extraordinary *meetings* of both firms' boards of directors. この問題は, 両社の臨時取締役会でそれぞれ決議された。

megabank 名 巨大銀行, 超巨大銀行, 巨大銀行グループ, メガバンク (⇒**alliance strategy, financial revitalization**)
▸The firm's securities division is seen as inferior to those other *megabank* groups. 同社の証券部門は, 巨大銀行グループと比べて見劣りがする。

megacompetition 名 大競争
megamerger 名 超大型合併, 超巨大合併
megastore 名 超大型チェーン店
melon 名 利益, 所得, 余剰利益, 特別配当, 多額の利益配当, メロン
  cut [carve, split] a melon 特別配当をする, 利益を分ける
  melon-cutting 特別配当
▸We cut a nice *melon* in the fourth quarter as profits skyrocketed. 利益が急増したので, 当社は第4四半期に多額の利益配当を行った。

meltdown 名 〈株価などの〉急落, 暴落, 下落, 市場の崩壊, 〈市場の〉暴落[急落] (crash), 経済の溶解, メルトダウン
  economic meltdown 経済のメルトダウン(溶解)
  market meltdown 市場崩壊
  meltdown in U.S. subprime mortgages 米国のサブプライム・ローン(低所得者向け住宅ローン)市場の崩壊
▸The *meltdown* in U.S. subprime mortgages has eroded earnings at financial firms. 米国のサブプライム・ローン(低所得者向け住宅ローン)市場の崩壊で, 金融機関の収益は減少している。

member 名 会員, 構成員, 社員, 部員, メンバー
  allied member 副会員
  associate member 準会員
  board member 役員, 取締役
  card member カード会員
  corporation member 法人会員
  external board member 社外取締役
  founder member 設立会員
  full member 正会員 (=regular member)
  group member グループ企業, グループ内企業
  management members 経営陣 (=members of management)
  member country 加盟国 (=member nation, member state)
  member firm 会員企業, 会員会社, 加盟企業
  Member of Congress 米下院議員
  Member of Parliament 英下院議員
  member store 加盟店 (=member's store)
  permanent member of the U.N. Security Council 国連安全保障理事会, 常任理事国
  private member 個人会員
  single-member districts 小選挙区制 (=single-member election districts)
  special member 特別会員
▸The average economic growth rate of the new EU *members* this year will exceed 4 percent, though the old *members* will see only sluggish growth. EU新加盟国の平均経済成長率は, 旧加盟国が伸び悩んでいるのに対して, 今年は4%を超える見通しだ。
▸The salary levels of our union *members* are generally low. 組合員の給与[賃金]水準は, 総じて低い。

member state 加盟国, 参加国 (=member country)
▸APEC *member* states are also leading members of the WTO. APEC (太平洋経済協力会議)参加国は, WTO (世界貿易機関)の有力メンバーでもある。
▸The WTO General Council meeting will be held from Tuesday with the participation of ambassadors of the 147 *member* states and regions. 147加盟国・地域の担当大使が参加して, 木曜日から世界貿易機関(WTO)の一般理事会が開かれる。

memorandum 名 覚書, メモ, メモランダム 条項
▶The company's president and heads of the two other companies signed a *memorandum* on the business tie-up agreement. 同社社長と他の2社のトップが, 業務提携契約に関する覚書に署名した.

memorandum of association 基本定款, 英国企業の通常定款 (米国企業の基本定款 (articles of incorporation) に相当)

memorandum of understanding 基本合意書, 予備的合意書, 意思表明状, 了解覚書, 協定覚書
▶In January 26, 2009, we signed a *memorandum of understanding* for the creation of a new company. 2009年1月26日に当社は, 新会社設立の協定覚書に調印しました.

mental handicap 知的障害
▶Managers tend to believe that employees with mental problems would be unable to work for the firm for long, compared with those with physical disabilities or *mental handicaps*. 身体障害者や知的障害者に比べて, 精神障害をかかえる従業員は長続きしない, と経営者は考えている傾向がある.

mental illness 精神病, 精神障害 (=mental ailment, mental disease)
▶Businesses have been unable to deal adequately with employees who displayed symptoms of *mental illness* after they were hired. 入社後に精神障害の症状を示した従業員に, 企業側はこれまで十分に対応しきれていない.

mental problems 精神病, 精神疾患, 精神障害
▶The number of salaried workers suffering from *mental problems*, such as manic depression, has risen lately. 最近は, 躁うつ病などの精神疾患をかかえるサラリーマンの数が増えている.

mentally disturbed 精神障害の
▶Due to the economic slowdown, the employment rate for the *mentally disturbed* people dropped. 景気低迷で, 精神障害者の雇用率 [就職率] は落ち込んだ.

mentally handicapped people 知的障害者
▶The law concerning the promotion of employment of handicapped people was revised to cover *mentally handicapped people*. 障害者雇用促進法は, 改正されて知的障害者にも適用されるようになった.

mentally ill people 精神障害者

menu 名 メニュー (コンピュータで実行できる機能の一覧表)
menu bar メニュー・バー (「ウインドウ」の上部にあるメニュー群のこと)
menu selection メニュー選択
menu system メニュー方式
on-screen menu 画面上のメニュー

mercantile 形 商業の, 貿易の, 商人の, 商売の, 利益目当ての
free mercantile policy 自由貿易政策, 自由商業政策
mercantile agency 商業興信所, 信用調査機関
mercantile bill 商業手形
mercantile capitalism 商業資本主義
mercantile credit 企業間信用, 商業信用貸し, 商業掛売り
mercantile emporium 商業の中心地, 貿易中心地
mercantile law 商事法, 商法
mercantile marine 商船, 海運力
mercantile risk 商品危険, 商品リスク
mercantile selling 業者間販売
mercantile trade [trading] 商取引

mercantile exchange 商業取引所, 商品取引所, マーカンタイル取引所
Chicago Mercantile Exchange シカゴ・マーカンタイル取引所《略 CME》
New York Mercantile Exchange ニューヨーク商業取引所《略 NYMEX》

merchandise 名 商品, 物品, 品物, 製品, モノ (⇒income account surplus)
basic merchandise 基本商品
merchandise assortment 商品品揃え
merchandise certificate 商品券 (=gift certificate)
merchandise control 商品管理, 商品統制 (=merchandise management)
merchandise cost 商品コスト
merchandise handling 商品取扱い, 商品輸送方法
merchandise inventory 商品在庫
merchandise knowledge 商品知識
merchandise manager 商品部長
merchandise mix 商品構成
merchandise on consignment 委託積送品
merchandise strategy 商品戦略
merchandise turnover 商品回転率 (=stock turnover)
merchandise warehousing 商品倉庫業務
non-merchandise account 貿易外収支
original merchandise オリジナル商品

private label merchandise プライベート・ブランド商品
seasonal merchandise 季節商品
staple merchandise 主力商品

merchandise trade モノの貿易, モノの取引, 商品貿易, 財の輸出入, 貿易取引
　merchandise trade gap モノの貿易赤字, 財の貿易赤字, 貿易収支の赤字額, 商品貿易の赤字, 貿易赤字（＝merchandise trade deficit）
　merchandise trade surplus モノの貿易黒字, 財の貿易黒字, 貿易収支の黒字額, 商品貿易の黒字, 貿易黒字

▸The surplus in *merchandise trade* climbed 30.8 percent in 2007 to ¥12.38 trillion as expanding exports outspaced rising imports. 2007年のモノの取引を示す貿易収支の黒字は, 輸出の拡大が輸入の増加を上回ったため, 30.8％増えて12兆3,800億円となった。

merchandiser 名 販売促進担当者

merchandising 名 商品化計画, 商品計画, 商品戦略, 商品売買, 計画的販売促進, マーチャンダイジング
　leader merchandising おとり商品戦略
　mass merchandising マス・マーチャンダイジング
　merchandising company [firm] 商社, 商事会社
　programed [programmed] merchandising 定型化された[定型的]マーチャンダイジング, プログラムド・マーチャンダイジング
　scrambled merchandising 多角化商品計画, よろず販売, スクランブルド・マーチャンダイジング

merchant system マーチャント・システム（インターネットで大規模な買い物のサービスを提供するシステム）

merchantability 名 商品性, 市販可能性, 市販性, 市場性（＝merchantable quality）

merchantable quality 商品性, 適商品質, 商品としての品質
　good merchantable quality 適商品質, 適商品質条件《略 GMQ》
　of merchantable quality 商品性がある, 適商品質を備えている

▸Seller represents and warrants that the goods covered by this sales order are of *merchantable quality* and fit and safe for consumer use. 売り主は, この売付け申込書に表示した物品は適商品質[商品としての品質]を備えており, 消費者の使用に適していると同時に安全であることを表示し, これを保証する。

merge 動 合併する, 吸収合併する, 経営統合する, 統合する（⇒**operation**）

▸Mizuho Financial Group Inc. will *merge* its two securities units in January 2008. みずほフィナンシャルグループは, 同社の証券会社2社を2008年1月に統合する。

▸Mizuho Securities Co. and Shinko Securities Co. will *merge* in May rather than January. みずほ証券と新光証券は, 1月ではなく5月に合併することになった。

merge operations 経営統合する, 事業を統合する（＝integrate operations）

▸TV stations are seeking tie-ups with Internet firms to *merge* their *operations* with Internet services. テレビ各局は, 放送事業とネット事業[通信事業]との融合を目指して, ネット企業との業務提携を求めている。

merged firm 合併会社

▸This newly *merged firm* will be formed within this year. この合併新会社は, 今年中に発足する。

merger 名 合併, 経営統合, 事業統合, 統合, 吸収合併, 併合, 融合（⇒**triangular merger**）
　acquisitions and mergers 企業取得と合併
　business merger 経営統合, 企業の合併（＝merger of businesses）
　corporate merger 企業合併, 会社合併
　debt-financed merger 借入れによる合併
　downstream merger 逆吸収合併（子会社による親会社の吸収のこと）
　horizontal merger 水平的合併, 同業他社との合併
　merger agreement 経営統合の合意書, 経営統合の契約・契約書, 合併協議書（＝merger deal）
　merger and acquisition 企業の吸収合併, 合併・買収, 企業取得と合併《略 M&A》（＝mergers and acquisitions; ⇒**M&A**, **mergers and acquisitions**）
　merger and acquisition deal M&A取引, M&A案件（＝M&A deal）
　merger on an equal basis 対等合併
　merger by purchase 合併
　merger consideration 合併の対価
　merger negotiation 合併交渉, 経営統合鉱床（＝merger talks）
　merger rate 統合比率, 合併比率（＝exchange ratio of merger, merger ratio）
　mergers and absorptions 吸収・合併
　mergers and realignments 統合や再編, 統合・再編
　multi-merger 多角的合併

stock-for-stock merger 株式交換による合併
vertical merger 垂直的合併
▶The people, assets and capital of the two firms won't change just because of this *merger*.　合併したからといって，両社の社員，資産と資本になんら変動はありません。

merger deal 合併協議書, 経営統合の合意書, 経営統合の契約[契約書]（＝merger agreement）
▶The two parties of Minshuto (Democratic Party of Japan) and Jiyuto (Liberal Party) signed a *merger deal*.　民主・自由両党は，合併協議書に調印した。

merger plan 統合計画, 吸収・合併計画, 合併計画
▶The *merger plan* likely will affect the realignment strategies of other companies in the banking and securities industries.　この統合計画は今後，銀行・証券業界の他企業の再編戦略に影響を与えそうだ。

merger proposal 経営統合案, 経営統合提案, 経営統合の提案書（＝business integration proposal）
▶AOKI Holdings Inc., the nation's second-largest menswear chain, has submitted a *merger proposal* to Futata Co.　紳士服関連チェーン国内2位のAOKIホールディングスが，（同業の）フタタに経営統合案を提出した。

merger talks 合併交渉, 統合交渉, 経営統合交渉（＝merger negotiation）
▶The two banks agreed to begin *merger talks*.　両行は，経営統合交渉を開始することで合意した。

mergers and acquisitions 企業の合併・買収《略 M&A》（＝merger and acquisition; ⇒ **corporate merger, M&A**）
▶Defects in the rules governing *mergers and acquisitions* are surfacing one after another.　M&A（企業の合併・買収）に関するルールの不備が，次々と表面化している。

merit-based pay plan [system] 業績連動型の報酬制度, 成果主義型の賃金制度[報酬制度]
▶A disparity in income between nonregular workers and regular workers is due to the establishment of *merit-based pay systems* at many firms.　正社員と非正社員との所得格差の原因は，多くの企業で成果主義型の賃金制度を採用したことにある。

message 名 通信文, 伝言, 文面,〈電子メールでの〉通信情報[伝達事項], メッセージ
　advertising message 広告メッセージ
　Budget Message 米大統領の予算教書
　commercial message コマーシャル, 広告文, 宣伝文句《略 CM》
　email message 電子メール
　message area call 市内通話
　online message board 出会い系掲示板
　presidential message 大統領教書（＝President's Message）
　Special Message 米大統領の特別教書
　State of the State Message 米州知事の施政方針演説
　State of the Union Message [Address] 米大統領の一般教書
　State of the World Message 米大統領の外交教書

metal 名 金属, 貴金属, メタル
　collection of rare metals 希少金属の回収, レア・メタルの回収
　fabricated metal product 加工金属製品
　mineral and metal materials 鉱物・金属材料
　non-ferrous metals 非鉄金属
　precious metal 貴金属
▶The city's budget proposes to halt the recycling of *metal*, glass and plastic to save money.　同市の予算案では，経費節約のため，金属とガラス，プラスチックのリサイクリング中止を提案している。

methane hydrate メタンハイドレート（天然ガスの主成分のメタンが低温高圧下で水に溶けたもので，石油や天然ガスに代わる新天然資源として注目されている。その氷のような形状から，「燃える氷（burning ice）」ともいわれる）
▶*Methane hydrate* is seen as a future energy source.　メタンハイドレートは，今後のエネルギー資源として注目されている。

method 名 方法, 手法, 方式, 手順, 順序, 筋道, 基準, 主義（⇒**accounting method, percentage of completion method, purchase method**）
　account method 帳簿控除方式
　accrued method 発生主義
　declining balance method 定率法
　full cost method 全部原価法
　interest method of amortization 利息法による償却
　liability method 負債法
　method of fixed percentage on cost 定率法
　method of historical cost 原価主義
　method of moving average 移動平均法
　method of price of last purchase 最終仕入原価法
　net of tax method 税引き後法
　normal stock method 基準棚卸し法

replacement cost method 取替原価法
tender panel method 競争入札制度
terminal funding method 年金現価充足方式
underwriting method 全額引受方式

▶Retailers are forced to adopt unconventional *methods* to improve their business, such as major mergers. 大胆な経営統合など，小売業界はこれまでに見られなかった手法での経営改革に迫られている。

▶We use the effective interest *method* of amortization. 当社は，実効利息法による償却法を採用しています。

mezzanine 形 メザニン型の，中間的［一時的］に介在する，中間に位置する

mezzanine bond メザニン債（優先債と劣後債の中間に位置する「メザニン債」は，一般にトリプルB（BBB）以下の格付けとなる）

mezzanine debt メザニン型負債［債務］メザニン負債，無担保ローンの借入金

mezzanine field 中間に位置する分野

mezzanine finance メザニン融資，メザニン型資金調達，メザニン・ファイナンス（=mezzanine financing, mezzanine funding: 企業買収の際に資金調達方法の一つとして高金利の無担保ローンを利用する方式。また，会社清算時の受取順位が，優先債権には劣後するが，普通株には優先する劣後債（subordinated debenture）などによる資金調達を意味する場合もある）

mezzanine funds メザニン投資ファンド
mezzanine money 転換社債
mezzanine subordination 準劣後請求権

▶Domestic and foreign insurance companies are scrambling to introduce new products in the so-called third sector—a *mezzanine* field between life and nonlife insurance, such as medical, cancer and nursing insurance. 国内外の保険各社は，第三分野（医療やがん，介護保険など生命保険と損害保険の中間に位置する保険分野）と呼ばれる医療保険の商品開発［商品導入］にしのぎを削っている。

middle manager 中間管理職，中間管理者，中堅幹部

middleman 名 仲買人，仲卸業者，仲介者
▶A major marine products wholesaler sold blowfish to an unlicensed *middleman* in violation to a Tokyo metropolitan ordinance. 大手の水産物卸売業者が，東京都条例に違反して，無認可の仲卸業者にフグを販売していた。

midterm 名 中間，中期（=medium term）
midterm account settlement 中間決算（=interim account settlement, midterm settlement of accounts, midterm results; ⇒**mark**）

midterm dividend 中間配当

midterm results 中間決算，半期の業績（=first-half results, interim results, midterm business results, semi-annual results; ⇒**product price**）

midterm business plan 中期経営計画，中期事業計画，中期経営構想，中期経営プラン

▶The company revealed a new *midterm business plan* for fiscal 2009-2012. 同社は，2009-2012年度の新中期経営構想を発表した。

midterm earnings report 中間決算，中間決算報告（=interim earnings report, midterm financial report）

▶In their *midterm earnings reports*, major banking groups revised initial loss projections resulting from bad loan disposal. 中間決算で，主要銀行グループは不良債権処理に伴う当初の予想損失額を修正した。

midterm management strategy 中期経営戦略

▶Under its *midterm management strategy*, the NTT group aims to further consolidate group companies and lessen duplication of services. 中期経営戦略によると，NTTグループは，グループ企業の一体化を強め，重複業務の解消を目指す。

midterm report 中間決算，中間決算報告，半期報告，中間報告（=interim report, midterm business report, midterm earnings report）

▶The fiscal 2008 *midterm reports* for most firms listed on the First Section of the Tokyo Stock Exchange have been released. 東京証券取引所の一部上場企業の2008年9月中間決算が，ほぼ出揃った。

-minded …志向の，…に熱心な，…好きの，…に強い関心がある，…重視［優先］の（=-oriented）

environmentally-minded 環境問題に強い関心がある

independence-minded 独立志向の

like-minded 考え方を共有する，似た考え方の，気質が同じな，同意見の

money-minded 金に執着する，金儲けへの執着心が強い

performance-minded 実績重視の

▶Like-*minded* partners such as the EU and Japan must work together. 欧州連合（EU）と日本のように考え方が似ているパートナーは，力を合わせなければならない。

minimum 名 最低，最小，最小限，最小値，ミニ

マム, 形 最低の, 最小の, 最小限の
minimum capital 最低資本金, 最低自己資本
minimum capital adequacy ratio 最低自己資本比率
minimum capital requirements 最低必要資本金額, 会社設立時に必要な最低資本金, 最低資本金の要件 (＝minimum capitalization requirements, minimum regulatory capital requirements; ⇒stock company)
minimum guarantee 最低保証金
minimum lease payments 最低リース支払い額, 最低賃借料等支払い額
minimum lending rate 最低貸出金利
minimum margin 最低利幅
minimum order size 最低発注量
minimum pension provision 最低年金計上額
minimum profit 最低利益, 最小利幅
minimum purchase 最低購入量
minimum royalty 最低ロイヤルティ, 最低使用料, ミニマム・ロイヤルティ
minimum stock 最低在庫量, 最低在庫
minimum subscription 最小株式引受限度
minimum tax ミニマム税, ミニマム・タックス (通常の法人税, 所得税に追加して課される税)
▶Under the rules of the Bank for International Settlements, the *minimum* capital adequacy ratio required of banks operating internationally is 8 percent. 国際決済銀行（BIS）の規則では、国際銀行業務を行っている銀行に要求される最低自己資本比率は、8％である。

mining 名 採掘, 採鉱, 鉱山業, 鉱業, 資源開発, 〈地雷などの〉敷設
gold mining company 金鉱開発会社
mining company 探鉱会社, 資源会社, 資源開発会社
mining engineer 鉱山技師
mining products 鉱産物
mining right 鉱業権, 採掘権
▶BHP Billiton Ltd. launched a hostile $147 billion bid for *mining* rival Rio Tinto Ltd. 英豪系資源最大手のBHPビリトンが、同業ライバルのリオ・ティントに対して1,470億ドルの敵対的TOBを開始した。

minority 名 少数, 少数派, 少数民族
minority buyout 少数持ち分の買取り
minority equity 少数株主持ち分, 少数株主権
minority shareholder 少数株主 (＝minority stockholder)
minority shareholders' equity 少数株主持ち分
▶A company's stock will be delisted if more than 80 percent of outstanding shares are held by a specified *minority* of owners for more than one year. 流通株式[上場株式数]の80％超を特定の少数株主が1年を超えて保有した場合、その会社の銘柄は上場廃止となる。
▶Our document describes programs in the United States for women, *minorities* and handicapped persons. 当社の小冊子には、女性、少数民族と身体障害者に対する当社の米国内プログラムが記載されています。

minority interest 少数株主持ち分, 少数株主持ち分利益, 少数株主損益, 少数利益, 過半数以下の出資, 少数株主権
income before income taxes, minority interest and cumulative effect of accounting changes 法人所得税, 少数株主損益[少数株主持ち分利益]および会計方針の変更による累積的影響額控除前利益
minority interest in common stock 少数株主持ち分—資本金
minority interest in consolidated subsidiaries 連結子会社の少数株主持ち分
minority interest in net income 少数株主持ち分利益
minority interests in earnings/loss 少数株主損益
▶*Minority interests* represent other companies' ownership interests in our net assets. 少数株主持ち分は、当社の純資産に対する他社の所有者持ち分を表します。

mint 名 造幣局, 発行したばかりの貨幣, 刷りたての紙幣, 巨額, 大量, 宝庫
mintage 名 貨幣鋳造, 貨幣
minutes 名 議事録, 議事要旨, 覚書, 訴訟記録 (＝minutes book)
misc. 雑, その他 (miscellaneous の略)
miscellaneous 形 種々雑多な, 雑, その他
misgiving 名 不安, 懸念, 心配, 疑念, 疑い, 疑惑, 不信の念
▶The most worrying thing, in terms of future, is the sense of *misgiving* in the financial system. 今後、最も懸念されるのは、金融不安だ。
mislabeling 名 不当表示, 不正表示, 偽装表示
misleading 形 紛らわしい, 誤解を招きやすい, 虚偽の
misleading advertisement 紛らわしい広告, 誤解を招きやすい広告, 虚偽の広告
▶The cell phone service provider ran *misleading advertisements*. この携帯電話サービス業者は、紛らわしい広告を出した。
misrepresentation 名 不当表示, 虚偽の表示

mismatch ミスマッチ（=mismatching）
▸We must address the improvement of employment situation, particularly in regard to jobs for young people and the *mismatch* between job seekers and job openings.　われわれとしては，特に若年層の雇用や求職者と新規雇用のミスマッチなどの面で，雇用状況の改善に取り組まなければならない。

Missile Technology Control Regime ミサイル関連技術規制《略 MTCR》
▸Exports of such machines are regulated by the *Missile Technology Control Regime*.　このような機器の輸出は，「ミサイル関連技術規制」で規制されている。

mission 使命，任務

misstatement 虚偽表示，虚偽記載，不実表示，誤表示（=misrepresentation）
　expected misstatement 予想虚偽表示
　known misstatement 既知の虚偽表示
　material misstatement 重大な虚偽記載，重要な虚偽表示
　tolerable misstatement 許容虚偽表示
▸These GAASs require that we plan and perform the audit to obtain reasonable assurance about whether the financial statements are free of material *misstatement*.　これらの一般に認められた監査基準は，連結財務書類に重要な虚偽表示がないかどうかについての合理的な確証を得るため，私どもが監査を計画して実施することを要求しています。

mix 構成，組合せ，混合，比率，内容，中身，ミックス（⇒**revenue mix**）
　asset mix 資産構成，資産配分
　business mix 事業構成，事業内容（=mix of business）
　currency mix of foreign exchange reserves 外貨準備の通貨構成
　distribution mix 流通ミックス（流通経路と物的流通が流通ミックスの主な構成要素）
　export mix 輸出構成
　factor mix 生産要素の組合せ
　marketing mix マーケティング手段の最適組合せ，マーケティング・ミックス
　merchandise mix 商品構成，商品ミックス
　policy mix 政策手段の最適組合せ，経済政策ミックス，ポリシー・ミックス
　portfolio mix ポートフォリオの構成，有価証券の中身，ポートフォリオ・ミックス
　product mix 商品構成，製品構成，製品組合せ，製品ミックス，プロダクト・ミックス
　sales mix 売上品構成，販売組合せ，セールス・ミックス
▸Pricing pressures and changes in our product sales *mix* caused the gross margin percentage to decline.　価格圧力［値下げ圧力］と当社製品の売上構成の変化で，売上総利益率は低下しました。

mobile Net services 携帯ネット・サービス
▸Competition in *mobile Net services* and the Net advertisement business likely will intensify in Japan as well.　今後は，日本でも携帯ネット・サービスとネット広告事業の競争が激化するだろう。

Mobile Number Portability (MNP) system 〈携帯電話の〉番号持ち運び制度
▸The *Mobile Number Portability system* was introduced in October 2007.　携帯電話の「番号持ち運び制度」は，2007年10月から導入された。

mobile phone 携帯電話，移動式電話，移動電話（=cell phone, cellular phone）
　mobile phone handset 携帯電話機，携帯電話端末機
　mobile phone manufacturer 携帯電話メーカー
　mobile phone number 携帯電話の番号
　mobile phone operator 携帯電話事業会社
　mobile phone provider 携帯電話会社，携帯電話プロバイダー
　mobile phone software 携帯電話専用ソフトウェア

mobile phone market 携帯電話市場，移動電話市場（=cell phone, cellular phone）
▸Japan's *mobile phone market* nears saturation.　日本の携帯電話市場は，ほぼ飽和状態だ。
▸The nation's largest cable television network operator has unveiled a plan to enter the *mobile phone market*.　ケーブルテレビ国内最大手が，携帯電話市場への参入計画を発表した。

mode 方式，様式，機能，〈統計で〉最頻値，並数，モード
　batch mode 一括処理方式
　compatible mode 互換モード
　conversational mode 会話様式
　enhanced mode 拡張モード
　real time mode 即時処理方式
　repeat mode リピート機能

model モデル，模型，型，型式，車種，機種，新案，模範（⇒**business model, patent**）
　buying behavior model 購買行動モデル
　consumer behavior model 消費者行動モデル
　corporate model 企業モデル
　decision model 意思決定モデル
　dynamic model 動態モデル，動学モデル

econometric model 計量経済モデル
elasticity model 弾力性モデル
existing models 現行機種
large models and smaller, lower priced models 大型機種と低価格の小型機種
leading model 主力車種, 主力車
linear model 線型［線形］モデル
linear program(m)ing model LPモデル
market model 市場モデル
Model Business Corporation Act 1984 1984年模範事業会社法
model change 型式変更, モデル・チェンジ
Model T T型フォード
performance model 業績モデル
pricing model 価格決定モデル
probability model 確率モデル
quantitative model 数量化モデル, 数量モデル
regression model 回帰モデル
role model 手本, 理想像, 理想の姿, 雛（ひな）型, 模範生, 優等生
simulation model シミュレーション・モデル
stock valuation model 株式評価モデル
successive model 後継機種
time series model 時系列モデル
utility model 実用新案
valuation model 評価モデル
working model 実用モデル, 実用模型

▶Behind the slump in the stock prices is a crisis of confidence in U.S. style capitalism, which until recently has served as a *model* of prosperity. 株価急落の背景にあるのは, 最近まで繁栄のモデルとされてきた米国型資本主義に対する信認の揺らぎだ.

▶In cooperation with its parts makers, Toyota has brought one new *model* after another to the market. 部品メーカーとの共同作業で, トヨタは新車種を相次いで市場に投入してきた.

▶Softbank Corp. will release 15 new mobile phone *models* in 64 different colors by the end of this year. ソフトバンクが, 年末までに携帯電話の新端末15機種(計64色)を発売する.

moderate 動 縮小する, 低下する, 下がる, 鈍化する, 減速する, 抑える, 弱める, 低下させる

▶The pace of U.S. consumer price increases *moderated* in June. 米国の6月の消費者物価の上げ幅は縮小した.

module 名 部品, モジュール (⇒**component**)

momentum 名 はずみ, 勢い, 余波, 惰性, 契機, 要素

add [spur] momentum to …に拍車をかける, …にはずみをつける
earnings momentum 収益力
gain cyclical momentum for a recovery 景気回復の循環にはずみをつける
gain momentum はずみをつける, 勢いを増す, 拡大する, 加速する
gather momentum 勢いを増す, 勢いがつく, 加速する, 拡大する, 本格化する, 上向きになる (＝gain momentum)
increase the political momentum 政治的はずみをつける
inflationary momentum インフレの勢い
lose momentum 失速する, 減速する, 勢いがなくなる, 息切れする, 下向きになる
momentum of the growth 経済成長の勢い
recovery momentum 景気回復の勢い
upward momentum 上昇の勢い, 上値の勢い

▶The economic recovery seems to be picking up *momentum*. 景気回復に, 勢いが出てきたようだ.

▶The economy is beginning to lose *momentum* as exports and capital investments are slowing. 輸出と設備投資が息切れを始め, 景気に減速傾向が出ている.

▶The market is gathering *momentum*. 市場は上向きだ.

▶With the economic recovery gaining *momentum*, U.S. companies have begun investing in the Japanese stock market again, giving a lift to stock prices. 景気回復が力強さを増していることから, 米国企業が日本の株式市場に再び投資するようになり, 株価を押し上げている.

monetary 形 金融の, 通貨の, 貨幣の, 財政上の, 金銭の, マネタリー

monetary authorities 金融当局, 通貨当局 (**joint market intervention**の項の文例参照)
monetary donations 企業献金
monetary easing 金融緩和
monetary easing policy 金融緩和政策, 金融緩和策 (＝monetary ease, monetary expansion, monetary relaxation)
monetary excess 過剰流動性
monetary gain and/or loss 貨幣利得および／または貨幣損失 (インフレで生じる貨幣項目の損益)
monetary liability 金銭債務
monetary market 通貨市場
monetary policy assessment 金融政策の判断
monetary restraint 金融引締め
monetary assets 貨幣性資産, 金銭債権 (＝money asset:「貨幣性資産」は, 貨幣そのものまた

は法令や契約によってその金額が固定している資産のことで、現金、預金、売掛金、受取手形、貸付金などが含まれる。これに対して、将来費用となる棚卸し資産などの資産を「費用性資産」という）

▸Current assets (excluding inventories and prepaid expenses), current liabilities, and long-term *monetary assets* and liabilities are translated at the exchange rates in effect at the balance sheet date. 流動資産（棚卸資産と前払い費用を除く）、流動負債と長期貨幣性資産および負債は、貸借対照表日[決算日]現在の実効為替レートで換算してあります。

monetary base マネタリー・ベース、貨幣的ベース （＝high-powered money base, money base: 日本銀行発行高、貨幣流通高と日銀当座預金（民間金融機関の中央銀行預け金）の合計で、日銀が金融市場に供給している資金の残高を示す）

▸The *monetary base* shrank 21.1 percent in January from a year ago. 1月のマネタリー・ベース（日銀券発行高、貨幣流通高、日銀当座預金の合計）は、前年同月比で21.1％減少した。

monetary base balance マネタリー・ベースの残高

▸The *monetary base balance* for May totaled ¥108.83 trillion. 5月のマネタリー・ベースの残高は、108兆8,300億円だった。

monetary items 貨幣性項目、貨幣項目 （貨幣性資産と貨幣性負債）

▸*Monetary items* in the balance sheets are translated at year-end rates. 貸借対照表の貨幣性項目は、期末レートで換算されています。

monetary policy 金融政策 （＝money policy）

▸The Bank of Japan decided to maintain its current *monetary policy*. 日銀は、金融政策の現状維持を決めた。

▸The U.S. Federal Reserve Board raised U.S. interest rates, leading the worldwide move to change current super-loose *monetary policy*. 米連邦準備制度理事会(FRB)が米国の金利を引き上げ、世界的な超金融緩和の政策転換の先陣を切った。

money 名 金、金銭、通貨、貨幣、資金、金融、マネー （⇒base money）

　borrowed money 借入金
　call money コール借入金、短期資金、銀行相互間の当座借入金、コール・マネー
　call money rate コール・レート
　easy money 金融緩和、低利の金、低金利
　hard money 硬貨
　hot money 短期資金、投機資金、ホット・マネー

　hush money 口止め料
　key money 権利金、保証金、礼金
　lose money 赤字を出す、損失を出す、損失を被る
　make money 利益を生み出す、利益を上げる、利益を得る、資金を稼ぐ
　money borrowed for long term 長期借入金
　money borrowed for short term 短期借入金
　money deposited from customers 得意先預り金
　money deposited from officers 役員預り金
　money easing 金融緩和
　money in hand 手元資金、手元現金預金
　money income 現金収入
　money management 投資運用
　money policy 金融政策 （＝monetary policy）
　money purchase plan 定額拠出年金
　money rate of interest 金利、利子率 （＝interest rate, money rate）
　money transaction 現金取引、直取引
　narrow money 狭義の通貨、狭義のマネー
　raise money 資金を調達する

▸The challenge in monetary policy for countries now is shifting toward finding a way to move away from ultra-loose *money* policies. 現在、各国の金融政策の課題は、超金融緩和政策からいかに転換するかに移りつつある。

money laundering 不正資金の洗浄、資金洗浄、マネー・ロンダリング （＝money washing: 犯罪で得た資金の出所や所有者を隠す行為）

▸The bank failed to adequately implement anti-*money-laundering* compliance programs. 同行は、マネー・ロンダリング（資金洗浄）防止の法遵守プログラムを適正に実施しなかった[同行のマネー・ロンダリングへの監視体制は、不十分だった]。

money-losing 形 赤字の、不採算の
　money-losing company 赤字企業、赤字会社 （＝loss-making company, red-ink firm）
　money-losing outlet 赤字店舗 （＝loss-making outlet）

money-losing operation 赤字の事業、不採算事業

▸The firm aims to turn its three core *money-losing operations* profitable in fiscal 2009. 同社は、2009年度から赤字の主力3事業の黒字化を目指している。

money-losing store 赤字店舗、不採算店舗

▸Daiei's group sales fell 22.3 percent to ¥672.11 billion in the March-August period due to closure of its *money-losing stores*. ダイエーの8月中間決算で[ダイエーの3-8月期決算で]、不

採算店舗[赤字店舗]の閉鎖により，連結売上高は22.3%減の6,721億1,000万円となった。

money market 金融市場, 短期金融市場, マネー・マーケット（長期金融市場はcapital market：「短期金融市場」は, 短期の金融資産であるコール, 手形, 譲渡性預金(CD), 現先などの資金取引が行われる金融市場のこと。⇒**capital market, inflow**）
  long-term money market 長期金融市場
  money market instruments 短期金融市場証券, 短期金融商品
  money market management 金融調節
  short-term money market 短期金融市場
▶The Bank of Japan uses the unsecured overnight call rate as the key target rate in the short-term *money market*. 日銀は, 無担保コール翌日物の金利を短期金融市場の誘導目標にしている。

money supply 通貨供給量, 資金供給, マネー・サプライ（中央銀行と市中金融機関が民間に供給する通貨の量で, 通貨にはM2（現金, 要求払い預金, 定期性預金）のほかにCD（譲渡性預金）が含まれる。⇒**key gauge**）
▶The *money supply* last year posted its lowest year-on-year growth in 10 years. 昨年の通貨供給量は, 前年比で10年ぶりの低い伸びにとどまった。

money transfer 振替え, 口座振替え, 振込み, 資金の移動, 送金（＝cash transfer）
▶Payments for items purchased through the Internet are primarily made by *money transfer* through specified banks and other institutions after the goods are delivered to the purchaser. インターネットで買った品物の代金の支払いは, だいたい商品が届けられてから購入者が指定された銀行などの金融機関に振り込む形になっている。

monitor 動 監視する, 管理する, 調査する, チェックする, 評価する, 把握する, 分析する, モニターする
▶Our internal auditors *monitor* compliance with the system of internal controls by means of an annual plan of internal audits. 当社の内部監査人は, 内部監査の年度計画により, 内部統制組織が守られているかどうかを監視しています。
▶We will continue to closely *monitor* the market and take appropriate actions as necessary. われわれとしては, 引き続き市場の動向に十分注意して, 必要に応じて適切な対応を取る。

monitoring 名 監視, 監視活動, 監理, モニタリング
▶The Tokyo Stock Exchange transferred Nikko Cordial stock to its *monitoring* post. 東京証券取引所は, 日興コーディアルグループの株式を，（投資家に上場廃止の可能性を知らせる）東証の監理ポストに移した。

monoline 名 単一の事業, 米国の金融保証保険会社, 金融保証会社, 金融保証専門会社, モノライン（＝bond insurer：「モノライン」は, 債券など金融商品の保証を専門に行う米国の保険会社で, 倒産などで社債購入者に元本と利息を支払えない場合に会社に代わってその支払いを保証する。生命保険や自動車保険, 火災保険などの各種保険を手がける保険会社を「マルチライン(multiline)」という）
  monoline bond insurer 債券専門保険会社
  monoline health insurer 健康保険専門会社
  monoline insurance company 専門保険会社（＝monoline insurer）

monopolization 名 独占, 専売
▶NTT's *monopolization* of subscribers' lines connecting NTT telephone stations and households has impeded fair competition among telecommunications companies. NTTの電話局と各戸を結ぶ加入者回線のNTTによる独占が, 通信事業者間の公正な競争を阻害している。

monopoly 名 独占, 売り手独占, 供給独占, 独占事業体, 独占企業体, 独占体
  monopoly goodwill 独占的営業権, 特許的営業権
  monopoly price 独占価格
  monopoly provider 独占企業
▶The three companies will sell their respective stakes in Sakhalin Energy Investment Co. to Russia's state-controlled natural gas *monopoly* OAO Gazprom. 3社はそれぞれ, 保有するサハリン・エナジー・インベストメントの株式を, ロシア国営の天然ガス独占企業体のガスプロムに譲渡する方針だ。

month-on-month 前月比で, 前月比（＝month-on-month figure, on the month）
▶The CPI continued to drop by close to 1 percent on a *month-on-month* basis. 消費者物価指数の下落幅は, 前月比で1％近い水準で終始した。

Moody's Investment Grade ムーディーズ投資等級《略 MIG》

Moody's Investors Service ムーディーズ, ムーディーズ・インベスターズ・サービス（米国の格付け会社）

moonlight 動 副業[夜間アルバイト]をする

morale 名 労働意欲, 勤労意欲, 勤労意識, 士気, モラール
  boost [improve, raise] morale 士気を高める
  morale survey 労働意欲調査, 勤労意欲調査, 士

気調査, モラール調査

morality 名 倫理, 道徳, 道義, 倫理性, 道徳性, 道義性, モラル
▸There is a need to improve the *morality* of corporate executives and more closely monitor companies. 経営者のモラルの向上と, 企業の監視を強化する必要がある。

moratorium 名 (債務の)支払い猶予, 支払い停止, モラトリアム(通常金融危機などの非常事態に際して法令などを定めて実施する)

mortgage 名 抵当, 担保, 担保不動産, 譲渡抵当, 抵当権, 抵当権設定, 抵当証書, 担保付き融資, 住宅ローン, モーゲージ (⇒subprime mortgage)
  adjustable mortgage [mortgage loan] 変動金利モーゲージ (=adjustable-rate mortgage, adjustable-rate mortgage loan)
  credits for mortgage payments 住宅取得控除
  home mortgage 住宅ローン
  home mortgage borrowing 住宅ローンの借入れ
  lower mortgage rate 住宅ローン金利の低下, モーゲージ金利の低下
  mortgage debenture 担保付き社債
  mortgage debt 担保付き長期債務, 抵当借り
  mortgage deed 担保証書
  mortgage loan 抵当貸し, 担保付き貸付け金 (mortgage loan receivable, secured loan), 住宅ローン
  mortgage note 担保付き長期手形
  mortgage rate 住宅ローン金利, モーゲージ金利
  mortgages payable 担保[抵当]付き借入金
  mortgages receivable 担保[抵当]付き貸付け金
  residential mortgage market 住宅ローン市場, 住宅用モーゲージ市場
  stripped mortgage securities 分離型モーゲージ証券
▸Japan Post is discussing an alliance with Suruga Bank to offer *mortgages* and other loans to individuals. 日本郵政は現在, 住宅ローンなど個人ローン商品の販売に向けて, スルガ銀行と業務提携協議を進めている。

mortgage-backed securities business 住宅融資証券事業, 不動産証券事業, 不動産証券化事業
▸Nomura will withdraw from the U.S. residential *mortgage-backed securities business*. 野村[野村ホールディングス]が, 米住宅融資の証券化事業[米国の住宅融資証券の関連事業]から撤退することになった。

mortgage-backed security 住宅融資証券, モーゲージ担保証券, モーゲージ証券, 不動産証券 《略 MBS》 (=mortgage-backed certificate)
▸Our quarterly net profit will be lower than the same period a year earlier because of losses tied to *mortgage-backed securities*. 当社の四半期純利益は, 不動産証券関連の損失で前年同期を下回る見込みです。

mortgage bond 担保付き債券, 抵当権付き[担保付き]社債, 不動産担保債
  first mortgage bond 第一順位抵当権付き社債, 一番抵当付き社債, 第一順位抵当付き債券
  junior mortgage bond 後順位物上担保付き社債
  second mortgage bond 第二順位抵当権付き社債, 二番抵当付き社債
▸The first *mortgage bonds* of the corporation are secured by a first mortgage and a floating charge on the company. 同社の第一順位抵当権付き社債は, 同社の第一順位抵当権と浮動担保権で保証されています。

mortgagor 名 抵当権設定者, 担保提供者

Mothers マザーズ (東京証券取引所のベンチャー企業向け市場で1999年11月に開設した)
▸The firm is listed on the *Mothers* market on the Tokyo Stock Exchange. 同社は, 東証マザーズ上場企業だ。

motion 提議, 提案, 動議, 発議, 申立て, 動き, 運動, 移動
▸Under the Commercial Code, to gain approval for an important resolution that directly affects corporate management, shareholders holding at least 50 percent of shares with voting rights must cast ballots, and two-thirds must back the *motion*. 商法で, 企業の経営に直接影響を及ぼす重要決議の承認を得るには, 議決権株式の少なくとも50％を保有する株主が投票し, 提案に対してその3分の2の支持を得る必要がある。

motivation 名 動機づけ, 刺激誘因, 意欲, 購買動機, 学習意欲, モチベーション
  buying motivation 購買動機 (=motivation of purchase)
  economic motivation 経済的動機づけ
  extrinsic motivation 外的動機づけ
  intrinsic motivation 内的動機づけ
  motivation control 動機づけ管理
  motivation information 動機づけ情報
  motivation level 動機づけ水準
  motivation research 動機調査, 購買動機調査, モチベーション・リサーチ 《略 MR》 (=motivational research)

motivation to spend 消費意欲
profit motivation 利潤動機, 利潤志向
movable [**moveable**] 形 動産の, 動かせる, 可動性の, 移動性の, 名 動産, 家具, 家財
　movable exchange 変動為替
　movable feast 移動祝祭日
　movable goods 可動商品
　movable insurance 動産保険
　movable property 動産
move 名 動き, 動向, 変動, 移動, 移行, 行動, 運動, 進展, 処置, 措置, 対応, 対策, 手段, 異動, 移転, 引っ越し
　best moves 最善の動き, 最善の措置, 最善の対応
　competitive moves 競争力
　international moves 海外進出
　limit move 値幅制限
　market move 市場の動き, 市場動向
　seasonal moves 季節要因
　speculative move 投機的な動き
　strategic moves 戦略的な動き
▶As seen in Seven-Eleven's *move* to reduce the price of seasonings, a price war between convenience stores is heating up. セブン・イレブンの調味料値下げなどの動きに見られるように, コンビニ業界では値下げ競争［価格競争］が激化している。
▶The situation will likely intensify *moves* behind the scenes among companies circulating to take over the company. このような状況から, 同社買収を狙った企業の動きが水面下で活発化する可能性が高い。
movement 名 動き, 行動, 活動, 運動, 移動, 動向, 流れ, 進展, 進行, 変化, 変動
　capital movement 資本移動
　consumer movement 消費者運動
　environmental movement 環境保護運動
　interest rate movement 金利動向, 金利変動（=interest rate move）
　market movement 市場の動き, 市場動向, 相場の動き, 相場変動
　movement of funds 資金移動（=fund transfer）
　price movement 価格変動, 物価動向
　price movement restriction 値幅制限
　quality movement QC運動
　stock price movement 株価動向, 株価変動
　zero defects movements 無欠陥運動, 無欠点運動, ZD運動
▶Sharp rises in the price of international commodities and other factors relating to price *movements* have changed significantly. 国際商品の価格高騰など物価動向をめぐる要因が, 大きく変化している。
▶The development of a market economy is possible only when there is a free *movement* of people, goods and capital. 市場経済の発展には, 人, モノ, 資本の自由な移動が前提となる。
moving average 移動平均, 移動平均線（株価の「移動平均線」は, 当日を起点に, 過去の一定期間をさかのぼって終値の平均値を算出する作業を毎日繰り返し, 値を線で結んだグラフ。株価変動の大まかな傾向をつかむのに有用とされている）
　moving average cost method 移動平均原価法
　moving-average method 移動平均法
moving strike convertible bond 転換社債型新株予約権付き社債《略 MSCB》
▶Fuji TV issued the *moving strike convertible bonds* (MSCBs) early this year for subscription by Daiwa Securities SMBC Co. to raise ¥80 billion for its NBS takeover bid. フジテレビは今春, ニッポン放送株の公開買付け(TOB)資金800億円を調達するため, 大和証券SMBCを引受先として転換社債型新株予約権付き社債(MSCB)を発行した。
MOX fuel プルトニウムとウランの混合酸化物(MOX)燃料, MOX燃料
▶If the spent nuclear fuel is reprocessed to extract plutonium, the plutonium can be processed into *MOX fuel* and the volume of stored spent fuel can be reduced. 使用済み核燃料を再処理してプルトニウムを取り出し, このプルトニウムをMOX燃料に加工すれば, 使用済み核燃料の貯蔵量を減らすことができる。
MPO 野村証券の登録商標（**multiple private offering**の略。新株予約権付き社債などを証券会社等への第三者割当てにより発行するという資金調達方法）
▶In *MPOs*, a firm issues zero-coupon convertible bonds to brokerages rather than directly to the market. MPOでは, 企業がゼロクーポン転換社債を市場に直接でなく証券会社などに発行する。
MSCB 転換社債型新株予約権付き社債（**moving strike convertible bond**の略。発行した企業の株価下落に伴って, 株式に換える価格を低く修正することができる特別条項が付いた社債）
multilateral accord 多国間合意
▶The new interpretation of the Foreign Exchange and Foreign Trade Law allows the government to suspend cash transfers and exports under an agreement between Tokyo and Washington, dispensing with the need for a U.N. resolution

and a *multilateral accord*. 外国為替・外国貿易法（外為法）の新解釈では，政府は，国連決議や多国間合意がなくても，日米間の合意に基づいて送金や貿易を停止することができる。

multilateral trade talks 多角的貿易交渉，多国間貿易交渉（＝multilateral trade negotiation）

multiple 形 多数の，多重の，複合の，複式の，多角式の，多種多様な，名 倍数，チェーン・ストア

cash multiples キャッシュ・フロー倍率

earnings multiple 株価収益率（＝price earnings multiple

multiple agriculture 多角式農業，多面農業

multiple growth model 多段階成長モデル

multiple listing 同時上場

multiple regression 重回帰

multiple store [shop] チェーン店，チェーン・ストア（＝chain store）

multiple private offering 転換社債の第三者割当て発行《略 MPO》（⇒**MPO**）

▸Especially companies with fragile capital bases are using schemes such as private placements of convertible bonds, known as *multiple private offerings* (MPOs). 特に資本基盤が弱い企業は，MPOと呼ばれる転換社債の第三者割当て発行のような資金調達方式を活用している。

municipal 形 地方自治体の，市制の，市の，市営の，名 市債，地方債

municipal bond 地方債，市債

municipal debt 地方債，市債（＝municipal loan）

municipal engineering 都市工学，都市計画

municipal enterprise 地方公営企業

municipal finance 都市財政

municipal management 都市経営，市営

municipal note 地方債，地方政府証券

municipal revenue bond 地方特定財源債

municipal security 地方債，地方証券，市債

municipal tax 市町村税

mutual 形 相互の，共通の，共同の

mutual company 相互会社

mutual fund 投資信託，ミューチュアル・ファンド

mutual insurance 相互保険

mutual ownership of shares 株式持ち合い，株の持ち合い（＝mutually held stocks）

mutual savings bank 相互貯蓄銀行

mutual aid pension plan 共済年金，共済年金制度

▸The main purpose of the integration of the corporate employees pension plan and the *mutual aid pension plan* is to eliminate the public-private disparities. 会社員の厚生年金と公務員が加入する共済年金の一元化は，官民格差の解消がその主な目的だ。

mutual relief operations 共済事業

▸Revenues from commissions of *mutual relief operations* were pooled in off-the-book accounts. 共済事業の手数料収入は，簿外口座に蓄えられていた。

MVNO 仮想移動通信事業者（**mobile virtual network operator**の略）

▸A mobile virtual network operator (*MVNO*) system enables companies without their own telecom networks to enter the cell phone business. 仮想移動体通信事業者(MVNO)の制度を利用すると，企業は自前の通信網を持たずに携帯電話事業に参入することができる。

N

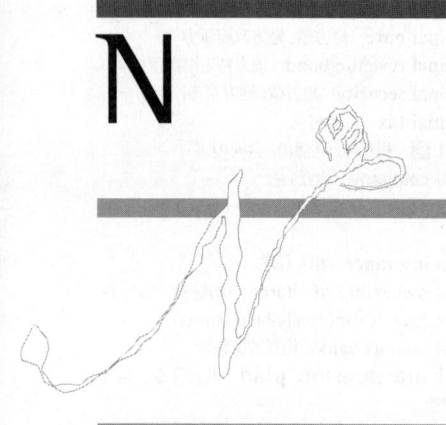

n

N/A 該当なし（**not applicable**の略）
NAFTA 北米自由貿易協定（**North American Free Trade Agreement**の略）
NAFTA 北大西洋自由貿易地域（**North Atlantic Free Trade Area**の略）
NAIC 全米保険監督官協会（**National Association of Insurance Commissioners**の略）
NAIC 全米投資家協会（**National Association of Investors Corporation**の略）
nail 名 くぎ，爪
 on the nail 即金で
name 動 指名する，任命する，選ぶ，指定する，命名する，…の名前を挙げる，公表する，決める
▸Under the agreement, France's Danone will *name* two people Yakult Honsha's board of directors and Yakult will *name* one to Danone's board. 合意事項では，仏ダノンがヤクルト本社に取締役2名を派遣し，ヤクルトはダノンに取締役1名を派遣する。
name 名 名称，名前，名義，知名度，銘柄，発行体，ネーム
 company name 会社名，社名（＝business name, corporate name, trade name）
 known name 有名銘柄，知名度の高い銘柄
 name borrowing 名義借り
 name gathering 名寄せ
 security name 銘柄名
 single name paper 単名手形（＝one-name paper）
 speculative name 仕手銘柄
 strong name 優良発行体
 top quality name 超優良銘柄，最優良銘柄
 top-rated name 超優良発行体
 trade name 商号，屋号，社名，商標，商標名，トレードマーク
 two-name paper 複名手形
▸After the management integration, the corporate *name* as well as the current management will be retained. 経営統合後も，社名や現在の経営体制はそのまま残る。
name lending 名義貸し
▸*Name lending* by doctors is illegal. 医師の名義貸しは，違法である。
name-list broker 名簿業者
▸A *name-list broker* has sold the leaked personal information. 名簿業者が，流出した個人情報を販売している。
name recognition 知名度
▸Greater *name recognition* will contribute to sales of the product in Japan. 日本での今後の知名度アップが，同製品の販売促進につながる。
nanometer 名 ナノメートル（1ナノメートル＝10億分の1メートル）
▸A *nanometer* is a billionth of a meter. 1ナノメートルは，10億分の1メートルである。
nanotech product ナノテク製品
▸Safety criteria for nanotechnology could be used to create standards for *nanotech products* and parts. ナノテク（超微細加工技術）の安全基準は，ナノテク製品や部品の標準化につながる可能性がある。
nanotechnology 名 超微細加工技術，超微細加工・計測技術，超微小技術，ナノ技術，ナノテク，ナノテクノロジー（1個の原子や分子を材料にしたり，部品として組み合わせてミクロ大の装置や機械などを作ったり，研究をする分野。極小半導体や

超小型ロボット, 燃料電池, 薬を直接病巣に運ぶ分子カプセルなど幅広い分野での応用が期待されている. ⇒**optical computer**)

naphtha 名 ナフサ (粗製ガソリン)
▶Polyethylene and polypropylene are made from *naphtha*. ポリエチレン (PE) とポリプロピレン (PP) は, ナフサ (粗製ガソリン) から作られる.

narrow 動 縮小する, 狭まる, 限定する, 狭める, 縮める
▶Japan Airlines' first-quarter loss *narrowed* by 30 percent. 日本航空の第1四半期赤字が, 30%縮小した.

NASD 全米証券業協会 (**National Association of Securities Dealers** の略)
▶*NASD* is the parent of the Nasdaq over-the-counter stock market. 全米証券業協会 (NASD) は, 米国の店頭株式市場「ナスダック」の運営母体である.

NASDAQ ナスダック, 米店頭株式市場, 全国店頭銘柄気配自動通報システム, 全国店頭銘柄建値自動通報システム, 店頭銘柄自動通報システム (**National Association of Securities Dealers Automated Quotations System** の略)

Nasdaq composite index ナスダック店頭市場の総合指数, ナスダックの総合指数

Nasdaq Stock Market ナスダック証券市場, ナスダック (マイクロソフトやインテルなど5千を超える銘柄が上場して取引され, これ以外に数千銘柄が店頭 (OTC) 市場で取引されている)

national 形 国民の, 全国民の, 国民的な, 国家の, 国家的な, (米国で) 連邦の, 国有の, 国立の

national economy 国民経済, 国の経済
▶In the age of the *national economy*, business activities were well geared to the goal of stabilizing employment and ensuring social security. 国民経済の時代には, 企業活動 [経済活動] は, 雇用の安定と社会保障の確保という二つの目標に向けられた.

national pension 国民年金
　national pension plan 国民年金, 国民年金制度 (= national pension program, national pension scheme, national pension system)
　national pension premiums 国民年金保険料
▶The *national pension* scheme mainly covers students aged 20 or older and the self-employed. 国民年金の加入対象は, 主に20歳以上の学生や自営業者だ.

national pension system 国民年金制度, 国民年金 (= national pension plan, national pension program, national pension scheme)

National People's Congress 中国の全国人民代表大会, 全人代 (= China's figurehead parliament: 中国の国会)
▶The *National People's Congress* opened its annual session in Beijing. 全国人民代表大会は, 年1回の全体会議を北京で開いた [全国人民代表大会の年1回の全体会議が, 北京で開幕した].

nationalize 動 国有化する, 国営化する

natural gas 天然ガス
　liquefied natural gas 液化天然ガス 《略 **LNG**》
　natural gas reserves 天然ガス埋蔵量
　solidified natural gas 固形化天然ガス
▶Production of *natural gas* likely will continue expanding for a few more decades. 天然ガスの生産は, 今後とも数十年間は拡大を続ける可能性が高い.

natural gas hydrate 天然ガス・ハイドレート 《略 **NGH**》
▶*Natural gas hydrate* (NGH) is an icelike solid material produced artificially by combining natural gas and water under high pressure. 天然ガス・ハイドレート (NGH) は, 高圧下で天然ガスと水を人工的に化合して, 氷状に固形化したものだ.

NAV 純資産価額 (**net asset value** の略)

navigate 動 水上輸送する

navigation system ナビゲーション・システム
▶KDDI and NEC have developed a mobile phone *navigation system* capable of showing directions to people inside buildings and underground. KDDIとNECが, ビル内や地下街でも道案内が可能な携帯電話用のナビゲーション・システムを開発した.

NB [nb] 留意せよ, 注意せよ (**nota bene** の略)

NBV 正味簿価 (**net book value** の略)

NCV 商業価値なし (**no commercial value** の略)

needs 名 必要, 必要量, 必要額, 要求, 需要, 必需品, 課題, ニーズ
　basic needs 一時的欲求, 最低生活費
　borrowing needs 借入需要, 資金調達需要, 調達額
　business needs 経営上の必要, 経営上の必要性
　capital needs 資金需要, 資本必要額, 必要資本
　energy needs エネルギー需要
　financing needs 資金調達需要, 資金調達のニーズ, 資金ニーズ, 調達額
　infrastructure needs インフラ需要
　investor needs 投資家のニーズ
　liquidity needs 流動性需要
　market needs 市場の需要, 市場のニーズ (⇒ **policy**)

net borrowing needs 純調達額
response to customer needs 顧客のニーズへの対応
working capital needs 運転資金の必要額, 運転資金のニーズ
▶We build enduring business relationships by understanding and anticipating our customers' *needs*. 当社は, お客さまのニーズを理解, 予測することにより, 長く続く取引関係を築いています。

NEET 無業者, ニート (Not in Education, Employment or Trainingの略。1990年代末のイギリスで生まれたことばで,「学校に行かず, 働いてもいないし, 職業訓練にも参加していない」若者)

negative 形 マイナスの, 負の, 逆の, 赤字の, 反対の, 弱含みの, 弱気の, 消極的な, 悪影響を与える, 有害な, 否定的な, 悲観的な, 成果が上がらない, ネガティブ, 名 弱気材料, 悪材料, マイナス要因 (⇒positive)
negative amortization 負の返済, 未収利息による元本の増加
negative assets 消極資産
negative growth マイナス成長
negative impact 負の側面, 負の効果, マイナス効果, マイナス影響, 悪影響, 悪材料 (＝negative effect; ⇒excessive competition)
negative income tax 負の所得税 (所得のない者や一定水準の所得しかない者に国が与える社会保障給付)
negative interest マイナス金利 (利息から差し引かれる金)
negative net gearing 純負債比率
negative yield 逆イールド, 逆ざや (＝negative spread)
negative yield curve 右下がりの利回り曲線, 逆イールド, 逆イールド・カーブ
structural negatives 構造的マイナス要因
▶Return on shareholders' equity was *negative* in 2008, compared with a return of 13 percent in 2007. 2008年度の株主持ち分利益率は, 前年度の13%に対して, マイナスに転じました。
▶The firm's net operating revenues for the first nine months of 2008 were a *negative* $104 million compared with a positive $41 million in the same period last year. 同社の2008年1－9月期の純営業収益は, 前年同期の4,100万ドルの黒字に対して, 1億400万ドルの赤字でした。

negative effect 悪影響, 悪材料, マイナス影響, マイナス効果, 負の効果, 負の側面 (＝negative impact)
▶If the yen starts to appreciate, this will have a *negative effect* on the revenues of exporting companies. 円高に転じれば, 輸出企業の収益は円高のマイナス影響を受けることになる。

negative factor 悪材料, 懸念材料, 売り材料, マイナス要因
▶*Negative factors* could affect these positive results, such as rapidly falling prices for printers. プリンターの売価急落などのマイナス要因が, これらの好決算に影響を及ぼす可能性がある。

negative goodwill 消極のれん, 消極的のれん, 負ののれん, マイナスの営業権
▶*Negative goodwill* is included in Shareholders' equity (Restricted reserves) or in Current liabilities. マイナスの営業権は, 資本の部(拘束予備金)または流動負債に含まれています。

negative legacy 負の遺産, ツケ (企業の「負の遺産」としては, 不良債権のほかに, 赤字続きの子会社, 値下がりした株や不動産, 退職金や企業年金の積立て不足といったものが挙げられる)
▶Banks should cut losses—nonperforming loans and other *negative legacies* of the bubble economy. 銀行は, 不良債権その他バブル期の「負の遺産」の損切りをしなければならない。

negative net worth 債務超過, 債務超過額, 税引き後利益の赤字
▶The subsidiary has actually had a *negative net worth* for three consecutive fiscal years. 子会社は, 実際は3期連続債務超過だった。

negative spread 逆ざや (＝negative yield: 運用利回りが保険契約者に約束した予定利率を下回ること; ⇒insurance policyholder)
▶Allowing insurers to lower the promised yields would solve the *negative spread* problem, thus serving as an effective measure to stave off collapse. 生命保険会社の予定利率の引下げを認めれば, 逆ざや問題の解消になり, その結果, 破綻回避の有力な手段になるはずである。

negative territory マイナス, マイナス基調
▶The CPI has remained in *negative territory* in recent years. 消費者物価指数は, ここ数年来マイナス基調が続いている。

negative wealth effect 逆資産効果 (土地や株その他の資産価格の下落)
▶The so-called *negative wealth effect* refers to the drop in the value of land, stocks and other assets. いわゆる「逆資産効果」とは, 土地や株その他の資産価格の下落のことをいう。

negligence 名 過失, 怠慢, 不注意, 手抜かり, 手抜き
gross negligence 重過失, 重大な過失

medical negligence 医療過失
negligence of duty 職務怠慢
negligence resulting in death 過失致死
negligence tax 過少申告加算税
ordinary negligence 通常過失
professional negligence 業務上過失
slight negligence 軽過失
▸The firm is suspected of professional *negligence* resulting in injury. 同社は, 業務上過失傷害の疑いが持たれている.

negotiable 形 流通可能の, 流通性のある,〈手形などを〉譲渡できる, 譲渡可能な, 買い取ることができる
negotiable asset 譲渡可能資産
negotiable bill of lading 譲渡可能船荷証券
negotiable certificate of deposit 譲渡性預金, 譲渡性預金証書《略 NCD》(＝negotiable CD)
negotiable instrument 有価証券, 流通証券, 換金可能証券 (＝negotiable securities)
negotiable paper 流通証券 (＝negotiable instrument)
Uniform Negotiable Instruments Law 統一流通証券法
▸The letter of credit set forth above shall be *negotiable* against a draft at sight signed by the seller upon the presentation of the following documents. 上記の信用状は, 次の船積み書類の提示がある場合には, 売り主が振り出した一覧払い手形と引換えに買い取られるものとする.

negotiate 動 交渉する, 協議する, 取り決める, 協定する,〈手形・小切手などを〉譲渡する, 換金する

negotiation 名 交渉, 協議, 商談, 取引, 流通, 権利の移転, 譲渡, 輸出地の取引銀行による荷為替手形の買取り, ネゴシエーション
conclude negotiations 交渉をまとめる
contract negotiation 契約交渉
enter into final negotiations with …と最終調整に入る
first-round negotiations 初協議, 第一回協議
multilateral negotiation 多国間交渉, 多角的交渉
negotiation charge 手形買取り手数料, 買取り手数料 (手形取組み時に銀行が請求する手数料)
negotiation of export bill 輸出手形の買取り
negotiations fall through 交渉が決裂する
negotiations on the capital increase 増資交渉
new round of multilateral trade negotiations 新多角的貿易交渉, 新ラウンド
second-round negotiations 2回目の協議
tie-up negotiation 提携交渉
unified wage negotiation 統一賃上げ交渉
▸Marubeni Corp. will soon enter into separate *negotiations* with Aeon Co. and Wal-Mart Stores Inc. to choose a partner to assist in the rehabilitation of Daiei. 丸紅は, ダイエー再建に協力する事業提携先として, イオン, 米ウォルマート・ストアーズとそれぞれ近く交渉に入る.

neighboring right 著作隣接権

net 動 相殺する, 純益を上げる, 獲得する, もたらす
▸We *netted* these prepaid costs with the liabilities. 当社は, この前払い費用を債務と相殺しました.

net 形 基本的な, 最終的な, 結局の, 正味の, 掛け値のない, 純粋の, 税引き後の (⇒**equity investment**)
net accounts receivable 売掛金純額
net advance 純貸出高
net amount 純額, 正味金額, 正味資産
net amount owed 正味負債額
net balance 純収支残高, 純収支尻
net basis 配当金[配当]課税後利益法, 純額ベース
net book value 正味帳簿価額, 正味簿価, 純簿価《略 NBV》(＝net carrying value)
net borrowing 正味借入金
net business profit 業務純益, 業務純利益 (⇒ **corporate income tax**)
net capital deficiency 債務超過, 純資本不足 (＝capital deficit; ⇒**going concern**)
net capital gain 純資本所得, 純キャピタル・ゲイン (資本利得), 純額キャピタル・ゲイン
net carrying amount 正味繰越し額, 簿価純額, 減価償却費控除後簿価
net carrying value 正味簿価, 正味帳簿価額
net current assets 正味流動資産, 純流動資産
net decrease in cash and cash equivalents 現金および現金等価物の純減少
net earned surplus forwarded 繰越し利益剰余金
net effects 正味の影響, 正味の影響額, 純影響額
net exports 純輸出 (純輸出＝輸出－輸入)
net external assets 対外純資産 (対外純資産＝日本の政府, 企業, 個人が海外に持つ資産(対外資産: external assets)－海外の政府, 企業, 個人が日本に持つ資産(対外負債: external debts, external liabilities)。net foreign assetsともいう)
net gain (loss) from operations 純事業利益(損失)

net gains on the sales of assets 資産売却による正味収益

net interest 純利息, 支払い利息純額（⇒ **general corporate expenses**）

net investment 純投資額

net investment hedges 純投資ヘッジ

net liabilities 正味負債, 債務超過額

net periodic pension cost 期間年金費用純額（⇒**expected long-term rate of return**）

▸Substantially increased investments in product and market development, combined with intense global competition, affected our *net financial performance*. 当社の業績は, 最終的に製品開発［商品開発］と市場開拓［市場開拓］に対する投資の大幅拡大とグローバル市場における競争［国際競争］の激化の影響を被りました。

net 名 純額, 税引き後金額, 純益, 正味, 正価, 純量, インターネット［ネット］

  accounts receivable—net 売掛金—純額

  net [Net] auction ネット・オークション（= Internet auction, online auction）

  Net buyer ネット購入者, ネット投資家, ネット・バイヤー

  Net-debit service ネット決済サービス, インターネット即時決済サービス

  Net posting ネット書き込み, インターネットの書き込み

  Net-related technologies ネット関連技術

  Net share trading ネット株取引, インターネットでの株取引（= online stock trading）

  Net shopping ネット・ショッピング（= electronic commerce, Internet shopping, on-line shopping）

  property, plant and equipment, net 有形固定資産（純額）

net asset 純資産, 正味資産, 正味財産（総資産から総負債を差し引いた資産残高）

  net asset value 純資産価値, 純資産額, 正味資産額, 純資産, 純財産《略 **NAV**》（= net worth: 貸借対照表上の資産総額から負債総額を差し引いた額で, 自己資本の額にあたる）

  net asset value per share 1株当たり純資産価値, 普通株式1株当たり純資産価値 (book value per share（1株当たり純資産, 1株当たり簿価）とか net tangible assets per share（1株当たり純有形資産価値）ともいう。会社が解散した場合, 株主は持ち株数に応じて残った財産が分配されるが, その時の1株当たり資産が「1株当たり純資産」で, 解散価値ともいわれている）

  net assets employed 純運用資産

net assets worth per share 1株当たり純資産（= net assets worth）

▸Amortization of the excess of cost over the *net assets* acquired is to be recorded over sixty months. 取得した純資産に対する取得価額超過額の償却は, 60か月にわたって行う予定です。

Net bank ネット銀行, ネット専業銀行, ネット・バンク（= Internet bank, Internet-based bank, Net-only bank）

▸The new *Net bank* whose initial capital is ¥20 billion started operations in the first half of fiscal 2007. 新ネット銀行は, 当初資本が200億円で, 2007年度上半期から業務を開始した。

Net business ネット事業, ネット・ビジネス

▸Yahoo Inc. is a pioneer in *Net businesses* founded in 1995. 米ヤフーは, 1995創業のネット事業の草分けだ。

net buying 〈株の〉買い越し, 買い越し額

▸Foreign investors' *net buying* so far has reached about ¥4 trillion this year. 外国人投資家のこれまでの株式の買い越し額は, 今年は約4兆円に達している。

net capital expenditures 資本的支出純額, 資本的支出（純額）

▸Operating cash flows covered our *net capital expenditures* and dividend payments for the two years. 過去2年間は, 営業活動によるキャッシュ・フローが, 当社の資本的支出（純額）と配当金支払いを賄いました。

net cash 純収支, 純キャッシュ, 正味現金, 現金純額, 正味キャッシュ, ネット・キャッシュ

  net cash flow 純収入, 純収支, 純資金収入額, 純キャッシュ・フロー, 正味キャッシュ・フロー（一定期間の現金収入と現金支出との差額, 一定期間の企業の営業活動から得られた資金（正味運転資本）, 投資の現金収入と現金支出との差額, 純利益から株式配当金を差し引いて減価償却費を加算した額, などの意味で用いられる）

  net cash from operating activities 営業活動により得た純キャッシュ, 営業活動による資金収入純額

  net cash provided by financing activities 財務活動により生じた正味現金, 財務活動［金融活動］による純現金収入［現金収入純額］, 財務活動により調達した資金（純額）

  net cash provided by investing activities 投資活動により得た純キャッシュ［現金預金純額］, 投資活動により生じた正味現金, 投資活動による純現金収入［現金収入純額］

  net cash provided by operating activities 営

業活動により生じた正味現金, 営業活動により得た純キャッシュ [現金預金純額], 営業活動による資金収入純額 [純現金収入]

net cash used in financing activities 財務 [金融] 活動に使用した現金預金純額 (＝net cash used for financing activities)

▸*Net cash* provided by operations reached a record $3 billion in 2008. 営業活動により調達した資金 (純額) は, 2008年度は過去最高の30億ドルでした。

net charge 純費用

▸Excluding this *net charge* and a fourth quarter restructuring charge, our per share earnings were $3.45 in 2008. この純費用と第4四半期の事業再編成費用を除くと, 当社の2008年度の1株当たり純利益は3.45ドルでした。

net creditor position 対外純資産残高

▸The nation's *net creditor position* is gauged by gross holdings of foreign assets by the government, business and individuals minus gross holdings of Japanese assets by foreigners. 日本の対外純資産残高は, 日本の政府や企業, 個人が海外に持つ資産の総保有額 (対外資産残高) から, 海外の政府や企業, 個人が日本国内に持つ資産の総保有額 (対外負債残高) を差し引いて算定される。

net debt 純債務, 純負債, 金融債務

net debt position 純負債額

ratio of net debt to net debt plus equity 金融債務比率, 金融債務対金融債務＋資本

▸The Company's ratio of *net debt* to net debt plus equity was 15.2 percent at December 31, 2008. 当社の金融債務比率 (金融債務対金融債務＋資本) は, 2008年12月31日現在で15.2%でした。

Net distribution ネット配信

▸For general viewers, there appears to be no difference between TV broadcasting and *Net distribution*. 一般の視聴者には, テレビ放送とネット配信に違いはないように見える。

net earnings 純利益, 当期純利益

net earnings before cumulative effect of accounting change 会計処理変更に伴う累積的影響額考慮前の純利益 [当期純利益], 会計原則変更の累積効果控除前純利益

net earnings per revenue dollar 売上高1ドル当たり純利益

net earnings per share 1株当たり純利益, 1株当たり当期純利益

▸Worldwide *net earnings* for the three months ended September 30, 2008 were $0.9 billion compared with 1.2 billion in 2007. 2008年9月30日終了四半期 [2008年7－9月期] の国内外の純利益 (連結純利益) は, 前年同期の12億ドルに対して9億ドルでした。

net earnings applicable to common shares 普通株式に帰属する当期純利益

▸*Net earnings applicable to common shares* were $330 million ($1.40 per common share) in 2008. 普通株式に帰属する当期純利益は, 2008年度は3億3,000万ドル (普通株式1株当たり1.40ドル) でした。

net financial liabilities 純金融負債

▸*Net financial liabilities* decreased as a result of our debts reduction. 純金融負債は, 当社の負債を削減した結果, 減少しました。

net income 純利益, 当期純利益, 税引き後利益, 純所得, 純収入, 〈日銀の〉剰余金 (＝net profit, profit after tax)

net income forecast 純利益 [税引き後利益] 予想, 純利益見通し

net income as percent of revenues 売上高当期純利益率

net income before taxes 税引き前当期純利益

net income (loss) 純利益 (損失), 当期純利益 (損失)

net income per share 1株当たり純利益

net income ratio 純利益率 (＝net income to sales ratio)

net income to sales ratio 売上高純利益率 (＝net income ratio)

net income to stockholders' equity ratio 自己資本利益率, 株主持ち分純利益率

net income to total assets ratio 総資本利益率, 総資産純利益率

▸Financing arm Ford Credit reported *net income* of $470 million. フォードの金融子会社フォード・クレジットは, 4億7,000万ドルの純利益を計上した。

net income applicable to common shares 普通株式に帰属する純利益 [当期純利益]

▸*Net income applicable to common shares* for the third quarter of 2008 was $223 million, compared with $283 million for the second quarter of 2008. 2008年第3四半期の普通株式に帰属する純利益は, 第2四半期の2億8,300万ドルに対して2億2,300万ドルでした。

net increase 純増, 正味増加

▸The *net increase* in gross margin was due principally to improved profit margins in the central office switching business. 売上総利益の純増は, 主に局用交換機事業の利益率改善によるも

のです。

net loss 純損失, 当期純損失, 税引き後赤字, 最終赤字, 赤字決算 （⇒**consolidated net loss, group net loss, quarterly net loss**）
▸Nikko Citigroup suffered a *net loss* of ¥6.86 billion in the April-December period. 日興シティグループ証券は，4－12月決算で税引き後利益が68億6,000万円の赤字となった。
▸The Company likely will dive into the red for the current business year with a group *net loss* of ¥55 billion. 当社は，当期は550億円の連結税引き後赤字[連結純損失]で，赤字に転落する見通しです。

net margin on sales 対売上高純利益率, 売上高純利益率, 売上利益率 （＝net profit on sales）
▸*Net margin on sales* was 6% for the full year 2008 compared with 5% a year ago. 対売上高純利益率は，前期の5％に対して，2008年度通期で6％でした。

net of …を除いて，…控除後，…差引後，…差引後純額
▸Our plant additions-related expenditures were at about the same level as depreciation, leaving property, plant and equipment, *net of* accumulated depreciation, essentially unchanged. 当社の工場増設関連支出は減価償却額とほぼ同水準で，減価償却累計額控除後の有形固定資産額は実質的に変動しませんでした。

net operating profit 純営業利益, 営業純利益, 金融機関の業務純益

業務純益とは➡銀行など金融機関の「本業によるもうけ」を，業務純益という。これは，貸出金と預金の利息の差から生じる「資金利益」，手数料などの「役務取引等利益」，債券の売買益などの「その他業務利益」の合計から，経費を差し引いて算出する。

▸Bad loan disposal at the end of March next year will be smaller than the *net operating profits* of all the seven major banking groups. 来年3月期の不良債権処理額は，大手銀行・金融7グループ各行の業務純益の範囲内になる見込みだ。

net operating revenues 純営業収益
▸The firm's *net operating revenues* for the second quarter were a negative $106 million compared with a positive $16 million in the same period last year. 同社の第2四半期の純営業収益は，前年同期の1,600万ドルの黒字に対して，1億600万ドルの赤字でした。

net premium revenues 正味収入保険料, 正味保険料収入 （「正味収入保険料」は，非金融機関の売上高に当たる）
▸*Net premium revenues* increased at four of the nation's nine major nonlife insurers. 正味収入保険料は，国内大手損保9社のうち4社で増加した。

net proceeds 正味入金額, 純売却益, 純資金, 受取金額
▸*Net proceeds* from the public offering were used to reduce notes payable. 公募による純資金[公募発行による受取金額]は，短期借入金の返済に充当しました。

net profit 純利益, 当期純利益, 税引き後利益, 最終黒字, 最終利益, 〈日銀の〉当期剰余金 （＝net income）

　net profit after tax 税引き後純利益, 税引き後の最終利益, 法人税控除後純利益

　net profit before tax 税引き前純利益, 法人税控除前純利益

　net profit from operations 営業純利益 （＝income from operations）

▸The confectionery maker managed to book a *net profit* of ¥1.4 billion through sales of fixed assets. この菓子メーカーは，固定資産の売却で，かろうじて14億円の税引き後利益を計上[確保]した。

net profit per share 1株当たり純利益
▸The Corporation's *net profit per share* in the April-September first half of fiscal 2008 year came to ¥19.95 from ¥34.05 a year before. 当社の2008年度上期（4－9月期）の1株当たり純利益は，前年同期の34円5銭に対して19円95銭だった。

net revenues 純収益, 営業利益
▸The decline in *net revenues* is mainly due to higher non-performing loans and reduced spread. 営業利益の減少は，主に不良債権[契約不履行債権]の拡大と利ざや（調達金利と貸出金利との差）の縮小によるものです。

net sales 純売上高
▸In recent years, a large and increasing portion of the Company's *net sales*, operating profits and growth have come from its international operations. ここ数年，当社の純売上高，営業利益，業績の伸びの相当部分が海外活動からもたらされ，その割合は年々高まっています。

net selling 売り越し
▸The amount of *net selling* of Japanese stocks further increased in September. 9月は，日本株の売り越しの額がさらに増えた。

net short-term borrowings 短期借入金純額
▸The Corporation's *net short-term borrowings*

amounted to $830 million at September 30, 2008.　当社の短期借入金純額は，2008年9月30日現在で8億3,000万ドルに達しました．

Net trading　ネット取引，ネット販売（＝Internet trading, online trading）
▸By offering electronic settlement services for *Net* shopping and *trading*, the firm wants to attract funds from Internet users.　同社のねらいは，ネット・ショッピングやネット取引の電子決済業務を行うことにより，インターネット利用者から資金を取り込むことにある．

net working capital　純運転資本，正味運転資本（＝net current assets: 正味運転資本＝流動資産－流動負債）
▸*Net working capital* refers to current assets less current liabilities.　正味運転資本は，流動資産から流動負債を控除した額です．

net worth　自己資本，資本，自己資金，株主持ち分，純資産，正味資産，正味財産（⇒negative net worth）
　net worth agreement　自己資本維持契約
　net worth of collateral　担保余力
　net worth ratio　自己資本比率，株主資本比率（＝capital adequacy ratio, capital-asset ratio, ratio of net worth）
　net worth shareholder's equity　所有者持ち分，株主持ち分，出資者持ち分
　ratio of total liabilities to net worth　負債対自己資本比率，負債比率（＝net worth to debts ratio）
　ratio of net worth to fixed assets　固定比率
　ratio of net worth to the total assets　株主資本比率
　return on net worth　株主資本利益率
　sales to net worth　株主資本回転率
　total liabilities and net worth　総資本
　turnover of net worth　株主資本回転率
▸Deferred tax accounting allows banks to calculate their *net worth* by assuming future refunding of excessive tax payments.　税効果会計では，銀行は，払いすぎた税金の将来の還付を見込んで自己資本を計算することができる．

network 名　網状組織，連絡網，通信網，回線網，回路網，網，ネットワーク
　branch network　支店網
　communications network　通信網，通信ネットワーク
　distribution network　流通網，流通ネットワーク，販売網
　global network society　インターネット社会，ネット社会
　human networks　人脈
　knowledge network　知識ネットワーク
　nationwide network　全国ネットワーク
　network appliance　ネットワーク家電
　network architecture　ネットワーク構成，網構成，ネットワーク・アーキテクチャー
　network distribution　ネットワーク配信，ネット配信
　network industry　ネットワーク産業
　network interconnection　ネットワーク相互接続
　network management system　ネットワーク管理システム
　network operating system　ネットワークOS《略 NOS》
　network service provider　ネットワーク回線接続プロバイダー
　neural network　神経回路網，神経回線網，ニューラル・ネットワーク
　retail network　小売販売網，リテール販売網
　sales network　販売網
▸Banks will develop larger sales *networks* for financial products than those of major securities companies.　今後は，銀行が大手証券会社をしのぐ金融商品の販売網を展開するようになる．

network configuration　ネットワーク構成
▸*Network configuration* can be shifted by the customer at will to accommodate growth, innovation, or changes in the telecommunications industry.　ネットワークの構成は，業務の拡張，通信技術の革新，通信業界の変革に対応して，顧客［ユーザー］が自由に変更できる．

networking 名　ネットワーク作り，ネットワーク化，提携，ネットワーキング
　backbone networking　基幹ネットワーク，ネットワークの基幹回線
　data networking products　データ通信ネットワーキング製品
　online networking system　オンライン提携

neutral 形　中立の，中性の，灰色の，ニュートラル
▸The Fed will take a *neutral* stance on future monetary policy.　米連邦準備制度理事会（FRB）は，今後の金融政策の運営方針について，（引締めと緩和の両にらみの）「中立」の姿勢を取る方針だ．

new 形　新規の，新しい，新…，ニュー
　new debt　新規借入金
　new debt issues　新発債の発行
　new fiscal year　新年度，新会計年度
　new funds　新規資金

new investment 新規投資
new issuance 新規発行, 新株発行, 新規発行額
new listing 新規上場
new issue 新規発行, 新規発行株式, 新発債
new issue of stock 新株発行
new lending 新規貸出
new loans 新規融資 （⇒sluggish performance）
new rating 新規格付け
new share issuance 新株発行 （＝issuance of new shares, new share issue）
new stock [share] issuing expenses 新株発行費
new technology 新技術, ニュー・テクノロジー
▶Not only must researchers develop *new* technologies, they must apply them to products which respond to specific customer requirements. 研究者は, 新技術の開発だけでなく, 開発した技術を製品に応用して顧客の特定の要求に応えなければならない。

new borrowing 新規借入れ, 新規資金調達
▶Ford Motor Co. will pledge its investment in Mazda Motor Corp. in its *new borrowing*. フォードは, 新規資金調達では保有するマツダ株を担保にする方針だ。

new economy 新しい経済, ニュー・エコノミー （インターネットを使った新しい経済システム。自動車, 建設, 不動産, 繊維, 流通などの成熟産業を指すオールド・エコノミーに対して, インターネット・ベンチャーやドットコム企業, IT関連の産業や企業を指す）

new generation Internet firm 新世代ネット企業
▶Many of these *new generation Internet firms* were established in about 2000, when the so-called IT bubble collapsed. これらの新世代ネット企業の多くは, いわゆるITバブルが崩壊した2000年前後に設立された。

new high 新高値, 最高記録, 空前の高値, 過去最高
▶Excluding these accounting changes, our net income and earnings per share were *new highs*. これらの会計上の変更を除くと, 当社の当期純利益と1株当たり利益は, 過去最高でした。

new market 新市場, 新規市場
▶Customers and competitors are making acquisitions, merging, and forming joint ventures and alliances to expand their geographic reach, enter *new markets* and gain scale. 当社の顧客と競争相手は, 企業買収や合併を行ったり, 合弁会社の設立や業務提携を行ったりして, 営業地盤の拡張や新規市場への参入と規模の拡大を目指している。

new middleman ニュー・ミドルマン（顧客の購買代理店の役割を果たすビジネスで, 顧客の特定のニーズに関連する商品や情報を集めて提供し, その購入を支援するビジネスのこと）

new product 新製品
▶The company started selling *new products*, including a single-lens reflex digital camera. 同社は, 一眼レフ・デジカメなど新製品の販売を開始した。

new share issue 新規株式発行, 新株発行, 増資 （＝new share issuance）
▶The company plans to use the proceeds from *new share issues* to increase its equity ownership in a staff dispatching company. 同社は, 新株発行で調達した資金［新株発行による手取金］を, 人材派遣会社の株式の追加取得にあてる計画だ。

new share offering 新株発行
▶The firm will raise ¥100 billion in a *new share offering*. 同社は, 新株発行で1,000億円を調達する。

new shares 新株, 増資
▶Hokuetsu Paper Mills Ltd. issued *new shares* worth about ¥30 billion to Mitsubishi as planned. 北越製紙は, 計画どおり, 三菱商事を引受先として約300億円の新株を発行した。

New York Commodity Exchange ニューヨーク商品取引所《略 Comex》
New York Mercantile Exchange ニューヨーク商業取引所《略 NYMEX》
New York Stock Exchange ニューヨーク証券取引所《略 NYSE》 （＝Big Board）
▶The bank debuted on the *New York Stock Exchange* in November 2006. 同行は, 2006年11月にニューヨーク証券取引所に上場した。

New York stock market ニューヨーク株式市場, ニューヨーク市場
▶Yahoo shares soared on the *New York stock market* as investors warmed to the prospect of realignment in the IT industry. IT業界再編見通しに対する投資家の関心が高まったため, ヤフー株がニューヨーク市場で急騰した。

newcomer [new comer] 新規参入企業, 新規参入組, 新規参入者, 新規参入業者, 新規事業者, 新任, 新人, 新入社員, 新メンバー, 初心者, ずぶの素人, 新たに台頭［出現］してきたもの （⇒latecomer）

▸*Newcomers* pay TEPCO an average of ¥2.57 per kilowatt to provide electricity to large factories via its transmission facilities. 東電の送電設備で大規模工場に電力を供給する場合，新規参入の電力会社は東電に1キロワット時当たり平均して2.57円支払う。

newly developing Big Five 新ビッグ・ファイブ，新ビッグ5（開発途上国のなかの経済大国。中国，インドネシア，ブラジル，インド，ロシアの5か国）

newly emerged industry 新興産業
▸Except for *newly emerged industries*, such as liquid crystal products, Japanese markets are already saturated. 液晶などの新興産業を除くと，日本の市場はすでに飽和状態だ。

newly emerging competitor 新規参入者
newly emerging technology 新技術
newly industrializing countries 新興工業国，中進工業国，新興工業国群，ニックス《略 **NICs**》（＝newly industrialized countries, newly industrializing countries: 1988年のサミットからNIEsと呼ばれるようになった）

newly industrializing economies 新興工業国，新興工業諸国，新興工業経済地域，新興工業経済群《略 **NIEs [NIES]**》（＝newly industrialized economies, newly industrializing countries）

newly issued bond 新発債
news conference 記者会見
▸The company is to hold a *news conference* to unveil a set of its programs to improve its corporate value. 同社は，記者会見を開いて，企業価値を高めるための一連のプログラムを発表する。

newsletter 名 社報，公報，回報，回報，PR誌，年報，月報，報告書，時事開説，時事通信，ニューズレター
▸The figures for earlier periods cited in this *newsletter* are restated. この報告書に記載されている当四半期以前の数値は，修正して再表示されています。

next-generation wireless communications system 次世代無線通信システム
NGH 天然ガス・ハイドレート（**natural gas hydrate**の略）
▸*NGH* stabilizes as a solid at around minus 20 C. 天然ガス・ハイドレート（NGH）は，マイナス20度前後で固形状態が安定する。

NGO 民間活動団体，非政府組織，非政府機関，非政府団体（**non-governmental [nongovernmental] organization**の略）

▸*NGOs* are playing a growing role in promoting Japan's diplomacy. 日本の外交を進めるうえで，NGOの役割は大きくなっている。

niche 名 特定分野，分野，領域，すき間，適所，適した場所[地位]，ニッチ
niche business 得意分野
niche market ニッチ市場，市場の特定分野，すき間市場
niche marketing すき間市場販売戦略，ニッチ・マーケティング（未開発のすき間市場・ニッチ市場への適応をめざすマーケティング）
niche strategy ニッチ戦略
specialized niche 得意分野（＝specialised niche）
▸We are ready to take on competitors in every *niche* of the marketplace. 当社は，市場のあらゆる分野でライバル企業と競争する態勢を整えています。

night mart 株の夜間市場，夜間取引市場（＝night market, nighttime market, nighttime marketplace）
▸Three securities firms will join kabu.com Securities Co.'s *night mart*. カブドットコム証券（ネット専業証券大手）が運営する株の夜間取引市場に，証券会社3社が参加する。

Nikkei index 日経平均，日経平均株価（＝Nikkei Index）
the benchmark Nikkei index 日経平均株価
the daily average for the Nikkei index 日経平均の月中平均株価
the key Nikkei Index 日経平均株価
Nikkei Stock Average 日経平均株価，日経株価平均，日経平均（＝the benchmark Nikkei index）

日経平均株価とは➡株式相場全体の動きを示す指標の一つ。東証一部上場の代表的な225社の株価合計を，一定の除数で割って算出する。除数は調整値で，株式分割や銘柄入れ替えのときに変更する。東証株価指数（TOPIX）が銀行株など時価総額の大きい株価の動きに敏感なのに対して，日経平均はハイテク株の組入れ比重が高く，ハイテク株の動きに左右されやすい。

▸The 225-issue *Nikkei Stock Average* plunged 646.26 points from the previous day to close at 13,099.24. 日経平均株価(225種)は，前日比646円26銭安の1万3,099円24銭で取引を終えた。

no-frills 形 余分なサービスを省いた，余分なサービスを提供しない，実利本位の，実質本位の，基本的な機能に限定した

nominal 形 名目の，名目上の，名目ベースの，名

義上の
nominal amount 額面金額, 名目元本
nominal bond yield 債券名目利回り
nominal capital 公称資本, 名目資本 (= authorized capital, nominal share capital)
nominal export 輸出額
nominal GDP growth 名目GDP成長率
nominal gross domestic product 名目国内総生産, 名目GDP
nominal growth 名目成長率
nominal interest 表面利率, 名目金利 (= nominal interest rate)
nominal owner 名義上の所有者
nominal rate 表面金利, 名目相場
nominal wage 名目賃金 (労働者が受け取る賃金の額を物価指数で割ったものが実質賃金)
nominal growth rate 名目成長率 (= nominal growth)
▶To reduce unemployment, the *nominal growth rate* must be boosted. 失業率を低くするためには, 名目成長率を高くしなければならない。
nominal interest rate 表面利率, 名目金利 (=nominal interest, nominal rate of interest)
▶The *nominal interest rate* for a 20-year government bonds stands at 2.3 percent. 20年債の表面利率は, 2.3%だ。
nominal terms 名目, 名目ベース (実質= real terms)
▶The GDP growth rate in *nominal terms* during the July-September period stood at zero on a quarter-on-quarter and a year-on-year basis. 7-9月期の名目GDPの成長率は, 前期比, 年率ともにゼロ%増だった。
nominee 图 候補者, 候補被指名者, 被指名者, 被任命者, 被推薦人, 株の名義人, 名義上の株式保有
▶Each of the 10 *nominees* named in the proxy statement who stood for election as a director received a plurality of the votes cast. 委任状に取締役選任候補者として記載された10名は, それぞれ投票総数の大多数[過半数]の支持を得ました。
nonassessable 形 追加出資義務のない, 追加払込み請求がない, 追加払込み義務を負わない, 追徴不能の
▶All shares of the new company issued pursuant to this agreement shall be validly issued, fully paid and *nonassessable* upon issuance. 本契約に基づいて発行する新会社の株式は, すべて有効に発行し, 発行時の全額払込み方式で追加出資義務はないものとする。
noncancelable [**noncancellable**] 形 解

約不能の, 中途解約不能の, 取消し不能の, 解約できない
noncancelable guarantee 取消し不能保証
noncancelable lease 解約不能リース, 中途解約不能リース
noncancelable operating lease 解約不能のオペレーティング・リース
▶The Company does lease certain office, factory and warehouse space, and land under principally *noncancelable* operating leases. 当社は, 一部の事業所, 工場, 倉庫や土地などを主に中途解約不能のオペレーティング・リースにより使用しています。
nonconforming goods 非適合品, 契約に適合しない商品[物品]
▶*Nonconforming goods* will be held by Buyer for disposition in accordance with Seller's instructions at Seller's risk. 非適合品は, 売り主の危険負担で売り主の指示に従って処分するため, 買い主が保持するものとする。
nonconsolidated 形 非連結, 非連結ベースの
nonconsolidated basis 非連結ベース, 単体ベース
nonconsolidated subsidiaries and affiliates 非連結子会社等
nonconsolidated subsidiary 非連結子会社
noncontributory 图 非拠出, 非拠出型の, 従業員でなく雇用者が負担する
noncontributory defined benefit (pension) plan 非拠出型確定給付年金制度, 非拠出型給付金規定方式による年金制度
noncontributory pension plan 非拠出型年金制度 (=noncontributory plan)
▶The Company's *noncontributory* pension plan covers most U.S. employees after one year of service. 当社の非拠出型年金制度は, 勤続1年以上のほとんどの米国内従業員を対象としています。
noncontributory plan 非拠出年金制度, 非拠出型退職金制度 (=noncontributory pension plan)
▶A *noncontributory plan* is funded by company contributions to an irrevocable trust fund. この非拠出型退職金制度の資金は, 会社の拠出金によって取崩し不能の信託基金に積み立てられています。
noncontributory supplemental retirement benefit plan 非拠出型追加的退職給付制度
▶The Corporation's *noncontributory supplemental retirement benefit plan* for its elected

officers contains provisions for funding the participants' expected retirement benefits. 当社の選任役員を対象とする非拠出型追加の退職給付制度には, 制度参加者の予定退職給付額を積み立てる旨の条項が含まれています。

nonconvertible bond 非転換社債

nonconvertible preferred stock 非転換優先株式

noncore assets 非中核的資産, 非中核的事業資産, 周辺資産

noncore business 非中核事業, 非主力事業
▸The company will withdraw from its *noncore businesses*. 同社は, 非中核事業から撤退する方針だ。

noncurrent 形 非流動的, 長期の, 固定した (=fixed)

  deferred tax asset/noncurrent 繰延べ税金資産・長期

  deferred tax liabilities/noncurrent 繰延べ税金負債・長期

  noncurrent assets 非流動資産, 固定資産 (=fixed assets)

  noncurrent liability 非流動負債, 固定負債 (=long-term liability)

  noncurrent tangible asset 長期の有形資産
▸Other assets include goodwill, patents, other intangibles, deferred taxes, and other *noncurrent* assets. その他の資産には, 営業権, 特許権, その他の無固定資産, 繰延べ税金と, その他の非流動資産が含まれています。

nonexclusive 形 非独占的, 非排他的, 非専属的

  nonexclusive agent 非独占代理店

  nonexclusive distributor 非独占販売店

  nonexclusive jurisdiction 非専属管轄[管轄権], 非専属的裁判管轄[管轄権]

  nonexclusive license 非独占的実施権, 非独占的ライセンス

  nonexclusive right 非独占的権利, 非独占, 非排他的権利
▸Supplier hereby grants to Distributor, and Distributor hereby accepts, a *nonexclusive* right to distribute Products in Territory. 供給者は本契約により販売店に対して販売区域内で本製品を販売する非独占的な権利を付与し, 販売店は本契約によりこれを受諾する。

nonlife insurance company 損害保険会社, 損保会社 (=casualty insurance company, nonlife insurance firm, nonlife insurer)
▸*Nonlife insurance companies* used to disperse the risk of large contracts with new corporate clients through reinsurance contracts with other insurance or reinsurance companies. 損保各社は従来, 他の保険会社もしくは再保険会社と再保険契約を結んで, 新規顧客企業と大型契約を結ぶリスクを分散してきた。

nonlife insurer 損害保険会社, 損保会社, 損保 (=nonlife insurance company)
▸Five major *nonlife insurers* saw their net profits decline in the first half of the fiscal year to Sept. 30 from a year earlier. 9月中間決算で, 損保大手5社の税引き後利益は前年同期を下回った。

nonmanagement Board member 経営権に関与しない取締役
▸The Board of Directors' Audit Committee consists entirely of independent *nonmanagement Board members*. 取締役会付属監査委員会は, 経営権に関与しない独立した取締役だけで構成されています。

nonmanufacturer 名 非製造業, 非製造業者 (=nonmanufacturing business)
▸A sense of restlessness and hopelessness still prevails among *nonmanufacturers*, small and midsize firms and regional economies. 非製造業や中小企業, 地方経済には, 焦燥と絶望感が広まったままだ。

nonmanufacturing sector 非製造業, 非製造部門, 非製造業セクター (=nonmanufacturing businesses)
▸The company will cut its payroll in the *nonmanufacturing sector* by 30 percent to 18,800 by the end of fiscal 2009. 同社は, 2009年度末までに非製造部門の総従業員[人員]を18,800人に3割削減する。

nonpar 名 無額面

  nonpar stock [share] 無額面株式

  nonpar value capital stock 無額面株式

  nonpar value stock 無額面株式 (=no-par-value stock)

nonpayment 名 不払い

  nonpayment of insurance benefits 保険金の不払い

  nonpayment of insurance money 保険金の不払い (=nonpayment of insurance benefits, nonpayment of insurance claims)
▸Instances of *nonpayment* involving third-sector insurance products totaled 1,140 for Mitsui Sumitomo Insurance Co. 第三分野(医療保険やがん保険など)の保険金不払い件数は, 三井住友海上火災保険が計1,140件もあった。

nonperforming loan 不良債権, 不良貸付け,

貸倒れ （=bad debt, nonperforming credits, uncollectible loan)
▶Corporate bankruptcies have led to the swelling of *nonperforming loans*, posing a heavy burden on banks. 企業倒産が不良債権の増大を生み，銀行に重くのしかかっている．

nonqualified plan 非適格年金

nonrecourse 形 遡求権なし，非遡求（= without recourse)
　nonrecourse loan 無償還融資，ノンリコース・ローン（担保物件の運用収益や売却代金で資金回収し，借手への償還請求権のない融資)
　nonrecourse obligation 非遡求債務
　on a nonrecourse basis 遡求権なしで
▶The receivables were sold on a *nonrecourse basis*. 債権は，遡求権なしで売却した．

nonregular contract employee 非正社員
▶About one-third of the Japan Federation of Service and Distributive Workers Unions' members are *nonregular contract employees*. サービス・流通連合の組合員の約3分の1は，非正社員だ．

nonregular employee 非正規雇用者
▶*Nonregular employees* are usually at a disadvantage when it comes to pay raises, compared with employees on a regular payroll. 非正規雇用者は，昇給面では，正社員に比べて一般に不利な条件にある．

nonstrategic business 非戦略的事業，非戦略的事業部門［業務部門］
▶We reported revenues from certain *nonstrategic businesses* of the firm last year. 前期は，同社の一部の非戦略的業務部門［事業部門］の売上高を計上しました．

nonstrategic division 非戦略的事業部門，非戦略部門
▶The revenues of these divested *nonstrategic divisions* were included in the second quarter of 2008. これらの非戦略的事業部門の売上高は，2008年第2四半期には計上されていました．

nontaxable 形 非課税の，無税の

nonvoting class B preferred stock 無議決権クラスB優先株式

nonvoting share 無議決権株，議決権のない株式（=nonvoting stock)

NOPAT 税引き後営業利益　（net operating profit after taxesの略)

norm 名 規範，標準，標準的方式，水準，規準，平均，典型，達成基準，要求水準，規準労働量，基準量，責任生産量，ノルマ

behavioral norms 行動規範，社会通念
cultural norms 文化の規範，社会規範
▶Since the bubble economy burst, low interest rates have been the *norm*. バブル崩壊以降，低金利が続いている．

normal course of business 通常の業務過程，通常の事業過程，通常の営業過程，通常の事業活動
▶We use various financial instruments, including derivatives, in the *normal course of business*. 当社は，通常業務で各種の金融商品を利用しており，これには金融派生商品も含まれています．

nosedive 動 急減する，急落する，暴落する，急速に悪化する
▶Imports of vegetables from China in the first three weeks of February have *nosedived* from a year earlier. 2月第1週〜3週に中国から輸入した野菜が，前年同期比で急減した．

notch 動 記録する，樹立する，収める，得る，獲得する
▶The Bank of England *notched* its benchmark rate lower to 5.25 percent from 5.5 percent. 英中央銀行のイングランド銀行は，政策金利を年5.5％から5.25％に引き下げた．

notch 名 段階，級，程度，順位，0.1ポイント，ノッチ（1ノッチ=0.1ポイント)
a top-notch hotel 高級ホテル
top-notch 第一級の，一流の
top-notch borrower 超優良発行体
▶Moody's Investors Service Inc. cut its rating on yen-denominated government bonds by two *notches* to A2 from Aa3. ムーディーズ・インベスターズ・サービスは，円建て国債の格付けをAa3からA2に2段階引き下げた．
▶The unemployment rate dipped down a *notch* to 5.5 percent last month, from 5.6 percent in June. 先月(7月)の失業率は，6月の5.6％から5.5％に1ノッチ(0.1ポイント)減少した．

note 名 手形，約束手形，証券，債券，債権表示証書，紙幣，通知書，伝票，覚書，注釈，注記，注意，ノート（証券の「ノート」は一般に中期の債務証券を指すが，米財務省証券に対して使うときは，償還期限が1年超10年以内の中期証券のことをいう)
auditing for note receivable 受取手形監査
bank note 中央銀行が発行する銀行券《略 BN》
contract note 契約書
delivery note 納品書
fixed and variable rate notes 確定および変動利付きノート
general notes of financial statements 財務諸

表[財務書類]の一般的注記
heading notes 頭注
loan on note 手形貸付け
loans on notes and bills 一般貸付け金
matured note 満期手形
notes and accounts receivable-trade, net of allowances 受取手形および売掛金, 貸倒れ引当金控除後
overdue note 期限経過手形
purchasing note 買約書
sales note 売約書
sight note 一覧払い約束手形, 一覧払い手形
three-year note auction 米国債3年物の入札, 3年物Tノートの入札
unlisted note 非上場債
unpaid note 不渡り手形
▸On October 1, 2008, we utilized the shelf registration program to issue US $300 million of 6.0% *Notes* due 2018. 2008年10月1日に当社は, 米証券取引所(SEC)の一括登録制度を利用して, 満期2018年・利率6.0%のノート3億米ドルを発行しました.

note payable 支払い手形, 手形債務, 手形借入金, 短期借入金, 借入金
note payable to subsidiary 子会社支払い手形
notes payable-trade 支払い手形 (=acceptance payable)
▸The Corporation has $1 million of *notes payable* due June 10, 2009. 当社は, 2009年6月10日期日の100万ドルの支払い手形を振り出している.
▸The difference was funded by increasing *notes payable* principally through the sale of commercial paper. 資金の不足分は, 主にコマーシャル・ペーパーを発行して手形借入金を増やして補填しました.

note receivable 受取手形
note receivable discount 手形割引
note receivable discounted 割引手形
note receivable due from employee 従業員手形貸付け金
notes receivable-trade 受取手形 (=acceptance receivable)

noteholder 手形所持人

notice 通知, 通知書, 通知方法, 通告, 通告書, 告知, 告知書, 予告, 広告, 公示, 告示, 表示, 認識
advance notice 事前通告, 予告 (=prior notice)
assessment notice 課税通知
copyright notice 著作権表示 (=notice of copyright)
dismissal notice 解雇通知
follow-up notice 督促状
legal notice 適法な通知, 法定通知, 擬制通知, 擬制認識
Notice of Annual Meeting 定時株主総会開催の通知, 年次株主総会招集通知
notice of demand 催告通知
notice of dishonor 不渡り通知, 拒絶の通知
notice of order 命令の通知, 判決通知
notice of proprietary rights 知的財産権の表示
notice of delisting 上場廃止の通告
public notice 公示, 公告, 告示
▸This agreement shall terminate on the date of dispatch of a *notice* of termination to such party by the other party hereto. 本契約は, 相手方[他方当事者]がこの当事者に契約解除の通知を行った日に終了する.

notification 通知, 通知書, 通報, 通告, 届け出, 告示, 公告, 告知, 催告
legal notification 法定公告
notification period 告示期間
notification of statute 設立文書
▸An employee of the Nikkei Shimbun made a profit by purchasing stocks after seeing the listed companies' legal *notification* in advance of their publication in the newspaper. 日経新聞の社員が, 新聞に掲載される前に上場企業の法定公告を見て株を買って, もうけていた.

novel business 事業の新規性
▸In May 2002, the TSE's Mothers market for start-up firms abolished its listing requirement that the new firm have a *novel business*. 2002年5月に, 東証の新興企業向け市場「マザーズ」は, 上場要件の一つである「新会社の事業の新規性」を排除した.

novelty 新規性, 斬新性, 斬新さ, 目新しさ, もの珍しさ, 新案品, 目新しい商品, 新型商品, アイデア商品, ノベルティ・グッズ, 贈答品, ノベルティ (=newness)
novelty advertising 贈呈広告, ノベルティ広告, 広告用新案商品
novelty merchandise 新案品, 新案商品, 新型商品, ノベルティ
novelty store アイデア商品の店
▸The licensor shall not warrant the *novelty* of the invention. ライセンサーは, 発明の新規性については保証しないものとする.

nuclear fuel 核燃料
nuclear fuel cycle 核燃料サイクル
nuclear fuel reprocessing plant 核燃料再処理

工場
▶The *nuclear fuel* cycle is a main pillar of the government's nuclear power policy. 核燃料サイクルは，政府の原子力政策の柱だ．
nuclear power 原子力，核保有国
 nuclear power generation 原子力発電
 nuclear power plant 原子力発電所（= nuclear power station）
 ▶Electric Power Development Co. plans to build a *nuclear power* plant in Aomori Prefecture. 電源開発は，青森県内に原子力発電所の建設を計画している．
nuisance e-mail 迷惑メール（=junk mail, spam mail）
null 形 無効な，価値のない，拘束力のない
number of shares 株式数
 number of shares authorized 授権株式数（= number of authorized shares）
 number of shares issued 発行済み株式数，発行済み株式総数（=number of stocks issued）
 number of shares of stock 株式数
 number of shares outstanding 発行済み株式数，社外流通株式数（=number of outstanding shares）
 number of weighted average shares outstanding 加重平均総発行株式数
number portability system 携帯電話の番号持ち運び制度（=mobile number portability system, MNP system）
 ▶In the *number portability system*, a cell phone user can switch a service provider without changing the cell phone number. 携帯電話の番号持ち運び制度では，携帯電話利用者は，携帯電話の番号を変更しないでサービス・プロバイダーを変えることができる．
nursing care 介護
 nursing care at home 在宅介護（=at-home nursing care）
 nursing care benefits 介護給付
 nursing care business 介護事業
 nursing care costs 介護費用
 nursing care hell 介護地獄
 nursing care insurance 介護保険
 nursing care plan 介護プラン
 nursing care premium 介護保険料
 nursing care program 介護計画
 nursing care taxi service 介護タクシー
 nursing care worker 介護福祉士
 ▶In many western European nations, *nursing care* is considered a welfare service to be provided by central or local governments. 西欧諸国の多くでは，介護は国や地方自治体が提供する福祉サービスと考えられている．
 ▶Traditionally, *nursing care* has been provided by family members. これまで，介護は家族が行ってきた．
nursing care facility 介護施設
 ▶The procedures taken to have an elderly person enter a *nursing care facility* are too cumbersome. 高齢者の介護施設への入所手続きが，煩雑すぎる．
nursing care insurance system 介護保険制度，介護保険（=nursing care system; ⇒ straits）
 ▶The public *nursing-care insurance system* began in April 2000. 国民介護保険制度は，2000年4月に始まった．
nursing care service 介護サービス，在宅介護サービス（=nursing services）
 ▶Home helpers play a key role in *nursing-care services*. ホーム・ヘルパーは，在宅介護サービスの担い手である．
nursing leave system 介護休業制度（= the holiday for nurse system）
nuts and bolts 基本，土台，基本問題，主眼点，実際面，詳細な段取り，実務面での細部，実地細目，形 基本的な，実践的な
N.V. 〈オランダ，ベルギーの〉株式会社（Naamloze Vennootschapの略）
NYMEX ニューヨーク商業取引所（New York Mercantile Exchangeの略）
NYSE ニューヨーク証券取引所（New York Stock Exchangeの略．通称でBig Boardともいう）
 NYSE Composite Index NYSE総合株価指数
 NYSE Group NYSEグループ
 ▶*NYSE* Group struck a deal to buy European bourse operator Euronext for $9.96 billion. （ニューヨーク証券取引所を運営する）NYSEグループは，欧州（パリやオランダなど）の証券取引所を運営する「ユーロネクスト」を99億6,000万ドルで買収する取引をした．
NYSE Euronext NYSEユーロネクスト（ニューヨーク証券取引所を運営するNYSEグループと，パリ，オランダなど欧州の取引所を統括するユーロネクストが合併して設立された持ち株会社）

O

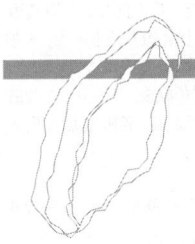

O&M 事務改善活動 (**organization and methods**の略)
OA 事務作業の機械化, オフィス・オートメーション (**office automation**の略)
  OA equipment OA機器 (=office automation product)
  OA interface OAインターフェース (=OA interface system)
  OA literacy OAリテラシー
OAPEC アラブ石油輸出国機構, オアペック (**Organization of Arab Petroleum Exporting Countries**の略)
OAS 米州機構 (**Organization of American States**の略)
OAU アフリカ統一機構 (**Organization of African Unity**の略)
o/b …以前 (**on or before** の略)
object 图 物体, 固体, 対象, 目的, 目標, ねらい, オブジェクト
  object and task method 目標基準法
  cost object 原価対象
  object code 機械語のコード, 目的コード, 目的プログラム, 実行用プログラム, オブジェクト・コード
  object language 対象言語, オブジェクト言語
  object product 対象製品
  policy object 政策目標
objective 图 目標, 目的, 対象, 目的地, 形 客観的な, 客観的目標に基づく, 事実に基づく, 実在の, 本当の, 目的の, 目標の
  business objective 経営目標, 経営目的
  company objective 企業目標, 会社目標
  control objective 内部統制目的
  cost objective 原価対象
  economic objective 経済目標
  financial policy objective 金融政策目標
  management by objectives 目標別管理, 目標管理, 目標管理制度《略 MBO》
  market objectives 市場目的
  marketing objectives マーケティングの目標, マーケティング目的
  objective basis 使途別分類, 対象別分類
  objective of financial reporting 財務報告の目的
  objective of financial statements 財務書類[財務諸表]の目的
  objective rationality 客観的合理性, 客観的合理点
  objective tax 目的税
  objective test 客観的基準
  objective validity 客観的妥当性
  organization objective 組織目標 (=objective of organization)
  overall company objectives 企業全体の目標
  performance against objectives 目標に反する達成度
  primary objective 最大の目標
▶One of our main *objectives* is to improve the value of our shareholders' investment. 当社の主要な経営目標の一つは, 株主の投資価値を高めることにあります。

objectivity 图 客観性
▶Management of the Corporation, in furtherance of the integrity and *objectivity* of data in the financial statements, has developed and maintains a system of internal accounting

controls. 当社の経営者は，財務書類に含まれる［財務書類上の］データの完全性と客観性を高めるため，会計に関する内部統制組織［内部会計統制組織］を整備・維持しています．

obligate 動 〈収入を〉債務の支払いにあてる

obligation 名 債務, 負債, 債務負担, 債務証書, 債権債務関係, 義務, 約束, 金銭
　customer obligations 顧客の債務
　debt obligation 債務, 債務負担, 債務証書, 債務契約書
　estimated future obligations 将来の予測支払い義務額, 予測される将来の支払い義務額
　fund obligation 基金債務, 資金負債
　interest obligation 金利債務
　lease obligation リース債務
　long term obligation 長期債務, 長期借入金
　obligation outstanding 未決済債務
　obligations hereunder 本契約に基づく義務, 本契約上の義務 (hereunder=under this agreement)
　obligations incurred 発生債務
　obligations under pension and deferred compensation plans 退職年金債務
　payment obligation 支払い債務, 支払い義務
　pension obligation 年金債務
　short term obligations 短期債務
　waiver of obligation 債務免除
▶The Corporation's finance subsidiary purchases customer *obligations* under long-term contracts from the Corporation at net carrying value. 当社の金融子会社は，当社との長期契約によって，顧客の債務を当社から帳簿価格で購入しています．
▶We placed this $13 billion liability on the books to reflect those estimated future *obligations* at January 1, 2009, expressed in today's dollars. 2009年1月1日現在の予測される将来支払い義務額を反映させるため，当社はこの130億ドル（現在のドル価値で）の債務を計上しました．

obligatory 形 義務的な (⇒**greenery on a rooftop, medical expenses**)

obsolescence 名 衰退, 退化, 減耗, 磨滅, 老朽化, 陳腐化, 旧式化, すたれること
　economic obsolescence 経済的磨滅［陳腐化］
　functional obsolescence 機能的陳腐化
　inventory obsolescence 棚卸し資産の陳腐化
　moral obsolescence 道徳的磨滅
　physical obsolescence 物理的陳腐化
　planned obsolescence 計画的陳腐化
　product and technology obsolescence 製品と技術の陳腐化
　product obsolescence 製品陳腐化
　style obsolescence スタイルの陳腐化
　technological [technology] obsolescence 技術の陳腐化, 技術的陳腐化

obsolete 形 陳腐化した, 老朽化した, 旧式の, 年代物の, 時代遅れの, 時代に取り残された, 一般に使われなくなった, すたれた, 退化した
　obsolete equipment 老朽設備, 老朽化した設備
　obsolete facilities 老朽設備, 老朽化した設備, 老朽化した施設
　obsolete goods 陳腐財
　obsolete inventory 陳腐化棚卸し資産, 陳腐化在庫 (=obsolete stock)
　obsolete items 陳腐化品
　obsolete property 陳腐化資産

obtain 動 取得する, 調達する, 入手する, 獲得する (=acquire)
　obtain funds 資金を調達する
　obtain in advance 前借りする
　obtain loan finance 借入れで資金調達をする, 借入れによる資金調達
▶We *obtained* a 20 percent stake in the company. 当社は，同社の株式の20%を取得した．

occupant 名 現住者, 占有者, 占拠者

occupation 名 従事, 業務, 職業, 占有, 占有権, 占有期間

occupational employee 非管理職従業員
▶Benefits for *occupational employees* are not directly pay-related. 非管理職従業員に対する給付は，給与と直接的な関係はありません．

occupy 動 占有する,〈地位を〉占める

ODA 政府開発援助 (**official development assistance**の略)
　ODA contribution ODA拠出金
　ODA donee ODA被供与国, ODA被援助国
　ODA donor 政府開発援助供与国, ODA供与国, ODA援助国
　ODA guidelines ODA大綱
　ODA loans 政府開発援助の円借款, 円借款
　ODA recipient ODA受入れ国
▶Japan's full-scale official development assistance (*ODA*) in this area began when it started helping Vietnam revise its Civil Code in 1994. 日本のこの地域での本格的な政府開発援助（ODA）は，1994年のベトナムに対する同国民法改正の支援から始まった．

OECD 経済協力開発機構 (**Organization for Economic Cooperation Fund**の略．自由な意見交換，情報交換を通じて経済成長，貿易自由化，途

上国支援への貢献を目的として，ヨーロッパ諸国を中心に日米を含めて30か国の先進国が加盟する国際機関）
▶*OECD* comprises Japan, the United States, European and other industrialized countries, as well as several newly emergent countries, including South Korea and Mexico. 経済協力開発機構（OECD）は，日本と欧米その他の先進諸国と，韓国，メキシコなどを含む一部の新興国とで構成されている。

OEM 相手先ブランド製造業者，相手先商標製造業者，生産委託契約 （original equipment manufacturerの略）

of counsel 顧問弁護士，弁護士，オブ・カウンセル

off-balance-sheet 貸借対照表に計上［表示］されない，簿外の，オフ・バランス，オフ・バランスシート
　off-balance-sheet activity オフ・バランス取引 （＝off-balance-sheet transaction）
　off-balance-sheet asset 簿外資産
　off-balance-sheet contingencies オフ・バランスの偶発債務
　off-balance-sheet financing 簿外資金調達，オフ・バランスシート資金調達，簿外金融，オフ・バランス金融，オフ・バランスシート・ファイナンシング （貸借対照表に負債が計上されない形での資金調達）
　off-balance sheet liability 簿外債務，簿外負債，オフ・バランス債務
　off-balance-sheet transaction 簿外取引，オフ・バランス取引，オフ・バランスシート取引 （＝off-balance sheet activity：貸借対照表上に表示されない取引のこと）
▶Other *off-balance-sheet* contingencies aggregated approximately $200 million at December 31, 2008. その他の偶発債務は，2008年12月31日現在で約2億ドルでした。

off-budget spending 予算外支出，オフ・バジェット予算

off-exchange market 店頭取引市場

off-hours trading 時間外取引

off-JT オフJT （＝off-the-job training）

off-market purchase of shares 株式の市場外買付け

off-market trading 取引所外取引，市場外取引 （＝off-market transactions）
▶Investors must use a public tender offer if they seek to acquire more than one-third of stocks issued by any listed corporation through *off-market trading*. 市場外取引で上場企業が発行した株式の3分の1超を投資家が取得する場合，投資家は株式公開買付け（TOB）を実施しなければならない。

off stream 生産停止，操業停止

off-the-book 形 帳簿外の，簿外の，記録されていない
　off-the-book account 簿外口座
　off-the-book deal 簿外取引
　off-the-book debts 簿外債務 （＝off-the-book liabilities）
　off-the-book property 含み資産
　off-the-book transaction 簿外取引 （＝off-the-book deal）
▶Andersen Consulting failed to uncover the massive *off-the-book* debts and dishonest accounting procedures of U.S. energy giant Enron Corp. アンダーセン・コンサルティングは，米エネルギー大手エンロンの巨額の簿外債務と不明朗な会計処理手続きを見抜けなかった。

off the job [off-the-job] training 職場外訓練，集合教育，オフJT （＝off-JT）

offending enterprise 加害企業

offensive 名 攻勢，攻撃 （⇒recruit）
　all-out offensive 全面攻勢
　spring labor offensive 春闘 （＝spring wage negotiations, spring wage offensive）
　spring offensive 春闘，春季労使交渉 （＝spring labor offensive）
　take [go on, go over to] the offensive against …に対して攻勢に出る
▶Microsoft's merger offer is the firm's attempt to take the *offensive* with Yahoo's help. マイクロソフトの買収提案は，ヤフーの支援で［ヤフーを取り込んで］攻勢に出る狙いがある。
▶This year's spring *offensive* will center around wage rises. 今年の春闘は，賃上げが焦点だ。

offer 動 申し込む，提供する，販売する，〈金利などを〉提示する，〈買収などを〉提案する，〈株式などを〉発行する，〈株式を〉売り出す （⇒mortgage）
　offered price 提示価格，買付け価格，売り呼び値
　offered rate 出し手レート，売り手レート，オファード・レート
▶One of our principal strategies is to *offer* customers the best value. 当社の主要戦略の一つは，顧客に最大の価値を提供することです。
▶The bank *offered* three types of preferred shares. 同行は，3種類の優先株を発行した。
▶The company does not *offer* income forecasts for the current business year. 同社は，今期の収

益予想を出していない。
▶The stock, *offered* at ¥235,000 a share in the initial public offering, closed at ¥295,000.　新規株式公開で1株235,000円で売り出された株[株式の新規公開で公開価格が1株当たり235,000円の同株]は，295,000円で取引を終えた。

offer 名　申込み，売申込み，募集，売出し，売呼び値，申し出，提案，提示，提示額，条件，オファー（⇒**public tender offer, takeover offer, tender offer**）

　　bid offer price　呼び値
　　block offer　一括売出し
　　buying offer　買い申込み，買いオファー
　　buyout offer　買収の申込み，買収提案（＝acquisition offer）
　　counter offer　修正申込み，逆申込み，カウンター・オファー
　　cross offer　交叉申込み
　　early retirement offer　早期退職提案
　　firm offer　確定申込み，ファーム・オファー
　　merger offer　買収提案
　　offer price per share　1株当たり買付け価格，1株当たり買取り価格
　　open offer　公募
　　selling offer　売り申込み，売りオファー
　　unseasoned offer　新規公開売出し

▶About 2,500 employees accepted the early retirement *offer*.　従業員約2,500人が，早期退職提案を受諾しました。
▶Negotiations fell through when Vodafone turned down TEPCO's *offer*.　東電側の提示額をボーダフォンが拒否して，交渉は決裂した。

offer price　募集価格，売出価格，発行価額，買付け価格，買取り価格，提示価格，TOB[株式公開買付け]価格

▶The offer will be completed four business days after the *offer price* is fixed.　売却は，株の売出価格決定の4営業日後に完了する。

offering 名　募集，売出し，〈株式などの〉発行，株式の公開[上場]，入札，〈教会などへの〉献金，提供（募集＝primary distribution, primary offering, 売出し＝secondary distribution, secondary offering；⇒**initial public offering, public offering, stock offering**）

　　equity offering　株式発行，株式公開
　　noncompetitive offering　非競争入札
　　offering circular　分売案内書
　　public offering bond　公募債
　　public stock offering　株式募集，株式公開，株式上場，公募増資（＝public equity offering, public offering, stock offering）
　　rights offering　株主割当て発行
　　security offering　有価証券の募集
　　shelf offering　一括募集
　　terms of the offering　発行条件
　　underwrite the offering　売出しを引き受ける

▶The company made a public stock *offering* on the Nasdaq Japan market on the Osaka Securities Exchange in March 2001.　同社は，2001年3月，大阪証券取引所のナスダック・ジャパン（現ヘラクレス）市場に株式を上場した。

offering price　公募価格，募集価格，売出価格（＝offer price：「募集価格」は新規発行の有価証券を募集する場合の価格，「売出価格」はすでに発行された有価証券を売り出す場合の価格）

office 名　事務所，仕事場，営業所，店舗，省[庁，課]，官職，公職，職務，任務，責任，要職，重要ポスト，在任期間，職員，オフィス

　　back office　バック・オフィス，事務部門，事務処理，後方部門，ディーリング管理業務
　　commercial office vacancy rate　賃貸オフィスの空室率
　　field office　営業所
　　foreign office　在外支店
　　front office　経営陣，幹部，本社
　　General Accounting Office　会計検査院《略 GAO》
　　head office　本社，本店，本部，本拠（＝home office, main office）
　　information office　案内所
　　inter-office account　本支店勘定
　　marketing office cost　営業事務費
　　office administration　事務管理
　　office clerk　事務員
　　office copy　公文書，公認謄本
　　office equipment　事務用設備，営業用什器（じゅうき）備品
　　office expenses　営業費，事務所費
　　office hours　営業時間，執務時間，勤務時間，診療時間（＝operating hours）
　　office lawyer　法律顧問
　　office machinery　オフィス機器，事務機器，OA機器
　　office management　事務管理
　　office tax　事業所税
　　office term　任期，在任期間，在職期間（＝term of office）
　　office worker　会社員，事務員，事務職員，職員
　　office workstation　多機能パソコン，オフィス・ワークステーション《略 OWS》

overseas offices 国外営業所, 海外拠点
principal office 本社事務所, 本店事務所, 主たる事務所, 本社, 本店, 本部
registered office 登記上の本社[本店], 登録事務所
registry office 登記所
representative office 駐在員事務所
▶Info technology has led to the downsizing of *office* administration sections. 情報技術(IT)は, 事務管理部門の縮小を招いている。

office work 事務, オフィス・ワーク
▶Streamlining of *office work* with the introduction of information technology will not only improve administrative services, but also lead to a reduction of the workforce. IT(情報技術)の導入による事務の合理化は, 行政サービスの向上だけでなく, 人員削減にもつながる。

officer 名 会社役員, 役員, 業務執行役員, オフィサー

> 米国企業の役員について➡ アメリカの会社では, 一般に取締役会の意思決定を受けて実際の業務執行をする会社役員(corporate officer)として最高業務執行役員(chief executive officer), 社長(president), 副社長(vice president), 秘書役(総務担当役員: secretary), 会計役(財務部長, トレジャラー: treasurer), 会計監査役(経理部長, コントローラー: controller, comptroller)やゼネラル・カウンセラー(法務部長: general counselor)などが置かれている。これらの役員(officers)と取締役(directors)は区別され, 取締役会のメンバーで業務執行についての意思決定をするのが取締役で, 日本の場合のように会社の役員はかならずしも取締役でなくてよい。

auditing officer 監査役
chief accounting officer 最高財務担当役員, 財務統括役員《略 CAO》
chief executive officer 最高業務執行役員, 最高経営責任者, 最高業務執行理事《略 CEO》(経営戦略や経営ビジョンを決める企業のトップ。米国では, CEOが会長を兼ねることが多い)
chief financial officer 最高財務担当役員, 最高財務責任者《略 CFO》
chief information officer 最高情報担当役員, 最高情報責任者, 情報戦略統括役員《略 CIO》
chief information security officer 最高情報セキュリティ担当役員《略 CISO》
chief knowledge officer 最高知識担当役員, ナレッジ担当統括役員, 知識統括役員《略 CKO》
chief operating officer 最高業務運営役員, 最高業務運営責任者, 業務執行役員, 最高執行責任者《略 COO》
chief privacy officer プライバシー保護担当役員, プライバシー統括役員, プライバシー保護最高責任者《略 CPO》
chief technical officer 最高技術担当役員, 最高技術責任者《略 CTO》
chief technology officer 最高技術責任者《略 CTO》
compliance officer 業務監査役, 法令[規則]遵守担当役員, コンプライアンス・オフィサー
corporate information officer 情報戦略統括役員《略 CIO》
corporate officer 株式会社の役員, 会社役員
elected officer 選任役員 (⇒pension cost)
executive officer 業務執行役員, 上席業務執行役員, 執行役員, 業務執行理事
intelligence officer 情報当局者
medical officer 保健担当者, 医療責任者, 嘱託医《略 MO》
officer and employee receivables 役員および従業員貸付け金
officers' bonuses 役員賞与, 役員賞与金
officers' remuneration 役員報酬
officers' salaries and bonuses 役員報酬[俸給]および賞与
senior executive officer 常務執行役員, 上席業務執行役員

▶The vice president of Mizuho Corporate Bank will take up the post of president and chief executive *officer* in the newly merged firm. 合併新会社の社長兼最高経営責任者(CEO)には, みずほコーポレート銀行の副頭取が就任する。

official 名 幹部, 指導者, 責任者, 役員, 経営者, 公務員, 職員, 当局者, 担当者, 関係者 (⇒action)
Asian affairs official at the U.S. Defense Department 米国防総省のアジア問題担当者
Obama administration official オバマ政権当局者
corporate official 会社役員, 経営者
current and former officials 現役職員とOB
deposit of accounting officials 預託金
finance official 財務当局者
financial market officials 金融市場関係者, 金融関係者
government officials 政府当局, 政府高官, 官僚, 政府職員 (⇒bribe)
high official 高官
high-ranking officials 上層部, 幹部
middle-ranked official 中堅幹部

monetary officials 金融当局
police officials 官憲
senior defense official 米国防総省高官
senior official 政府高官, 企業の幹部[役員]
senior official in the Islamic militant Hamas group イスラム過激派組織ハマス幹部
top corporate official 経営者, 企業のトップ
top official meeting 首脳会談, 首脳懇談会
top U.S. officials 米政府高官
top officials 高官, 首脳
US Defense Department officials 米国防総省当局者
U.S. intelligence officials 米国の情報機関当局者
U.S. officials 米政府当局者

▸High-ranking *officials* at TEPCO headquarters were involved in systematically falsifying inspection records for 13 nuclear reactors at the company's three nuclear power plants. 東京電力(東電)の3原子力発電所の原子炉13基の点検記録の組織ぐるみの改竄には, 東電本社の上層部が関与していた。

official 形 公の, 公的な, 公式の, 正式の, 公認の, 公示の, 公用の, 公務上の, 表向きの, 一般に公開されていない

file an official complaint 正式に苦情申立てをする
official barriers 法律上の制約, 法的な障壁
official document 正式文書
official duties 公務
official exchange rate 公定レート
official explanation 表向きの説明
official figures 公式発表の数字
official gazette 官報
official interest rate 政策金利 (＝official rate)
official land prices 公示地価
official receiver 破産管財人
official report 正式な報告
official retail price 公定小売価格
Official Score Certificate 公式認定証
Official Secrets Act 英国の国家機密保護法
official statement 公式声明
official telecommunications equipment supplier 公認通信機器納入業者
official website 公認ホームページ

official development assistance 政府開発援助《略 ODA》

▸Japan's *official development assistance* has been criticized as wasteful. 日本の政府開発援助(ODA)は, ムダが多いと批判されている。

official discount rate 公定歩合 (＝bank rate, discount rate, official bank rate)

公定歩合→「公定歩合」は, 中央銀行が金融機関に直接資金を貸し出すときの基準金利のこと。米国の場合は, 米連邦準備制度理事会(FRB)が「最後の貸し手」として金融機関に貸し付けるときの金利で, フェデラル・ファンド(FF)金利より高めとなる。なお, 日銀は, 2006年8月11日から公定歩合の名称を「基準割引率および基準貸付け利率」に変更した。⇒ **Federal [federal] funds rate, key rate**

▸The current *official discount rate* of 0.1 percent per annum is expected to be raised to between 0.35 percent and 0.5 percent. 年0.1%の現行の公定歩合は, 0.35－0.5%程度に引き上げられる見通しだ。

offline [off-line] 形 非連結, オフライン式, 実店舗, オフライン (ホスト・コンピュータやネットワークに端末が接続されていない状態)

offline business オフライン・ビジネス
offline meeting オフライン・ミーティング (取引相手などと直接顔を合わせて話をすること)
offline processing オフライン処理
offline storage media オフライン記憶媒体, オフライン記憶装置 (＝offline storage device)

offset 動 相殺する, 埋め合わせをする, 帳消しにする, 吸収する, 吸い上げる, 解消する, 打ち消す, 〈リスクなどを〉カバーする, 名 相殺, 相殺額, 差引勘定, 埋め合わせ (⇒discount plan)

be partially offset by …で一部相殺される, …で部分的に相殺される
more than offset 十分相殺する, かなり相殺する
offset market risk 市場リスクを吸収する, 市場リスクを相殺する, 市場リスクをカバーする
offset the loss 損失の穴埋めをする, 損失をカバーする

▸An account payable can be *offset* against an account receivable from the same company. 買掛金は, 同じ会社の売掛金と相殺することができる。

offshore 形 海外[域外]の, 沖合いの, オフショア

offshore assembly plant 海外組立工場
offshore banking facility オフショア市場 (＝offshore market, offshore banking center)
offshore fishing 沿海漁業, 沖合漁業 (＝offshore fisheries)
offshore fund 海外投信
offshore drilling 海底石油掘削
offshore investment 海外投資

offshore oil drilling 海底石油掘削
offshore production area 経済特区
offshore purchase 域外調達

offshoring 名 海外への業務委託, オフショアリング

oil 名 石油, 原油, オイル (⇒crude oil)
  buyback oil 買戻し原油
  exchanges-crude oil 原油交換
  fuel oil market 燃料油市場
  heating oil 暖房用燃油
  heavy crude oil 重質原油 (=heavy crude)
  heavy oil products 重油製品
  lubricating oil 潤滑油
  offshore oil drilling 海底石油掘削
  offshore oil field 海底油田
  offshore oil storage 石油洋上備蓄
  oil concession 石油採掘権
  oil crunch 石油危機, 石油逼迫, 石油ショック, オイル・ショック (=oil crisis)
  oil demand 石油需要, 原油需要
  oil distributor 石油元売り
  oil drilling rig 油井掘削装置
  oil field concession 油田採掘権, 油田の権益
  oil floor price 石油下限価格
  oil glut 石油供給過剰
  oil industry 石油産業, 石油業界 (=petroleum industry)
  oil infrastructure 原油の関連設備
  oil money 石油資本, オイル・マネー
  oil platform 石油基地
  oil pollution 石油汚染
  oil producing area 産油地域
  oil producing country 産油国 (=oil producer)
  oil product 石油製品
  oil production 原油生産, 石油生産
  oil-refiner distributor 石油元売り会社
  oil refinery 製油所
  oil refining capacity 石油精製能力
  oil sand 油砂, オイル・サンド
  oil shale 油母頁岩(けつがん), オイル・シェール
  oil slick 流出原油, 油膜
  oil spill 石油流出
  oil stockpile 石油備蓄
  residual oil 残渣(ざんさ)油, かま残油
  shale oil 頁岩油 (オイル・シェールから採取する石油のこと)

oil consuming country 石油消費国 (=oil consuming state)
▸To prevent the economic recovery from stalling, coordination among *oil* producing and consuming *countries* is needed. 景気回復の失速を防ぐには,産油国と石油消費国の協調が必要だ。

oil development 石油開発
▸The current high price of crude oil stems partly from the lack of investment in *oil development* for a long period. 現在の原油高の一因は,長期にわたる石油開発投資の不足だ。

oil field 油田
▸Unocal Corp. has sophisticated drilling technology and succeeded in developing deep-sea *oil fields* in the Gulf of Mexico. ユノカル(米国の独立系石油会社)は高度な掘削技術を持っており,メキシコ湾の深海油田開発に成功している。

oil-for-food program 石油・食糧交換プログラム
▸Under the U.N. *oil-for-food program*, Iraq must obtain U.N. approval to import hundreds of dual-use items. 国連の石油・食糧交換プログラムに基づいて,数百品目ある軍民両用物資を輸入するには,イラクは国連の承認を得なければならない。

oil inventory 原油在庫
▸*Oil inventory* in the United States as of the end of July was up 6.5 percent on the year-ago figure. 米国の7月末現在の原油在庫は,前年より6.5%多い。

oil majors 国際石油資本, 石油メジャー, 石油資本
▸In China, *oil majors* have been building ethylene plants in joint ventures as well. 中国では,国際石油資本(メジャー)が合弁エチレン・プラントの建設も進めている。
▸Venezuelan President Chavez survived a recall referendum, but he remains at loggerheads with *oil majors*. ベネズエラのチャベス大統領は解任の国民投票で信任されたが,石油資本との対立が続いている。

oil output limits 原油生産枠
▸The Organization of Petroleum Exporting Countries decided to keep *oil output limits* on hold. 石油輸出国機構(OPEC)は,現行の原油生産枠を据え置くことを決めた。

oil price 原油価格, 石油価格
  global oil price 国際原油価格
  rising oil prices 原油価格の高騰, 原油高
▸The rising *oil prices* basically reflect increases in oil demand driven by a recovery in the world economy. この原油高は,基本的に世界経済の回復による原油の需要増を反映している。

oil shock 石油危機, 石油ショック, オイル・

ショック
▶In fiscal 1979, during the second *oil shock*, the average price of imported crude oil was ¥33.5 per liter.　第二次石油ショックに見舞われた1979年度の輸入原油の平均価格は，1リットル＝33.5円だった．

oil tanker　原油タンカー
▶Pirates are threatening the safe navigation of *oil tankers* and other ships in Southeast Asian waters.　東南アジアの海域では，海賊が原油タンカーなどの船舶の安全な航行を脅かしている．

oil wholesalers　石油元売り各社，元売り各社
▶*Oil wholesalers* are tightening supplies due to production cuts by oil producing countries.　石油元売り各社は，産油国の減産で供給を引き締めている．

old economy　オールドエコノミー（＝t-economy: IT関連の産業や企業を指すニューエコノミーに対して，自動車，建設，不動産，繊維，流通などの成熟産業を指す）

omnibus bill　総括的法案，包括法，オムニバス法案（＝omnibus legislation）

Omnibus Trade and Competitiveness Act of 1988　1988年包括通商・競争力法

on shore business　国内事業

on-site service　出張修理サービス，現場修理サービス

on stream　生産中，操業中

on-site demonstration　現地実証試験（⇒demonstration）

on the job [on-the-job] training　職場内訓練，職場研修，社内の職業訓練《略 OJT》
▶Under a new system introduced in April 2004, all new doctors are required to undergo *on-the-job training* at designated hospitals for two years after graduation.　2004年4月から導入された新制度では，新人医師は全員，指定病院で2年間の卒業後研修［職場研修］を受けなければならない．

on-the-run issue　指標銘柄

on-the-spot inspection　現場検証，現地調査，立入り検査，立入り考査，立入り調査
▶The agency obtained records of operations at the facility and copies of the unauthorized operations manual in an *on-the-spot inspection*.　同庁は，立入り検査で施設の作業記録や違法な作業マニュアルを入手した．

on-the-spot payment　即時決済

one-bank holding company　単一銀行持ち株会社

one-month money　1か月物資金

one-off 形　一時的，一回限りの
　one off [one-off] charge　特別損失，一時的費用，一時的費用計上，一括処理
　one-off gains　特別利益，一回限りの利益
　one-off payment　一時金，一時支払い，一回限りの支払い
▶Sumitomo Metal Industries Ltd. raised its annual profit forecast by 38 percent on strong demand and *one-off* gains.　需要急増と特別利益で，住友金属工業は年間業績予想を38％上方修正した．

one-off losses　特別損失，一回限りの損失
▶Earnings fell sharply on *one-off losses* related to changes in accounting standards for fixed assets and a switch in our employee pension system.　固定資産と当社の従業員年金制度変更の会計基準変更に伴う特別損失で，利益が大幅に減少した．

one-price policy　単一価格政策，均一価格制，単一価格制

one-price retailer　均一価格店，均一価格小売店，ワンプライス店

one-segment broadcasting　ワンセグ（ワンセグは，「1セグメント放送」の略称）

one-shot decision making　1回限りの意思決定

one-shot promotion　単発プロモーション

one-stop 形　一点集中の，ワンストップの，1か所でいろいろなこと［いろいろな買い物］ができる
　one-stop banking　総合銀行サービス
　one-stop service of administration　ワンストップ行政サービス

one-stop service　ワンストップ・サービス（消費者のニーズを満たすため，主力製品と関連商品をすべて一つのサイトで提供するサービスのこと）
▶We form a global alliance and offer *one-stop service* for multinationals.　当社は，グローバルな提携関係を築いて，多国籍企業にワンストップ・サービスを提供します．

one-stop shopping　一点集中購買，関連購買，1か所での同時まとめ買い，1か所ですべて済ませる買い物，ワンストップ・ショッピング
▶For our customers, our partnership means *one-stop shopping* for service ordering, maintenance and billing.　当社の顧客にとって，当社の提携関係は，サービスの発注，保守と課金がすべてワンストップ・ショッピング（1か所の窓口ですべて済ますことができること）を意味します．

one-time 形　1回限りの，単発の，一時的な，臨時の

one-time buyer 単発購入者
one-time password 使い捨てパスワード, ワンタイム・パスワード
one-time rate 単発料金 (=open rate)
one-time repayment 一括完済 (=repayment at one time)

one-time [onetime] charge 一時的費用, 臨時費用
▸The first-half loss of the company widened because of a *onetime charge* from writing down the value of its assets to meet new accounting rules. 同社の上期の赤字は, 新会計基準に対応するため同社の資産価値の評価減による一時的費用を計上したため, 拡大した。

one-time credit 一括払戻し金
▸Our financing requirements for 2008 include the permanent financing requirement of approximately $150 million as a result of the payment of the *one-time credit* to our subscribers. 当社の2008年度の資金調達必要額には, 電話加入者への支払いに要する一括払戻し金額約1億5,000万ドルの長期的な資金調達必要額が含まれています。

one-time pretax charge 税引き前臨時費用, 臨時税引き前費用
▸We elected to record a *one-time pretax charge* of $11,000 million to record the unfunded portions of these liabilities. 当社は, この債務の未拠出部分を記録するため, 110億ドルを税引き前の臨時費用として計上することにしました。

one-to-one marketing ワン・トゥ・ワン・マーケティング (マス・マーケティングに代わり, インターネットを利用して各顧客のニーズに応じた商品を提供して販売促進を図るマーケティング手法。具体的には, 顧客の注文やアクセス・データに基づいて顧客1人ひとりのニーズを把握し, それぞれのニーズに合った商品を電子メールで知らせたり, 商品の最新情報をホームページに表示したりすること)

one yen capital's company 1円起業
ongoing concern 継続企業
online [on-line] 形副 オンライン, オンライン式, 直結, 回線接続中, コンピュータ回線で, コンピュータ回線を使って, コンピュータのネットワークで, インターネットで, ネット上で, ネットで 《略 OL》
 online bank ネット銀行, ネット専業銀行 (=e-banking, Internet bank, Internet-based bank, Net bank, Net-only bank)
 online brokerage オンライン証券, ネット専業証券, ネット専業証券会社 (=e-broker, online broker, online securities brokerage)
online business オンライン業務, オンライン・ビジネス
online debit service インターネット即時決済サービス, オンライン即時決済サービス
online finance ネット金融, オンライン金融
online grocery ネット・スーパー
online home delivery retailer オンライン宅配小売業者
online job-search service オンライン求職システム
online mall 仮想商店街, オンライン・モール (=virtual mall)
online music distribution services インターネットを通じた音楽配信
online networking オンライン提携
online procurement オンライン調達
online securities brokerage ネット専業証券会社, オンライン証券会社 (=e-broker, online broker, online brokerage)
online stock trading business 株のインターネット取引業務
online trading ネット取引, ネット専業取引, オンライン取引 (=Internet trading, Net trading)
online voting 電子投票 (=e-vote, electronic voting)
▸Shareholders must send a report *online* to the FSA when their stake in a listed company exceeds 5 percent of issued shares. 上場企業に対する株式の保有比率が発行済み株式の5%を超えた場合, 株主は金融庁にインターネットで報告書を提出しなければな, らない。

online advertising オンライン広告, ネット広告 (=online ad, online advertisement, Web advertisement)
▸The company is also likely to enjoy an expected rise in *online advertising* revenue. 同社の場合は, 予想されるオンライン広告の増益も期待できる。

online auction ネット・オークション (=Net auction: オンライン・オークションには, 個人対個人, 企業対個人と企業対企業の3種類のオークションがある)
▸Google Inc. plans to go public by selling $2.7 billion in stock through an *online auction*. 米インターネット検索サービス最大手のグーグルが, ネット・オークションによる27億ドルの株式発行で新規株式公開を計画している。

online fraud オンライン詐欺
▸We must change our personal identification

number first to prevent the recurrence of *online fraud*. オンライン詐欺の再発を防ぐには，まずパスワードを変えなければならない。

online shopping mall 仮想商店街
▸Thirty percent of the goods the company sold in the first quarter of this fiscal year were sold through the *online shopping mall*. 同社が今年度第1四半期に販売した商品の3割は，仮想商店街を通じて販売された。

online shopping mall business 仮想商店街事業（＝Internet shopping mall business）
▸Amazon Japan's entry into the *online shopping mall business* may shake up the customer bases of its forerunners, including Rakuten Inc. and Yahoo Japan Corp. アマゾンジャパンの仮想商店街事業への参入は，同事業で先行する楽天やヤフーの顧客基盤を揺るがしかねない。

online stock brokerage ネット証券会社（＝online brokerage, online securities brokerage）
▸Kabu.com Securities Co. is an *online stock brokerage* headquartered in Chuo Ward, Tokyo. カブドットコム証券は，東京都中央区に本社を構えるネット証券会社だ。

onstream 形 操業中の，稼動中の，すぐに操業できる
▸Central Motor is building a vehicle assembly factory in Miyagi Prefecture that will come *onstream* in 2010. セントラル自動車は，2010年に稼動予定の車両組立工場を宮城県に建設している。

OPEC 太平洋地域経済協力機構（Organization of Pacific Economic Cooperationの略）

OPEC 石油輸出国機構，オペック（Organization of Petroleum Exporting Countriesの略）
▸*OPEC* held production levels steady. 石油開発機構（OPEC）は，原油の生産目標水準を据え置いた。

open 動 開く，開設する，出店する，〈市場などを〉開放する，初値を付ける
　open an account with …に口座を開く，…に口座を開設する
　open up to public ownership 株式を公開する
　opened package 開封後のパッケージ
　opened product 開封後の商品
▸Stock in J-Com *opened* at ¥672,000, but it plunged to its lower limit of ¥572,000. ジェイコム株は，1株67万2,000円の初値が付いたが，値幅制限（ストップ安）の下限の57万2,000円に下落した。

open 形 開かれた，開放的な，制限のない，自由な，公開の，周知の，営業中の，開会中の，未決定の，未解決の，未定の，非武装の，無防備の，オープン

open architecture 仕様公開，オープン・アーキテクチャー
open bid 一般競争入札，公開入札
open check 普通小切手
open college 成人教育大学
open competition 自由競争
open contract 未決済契約，予定契約，先渡し契約，暫定契約，仮契約
open corporation 公開会社，株式公開会社
open credit 無条件信用状，買取銀行不指定信用状
open collar worker 在宅勤務者
open date 賞味期限（＝harmless period of food）
open day 公開日
open demerit デメリット表示
open display 裸陳列，オープン・ディスプレー
open-door policy 門戸開放政策，機会均等政策，ドア開放政策，自由入室制度
open enrollment [admission] 大学全入方式
open for business 営業している
open house 建売り住宅の内覧日，授業参観日，私宅開放日
open housing 公正住宅取引
open letter 公開状
open mortgage 一番抵当
open price 公開価格，始め値，寄り付き値段
open question 未解決の問題
open rate 基本料金
open sea 公海
open season 解禁日
open shop オープン・ショップ（非組合員労働者も雇う会社）
open society 開かれた社会
open source オープン・ソース（ソース・コードを無償で公開して，そのソフトウエアを改良したり再配布したりできるようにすること）
open tendering 一般競争入札，公開入札
▸The Business Day means any day on which the banks are *open* for business in both cities of Tokyo and London. 「営業日」とは，東京とロンドンの両市で銀行が営業している日を意味する。

open account 当座勘定，精算勘定，未決算勘定，無条件信用取引勘定，売掛金
▸We made the sale on 60-day *open account* because the company was a customer of good credit standing. 同社は信用度の高い得意先なので，当社は60日後払いの掛売りで販売した。

open-end 形 開放式の，無制限の，限度のない，変更自由な，オープンエンド型，オープンエンド

(=open-ended)
open-end contract 未定数量契約, 一部条項未定契約, 不定契約
open-end credit system 開放信用体系
open-end investment company オープンエンド型投資会社
open-end mortgage 開放担保, 開放式譲渡抵当, 開放型担保付き社債
open-end policy 可変保険証券
open-end transaction 変更自由な取引

open-ended 形 開放式の, 拡張可能な
open-ended digital communication system 開放式デジタル通信システム
open-ended fund オープンエンド型ファンド
open-ended multilevel marketing method マルチ商法, ネズミ講
▶This cable network is based on an *open-ended* digital communication system complying with a standard ISO model. このケーブル・ネットワークは, ISOの標準化モデルに適合する開放式デジタル通信システムをベースにしている。

open market 公開市場, 自由市場, 一般市場
open market forces 市場原理
open market operation 公開市場操作
open market policy 市場開放政策 (=market opening policy)
open market rate 市中金利
▶The Bank of Japan's conventional *open market* operation of buying short-term government notes without repurchase agreements is limited in its effect. 日銀のこれまでの売戻し条件を付けない短期国債の買切りオペ(公開市場操作)だけでは, その効果に限界がある。

open system 開放型システム, 開システム, 開放系, 汎用性のあるシステム, オープン・システム
open systems interconnection 開放型システム相互接続《略 OSI》
open systems interconnection reference model OSI参照モデル

opening 名 開始, 開会, 開会式, 開通, 開幕, 開店, 開場, 冒頭, 序盤, 初日, 寄り付き, 期首, 就職口, 求人, 空席, 空き, 欠員, 定員, 機会, 好機, 〈弁護人の〉冒頭陳述, オープニング
opening balance 期首残高, 開始残高
opening bank 信用状発行銀行, 信用状の開設銀行 (=issuing bank)
opening charge 発行手数料 (=opening commission)
opening hours 営業時間, 一般開放時間
opening inventory 期首棚卸高
opening price 寄り付き価格, 寄り付き相場, 寄り付き値, 寄り付き, 始め値, オープニング・プライス (=opening quotation)
opening trial balance 繰越し試算表
▶Reducing the number of hours of overtime may not only help those workers retain their jobs, but also increase job *openings*. 残業時間数の削減は, 雇用の維持だけでなく, 新規の雇用を増やす可能性がある。

operate 動 経営する, 運営する, 操作する, 事業を展開する, 営業する, 操業する
continue to operate 営業を続ける, 運営を続ける, 操業を続ける
operate at capacity フル稼働を維持する
operate businesses 各種事業を展開する, 事業を進める
▶Financial institutions *operate* diverse businesses cross-sectionally. 金融機関は, 多様な業務を横断的に展開している。
▶The company *operates* an auction sites and collects charges from users. 同社は, オークション・サイトを運営して, (落札時に)利用者から手数料を徴収している。
▶The company's stores, including the 263 it runs directly, will continue *operating*. 同社の店舗は, 263の直営店を含めて営業を続ける。

operating 形 経営上の, 営業上の, 業務の
operating activities 営業活動, 経営活動
operating capital 運転資金, 運用資本 (=working capital)
operating earning rate 営業利益率, 経営資本利益率 (=operating income to operating assets ratio)
operating funds 運転資金, 営業資金 (=operating capital, working capital, working funds)
operating leverage 営業レバレッジ, オペレーティング・レバレッジ
operating liabilities 営業負債
operating margin percentage 営業利益率
operating rate 操業度
operating receipt 営業収入
operating assets 運用資産, 運転資産, 営業資産, 営業用資産
▶After deduction for noninterest-bearing current liabilities, the return on *operating assets* was 5 percent. 運用資産[運転資産]の利益率は, 無利息流動負債の控除後で5%でした。
operating cash flow 営業活動によるキャッシュ・フロー, 営業キャッシュ・フロー(企業が本

業で生み出した現金などの出入りを「営業キャッシュ・フロー」という）
▸The decline in *operating cash flows* was mainly due to higher inventories and accounts receivable. 営業活動によるキャッシュ・フローの減少は，主に在庫と売掛金の水準が前期比で高かったためです。

operating company 事業会社
▸We forged this new entity out of three *operating companies*. 当社は，三つの事業会社を統合してこの新会社を設立しました。

operating cost 営業費，営業コスト，営業上の費用，営業費用，営業経費，業務費，創業費，運営費 （＝operating expense）
▸About 70 percent of the bank's *operating costs* were its nonpersonnel expenses. 同行の物件費［非人件費］の約7割が，営業経費だった。

operating deficit 営業赤字
▸We posted an *operating deficit* of about ¥25 billion at a settlement term ending March 2009. 当社は，2009年3月期決算で約250億円の営業赤字を計上しました。

operating earnings 営業利益，業務純益
▸Nissan Motor Co. reported a loss of *operating earnings*. 日産自動車は，営業減益となった。
▸Operating earnings represent total revenues less *operating expenses*. 営業利益は，総収益から営業費用を控除したものです。

operating expense 営業費用，営業費，経常経費 （＝operating cost）
▸*Operating expenses* grew 8% in 2008 mainly because of marketing and sales efforts. 2008年度の営業費用は，主にマーケティングと販売努力により8％増加しました。
▸This increase in *operating expenses* was primarily due to higher depreciation expenses. この営業費用増加の主な要因は，減価償却費の増加です。

operating income 営業利益，営業収益，営業損益 （＝income from operations, operating profit, total sales; ⇒from a year ago）
　operating income and loss 営業損益
　operating income (loss) 営業利益（損失）
　operating income margin 売上高営業利益率，営業利益率
▸Our *operating income* has decreased since 2007. 当社の営業利益は，2007年度以来減少しています。

operating lease 営業型リース，営業リース契約，賃貸性リース，オペレーティング・リース

▸Our rental expense under *operating leases* was $1,500 million in 2008. 当社のオペレーティング・リースの賃借料は，2008年度は15億ドルでした。
▸We lease equipment to others through *operating leases*. 当社は，設備をオペレーティング・リース方式で他社に提供しています。

operating loss 営業損失，事業損失，営業赤字，営業欠損金，欠損金 （＝operational loss）
▸The company's half-yearly performance until the end of February showed an *operating loss* of ¥4 billion. 同社の2月中間決算は，40億円の営業赤字だった。
▸We reported an *operating loss* in our operations outside the U.S. in 2008. 2008年度は，当社の米国外事業で営業損失を計上しました。

operating margin 営業利益率
▸Nissan Motor Co.'s *operating margin* was the highest among domestic automobile manufacturers at midterm settlements that ended Sept. 30. 9月中間期［今年の9月中間決算］で，国内自動車メーカーでは日産の営業利益率が最高だった。

operating plan 業務計画，事業計画，営業計画
▸We have reviewed the Corporation's *operating plans* for 2009. 私ども経営陣は，2009年度の当社の事業計画の見直しをしました。

operating profit 営業利益，営業収益，金融機関の業務純益 （＝income from operations, operating income: 売上高から販売・管理費を差し引いた収益で，本業のもうけを示す）
　operating profit and loss 営業損益 （＝operating profit or loss）
　operating profit before exceptional items 特別項目前の営業利益，特別損益計上前の営業利益
▸*Operating profit* from the company's core businesses was ¥5.2 billion. 同社の主力事業の営業利益は，52億円だった。
▸The firm's *operating profits* show the earnings of its core business. 同社の営業利益は，本業のもうけを示す。
▸These banks submitted management restructuring plans with stated targets for net and *operating profits* and other areas. これらの銀行は，当期純利益や業務純益などの目標を掲げて経営健全化計画を提出した。

operating profit forecast 営業利益予想
▸Sanyo revised downward its *operating profit forecast* by a steep 72 percent to ¥18 billion for this business year. 三洋電機は，今年度の営

業利益予想を72%急減の180億円に下方修正した。

operating results 営業成績, 経営成績, 営業損益, 業績 (=business results)
▸When we dispose of assets that were depreciated using the unit method, we include the gains or losses in *operating results*. 個別償却法で償却した資産を処分する場合, 当社はその利益または損失を営業損益に含めています。

operating revenue 営業収益, 営業収入, 売上高, 〈銀行などの〉経常収益 (⇒accumulated losses)
▸The bank's *operating revenue*, generated by interest payments and profits from investments in national bonds, is the equivalent of sales revenues at regular companies. 同行の経常収益は, 貸出金の利息や国債の運用益などで, 一般企業の売上高にあたる。
▸We had an *operating revenue* of ¥224.7 billion in fiscal 2008. 当社の2008年度の営業収益は, 2,247億円でした。

operating system 基本ソフト, システム・ソフト, オペレーティング・システム《略 OS》
▸Microsoft dominates the market for personal computer *operating systems*. 米マイクロソフトは, パソコンの基本ソフト(OS)市場で圧倒的な強さを示している。

operation 名 営業, 営業活動, 事業, 業務, 作業, 経営, 活動, 操業, 操作, 運用, 公開市場操作, 介入操作, 部門, 子会社, 関係会社, オペ, オペレーション
  business operation 業務運営, 企業運営, 企業経営, 経営, 営業活動, 営業運転, 業務, 事業, 業容
  buying and selling operations by hedge funds ヘッジ・ファンドの売り買い操作
  continuing operations 継続事業
  corporate operations 企業経営, 企業の営業活動, 企業の業務
  discontinued operations 廃止事業
  domestic sales operations 国内営業部門
  financial operation 財務活動
  foreign operation 海外事業, 在外事業
  full operation 本格稼動, 完全操業, フル稼働
  go into operation 操業を開始する
  international operations 国際業務
  merge operations 経営統合する (=integrate operations)
  net operation loss 営業純損失
  normal operations 通常業務
  operation of a pension plan 年金制度の運用
  operations located outside the U.S. 米国外子会社, 米国外の関係会社
  reduction of operation 操業短縮
  safe operation 安全操業
  take over operations 経営を受け継ぐ
  transfer operation 振替操作
  treasury operation 財務運用
  wholly owned operations 完全所有子会社, 100%子会社
  yen-selling, dollar-buying operation 円売り・ドル買い介入操作
▸The Bank of Japan asked the Federal Reserve Bank of New York to intervene in the New York foreign exchange market on its behalf through yen-selling, dollar-buying *operations* for the first time in 15 months. 日銀は, 1年3か月ぶりにニューヨーク連銀に委託して, ニューヨーク外国為替市場で円売り・ドル買いの介入に踏み切った。
▸The two companies will merge their *operations* under a holding company to be set up next September. 両社は, 来年9月に持ち株会社を設立して経営統合する。
▸We expect to meet our cash requirements in 2009 from *operations*, complemented, if necessary, by external financing. 当社は, 業務活動によってもたらされる資金で2009年度の必要資金を確保し, 必要に応じて外部資金を調達してこれを補う方針です。

operational 形 操作[運転]上の, 運用[運用上]の, 経営[経営上]の, 業務上の, 営業[営業上]の, 戦略[作戦]上の, 機能している, 使用できる
  operational data 業務データ
  operational decision 業務的意思決定
  operational diversification 営業活動の多様化
  operational experience 業務実績
  operational profit 営業利益
  operational research 作戦研究, 業務調査, オペレーションズ・リサーチ《略 OR》(=operations research)
  operational revenues 営業収益

operational efficiency 経営効率, 業務効率, 業務[作業]の効率性
▸The serious deterioration of *operational efficiency* is caused by excess output capacity and burgeoning workforces. 極端な経営効率の悪化は, 生産設備と従業員の過剰によるものだ。

operational funds 営業資金, 運転資金 (=operating funds)
▸We were provided with ¥10 billion in *operational funds*. 当社は, 運転資金として100億円の融資を受けました。

operational integration 経営統合 (= business integration, management integration)
▶*Operational integration* and merger have become two major options to shore up the foundations of companies. 経営統合と合併が, それぞれ企業の経営基盤を強化する有力な選択肢になってきた。

operational loss 営業損失, 営業赤字
▶The company's confectionery division has been recording *operational losses* since the year ending in March 2006. 同社の洋菓子部門は, 2006年3月期から営業赤字が続いている。

operator 名 運営者, 経営者, 事業主, 事業者, 事業会社, 運営会社, 会社, 電気通信事業者, 電話交換手, 交換取扱い者, コンピュータを操作する人, 運転者, 株の相場師, 仕手, 演算子, 演算記号, オペレータ (⇒Internet shopping mall operator)
　auction site operator オークション・サイト運営会社, 競売サイト運営業者
　business operator 事業者
　company operator 会社経営者
　major operators 大企業
▶InterContinental Hotels Group PLC is the world's biggest hotel *operator*. インターコンチネンタル・ホテルズ・グループ(IHG)は, 世界最大手のホテル運営会社だ。

opinion 名 意見, 監査意見, 意見表明, 判断, 見解, 鑑定, 評価, 〈弁護士の〉意見書, オピニオン (⇒legal opinion)
　accountant's opinion 会計士の意見, 監査意見書
　audit opinion 監査意見 (=auditors' opinion)
　collective opinion 統一意見
　credit opinion 格付け見解 (=rating opinion)
　express an opinion 意見を表明する
　legal opinion 法律専門家の意見, 法律意見書, 法的見解, 弁護士意見[意見書]
　opinion date 監査報告書の日付
　opinion of independent (public) accountants 独立会計士の意見, 独立会計士の監査意見
　opinion of management 経営陣の見解, 経営者の見解
　Opinions of Accounting Principles Board APB (会計原則審議会)意見書
　overall opinion on the financial statements as a whole 財務書類[財務書類]全体についての総合意見
　professional opinion 職業専門家の意見
▶Corporations have been limiting shareholders' right to express *opinions* at shareholders' meetings. 企業は, 株主総会での株主の発言権を抑えてきた。
▶Our responsibility is to express an *opinion* on these financial statements based on our audits. 私どもの責任は, 私どもの監査に基づいてこれらの財務書類[財務諸表]について意見を表明することにある。

opportunity 名 機会, 事業機会, 商機, 好機, 場, 環境, 可能性, ビジネス・チャンス, チャンス
　business opportunity ビジネス機会, 事業機会, 商機会, 商機, ビジネス・チャンス (=business chance)
　capitalize on a market opportunity 市場の機会をとらえる, 市場の機会を生かす
　creation of job opportunities 雇用機会の創出
　employment opportunity 雇用機会, 就労機会
　growth opportunity 成長の機会 (⇒community of interest)
　investment opportunity 投資機会, 投資対象, 運用先
　job opportunity 雇用機会, 就労機会, 就業機会, 就業のチャンス, 求人
　market opportunity 市場機会, ビジネス機会, 事業機会
　merit-based opportunity 実力主義
　opportunity assessment 市場機会の分析・評価, オポチュニティ・アセスメント
　opportunity cost 機会原価
　opportunity loss 機会損失 (=conditional loss, cost of prediction error)
　opportunity of advancement 昇進の機会
　take advantage of opportunities 機会をとらえる, 機会をつかむ, 機会を利用する
　window of opportunity 機会の窓, 機会の手段, 瞬時の好機, 好機
▶We make an acquisition when that seems the most effective way to take advantage of a particular market *opportunity* to further our growth goals. 当社が企業を買収するのは, 特定の市場機会をとらえて当社の成長目標をさらに推進する上で, それが最も効果的な方法であると思われるときです。
▶We see an abundance of *opportunities* for these new lines of business. これらの新事業部門には, 事業機会が豊富にあります。
▶We sell equity interests in our subsidiaries only when *opportunities* or circumstances warrant. 当社が子会社の株式持ち分を売却するのは, 商機が到来した時または環境が良好な場合に限られています。

opportunity cost 機会原価, 機会費用 (=

imputed cost: ある特定の目的に資源を使う際, 選択可能な複数の方法からその一つを選択した場合, 断念した他の方法を選択した場合に得られたと思われる収益のことを「機会原価・費用」という)
▶We reduced our cash balance and working capital to lower our *opportunity costs* of maintaining that capital. 当社は，現金残高と運転資本を減らして，当該資本を維持するための当社の機会費用を削減しました。

opposition 名 反対, 抵抗, 反発, 反撃
▶There was unexpectedly strong *opposition* within and outside the company to the plan to sell off the company's main earner. 同社のドル箱である事業の全面売却案には，社内外から予想外の強い反発があった。

optical computer 光コンピュータ
▶Nanotechnology has been used to create a number of next-generation products, including a drug delivery system and *optical computers*. ナノテクノロジー（超微細加工技術）は，薬物送達システム（DDS）や光コンピュータなど，多くの次世代製品の開発に使われている。

optical fiber 光ファイバー
  optical fiber cable 光ファイバー・ケーブル (=optical cable)
  optical fiber communications 光ファイバー通信, 光通信 (=optical communications)
  optical fiber composite cable 光複合ケーブル
  optical fiber industry 光ファイバー工業
  optical fiber transmission 光ファイバー伝送

optical magnetic disk 光磁気ディスク (=magneto-optical disk, MO disk)
▶The personal data is stored in one of six files on an *optical magnetic disk* that the company created in December. この個人データは，同社が12月に作成した光磁気ディスク（MO）に収められている六つのファイルのうちの一つにある。

optimal 形 最適の, 最高の, 申し分のない (=optimum)
  optimal capital structure 最適資本構成 (=optimal leverage)
  optimal output 最適生産量, 最適産出量
  optimal production lot size 最適生産ロット・サイズ
  optimal purchasing lot size 最適購入ロット・サイズ, 最適発注量 (=economic order quantity, optimal order quantity)

optimal place production 最適地生産（各国で部品生産を分業して相互供給する方式）
▶An *optimal place production* method is now applied by Japan's major automakers in ASEAN countries. ASEAN（東南アジア諸国連合）域内の日本の大手自動車メーカーは現在，最適地生産方式をとっている。

optimization 名 最適化
  optimization model 最適化モデル
  portfolio optimization ポートフォリオの最適化

optimum 形 最適の, 適正な, 最善の, 最上の
  ex ante optimum program 事前最適計画
  ex post optimum program 事後最適計画
  optimum capacity 最適操業度
  optimum conditions 最適条件
  optimum resources allocation 最適資源配分 (=optimum allocation of resources)
  optimum stock 最適在庫量
  optimum size 適正規模, 最適規模

option 名 選択, 選択肢, 選択手段, 選択の余地, 選択科目, 選択権, 優先的選択権, 購入選択権, 売買選択権, 商品の有料付属品, 付加的機能, オプション取引, オプション (⇒exercise 名, stock option)
  exercise of option オプションの行使
  funding option 資金調達の選択肢, 調達手段の選択肢
  option holder オプション保有者, オプションの買い手
  option price オプション価格
  option trading オプション取引 (=option transaction)
  options cancelled 失効したオプション
  options exercisable 行使可能オプション
  options exercised 行使されたオプション
  options forfeited 失効オプション
  options granted オプション付与[授与], 許諾オプション
  options outstanding 未行使オプション, オプション残高
  options terminated 期限切れオプション
  put option 売付け選択権, 売る権利, プット・オプション
  stock option transaction ストック・オプション取引

▶Certain land and building leases have renewal *options* for periods ranging from three to five years. 特定の土地と建物のリースには，3−5年の期間の更新選択権がついている。
▶The right to exercise *options* generally accrues over a period of four years of continuous employment. オプションを行使する権利は，原則として勤務[在任]期間が4年を経過した時点で発

生します。

order 動 命じる, 命令を出す, 指示する, 指図する, 注文する, 発注する, 並べる, 陳列する
▸Mitsui Sumitomo Insurance Co. was *ordered* to halt sales of medical insurance products for an indefinite period from July 10.　三井住友海上火災保険が, 7月10日から医療保険商品販売の無期限停止命令を受けた。

order 名 注文, 注文書, 注文品, 受注品, 受注高, 命令, 順序, 秩序, オーダー
 administrative order　行政命令
 blanket order　一括注文
 budget for order-filling cost　注文履行費予算
 cash with order　現金注文, 注文時支払い条件《略 cwo》
 construction order　建設工事受注, 建設受注
 contingent order　条件付き注文 (= contingency order)
 delivered to order　指図人渡し
 delivery order　荷渡し指図書
 factory orders　製造業受注, 製造業受注高, 製造業新規受注高
 fill and kill order　即時執行注文
 firm order　確定注文, ファーム・オーダー
 good till canceled order　取消しまで有効注文, 出合い注文, オープン注文
 job order　製造指図書
 large order　大口注文 (=block order)
 limit order　指し値注文
 mail order business　通信販売事業 (=mail order activity)
 main order　主指図書 (=main production order)
 manufacture order　製造指図書, 生産指図書
 market order　成り行き注文
 new orders　新規受注高
 order and advance　前払い注文
 order-filling cost　注文履行費, 注文処理費 (包装費や輸送費など)
 order-getting cost　注文獲得費 (市場調査や製品計画, 広告宣伝販売促進などの費用)
 order size　発注量 (=order quantity)
 overseas orders　海外からの受注
 parts production order　部品製造指図書
 place a block order　大口注文を出す
 place a limit order　指し値注文を出す
 place a market order　成り行き注文を出す
 production order　製造指図書
 sales order　販売注文
 shipping order　船積み指図書
 specific order costing　個別原価計算 (= specific-order cost system)
 spread order　スプレッド注文
 standing order　継続製造指図書
 stop order　逆指し値注文, ストップ・オーダー
 tool order　工具指図書
 unfilled orders　受注残高, 受注残
 work order　製造指図書
▸At the TSE, securities firms input their *orders* for trading on computer terminals. The order is then transmitted via the computer system to the TSE, where the transaction is completed.　東証では, 証券会社がコンピュータ端末で株式売買の注文を入力すると, コンピュータ・システムを通じてその売買注文が東証に送られて, 取引が成立する。
▸The administrative *order* by the Financial Services Agency included the suspension of sales of nonlife insurance products at all of the company's outlets for two weeks.　金融庁の行政命令には, 同社全店舗での2週間の損保商品の販売停止が含まれている。

order backlog　受注残高, 受注残
▸*Order backlog* at December 31, 2008 was up six percent to $1.8 billion.　2008年12月31日現在の受注残高は, 6%増の18億ドルに達しました。

orders on hand　受注残高, 手持ちの受注分
▸Nearly half of the *orders on hand* are scheduled for delivery in 2009.　受注残高の半分近くは, 2009年中に納入することになっています。

ordinary 形 普通の, 通常の, 経常的
 ordinary annuity　普通年金, 期末年金, 年金
 ordinary dividend　普通配当
 ordinary expenditure　経常支出, 経常費用
 ordinary expenses　経常費, 通常費用 (= ordinary charges)
 ordinary income　経常利益, 経常損益, 通常の所得
 ordinary income and loss　経常損益
 ordinary loss　経常損失
 ordinary profit　経常利益
 ordinary profit and loss　経常損益, 経常損益の部
 ordinary share　普通株 (=common share, common stock, ordinary stock: 優先株や後配株のように特定の権利が与えられていない一般の株式)
 ordinary stock dividend　通常の株式配当
▸During the first nine moths of 2008, we invested $380 million in *ordinary* shares of the

company. 2008年1-9月期に，当社は3億8,000万ドルを投資して，同社の普通株式を取得しました。

organic 形 有機的な，組織的な，系統的な，有機体の，有機物質の
  organic beer 有機ビール
  organic farming 有機農業
  organic food 有機食品，自然食品
  organic organization 有機的組織，有機的システム
  organic vegetables 有機野菜，有機栽培野菜 (=organically grown vegetables)
  ▶Demand for *organic* beer brewed from hops grown without pesticides or fertilizers has grown amid deepened public concern over food safety. 食品の安全性への懸念が深刻化するなか，殺虫剤や化学肥料を使わないで栽培したホップで醸造する有機ビールの需要が高まっている。

organic electroluminescent screen 有機EL（エレクトロルミネッセンス）ディスプレー
  ▶*Organic electroluminescent screens* can display high-quality moving image. 有機EL（エレクトロルミネッセンス）ディスプレーは，高画質の動画を表示できる。

organic growth 有機的成長，有機的成長率，内部成長 (=organic: M&Aによる成長でなく，自社内で新規事業を成長させること)
  ▶Above 6% *organic growth* was achieved in the United States, with good performances in all key markets. すべての主要市場で業績が好調で，米国では6％以上の有機的成長率を達成しました。

organization 名 組織，機関，機構，団体，組織体，企業，会社，組織化，企画，企画力，段取り，構造，構成
  business organization 企業，企業組織，業務組織，実業団体，経済団体，財界団体
  consumer organization 消費者組織，消費者団体
  corporate organization 企業組織，企業の組織
  cost accounting organization 原価計算組織
  divisional organization 事業部制，事業部制組織
  financial organization 金融機関
  functional organization 機能的組織
  global organization グローバル企業
  governmental regulatory organization 政府規制機関
  human service organization 人的サービス機関
  interconnected organization ネットワーク型組織
  investment organization 投資機関
  marketing organization 販売組織，マーケティング組織
  member organization 会員会社
  organization chart 組織図，会社組織図
  organization climate 組織風土
  organization cost 創業費，創立費，開業費，設立費用 (=formation expense, organization expense, preliminary expense, promotion expense)
  organization development 組織開発
  organization form 組織形態
  organization goal 企業目標
  organization planning 組織計画
  organization structure 組織構造
  profit organization 営利企業，営利事業体，営利組織，営利団体 (=profit corporation)
  sales organization by product 製品別販売組織
  sales organization on markets 市場別販売組織
  service organization サービス提供機関
  voluntary organization 任意組合
  ▶Many major companies have been streamlining their *organizations*—selling operations, laying off employees, and so forth. 大企業の多くは，事業の売却，従業員解雇など，組織の合理化を進めてきた。

Organization of Petroleum Exporting Countries 石油輸出国機構《略 OPEC》

organizational 形 組織的な，組織上の，組織全体の，構造上の
  organizational behavior 組織行動
  organizational buyer 組織購買者
  organizational change 組織改革，組織改編，組織変更
  organizational climate 組織風土，経営風土，社風
  organizational code 組織規範
  organizational decision 組織的意思決定
  organizational design 組織設計，組織編制，組織計画，組織デザイン
  organizational development 組織開発，組織的発展
  organizational hierarchy 組織の階層，組織の序列，組織の上下関係
  organizational motivation 組織の動機づけ
  organizational orientation 組織志向
  organizational philosophy 組織理念
  organizational planning 組織計画
  organizational slack 組織スラック，組織上のたるみ
  organizational strategy 組織戦略
  organizational structure 組織構成，組織構造，

組織形態
organizational unit 組織単位
▶The biggest difference between the two reports on reforming NHK lies in the proposed *organizational* structure of NHK. NHK改革に関する両報告書の最大の相違点は，NHKの組織形態に関する提案だ．
▶The Corporation routinely reviews its business strategies, *organizational* structure and asset valuations, and implements changes deemed appropriate by management. 当社は，事業戦略，組織構成，資産評価をつねに見直し，経営陣が適切と判断した変更についてはそれを実施しています．

organize 動 組織化する，系統立てる，体系化する，まとめる，編成する，設立する，結成する，〈催しなどを〉準備する，用意する，手配する，運営する，開催する，主催する
　organize protests against a company 会社に対して抗議行動［運動］を組織する
　organized activity 組織的活動
　organized behavior 組織的行動，組織された行動
　organized boycott 組織的不買運動［行動］
　Organized Crime Control Act 米国の組織犯罪取締法
　organized decision making 組織的意思決定
　organized financial market 組織金融市場
　organized labor 組織労働，組織労働者
　organized market 規制市場
　organized speculation 組織的投棄
　organized worker 組織労働者
　organizing committee 組織委員会，発起人会
　right to organize 団結権

organizer 名 設立者，〈大会やイベントの〉組織者，主催者，開催団体，立案者，企画運営者，幹事，まとめ役，整理するもの，整理箱
　electronic organizer 電子手帳，システム手帳（＝personal organizer）
　event organizer イベント主催者，催し物の主催者
　political organizer 政治のまとめ役
　seminar organizer セミナー主催者，セミナー主催団体
Ford Motor Co. closed its five North American plants as part of its *overhaul plan*. 米フォード・モーターは，リストラ策の一環として同社の北米5工場を閉鎖した．
The weak dollar may decrease *overseas* investment in the U.S. market. ドル安で，海外の対米投資が減少する恐れがある．

orientation 名 方針，方針決定，方向，方向性，方向づけ，適応［順応］指導，進路指導，科目履修案内，態度，志向，オリエンテーション
　business orientation 事業の方向
　commercial orientation 経済的利益の追求
　consumer orientation 消費者志向
　customer orientation 顧客志向，顧客のニーズ
　export orientation 輸出志向，輸出主導型
　managerial orientation 経営者の志向
　marketing orientation マーケティング志向（＝marketing concept orientation）
　orientation for new recruits 新入社員に対するガイダンス
　production orientation 生産志向
　profit orientation 利益志向
　supply orientation 供給側志向
　sales orientation 販売志向

-oriented …志向の，…志向型，…集約型，…追求型の，…重視の，…に重点を置く，…中心の，…優先の，…偏重の，…向けの（＝-driven, -led, -minded）
　academic-oriented society 学歴偏重社会
　commodity-oriented area 市況商品的性格の強い分野
　consumer-oriented 消費者志向の，消費者重視の
　customer-oriented organization 顧客志向型組織
　domestic demand-led economy 内需主導型経済
　export-oriented companies 輸出企業，輸出志向型企業
　food-oriented supermarket 食品スーパー，食品重視のスーパー
　growth-oriented business strategy 成長志向型戦略，拡大志向型戦略
　high-tech oriented industries ハイテク企業
　import-oriented economy 輸入依存型経済
　labor-oriented 労働集約型
　market-oriented 市場原理に基づく，市場重視型，市場経済志向の
　marketing-oriented マーケティング志向
　needs-oriented ニーズ志向
　personal-oriented 個人専用の，個人重視の，個人優先
　problem-oriented language 問題向き言語
　production-oriented 生産志向
　urban-oriented industry 都市型産業
　user-oriented ユーザー志向，顧客志向，顧客第一主義
　value-oriented investor 価値志向の投資家

value-oriented management 価値重視の経営
▶Daiei will restructure its business to concentrate on food-*oriented* supermarkets and management of rental commercial complexes. ダイエーは，事業を再編して食品スーパーと賃貸複合商業ビルの管理事業に特化する方針だ。
▶Everyone connected with the Corporation, or the people we call our "stakeholders" will also benefit from value-*oriented* management. 当社とかかわりのある人たち，つまり当社の「ステークホルダー」といわれる人たち全員も，価値重視の経営によって利益を受けることになる。

original cost 取得原価，取得価額，原始原価，原初原価，歴史的原価，仕入原価，簿価
▶When we sell or retire plant that was depreciated using the group method, we deduct the *original cost* from the plant account and from accumulated depreciation. グループ償却法を用いて償却した工場を売却もしくは除却する場合，当社は当該工場の取得原価を当該資産勘定と減価償却累計額から控除します。

original equipment manufacturer 相手先ブランド［商標］製造業者《略 OEM》
▶"OEMs" refer to original equipment manufacturers. 「OEM業者」とは，相手先ブランド製造業者のことをいう。

original equipment manufacturing 相手先ブランドでの生産，相手先ブランドによる生産方式，生産委託契約

original equipment manufacturing arrangements OEM（相手先ブランドでの生産）契約
▶Under the latest corporate rebuilding plan, MMC intends to supply products through *original equipment manufacturing arrangements* to Nissan Motor Co. and Peugeot Citroen group. 今回の再建計画では，三菱自動車は，OEM（相手先ブランドでの生産）契約により日産自動車やプジョー・シトロエンに製品を供給する方針だ。

originate 考案する，発明する，開発する，創造する，創設する，実行する（＝create, develop, invent）
▶LICENSOR has *originated* or acquired sole licensing rights to certain computer software products and user's manuals. ライセンサーは，特定のコンピュータ・ソフトウエア製品とユーザー・マニュアルをすでに開発しているか，その独占的使用許諾権［ライセンス許諾権］をすでに取得している。

origination 考案，発明，開発，創造，創作，創設，発生，開始，起点，起因，実行，オリジネーション

loan origination fee 融資取組み手数料（＝origination fee）

origination fee 融資取組み手数料，取組み手数料，貸付け手数料，不動産担保ローン（mortgage loan）の取扱い手数料（＝loan origination fee）

origination standards 審査基準

OTC 店頭，店頭市場（＝over the counterの略）
Nikkei OTC stock average 日経店頭平均株価
OTC dealer 店頭ディーラー
OTC derivatives 店頭派生商品
OTC firm 店頭取引銘柄
OTC market 店頭市場
Tokyo OTC 東京店頭市場

outbid …よりも高い値を付ける
outfit 装い，装束
outflow 流出，流出額，アウトフロー（⇒capital outflow, inflow）
asset outflow 資産の流出，資産流出額
capital outflows 資本の流出，資本の海外流出，資本流出，対外投融資（＝outflows of capital）
cash outflow 支出，支払い額，キャッシュ・アウトフロー
investment outflow 投資支出額
long-term capital outflow 長期資本流出
net cash outflow 純支払い額
net inflow or outflow of capital 資本収支
outflow of funds 資金の流出，資金の海外流出
outflow of technology 技術の流出，技術の輸出
short-term capital outflows 短期資金の流出
▶The *outflow* of Japan's technical skills began in the late 1990s. 1990年代後半から，日本の技術力の流出が始まった。

outlay 支出，経費，出費（＝outgo; ⇒capital outlay）
budget outlays 財政支出
cash outlay cost 現金支出原価
consumer outlays 消費支出
discretionary outlays 裁量的支出
entitlement outlays 義務的経費
initial cash outlay 当初支出額
outlay for advertisement 広告費
outlays for capital equipment 設備投資（＝capital outlays）
outlays for plant and equipment (progress base) 設備投資（進捗ベース）
public works outlays 公共工事支出
▶The company's group net profit increased

significantly against the backdrop of Japanese firms' greater capital *outlays* on factories.　同社の連結税引き後利益は，日本企業の設備投資拡大を背景に，大幅に増加した。

outlet 名　販路, 市場, 小売店, 特約店, 出店, 店舗, 商店, …店, 発表の場, アウトレット
　affiliated sales outlet　系列販売店
　distribution outlet　販路
　giant outlet　大規模小売店
　outlet store　系列販売店
　retail outlet　小売店
　unprofitable outlet　不採算店舗
▸The company is expected to close its unprofitable *outlets* and divisions.　同社は，不採算店舗や事業部門を閉鎖する見通しだ。

outlook 名　見通し, 予測, 予想, 展望, 先行き, …観, 予報
　business outlook　景気見通し, 企業見通し, 業績見通し（＝business projection）
　financial outlook　財務見通し
　negative outlook　弱含みの見通し, ネガティブの見通し
　rating outlook　格付け見通し
　strong earnings outlook　力強い増益見通し, 高収益見通し
▸Moody's lowered Merrill Lynch's rating *outlook* to "negative" from "stable."　ムーディーズは，メリルリンチの格付け見通しを，「安定的」から「ネガティブ（弱含み）」に引き下げた。
▸Sony left unchanged its fiscal year sales *outlook* at ¥8.23 trillion.　ソニーは，今年度の売上高見通しを8兆2,300億円に据え置いた。

outplacement 名　転職斡旋, 再就職斡旋
▸The remaining provisions include $35 million for employee relocation and *outplacement* services.　残りの引当金には，従業員の配置換えや転職斡旋サービスの費用としての3,500万ドルも含まれています。

output 名　生産, 生産量, 生産高, 製作, 産出量, 産出高, 出力, アウトプット（⇒ **industrial output**）
　aggregate output　総生産高, 総生産量, 総産出高
　capital-output ratio　資本・産出量比率, 資本産出高比率
　optimum output　最適操業度（＝optimum capacity）
　output capacity　生産能力, 生産設備（＝production capacity）
　output cost　製造原価, 製作費
　output method　生産高比例法, アウトプット法
　output volume　生産量
　per-worker output　従業員1人当たり生産高
　real output　実質生産高, 実質産出高, 実質GDP
▸*Output* at domestic factories rose 0.2 percent in April from March.　4月の国内鉱工業生産は，前月比で0.2%増加した。
▸Toyota's global auto *output* is expected to increase 5% from a year earlier to reach 9.95 million units on a group basis in 2008.　トヨタの（子会社を含めた）グループ・ベースでの世界全体の自動車生産台数は，2008年には前年比5％増の995万台に達する見込みだ。

output adjustment　生産調整
▸There has been a conspicuous trend of *output adjustments* in industrial production, particularly for such products as semiconductors and electronic parts.　鉱工業生産は，半導体や電子部品を中心に，生産調整の動きが目立つ。

output ceiling　生産枠
▸The OPEC's oil production in July stood at 27.11 million bpd, 1.11 million bpd more than the *output ceiling* set for August.　石油輸出国機構（OPEC）の7月の原油生産高は日量2,711万バレルで，8月の生産枠を111万バレル（日量）上回った。

outright 形　無条件の, 即座の, 徹底的な, 完全な, 絶対的な, 公然の, まぎれもない, はっきりした, あからさまな, アウトライト
　outright buyouts of government bonds　国債の買切りオペレーション, 国債の買切りオペ（＝outright purchases of government bonds）
　outright exchange rate　アウトライト為替相場
　outright forward　アウトライト先物, 確定日渡し
　outright forward operation　先物操作
　outright loss　丸損
　outright majority　絶対多数
　outright recession　完全な景気後退
　outright sale　売切り（金融引締め策として，市中銀行の支払い準備を減少させるため，ニューヨーク連邦準備銀行が公開市場で財務省証券（Treasuries）などを買戻し条件なしで売却すること）
　outright transaction　アウトライト取引（売りっぱなし, 買いっぱなしの外国為替取引。外国為替の受渡しの時期によって直物と先物取引に分かれる）

outright purchase　無条件購入, 買切り, 買切りオペ, 買切りオペレーション（＝outright purchase operation: 金融緩和策として，市中銀行の支払い準備を増加させるため，ニューヨーク連邦準備銀行が公開市場で財務省証券（Treasuries）など

を売戻し条件なしで買い入れること）
implementation of outright purchase operations 買切りオペの実施
outright purchases of long-term government bonds 長期国債買切りオペレーション
the Bank of Japan's outright purchases of government bonds 日銀の国債買切りオペレーション
▶A likely measure to be adopted by the Bank of Japan's Policy Board is an increase in the central bank's *outright purchases* of long-term government bonds. 日銀政策委員会が取る措置として，日銀の長期国債買切りオペ（公開市場操作）の額の引上げが予想される。

outside director 社外取締役，外部取締役
（＝outside board director, outside board member）

社外取締役について➡米国企業の場合，取締役会のメンバーで業務執行の意思決定をするのが取締役（director）である。この意思決定を受けて実際の業務執行をするのが役員（officer）であるが，取締役のうち役員を兼務している者を内部取締役（inside director）といい，外部取締役（outside director）と区別している。外部取締役は，経営のチェック機能を高めるために置かれる社外の取締役で，アメリカの会社では取締役の半数を外部取締役にしなければならないことになっている。外部取締役は，一般に大手企業の社長，会長や経営コンサルタント，弁護士，会計士などが株主により選任されることが多い。

▶General Electric Co. has asked two of its *outside directors* to leave as of the end of December. ゼネラル・エレクトリック（GE）は，12月末日付で社外取締役2名の退任を求めた。

outsource 動 外部資源を活用する，外部委託する，外注する，社外調達する，業務委託する
▶Sanyo Electric Co. has decided to *outsource* all of its domestic refrigerator production to the top Chinese refrigerator maker. 三洋電機は，冷蔵庫の国内生産をすべて中国の家電大手に委託することを決めた。

outsourcing 名 外部資源の活用，外部委託，外注，社外調達，海外調達，業務委託，アウトソーシング（企業が周辺業務を外部に委託すること；⇒**business resources, human resources**）
outsourcing costs 業務委託料
outsourcing deal 業務委託契約
outsourcing of frozen food production 冷凍食品の生産委託
▶Japan Tobacco Inc. will cut *outsourcing* of frozen food production to China. 日本たばこ産業（JT）は，中国への冷凍食品の生産委託を縮小する方針だ。

outspoken shareholder もの言う株主
▶The firm is known as an *outspoken shareholder* because it has been involved in the reorganization of stock exchanges and financial institutions in Europe. 同社は，欧州での証券取引所や金融機関の再編にかかわるなどして，「もの言う株主」として知られている。

outstanding 形 未払いの，未決済の，未償還の，未履行の，未解決の，未決定の，未処理の，発行済み，すでに発生している，傑出した，とび抜けた，顕著な，目立った，特に優れた （⇒**debt outstanding**）
amount outstanding 残高，未払い金，発行残高，市中売却残高
average number of shares outstanding 期中平均発行済み株式数
bond outstanding 債券発行残高
commercial paper outstanding CP発行残高
contracts outstanding 事業年度末約高
loans outstanding 借入金残高，融資残高，貸付け残高
long term debt outstanding 長期負債残高
number of shares of stock outstanding 発行済み株式数
outstanding capital stock 株式発行高
outstanding checks 未決済小切手
outstanding common stock 外部発行済み普通株式，社外流通の普通株式 （＝outstanding common shares）
outstanding company 超優良企業
outstanding current accounts 当座預金残高
outstanding equities 発行済み株式，発行済み株式数
outstanding loan 融資残高，貸出残高，未決済貸付け金，借入金残高 （＝outstanding debt）
outstanding nonperforming loans 不良債権残高 （＝outstanding bad loans）
outstanding ordinary shares 発行済み普通株式
outstanding shares 発行済み株式，発行済み株式数，社外株式，社外発行株式，流通株式数 （＝outstanding capital stock, outstanding equities）
outstanding voting stock 発行済み議決権株式
principal outstanding 残存元本額
warrant outstanding 発行済みワラント
▶Unexercised stock options to purchase 30,000 shares of common stock at $22 per share were *outstanding* at the beginning and end of 2008.

2008年期首および期末には，1株当たり22ドルで普通株式3万株を購入できる未行使のストック・オプションが存在していた。

outstanding balance 未払い残高，残高
 outstanding balance of contracts 保有契約高，保有契約，保険の総額（＝outstanding）
 outstanding balance of current account deposits 当座預金残高（＝outstanding balance of current accounts）
 outstanding balance of government bonds 国債発行残高（＝outstanding balance of government bond issues）
 outstanding balance of lending 銀行の貸出残高
 outstanding balance of nonperforming loans 不良債権の残高（＝outstanding nonperforming loans）
 ▶The 10 life insurers reported a fall in the combined *outstanding balance* of individual life insurance and annuity contracts for five straight years. 生命保険10社の個人保険・年金の10社合計での保有契約高[保障の総額]が，5年[5期]連続で減少した。

outstanding debt 借入金残高，借入残高，債務残高，未払い残高，残高，未払い負債額，未償還負債，既存の債務（＝outstanding loan）
 ▶We unconditionally guaranteed all of the firm's *outstanding debt* at the end of March 2009. 当社は，2009年3月末現在の同社の未払い負債額をすべて保証しました。

outstanding letters of credit 信用状未使用残高
 ▶*Outstanding letters of credit* aggregated approximately $450 million and $190 million at December 31, 2008 and 2007, respectively. 2008年および2007年12月31日現在の信用状未使用残高は，それぞれ総額約4億5,000万ドルと1億9,000万ドルとなっています。

outstanding performance 際立った業績
 ▶Canon's *outstanding performance* is based on a rapid increase in the sales of digital cameras and equipment for the production of semiconductors and liquid crystal monitors. キヤノンの際立った業績は，基本的にデジタル・カメラや半導体・液晶パネル製造装置の販売の急成長にある。

outweigh 動 上回る，…より大きい，…より価値がある
 ▶Increases in interest payments on deposits *outweighed* credit cost falls. 預金の支払い増加のほうが，与信費用の低下より大きかった。

over-indebtedness 名 債務過多
over-the-counter 形 店頭の，店頭市場の，店頭売買の，店頭取引の《略 OTC》
 over-the-counter dealing 店頭取引
 over-the-counter market 店頭市場，店頭株市場，場外市場（＝OTC market, over-the-counter stock market）
 over-the-counter sale 店頭販売，店頭売買，窓口販売（＝OTC sale）
 over-the-counter services 窓口サービス
 over-the-counter stock market 株式店頭市場
 ▶FX margin trading can be conducted via *over-the-counter* dealings at securities companies and other financial institutions. 外国為替証拠金取引は，証券会社など金融機関の店頭取引で行うことができる。

over-the-counter drug 薬局[薬店]で購入できる一般用医薬品
 ▶Ten reports of deaths are suspected to be linked to eight types of *over-the-counter drugs*. 10件の死亡報告例は，薬局・薬店で市販されている8種類の一般用医薬品との関係が疑われている。

overage 名 余剰高，過多量
overallotment 名 追加割当て，オーバーアロットメント
overborrowed 形 借金しすぎた，金を借りすぎた
overbought 形 買い上がりすぎた《株・相場》
overcapacity 名 過剰設備，設備過剰，過剰生産能力
 ▶The U.S. auto industry has been reeling from the U.S. recession, quality problems, *overcapacity*, and stiff competition from Asian and European automakers. 米自動車業界は，景気後退や品質問題，過剰設備，アジアや欧州の自動車メーカーとの激しい競争で浮き足立っている。

overcapitalized 形 資本が過大評価された，資本をかけすぎた
overdraft 名 当座貸越し，当座借越し
overdrive the economy 景気を過熱する
 ▶Steel, cement and other manufacturers as well as construction companies are blamed for *overdriving the Chinese economy*. 鉄鋼，セメントなどの産業や建設業界が，中国の景気過熱[中国経済の過熱]の主因だ。

overdue 形 期限の経過した，満期の経過した，支払い遅延の，支払い期限の過ぎた，延滞の
 overdue charge 延滞金
 overdue interest 延滞利子，延滞金利
 overdue loan 延滞債権，返済期限経過貸付け金

overdue penalty 支払い遅延違約金
▸Ninety-one social insurance offices illegally reduced *overdue* charges by a total of about ¥1.09 billion to improve premium collection. 社会保険庁事務所91か所で，(健康保険や厚生年金の)保険料の徴収実績を上げるため，延滞金総額約10億9,000万円を不正に減額していた。

overfunding 名 財政資金過調達，オーバーファンディング

overhaul 名 再編，改革，見直し，リストラ
　financial overhaul plan 金融改革案，金融再編案
　overhaul of production processes 生産工程の見直し
　radical overhaul 抜本的改革 (= radical reform)
　structural overhaul 構造改革，機構改革 (= structural reform)

overhaul plan 改革案，リストラ策，再編策
▸U.S. Treasury Secretary Henry Paulson unveiled the *overhaul plan* of the U.S. financial regulatory system. ヘンリー・ポールソン米財務長官は，米国の金融監督制度の改革案を発表した。

overhead 名 間接部門，間接費，製造間接費，総経費，固定費
　administration overhead 一般管理費
　expenses and overhead 費用と経費
　general overhead 一般間接費，販売費・一般管理費 (= general expense, selling and administrative expenses)
　production overheads 製造間接費
　purchasing overhead 仕入間接費
▸Since early 2005, the *overhead* has decreased by more than 20,000 people. 2005年初め以降，間接部門の従業員は3万人以上減少しました。

overhead costs 間接製造費，間接費 (間接労務費，間接材料費と間接経費から成る)
▸The company plans to slash *overhead costs* both at home and abroad by such measures as reducing advertising expenses, and cutting expenses at its head office and in research and development departments. 同社は，宣伝費の削減，本社と研究開発部門の経費削減などで，国内・海外の製造間接費を削減する方針だ。

overheat 動 過熱する，インフレを起こす，オーバーヒートする
　cool down the overheated economy 景気の過熱感を沈静化する，過熱した景気を冷ます
　overheated economy 過熱した景気，過熱景気，景気の過熱，景気の過熱感
▸The U.S. policy of precautionary tight-money measures was taken to cool down the *overheated* economy and ease inflationary pressures. 景気の過熱感を沈静化し，インフレ圧力[インフレ懸念]を和らげるために，米国は予防的金融引締め策を取った。

overheating 形 過熱，景気過熱，オーバーヒート
　economic overheating 景気の過熱
　signs of overheating 過熱気味の様相，過熱気味の兆し
▸The growing U.S. economy is showing signs of *overheating*. 拡大している米景気は，過熱気味に推移している。

overkill 名 景気の冷やしすぎ

overlap 名 重複，重複部分，重複関係
▸Material interdependencies and *overlaps* exist among the Company's operating units. 当社の各事業体の間には，重要な相互依存と重複の関係が存在します。

overmanning 名 過剰雇用，雇用過剰，過剰人員配置

overnight loan 翌日物，翌日返済証券担保貸付け
▸Policymaking members of the U.S. FOMC voted unanimously to keep its trendsetting federal funds rate for *overnight loans* between banks at 1 percent. 米連邦公開市場委員会(FOMC)の政策決定メンバーは，銀行同士の翌日物のフェデラル・ファンド(FF)金利の誘導目標を，現行の1%に据え置くことを全会一致で決めた。

overseas 形副 海外[外国]の，海外向けの，海外への，対外，海外からの
　overseas borrowing 対外借入れ
　overseas branch 海外支店
　overseas debt 対外債務
　overseas demand 外需
　overseas investment 対外投資，海外への直接投資，海外投資，海外からの投資
　overseas operations 海外事業
　overseas shipments 輸出
　overseas subsidiary 海外子会社
　overseas transaction 海外取引

overseas earnings 海外収益
▸A weaker yen boosted *overseas earnings*. 円安が，海外収益を押し上げた。

overseas production 海外生産
▸Toyota now has 53 bases in 27 countries and territories by expanding its *overseas production*. トヨタは現在，海外生産を拡大して，生産

拠点が27国・地域で53拠点に達している。

overseas sales 海外売上高
▶The Corporation's goal is to expand its *overseas sales* to ¥50 billion within three years through mergers and acquisitions. 当社は、M&A（企業の合併・買収）を通じて3年以内に海外の売上高を500億円に拡大する目標を掲げています。

oversight 名 監視，監督，手落ち，手抜かり，見落とし，失策
　internal independent oversight board 社内独立監視委員会
　oversight agency 所轄官庁
　oversight body 監督機関
▶In order to stem a series of client defections, the internal independent *oversight* board of the accounting firm rushed out an initial set of management reforms for the firm. 一連の顧客離れを食い止めるため、同会計事務所の社内独立監視委員会は、最初の経営改善策を急きょ取りまとめた。

overstatement 名 過大表示，過大評価，過大計上，実際より多く計上すること
▶Freddie Mac revealed its earnings manipulation including billions of dollars of *overstatements* and understatements. フレディマック（米連邦住宅貸付抵当公社）は、数十億ドルの過大計上と過小計上を含めて利益の不正操作をしていたことを明らかにした。

overstock 名 過剰在庫
oversubscribed 形 申込みが募集額［発行数］を上回った
oversupply 名 供給過剰
overtime 名 残業，超過勤務，時間外労働（＝overtime work）
　overtime allowance 残業手当，時間外勤務手当（＝overtime pay, overtime premium）
　overtime pay 残業手当，超過勤務手当
　overtime premium 残業手当，超過勤務手当，時間外手当（＝overtime allowance）
　overtime work 残業，超過勤務，時間外労働
▶Wage earners' average *overtime* pay, a barometer of income conditions, rose 0.4 percent in September from the same month last year to ¥18,452. 9月の賃金労働者の平均残業手当（所得動向の指標）は、前年同月比で0.4％増の18,452円だった。

overtrade 動 能力以上の取引をする，支払い能力以上に購入する
overvalue 動 過大評価する（＝overstate）
　overvalued dollar ドル高，ドルの過大評価（＝strong dollar）
　overvalued stock 割高な株式
▶An *overvalued* dollar is seriously crimping U.S. manufacturers' ability to export. ドル高が、米国の製造業界の輸出力を大いに妨げている。
▶In spite of Mixi's robust performance, traders fear the company has been *overvalued*. ミクシィの業績好調にもかかわらず、証券業者は同社への過大評価を警戒している。

overweight 名 組入れ比率が高いこと，オーバーウエイト
overwork 名 過重労働，過度の労働，過労，超過勤務，オーバーワーク
　break down through overwork 過労で健康を害する，過労で病気になる
　death resulting from overwork 過労死（＝death by overwork, death from overwork）
▶*Overwork* has become a particularly serious issue due to recent corporate restructuring. 最近の企業のリストラで、過重労働は深刻な事態になっている。

ovno あるいは付け値に非常に近い最高額（or very near offer の略）
owe 動 …の支払い義務がある，…に借金がある，〈借金・義務を〉負っている
own 動 所有する，保有する，持つ（⇒**wholly owned subsidiary**）
　equally owned 折半出資している，共同所有している（＝jointly owned）
　family-owned company 同族経営企業
　fifty-percent-owned company 50％所有会社
　fully owned subsidiary 完全所有子会社，全額出資会社，100％子会社
　government-owned corporation 政府出資企業
　jointly owned 共同所有の，折半出資の（＝equally owned）
　less than 20% owned company 20％未満所有の会社
　majority owned company 過半数所有子会社（＝majority owned subsidiary）
　owned capital 自己資本
　privately owned company 株式非公開企業，非上場会社（＝privately held company）
　publicly owned company 株式公開企業，上場会社（＝publicly held company, publicly owned corporation）
　real estate owned 所有不動産，保有不動産
　state-owned company 国有企業
　wholly owned foreign firm 100％外資企業
▶Mitsubishi UFJ Merrill Lynch PB Securities Co.

is an equally *owned* private banking venture between Mitsubishi UFJ Financial Group and Merill Lynch Japan Securities. 三菱UFJメリルリンチPB証券は, 三菱UFJフィナンシャル・グループとメリルリンチ日本証券が折半出資している合弁会社だ.
▸On January 31, 2009, over 15,000 registered shareholders *owned* the remaining 47.2 percent of the outstanding common shares of the firm. 2009年1月31日現在, 15,000名余りの登録株主が, 同社の発行済み普通株式の残りの47.2%を所有しています.

owner 名 所有者, 所有権者, 権利者, 株主, 出資者, 企業主, 荷主, 船主, 〈プラント輸出契約の〉注文者, 発注者, 施主, オーナー
  at owner's risk 荷主危険持ちで
  beneficial owner 受益者, 実質所有者, 受益株主
  cargo owner 荷主, 貨物所有者
  factory owner 工場主
  joint owner 共有者
  majority owner 過半数株主
  managing owner 経営所有者
  owner control 所有者支配
  owner-manager 社主経営者, 所有者経営者
  owner of record 名義上の株主
  owner of the business 社主, 事業主, 店主
  owner's capital 自己資本, 株主資本, 株式資本
  owner's claims 株主の請求権
  owner's equity 自己資本, 株主資本, 資本, 所有者持ち分, 株主持ち分, 持ち分権, 所有権 (= net assets, net worth, owners' equity, shareholders' [stockkolders'] equity)
  owners' equity to total assets 自己資本比率
  owners' interest 所有者持ち分 (= owners' equity, ownership interest)
  stock owner 株式所有者
  virtual owner 実質的な所有者, 実質的な保有者, 事実上の保有者
▸Legally speaking, the shareholders are the *owners* of a joint stock company. 法律上, 株主が株式会社の所有者だ.

ownership 名 所有, 所有権, 所有者, 所有比率, 出資比率, 持ち株比率, 経営権
  acquire full ownership 完全子会社化する
  acquire ownership stakes in …へ資本参加する, …へ一部出資する, …株を一部取得する
  capital ownership 出資比率
  change of ownership 所有権の移転, 株式の譲渡
  control of ownership 経営権
  equity ownership 株式所有, 株主所有権, 自己資本, 持ち株比率
  equity ownership conditions 持ち株比率状況
  foreign ownership 外国人持ち株比率, 外国人保有比率, 外国資本の所有
  initial ownership 会社設立時の出資比率, 当初の出資比率 (= initial ownership interest)
  joint ownership 共同所有, 共有権
  majority ownership 過半数支配
  management ownership 経営所有
  ownership of affiliates 関連会社[関係会社]株式の所有比率
  ownership capital 株主資本
  ownership interest in subsidiaries 子会社所有持ち分
  ownership interest in the assets 資産の所有権
  ownership structure 出資構成, 株主構造, 株主構成
  public ownership 株式公開, 上場企業
▸Minority interests increased mainly because of the sale of 15% *ownership* in the company in June 2008. 少数株主持ち分は, 主に2008年6月に同社所有権の15%を売却したため, 増加しました.
▸Our *ownership* in the company will increase to 80 percent in 2009. 同社に対する当社の持ち株比率は, 2009年度には80%に増加します.

ozone-depleting solvent オゾン層を破壊する溶剤
ozone-depleting substance オゾン層破壊物質
▸The fulfillment of a commitment to eliminate an *ozone-depleting substance* from manufacturing facilities put the Corporation in the forefront of corporate environmental responsibility. 製造施設からオゾン層を破壊する物質を取り除く公約を果たして, 当社は環境保護に対する企業責任の面でも業界をリードしています.
ozone depletion オゾン破壊, オゾン層破壊
▸We will support industry cooperative efforts to solve industry problems, such as *ozone depletion*. 当社は, オゾン層破壊など業界が抱える問題を解決するための業界全体の協調努力を支援していく方針です.
ozone layer オゾン層

P

P&A 資産と負債の承継[継承], 資産・負債承継, P&A方式 (**purchase and assumption**の略)
- *P&A* has been used in more than 80 percent of all liquidation cases in the United States. アメリカでは, P&A(資産と負債の継承)方式が, 破綻処理全体の8割以上で活用されている.

P&I insurance 船主責任保険 (＝maritime protection and indemnity insurance: P&Iは**protection and indemnity**の略)
- Of 1,344 North Korean ships that entered Japanese ports last year, only 38 (2.8 percent) were covered by *P&I insurance.* 昨年日本に入港した北朝鮮の船舶1,344隻中, PI保険に加入していたのは38隻(2.8%)に過ぎなかった.

P&L 損益 (**profit and loss** の略)

pace 名 速度, 速さ, スピード, テンポ, 伸び, 足並み, 足どり, ペース (⇒moderate)

 be gathering pace スピード[ピッチ]が上がっている, 増えている, 本格化している, 激化している

 keep pace with inflation インフレと足並みを揃える

 pace of economic recovery 景気回復の足どり, 景気回復のピッチ

 pace of competition 競争のスピード

 pace of growth 成長のペース

 pace of rate reduction 利下げのテンポ

 pace of stockbuilding 在庫積上げのペース, 在庫増加のペース

- High energy and raw material prices as well as slumping housing investment have slowed the *pace* of growth. 住宅投資の落ち込みやエネルギー・原材料価格高の影響で, 景気が減速している.
- We increased our *pace* of growth with revenue increasing nine percent in 2008. 当社の成長のペースは上がっており, 2008年度の売上高は9%増加しました.

pace-setting innovation 先駆的な技術革新
- We are a company that not only embraces change, but leads it through *pace-setting innovations.* 当社は, 変化に対応するだけでなく, 先駆的な技術革新を通して変革をリードしています.

package 名 対策, 政策, 策, 案, 計画, プラン, 制度, 包括法案, 一括法案, 装置, 包装, 梱包, パッケージ

 a new package of antideflationary measures 第二次デフレ対策

 aggressive stimulus package 大型の財政出動

 aid package 支援策, テコ入れ策 (＝assistance package, rescue package)

 bailout package 救済策, 金融支援策, 緊急救助策

 combination package 組合せ包装

 deficit reduction package 赤字削減策

 early retirement and buyout packages 早期退職優遇制度

 economic package 景気対策, 経済対策

 economic stimulus package 景気刺激策

 employment package 一括雇用対策

 exceptional measure 例外的な措置, 特例

 fiscal package 財政刺激策, 財政面からの景気対策, 財政出動

 fiscal stimulus package 財政刺激策, 財政面での景気刺激策, 景気刺激策, 景気対策

 integrated package 総合対策, 統合対策, 総合政策, 統合政策

 loan package 円借款

package appearance 包装の外観, 包装の体裁
package consolidating agency 小口運送業者 (=freight forwarder)
package cost 包装費 (=packing cost)
package deal 一括取引, 一括購入, セット販売, 抱き合わせ商品, 抱き合わせ契約, 包括案 (=packaged deal)
package express 急送小荷物
package freight 小口扱い貨物運送
package goods 容器入り商品
package of antideflationary measures 総合デフレ対策
package program 既製番組
package service 一括サービス, セット・サービス
package software 既製のソフト, 市販ソフト, 汎用パッケージ・ソフトウエア
remuneration package 報酬, 給付, 謝礼, 代անあ, 報償
rescue package 支援策 (=aid package)
restructuring package 再建計画, リストラ策
retirement packages for executives 執行役員の退職金
software package ソフトウエア・パッケージ, 汎用ソフトウエア製品
stimulus package 景気刺激策, 経済対策
supplementary fiscal package 補正予算
supplementary package 景気対策
videoconferencing package テレビ会議装置

▶A financial aid *package* that includes a debt-for-equity swap and debt forgiveness was considered by the main banks. 債務の株式化 (銀行にとっては債権の株式化) や債権放棄などの金融支援策を, 主力取引銀行が検討した。

▶The U.S. government hammered out an emergency economic stimulus *package*. 米政府は, 緊急景気対策をまとめた。

▶This is a desktop videoconferencing *package* that lets remote computer users meet and work together without leaving their desks. これはデスクトップ型テレビ会議装置で, 遠隔地のコンピュータ・ユーザーは, それぞれデスクを離れることなく顔をつき合わせて共同作業をすることができます。

packaging 名 包装, 荷造り, 梱包, 内装, 包装材料, 梱包材料, 組合せ, 一括すること, パッケージング
  cross packaging 共通意匠包装
  dual-use packaging 二重用途包装
  novelty packaging 変わり包装
  packaging materials 包装材料, 包装資材
  sample packaging 見本包装

▶The make-up, packing, *packaging* and marking shall be at Seller's option. 組立て, 外装, 内装とマーキングは, 売り手の選択によるものとする。

packet 名 小さな包み, 束, パケット, 郵便物, 郵便船, 定期船, 動〈データ・情報を〉パケット単位に区切る

packing 名 包装, 梱包, 外装, 食品包装, 缶詰工業, パッキング
  bad packing 不良包装
  bale packing 俵包装
  case packing 木箱包装
  export packing 輸出包装
  inferior [inadequate] packing 不適当包装
  inner packing 内部包装
  outer packing 外装
  packing credit 前貸信用状, 輸出前貸付け信用状
  packing house 包装出荷工場, 包装出荷場, 食品包装工場, 缶詰工場, 小口運送業者
  packing inspection 包装検査
  packing list 包装明細書, 荷造目録
  packing note 包装指図書
  waterproof packing 耐水包装

▶Supplier shall, at its expense, pack all Products in accordance with Supplier's standard *packing* procedure. 供給者は, 供給者の費用で, 供給者の標準梱包手続きに従って本製品をすべて梱包する。

pact 名 国際間の協定, 条約, 協約, 契約, 約束, 議定書 (=protocol, treaty)
  alliance pact 提携契約
  commercial pact 通商条約
  free trade pact 自由貿易協定
  solidarity pact 連帯協定

▶The *pact*, formally called the Kyoto Protocol to the U.N. Framework Convention on Climate Change, was adopted by an international conference in Kyoto in 1997. 正式には気候変動枠組み条約京都議定書と呼ばれているこの条約は, 1997年に京都で開かれた国際会議で採択された。

▶The strategic alliance *pact* is aimed at strengthening their leadership in probiotics. この戦略的提携契約は, 腸内乳酸菌 (プロバイオテクス) 市場での主導的地位の強化を目指している。

paid-in capital 払込み資本, 払込み資本金, 発行済み資本金 (=paid-up capital: 株主が会社の株式取得に払い込んだ金額で, これまで発行した株式の総発行価額に相当する。資本金 (capital stockまたはcommon stock) と払込み剰余金 (paid-in surplusまたはcapital in excess of par value) を合わせたもの)
  additional paid-in capital 株式払込み剰余金,

払込み剰余金, 資本剰余金
initial paid-in [paid-up] capital　設立時の払込み剰余金, 当初払込み資本金
paid-in capital in excess of par　額面株式払込み剰余金
paid-in surplus　払込み剰余金　(=contribution surplus)
▶An amount equal to the par value of the additional shares issued has been transferred from additional *paid-in capital* to common stock due to the two-for-one stock splits.　追加発行株式の額面価額相当額が, 1対2の株式分割により, 株式払込み剰余金から普通株式に振り替えられました。

panel 名　討論会, 座談会, 委員会, 小委員会, 審査会, 審議会, 委員団, 審査団, 調査団, 講師団, 専門家集団, 制御盤, 計器盤, パネル　(⇒**WTO panel**)
consumers' panel　消費者パネル, 消費者グループ
control panel　制御盤, コントロール・パネル
corporate reform panel　経営改革委員会
disciplinary panel　懲罰委員会
front panel　前面操作盤, フロント・パネル
government advisory panel　政府諮問委員会
independent panel　独立委員会
management reform panel　経営改革委員会
panel arbitrator　名簿仲裁人
panel conference　公開検討会, パネル・コンファレンス
panel discussion　公開討論会, 代表討論会, 討論会, パネル・ディスカッション
panel research　パネル調査　(=panel survey)
panel survey　パネル調査, パネル・サーベイ（マーケティング調査法の一つ）
tender panel method　競争入札制度
working-level panel　事務レベルの委員団
▶The management reform *panel* will seek help from major creditors for the capital increase at the company.　経営改革委員会は, 同社の増資に対する支援を, 主要取引行に要請する方針だ。

panelist 名　〈パネル・ディスカッションの〉講師［討論者］, パネラー, パネリスト

paper 名　手形, 証券, 債券, 文書, 書類, 資料, 論文, 新聞, 紙, ペーパー　(⇒**commercial paper**)
accommodation paper　融通手形　(=accommodation bill)
business paper　業務書類, 商用手形, 商業手形
corporate paper　社債
export paper　輸出手形
financial paper　有価証券報告書, 金融手形
fine paper　優良手形
government paper　国債, 政府発行有価証券
original papers　原本書類
paper loss　含み損, 評価損
paper profit　含み益, 架空利益
paper profit or loss　含み損益, 評価損益
primary paper　新発債　(=new paper)
recycled paper　再生紙
short paper　短期証券
valuable paper　有価証券
white paper　白書

paperwork 名　文書業務, 文書処理, 事務処理, 書類事務, 事務の仕事, 書類
▶Taking into account a few extra days to complete *paperwork*, the two companies expect to finalize the tender procedure by their general shareholders meetings.　事務処理にかかる数日間を考慮して, 両社は, 株主総会までに株式公開買付け(TOB)の手続きを完了したいとしている。

par value　額面（「額面」は, 株式や社債の券面に記載されている払込みの最低単位）, 額面価格, 額面額, 額面金額（「額面金額」は, 株主が払い込んだ金額のうち法定資本金(legal capital)に組み入れる金額）, 為替平価
change in par value　額面変更
par-value capital stock　額面株式, 額面額資本金　(=par value capital)
par value of the stock　株式の1株当たり額面
par value stock　額面株式, 額面株　(=share with par value, stock at par, stock with par value)
stock with par value　額面株
stock without par value　無額面株
under-par value investment trust　額面割れ投信
▶The Board of Directors declared a two-for-one stock split in the form of a 100% stock dividend for $1.5 *par value* common stock.　取締役会は, 100％株式配当形式で額面1.5ドル普通株式の1株を2株にする株式分割を行うことを公表した。

parachute 名　解雇手当, 退職金　(⇒**golden parachute**)

paradigm 名　理論的枠組み, 枠組み, 構図, 模範, 範例, 典型, 例, 実例, パラダイム　(=example, framework, pattern, typical example)
conventional paradigm　従来の枠組, 従来のパターン
paradigm of bid rigging　談合の構図
paradigm shift　根本的変化, 抜本的変革, 社会の価値観の移行, 社会全体の枠組みの転換［変

化], パラダイムの転換, パラダイム・シフト （= paradigm change）
regulatory paradigm 規制の枠組
scientific paradigm 科学的パラダイム
the norms and paradigms of human lives 社会の規範とパラダイム
▶The challenge for the management of international companies is that all the aspects of the rapidly changing global economy have driven a *paradigm* shift from an industrial to an information society. 国際企業経営者の課題は, 急速に変化する世界経済のあらゆる側面が, 工業社会から情報化社会へパラダイムが移行してしまったことである。

parallel 形 並行の, 平行の, 並列の, 同時並行的, パラレル
parallel clearing 相互決済
parallel computer 並行処理計算機, 並列計算機, パラレル・コンピュータ
parallel development 並行開発
parallel import 並行輸入
parallel issue 並行起債
parallel loan 並行借款, 並行借入れ, パラレル・ローン
parallel market 並行市場 （= parallel money market）
parallel price 並行価格
parallel pricing 並行的価格設定, 追随的価格設定
parallel processing 並行処理, 並列処理
parallel rate 並行為替相場
parallel shift 平行移動
parallel transfer 並列転送, パラレル転送

parameter 名 要素, 要因, 係数, 母数, 助変数, 媒介変数, パラメーター
adjustment parameter 調整パラメーター
parameter space 母数空間
planning parameter 計画パラメーター
population parameter 母数
qualitative parameter 質的要因
scale parameter 尺度パラメーター

parent 名 親会社, 母体, 根源, 単独ベース
at the parent base [basis] 単独ベースで
on a parent-only basis 単独ベースで
parent-basis earnings forecast 単独ベースの収益見通し （= parent-only earnings forecast）
parent basis EBITDA multiple 単独ベースのEBITDA倍率
parent capex 単独ベースの設備投資 （= parent capital spending）
parent operating profit 単独ベースの営業利益
parent recurring profit 単独経常利益
parent sales 単独ベースの売上高
▶Under the new Corporate Law, a subsidiary of a foreign company is allowed to use shares of the *parent* to acquire a Japanese company. 新会社法では, 外国企業の子会社が親会社の株を用いて日本企業を買収することができる。

parent company 親会社
▶All companies that have been listed on the TSE from January 1996 are required to provide management information on their *parent companies* and affiliates. 1996年1月以降に東証に上場した企業は, すべて親会社とグループ企業［関連会社］の経営情報を提供するよう義務付けられている。

parent-only pretax profit 単独ベースの税引き前利益, 単独ベースの経常利益
▶The firm posted a *parent-only pretax profit* of ¥302 million for the March-August period. 同社は, 8月中間決算で［3-8月期に］3億200万円の連結経常利益［連結税引き前利益］（単独ベース）を計上した。

Paris Club パリ・クラブ, 主要債権国会議 （開発途上国の公的債務の救済策について非公式に話し合う日米欧19か国の定期会議。パリにある仏財務経済産業省で行われるため, パリ・クラブと呼ばれている）

parity 名 平衡, 平価, 為替平価, 等価, 等量, 同等, 同格, 対応, 類似, パリティー
exchange parity 為替平価, 為替交換平価
income parity 所得均衡, 所得パリティー
interest parity 金利平価
international parity 国際比価
parity adjustment 平価調整
parity index パリティー指数
parity of treatment 均等待遇
parity price パリティー価格
parity ratio パリティー比率
purchasing power parity 購買力平価

park 名 公園, 地区, …街, 遊園地, テーマ・パーク, イベント広場, 試合場, 競技場, パーク （特定用途に使うように設計された区画）
car park 駐車場
industrial park 工業団地
marine park 海中公園
theme park テーマ・パーク

participant 名 参加者, 参加企業, 参加行, 参加国, 加入者, 受講者, 出席者, 関係者
active plan participants 在職制度加入者

industry participant 業界参加者
market participant 市場参加者, 市場参入企業, 市場関係者 （＝market player）
participant in the dividend reinvestment plan 配当金再投資制度加入者
transaction participant 取引参加者

▶Market *participants* pointed out the issuance of new shares would dilute the value of the company's existing shares. 市場関係者は, 増資［新株発行］によって同社の既存株式の価値が損なわれる, と指摘している.

▶The proxy form indicates the number of shares to be voted, including any full shares held for *participants* in the Employee Stock Purchase Plan. 委任状用紙には, 従業員株式購入制度加入者のために保有している株式をすべて含めて, 行使される議決権数が記載されています.

participate 動 参加する, 参入する, 進出する, 加入する, 関与する
nonparticipating preferred stock 非参加優先株式
nonparticipating stock 非参加株
participating bond 利益参加社債
participating capital stock 参加株式
participating dividend 参加配当
participating preferred stock 参加優先株式

▶In order to *participate* in this market in a major way, we are devoting substantial resources to aggressive product development programs. この市場に本格的に参入するため, 当社は現在, 大型の製品開発計画に多くの経営資源を投入しています.

participation 名 参加, 参入, 進出, 加入, 関与, 貢献, 出資 （＝involvement）
capital participation 資本参加 （＝equity participation）
equity participation 資本参加, 出資（capital participation）, 株式投資
equity participation rates 出資比率
human participation 人的貢献
management participation 労働者の経営参加
participation financing 複数の銀行による協調融資, 共同融資, 参加融資 （＝participation loan）
participation loan 複数の銀行による協調融資, 共同融資, 参加融資 （＝participation financing）
participation right 参加権, 配当権
profit participation 利益分配

▶This program encourages *participation* and sharing of our results by each employee in the company. この制度は, 当社の業績に各従業員が参加し, その成果をそれぞれが分かち合うことを奨励しています.

particulars 名 詳細, 明細書
particulate matter 粒子状物質《略 PM》

▶Plans to reduce the overall amount of nitrogen oxides and *particulate matter* emitted by automobiles were approved by a government council on environmental pollution control. 自動車から排出される窒素酸化物と粒子状物質(PM)の総量削減計画が, 政府の公害対策会議で了承された.

partner 名 共同経営者, 共同出資者, 共同所有者, 提携者, 提携先, 事業提携先, 提携企業, 組合員, 社員, パートナー （⇒business partner）
capital partner 資本提携先 （⇒change of control）
dormant partner 匿名組合員
equity partner 資本参加者, 出資者
general partner 無限責任社員
interested parties 利害関係者 （＝interest group, interest parties, interested persons: 株主や債権者, 取引先, 顧客などをいう）
joint partner 共同出資者, 共同パートナー
social partner 労使団体, ソーシャル・パートナー
strategic partner 戦略的パートナー

partnership 名 共同出資, 共同所有, 共同経営, 提携, 連携, 協力, 組合, 合名会社, パートナーシップ （⇒capital and business partnership）
business partnership 業務提携 （＝business alliance, business tie-up）
equal partnership 折半出資, 対等提携, 対等な協力関係
form a partnership 提携する, 提携を結ぶ
interests in certain partnership 特定パートナーシップの持ち分
limited liability partnership 有限責任事業組合, 有限責任パートナーシップ《略 LLP》
partnership shares パートナーシップの株式
public private partnership パブリック・プライベート・パートナーシップ《略 PPP》（民間の資金やノウハウを導入して税金の効果的で効率的な活用を図るため, 企業や非営利組織が参加して公共サービスを提供する手法の総称）
three-way partnership 3社共同契約
voluntary partnership 任意組合

▶Limited liability *partnership* (LLP) is a new form of business entity that is not a joint stock company or business union. 有限責任事業組合

(LLP) は，株式会社でもなく，事業組合でもない新しい事業体だ。
▶We have continued to strengthen our *partnership* with our customers. 当社は，継続してお客さまとの連携を強化してきました。

partnership interest パートナーシップ持ち分，パートナーシップの利権
▶*Partnership interests* are recorded at equity. パートナーシップ持ち分は，持ち分価額で評価しています。

party 名 当事者，契約当事者，関係者
　both parties 両当事者 (=the two parties)
　each party 各当事者 (=each of the parties)
　either of the parties hereto 本契約のいずれか一方の当事者 (=either party)
　one of the parties 当事者の一方
　other party 他方の当事者，相手方，相手方当事者
　the concerned parties 利害関係人
　the parties hereto 本契約当事者，当事者

pass 動 〈法案などを〉可決する，〈判断[判決]を〉下す，伝える，回す，委ねる，譲渡する，〈範囲を〉越える
　pass a bill 法案[議案]を可決する
　pass along [on] to consumers 消費者に還元する，価格に転嫁する
　pass higher costs to customers コスト増を顧客に転嫁する
　pass on credit risk 信用リスクを回避する
　pass on the lower prices of crude oil to users 原油価格の低下をユーザーに還元する
　pass sentence on …に判決を下す，…に判決を述べる
▶Japan's banking groups were not able to *pass* on the higher fund-raising costs fully to borrowers by raising lending rates. 日本の銀行・金融グループは，貸出金利を引き上げて資金調達のコスト増を融資先に十分転嫁することができなかった。

pass-along 形 二次的…，回読による，パス・アロングの

passenger transportation 旅客輸送
▶*Passenger transportation* on international flights has been sluggish. 国際線の旅客輸送は，低迷している。

passive 形 受動的な，受け身の，不活発な，活気のない，〈借金が〉無利息の，無配当の，利息を生まない，パッシブ
　passive balance 国際収支の赤字 (=adverse balance, balance of payments deficit, unfavorable balance)

passive belt 自動シートベルト
passive business 受動的事業
passive damages 逸失利益
passive debt 無利息の負債，受動的公債
passive income 受動的所得
passive investment 受動的投資
passive loss 受動的損失，パッシブ損失
passive management パッシブ運用
passive protection 受動的保護装置，自動式搭乗者保護装置
passive restraint 自動保護装置，安全装置 (エアバッグやシートベルトなど)
passive smoking 受動喫煙
passive trust 受動信託，消極信託

past service 過去勤務，原始過去勤務
　past service cost 過去勤務年金費用，過去勤務費用，原始過去勤務原価
　past service liability 過去勤務債務
▶When we adopted the new standard, we had an accumulated liability for benefits related to the *past service* of active employees. 新基準を採用した時点で，当社は現従業員の過去勤務に関連した給付について，累積債務がありました。

patent 名 特許，特許権，特許物件，特許証，特権，権利，公有地譲渡証書，パテント，形 明白な，公開の
　BM patent ビジネス・モデル特許，BM特許，ビジネス方法の特許 (=business model patent, business method patent, patent for a business model)
　cession of a patent 特許権の譲渡
　dominant patent 基本特許
　patent agent 弁理士，特許弁理士 (=patent attorney)
　patent application 特許出願
　Patent Cooperation Treaty 特許協力条約
　patent defect 明白な瑕疵(かし)，明白な欠陥
　patent description 特許明細，特許説明書
　patent dispute 特許紛争
　patent examination 特許審査
　patent license agreement 特許ライセンス契約，特許実施許諾契約
　patent licensing 特許許諾，特許実施許諾
　patent management 特許管理
　patent marking 特許表示
　patent on one-click technology ワンクリック特許
　patent owner 特許権者 (=patent holder)
　patent pending 特許出願中，特許審査中
　patent property 特許権 (=patent right)

pioneer patent 基本特許, 開拓特許, パイオニア特許
process patent 方法特許, 製法特許
product patent 製品特許
pro-patent policy 特許重視政策, プロパテント政策
share patents on basic techniques 基本技術に関する特許を相互利用する
use of a patent 特許権の使用
▶Under the deal, Toyota will license to Volkswagen all its *patents* concerning direct-injection gasoline engines. 両社の取決めによると, トヨタが直噴型ガソリン・エンジンに関するすべての特許をフォルクスワーゲン(VW)にライセンス供与する。

patent infringement 特許侵害, 特許権侵害, 特許抵触 (=patent violation)
▶Sony Corp. has agreed to pay $40 million to Ampex Corp. to settle a lawsuit filed by the U.S. visual information technology company over *patent infringement* on its digital camera-related technology. デジタル・カメラ関連技術の特許権侵害をめぐって米国の視覚情報技術会社のアンペックスが起こした訴訟を和解で解決するため, ソニーは, アンペックスに4,000万ドル支払うことに同意した。

patent protection 特許保護
▶Our basic stance toward *patent protection* is to fight such paten infringements openly and squarely. このような特許侵害については正々堂々と対応するのが, 当社の特許保護に対する基本姿勢だ。

patent violation 特許侵害, 特許権侵害, 特許抵触 (=patent infringement)
▶We have discussed the *patent violation* problem with the company in Taiwan, which has been manufacturing the LCDs in question. 問題の液晶パネルを製造している台湾の同社とは, 特許侵害問題で交渉している。

pattern 様式, 形式, 様相, 動向, 傾向, 方向性, 型, 類型, モデル, 見本, 手本, サンプル, 範疇, デザイン, 模様, パターン
behavior [behaviour] pattern 行動様式
consumption pattern 消費パターン (=pattern of consumption)
cost behavior pattern 原価変動の動向
flying geese pattern 雁行型
investment pattern 投資パターン
pattern of forecast returns 予想収益率
pattern recognition パターン認識
remain in a holding pattern 模様眺めになる
social patterns 社会の様式, 社会の構造
▶The subprime issue means individual consumption *patterns* in the United States are inevitably going to change. サブプライム問題で, 米国の個人の消費パターン[消費行動]が今後変調することは避けられない。

pave the way for …に道を開く, …への道を開く, …を可能にする
▶The agreement *paves the way for* the firm to fully enter the aviation business through the partnership with GE. この契約で同社は, ゼネラル・エレクトリック(GE)との提携により航空事業に本格的に参入することが可能になる。

pawn 質(しち), 抵当物, 入質
pawnbroker 質屋, 質店営業者

pay 支払う, 支出する, 負担する, 返済する, 弁済する, 利潤をもたらす, 利益になる, 採算が取れる, もうかる
capital paid in 払込み資本
capital paid-in excess of par value 株式払込み剰余金, 額面超過金 (=share premium, paid-in surplus)
pay at sight 一覧払い
pay for losses 損失を補填する
pay in advance 前払いする
pay in full [part] 全額支払う, 全額払い込む, 完納する
pay up 完済する, 全額支払う, 決済する
pay when due 期限どおりに支払う, 支払い期日どおりに支払う
▶Foreign firms were allowed to *pay* the merger consideration only in the form of shares of the subsidiary. 外国企業の場合, 合併の対価は(日本に設立した)子会社の株式でしか支払うことができなかった。
▶We will *pay* a dividend of ¥50 per share for the first half. 当社は, 上半期の配当支払い額を1株当たり50円にする方針です。

pay 賃金, 給料, 手当, 報酬
maternity pay fund 出産手当基金
pay according to ability 能力給
pay according to function 職務給
pay-as-you-earn 源泉課税, 即金主義, 現金払い主義, 現金払い方式《略 PAYE》 (=pay-as-you-go)
pay cut 減給, 賃金カット, 報酬カット, 減俸
pay-for-age structure 年功序列賃金構造
pay level 賃金水準, 給与水準
pay rise 賃上げ, 昇給 (=pay hike, pay in-

crease, pay raise)
pay structure 賃金構造, 給与構造
pay system 賃金制度, 賃金体系, 給与制度 (＝wage system; ⇒**merit-based pay plan [system], performance-based**)
▸The company imposed 30 percent *pay* cuts for three months on two senior executive officers. 同社は, 常務執行役員2人について3か月間3割減給の処分にした.

pay-as-you-go 名 現金払い方式, 現金払い主義, 源泉課税方式, 源泉徴収方式, 独立採算制, 無借金の (＝pay-as-you-earn)
pay-as-you-go financing plan 賦課方式 (＝pay-as-you-go system)
pay-as-you-go formula 賦課方式, 源泉課税方式, 現金払い方式 (＝pay-as-you-go basis, pay-as-you-go plan)
pay-as-you-go method 源泉徴収方式, 源泉課税方式 (＝pay-as-you-earn method, pay-as-you-go basis)

pay-as-you-go accounting 現金主義会計
▸In our former *pay-as-you-go accounting*, we booked our contribution to trust funds for life insurance benefits as they occurred. 従来の現金主義会計では, 生命保険給付についての信託基金への拠出額は, その発生時に計上していました.

pay-as-you-go basis 現金主義, 現金基準, 現金払い方式, 現金払い主義, 独立採算制
▸This table shows our actual postretirement benefit costs on a *pay-as-you-go basis* in these years. この表は, これら各年度の実際の退職後給付費用を, 現金基準で表示したものです.

pay down debt 債務を返済する
▸New York Times will sell its nine TV stations for $575 million to *pay down debt*. ニューヨーク・タイムズは, 債務返済のため, 傘下のテレビ9局を5億7,500万ドルで売却する.

pay hike 賃上げ, 賃金引上げ (＝pay increase)
▸The union of Mitsubishi Heavy Industries Ltd. requested a basic monthly *pay hike*. 三菱重工業の労組は, 月給の基本給引上げを要求した.

pay off 〈借金などを〉完済する, 借金を返す, 返済する, 返還する, よい結果を生む, うまく行く, 実を結ぶ, 引き合う
pay off a loan 借入金[ローン]を返済する
pay off the public funds 公的資金を返済する
▸Maturing commercial paper was *paid off*. 満期を迎えたコマーシャル・ペーパー (CP) が, 償還された.
▸The bank has already *paid off* the injected public funds. 同行は, (国から) 注入を受けた公的資金をすでに完済している.

pay out 支払う, 〈積立金を〉払い戻す
pay out a larger percentage of earnings 配当性向を高める
pay out dividends 配当金を支払う
▸A payout ratio refers to the percentage of a company's profits to be *paid out* to shareholders in the form of dividends. 配当性向とは, 配当の形で株主に支払われる企業の利益の比率[企業の利益のなかから株主への配当に回す比率]のことだ.

pay plan 賃金制度, 報酬制度
▸In return for abolishing retirement allowances for directors, more companies are introducing a merit-based *pay plan*. 役員退職慰労金[役員退職金]を廃止する代わりに, 業績連動型の報酬制度を導入する企業が増えている.

payable 形 支払うべき, 支払い満期の, 支払い期限に達した, 支払い期日の到来した, 支払われる, 名 未払い勘定, 仕入れ債務, 買掛金
bill payable at a fixed period after sight 一覧後定期払い手形
bill payable at sight after a fixed period 確定日後一覧払い手形
estimated taxes payable 見積り未払い税額
loan payable from officer 役員借入金
note payable to subsidiary 子会社支払い手形
payable period 回収期間 (＝payback period)
payables 債務, 支払い債務, 未払い金, 未払い勘定 (＝debt, liability)
payables in foreign currency 外貨建て債務
rent payable account 未払い賃借料勘定
▸Interest is *payable* semiannually on December 1 and June 1. 利息は, 12月1日と6月1日の6か月ごとに支払われる.

payback 名 現金回収, 資本回収, 投資利益, 投資利益を上げるまでの期間, 返済
payback agreement ペイバック・アグリーメント (社員が短期間で退職する場合, 会社が負担した経費の一部を社員が返済する雇用契約)
payback period 現金回収期間, 投資回収期間, 回収期間, 返済期間
payback reciprocal 回収期間逆数

paycheck 名 給料支払い小切手, 給料小切手, 給料
payday 名 給料日, 支給日
PAYE 源泉課税[徴収] (**pay as you earn** の略)
payload 名 給与支払い用経常負担(金), 料金徴収荷重, 有償荷重, 有償搭載量, 有償重量

payment 名 支払い, 払込み, 振込み, 決済, 納入, 返済, 弁済, 支払い金額, 債権 (⇒ **interest payment**)
 automatic payment 自動振込み, 自動支払い
 commission payments 手数料収入
 debt payment 債務支払い, 債務返済
 deferred payment 延べ払い, 後払い
 initial payment 頭金, 一時金, 契約金 (＝initial sum)
 installment payment 分割払い, 割賦返済 (＝payment in installment)
 loan principal payments 借入金返済額
 means of payment 支払い方法
 on-the-spot payment 即時決済
 payment against documents 書類[船積み書類]引換払い, 証券引換払い
 payment at full 全額払い (＝payment in full)
 payment at sight 一覧後払い
 payment by bill 手形払い
 payment by cash 現金払い
 payment by check 小切手払い
 payment by results 業績給, 能率給, 成果分
 payment commission 支払い手数料
 payment day 支払い日, 支払い期日, 払込み日, 配当支払い日
 payment(s) due 満期支払い金, 満期支払い額, 未払い金
 payment in advance 前払い, 前金払い
 payment in part 内払い, 部分返済, 一部返済
 payment in suspense 仮払い金
 payment on delivery 引換え払い, 受渡し払い
 payment on demand 要求払い
 payment statement 支払い明細書 (＝payment slip)
 payment system 代金決済方法
 payment terms 決済条件, 支払い条件, 支払い期限
 principal payment 元本返済, 元金返済
 security payment 保証金, 敷金
 sight payment 一覧払い
▸Common shares may be purchased at the average market price by voluntary cash *payments* of as little as US $40 to a maximum of US $4,000 during a quarter. 当社の普通株式は, 1四半期に最低40米ドルから最高4,000米ドルまでの範囲で任意現金支払いにより, 平均市場価格で購入することができます.
▸The newly introduced installment plan allows purchasers to pay no initial *payments*. 新たに導入された割賦制度では, 購入者は頭金[契約金]の支払いが不要となっている.

payment transaction 支払い事務
▸Local governments have designated local banks, shinkin banks and other establishments as financial institutions to handle public money and *payment transactions*. 地方自治体は, 地元の銀行や信用金庫などを, 公金の収納や支払い事務を取り扱う金融機関に指定している.

payoff 名 〈給料などの〉支払い, 〈借金などの〉完済, 決済, 〈預金の〉払戻し, 報酬, 利得, 利益, 利益供与, 賄賂(わいろ), 回収, 成果
 payoff of market reform 市場改革の成果
 payoff period 回収期間
 payoff scandal 贈収賄事件, 利益供与事件 (＝payoff case)
 political payoffs 政治献金
▸The *payoff* for this heavy investment in research and development is the acceptance of our products by customers around the world. この大幅な研究開発投資の成果として, 当社の製品は世界中のお客さまに受け入れられています.
▸There were the *payoff* and falsification of financial statements in a series of scandals involving the company. 同社の一連の企業不祥事としては, 利益供与や有価証券報告書の虚偽記載などがあった.

payoff system ペイオフ制度
▸Under the *payoff system*, the guaranteed refund in the event of a bank's failure will be capped at ¥10 million of principal plus accrued interests in savings deposits. ペイオフ制度では, 銀行が破綻した場合, 預金払戻しの保証額は元本1,000万円までと貯蓄預金の利息[発生利息]となる.

payout 名 支払い, 支出, 支出金, 〈株式などの〉配当[配当金], 〈保険金の〉支払い, 支払い保険金, 〈社会保障の〉給付金, 回収
 expected payout ratio 期待配当性向
 payout percentage 配当性向, 配当支払い率, 配当比率 (＝payout ratio)
 pension payout 年金の支払い
 payout period 投資回収期間 (＝payback period)
 payout ratio [rate] 配当性向, 実質引受手数料率, ペイアウト比率 (＝dividend payout, payout percentage: 企業の利益のなかから株主への配当に回す比率のこと)
▸There are moves among listed companies to raise *payout* ratios. 上場企業に, 配当性向を引き上げる動きがある.

payroll 名 給与表, 給与総額, 給与支払い簿, 人件

費, 従業員名簿, 雇用者数, 総従業員数, 職員定数
direct payroll deduction 給与天引き方式
full time payroll 正規雇用
meet a payroll 給与を支払う
off the payroll 失業中
on the payroll 雇用されている
payroll and benefit-related liabilities 給与および給付関連債務
payroll cost 人件費, 労務費
payroll deduction 天引き, 賃金控除
payroll distribution 給与配賦, 給与記録
payroll expense 給料, 賃金, 給与支払い経費
payroll fringe benefit 労務副費
payroll funds 給与支払い資金
payroll savings plan 賃金貯蓄プラン, 賃金貯蓄制度
payroll structure 賃金構造 (=pay structure)
payroll taxes 賃金税, 給料税, 社会保障税, 社会保険料
ratio of payroll to gross profit 労働分配率
taxable payroll 課税給与総額
PBR 株価純資産倍率 (株式投資の主な投資指標の一つ。PBR(倍)は, 株価を1株当たり純資産で割って算出する。純資産は企業の解散価値で, PBRが1倍の企業の場合, その企業を解散したときに株主に分配される額と株価は同じということになる)
PBX 構内交換 (**private branch exchange** の略)
PC パソコン, パーソナル・コンピュータ (**personal computer**の略。⇒performance)
P.C. 専門職法人, 職能法人, 知的職業法人 (**professional corporation**の略)
PCAOB 米上場企業会計監視委員会, 公開企業会計監視委員会 (**Public Company Accounting Oversight Board**の略。民間の独立機関(SECの会計事務局(Chief Accountant Office)の直轄)で, 2002年に制定された企業改革法に基づいて2003年に発足。米上場企業を扱う監査法人は, 国内外を問わずPCAOBへの登録を義務付けられている)
▶The *PCAOB* was created by the Sarbanes-Oxley Act of 2002. 米上場企業会計監視委員会 (PCAOB)は, 2002年サーベンス・オクスレー法(企業改革法)により設置された。
PDA 携帯情報端末 (**personal digital assistant**の略)
PDCA cycle PDCAサイクル (マネジメントの基礎サイクル。PDCAは, plan (計画), do (実行), check (検証)と action (改善)の頭文字)
P/E 株価収益率 (=P/E ratio, PER)
peak 動 〈活動・生産などが〉頂点に達する
pecuniary 形 金銭の

peer 名 同業者, 同業他社, 同業他行, 競合他社, ライバル, 仲間, 同僚, ピア
peer companies 同業他社, 競合他社
peer group 同業他社, 競合他社, ライバル, 仲間集団, 仲間グループ, ピア・グループ
peer pressure 同等集団圧力, 張り合い圧力, ピア・プレッシャー
peer review 相互検査, 専門家による相互審査, 相互評価, 同僚評価, 相互批判, ピア・レビュー
private peers 民間の競合他社, 競合する民間企業
▶The bank has a stronger balance sheet than some of its bigger *peers*. 同行の財務基盤は, 一部の大手の同業他行よりも強固だ。
peg 動 安定させる, 固定させる, 一定にさせる, 釘付けにする, 連動させる, 凍結させる, リンクさせる, 名 株価などの設定水準, 固定相場制, ペッグ
adjustable peg rate system 調整可能な釘付け相場制
crawling peg 小刻みな為替変更, クローリング・ペッグ
dollar-pegged currency system 対ドル固定為替相場, 対ドル固定相場制
peg one's exchange rates to the dollar …の為替レートをドルに連動させる
peg point 基準点
pegged exchange 固定為替相場, 釘付け為替相場
pegged exchange rate system 固定為替相場制, 釘付け為替相場制 (=fixed exchange rate system, pegged exchange, pegged exchange rate)
pegged market 釘付け相場, 釘付け市場
pegged stock 釘付け株
sliding peg スライディング・ペッグ
the peg to the U.S. dollar 米ドルに合わせた通貨基準の設定, 米ドルへの連動, 対ドル固定相場制
▶China has ended the yuan's *peg* to the U.S. dollar. 中国は, 対ドル固定相場制を廃止した。
pegging 名 釘付け, 安定操作, 釘付け政策
exchange pegging 為替の釘付け
exchange pegging policy 為替釘付け政策
pegging operation 釘付け操作, 安定操作
pegging policy 釘付け政策
penalty 名 処罰, 処分, 罰金, 違約金, 延滞金, 反則金, 制裁金, 制裁, 罰則, 刑罰, ペナルティ
penalty charge 遅延損害金
penalty interest 遅延利息
penalty rate 延滞金利
penalty tax 追徴課税, 加算税
▶Kajima Corp. was ordered to pay about ¥800

million in additional tax, including a *penalty*. 大手ゼネコンの鹿島は，重加算税を含めて約8億円の追徴税の支払い命令を受けた．
▸*Penalties* against insider trading and market manipulation have been strengthened. インサイダー取引や相場操縦などに対する罰則が，強化された．

penetration 名 浸透，参入，加入，進出，普及率，侵入，侵略，ペネトレーション
  cellular penetration 移動電話の普及率
  economic penetration 経済侵略
  household penetration 家庭普及率，家庭への普及率
  import penetration 輸入浸透度，輸入品の浸透度
  market penetration 市場参入，市場進出，市場浸透
  market penetration rate 市場浸透度
  penetration price 浸透価格，市場浸透価格，ペネトレーション価格
  penetration rate 加入率，普及率

pension 名 年金
  annual pension 年金
  basic pension 基礎年金
  corporate pension 企業年金，厚生年金
  earnings-related pension 所得比例年金
  full pension 完全年金
  group pension 団体年金
  occupational pension 雇用年金
  pension beneficiary 年金受給者
  pension defaulter 年金未納者
  pension income 年金利益 (⇒**prepaid pension cost**)
  pension obligations 年金債務 (⇒**fair value**)
  pension plan for company employees 厚生年金 (=company employees' pension plan, corporate employees' pension insurance plan)
  pension provision 年金計上額，年金引当金
  pension reserve 年金引当金，年金積立金
  pension subscription period 年金加入期間
  pension system benefits 年金の給付金 (⇒**pension**)
  private pension 企業年金保険，私的年金
  public pension 公的年金
  retirement pension 退職年金
  supplementary pension 補足年金
  transitional pension 経過年金
  universal pension 一律給付年金
▸Just as the number of people qualifying for *pensions* is on the rise, the working population, which underpins the pension scheme, is on the decline. 年金受給の資格者は増える一方，年金制度を支える現役世代は減っている．

pension asset 年金資産
▸About ¥21 billion in *pension assets* belonging to more than 80,000 subscribers to defined-contribution pension plans were left unmanaged as of March 2007. 2007年3月末現在で，8万人を超える確定拠出年金加入者の年金資産約210億円が，運用されないままになっている．

pension benefits 年金給付，受取年金，退職年金給付 (=pension payments)
▸In addition to *pension benefits*, the Corporation and its subsidiary companies provide certain health care and life insurance benefits for retired employees. 当社と当社の子会社は，年金給付のほかに，退職者を対象に医療給付と生命保険給付を提供しています．

pension contributions 年金拠出額
▸*Pension contributions* are principally determined using the aggregate cost method. 年金拠出額は，基本的に総額原価法を用いて決定される．

pension cost 年金費用，年金原価，年金コスト (=pension expense)
▸The net U.S. *pension cost* for the elected officers' supplemental retirement benefit plan was $27 million in 2008. 選任役員の追加の退職給付制度に対する米国内の純年金費用は，2008年度は2,700万ドルでした．

pension expense 年金費用 (=pension cost)
▸Increases in salaries, wages, and depreciation expenses were partially offset by lower *pension expenses* and by the effect of the strike. 給料・賃金と減価償却費の増加分は，年金費用の減少とストの効果［影響］で一部相殺されています．

pension fund 年金基金，年金資金，年金積立金
  employee's [employees'] pension fund 従業員年金基金，厚生年金基金
  investment management for pension funds 年金基金の運用
  pension fund investment 年金積立金の運用 (⇒**corporate pension plan**)
  pension fund reserve 年金基金積立金
▸The *Pension Fund* Association manages about ¥9.9 trillion in pension funds for employees pension fund plans. 厚生年金基金連合会［企業年金連合会］は，厚生年金基金［企業年金］の年金資金約9兆9,000億円を運用している．

pension insurance sales 年金保険の販売
▸Mizuho Financial Group Inc. enjoyed healthy

nonfinancial earnings such as commissions on *pension insurance sales*.　みずほフィナンシャルグループは，年金保険の販売手数料など，(貸出以外の)非金利収入が好調だった．

pension liability　年金債務，年金負債（⇒ **pension plan assets**）
▶The prepaid pension costs are net of *pension liabilities* for plans where accumulated plan benefits exceed assets.　この前払い年金費用は，累積給付債務額が資産額を超過している場合の年金債務純額を控除したものです．

pension payments　年金支給額，年金給付，年金給付額（＝**pension benefits**）
▶In times of inflation, *pension payments* increased in step with price increases.　インフレの時代は，物価の上昇に伴って年金支給額も上昇した．
▶The current level of *pension payments*, which cover more than 90 percent of average monthly consumption by senior citizens, are too high.　高齢者の平均消費月額の9割以上もカバーしている現在の年金の給付水準は，高すぎる．

pension payout　年金の支払い
▶Under the defined-contribution annuity scheme, workers who will receive *pension payouts* in the future decide how the pension fund is invested.　確定拠出年金制度では，将来年金の支払いを受ける従業員が年金積立金の運用方法を決める．

pension plan　年金制度（＝**pension program, pension scheme, pension system**; ⇒ **corporate pension plan**）
　basic pension plan　基礎年金制度，基礎年金
　company-run pension plan　企業年金制度
　defined benefit pension plan　給付建て年金制度
　defined contribution pension plan　拠出建て年金制度
　employee pension plan　従業員年金制度
　insured pension plan　保険型年金
　liability under pension plan　未払い年金債務
　qualified pension plan　適格年金制度
　the operation of a pension plan　年金制度の運用
▶It is extremely unusual for a company to take action against the government over company-run *pension plans*.　企業年金制度をめぐって企業が行政を訴えるのは，極めて異例だ．

pension plan assets　年金制度資産，年金資産（⇒**fair value**）
▶Our *pension plan assets* are earning a return that exceeds the growth in pension liabilities.　当社の年金制度資産は，年金債務の増大を上回る収益を上げています．

pension premium　年金保険料
▶The instability of the pension system has repeatedly experienced increases in *pension premiums* and decreases in pension benefits.　年金制度が不安定なため，年金保険料の負担増と年金給付減が繰り返されてきた．

pension scheme　年金制度，年金供給協定（＝**pension plan**）
　approved pension scheme　適格年金制度
　company employees' pension scheme　厚生年金制度，厚生年金（＝**company employees' pension system**）
　occupational pension scheme　従業員年金制度
▶Under the company employees' *pension scheme*, subscribing is mandatory for all firms with five or more employees.　厚生年金制度では，従業員5人以上の法人すべてに加入が義務付けられている．

pension subscriber　年金加入者
▶The Pension Fund Association was found not to have paid a total of ¥154.4 billion in pension benefits to 1.24 million *pension subscribers*.　企業年金連合会が，年金加入者124万人に対して計1,544億円の年金を未払いにしていることが分かった．

pension system　年金制度，年金システム（＝**pension scheme**）
▶The *pension system* may collapse before people qualify as beneficiaries.　年金をもらう前に年金制度が崩壊する可能性がある．

pensioner 名　年金受給者，年金生活者

pentagon management　ペンタゴン(五角形)経営，多角経営
▶The firm's poor business performance is a result of its *pentagon management* that saw a lack of coordination between businesses.　同社の経営不振の一因は，ペンタゴン経営と呼ばれる多角経営で，事業部門間の連携が行き詰まったことにある．

people 名　社員，従業員，人々
▶We invest almost $3 million a day in the continuing education, training and development of our *people*.　継続している当社従業員の教育，訓練と開発に，当社は1日当たり約300万ドルを投じています．

People's Bank of China　中国人民銀行（中国の中央銀行に当たる）

PER　株価収益率（＝**P/E, P/E ratio**: **price earnings ratio**の略）

株価収益率について➡「株価収益率(PER)」は、株式投資の主な投資指標の一つで、株価が1株当たり利益(税引き後利益)の何倍に相当するかを示す。PERは、株価を1株当たり利益(earnings per share)で割って算出する。自分の投資した代金を利益で回収すると何年かかるか、が分かる。回収期間は短いほうがよいので、PERは小さいほうがよい。

▶Price earnings ratio (*PER*) is obtained by dividing price per share by earnings per share. 株価収益率は、1株当たりの株価を1株当たり利益で割って[除して]求められます。

per 前 …につき、…ごとに、…で、…によって、…によれば

per annum rate 年利

per capita 1人当たり、国民1人当たり
▶More than ¥10 million in assets has been lost on a *per capita* basis due to deflation. デフレで、国民1人当たり1,000万円以上の資産を失った。

per share 1株当たり (⇒book value, dividend per share, earnings per share, net profit per share)
▶Hewlett-Packard earned $1.55 billion, or 55 cents *per share*, for the first quarter ended Jan. 31. ヒューレット・パッカードは、第1四半期(11 −1月期)に15億5,000万ドル(1株当たり55セント)の利益を上げた。

▶The company increased the projected dividend *per share* to ¥6 for fiscal 2008 from the ¥5 paid the previous year. 同社は、2008年度の1株当たり予想配当を前年度の5円から6円に引き上げた[増配した]。

per-share group net profit 1株当たり連結純利益
▶*Per-share group net profit* plunged to ¥85.95 from the preceding fiscal year's ¥37,983.95. 1株当たり連結純利益は、前年度の37,983円95銭から85円95銭に激減した。

per-share net loss 1株当たり純損失
▶*Per-share net loss* came to ¥77.92 in a sharp downswing from a profit of ¥10.06 the previous year. 1株当たり純損失は、前期の10.06円の利益から急落して77.92円となった。

per-share net profit 1株当たり純利益
▶The company's *per-share net profit* came to ¥18.24, down from ¥40.12 a year earlier. 同社の1株当たり純利益は、前年同期の40円12銭から減少して18円24銭となった。

per-share value 1株当たり価値
▶The massive issuance of new shares will result in the dilution of the *per-share value* of existing stock, which will then depress share prices on the stock market. 新株が大量に発行されると、既存株式の1株当たり価値の希薄化を招いて、株式市場の株価が下がることになる。

percent 名 百分率、率、割合、パーセント
  net income as percent of average stockholders' equity 自己資本当期純利益率
  percent depreciated 償却率、償却累計
  percent of capacity use 稼動率

percentage 名 比率、割合、部分、分け前、歩合、歩合制、百分率、利益、利点、得、パーセント
  annual percentage rate 実質年率
  cost percentage 原価率
  fixed percentage method 定率法
  gross margin [profit] percentage 粗利益率
  net income (loss) as a percentage of revenues 純利益(損失)率
  nonperforming loan percentage 不稼動債権の比率
  percentage of capital structure 資本構成比率
  percentage profit on turnover 売上高利益率

▶As a *percentage* of revenues SG&A expenses in the second quarter of 2008 decreased to 19.5 percent from 21.0 percent last year. 売上高に占める2008年第2四半期の販売費および一般管理費(SG&A)の比率は、前年同期の21%から19.5%に低下しました。

▶Cost controls, coupled with our revenue growth, caused our gross margin *percentage* to improve the past two years. コスト管理と増収により、当社の売上総利益率は過去2年間上昇しました。

percentage gain 伸び率
▶Our business communications systems and cable group product lines had strong *percentage gains* in revenue growth. ビジネス通信システムと通信ケーブル・グループの製品系列は、増収の伸び率が大幅に上昇しました。

percentage of completion method 工事進行基準、進行基準 (=percentage of completion accounting)
▶The Company accounts for this construction work contract under the *percentage of completion method*. 当社は、この請負工事契約については、工事進行基準にしたがって会計処理しています。

percentage point パーセント・ポイント、ポイント、厘、パーセンテージ・ポイント(one percentage point=1パーセント)
  a quarter percentage point 0.25%
  half a percentage point 0.5%

▶The tax rate was reduced by 1.5 *percentage points* in 2008 due to the inclusion of the company's after-tax earnings in the Corporation's earnings before tax. 2008年度の税率は、同社の税引き後利益を当社の税引き前利益に含めたため、1.5％低下しました。

perform 動 遂行する, 実行する, 行う, 〈約束などを〉果たす, 機能する, 作動する, 〈投資などが〉収益を生む

performance 名 実績, 業績, 成果, 義務[債務]の履行, 運用, 運用成績, 動向, 値動き, 収益性, パフォーマンス (⇒business performance, corporate performance, good performance, high performance, robust performance, strong performance)

- after-market performance 公開後の値動き
- brisk business performance 好決算, 好業績 (＝buoyant performance)
- company's performance 企業の業績, 業績 (＝company's results)
- consolidated performance 連結決算
- cost performance コスト効率, 対原価性能比
- cost/performance ratio 費用・性能比
- disappointing performance 期待外れの業績, 予想を裏切る業績
- earnings performance 利益実績, 業績
- economic performance 経済実績, 経済成長率, 景気動向
- financial performance 財務状態, 業績
- high-performance data communications service 高性能データ通信サービス
- historical performance 過去の運用成績, 過去の運用実績
- inflation performance インフレ動向
- investment performance 投資実績, 運用成績, 運用実績
- job performance 職務遂行, 職務能力
- management performance 経営実績, 経営成績, 経営業績, 運用実績
- market performance 市場成果, 相場の動き
- operating performance 営業成績, 経営成績, 営業業績, 業績, 事業効率
- operational performance 業績
- past performance 実績
- performance audit 業績監査
- performance evaluation 業績評価, 業績査定 (＝performance appraisal)
- performance measurement 業績測定
- performance rating 人事考課, 職務考課, 達成度査定
- performance review 勤務評定, 人事考課
- poor performance 業績不振, 業績低下, 業績低迷, 業績悪化 (＝weak performance)
- portfolio performance 資産運用実績, 資産運用成績, ポートフォリオの運用成績
- price performance 値動き, インフレ動向
- product performance 製品性能, 製品成果
- profit performance 利益率, 収益性, 利益実現, 利潤成果
- stable performance 安定した業績[実績], 安定運用
- stock performance 株価の値動き, 株価パフォーマンス, 株価動向 (＝share price performance, stock price performance)
- strong financial performance 好業績 (＝strong performance)

▶The downgrade reflects Standard and Poor's concern over the company's ability to avoid a further deterioration in its operating *performance*. この格下げは、同社の一段の業績悪化は避けられないとのスタンダード＆プアーズの懸念を反映している。

▶The firm's financial situation has been aggravated by recent poor *performance* in its main business of developing resorts. リゾート開発の本業がこのところ不振で、同社の財務状況が悪化している。

▶This improved *performance* is due both to steady growth in demand, reflecting a generally prosperous economy, and to efficient management. この業績改善は、好景気を背景にした需要の着実な伸びと経営の効率化によるものです。

▶Today, the *performance* of new PCs has improved so much that customers can now use new software without problems, even with two- or three-year-old PCs. 今では、新品パソコンの性能がかなり向上したため、2,3年前のパソコンでも、ユーザーは新発売のソフトを問題なく[不自由なく]使用できるようになった。

performance-based 形 成果主義の

- performance-based fiscal budget system 成果主義の年度予算制度
- performance-based pay system 能力給制度, 成果主義型給与制度, 成果主義型賃金体系 (＝merit-based pay system)

▶We plan to make a full-scale shift to a *performance-based* pay system next April. 当社は、来年4月から成果主義型の給与制度に全面的に移行する方針です。

performance plan パフォーマンス制度, パ

フォーマンス・プラン
▸The long-term *performance plan* provides for incentive awards to be made to officers and other key employees. この長期パフォーマンス・プランは，役員と幹部社員に奨励報酬を与える制度です。

peril 名 危険，危難

period 名 期間，時期，局面，…期，年度，年数，会計期間，会計年度，事業年度，ピリオド（⇒**accounting period, for the period**）
　amortization period 元本償還期間，元利払い期間
　at fixed period after date 日付後定期払い
　at fixed period after sight 一覧後定期払い
　base period 基準年度
　beginning of the period 期首
　claim period 請求期間
　cooling-off period クーリング・オフ期間
　current period 当事業年度，当期（⇒**reverse**）
　exercise period 権利行使期間
　fiscal period 会計期間，会計年度（＝accounting period）
　grace period 猶予期間，保険料払込み猶予期間，据え置き期間
　interest period 金利期間
　investment holding period 投資期間（＝holding period）
　July-September period 7−9月期（⇒**rack up**）
　limitation period 出訴期限
　over the same period last year 前年同期比で
　payment period 返済期間
　performance period 当該期間
　period benefited 利益発生期間（⇒**goodwill**）
　period under review 当期
　phase-in period 経過期間
　portfolio period 資産運用成績
　pricing period 価格設定期間
　prior period 過去の事業年度，過年度，前期
　production period 生産期間，製造期間
　purchases for the period 当期仕入高
　quarterly period 四半期
　settlement period 決済期間
　share price performance 株価動向，株価の値動き，株価パフォーマンス
　subscription period 募集期間，販売期間
　test period 検討対象期間
　the last period of settlement of accounts 最終決算期
　wind-down period 元利払い期間

▸Goodwill is amortized on a straight line method over the *periods* estimated to be benefited, currently not exceeding five years. 営業権は，その効果が及ぶと見込まれる期間にわたって(現在は5年を超えない期間にわたって)，定額法で償却されています。

▸The company's auditing firm approved the firm's accounting for the suspected *periods*. 同社の監査法人は，問題となっている時期の同社の決算処理を承認していた。

▸The firm posted a pretax profit of ¥30 billion for the April-September *period*. 同社の4−9月期の税引き前利益は，300億円となった。

periodic 形 定期的な，周期的な，期間の
　periodic cost 期間費用
　periodic income 期間利益，期間収益
　periodic inventory 定期の棚卸し
　periodic loss 期間損失
　periodic pension cost 期間年金費用，毎期の年金費用（⇒**expected long-term rate of return**）
　periodic physical count 定期的数量カウント
　periodic physical inventory 定期実地棚卸し
　periodic profit 期間利益
　periodic stock-checking system 定期的在庫チェック・システム

▸Cost for inventory purposes should be determined by the inventory cost flow method most clearly reflecting *periodic* income. 棚卸し資産の原価は，期間利益を最も明確に反映する棚卸し資産原価算定の方法によって算定すべきである。

peripheral 形 周辺の，付随する，名 周辺機器，周辺装置（＝peripheral device, peripheral unit）
　peripheral and terminal units 周辺・端末装置
　peripheral control unit 周辺機器制御装置
　peripheral equipment 周辺機器，周辺装置
　peripheral transaction 付随的取引

perishable food 生鮮食品，生鮮食料品（＝perishables）

▸The nationwide consumer price index, excluding *perishable food* prices, came to 98.0 for the year ended March 31 against the base of 100 set in 2000. 当年度(4−3月期)の全国の消費者物価指数(2000年＝100)は，生鮮食品の価格を除いた総合物価指数で98.0と下落した

perishable goods 生鮮食品，生鮮食料品，腐敗性商品（＝perishables）

perishables 名 腐敗性商品

perk ＝perquisite

permanent 形 永久の，永久的，恒久的，長期的

な，常設の
permanent committee 常設委員会
permanent debt 永久公債，永久債
permanent differences 永久差異，永久差異項目
permanent establishment 恒久的施設《略 P.E.》
permanent financing 永久資本
permanent financing requirement 長期的な資金調達必要額（⇒one-time credit）
permanent investment 恒久的投資，永久証券
permanent income 恒常所得
permanent preferred stock 永久優先株
▸The Corporation has established *permanent* committees of the board of directors to permit continuing review of the areas of auditing, management resources and compensation, pension fund policy, and investment. 当社は，監査，役員人事・報酬，年金基金対策と投資の各分野に関する検討を継続的に行うため，常設の取締役会付属委員会を設置しています．

permission 名 許可，許し，認可，承認，同意
▸Music and images may not, in principle, be copied or used without the artists' prior *permission*. 音楽や映像は，原則として著作者の事前許可なしに複製・利用することはできない．

permit 名 許可，認可，免許，許可書，許可証，免許証，免許状
building permits 住宅着工許可件数，建設許可件数
export permit 輸出許可，輸出許可書
new permits 住宅着工許可件数
permits and licenses 許認可費用
residence permit 居住許可書
trading permit 取引の認可

perpetuity 名 永続物，終身年金，永久所有権，財産永久拘束，永続，パーペチュイティー

perquisite 名 臨時収入，役得，チップ

personal 形 個人の，個人的，私的の，本人自らの，人的な，対人の，動産の，名 個人広告，個人情報，個人消息
personal assistant 個人秘書
personal belongings 身の回り品，所持品（＝personal effects）
personal check 個人小切手，パーソナル・チェック
personal column 求人広告欄，個人広告欄，個人消息欄，身の上相談
personal communicator 携帯通信端末
personal computer パソコン，個人用小型コンピュータ，パーソナル・コンピュータ《略 PC》
personal counseling 個人相談，パーソナル・カウンセリング
personal data 個人情報（＝personal information）
personal deposits 個人預金
personal digital assistant 携帯情報端末，携帯情報通信端末《略 PDA》
personal electronic device 携帯用電子機器
personal equity plan 個人投資計画
personal exemption 個人の所得税控除
personal finance company 消費者金融会社
personal history 履歴書（＝curriculum vitae, resume, résumé）
personal holding company 個人的持ち株会社，同族持ち株会社
personal identification number 暗証番号，個人の識別番号（＝password, PIN number）
personal letter [message] 親書，私信
personal loan 個人ローン，個人向け融資，消費者ローン
personal organizer 電子手帳
personal outlays 個人支出
personal product 家庭用品
personal property 動産，人的財産
personal savings 個人貯蓄
personal selling 人的販売
personal service 個人サービス
personal shopper 買い物相談員，買い物相談係

personal consumption 個人消費（＝personal spending, private consumption）
▸Together with exports, *personal consumption* was the biggest contributor to the GDP growth. 輸出とともに個人消費が，国内総生産（GDP）の伸び率にとくに大きく寄与した．

personal handy-phone system 簡易型携帯電話システム，簡易携帯電話《略 PHS》
▸Cell phone and *personal handy-phone system* companies have been engaged in a fierce competition. 携帯電話，PHS各社が，激しい競争を繰り広げている．

personal information 個人情報（＝personal data）
▸A sizable amount of *personal information* leaked from a telecommunication company. 通信会社から，大量の個人情報が流出した．

Personal Information Protection Law 個人情報保護法
▸The *Personal Information Protection Law* regulates the use of personal information by private firms. 個人情報保護法は，民間企業による個人情報の使用を規制している．

personal spending 個人消費（＝personal

consumption)
- It is highly unlikely *personal spending* will fully recover. 個人消費の本格回復は、望み薄だ。

personnel 名 人員, 要員, 従業員, 職員, 人事
　key personnel 基幹人員, 主要人員
　management personnel 経営陣
　personnel costs 人件費 (⇒**cash flow problems**)
　personnel cuts 人員削減
　personnel exchange 人事交流
- In the closing phases of economic upturns, rises in *personnel* costs and other fixed expenditures caused profits to shrink, leading to a recession. 景気回復期[景気拡大期]の最終局面では、企業の人件費など固定費の上昇が収益を圧迫して、景気後退につながった。

　personnel change 人事刷新
- The bank will conduct a drastic *personnel change* and replace about 20 senior officials. 同行は、大幅な人事刷新を行い、幹部約20人を更迭する方針だ。

PERT パート法, パート(法) (**project evaluation and review technique** の略)

petrochemical 名 石油化学製品
　petrochemical and plastics industries 化学品・プラスチック産業[業界]
　petrochemical complex 石油化学コンビナート
　petrochemical plant 石化プラント

petrochemical product 石油化学製品
- Production costs for *petrochemical products* such as polyethylene have risen. ポリエチレンなど石油化学製品の製造コストが、上昇している。

petroleum 名 石油
　international petroleum cartel 国際石油カルテル
　petroleum exploration 石油の探鉱, 石油探査
　petroleum refining 石油精製
　petroleum refining industry 石油精製業
　petroleum reserves 石油埋蔵量, 原油埋蔵量, 可採埋蔵量
　refined petroleum products 石油精製品
　storing of petroleum 石油備蓄

petroleum product 石油製品
- Due to soaring crude oil prices, distributors' *petroleum product* sales sections have been suffering from a downturn in their businesses. 原油価格の高騰で、石油元売り各社の石油製品販売部門は最近、業績が悪化している。

PFI プライベート・ファイナンス・イニシアチブ, PFI方式, 民間資金による社会資本整備 (**private finance initiative** の略)
- In Britain, bridges, subways and prisons are constructed with *PFI*. 英国では、橋や地下鉄、刑務所などもPFI方式で建設されている。

pharmaceutical disaster 薬害
pharmaceutical firm 製薬会社
phase 名 段階, 局面, 動 段階的に実行する, 漸次導入する
phase in 段階的に[徐々に]取り入れる, 導入する, 投入する, 実行する
phase out 段階的に撤退する, 段階的に廃止する, 段階的に削減する, 段階的に閉鎖する, 段階的に解消する
- During the fourth quarter of 2007, the Corporation announced a plan to *phase out* certain manufacturing plants. 2007年第4四半期に当社は、一部の製造施設を段階的に閉鎖する計画を発表しました。

philanthropy 名 慈善, 慈善行為, 慈善活動, 慈善事業, 慈善団体, 寄付活動, 企業の文化・社会への貢献, フィランソロピー活動, フィランソロピー

philosophy 名 理念, 方針, 主義, 哲学, 基本的な考え方
　business philosophy 経営理念
　company philosophy 企業理念, 経営哲学, 経営方針
　financing philosophy 資金調達方針, 財務についての考え方
　investment philosophy 投資方針
　management philosophy 経営理念, 経営方針, 経営哲学, 経営思想, 経営者精神 (＝**management thought, managerial philosophy**)
- Any listed corporations must convince their customers, business partners and other stakeholders of their business *philosophy* and strategies. 上場企業は、顧客や取引先などのステークホルダー(利害関係者)に対して、経営理念と戦略をきちんと説明する必要がある。

phishing 名 ウェブ偽装詐欺, フィッシング (銀行やクレジット・カード会社などの偽のホームページを使って、口座番号やパスワードなどの個人情報を盗むこと)

physical 形 物理的な, 物的な
　physical checkup 健康診断, 人間ドック
　physical control 物量管理
　physical counts 実地棚卸し, 実査
　physical delivery 現物受渡し, 現渡し, 現引き
　physical distribution management 物的流通管理, 物流管理《略 **PDM**》
　physical distribution value added network

物流VAN
physical evidence 物的証拠
physical inspection 実査
physical life 物理的耐用年数
physical market 実物市場
physical production 物的生産
physical resources 物的資源

pick up 景気づく，〈景気などが〉回復する，復調する，勢い[はずみ]をつける，増える，盛り上がる，上向く，改善する
▸Japan's business leaders believe the economy is *picking up* steam. 日本企業のトップ[経営者]は，景気は上向いていると見ている。

picket 名 〈スト破りを阻止するための〉ピケ隊員，スト破り監視員
▸Workers could return to the *picket* lines if the company rejects the new agreement. 新協約を拒否したら，労働者はピケライン[監視線]に戻る可能性がある。

pickup [pick-up] 名 回復，改善，向上，増加，伸び，上昇，拡大，活発化
economic pickup 景気拡大 (＝pickup in economic performance)
equity pickup 株価の値上がり
pickup in demand 需要の高まり，需要の回復
pickup in inflation インフレ率の上昇
pickup in production 生産の回復
▸We reported a 5% increase in total revenues in 2008, a *pickup* from the 3% increase in 2007. 当社の2008年度の総営業収益は5%の伸びで，前年度の3%の伸びを上回りました。

pictogram 名 絵画図表，絵表示統計図，ピクトグラム

pie 名 全体，総額，わいろ，不正利得，理想郷，パイ
division of the economic pie パイの分配
pie chart 円グラフ，パイ図表 (＝circle graph)
pie in the sky 絵に描いた餅，夢のような計画，あてにならない計画，希望的観測，天国，ユートピア
the size of employment pie 雇用全体の規模
▸The size of employment *pie* has shrunk amid the lingering recession. 長引く不況のなかで，雇用全体の規模が縮小した。

piecework 名 請負仕事，出来高払いの仕事，手間仕事

piggyback 名 台車輸送，ピギーバック；動 …に便乗する，…を背負う，…を借りる，貨車・鉄道で運ぶ
piggyback and impersonation 便乗と偽装
piggyback system ピギーバック方式，ピギーバック・システム (荷物を積んだトラックなどを，そのまま貨物列車に載せて運ぶ方式)
▸Walt Disney Co. (Japan) has started a cell phone service in Japan that *piggybacks* on the telecommunications networks of Softbank Mobile Corp. ウォルト・ディズニー・ジャパンが，ソフトバンクモバイルの通信網を借りて，日本で携帯電話サービスを開始した。

pilot 形 試験的，実験的，予備の，事前の，先行的，指標となる，補助の，パイロット
pilot assembly plant 試験的組立工場
pilot experiment 先行的実験，予備実験
pilot film 見本用フイルム，見本フイルム
pilot plant 実験工場，試験工場，試験的生産工場，試験設備，パイロット・プラント
pilot production 試験的生産，試験生産，試作，パイロット生産
pilot project [scheme] 予備計画，先行的プロジェクト，パイロット・プロジェクト
pilot store 実験店，実験店舗，パイロット店，パイロット・ストア
pilot survey 予備調査，パイロット・サーベイ
pilot system パイロット・システム
pilot test 事前調査，予備テスト，先行的試験，パイロット・テスト
▸The chain store opened a *pilot* store in Tokyo in late March. このチェーン・ストアは3月末，東京都内に実験店を出した。

PIN 暗証番号 (＝personal identification number, PIN number)

pioneer 草分け，先駆者，創始者，首唱者，率先者，開拓者，新規事業開発者，パイオニア (⇒Net business)
pioneer invention 画期的な発明，革新的な発明
pioneer patent 基本特許，開拓特許，パイオニア特許
▸The *pioneer* of the move by convenience stores to sell a wide variety of perishable foods was the Shop 99 chain, which sells everything for ¥99 (excluding consumption tax). 生鮮コンビニ(広範な生鮮食品を販売するコンビニ)の動きの草分けは，商品を99円(消費税抜き)均一で売る「ショップ99」のチェーン店だ。

pipeline 名 〈原油や天然ガスなどの〉パイプライン，〈輸送用あるいは荷役用の〉鉄製配管，供給ルート，流通ルート，情報ルート，機密ルート，入手経路，パイプ，パイプライン

石油事業の各種パイプライン:

| feeder line | フィーダー・ライン(数か所の地点から石油を集めて幹線パイプラインに直接送油するパイプライン) |

flow line	フロー・ライン（油井から貯蔵タンクまでのパイプライン）
gathering line	集油パイプライン（数ヵ所の地点から集油センターまで送るパイプライン）
lease line	リース・ライン（賃貸契約により生産井からタンクまで全石油生産物を集めて送るパイプライン）
trunk line	幹線パイプライン，トランク・ライン（石油生産地から精製センターに送油するパイプライン，または精製した製品を販売市場に送油するパイプライン）

in the pipeline　輸送中，準備中，進行中
pipeline transportation　パイプライン輸送
play the role of a pipeline　パイプの役割を果たす
Trans-Alaska Pipeline System　アラスカ縦断パイプライン《略 TAPS》
▸Plans to strengthen regulations covering operators that send out spam also are *in the pipeline*.　現在，迷惑メール送信事業者への規制を強化する計画も準備している。

piracy 名　著作権侵害，特許権侵害，海賊版，模造品，模倣品
pirate 動　著作権を侵害する，名　著作権侵害者
pirate copy　侵害品，模造品，違法コピー，海賊版コピー，著作権［特許権］侵害のコピー（＝pirate product, pirated copy）
pirated designer goods　偽ブランド品（＝counterfeit brand product）
pirated product　特許権侵害の製品，著作権侵害のコピー，違法コピー（＝bogus goods, fake product）
▸*Pirated products* are said to have grown into a global market worth ¥50 trillion per year.　コピー製品は，全世界で年50兆円に達するといわれる。
pirated software　海賊版ソフト
▸The export of *pirated software* is deemed an act of copyright infringement.　海賊版ソフトの輸出は，著作権を侵害する行為と見なされる。
pitch 動　〈商品を〉市場に出す，陳列する，名　コマーシャル
place 名　場所，職，役職，座席
　business place tax　事業所税
　investment in place　投資実績
　place of origin　原産地
　place of work　職場，仕事場（＝place to work, workplace）
　put production facilities in place　生産拠点をつくる
▸The Japanese Agricultural Standards (JAS) Law requires the producers of perishable foods to ensure that labels mention *place* of origin.　日本農林規格(JAS)法は，生鮮食品の生産者に原産地表示を義務付けている。

placement　〈株式・債券の〉募集［販売］，売出し，販売先，職業紹介，職業斡旋，人員配置（⇒private placement）
　direct placement　直接募集，直接販売，私募（＝private offering, private placement）
　indirect placement　間接募集，間接販売
　initial placement　募集業務
　public placement　公募発行，公募，公募債
　raise cash by a private placement　第三者割当てで資金を調達する
　retail placement　個人投資家への販売
▸Hokuetsu Paper Mills Ltd.'s private *placement* of new shares to allocate a stake of more than 30 percent to trading house Mitsubishi is scheduled for Monday.　三菱商事に30%超を割り当てる北越製紙の第三者割当て増資は，月曜日に予定されている。

plan 動　計画する，計画を立てる，立案する，設計する
　planned capital increase　増資計画
　planned capital spending　設備投資計画（＝capital spending plan, planned capex）
　planned expansion　設備拡張計画
　planned listing　上場計画，計画していた上場
▸Nissan *plans* to put about 100,000 units of its Altima Hybrid model on the U.S. market early next year.　日産は来年はじめ，「アルティマ・ハイブリッド」車約10万台を米国で発売する計画だ。

plan 名　計画，構想，提案，案，政策，策，制度，方式，方法，予定，段取り，平面図，プラン（⇒business plan, noncontributory plan, pension plan, stock purchase plan）
　accumulation plan　積立てプラン
　acquisition plan　買収計画（＝acquisition planning）
　audit plan　監査計画
　bonus plan　ボーナス制度
　capex plan　設備投資計画（＝capital spending plan）
　compensatory plan　報酬制度
　contributory plan　拠出型制度，拠出制年金制度
　deferred compensation plan　報酬据え置き方式
　defined benefit plan　給付金制度
　defined contribution plan　拠出金制度
　employee capital accumulation plan　従業員の資本蓄積プラン
　fixed benefit plan　定額給付制度

incentive compensation plan 奨励報償制度
insured pension plan 保険型年金
investment plan 投資計画
management plan 経営計画 （=management planning）
production plan 生産計画
profit plan 利益計画 （=profit planning）
reserve financing plan 積立て方式
stock award plan 株式報奨制度
stock bonus plan 株式賞与制度

▶Fujita Corp. scrapped a *plan* to merge with Sumitomo Mitsui Construction Co. 2005年3月にフジタは，三井住友建設との経営統合計画を白紙撤回した。

▶The *plan* will be officially decided upon at a meeting of representatives of policyholders in July. この案は，7月の総代会で正式に決定される。

plan assets 年金資産, 制度資産, 年金制度資産, 基金資産 （=pension plan assets; ⇒**expected long-term rate of return, secured mortgage**）

actual return on plan assets 制度資産の実際運用益
estimated market value of plan assets 基金資産の見積り市場価値
expected return on plan assets 制度資産の期待収益, 年金資産の予想収益
net plan assets 年金プラン純資産
plan assets at fair value 公正価額による年金資産, 年金資産の公正価額, 制度資産時価
plan assets in excess of projected benefit obligation 基金資産の見積り給付債務超過額

▶Our *plan assets* consist primarily of listed stocks, corporate and governmental debt, real estate investments, and cash and cash equivalents. 当社の年金制度資産は，主に上場株式，事業債，国債，不動産投資と現金および現金等価物で構成されています。

plan benefits 年金給付
accrued plan benefits 年金給付債務額
accumulated plan benefits 年金給付累積額, 年金給付債務額, 年金未支給額

▶The actuarial present value of the accrued *plan benefits* and the net assets available to discharge these benefits at December 31 are as follows: 12月31日現在の年金給付債務額の年金数理原価と年金給付債務に充当可能な年金純資産は，以下のとおりです。

plan participant 制度加入者
▶The new shares of common stock are being allocated to *plan participants* over ten years as contributions are made to the plan. この普通株式新株は，制度への資金拠出と並行して，10年にわたり制度加入者に割り当てられています。

plan to …する計画だ，…する方針だ，…する方向だ，…する考えだ

▶The firm *plans to* spend about ¥500 billion by 2009 to build one of the world's largest DRAM plants. 同社は，2009年までに約5,000億円を投資して世界最大規模のDRAM（記憶保持動作が必要な随時書込み読出しメモリ）工場を建設する方針だ。

planner 名 計画立案者, 企画者, 設計者, プランナー
corporate planner 企業の企画部門
financial planner フィナンシャル・プランナー （=financial planning specialist）

▶A financial *planner* plans and manages total financial assets of individuals and corporations. フィナンシャル・プランナーは，個人や法人の金融資産の総合設計と管理をする。

planning 名 企画, 立案, 企画立案, 計画, 計画策定, プランニング
accounting for planning 計画会計
audit planning 監査計画
budget planning 予算計画
business planning 経営計画, 事業計画, ビジネス・プランニング
cash planning 資金計画
corporate planning 経営計画, 企業計画立案
distribution planning 流通計画
financial planning 財務計画, ファイナンシャル・プランニング
intermediate planning 中期経営計画, 中期計画
managerial planning 経営計画 （=management planning）
manufacturing planning 製造計画
master plan 基本計画, 総合計画, マスター・プラン
office planning 事務計画, 事務改善計画
operational planning 業務計画
organization planning 組織計画 （=organizational planning）
periodic planning 期間計画 （=period planning）
planning, program(m)ing, budgeting system 企画計画予算制度, 全計画予算方式, 費用対効果分析予算方式《略 **PPBS**》
product planning 製品計画, 商品企画, 商品企画力
production planning 生産計画
profit planning 利益計画 （=profit plan）

scenario planning シナリオ・プランニング
short-term planning 短期経営計画, 短期計画 (=short-range planning)
strategic planning 戦略計画, 戦略企画, 戦略策定, ストラテジック・プランニング
tax planning 節税計画
tax planning strategy 戦略的税務計画, 税計画戦略, 税務戦略

▶We are working with employees and the unions to increase their involvement and input in *planning* and decisions. 私たちは，従業員・組合と共に，従業員と組合が会社の企画立案や意思決定に参加して意見を述べる機会の拡大に努めています。

▶We forecast our expenses and capital expenditures for existing and planned compliance programs as part of our regular corporate *planning* process. 当社の定期的な企業計画立案作業の一環として，私たち経営陣は，現在および将来の規制遵守プログラムの費用と資本的支出を予測しています。

plant 名 工場, 生産設備, 工場設備, 施設, 植物, プラント
  assembling plant 組立工場 (⇒assembly plant)
  idle plant 遊休設備, 遊休施設, 遊休工場設備
  industrial plant 工場設備, 工場
  LCD panel plant 液晶パネル工場, 液晶ディスプレー・パネル工場
  new plant startup 新工場の稼働, 工場の操業開始
  nuclear power plant 原子力発電所 (=atomic power station, nuclear power station)
  petrochemical plant 石油化学プラント
  plant additions 工場増設 (⇒net of)
  plant asset 工場設備資産, 設備資産
  plant builder プラント・メーカー
  plant capacity 設備能力
  plant closure 工場閉鎖
  plant expansion 工場拡張
  plant in service 稼動施設
  plant investment 設備投資
  processing plant 加工工場, 加工処理工場
  subcontracting plant 下請工場
  title plant 権原プラント
  utility plant 公益設備

▶The firm's *plants* will be sold or liquidated. 同社の工場は，売却または清算される。

▶This joint venture *plant* started operating in 1984 with Toyota and GM each providing half the capital. この合弁工場は，トヨタとGMが折半出資して1984年に生産を開始した。

▶Toyota is estimated to have invested an initial ¥15 billion in the *plant*. トヨタの同工場への初期投資額は，推定で150億円と見られる。

plant and equipment 工場設備, 生産設備, 設備, 設備装置, 有形固定資産 (⇒investment in plant and equipment)
  existing plant and equipment 既存設備
  new plant and equipment 新規設備
  plant and equipment investment 設備投資 (=investment in plant and equipment, plant and equipment funding, plant and equipment spending, spending for plant and equipment)
  producer's plant and equipment 生産設備
  spend on plant and equipment 設備投資する

▶As companies are cautious about the future outlook on exports and business performance, a slowdown of their investment in *plants and equipment* will be avoidable. 企業が輸出や業績の先行きについて慎重なため，企業の設備投資の減速は今後，避けられないだろう。

plasma 名 プラズマ, 粒子 (物質の原子核と電子が分離して，激しく飛び回る状態をプラズマという)

▶The extreme heat observed on the shuttle Columbia's left wing during its reentry could have been caused by hot *plasma* penetrating the craft's wheel well. スペース・シャトル「コロンビア」が大気圏に再突入している間，機体の左翼に観察された異常な温度上昇の原因は，機体の車輪収納部に浸透した高温プラズマ(粒子)だった可能性がある。

plasma display panel プラズマディスプレー・パネル《略 PDP》(薄型テレビの中核部品)

▶Hitachi Ltd. and Matsushita Electric Industrial Co. will tie up to develop *plasma display panels* (PDPs). 日立製作所と松下電器産業が，プラズマディスプレー・パネル(PDP)の開発で提携する。

plasma-display panel TV プラズマテレビ

▶The market share for *plasma-display panel TVs* larger than 40 inches will remain at less than 3 percent. 40インチ型以上のプラズマテレビの市場シェアは，3%未満にとどまるだろう。

plasma duration time プラズマの持続時間

▶The Japan Atomic Energy Agency's JT-60 Tokamak has extended its *plasma duration time* to 28.6 seconds. 日本原子力研究開発機構の臨界プラズマ試験装置「JT-60」で，プラズマの持続時間を28.6秒に延ばした。

plasma television プラズマ・テレビ

▶The company has slashed production costs of

plasma televisions while keeping them compatible with the "full high vision" standard.　同社は，画像規格の「フルハイビジョン」に対応しながら，プラズマテレビの生産コストを大幅に削減した。

plastic 形 可塑性のある，柔軟な，合成樹脂製の，ビニール製の，プラスチック製の，人工の，形成の，名 合成樹脂製品，ビニール，クレジット・カード，プラスチック

　optical plastic fiber プラスチック光ファイバー《略 POF》
　plastic bag ビニール袋，ポリ袋
　plastic card プラスチック・カード
　plastic credit クレジット・カードによる支払い，クレジット・カードの利用
　plastic injection molding プラスチック射出成形
　plastic money クレジット・カード，プラスチック・マネー
　plastic product プラスチック製品（＝plastic goods）
　plastic surgery 形成外科
　plastic tray 食品用のトレー
　plastic waste 廃プラスチック
　plastic wrap 台所用品のラップ（＝cling film）
▶Polyethylene is used to make *plastic* bags and plastic trays.　ポリエチレンは，レジ袋や食品用のトレーを作るのに使われる。

plastics industry 合成樹脂業界，樹脂業界，樹脂産業，プラスチック産業

plateau 名 踊り場，横ばい状態，安定状態，安定水準，安定期，高水準，停滞，停滞期，伸び悩み，高原，高原現象，台地

　economic plateau 高原景気
　reach a plateau 横ばい状態［安定水準］に達する，伸び悩む，停滞期に入る
　remain on a plateau 高水準にとどまる
▶The economy has climbed out of a *plateau*.　景気［経済］が踊り場から脱出した。

platform 名 演壇，舞台，場所，場，席，足場，足がかり，土台，基地，〈政党の〉政策綱領，綱領，〈米大統領選候補者選びでの〉綱領宣言，政策方針，公約，〈コンピュータの〉基盤，（ソフトウエアやハードウエアなど）コンピュータの基盤となるシステム，基本システム，掘削の足場，プラットフォーム

　drilling platform 掘削プラットフォーム（海底掘削装置を支える構造基台）
　e-procurement platform 電子調達プラットフォーム
　moving platform 自動作業台
　multi-platform operating system マルチプラットフォームの基本ソフト（OS）
　officers platform 役席
　platform for the comeback 復活の切り札
　platform frame construction 枠組壁工法，ツーバイフォー工法
　platform officer 役席者
　platform service プラットフォーム・サービス（ネットワーク上に取引のための場を提供するサービス）
　production platform 生産基地
　software platform 基本ソフト，ソフトウエア・プラットフォーム
　technology platform 技術基盤
▶Republicans at their national convention adopted a *platform* endorsing President George W. Bush's agenda.　米共和党全国大会で共和党員は，ブッシュ大統領の政策を承認する綱領を採択した。

play 動 〈投資・事業機会などを〉利用する，取引する

player 名 参加者，関係者，投資家，トレーダー，専門家，企業，要因，プレーヤー（playersで「企業グループ」，「勢力」を意味する場合もある）

　major player 主流，大手企業
　major players in the industries 業界大手，業界の大手企業
　market player 市場関係者，市場参加者，市場筋，マーケット・プレーヤー（＝market participant）
　professional players ディーラー筋
　strong player 有力企業
　top player 最大手
▶*Players* on the country's stock markets responded to the preliminary GDP report favorably.　国内の株式市場関係者は，国内総生産（GDP）の速報に好感した。
▶The firm's Japanese unit is the dominant *player* in online search services in this country.　同社の日本子会社は，日本国内のオンライン検索サービスでは他者をリードしている。

playing field 事業環境，競争条件，競争の場，土俵

Plaza Accord プラザ合意（＝Plaza Agreement: 1985年にニューヨークのプラザ・ホテルで行われたG5での合意）
▶*Plaza Accord* served as demand by these four countries for Japan to boost domestic demand as a means of curtailing its trade surplus.　プラザ合意は，日本の貿易黒字を減らす手段として，これら主要4か国（米英独仏）が日本に内需拡大を要求

PLC 英国の公開有限会社，公開有限責任会社 （= plc, p.l.c.: **public limited company**の略。株式会社(company limited by shares)と保証有限責任会社(company limited by guarantee)のうち，公開会社(public company)として登録している会社の社名の末尾に表示することになっている）
▶HSBC Holdings *PLC* will shut its subprime mortgage unit and eliminate 750 jobs. 英銀行大手のHSBCホールディングスは，低所得者向け住宅融資「サブプライム・ローン」事業の米国子会社を閉鎖して，従業員750人を解雇する。

PLC 製品ライフサイクル （**product life cycle** の略）

plead 動 弁護する，…に抗弁する，主張する，申し立てる，答弁する，嘆願する，要請する
　plead against wrong 不正に対して抗弁する
　plead guilty to …に対して罪を認める，…に対して有罪を認める
　plead innocent [not guilty] to …に対して無罪を申し立てる，…に対して無罪を主張する
　plead one's case …の事件を弁護する
　plead with the jury to …するよう陪審に嘆願する

plebiscite 名 住民投票，国民投票 （= public vote, referendum）
▶A majority of residents of the village objected to a plan to use plutonium-uranium mixed oxide (MOX) fuel at a local nuclear power plant in the nation's first *plebiscite*. 全国初の住民投票で，同村住民の過半数が，プルトニウムとウランの混合酸化物(MOX)燃料を地元原子力発電所で利用する計画（プルサーマル計画）に反対した。

pledge 動 入質する，質入れする，質を置く，抵当に入れる，担保に入れる，担保に供する，誓約する，公約する，確約する
　amount pledged 譲渡済み金額
　assets pledged 担保資産，担保提供された資産，担保として差し入れられた資産
　negative pledge 担保制限
　pledge as collateral for financing 資金調達の担保として提供する［担保として差し出す］
　pledge collateral 担保を差し入れる，担保を差し出す
　pledged asset 担保資産，買入資産
　pledged collateral 担保の裏付け，担保の差し入れ，差し入れ担保
▶An advance of $100,000 was received from the bank by *pledging* $120,000 of the company's accounts receivable. 同社は，同社の売掛金12万ドルを担保に供して，同行から借入金10万ドルを受領した。

pledge 名 担保，抵当，質権設定，入質，担保［抵当］品，誓約，公約，確約，プレッジ
　negative pledge [clause] 担保提供制限条項，ネガティブ・プレッジ条項
　right of pledge 担保権
　unconditional pledge [clause] 無条件の担保条項

plenary 形 全員出席の，完全な，全権の，正式の

plight 名 窮状，苦境，深刻な状況，悪状況
▶The latest financial reorganization drama was triggered by UFJ Holdings' corporate *plight*. 今回の金融再編劇の引き金となったのは，UFJホールディングスの深刻な経営状況だ。

plot 名 陰謀，策略，小区画，動 …の設計図を作る，図をかく，たくらむ，計画する

plug 名 店(たな)ざらし品，売れ残り，宣伝，推薦，栓，詰め物，動 こつこつ働く，…に栓をする，プラグを差し込む

plummet 動 急落する，暴落する，大幅に減少する
▶Stock prices have *plummeted* and the yen's value has risen in the wake of the subprime loan fiasco. サブプライム・ローン(米低所得者向け住宅ローン)問題を受けて，株価が急落し，円高が進んでいる。

plunder 動 略奪する，収奪する，名 略奪品

plunge 動 減少する，下落する，低下する，低迷する，急落する，安値を付ける，転落する （= drop）
　plunge into loss 赤字に転落する
　plunge to a five month low 5か月来の安値を付ける
▶Citigroup's third-quarter profit *plunged* 57 percent mainly due to fixed-income trading losses and mortgage-backed securities losses. シティグループの第3四半期の利益は，主に債券取引の損失や住宅融資証券[不動産証券]関連の損失で，57%減少した。

plunge 名 〈市場の〉低迷，〈株価の〉急落，下落，激減，減少，急降下，落ち込み，突入
　plunge in demand 需要の落ち込み
　stock market's plunge 株式市場の低迷
　the sharp plunge in the dollar's value 急激なドル安
▶If Japanese stock prices continue to fall whenever there is a *plunge* in U.S. stocks, the country might be hit by another financial crisis. 米国株の下落に連動して日本の株価の下落が続けば，日本は再び金融危機に見舞われかねない。

plus 前 …を加えて[加えた], 形 プラスの, 正の, 名 加符号, プラス記号, 正数, プラスアルファ, 余り, 利益

ply 動 精出して働く, 営む, 〈交通機関が〉定期的に往復する

POD 現物引換え払い (**payment on delivery** の略)

point 名 〈為替相場などの〉騰落単位, 水準, 地点, 時点, 時期, 問題, 要点, 論点, 趣旨, 事項, 材料, ポイント (⇒**Nikkei Stock Average**)
　appeal point 訴求点
　basis point ベーシス・ポイント (1ベーシス・ポイント=0.01%, 100ベーシス・ポイント=1%)
　breakdown point 損益分岐点, 採算点 (= break-even point)
　commercialization point 商業化点
　ex point of origin 現地渡し
　half a percentage point 0.5%
　negative points 悪材料, マイナス面
　ordering point 発注点
　pension point system 年金ポイント制
　percentage point パーセント・ポイント, ポイント, % (1パーセント・ポイント=1%)
　point and figure charting 株式相場の罫線方式
　point card service カード・サービス
　point man 代表交渉人
　point of origin price 現場渡し価格
　point of purchase 購買時点《略 POP》
　point system ポイント制
　points of concern 懸念材料
　positive points 好材料, プラス面
　sales point セールス・ポイント
　shipping point 出荷地渡し
　tax point 課税時期
　three-quarters of a point 0.75%, 0.75ポイント (⇒**key interest rate**)

▶The broader Tokyo Stock Price Index dropped 56.72 *points* to 1,017.03, the largest drop this year. 東証株価指数(TOPIX)は, 前日より56.72ポイント低い1,017.03で, 今年最大の下げ幅を記録した.

▶The Dow Jones industrials plunged 370 *points* after the ISM's index of service sector activity dropped below 50. ダウ平均株価(工業株30種)は, 全米供給管理協会(ISM)のサービス業景況感指数が50を割り込んだことを受けて, (前日比で)370ドル急落した.

▶The economy reached its lowest *point* at the beginning of this year. 景気は, 今年の初めに「谷」を付けた.

▶The Ito-Yokado Co. retail group issues the IY Card, with which users can accumulate *points* paying with both cash and credit card. イトーヨーカ堂グループは, 現金購入でもクレジット・カードでの購入でも利用者がポイントをためることができるアイワイカードを発行している.

▶There are several *points* of concern regarding the future prospects of the nation's economy. 日本経済の先行きに, いくつか懸念材料がある.

point of origin 源泉地, 原産地点, 現場渡し

▶The *point of origin* (the location of the selling organization) of revenues and the location of the assets determine the geographic areas. 地域別区分は, 収益の源泉地(販売組織の所在地)と資産の所在地に基づいて行われています.

point of sales 販売時点情報管理《略 POS》

point-of-sale 名 小売店, 特約店, 形 店頭の, 販売時点の《略 POS》
　point-of-sale advertising 店頭広告, POS広告
　point-of-sales equipment POS機器
　point of sales system 販売時点情報管理システム, POSシステム

poised to …する用意[準備]ができている, …する覚悟だ, …する構えを見せている, …する方針だ, …しそうだ, …する見通しだ (=ready to)

▶The IAEA is *poised to* cut the frequency of inspections at the Japan's 50 or so light-water nuclear reactors from quarterly to once a year. 国際原子力機関(IAEA)が, 日本の軽水炉約50基の査察回数を年4回から1回に削減する見通しとなった.

poison pill 毒薬条項, 敵対的買収に対する防衛手段, 買収防衛策, ポイズン・ピル (敵対的買収に対する防衛策の一つ.「毒薬条項」は, 既存株主に対して転換優先株式を株式配当の形で発行することを定めた条項を指す)
　poison pill strategy ポイズン・ピル戦略
　poison pill variant 毒薬条項の一種, ポイズン・ピルの一種

▶If Hokuetsu Paper Mills decides to carry out the *poison pill*, Oji Paper Co. is likely to take legal action against it. 北越製紙が買収防衛策を実施したら, 王子製紙は法的措置を取る可能性が高い.

poison pill defense [defence] ポイズン・ピル防衛, 毒薬条項防衛, 毒入り避妊薬

▶The Business Organization Law, which went into effect in fiscal 2006, allows companies to use *poison pill defense* tactics more easily. 2006年度から施行された「会社法」で, 企業は, ポイズン・ピル(毒薬条項)防衛策を以前より容易に講

じられるようになった。

poison pill plan ポイズン・ピル方式（＝poison pill scheme）
▶Companies can resort to corporate defense schemes, including a *poison pill* plan to issue new shares, to fight hostile takeover bids. 敵対的買収への対抗策として，企業は新株発行（増資）のポイズン・ピル（毒薬）方式などの企業防衛策をとることができる。

poison pill scheme ポイズン・ピル防衛策，ポイズン・ピル方式（＝poison pill plan）
▶The firm has scrapped its plan to invoke the nation's first *poison pill scheme* to ward off hostile takeover bids. 同社は，敵対的TOB（株式公開買付けによる企業買収）を防ぐための日本で最初のポイズン・ピル防衛策の実施計画を白紙撤回した。

policy 图 政策，対策，方針，施政方針，経営方針，規定，保険証券，保険証書，保険契約，ポリシー（⇒production）
　acceptable use policy ネットワークやコンピュータ・システムを利用する際の方針や約束事《略 AUP》
　accounting policy 会計方針，経理方針
　administrative policy 業務方針
　advertising policy 広告政策
　bank rate policy 金利政策
　basic policy 基本政策，基本方針
　budgetary policy 財政政策
　business policy 経営方針，経営政策，営業政策，営業方針，企業政策
　cheap money policy 低金利政策
　collateral policy 担保方針
　consolidated policy 連結方針（＝consolidation policy）
　credit policy 信用方針，金融政策
　credit underwriting policy 与信基準
　dividend policy 配当方針，配当政策
　economic policy 経済政策
　endowment policy 養老保険証券
　environmental policy 環境政策
　exchange rate policy 為替政策（＝exchange policy）
　expansionary policy 景気刺激型の政策
　financial policy 金融政策，財政政策，財務政策，財務方針，資金調達方針（資金の調達と運用についての基本方針）
　financing policy 資金調達方針（＝financing philosophy）
　fire policy 火災保険証券
　fiscal policy 財政政策
　income policy 所得政策
　insurance policy 保険証券，保険証書，保険契約，保険商品，保険
　interest rate policy 金利政策
　investment policy 投資政策
　labor [labour] market policy 労働政策
　liberal policy 自由化政策
　life policy 生命保険証券
　management policy 経営方針，経営政策，経営姿勢（＝managerial policy）
　marine insurance policy 海上保険証券
　marketing policy マーケティング政策，マーケティング方針
　monetary policy 金融政策
　open policy 予定保険証券
　pay-as-you-go policy 無借金経営
　personnel policy 人事方針
　policy address 施政方針演説（＝policy speech）
　policy-based financing 政策金融（＝policy-based finance）
　policy bulletins 業務方針書
　policy cancellation 保険の解約
　policy committee 政策委員会
　policy conditions 保険約款
　policy dividend 契約者配当
　policy formulation 方針策定
　policy maker [policymaker] 政策立案者，政策策定者，政策決定者，政策当局［当局者］
　policy making [policymaking] 政策立案，政策策定，政策決定
　policy obligations 保険契約債務（⇒unforeseen loss）
　policy rate 政策金利
　policy reserve 保険契約準備金，責任準備金
　policy-setting panel 政策決定委員会
　policy shift 政策転換，方針転換
　policy speech 施政方針演説
　price policy 価格政策，売価政策
　pricing policy 価格決定方針，価格決定政策，価格政策
　product differentiation policy 製品差別化政策
　product diversification policy 製品多角化政策
　promote-from-within policy 社内人材登用方針
　regulatory policy 規制政策
　restrictive monetary policy 金融引締め政策
　risk management policy リスク管理政策
　stock policy 株価対策

time policy 期間保険
unemployment insurance policy 失業保険証券
valued policy 確定保険証券
wage policy 賃金政策
write-off policy 償却方針

▶During the bubble economy, life insurers sold a large number of *policies* by promising high yields. バブル期に生保各社は、高い予定利率を約束して多くの保険契約を獲得した。

▶*Policies* are only implemented after relevant bills have been enacted by the Diet into law. 政策は、関連法案が国会で立法化されて初めて実行に移される。

▶U.S.-based fund Steel Partners is happy at changes in Yushiro Chemical Industry Co.'s dividend *policy* taken to fend off the hostile takeover bid. 米系投資ファンドのスティール・パートナーズは、ユシロ化学工業が敵対的株式公開買付け(TOB)の防衛策として行った配当方針の変更に満足している。

policy-based financing operations 政策金融の運営

▶*Policy-based* financing operations, which take advantage of government subsidies, are adversely affecting the price mechanism in the financial market. 政府の補助金を受けて運営される政策金融は、金融市場の価格メカニズムを歪めている。

policy firming 政策の引締め

▶The U.S. central bank's Federal Open Market Committee emphasized that the extent and timing of any further *policy firming* would depend on the evolution of the economic outlook. 米連邦準備制度理事会(FRB)の連邦公開市場委員会(FOMC)は、「一層の金融政策引締め[一層の金融引締め]の程度やタイミングは、経済見通しの成り行きによる」と強調した。

policy meeting 政策会議

▶The U.S. Federal Reserve Board left U.S. rates unchanged at a key *policy meeting*. 米連邦準備制度理事会(FRB)は、重要な政策会議(公開市場委員会)で、米国の金利(公定歩合とFF金利の誘導目標)を据え置くことを決めた。

policyholder 名 保険契約者, 契約者, 保険加入者 (⇒insurance policyholder)
dividend to policyholders 契約者配当 (= policyholder dividend)
insurance policyholder 保険契約者
meeting of representatives of policyholders 総代会
policyholder benefits 契約者給付金

▶Life insurance companies invest *policyholders'* premiums in stocks. 生命保険会社は、保険契約者の保険料を株式に投資している。

policyholders' representative meeting 総代会, 保険会社の総代会 (=the meeting of representatives of policyholders:「総代会」は、株式会社の株主総会にあたる。総代は取引先などから選ばれることが多く、経営へのチェック機能が乏しいとの批判がある)

▶A *policyholders'* representative meeting is akin to a general shareholders meeting for a stock company. 総代会は、株式会社の株主総会にあたる。

policymakers of the FRB 米連邦準備制度理事会(FRB)の政策決定者 (=the FRB's policy-makers)

policymaking members of the U.S. Federal Open Market Committee 米連邦公開市場委員会(FOMC)の政策決定メンバー [政策決定者]

policy-setting meeting 政策決定会合

▶The Bank of Japan kept its ultra-loose monetary policy unchanged at Friday's *policy-setting meeting*. 日銀は、金曜日の政策決定会合で、極端な金融緩和政策を見直さない[据え置く]ことにした。

Political Funds Control Law 政治資金規正法

poll 名 世論調査, 投票, 選挙, 投票所, 投票数
exit poll 出口調査
Gallup poll ギャラップ調査
heavy poll 高い投票率
light poll 低い投票率
nationwide poll 全国世論調査
opinion poll 世論調査 (=public opinion poll)
straw poll 非公式投票

pollution 名 汚染, 公害
air pollution 大気汚染
Air Pollution Control Law 大気汚染防止法, 大気汚染規制法
atmospheric pollution control 地球環境保護
combined pollution 複合汚染
environmental pollution 環境汚染
Federal Air Pollution Regulations 連邦大気汚染防止規制
information pollution 情報公害
noise pollution 騒音公害
pollution control 汚染防止, 公害防止
pollution export 公害輸出

pollution tax 公害税, 汚染税
road-related pollution 道路公害
soil pollution 土壌汚染
Water Pollution Control Law 水質汚濁防止法
▸Air and other road-related *pollution* is mainly caused by the exhaust from cars and other vehicles, and particularly by particulate matter (PM) emitted in the exhaust from diesel-powered vehicles. 大気汚染や他の道路公害の主因は, 自動車排ガス, とりわけディーゼル車の排ガスから出る粒子状物質 (PM) だ。
▸In the process of Japan's rapid economic growth after the war, many *pollution*-related lawsuits were filed around the country. 戦後日本の高度経済成長の過程で, 公害訴訟が全国各地で起きた。

polypropylene 名 ポリプロピレン
▸*Polypropyren* is used for automobile bumpers and snack bags. ポリプロピレンは, 自動車のバンパーやお菓子の袋を作るのに使われる。

pool 名 企業連合, カルテル, 共同出資, 共同管理, 共同資金, ストック, プール, 動 共同計算する, 共同の利権とする, 共同負担する, プールする

pooling of interest [interests] 持ち分プーリング, 持ち分プーリング法 (＝pooling of interest method)
▸We accounted for the merger as a *pooling of interests*. This means we combined the financial statements for the two companies. 当社は, この合併を持ち分プーリング法で会計処理しました。これは, 2社の財務書類を結合したということです。

poor 形 不振の, 低迷した, 伸び悩みの, 不利な, 厳しい, 乏しい, 悪い
poor earnings 減益
poor economic conditions 景気低迷, 景気の悪化
poor operating revenue 営業収入の低迷
poor operational performance 業績低迷, 業績の悪化
poor performance 業績不振, 業績の伸び悩み
poor-performing company 業績不振の会社 [企業]
poor profitability 収益性の低迷
poor sales 販売低迷, 販売不振, 売上低迷 (＝weak sales)
▸In 2008, we were hit by poor sales of digital devices. 2008年度は, デジタル製品 [デジタル機器] の販売不振に見舞われました。

poor profitability 収益性の低迷, 低収益性
▸The firm entered the U.S. cell phone service market as an MVNO, but withdrew due to poor *profitability*. 同社は, MVNO (仮想移動体通信事業者) として米国の携帯電話サービス市場に参入したが, 採算が取れないため撤退した。

POP 購買時点 (**point of purchase** の略)
pop industry 文化産業
▸*Pop industries*, which engage in the production and marketing of such popular cultural items as manga, anime, TV dramas and video games, have grown into one of the biggest industrial sectors of East Asia. マンガやアニメ, テレビ・ドラマ, テレビ・ゲームなど人気のある文化商品を生産し販売する文化産業が, 東アジアの一大産業に成長した。

pop item 文化商品
▸*Pop items* have been produced and marketed with such middle-income people in urban centers as targets. 文化商品は, このような都市中心部の中産階級の人たちを対象として生産, 販売されている。

population 名 人口, 住民数, 全住民
populist 形 大衆迎合的な
port 名 港, 通関港, 空港, 荷役口
cargo port 貨物港
commercial port 商港, 商業港
container port コンテナ港
discharge port 荷揚げ港
fishing port 漁港
free port area 自由港区
industrial port 工業港
lading port 船積み港
port authority 港湾管理者, 港湾当局
port charges 港湾諸掛り (港税 (port rates), 港湾使用料 (port dues), 灯台料 (light dues), 水先料 (pilotage), トン税 (tonnage dues), 桟橋使用料 (pier dues) など)
port clearance 通関手続き, 出港手続き, 出港許可
port facilities 港湾施設
port industry 港湾産業
port mark 仕向け港マーク, 揚げ地荷印
port of call 寄港地
port of destination 仕向け港
port of entry 輸入港, 通関港, 手続き港
port of exit 輸出港, 仕出し港
port warehouse 港湾倉庫
quarantine port 検疫港
shipping port 積出し港
trade [trading] port 貿易港
way port 中間港

port state control ポート・ステート・コント

ロール制度《略 PSC》(一般に老朽化した外国の船舶や新造船について，入港を許可する寄港国がその監督を行う制度)
▸The real purpose of the *port state control* (PSC) system is to check the safety of ships. ポート・ステート・コントロール(PSC)の本来の目的は，船舶の安全性の検査にある．

portable 形 携帯用の，持ち運びできる，移動式，移植可能な，通算可能な年金制度の

porter 名 運搬人

porterage 名 運搬，運送業，運賃

portfolio 名 所有有価証券，保有株式，有価証券明細表，有価証券報告書，資産内容，資産構成，資産管理，金融資産，投資資産，ポートフォリオ
  bond portfolio 債券ポートフォリオ
  equity portfolio 株式投資
  financial portfolio ローンや証券投資
  investment portfolio 投資ポートフォリオ，投資資産，投資資本構成，投資の内容
  loan portfolio 貸出残高，貸出金ポートフォリオ
  optimal portfolio 最適ポートフォリオ
  portfolio diversification ポートフォリオの分散投資
  portfolio gains 資産売却益
  portfolio investment 有価証券投資，証券投資，株式・債券投資，資産運用投資，間接投資，ポートフォリオ投資，投資有価証券
  portfolio management 資産管理，最適資産管理，資産運用，資金運用，ポートフォリオ管理，ポートフォリオ運用
  portfolio of products 製品ポートフォリオ，製品ライン (＝product portfolio)
  portfolio selection 資産選択，資産選好，資産管理，株式銘柄選択
  product portfolio management 製品ポートフォリオ管理《略 PPM》
  receivables portfolio 債権ポートフォリオ
  troubled loan portfolio 不良債権ポートフォリオ
▸The investment *portfolio* was predominantly long-term bonds and equity investments as of December 31, 2008. 投資ポートフォリオは，2008年12月31日現在，長期債券と株式投資が中心になっています．
▸We are building on the skills of our people and our growing *portfolio* of technologies to create the platforms upon which whole new global industries will be born. 当社は，社員の技能と発展を遂げる当社の各種製品技術を構築して，まったく新しいグローバル産業を生み出す基盤を創造しています．

position 動 位置につける，据える，特定の場所に置く，配置する (⇒research and development)
  be favorably positioned to …する上で有利な立場にある
  be positioned to …する体制を築く，…する態勢を整える
  be well positioned to …する上で有利な立場にある，…する好位置につける，…できる力がある (⇒well positioned)
  position oneself to [for] …への準備を進める，…への対応を進める，…を推進する，…に取り組む
▸Today, the Corporation is favorably *positioned* to capture an increasing share of the global market for telecommunications equipment and associated services. こんにち当社は，通信機器と関連サービスのグローバル市場でシェアを拡大するうえで，有利な立場にあります．
▸We will *position* ourselves for new opportunities in Europe. 当社は，欧州での新たな事業機会に備える方針です．

position 名 有価証券の保有状態，証券保有高，持ち高，経営基盤，事業基盤，位置，地位，役職，状態，地歩，足場，勤め口，職，ポジション (⇒financial position)
  bear position 売り持ち，投機的売り持ち，空売り
  bedrock position 基本的立場
  bull position 買い持ち，投機的買い持ち，空買い
  cash position 現金持ち高，現預金，直物ポジション，キャッシュ・ポジション
  competitive position 競争力，競争上の地位
  credit position 信用状態
  debt position 借入れ状況，債務状況
  ensure market position 市場での地位を強化する
  enter the market 市場に参入する，市場に進出する，市場を利用する
  equity position 持ち株比率，出資比率
  exchange position 為替持ち高，為替ポジション
  hedge position ヘッジ・ポジション
  leading position 主導的地位
  leverage position 財務状況
  long position 買い持ち，買い建て，ロング・ポジション
  management position 管理職，上級管理職
  market position 市場での地位，市場での立場
  negotiating position 交渉力
  operating position 営業状況，事業基盤
  overbought position 買い持ち
  oversold position 売り持ち

position paper 特定の問題に関する方針説明書
short position 売り持ち, 売り建て, ショート・ポジション
strengthen our position 当社の経営基盤[事業基盤]を強化する
take long positions in securities 証券の買い持ちをする, 証券のロング・ポジションを取る
take short positions in securities 証券の空売りをする, 証券のショート・ポジションを取る

▶A derivative contract is also used to hedge an investor's *position*. デリバティブ契約は, 投資家のポジションをヘッジするために使われることもある。

▶At the end of the year, women held 20 percent of U.S. management *positions*. 当期末の時点で, 女性は米国の当社管理職の20%を占めています。

▶Following the merger, Nichiro's president will assume the *position* of chairman of the new holding company. 経営統合に伴って, ニチロの社長が新持ち株会社の会長に就任する。

▶We will strengthen our *position* by reducing costs and improving productivity. 当社は, コスト削減と生産性の向上により, 当社の経営基盤を強化する方針です。

positive 形 プラスの, 正の, 黒字の, 強含みの, 強気の, 好影響を与える, 明るい, 上昇傾向にある, 積極的な, ポジティブ, 名 強気材料, 好材料, プラス要因 (⇒**negative**)
  positive earnings 好業績, 好決算
  positive factor 強気の材料, 好材料, 買い材料, プラス要因, 重要なポイント
  positive goodwill 積極的のれん, 積極的営業権
  positive growth プラス成長
  positive implications 好材料, プラス要因, 格上げの方向
  positive results 好業績, 好決算 (=good results, positive earnings, robust performance)
  revise upward the rating outlook from negative to positive 格付け見通しを「ネガティブ(弱含み)」から「ポジティブ(強含み)」に上方修正する

▶The gross domestic product in the October-December period marked *positive* growth for the second consecutive quarter. 10−12月期の国内総生産(GDP)は, 2四半期連続でプラス成長を示した。

positron emission tomography 陽電子放射断層撮影装置《略 PET》

▶*Positron* emission tomography (PET) is an up-to-date technology that can detect tiny cancer cells. 陽電子放射断層撮影装置(PET)は, 微細ながん細胞も発見できる最新技術だ。

possess 動 所有する, 占有する, 入手する
possession 名 所有, 保有, 占有, 所持, 所有物, 所持品, 財産, 所有権, 支配権
  actual possession 現実の占有
  bond yield in the possession period 所有期間利回り
  chose in possession 動産
  debtor in possession 継承破産人
  estate in possession 現有不動産権, 現有不動産物件
  exclusive possession 排他的占有
  hostile possession 自主占有
  in one's possession …が所有する, …が占有する
  personal possessions 個人財産
  possession in deed [fact] 現実の占有
  right of possession 占有権, 所有権
  take into possession 抵当権を実行する
  take possession of …を取得する

▶In the temporary nationalization, the government will take *possession* of all shares from the bank's holding company at no cost. 一時国有化で, 政府は同行の持ち株会社から株式をゼロ円で全株取得することになる。

post 動 …を示す, 提示する, 〈赤字や黒字などを〉計上する, 転記する, 〈担保や証拠金などを〉差し入れる, 〈担保を〉設定する (⇒**row**)

▶In the previous year, we *posted* a group net profit of ¥37.3 billion. 前期に当社は, 373億円の連結税引き後利益[連結純利益]を計上した。

post 名 職, 地位, 部署, 持ち場, 任務, ポスト (⇒**president, representative**)
  be at one's post 持ち場についている, 任務についている
  be relieved of one's post 解任される
  liquidation post 整理ポスト
  monitoring post 監理ポスト, 監視ポスト (=supervision post)
  presidential post 社長ポスト
  trading post 取引ポスト

▶Tokyo, Osaka and Nagoya bourses placed Nikko Cordial stock on their respective supervision *posts* for possible delisting. 東京, 大阪, 名古屋の3証券取引所が, それぞれ日興コーディアルの株式を, 上場廃止の可能性があるため監理ポストに割り当てた。

post-balance sheet day 決算日後
post-balance sheet event 後発事象
post industrial society 脱工業化社会, 脱工

業社会
post-office box 私書箱《略 POB》
post-tax profit 税引き後利益（＝after-tax profit, net profit）
post test [**post-test**] 事後調査
postal business 郵政事業, 郵便事業
▸Privatization of the *postal businesses* started in April 2007.　郵政事業の民営化は，2007年4月にスタートした。
postdate 動 日付を実際より遅らせる，…に後の日付を書き込む，名 先日付, 事後日付
postemployment [**post-employment**] **benefits** 雇用後給付
▸*Postemployment benefits* include payments for separations and disabilities.　雇用後給付には，休職と疾病に対する支払いも含まれています。
postindustrialism ポスト工業化, 脱工業化
posting 名 書き込み(online chat),〈ニュースグループに送られる〉メッセージ, 担保の差し入れ, 担保の供与, 転記, 登記,〈職務などの〉任命, 派遣
　collateral posting 担保の差し入れ, 担保供与（＝posting of collateral）
　Net posting インターネットの書き込み
　direct posting 直接転記
　multiple posting 複数転記
　unit posting 個別転記
postpone 動 延期する
▸It is the first time in Japan that a company has *postponed* a planned listing due to the sub-prime crisis.　サブプライム・ローン（米国の低所得者向け住宅融資）問題で企業が上場計画を延期したのは，日本では初めてだ。
postponement of credits 債権の棚上げ
postretirement 名 退職後
　postretirement award 退職年金増加額
　postretirement benefit plan 退職後給付制度
　postretirement liabilities 雇用後債務
▸Our net liabilities for *postretirement* and post-employment liabilities are now combined on our balance sheet.　当社の正味の退職後債務と雇用後債務は現在，貸借対照表で合算されています。
postretirement benefit 退職後給付（＝benefit plan for retirees）
▸The cost of providing *postretirement benefits* is accrued over an employee's service period.　退職後給付費用は，従業員の勤続年数にわたって引当計上されています。
postretirement benefit cost 退職後給付費用
▸It is the company's practice to fund *postretirement benefit costs*, with an independent trustee, to the extent it is tax deductible.　税務上損金として認められる範囲内で，退職後給付費用を独立した信託機関に積み立てるのが，当社の慣行です。
postretirement benefit obligation 退職後給付債務
▸The Company recognized as expense in 2008 the entire accumulated *postretirement benefit obligation* as of January 1, 2008.　当社は，2008年1月1日現在の退職後給付債務累積額を2008年に費用として全額認識しました。
postretirement health care benefit 退職後の健康保険給付金, 退職後の健康管理給付
▸*Postretirement health care* and life insurance *benefits* are fully accrued, principally at retirement.　退職後の健康保険と生命保険の給付金は，主に従業員の退職時に全額計上されています。
potential 形 可能性がある, 潜在的な, 将来起こりそうな, 名 可能性, 将来性, 潜在能力, 潜在力, 潜在成長率, 余力, 余地, 素質, ポテンシャル（⇒ **strategic investment**）
　borrowing potential 借入れ余力
　cost cutting potential コスト削減の余地
　earnings growth potential 増益力, 増益の余地, 収益増加の可能性
　earnings potential 潜在収益力
　growth potential 成長潜在力, 潜在成長力, 成長余地, 成長能力, 成長ポテンシャル
　investment potential 投資収益力
　market potential 市場の可能性, 市場としての可能性
　potential acquisition 買収計画
　potential common stock 潜在株式
　potential demand 潜在需要
　potential growth 潜在成長力
　potential liability 潜在的債務額
　potential loss 予想損失, 潜在的損失額
　potential market 潜在市場
　potential seller 売却を考えている人
　production potential 生産能力
　sales potential 販売可能性, 販売可能量, 販売見込み高
▸Japanese automakers are considering hiking prices for their new models to be released in the U.S. market to compensate for *potential* foreign exchange losses.　日本の自動車メーカー各社は，将来の為替差損を穴埋めするため，米国市場に投入する新型車の値上げを検討している。
potential loan losses 予想貸倒れ損失, 予想

貸倒れ損失額
▸We took out provisions against *potential loan losses* from non-accrual loans. 不稼動資産から生じる予想貸倒れ損失に備えて、準備金を引き当てました。

pound 名 ポンド(重量単位), ポンド (英国などの通貨単位)

poundage 名 1ポンド当たりの料金[税金] (このポンドは金額・重量)

power 名 力, 能力, 権力, 権能, 権限, 法的権限, 支配力, 指名権, 電力, エネルギー, パワー (⇒ **earning power**)
 borrowing power 借入能力
 buying power 購買力 (＝purchasing power)
 excess earnings power 超過収益力
 financial power 金の力
 gain or loss in purchasing power 購買力損益
 historical cost/constant purchasing power accounting 取得原価・統一購買力会計
 hydroelectric power 水力発電
 nuclear power 原子力
 power breakfast 朝食会, 朝食会議 (朝食をとりながらのビジネス会議)
 power lunch 昼食会, 昼食会議 (昼食をとりながらのビジネス会議)
 power of attorney 委任状, 委任権 (＝letter of attorney)
 power producer and supplier 特定規模電気事業者《略 PPS》
 power-sharing 権限分担, 権限分有
 pricing power 価格支配力, 価格交渉力
 shifting power to price 価格転嫁力
 tidal power 潮汐（ちょうせき）発電
▸Nissan Motor Co.'s board of directors has delegated all the necessary *powers* to Nissan/Renault Chief Executive Officer Carlos Ghosn to conduct any discussions and negotiations with General Motors. 日産自動車の取締役会は、GMとの協議や交渉を行うのに必要な全権限を、カルロス・ゴーン日産／仏ルノー最高経営責任者に委任した。

power accommodation 電力の融通
▸There are more than 20 power generating companies in the area hit by the power outage, with five Independent System Operator organizations monitoring glitches involving *power accommodations* and transmission among the companies. 停電が起きた地域には発電会社が20社以上あり、五つある独立系運用機関が各社間の電力の融通や送電トラブルなどの監視をしている。

power game 駆け引き, 権力闘争, 権力奪取競争, 支配力獲得競争, パワー・ゲーム
▸The negotiations on measures to combat global warming are a *power game* in which developed, emerging and developing countries pursue their own national interests. 地球温暖化対策の交渉は、先進国や新興国、途上国がそれぞれ国益をかけるパワー・ゲームだ。

power generation 発電
 binary cycle power generation バイナリー・サイクル発電
 coal burning thermal power generation 石炭火力発電
 electric power generation 電力発電, 発電
 geothermal power generation 地熱発電 (＝geothermal generation)
 magnetohydrodynamic power generation MHD発電, 電磁流体力学発電
 nuclear power generation 原子力発電
 ocean current power generation 海流発電
 photovoltaic power generation 太陽光発電
 power generation by blast furnace top gas pressure 炉頂圧発電
 power generation by combined cycle 複合サイクル発電, 複合発電 (＝combined cycle generation)
 power generation by methanol reforming メタノール改質型発電
 power generation by pumped up water 揚水発電
 power generation combined with refuse incinerator ゴミ発電システム
 power generation from urban waste ゴミ発電
 power generation system by refuse incinerator ゴミ発電システム
 pumped-power generation 揚水発電 (＝pumping-up hydraulic power generation)
 solar energy power generation 太陽光発電
 solar thermal power generation 太陽熱発電 (＝solar thermal electric generation)
 steam power generation 火力発電
 superconducting power generation 超電導発電
 terrestrial geothermal power generation 地熱発電
 terrestrial heat power generation 地熱発電
 thermoelectric power generation 熱電気発電
 thermionic power generation 熱電子発電
 tidal power generation 潮流発電, 潮汐発電
 volcanic power generation 火山発電

wind-power generation 風力発電

power liberalization 電力自由化 (=liberalization of the electricity market)
▶The expanded *power liberalization* allows new firms set up by trading houses and gas companies to sell electricity to companies that consume more than 50 kilowatts of electricity at a time.　この電力自由化拡大で，商社やガス会社などが設立した新規参入の電力会社が，瞬間使用料50キロ・ワット以上の電力供給ができるようになった。

power outage 停電 (=power blackout)
▶The massive *power outage* affected the northern United States as well as southern Canada.　米国北部とカナダ南部で，大停電の影響が出た。

power plant 発電装置，発電設備，発電所，動力装置 (=power station, powerhouse)
▶The weak U.S. power system, incapable of controlling its *power plants*, and transmission and distribution companies of different sizes are believed to be behind the disaster.　規模の違う複数の発電所と送電・配電会社を統御できない米国の電力システムの弱さが，被害の背景にあると見られる。

powerhouse 名 発電所，原動力，強豪チーム，強力なチーム［組織］

PPI 生産者価格指数 (producer price indexの略)

PPP パブリック・プライベート・パートナーシップ (⇒partnership)

practice 名 実行，実践，実務，行為，営業，開業，業務，慣行，慣習，習俗，手法，仕組み，法律事務，訴訟実務，訴訟手続き (⇒business practice)
　accounting practices 会計実務，会計慣行，会計処理
　banking practice 銀行業務
　best practice 最善の手法，最良の方法，卓越した事例，最善の実施例，最善の業務慣行，最善の慣行，ベスト・プラクティス (⇒come up with)
　business practice 商慣習，商慣行，企業慣行，取引慣行，取引慣習，営業手法，業務
　collection practice 回収業務
　commercial practices 商慣習，商慣行，商慣習
　current practice 現行業務，現行実務
　fair practice 公正慣行，公正慣習
　financial practice 金融措置
　financial reporting practice 財務報告実務
　Foreign Corrupt Practices Act 海外不正行為防止法
　labor practice 労働慣行，労働行為，労働習慣 (=working practice)
　lending practice 融資慣行
　market practice 市場慣行
　marketing practices マーケティング慣行，マーケティング実践
　practice management 経営手法 (=operating management)
　practice of law 法律実務，弁護士業務
　practice standards 業務基準
　present practice 現行業務，現行実務 (=current practice)
　product development practice 製品開発戦略
　restrictive practices 制限的慣行，制限的取引慣行
　Rules of Fair Practice 公正慣習規則，公正慣行ルール (全米証券業協会の業界規則)
　theory and practice 理論と実践
　trade practices 貿易慣行，取引慣行，商慣行
　unfair business practices 不公正取引慣行，不公正商慣習
　uniform practice code 統一慣習規則
　usual practice 慣例 (⇒proceedings)
▶Our *practice* to raise the dividend every year is a signal to investors of our confidence in our future earning power.　毎年増配する当社の慣行は，投資家にとって，当社の将来の収益力に当社が確信をもっていることを裏付けるものです。
▶There have been inappropriate accounting *practices* at the subsidiary over the past several years.　過去数年間，子会社で会計処理の不正が行われてきた。

practice improvement plan 業務改善計画
▶This *practice improvement* plan must include steps to prevent such failures or breaches.　この業務改善計画には，このような義務の不履行や違反の防止策を盛り込むことになっている。

precaution 名 予防措置，警戒

precedent 名 先行，上位，優先権

precision 名 正確，精密，精度，形 正確な，精密な

precision equipment manufacturer 精密機器メーカー

precision machinery 精密機械
▶Many of Electrical and *precision machinery* companies in the country have shifted their production bases overseas to improve their competitiveness in prices.　国内電機・精密機械企業の多くは，価格競争力の向上をめざして生産拠点を海外に移している。

predecessor 名 前任者

predominantly 副 優位に，優勢に，主に

▶The Company operates *predominantly* in the wireless communication, semiconductor technology and advanced electronic industries. 当社は，無線通信，半導体技術と高度電子機器の各分野で優位に事業を展開しています。

preempt 動 先買権を得るために占有する，先制する

preemptive right 新株優先引受権，新株引受権，新株先買権，新株予約権，先取特権

preference 名 優先，優遇，特恵，優先権，先取権，好み，選好，選択，志向
　asset preference 資産選好
　buying preferences 消費者の好み
　dollar preference ドル選好
　liquidation preference 清算優先権
　liquidity preference 流動性選好
　preference dividend 優先配当
　preference measurement 選好測定
　preference segmentation 選好による細分化
　preference share [stock] 優先株
　preference test 選好テスト，好みテスト
　risk preference リスク選好
　risk/return preference リスクとリターンに関する選好，リスク・リターン輪郭についての選好
▶Voters have shown a *preference* for small government. 有権者は，「小さな政府」への志向を示している。

preferential 形 優先的な，先取権のある，優遇する，特恵的な，選択的な，差別制の
　general preferential duties 一般特恵関税
　preferential bill 優遇手形
　preferential creditor 優先債権者
　preferential duties 特恵関税
　preferential hiring 組合員優先雇用
　preferential interest rate for companies 企業向け融資の優遇金利
　preferential right 先取特権
　preferential tax system 優遇税制 (＝preferential taxation system)
▶The government and ruling parties will drastically review the *preferential* tax system for public entities. 政府・与党は，公益法人への優遇税制の抜本的見直しをする方針だ。

preferential nonvoting share 議決権のない優先株式
▶Sanyo will issue *preferential nonvoting shares* worth about ¥50 billion to Sumitomo Mitsui Banking Corp. 三洋電機は，三井住友銀行を引受先として約500億円の議決権がない優先株式を発行する。

preferential tax system for housing loans 住宅ローン減税制度，住宅ローン減税，住宅減税
▶The *preferential tax system for housing loans* has taken root as a way of promoting housing investment and sustaining economy. 住宅ローン減税制度は，住宅投資を促し，景気を支える手段として定着している。

preferential tax treatment 優遇税制措置，税制優遇
▶Businesses that are recognized as having a highly public nature will be entitled to receive *preferential tax treatment*. 高い公益性を認められた事業は，優遇税制措置を受けることができる。

preferred 形 優先権を与えられた，優先権を持つ，優先的，優先…
　preferred dividends 優先配当金
　preferred dividends declared 優先株式の配当宣言額
　preferred operating rate 最適操業度
　preferred resource 優先的供給源
　preferred securities 優先出資証券

preferred share 優先株式，優先株（＝preferred stock: 利益の配当や会社解散時の残余財産の分配が普通株式に優先して与えられる株式で，一般に議決権（経営参加権: voting right）は与えられない。⇒**preferred stock, priority**）
　convertible preferred shares 転換型優先株
　cumulative preferred shares 累積優先株
　first preferred shares 第一優先株式
　limited-life preferred shares 期限付き優先株
　nonconvertible preferred shares 非転換型優先株
　non-voting preferred shares 無議決権優先株
　participating preferred shares 参加型優先株，受益権付き優先株
　preferred share dividends 優先株式配当金
　preferred shares redeemed 優先株式の償還
　redeemable preferred shares 償還優先株，償還可能優先株
▶During the first nine months of 2008, the Corporation raised $600 million by the issuance of *preferred shares*. 2008年1－9月期に当社は，優先株式を発行して6億ドルを調達しました。

preferred stock 優先株式，優先株（＝preferred share; ⇒**common stock**）
　accumulated preferred stock 累積的優先株式
　adjustable rate preferred stock 配当率調整型優先株式
　auction rate preferred stock 配当率入札方式

優先株式
- **authorized preferred stock** 授権優先株式数
- **callable preferred stock** 償還優先株式
- **convertible preferred stock** 転換優先株式
- **cumulative preferred stock** 累積優先株式, 累加優先株式
- **dividend on preferred stock** 優先株式配当, 優先株配当
- **dividend preferred stock** 配当優先株式
- **increasing rate preferred stock** 配当率逓増優先株式
- **limited-life preferred stock** 期限付き優先株式
- **nonredeemable preferred stock** 非償還優先株式
- **nonvoting redeemable preferred stock** 無議決権償還優先株式
- **participating preferred stock** 参加型優先株式
- **perpetual preferred stock** 永久優先株式 (= permanent preferred stock)

▶No *preferred stock* is currently issued and outstanding. 現在, 優先株式は発行されておらず, 残高もありません。

prejudice 名 不利益, 損なうこと, 害すること, 侵害, 損害, 損傷, 動 損なう, 害する, 損害を与える, 傷つける
- **without prejudice** 権利を損なわずに, 権利を侵害しないで, 権利関係に不利益を与えることなく
- **without prejudice to any other rights or remedies** 他の権利または救済手段を侵害することなく
- **without prejudice to claim damages** 損害賠償の請求権を損なわないで

▶Such inspection shall not, in any way, *prejudice* the purchaser's right of inspection of the products after the delivery at the final destination or rejection of the defective products. この検査は, 最終目的地での引渡し後に本製品を検査する買い主の権利, または瑕疵(かし)ある製品を拒絶する買い主の権利を, いかなる意味でも損なわないものとする。

preliminary 形 予備の, 予備的な, 暫定的な, 仮の
- **preliminary announcement** 業績発表
- **preliminary application for listing** 上場の仮申請
- **preliminary data** 速報値
- **preliminary estimate** 暫定推定値
- **preliminary expenses** 創立費
- **preliminary exploration** 予備調査
- **preliminary prospectus** 仮目論見書
- **preliminary rating** 予備格付け
- **preliminary report** 速報, 速報値
- **preliminary research** 予備調査, 予備的調査
- **preliminary talks** 予備会談

▶A *preliminary* report on the GDP growth rate was released by the Cabinet Office. 内閣府が, GDP成長率の速報を発表した。

premarket trading 発行前取引, 通常取引前の時間外取引

▶New York oil prices quickly rose into $105 range in *premarket trading*. ニューヨーク(ニューヨーク商業取引所)の原油価格が, 通常取引前の時間外取引で105ドル台まで急騰した。

premarketing period [phase] 事前販売期間

premier 名 首相, 形 最初の, 第1位の

premises 名 〈契約の〉前文, 頭書, 既述事項, 前記[上記]事項, 不動産, 土地, 建物, 施設, 構内, 家屋, 不動産物件, 根拠, 前提

▶NOW, THEREFORE, in consideration of the *premises* and mutual agreements herein contained, the parties hereto agree as follows. そこで, ここに記載した上記事項と相互の合意事項を約因として, 本契約当事者は以下のとおり合意する。

premium 名 保険料, 保険金, 額面超過額, 割増価格, 割増金, 上乗せ, 手数料, 打ち歩(うちぶ), 権利金, オプション料, 報奨金, 奨励金, 賞金, 景品, プレミアム (⇒ net premium revenues, pension premium)
- **bond premium** 社債発行差金, 社債発行割増金, 社債割増金, 社債プレミアム, 打ち歩(ぶ)料 (「社債発行差金」=発行価額−額面金額。社債の発行価額(売買価格)が額面金額(額面価格)を上回ったときの差額)
- **call the preferred issue at a premium** プレミアムを払って優先株を償還する
- **estimated property premium** 推定損害保険料, 概算損害保険料
- **insurance premium** 保険料 (=insurable expense, insurance expense)
- **overtime premium** 超過勤務手当
- **premium borrower** 優良発行体
- **premium income** 保険料収入, 収入保険料
- **premium jobber** 景品取扱い卸売り業者, プレミアム・ジョバー
- **premium money** 奨励金, 報奨金, プレミアム・マネー (=push money)
- **premium on bonds payable** 社債割増発行差金
- **premium product** プレミアム付き製品
- **premium representative** プレミアム取扱い代

理人
- **redemption premium** 償還プレミアム
- **reinsurance premium** 再保険料
- **risk premium** 危険負担割増料, 危険度に対する割増金, 危険打ち歩, リスク・プレミアム
- **single premium** 一括払い保険料, 一時払い保険料
- **term premium** 期間プレミアム
- **up-front premium** 前払い保険料, 前払いプレミアム

▸The *premium* revenues are comprised of *premiums* from both individual and collective insurance contracts. この保険料収入は, 個人保険契約による収入と集団保険契約による収入から成る。

premium revenue 保険料収入(一般事業会社の売上高に相当。⇒**net premium revenues**)

▸*Premium revenues* slipped at seven of the nine major life insurers. 保険料収入が, 主要生命保険9社のうち7社が減少した。

prepaid 形 支払い済みの, 前払いの, プリペイド

prepaid book card プリペイド式図書カード

▸*Prepaid book cards* are the same size as business cards. プリペイド式図書カードは, 名刺と同じサイズだ。

prepaid cell phone プリペイド式携帯電話, プリペイド携帯 (=prepaid mobile phone)

▸A *prepaid cell phone* is one whose user fees are paid in advance, with no monthly basic charge. プリペイド式携帯電話は, ユーザーの使用料が前払い制で, 毎月の基本料金も不要だ。

prepare 動 作成する, 準備する, 用意する (⇒**accounting principle**, **GAAP**)

▸Small and midsize companies have been stepping up equity financing to fund capital investments and *prepare* for M&A deals. 中小企業は, 設備投資の資金調達とM&A取引に備えて, 株式発行による資金調達を急いでいる。

▸These financial statements have been *prepared* in accordance with the U.S. GAAP consistently applied throughout the periods indicated. これらの財務書類は, 当該期間中に一貫して適用した米国の一般に公正妥当と認められた会計原則[米国の会計基準]に従って[準拠して]作成されています。

prepay 動 前払いする, 前納する, 期限前償還する, 期限前弁済する

- **prepaid card** 代金前払い式カード, プリペイド・カード
- **prepaid cell phone** プリペイド式携帯電話, プリペイド携帯 (=prepaid mobile phone)
- **prepaid expenses** 前払い費用 (=prepaid costs)
- **prepaid expenses and other receivables** 前払い費用およびその他の債権
- **prepaid income** 前受け収益
- **prepaid pension cost** 前払い年金費用, 前払い年金原価, 前払い年金コスト (=prepaid pension expense)
- **prepaid postretirement healthcare costs** 前払い退職後健康保険費用
- **prepaid rental** 前払い賃借料 (=prepaid rental expense)
- **prepaid royalty** 前払い特許権使用料, 前払いロイヤルティ
- **prepay all or part of the mortgage** モーゲージの全部または一部を期限前償還する
- **prepay debt** 繰上げ償還する

▸The *prepaid* pension costs shown above are net of pension liabilities for plans where accumulated plan benefits exceed assets. 上記の前払い年金費用は, 累積給付債務額が資産額を超過している場合の年金債務純額を控除してあります。

prepayment 名 前払い, 前払い費用, 期限前償還, 期限前返済, 借換え

- **deferral of prepayments for future services** 短期繰延べ法
- **income tax prepayments** 前払い法人税等, 前払い税金
- **long term prepayments** 長期前払い費用 (=long-term prepaid expenses)
- **prepayment paid** 前払い費用
- **prepayment received** 前受け収益
- **prepayment speed** 期限前償還率 (=prepay speed, prepayment rate)
- **prepayment assumed** 期限前返済推定額
- **surge in prepayments** 期限前償還の急増 (=prepayment surge)

prerequisite 名 前提条件, 必要条件, 先行条件

▸Enhancing of the quality of graduate schools is a *prerequisite* for boosting Japan's international competitiveness in business and technology. 大学院の質向上が, ビジネスや技術の国際競争力を高めるための前提条件だ。

presale 名 前販売, プリセール(一般販売より先に行う得意客向けの特別販売)

presence 名 存在, 存在感, 影響力, 地位, 立場, 事業基盤, 経営基盤, 拠点, 進出, 営業網, ポジション, 態度, 姿勢, プレゼンス (⇒**international market**)

- **economic presence** 経済的影響力, 経済力
- **establish a presence in the market** 市場での

地位を確立する, 同市場で地位を築く
expand one's presence in …で事業基盤を拡大する
global presence 世界の営業網
market presence 市場での地位, 市場でのプレゼンス, 市場進出
political presence 政治的影響力
▶Leading banks may utilize the banking agent system to increase their *presence* in regional areas. 大手行は, 地方で拠点を増やすため銀行代理店制度を活用する可能性がある。
▶Oji Paper Co. ignored the *presence* of the anti-takeover measures and launched a tender offer for Hokuetsu Paper Mills Ltd. 王子製紙は, 買収防衛策の提示を無視して, 北越製紙に対してTOB (株式の公開買付け) に踏み切った。

present 動 表示する, 提示する, 示す, 開示する, 作成する, 提出する, 提供する, 贈呈する, 口頭で説明する, 申し立てる
　fairly present 適正に表示する (=present fairly; ⇒**closing balance sheet**)
　present consolidated financial statements 連結財務書類[連結財務諸表]を作成する[表示する]
▶In our opinion, these consolidated financial statements *present* fairly the financial position of the corporation as at December 31, 2008. 私どもの意見では, これらの連結財務書類は, 同社の2008年12月31日現在の財政状態を適正に表示しています。

present value 現在価値, 現価 《略 PV》 (=present worth)
▶The net *present value* of capital lease payments was $160 million after deducting estimated executory costs of $1 million and imputed interest of $23 million. キャピタル・リース支払い額の純現在価値は, 見積り管理費用100万ドルと帰属利子2,300万ドルの控除後で, 1億6,000万ドルです。

presentation 名 表示, 表示方法, 表示形式, 提示, 提案, 提出, 手形の提示, 発表, 公開, 説明会, 上演, 贈呈, 進呈, 授与, プレゼンテーション
　fair presentation 適正表示, 公正表示
　financial presentation 財務情報の表示
　financial statement presentation 財務書類[財務諸表]の表示, 財務書類の作成
　graphic presentation 図表による表示, 図表による報告
　manner of presentation 表示方法
　net presentation 純額表示
　presentation of current assets and liabilities 流動資産と流動負債の表示
▶An audit includes evaluating the overall financial statement *presentation*. 監査には, 財務書類全体の表示についての評価も含まれています。

president 名 社長, 会長, 会頭, 頭取, 総裁, 議長, 委員長, 学長, 総長, 大統領, 国家主席
　co-president 共同頭取
　company president 会社社長
　president and chief executive officer 社長兼最高経営責任者
　president-designate 次期社長, 新任社長
　president-elect 次期大統領
　president emeritus 名誉会長
　President's Letter 社長の書簡, 株主各位, 株主の皆様へ, ご挨拶
　President's Message 社長の挨拶, 株主各位, 株主の皆様へ, ご挨拶
▶Following the merger, Maruha's *president* will take the post of *president* of the new holding company. 経営統合に伴って, マルハの社長が新持株会社の社長に就任する。
▶Takafumi Horie quit his post as the *president* of Livedoor Co. 堀江貴文氏が, ライブドアの社長を辞任した。

press 動 押す, 押しつける, 圧する, プレスする, 名 圧迫, 押し, 報道機関, 出版物, 印刷機, プレス
press conference 記者会見 (=news conference)
▶The joint *press conference* was held at the firm's headquarters in Osaka. 共同記者会見は, 大阪市内の同社の本社で行われた。

pressure 名 圧力, 圧迫, 逼迫, 強要, 強制, 反発, 縮小, 減少, 低下, 悪化, 下落, 伸び悩み, ストレス (⇒**financial pressure, last half**)
　add to the upward pressure on prices 物価上昇圧力を強める
　asset quality pressures 資産内容の悪化
　be under further pressure 続落する
　business pressure 業務上のストレス, 業務の繁忙 (=pressure of business)
　come under heavy pressure 重圧[強い圧力]がかかる
　competitive pressure 競争圧力
　inflationary pressure インフレ圧力 (=inflation pressure)
　pressure on margins 利益率低下, 利益率への圧力 (=margin pressure)
　pressure on pricing 価格圧力, 値下げ圧力 (=pricing pressure)

pressure on profitability 収益性の悪化
price pressure 値下げ圧力, 価格低下圧力, インフレ圧力
pricing pressure 価格圧力, 値下げ圧力 (= pressure on pricing; ⇒**mix**)
profit pressure 収益への圧迫
put [apply, exert, place] pressure on …に圧力をかける, …に圧力を加える
revenue pressure 減収圧力
sales pressures 販売の伸び悩み
selling pressure 売り圧力
upward pressure 上昇圧力, 引上げ圧力, 上昇傾向, 上昇要因

▸Dollar-selling *pressure* remains strong due to concerns over the outflow of funds from the United States. 米国からの資金流出に対する懸念で, ドル売り圧力は依然として強い.

▸Gross margins for all of 2008 were essentially maintained despite severe price *pressures*. 2008年度全体の売上利益率は, 値下げ圧力にもかかわらず, 実質的に従来と同水準を維持しました.

▸Prices and technology are under continual *pressure*. 価格と技術は, 絶えず圧力にさらされています.

prestige 名 威信, 名声, 信望, 格式
　international prestige 国際的地位
　national prestige 国威, 国家の威信 (= the prestige of the nation)
　personal prestige 個人の威信
　prestige advertising 威信広告, 名声広告
　prestige brand 有名ブランド, 高級品, 銘柄品 (= prestigious)
　prestige effect 威光効果, ハロー効果
　prestige pricing 名声価格, 威光価格, 名声価格 [威光価格] 設定
　prestige school 名門校, 一流校
　prestige store 有名店, 高級店, 名声店, 高級百貨店

prestigious 形 名声 [威信] のある
pretax 形 税引き前の, 課税前の, 税込みの
pretax loss 経常損失, 経常赤字, 課税前損失, 税引き前損失 (⇒**group pretax loss**)

▸UBS SA will post a *pretax* loss of about $690 million in the third quarter mainly because of losses linked to the U.S. subprime mortgage crisis. スイス最大手銀行UBSは, 主に米国のサブプライム・ローン問題の関連損失で, 第3四半期は約6億9,000万ドルの税引き前損失を見込んでいる.

pretax profit 経常利益, 経常収益 (民間企業の税引き前利益に相当), 税込み利益, 課税前利益, 税引き前利益 (= current profit, recurring profit; ⇒**group pretax profit**)

▸This *pretax profit* is mainly due to earnings from our asset management business. この計上利益 [税引き前利益] は, 主に当社の資産運用業務の収入によるものです.

pretax provision 税引き前引当金

▸The decrease in 2008 net earnings and earnings per share was due mainly to the *pretax provision* of $500 million for restructuring costs. 2008年の純利益と1株当たり純利益が減少したのは, 主に事業再編成費用に対する税引き前引当金5億ドルによるものです.

prevailing rate 市場の実勢金利, 市場金利, 実勢相場, 中心相場, 中心レート, 一般賃金, 一般賃率

▸The *prevailing rate* of interest for a note payable of this type is 12%. この種の支払い手形の通常 [現行] の利子率は, 12%である.

preventive 形 予防の, 名 予防手段
　preventive maintenance 定期保守, 予防的保守
　preventive measures 予防策, 予防の対策, 防止策, 対策

prey 名 餌食, 犠牲
price 動 価格 [値段] をつける, 価格 [値段] を決める, 価格形成する
　be fairly priced 適正価格がつけられている, 適正な価格形成が行われている
　be priced in dollars ドル建てである
　be priced into …に織り込まれる

▸Interarea transfers are generally *priced* at cost plus an appropriate service charge. 地域間振替えは, 原則として原価に適正サービス料を加えた価格で行われています.

price 名 価格, 値段, 物価, プライス (⇒**market price, offer price, share price, stock price**)
　adjusted selling price method 修正売価法
　advertising prices 広告費
　agreed price 協定価格
　at constant prices 実質値
　at current prices 当期価格表示
　base period price 基準年の価格
　basis of price 価格条件
　cash price 現金価格
　closing price 終値, 引け値 (= closing market price)
　competitive price 競争価格, 安い価格 [値段]
　consumer prices 消費者物価
　current price 通り相場, 時価, 現行価格
　firm price 確定価格

issue price 発行価格
list price 表示価格
market price of stock 株式相場
price before tax 税込み前値段, 税金を含めた価格
price book-value ratio 株価純資産倍率《略 PBR》(=株価を1株当たり純資産(book value per share)で割ったもの。⇒**price-to-book value**)
price cartel 価格カルテル (=price agreement)
price earnings ratio 株価収益率《略 PER》(=market multiple, multiple, P/E, P/E ratio: 株式の市場価格(common stock market price)÷1株当たり利益(earnings per common share)=株価収益率)
price fixing 価格維持, 価格固定, 価格決定, 価格操作, 価格協定, 価格についての取決め, 物価安定
price fluctuation 物価の変動, 価格騰落, 相場変動, 株価の乱高下, 株価変動
price maintenance 価格維持
price margin 売上総利益, 価格差益
price minus tax 税引き価格, 税引き値段 (=price less tax)
price war 価格戦争, 価格競争, 値引き競争, 値引き販売
public utility price 公益事業料金
reacquisition price 買戻し価格
replacement price 取替え価格
selling price 販売価格, 売却価格, 売価, 売り値
share price on the first day 初値
standard price 標準価格, 標準物価, 基準価格
sticker price メーカー小売希望価格
stop price 最低落札価格
strike price 行使価格, 権利行使価格

▶In the transportation industry, the *price* hike in crude oil has led directly to drops in profits. 運輸業界では, 原油価格の値上りが収益減に直結している。

price competition 価格競争, 価格引下げ競争, 価格競争力

▶Despite a weak global economy and intense *price competition*, our sales grew 9% in 2008. 世界経済の低迷や激しい価格競争にもかかわらず, 2008年度の当社の売上高は9%増加しました。

price competitiveness 価格競争力

▶Seven-Eleven Japan Co. has boosted its *price competitiveness* by mass-purchasing supplies. セブン−イレブン・ジャパンは, 商品の大量仕入れで価格競争力を高めてきた。

price cut 値下げ, 価格引下げ (=price cutting, price reduction)

▶*Price cuts* are afoot in other convenience stores. 値下げは, 他のコンビニでも行われている。

price fluctuation 物価変動, 価格騰落, 相場変動, 株価の乱高下, 株価変動

▶Nominal GDP reflects *price fluctuations* and is said to more accurately reflect the sentiment of households and companies. 名目GDPは, 物価変動を反映し, 家計や企業の実感に近いものを反映しているとされる。

price hike 値上げ, 価格引上げ, 物価上昇

▶For JAL, a *price hike* of jet fuel by $1 per barrel means a drop of ¥5.5 billion in its recurring profit on a consolidated basis a year. 日航システムの場合, ジェット燃料の価格が1バレル当たり1ドル上昇すると, 年間の連結経常利益が55億円減る。

price increase 値上げ, 価格上昇, 物価上昇 (=price hike)

▶We filed for *price increases* of $800 million on an annual basis in late December. 12月末に当社は, 年ベースで8億ドルの値上げを申請しました。

price reduction 値下げ, 価格の引下げ (=price cut)

▶The increase in revenues occurred despite *price reductions* in 2008. 2008年度は, 製品価格の引下げにもかかわらず売上高が増加しました。

price-to-book value 株価純資産倍率 (=price book-value ratio)

▶*Price-to-book value* is obtained by dividing price per share by assets per share. 株価純資産倍率は, 1株当たり株価を1株当たりの資産額で割って[除して]求められます。

price war 価格戦争, 価格競争, 値引き競争, 値引き販売

▶A *price war* between convenience stores is heating up. コンビニ業界では, 価格競争が激化している。

pricing 名 価格設定, 価格決定, 価格計算, 価格政策, 値付け, 価格
basing point pricing 基点価格政策
capital asset pricing model 資本資産評価モデル
cost-based pricing 原価に基づく価格決定
cost-plus pricing 原価加算法, 原価加算価格決定
flat-rate pricing scheme 定額料金制
incremental profit pricing 増分利益方式
intra-company transfer pricing 振替価格の決定

primary

- marginal cost pricing 限界費用価格形成, 限界費用運賃
- option pricing オプションの値付け
- pricing behavior 価格方針
- pricing policy 価格決定方針, 価格政策
- reasonable pricing 手頃な値段
- return on assets pricing 資本利益率に基づく価格設定
- skimming pricing 初期高価格政策, 上澄み吸収価格政策 (＝skim-the-cream pricing)

primary 形 基本的, 第一順位の, 希薄化前, プライマリー
- primary balance プライマリー・バランス, 財政の基礎的収支 (国債発行による収入と国債の元利払い費を除いた基礎的収支。基礎的財政収支が赤字だと, 国の借金が増えるため, 財政再建には黒字化が必要になる)
- primary dealer プライマリー・ディーラー (米国の場合は, ニューヨーク連邦準備銀行との直接取引を認められている政府証券ディーラーのこと)
- primary EPS 基本的1株当たり利益 (＝primary earnings per share)
- primary market 発行市場, プライマリー市場 (新規株式公開や公募など, 企業や国が株や債券を新規発行して資金調達をする市場。⇒capital market)
- primary materials 原材料
- primary offering 募集 (新規発行される有価証券の取得申込みを勧誘すること)

▸Average *primary* common and common equivalent shares outstanding for 2008 includes the dilutive effects of the convertible zero coupon notes. 2008年度の期中平均発行済み普通株式および普通株式相当証券数には, 転換可能なゼロ・クーポン債の希薄化効果も含まれています。

primary commodity 第一次産品, 一次産品, 基本財

▸The prices of *primary commodities* such as crude oil and coal are rapidly increasing. 原油, 石炭など一次産品の価格が, 高騰している。

prime 形 首位の, 最重要の, 優良な, 最高級の, 第一等の, 極上の, 信用等級が最高の, 主要な, 素数の, 名 最上等, 素数
- prime bank 有力銀行, 一流銀行
- prime banker's acceptance 一流銀行引受手形
- prime bill 優良手形, 一流手形
- prime business 優良企業
- prime contractor 元請業者, 元請人
- prime cost 仕入値段, 直接原価, 直接費, 主要費用

principal

- prime credit 原信用状
- prime debtor [issuer] 優良発行体
- prime entry 仮輸入手続き
- prime force 原動力
- prime meridian (グリニッジ)子午線
- prime mover 原動力, 牽引力, 推進力, 主唱者, 動力機械, 原動機
- prime number 素数
- prime paper 一流手形
- prime quality 優良品, 最上品
- prime rating 高格付け
- prime stock 花形株, 主力株

prime rate 一流企業向け最優遇貸出金利, プライム・レート (＝primary interest rate, prime, prime bank rate, prime lending rate)

▸Short-term *prime rate* is a benchmark for interest rates on loans to small and midsize firms and home buyers. 短期プライム・レートは, 中小企業と住宅取得者向けローンの基準金利である。

▸The long-term *prime rate* is charged on loans of one year or longer to the bank's most creditworthy corporate clients. 長期プライム・レートは, 最も信用力がある銀行の顧客企業に対する1年超の貸付け金に適用される。

principal 名 元本, 元金, 基本財産, 株式の額面価額, 主債務者, 本人
- collateral principal payment 担保からの元本支払い[元本返済]
- collection of principal 元本回収
- exchange of principal 元本の交換
- guaranteed principal 元本保証
- payment of principal and interest 元利の支払い, 元利払い, 元利の返済, 元利返済
- principal guarantee 元本保証
- principal outstanding 残存元本額
- principal payment 元本返済, 元本の支払い, 元本返済額
- remaining principal balance 元本残存額, 残存元本額 (＝principal outstanding)
- repayment of principal 元本の償還, 元本返済

▸Stocks and foreign currency-denominated bonds are financial products which may reduce the *principal*. 株式や外貨建て債券は, 元本割れの恐れがある金融商品だ。

▸We must consider delays or reduced payments of interest as well as *principal* when we value loans that may not be fully repaid. 100％返済されない可能性がある債権を評価するにあたって, 利息や元本の遅延や減額返済を考慮する必要があります。

principal amount 元本, 元金, 額面価額, 額面
▸These convertible debentures are redeemable as of December 2008 at a price of 105% of the *principal amount*. この転換社債は, 2008年10月時点で, 元本の105%の価格で償還できます。

principal and interest 元本と利息, 元利
▸Debt-servicing costs are payments on the *principals and interests* on previously issued government bonds. 国債費は, 過去に発行した国債の元利払いに使われる金だ。

principle 名 原理, 原則, 主義, 方針, 基準, 道義
  accrual principle 発生主義の原則
  alternative accounting principle 代替的会計基準
  arm's length principle 独立企業原則
  business accounting principle 企業会計原則
  cost principle 原価主義
  equal value principle 等価交換の原則
  full cost principle 総括原価主義, フルコスト原則
  income statement principle 損益計算書原則
  market principles 市場原理
  principle of consistency 継続性の原則
  principles of consolidation 連結方針, 連結の基準 (=consolidation policy)
  principle of current operating performance 当期業績主義の原則
  principle of matching costs with revenues 費用収益対応の原則
  profit-first principle 利益至上主義
  utility maximization principle 効用最大化の原理
▸We operate on the *principle* that management is accountable to shareholders. 経営者は株主に対して責任がある, というのが当社の経営方針です。

print 動 印刷する, 名 印刷, 印刷物
prior 形 事前の, 前の, 先の, …より上の, 重要な
  prior art 先行技術, 既存の技術, 既知の発明
  prior bond 優先権付き債券
  prior claim 優先請求権
  prior consultation 事前協議
  prior endorser 〈手形の〉前裏書人
  prior engagement 先約
  prior knowledge 予備知識, 予備的知識
  prior mortgage 上位抵当
  prior permit 事前承認
  prior preferred [preference] stock 第一優先株, 最優先株式
  prior redemption 優先権付き償還, 満期前償還
  prior stock 先順位優先株

prior use 先使用
prior service 過去勤務 (=past service)
  prior service cost 過去勤務費用, 過去勤務原価, 過去勤務債務 (=prior service pension cost)
  prior service liability 過去勤務債務
  prior service pension cost 過去勤務費用 (=prior service cost)
▸We amortize *prior service* costs primarily on a straight-line basis. 過去勤務債務は, 主に定額法で償却しています。

priority 名 優先, 優先事項, 優先権, 優先順位, 先取権
  cost priority コスト優先, コスト重視
  creditors by priority 優先債権者 (=priority creditors)
  first priority 最優先
  payment priorities 支払いの優先順位, 元本返済の優先順位
  priority between mortgages 担保権の順位
  priority of claims 請求優先権, 債権先取り権
  top priority 最優先課題
▸Existing convenience stores put *priority* on efficiency and forgot about customers. 既存のコンビニは, 効率を重視するあまり顧客のことを忘れていた。
▸Suits are usually a low-*priority* item in household spending. 紳士服は, 家族の消費支出の中では一般に後回しにされる商品だ。
▸Toyota has put *priority* on reducing trade friction with the U.S. トヨタは, 米国との貿易摩擦回避を優先した。

privacy 名 私的自由, 個人的自由, 私生活, 秘密, プライバシー
  privacy enhanced mail 暗号化した電子メール《略 PEM》
  privacy infringement プライバシーの侵害
  privacy policy プライバシー規定 (ウェブ上の法的通知)
  privacy protection プライバシー保護, 個人情報保護
  privacy statement プライバシー規約
▸The points of contention in the violation of *privacy* rights have been diverse, ranging from the publication of personal secrets, personal background and love affairs, to the publication of pictures without permission. プライバシー(権)の侵害の争点も, 最近は私生活上の秘密や個人の経歴, 異性関係の公表から写真の無断掲載など, 多岐にわたっている。

private 形 私的な, 個人的な, 私有の, 私設の, 民

営の, 民間の, プライベート
- **private allocation** 縁故者割当て
- **private banking** プライベート・バンキング
- **private brander** 自家銘柄業者
- **private consumption** 個人消費, 民間消費支出, 民間最終支出（＝personal consumption）
- **private corporation** 非公開会社（＝private enterprise）
- **private delivery system** 自社配送システム
- **private demand** 民需, 民間需要
- **private enterprises annuity** 企業年金
- **private financing** 民間資金
- **private investment** 民間投資, 民間設備投資, 民間企業による投資, 非公開投資
- **private label** 商業者ラベル, 商業者商標, 自家商標（＝private brand）
- **private limited company** 有限責任会社, 有限会社
- **private placing** 私募発行
- **private sector businesses** 民間企業
  ▶There has been no sign of increases in the two chief components of private sector demand — *private* consumption and capital investment. 民間需要の2本柱である個人消費と設備投資に, 回復の兆しが見えない。
- **private brand** 自家商標, 商業者商標, 自主企画商品, プライベート・ブランド《略 **PB**》（＝dealer brand, dealer's brand, private label）
  ▶Leading department stores are stepping up efforts to develop their own *private brands* that can respond to consumers' opinions and desires. 主要百貨店各社は, 顧客の意見や要望を取り入れた独自の自主企画商品（プライベート・ブランド）の開発を進めている。
- **private brand product** 自主開発商品, 自主企画商品, 自社開発商品, プライベート・ブランド商品
  ▶Aeon's proposal for business tie-up with Lawson includes installing Aeon automated teller machines at Lawson stores and joint development of *private brand products*. イオンのローソンとの業務提携案には, イオン銀行のATM（現金自動預け払い機）のローソン店舗への設置や自主開発（プライベート・ブランド）商品の共同開発などが含まれている。
- **private company** 民間企業, 民営会社, 私会社, 非公開会社, 閉鎖会社（＝private corporation）
  ▶Japan Post became a *private company* on Oct. 1, 2007. 日本郵政公社は, 2007年10月1日付けで民間企業になった。
- **private offering** 株式の直接募集, 縁故募集, 私募（＝private placement, private placing）
  ▶The bonds were for sale by *private offering* and issued by Princeton Global Management Ltd. この債券は, プリンストン・グローバル・マネジメントが発行した私募債である。
- **private placement** 私募発行, 私募, 私募債, 第三者割当て（＝direct placement, private offering, private placing）
  　私募発行とは⇒公募（public offering）と違って, 私募（private placement）は株主や取引先, 機関投資家など特定少数の投資家を対象に新株を発行, 募集するもの。米国では, 一定以上の資産・収入のある投資家（accredited investor）に私募発行する場合には, 証券取引委員会（SEC）に登録する必要がない。
- **bonds offered through private placement** 私募債
- **debt private placement** 私募債発行
- **private placement bond market** 私募債市場
  ▶During the first quarter 2008, the Company issued, in *private placements* in Canada, $325 million of preferred shares. 2008年第1四半期に, 当社は優先株式をカナダで私募発行して3億2,500万ドルを調達しました。
- **private sector** 民間部門, 民間セクター, 民間企業, 民間
  ▶The *private sector* has tackled necessary restructuring efforts earnestly. 民間は, 必要なリストラ策に懸命に取り組んできた。
- **privately held company** 非公開会社, 株式非公開会社, 株式未公開企業, 非上場会社
- **privately place** 私募発行する, 第三者割当て発行する, 第三者割当て増資する（＝privately issue）
  ▶In July 2008, the Company *privately placed* two million special warrants to purchase new common shares of the corporation. 2008年7月に当社は, 同社の新規発行普通株式引受権付き特別ワラント債200万単位を, 私募発行しました。
- **privatization** 图 民営化
  ▶Japan Post turned into the state-funded Japan Post Holdings Co. as part of the *privatization* of postal services. 日本郵政公社は, 郵政民営化の一環として政府出資の持ち株会社, 日本郵政グループ[日本郵政株式会社]に生まれ変わった。
- **privatize** 動 民営化する, 非国有化する
  ▶The operator of Narita Airport will be fully *privatized* and listed on the Tokyo Stock Exchange probably in fiscal 2009. 成田空港の運営会社は,

2009年度にも完全民営化され東証に上場される予定だ。

pro forma standard tax 外形標準課税 (＝corporate tax on gross operating tax:「外形標準課税」は, 法人事業税(都道府県税)について, 現行の企業所得(黒字分)ではなく, 資本金や人件費, 売上高などの事業規模を基準に課税する方法)
▶ Under the *pro forma standard tax*, corporate tax is levied on the basis of the number of employees, combined wages, and the size of capital. 外形標準課税では, 法人事業税は従業員数や給与総額, 資本金の規模などを基準にして課税される。

pro rata 比例して, その割合に応じて, 一定の割合に従って, 按分(あんぶん)に (＝according to a certain rate, according to the rate)
　be refunded pro rata 一定比率払い戻される
　on a pro rata basis 一定の割合[比率]に応じて, 出資割合[比率]に応じて, プロラタ・ベース
　pro rata allocation 比例配分 (＝proration)
　pro rata share of the expenses 費用の比例配分, 費用の按分負担
▶ Such dividends will be distributed between the parties on a *pro rata* basis in accordance with the respective number of shares of Stock owned by each of them. この配当金は, 各当事者が所有する本株式のそれぞれの株式数の割合に応じて当事者間に配分するものとする。

pro rata hiring system 雇用率制度 (＝pro rata hiring rate system)
▶ Businesses are subject to the so-called *pro rata hiring system*, whereby physically or intellectually handicapped people must account for a proportion of the overall payroll. 企業に対して従業員全体の一定割合の身体障害者や知的障害者の雇用を義務付けるいわゆる「雇用率制度」に, 企業は従わなければならない。

proactive 形 先行的, 先行型の, 事前の, 事前行動の, 予備措置の, 主体的な
　proactive involvement in the bid-rigging 談合への主体的関与
　proactive strategy 先行型戦略, 事前行動戦略

proactively 副 前向きに, 先のことを考えて, 事前に対策を講じて
▶ Corporate leaders should not only focus on belt-tightening, but also should *proactively* deal with replacing aging plants and equipments. 企業経営者は, 緊縮経営一辺倒ではなく, 老朽化が進む設備の更新にも前向きに対応する必要がある。

probation 名 試験, 検定, 見習い, 実習, 試用期間, 仮採用期間, 保護観察期間

probationary 形 試みの, 試練の, 見習い中の

problem 名 問題, 課題, 難問
▶ Canon's president and other executives hold a meeting every morning to exchange views about management *problems* and the economic situation. キヤノンの社長以下役員は毎朝, 会議を開き, 経営課題や経済状況について意見交換をしている。

problem borrower 問題融資先 (＝problematic borrower)
▶ These *problem borrowers* were either consolidated or reorganized. これらの問題融資先は, 整理, 再編された。

problem loans 問題債権, 不良債権, 不良債権額, 貸倒れ (＝bad loans, loans to questionable borrowers, problem debts)
▶ Shinsei Bank set aside an extra ¥8 billion in provisions for *problem loans* to U.S. mortgage business operators. 新生銀行は, 米国内の住宅ローン事業を営む融資先に対する貸倒れ引当金として, 新たに80億円を積み増した。

procedure 名 手続き, 手順, 処理手順, 慣行, 方式 (⇒test)
　accounting procedure 会計手続き, 会計慣行, 会計処理方法
　auditing procedure 監査手続き (＝audit procedure)
　budgetary procedure 予算手続き
　clearing procedure 決済手続き
　closing procedure 決算手続き
　complaint procedures 苦情処理手続き
　control procedure 内部統制手続き
　credit procedures 与信手続き
　external auditing procedure 外部監査手続き
　internal procedures 内部規定
　judicial procedures 裁判手続き
　management procedures 管理手続き
　procedures manual 手続きマニュアル, 業務マニュアル
　settlement procedure 決済手続き, 決済方式
▶ We have to admit there has been an inappropriate accounting *procedure*. 不適切な会計処理であったことは, 認めざるを得ない。

proceedings 名 議事進行, 議事録, 決議録, 会議録, 会報, 訴訟手続き, 法的手続き, 手続き, 措置, 訴訟, 弁論
　administrative proceedings 行政手続き, 行政訴訟
　legal proceedings 法律手続き, 法的手続き, 裁

判手続き, 法的手段
receivership proceedings 破産手続き
take [bring, institute, start] proceedings against …に対して訴訟を起こす
the proceedings of an annual shareholders meeting 年次株主総会の議事進行

▶In accordance with our usual practice, a summary of the *proceedings* of the annual meeting will be mailed to all shareholders.　当社の慣例に従って，株主総会の議事要項は株主全員に後日，郵送いたします。

▶In the normal course of business, we are subject to *proceedings*, lawsuits and other claims, including proceedings under government laws and regulations related to environmental and other matters.　通常の業務過程で当社は，環境その他の問題に関する政府の法律や規則に基づく措置を含めて，法的手続きや訴訟その他の請求の対象になります。

proceeds 名　代金, 手取金, 売上, 売上高, 売却収入, 売却益, 所得, 収益, 純利益, 収入, 調達資金, 資金　(⇒**net proceeds**)
by-product proceeds 副産物からの手取金
export proceeds 輸出代金
historical proceeds 実際現金受領額
IPO proceeds 公募による手取金
proceeds of the sale 売却代金
use of proceeds 資金の使途

▶The company will use the *proceeds* from selling its nine TV stations for debt repayment.　同社は，テレビ9局を売却して得た資金を，債務返済に充てる予定だ。

▶We had net *proceeds* of $600 million from selling our shares in the company.　当社は，同社株を売却して純額で6億ドルの売却益を得ました。

proceeds from exercising stock options ストック・オプションの行使による利益, ストック・オプション実行受取金　(=proceeds from the exercise of stock options)

▶*Proceeds from exercising stock options* are compensation for labor and service rendered and constitute salary income.　ストック・オプション（自社株購入権）を行使して得た利益は，職務遂行の対価なので，給与所得に当たる。

proceeds from the public offering 株式公開による手取金, 公募による手取金

▶The net *proceeds* of $973 million *from the public offering* were used to reduce notes payable.　公募による純手取金9億7,300万ドルは，短期借入金の返済に充当しました。

proceeds from the sale 売却益, 売却代金

▶*Proceeds from the sale* were in cash.　売却代金は，現金で入手しました。

process 名　過程, 工程, 流れ, 段階, 部門, 製法, 手続き, 訴訟手続き, プロセス
beginning work in process 期首仕掛(しかけ・しかかり)品　(=initial goods in process)
business process 業務の流れ
closing process 決算手続き
construction in process 建設仮勘定　(=construction in process account)
cost-cutting process コスト削減計画
decision-making process 意思決定の過程, 政策決定の過程
deflationary process デフレ
issuing process 起債手続き
labor-intensive manufacturing process 労働集約型の製造部門
loan making process 融資手続き
management process 管理過程, マネジメント・プロセス
manufacturing process 製造工程, 製造部門
planning process 計画策定のプロセス
process center 生鮮加工センター
process control 工程管理
process industry 加工産業, 装置産業
process production order 継続製造指図書
process sheet 工程表
production process 生産工程, 製造工程, 生産過程, 製造段階, 生産体制　(=manufacturing process)
quality processes 品質管理手続き
rating process 格付けの過程

▶The increase in R&D spending reflected new and ongoing programs for new products and *process* developments.　研究開発費の増加は，新製品とプロセスの開発をめざして，従来から継続している計画に加えて新規計画を実施したことを反映しています。

processing 名　処理, 加工, 事務処理, 手続き
advanced processing 二次加工
batch processing バッチ処理, 一括処理
computer processing コンピュータ処理
data processing データ処理, 情報処理, データ処理業務
food processing 食品加工
information processing 情報処理
information processing equipment 情報処理機器
inhouse processing 内製, 内製比率

online processing オンライン処理
outside processing 外注加工
overnight processing 翌日処理
planning process 計画策定プロセス
primary processing 一次加工
processing cost 加工費 (＝manufacturing cost, processing expense, production cost)
processing industry 加工産業, 食品加工業
return generating process 収益生成過程
▸The plastic parts-*processing* industry and film manufacturers will not be able to shift the raised costs onto product prices. プラスチック部品の加工業界やフィルムのメーカーは, コスト高 [コスト上昇分] を製品価格に転嫁できないようだ。

procure 動 調達する, 購入する, 仕入れる, 取得する, 入手する, 獲得する, 引き起こす
▸We need to *procure* funds by the end of May. 当社は, 5月末までに資金調達 [資金繰り] を迫られている。

procurement 名 調達, 購入, 仕入れ, 機器調達, 取得, 入手, 獲得, プロキュアメント
competitive procurement 一般競争による調達
e-procurement 電子調達, eプロキュアメント
enterprise procurement automation software 企業調達オートメーション・ソフト
fund procurement 資金調達, 資本調達 (＝fund raising)
government procurement 政府調達
Internet procurement インターネット調達, ネット調達
local procurement of components 部品の現地調達 (⇒local procurement)
mutual procurement 相互調達
noncompetitive procurement 非競争調達
outside procurement 外部調達, 外部からの調達
procurement cost 調達費, 調達コスト, 仕入コスト (⇒profitability)
procurement department 調達部門
procurement of funds 資金調達 (＝fund procurement, fund raising)
procurement of materials 原材料の調達, 原料の調達 (＝material procurement, procurement of raw materials, raw material procurement)
special procurements 特需
▸Pioneer Corp. will stop making plasma display panels and switch to outside *procurement*. パイオニアは, プラズマテレビの基幹部品 [中核部品] であるパネルの生産を中止して, その後は外部調達に切り替える。
▸The two companies can save a combined ¥15 billion in distribution costs a year through mutual *procurement* of oil products. 両社は, 石油製品の相互調達で, 物流コストを両社合わせて年間150億円節約できる。

produce 動 生産する, 製造する, 製作する, 作成する, 提出する
goods produced 製品
income-producing real estate 稼動不動産
income-producing stock 所得を生む株式
national income produced 生産国民所得
producing country 生産国, 製造国
producing department 製造部門
revenue-producing enterprise 営利事業体
▸Import growth outpaced export growth, thus *producing* the trade imbalance. 輸入の伸びが輸出の伸びを上回ったため, 貿易の不均衡が生じた。
▸This increase in recurring profits is largely due to an expansion in domestic demand for steel sheets used to *produce* automobiles and favorable steel exports to the Chinese market. この経常利益の増加は, 主に自動車生産用鋼板の内需拡大と中国向け鉄鋼輸出の好調によるものだ。

producer 名 生産者, 製造業者, 生産国, 供給者, 企業, メーカー (＝maker, manufacturer)
auto producer 自動車メーカー (＝car maker, car producer, vehicle producer)
income producer 収益源, 収入源 (＝income source)
industrial commodity producer 素材メーカー
leading producer 最大手のメーカー, トップ・メーカー, 主力メーカー
low price producer 低価格品メーカー
producer goods 工業製品, 生産財
producer organization 生産者団体
Producer Price Index 生産者物価指数
producer prices for [of] finished goods 生産者物価指数 (最終財)
producers' product inventories 生産者製品在庫
synthetic fiber producer 合成繊維メーカー
▸The new tariff on beef imports favors *producers* rather than consumers. 牛肉の輸入に対する新関税は, 消費者ではなく生産者寄りの対応だ。
▸Toyota overtook General Motors Corp. to become the world's No.1 car *producer* in terms of units produced. トヨタは, 生産台数でGMを抜いて [追い越して] 世界一の自動車メーカーになった。

product 名 製品, 生産品, 産物, 商品, 結果, 成果, プロダクト

accumulation product 年金商品
consumer product 消費財
core product lines 主要製品, 主力製品
finished product 製品, 最終製品
foreign currency product 為替商品 （＝foreign exchange product）
high-margin product 利益率が高い製品
high-tech product ハイテク製品, ハイテク商品
high value-added product 付加価値の高い製品
insurance product 保険商品 （＝insurance instrument）
investment product 金融商品, 投資商品, 投資対象商品
IT-related products IT関連製品
Joint products costing 連産品原価計算
low-end product 低価格製品
manufactured product 工業製品 （＝manufacturing industry product）
medical insurance product 医療保険商品
popular product 人気商品
product category 製品分野, 製品カテゴリー
product cost 製品原価, 生産物原価, プロダクト・コスト
product design 製品デザイン, 製品設計, 製品計画, 生産デザイン, プロダクト・デザイン
product financing 製品金融, 製品による資金調達
product financing arrangement 製品による資金調達方法 （製品を買戻し条件付きで販売することで資金を調達する方法）
product improvement 製品改良, 製品改善
product information 製品情報, 商品情報
product innovative strategy 製品イノベーション戦略
product item 製品種目
product launch 新製品の売出し［発売, 導入］
product liability 製造物責任, 製造責任, 製造者責任《略 PL》
product placement プロダクト・プレースメント （映画などに商品を登場させる宣伝手法）
product quality 製品の品質
product recall 製品回収
product testing 製品テスト, 商品テスト （＝product test）
structured financial product 仕組み商品
variable product 変額商品

▸Our strategy of listening to our customers and improving the competitiveness of our *products* and services is working. お客さまのご意見を取り入れ, 製品とサービスの競争力強化に取り組んで いる当社の経営戦略が, 功を奏しています。

▸The good results of the past quarter are the *product* of our people. 当四半期に高水準の業績を記録できましたことは, ひとえに各社員の努力の賜物です。

product development 製品開発, 商品開発 （⇒**participate**）

▸Restructuring allows us to refocus our resources on *product development*. 事業再編を通して, 当社は経営資源を製品開発に新たに集中することができます。

▸This nonlife insurance company provides the company with know-how on damage assessment and *product development*. この損害保険会社は, 同社に損害査定や商品開発に関するノウハウを提供している。

product line 製品ライン, 商品ライン, 商品群, 製品系列, 製品種目, 製品品目, 製品構成, プロダクト・ライン （⇒**focus on**）

▸*Product line* revenue growth was led by strong percentage gains in business communications systems and terminals. 製品系列の売上高の伸びは, 主にビジネス通信システムと端末機器の大幅な伸び率によるものです。

▸*Product lines* have been refreshed from top to bottom. 製品ラインが, 全面的に一新された。

product performance 製品性能

▸Competitive factors include price, *product performance*, product quality, and service and systems quality and availability. 競争要因としては, 価格, 製品の性能, 製品の品質のほかに, サービスおよびシステムの品質や利用度などもあります。

product portfolio 製品ポートフォリオ, 製品構成, 製品群, 製品一覧表, 製品明細表, プロダクト・ポートフォリオ

▸We invest internationally in order to be able to provide our customers with a global *product portfolio*. 顧客にグローバルな製品群を提供するため, 当社は国際投資を行っています。

product price 製品価格

▸What is noteworthy in the midterm results is the 6 percent increase in sales resulting from an increase in *product prices* and sales volumes. 中間決算で特筆できるのは, 製品の価格の上昇と販売数量の拡大で, 売上高が6％伸びたことです。

product related expenses 製品関連費用

▸Expenditures for advertising and sales promotion and for other *product related expenses* are charged to costs and expenses as incurred. 宣伝・販売促進費とその他の製品関連費用は, その発

生時に費用に計上されます。

product sales 製品販売
▸For other *product sales*, revenue is recognized at the time of shipment.　その他の製品販売については、収益は出荷時に認識されます。

production 名　生産, 製造, 製作, 制作, プロダクション

　assembly production　組立生産
　industrial production　工業生産, 鉱工業生産, 工業出荷, 鉱工業生産高
　job order production system　個別生産システム
　just-in-time production system　かんばん方式, ジャスト・イン・タイム, JIT
　license production　ライセンス生産
　line production　直線生産, 流れ作業生産, 流れ作業
　local production　現地生産, 国内生産
　offshore production　海外生産（＝overseas production）
　production center　生産拠点, 製造拠点, 生産センター, 生産中心点, 生産の中核拠点
　production control　生産管理, 工程管理
　production labor　製造労務費, 生産労務費, 直接労務費
　production level　操業度
　production management　生産管理
　production method　生産高比例法 (activity method, production output method, service yield basis, unit of production method), 製造方法, 生産方法, 生産方式
　production of content　コンテンツ（情報の中身）の制作
　production output method　生産高比例法（＝productive output method）
　production overhead cost　製造間接費（＝production overheads）
　production process　生産工程, 製造工程, 製造段階, 生産過程, 製造過程, 製造部門（＝manufacturing process, process of production）
　production sharing contract　石油会社と政府間の生産分与契約, 生産物分与契約, 生産契約
　round-about production　迂回生産
　surplus production　余剰生産

▸Canon has stuck by its policy of keeping *production* within Japan.　キヤノンは、国内生産を維持する方針にこだわり続けている。
▸Ford Motor Co. will temporarily halt *production* at its assembly plants to reduce bloated inventories.　米フォードは、増大した在庫を削減 [圧縮] するため、組立工場での生産を一時中止する。

production activity 生産活動
▸A rise in borrowing costs will curb consumer spending as well as *production activity* in industrial sectors.　借入コストの増大は、産業の生産活動や個人消費を抑えることになる。

production base 生産拠点, 製造拠点（＝production center）
▸Canon already has moved its *production base* overseas for products that require a lot of labor but must have a low selling price, such as digital cameras.　キヤノンは、デジカメなど手間の割に販売価格が安い製品の生産拠点はすでに海外に移している。

production capacity 生産能力, 生産余力, 生産設備（＝output capacity）
▸Rapid growth in demand for digital electric appliances led leading electronic and precision equipment manufacturers to enhance investment in their *production capacities*.　デジタル家電の需要急増で、電機、精密機器などの大手メーカーが、生産設備への投資を増やした。

production cost 製造費, 製造原価, 製品原価, 生産コスト, 製造コスト（＝cost of production, production expense）
▸Steady efforts toward technological improvement and cuts in *production costs* were the driving forces behind our record net profit for the year ended Dec. 31, 2008.　技術力の向上や生産コスト削減に向けた地道な取組みが、当社が2008年12月期決算で記録した過去最高の税引き後利益の原動力です。

production cycle 生産サイクル
▸*Production cycles* have been shortened to enable the company to deliver solutions faster.　（お客様に対する）ソリューション（問題解決策）の早期提供をめざして、当社は生産サイクルを短縮しています。

production efficiency 生産効率
▸Canon's cell production system has contributed to the improvement of *production efficiency*.　キヤノンのセル生産方式は、生産効率の向上に貢献している。

production facilities 生産設備, 生産拠点（＝manufacturing facilities）
▸The company will gradually transfer *production facilities* currently in operation to the industrial complex.　同社は、現在稼動している生産設備を順次、この工業団地に移していく方針だ。

production line 生産ライン, 製造ライン, 生

産系列, 流れ作業, 生産線 （=assembly line; ⇒ sales efforts, workweek)
▶Toyota and GM will introduce new *production lines* by investing tens of billions of yen in their joint venture plant. トヨタとGMは, 両社の合弁工場に数百億円を投資して, 新生産ラインを導入する。

production support company 生産支援会社
▶With the addition of the *production support company* in Thailand, Toyota has strengthened the integration of its development, production and distribution process. タイに生産支援会社を新たに設立して, トヨタは開発, 生産と販売の各部門を一体化する体制を強化した。

production system 生産方式, 生産体制, 生産システム （⇒**local production system**)
▶Canon's successful cost-cutting efforts through *production system* reforms of its traditional core products significantly contributed to the company's high performance. キヤノンの伝統的な主力商品の生産方式の改革によるコスト削減策の成功が, 同社の高収益の大きな要因だ。

productive 形 生産的な, 生産力のある, 生産上の, 営利的な
 productive factor 生産要素 （=production factor)
 productive force 生産力
 productive life 生産年数
 productive resources 生産資源

productivity 名 生産性, 生産力, 生産効率, 多様性, プロダクティビティ （⇒**labor productivity, position**)
 capital productivity 資本生産性 （=productivity of capital)
 corporate productivity 企業の生産性
 comparative productivity 比較生産性
 distribution productivity 流通生産性
 green productivity 環境にやさしい生産性, グリーン・プロダクティビティ
 gross productivity 粗生産力, 粗生産性
 improved productivity 生産性向上, 生産性の向上 （=increased productivity)
 marginal productivity 限界生産力, 限界生産性
 net productivity 純生産性, 純生産力
 productivity improvement 生産性向上, 生産性上昇 （=improved productivity, increased productivity)
 productivity of added value 付加価値生産性 （=productivity of value added)
 productivity of labor 労働生産性 （=labor productivity)
 sales productivity 販売効率
 total-factor productivity 全要素生産性
 value productivity 価値生産性
▶We will strengthen our position by reducing costs and improving *productivity*. 当社は, コスト削減と生産性の向上により, 当社の経営基盤を強化することになりました。

profession 名 職業, 知的職業, 専門的職業, 専門職, 公言, 宣言
 auditing profession 職業監査人
 learned profession 知的職業
 profession permitted to be incorporated 知的職業法人, 職能法人, 専門職法人, 法人化を許された専門職 （=professional corporation: 弁護士や医師, 会計士, 建築家など知的職業に従事するために設立される法人)

professional 形 職業の, 職業上の, 業務上の, 専門職の, 本職の, プロの, 専門的な, 熟練した, 巧妙な
 code of professional conduct 職業行為規程
 code of professional responsibility 職業責任規範
 professional bank 専業銀行
 professional corporation 知的職業法人, 職能法人, 専門職法人《略 P.C.》 （=profession permitted to be incorporated)
 professional discipline 職業上の規範
 professional ethics 職業倫理
 professional investor 機関投資家
 professional manager 専門経営者
 professional negligence resulting in death and injury 業務上過失致死障害
 professional occupation 専門職
 professional opinion 職業専門家の意見
 professional skill 本職の腕, プロの技, 専門技能, 特技
 professional specialty occupation 専門職
 unethical professional conduct 職業倫理違反行為

professional 名 職業人, プロ, 専門家, 本職, 玄人（くろうと）, プロフェッショナル
 accounting professional 職業会計人, 公認会計士
 credit professional 信用分析の専門家
 highly trained professional 高度な訓練を受けた専門家
 industry professionals 業界関係者
 money market professional 金融市場専門家

professionals and institutional investors ディーラーと機関投資家
qualified professional 有資格専門家
skilled professional 熟練労働者

professional negligence resulting in a fire 業務上失火
▶Officers from the Hokkaido prefectural police searched Idemitsu Kosan Co.'s oil refinery on suspicion the company was guilty of *professional negligence resulting in a fire* in a naphtha tank. 北海道警は,ナフサ・タンクの火災で,出光興産の製油所を業務上失火の疑いで捜索した。

professional regulation 職業規則
▶In Germany, doctors who have violated *professional regulations* stipulated by the doctors association are tried at a vocational court. ドイツでは,医師会が定めた職業規則に反した医師は,職業裁判所で裁かれる。

professionalism 名 プロ意識,プロ根性,職人気質(かたぎ),専門家気質,優れた専門技術,玄人(くろうと)芸
▶It has been pointed out that morale and *professionalism* are lacking in engineers in the nuclear power industry. 最近,原子力産業の技術者の士気やプロ意識が低下している,と指摘されている。

profile 名 構成,構造,輪郭,概要,案内,見通し,予測,特性,地位,方針,プロフィール[プロファイル]
business profile 事業構成
credit profile 信用情報,信用力
earnings profile 収益見通し
financial profile 財務力見通し
investment profile 投資方針
market profile 市場プロフィール,市場特性,市場情報
product profile 製品構成
risk profile リスク特性,リスク構造,リスク輪郭
the dollar's profile ドルの地位
▶The credit *profiles* of major Japanese bank groups have improved through falling balance-sheet risk, a plan to repay public funds and other factors. 財務リスクの軽減や公的資金の返済計画などの要因により,日本の大手金融グループ各行の信用力は改善している。

profit 動 利益を得る,教訓を得る,利益になる,役に立つ
▶In foreign exchange margin trading, investors repeatedly trade U.S. dollars, euros and other currencies, aiming to *profit* from fluctuations in exchange rates. 外国為替証拠金取引では,為替の変動による利益を狙って,投資家が米ドルやユーロなどの外貨を繰り返し売買する。

profit 名 利益,収益,利得,利潤,黒字,プロフィット (⇒consolidated net profit, current account profit, current profit, group net profit, net profit, operating profit)
absolute profit 純利益
accounting profit 会計上の利益
advance in profits 増益
all-inclusive profit 包括主義利益
average profit growth 年平均増益率
book profits 評価益
business profit 企業収益,企業利益,業務利益 (=business income)
capital profit 資本利潤
corporate profit growth 企業増益率
corporate profits 企業収益,企業利益
excessive profit 超過利潤,不当利得,暴利
increase [improve] profit margins 利益率を高める
internal profit 内部利益
maximum profit 最大利潤,最大の利益,利益の極大化
move into profit 黒字に転換する (=return to profit)
not-for-profit organization 非営利団体 (=non-profit organization)
pre-depreciation profit 償却前利益
profit after taxation 税引き後利益
profit before taxation 税引き前利益
profit brought forward from the previous (business) term 前期繰越し利益金
profit center 利益中心点,プロフィット・センター
profit-earning capacity 収益力 (=profit-making capability)
profit expectation 利益予想 (=profit forecast, profit forecasting)
profit from capital reduction 減資差益
profit from redemption 償還利益
profit from securities revaluation 有価証券評価益 (=profit from revaluation of securities)
profit on foreign exchange 為替差益,外国為替差益
profit on securities sold 有価証券売却益
profit on treasury stock 自己株式処分益
profit outlook 利益予想,収益見通し,業績予想 (=earnings forecast, profit forecast)
profit-padding 利益の水増し

profit prior to consolidation 連結前利益
profit sharing 利益配分, 利益分配, 利益配当
profit taking 利益を確定するための売り, 利益確定売り, 利食い, 利食い売り (=profit taking sales)
profit target 収益目標, 運用益の目標
profits for the term 当期利益金
profits from redemption 償還差益 (=gains from redemption)
rake in massive profits 巨額の収益を上げる, 大もうけする
realize a profit 利益を得る
return to profit 黒字に転換する, 黒字に戻る
squeeze profits 利益を圧迫する
take profits 利食い売りをする, 利食いに出る, 利食う
target profit 目標利益
trading profit 売買益
undivided profit 未処分利益

▶Major electric appliance manufacturers and 10 telecommunication companies turned *profits* for the year ended March 31. 3月期決算では, 大手電機と情報通信10社が, 黒字に転換した。

▶Mizuho Financial Group Inc. booked as *profit* a combined ¥180.5 billion from loan-loss reserves at the group's three banks. みずほフィナンシャルグループが, 傘下3銀行の貸倒れ引当金のうち合算で計1,805億円を利益として計上した。

profit and [or] loss 損益

extraordinary profit and loss 特別損益, 臨時損益, 非経常的損失 (=special profit and loss)
intercompany profit and loss 内部損益
operating profit and loss 営業損益
ordinary profit and loss 経常損益
profit and loss break-even point 損益分岐点 (=profit and loss point)
profit and loss statement 損益計算書 (=income account, income statement, profit and loss account, statement of earnings, statement of income, statement of operations)
profit or loss for the financial year 当期損益
unrealized profits and losses 含み損益, 未実現損益

▶Under the consolidated return system, a company pays corporate tax after totaling the *profits and losses* of its affiliated companies. 連結納税制度では, 企業はグループ企業[系列企業]の損益を合算して法人税を納める。

profit decline 減益

▶Pulp and paper makers have seen their year-on-year *profits decline*. 製紙業界は, 前年比で減益となっている。

profit driver 収益の原動力, 収益を押し上げる原動力

▶Equities once again were a main *profit driver* for Nomura. 野村の収益を押し上げる原動力[主な要因]は, 再び株式となった。

profit-first principle 利益至上主義

▶The *profit-first principle* may have overpowered the law-abiding spirit in the case of the company. 同社の場合は, 利益至上主義のほうが順法精神より強すぎたかもしれない。

profit forecast 利益予想, 収益見通し, 業績予想, 業績見通し (=earnings forecast, profit outlook)

▶The financial group halved its *profit forecast* for fiscal 2009. 同フィナンシャル・グループが, 2009年度の業績予想を(前回予想より) 50%引き下げた。

profit growth 収益の伸び, 増益

▶Although corporate sector is enjoying *profit growth*, businesses generally have yet to relax their restructuring measures to transform them into highly profitable companies. 企業部門[企業]は収益が伸びているが, 一般に高収益企業[高収益体質]に転換するためのリストラの手をまだ緩めていない。

profit making 利益を上げること, 利益を得ること, 収益, 営利

profit-making business 収益事業, 営利事業
profit-making capability 収益力 (=profit-earning capacity)
profit-making corporation 営利法人
profit-making sources 収益源

▶The group aims to strengthen its *profit-making* capability by establishing joint frameworks in product delivery and development. 同グループは, 商品の配送と商品の開発を共同化して, グループ全体の収益力を強化する計画だ。

profit margin 売上利益率, 売上純利益率, 利益率, 利ざや, 利幅(売上純利益率(%) = (純利益÷純売上高)×100。「利ざや」は, 金融機関の資金の調達金利と貸出金利の差をいう)

operating profit margin 営業利益率 (=the ratio of operating profit to sales)
profit margin on sales 売上高利益率, 売上高純利益率, 売上総利益

▶Hitachi Ltd. aims to achieve a group operating *profit margin* of 5 percent by the end of fiscal 2009. 日立製作所は, 2009年度末[2010年3月期]

までに連結営業利益率5%の達成を目指している。

profit prediction
利益予想, 業績見通し (= profit projection)
- A growing number of firms have begun revising their *profit predictions* downward. 利益予想を下方修正する企業が, 増えている。

profit projection
利益予想, 業績見通し (= earnings forecast, profit forecast, profit outlook)
- The company may need to further lower its *profit projections* as losses related to the battery recall may grow. 充電池回収の関連損失が拡大することもあるため, 同社はさらに業績見通しの下方修正を迫られる可能性がある。

profit ratio 利益率
- **profit ratio of gross capital** 総資本利益率
- **profit ratio of net worth** 自己資本利益率
- **profit ratio of operating capital** 経営資本利益率
- **profit ratio of paid-up capital** 払込み資本収益率

profit sharing plan
利益配分制度, 利益分配制度
- ESOP resembles a *profit-sharing plan*. ESOP(従業員持ち株制度)は, 利益分配制度に似ている。

profitability
収益性, 収益力, 営利性, 採算性, 利益率, 収益率 (= earning power)
- **achieve profitability** 黒字転換を果たす, 黒字化する
- **core profitability** コア収益性
- **corporate profitability** 企業収益性, 企業の収益性
- **expected profitability of new investment** 新規投資の期待収益力
- **increased profitability** 収益性の改善, 収益性の向上, 収益力の高まり (= improved profitability)
- **investment profitability** 投資収益性, 投資利益率, 投資収益率
- **potential profitability** 採算性
- **regain profitability** 収益力を回復する
- **return to profitability** 黒字に転換する
- **segment profitability** 事業部門別収益性
- **weakened profitability** 収益性の低下 (= decreased profitability)
- There are pressures on prices, margins and *profitability*. 価格や利益率, 収益性が悪化している。
- We expect the deal to help slash procurement costs and raise *profitability*. 当社は, 今回の提携で, 仕入コスト[調達コスト]の削減と収益性の向上[収益力の改善]を見込んでいます。

profitable 形
儲かる, 利益を生む, 収益性[収益力]がある, 収益性が高い, 有利な, 有益な, ためになる, 役に立つ
- **highly profitable company** 高収益企業, 収益力[収益性]が高い企業
- **most profitable season** 書き入れ時
- **profitable basis** 会社の収益基盤
- **profitable business** 収益性の高い事業, 儲かる商売[仕事], 利益が出る商売
- **profitable goods** 利益率の高い商品, 収益性の高い商品, 収益商品
- **profitable investment** 有利な投資
- **profitable opportunity** 有利な機会
- **turn profitable** 黒字に転換する
- Mitsubishi Motors Corp. expects to be *profitable* for the first time in four years with the introduction of new models. 三菱自動車は, 新型車の導入で, 4年ぶりの黒字転換を見込んでいる。

program 名
計画, 予定, 政策, 対策, 策, 措置, 政党の綱領, 政治要項, 制度, 番組, コンピュータ・プログラム, プログラム (⇒protection, stock option program)
- **affirmative action compliance program** 積極的優遇措置遵守プログラム
- **asset disposal program** 資産売却計画
- **audit program** 監査計画, 監査プログラム, 監査指示書, 監査実施手続き書
- **cost containment program** コスト削減計画
- **economic program** 経済計画
- **engineering program** 開発体制
- **expansion program** 事業拡大計画
- **funding program** 資金調達計画
- **investment program** 投資計画, 投資プログラム
- **loan program** 融資枠
- **product program** 商品計画
- **program trading** プログラム売買
- **savings-stock purchase program** 貯蓄株購入制度
- **streamlining program** 合理化計画
- **training program** 研修計画, 研修制度, 教育訓練計画, 教育訓練制度
- Managers of companies with such stock option *programs* are discouraged from holding a long-term view. このようなストック・オプション制度を設けている企業の経営者は, 長期的な視点で企業経営に当たらなくなる。
- We support *programs* that relieve job-family stress so our people can concentrate on doing

their jobs and satisfying our customers. 当社は，社員が業務の遂行と顧客を満足させることに専念できるよう，仕事と家族のストレスを和らげるプログラムを支援しています。

programing [programming] 名 計画法, 番組編成, プログラミング
　dynamic programing 動的計画, 動的計画法
　goal programing 目標プログラミング, 目標計画法, ゴール・プログラミング
　integer programing 整数計画法
　linear programing 線型［線形］計画法, リニア・プログラミング
　mathematical programing 数理計画法
　nonlinear programing 非線型［線形］計画法
　parametric programing パラメトリック計画法
　quadratic programing 二次計画法
　stochastic programing ストカスティック・プログラミング

progress 名 進歩, 発展, 成長, 進捗状況, 未成工事
　biased technological progress 偏向的技術進歩
　capital-using technical progress 資本使用的技術進歩
　earnings progress 増益
　economic progress 経済発展, 経済進歩, 経済成長
　labor-saving technical progress 労働節約的技術進歩
　long-term contract work in progress 長期請負契約
　product in progress 仕掛(しかけ・しかかり)品 (＝goods in process, stock in process, work in process)
　progress control 製造工程の進度管理, 進度統制
　progress payment 分割払い, 分納
　progress payments 未成工事支出金, 未成工事の前受金
　progress report 経過報告, 経過報告書
　technical progress 技術進歩
　work in progress 仕掛品 (＝product in progress, work in process)
▸2008 was a year of steady *progress* for the Corporation, as was 2007. 2008年度は，当社にとって2007年度と同様に着実な発展を遂げた年でした。
▸We continue to make *progress* in Asian markets. 当社は，アジア市場で拡張を続けています。

prohibit 動 禁止する, 妨げる
prohibitive 形 禁止する, 禁制の, 〈値段が〉法外な

　at a prohibitive price 法外な値段で, 高値で
　prohibitive duty [tariff] 禁止［禁止的］関税, 高率輸入関税, 禁止的輸入税
　prohibitive tax 高率輸入税, 禁止的重税, 法外な重税

project 動 計画する, 企画する, 予測する, 予想する, 見積もる
　projected deficit 赤字見通し
　projected dividend 予想配当
　projected P/e 予想PER
　projected pension obligations 予想年金債務額 (⇒**fair value**)
▸For the full business year through next March, the company *projects* ¥27 billion in group net profit. 来年3月までの通期で，同社は270億円の連結税引き後利益を予想している。
▸The combined sales of the firm's large hotels and resort facilities are *projected* to top ¥150 billion. 同社の大型ホテルとリゾート施設の売却総額は，1,500億円を超える見通しだ。

project 名 計画, 企画, 対策, 案件, 事業, 開発事業, 公共事業計画, 長期目標, プロジェクト (⇒**turnover**)
　approved project 認可済み案件
　development project 開発計画, 開発プロジェクト
　integrated project management 総合プロジェクト管理
　joint project 共同事業
　large project 大型プロジェクト (＝high-profile project)
　pilot project 予備計画
　project control プロジェクト管理 (＝project management)
　project finance プロジェクト金融, 特定事業に対する金融, プロジェクト・ファイナンス
　project management プロジェクト管理, 計画管理, プロジェクト・マネジメント
　project plan 事業計画
　project planning 個別計画, 個別計画設定, プロジェクト・プランニング
　R&D project 研究開発プロジェクト
　raw material development project 資源開発事業
▸A joint venture including Penta-Ocean won a contract for about ¥2.6 billion in this construction *project*. この建設工事では，五洋建設などの共同事業体(JV)が約26億円で受注した。
▸The construction industry received no large *projects* in the quarter compared with the pre-

vious quarter.　建設業界は，前期に比べて当期は大型案件がなかった。
▶The lease-financing *project* targets individual investors such as company operators and other affluent people.　このリース金融事業の対象は，会社経営者や資産家などの個人投資家だ。
▶The Sakhalin-2 *project* would meet about 10 percent of Japan's natural gas requirements.　「サハリン2」事業は，日本の天然ガス需要の約1割をまかなう。

projected benefit obligation　予測給付債務，見積り給付債務，予定給付債務，予測給付債務制度，退職給付債務
▶Measurement of the *projected benefit obligation* was based on a discount rate of 8.5% and a 5% long-term rate of compensation increase in 2008.　予測給付債務は，2008年度の8.5％の割引率と5％の長期昇級率に基づいて算定されています。

projected loss　赤字予想，予想赤字
▶Reflecting the *projected losses*, the company will pay no dividends for fiscal 2009.　赤字予想を反映して，同社は2009年度を無配とする［配当金を支払わない］方針だ。

projected unit credit　予測単位給付，予測単位年金積増し
▶Annual pension cost is determined using the *Projected Unit Credit* actuarial method.　年間年金費用は，予測単位年金積増方式による年金数理計算方式で決定されています。

projection 名　見積り，予測，推定，予想，想定，見通し，推計　(⇒initial projection)
　business projection　業績見通し
　cash flow projection　資金繰りの見通し，キャッシュ・フロー予測
　earlier projection　当初予想　(＝earlier forecast, original projection)
　earnings projection　業績予想，業績見通し，収益予想，収益見通し　(＝earnings estimate, earnings forecast)
　financial projection　財務計画，財務見通し
　preliminary projections　暫定値
　sales projection　売上予想，販売見通し，予想売上
▶Banks have to set aside loan loss reserves based on *projections* of future revenues of their borrowers, not based on bankruptcies in the past.　銀行は，過去の倒産実績ではなく，融資先企業［貸出先］の将来の収益予想などを基にして，貸倒れ引当金を積み立てるべきだ。
▶The Japanese currency is about ¥5 lower than its initial *projection* of ¥115 to the dollar.　円は，当初想定した1ドル＝115円より5円程度安く推移している。

prolonged 形　長引く，長期の，長期にわたる，慢性的な
　prolonged deflation　長引くデフレ，長期デフレ，デフレの長期化　(＝protracted deflation)
　prolonged economic malaise　長引く景気低迷
　prolonged economic slump　長期不況　(＝prolonged recession)
　prolonged losses　慢性赤字，慢性的な赤字
　prolonged recession　長引く不況，長期不況，不況の長期化，後退局面の長期化
▶The main cause of the *prolonged* deflation is that consumer demand has been weak due to the current economic slump.　デフレ長期化の主因は，現在の不況で消費需要が低迷していることだ。

promised yield rate　予定利率　(＝promised yield, prospective yield rate: 生命保険会社が保険契約者に約束した利回り。⇒insurance contract)

promising area　有望な分野，期待できる分野，成長分野
▶Sanyo plans to shift resources to more *promising areas* such as rechargeable batteries and industrial-use air conditioners, where it still earns healthy profits.　三洋電機は，充電式電池や業務用エアコンなど，同社が現在も順調に利益を上げている有望な分野に経営資源を振り向ける計画だ。

promising market　期待できる市場，有望市場，成長市場

promote 動　促進する，推進する，振興する，助長する，奨励する，販売を促進する，宣伝する，売り込む，昇進させる，昇格させる，主催する，発起する，議案の通過を促す　(⇒consumers' interests, internal growth, representative)
▶Board members who were *promoted* from within the company have been managing firms in Japan　日本では，社内から昇進した取締役［従業員から持ち上がった取締役］が企業を経営している。

promotion 名　昇進，昇級，昇格，昇任，促進，推進，増進，助長，振興，奨励，販売促進，販売促進活動，創設，創立，発起，プロモーション　(⇒sales promotion)
　advertising and promotion costs　広告宣伝費
　employment promotion　雇用促進
　export promotion　輸出振興，輸出促進
　job promotion　職種内昇進
　productivity promotion　生産性向上
　promotion department store　大衆路線型百貨店，大衆百貨店　(＝promotional department

store)
promotion expense 販売促進費 (sales promotion cost), 創業費 (organization cost), 創立費, 設立費用
promotion strategy プロモーション戦略 (= promotional strategy)
promotion system 昇進制度
sales promotion cost 販売促進費, 販促費用
trade promotion 貿易振興, 貿易促進
▸Selling, general and administrative expenses increased largely because of advertising and promotions. 販売費および一般管理費は、主に広告宣伝と販売促進活動により増加しました。

promotional 形 宣伝の, 宣伝用の, 販売促進用の, 販売促進のための, プロモーショナル
promotional advertising 販売促進広告, 販促広告, 促進広告, 宣伝広告 (= product reputation advertising)
promotional allowance 促進割引き, 促進奨励金 (= promotion allowance, promotional discount)
promotional display プロモーショナル陳列
promotional item 特売品目
promotional marketing プロモーショナル・マーケティング
promotional merchandise 促進商品, 特売商品
promotional mix 販売促進ミックス, プロモーション・ミックス (= promotion mix: 一般に人的販売, 広告, 販売促進, パブリシティのプロモーション手段から成る)
promotional policy プロモーション政策
promotional pricing 特売価格設定
promotional program プロモーション実施計画
sales promotional program 販売促進計画

promotools 名 プロモーション用具

prompt 形 即座の, 即時の, 迅速な, 素早い, 機敏な, 即時払いの, 名 支払い期日, 期限付き契約, 即時払い
prompt cash 4, 5日以内に支払う決済条件, 即金払い, 直払い
prompt cash discount 直払い割引
prompt day [date] 支払い期日, 受渡し日, 延べ渡し日
prompt delivery 直渡し
prompt exchange 直物為替 (= spot exchange)
prompt neutron 触発中性子
prompt note 買上票
prompt payment 即時払い
prompt sale 延べ取引
prompt shipment 直(じき)積み, 即時船積み

[船積み条件], 即時出荷 (= as soon as possible shipment, immediate shipment)
your prompt reply 貴社の迅速なご返事

prop up 支える, 支持する, 買い支える, 後援する, テコ入れをする
prop up the economy by fiscal means 財政面でのテコ入れをする
prop up the sagging dollar 下落するドルを買い支える
▸He siphoned off the money to *prop up* his consulting firm. 同氏は, 自らのコンサルタント会社の経営を支えるために資金を流用していた。

propensity 名 性向, 傾向, 好み, 選好
average propensity to import 平均輸入性向
marginal propensity to expend 限界支出性向
marginal propensity to save 限界貯蓄性向
propensity to consume 消費性向
risk propensity リスク選好
▸It also is of great concern that the average *propensity* to consume has begun to decline. 平均消費性向が下がり始めたことも, 大いに気がかりだ。

property 名 財産, 有体財産, 資産, 固定資産, 有形固定資産, 所有, 所有権, 所有地, 所有物, 財産権, 特性, 属性, 物件
after-acquired property 事後取得財産
basic property 基本財産
gain on property dividend 現物配当処分益
immovable property 不動産 (= immovables)
inventories and property 棚卸し資産および有形固定資産
investment property 投資不動産, 投資資産
leased property リース資産
movable property 動産 (= movables)
negative property 消極財産(負債や支払い勘定)
personal property tax 動産税
property additions 固定資産の増設額, 固定資産の新規取得
property and equipment 有形固定資産
property development project 不動産開発事業, 不動産開発プロジェクト (⇒ turnover)
real property tax 不動産税, 固定資産税
residential property price 住宅用不動産価格
total property 有形固定資産合計
▸Plant, rental machines and other *property* are depreciated over their estimated useful lives using the straight-line method. 工場設備, 賃貸機械, その他の固定資産は, それぞれの見積り耐用年数にわたって定額法を用いて償却されています。

property right 所有権, 財産権, 財産所有権, 資産権利

▸The expanded application of the Copyright Law to the Net means the curtailment of the *property right* of copyright holders such as music producers, composers and singers.　著作権法のネットへの拡大適用は，音楽会社や作曲者，歌手など著作権者の所有権[知的所有権]の縮小を意味する．

property, plant and equipment　有形固定資産，土地，建物および設備，不動産・工場設備
(＝tangible fixed assets)

▸For the three years, operating cash flows covered our additions to *property, plant and equipment* and dividend payments.　過去3年間は，営業から生じるキャッシュ・フローで有形固定資産に対する追加投資額と支払い配当金をまかないました．

proportion 名　割合，比率，比例，釣合い，均衡，バランス，大きさ，広さ，規模，部分，割当て，分け前

factor proportion　要素比率（＝proportion of factors)

inverse proportion　反比例

proportion defective　不良率

proportion of work carried out　工事進行度，工事進捗度

▸To promote the internal growth of ABC Inc. and the value of its shares, the *proportion* of earnings invested in the corporation should be permitted to grow.　ABC社の内部成長を促し，当社株式の価値を高めるためには，収益のうち当社自体に対する投資比率を引き上げる必要があります．

proposal 名　提案，案，企画，構想，計画，申込み，オファー

management integration proposal　経営統合の提案

proposal for appropriation of retained earnings　利益処分案

shareholder proposal　株主提案

▸Oji lowered its offer price per share from ¥860 to ¥800 under its latest *proposal*.　王子製紙は，今回の提案で1株当たり買付け価格[買取り価格]を860円から800円に引き下げた．

▸On the stockholder *proposal* requesting detailed reporting on animal experimentation, 92% of the votes cast were voted against.　動物実験に関する詳細な報告を要求する株主提案については，投票総数(投票株式総数)の92％が反対で否決された．

▸Rakuten Inc.'s management integration *proposal* will not increase TBS's corporate value.　楽天からの経営統合の提案は，TBSの企業価値の向上にはつながらないだろう．

propose 動　提案する，提唱する，企画する，申し出る，提出する，提示する，指名する，推薦する

▸*Proposed* purchase price is still far from what the investment fund is expecting.　提示された(TOBの)買付け価格は，投資ファンドの想定価格とまだ開きがある．

proprietary 形　所有者の，所有権者の，独占の，専売の，特許の，財産の価値のある

proprietary article　専売品

proprietary company　管理会社，親会社，土地会社，閉鎖会社

proprietary dealing　自己売買，自己勘定取引，ディーリング業務

proprietary information　有価値情報，専有情報，財産たる情報，財産価値のある情報

proprietary interest　所有権限，所有権，所有者の権利

proprietary knowhow　財産的ノウハウ

proprietary material　財産的権利のある資産

proprietary right　所有権，財産権，知的所有権，知的財産権，財産価値のある権利

proprietary trade name　特許商標名

proprietary trading system　私設取引システム《略PTS》(米国のalternative trading system (代替取引システム)，EUのmultilateral trading facility (多角的取引システム)に相当する)

trading of proprietary books　自己勘定取引

▸The confidential information includes, but not limited to, business plans, price lists, pricing data, technical data, and documents marked "Confidential" or "*Proprietary*."　秘密情報には，事業計画，価格表，価格設定資料，技術資料と「秘密」または「専有」と表示した書類などが含まれる．

proprietary technology　特許技術（＝proprietary technique)

▸Hitachi will establish a new company to develop PDP *proprietary technology* and Matsushita will provide up to 20 percent of the new firm's capital.　日立がプラズマ・ディスプレー・パネル(PDP)の特許技術を開発する新会社を設立し，松下電器が新会社の資本金の最高で2割ほど出資する見込みだ．

proprietor 名　事業主，経営者，所有者，所有主，出資者，資本主，オーナー

▸A fairly large number of *proprietors* gave up their business despite their companies enjoying good financial health.　会社の経営状況が良くても，事業承継を断念した(中小企業の)経営者はかなりいる．

proprietorship 名 自己資本, 出資者持ち分, 資本主, 資本主勘定, 正味財産, 個人企業, 自営業者
   individual proprietorship 個人企業 (=single proprietorship, sole proprietorship)
   single proprietorship 個人企業, 個人事業主, 個人事業

prorate 動 配賦する, 割り当てる, 比例配分する
▸Actual indirect factory overhead was *prorated* to producing and service departments. 実際製造間接費は, 製造部門とサービス部門に比例配分しました。

proration 名 配賦, 比例配分 (pro rata allocation), 割当て (=prorating)

prosecute 動 起訴する, 訴追する, 遂行する, 追及する

prosecutors 名 検察当局, 検察側
▸*Prosecutors* searched the Tokyo headquarters of the firm one day after three of its officials were arrested on suspicion of involvement in a bid-rigging scheme. 検察当局は, 同社の社員3人が不正入札にかかわった疑いで逮捕された翌日, 同社の東京本社を捜索した。

prospective 動 未来の, 将来の, 今後の, 予想される, 予期される, 期待される, 見込みのある, …になる予定の
   prospective buyer 見込み客, 見込み購買者
   prospective candidate 立候補予定者
   prospective customer 見込み客, 見込み顧客 (=prospective buyer)
   prospective financial information 将来財務情報
   prospective PE [P/E] 予想株価収益率, 予想PER (=prospective PE multiple, prospective price/earnings ratio)
   prospective profits 予想収益, 収益見通し
   prospective retirees 退職予定者, 予想される退職者
   prospective site 候補地
   prospective yield 予想利回り
   prospective yield rate 予定利率 (=promised yield rate)
▸Under the existing Insurance Business Law, life insurance companies are not allowed to revise *prospective* yield rates unless they go bankrupt. 現行の保険業法では, 生保各社が破綻しないかぎり, 予定利率は変更できない。

prospects 名 見通し, 予想, 先行き, 将来性, 見込み, 可能性, 期待, 目処
   demand prospects 需要見通し
   earnings prospects 収益見通し, 収益予想
   economic prospects 経済見通し, 景気見通し
   future prospects 将来の見通し, 将来性
   prospects for growth 成長見通し, 成長力, 業績見通し, 景気見通し, 景気の先行き (=growth prospects)
   short-term prospects 短期見通し
▸Financial institutions, concerned about MMC's future *prospects*, began calling in the company's loans. 金融機関は, 三菱自動車の先行きを懸念して, 同社への融資回収に動いた。
▸We are confident about the long-term *prospects* for our business. 当社の長期事業見通しについては, 私ども経営陣は自信を持っております。

prospectus 名 目論見書, 発行目論見書, 会社の設立趣意書, 事業要綱, 保険案内書, 案内, 内容見本 (=listing particulars)
   目論見書とは➠有価証券の募集や売出しの際, 有価証券や発行者の内容を説明した文書。株式や投資信託など有価証券を購入する投資家のための資料として, 証券取引法で販売会社に交付が義務付けられている。投資信託の場合は, 約款の内容や運用体制, リスク要因, 申込手数料などが記載される。
   final prospectus 最終目論見書
   listing prospectus 上場目論見書
   pathfinder prospectus 募集目論見書
   preliminary prospectus 仮目論見書
   prospectus issue 目論見書の発行
   prospectus of promotion 会社設立趣意書, 会社設立目論見書
▸A *prospectus* must include certain details stipulated by the Banking Commission, such as shareholdings, a comparison of the last five annual reports, capital review and others. 目論見書には, 株主情報や過去5年間の年次報告書比較, 資本金の推移など, 銀行委員会が定めた特定の詳細事項も記載しなければならない。

protect 動 保護する, 保全する, 保証する
▸Financial authorities should stiffen the penalties for illegal transactions to *protect* the financial system from rumors and speculative investment. 金融当局は違法取引[違法行為]に対する罰則を強化して, 金融システムを風評や投機[投機的投資]から守らなければならない。

protection 名 保護, 保全, 保証, 保障, 補償, 対策
   apply for protection from creditors 会社更生手続きを申請する, 資産保全を申請する
   asset protection 財産保全
   blanket protection on bank deposits 銀行預金全額保証

call protection　任意償還権不行使期間
consumer protection　消費者保護
court protection from creditors under the Civil Rehabilitation Law　民事再生法に基づく資産保全　(⇒civil)
customer protection　顧客保護
debt protection　債権保護水準, 債権者保護, 債務返済能力
environmental protection　環境保護
income protection　利益保護
debtholder [debt holder] protection　債権保有者保護
insurance protection　保険保障
lien protection　先取特権
price protection　価格保全
protection from creditors　資産保全
protection of intellectual property　知的所有権の保護, 知的財産の保護
protection of personal information　個人情報保護

▶Domestic industries harmed by dumping require urgent protection.　ダンピングによる損害を受けている国内産業は, 緊急保護を必要としている。

▶Reserves are established for price protection and cooperative marketing programs with distributors.　価格保全や販売業者との協調販売計画のために, 引当金が設定されています。

▶The firm filed for court protection from creditors under the Civil Rehabilitation Law with debts of about ¥60 billion.　同社は, 約600億円の負債をかかえて, 民事再生法に基づく資産保全を［民事再生法の適用を］申請した。

protectionism 名　保護主義, 保護貿易主義

▶Chinese local protectionism also has made it difficult for suppliers to collect payments and eliminate piracy.　中国の地方保護主義も, サプライヤーにとって債権の回収や模造品の排除［摘発］を難しくしている。

protectionist policy　保護貿易政策, 貿易保護政策, 保護政策

▶Japan's protectionist policies impose high tariffs on imports of agricultural products.　日本の保護政策は, 輸入農産品に高率の関税をかけている。

protective 形名　保護する(もの), 保護貿易主義に基づく
　protective duties　保護関税 (= protective tariff)
　protective features　保護措置
　protective measures　保護措置, 対応策
　protective tariff　保護関税

protest 名　抗議, 異議申立て, 〈手形の〉拒絶証書
　notice of protest　支払い拒絶証書
　protest charges [fee]　〈手形の〉拒絶証書作成料
　waived protest　拒絶証書不要文言 (= protest waived)

▶The company intends to lodge a protest with the Tokyo District Court immediately.　同社は, 東京地裁に直ちに異議申立てを行う方針だ。

protocol 名　〈契約・条約などの〉原案［原本], 議定書, 条約議定書, 〈協定・条約の〉付随書, 〈国家間の〉補足協約, 〈国家間の〉協定［協約], 〈自治体などの〉規定, 議事録, 外交上の儀礼書, 外交文書, 外交慣習, 通信規約, プロトコル
　authentication protocol　認証プロトコル
　Kyoto Protocol　京都議定書
　Internet Protocol　インターネット・プロトコル

prototype 名　原型, 見本, モデル, 模範, 手本, 典型, 試作品, 試作車, プロトタイプ
　prototype model　原型モデル
　working prototype　動作可能な試作品［試作機]

provide 動　提供する, 供給する, 与える, 付与する, 販売する, 創出する, 調達する, 発生する, 設定する, 定める, 算定する, 計上する, 引当計上する, 発表する (⇒contingency)
　cash provided from financing activities　財務活動に伴う資金の調達, 財務活動から生じた資金
　provide for　…に備える, …に引き当てる, …を算定する, 定める, 規定する, 計上する
　provide liquidity　流動性を提供する, 流動性を供給する
　provide the required capital　必要資本を調達する
　working capital provided from other sources　その他から得た運転資本

▶Our business is asset management and we do not directly provide any service or manufacture any product.　当社の業務は資産の運用であり, サービスを提供するとか製品を製造するということは, 直接的にはしておりません。

▶We did not provide for deferred taxes on the gain.　当社は, この利益に対して繰延べ税金は計上しませんでした。

provider 名　提供者, 請負業者, 業者, 企業, インターネット接続業者, ネット接続会社, プロバイダー
　cash provider　資金提供者 (= capital provider)
　content provider　出店企業, コンテンツ・プロバイダー
　credit enhancement provider　信用補強提供者
　credit support provider　信用補填提供者, 信用

補完提供者
e-mail service provider 電子メール・サービス会社
information provider 情報提供者《略 IP》
internet provider インターネット・プロバイダー，プロバイダー《略 IP》
internet service provider インターネット接続サービス業者《略 ISP》
monopoly provider 独占企業
service provider サービス会社，サービス企業
solution provider ソリューション請負業者，ソリューション・サービス業者
terminal equipment provider 端末機器提供業者，端末プロバイダー
▶To avoid sinking into a negative net worth, the firm is seeking ¥300 billion in financial aid from capital *providers*.　債務超過に陥るのを避けるため，同社は資金提供者に3,000億円の金融支援を要請している。

provision 動　引当金を計上する，引当金を繰り入れる
▶Banks have *provisioned* sufficiently against bad loans.　これまでのところ，銀行は不良債権に対して引当金［不良債権引当金，貸倒れ引当金］を十分計上している。

provision 名　準備金，引当金，引当金繰入れ，引当金繰入れ額［充当額］，引当金計上，計上，拠出，提供，用意，準備，規定，条項　(⇒housing loan)

準備金と引当金について➡「準備金」には，一般にprovisionよりreserveやallowanceが使用されることが多い。日本の場合，「準備金」は法定準備金(legal capital reserves, legal reserves, legally required reserves)である資本準備金(capital reserve)，利益準備金(profit reserve)や価格変動準備金(reserve for price fluctuation)などにだけ用いられている。これに対して「引当金」は，将来の支出にあてるためにあらかじめ準備しておく資金のことである。

bolster provisions 引当金を積み増す　(=increase provisions)
establish a provision for …の引当金を設定する
life insurance provision 生命保険準備金
loss provision 損失引当金，損失準備金　(=loss reserve)
provision for depreciation 減価償却引当金
provision for doubtful debts 貸倒れ引当金，貸倒れ引当金繰入れ額　(=bad debt provision, provision for bad debts, provision for doubtful accounts)
retirement provisions 退職給与引当金繰入れ額

risk provision 危険引当金，リスク引当金
▶Nonbank firms are forced to raise *provisions* by a recent accounting rule change.　今回の会計規則の変更で，ノンバンク（銀行以外の金融機関）各社は引当金の積み増しを迫られている。

provision for business restructuring activities 事業再編成作業の引当金
▶In the third quarter of 2008, we recorded $300 million in *provision for business restructuring activities*.　2008年第3四半期に，当社は事業再編成作業の引当金として3億ドルを計上しました。

provision for income taxes 法人税等引当金，法人税等充当額，法人税繰入れ額，法人税等計上額，納税引当金
▶The 2008 *provision for income taxes* was $142 million (effective tax rate of 22 percent) compared with a 2007 provision of $128 million (effective tax rate of 29 percent).　2008年の法人所得税等引当金［法人税等計上額］は，2007年の1億2,800万ドル（実効税率29％）に対して，1億4,200万ドル（同22％）でした。

proxy 名　代理人，代行者，代理行為，代理権，代理委任状，委任状，議決権行使委任状，指標，比較対象，プロキシ［プロクシー］
by proxy 代理人を立てて，代理で，委任状で
form of proxy 代理人様式，委任状用紙，委任状カード　(=proxy form)
index proxy 指標
joint proxy 共同委任状
proxy card 代理人カード，代理投票カード，代理投票用紙　(=proxy voting card)
proxy committee 議決権代理行使委員会
proxy fight [battle, contest] 委任状争奪戦，委任状合戦，代理人競争
proxy for the market 市場の指標
proxy form 代理人様式，委任状用紙，委任状カード，委任状　(=form of proxy; ⇒**participant**)
proxy material 委任状参考資料
proxy regulation 委任状規制
proxy rule 委任状規則
proxy server 代理サーバー，プロキシ・サーバー
proxy solicitation 委任状勧誘
proxy statement 代理勧誘状，代理権勧誘状，委任状，委任状説明書，議決権代理行使勧誘状，プロクシー・ステートメント
proxy vote 代理投票
proxy voting card 投票委任用紙，代理投票用紙　(=proxy card)
single proxy 単独委任状
solicitation of proxies 議決権行使委任状勧誘，

委任状勧誘
standing proxy 常任代理人
voting by proxy 代理人による議決権の行使
▸Over 180 million shares, or about 62 percent of total shares outstanding, were represented at the annual meeting in person or by *proxy*. 定時株主総会には，1億8,000万株(発行済み株式総数の約62%)以上を所有する株主が出席，または委任状を提出しました。

PTO 次ページに続く (**please turn over** の略)

public 名 一般の人々，公衆，社会，顧客，…界，…層
▸Japan Airlines Corp. decided to issue new shares to the *public* at ¥211 per share. 日本航空は，公募増資の新株発行価格を1株当たり211円とすることを決めた。
▸Sale to the *public* of shares in our subsidiaries will reinforce the Corporation's value. 当社子会社の株式公開で，当社の資産価値は今後，拡大するものと思われます。

public 形 公の，公的，公共の，社会的
  public bidding 入札
  public company 上場企業，株式公開企業
  public corporation 公共企業体，公団，公社
  Public Company Accounting Oversight Board 米上場企業会計監視委員会 《略 PCAOB》
  public debt 公債
  public elderly care service 公的高齢者介護サービス，高齢者介護サービス
  public fund injection 公的資金の注入 (= **public fund infusion**)
  public goods 公益
  public interest corporation 公益法人
  public investment spending 公共投資関係費
  public knowledge 公知，公知の事実 (= **public domain**)
  public limited company 公開有責任会社，株式会社
  public ownership 株式公開，上場企業
  public pension benefits 公的年金給付
  public pension plan 公的年金制度，公的年金 (= **public pension system**)
  public tender period 株式公開買付け[TOB]期間 (= **public tender offer period**)

public funds 公的資金，公金，公費 (= **public money, taxpayers' money**)
▸The United States should use *public funds* to settle the subprime problem. サブプライム問題を解決するために，米国は公的資金を利用[投入]すべきだ。

public listing 株式上場
▸The *public listing* of the firm, with the market value this creates, helps to reinforce the value of ABC Inc.'s own shares. 同社の株式上場は，ABCの市場価値を高めるとともに，ABCの自社株の株価強化にも役立っている。

public offering 株式公開，株式公募，公募，公募増資，売出し (= going public, primary offering, public stock offering: 一般投資家を対象に，有価証券の取得の申込みを勧誘すること。有価証券が新規発行の場合は primary offering (募集・公募)，既発行の場合は secondary offering (売出し) と呼ばれる。私募 = private placement。⇒ **initial public offering, net proceeds, proceeds from the public offering**)
  public offering bond 公募債
  public offering of bonds on fixed conditions 定率公募
▸During the first nine months of 2008, the Company completed a *public offering* in Canada of $150 million in Debentures, due 2019. 2008年1-9月期に，当社はカナダ国内で満期2019年の社債1億5,000万ドルの公募発行を完了しました。

public offering price 公募価格
▸We have signed an underwriting agreement with Merrill Lynch Canada Inc. for the issue of three million common shares at a *public offering price* of $18 per share. 当社は，普通株式300万株を1株18ドルの公募価格で発行するため，メリルリンチ・カナダ社との募集引受契約に調印しました。

public tender offer 株式公開買付け 《略 TOB》 (= **takeover bid, tender offer, TOB**)
▸Investors must use a *public tender offer* if they seek to acquire more than one-third of stocks issued by any listed corporation through off-market trading. 市場外取引で上場企業が発行した株式の3分の1超を投資家が取得する場合，投資家は株式公開買付け(TOB)を実施しなければならない。
▸The Murakami Fund responded to the *public tender offer* by selling all of its Hanshin shares to further the integration of Hanshin and Hankyu. 村上ファンドは，阪神と阪急の経営統合を促進するため，保有する阪神株を全株売却して株式公開買付け(TOB)に応じた。

publicity 名 公表，広報，宣伝，広告，パブリシティー

publicly held company 公開会社，株式公開企業，上場会社，上場企業 (= **publicly owned**

company, publicly traded company)
▶Web search leader Google Inc., in its first earnings report as a *publicly held company*, posted quarterly net income and revenue that more than doubled on strong advertising revenues. インターネット検索最大手のグーグルは，上場会社として初の決算(7-9月期決算)で，広告収入が伸びたため四半期純利益と売上高が前年同期の2倍超となった．

publicly owned company [corporation] 株式公開企業，公開会社，上場企業 (＝publicly quoted company, publicly traded company)
▶After an initial public offering of its common stock in September 2006, the firm became the largest *publicly owned* equipment leasing and financing *company*. 2006年9月の普通株初公開後，同社は機器リースおよび金融部門で国内最大の公開会社になった．

publish 動 出版する，刊行する，発行する，掲載する，公表する，公開する (⇒source(s))
pull distribution strategy プル販売戦略
pull out of …から撤退する，…から手を引く
▶The firm effectively *pulled out* of the energy market. 同社は事実上，エネルギー市場から撤退した．
pull promotion strategy 引くプロモーション戦略
pull strategy 引く戦略，プル戦略
pulsing 名 パルシング (一定間隔で広告費の投入を増やすこと)
pump priming 呼び水，誘い水，予算ばらまき，呼び水用の財政支出，呼び水的支出政策，呼び水経済政策，景気刺激策，景気振興策
pump-priming effect 呼び水効果
pump-priming measures 景気テコ入れ策，景気刺激策，景気振興策，呼び水政策
pump-priming money 呼び水用の資金
pump-priming policy 呼び水政策，誘い水政策
▶The $150 billion *pump-priming* package is being negotiated between the U.S. administration and Congress. 米政府と議会は現在，1,500億ドルの景気刺激策について調整を進めている．
punish 動 処分する，処罰する，罰する，手荒く扱う，酷使する
▶The company has *punished* 29 employees over the cover-up of vehicle defects. 同社は，自動車の欠陥隠し問題で社員29人を処分した．
punitive 形 懲罰的な，制裁の，報復の(retaliatory)，報復的な，刑罰の，因果応報の(retributive)，厳しい，過酷な

punitive action 処罰行為，制裁措置
punitive duties [tariffs] 報復関税，制裁課税 (＝retaliatory tariffs, tit-for-tat tariffs)
punitive justice 因果応報，当然の報い
punitive measures 制裁措置，懲罰手段
punitive regulation 懲罰的規制
take punitive measures [action, steps] against …に対して制裁措置を取る
punitive damages 懲罰的損害賠償，懲罰的損害賠償金，懲罰的賠償，制裁的慰謝料
▶*Punitive damages* have been claimed by a group of victims of food poisoning involving Snow Brand Milk Products Co.'s dairy products. 制裁的慰謝料は，雪印乳業の乳製品による集団食中毒事件の被害者が請求したことがある．

purchase 動 買い取る，買い付ける，購入する，引き受ける，仕入れる，買収する，取得する (＝buy)
purchased cost 仕入原価
purchased fund 取得資金，市場性資金
▶The company is considering directly *purchasing* a majority stake in Japan Telecom Co. 同社は，日本テレコムの過半数株式の直接取得を検討している．
▶We *purchase* essentially all cardholder receivables under an agreement with the company which issues the cards. 当社は，基本的にカード発行会社との契約に基づいてカード保有者に対する債権をすべて買い取っています．
▶We *purchased* the net assets of the company for $600,000 during 2008. 当社は，2008年度に同社の純資産を60万ドルで取得しました．

purchase 名 買取り，買付け，買入れ，購入，購買，調達，調達先，引受け，仕入れ，買収，取得，獲得，パーチェス (⇒stock purchase plan)
bulk purchase 一括購入
corporate purchase 企業買収
equity purchase 株式投資，株式取得
gross purchases 総仕入高
material purchase 材料購入，材料購買，材料仕入れ，材料受入れ
offshore purchase 域外調達
purchase and assumption method [system] 資産・負債継承方式，P&A方式
purchase and operating expenses 売上原価および営業費
purchase cost 仕入原価，購入原価 (＝purchasing cost)
purchase goodwill 買入のれん
purchase of business 企業取得，企業買収，買収，

営業の譲り受け

purchase of common shares for cancellation 消却のための普通株式の購入

purchase of loans 債権買取り （＝purchase of debts）

purchase price 購入価格, 買入価格, 買取り価格, 買付け価格, 取得価格, 買収価格, 仕入価格, 仕入値段 （＝purchasing price）

purchases and sales of treasury stock 自己株式の取得および売却

redemption by purchase 買入償却

replacement purchase 買替え

returned purchase 仕入戻し品

▸*Purchases* of our strongest product line were deferred by some of our major customers. 当社の最も強力な製品ラインの購入を，一部の顧客が延期しました。

purchase method パーチェス方式, パーチェス法, 買収法, 買収方式 （＝purchase method of combination）

▸Acquisitions of companies are accounted for using the *purchase method*. 企業の取得は，パーチェス法を採用して会計処理されています。

purchase order 発注書, 注文書, 購入注文書, 購入指図書, 仕入注文書

▸We issued a *purchase order* of merchandise to the company at a total price of US $1,000,000. 当社は，同社に総額で100万米ドルの商品注文書を発行した。

purchase right 購入権

▸Each outstanding share of the Company's common stock carries with it one-quarter of a preferred share *purchase right*. 当社の発行済み普通株式には，1株に付き0.25単位の優先株式購入権が付与されています。

purchaser 買い主, 買い手, 買取り人, 購買者, 得意先

▸*Purchasers* are able to make on-the-spot payments through various financial institutions. 購入者は，各種金融機関を通じて即時決済することができる。

purchasing 購入, 購買, 仕入れ, 買取り, 取得

mass purchasing 大量購入, 大量仕入れ

purchasing conditions 取引条件

purchasing expenses 仕入費用

purchasing price 購入価格, 取得価格, 買取り価格 （＝purchase price）

▸The RCC's main function was *purchasing* of loan credits from failed financial institutions and then collecting the money. 整理回収機構（RCC）の主な業務は，破綻金融機関からの債権買取りとその金（債権）の回収であった。

purchasing power 購買力, 貨幣購買力 （＝buying power）

common purchasing power units of measurements 共通購買力測定単位

constant purchasing power 恒常ドル, 恒常購買力, 統一購買力

consumer purchasing power 消費購買力

current purchasing power 現在購買力

external purchasing power of money 貨幣の対外価値

general purchasing power 一般購買力

household purchasing power 家計の購買力

National Purchasing Managers' data [index, survey] 全米購買部協会の景気総合指数

purchasing power bond 購買力債券

purchasing power gain or loss 購買力損益, 購買力利得または損失, 貨幣購買力損益 （＝monetary gain or loss）

purchasing power of money 貨幣の購買力

purchasing power parity 購買力平価

purchasing power risk 購買力リスク, インフレ危険

purpose 名 目的, 意図, 決意, …上, 用途 （⇒ temporary differences）

allowance for special purpose 特別引当金, 特別用途引当金

business purpose 事業目的, 経営目的 （＝purpose of business）

cash flow purpose 資金繰りの目的

for financial reporting purposes 財務報告上, 財務会計上

for financial statement and income tax reporting purposes 会計上および税務上

for financial statement purposes 財務諸表上の, 財務書類上の, 財務会計上

for income tax purposes 税務会計上, 税務上

for plan purposes 年金制度の目的上

for tax purposes 税務上

general corporate purposes 一般事業目的

general purpose financial statements 一般目的財務書類

multi purpose card 汎用カード

purpose loan 目的貸付け, 目的融資, 証券購入目的融資

purpose of loan 資金使途

purpose statement 目的申告書

▸We consider temporary cash investments to be cash equivalents for cash flow reporting

purposes. 当社は, キャッシュ・フロー報告上, 短期投資を現金等価物と見なしています。
purse 名 財布, 金銭, 財力, 資力, 寄付金
purveyor 名 調達人, 提供者, 供給元
push distribution strategy プッシュ販売戦略
push money 報奨金, 販売奨励金
push/pull technology プッシュ・プル技術
push strategy 押す戦略, プッシュ戦略
push technology プッシュ技術, プッシュ型サービス (インターネットを利用して, ニュースや株価情報などユーザーが求める情報を自動的に配信するシステム)
put 動 〈信任などを〉置く, 預ける, 委ねる, 記入する, 評価する, 見積もる, 投入する, 付ける
put 名 買取り請求権, 株式売付け選択権, 償還請求権, 売戻し選択権, プット・オプション, プット
　buy a put プットを買い建てる
　long put プットの買い
　put bond 償還請求権付き社債, プット・オプション付き債券
　put date プット・オプション行使日
　put option 売付け選択権, 株式売渡し選択権, プット・オプション

short put プット売り
pyramid 名 ピラミッド型組織, 株式の買い乗せ[売り乗せ], 利乗せ(pyramiding), ピラミッド式価格[賃金]の決定, ピラミッド, 動 〈コストを〉価格に上乗せする, 徐々に上げる, 漸増する, 〈議論などを〉着々と進める[次第に高める], 取引を拡大して利ざやを稼ぐ, 〈株式を〉利乗せする, 〈信用取引で未実現利益を利用して〉買い乗せをする
population pyramid 人口分布グラフ
pyramid control ピラミッド型管理
pyramid investment scheme ネズミ講式投資計画
pyramid selling マルチ商法, ネズミ講式販売(方式)
pyramid [pyramidal] structure ピラミッド構造, ピラミッド型組織
pyramid structure ratio analysis ピラミッド型経営比率分析
pyramid scam マルチ商法詐欺
▸The chairman of health food marketing company was arrested on suspicion of ¥50 billion *pyramid scam*. 健康食品販売会社の会長が, マルチ商法による500億円の詐欺容疑で逮捕された。

Q q

Q1 第1四半期 （＝first quarter: 12月期決算企業の1−3月期。日本企業に多い3月期決算企業の場合は、4−6月期を指す）
▶In the *Q1* of 2008, we issued 19 million common shares for net cash proceeds of $244 million. 2008年第1四半期に，当社は普通株式1,900万株を発行して，2億4,400万ドルの純資金を調達しました。

Q2 第2四半期 （＝second quarter）
▶*Q2* operating revenues were $1,819 million. 第2四半期の営業収益は，18億1,900万ドルでした。

Q3 第3四半期 （＝third quarter）
▶The Corporation's *Q3* consolidated net income improved 8.7 percent to $301 million. 当社の第3四半期の連結純利益は，前年同期比8.7％増の3億100万ドルでした。

Q4 第4四半期 （＝fourth quarter）
▶Net income for the *Q4* of 2008 was higher than for the same period last year. 2008年第4四半期の純利益は，前年同期の水準を上回りました。

QA 品質保証 （**quality assurance** の略）
QC 品質管理 （**quality control**の略）
　QC circle 品質管理サークル，QCサークル
　total QC 総合品質管理，総合的品質管理，全社的品質管理
Q.C. 勅選弁護士 （**Queen's Counsel**の略）
QSPE 適格特別目的事業体 （**qualifying special purpose entity**の略）
quadrilateral trade talks 4極通商会議
quadrillion 名 1,000兆
quadruple 動 4倍にする，4倍増にする，4倍になる，4倍増になる
▶Operating revenues of our telecommunications operating subsidiaries in the first quarter of 2008 *quadrupled* over the same period last year. 通信事業子会社の2008年第1四半期の営業収益は，前年同期比で4倍増加しました。

qualified 形 限定付き，条件付きの，適格の，有資格の
　qualified acceptance 手形の条件引受け，制限引受け
　qualified auditor's report 限定付き監査報告書，限定意見監査報告書，限定意見報告書 （＝**qualified audit report, qualified auditor report, qualified opinion report**）
　qualified bond 適格債券
　qualified indorsement 無担保裏書き
　qualified institutional investor 適格機関投資家
　qualified opinion 限定意見，限定付き適正意見
　qualified pension plan 適格年金制度，適格退職年金
　qualified personnel 適格従業員，有資格者 （⇒**judgment**）
　qualified plan 適格退職年金 （＝**qualified pension plan**）
　qualified resident 適格居住者
　qualified security 適格証券
　qualified stock option 条件付きストック・オプション
　tax qualified pension plan 適格退職年金
qualify 動 …に資格を与える，権限を与える，適格にする，制限する，限定する （⇒**lease** 名）
qualifying 形 適格の，資格を与える，資格取得の
　qualifying capital interest 適格資本持ち分
　qualifying condition 資格条件

qualifying corporate bond 適格社債
qualifying dividend 適格配当
qualifying facilities 適格設備, 適格設備電気事業者《略 QF》
qualifying lender 適格融資者
qualifying special purpose entity 適格特別目的事業体《略 QSPE》
qualifying stock option 自社株購入権
qualitative 形 質的な, 定性的な
　qualitative analysis 質的調査, 定性的評価
　qualitative information 定性情報
　qualitative research 質的調査, 定性的調査
quality 名 質, 品質, 品位, 特質, 特性, 良質, 優良, 高級, 内容, 優良品, クオリティ
　asset quality 資産内容, 資産の質
　best quality 最高の品質, 最優良品質, 最上品 (=top quality)
　credit quality 信用の質, 信用度, 信用力
　debt quality 債券の質, 債券の信用力
　environmental quality improvement 環境の質改善, 環境改善
　fine quality 優良品質, 優良品
　higher quality 品質向上
　low quality earnings 低質の利益
　management quality 経営の質
　merchantable quality 商品性
　order quality 受注内容
　product quality 製品の品質
　quality assurance 品質保証 (=product guarantee)
　quality competition 品質競争
　quality function deployment 品質機能展開
　quality improvement 品質改善, 品質向上
　quality magazine 高級誌, クオリティ・マガジン
　Quality Management Institute 品質管理協会《略 QMI》
　quality movement QC運動 (=quality control activity)
　quality name 優良銘柄 (=quality stock)
　quality of earnings 利益の質, 収益の質, 収益内容
　quality of life 生活の質, 生命の質, クオリティ・オブ・ライフ《略 QOL》
　quality of work [working] life 労働生活の質, 働き甲斐, 労働の人間化《略 QWL》
　quality paper 高級紙
　quality review 品質検査, 品質調査
　quality standards 品質基準
　shipped quality terms 船積み品質条件
▶GM has been intensifying efforts to reduce costs and improve *quality*. GMは, コスト削減策と品質改善策を強化している.
▶The bank's planned acquisition of a controlling stake in Nippon Shinpan Co. will only have a limited impact on the credit *quality* of the bank. 同行が日本信販の支配持ち分(発行済み株式の50%超)の取得を計画しているが, これによる同行の信用力への影響はごく限られるものと思われる.
▶Which can provide higher-*quality* service at a lower cost, the public sector or the private sector? 官と民で, どちらが安くて質の高いサービスを提供できるか.
quality control 品質管理《略 QC》(=quality management)
　companywide quality control 全社的品質管理
　quality control activity QC運動 (=quality movement)
　quality control circle QCサークル (=quality circle)
　quality control engineering 品質管理工学《略 QCE》
　quality control reliability 品質管理審理度《略 QCR》
　quality control technology 品質管理技術《略 QCT》
　Statement on Quality Control Standards 品質管理基準書
　total quality control 全社的品質管理, 総合品質管理
▶Mitsubishi Fuso will strive to regain lost consumers' confidence by drastically restructuring its *quality control* section. 三菱ふそうは, 品質管理部門の抜本改編により, 失った消費者の信頼回復に取り組む方針だ.
quality management standards 品質管理基準
▶Fujiya and Yamazaki Baking Co. signed a memorandum of understanding on Yamazaki's assistance, which will be based on U.S. *quality management standards*. 不二家と山崎製パンは, 米国の品質管理基準に基づく山崎製パンの支援に関する基本合意書に署名した.
quango 名 特殊法人
quantitative 形 量の, 量的な
　quantitative analysis 数量分析, 定量分析, 量的分析
　quantitative boom 数量景気
　quantitative information 数量的情報, 定量情報
　quantitative market model 定量的市場分析

quantitative model　数量モデル, 数量化モデル
quantitative easing　量的緩和, 量的金融緩和　(金融の量的緩和政策は，デフレ経済からの脱却をめざして，日銀が2001年3月から2006年3月まで実施した異例の金融政策)
- **quantitative easing framework**　量的金融緩和体制, 量的金融緩和策
- **quantitative easing monetary policy**　金融の量的緩和政策
- **quantitative easing policy**　量的緩和策, 量的金融緩和策, 量的緩和政策　(=quantitative monetary easing policy)
- **quantitative easing step**　量的緩和策　(=quantitative easing policy)
- **quantitative monetary easing policy**　量的緩和政策, 量的金融緩和政策　(=quantitative easing policy)
▸In March 2006, the Bank of Japan ended its *quantitative easing* monetary policy. 2006年3月に，日本銀行は金融の量的緩和政策を解除した。

quantitative standard　物量標準
quantity 名　量, 数量, 大量
- **contract quantity**　契約数量
- **economic batch quantity**　経済バッチ数量, 経済的バッチ数量《略 EBQ》
- **economic manufacturing quantity**　経済的生産数量, 最適生産量《略 EMQ》
- **economic order quantity**　経済的発注量, 最適発注量《略 EOQ》
- **increase the quality and quantity of products**　製品の品質向上 [高級化] と量の拡大を図る
- **inventory quantities**　棚卸し資産数量
- **minimum order quantity**　最低発注量, 最低発注数量
- **order quantity**　注文量, 注文数量
- **output quantity**　生産量, 生産数量　(=production quantity)
- **production quantity**　生産量
- **quantity adjustment**　数量調整
- **quantity buying**　大量仕入れ, 大量購入　(=large lot buying)
- **quantity discount**　数量割引き　(=volume discount)
- **quantity production**　大量生産
- **quantity shipped**　出荷数量, 積載数量, 積送数量
- **quantity system**　定量発注システム
- **sales quantity**　販売数量
- **unit quantity**　単位量, 単位数
▸Labor is now evaluated only in terms of *quantity*, or how many hours a worker toils, by the homogenization of labor. 労働の均質化により，労働は現在，量によって，つまり労働時間の長さによってだけ評価されるようになった。

quarter 名　四半期　(1年の4分の1，つまり3か月を指す。暦年の第1四半期は，1月1日から3月31日までの3か月のこと)
- **fiscal quarter**　会計四半期
- **for the quarter**　当四半期
- **for three consecutive quarters**　3四半期連続して, 3四半期連続
- **from the previous quarter**　前期比
- **on a quarterly basis**　四半期ごとに, 四半期ベースで
- **quarter-end close**　四半期末終値
- **the April-June quarter**　4-6月期 (日本の3月期決算企業の第1四半期にあたる)
- **the first quarter**　第1四半期
- **the first quarter as a whole**　四半期全体
- **the fourth quarter**　第4四半期
- **the last quarter**　第4四半期, 前期
- **the preceding quarter**　前期　(=the previous quarter)
- **the second quarter**　第2四半期
- **the third quarter**　第3四半期
▸For the *quarter*, shipments, revenues and earnings exceeded those of a year ago. 当四半期は，出荷高，収益と利益が前年同期を上回りました。

quarter point　0.25%
▸The latest rate increase marked the 15th consecutive *quarter-point* adjustment since June 2004. 今回の利上げで，2004年6月から15回連続0.25%の調整となった。

quarterly 形　四半期の, 四半期ベースの, 四半期別, 四半期ごとの, 年4回の, 前期比, 副 年4回, 四半期ごとに, 3か月ごとに, 毎季に
- **on a quarterly basis**　四半期ベースで　(⇒ straight bond)
- **quarterly consolidated business results**　四半期連結決算　(=quarterly consolidated settlement of accounts)
- **quarterly earnings**　四半期利益
- **quarterly earnings report**　四半期決算, 四半期決算報告, 四半期報告
- **quarterly earnings statement**　四半期決算, 四半期報告　(=quarterly statement of earnings)
- **quarterly financial data**　四半期財務情報
- **quarterly financial information**　四半期財務情報
- **quarterly financial reporting**　四半期財務報告
- **quarterly financial statements**　四半期財務諸

表, 四半期財務書類

quarterly group net profit 四半期連結純利益, 四半期連結税引き後利益 (⇒**strong sales**)

quarterly income statements 四半期損益計算書

quarterly increase 四半期の伸び率, 前期比伸び率

quarterly information (unaudited) 四半期情報(未監査)

quarterly operating profit 四半期営業利益

quarterly release system 四半期開示制度

quarterly reporting of interim earnings 四半期報告

quarterly results 四半期業績, 四半期決算 (= quarterly business results, quarterly settlement of accounts)

quarterly settlement 四半期決算

quarterly statement 四半期報告書 (=quarterly report)

quarterly statement of earnings 四半期報告, 四半期報告書
▶Some listed companies have already started issuing earnings reports *quarterly*. 上場企業の一部は, 業績報告書の四半期発表をすでに開始している。

quarterly dividend 四半期配当, 四半期配当金 (⇒**during the year**)
▶On November 1, 2008, the board of directors approved a 45% increase in the *quarterly dividend* on common stock. 2008年11月1日, 取締役会は, 普通株式の四半期配当の45%増額を承認しました。

quarterly earnings per common share 普通株式1株当たり四半期純利益, 1株当たり四半期純利益
▶The sum of *quarterly earnings per common share* may not be the same as earnings per common share for the year. 普通株式1株当たり四半期純利益の合計は, 年度の普通株式1株当たり純利益と同額とならない可能性もあります。

quarterly growth 四半期の伸び, 四半期の伸び率, 四半期の成長[成長率]
▶The latest GDP figures marked the fifth consecutive *quarterly growth* in the domestic economy. GDP速報値によると, 国内経済は5四半期連続のプラス成長となった。

quarterly net loss 四半期純損失, 四半期税引き後損失, 税引き後四半期赤字
▶UFJ Holdings, Inc. posted a *quarterly net loss* of ¥91 billion as costs to clean up its bad loans mounted. UFJホールディングスは, 不良債権処理費用が増加したため, 税引き後で910億円の四半期赤字となった。

quarterly net profit 四半期純利益, 四半期税引き後利益, 税引き後四半期黒字
▶Citigroup's *quarterly net profit* will be significantly lower than the same period a year earlier. 米大手銀行シティグループの四半期純利益は, 前年同期を大幅に下回る見込みだ。

quarterly performance 四半期業績
▶This improved *quarterly performance* was due mainly to the company's contribution. 当四半期の業績改善は, 主に同社の貢献によるものです。

quarterly profit 四半期利益
▶*Quarterly profit* for the period ending Aug.31 rose to $2.85 billion, or $6.13 per share, compared to $1.55 billion, or $3.26 per share, a year earlier. 6－8月期決算の四半期利益は, 前年同期の15億5,000万ドル(1株当たり3.26ドル)に対して, 28億5,000万ドル(1株当たり6.13ドル)に増加しました。

quarterly report 四半期報告書, 四季報 (=quarterly statement:「四半期報告書」は, 四半期ごとの企業の決算報告書。⇒**annual report, Form 10-Q**)
▶Though these changes are not yet reflected in this *quarterly report*, their impact will be felt in the performance of tomorrow. これらの変革[改革]の成果は, 当四半期の業績にはまだ反映されていませんが, そのインパクトは今後の業績に現われることと思います。

quarterly results 四半期業績
▶We are always reminded of our long-term corporate goals when we look to our *quarterly results*. 各四半期の業績を検討するにあたって, 私たちがつねに想起するのは, 当社の長期的な企業目標です。

quartile 形 四分位の, 名 四分位数
quash 動 抑える, 鎮める, 無効にする, 却下する, 廃棄する
quasi money 準通貨
▶*Quasi money* refers to time deposits and other types of savings at banks that can not be immediately cashed. 準通貨とは, 定期性預金のほかに, 即時に換金できない銀行預金のことをいう。
quasi subsidiary 準子会社
query 名 質問, 疑問, 問い合わせ
question 名 質問, 質疑, 問題, 論点, 議題, 案件, 動 …に問う, 疑う, …に異議を唱える
questionnaire 名 質問事項, 調査票, アンケ

ート

queue 名 列, 待ち行列
queuing model 待ち行列モデル
queuing theory 待ち行列理論, 待ち合わせ理論
queuing time 待ち時間, 待機時間
quick 形 素早い, 迅速な, 即時の, 即座の, 当座の, すぐ現金化できる, 敏感な
  quick asset ratio 当座比率
  quick assets 当座資産, 当座資金 (現金・預金のほか, すぐに現金化できる受取手形, 売掛金, 有価証券など)
  quick cash 即時現金
  quick deposit 当座預金
  quick estimation 速報, 四半期速報
  quick die change system 金型迅速交換システム, QDCシステム
  quick fix 応急措置, 緊急措置, 応急の解決策, 当座の(問題)解決策, 即効薬, 即効
  quick fund 当座資金
  quick liabilities 短期負債
  quick loan 急速回収貸付け[融資], クイック・ローン
  quick ratio 当座比率 (＝acid-test ratio)
  quick response 速答, 迅速[素早い]対応, 納期短縮
  quick returns and small margin 薄利多売
  quick sale 飛ぶような[爆発的]売れ行き
  quick estimation 速報, 四半期速報
quiet 形 不活発な, 閑散とした
quit 動 やめる, 放棄する, 明け渡す, 立ち退く, 辞職する
quorum 名 定足数
quota 名 割当て, 割当数量, 持ち分, 枠, 分担
  catch quotas 漁獲割当て
  emission quotas 排出枠
  import quota system 輸入割当制度
  on a quota share basis 比例配分ベース
  production quota 生産割当て
  tariff quota 関税割当て
▸The actual oil outputs of Nigeria, Venezuela, Iran and other OPEC members have been below allocated country-by-country *quotas*. ナイジェリアやベネズエラ, イランなどOPEC (石油輸出国機構) 加盟国の実際の石油生産量は, OPECの国別生産枠を下回っている。
▸The fund will take advantage of a Kyoto mechanism that allows industrialized countries to purchase excess *quotas* for carbon dioxide and other greenhouse gas emissions from developing countries to gain emission rights. この基金(日本温暖化ガス削減基金)は, 途上国の二酸化炭素など温室効果ガス排出量の削減分を先進国が購入できる「京都メカニズム」を利用して, 排出権を獲得することになっている。

quotation 名 相場, 時価, 建て値, 提示価格, 見積り, 見積り価格, 見積り額, 価格見積り書, 引用
  flat quotation 裸相場
  market quotation 市場相場, 相場表
  price quotation 自国通貨建て, 時価, 相場, 建て値
  spot quotation 直物相場
  volume quotation 外貨建て建て値
quote 動 見積もる, 値段[相場]をいう, 値を付ける, 取引される, 価格を提示する, 上場する
  be quoted at …の値を付ける
  quoted company 上場会社, 上場企業 (＝listed company, publicly quoted company)
  quoted investment 上場有価証券 (＝listed investment)
  quoted market price 時価, 市場相場
  quoted price 相場, 市場相場価格
▸At 5 p.m., the U.S. dollar was *quoted* at ¥97.36-39 in New York. 午後5時, ニューヨークの外国為替市場では, 米ドルが1ドル＝97円36－39銭の値を付けた。
▸The fair values of the Company's financial instruments have been determined based on *quoted* market prices and market interest rates, as of December 31, 2008. 当社の金融手段の公正価格は, 2008年12月31日現在の市場の相場と市中金利に基づいて決定されています。
quote 名 見積り, 値付け, 相場, 建て値, 気配値, 呼び値, 引用
  best quote 最低価格の見積り (＝best price quote, lowest quote)
  bond quote 債券相場
  closing quote 終値(おわりね)
  direct quotes 直接呼び値
  mandatory quote period 値付け義務時間
  opening quote 始値(はじめね)
  price quote 見積り (＝quote)
  stock quote 株価
▸The euro traded $1.5763-5766 against late Friday's *quotes* of $1.5670-5680 in New York. ユーロは, ニューヨークの外国為替市場では, 前週末(午後5時)の相場1ユーロ＝1.5670－5680ドルに対して, 1ユーロ＝1.5763－5766ドルで取引された。
QWL 労働生活の質 (**quality of working life**の略)

R r

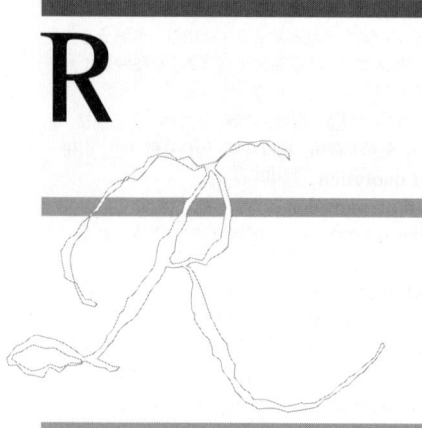

R&D 研究開発 （research and developmentの略）
  R&D base 研究開発拠点
  R&D expenditures 研究開発費
  R&D expense 研究開発費
  R&D functions 研究開発部門
  R&D intensive industry 研究開発集約型産業
  R&D project 研究開発プロジェクト
  R&D ratio R&Dレシオ（1株当たり研究開発費を株価で割った比率）
▶Investing about $30 million in *R&D*, we created new manufacturing techniques that eliminated ozone-depleting substances. 研究開発に約3,000万ドルを投じて，当社はオゾン層破壊物質を削減する新製造技術を開発しました。

R&D spending 研究開発費 （＝R&D expense, spending on research and development）
▶Most of our *R&D spending* is incurred in Canada. 当社の研究開発費の大半は，カナダで発生しています。

race 名 競争，戦い，レース
  a race against time 時間との競争
  a race for cost savings コスト削減競争
  a race for promotion 出世競争
  a rat race 激しい出世競争，出世争い，激烈な競争，自転車操業，悪循環，イタチごっこ
▶A global *race* to secure energy resources is becoming increasingly intense. 国際的なエネルギー資源確保競争が，激しさを増している。

rack up 達成する，確保する （＝achieve）
▶In the July-September period, the company will *rack up* an extra cost of ¥51 billion for recalls of lithium-ion batteries for laptops. 7－9月期は，同社のノート型パソコン用リチウムイオン電池回収の特別費用が510億円に達する見込みだ。

racketeer 名 ゆすり，ゆすり屋，恐喝者，脅迫者，てき屋，暴力団員，詐欺師，ペテン師
  corporate racketeer 総会屋，企業ゆすり
  Racketeers Influence and Corrupt Organizations Act 集団暴力腐敗組織法
▶The company's three board members were arrested on suspicion of paying off corporate *racketeers* known as "sokaiya." 同社の役員3人が，「総会屋」と呼ばれる企業ゆすりに金を支払った容疑で逮捕された。

racketeering 名 不正取得，ゆすり，密造，密売，密輸
  racketeering group ゆすり屋グループ

radiation 名 放射，放射能，放射線，放射エネルギー，放射熱，放射能漏れ
  radiation chemistry 放射線化学
  radiation exposure 放射線被曝，放射能被爆
  radiation therapy 放射線療法
▶No *radiation* escaped in the accident at a Japanese nuclear power plant. 日本の原子力発電所の事故で，放射能漏れはなかった。

radioactive leak 放射能漏れ
▶There are no concerns about a possible *radioactive leak* from the facility. 施設からの放射能漏れの心配はない。

radioactive materials 放射性物質
▶Gathered air samples contained *radioactive materials*. 採取した空気中のサンプルは，放射性物質を含んでいた。

raid 名 従業員引き抜き，売り崩し，売り浴びせ，会社乗っ取り，乗っ取り行為，横領，手入れ，捜査，踏み込み，襲撃，強盗，不法侵入

bear raid 売り崩し (＝bear raiding)
bull raid 強気筋の市場かく乱
raider 名 乗っ取り屋, 企業買収家, 敵対的買収者, 買占め屋, 市場荒し, 強盗, 不法侵入者, 急襲者
　bear raider 現在より低い価格で買い戻す予定で株式を売却する者
　corporate raider 企業乗っ取り屋, 企業買収家
　raider alert 企業乗っ取り警報
raise 動 〈資金などを〉調達する, 〈料金, 価格, 資金などを〉引き上げる, 上方修正する
　amount raised 調達額
　raise capital 資金を調達する, 資本を調達する, 資金を引き上げる, 増資する, 資金繰りをする
　raise cash through a private placement 第三者割当てで資金を調達する
　raise earnings substantially 収益を大幅に増やす
　raise equity 増資する
　raise external funds 外部資金を調達する (＝raise capital, raise money)
　raise prices 値上げする
　raise tier-one capital ティア1自己資本を調達する
　raised costs コスト高, コスト上昇
▶JAL plans to *raise* about ¥200 billion by issuing up to 750 million new shares both at home and abroad. 日航は, 最終的に国内と海外で7億5,000万株の新株を発行して, 約2,000億円調達する計画だ。
▶These ongoing efforts to *raise* productivity are part of our commitment to meet the challenge of intense competition. 現在実施しているこれらの生産性向上策は, 熾烈な競争という課題に対応するための当社の取組みの一環です。
▶Time Warner had been seen as the front-runner for MGM, but Sony *raised* its offer. タイム・ワーナーがMGM買収の最有力候補とみられていたが, ソニーが提示額を引き上げた。
raise funds 資金を調達する, 資金を集める (＝raise capital, raise money)
▶The funds were *raised* via loans from private-sector banks. 資金は, 民間銀行からの借入金で調達された。
raise one's capital 増資する (＝increase one's capital)
▶The bank is scheduled to *raise its capital* by ¥1 trillion by the end of March. 同行は, 3月末までに1兆円規模の増資を行う方針だ。
raise the dividend 増配する, 配当を引き上げる

▶It has been our practice since 1975 to *raise the dividend* every year. 1975年以来の慣行として, 当社は毎年, 配当引上げを実施してきました。
raising 名 資金の調達, 募集, 値上げ, 延長
　capital raising plan 資本調達計画, 資金調達計画
　fund raising 資金調達, 資本調達, 募金 (＝fund procurement, raising of fund)
　new equity raising 新株発行, 増資 (＝equity raising)
　new fund raising 新規資金調達, 新規調達額
　price raising 値上げ
　raising of dividend payments 増配
▶Banks' fund-*raising* costs have increased, reflecting the rise in market rates after the Bank of Japan abandoned its zero-interest policy. 日銀のゼロ金利政策解除に伴って市場金利が上昇したのを反映して, 銀行の資金調達コストが増大した。
rally 名 〈株価の〉反騰, 反発, 急反, 上げ相場, 強気相場, 〈景気などの〉持ち直し, 回復, 上昇, 上昇局面, 動 反騰する, 回復する, 盛り返す, 上昇する, 急騰する (＝rebound)
　bond rally 債券相場の上昇, 債券相場の急騰, 債券市場の上げ相場 (＝bond market rally, rally in the bond market)
　modest rally 穏やかな上昇局面
　rally against the U.S. dollar 対米ドルで回復する
　rally in stocks 株価の持ち直し
　rally through the old highs 最高値を更新する
　secondary rally 中間戻し
　sustainable rally 本格的上げ相場
　the U.S. dollar's rally 米ドル高
　the U.S Treasury rally 米国債の急騰, 米国債相場の上昇[急騰], 米国債の価格上昇
▶The recent stock market *rally* has boosted returns on the insurance premium management of four major life insurers. 最近の株式相場の上昇[株高]で, 4大生保各社の保険料運用収益が増加した。
Ramsar Convention ラムサール条約, 国際湿地条約, 水鳥湿地保全条約(正式名称は「特に水鳥の生息地として国際的に重要な湿地に関する条約」で, 1971年に採択された。締約国会議は, 3年ごとに開催される)
random 形 無作為の, 任意の, 手当たり次第の, ランダム
　random access 等速呼出し, 即時呼出し, 直接アクセス, 随時書込み読出し可能, ランダム・アクセス

random access memory 等速呼出し記憶装置, 即時呼出し記憶装置, 任意抽出記憶装置, ラム, ランダム・アクセス・メモリ《略 RAM》
random development 乱開発
random drug testing 無作為薬物検査
random error 測定誤差
random numbers 乱数, 乱数表
random sample 無作為抽出標本
random sampling 無作為抽出法, 任意抽出[抽出法], ランダム・サンプリング
random selection 無作為選択, 無作為抽出
random table 乱数表
random variable(s) 確率変数
range 名 範囲, 幅, 領域, 種類, 品揃え, 製品群, 限界, 射程, 射程距離, レンジ (⇒**real growth rate**)
　a new range of PCs パソコンの新製品群
　a wide range of product range 幅広い製品構成
　asset depreciation range 可能法定耐用年数, 法定耐用年数
　full [broad, whole, wide] range of 広範な, 広範囲の, 多種多様な, 幅広い
　in the range of …の範囲内で
　long-range cash [fund] planning 長期資金計画
　middle range technology 中間技術
　price range 価格帯, 値幅, 協定価格帯
　product range 製品構成, 製品の機種[種類], 製品群, 品揃え, 製品の幅, 車種
　range of funding options 資金調達の選択の幅
　range of industries 業種
　range of loss 損失の範囲, 損失の範囲額
　range trading もみ合い
　short-range business planning 短期経営計画
　target range 目標圏, 目標レンジ
　trading range 取引圏, 相場圏, ボックス圏, 取引レンジ
▶We offer the full *range* of telecommunications services. 当社が提供している電気通信サービス[通信サービス]は, 広範にわたっています。
rank 動 地位を占める, 並ぶ, 評価する, 位置づける, …の順位を決める, 等級をつける
　be ranked as …と位置づけされる, …と評価される
　be ranked top among …でトップにランクされる, …でトップを占める
　rank with …と肩を並べる
▶Toyota *ranks* fifth, when compared with the U.S. magazine Forbes' ranking of global companies in terms of profits. 米フォーブス誌世界企業利益ランキングと比較して, トヨタは5位にランクされる。
rank 名 地位, 身分, 階級, 等級, 順位, レベル, ランク
　break ranks 組織に刃向かう, 隊列を乱す
　rank and file 平社員, 一般従業員, 一般職員, 一般労働者, 一般組合員, 一般大衆
　the ranks 一般大衆
　upper rank 上位階級
rank-and-file employee 一般社員, 一般従業員, 平社員, 一般職員
▶Larger-than-planned *rank-and-file employees* have applied for early retirement in a program designed to cut 1,100 jobs. 1,100人の人員削減計画で, 計画を上回る数の一般従業員が希望退職に応募した。
ranking 名 順位, 番付け, 序列, 格付け, ランキング
　ranking official 幹部職員, 役職員, 高官
ratable 形 比例した(proportional), 評価できる, 課税可能な
　ratable distribution 比例配分, 比例配当
　ratable value 課税評価額
ratchet effect ラチェット効果, 歯止め効果(不況期に消費や投資がそれまでの水準を保つこと)
rate 名 割合, 率, 金利, 歩合, 料金, 値段, 運賃, 相場, 等級, 速度, 進度, 程度, レート (⇒ **exchange rate, interest rate, prime rate**)
　basic rate 基本料金, 基本給(base salary), 基礎賃率(basic wage rate), 基準率, 所得税の基礎税率
　hourly rate plan 時間給制, 時間給制度
　loan rate 貸出金利
　market rate 市場金利, 市場相場, 市場レート, 銀行間相場
　rate cutting 料率引下げ, 賃率引下げ
　rate hike 利上げ, 金利引上げ, 料金引上げ, 値上げ
　rate of depreciation 減価償却率, 減価償却費率 (=depreciation rate)
　rate of earnings 収益率
　rate of earnings on total capital 総資本純利益率
　rate of exchange 為替相場, 為替レート, 交換比率 (=exchange rate, foreign exchange rate)
　rate of interest 利率, 金利, 利子率 (=interest rate)
　rate of operation 操業度, 操業率 (=rate of output)
　rate of pension premiums 保険料率, 保険料の料率

rate of stock turnover 棚卸し資産回転率, 商品回転率 (=rate of stock-turn)
rate sensitive assets and liabilities 金利感応資産・負債
selling rate 売り相場
yen rate 円相場, 円為替レート
▶Japan Airlines System Corp. plans to raise *rates* for international freight. 日本航空システムは, 国際線の貨物運賃を値上げする方針だ.
▶Leading moneylending businesses make huge profits by securing loan funds from financial institutions at annual average *rates* of less than 2 percent. 大手の貸金業者は, 金融機関から平均年2％以下の金利で融資資金を調達して, 高い収益を上げている.

rate of economic expansion 経済成長率 (=economic growth rate, pace of economic expansion, rate of business expansion)
▶The *rate of economic expansion* in the current phase of recovery is much smaller than previous expansionary phases. 現在の景気拡大期［景気拡大局面］の経済成長率は, 過去の景気拡大期よりかなり低い.

rate of return 利益率, 収益率, 〈株式の〉配当利回り, 〈債券の〉直接利回り, 利回り
rate of return on asset 資産利益率
rate of return on equity 株主資本利益率, 資本利益率
rate of return on invested capital 投下資本利益率
rate of return on investment 投資収益［利益］率, 資本利益率, 投資の運用利回り
rate of return on plan assets 年金資産の運用利益率［収益率］
▶The weighted average discount rate used in determining the weighted average assumed long-term *rate of return* on plan assets was 8 percent for 2008. 年金資産の加重平均長期予想利益率［長期予想収益率］の算定に用いた加重平均割引率は, 2008年度は8％でした.

rating 图 格付け, 評価, 信用度, 視聴率 (⇒credit rating, debt rating)
assign a rating of B2 B2の格付けを付与する
base rating 基礎格付け, 基本格付け
BBB long-term rating トリプルBの長期格付け
bond rating 債券格付け, 社債格付け (=debt rating)
credit-risk rating 信用リスク格付け
experience rating 実績格付け, 実績格付け方式, 経験料率方式
financial strength rating 財務力格付け, 支払い能力格付け
implicit rating 間接格付け
independent rating agency 独立格付け機関, 独立した格付け機関 (=independent credit rating agency)
insurance rating 保険格付け
investment-grade rating 投資適格の格付け
issuer's debt ratings 発行体の債券格付け
long-term rating 長期格付け
performance rating 人事考課 (=service rating)
preliminary rating 予備格付け (=provisional rating)
rating agency 格付け機関, 信用格付け機関, 格付け会社 (=credit rating agency, rating company, rating firm, ratings service agency)
rating outlook 格付け見通し
seek a rating 格付けを申請する
▶Standard & Poor's kept its *rating* on the two bond insurers of MBIA Inc. and Ambac Financial Group Inc. スタンダード＆プアーズは, MBIAとアムバック・ファイナンシャル・グループ(AMBAC)のモノライン2社の格付けを, 据え置いた.

rating cuts 格下げ, 信用格付けの引下げ
▶*Ratings cuts* by rating firms can boost borrowing costs. 格付け会社が行った格下げ［信用格付けの引下げ］で, 借入コストが増大する可能性がある.

rating firm 格付け会社
▶Both *rating firms* put Ford Motor Co. on review for possible downgrade. 両格付け会社は, フォードに対して［フォードの格付けを］格下げの方向で見直しに入った.

ratio 图 割合, 比率, 利益率, 収益率, 指標 (⇒capital adequacy ratio)
equity ratio 株主資本比率, 自己資本比率, 株主持ち分比率
liquidity ratio 流動性比率, 流動比率
ratio of debts to assets 資産に対する負債の比率, 負債・資産比率 (=debt-asset ratio, debt to asset ratio: 総資産に対する総負債の比率)
ratio of gross profit to net sales 売上総利益率
ratio of net debt to net debt plus equity 金融債務比率 (=金融債務対金融債務＋資本)
ratio of net profit to capital 資本利益率
ratio of net worth to the total assets 株主資本比率
ratio of operating profit to sales 売上高に対する営業利益の比率［割合］, 営業利益率
ratio of profit to capital 資本利益率

ratio of shareholders' [stockholders'] equity 株主資本比率
▶Through continuing gains in annual earnings, it will be possible, over time, to adjust the payout *ratio* while still maintaining our dividend record. 年間利益の増大を続けることによって、当社の配当実績を今後とも維持しながら、時期が来たら配当性向を調整することは可能である。

rationalization 名 合理化, 効率化
　capacity rationalization 生産合理化, 設備合理化
　distribution rationalization 流通合理化
　industrial rationalization 産業合理化
　labor rationalization 労働力の合理化
　rationalization of distribution 流通合理化
　rationalization of management 経営合理化
　thorough rationalization 徹底した合理化
▶The firm made a $90 million provision, related to restructuring and *rationalization* of international operations. 同社は、国際事業部門の再構築(リストラクチャリング)と効率化[合理化]に関連して、9,000万ドルの引当金繰入れを行った。

rationing 名 配給, 割当て, 制限
　capital rationing 資本割当て, 資本制限
　consumer rationing 消費者割当て
　producer rationing 生産者割当て
　water rationing 給水制限

raw 形 生(なま)の, 未加工の, 未処理の, 精製していない
　raw data 生のデータ, 未調整データ, 原資料
　raw labor [labour] 未熟練労働
　raw oil 原油
　raw procurement 原料調達
　raw rubber 生ゴム
　raw wool 原毛

raw material 原料, 材料, 原材料, 素材, 資源 (⇒material)
　raw material cost 原材料費
　raw material prices 原材料価格
　raw materials consumption 原材料消費
▶Escalating *raw material* prices and a recent appreciation in the yen are beginning to cast a shadow on corporate performances in Japan. 原材料価格の高騰や最近の円高が、日本の企業業績に影を落とし始めている。

RDF ごみ固形燃料, 固形化燃料 (refuse-derived fuelの略)
▶The heat of fermentation by microorganisms and oxidation processes raised the temperature of the *RDFs* to ignition level. 微生物による発酵熱や酸化の過程で発生した熱で、ごみ固形燃料の温度が発火温度まで上昇した。

reach 名 届く範囲, 到達, 到達数, リーチ
　media reach 媒体到達
　out of reach of the budget 予算の範囲外で
　reach and frequency 到達度と到達回数
　the economic reach 経済圏

reaction 名 反応, 反動, 反発, 対応, 反響, 逆行, リアクション (=response)
　customer reaction 顧客の反応
　negative reaction 反発
　quick reaction 素早い対応, 迅速な対応

reactor 名 原子炉, リアクター
　advanced boiling water reactor 改良沸騰水型炉《略 ABWR》
　advanced thermal reactor 新型転換炉《略 ATR》
　boiling water reactor 沸騰水型軽水炉《略 BWR》
　commercial reactor 実用炉
　corrosion of the reactors' cores 炉心崩壊
　fast breeder reactor 高速増殖炉《略 FBR》
　fast neutron reactor 高速中性子炉
　fast reactor 高速炉
　heavy water reactor 重水炉《略 HWR》
　high temperature engineering test reactor 高温工学試験研究炉《略 HTTR》
　high temperature gas-cooled reactor 高温ガス炉《略 HTGR》
　light water reactor 軽水炉《略 LWR》
　nuclear power reactor 原子炉
　pressurized water reactor 加圧水型原子炉, 加圧水型軽水炉《略 PWR》
　research reactor 研究炉
　thermal neutron reactor 熱中性子炉
▶The blast in Chernobyl's fourth *reactor* contaminated large swaths of territory in Ukraine, Belarus and Russia. チェルノブイリ原発の4号炉で起きた爆発で、ウクライナ、ベラルーシとロシアが広域にわたって汚染された。
▶The Monju fast breeder *reactor* has been shut down since a leak of sodium coolant in 1995. 高速増殖原型炉「もんじゅ」は、1995年に冷却剤のナトリウムが漏れた事故以来、運転が中止されている。

reading 名 数値, 指標, 指数, 議案の読会
　core inflation reading 基礎インフレ率の数値
　DI reading DIの数値
　first reading 第一読会, 第一回読会
　index reading for small companies' sentiment

中小企業景況判断指数
positive reading プラスの数値
second reading 第二読会, 第二回読会
third reading 第三読会, 第三回読会

ready 形 持ち合わせの, 手持ちの, 手近の, 名 現金

real 形 実際の, 実体の, 現実の, 実質の, 実質上の, 重大な, 不動産の, リアル
  real deficit 実質赤字
  real effective exchange rate 実質実効為替レート
  real expenditure 実質的経費
  real growth 実質経済成長, 実質伸び率 (=real economic growth)
  real profit 実質利益
  real rate of return 実質収益率, 実質利回り
  real value 実質価値, 実質値

real economy 実体経済
▶Capital investment in the private sector is still sluggish and this will delay a full-fledged recovery in the *real economy*. 民間設備投資の動きがまだ鈍いので, 実体経済の本格的な回復は遅れる。

real estate 不動産 (⇒slump)
  real estate acquisition tax 不動産取得税
  real estate developer 不動産開発業者, 不動産開発会社, 不動産デベロッパー (=property developer)
  real estate gain 不動産売却益
  real estate investment 不動産投資
  real estate investment trust 不動産投資信託 《略REIT》
  real estate lending 不動産融資
  real estate loss 不動産関連損失
  real estate operations 不動産事業
▶The company earns revenue through *real estate* investment and through resuscitating failed financial institutions. 同社は, 不動産投資と経営破綻した金融機関を再生させることで収益を上げている。

real estate appraiser 不動産鑑定士, 不動産鑑定業者
▶The public corporation asked a Tokyo-based *real estate appraiser* to assess the value of the forested land in Ichihara. 同公社は, 東京都内の不動産鑑定業者に市原市の山林の鑑定(山林の評価額算定)を依頼した。

real estate investment fund 不動産投資ファンド, 不動産ファンド (投資家から資金を集めて, 不動産などへの投資事業で運用している投資ファンド)
▶A *real estate investment fund* was alleged to have failed to report about ¥18 billion in income from transaction involving land and property taken as collateral for nonperforming loans. 不動産投資ファンドが, 不良債権の担保に取った不動産関連の取引で得た所得約180億円の申告漏れを指摘されていた。

real growth rate 実質成長率
▶The government revised downward the *real growth rate* in gross domestic product for the July-September quarter to 0.2 percent rise on an annualized basis. 政府は, 7-9月期のGDP(国内総生産)の実質成長率を年率換算で0.2％増に下方修正した。
▶The *real growth rate* will reach the 3 percent range. 実質成長率は, 3％台に達するだろう。

real term growth 実質成長率
▶The *real term growth* of the U.S. economy during the April-June quarter slowed to 3 percent on an annualized basis. 米国経済の4-6月期の実質成長率が, 年率3％と鈍化した。

real terms 実質
▶The Chinese economy registered an annualized growth rate of 9.1 percent in *real terms* during the July-September quarter. 7-9月期の中国経済は, 実質で9.1％の伸び率を示した[7-9月期の中国の実質経済成長率は, 年率9.1％だった]。

real time 実時間, 同時, 即時, 即時処理, 実時間処理, リアルタイム処理, リアルタイム (=real-time)
▶Some information is transmitted in *real time* globally. 情報の一部は, リアルタイムでグローバルに伝達される。

realign 動 再編成する, 再編する, 再調整する, 再統合する, 再提携する, 変更する
▶The media and communications industry hasn't been *realigned* for some time. マスコミ業界は最近, 業界再編がなかった。

realignment 名 再編成, 再編, 再調整, 再統合, 再提携, 組替え
  mergers and realignments 統合や再編
  business realignment 企業再編, 再編
  company realignment 企業再編
  currency realignment 通貨調整, 通貨再調整
  general realignment 全面的再調整, 全面調整
  industry realignment 業界再編
  realignment of business units 事業部門の組替え
  realignment of management structure 経営

組織の再編
realignment strategy　再編戦略
▶The two years have been reclassified to reflect the *realignment* of various business units.　両年度は，事業部門の組替えを反映させるため，修正して再表示されています。
▶The new Corporate Law that went into effect in May 2006 has made company *realignment* much easier.　2006年5月から実施された新会社法で，企業再編が以前よりはるかに容易になった。

realignment of the industry　業界再編
▶The liberalization of brokerage commissions on commodity futures trading has paved the way to potentially dramatic *realignment of the industry*.　商品先物取引の委託手数料の自由化で，業界が劇的に再編される可能性が出てきた。

realization 名　実現，理解，認識，現金化，換金
　実現 ➡ 実現（realization）は，一般に「収益の実現」（realization of revenue）を意味することが多い。「収益」は，財・サービスの引渡しが完了し，その対価として現金または現金等価物を受領したときに「実現」する
　income realization　利益の実現，収益の実現
　revenue realization　収益の実現　（＝realization of gains, realization of revenue）
　realization of profit and loss　損益の実現
realize 動　実現する，換価する，現金に換える
　realize a profit on the property　財産を処分して利益を得る
　realize capital losses　キャピタル・ロスを実現する
　realize latent capital gains　含み益を実現する
▶Such income is not *realized* in cash currently but will be *realized* over the service life of the plant.　これらの収益は，当該期間に現金収益としては実現せず，当該設備の耐用年数にわたって実現します。
realized 形　実現した，実現の要件を満たした，実現済みの，換価した
　realized capital gains　実現資本利得，キャピタル・ゲインの実現額，キャピタル・ゲイン実現額，実現キャピタル・ゲイン
　realized gain (loss)　実現利得（損失），実現利得（損失）
　realized gain on investment activities　投資活動による実現益
　realized income　実現利益，利益の実現　（＝realized profit）
　realized loss　実現損失，損失の実現
　realized profit　実現利益　（＝realized income）

realized revenue　実現利益，実現収益，利益の実現
realized value　実現価値，実現価額
realized yield　実効利回り
▶The bank's decline in net revenues reflects lower *realized* capital gains and non-accrual loans.　同行の営業利益の減少は，キャピタル・ゲインの実現額の低下と利息計上を停止した貸付け金の増大を反映しています。

realtor 名　不動産業者　（＝real estate agent）
▶Battles between *realtors* over small lots of land have become increasingly fierce.　狭い土地をめぐる不動産業者の競争が激化している。

realty 名　不動産
reason　理由，根拠，要因，材料，事由
　cyclical reason　循環要因
　for speculative reasons　投機的な思惑で
　good reason　十分な根拠，根拠が十分にあること
　main reason　主な要因，主因
　major reason　大きな要因，主因，最大の要因
　seasonal reason　季節要因
　secular reason　構造要因
　speculative reasons　投機的な思惑
▶The weak yen is likely to be the main *reason* for profits increasing by about ¥150 billion in the first half of the business year alone.　円安が，上半期だけで約1,500億円の主な増益要因となる見通しだ。

reasonable 形　合理的な，妥当な，根拠のある，相当な，公正な，適切な
　reasonable assurance　合理的な確証，合理的保証　（⇒misstatement）
　reasonable basis　合理的な基礎，合理的根拠
　reasonable care　相当な注意
　reasonable estimate　合理的見積り，根拠のある見積り
　reasonable level　妥当な水準
　reasonable period　相当期間
　reasonable possibility　論理的可能性
　reasonable price　適正価格，合理的価格，手頃な値段，納得できる価格，相当の代価
　reasonable step　適正措置，合理的な措置
　reasonable time　相当な期間，相当の期限，合理的な期間
▶Each party shall take all *reasonable* steps to ensure the confidentiality of all the confidential information.　各当事者は，すべての秘密情報の守秘義務[秘密性]を維持するため，あらゆる合理的な措置を取るものとする。
▶Our audits provide a *reasonable* basis for our

opinion. 私どもの監査は，私どもの意見表明のための合理的根拠となっています．

rebate 名 割戻し，払戻し，現金割戻し，返金，還付金，奨励金，報償金，手数料，戻し税，割引，控除，リベート
  allowance for sales rebate 売上割戻し引当金（＝reserve for sales rebate）
  cash rebate 現金割戻し，現金払戻し
  purchase rebate 仕入割戻し
  quantity rebate 大量購入払戻し
  rebate business リベート商法
  sales rebate 売上割戻し，販売奨励金，リベート（＝rebate on sales）
  tax rebate 税金の還付，戻し減税，戻し税
▶General Motors Corp. and Ford Motor Co. scaled back *rebates*. ゼネラル・モーターズ（GM）とフォード・モーターは，リベート（現金割戻し額）を引き下げた．
▶The $150 billion pump-priming package centers on income tax *rebates* and tax incentives for corporations to make investments. 1,500億ドルの景気刺激策は，納付した所得税の還付［戻し税］と投資を促進する企業減税を柱としている．

rebound 動 回復する，反発する，はね返る，持ち直す，〈下落後に〉再び上昇する，〈減少から〉増加に転じる，好転する
▶The 225-issue Nikkei Stock Average has *rebounded* by about 60 percent since then. 日経平均株価（225種）は，それ以来ほぼ6割値を戻した．

rebound 名 回復，反発，〈株価の〉持ち直し，好転
  economic rebound 景気回復
  modest rebound 穏やかな回復，穏やかな景気回復
  rebound in economic activity 景気回復
  rebound in profits 収益の回復
  slight rebound 小幅反発（＝small rebound）
  strong rebound of spending 消費の力強い回復
  the dollar rebound against the yen 円に対するドルの反発
▶There have been no signs of a *rebound* in the amount of outstanding loans, which continues on an abated decline. このところ引き続き減少傾向にある銀行の貸出残高に，反転の兆しは見えない．

rebuild 動 再構築する，再建する，再興する，再生する，回復する，〈在庫などを〉積み増す，建て替える，復元する，立て直す
▶Aeon Co. is a potential key player in efforts to *rebuild* Daiei Inc. イオンは，ダイエー再建を支援する有力な提携候補だ．

recall 動 リコール［無料回収・修理］する，回収する，撤回する，取り消す，召喚する，呼び戻す，解任［解職］する，思い出す，回想する
▶About 163,700, or 156,400 vehicles sold at home and about 7,300 vehicles exported, will be *recalled*. 国内販売約156,400台と海外輸出分約7,300台の合計163,700台ほどがリコール（改修・無償交換）される予定だ．
▶Three domestic drugmakers have begun *recalling* 17 heparin sodium products. 国内の製薬会社3社が，ヘパリンナトリウム製剤17製品の自主回収を開始した．

recall 名 欠陥車［欠陥品の］回収，リコール［無料回収・修理］，無償修正，撤回，取消し，召喚，呼び戻し，復職，〈公職者の〉解任請求，解任［解職］権，回想
  loan recall 貸出回収
  recall cost [expense] 回収費用
  recall of advance 貸出回収
▶Sony booked the ¥51.2 billion battery *recall* cost for the July-September quarter. ソニーは，7−9月期に（パソコン用）充電池のリコール費用［回収費用］として512億円を計上した．

recapitalization 資本再編，資本の再構成，資本変更，資本組入れ，増資（「資本の再構成」は，増資や減資のほかに，普通株の一部を優先株と組み替えたり，債券を株式と組み替えたりするなど，会社の資本構成（capital structure）を変更すること）
▶The firm plans *recapitalization* to raise funds for the construction of a new headquarters building. 同社は，新社屋の建設費用を調達するため，資本の再構成（増資）を計画している．

recapitalize 動 資本を再編する，資本構成を修正［変更］する，〈法定準備金などを〉資本に組み入れる
▶In an attempt to *recapitalize* itself, we raised ¥13 billion through a third-party share allotment. 資本再編のため，当社は第三者株式割当で130億円を調達しました．

recede 動 撤back する，取り消す，手を引く，縮小する

receipt 名 受領，受取り，領収，収納，受取証，領収書，証書，受領額，収入，収入金額，収入高，入荷高
  air receipt 航空貨物受取証
  American depositary receipt 米国預託証券
  cash receipt 現金収入，現金収入額
  deposit receipt 預金証書
  depositary receipt 預託証券《略 DR》
  foreign currency receipts 外貨収益
  official receipt 受領書
  ordinary receipts and payments 経常収支

revenue receipt 売上収入
store receipts 小売売上高
tax receipts 税収
Uniform Warehouse Receipt Act 統一倉庫証券法
▶This accounts book indicates *receipts* and payments totaling about ¥80 million made between September and October. この会計帳簿には，9月と10月の収支状況(約8,000万円)が記載されている。

receivable 形 受け取るべき，受領できる，支払われるべき，支払いを待っている（⇒account receivable）
bill receivable 受取手形
commission receivable 未収手数料
dividends receivable 未収配当金
interest receivable 未収利息
loan receivable 貸付け金
mortgage loan receivable 担保付き貸付け金（＝mortgage receivable）
note receivable 受取手形
rent receivable 未収賃料
sales contract receivable 売渡し契約未収金
▶Accounts *receivable* balances were $1.3 million and $1.5 million at December 31, 2007 and December 31, 2008, respectively. 2007年12月31日および2008年12月31日現在の売掛金残高は，それぞれ130万ドルと150万ドルでした。

receivable 名 債権，受取債権，売上債権，売掛債権（「受取債権[売上債権]」には，企業の全取引から生じた売掛金や受取手形，貸付け金，未収金，立替金などの受取勘定が含まれる）
assignment of receivables 債権譲渡
consumer receivables 消費者向け債権
credit card receivables クレジット・カード債権
delinquent receivables 支払い遅延債権
dollar-denominated receivables ドル建て債権
eligible receivables 適格債権
finance receivables 金融債権，貸出債権
net receivables 純債権
nonperforming receivables 不良債権
outstanding receivables 債権残高
receivable from customers 顧客への債権
receivables financing 債権融資
receivables management 売掛債権の管理
receivables turnover 売上債権回転率，受取勘定回転率
sales of lease receivables リース債権の売却
term receivables 長期債権，ターム債権
unsecured receivables 無担保債権

▶Days sales outstanding in our core business declined because of improved *receivables* management. 当社の主力事業の平均売上債権回転日数は,売掛債権の管理が改善したため,減少しました。
▶The improved gross margin percentage mainly reflects the maturation of the credit card *receivables* portfolio. 売上総利益率の改善は，主にクレジット・カード売掛債権ポートフォリオが成熟してきたことを反映しています。

receive 動 受け取る，受領する，受け入れる，認める，受け付ける，〈資金を〉調達する，〈損害などを〉被る，歓迎する
receive accrual accounting 発生主義会計で処理される
receive dividends 配当金を受け取る
receive funding from …から資金を調達する
▶GM expects to *receive* about $14 billion from the sale of General Motors Acceptance Corp. GMは，金融子会社GMACの売却により，約140億ドルを確保する見通しだ。
▶The Corporation *received* some $200 million upon disposal of certain noncore assets. 当社は，一部の非中核的事業資産を売却して，2億ドル余りを受領しました。

recession 名 景気後退，不景気，不況，リセッション
景気後退について➡「景気後退」は，景気の回復・拡大期が終わって底を打つまでの状態をいう。米国では，一般に実質国内総生産(GDP)が2四半期連続でマイナス成長になると，景気後退と見なされる。日本の場合は，鉱工業生産指数や有効求人倍率などの経済指標に基づいて，景気動向指数研究会が判定している。
be heading into [towards] recession 景気後退に向かっている
deep recession 深刻なリセッション（＝severe recession）
double dip recession 景気の二番底
economic recession 景気後退，不況
economic recession caused by the string yen 円高不況（＝yen-caused recession）
financial recession 金融不況
go [fall] into recession 景気後退局面に入る，景気後退期に入る
lingering recession 長引くリセッション
move [climb] out of recession 景気後退から抜け出す
prolonged recession 長引く不況，不況の長期化，リセッションの長期化
renewed recession 不況への逆戻り

severe recession 厳しいリセッション, 深刻なリセッション
sink into a double-dip recession 景気が底割れする
worldwide recession in the steel industry 世界的な鉄鋼不況
▸The economy could sink into a double-dip *recession* due to the clouds hanging over the U.S. economy and rising deflationary pressures that will accompany the accelerated disposal of nonperforming loans. 米国経済の行方（米国経済への先行き不安）や, 不良債権処理の加速に伴うデフレ圧力の高まりなどで, 景気が底割れする恐れがある。
▸The U.S. economy is sinking into *recession*. 米経済は現在, 景気後退局面に入っている。

recipient 名 受取人, 受領者, 受給者, 情報開示を受けた者
▸During the term of this agreement, *Recipient* shall keep the Secret Information in confidence. 本契約期間中, 受領者[情報開示を受けた者]は, この秘密情報を秘密にするものとする。

reciprocal 形 相互の, 互恵的な, 逆の, 相対応する, レシプロカル
  reciprocal account 対応勘定, 相互勘定
  reciprocal arrangement 相互協定
  reciprocal assistance 相互援助
  reciprocal bargaining 相互取引
  reciprocal business 相互主義
  reciprocal contract 相互契約, 双務契約
  reciprocal demand 相互需要
  reciprocal duties [tariff] 互恵関税
  reciprocal function 逆関数
  reciprocal (letter of) credit 同時開設信用状, 相殺信用状, 抱き合わせ信用状 （＝reciprocal L/C)
  reciprocal recognition 相互承認
  reciprocal share holding 株式の相互保有, 株式持ち合い
  reciprocal supply 相互供給
  reciprocal trade 互恵貿易, 互恵通商
  Reciprocal Trade Agreement Act 米国の互恵通商協定法
  reciprocal treaty 互恵条約

reckon 動 計算する, 総計する, 支払う, 清算する （⇒entertainment)

reclaim 動 開発する, 開拓する,〈天然資源を〉利用する

reclassification 名 組換え, 組換え再表示, 振替え, 再分類

reclassify 動 組み替える, 組替え再表示する, 振り替える, 再分類する
▸We *reclassified* certain amounts for previous years to conform with the 2008 presentation. 当社は, 2008年度の表示方法[表示形式]に合わせて, 過年度の金額の一部を組み替えました。

recognition 名 認識, 計上, 認可, 許可, 認知, 認定, 承認 （会計上の「認識」は, ある会計項目を, 資産, 負債, 収益, 費用などとして会計帳簿や財務書類に正式に記帳・記載すること）
  basis of recognition 認識基準
  brand recognition ブランド認知
  expense recognition 費用の認識
  immediate recognition 即時認識, 発生即費用, 発生即費用原則
  immediate recognition as an expense 費用としての即時認識
  income recognition 利益の認識, 利益計上
  loss recognition 損失の認識
  profit recognition 利益の認識
  recognition of gain and loss 損益の認識, 利得と損失の認識
  recognition of latent reserves 含み益の実現
  recognition of pension liability 年金債務の計上
  revenue recognition 収益の認識 （＝recognition of revenue)
▸Our *recognition* of these liabilities created additional deferred tax assets. 当社がこれらの債務を認識したことで, 追加的な繰延べ税金資産が生じました。

recognition of revenue and expense 収益と費用の認識
▸There are timing differences in the *recognition of revenue and expense* for tax and financial statement purposes. 税務上と財務会計上とで, 収益と費用の認識に期間差異がある。

recognize 動 認識する, 計上する, 費用処理する, 認可する, 許可する, 認定する, 承認する （＝recognise; ⇒long term contract)
  be recognized on a straight-line basis 定額法で費用処理する
  recognize income when the contract is completed 工事完成時に利益を認識する
  recognized agency 公認広告代理店
  recognized company 優良企業
  recognized in the statement of financial position 貸借対照表に計上した
▸Previously, we *recognized* costs for separations when they were identified. これまで当社は, 休

職については，休職が確認された時点でその費用[休職手当支払いの費用]を認識していました。

recommend 動 推薦する，推奨する，勧める
- Hokuetsu Paper Mills' independent panel *recommended* that the company initiate measures to try to foil a hostile takeover bid by Oji Paper Co. 北越製紙の独立委員会は，王子製紙の敵対的TOB（株式の公開買付け）に関して北越が防衛策を発動すべきだと勧告した。
- The Board of Directors *recommends* a vote AGAINST this proposal. 当取締役会は，この提案を否決されるようお願い致します。

recompense 動 …に報いる

reconcile 動 和解させる，調停する，一致させる

reconstruct 動 再建する，再構築する，立て直す，再現する，復元する，改築する
- The company's group has chosen to *reconstruct* itself under a holding company. 同社グループは，持ち株会社での再建を選択した。

reconstruction 名 再建，再構築，立て直し，復興，復元，再現，改築
- **corporate reconstruction plan** 企業再建計画，再建計画
- **economic reconstruction plan** 経済再建計画
- **fiscal reconstruction** 財政再建
- The firm currently is in the process of *reconstruction*. 同社は現在，経営再建中だ。

reconstruction plan 再建計画，再建策（= reorganization plan）
- Crisis-stricken giant supermarket chain operator announced a fresh *reconstruction* plan. 経営危機に陥っている巨大スーパーが，新たな経営再建策を発表した。
- The *reconstruction* plan was approved at a meeting of the company's board of directors. 再建策は，同社の取締役会で承認された。

record 動 記録する，記帳する，計上する，評価する，登記[登録]する，表示する，示す（⇒**partnership interest**）
- Amortization of the bond premium is *recorded* on the straight-line method. 社債プレミアムの償却は，定額法で行われています。
- The seven major banking groups' midterm settlement of accounts is expected to *record* an estimated ¥1.95 trillion in latent gains. 大手7行・金融グループの中間決算では，推定で1兆9,500億円の含み益が出る見込しだ。

record 名 記録，最高記録，過去最高，過去最大，成績，登記，登録，動向， 形 記録的な，過去最高の，空前の （⇒**financial records**）

- **accounting record** 会計記録，会計帳簿
- **dividend record** 配当実績
- **hit a record high** 過去最高を記録する，過去最高に達する
- **original record** 原本記録
- **post a record quarterly deficit** 過去最高の四半期赤字を記録する，四半期ベースで過去最高を記録する
- **record date** 配当基準日，基準日，名義書換え停止日，登録日 （= date of record）
- **record earnings** 過去最高益，過去最高の利益
- **record high** 記録的な高さ，空前の高さ，過去最高，過去最悪，史上最高，最高値
- **record low** 記録的な低さ，記録的な低水準，空前の低さ，過去最低，過去最悪，史上最低
- **record net profit** 過去最高の純利益 （= record-high net profit）
- **record profit** 最高益，過去最高の利益
- **stock record date** 株式の名義書換え停止日
- The FSA will issue an order to a consumer loan company to suspend business at all its branches for falsifying customers' *records*. 金融庁は，消費者金融会社に対して，顧客の取引履歴改竄で全営業店を対象とする業務停止命令を発動する見通しだ。
- Total revenues were a *record*. 総収益は，過去最高となりました。
- Toyota Motor Corp. announced *record* group sales and net profit for the half year to Sept. 30. トヨタ自動車は，9月中間決算として過去最高の連結売上高と税引き後利益[純利益]を発表した。

record-high net profit 過去最高の純利益，過去最高の税引き後利益
- The firm recorded a *record-high* group *net profit* in the business year to Feb. 29, 2008. 同社の2008年2月期決算は，過去最高の連結税引き後利益となった。

recoup 動 控除する，差し引く，償う，埋め合わせる，取り戻す

recourse 名 償還請求，償還請求権（手形などの振出人または裏書人に支払いを請求する権利），二次的請求，二次的支払い義務，遡求，依頼，頼みの綱
- **by recourse to** …に訴えて
- **endorsement without recourse** 無担保裏書き，遡求に応じない裏書き
- **last recourse** 最後の手段
- **limited recourse** 限定付き[制限付き]償還請求権
- **recourse fund** 不渡り手形の償還準備積立金
- **without recourse** 遡求なし，遡求権なし，二次的支払い義務なし，償還請求に応ぜず

recourse loan 遡求請求権付き貸付け金
recourse obligation 償還義務, 二次的支払い義務
right of recourse 償還請求権
with recourse 買戻し請求権付き, 償還請求権付き
without recourse to …に頼らずに, …に訴えることなく, …に償還請求することなく
▸ ABC shall have no *recourse* against XYZ for any obligations under the original agreement assigned pursuant to this assignment agreement. ABCは, この譲渡契約に従って譲渡された原契約上の債務については, XYZに履行の請求を一切求めないものとする。
▸ This loss came from deducting *recourse* loans made to our senior management. この損失は, 当社の上級経営陣に対して行った遡求請求権付き貸付け金を控除したことで生じました。

recover 動 回復する, 〈貸出金などを〉回収する, 〈債権などを〉取り立てる
▸ None of the loans were *recovered*. 融資額は全額, 回収されなかった。
▸ We expect to *recover* our negative net worth by the end of fiscal 2009. 2009年度末には, 当社の債務超過は解消できる見通しです。

recovery 名 回復, 景気回復, 〈景気や市場の〉持ち直し, 相場の回復, 回収, 再建, 復興 (⇒economic recovery)
bad debt recovery 償却債権の取立て, 償却済み債権取立益
be on a recovery trend 回復傾向にある
capital recovery 資本の回収
cost recovery basis [method] 原価回収法
cyclical economic recovery 景気回復 (=cycle recovery, cyclical recovery, economic recovery)
earnings recovery 業績回復, 収益の回復
enter a recovery course 回復軌道に入る
full economic recovery 景気の本格回復, 景気の全面的回復
full-fledged recovery 本格復調, 本格回復
full scale recovery 本格的な回復
incipient recovery 回復局面, 景気持ち直しの局面
investment recovery 投資回収
movement toward a recovery 景気回復の動き, 景気持ち直しの動き
production recovery 生産の回復 (=recovery in production)
put the economy on a steady recovery track 景気を順調な回復軌道に乗せる
recoveries of write-offs 償却債権取立益
resource recovery 資源回収, 資源の再利用
self-sustaining recovery 自律回復, 自力回復
sustainable recovery 本格的な景気回復 (=full scale recovery)
signs of recovery 回復の兆し
V-shaped recovery V字型回復
zero recovery 全額回収不能
▸ Japan's imports are also climbing because the economic *recovery* is fueling domestic demand. 景気回復で国内需要が拡大しているため, 日本の輸入も伸びている。
▸ The company literally achieved a V-shaped *recovery* after recording a net loss in fiscal 2006. 同社は, 2006年度に赤字に転落した後, 文字どおりV字型回復を達成した。

recovery track 回復軌道 (=recovery course, recovery path)
▸ The U.S. economy has gotten back on the *recovery track* since the latter half of last year. 米国の景気は, 昨年後半からまた回復軌道に乗り始めた。

recruit 動 新規採用する, 採用する, 雇い入れる, 募集する, 補充する, 名 新入社員, 新入生, 新会員, リクルート
recruit more new graduates 新卒採用を増やす
recruit new employees 新入社員を採用する, 新入社員を雇い入れる
recruit staff 職員を募集する
▸ Firms are going on the offensive to *recruit* new graduates. 企業各社は, 新卒採用で攻めに転じている。

recruiting 名 採用, 募集, 補充 (=recruitment)
campus recruiting 新卒者募集
midcareer recruiting 中途採用
recruiting company 人材会社, 求人企業
recruiting station 志願者受付局
recruiting test 採用テスト, 採用検査, 採用試験
▸ As for midcareer *recruiting*, some companies will hire more experienced workers to make up for a lack of new graduate recruitment. 中途採用については, 一部の企業は, 経験者を増やして新卒採用の人員不足を補う方針だ。

recruitment 名 新規採用, 求人, 新入社員募集, 人員補充, 人材登用, 人材開発, リクルートメント
campus recruitment 新卒者募集
employee recruitment 社員募集
hold back on recruitment 新規採用を抑える

in-house staff recruitment system 社内公募制度
labor recruitment 従業員の採用
mass recruitment 大量採用
new graduate recruitment 新卒採用
recruitment advertising 求人広告, 募集広告 (=job advertisement)
recruitment magazine 求人情報誌 (=job magazine)
recruitment of temporary employees 期間従業員の採用
staff recruitment 職員募集
year-round recruitment 通年採用
▸Companies' mass *recruitment* efforts are intended as a hedge against possible manpower shortages. 企業各社の大量採用の動きは, 予想される人材不足に備えてのものだ[人材不足を補充するためのものだ].

recruitment activity 採用活動, 新規採用活動, 新規募集活動
▸The *recruitment activity* next spring will be even more competitive than this year. 来春の採用活動は, 今年以上に活発になるだろう。

recuperate 動 回復させる, 〈損失を〉取り返す
recurrence of deflation デフレの再燃
▸A slight rise in consumer prices will not eliminate fears of a *recurrence of deflation* and public anxiety over the future of the economy. 消費者物価の小幅な上昇だけでは, デフレ再燃への懸念や景気の先行き不安を払拭(ふっしょく)できない。

recurring 形 経常的な, 定期的な
recurring loss 経常赤字
recurring operating losses 経常的な営業損失
recurring payment 定期循環払い
▸The Corporation incurred ¥3 billion of *recurring* losses in its semiannual settlement of accounts. 当社は, 9月の中間決算で30億円の経常赤字となりました。

recurring profit 経常利益 (=current profit, income before extraordinary items; ⇒stream)

経常利益について➡「経常利益」は, 売上高から販売・管理費を差し引いた営業利益に, 預金の受取利息や保有株式の配当収入を加えたり, 借入金の支払い利息などを差し引いたりして計算する。ただし, メーカーの工場売却や保有株式の売却による利益, リストラのための割増退職金の費用などは特別利益または特別損失と呼ばれ, 経常利益には含まれない。経常利益は, 日本では, 企業の業績や中長期的な業況を知るのに最も適した指標とされている。

▸Companies listed on the First Section of the TSE are predicted to post the highest *recurring profits* ever for the fifth straight year in their earnings reports for the business year ending in March 2008. 東証1部上場企業は, 2008年3月期決算で5年連続, 過去最高の計上利益を計上する見通しだ。

recycle 動 再利用する, 再生利用する, 循環処理する, 循環使用する, 〈資金などを〉還流する, 〈利益などを〉還元する, 修復する, リサイクル
recycle funds 資金を還流させる
recycled paper 再生用紙, 再生紙
recycle resources 資源を再利用する, 資源をリサイクルする
▸The Education, Science and Technology Ministry also proposed a research and development project on *recycling* biomass. 文部科学省も, バイオマス(生物資源)の再資源化に関する研究開発事業を提案した。

recycling 名 資源循環, 再生利用, 再利用, 再処理, 再生事業, 循環使用, 循環, 還流, 還元, リサイクリング (⇒corporate image)
automobile recycling law 自動車リサイクル法
financial recycling 資金還流
recycling cost リサイクル費用, リサイクル料 (=the cost of recycling)
recycling plant 再処理工場
the recycling of metal, glass and plastic 金属とガラス, プラスチックのリサイクリング
▸The market for services related to *recycling* and waste disposal is expected to grow 20 percent to ¥29 trillion by 2015. 資源再利用や廃棄物処理事業の市場は, 2015年には20%増の29兆円に達する見込みだ。

recycling fee リサイクル費用, リサイクル費, リサイクル料金 (=recycling cost)
▸Under the current system, companies are required to pay *recycling fees* when they scrap PCs. 現在の制度では, パソコンの廃棄時に企業がリサイクル費用の支払いを義務付けられている。

red 名 赤字 (=red ink; ⇒black)
be forced into the red 赤字に追い込まれる
company in the red 赤字企業, 赤字法人 (=company operating in the red)
go into the red 赤字になる (=fall into the red)
operate in the red 赤字経営する
out of the red 赤字を脱して
plunge into the red 赤字に転落する
remain in the red 赤字にとどまる

slip into the red 赤字に転落する（＝fall into the red）
▶Nomura is the first major Japanese financial institution to fall into the *red* because of problems stemming from U.S. subprime mortgage loans. 米国でのサブプライム・ローン問題で赤字に転落するのは，野村が［野村ホールディングス］が日本の大手金融機関では初めてだ．
▶The company remained in the *red* for the fiscal year ended March 31, 2009 due to appraisal losses on its stockholdings. 同社の2009年3月期決算は，保有株式の含み損［評価損］で赤字にとどまった．

red herring 仮目論見書，予備目論見書，レッド・ヘリング（＝preliminary prospectus, red herring prospectus）

red ink 赤字（＝red figure, red-ink figure）
 bleeding red ink 巨額の赤字
 budgetary red ink 財政赤字
 red-ink firm 赤字企業，赤字会社（＝money-losing company）
▶The company is likely to post a group net loss of ¥50 billion for the current business year, its third straight year of *red ink*. 同社の今年度の連結税引き後利益は，500億円の赤字(3年連続の赤字)になる見込みだ．

red tape 官僚的形式主義
▶The agency is hobbled by *red tape*. 同局は，官僚的形式主義で身動きが取れなくなっている．

redeem 動 買い戻す，償還する，補填する，埋め合わせる
▶The company elected to *redeem*, prior to maturity on June 3, 2009, $120 million of first mortgage bonds on May 1, 2009. 同社は，満期が到来する2009年6月3日以前の2009年5月1日に，第一順位抵当権付き社債1億2,000万ドルを償還することを決定した．

redeemable 形 償還可能な，買戻しできる，交換できる
 redeemable bond 随時償還社債，償還社債，随時償還公債
 redeemable stock 償還株式（＝redeemable share）
▶Debt and preferred shares (*redeemable*) denominated in currencies other than the U.S. dollar are regarded as partial hedges of the corporation's net investments in related non-U.S.-based self-sustaining operations. 米ドル以外の通貨建て債務と償還可能優先株式は，米国外に拠点を置く自立した関連事業に対する当社の純投資額の為替リスクを一部ヘッジするためのものです．

redeemable convertible preferred share 償還・転換可能優先株式
▶As at June 30, 2008 ABC Inc. owned 100 percent of the *redeemable* convertible preferred shares of XYZ Corp. convertible into 75,000,000 common shares. 2008年6月30日現在，ABCは，XYZ社の普通株式7,500万株に転換できる同社の償還・転換可能優先株式を100％所有しています．

redemption 名 〈株式などの〉償還，〈投信などの〉解約（＝refundment, repayment）
 advanced redemption 繰上げ償還，期日前償還，期限前償還，期中償還（＝early redemption）
 capital redemption 資本償還
 debenture redemption 社債償還
 mandatory redemption 定時償還，強制償還
 optional redemption 任意償還，随時償還
 premium on redemption 償還プレミアム
 redemption at fixed date 定時償還
 redemption before maturity 期限前償還
 redemption fee 解約手数料
 redemption of maturity 満期償還
 redemption period 償還期間
 stock redemption 株式償還，株式の償還（＝redemption of stock）
▶In respect of our capital stock, there has not been any direct or indirect *redemption*, purchase, or other acquisition of any such stock. 当社の株式に関して，当社はこれまで当該株式の直接・間接の償還，買取りやその他の取得も行っていません．

redenomination 名 通貨単位の呼称変更，券面額の変更，デノミ，デノミネーション（＝currency redenomination, renaming monetary units）
 carry out currency redenomination デノミを実施する
 downward redenomination 呼称の下方変更，デノミ
 redenomination of the yen 円の呼称変更，デノミ
 upward redenomination 呼称の上方変更
▶If we carry out the currency *redenominations*, $1 will be worth about ¥1, and figures indicating the exchange rates of the dollar, the euro and the yen will be almost the same. 通貨のデノミを実施すれば，1ドルが約1円となり，(世界3大通貨の)ドル，ユーロと円の為替レートの単位がほぼ同じになる．

redeploy 動 配置転換する，再配置する，再配分する，移動する，改善する，有効利用する（＝

relocate; ⇒**focus on**)
▸Operating internationally is forcing firms to reinvent their internal environments, reassess their markets, *redeploy* their resources, and change their thinking.　国際的に業務展開するにあたって、企業は社内体制の再検討や市場の再評価、経営資源の再配分、発想の転換などを迫られています。

redeployment 名　配置転換, 再配備, 再配置, 配置替え, 再配分, 工場施設[工場, 設備]の移動, 工場施設の改善, 有効利用, 転用, 移動, 転進　(=relocation)
▸Our strategy is to focus on those product lines vital to our future by streamlining our operations and assets *redeployment* to position the Corporation to serve its customers more effectively.　当社は、業務の効率化と資産の有効利用により、一段と効率的な顧客サービスの体制確立をめざして当社の将来を支える製品ラインに焦点をあてる経営戦略を展開しています。

redevelopment 名　再開発
▸We will establish a good, constructive relationship of trust with an eye to the *redevelopment* of the Hibiya area.　今後は日比谷地区の再開発を視野に入れて、良好で建設的な信頼関係を両社で築いて行きます。

redistribution 名　再配分, 再分配

redress 動　是正する, 矯正する, 正す, 〈均衡などを〉取り戻す
▸The wage disparity with some private sector workers must be *redressed*.　民間従業員との賃金格差は、是正しなければならない。

reduce 動　減らす, 削減する, 低下させる, 押し下げる, 引き下げる, 下げる, 減少させる, 低減する, 緩和する, 軽減する, 解消する, 控除する, 短縮する
　reduce capital　減資する
　reduce funding costs　調達コストを引き下げる
　reduce gearing　負債比率を引き下げる
　reduce inventories　在庫を圧縮する
　reduce investment　投資を抑制する
　reduce overhead costs　製造間接費を削減する, 経費を切り詰める
　reduce the profitability　収益性を低下させる
　reduced borrowing costs　調達コストの削減
　reduced losses　損失の減少, 赤字縮小
　reduced profit　減益, 利益の減少, 利益逓減
　reduced sales　販売低下, 販売の落ち込み, 売上高の減少
▸Sony wants to turn around the performance of the electronics division by *reducing* the number of products.　ソニーは、製品の数を減らしてエレクトロニクス事業部の業績回復を目指している。
▸The company hopes to *reduce* production costs by boosting output volume.　同社は、生産量を大幅に増やすことで、生産コストの削減を目指している。
▸The Company's share of each associated company's income after tax is *reduced* by amortization of excess values and by the amount of dividends received.　各関連会社の税引き後利益に対する当社の持ち分は、投資超過差額の償却額と受取配当金が控除されています。
▸U.S. and European banks gradually *reduced* their lines of credit to Japanese banks.　欧米の銀行は、邦銀に対するクレジット・ライン(貸出限度)を次第に引き下げた。

reduction 名　削減, 軽減, 圧縮, 短縮, 引下げ, 縮小, 低下
　debt reduction　債務削減, 債務減らし
　deficit reduction　赤字削減, 財政赤字削減, 赤字縮小
　expense reduction　経費削減
　income tax reductions　所得税減税
　inventory reduction　在庫圧縮, 在庫整理, 在庫削減　(=reduction of inventories)
　personnel reduction　人員削減, 従業員削減　(=staff reduction)
　price reduction　価格低下, 価格の引下げ
　reduction in [of] capital　減資, 資本金の減額　(=capital decrease, capital reduction)
　reduction in operating expenses　営業経費の削減
　reduction of capital stock　減資　(=reduction of capital)
　reductions of long-term debt　長期債務の返済, 長期債務減少
　risk reduction　リスク軽減, リスクの低下
　tax reduction　減税
　wage reduction　賃金引下げ
▸This economic recovery is mainly due to the increased exports and corporate restructuring efforts centered on debt *reduction*.　今回の景気回復の主な要因は、輸出拡大と債務減らしを中心とした企業のリストラ努力だ。

redundancy 名　解雇, 一時解雇, レイオフ, 余剰, 余剰人員, 人員過剰, 被解雇者, 割増退職金, 失業　(⇒**downsizing target**)
▸In the last two years, the number of people working for the Corporation has been reduced

with no *redundancies* required.　過去2年間，当社は人員過剰による解雇に踏み切るまでもなく，従業員の削減に取り組んできました。

reemployment 名　再雇用，再就職
reemployment of retired workers　雇用延長
reemployment opportunities for people of middle and advanced age　中高年の再雇用機会
▸Pasona Inc., a major temporary staffing agency, will start a new service to support the *reemployment* of retired central government employees from autumn.　人材派遣大手のパソナが，中央省庁を退職した国家公務員の再就職を支援する新サービスを今秋から開始する。

reengineer 動　業務を革新[変革]する，業務を根本的に革新する，リエンジニアリング（＝business reengineering）
▸We are *reengineering* and centralizing support services for telecommunications services.　当社は現在，通信サービス部門に対する支援業務の根本的変革と集中化を進めています。

reengineering 名　業務革新，業務の根本的革新，リエンジニアリング（＝business process reengineering, business reengineering）
business process reengineering　業務革新
business reengineering　業務革新，経営再建

reenter the workforce　再就職する
▸Currently, job training for those trying to *reenter the workforce* is offered mainly at skills development facilities.　現在，再就職のための職業訓練は，主に職業能力開発施設で行われている。

reference 名　参考，参照，参照番号，照会，照会番号，照会人，身元保証，問合せ，問合せ先，委託，付託，関連，関係，参考人，参考文献，言及，論及
accounting reference date　会計基準日
bank reference　銀行信用照会先
credit reference　信用照会先
cross reference　前後参照，相互参照
examination by reference　照査
incorporation by reference　参照による組込み，参照による編入
reference data　参照データ
reference level　基準レベル
reference number　参照番号，照会番号
reference rate　指標金利
reference room　資料室
trade reference　信用照会先，同業者信用照会先
▸All *references* to shares outstanding, dividends and per share amounts have been adjusted on a retroactive basis.　発行済み株式数と配当，1株当たりの金額については，すべて過去に遡及して調整してあります。

refinance 動　借り換える，切り換える，資金を補充する，再融資する
ability to refinance　借換え能力
refinance existing debt　債務[既存の債務]を借り換える（＝refinance outstanding debt）
▸Interest expense declined because of benefits from *refinancing* long-term debt at favorable rates.　利息費用は，長期負債の低金利での借換え効果で減少しました。

refinance 名　借換え，再融資，リファイナンス（＝refinancing）
refinance of existing exposure　融資の借換え
refinance of redemption　借換え発行

refinancing 名　借換え，資金の再調達，再融資，リファイナンス（＝refinance, refunding;⇒**call premium**）
bank refinancing　銀行融資の借換え
market access for refinancing　借換え目的の市場からの資金調達，市場から資金調達して借り換える
mortgage refinancing　モーゲージの借換え，住宅ローンの借換え
refinancing bonds　借換え債
the benefits of refinancing　借換えの効果
▸The benefits of *refinancing* were responsible for about half of the decline in interest expense in 2008.　借換えの効果は，2008年度の支払い利息減少の約半分を占めています。

refinery 名　製油所，精錬所，精糖所
oil refinery margin　石油精製マージン
refinery switchover　製油所の生産変更
refinery utilization rate　製油所の利用率
▸The business tie-up does not include the firms' sales divisions or the abandonment and consolidation of *refineries*.　今回の業務提携には，両社の製油所の統廃合や販売部門は含まれていない。

refining 名　精製

reflationary policy　景気刺激策，景気浮揚策
▸Japan's *reflationary policy* in recent years has centered around interventions in the foreign exchange market by the Finance Ministry and the Bank of Japan.　近年の日本の景気刺激策は，財務省と日銀による為替市場介入を軸としている。

reflate 動　〈通貨などを〉再び膨張させる

reflect 動　反映する，示す，記載する，反映させる，織り込む，組み入れる，適用する
▸The financial statements *reflect* the consolidated accounts of the Corporation and its sub-

sidiaries. この連結財務書類は，当社と子会社の財務書類を連結したものです。
▶We did not restate our 2006 and 2007 financial statements to *reflect* the change in accounting for retiree benefits. 当社は，2006年度と2007年度の財務書類[財務諸表]については，退職者給付に関する会計処理の変更を反映させるための修正・再表示をしておりません。

reform 動 改革する，改正する，改善する，改良する，矯正する，改める
▶In a move to *reform* its board of directors into a U.S.-style system of corporate governance, Sony Corp. will introduce a committee-based management system along with the revised Commercial Code. 取締役会を米国流の会社管理・運営方式に改革する動きとして，ソニーでは，商法改正に伴って委員会ベースの経営システムを導入する。

reform 名 改革，革新，改正，改善，改良，矯正，リフォーム
　economic reform 経済改革
　financial reform 金融改革
　market reform 市場改革
　production reform 生産革新
　structural reform 構造改革
　tax reform 税制改革
▶Out of the total reduced costs of about ¥110 billion, about ¥55 billion was attributed to the production *reforms*. コスト削減総額約1,100億円のうち，約550億円は生産革新によるものだ。
▶Sony was the first company to announce a *reform* of its board under the revised Commercial Code. 改正商法に従って取締役会の改革を発表した会社は，ソニーが初めてだ。

refund 動 払い戻す，返済する，還付する，弁済する，借り換える，償還する （=repay）
▶Deferred tax assets are essentially taxes paid in advance, which are expected to be *refunded* when the bank incurs losses. 繰延べ税金資産は本質的に前払いした税金で，銀行が損失を被った時点で戻ってくる。

refund 名 返済，払戻し，税金の還付，弁済，弁償，返済金，弁済金，借換え （=repayment）
　income tax refunds 還付税金，法人税等の還付金
　submit refund claims 税金の還付請求書を提出する，税金の還付請求をする
　refund claim 還付申請書 （=refund form）
　tax refund 税金還付
　the guaranteed refund of savings deposits 普通預金[貯蓄性預金]の払戻し保証額
　withholding tax refund 源泉税還付，源泉課税還付

refunding 名 借換え，払戻し，税金などの還付，償還，国債入札 （=refinancing）
　advance refunding 期前償還
　bond refunding 社債借換え，社債の借換え（発行済み社債の償還資金を得るため，新規社債を発行して相互交換すること）
　debt refunding 債務借換え，債務の借換え
　issuance of refunding bonds 借換え債の発行
　quarterly refunding 米国債の四半期入札
　Treasury refunding 国債入札
▶The burden of interest payments on *refunding* bonds will accumulate year after year. 借換え債の利払い負担[金利負担]は，年ごとに増える。

region 名 地域，領域，体の部分
regional 形 地域の，地域的な，地域全体の，地方の，局地の，局所の，局部的な
　regional bank 地方銀行，地銀
　regional cooperation 地域協力，地域連携
　regional development banks 地域開発国際金融機関（米州開発銀行，カリブ開発銀行，アジア開発銀行，アフリカ開発銀行などを指す）
　regional development project 地域開発計画
　regional economic partnership 地域経済連携，地域経済連携協定
　regional economic zone 局地経済圏
　regional economy 地域経済
　regional government 地方自治体，地方政府
　regional unity 地域の一体化，地域統合
▶A recovery in the performance of small and midsize companies and *regional* economies has yet to be seen. 中小企業の業績や地域経済の回復は，まだ見られない。

regional integration 地域統合，地域的の統合，域内統合
▶ASEAN countries set a new milestone in *regional integration* by agreeing to fuse into a European-style single market by 2015. ASEAN（東南アジア諸国連合）諸国は，2015年までに欧州型単一市場に統合することで合意したことで，域内統合の新たな一里塚を打ち立てた。

regional tax 地方税
▶In Japan, the tax rate for proceeds from selling shares by a company is about 45 percent, including the corporate and *regional taxes*. 日本では，法人による株売却益への税率は，法人税と地方税を含めて約45％となっている。

regionwide agreement 地域協定

register 【動】登録する, 登記する, 届け出る, 正式に記録する, 示す, 表す, 書留にする
- **-registered** …船籍の
- **registered bond** 記名債券, 記名社債, 登録社債
- **registered capital** 登録資本, 登録資本金 (= authorized capital)
- **registered common shareholder** 普通登録株主
- **registered company** 登記会社, 上場会社
- **registered corporation** 登録会社
- **registered design** 登録意匠
- **registered director** 登録役員
- **registered holders of common shares** 登録済み普通株主, 登録普通株主
- **registered instrument** 登録証券
- **registered investment adviser** 登録投資顧問
- **registered letter** 書留書簡
- **registered mail** 書留郵便
- **registered office** 登記上の事務所, 登記上の本社[本店], 登録事務所
- **registered security** 登録証券, 記名証券 (「記名証券」は, 株式や債券などの保有者の名義が, 発行会社や登録機関の原簿に登録されているもの。登録証券は, 米国の場合は, 米証券取引委員会(SEC)に登録されている有価証券のこと)
- **registered shareholder** 登録株主
- **registered stock** 記名株式, 登録済み株式 (無記名株=non-registered stock)
- **registered trademark** 登録商標
▸All business sectors *registered* year-on-year increases in earnings and profit for the account settlement term ending in March. 3月期は, 前年同期比で全業種が増収増益だった。
▸The Securities and Exchange Law requires investment funds to *register* and report the names of their representatives and their locations. 証券取引法は, 投資ファンドに対して, 投資ファンドの代表者名や所在地などの登録・届け出を義務付けている。

register 【名】登録, 登記, 記録, 登録簿, 登記簿, 記録簿, 名簿, 自動登録機, 通風装置
- **cash register** 金銭登録機, レジ
- **certified copy of the commercial register** 登記簿謄本
- **check register** 小切手記入帳
- **insurance register** 保険契約台帳
- **payroll register** 賃金支払い帳
- **register of members** 株主名簿 (=record of shareholders, stock register)
- **register office** 戸籍登記所, 登記所, 職業紹介所
- **register tonnage** 登録トン数 (=registered tonnage)
- **subsidiary register** 補助記入帳

registrar 【名】登録機関, 株主名簿登録機関, 株式登録機関, 名義書換え機関, 名義書換え代理人, 登記官, 登録事務官, 記録係
- **registrar for stock** 株式登録機関
- **Registrar of Companies** 会社登記官
- **registrar of company** 会社登記担当役員

registration 【名】登録, 登記, 正式記録, 登録事項, 記録事項, 登録物件, 名義書換え (⇒ shelf registration)
- **accessory registration** 付記登録
- **application for registration** 登録申請, 登記申請
- **commercial registration** 商業登録, 商業登記
- **corporate registration** 法人登記
- **issuer registration** 発行者登録
- **land registration** 土地登記, 不動産登録・登記
- **provisional registration** 仮登録, 仮登記
- **registration and license taxes** 登録免許税
- **registration of one's seal impression** 印鑑登録
- **registration statement** 米証券取引委員会(SEC)への登録届出書, 有価証券届出書(有価証券を公募発行する際, 発行者が米取引委員会に事前に提出する書類。⇒shelf registration statement)
- **shelf registration** 一括登録, 一括登録制度, 発行登録, シェルフ登録
- **trade registration** 売買登録
- **Trade Registration and Matching System** 売買登録システム
▸Through this shelf *registration*, the Corporation will be able to offer, from time to time, up to U.S. $300 million of its debt securities and warrants to purchase debt securities. この発行登録により, 当社は3億米ドルを上限として, 債務証券と債務証券の引受権付きワラントを随時, 発行することができます。

registration fee 登録料, 登記料
▸With ¥240,000 in *registration* fees and other costs in addition to 1 yen, anyone can become a company president under the new Corporate Law. 新会社法では, 資本金1円のほかに登記料など24万円で, 誰でも会社の社長になれる。

registration system 登録制
▸Three kinds of trust services will be introduced under a *registration system*. 今後は, 信託3業務が登録制で導入される。

registry 【名】登録, 登記, 記録, 船籍, 登録簿, 登記簿, 記録簿
▸According to the company *registry*, the firm

was established in September 2005 with a capital value of ¥30 million. 会社登記簿によると，同社は2005年9月に資本金3,000万円で設立された。

regular 形 一定の, 正規の, 定期的な, 定期の, 定例の, 習慣的な, 通常の, 一般の, レギュラー (⇒operating revenue)
　regular assortment 定番商品
　regular audit 正規監査
　regular board meeting 定例取締役会
　regular checkup 定期検診
　regular employee 正社員, 常雇い, 常用雇用
　regular dividend 普通配当
　regular employment 正規雇用
　regular general stock meeting 定例株主総会
　regular meeting 定例総会, 定例理事会
　regular member 正会員
　regular operating hours 通常の営業時間
　regular wage 基本給, 基準内賃金

regular pay hike 定期昇給
▸In the system of *regular pay hike*, salaries rise in step with the age and the length of service of employees. 定期昇給制では，従業員の年齢や勤続年数に連動して給与が上がる。

regular workers 正規雇用者, 正社員, 常用労働者
▸A disparity in income between *nonregular* workers and regular workers is due to the establishment of merit-based pay systems at many firms. 正社員と非正社員との所得格差の原因は，多くの企業で成果主義型の賃金制度を採用したことにある

regulate 動 規制する, 取り締まる, 統制する, 調整する, 調節する
　non-regulated company 規制対象外の企業
　regulated company 規制対象企業
　regulated industry 規制を受ける業界
　regulated market 規制市場, 市場の規制
▸A steady annual improvement in earnings of five percent or more is a reasonable goal given the weight of *regulated* companies in our asset base. 年5％以上の利益増加率の安定確保は，規制対象企業が当社の資産構成で大きな比重を占めていることから，妥当な目標と言えるでしょう。

regulation 名 規則, 規定, 規制, 管理, 法規, 令, 行政規則, レギュレーション
　advertising regulation 広告規制
　business regulations 業務規定, 業務規則
　comprehensive regulation 包括規制
　financial quantitative regulation 金融の量的規制
　lending regulation 貸出規制
　premium regulation 景品規制
　regulation of illegal and harmful contents 違法有害コンテンツ規制
　regulation on exhaust gas and noise emission 排ガス騒音規制
　SEC Regulation S-X 米証券取引委員会規則S-X, SEC財務諸表規則S-X, 米証券取引委員会の連結財務書類［連結財務諸表］作成規定, レギュレーションS-X
　self-regulation 自主規制

regulators 名 規制当局, 規制機関, 規制責任者, 監視官
　antitrust regulators 独占禁止規制当局, 反トラスト規制当局
　banking regulators 銀行規制当局
　financial regulators 金融当局
　independent regulators 独立規制当局
　securities regulators 証券業務規制当局, 証券規制機関
　U.S. federal and state regulators 米連邦・州規制当局

regulatory body 規制機関
▸Three *regulatory bodies* of the Stock Exchange Commission, the Listing Committee and the Banking Commission have been set up to ensure that stock market operators abide by a strict code of ethics and that transactions run smoothly. 証券取引所［株式市場］で業務を行う者が厳格な倫理規定を守り，取引を円滑に行うため，証券取引委員会，上場委員会と銀行委員会の三つの規制機関が設置されている。

rehabilitate 動 再建する, 再生する, 立て直す (＝reconstruct)
▸It will not be easy to *rehabilitate* the company, which has been driven into the red by multiple factors. 同社は，複合的な要因による赤字転落なので，再建は容易ではない。

rehabilitation 名 〈信用などの〉回復, 修復, 再建, 経営再建, 再生, 立て直し, 再興, 復興, 健全化, 更生, 復権, 復職, 復職, 社会復帰, リハビリ
　financial rehabilitation 金融再生
　management rehabilitation 経営再建
　rehabilitation plan 再建計画, 再生計画, 経営健全化計画 (＝restructuring plan)
　self-rehabilitation 自主再建
▸Corporate *rehabilitation* funds are established by creditor banks and other investors to bail out heavily indebted companies. 企業再建ファ

ンドは，巨額の債務を抱えた企業を救うため，取引銀行や投資家などが設立する基金だ。
▶Sanyo Electric Co. is under *rehabilitation*. 三洋電機は，経営再建中だ。
▶The company is undergoing management *rehabilitation*. 同社は現在，経営再建に取り組んでいる。

reimbursement 名 返済，弁済，償還，払戻し，精算，返還，補償，弁償，賠償
　reimbursement claim 還付請求
　reimbursement obligation 補償債務
　reimbursement of expenses 経費の弁済（＝expense reimbursement）
▶Through 2006 we expensed these *reimbursements* as incurred. 2006年度までは，この返済額を発生時に費用計上していました。

reinforce 動 強化する，強める，補強する，増強する，一段と固固にする，テコ入れする
▶GM and Toyota reaffirmed that they would *reinforce* cooperative relationship. GMとトヨタは，両社の協力関係を強化する方針を改めて確認した。

reinstate 動 復帰させる，復職させる
reinsurance 名 再保証，再保険
　excess of loss reinsurance 超過損害額再保険
　excess [surplus] reinsurance 超過額再保険（＝reinsurance for excess, surplus relief reinsurance）
　facultative reinsurance 任意再保険
　life reinsurance 生命保険の再保険
　non-proportional reinsurance 非比例配分式の再保険，非比例式再保険
　quota share reinsurance 比例再保険，比例配分式再保険（＝proportional reinsurance）
　reinsurance claims 再保険金
　reinsurance contract 再保険契約（⇒nonlife insurance company）
　reinsurance losses 再保険金
　reinsurance premiums assumed 受再保険料
　reinsurance premiums ceded 再保険料
　reinsurance rate 再保険料率（＝reinsurance premium rate）
　reinsurance recovery 再保険金，再保険回収金
　reinsurance treaty 再保険特約
　reinsurance with risk premium 危険保険料式再保険
　treaty reinsurance 特約再保険
▶Under *reinsurance* schemes, nonlife insurers pay premiums to other nonlife insurers or *reinsurance* companies in return for their sharing the burden of future claims. 再保険制度に従って，損保各社は，他の保険会社や再保険会社が将来の保険金を共同負担する見返りに，これらの保険会社に保険料を支払っている。

reinsure 動 再保証する，再保険をかける
▶American investor Warren Buffet has offered to *reinsure* up to $800 billion in municipal bonds to help out three troubled bond insurers. 経営難の米金融保証会社3社を支援するため，米投資家のウォーレン・バフェット氏が，3社が保証する地方債のうち最大8,000億ドルを再保証する申し入れを行った。

reinvent 動 作り直す，再発明する，再検討する，考え直す，出直す（⇒redeploy）

reinvest 動 再投資する
　earnings reinvested 留保利益，利益剰余金
　reinvested income 利益剰余金
▶Quarterly dividends may be *reinvested* automatically to purchase additional common shares at a discount from the average market price. 四半期配当金は，自動的に再投資して，平均市場価格から割り引いた価格で当社の普通株式を追加購入することができます。

reinvestment 名 再投資，社会還元
　Community Reinvestment Act 地域社会還元法
　dividend reinvestment 株主配当再投資，配当再投資，配当金株式再投資，配当金再投資
　reinvestment in business 事業への再投資
　reinvestment in financial assets 金融資産への再投資
　reinvestment income 再投資収益
　reinvestment of earnings 利益の再投資
▶ABC Inc. raised $100 million of common equity by means of its Dividend *Reinvestment* and Stock Purchase Plan and the Employees' Savings Plan. ABC Inc.は，株主配当再投資・株式購入制度と従業員社内預金制度により普通株式を発行して1億ドルを調達しました。

REIT 不動産投資信託，リート（**real estate investment trust**の略）

reject 動 拒否する，拒絶する，否認する，否定する，棄却する，退ける，否決する，断る
▶Yahoo Inc. has *rejected* Microsoft Corp.'s unsolicited $41.6 billion takeover offer as too low. 米ヤフー（インターネット検索世界第2位）は，米マイクロソフト（ソフトウエア世界最大手）による416億ドルの敵対的買収提案を，過小評価しているとして拒否した。

related 形 関係のある，関連した，…関係の，…系の，同族の，同種の

related business 関連事業
related business units 関連事業部門
related company 関連会社, 関係会社, 系列会社
related facilities 関連施設
related materials 関連資料
related papers 関係書類
related party 関連当事者, 利害関係者
related products 関連商品
related stories 関連記事
securities-related lines of business 証券関連業務
transaction-related contingencies 取引関連偶発債務

relations 名 関係, 関連, 広報, リレーション (⇒investor relations)
  business relations 取引関係, 業務上の関係, 事業上の関係, ビジネス関係
  capital and business relations 資本・業務関係
  community relations 地域社会との関係, 対地域社会関係, 地域社会PR, 地域社会《略 CR》
  customer relations 顧客関係
  economic relations 経済関係, 経済交流
  employee relations 従業員との関係, 従業員PR
  employer-employee relations 雇用者対従業員の関係, 従業員PR
  industrial relations 労使関係
  job relations 職場従業員関係
  labor relations 労使関係, 労働関係
  partner relations 提携先との関係
  public relations 広報, 広報活動, 広報宣伝活動, パブリック・リレーションズ, ピーアール《略 PR》(企業や各種団体などの業務・活動内容や商品, サービスに関する情報を社会, 消費者に伝える仕事)
  public relations officer 広報担当者, 渉外係《略 PRO》
  stockholder relations 株主PR
  subcontractor relations 下請企業との関係
  supplier relations 納入業者との関係
▶In terms of market value, the *relation* between Ito-Yokado and Seven-Eleven is a contradiction. 時価総額(株価による企業価値を示す)では, イトーヨーカ堂(親会社)とセブン-イレブン(子会社)との関係が逆転している.

relationship 名 関係, 関連, 結びつき, 取引先
  arm's length relationship 商業ベースの取引関係
  capital relationship 資本関係
  competitive relationship 競争関係
  contractual relationship 契約関係
  cooperative relationship 協力関係
  corporate relationship 企業関係
  currency relationships 為替相場, 為替レート
  customer relationship 顧客関係
  economic relationship 経済関係
  financial relationship 財務比率
  foreign relationships 外交関係
  legal relationship 法的関係
  relationship bank 取引銀行, 協力銀行
  relationship management 取引先総合管理《略 RM》
  symbiotic relationship 共生の関係, もちつもたれつの関係
  vertical and horizontal human relationships 縦と横の人間関係
  vertical keiretsu relationships 垂直型の系列関係
  vertical price relationship 垂直的価格関係
▶Mitsubishi Corp. intends to reinforce its business through the *relationship* with Hokuetsu Paper in such areas as material procurement and trading of paper-pulp products. 三菱商事は, 原材料の調達や紙パルプ製品の取引などの面での北越製紙との関係により, 同社事業のテコ入れを目指している.
▶While maintaining a conventional competitive *relationship*, Yomiuri, Nikkei and Asahi aim to bolster their ability to disseminate information as news media. 従来の競争関係を維持しながら, 読売, 日経, 朝日の3社は, 報道機関としての情報発信力の強化を目指している.

release 動 発売する, 販売する, 公表する, 発表する, 公開する, 〈映画を〉封切る, 解放する, 放出する, 〈借金などを〉免除する, 〈権利などを〉放棄する, 〈財産を〉譲渡する, リリースする
▶Apple Computer Inc. *released* their new desktop computer, the iMac G5. 米アップルコンピュータは, デスクトップ・パソコン「iMac G5」を発表した.
▶Now is the peak period for listed companies to *release* their business reports for the business year ending in March. 上場企業の3月期決算の発表が, ピークを迎えている.

reliability 名 信頼, 信頼性, 信頼度, 確実性, 信憑性
  automobile reliability survey 自動車信頼度調査
  consistency and reliability 一貫性と信頼性
  integrity and reliability of the financial statements 財務書類の完全性と信頼性
  product reliability 製品[商品]の信頼性

▸These capital additions provide for growth, modernization and *reliability*. これらの追加投資は，成長，近代化と信頼性向上が目的です。

reliable 形 信頼できる，信用できる，確かな，確実な，期待どおりの
▸The firm's financial data is not *reliable*. 同社の財務データは，信頼性が薄い。

relief 名 救済，救助，救援，緩和，軽減，除去，控除，給付金，生活保護手当，職務の交替要員，代行者
  debt relief 債務救済，債務削減 （＝debt forgiveness）
  double taxation relief 外国税額控除
  personal relief 人的控除
  regulatory relief 規制の適用除外
  relief fund 救済基金
  relief measures 救済措置
  relief works 失業対策事業
  tax relief measures 税金の減免措置
  temporary relief 一時救済
  U.K stock relief 英国税法の棚卸し資産税額控除，英国棚卸し資産控除

relocate 動 配置転換する，再配置する，移動する，移転する，移す （＝redeploy）
▸Our provisions for business restructuring cover the costs of closing facilities and *relocating* employees. 当社の事業再編成引当金には，施設閉鎖や従業員再配置などの費用も含まれています。

relocation 名 配置転換，再配置，移動，移転，立地変更 （＝redeployment）
  employee relocation 従業員再配置，従業員の配置転換
  relocation allowance 引っ越し手当
  relocation of production facilities 生産拠点の移設［移転］
▸Costs of $500 million associated with employee separations and *relocations* are also induced in selling, general and administrative expenses. 従業員の退職と配置転換に関連する費用5億ドルも，販売費および一般管理費に含まれている。

remainder 名 残余，残り，余り，残余権
remaining 形 残りの，残存する，残余の
  remaining cash flow 残存キャッシュ・フロー
  remaining depreciable lives 残存償却年数
  remaining economic life 経済的残存耐用年数 （＝remaining economic age）
  remaining interest 残存持ち分，残りの持ち分
  remaining life 残存期間，残存年数，残存耐用年数
  remaining service 残余勤続年数，残存勤続年数 （＝remaining service period）

  remaining useful life 残存耐用年数
▸MUFG obtained the *remaining* 38.8 percent stock in Mitsubishi UFJ Securities through a stock swap deal. 三菱UFJフィナンシャル・グループ（MUFG）は，株式交換取引で三菱UFJ証券の残りの株式の38.8％を取得した。

remit 動 送達する，送金する，免除する，延期する，譲渡する，差し戻す
remittance fees 送金手数料，振込み手数料
▸Overseas *remittance fees* are currently several thousand yen per transfer. 海外への送金手数料は現在，送金1回に付き数千円かかる。

remote 形 遠隔の，遠隔操作による
remote control 遠隔制御，遠隔操作，遠隔操縦，リモート・コントロール，リモコン
▸The arrival of such a ubiquitous computing society will see technology allow consumers to operate such home appliances as air-conditioners and washing machines by *remote control* while far from home. このようなユビキタス社会が到来すると，技術の進展により，消費者は外出先からリモコンでエアコンや洗濯機などの家電製品を操作できるようになる。

remuneration 名 報酬，給料，代償，報償，謝礼，対価
  auditor's remuneration 監査報酬
  entrepreneur's remuneration 事業主報酬
  management remuneration 経営者報酬
  monetary remuneration 金銭的報酬
  officers' remuneration 役員報酬
  remuneration cost 支払い報酬，報酬，代償
  remuneration package 報酬，給付，謝礼，代償，報償

renege 動 〈約束を〉破る，違反する
renewable 形 更新できる，継続できる，延長できる
renewal 名 刷新，更新，書換え，書換え継続，期限延長，自動継続，再開，再生，復活，再開発，リニューアル
  automatic renewal 自動更新
  card renewal カード更新
  renewal expenses 更新費用，書換え費用
  renewal fee 更新手数料，書換え手数料
  renewal fund 設備の更新資金
  renewal option 更新選択権
  renewal or extension 更新または延長
  renewal term 更新期間
  renewals and betterments 更新・改良
  urban renewal 都市再開発
▸Certain land and building leases have *renewal*

options for periods ranging from three to five years.　特定の土地と建物のリースには，3−5年の期間の更新選択権がついている。

renminbi 名　人民幣, 人民元《略 RMB [Rmb]》

renovate 動　修理する，修復する，修繕する，改装する，刷新する，革新する，新しくする
▶The draft assumes the ¥100 billion needed to open new stores and *renovate* old outlets can be obtained from sponsor companies.　新規出店や老朽化店舗の改装に必要な費用1,000億円はスポンサー企業から確保できる，と原案は想定している。

renovation 名　修復，修復作業，修復，修繕，改装，刷新，革新，最新設備の導入
▶The factory will implement its first *renovation* before April.　同工場では，4月までにまず最新設備の導入を実施する。

rent 名　地代，家賃，賃料，賃借料，不動産使用料（＝rental）
▶The monthly *rent* per tsubo (3.3 square meters) on the first floor is about ¥200,000 or more.　1階部分の坪（3.3平方メートル）当たり賃料は，月20万円以上だ。
▶The *rent* is about twice the market price.　賃借料は，相場の約2倍だ。

rental 名　賃貸料，賃借料，リース，レンタル
　annual rental　年間リース料，年間レンタル料
　lease rentals receivable　受取リース料
　rental commitments　賃借料
　rental expense　賃借料, 賃借費用，リース料（＝rent expense）
　rental income　賃貸料，賃貸収入，受取賃貸料，リース料収入
　rental payments　リース支払い額，リース料
　rental revenues　賃貸料，レンタル収益，リース料
　rental store　レンタル店（＝rental shop）
　rentals and other services　レンタルその他のサービス
▶The revenues of *rentals* and other services were about level the last three years.　レンタルその他のサービス部門の収益は，過去3年間ほぼ同水準でした。

reorganization 名　再編成，再編，改編，改造，改組，改革，再生，再建，会社再建，事業再編，組織再編，組織変更，会社更生（＝realignment; ⇒ **repositioning program, retail industry**）
　capital reorganization　資本再編
　corporate reorganization　企業再編，再編，会社更生
　industrial reorganization　産業再編，産業再編成
　financial reorganization　金融再編成
　large-scale reorganization of the retail industry　流通業界［小売業界］の大規模再編，流通業界の大がかりな再編
　major corporate reorganization　大規模な企業再編
　quasi-reorganization　準更生
　reorganization of debt　債務再構成（＝debt reorganization）
　reorganization scheme　再建計画（＝reorganization plan）
　structural reorganization　組織改革
▶Northwest's board is scheduled to meet Wednesday to decide on a Chapter 11 bankruptcy *reorganization*.　ノースウエスト航空（米航空4位）の取締役会は，水曜日に会合を持って，米連邦破産法第11章による会社再建を決定する予定だ。

reorganize 動　再編成する，再編する，改造する，改組する，改革する，再生する，再建する，組織変更する
▶In the United States, a troubled company is afforded the opportunity to *reorganize* under Chapter 11 of the federal Bankruptcy Code.　米国では，経営破綻した企業は，米連邦破産法11章に基づいて企業を再建する機会が与えられる。

reparation 名　賠償，償い，補償，賠償金

repatriation 名　海外投資資金の引揚げ，対外投資資金の本国送金

repay 動　払い戻す，返済する，返還する，返金する，償還する（＝refund）
　repay bank borrowings　銀行借入れを返済する，銀行借入金を返済する
　repay debt　債務［負債］を返済する，借入金を返済する
　repay maturing CP　満期を迎えた［満期が来た］CPを償還する
　repay principal　元本を返済する，元本を償還する
　repay the loan　ローンを返済［弁済］する，借入金を返済する
▶Proceeds from the new share issue will be used to *repay* $300 million of 10% Series 3 Notes, maturing in May 2008.　この起債［新株発行］による手取金は，2008年5月満期・利率10％のシリーズ3ノート3億ドルの償還に充てられます。
▶We *repaid* $823 million of long-term debt during the first nine months.　当社は，1−9月期に長期債務8億2,300万ドルを返済しました。

repayment 名　返済，払戻し，償還，返金（⇒ **cash flow problem, debt repayment**）
　debt repayment　債務返済，借入金の返済（＝

repayment of debt)
early repayment (before due date) 早期返済, 早期完済
loan repayment 債務返済, 融資の返済, 借入金の返済, ローンの返済 (＝repayment of the loan)
lump sum repayment 一括返済
principal repayment 元本の償還 (＝repayment of principal)
raising and repayment of funds 資金の調達と償還
repayment of debt 債務返済, 債務の支払い, 借入金返済額
repayment of long term debt 長期債務の返済, 長期債務支出, 長期借入金返済額
repayment of public funds 公的資金の返済 (＝public fund repayment)
repayment of the loans 借入金の返済, ローンの返済 (＝loan repayment)
▸The company will raise more funds for loan *repayment*. 同社は，さらに債務返済の資金を調達する。
▸The financial group has already completed the *repayment* of all the public funds it received from the government. 同フィナンシャル・グループは，国から調達した公的資金をすでに完済している。

repeal 動 〈法律・決議などを〉廃止する, 無効にする, 撤回する, 名 廃止, 廃棄, 取消し, 撤回

replacement 名 交換, 補充, 代替, 取替え, 再取得, 再調達, 後任者, 後継者, 交換要員, 代替品, 返却, 返却, 復職
card replacement カード再発行
replacement cost 代替コスト, 再取得原価, 再調達原価, 再調達コスト, 取替え原価
replacement demand 買替え需要
replacement purchase 買替え
▸The company carried out a sweeping management reshuffle, including the *replacement* of three top managers. 経営トップ3人の一新 [交替] を含めて，同社は経営陣の全面入れ替え実施を決めた。

repo 名 レポ取引, 買い戻し条件付き売却契約

report 動 報告する, 報告書を提出する, 表示する, 記載する, 公表する, 計上する, 申告する, 報道する, 連絡する (⇒advisory)
as previously reported 前期報告額, 前年度報告額
net assets at year end—as reported 期末現在の純資産: 公表額, 期末純資産: 公表額

report as liability 負債として計上する
report at a market value 時価で表示する, 市場価格で表示する
report huge losses 巨額の損失を計上する
report net income 純利益を計上する
report recurring losses 経常赤字になる, 経常赤字に転落する
▸Firms are allowed to annually *report* their profits from large construction projects that last several years. 複数年にまたがる大規模工事の場合，企業は（完工前でも）単年度ごとに利益を計上することができる。
▸The firm failed to *report* a total of about ¥7 billion in taxable income. 同社は，課税総額約70億円を申告しなかった。

report 名 報告, 報告書, 申告書, 報道, レポート (⇒annual report, consolidated earnings report, earnings report)
accountant's report 監査報告書, 会計士報告書 (目論見書添付書類)
accounting reports 会計報告書, 財務諸表, 有価証券報告書, 財務情報
advisory report 意見書
annual meeting report 株主総会報告書
business report 事業報告, 事業報告書, 営業報告書, 業務報告書, ビジネス・レポート
consumer report 個人信用情報
extraordinary report 臨時報告書
financial report 財務報告, 財務報告書, 業績報告, 有価証券報告書
flash report 営業速報
fund report 資金報告, 資金報告書
import and export report 輸出入申告書
operating report 業務報告
performance report 業績報告書
periodic report 定期報告, 定期報告書
press report 新聞報道
preliminary report 速報
report of management 経営者の報告, 経営陣の報告
report on large shareholders 大量保有報告書
sales report 売上報告書
securities report 有価証券報告書 (＝securities statement)
segmental report セグメント情報
tentative report 中間報告
▸Those stockholders who attended the annual meeting received a report on the Corporation's current business, as well as its plans for the future. 株主総会に出席された株主の皆さま

には，当社の現在の事業と将来の計画についてご報告しました。

reported 形　財務報告上の，決算報告上の，報告された，計上された，公表された，計上…，公表…
　reported earned premium　公表経過保険料
　reported earnings　決算報告上の利益，財務報告上の利益，公表利益，計上利益
　reported earnings per share　1株当たり計上利益
　reported equity　財務報告上の株主資本
　reported figures　報告書上の数値，報告書に掲げた数値
　reported income　公表利益，計上利益
　reported numbers　決算　(=financial figures)
▶There is no change in the current or previously *reported* net earnings.　当年度の当期純利益と過年度に計上した当期純利益に，変動はありません。

reportedly 副　報道によると，伝えられるところによれば，評判では，うわさによると，…という，…したそうだ
▶The ruling was *reportedly* the first ever to suspend ongoing merger talks between financial institutions.　継続中の金融機関の統合交渉を差し止める決定は，前例がないという。

reporting 名　報告，表示　(⇒financial reporting)
　accounting for external reporting　外部報告会計
　employee reporting　従業員に対する報告
　for financial statement reporting　財務書類上，財務諸表上
　for income tax reporting　税務上，税務会計上
　functional reporting of expenses　職能別報告書，職能別計算書
　income reporting　損益報告
　net of tax reporting　税引き後純額の報告，正味税効果の報告，税効果考慮後の報告
　periodic reporting　定期報告，期間報告
　principle of true and fair reporting　真実性の原則
　production reporting　生産報告
　reporting currency　報告通貨　(財務諸表などで金額表示の単位として用いる通貨)
　reporting period　報告期間，決算報告期間，財務報告期間，報告事業年度　(文脈に応じて [当期] や [当四半期] を指す場合もある)
　reporting year　報告事業年度，報告年度，当年度，当期
　segmental reporting　セグメント情報　(=segmental report)

　standard of reporting　報告基準
▶*Reporting* in U.S. dollars provides the most meaningful presentation of our consolidated results and financial position.　米ドルで計上 [報告] したほうが，当社の連結経営成績 [連結業績] と財政状態を最も適切に表示することになります。

reporting quarter　当四半期，報告四半期
▶The pretax profits of nonmanufacturers climbed 9.1 percent in the *reporting quarter* (April-June quarter), up for the 13th consecutive quarter.　非製造業の当四半期 (4－6月期) の経常利益は，9.1％の上昇で，13期連続増加した。

repositioning 名　事業基盤の再構築，事業基盤の強化，企業再編，再位置付け，再ポジショニング，ポジションの再設定，リポジショニング
▶European and U.S. automakers repeated consolidation and *repositioning* as part of attempted business expansion.　欧米の自動車メーカーは，経営の規模拡大を求めて合従連衡を繰り返した。

repositioning program　事業基盤の強化プログラム
▶Our reorganization plan is compatible with a worldwide *repositioning program* initiated earlier in the year, aimed at strengthening our structures and procedures.　この組織再編計画は，事業機構と業務運営の強化をめざして当社が年初から世界的な規模で進めてきた事業基盤強化プログラムに沿うものです。

repossess 動　〈商品を〉回収する，引き取る，再入手する，回復する

represent 動　表示する，表明する，意味する，示す，…を表章する，…を表す，…の代理をつとめる，…を代表する，…を代行する，…に相当する，…に当たる　(⇒secured mortgage)
▶Many of our employees are *represented* by unions.　当社従業員の多くは，組合に加入しています。
▶Research and development expenses *represented* 12.0 percent of revenues in the third quarter of 2008.　2008年第3四半期の研究開発費は，売上高の12％を占めました。

representative 名　代表者，代理人，代行者，代議士，米下院議員，事務所，駐在員事務所，セールスマン，販売員，外務員，駐在員，担当者　(⇒policyholders' representative meeting)
　account representative　証券会社のセールスマン
　customer service representative　顧客サービス担当者　(=customer service staff)

duly authorized representative 正式に権限を与えられた代表[代表者・代理人]
legal representative 法律上の代表者（法定代理人や遺言執行者など）
media representative 媒体代表
medical representative 医療情報担当者
Office of the United States Trade Representative 合衆国通商代表部, 米通商代表部
registered representative 登録外務員, 登録販売員, 証券外務員, 登録取引会員
sales representative 販売外交員, 販売担当者, 営業部員, セールスマン, 外商, 製造業者の代理人

representative 形 代表的な, 典型的な, 代理の, 代表する
representative action 株主の代表訴訟, 集団訴訟（＝representative suit）
representative director 代表取締役
representative office 駐在員事務所, 在外公館
representative rights 代表権

▶He was promoted to the position of *representative* director of the company. 氏は, 同社の代表取締役に昇格した.

reprimand 名動 叱責(する), 懲戒(する)
repurchase 動 買い戻す, 再購入する（＝buy back）

▶Shares were *repurchased* for cancellation in 2008. 株式は, 2008年度に買い戻して消却しました.
▶The *repurchased* shares were retired and restored to the status of authorized but unissued shares. 買戻し株式は消却して, 授権未発行株式の状態に戻っています.

repurchase 名 買戻し, 再調達
equity repurchase 株式の買戻し
repurchase agreement 現先取引, 現先, レポ, 売戻し条件付き買いオペ
repurchase and reverse repurchase agreements 買戻し・売戻し条件付き売買契約, レポおよびリバース・レポ契約
repurchase cost 再調達原価, 再調達価格
repurchase of bonds 社債の買戻し
share [stock] repurchase 株式の買戻し, 自社株買い（＝share buyback, stock buyback, stock repurchase）

▶Under our stock *repurchase* programs, we repurchased 11,252,000 shares during 2008 at a cost of $1,425 million. 当社の自社株買戻しプログラムに従って, 当社は2008年度に11,252,000株を14億2,500万ドルで買い戻しました.

reputation 名 評価, 名声, 地位, 信望, 知名度, 評判, 名誉, イメージ

▶Courts have handed down decisions that emphasized the importance of an individual's *reputation* and privacy. 一連の裁判では, 個人の名誉やプライバシーを重視する判断が示されている.
▶Restructuring allows us to maintain our *reputation* as the world's most innovative telecommunications corporation. 事業再編を通して, 当社は, 世界でもっとも革新的な通信機器メーカーとしての当社に対する評価を維持することもできます.
▶Toyota's success has been built on a *reputation* for high-quality and economical cars. トヨタの躍進は, 高品質・低燃費車のブランド・イメージを定着できたことが大きい.

request 名 要求, 要求書, 請求, 要請, 要請書, 依頼, 依頼書, 委任, リクエスト

▶Major unions submitted their *requests* to their companies. 主要労組が, それぞれ会社側に組合の要求書を提出した.

requirement(s) 名 要件, 条件, 必要条件, 基準, 規定, 制度, 資格（⇒capital requirements, cash requirements）
accounting requirement 会計基準, 会計処理方法, 会計義務
cash capital requirements 資金需要
employee contribution requirements 従業員拠出義務
financial requirement 資金需要
financing requirements 資金需要, 借入需要, 資金調達の必要額
funding requirements 資金需要（＝funding needs）
initial margin requirement 当初証拠金率
meet one's cash requirements 必要資金を確保する, 必要資金を賄う
reporting requirements 報告制度
requirement for funds 資金需要（＝capital requirements）
sinking fund requirements 減債基金積立額
transparency requirement 透明性の規定
underwriting requirements 引受基準
working capital requirements 必要運転資金

▶We will refinance debt maturing in 2009 to meet our cash *requirements* in 2009. 当社は, 2009年に満期が到来する債務の借換えで, 2009年度の必要資金を確保する方針です.

resale price maintenance 再販価格維持, 再販売価格維持[維持制度]
reschedule 動 債務返済を繰り延べる, 債務の支払いを繰り延べる, 債務を再編する

▶The Paris Club of credit countries struck a deal with Russia to *reschedule* about $8.1 billion in debts.　パリ・クラブ(主要債権国会議)は，約81億ドルの債務について支払いを繰り延べることでロシアと合意した．

rescheduling 名　債務返済繰延べ，債務再編，リスケジューリング
　debt rescheduling　債務再編，債務返済の繰延べ，債務リスケジューリング　(＝rescheduling of debt)
　rescheduling program　債務再編計画

rescind 動　〈規則などを〉廃止する，無効にする，〈命令などを〉撤回する，取り消す，〈上告などを〉取り下げる
▶NTT Corp. filed a lawsuit against the Health, Labor and Welfare Ministry, demanding that the ministry *rescind* its disapproval of NTT plans to cut pension payments to NTT retirees.　NTTは，NTTのOBに対する企業年金減額計画の不承認処分取消しを求めて，厚生労働省を提訴した．

rescue 名　救援，支援，救済，救出，救助，レスキュー，動　救う，救助[救出]する，支援する，救済する
　financial rescue　金融支援，経営支援
　rescue package　支援策，救済策，支援計画，救助計画　(＝rescue plan)
　rescue plan　支援計画，支援策　(＝rescue package)
　rescue team　救助隊　(＝rescue crew [squad, unit])
　rescue work　救助作業
▶The bank is orchestrating a ¥470 billion *rescue* package for ailing condominium builder Daikyo Inc.　同行は，経営再建中のマンション分譲大手の大京に対する4,700億円の金融支援策の最終調整に入った．

research 名　研究，調査，研究開発，リサーチ
　applied research　応用研究
　basic research　基礎研究　(＝fundamental research)
　development research　開発研究
　equity research　株式調査
　ex post research　事後的研究
　experiment research　実験研究
　image research　イメージ調査
　market research　市場調査，販路調査，マーケット・リサーチ　(＝marketing research)
　modified research　改良研究
　motivation research　動機調査，購買動機調査，モチベーション・リサーチ《略 MR》
　operational research　作戦研究，業務調査，オペレーションズ・リサーチ　(＝operations research)
　opinion research　意見調査
　product research　製品調査，製品研究
　pure research　基礎研究
　rating research　視聴率調査
　research activities　リサーチ業務，調査研究業務
　research and experimentation　試験研究
　research approach　調査方法
　research cost　研究費，試験研究費
　research design　調査設計，調査計画
　research facilities　研究施設
　research finding　調査結果
　research kitchen　食品関係の調査・開発研究所
　research policy　調査方針
　video research　ビデオ・リサーチ
▶*Research* facilities will expand over the next five years, with increases in both laboratory space and research staff.　研究所のスペース拡張と研究スタッフの増員に伴って，研究施設は今後5年にわたって拡大する見込みです．

research and development 研究開発《略 R&D》
　research and development cost　研究開発費
　research and development expense　研究開発費，試験研究費　(＝R&D expense, research and development expenditure)
　research and development investment　研究開発投資，研究開発投資額
　research-and-development-related industry　研究開発型産業
▶We have positioned ourselves well with our increasing investments in *research and development* and improving product line.　当社は，研究開発投資の拡大と製品ラインの充実に取り組んできました．

reserve 動　引当金を積む，権利を留保[保有]する，保留する，延期する，予約する
　be under-reserved　準備金不足になる
　reserve for future losses　将来の損失に対して引当金を積む
　reserve for possible future losses　将来の偶発損失に対して引当金を積む
　reserved profit　留保利益，未処分利益　(＝retained earnings, retained surplus)
　reserved stock　予備在庫
　reserved surplus　処分済み剰余金，処分済み利益剰余金　(＝appropriated earned surplus, appropriated retained income)

reserve 名 準備金, 積立金, 引当金, 充当金, 支払い準備, 予備品, 保存品, 保留, 留保, 保存, 制限, 条件 (⇒**capital reserve, loan loss reserves**)
 accumulated reserves 累積積立金
 catastrophe reserve 異常損失準備金
 depreciation reserves 減価償却引当金
 earned surplus reserve 利益準備金
 financial reserves 財政基盤
 general reserve 一般引当金, 別途積立金 (＝other reserve, special reserve, unconditional reserve)
 internal reserves 内部留保, 内部留保金
 inventory reserve 棚卸し資産評価引当金
 legal capital reserves 法定準備金 (＝legal reserves, legally required reserves)
 legal reserves 法定準備金, 準備金, 利益準備金 (＝legal earned reserves)
 liability reserve 責任準備金, 負債性引当金
 loan redemption reserve 借入金償還引当金
 loan reserves 融資引当金, 金融機関の債権に対する引当金, 債務引当金
 loss reserves 責任準備金, 損失準備金
 mathematical reserve 保険料積立金
 optional reserve 任意準備金, 任意積立金
 other reserves その他積立金, 別途積立金 (＝general reserves, special reserves, unconditional reserves)
 pension reserve 年金積立金
 petroleum reserve 石油備蓄
 profit reserve 利益準備金
 reserve for amortization 償却引当金
 reserve for bad debts 貸倒れ引当金 (＝reserve for possible loan losses)
 reserve for depletion 減耗償却引当金
 reserve for depreciation 減価償却引当金, 減価償却累計額 (＝accumulated depreciation, allowance for depreciation)
 reserves for losses 損失引当金
 reserve for retirement allowances 退職給与引当金
 reserve for retirement fund 退職給与積立金
 reserve production ratio 可採年数《略 R/P》
 reserve recognition accounting 埋蔵量認定計算《略 RRA》
 reserve requirements 支払い準備, 預金準備, 預金準備率
 reserves-dedicated 売り先指定ガス埋蔵量
 reserves-prospective 推定埋蔵量
 reserves-proved 確認埋蔵量
 revenue reserve 利益準備金, 利益剰余金, 任意積立金
▸Regular FSA inspections focus on whether banks' loan *reserves* are adequate. 金融庁の通常検査は, 主に銀行の債権に対する引当金が十分かどうかを検討する。
▸We provide *reserves* for these potential costs and regularly review the adequacy of our *reserves*. 当社は, これらの潜在的費用に対して引当金を設定し, その妥当性を定期的に検討しています。

reservoir 名 貯留岩 (石油やガスが流動して満たされている多孔質浸透性の地下岩層)

reshape 動 刷新する, 再編成する, 立て直す, 作り直す, 作り変える, 新生面を開く
▸We have slimmed down and *reshaped* our worldwide organization. 当社は, 当社の世界各国の組織をスリム化して再編成しました。

reshuffle 動 人員を入れ替える, 刷新する, 更迭する, 改革する, 再編する
▸The company *reshuffled* its management. 同社は, 経営陣を刷新した。

reshuffle 名 内閣改造, 人員の入れ替え, 人事刷新, 更迭, 〈構造などの〉改革, 再編
 industry reshuffle 業界再編
 major reshuffle 大幅入れ替え
 management reshuffle 経営人事刷新, 経営陣の刷新, 経営陣の全面入れ替え
 sweeping reshuffle 全面的入れ替え
▸This could lead to an industry *reshuffle*. これは, 業界再編につながる可能性がある。

resident 名 居住者, 形 居住している, 駐在している, 専任の
▸**Canadian resident** カナダ居住者
 non-resident 非居住者
 nursing home resident 老人ホーム入居者
 qualified resident 適格居住者
 resident advisor [adviser] 専任アドバイザー
 resident card 住民票
 resident identification number 住民コード番号
▸Dividends paid to owners of the Corporation's common shares who are not *residents* of Canada are subject generally to a 25 percent withholding tax. 配当金がカナダ居住者でない当社の普通株主に支払われた場合, その配当金には一般に25％の源泉所得税[源泉徴収税]が課されます。

residual 形 残余の, 余りの, 名 残余, 残留物, 残差
 residual interest 残余権
 residual maturity 残余期間

residual useful life 残存耐用年数
resign 動 辞職する，辞任する，退職する，退任する，〈権利などを〉譲り渡す（＝step down）
▸All three representative directors of the firm decided to *resign*. 同社の代表取締役3人が，すべて退陣することになった。

resignation 名 辞職，辞任，退任，辞表
　a letter of resignation 辞表，辞職願い（＝a resignation letter）
　tender [give in, hand in, send in] one's resignation 辞表を提出する
▸JAL's internal conflict has been halted at least for a while by the *resignation* of its president and chief executive officer. 日本航空の内紛は，同社の社長兼最高経営責任者の退任でひとまず決着した。

resilient 形 弾力のある，立ち直りの早い，快活な
resize 動 合理化する，…の大きさ[サイズ]を変える，再編する
▸We have focused on our strengths, honed our strategies, seized opportunities, trimmed costs and *resized* our operations. 私どもは，自分たちの強い分野に的を絞り，戦略を磨き，機会をとらえ，費用を削減するとともに，経営の合理化に努めてきました。

resolution 名 決議，決議案，議案，決断，決意，決定，裁決，判定，解決，解答，解明，決着，〈映像の〉鮮明度，〈光の〉解像
　extraordinary resolution 特殊決議，非常決議（議決権を持つ株主の半数以上，かつ議決権で3分の2以上の支持がなければ成立しない決議）
　important resolution 重要決議
　special resolution 特別決議
　stockholder resolution 株主決議（＝shareholder resolution）
▸On the *resolution* to ratify the appointment of auditors, 99% of the votes cast were voted for. 監査人の選任を承認する議案については，投票総数(投票株式総数)の99%が賛成しました。

resolve 動 解決する，決心する，決議する，分解する，分離する
resort 名 手段，頼みの綱，頼ること，訴えること
▸The EU considers retaliatory measures as a last *resort*. 欧州連合(EU)は，報復措置を最後の手段と考えている。

resource(s) 名 資源，経営資源，財源，資金，源泉，供給源，教材，資料，手段，方策，兵力（⇒**human resources, management resources, promising area**）
　air resources 大気資源
　allocation of resources 資源の配分（＝resource allocation）
　business resources 経営資源
　capital resources 資金の源泉
　commitment of resources 融資承認額
　corporate resources 経営資源，会社の資源
　financial resource(s) 資金，資本，資金力，金融力，金融資産，財務資源，財源，資金の源泉，資金源，原資（⇒**trend**）
　fishing resources 漁業資源
　funding resources 資金調達源（⇒**financial base**）
　human resources 人的資源，人材，人事源
　industrial resources 工業資源
　internal resources 内部資金，手元資金
　labor resources 労働資源
　management resources 経営資源，役員人事（＝managerial resources）
　marine resources 海洋資源（＝ocean resources）
　mineral resources 鉱物資源
　natural resources 天然資源
　productive resources 生産資源
　recycled resources リサイクル資源
　resource allocation 資源配分（＝allocation of resources）
　resource exploitation 資源の活用，資源開発
　resource library 資料図書室
　resource mobilization 資源活用
　resource-probing vessel 資源探査船
　resource recovery 資源回収，資源再利用
　resource room 資料室
　resource utilization 設備と労働力の稼動率
　scarce resources 希少資源
　the development and use of ocean resources 海洋資源の開発・利用
　timber resources 森林資源
　water resources development 水資源の開発
▸Now is time for businesses to inject their corporate *resources* into promising areas as a new source for earnings. 今は，新たな収益源として企業がその経営資源を有望な分野に投入する時期だ。
▸To meet customer needs, we coordinate *resources* across business unit lines. 顧客のニーズを満たすため，当社は事業部門の境界を越えて経営資源の調整を図っています。

resource-conserving product 省資源製品，省資源を心がけた商品
▸The decline of excessive packaging used at

supermarkets and shops might prompt manufacturers into producing more *resource-conserving products*.　スーパーや小売店の過剰包装が減少すれば，メーカー側がもっと省資源を心がけた商品作りをするようになる可能性がある．

resource-conserving society　省資源社会
▶Charging for the collection of ordinary garbage, including household wastes, is a price we have to pay to create a *resource-conserving society*.　家庭ゴミなど一般廃棄物回収の有料化は，省資源社会に向けてわれわれが支払わなければならない代価の一つだ．

respond to　…に応じる，…に応える，…に対応する，…に反応する
▶GM failed to *respond* to consumers' growing disenchantment with large, gas-guzzling vehicles.　GMは，消費者のガソリンを食う大型車離れへの対応が遅れた．

response　名　回答，応答，反応，対応
　consumer response　消費者反応
　demand response　需要反応
　market responses　市場の反応
　response rate　回答率
　response time　応答時間
　response to customer needs　顧客ニーズへの対応
　supply response　供給反応

responsibility　名　責任，職責，義務，債務，負担，契約義務，履行能力，支払い能力（⇒**corporate social responsibility**）
　management responsibility　経営責任，管理責任（＝responsibility of management）
　public responsibility　公共責任，社会的責任，公共性
　resignation to take responsibility　引責辞任
　responsibility for financial reporting　財務報告に対する責任
　responsibility of the Company's management　会社の経営者の責任
　shareholders' responsibility　株主責任
▶Ashikaga Financial Group Inc. must assume some *responsibility* for the bank's failure as the bank's only shareholder.　あしぎんフィナンシャルグループは，同行の唯一の株主として，同行破綻の責任を負わなければならない．
▶Our management executive committee has *responsibility* for policy, strategy and values.　当社の経営執行委員会は，会社の政策，戦略と価値観などについての責任を負っています．

responsible　形　責任がある，責任を負う，責任の重い，報告義務がある
▶ChuoAoyama PricewaterhouseCoopers was *responsible* for auditing the accounts of about 5,600 companies as of the end of January 2006.　中央青山監査法人は，2006年1月末時点で，約5,600社の会計監査［財務書類の監査］を担当していた．
▶Management is *responsible* for maintaining a system of internal controls as a fundamental requirement for the operational and financial integrity of results.　経営者は，営業成績および財務成績の適正性を保つ基本的条件として，内部統制組織を維持する責任を負っています．

restate　動　修正する，再表示する，修正再表示する，更新する（⇒**International Financial Reporting Standards**）
▶Income taxes for 2008 have not been *restated* for this change.　2008年度の法人所得税額は，この変更による修正・再表示を行っていません．

restatement　名　修正，再表示，修正再表示，更新，改訂，言い換え，再陳述，リステートメント

restrict　動　制限する，限定する，制止する，禁止する

restriction　名　制限，規制，制約
　dividend restriction　配当制限
　foreign exchange restrictions　外国為替規制
　lending restrictions　貸出規制
　loan restrictions　融資規制
▶*Restrictions* on share buybacks were eased in October 2001.　2001年10月に，自社株買戻しに対する規制が緩和された．
▶Some *restrictions* must be imposed on foreign investment in major domestic airport operations.　国内空港の運営に対する外国からの投資には，ある程度，制限を設ける必要がある．

restructure　動　再編成する，再構築する，再構成する，再建する，立て直す，組織替えする，リストラする，改編する
▶We need to *restructure* some of our overseas operations.　当社は，海外事業の一部再編成を迫られています．

restructuring　名　事業の再構築，事業の再編成，再構成，再建，経営再建，再編，改革，解雇，リストラ，リストラクチャリング（⇒**business restructuring**）
　balance sheet restructuring　財務再編
　capital restructuring　資本再構成，資本の再編成
　corporate debt restructuring　企業債務の再編
　corporate restructuring　企業再編成，企業再編，会社再建，企業リストラ，事業機構の再編，経営再建，リストラ

debt restructuring 債務再構成，債務の特別条件変更（＝refinancing debt）
financial restructuring 財務再編，財務再構築，金融のリストラ
large scale restructuring 大規模再建計画
restructuring costs 事業再編成費用，リストラクチャリング費用，リストラ費用，リストラ経費（＝restructuring charges; ⇒pretax provision）
restructuring efforts 経営再建策，リストラ策（⇒sale）
restructuring measures 再建策，再編策，リストラ策
restructuring of debt 債務再編，債務再構築，債務の再構築（＝debt restructuring）
restructuring program 再建計画，再編計画，再生計画，事業再編成計画，事業再構築計画，再建策，再建案，リストラ計画（＝restructuring package, restructuring plan）
restructuring provision 事業再編引当金，事業再編に伴う引当金繰入れ

▸In the fourth quarter, we decided to establish a provision of $300 million for *restructuring*. 第4四半期に当社は，事業再編成のため3億ドルの引当金設定［3億ドルの事業再編引当金の設定］を決定しました。
▸*Restructuring* should strengthen our position as the industry's low-cost manufacturer. 事業再編によって，業界の低コスト・メーカーとしての当社の地位［経営基盤］は強化されるはずです。

restructuring plan 再建計画，再編計画，再生計画，再建策，再編案，リストラ計画（＝restructuring package, restructuring program）

▸The firm will ax 10,000 jobs worldwide and cut ¥200 billion in costs by the end of fiscal 2009 in a sweeping *restructuring plan*. 同社は，抜本的な再建策として，2009年度末までに全世界の人員10,000人の削減と2,000億円のコスト削減を図る。

results 成績，業績，決算，決算内容，実績，成果，結果，効果，影響，影響額，統計（⇒business results, earnings results, financial results）
annual results 年間成績，通期決算，年次決算（＝full year results）
company's results 会社の業績，会社の決算（＝corporate business results, corporate results）
consolidated results 連結業績，連結経営実績，連結経営成績，連結決算（＝group results）
corporate results 企業業績，決算
economic results 景気指標
gross results 経常収益
interim results 中間決算（＝first-half results, interim financial results, semi-annual results）
investment results 投資成績，投資実績，運用成績［実績］，投資の成果（＝investment performance）
net result 当期利益
payment by results 業績給，能率給
poor results 業績の落ち込み，業績低迷（＝stagnant results）
results announcement 決算発表
results for the year 当期業績，当年度の業績
results of business 営業成績，営業実績，業績（＝business results）
results of operating activities 経営成績
results of [from] operations 経営成績，営業成績，営業活動の成果，損益計算書
results season 決算期，決算シーズン，決算発表シーズン
successful results 好業績，好結果，上首尾

▸Of First Section-listed companies, 819 firms excluding financial institutions and brokerages have released their annual *results*. 東証1部上場企業のうち，金融機関と証券業を除く819社が年次決算の発表を終えた。
▸Other income-net depends mostly on our cash balance and the *results* and changes in our investments and joint ventures. 「その他の収益—純額」の大半は，当社の現金残高と当社の投資および合弁事業の成果と変更により生じています。
▸The company's business *results* for fiscal 2009 are expected to result in a massive loss. 同社の2010年3月期決算［2009年度］の業績は，大幅赤字［損失］が見込まれる。

resume 動 再開する，取り戻す，回復する，要約する

▸The bank *resumed* donations to political parties. 同行は，政党への献金を再開する予定だ。

retail 名 小売り，売価，個人投資家，小口投資家，個人向け取引，リテール
large-scale retail store 大型小売店，大規模小売店
major retail store operators 流通大手（⇒discount sales [sale]）
retail basis 売価基準
retail business 小売業，小売ビジネス
retail conglomerate competition 小売コングロマリット間競争
retail cost 小売原価
retail demand 小口需要，消費需要
retail distribution 小売流通
retail establishment 小売店舗，小売事業所

retail inventory method 売価還元法, 小売棚卸し法, 売価棚卸し法（＝retail inventory method of accounting, retail method）
retail investor 個人投資家
retail lending 消費者向け融資, 個人向け融資, 個人向けローン, 消費者向け貸付け
retail management 小売経営, 小売業管理
retail method 売価法, 売価基準法, 売価還元法
retail sales volume 小売売上数量 小売売上高, 小売販売高, 小売販売額
retail services 小売サービス, 小売業務, 個人向け取引業務, リテール業務
retail store 小売店舗
retail therapy ショッピング・セラピー（買い物をして憂うつな気分を治すという意味）
retail trade 小売業
retail trade area 小売商圏, 小売販売圏
▶The tie-up of Fukuta and Konaka will produce the third-largest firm in this sector of the menswear *retail* market. フタタとコナカが経営統合すると, 紳士服小売市場［業界］で第三位の会社が誕生する。

retail banking operations リテール銀行業務, 小売銀行業務, 小口取引銀行業務（＝retail banking, retail operations）
▶The bank has been relatively weak in *retail banking operations* dealing with individuals and small and medium-sized firms. 同行は, 個人や中小企業向けの小口取引銀行業務が比較的弱い。

retail industry 小売業, 小売業界, 流通業界
▶The tie-up negotiations with the firm are expected to lead to a large-scale reorganization of the *retail industry*. 同社との提携交渉は, 流通業界の大規模再編につながる見通し。

retail operations 個人向け営業
▶The firm has a competitive edge in *retail operations* thanks to its 110 outlets across the country. 同社の競争上の強みは, 全国110店の店舗を生かした個人向け営業［リテール部門］だ。

retail price 小売価格, 小売物価, 販売価格
  actual retail price 実売価格
  official retail price 公定小売価格
  retail price figure 小売物価指数（＝retail price index）
  retail price index 小売物価指数《略 RPI》
  retail price inflation 小売物価上昇率
  retail price structure 小売価格構造
▶Increased discounting and imports from China and other developing countries have helped compound the downward pressure on *retail prices*. 値引き競争の激化や中国その他の開発途上国からの輸入品の増加が, 小売価格押し下げ圧力として働いている。

retail sales 小売販売, 小売販売高, 小売売上高
▶The U.S Commerce Department reported that *retail sales* rose by 0.3 percent in January 2008 after having fallen 0.4 percent in December. 米商務省の報告によると, 2008年1月の小売売上高の伸び率は, 前月に0.4％減少したものの0.3％上昇した。

retailer 小売業, 小売企業, 小売業者, 小売商, 小売店, スーパー, リテーラー（⇒method）
  Big Retailer Law 大規模小売店舗法
  mass retailer 量販小売業, 量販店
  producer-retailer alliance 製販同盟
  retailer-owned brand プライベート・ブランド
▶The chain of large-scale *retailers* of home appliances finally became unable to procure funds. この家電量販店は, 最終的に資金調達ができなくなった［資金繰りに行き詰まってしまった］。
▶There is slow progress in economic improvement among nonmanufacturing businesses, largely as a result of sluggish sales at *retailers* due to the ongoing deflation. デフレの進行で主に小売業の売上が低迷しているため, 非製造業は景気回復の足取りが弱い。

retailing 名 小売り, 小売活動, 小売業, 販売, 流通
  nonstore retailing 無店舗販売
  retailing company 小売企業
  retailing competition 小売競争
  retailing management 小売業経営
  retailing sector 流通業界, 小売業界
  retailing strategy 小売戦略
  rural discount retailing 郊外型ディスカウント・ショップ
▶With the exception of its core businesses, including *retailing*, the firm will close and sell as soon as possible affiliated companies and other assets. 小売りなどの中核事業を除いて, 同社は関連会社やその他の資産をできるだけ早期に閉鎖・整理し, 売却する。

retain 動 維持する, 留保する, 保持する, 保有する, 確保する, つなぎとめる
  income retained in the business 企業内留保利益
  retain earnings 利益を留保する
  retain ownership 経営権を握る
  retained cash flow 手元キャッシュ・フロー

retained income 任意積立金, 留保利益, 留保利益金, 留保利益剰余金
retained profit 留保利益, 繰越し利益
retained surplus 留保利益, 留保利益剰余金
▶For the year to March 2009, the Company has *retained* its forecasts for operating profit of ¥900 billion and net profit of ¥550 billion. 当社は, 営業利益9,000億円, 税引き後利益5,500億円の2009年3月期の業績予想を変えていません。

retained earnings 剰余金, 利益剰余金, 留保利益, 社内留保利益金, 社内留保, 内部留保 (= earned surplus, retained income: 過去の利益の積立てで, 企業の税引き後利益から配当金や役員賞与金など社外流出分などを控除した残額をいう。イギリスではprofit and loss accountともいう。⇒ **capital reserve**)
legal retained earnings 利益準備金
retained earnings appropriated for bond 減債積立金
retained earnings appropriated for contingency 偶発損失準備金
▶The company plans to dig into its *retained earnings* to prevent its net balance from sinking into the red. 純収支残高が赤字に転落するのを防ぐため, 同社は内部留保を取り崩す方針だ。

retaliatory measures 報復措置
▶Elpida Memory Inc. applied to the government for *retaliatory measures* against exports of dynamic random access memory chips made by South Korean Hynix Semiconductor Inc. エルピーダメモリ (日本最大の半導体メーカー) は, 韓国のハイニックス社製DRAM (記憶保持動作が必要な随時書き込み読み出しメモリ) の輸出品に対する報復措置の適用を政府に申請した。

retaliatory tariffs 報復関税 (= punitive tariffs, tit-for-tat tariffs)
▶China's *retaliatory tariffs* on Japanese cars, cellular phones and air conditioners clearly ran counter to WTO rules. 日本の自動車, 携帯電話とエアコンに課した中国の報復関税は, 明らかにWTOルールに違反していた。

retention 名 保持, 保有, 保留, 留保, 維持, 保存, 保管, 記憶, 記憶力
capital retention 留保利益
retention bond 留保金保証 (= retention money bond)
retention fund 保留金
retention of earnings 利益の留保, 利益留保
retention of employees 従業員[社員]の離職防止, 社員の定着率
retention of title 所有権留保 (= title retention)
retention rate [ratio] 定着率, 内部留保率, 留保率, 継続率, 記憶把持率
▶It is necessary for firms to enhance their employee *retention* rate and to ensure that their staff are the main pillar of the company. 企業は, 社員の定着率を高め, 社員を会社の主柱に育てる必要がある。
▶The second copy is for your *retention*. もう一部は, 貴社の保管用です。

retire 動 〈株式を〉消却する, 〈株式を〉償還する, 〈債務[借入金]などを〉返済する, 〈工場などを〉除却する, 〈紙幣などを〉回収する, 撤退する, 引き下がる, 退職する, 退任する, 引退する (⇒**original cost**)
retire early 早期退職する
retire from the board 取締役を退任する
retire maturing CP 満期がきたCPを償還する
retire repurchased shares 買い戻した株式を消却する
retire [withdraw] from unprofitable operations 不採算事業から撤退する, 不採算事業を整理する (unprofitable operations = unprofitable businesses)
retired employees 退職従業員
retired life fund 退職終身基金
sell or retire plant 工場を売却もしくは除却する
▶This year, two long-serving directors are *retiring* from the board. 今年は, 長年にわたって当社の取締役を務めてきた取締役数名が退任します。

retiree 名 退職者, 定年退職者, 引退者, 年金受給者, 年金生活者 (⇒**retirement incentive program**)
cost of health care benefits for retirees 退職者に対する医療給付費用
cost of life insurance benefits for retirees 退職者に対する生命保険給付費用
Retiree Benefit Bankruptcy Act 退職者給付破産法
retiree benefits 退職者給付
retiree health benefits 退職者健康保険
retiree health care benefits 退職者健康管理給付, 退職者医療給付
▶For the years ended December 31, 2008 and 2007, the costs of *retiree* benefits amounted to $7.2 million and $5.7 million, respectively. 2007年および2008年12月31日に終了した事業年度の退職者への給付費用総額は, それぞれ720万ドルと570万ドルでした。

retirement 名 退職, 引退,〈株式の〉消却, 償還, 返済, 除却, 処分, 廃棄 (「除却」は, 耐用年数の到来や陳腐化などで使用に耐えられなくなった有形固定資産を, 処分して固定資産台帳から抹消すること)
  allowance for retirement and severance 退職給与引当金
  bond retirement 社債償還, 社債の買入れ消却 (=retirement of bond)
  mandatory retirement 定年退職
  probability of retirement 退職確率
  property retirement 有形固定資産の売却, 有形固定資産の廃棄
  rate of debt retirement 償還率
  regular retirement 正規退職, 自然減
  reserve for retirement of preferred stock 優先株式償還準備金
  retirement age 退職年齢
  retirement annuity 退職年金
  retirement benefit plan [scheme] 退職給与制度
  retirement benefits 退職給付, 退職給与 (⇒**service** 名)
  retirement bonus 退職一時金
  retirement of debt 負債の返済, 債務返済, 債務償還 (=debt retirement)
  retirement of fixed assets 固定資産の処分, 固定資産の除却
  retirement of shares 株式の消却, 株式の償還, 株式の買入れ消却 (=retirement of stocks, share retirement, stock retirement: 発行済み自己株式を取得して消滅させること)
  retirement plan reserves 退職給付引当金 (⇒**indemnity**)
  retirement system 除却法 (=retirement method, retiring method)
  self-employment retirement plan 自営業者退職金制度
  Social Security retirement benefits 社会保障退職給付
  voluntary retirement 希望退職
▸Seibu Department Stores reduced its 5,400 regular staff by 40 percent last year through regular *retirement* and the encouragement of early *retirement*. 西武百貨店は, 自然減[正規退職]と希望退職[早期退職の勧奨]で, 昨年1年で正社員5,400人を4割減らした。
▸The reconstruction plan includes the *retirement* of 50 percent of the firm's common shares. 経営再建には, 同社の普通株式の5割消却も含まれている。

retirement allowances 退職金, 退職給与, 退職慰労金, 退職給与引当金 (⇒**serve**)
▸The company will forgo paying *retirement* allowances to directors. 同社では, 役員の退職慰労金の支給を見送る方針だ。

retirement incentive program 退職勧奨制度
▸The retiree increase was a result of the *retirement incentive programs* offered in 2008. 退職者の増加は, 2008年度に実施した退職勧奨制度によるものです。

retract 動 撤回する, 取り消す

retraining 名 再教育, 再研修, 再訓練 (⇒**support** 名)
▸We are very active in the *retraining* of our employees. 当社は, 従業員の再教育を積極的に行っています。

retreat 名 退却, 撤収, 避難, 下落, 引退, 動 退く, 退却する, 撤収する,〈株価が〉下がる (⇒**sideline**)

retroactive 形 遡及力のある, 遡及する, 過去にさかのぼる (=retrospective)
  on a retroactive basis 過去に遡及して (⇒**reference**)
  retroactive adjustment 遡及修正, 遡及修正項目
  retroactive application 遡及適用, 遡及的適用 (=retroactive imposition, retrospective application)
▸The accounting change was made *retroactive* to January 1, 2005. 会計処理の変更は, 2005年1月1日に遡及して行いました。

retrospective application 遡及適用, 遡及的適用 (=retroactive application; ⇒**International Financial Reporting Standards**)

return 動 返す, 戻す, 返還する, 還元する,〈資本などを〉還流する,〈利益などを〉生む,〈収入などを〉申告する, 戻る, 復帰する, 転換する
  return to a rising trend 上昇基調に戻る
  return to break-even 収支とんとんに戻る, 赤字が解消する
  return to profit 黒字に転換する, 黒字回復する
  return to work 職場に復帰する
  returned purchase 仕入戻し, 仕入戻し品, 戻し品, 返送品
  returned sales 売上戻り, 戻り品
▸Roughly half of the earnings in 2008 were *returned* to the stockholders in dividends. 2008年度の利益の約半分は, 配当金として株主に還元されています。

return 名 利益, 利益率, 収益, 収益率, 利回り,

運用成績, 運用収益, 戻り益, 還元, 返却, 返品, 申告, 申告書, 報告書, 投票結果, 改行キー, リターン
accounting return on equity 株主資本利益率
added return 追加収益
after-tax return 税引き後収益率, 税引き後利益
asset return 資産収益率, 資産利回り
annual return 年次届出書, 年次報告書
blue return 青色申告 （＝blue form income tax return, blue form return）
cash return on investment 現金投資収益率
census returns 国勢調査結果
earn a return 利益を上げる, 利益率を上げる
expected return 期待収益, 予想収益, 期待収益率, 予想利益率
external rate of return 外部収益率
financial returns 配当金, 投資収益
horizon return 所有期間利回り （＝holding period return）
income tax return 所得税申告書, 所得税納入申告書, 法人税申告書
interim return 中間申告, 中間申告書
investment return 資本利益率, 投資収益率, 運用益 （＝return of investment, return on investment）
price returns 価格収益
rate of return on invested capital 投下資本利益率
return of profits to shareholders 株主への利益還元 （⇒review 動）
rerurn of the loan 借金の返済, ローンの返済
return on average equity 平均株主資本利益率
return on capital 資本利益率, 自己資本利益率, 資本の見返り, 資本運用利回り （⇒**average return on capital**）
return on insurance premium management 保険料運用収益 （⇒rally）
return on net assets employed 純資産利益率 《略 RONA》
return on net worth 株主資本利益率, 自己資本利益率
return on sales 売上高利益率, 純利益率 （純利益率＝純利益÷売上）
revised return 修正申告
sales return 売上戻り高, 売上戻り品
stock returns 株式総合利回り

▶The expected *return* on an investment can be estimated on the basis of its historical performance. 投資の期待収益率は, 過去の運用成績に基づいて予測することができる。
▶The rate of *returns* across the publishing industry has not entered the danger zone of 40 percent. 出版業界の書籍の返品率は, まだ危険水域の4割に達していない。
▶We are trying as hard as we can to improve the sales, efficiency and financial *returns* of the Corporation. 私どもは, 当社の売上, 効率性の向上・改善と増utilities全力投球しています。

return on assets 資産利益率, 総資産利益率 《略 ROA》 （＝return on capital employed）
▶*Return on assets* is obtained by dividing net income (minus preferred stock dividends) by average total assets. 総資産利益率(ROA)は, 純利益(優先株式配当金控除後)を平均総資産価額で割って[除して]求められます。

return on average shareholders' equity 平均普通株主持ち分利益率
▶The *return on average shareholders' equity* in 2008 was seven percent compared with 15 percent in 2007. 2008年度の平均普通株主持ち分利益率は, 前年度の15％に対して7％でした。

return on capital employed 資本利益率, 使用資本利益率 《略 ROCE》
▶*Return on capital employed* is calculated as income divided by average total assets less average noninterest-bearing current liabilities. 使用資本利益率は, 利益を平均総資産から平均無利息流動負債を控除した金額で割って[控除した金額で除して]算出されています。

return on equity 株主資本利益率, 自己資本利益率 《略 ROE》(資本金などをどれほど有効に使って利益を生んだかを示す経営指標)。⇒ROE)
▶*Return on equity* was 19% in 2008, compared with 21% in 2007. 2008年度の株主資本利益率[自己資本利益率]は, 前年度の21％に対して19％でした。

return on investment 投下資本利益率, 使用総資本利益率, 投資収益, 投資利益率, 投資収益率, 投資利回り, 運用利回り, 投資リターン, 投下資本利益率 《略 ROI》
▶We improved our *return on investment* in 2008. 2008年度は, 投下資本利益率も向上しました。

return on plan assets 年金資産運用益, 年金資産の長期収益率
▶We assumed a long-term rate of *return on plan assets* of 8.6% in 2008. 年金資産の長期収益率は, 2008年度は8.6％でした。

return on stockholders' [shareholders'] equity 株主資本利益率, 株主持ち分利益率
▶*Return on stockholders' equity* is calculated as Net income divided by average average equity

capital. 株主持ち分利益率は，当期純利益を平均株式資本で割って［平均株式資本で除して］算出します。

return to stockholders [shareholders]
株主還元, 株主の利益
▸We are mindful about *return to our stockholders*. 株主への還元［利益還元］については，絶えず念頭に置いています。

revaluation 名 再評価, 評価替え, 見直し, 平価切上げ
  asset revaluation 資産再評価, 資産評価替え（＝revaluation of assets）
  equity revaluation 持ち分評価替え, 株式評価替え
  investment revaluation 投資再評価
  investment revaluation reserve 投資再評価積立金
  loss from inventory revaluation 棚卸し評価損
  loss from securities revaluation 有価証券評価損
  revaluation of the dollar ドル高（＝dollar revaluation）
  revaluation reserve 再評価準備金, 再評価積立金
  stock revaluation 株式評価替え（＝equity revaluation）
▸Higher interest rates would increase the pressure for a *revaluation* of the Chinese yuan. 中国の利上げは，人民元の切上げ圧力を高めることになる。

revalue 動 再評価する, 〈平価を〉切り上げる

revamp 動 見直す, 立て直す, 刷新する, 改良する, 改造する, 改訂する, 修正する
▸We are forced to *revamp* our management system. 当社は，経営体制の見直しを迫られています。

reveal 動 発表する, 公表する, 示す, 開示する, 明らかにする
▸The company *revealed* a new medium-term business plan for fiscal 2008-2011. 同社は，2008-2011年度の新中期経営構想を発表した。
▸The company *revealed* the annual salaries of its four top executive officers at this year's general shareholders meeting. 同社は，今年の株主総会で代表取締役4人の年間報酬額を開示した。

revenue 名 収益, 営業収益, 売上, 売上高, 収入, 歳入
  収益とは➡商品の販売，サービスの提供，その他企業の営業活動から生じる現金または現金等価物（cash equivalents: 売掛金や受取手形などを含む）の流入額，投資から得た利子，配当ならびに固定資産の売却や交換に基づく利得，負債の減少額をいう。資本の払込みや借入金の受入れなどは，収益とはならない。なお，会計上「現金」は，銀行預金のほかに小切手，手形，郵便為替証書などを含むが，流動資産に含まれるcashは手元現金と銀行の要求払い預金を指す。
  capital revenue 資本的収入
  corporate revenue 企業収益
  dividend revenue 受取配当金
  financial revenue 財務収益, 金融収益
  geographic revenues 連結売上高
  incremental revenues 増分収益
  nonoperating revenue 営業外収益
  nonrecurring revenue 経常外利益
  other revenue (expenses) 営業外収益（費用）
  other revenues and gains 営業外収益および利得
  revenue from investment 投資収益
  revenue income 売上収入
  revenue shortfall 歳入不足, 歳入欠陥
  revenue standard 収益基準
  revenues and earnings 収益と利益［純利益］, 営業収益と利益［純利益］
  revenues and earnings losses 減収減益（＝losses in revenues and earnings）
  segment revenue セグメント収益
▸The increase in *revenues* in 2008 was mainly due to increased demand for business communications products in Europe. 2008年度の売上高の増加［2007年度の増収］は，主に欧州でのビジネス通信機器の需要拡大によるものです。

revenue base 収益基盤（＝revenue basis; ⇒enhancement）
▸The enhancement of the major banks' *revenue bases* is essential for the final disposal of bad loans. 不良債権の最終処理には，大手銀行の収益基盤の強化が欠かせない。

revenue growth 売上高［営業収益］の伸び, 収益の伸び, 増収（⇒introduction）
▸*Revenue growth* from 2006 to 2008 occurred across all product lines. 2006年から2008年まで3期連続の売上高の伸びは，全製品系列にわたっています。

revenue mix 売上構成
▸The shift in *revenue mix* to other services from higher-margin rentals led to a decline in the margin percentage in 2007. 2007年度は，高収益のレンタル事業からその他の事業に売上構成が変化したため，利益率が低下しました。

revenue source 収益源

▶Microsoft plans to make Net businesses a new *revenue source*.　マイクロソフトは，ネット事業を新たな収益源にする方針だ。

reversal 名　逆転，反転，どんでん返し，転換，破棄，取消し
　reversal auction　逆入札
　reversal of the transfer　復帰人事

reverse 動　振り戻す，戻し入れる，入れ替える，取り崩す，再修正する，再整理する，覆す，逆転させる，〈方向などを〉逆にする，〈判決などを〉破棄する，無効にする，取り消す

▶The Supreme Court *reversed* a high court decision.　最高裁は，東京高裁決定を破棄した。

▶The tax effects of timing differences originating in prior periods and *reversing* in the current period are determined at the applicable income tax rates reflected in the accounts as of the beginning of the current period.　過年度に発生し，当期に取り崩される期間差異の税効果は，当期首現在の勘定に反映されている当該所得税率で算定されます。

reverse 形　逆の，反対の，逆方向の，裏の，裏側の，裏面の
　reverse assets effect　逆資産効果
　reverse auction　逆オークション，リバース・オークション（買い手の購入希望価格に対して売り手が入札して，最も安い値段で入札した売り手が商品を販売するもの）
　reverse commuting　都市から郊外への逆方向通勤
　reverse distribution channel　逆流通チャネル
　reverse engineering　逆行分析，分解工学，逆分析工学，リバース・エンジニアリング（他社製品の分析・調査をとおして自社製品にその技術を導入すること）
　reverse imports　逆輸入品
　reverse leverage　逆レバレッジ（借入金による投資で，投資収益より借入金利息のほうが高い状態）
　reverse repo　リバース・レポ，リバース・レポ取引
　reverse split　株式併合，株式分割（＝reverse split of stocks, reverse stock split, share split-down）
　reverse takeover　逆買収（小企業による大企業の買収や非公開企業による上場企業の買収のこと）

▶The company is considering a *reverse* split of stocks by combining two shares into one.　同社は現在，2株を1株にまとめる株式併合を検討している。

review 動　査閲する，評価する，検討する，監査する，調査する，審査する，レビューする（監査が一般に公正妥当と認められる監査基準に従って実施されているかどうか，また所定の監査方針が遵守されているかどうかを確かめることを「査閲」という）

▶An increase in the number of foreign shareholders prompted the company to *review* the return of profits to shareholders.　外国人株主が増えているため，同社は株主への利益還元を見直した。

▶The audit committee reviews the corporation's annual consolidated financial statements and recommends their approval to the board of directors.　監査委員会は，当社の年次連結財務書類を査閲して，取締役会にその承認を求めます。

review 名　〈監査調書の〉査閲，〈監査技術としての〉閲覧，調査，審査，再調査，検討，見直し，再考，再審理，報告，報告書，評論，レビュー
　business review　営業概況
　chairman's review　会長報告書
　legal review　法律見解書
　limited review　限定監査
　management review　経営監査
　peer review　相互検査，専門家による相互審査，相互評価，相互批判，同僚評価
　rating review　格付け見直し
　review of financial statements　財務諸表［財務書類］のレビュー
　review of internal control　内部統制の調査
　review of operations　営業報告書

revise 動　修正する，改正する，改定する，改訂する，見直す，校正する，校閲する（⇒**business projection**）

▶Losses related to U.S. subprime mortgages forced Mizuho Financial Group Inc. to *revise* terms for merging Mizuho Securities and Shinko Securities.　米国のサブプライム・ローン（低所得者向け住宅融資）関連の損失で，みずほフィナンシャルグループ（FG）は，みずほ証券と新光証券の合併条件の修正を迫られた。

▶The company was forced to *revise* an original revitalization plan.　同社は，当初の再生計画の見直しを迫られた。

revise downward　下方修正する（＝downgrade, revise down, slash）

▶Other banks are likely forced to *revise* their earnings projections *downward* because of the accelerated disposal of bad loans, business deterioration of borrowers due to the lingering recession and further decline in stock prices.　不良債権処理の加速や長引く不況による融資先の業

績悪化，株安などの影響で，他行も業績予想の下方修正を迫られている。

revise upward 上方修正する （＝revise up, upgrade）
▸Standard & Poor's *revised upward* the outlook on its ratings on six major Japanese insurance companies against the backdrop of their improved financial profiles. スタンダード＆プアーズは，日本の大手保険会社6社の財務力見通し改善を背景に，6社の格付け見通しを上方修正した。

revision 名 修正, 改正, 改訂, 変更, 見直し
  downward revision 下方修正
  massive [large, substantial] upward revision 大幅な上方修正
  slight upward revision 小幅な上方修正
  upward revision 上方修正
▸Many expect losses from bad loan disposals to increase drastically, leading to an inevitable downward *revision* of banks' business performance. 大方の予想では，不良債権処理に伴う損失額は今後大幅に増え，銀行の業績の下方修正は避けられない状況だ。

revitalization 名 再生, 活性化, 再活性化, 健全化, 復興, 回復
  corporate revitalization 企業再生
  management revitalization plan 経営健全化計画
  revitalization firm 企業再生会社 （＝revitalizing firm）

revitalization of the economy 経済の活性化
▸These tax reforms are aimed at shifting capital from savings to investment, seen as vital in promoting the *revitalization of the economy*. これらの税制改革のねらいは，経済活性化を促すうえで必要とみられる「貯蓄から投資への資金移動」にある。

revitalization plan 再生計画, 再活性化案
▸The company was forced to revise an original *revitalization plan*. 同社は，当初の再生計画の見直しを迫られた。
▸The government demanded banks seeking public funds to submit management *revitalization plans*. 政府は，公的資金[資金注入]を受ける銀行に経営健全化計画の提出を求めた。

revitalize 動 回復させる, 再生する, 活性化する, 復興させる
▸Breaking this vicious circle could be the key to *revitalizing* the economy. この悪循環を断ち切ることが，景気浮揚へのカギになる。

▸Government efforts to help *revitalize* the nation's industrial sector are gathering momentum. 政府の産業・企業再生支援策の準備が，本格化している。

revival 名 再生, 事業再生, 再建, 復活, 回復, 再燃
  economic revival 景気回復, 経済再生
  industrial revival 産業再生
  revival in demand 需要の回復
  revival of inflation インフレ再燃
  revival of the financial system 金融再生 （＝financial revitalization）
▸Development of new products will be key to the company's *revival*. 新商品の開発が，同社再建のカギを握っている。

revival account 再生勘定
▸The bank announced a plan to introduce *revival accounts* to manage its ¥2.3 trillion nonperforming loans separately from the healthier loans. 同行は，2兆3,000億円の不良債権を正常債権とは別個に管理する「再生勘定」を導入する方針を発表した。

revival plan 再生計画, 事業再生計画, 再建計画
▸Under the *revival plan*, the firm intends to issue ¥30 billion worth of preferred shares to Sumitomo Mitsui Banking. この再生計画では，同社は，三井住友銀行を引受先として300億円の優先株式を発行する。

revive 動 再生する, 再建する, 立て直す, 再び活性化する, 〈景気などを〉刺激する, 回復する, 再燃する
▸The firm closed some plants as part of a strategy to *revive* its struggling operations. 同社は，不振の事業部門再建策の一環として，工場の一部を閉鎖した。

revolution 名 革命
  agricultural revolution 農業革命
  consumption revolution 消費革命
  digital revolution デジタル革命
  distribution revolution 流通革命
  financial revolution 金融革命
  genetic revolution 遺伝子革命
  green revolution 緑の革命
  information revolution 情報革命
  periphery revolution 周辺革命
▸The information and telecommunications *revolution* has enabled the instantaneous transmission of information to every corner of the world. 情報通信革命は，情報をリアルタイムで[即時に]世界中に伝えることを可能にした。

revolving 名形 回転, リボルビング
　revolving commitment 回転契約
　revolving fund 回転資金
　revolving letter of credit 回転信用状 (＝revolving L/C)
　revolving line of credit 回転信用供与枠, 回転信用貸出枠
　revolving loan 回転貸付け, 回転融資
　revolving system 回転信用方式
▸The Company and its finance subsidiary entered into one- and five-year *revolving* domestic credit agreements totaling $1.5 billion with a group of banks. 当社と当社の金融子会社は, 銀行グループと総額15億ドルの1年および5年満期の国内回転信用契約を締結しました。

revolving credit 回転信用
　revolving credit agreement 回転信用契約
　revolving credit facility 回転信用供与枠, 回転融資枠, 回転信用ファシリティ
▸These *revolving credit* facilities were unused at December 31, 2008. これらの回転融資枠は, 2008年12月31日現在, 使用されていません。

revolving repayment 回転返済, リボルビング方式の返済
　revolving repayment contract 回転返済契約, リボルビング方式の返済契約 (契約で定めた限度額の範囲内で何回でも借入れと返済を繰り返せる仕組みで, 包括契約方式とも呼ばれる)
　revolving repayment method 回転返済方式, リボルビング返済方式, リボルビング方式
▸A *revolving repayment* method allows consumers to borrow money a number of times under a certain credit line while repaying earlier loans. リボルビング方式だと, 消費者は前の借入金を返済している間, 特定の融資枠に基づいて何回でも金を借り入れることができる。

reward 名 報酬, 報償, 報奨金, 褒賞金, 謝礼, 対価, 成果, リターン
　financial rewards 金銭的な報酬
　reward to shareholders [stockholders] 株主の利益, 株主への利益還元, 株主還元
　rewards of investment 投資の成果
　rewards system 報奨金制度
　risk and reward リスクとリターン
▸Gain from stock options is a *reward* for dedicated work by an employee. ストック・オプション(自社株購入権)の利益は, 従業員が熱心に勤務したことへの対価である。

rig 名 詐欺, 市場操作, 相場操作

right 名 権利, 権限, 所有権, 新株引受権, 正当,公正 (⇒management right, stock appreciation right)
　business right 営業権
　dividend right 配当請求権
　minority stockholders' right 少数株主権
　operating right 営業権
　pension right 年金権
　right of beneficiary 受益権
　right of claim 請求権
　right of minority shareholders 少数株主権
　right to benefits 受給権
　rights issue 株主割当て発行, 株主割当て発行増資
　rights offering 株主割当て, 株主割当て発行, 株主割当て発行増資 (新株発行の際, 一定の割合で株主に優先的に新株を引き受ける権利を与えることをいう)
　security right 担保権
　shareholders' right 株主権 (＝stockholders' right)
　stock acquisition right 新株予約権
　stock right 新株引受権, 株式引受権, 株式買受権 (＝subscription right)
　stockholder rights plan 株主権利制度
▸Corporations have been limiting shareholders' *right* to express opinions at shareholders' meetings. 企業は, 株主総会での株主の発言権を抑えてきた。
▸During 2008, various holders of these zero coupon notes exercised conversion *rights* for approximately 614,000 notes. 2008年度に当社は, このゼロ・クーポン債所有者から約61万4,000の債券について転換権が行使されました。

right of indemnity 求償権
▸A nonlife insurer has used its *right of indemnity* concerning the series of faults in MMC-made vehicles. 一連の三菱製自動車の欠陥問題に関して, 損保会社が求償権を行使した。

rightsize 形 〈人員を〉適正規模にする, 人員整理する

ring 名 買占め同盟, 立会場, 取引, 立会い

ripple effect 波及効果
▸Housing starts have a tremendous *ripple effect* on the overall economy. 住宅着工件数は, 景気全体への波及効果が大きい。

rise 動 増加する, 拡大する, 伸びる, 上昇する, 高まる
▸Against the backdrop of the *rising* prices of crude oil, prices of raw materials are likely to continue *rising*. 原油高を背景に[原油高で], 原

材料価格の上昇は続きそうだ。
- Net income *rose* to ¥143 billion, or ¥78 per share, in the three months ended June.　4－6月期は、純利益［税引き後利益］が1,430億円（1株当たり78円）に増加した。
- The company's sales in the first quarter *rose* 12.6 percent to ¥693.7 billion.　同社の第1四半期の売上高は、（前年同期比）12.6％増の6,937億円だった。

rise 名　増加, 拡大, 伸び, 上昇, 高騰, 向上
　rise in corporate profits　企業収益の増加
　rise in deficit　赤字の増加
　rise in oil prices　原油価格の高騰
　rise in the yen　円高
- We recorded a strong 12 percent *rise* in the third-quarter net income.　当社の第3四半期の純利益は、12％増と高水準の伸びを記録しました。

rise in the yen's value　円高
- The *rise* in the yen's value is accelerating.　円高が加速している。

rising cost　コストの上昇
- Pulp and paper makers have a hard time passing the *rising cost* of their materials onto customers.　製紙業界は、原材料コスト上昇の価格転嫁に難航している［製紙業は、原材料のコスト増を顧客に転嫁するのが難しくなっている］。

rising interest rate　金利の上昇
- *Rising* long-term *interest rates* will lead directly to higher interest payments for government bonds.　長期金利の上昇は、国債の利払い費増に直結する。

rising sea level　海面上昇
- The most easily measured effect of *rising sea level* is the inundation of coastal areas.　最も簡単に測定できる海面上昇の影響は、海岸地域の冠水である。

risk 名　危険, 危険性, 危険負担,〈価格などの〉値下がり確率, リスク
　avoid prepayment risk　期限前償還リスクを避ける
　balance sheet risk　財務リスク
　bear the risk　リスクを負う（＝assume the risk）
　capital risk　元本リスク, キャピタル・リスク
　collection risk　回収リスク
　credit risk　信用リスク
　diversify investment risks　投資リスクを分散する
　diversification of risks　リスク分散（＝diversity of risks）
　exchange risk　為替リスク（＝currency risk, foreign exchange risk）
　failure risk　倒産リスク
　financial risk　金融リスク, 財務リスク, 財務上［金融上］のリスク
　financing risk　資金調達リスク
　hedge risks　リスクを相殺する, リスクをヘッジする
　high-risk high-return　ハイリスク・ハイリターン, リスクを回避［防止, 軽減］する（危険性の高い金融資産ほどその高い運用益が期待できること）
　hostile acquisition risk　敵対的買収リスク
　lay off financial risk　金融リスク［財務リスク］を回避する, 金融リスクを低減する, 金融リスクをヘッジする
　liquidity risk　流動性リスク
　manage the risk exposure　リスクを管理する（＝control the risk exposure）
　management risk　経営リスク, 経営者リスク, マネジメント・リスク（＝managerial risk）
　rating risk　格付けリスク
　reduce the default risk　不履行リスクを軽減する［低減する, 低下させる, 抑える］
　risk capital　危険資本, 危険負担資本, 危険投下資本, 危険資本投資（＝venture capital）
　risk exposure　リスク, リスク・エクスポージャー
　risk hedge　リスクの防止・軽減, 危険［リスク］回避手段, 損失リスクからの防衛手段［防衛策］, リスク・ヘッジ
　risk management　危機管理, リスク管理, リスク・マネジメント
　risk reduction　リスクの軽減
　risks and rewards approach　リスク経済価値アプローチ
- Management believes that these forward contracts should not subject the Company to undue *risk* to foreign exchange movements.　これらの先物取引契約で当社が過大な為替相場の変動リスクを負うことはない、と経営陣は考えております。
- We can hedge exchange *risk* through forward markets.　為替予約で、為替リスクをヘッジすることができる。

rival 名　競争相手, 競争相手国, 同業他社, 好敵手, ライバル
　catch up with a rival　ライバルに追いつく
　compete with one's rivals　同業他社と競争する
　trading rivals　貿易競争相手国
- The company wants to acquire a controlling

stake in the smaller *rival* as part of its efforts to prepare for intensifying international competition.　同社は，激化する国際競争への対応策の一つとして，この中小ライバル企業の経営支配権の取得を目指している。

rivalry 名　競争，拮抗
RMBS　住宅ローン担保証券，住宅ローン債権担保証券（residential mortgage-backed securities の略）
ROA　総資産利益率，総資本利益率（当期利益を総資本で割った比率．⇒return on assets）
road map　ロード・マップ，行程表，道路地図，案内役
roadshow 動　投資家説明会を行う，投資家向け説明会を行う
▶The firm will *roadshow* for the bond issue in Japan.　同社は，日本での債券発行［社債発行］の投資家説明会を行う。
roadshow 名　投資家説明会，投資家向け説明会，募集説明会，巡回説明会，巡回キャンペーン，ロードショー（＝road show: 証券発行会社の経営者と引受業者の担当者が，機関投資家や有力な個人投資家（アナリストやファンド・マネージャーなど）を対象にして行う証券購入のメリットに関する説明会．一般に，発行会社の財務状況や将来の収益見通しなどを説明する．⇒investor relations, IR）
roadside land price　路線価（＝price of land facing main streets）
▶This *roadside* land price is being used by tax authorities to assess inheritance, gift and landholding taxes for 2008.　この路線価は，2008年の相続税や贈与税，土地保有税の評価基準として税務当局が使用している。
robot 名　ロボット，自動装置
　autonomous mobile robot　自律移動ロボット
　biped robot　歩行ロボット
　direct drive robot　ダイレクト・ドライブ・ロボット，DDロボット
　fuzzy robot　ファジー・ロボット
　guide dog robot　盲導犬ロボット
　human care robot　介護ロボット
　humanoid robot　2足歩行ロボット
　industrial robot　産業ロボット，産業用ロボット
　intelligent robot　知能ロボット
　micro robot　マイクロ・ロボット（＝microrobot）
　numerical control robot　NCロボット
　personal robot　パーソナル・ロボット
　pet robot　ペット・ロボット
　robot-operated factory　ロボット制御の工場
　robot with the mission of mine　地雷撤去ロボ
　self-recovery robot　自己修復ロボット
　surgical robot　手術ロボット，手術支援ロボット
　underwater robot　潜水ロボット，潜水ロボ
　vacuum cleaner robot　掃除ロボット
　welfare robot　福祉ロボット
▶This *robot* "guide dog" is able to recognize obstacles on roads as well as traffic and pedestrian signals through a video camera and a sound sensor.　この「盲導犬」ロボットは，ビデオ・カメラとサウンド・センサーにより，路上の障害物や交通信号等，横断歩道の信号などを認識できる。
robotic rover　無人探査車
robotics 名　ロボット技術，ロボット工学，ロボット
▶*Robotics* is used for delivery of mail and office supplies in this campus.　この事業施設では，郵便物や事務用品の取扱にロボットを使っています。
robotization 名　無人化，ロボット化，自動化，ロボットの導入
▶The company uses automation and *robotization* in factories to reduce costs within Japan.　同社は，国内コストを削減するため，工場での自動化と無人化を進めている。
robust 形　好調な，活発な，活況の，目覚しい，大幅な，著しい，底堅い
　robust earnings　好業績，業績好調（＝robust performance, robust results）
　robust economy　経済の活況，景気好調，底堅い景気
　robust growth　大幅な伸び
　robust sales　販売好調，好調な販売
▶*Robust* sales in overseas markets, including North America, contributed to the growth in profits and sales.　北米など海外市場での販売好調が，増収増益［利益と売上高の増加］の要因だ。
robust performance　好業績，好調な業績，業績好調（＝robust earnings）
▶The company traced the overall sales surge to *robust performances* at new subsidiaries.　同社は，総売上高急増の主因として新子会社の業績好調を挙げた。
rock bottom　最低，最低レベル，どん底，大底
▶Japan's economy has risen slightly above rock bottom.　日本経済は，大底圏からかろうじて浮び上がった。
rock-bottom 形　最低の，最低レベルの，どん底の，大底の
　rock-bottom interest rate　超低金利（＝extremely low interest rate）

rock-bottom price 底値

rocket 名 ロケット
- **booster rocket** 打上げロケット, 補助ロケット, 補助推進装置
- **liquid-fuel rocket** 液体燃料ロケット
- **rocket carrying a state-of-the-art solar observation satellite** 最新技術の太陽観測衛星を搭載したロケット
- **rocket warhead** ロケットの弾頭
- **solid-fuel rocket** 固体燃料ロケット
- **supply rocket** 補給機
- **the third H-2A rocket** H2Aロケット3号機
  ▶The new H-2A *rocket* will be able to place about 16 tons of materials at the altitude at which the ISS is orbiting. 新型H-2Aは, 地球軌道を周回している国際宇宙ステーション(ISS)の高度に約16トンの物資を打ち上げることができる。

ROE 株主資本利益率, 自己資本利益率, 持ち分資本利益率, 株式投資収益率 (**return on equity**, **return on owners' equity**の略。株主資本利益率(自己資本利益率)＝純利益(net income)÷純資産(owners' equity)。⇒**return on equity**)
  ▶Return on equity (*ROE*) is a key gauge of a company's stock investment efficiency. 株主資本利益率(ROE)は, 企業の株式投資効率を示す重要な経営指標だ。

ROI 投下資本利益率, 使用資本利益率, 投資利益率, 資本利益率 (⇒**return on investment**)

role model 手本, 理想像, 理想の姿, 雛型, 模範生, 優等生
  ▶The FTA with Mexico can serve as a *role model* for Japan's future FTAs with countries such as Korea, Thailand and the Philippines. メキシコとの自由貿易協定は, 韓国, タイ, フィリピンなどとの日本の今後の自由貿易協定のひな型[手本]にもなり得る。

roll off the assembly line (完成して)組立ラインを離れる, 流れ作業で完成する, 生産第1号が工場出荷される, 生産が開始される, 生産がスタートする
  ▶The first Kentucky-made Camry Hybrid of Toyota *rolled off the assembly line*. トヨタのケンタッキー州の工場(ジョージタウン工場)で, 米国初の「カムリ・ハイブリッド」車生産がスタートした。

roll out 大量生産する, 量産する, 生産する, 発表する, 公表する, 初公開する, 発売する
  ▶Microsoft *rolled out* an external high-definition DVD player for its Xbox 360 in an effort to match the PlayStation3. マイクロソフトは, 「プレイステーション(PS) 3」(ソニーの次世代ゲーム機)への対抗策として, 同社の「Xbox360」用のHD(高品位)DVDドライブを発売した。

roll over 繰り越す, 借り換える, 乗り換える, 書き換える (＝carry over)

rollback strategy 巻き返し戦略

rollout 名 大量生産, 量産, 生産, 発表, 初公開, 発売, 新製品の紹介, 〈事業などの〉展開
  ▶The chain is awaiting the opportunity for a full-scale *rollout* of the new business by opening a pilot store. 同チェーン店では, 実験店を出して, 新事業の本格展開の機会をうかがっている。

rollover 名 更新, 更改, 満期書替え, 資金の回転調達, 借りつなぎ, 借換え, 支払い繰延べ, ロールオーバー
- **debt rollover** 債務返済の繰延べ, 債務再構成, 債務の特別条件変更 (＝refinancing debt)
- **lease rollover** リース契約更新, 賃貸契約更新
- **rollover lending** ころがし貸付け
- **rollover loan** 借換え融資
- **rollover of an existing debt** 既存の債務の借換え, 借換え
- **rollover of liabilities** 負債の借換え

RONA 純資産利益率 (**Return On Net Assets employed**の略)
- **RONA awards** RONA報奨金, 純資産利益率報奨金
- **RONA incentive program** 純資産利益率報奨金制度
  ▶The *RONA* Incentive Program is available to eligible employees who are not participating in the Company Executive Incentive Plan. 純資産利益率報奨金制度は, 会社幹部報奨金制度に参加していない有資格従業員が利用できます。

rotate 動 〈人を〉交替させる, 交替で勤務させる

rotation 名 転換, 回転, 輪番, 交替, 循環, ローテーション
- **by rotation** 交代で, 輪番で
- **crop rotation** 輪作
- **job rotation** 配置転換, 職務転換, ジョブ・ローテーション
- **rotation of capital** 資本の回転
- **rotation system** 輪番制 (＝rotational system)

round-the-clock service 24時間営業

route 名 配達路, 販売路, 路線, 航路

routine 名 日常業務, 日課, 慣例

royalty 名 ロイヤルティ, 〈著作権・特許権・鉱区などの〉使用料, 工業権使用料, 〈権利の〉実施料, 許諾料, 採掘料, 印税
- **maximum royalty** 最高実施料

minimum royalty 最低ロイヤルティ
royalties revenue 使用料収益, 受取使用料
royalty cost 支払い使用料, 使用料原価
royalty fees on recorders レコーダーの補償金 [著作権使用料]
royalty income ロイヤルティ収入
royalty of patent rights 特許権使用料 (= patent right royalty)
royalty payment ロイヤルティの支払い, ロイヤルティの支払い金
running royalty 継続的使用料, 継続的実施料, ランニング・ロイヤルティ

▶For financial statement reporting, the *royalties* are recognized as income in the period earned. 財務書類上[財務諸表上], ロイヤルティは, それを稼得した期の利益として認識される。

▶Sharp Corp. revised its rewards system for inventors, allowing retired employees to receive *royalties*. シャープは, 発明者に対する報奨金制度を改定して, 退職者もロイヤルティを受け取ることができるようになった。

RPI 小売物価指数 (retail price index の略)
RPM 再販売価格維持 (retail price maintenance の略)

Rubicon 名 ルビコン川
　cross [pass] the Rubicon 背水の陣を敷く, 重大な決意をする, 断固たる手段をとる, (後退を許されない)思い切った処置をとる
　psychological Rubicon 心理的な壁

rule 名 規則, 規定, 規約, 通則, 法, 法規, 原則, 慣例, 通則, 支配, 〈裁判所の〉裁定[命令], 基準, 規準, ルール
　capital adequacy rule 自己資本規制, 自己資本比率規制
　client money rules 顧客資金規則, 顧客資金ルール
　compliance rules 法令・規則の遵守規則
　conduct of business rule 業務遂行基準
　cost or market rule 低価基準
　exclusionary rules 排他的規則
　home country rules 原籍国のルール
　host country rules 営業国のルール
　house rules 社内取扱い規則
　investor protection rules 投資家保護規則
　listing rules 上場基準, 上場規則, 上場要件
　net capital rule 自己資本規制比率
　one-share/one-vote rule 1株=1議決権ルール
　proxy rule 委任状規則
　Rule 415 shelf registration SEC規則415に基づく一括登録
　rule of fair practice 公正慣習遵守の原則
　rules of conduct 行為規則, 紀律規則
　trade rules 貿易規則
　work rules 業務規定
　working rules 就業規則, 準則

▶According to the NYSE's new *rules*, corporate boards must be composed of a majority of independent directors. ニューヨーク証券取引所(NYSE)の新上場基準によると, 企業(上場企業)の取締役の過半数は社外取締役にしなければならない。

▶China is breaking trade *rules* by taxing imports of auto parts at the same rate as foreign-made finished cars. 中国は, 輸入自動車部品に外国製完成車と同じ税率で課税して, 貿易規則に違反している。

ruling 名 決定, 判断, 判決, 判定, 裁定, 回答, 通達 (⇒antidumping probe)

▶When Washington refuses to comply with the WTO's *ruling*, the EU will impose retaliatory tariffs on U.S. products. 米国が世界貿易機関(WTO)の決定に従わなかった場合, 欧州連合(EU)は米国製品に報復関税を発動する方針だ。

run 他動 経営する, 指揮する, 管理する, 運営する, 運営する, 提供する, 操作する, 動かす, 実行する, 行う, 掲載する, 載せる, 自動 …の状態になる, 〈契約などが〉有効である, 動く, 作動する, 稼働する, 進行する, 進む, 行われる, 上演される

▶With the collapse of the economic bubble in the early 1990s, many corporate managers had to devote themselves to *running* their own companies. 1990年代はじめのバブル崩壊とともに, 企業経営者の多くは自社の経営に専念せざるをえなくなった。

run 名 〈銀行などに対する〉取付け, 取付け騒ぎ, 〈証券価格の〉急上昇, 盛んな売行き, 注文殺到, 大量需要, 情勢, 趨勢, 成り行き, 流れ, 市場の気配, 気配値 (「取付け」は, 経営破綻した銀行などに預金払戻しの請求者が殺到することをいう)
　broker's run ブローカーの気配値
　off-the-run issue 周辺銘柄
　on-the-run curve 新発債の利回り曲線
　on-the-run issue 指標銘柄
　run of the market 市場の気配, 市場の成り行き, 市況の情勢
　run on a bank 銀行の取付け騒ぎ, 銀行に対する取付け (=bank run)
　run on the dollar ドルに対する大量需要

▶Since total deposits are currently guaranteed, there are few fears of *runs* on banks, even if

they face failure. 預金は現在，全額保証されているので，銀行が破綻しても，銀行の預金払戻しの取付け騒ぎが起きる心配は少ない。
▸There has been a *run* on the dollar today. 今日は，ドル売りが殺到した。

running 形 連続している，連続する，絶え間のない，運転中の，現在の
　running average method 移動平均法（＝moving average method）
　running bill 未決済手形
　running cost 運転費，運転コスト，運営費，操業費，経営費，営業経費，ランニング・コスト
　running expense 操業費，経常費
　running price 時価，市価
　running stock 適正在庫，正常在庫，運転在庫，ランニング・ストック
▸Group sales also hit a record high for the fourth year *running*. 連結売上高も，4年連続，過去最高となった。
▸The total *running* costs of Shinginko Tokyo bank were equivalent to nearly 40 percent of the ¥126 billion in its accumulated losses. 新銀行東京の営業経費（物件費や人件費）が，同行の累積損失1,260億円の約4割に上った。

S

S&L 米貯蓄貸付け組合（Savings and Loan Associationの略）
S&P 500 S&P500総合指数, スタンダード＆プアーズ総合500種株価指数（Standard&Poor's 500の略。ダウ平均（ダウ工業株30種）とともに, 米株式市場の動向を反映する標準的な経済指標）
S.A. [SA] スペインの株式会社（sociedad anónimaの略）, イタリアの株式会社（società anònimaの略）, フランスの株式会社（société anonymeの略）
▸Mittal Steel Co. has acquired half of the shares of Arcelor *SA*. 鉄鋼世界最大手のミッタル・スチールが,（同世界2位の）アルセロールの株式の半数を取得した。
sack 名 解雇, 免職
saddled with …を抱えて, …を背負って, …で手いっぱい
▸The firm went bankrupt *saddled with* a ¥300 billion debt in June 2008. 同社は, 3,000億円の負債を抱えて2008年6月に破産した。
safe 形 安全な, 信頼できる
safe harbor 安全港, 避難港, 避難場所, セーフ・ハーバー
　safe harbor leasing セーフ・ハーバー・リース
　safe harbor rule 安全条項（規則や法律に抵触しないためのガイドライン）, 避難条項, 安全港規則, 安全港ルール, セーフ・ハーバー・ルール（「セーフ・ハーバー・ルール」は, 会社が自社株を買い戻すときの規則を定めた米証券取引委員会（SEC）規則10-bの通称）
safe haven 安全投資先, 資金避難先
safeguard 名 緊急輸入制限, 緊急輸入制限措置, セーフガード措置, 予防手段, 保護手段, 安全装置, 保障条項, 保障規約, セーフガード
　a safeguard against hostile takeovers 敵対的買収の防衛策
　a safeguard measure to raise tariffs 関税引上げのためのセーフガード措置
　corporate safeguards 企業防衛策
　impose safeguard on …に緊急輸入制限を課す
　resort to safeguard measures セーフガード措置を発動する
　safeguard clause 緊急輸入制限条項, 緊急避難条項, 例外条項
　safeguard tariffs 緊急輸入制限のための関税, セーフガード関税
▸Each member nation of the WTO may resort to *safeguard* measures if it has been determined that a rapid growth in imports is seriously affecting its domestic industries. WTO（世界貿易機関）加盟各国は, 輸入製品の急増で国内産業に重大な影響が出ていると判断された場合に, セーフガード措置を発動することができる。
safety 名 安全, 安定, 安全性, 安全装置
　financial safety 財政安定
　food safety 食の安全, 食品の安全性
　industrial safety 産業安全
　margin of safety 安全余裕率, 安全余裕度, 安全比率, MS比率
　product safety 製品の安全, 製品の安全性
　public safety 公安, 公共の安全, 治安
　safety catch 安全装置
　safety control 安全管理
　safety criteria 安全基準
　safety mark 安全基準合格マーク, Sマーク
　safety net 安全網, 安全策, 安全装置, 救済, 救済

策, 社会保障, 安全ネット, セーフティ・ネット
safety standards 安全基準
safety stock 安全在庫, 安全在庫量
the safety of U.S. beef 米国産牛肉の安全性
the safety valve effect of import 輸入の安全弁効果
▸*Safety* and disaster prevention are the absolute conditions for a company's survival. 安全と防災は, 企業存続のための絶対条件だ。

sag 動 下落する, 低下する, 落ち込む, 沈下する
sagging economy 景気低迷, 景気鈍化, 下降景気
sagging profits 利益の低下, 利益の低迷, 利益の落ち込み
▸The Bank of Japan's capital adequacy ratio *sagged* to 7.33 percent as of March 31, 2004. 日銀の自己資本比率は, 2004年3月31日時点で7.33%に低下した。

salad bowl サラダ・ボウル (多民族国家アメリカの別称)

salaried employee 月給制従業員 (＝salaried worker)
▸GM's UAW members now pay 7 percent of their health care costs, while the company's *salaried employees* pay 27 percent. GMの全米自動車労組(UAW)組合員は現在, 医療費の7%を負担しているのに対して, 同社の月給制従業員は27%負担している。

salaried worker サラリーマン

salary 名 給与, 給料, 月給, 俸給, 報酬
annual salaries of a company's executives 企業役員の年間報酬額
annual salary system 年俸制
bonus and salary 賞与・給与
executive salaries 役員報酬
salaries and allowances 給料手当
salaries and salary related expenses 給料および給料関連費用
salaries and wages 給料賃金, 給与・賃金 (⇒ wage)
salaries expense 給料, 給与
salaries payable 未払い給与
salary day 給料日
salary income 給与所得
salary payment 給与振込み, 給与支払い
salary plan 固定給制
salary projection 給与計画
salary roll 給与簿
salary structure 給与体系 (＝salary system)
salary system 給与体系
salespeople salaries 販売員給与

▸*Salaries* for the managerial employees can go up or down in accordance with each employee's performance and contribution to the company. 管理職の給与は, 各社員の能力[成果]と会社貢献度に応じて上下する可能性がある。
▸The firm's shareholders submitted proposals to disclose individual executive *salaries* at their general shareholders meetings. 同社の株主から は, 株主総会で役員報酬の個別開示を求める案が出された。

salary disparity 給与格差
▸The *salary disparity* between managers and workers is widening. 経営側と労働側の給与格差は, 広がりつつある。

salary reduction 減俸
▸The company will soon announce *salary reductions* for its president and chairman after a series of recalls conducted by the company. 同社が行った一連のリコール(回収・無償交換)を受けて, 同社は近く社長と会長の減俸を発表する。

sale 名 販売, 売買, 売却, 〈証券などの〉発行, セール
approval sale 試用販売
auction sale 競売
bulk sale 一括売却[販売], 全量販売[売買], 包括譲渡, 事業用資産包括譲渡 (＝bulk transfer)
credit sale クレジット販売
executive salaries 役員報酬
funds gained from the sale of shares 株式売却で調達した資金, 株式発行で調達した資金
gain on sale of bonds 社債売却益
offer for sale 売出発行, 間接発行
profits from the sale of businesses 営業譲渡益
public sale 公売
sale and leaseback transaction 売却後借戻し取引, セール・リースバック取引, セール・アンド・リースバック取引 (＝sale-leaseback transaction)
sale as it is 現状のままの売買
sale by sample 見本売買
sale of a business ビジネスの取引
sale of bonds 社債発行
sale of commercial paper コマーシャル・ペーパーの発行
sale on commission 委託販売
sale value 販売価格, 売却価額, 売却価値, 売上高
share sale 株式発行
▸The planned *sale* of GM's stake in Suzuki Motor Corp. is believed to be part of GM's restruc-

turing efforts. GMが保有するスズキ株の売却計画は，GMの経営再建策の一環と見られる。

sale and purchase 売買
▶The closing of the *sale and purchase* of the Shares took place at the offices of ABCD Corp. on June 10, 2008. 本株式の売買取引の実行［本株式のクロージング］は，2008年6月10日にABCDコーポレーションの事務所で行われた。

sales 名 売上, 売上高, 取引高,〈航空会社などの〉営業利益, 販売, 売買, 売却, 商ло, セールス（⇒ consolidated sales, group sales）
bogus sales 架空の売上, 虚偽の売上
business sales 企業売上高, 事業売却
cost of sales 売上原価（＝cost of goods sold）
credit sales 掛売り, 信用販売, 掛売高, 掛売上高
foreign sales 海外販売, 海外売上高, 国外売上高
gross sales 総売上高
installment sales 割賦販売, 割賦売上高, 延べ払い
intercompany sales 内部取引高
property sales 資産の売却
sales activities 販売活動
sales administrative expense 販売管理費
sales and administrative expense 販売費および一般管理費, 販売費・一般管理費
sales and earnings gains 増収増益
sales base 営業拠点, 販売拠点
sales cost 販売費, 販売原価, 売上原価
sales department 営業部門
sales forecast 売上高予想, 売上高の見通し, 販売見通し
sales mix 売上品目構成, 商品構成
sales profit ratio 売上利益率
sales through the Internet ネット販売, インターネット販売
stock sales 株式売却, 株式の売買, 株式譲渡
unscrupulous sales 悪徳商法（＝unscrupulous business）
Web sales ネット販売, ホームページ販売
▶NEC Corp.'s *sales* of semiconductors and mobile phones have been sluggish. NECの半導体や携帯電話の販売は，低迷していいる。
▶*Sales* and earnings again set record, with all three our major business segments contributing to the continuing growth. 売上高と純利益は，当社の主力3事業部門が成長の持続に貢献し，過去最高を更新しました。
▶*Sales* of stock by our subsidiaries produced $45 million gain in 2008. 当社の子会社による株式の売出しで，2008年度は4,500万ドルの利益が生じました。

sales efforts 販売努力, 営業面の努力
▶Toyota's operating profit was pushed up mainly due to *sales efforts* and cost-reduction efforts in its production lines. トヨタの営業利益を押し上げた主な要因は，販売努力［営業面の努力］と生産ラインのコスト削減［従業員による生産コスト削減］だ。

sales network 販売網
▶Aoki Holdings Inc. was forced to revise its plan to establish a nationwide *sales network* by taking Futata under its umbrella. AOKIホールディングス（アオキ）は，フタタを傘下に収めて全国販売網を確立する計画の見直しを迫られた。

sales operations 営業, 営業活動, 営業部門
▶The firm plans to spin off its domestic *sales operations*. 同社は，国内営業部門の分社化を計画している。

sales promotion 販売促進, 販促, セールス・プロモーション
▶All cell phone service providers spend hefty sums on *sales promotions* to bring in new subscribers. 携帯電話会社はいずれも，新規加入者の獲得のため，多額の販売促進費を投入している。

sales revenue 売上高, 売上収益, 総売上高, 販売収入, 販売収益（⇒operating revenue）
▶The firm's *sales revenue* for the first quarter totaled ¥4.51 trillion, an increase of 10.2 percent compared with the same period the previous year. 同社の第1四半期の売上高は，前年同期比10.2％増の4兆5,100億円となった。

sales-type lease 販売型リース, 販売金融リース
▶We lease our products to customers under *sales-type* leases. 当社は，自社製品を販売型リースで顧客にリースしています。

salesman 名 販売員, 販売係, 店員, 売り子, 販売外交員, 営業マン, セールスマン（＝salesclerk, salesperson, sales）
missionary salesman 宣伝販売員
retail salesman 小売販売員, 店員
salesman training 販売員訓練

salespeople 名 販売員, 店員, 営業スタッフ, 販売スタッフ（＝salespersons）
▶The company has set up blogs on its Web site, through which consumers can chat with *salespeople* and consult with them on makeup. 同社は，同社のホームページにブログを開設して，消費者が販売員と会話をしたり，美容相談したりすることができるようにした。

salvage 名 救済,〈沈没船の〉引揚げ, 海難救助
salvage value 残存価格, 残存価額, 転用価額（＝residual value, scrap value; ⇒**useful life**）
same-day 形 同日の, 当日の
same store sales 既存店ベースの売上高, 既存店ベースの売上
sample 名 見本, 試供品, 標本
Samurai bond 円建て外債, サムライ・ボンド（日本の債券市場で国外の発行者が円貨表示で発行する債券）
sanctions 名 制裁, 制裁措置
  impose economic sanctions against …に対して経済制裁を課す, …に対して経済制裁に踏み切る, …に対して経済措置を取る
  lift economic sanctions against …に対する経済制裁を解除する
  trade sanctions 貿易制裁, 貿易制裁措置
  U.N. sanctions against Iraq 対イラク国連制裁
  unilateral N. Korea sanctions 対北朝鮮単独経済制裁
▸This kind of rocket engine is on the list of items whose exporters are subject to U.N. *sanctions*. この種のロケット・エンジンは, その輸出業者が国連の制裁を受けることになっている品目のリストに入っている。
SAR 株式評価益権, 株式評価受益権（⇒**exercisable, stock appreciation right**）
Sarbanes-Oxley Act 企業改革法, 企業会計改革法, サーベンス・オクスレー法, SO法（＝Sarbanes-Oxley Act of 2002）
satellite 名 衛星, 人工衛星, 衛星放送, 近郊都市
  broadcasting satellite 放送衛星《略 BS》
  commercial satellite 商業衛星
  communication satellite 通信衛星《略 CS》
  Data Relay Test Satellite データ中継技術衛星《略 DRTS》
  geostationary meteorological satellite 静止気象衛星
  Geostationary Operational Environmental Satellite 静止環境観測衛星, ゴーズ《略 GOES》(日本での愛称は「パシフィック・ゴーズ」)
  information-gathering satellite 情報収集衛星
  meteorological satellite 気象衛星
  Multifunctional Transport Satellite-1R 運輸多目的衛星新1号《略 MTSAT-1R》
  multipurpose satellite 多目的衛星
  nuclear reactor satellite 原子炉衛星
  optical satellite 光学衛星
  quasizenith satellite 準天頂衛星
  radar satellite レーダー衛星（＝radar-sounding satellite）
  satellite broadcasting 衛星放送
  satellite television 衛星テレビ
  solar power satellite 太陽発電衛星
  spy satellite 偵察衛星, 情報衛星
  weather satellite 気象衛星
satellite launch business 衛星打上げ事業
▸The government transferred the state-run *satellite launch business* using H2A rockets to Mitsubishi Heavy Industries Ltd. H2Aロケットによる国営の衛星打上げ事業は, 国から三菱重工に移管された。
saturate 動 飽和させる
▸The PC market is *saturated*. パソコン市場は, 飽和状態にある。
saturation 名 飽和, 飽和度, 飽和状態, 飽和感, 成熟化, 集中キャンペーン, サチュレーション
  market saturation 市場の成熟化
  saturation campaign 集中キャンペーン, 集中スポット
  saturation level 飽和水準, 普及水準
  saturation spot 集中スポット
▸The current business environment has seen a *saturation* of domestic market due to the nation's low birthrate. 現在の企業環境は, 少子化で国内市場が飽和状態にある。
save 動 貯蓄する, 蓄える, 節約する, 保存する
savings 名 貯蓄, 貯金, 預金, 年金
  savings account 貯蓄預金, 貯蓄口座, 銀行預金, 普通預金
  savings deposit 貯蓄預金, 貯蓄性預金, 普通預金
  retirement savings 退職年金
  savings and loan association 貯蓄金融機関, 米国の貯蓄貸付け組合(S&L)
  savings from a debt waiver 債務免除益
  savings incentive plan 貯蓄奨励制度
  savings plan 貯蓄制度
▸We contributed $350 million to the *savings* plans for our employees in 2008. 当社は, 当社従業員のための貯蓄制度に2008年度は3億5,000万ドル拠出しました。
▸When the freeze on the payoff system was partially lifted, clients shifted their funds from time deposits to *savings* deposits that will be protected fully. ペイオフ制度凍結の一部解禁が行われた際には, 顧客が預金を定期預金から全額保護される普通預金に預け替えた。
savvy 名 実際的な知識, 実務知識, 知識, 能力, 手腕, 理解力, 勘, 形 事情通の, 精通した, 物知り

の, 博識の, 抜け目のない, やり手の, しっかりした, 経験[知識]の豊富な, ベテランの
▸The ratio of Net-*savvy* Japanese to the nation's overall population hit a new high of 67 percent last year. 日本全国の人口に対するインターネットを利用している日本人の割合は, 67％で過去最高となった。

SBA 米中小企業庁 (Small Business Administration の略)

scale 名 規模, 基準, 尺度, 段階, 金利体系, 発行条件, 目盛り, スケール
  corporate scale 企業の規模
  diseconomy of scale 規模の不経済, 規模の不経済性 (＝diseconomies of scale)
  economy of scale 規模の経済, 規模の経済性, 規模の利益, 数量効果, スケール・メリット (＝economies of scale, scale economies)
  gain scale 規模を拡大する
  left scale 左目盛り (右目盛り＝right scale)
  manufacturing scale 生産規模
  optimal scale 最適規模
  ratio scale 対数目盛り
  scale economies 規模の経済
  scale merit 規模の利益, 規模拡大によるメリット[利益], スケール・メリット
  the scale of revision 改定幅
  world scale facility 世界規模の設備, 世界規模の生産設備
▸A merger can bring about *scale* merits and multiple benefits to both parties. 経営統合で, 両当事者は, 規模の利益と相乗効果を期待することができる。

scalp 名 利ざや

scan 動 精査する, 走査する

scanner 名 読取り機, 映像走査機, 走査機, 走査装置, スキャナー (⇒**cardholder**)

scarce 形 乏しい, 不足している, 珍しい, 希少の
  scarce currency 希少通貨
  scarce goods 希少品, 品薄
  scarce resources 希少資源, 資源不足 (＝scarcity of resources)
  scarce share [stock] 品薄株
▸The average retail price of Japanese beef rose to a fresh record high in the week through Friday due to *scarce* shipments. 国産牛肉の全国平均小売価格は, 出荷量が落ち込んだため, 金曜日までの1週間で最高値を更新した。

scenario 名 シナリオ, 台本, 筋書き, 事態, 状況, 脚本, 予測, 予定の計画, 行動計画, 計画案
  alternative scenario 代替プラン, 予備のプラン
  economic scenario 経済予測, 景気予測, 景気シナリオ
  every possible scenario 想定されるあらゆる事態
  most likely scenario 最も実現しそうなシナリオ
  optimistic scenario 楽観的シナリオ
  political scenario 政情, 政局
  worst case scenario 最悪の事態, 最悪のシナリオ (＝nightmare scenario)

scene 名 光景, 景色, 風景, 眺め, 舞台, 場面, 背景, 状況, 事情, 事態, 出来事, 現場, 現地, 場所, 場, 業界, 分野, …界, 大騒ぎ, 醜態, シーン (⇒**strong player**)
  behind the scenes 舞台裏で, 裏側で, 秘密裏に, ひそかに, 内密に, 陰で, 黒幕として, 内幕に通じて, 内情に詳しい
  behind-the-scenes talks 水面下の話し合い
  change of scene 転地, 状況の変化
  economic scene 経済界
  education scene 教育界
  international scene 国際舞台
  make a scene 大騒ぎをする, 醜態を演じる
  make the scene 登場する, やってくる, 派手にやる, 人目を引く, 参加する, 加わる
  medical scene 医学界
  moves behind the scenes 水面下の動き
  operate from behind the scenes 陰で糸を引く
  political scene 政界, 政治の舞台
  rush to the scene of …の現場に急行する
  steal the scene 人気をさらう

schedule 名 別表, 別紙, 付属書類, 明細表, 一覧表, 予定表, 法律の付則, 予定, 計画, スケジュール
  attached schedule 付表, 添付の付属書類
  delivery schedule 納期
  maturity schedule 償還計画
  production schedule 生産予定表
  Schedule 13D 届出様式13D
  schedule of concessions 関税譲許表
  schedule of terms and conditions 取引条件書
  schedule of values 価格表
  supplementary schedule 付属明細書
  tariff schedule 関税表, 料金表

scheme 名 事業, 計画, 企画, 案, 策, 仕組み, 制度, 体系, 方式, 組織, 機構, 体制, 概要, 基準, スキーム (⇒**triangular merger scheme**)
  business scheme 業務体制
  classification scheme 分類基準
  corporate defense schemes 企業防衛策
  defined benefit scheme 確定給付年金
  occupational pension scheme 従業員年金制度

pension scheme 年金制度
regulation scheme 規制策
retirement benefit scheme 退職給与制度
share buyback scheme 自社株買い
▶The new triangular merger *scheme* was introduced in Japan in May 2007. この新三角合併方式は，2007年5月に日本で導入された。

SCM サプライ・チェーン・マネジメント (**supply chain management** の略)

scope 名 範囲, 領域, 枠組み, 構成, 区分, 余地, 機会, 可能性
　audit scope 監査の範囲 (= scope of audit, scope of examination)
　economy of scope 範囲の経済
　geographic scope 営業地域
　product scope 製品構成
　scope of business 業務範囲
　scope of consolidation 連結の範囲 (= consolidation criteria:「連結の範囲」の基準としては，基本的に「他社の発行済み議決権株式(outstanding voting stock)の50%超(過半数)を直接間接に所有している場合，その会社を連結の範囲に含める」ことになっている)
　scope of opinion 意見区分
▶To improve their business performance, news organizations are working to expand the *scope of news distribution* through the Net. メディア各社は，経営改善に向けて，ネットによるニュース配信の拡充を進めている。

scorched-earth defense 焦土作戦 (= scorched-earth tactic: 敵対的買収を仕掛けられた会社が，買収者にとって魅力的な会社の最優良資産などを売却して会社の価値を減少させ，買収意欲をそぐ手法のこと。crown jewels (クラウン・ジュエル)と同じ意味で使われることが多い)

scrap 動 撤回する, 撤廃する, 打ち切る, 中止する, 廃案にする, 捨てる, 廃品にする, スクラップにする
　scrap and build スクラップ・アンド・ビルド (採算の合わない店舗などを閉鎖して効率のよい新店に切り換えること)
　scrap the law 法律を廃案にする
　scrap the consumption tax 消費税を撤廃する
▶The companies *scrapped* the merger plan. 両社は，合併計画を撤回した。

scrap value 残存価格, 残存価額, 廃材価額 (= residual value, salvage value)
▶The asset has a useful life of 5 years and no *scrap value*. この資産の耐用年数は5年で，残存価額はゼロである。

screen 名 画面, 遮蔽物, スクリーン, 映写幕, 動 審査する, ふるいにかける, 選抜する, 遮蔽する
　on-screen instruction 画面上の指示
　on-screen menu 画面上のメニュー
　on-screen window 画面上のウインドウ
　organic electroluminescent screen 有機EL(エレクトロルミネッセンス)ディスプレー
　screen dump 画面コピー
　screen design 画面設計
　screen image 出力イメージ
　screen layout 画面レイアウト
　screen scrolling 画面スクロール
　screen trading 画面取引, スクリーン取引 (= screen-based trading)

screening 審査, 検査 (⇒**credit guarantee**)
　customer screening 顧客審査
　lax screening 手薄な審査
　screening division 審査部門
　the overlenient screening of borrowers 融資先のずさんな審査

scrip 名 仮証券, 仮株券, 受取証, スクリップ
　bearer scrip 無記名仮証券
　scrip dividend 株式配当, 手形[仮証券]配当, スクリップ配当
　scrip issue 無償増資, 特別配当, 特別配当株 (= bonus [capitalization, free] issue)
　stock scrip 株式仮証券

SDR 〈IMFの〉特別引出し権 (**special drawing right(s)** の略)

sea change 大きな変化, 大変化, 大変革, 著しい変貌
▶The Internet has brought about a *sea change* in communications. インターネットは，通信に大変革をもたらした。

seal 名 印章, 印鑑, 捺印, 社印, 封印, シール, 動 捺印する, 調印する, 保証する, 照明する
　common seal 共通印章, 社印
　corporate seal 社印
　great seal 国印, 州印
　marginal seal 捨て印
　place of seal 捺印箇所 (ラテン語でlocus sigilli [L.S.]という)
　registration of one's seal impression 印鑑登録
　seal impression 印鑑
▶*Seal* means the common *seal* of the Company and includes every official *seal*. 社印とは，当会社の共通印章をいい，公式印章をすべて含むものとする。

seamless 形 継ぎ目のない, 部位と部位との継ぎ

目を感じさせない, ぎくしゃく感がない, 滑らかな, 完全に一体化した, 一貫した, シームレス
▸The firm aims at transforming itself into a *seamless* oil company engaged in both upstream and downstream operations. 同社は, 原油の採掘［原油生産］から精製・販売まで一貫して手がける石油会社への脱皮を目指している.

SEAQ 証券取引自動通報システム (Stock Exchange Automated Quotations (system) の略)

search 名 調査, 精査, 検査, 探査, 捜索, 分析, 探求, 追求, 開発, 検索, 情報検索, サーチ
  executive search 社長クラスの人材のスカウト業
  job search 職探し
  market search 市場探求
  Net search services ネット検索サービス
  run [do, perform] a search on the Internet インターネットで検索する
  search and rescue system 捜索救難システム
  search by brand ブランドによる検索
  search by keyword キーワードによる検索
  search engine 検索エンジン, サーチ・エンジン
  search for alternative sources of energy 代替エネルギー源［代替エネルギー］の開発
  Search for Extra-Terrestrial Intelligence 地球外文明探査計画, セティ《略 SETI》
  search function 検索機能
  title search 権原調査

searcher 検索専門家, 情報検索代行業者
searching the Net ネット検索, ネット・サーチング
searching the Web ウェブ検索
season 名 季節, 時期, 最盛期, 活動期, …期, シーズン
  bonus season ボーナス・シーズン
  busy season 繁忙期
  Christmas season クリスマス・シーズン (= holiday season)
  Christmas shopping season クリスマスの買い物シーズン
  holiday season 米国の祝祭シーズン (11月第4木曜日の感謝祭(Thanksgiving Day)から正月までの休暇期間)
  most profitable season 書き入れどき
  off-demand season 需要減退期
  off season 閑散期, 商売の霜枯れ時, シーズンオフ (= dead season, dull season)
  results season 決算シーズン, 決算発表シーズン
  tourist season 観光シーズン
▸U.S retailers suffered through their worst Christmas shopping *season* in five years. 米国の小売業界は, 過去5年で最悪のクリスマス・ショッピング・シーズンとなった.

seasonal 形 季節の, 季節的な, 季節ごとの
  seasonal adjustment 季節調整
  seasonal business 季節的事業, 季節変動事業
  seasonal demand 季節需要
  seasonal factors 季節要因 (= seasonal influences, seasonal reasons)
  seasonal model 季節変動型モデル
  seasonal product [goods, merchandise, moves] 季節商品, 季節的商品
  seasonal stock 季節在庫品
  seasonal variation 季節変動, 季節的変動 (= seasonal fluctuation)
  seasonal worker 季節労働者 (= seasonal laborer)

seasonally adjusted 季節調整済みの, 季節調整後の, 季節調整値
▸The *seasonally adjusted* unemployment rate hit a 45-month low of 4.6 percent in May, down 0.1 percentage point from April. 5月の完全失業率(季節調整値)は, 前月より0.1ポイント低下の4.6%で, 45か月ぶりの最低水準となった.

seasonally adjusted basis 季節調整値, 季節調整済み, 季節調整ベース
▸The economy grew by 0.4 percent in real terms on a *seasonally adjusted basis* during the April-June quarter from the previous quarter, or an annualized 1.7 percent. 4-6月期の経済成長率(季節調整期)は, 物価変動の影響を除いた実質で前期(1-3月期)に比べて0.4%増, 年率換算で1.7%増加した.

seat 名 会員権, 取締役の地位
SEATS 証券取引所別途売買サービス(Stock Exchange Alternative Trading Service の略)
SEC 米証券取引委員会 (⇒ Securities and Exchange Commission)
second half 下半期, 下期 (= the second half of the fiscal [business] year, the second half of the year)
▸Kajima Corp., the nation's largest general contractor, returned to profit in the *second half* of the last business year. 国内ゼネコン最大手の鹿島建設が, 前期［前年度］の下半期［下期］から黒字に転換した.

second-hand smoke 受動喫煙 (= passive smoking)
▸*Second-hand smoke* in the workplace causes health problems. 職場での受動喫煙は, 健康上の問題を引き起こす.

second quarter

second quarter 第2四半期
- **gross profit margins for the second quarter of 2009** 2009年[2009年度]第2四半期の売上利益率
- **second-quarter operating loss** 第2四半期の営業損失, 第2四半期の営業赤字
- **second-quarter operating revenues** 第2四半期の営業収益
- ▶The Corporation's wholly owned telecommunications subsidiary posted net income of $211 million for the *second quarter* of 2008. 当社が全額出資している通信事業部門子会社が、2008年度第2四半期は2億1,100万ドルの純利益を計上しました。

second-tier 形 準大手の, 中堅の, 中位の, 二流の (⇒tier)
- **second-tier life insurer** 準大手の生命保険会社, 中堅生命保険会社
- **second-tier regional bank** 第二地銀, 第二地方銀行 (=second regional bank)
- **second-tier securities firm** 準大手の証券会社 (=second-tier securities house)

secondary 形 第二位の, 二流の, 二次的な, 派生的な, 間接的な
- **secondary bonds** 既発債
- **secondary distribution** 売出し, 第二次分売 (=secondary offering: 不特定多数の投資家に対して, 均一の条件で, すでに発行された有価証券の取得の申込みを勧誘すること)
- **secondary industry** 二次産業, 第二次産業
- **secondary offering** 売出し, 第二次分売 (=secondary distribution: すでに発行されている有価証券(大口株主の保有株式など)を一般投資家に売り出すこと)
- **secondary placement** 売出し
- **secondary product** 二次製品
- **secondary public offering** 上場後の公募
- **secondary yield** 流通市場利回り (=secondary market yield)

secondary market 流通市場, セカンダリー市場, 短期金融市場 (「流通市場」は、投資家が発行済みの株式や債券を売買する市場で trading market ともいう。また「短期金融市場」は、銀行引受手形や譲渡可能定期預金証書などの短期金融市場証書(money market instruments)を売買する市場)
- **liquidity of secondary market** 流通市場の流動性 (=secondary market liquidity)
- **secondary market in public debt** 国債流通市場
- **secondary market share offering** 株式売出し
- **secondary market price** 流通市場価格

secretary 名 秘書役, 総務部長

section 名 区分, 部, 部門, 部分, 課, 条項, 条, セクション
- **cross-section analysis** 横断面分析, クロス・セクション分析
- **equity section** 資本の部
- **financial section** 財務区分, 年次報告書の「財務の部」
- **Section 301 of the Trade Act of 1974** 1974年米通商法301条
- **Section 1244 stock** (内国歳入法)第1244条の株式
- **section of stockholders' equity** 資本の部

sector 名 部門, 分野, 業界, 地域, 市場, 株, セクター
- **agricultural financial sector** 農林系金融機関
- **all business sectors** 全業種
- **banking sector** 銀行業界, 銀行セクター
- **business sector** 事業分野, 業種, 企業セクター, 企業, 産業界, 業界
- **construction sector** 建設部門, 建設業界
- **corporate finance sector** 企業金融部門
- **corporate sector** 企業部門, 法人部門, 企業セクター, 企業
- **corporate sector's performance** 企業業績
- **domestic-demand dependent sectors** 内需依存株
- **factory sector** 製造業
- **financial sector** 金融部門, 金融業界, 金融・保険業, 金融セクター
- **household sector** 家計部門
- **information and telecommunications sector** 情報通信部門
- **labor-intensive sectors** 労働集約型産業
- **leasing sector** リース部門
- **life insurance sector** 生命保険業界, 生保業界 (=life insurance industry)
- **manufacturing sector** 製造業, 製造業セクター
- **mining sector** 鉱業株
- **motor sector** 自動車株
- **other sectors** 異業種
- **primary sectors** 第一次産業
- **private sector** 民間部門, 民間セクター, 民間企業
- **public sector** 政府部門, 公共部門, 公共セクター
- **retail and wholesale sector** 流通業
- **service sector** サービス部門, サービス産業
- **steel sector** 鉄鋼部門, 鉄鋼業界
- **T-bill sector** Tビル市場, 米財務省短期証券市場

technology sector ハイテク株
▶Carbon dioxide from cars accounts for 90 percent of various greenhouse gas emissions from the transportation *sector*. 自動車から排出される二酸化炭素は、運輸部門全体が排出する各種温室効果ガスのうち、9割を占めている。

secure 動 獲得する、確保する、達成する、実現する、設定する、固定する、保証する
　be secured by …によって保証される、…で担保されている、…を担保にして、…を裏付けとする
　be secured on …を担保とする
　secure bank financing 銀行融資を受ける
　secured debt instrument 有担保債券
　secured financing 担保付き資金調達
　secured liability 担保付き負債
　secured loans 担保付き融資
　secured obligation 担保付き社債（＝secured bond）
　secured party 担保権者
▶The bank had already *secured* it as fixed collateral. 同行は、それにはすでに根（ね）抵当権を設定していた。
▶The company was unable to *secure* sufficient funding for redemption of its corporate bonds. 同社は、社債の償還資金の手当てがつかなかった。

secured mortgage 抵当権付き債権
▶Plan assets are represented by common and preferred shares, bonds and debentures, cash and short-term investments, real estate and *secured mortgages*. 年金資産は、普通株式・優先株式や債券・社債、現金・短期投資証券、不動産、抵当権付き債権などで構成されています。

securities 名 有価証券、証券、債券、証書、権利証書
　annual securities report 有価証券報告書
　cash and marketable securities at the end of the year 現金預金および有価証券期末残高
　debt and equity securities 債券および持ち分証券
　income before securities transactions 有価証券売買益前利益
　income from cash and securities 金融収益と有価証券売買益
　increase (decrease) in cash and marketable securities 現金預金および有価証券の増加額（減少額）
　investment securities with remaining maturities of one year or less 1年以内に満期を迎える投資有価証券
　loss from securities revaluation 有価証券評価損
　loss on securities sold 有価証券売却損
　other securities その他の有価証券
　profit from securities revaluation 有価証券評価益
　Securities and Exchange Surveillance Commission 日本の証券取引等監視監視委員会
　securities company 証券会社（＝securities firm, securities house）
　securities exchange 証券取引所
　securities gains 証券売却益、投資有価証券売買益
　securities holdings 保有証券、保有有価証券（保有する株式や債券のこと）
　securities investment 証券投資、有価証券投資
　Securities Investor Protection Act of 1970 1970年証券投資家保護法
　securities losses 有価証券の評価損、投資有価証券売買損
　securities of affiliated company 関係会社有価証券
　unrealized gains on securities 証券含み益、有価証券含み益
▶Before we invest in *securities* such as stocks, bonds and mutual funds, we must consider our investment time horizon. 株式、債券やミューチュアル・ファンドなどの有価証券に投資する前に、自分の投資資産の運用期間も検討しなければならない。

Securities and Exchange Commission
米証券取引委員会《略 SEC》

米証券取引委員会とは ➡ 証券関連法の運用と公正な証券取引の維持および投資家保護を目的として、1934年証券取引法に基づいて創設された米国の独立した連邦政府機関。インサイダー取引（insider trading）や相場操縦（manipulation）などの不公正取引を監視・摘発するための強力な行政権限をもっている。委員会は、上院の同意を得て大統領が任命する任期5年の委員5人で構成されている。
　SEC（米証券取引委員会）に登録している企業がSECへの提出を義務付けられている財務書類は、consolidated balance sheet（連結貸借対照表）、consolidated income statement（連結損益計算書）、consolidated statement of stockholders' equity（連結キャッシュ・フロー計算書）とnotes to financial statements（財務書類注記）で構成されている。

SECの主な組織構成：

Directorate of Economic and Policy Analysis 経済分析室

Division of Corporation Finance	企業財務局, 法人金融部
Division of Enforcement	法規執行局, 執行部
Division of Investment Management	投資管理局, 投資管理部
Division of Market Regulation	市場規制局, 市場規制部
Office of Administrative Law Judges	行政訴訟審判官室, 行政法審判官室
Office of EDGAR Management	エドガー管理室
Office of International Affairs	国際問題室, 国際問題課
Office of Opinions and Review	意見起草室
Office of the Chief Accountant	主任会計官室
Office of the General Counsel	法律顧問室

Securities and Exchange Law 証券取引法
▶Financial statements are required to go through an external auditing by certified public accountants under the *Securities and Exchange Law*. 有価証券報告書は, 証券取引法で公認会計士による外部監査を受けなければならない。

Securities and Exchange Surveillance Commission 証券取引等監視委員会《略 SESC》
▶The *Securities and Exchange Surveillance Commission* (SESC) was established in July 1992 after a series of crimes involving major securities firms illegally compensating clients for losses came to light the previous year. 証券取引等監視委員会(証券監視委)は, 1991年に明らかになった損失補填事件など大手証券会社の一連の不祥事を契機に, 1992年7月に発足した。

securities brokering 証券仲介業 (= securities brokerage business, stock brokerage business)
▶The wall separating banking and securities businesses has been lowered through such moves as the liberalization of banks' *securities brokering*. 銀行と証券業の垣根は, 銀行に対する証券仲介業の規制緩和などの動きで, 低くなっている。

securities market 証券市場, 証券市況, 有価証券市場 (= security market: 「証券市場」は, 長期金融資産である株式や債券を取引する金融市場で, 日本では資本市場(capital market)と同義)
debt securities market 債券市場
mortgage-backed securities market モーゲージ証券市場
public securities market 公募証券市場

secondary securities market 流通市場 (= secondary market)
unlisted securities market 非上場証券市場
▶Insider trading distorts share prices and undermines the fairness of the *securities market*. インサイダー取引は, (適正な)株価をゆがめ, 証券市場の公正さを損なう。

securities report 有価証券報告書
▶To maintain the listing, the company had paid other costs totaling about ¥20 million annually, including translating *securities reports* into Japanese. 上場を維持するため, これ以外に同社は, 有価証券報告書の日本語への翻訳などを含めて, 年間約2,000万円の諸経費も払っていた。

securitization 名 証券化, 金融の証券化, セキュリタイゼーション
bad loan securitization 不良債権の証券化 (= securitization of bad loans)
car loan securitization 自動車ローンの証券化
credit card securitization クレジット・カード債権の証券化, クレジット・カードの証券化 (= securitization of credit card receivables)
real estate securitization 不動産の証券化
securitization of government assets 政府資産の証券化
securitization of housing loans 住宅ローンの証券化, 住宅ローン債権の証券化 (= housing loan securitization)
securitization of real estate assets 不動産資産の証券化
▶The two prospective partners have extensive expertise in mergers and acquisitions, as well as the *securitization* of bad loans. 提携する予定の両社は, 企業の合併・買収(M&A)や不良債権の証券化などに豊富なノウハウを持っている。

securitize 動 証券化する
securitized assets 証券化資産, 証券化した資産
securitized borrowings 借入れの証券化
securitized debt 証券化した債権, 債権の証券化
securitized home mortgages 証券化した住宅モーゲージ
▶The Japan Housing Finance Agency plans to *securitize* housing loan claims bought from financial institutions. 住宅金融支援機構(独立行政法人で, 旧住宅金融公庫が2007年4月1日に改称)は, 金融機関から買い取った住宅ローンの債権を証券化する方針だ。

securitized product 証券化商品 (⇒Financial Stability Forum)
▶*Securitized products* have been a major cause

of worsening the subprime problem.　証券化商品が，サブプライム問題拡大の主な要因となっている．

security 名　安全, 安全性, 保証, 保障, 保証人, 担保, 抵当, 証券, 債券, 銘柄, 保険, セキュリティ
　as security for　…の抵当[担保・保証]として（= in security for）
　benefit security　給付保障
　creation of a security interest　担保権の設定
　energy security　エネルギー安全保障
　financial security　支払い能力, 財務上の安全性
　food security　食糧安全保障
　job security　雇用の安定, 雇用保障, 職務保証, 職の安全
　listed security　上場証券, 上場有価証券
　security advisor　証券顧問業者, 証券アドバイザー
　security control　機密管理
　security income and expenses　有価証券損益
　security money　保証金, 手付け金
　security right　担保権
　unemployment security　失業保険
▶We are considering using the company's shares as *security* to secure the necessary funds.　当社は，同社株を担保にして必要資金を確保することを検討している．
▶We need to enhance the *security* of information networks by preventing leaks of personal information and averting the spread of computer viruses.　われわれは，個人情報の漏洩を防ぎ，コンピュータ・ウイルスの流行を回避して，情報ネットワークの安全性を高める必要がある．

security holes　安全対策の盲点, セキュリティ・ホール
▶In a test hack, the hacker team will probe for *security holes* in operating systems and installed software and launch an attack over the Internet.　テストの不正アクセスでは，ハッカー・チームが，インターネットを通してOS(基本ソフト)や応用ソフトのセキュリティ・ホール(安全対策の盲点)をつき，攻撃を仕掛ける．

SED　表面伝導型電子放出ディスプレー(**surface-conduction electron-emitter display**の略)
▶In 2004, Canon and Toshiba formed SED Inc. with a capital of ¥10.5 billion, to release *SED* television sets in Japan in the fourth quarter of 2007.　2004年にキヤノンと東芝は，2007年第4四半期にSEDテレビを国内販売するため，資本金105億円で合弁会社のSEDを設立した．

seed capital　着手資金, 元手

segment 名　事業区分, 事業分野, 事業部門, 営業区分, 区分単位, セグメント, 動　区切る, 区分する, 細分化する（⇒expect, industry segment）
　business segment　事業分野, 事業部門, 営業区分（=segment of business）
　customer segment　顧客層
　geographic segments　地域別セグメント（=geographical segments）
　industry segments　事業別セグメント, 産業別セグメント, 産業セグメント
　information on business segment by geographic areas　地域別セグメント情報
　market segment　市場区分, 市場分野
　segment information (unaudited)　セグメント情報(未監査)
　segment results　セグメント業績, セグメント別業績
　single industry segment　単一の事業区分
　supplying segment　供給部門
▶For the first six months of fiscal 2009, the Company's power and industrial systems *segment* is likely to book an operating loss of ¥50 billion.　2009年度上期の当社の電力・産業設備事業部門は，500億円の営業損失[営業赤字]になる見通しです．
▶Revenues between industry *segments* are not material.　産業セグメント間の収益に，重要性はありません．

self-declared bankruptcy　自己破産
self-employed people　自営業者（=the self-employed）
▶Both salaried workers and *self-employed people* in the United States report their respective earnings in detail to tax offices, quoting their Social Security number.　米国のサラリーマンや個人事業主は，社会保障番号を示して，個々の所得を詳細に税務署に申告する．

self-funding department　独立採算の事業部
▶The company has expanded its business by encouraging competition between self-funding departments within the group.　同社はこれまで，独立採算の事業部をグループ内で競争させて事業を拡大してきた．

self-management 名　自主管理
self-rehabilitation 名　自主再建, 自力再建
self-service gas station　セルフサービスのガソリン・スタンド, セルフサービス方式のガソリン・スタンド, セルフのガソリン・スタンド
▶Regular gasoline sells at a *self-service gas station* for ¥124 per liter.　レギュラーガソリン

は，セルフのガソリン・スタンドでは1リットル124円(店頭価格平均は135円)で販売されている。

self-sufficiency rate 自給率
▶Japan has the lowest food *self-sufficiency* rate among industrialized countries. 日本の食糧自給率は，先進国で最低となっている。

self-supporting accounting system 独立採算制

self-sustainable growth 自律的な成長
▶The Japanese economy is entering into a virtuous cycle of *self-sustainable growth* led by private demand. 日本経済には，民需主導の自律的な成長という好循環が生まれている。

sell 動 販売する，売る，売却する，売り渡す，売り込む，納入する，処分する，〈債券などを〉発行する，譲渡する
▶Some subsidiaries were *sold* in 2008, while new investments were made in others. 2008年には一部の子会社を売却するとともに，他の事業に新規投資を行いました。
▶The financially troubled company *sold* its operating rights to a joint company set up with GE Capital Co. 経営難に陥った同社は，GEキャピタルと設立した合弁会社に営業権を譲渡した。
▶We *sold* our 8% bonds that had a face value of $1,000,000. 当社は，額面100万ドルの8％利付き社債を発行しました。

sell-by date 販売妥当期限

sell off 売却する，投げ売りする，安く売り払う，見切り品として処分する
▶We *sold off* our U.S. plants to the firm. 当社は，同社に米国工場を売却した。

sell-off 名 投げ売り，大量売り，売却，売り，大量売りによる急落，急落 (⇒collapse 動)
  dollar sell-off ドル売り
  sell-off in the market 市場の急落，売り局面
  stock market sell-off 株式相場の急落
  triple sell-off トリプル安
▶Tokyo stocks fell to a three-month low as foreign investors sparked a *sell-off*. 東京株[東京株式市場の株価]は，外国人投資家が株を売り進めたため3か月ぶりに急落した。

sell order 売り注文
▶It's not a beautiful story for securities firms to snap up stocks while being aware of the erroneous *sell order*. 誤発注と認識しながら，証券会社が間隙を縫って株を取得するのは，美しい話ではない。

seller 名 売主，販売人，売れるもの
selling 販売，売込み，売り，売り越し，商法

  automatic selling 自動販売
  direct selling 直接販売，直販，無店舗販売
  panic selling 狼狽売り
  selling and administrative expenses 販売費および一般管理費 (=general overhead)
  selling and marketing expenses 販売・マーケティング費 (⇒SG&A)
  selling, general and administrative expenses [expenditures] 販売費および一般管理費《略 SG&A》(=SG&A expenditures, SG&A expenses)
  selling pressure 売り圧力，売り注文の殺到，売り優勢の展開
  short selling 空売り
  spot selling 現物売り
  yen-selling intervention 円売り介入
▶Shares of leading banks came under *selling* pressure across the board. 大手銀行株は，軒並み売られた(売り圧力がかかった)。
▶The securities company repeatedly alternated spot and short *selling* of shares of a regional bank. この証券会社は，地方銀行株の現物売りと空売りを交互に繰り返した。

semiconductor 名 半導体
  compound semiconductor 化合物半導体
  gallium nitride semiconductor laser 窒化ガリウム系半導体レーザー
  metal oxide semiconductor 金属酸化膜半導体，金属酸化物半導体《略 MOS》
  semiconductor chip 半導体素子，半導体チップ，半導体
  Semiconductor Chip Protection Act 半導体チップ保護法
  semiconductor equipment 半導体装置
  semiconductor laser 半導体レーザー
  semiconductor memory 半導体メモリ
  semiconductor production [manufacturing] equipment 半導体製造装置
  semiconductor related names 半導体関連銘柄

semiconductor business 半導体事業
▶Sanyo abandoned its decision to divest part of its *semiconductor business* to an investment fund. 三洋電機は，半導体事業の一部を投資ファンドに売却する決定を破棄した。

semiconductor industry 半導体産業，半導体業界
▶The so-called silicon cycle, a phenomenon unique to the *semiconductor industry*, describes changes in the marketplace. いわゆる「シリコン・サイクル」とは，半導体産業に特有の現象

で，市況変動の繰り返しをいう。

semiconductor maker 半導体メーカー（= semiconductor company, semiconductor manufacturer）
▶Elpida Memory Inc. is the nation's largest *semiconductor maker*. エルピーダメモリは，日本最大の半導体メーカーだ。

semifinished goods 半製品，中間製品（= semimanufactured goods）

semimanufactured goods 半製品（= semifinished product）

send 動 送る，届ける
　send in a bid 入札に応じる
　send up the price 価格を上げる
▶The two companies will *send* board members to each other. 両社は，役員を相互派遣する。

senior 形 上級の，上位の，優先の，優先順位の，首席の，先任の，シニア（⇒**junior**）
　senior claim 上位請求権，優先請求権
　senior creditor 優先順位の高い債権者
　senior debt 上位債，上位社債，優先弁済債務
　senior debt obligations 上位債務，一般債務
　senior debt rating 上位社債格付け
　senior director 上位取締役
　senior loan 優先貸付け
　senior management 経営陣，経営幹部，上級経営者，上級幹事，上席副社長
　senior official 政府高官
　senior policyholder 上位保険契約者，上位保険加入者
　senior security 上位証券
　senior subordinated note 上位劣後債，上位劣後社債
　senior unsecured bond 上位無担保社債
　senior unsecured debtholder 上位無担保債保有者

seniority 名 年功，年功序列，先任順，先任権，年長，古参

seniority-based wage system 年功序列賃金制度，年功序列型賃金体系，年功序列型給与制度（= seniority-based pay system, seniority order wage system, seniority-oriented wage system）
▶With the globalization of society, the conventional *seniority-based wage system* has started to collapse. 国際化とともに，従来の年功序列賃金制度は崩れはじめている。

seniority system 年功，年功序列制度，年功序列賃金制度
▶The current *seniority system* assures a certain level of promotion for career bureaucrats. 現行の年功序列制度は，キャリア官僚に一定の昇進を保証している。

sensitive 形 敏感な，左右されやすい，高感度の，要注意の，機密の，重要な
　consumer-sensitive 消費者動向に敏感な
　cost-sensitive コストに敏感な，コストに左右されやすい
　data-sensitive error データ依存型誤り
　interest-sensitive instrument 金利感応商品（= interest-rate sensitive instrument）
　market-sensitive 市場に敏感な，市場に左右されやすい
　price-sensitive consumer 価格に敏感な消費者
　sensitive film 高感度フィルム
　sensitive intelligence 機密情報
　sensitive item 輸入要注意品目，センシティブ品目
　sensitive product 重要品目
▶*Sensitive products* include rice in Japan's case. 重要品目には，日本の場合のコメが含まれる。

sensitivity 名 感度，感応度
　sensitivity analysis 感応分析，感度分析
　sensitivity training 集団感受性訓練，感受性訓練《略 ST》

sentiment 名 景況感，市場の地合い，所感，心理，意見，感情，意識，人気，マインド，傾向（⇒**business sentiment**）
　bearish market sentiment 市場の弱気の地合い，市場の弱気ムード
　bullish market sentiment 市場の強気の地合い，市場の強気ムード
　consumer sentiment 消費者マインド，消費マインド，消費者心理，消費意欲
　consumer sentiment index 消費者マインド指数
　corporate sentiment 企業の心理，企業の景況感，企業の業況判断
　inflationary sentiment インフレ心理，インフレ・マインド
　investor sentiment 投資マインド，投資家心理，投資家の地合い
　negative sentiment マイナスの業況判断，マイナスの景況感，景況感の悪化
　selling sentiment 売り気
　sentiment index 業況判断指数

separate 動 切り離す，分離する
▶The company is *separating* its information-processing and distribution affiliates from its group to reduce its debts. 同社は，負債を削減

するため，情報処理子会社と物流子会社を同社グループから切り離す方針だ．

separation 名 退職，離職，休職，分離，分割，分解
  corporate separation 会社分割（＝corporate divestiture, demerger）
  separation of capital and administration 資本と経営の分離（＝separation between capital and management）
▸We must book expenses for future *separations* during the years employees are working and accumulating services with the company. 社員が勤務して会社にサービスを提供し続けている期間にわたって，当社は将来の休職に関する費用を計上しなければなりません．

separation payments 休職手当の支払い，中途退職金の支払い
▸Provisions for business restructuring also cover *separation payments* made as a result of special offers related to defined benefit plans. 事業再編成引当金には，確定給付年金制度に関する特別提案を受けて行われる中途退職金の支払いも含まれています．

serial 形 連続した，順次の，逐次の，系列の，シリーズの
  serial bond 連続債券［社債］，連続償還債券［社債］，順次償還社債，シリーズ債券
  serial issue 連続発行，連続償還発行
  serial securities 連続償還証券
▸A *serial* bond progressively matures at a series of stated installment dates. 連続社債とは，記載された一連の分割日に一定数の社債の償還期限が連続して到来する債券のことである．

series 名 連続，順次，系列，分割発行，指標，指数，シリーズ（⇒repay）
  Accounting Series Release 会計連続通牒
  data series 指標
  domestic WPI series 国内卸売り物価指数
  economic series 景気指標
  import WPI series 輸入物価指数
  manufacturing business conditions series 製造業の業況判断
  series advertising シリーズ広告
  series bond 分割発行社債
  series discount 連続割引
  series H bond シリーズH債券
  time series 時系列
▸In Canada, the Corporation issued $300 million of 9% *Series* 7 Notes, due 2012. カナダで当社は，満期2012年・利率9％のシリーズ7ノート3億ド

ルを発行しました．
▸The articles of incorporation authorize the Directors to issue such shares in one or more series and to fix the number of shares of each *series* prior to their issue. 定款では，これらの株式をシリーズで1回以上発行する権限と，その発行前に各シリーズの発行株式数を決定する権限は，取締役会に与えられています．

serve 動 務める，勤務する，働く，仕事をする，〈サービスなどを〉提供する，供給する，〈商品などを〉売る，運航する，文書を渡す，送付する，…の役に立つ，奉仕する，貢献する，利用できる，…の目的にかなう，…の要求などを満たす，…の機能を果たす，…の任務［職務］を果たす，…の手段として機能する，助長する，促進する，推進する，高める
  better serve customers' needs 顧客のニーズへの対応を改善する
  serve as a hedge against inflation インフレ・ヘッジの手段［インフレに対するヘッジ手段］として機能する
  serve one's debt 債務を返済する
  serve one's interests …の利益に十分見合う
  serve one's purpose …の目的にかなう
  serve the community 地域社会に貢献する，地域社会に奉仕する，地域社会に尽くす
▸The amount of retirement allowances usually is determined by the length of time directors *serve* in their post. 役員退職慰労金の金額は通常，役員の在任期間によって決められる．
▸We streamlined our operations and redeployed assets to position the Corporation to *serve* its customers more effectively. 顧客サービスの効率改善［一段と効率的な顧客サービスの体制確立］をめざして，当社は業務の効率化と資産の有効利用に取組みました．

serve as …を務める，…として勤務する，…として機能する，…の機能を果たす，…としての役割を担う，…として役立つ，…に使える，…になる
▸He is scheduled to *serve as* the chairman of Japan Automobile Manufacturers Association, Inc. through May. 同氏は，5月まで，日本自動車工業会会長の任期を務める予定だ．

serve on a committee 委員を務める，委員会に所属する
▸These two directors have *served on* several different *committees* and their business experience and judgment have proved invaluable to the corporation. 両取締役は，（取締役会のもとに設置された）各種委員会の委員を務め，その企業経営の豊かな経験と適切な判断によって当社に大い

service 動　〈借金や利子などを〉支払う，〈債務を〉返済する，〈債務を〉履行する，〈債権を〉回収する，〈役務を〉提供する
▶An insurance agent is a sales person who represents a life insurance company for the purpose of soliciting applications, collecting initial premiums, and *servicing* insurance contracts.　保険募集人は，生命保険会社を代表して保険契約の勧誘，初回保険料の徴収，保険契約に関する役務を提供する販売員である。

service 名　事業，業務，サービス，役務（えきむ），労務，勤務，服務，公務，〈借入金の〉定期返済，公債利子，〈訴状や呼出状の〉送達　(⇒**Internal Revenue Service, length of service**)
　advisory services　顧問業務
　after-sales service　販売後サービス，アフター・サービス
　auditing services　監査業務
　before service　販売前サービス，ビフォア・サービス
　debt service　債務返済，元利払い
　employee's service period　従業員の勤務年数
　management services　経営者への提案業務，経営指導，マネジメント・サービス《略 **MS**》(= management advisory services)
　service area　供給区域，放送区域，通話区域，有効範囲，サービス・エリア
　service balance　貿易外収支
　service capability　サービス能力，供給能力，用役能力
　service contract　保守サービス契約，保守業務契約，労務供給契約，サービス契約
　service economy　サービス経済
　service fee　サービス手数料，受取手数料
　service industry　サービス産業
　service life　耐用年数，耐用期間，試用期間，有用期間　(= depreciable life, durable years, useful life)
　service of notices　通知の送達
　service of process　訴状［呼出状］の送達
　service potentials　将来収益獲得能力，潜在的用益，サービス・ポテンシャルズ
　service station　給油所，ガソリン・スタンド
　service-through-people　人を通じてのサービス
　service trade　サービス貿易
　service yield basis　生産高比例法，生産高基準法　(= production method, service output basis)
　year of service　勤続年数，在職年数
▶Retirement benefits are based on years of *service* and the employee's compensation.　退職給付は，勤続年数と従業員の給与額に基づいて算定されています。
▶We will continue to develop innovative new *services* and offer pricing packages that add up to greater value for our customers.　当社は，今後とも革新的な新サービスを開発して，顧客に一段と高い価値をもたらす価格パッケージを提供していく方針です。

service charge　手数料，サービス料金，サービス料
▶There are no brokerage fees or other *service charges*.　仲介手数料やその他のサービス料金は，一切不要です。

service cost　勤務費用，補助部門費，補助原価，用役原価，サービス部門原価　(⇒**current service cost, prior service cost**)
　past service cost　過去勤務費用　(= prior service cost)
　service cost—benefits attributed to service during the period　勤務費用—期中の勤務により発生した給付［給付費用］
▶Net transition amounts and prior *service costs* are being amortized over periods ranging from 10 to 15 years.　移行時差額と過去勤務費用は，10−15年の期間にわたって償却されています。

service pensions　年金額
▶Non-contributory defined benefit plans provide for *service pensions* based on length of service and rates of pay.　非拠出型確定給付年金制度［非拠出型給付金規定方式による年金制度］は，勤続年数と給与額に基づいて年金額を決定する。

service period　勤務期間，勤務年数
▶Prior service costs resulting from improvements in the retirement plans are amortized over the average remaining *service period* of employees expected to receive benefits.　退職金制度の改善によって生じた過去勤務費用は，受給が予想される従業員の平均残存勤続期間にわたって償却されます。

servicer 名　債権回収会社，サービサー

servicing 名　債務返済，債務履行，利払い，債権回収，事務処理，サービシング　(⇒**debt servicing**)
　government bond-servicing expenditures　国債利払い費
　loan servicing　利払いなどの融資処理，貸出金サービシング
　loan servicing fee　融資処理手数料，貸出金サービシング手数料

mortgage servicing right モーゲージ・サービス権
servicing burden 債務返済負担
▶This joint venture will offer sales financing and *servicing* as well as raise funds for auto loans. この合弁会社は，自動車ローンの資金調達や販売金融，債権回収などを手がける。

session 名 会議，会談，会合，集会，集まり，議会，開会，会期，〈株式取引所の〉立会い[場]，セッション
afternoon session 後場，午後の授業
drinking session 飲み会
during the current session 今会期中
final session of a year 大納会
first session of a year 大発会
in full session 総会で
in session 会議[開会，開廷]中
IR session 投資家説明会，IR説明会，会社説明会（＝IR meeting）
morning session 前場，午前の授業
night session 夜間取引
photo session 撮影会
working session 会議

set aside 〈準備金などを〉積み立てる，蓄えておく，蓄える，引き当てる，設定する，繰り入れる，用意する，〈考えや問題を〉捨てる，無視する，棚上げする，取り除く，除外する
▶Insurers *set aside* provisions for disasters. 保険会社は，災害準備金[異常危険準備金]を積み立てている。
▶The consumer loan company set aside ¥150 billion in provisions to return excessive interest charges to customers. 顧客に超過支払い利息[超過利息]を返還するため，この消費者金融会社は1,500億円の引当金を積み増した。

set to …に取り掛かろうとしている，…する用意ができている，…する方針だ，…する方針を固める，…する見通しだ，…する恐れがある
▶GM and Toyota are each *set to* invest tens of billions of yen in a plant they jointly own in California. GMとトヨタはそれぞれ，両社が共同出資する米カリフォルニア州の工場に数百億円を（追加）投資する方針だ。
▶JAL is *set to* raise international freight fares, primarily due to hikes in fuel prices. 日航システムは，主に燃料価格の上昇で，国際貨物運賃を値上げする方針を固めた。

set up 設立する，設定する，準備する，用意する，組み立てる，築く，始める，〈ホームページなどを〉開設する，開く，創業する（⇒**site**）
▶Hitachi, Toshiba and Renesas Technology will *set up* a planning company to look into the feasibility of a microchip foundry. 日立製作所，東芝，ルネサステクノロジーの3社が，企画会社を設立して，半導体ファウンドリ計画の実行可能性を調査する。

setback 名 後退，景気後退，下落，がた落ち，落ち込み，減少，反落，逆行，逆風，挫折，失敗，敗北，調整局面
business setbacks 景気後退（＝economic setbacks）
earnings setback 収益の落ち込み
face setbacks 逆風にぶつかる
setback in the stock market 株式相場の下落
▶Among other factors that could adversely affect the national economy are possible *setbacks* in the Chinese and U.S. economies as well as high oil prices. 国内景気に悪影響を及ぼす恐れがある他の要因として，中国や米国の景気後退や原油高がある。

settle 動 決済する，清算する，処分する，処理する，解決する，決定する，決議する，和解する
▶Banks are about to *settle* their midyear accounts. 銀行は，これから中間決算をまとめるところだ。
▶Companies should not *settle* for good results for the first half of fiscal 2007. 企業は，2007年度上期の好決算に安住してはならない。

settlement 名 決済，清算，決算，処分，解決，決着，決定，妥結，和解，調停，示談，財産の譲渡，贈与財産，定食
abnormal settlement of accounts 異常決算
account settlement term 決算期
asset settlement 資産決済
automatic settlement 自動決済
biannual settlement 半期決算，中間決算，半期決済（＝semiannual settlement）
business settlement 取引決済
cash settlement 現金決済，現物決済，差金決済，即日決済
consolidated midterm financial settlement 中間連結決算
disruption of settlements 決済マヒ
electronic settlement 電子決済
electronic settlement services 電子決済業務（⇒**Net trading**）
final settlement 債務の完済
financial settlement 決算
IC card cashless account settlement system ICカード・キャッシュ決済システム，キャッシュレス決済システム

installment settlement 分割払い
legal settlement 訴訟和解金
midterm settlement in May 5月中間決算
out-of-court settlement 示談による和解
settlement account 決済用預金，決済口座（＝settlement deposit, settlement-specific deposit)
settlement accounts for fiscal 2009 2009年度決算
settlement gain and loss 決算差損益
settlement of balance 帳尻決算
▶Disruption of *settlements*, including payments to credit card companies and encashing of promissory notes, must be prevented in case of a bank collapse. 銀行が破綻した場合，クレジット・カード会社への支払いや約束手形の現金化などの決済マヒを防がなければならない。
▶The firm has announced its *settlement* accounts for fiscal 2008. 同社は，2008年度の決算（2009年3月期決算）を発表した。

settlement of accounts 決算，収支決算，決算報告（＝account settlement)
  the consolidated settlement of accounts 連結決算（＝consolidated account settlement, consolidated results)
  the deficit settlement of accounts 赤字決算
  the provisional settlement of accounts 仮決算
  the settlement of accounts for the April-June period 4–6月期決算
  the settlement of accounts for the business year that ended in March 3月期決算
  the settlement of accounts for the half year to September 9月中間決算
  the settlements of accounts in the business year ending March 31 3月期決算
  the term-end settlement of accounts 期末決算（⇒term-end settlement of accounts)

set-up [setup] 名 編成，構成，セットアップ，インストール
sever 動 分離する
severance 名 分割，切断，断交，雇用契約解除，契約条項の分離独立性，退職，離職，解散
  severance indemnity plan 退職金制度（＝severance plan)
  severance pay 退職金，退職［離職，解職］手当（＝separation pay, severance payment)
  severance tax 鉱産物税，資源分離税（石油生産業者が石油やガスの採取にあたって米国の州に支払う事業税）

SG&A 販売費および一般管理費（＝SG&A expenses: selling, general and administrative expenses [expenditures]の略）
▶The increase in *SG&A* expenses over the last three years reflects higher selling and marketing expenses. 過去3年にわたる販売費および一般管理費の増加は，販売・マーケティング費の拡大を反映しています。

shakeout 名 企業合理化，再編，〈組織などの〉刷新，改組，大改造，大改変，立て直し，再編成（＝shake-up)
  industry shakeout 業界再編
  inventory shakeout 在庫整理，在庫削減
  management shakeout 経営刷新，経営体制の刷新

shake-up 名 再編，大変革，大刷新，大改革，大改造，抜本的改革，抜本的改組（＝shakeout)
  Cabinet shake-up 内閣改造（＝Cabinet reshuffle)
  industry shake-up 業界再編（＝shake-up in the industry)
  management shake-up 経営刷新，役員交代（＝management reshuffle)
  shake-up within the house 機構改革
▶The firm's decision to stop the development and production of cell phone handsets is likely to further accelerate the *shake-up* of the domestic mobile phone industry. 携帯電話機の開発・生産を中止する同社の決定で，国内携帯電話業界の再編が一段と加速する可能性がある。

shall 助 …しなければならない，…するものとする，…と定める（契約書や法律文書でshallが使われる場合は，単純未来を表す助動詞ではなくmustの意味で，現在あるいは未来の義務，命令を表す）
▶For the purpose of this Agreement, each of the following terms *shall* have the following meaning respectively. 本契約の目的上［本契約上］，次の各用語はそれぞれ下記の意味を持つものとする。

shall not …してはならない，…しないものとする，…を禁止する（＝must not: 契約書や法律文書でshall notは禁止を表し，may notと同じく「…してはならない」の意味になる）
▶During the term of this agreement, each party *shall not* divulge any commercial or manufacturing secrets obtained from the other party. 本契約期間中，いずれの当事者も，相手方［他方の当事者］から取得した商業上または製造上の秘密を開示してはならない。

share 動 共有する，相互利用する，分配する，共

同負担する, 共同分担する, 分担する, 支持する, 参加する
‣The expected development cost of ¥50 billion is to be *shared* fifty-fifty between the government and the manufacturers. 500億円が見込まれている開発費は, 国とメーカーが折半する予定である.
‣The three companies aim to cut the cost of manufacturing steel products and enhance their products' quality by *sharing* some of their patents. この3社は, 特許の一部を相互利用することによって鉄鋼製品の製造コストを下げるとともに, 鉄鋼製品の品質向上も目指している.
‣The two chains will provide each other with merchandise and *share* distribution centers. 両チェーン店は今後, 相互に商品を提供するとともに, 物流センターの共通化を図る.

share 名 株, 株式, 株券, 持ち分株, 市場占有率, 市場占拠率, 負担分, シェア (=stock; ⇒**golden share, lion's share, market share, net profit per share, new share issue**)
　additional share 増資株
　all shares issued and outstanding 発行済み社外株式総数
　capital share 資本金, 株式, 資本分配率, キャピタル・シェア
　equity share 持ち分有価証券, 持ち分株式
　fund flow per share 1株当たり資金フロー
　market share gain 市場シェアの拡大 (=expansion of market share)
　ownership share 所有権株
　share allotment 株式割当て (=allotment of shares, share allocation)
　share earnings 1株当たり利益
　share exchange 株式交換
　share exchange rate 株式交換比率 (=stock exchange rate)
　share issue 株式発行, 新株発行
　share ownership 株式所有, 持ち株数
　share purchase 株式購入, 株購入, 株式買取り, 株式の買入れ, 株式取得 (=stock purchase)
　share purchase system 株式買取り制度
　share register 株式名簿, 株主名簿 (⇒**shareholders list**)
　shares authorized 授権株式数
　shares in thousands 単位: 千株
　shares in treasury 自己株式数, 金庫株数
　shares issued 発行済み株式数
　total number of shares 株式総数
‣Sanyo's rechargeable battery and photovoltaic power generation businesses have the largest *share* of their respective global markets. 三洋電機の充電池と太陽光発電の2事業は, 世界の市場でそれぞれ最大のシェア [市場占有率] を誇っている.
‣The company increased the number of its *shares* on the market with a stock split. 同社は, 株式分割で同社の流通する株式数を増やした.
‣The stock, offered at ¥235,000 a *share* in the initial public offering, opened 28 percent higher at ¥301,000. IPO (新規株式公開) で公開価格 [公募価格] が1株235,000円の同株は, 公開価格を28%上回る301,000円の初値を付けた.

share buyback 株式の買戻し, 自社株発行済み株式の買戻し, 自社株買戻し, 自社株買い, 自社株取得 (=share repurchase, stock buyback)
‣*Share buybacks* are commonly aimed at raising profits per share and enhance dividend payouts to shareholders. 株式買戻しの狙いは, 一般に1株当たり利益の引き上げと株主への配当支払いの増額にある.

share capital 株式資本, 株式資本金, 資本金 (=capital stock: 株式会社の資本金)
　equity share capital 持ち分株式資本, 普通株式資本
　issued share capital 発行済み株式資本
　ordinary share capital 普通株式資本, 普通株資本
　paid-up share capital 払込み資本金
　preference share capital 優先株式資本

share issue limit 株式発行枠, 株式の発行可能枠 [授権株式数]
‣Almost 100 companies listed on the Tokyo Stock Exchange are expected to propose a revision to their articles of incorporation to expand their respective *share issue limits* at their annual general shareholders meeting. 東証上場企業の約100社が, 年次株主総会で, 株式発行枠 [授権株式数] 拡大のための会社定款の変更を提案する見通しだ.

share of profits 利潤分配率, 利益分配率 (=profit share)
‣The labor distribution rate is an indicator of labor's *share of profits*. 労働分配率は, 利益がどの程度, 労働者に還元されているかの指標である.

share price 株価 (=stock price)
　share price level 株価水準
　share price performance 株価パフォーマンス, 株価動向, 株価の値動き
‣Signs of recovery have become visible, with

an upturn in *share prices* and an increase in consumer spending. 株価上昇と個人消費の伸びを背景に，景気回復の兆しも見えるようになった．

share purchase price 株式の買付け価格，株の買取り価格
▶The company set the *share purchase price* at ¥800 per share for the tender offer. 同社は，株式公開買付け(TOB)の株の買付け価格を1株800円に設定した．

share purchase unit 株式の購入単位
▶A stock split is a measure designed to enable investors, including those with only limited funds, to invest in a company by reducing the *share purchase unit*. 株式分割は，株式の購入単位を小口化して，少額の資金しかない投資家でも企業に投資できるようにするための手段[資本政策]だ．

share split 株式分割 (=share splitting, stock split；株式分割は，一時的な株価上昇を招く特徴がある．⇒**stock split**)
  share split-down 株式併合 (=reverse split, reverse stock split, stock split-down)
  share split-up 株式分割 (=stock split-up)
▶Earnings per share in 2007 are restated for a two-for-one *share split* on April 20, 2008. 2007年度の1株当たり純利益は，2008年4月20日の1対2の株式分割により修正・再表示されています．

share swap 株式交換 (=equity swap, stock swap；「株式交換」は企業買収を行う際に買収相手と自社の株式を交換することで，現金がなくても企業買収を進められる)
▶The company acquired six firms via a *share swap* in 2007. 同社は，2007年に株式交換で六つの会社を買収した．

shareholder 🔲 株主 (=stockholder)
  boost shareholder value 株主価値を高める
  equity shareholder 普通株主
  individual shareholder 個人株主
  institutional shareholder 機関投資家
  ordinary shareholder 普通株主 (=equity shareholder)
  shareholder approval 株主の承認
  shareholder structure 株主構成 (株主を機関別や所有株数別に区別した割合のことで，一般に1社の株式分布状況をいう)
  shareholder value 株主価値，株主利益 (=shareholders' value, value for shareholders)
  shareholders' assets 株主資本
  shareholders' interest 株主の権利，株主利益 (⇒**trading unit**)

shareholders' lawsuit 株主代表訴訟
shareholders' representative suit 株主代表訴訟 (=shareholders' lawsuit)
▶These transactions made the Corporation the second-largest shareholder in the company. これらの取引[株式取得]で，当社は同社の第2位株主になりました．

shareholder dividend reinvestment and stock purchase plan 株主配当再投資・株式購入制度
▶Shareholders wishing to acquire additional common shares of the Corporation can take advantage of the *Shareholder Dividend Reinvestment and Stock Purchase Plan*. 当社の普通株式の追加購入を希望される株主は，株主配当再投資・株式購入制度を利用することができます．

shareholder equality 株主平等
▶Golden shares violate the principle of *shareholder equality*. 黄金株は，「株主平等の原則」に反する．

shareholder interest 株主の利益，株主の権利
▶Steel Partners' takeover offer may seriously harm *shareholder interests*. スティール・パートナーズ(米系投資ファンド)の買収提案は，株主の利益を著しく損なう怖れがある．

shareholder of record 登録株主，株主名簿上の株主，株主 (=stockholder of record)
▶The board of directors declared the corporation's regular quarterly dividend of $.08 per common share, payable June 29, 2009 to *shareholders of record* at the close of business on June 11, 2009. 取締役会は，当社の普通株式1株当たり通常四半期配当を0.08ドルとし，2009年6月11日営業終了時の登録株主に対して2009年6月29日に支払うことを発表しました．

shareholder vote 株主投票
▶In the *shareholder vote*, there was substantial focus on whether the chair and CEO functions at the company should be split. 株主投票では，とくに同社の会長職とCEO(最高経営責任者)の職を分離すべきかどうかが大きな関心事だった．

shareholders incentives 株主優待，株主優待制度
▶*Shareholders incentives* are designed to encourage shareholders to hold onto their stocks over the long term. 株主優待の狙いは，株主の株式の長期保有促進にある．

shareholders list 株主名簿 (=list of shareholders, share register)

▶The ratio of voting rights held by the company is based on the *shareholders list* as of the end of February. 同社が保有する議決権の比率は，2月末時点の株主名簿をもとにしている。

shareholders meeting 株主総会 (=general meeting of shareholders, general meeting of stockholders, shareholders' meeting, stockholders' meeting)

annual shareholders meeting 年次株主総会
emergency shareholders meeting 緊急株主総会，臨時株主総会

▶The company has yet to receive approval for the action at its *shareholders meeting*. 同社は，同社の株主総会でこの措置の承認はまだ得ていない。

shareholders' equity 株主資本，株主持ち分，自己資本，資本，資本の部 (⇒**stockholders' equity**)

▶Only income arising after the date of acquisition is included in *shareholders' equity*. 企業取得日後に生じた利益だけが，資本の部に含まれています。

shareholders' value 株主価値 (=shareholders value)

create shareholders' [shareholders] value 株主の価値を高める (=create value for shareholders)
increase shareholders' value 株主の価値を高める
maximize shareholders' value 株主価値の極大化を図る

▶The U.S. businesses give priority to maximizing *shareholders' value*. 米国の企業は，株主の価値の極大化を第一に考えている。

shareholding 株式所有，株式保有，株式保有率，出資比率，持ち株比率，持ち株，保有株，保有株式 (=equity holding; ⇒**stockholding**)

foreign shareholding ratio 外国人持ち株比率
interlocked shareholdings 株式の持ち合い，株式持ち合い (⇒**cross shareholding**)
public shareholding 株式公開
shareholding ratio 持ち株比率，株式保有比率

▶Toyota will purchase some of General Motors Corp's *shareholding* in Fuji Heavy Industries Ltd. トヨタが，米ゼネラル・モーターズ(GM)が保有している富士重工の株式の一部を取得することになった。

shareowner 名 株主

common shareowners' equity 普通株式株主持ち分

Dear shareowner: 株主各位，株主の皆さまへ

▶For the past three years we have issued new shares of common stock in our *shareowner* and employee savings plans. 過去3年間，当社は，当社の株主制度と従業員貯蓄制度のために普通株式の新株を発行してきました。

shareowner services 株主サービス

▶First Chicago Trust is our *shareowner services* and transfer agent. ファースト・シカゴ・トラストが，当社の株主サービスおよび名義書換取扱い機関です。

sharing 名 分配，配分，共同分担，共同負担，シェアリング (⇒**participation, profit sharing plan**)

cost sharing 費用分担，原価負担
job-sharing ジョブ・シェアリング (=work-sharing)
profit sharing 利益分配，利益配分
tax sharing 租税分担
work sharing (system) ワークシェア，ワーク・シェアリング（1人当たりの労働時間を短縮して，雇用を分かち合う制度）

▶The work *sharing* system may lead to a decline in productivity. ワーク・シェアリングは，生産性の低下につながる可能性がある。

shares outstanding 社外流通株式数，発行済み株式，社外発行株式，発行株式 (=outstanding shares)

▶The number of weighted average *shares outstanding* increases as we issue new common shares for employee plans, shareowner plans and other purposes. 加重平均総発行株式数は，従業員貯蓄制度や株主制度その他の目的で当社が発行する新株に応じて増加します。

shark 名 高利貸し，ヤミ金融業者，サメ

loan shark 高利貸し，ヤミ金融業者
shark repellent [repellant] サメ駆除剤（定款の改正や転換優先株の発行など，敵対的買収への防衛策の一つ）
shark watcher サメ監視人（企業買収の動きを専門に監視する会社）

sharp 形 急激な，急速な，急な，大幅な

sharp drop in earnings 業績の急激な悪化
sharp rise in stock prices 株価の急騰，株価の急上昇
sharper competition 競争激化

▶The company posted a group pretax profit of ¥57.6 billion in the nine months to Dec. 31 in a *sharp* turnaround from a loss of ¥30 billion a year earlier. 同社の4－12月期決算は，576億円

の連結経常利益[連結税引き前利益]を計上し，前年同期の300億円の赤字から大幅黒字に転換した．

sharp increase 急増
▶Net profit per share in the period dived to ¥6.07 from ¥41.95 in the same period a year earlier as a result of a *sharp increase* in the number of the company's outstanding shares. 当期の1株当たり純利益は，同社の発行済み株式数の急増で，前年同期の41円95銭から6円7銭に急落した．

shed 名 上屋(うわや)
　bonded shed 保税上屋
　ex-quay shed 上屋渡し

shelf life 賞味期間，有効保存期間，棚ざらし期間，陳列許容期間

shelf offering 一括募集

shelf registration 一括登録，一括登録制度，発行登録，シェルフ登録，シェルフ・レジストレーション(「一括登録制度」では，将来発行予定の有価証券について，米証券取引委員会(SEC)に前もって登録しておくと，SEC Rule 415 (米証券取引委員会規則415)に基づき，実際の発行時に届け出をする必要はない)
▶No securities have been issued under this *shelf registration*. この一括登録制度に基づいて，有価証券はまだ発行されていません．

shelf registration program 一括登録制度，発行登録制度
▶We have U.S. $500 million of debt securities registered with the U.S. Securities Exchange Commission pursuant to a *shelf registration program*. 当社は，米証券取引委員会(SEC)の一括登録制度[発行登録制度]に基づき，5億ドルの債務証券発行予定額をSECに登録しています．

shelf registration statement 一括登録届け出書，発行登録届け出書
▶During September 2008, the Corporation filed a *shelf registration statement* with the U.S. Securities and Exchange Commission. 2008年9月に，当社は有価証券の一括登録届け出書を米国証券取引委員会(SEC)に提出しました．

shift 動 移す，変更する，変える，転嫁する，入れ替える，繰り上げる，シフトさせる，移る，移動する，変わる，変化する，シフトする
　shift downward 下降に転じる
　shift funds into other financial products 資金を他の金融商品に変える
　shift production base overseas 生産拠点を海外に移す
　shift upward 上昇に転じる (⇒**manager**)
▶In 2008, we *shifted* some people and responsi-

bilities on our Management Executive Committee, with an eye to increasing the pace of growth and globalization. 2008年に当社は，成長速度とグローバル化の促進をめざして，当社の経営執行委員会メンバーの一部とその担当分野の入れ替えを行いました．
▶We are not able to *shift* the raised costs of plastic parts onto product prices. プラスチック部品のコスト高[コスト上昇分]を，製品価格に転嫁できない状況にある．

shift 名 変化，変動，移行，移動，転換，配置転換，交替，交替勤務時間，傾斜，転嫁，手段，方法，策，シフト (⇒**revenue mix**)
　do [work] a shift 交替勤務をする
　equity structure shift 資本再編成
　night shift 夜勤組
　shift in interest rate 金利の変動
　shift in market rates 相場の変動
　shift in [of] sentiment 市場の地合いの変化
　shift in the total workforce 従業員全体の配置転換
　temporary shift in money demand 資金需要の一時的なシフト
　two shifts of eight hours 8時間の2交替勤務
▶By shrinking corporate, group, division and country headquarters, we have produced a fundamental *shift* in the total workforce. 本社，グループ，部門と各国の本社機構を縮小することによって，当社は従業員全体の重要な配置転換を行いました．

shift of funds 資金の移動，資金移動，資金シフト
▶A sudden, huge *shift of funds* could bring even healthy financial institutions to the verge of collapse. 急激かつ大量の資金の移動は，健全な金融機関までも破綻に追いやる可能性がある．

shifting loan 借換え

ship 動 出荷する，発送する，発売する，船で送る，輸送する，輸出する
▶Revenue is recognized from sales or sales-type leases when the product is *shipped*. 売上または販売型リースの収益の計上時期は，製品の出荷時となっています．

ship 名 本船，船側
　ship's agent 船舶代理店
　ship's flag certificate 船籍証明書
　ship's flag of convenience 便宜置籍船
　ship's rail 船の舷側欄干，本船の欄干，本船舷側欄干
▶Risks of and title to the products shall pass

from the seller to the purchaser at the time when the products or any part of the products passes the *ship*'s rail of the vessel at the port of the shipment. 本製品の危険負担と所有権は，本製品または本製品の一部が船積み港で本船の舷側欄干を通過した時点で，売り主から買い主に移転するものとする。

shipment 名 出荷, 出荷量, 出荷台数, 発送, 輸出, 船積み, 船積み品, 船積み量, 積み荷, 船積
  inventory to shipment ratio 在庫率, 在庫率指数
  shipment in installment 分割船積み
  shipment of goods 商品の出荷, 商品の発送, 商品の船積み
  shipment procedures 輸出入手続き
  the conclusive date of shipment 船積みの確定日
  the date specified for shipment 船積みの特定日
  unit shipments 販売台数
  ▸Partial *shipment* and/or transhipment [transshipment] shall be permitted. 分割船積みや積み替えも可能とする。

shipping 名 船積み, 出荷, 港湾荷役
  Shipping Act 米海運法
  shipping agent 船舶代理店, 荷受業者
  shipping arrangement 船積み手配
  shipping cost 発送費
  shipping documents 船積み書類
  shipping firm 海運会社
  shipping industry 海運業, 海運業界
  shipping space 船腹
  ▸This letter of credit shall be opened not less than 30 calendar days before the first scheduled *shipping* date for each order. この信用状は，各注文の最初の出荷予定日から30暦日以上前に開設するものとする。

shop 名 小売店, 商店, 専門店, 職場, 作業場, 作業所, 工場, ショップ
  antenna shop アンテナ・ショップ（情報収集が主な目的のメーカー直営店）
  cash shop 現金店
  closed shop クローズド・ショップ（労働組合員だけを雇う会社）
  investment shop 投資銀行
  job shop 注文生産工場, 注文生産メーカー, 職業紹介所, ジョブ・ショップ
  open shop オープン・ショップ（非労働組合員も雇う会社）
  post-entry closed shop 入社後のクローズド・ショップ
  shop committee 職場委員会
  shop in shop 大型店に設けられる別の店舗, ショップ・イン・ショップ
  shop layout 店舗レイアウト（＝store layout）
  shop right 使用権, 使用者実施権, 社員発明の実施権, ショップ・ライト
  shop steward 労組の職場代表, 職場委員
  union shop ユニオン・ショップ（雇用者と労働組合の協定で，従業員の組合加入を条件とする会社）

shop front 店先, 店頭
shoplifting 名 万引き
shopping 名 買い物, 購買, 商戦, ショッピング (⇒one-stop shopping)
  Christmas shopping season クリスマス商戦
  Easter shopping season イースターの買い物シーズン
  holiday shopping season 米国のクリスマス商戦, クリスマスの買い物シーズン
  Internet shopping ネット・ショッピング（＝online shopping, virtual shopping）
  Net shopping ネット・ショッピング（＝Internet shopping）
  online shopping オンライン・ショッピング
  shopping district 商業地区
  shopping goods 買回り品（ファッション関連や耐久消費財などの商品）
  shopping mall 商店街, ショッピング・センター（＝shopping center, shopping complex）
  shopping on the web ネット・ショッピング
  shopping radius 買い物範囲
  treaty shopping 租税回避, 節税行為, トリーティ・ショッピング
  TV shopping テレビ・ショッピング
  virtual shopping バーチャル・ショッピング
  year-end shopping season 年末商戦
  ▸We are considering creating a *shopping* mall on the Web site we currently operate. 当社は，現在運営している自社サイト上に仮想商店街を設けることを検討している。

short-covering 名 買戻し
  ▸The dollar inched up on short-covering in afternoon trading. ドル相場は，午後の取引でドルが買い戻されて徐々に上昇した。

short-hour 名 臨時雇用
short-range profit planning 短期利益計画
short-run fund planning 短期資金計画（＝short-range fund planning, short-run cash

short selling 空売り (=short sale)
▶ *Short selling* is the practice of borrowing stocks from securities and financial companies and other investors to sell them and then buy them back when their prices drop. 空売りは、証券金融会社や他の投資家(機関投資家など)から株を借りて売り、その株が値下がりした時点で買い戻すことをいう。

short-term 形 短期の

short-term borrowings 短期借入金, 短期債務 (=short term loans, short term obligations)
▶ The firm sold 50-year debt to refinance its *short-term borrowings*. 同社は、短期債務[短期借入金]の借換えのため、満期50年の債券を発行した。

short-term liability 短期負債, 短期借入金, 短期貸付け金, 短期債権
▶ Net working capital—current assets less current liabilities—is a measure of our ability to cover *short-time liabilities* with assets that we expect to convert to cash soon. 正味運転資本(流動資産から流動負債を控除した額)は、短期債務を直ちに現金化できる資産で賄う能力を表します。

short-term profits 短期利益, 短期的利益
▶ The firm reportedly has a strong corporate culture of seeking *short term profits*. 同社は、短期的利益を追求する企業体質が強いとされる。

shortage 名 不足, 欠乏, 払底, 不足額, 不足高, 欠陥
- manpower shortage 人材不足, 人手不足, 労働力不足
- power shortage 電力不足

shortfall 名 不足額, 不足量, 不足分
- capital shortfall 資本不足, 資金不足, 自己資本不足
- revenue shortfall 歳入不足, 歳入欠陥

showing 名 成績, 出来, 出来栄え, 表示, 展示, 上映, 上演, 外観, 体裁, 供述, 申立て
- business showing 業績
- economy's better showing 景気回復, 景気の上向き, 景気回復
- improved showing 業績改善
- strong showing 好成績, 好決算
- upturn in the business showing 業績回復

▶ So far there are few promising signs of an upturn in the business *showing*. 今までのところ、業績回復の明るい兆しは見られない。

▶ The firm attributed the improved *showing* to stepped-up cost-cutting efforts and sales promotion. 同社は、業績改善の要因として、コスト削減努力の促進と販促を挙げた。

shrink 動 減少する, 低下する, 縮小する (⇒ shift 名)
▶ The firm's quarterly net loss *shrank* by more than 60 percent to ¥21.65 billion. 同社の四半期純損失は、60%以上縮小して216億5,000万円となった。

shrinkage 名 減少, 縮小, 低下, 下落, 減耗, 減耗費, 減耗損, 減損
- estimated normal shrinkage 通常の減耗見積り高
- inventory shrinkage 棚卸し減耗
- shrinkage loss 棚卸減耗費, 棚卸減耗損
- the shrinkage of the market 市場縮小

shut down 〈工場などを〉閉鎖する, 〈操業を〉停止する (⇒close 動)
▶ The firm will *shut down* and sell 20 percent of its plants in Japan. 同社は、日本国内工場の20%を閉鎖して売却する。

side 形 側面の, 主要でない, 副次的な, 付加的な
- farmer with a side job 兼業農家
- side benefit 付加的な利点, 副次的効果
- side business 副業, サイド・ビジネス
- side business sales 副業斡旋商法
- side-by-side form 左右対照式
- side-by-side sales 側面商法
- side effects 副作用, 予想外の副産物, 副次的効果
- side issue 副次的問題, 派生的問題
- side job 内職, アルバイト
- side view 側面図, 横顔, プロフィール

▶ Possible *side* effects drugs have on humans have been examined before. これまでの医薬品の審査対象は、人間への潜在的な副作用だった。

side with …に味方する, …の側に立つ, …の側につく, …を支持する (=take sides with, take the side of)
▶ The World Trade Organization *sided with* the United States, the European Union and Canada in a dispute over car parts. 世界貿易機関(WTO)は、自動車部品をめぐる紛争で、米国、欧州連合(EU)とカナダを支持した。

sideline 名 専門外取扱品, 副業, 内職, 側線, 様子見(複数形), 模様眺め, サイドライン
- on the sidelines 傍観者として
- remain on the sidelines 様子見の姿勢を崩さない
- retreat to the sidelines 手控える

sit on the sidelines 模様眺めの状況[状態]にある, 様子見のスタンスをとる (=take a wait-and-see attitude)
stay on the sidelines 様子見の状況にある, 模様眺めの状態にある, 模様眺めの姿勢に回る
wait on the sidelines 出番を待つ
▸Foreign investors retreated to the *sidelines*. 外国投資家は, 手控えた.

sight 名 一覧, 一見, 閲覧
at sight 提示のあり次第, 一覧で
sight bill 一覧払い為替手形 (=sight draft)
sight draft 一覧払い為替手形 (=sight bill)

sign 動 署名する, 署名調印する, 調印する, …と契約する
sign a memorandum 覚書に調印する
sign an agreement 契約書に署名する, 契約書に調印する, 合意書に署名する, 基本合意する (=sign a contract)
sign and seal 署名・捺印する
sign on the dotted line 文書に署名する, 無条件に同意する
▸The major Japanese automaker and the U.S. conglomerate *signed* a basic agreement to produce and sell jet engines developed by Honda for light business planes. 日本の大手自動車メーカー (ホンダ) と米国のコングロマリット (GE) は, ホンダが開発した小型ビジネス・ジェット機用ジェット・エンジンを生産・販売する基本契約書に署名した.

sign 名 兆し, 兆候, 動き, 様相, 気味, 標識, 署名
amid emerging signs of …の兆しが見られるなか
sign of recovery 景気回復の兆し, 回復の兆し
signs of instability 不安定な動き
signs of overheating 景気過熱の様相, 景気過熱気味
"sign of recovery" from "unchanged" 「横ばい」から「持ち直しの動き」
with no sign of an end to deflation デフレ克服の道筋は見えない
▸The economies in the U.S. and China that have aided the Japanese companies' recovery have now started to show *signs* of change. 日本企業の回復を支えてきた米国と中国の経済が, 今は変調の兆しが見え始めている.

sign up 契約[協定]を結ぶ, 参加する, 応募する
▸We expect to *sign up* other distributors for the product. 当社は, 他の販売代理店とも本製品の契約を結ぶ予定です.

signatory 形 参加調印した, 名 調印者, 署名者, 締約国
authorized signatory 正当な署名人

significant 形 重要な, 重大な, 大きな, 著しい, 際立った, 目立った, 本格的な, 相当な, かなりの, 大量の, 多額の, 大幅な, 大型の
significant accounting policies 重要な会計方針
significant acquisition 大型買収
significant earnings gains 大幅な増益
significant losses 巨額の損失, 巨額の赤字
significant subsidiary 重要な子会社
▸During 2008, the Corporation experienced a *significant* increase in its cash requirements because of higher fixed asset expenditures. 2008年度は, 固定資産支出額が増えたため, 必要資金がかなり増加しました.

simultaneous 形 同時の
simultaneous stock market plunges 同時株安
▸The worldwide *simultaneous stock market plunges* triggered by the United States have dealt a major blow to Japan 米国を震源とする世界同時株安が, 日本に大きな影響[打撃]を与えている.
simultaneous interpretation 同時通訳 (=simultaneous translation)
simultaneous transmission 同時送信

Singapore Exchange Ltd. シンガポール取引所《略 SGX》
▸The *Singapore Exchange Ltd.* (SGX) was inaugurated in December 1999 following the merger of the Stock Exchange of Singapore and the Singapore International Monetary Exchange. シンガポール取引所(SGX)は, シンガポール証券取引所とシンガポール国際金融取引所(金融先物取引所)が合併して, 1999年12月に設立された.

sinking fund 減債基金, 償却基金, 償却積立金, 別途資金 (「減債基金」は, 債券発行者が, 債券の償還に備えて償還期限前から一定額を定期的に積み立てる基金のこと)
reserve for sinking fund 減債基金積立金, 減債積立金 (=sinking fund reserve)
sinking fund for plant expansion 工場拡張基金
sinking fund for redemption of bonds 社債償還基金
sinking fund payments 減債基金の積立て, 減債基金の繰入れ
sinking fund requirements 減債基金への支払

い額, 減債基金積立額
▶Annual maturity and *sinking fund* requirements in millions of dollars on long term debt outstanding at December 31, 2008 are as follows: 2008年12月31日現在の長期負債残高の年度別返済額と減債基金への支払い額(単位:百万ドル)は, 次のとおりです。

site 名 拠点, 施設, 事業所, 工場, 用地, 設置先, 現場, サイト, インターネット上の場所, ホームページ (⇒**Web site**)
  auction site オークション・サイト
  community site コミュニティ・サイト
  construction site 建設用地, 建設現場
  dating site 出会い系サイト (=dating Web site, online dating site)
  e-commerce site eコマース・サイト
  EC site ECサイト
  harmful site 有害サイト
  investment site 投資先
  joint Web site 共同サイト
  mirror site ミラー・サイト
  portal site ポータル・サイト
  production site 生産拠点, 生産施設, 生産先
  search site 検索サイト (⇒**search**)
  shopping site ショッピング・サイト
▶In August 2009, 3,500 local employees, now located in 14 separate *sites*, will finally be consolidated into the new facility. 2009年8月から, 現在14か所の事業所に配置されている3,500人の従業員が, 最終的にこの新事業施設に移転する予定です。
▶To support Toyota's assembly plant, Japanese auto component and material suppliers are expected to set up production *sites* in Russia. トヨタの組立工場を支援するため, 日系部品・材料メーカーがロシアに生産拠点を設けることが予想される。

situation 名 状況, 状態, 情勢, 事情, 事態, 場面, 環境
  business situation 景況
  cash situation 資金繰り
  employment situation 雇用環境, 雇用情勢, 雇用状況
  financial situation 財政状態, 財政状況, 財政情勢, 財務状態, 財務体質, 金融情勢 (=financial condition, financial position)
  inflation situation インフレ環境
  market situation 市況
  monetary situation 金融事情, 金融情勢, 金融状態

  over-borrowed situation オーバー・ローン (=over-loaned situation)
  political situation 政局
  profit situation 収益状況
  situation management 状況管理
  situation wanted 求職
  supply and demand situation 需給状況, 需給バランス
  technical situation テクニカル要因
  turnaround situation 業績回復
▶The employment *situation* has improved in line with the economic recovery. 景気回復に伴って, 雇用環境は良くなっている。
▶The *situation* is that it is difficult to acquire more than 50 percent of shares in the firm. 今の状況では, 同社株の50%超を取得するのは厳しい。

six months ended Sept. 30 4-9月期, 3月期決算企業の上半期, 上期, 9月中間期 (=six months through Sept. 30, six months up to September)
▶The loss totaled ¥2.8 billion in the *six months ended Sept. 30*, compared with a loss of ¥18 billion a year earlier. 上半期[4-9月期]の損失総額は, 前年同期の180億円に対して28億円となった。

six months through June 1-6月期, 上半期, 上期
▶Mergers and acquisitions involving Japanese companies reached an all-time high in the *six months through June* 2006. 2006年上期(1-6月期)の日本企業関連のM&A(企業の合併・買収)件数は, 過去最高に達した。

six sigma シックス・シグマ (=6σ)
  シックス・シグマ➡業務改革の一環として, 製品やサービスの品質向上のために米モトローラ社が開発した手法で, 組織全体で製品, サービスのエラーやミスの発生確率を100万分の数回[3.4回]に抑えること。GEやIBMのほか, 日本のソニー, NECや東芝も導入している。シックス・シグマは, 測定・分析・改善と管理のプロセスを経て実現される。
▶Motorola's *Six Sigma* shows its corporate culture that strives to achieve perfection in quality. モトローラ社の「シックス・シグマ」は, あくまでも品質面での完璧さを追求する同社の企業文化を示している。

size 名 規模, 大きさ, 寸法, 大量, 大規模, 型, 番, サイズ
  economic size 経済規模 (=size of the economies)
  issue size 発行規模

lot size 取引規模
market size 市場規模, 取引規模
offering size 入札総額
optimal production lot size 最適生産ロット・サイズ
optimal purchasing lot size 最適購入ロット・サイズ
regular size advertising 規格広告
sample size 標本数, サンプル数
size effect 規模の効果
size of capacity 生産能力
size of the firm 企業規模 (＝the firm size)
▶The *size* of the global market for photovoltaic power generation is expected to double in the 2006 to 2010 period. 太陽光発電のグローバル市場の規模は, 2006年から2010年の5年間で2倍になる見通しだ。

skill 名 能力, 手腕, 技術, 技能, 熟練, 職業能力, スキル
　bargaining skill 交渉術
　business skills 経営技術
　communication skills コミュニケーション技能, コミュニケーション力
　conceptual skills 総合管理技術
　decision-making skill 意思決定能力
　entrepreneurial skills 経営技術, 経営のノウハウ
　industrial skills 産業技術
　managerial skills 経営技術, 経営の手腕
　management skills 経営手腕, 経営技術
　sales skills 販売能力, 販売技術
　skill test 技能検定 (＝skills testing)
　skills assessment 技能評価
　skills center 技能センター
　skills development 職業能力開発 (⇒**reenter the workforce**)
　technical skills 技能, 技術力 (⇒**transfer of technical skills**)
▶We are investing in enhancing the *skills* of our people and in the development of improved tools of productivity. 当社は, 社員の技能向上と生産性向上に役立つツールの開発に投資しています。

skilled 形 熟練した, 熟練［特殊技術］を要する, 特殊技術［特殊技能］を持った, 老練な
　skilled craftsman 熟練した職人, 職人
　skilled employee 熟練社員, 貴重な人材
　skilled labor 熟練労働, 熟練労働者, 熟練工 (＝skilled worker)
　skilled work 熟練を要する仕事
　skilled worker 熟練工, 熟練労働者 (＝skilled hand, skilled labor)
　skilled workman 熟練工
▶Toyota is considering accepting some *skilled* assembly workers of Mitsubishi Motors Corp.'s factory in Okazaki. トヨタは現在, 三菱自動車の岡崎工場の熟練組立工受入れを検討している。

skim 動 〈所得を〉隠す, ごまかす, 名 所得隠し, 隠し所得

skyrocket 動 急増する, 急騰する, 急上昇する, 跳ね上がる (⇒**melon**)
▶Sovereign wealth funds have grown to $2 trillion ?3 trillion globally as a result of *skyrocketing* crude oil prices and accumulation of foreign exchange reserves in emerging market economies. 政府系投資ファンドの運用総額は, 原油価格の急騰と急成長市場国の外貨準備高の増加で, 世界全体で2兆－3兆ドルに拡大している。

slack 形 不活発な, 不景気な, 副 不振で, 名 不振 (⇒**wage growth**)
　slack demand 需要低迷, 需要不振

slash 動 削減する, 減らす, 低減する, 引き下げる, 下方修正する (⇒**employer, profitability**)
　slash capital expenditures 設備投資を減らす, 設備投資を削減する
　slash profit forecasts 業績見通し［業績予想］を下方修正する
▶GM has posted losses and its credit rating has been *slashed* to junk status. GMは最近赤字に陥り, 信用格付けが「投機的」に落とされた。
▶The company *slashed* its profit forecasts because of costs from a massive global recall of laptop batteries. 同社は, 全世界でのパソコン用充電池の回収費用が巨額なため, 業績見通しを下方修正した。
▶The firm is giving up its assets in an attempt to *slash* its interest-bearing liabilities. 同社は, 有利子負債を削減するため, 資産を手放している。

slide 名 下降, 下落, 値崩れ
sliding scale system 物価スライド制
▶The *sliding scale system* for pension payments is aimed at guaranteeing pensioners the real value of their pension payment. 年金支給額の物価スライド制の目的は, 年金受給者に年金支給の実質的な価値を保証することにある。

slip 動 落ち込む, 低下する, 水準から外れる, 名 紙片, 伝票
　debit slip 借方票, 借方伝票, 債務覚書, 代金請求書
　payment slip 支払い明細書
　slip into the red 赤字に転落する (＝fall into

the red)

slot 名 位置, 場所, 地位, 放送番組の時間帯, 硬貨の差入れ口, スロット
▸Sony has held the top *slot* seven times in the last 10 years in the Harris Interactive's poll of corporate brands. 米国の世論調査会社ハリス・インタラクティブの企業ブランド意識調査で, ソニーが過去10年で7回, 1位(トップ)となった。

slow down 減速する, 後退する, 鈍化する, 停滞する, 低迷する
▸The growth rates of sales and profits are expected to *slow down* in the second half of the year. 売上高と利益の伸び率は, 下半期は鈍化しそうだ。

slowdown 名 〈景気などの〉減速, 後退, 沈滞, 低迷, 低下, 減産, 操業短縮, 怠業 (⇒housing investment)
　demand slowdown 需要の伸びの鈍化, 需要減速, 需要低迷
　economic slowdown 景気減速, 景気後退, 景気低迷, 景気鈍化
　global slowdown 世界的な景気低迷, 世界的な景気減速
　inflationary slowdown インフレ率の低下
　seasonal demand slowdown 季節要因による需要減速
▸Many analysts expect a *slowdown* in January-March 2009. アナリストの多くは, 2009年1-3月期に景気が減速すると見ている。
▸There are signs of a *slowdown* in the U.S. economy. 米国経済に, 陰りが見えてきた。

sluggish 形 不振の, 低迷した, 不活発な, 不景気な, 動きが鈍い, 足どりが重い, 軟調な
　sluggish demand 需要低迷 (＝weak demand)
　sluggish economy 景気低迷 (＝sluggish economic conditions)
　sluggish sales 販売低迷
　sluggish stock market 低迷した株式市場, 株式市場の低迷, 株式相場の低迷 (＝slumping stock market)
▸Our business in the United States continued to be *sluggish* and showed no growth over the previous year. 米国内での当社の業績は伸びず, 前年度を上回る成長を見ることができませんでした。

sluggish consumption 消費の低迷
▸This wide gap between supply and demand was caused by such factors as a plunge in demand in IT-related industries and *sluggish consumption*. この大幅な需給ギャップは, IT関連産業の需要の落ち込みや消費低迷によるものだ。

sluggish performance 業績不振
▸Banks refused to extend new loans to the company due to its *sluggish performance*. 業績不振で, 銀行は同社への新規融資に応じなかった。

slump 名 暴落, 急落, 落ち込み, 減少, 低迷, 不振, 不況, 不景気, 景気沈滞, スランプ (＝sluggishness)
　business slump 景気低迷, 景気沈滞, 経営不振, 業績不振 (＝slump in business)
　demand slump 需要低迷
　economic slump 景気低迷, 景気後退, 不景気, 不況
　economic slump triggered by the yen's sharp appreciation 円高不況
　slump in the dollar ドル安
　slump in the stock prices 株価急落
　slump-ridden industry 不況業種
　worldwide slump 世界的不況
▸A housing investment *slump* results from the enforcement of the revised Building Standards Law. 住宅投資の落込みは, 改正建築基準法の施行によるものだ。
▸The prolonged *slump* in the real estate market is maintaining the decline in land prices. 不動産取引市場の長期低迷が, 引き続き地価の下落を招いている。

slumping stock market 株式市況の低迷
small business 中小企業
small-business operator 零細事業主
▸People indebted to multiple consumer loan firms and financially strapped *small-business operators* have been the main targets of loan sharks. 多重債務者や資金繰りが苦しい零細事業主が, ヤミ金融業者の主な標的になっている。

small-cap 名 小型株
soar 動 急騰する, 急増する, 大きく上回る
　soaring euro ユーロの急騰
　soaring prices 物価高騰
　soaring profits 利益の急増
▸The company's group operating profit *soared* 35.1 percent from a year before. 同社の連結営業利益は, 前年比で35.1％の急増となった。
▸The yen *soared* to ¥109 to the dollar recently. 円は最近, 1ドル＝109円に急騰した。

social insurance labor consultant 社会保険労務士
▸A certified *social insurance labor consultant* specializes in annual pensions. 公認社会保険労務士は, 年金相談を専門とする。

social insurance premium 社会保険料

▸Taxes and the portion of *social insurance premiums* charged to Japanese corporations' employers are considered costs. 日本企業の事業主が負担する税金や社会保険料も，コストになる．

social networking service ソーシャル・ネットワーキング・サービス《略 SNS》(日記や個人情報などを，特定の仲間うちなどに限ってネット上で公開するサービス．原則としてお互いの名前や肩書などを公開して，意見交換や交流などを行うことができる)
▸The number of users of *social networking services* has been rapidly increasing in recent years. 近年，ソーシャル・ネットワーキング・サービス(SNS)の利用者が急増している．

social responsibility 社会的責任
▸From the perspective of corporate *social responsibility*, the distribution industry should pay more attention to intellectual property rights in the future. 企業の社会的責任の観点から，流通業界は今後，知的財産権にも一段と配慮しなければならない．

social security 社会保障
 Social Security Act 社会保障法
 social security allowance budget 社会保障給付費
 social security benefits 社会保障給付
 social security number 社会保障番号《略 SSN》
 social security outlays 社会保障関係費 (＝social security spending, social welfare costs)
 social security taxes payable 社会保険税預り金

social security insurance premium 社会保険料
▸*Social security* insurance premiums are paid by employers. 社会保険料は，雇用主が負担している．

social security system 社会保障制度 (＝social security plan)
▸The sharp decline in the birthrate and the rapid graying of society are shaking the very foundation of the nation's *social security system*. 急速な少子高齢化が，日本の社会保障制度の土台そのものを揺るがしている．

social service 社会福祉事業
social service leave 社会福祉休暇，ボランティア休暇
soft 形 楽な，楽に儲かる，低利長期の，軟調の
 soft goods 非耐久財
 soft loan 長期低利貸付け
soft drinks industry 清涼飲料産業，清涼飲料業界

▸Industries in which two leading companies compete head-to-head to the exclusion of all others, such as in the U.S. *soft drinks industry*, are relatively rare. 米国の清涼飲料業界などのように，大手2社が他社を除外して激烈な競争を繰り広げている産業は，あまり多くはない．

soft landing 軟着陸 (⇒hard landing)
▸The Chinese central bank's recent interest rate hikes is an important move to cool the overheating Chinese economy and guide it toward a *soft landing*. 中国の中央銀行である人民銀行の今回の利上げ[貸出金利の引上げ]は，景気の過熱[中国経済の過熱]を鎮め，中国経済を安定成長に軟着陸させるための重要な動きである．

software 名 ソフトウエア，コンピュータ・プログラム，コンピュータの運用操作技術，利用技術，視聴覚教材，ロケット[宇宙船]の燃料，ソフト
 accounting software 財務会計ソフト
 antivirus software ウイルス防止ソフト
 audit software 監査ソフト
 bundled software 添付ソフト
 business software 業務ソフト，ビジネス・ソフト
 communication software 通信ソフト
 financial software 金融ソフト
 image processing software 画像処理ソフト
 integrated software 統合ソフト
 operating software 基本ソフト，基本ソフトウエア (＝operating system)
 package software 市販ソフト，パッケージ・ソフト
 proprietary software 専用ソフト
 software devices ソフトウエアの記憶媒体，ソフトウエアの媒体
 software platform 基本ソフト
 software product ソフトウエア製品，ソフトウエア
 software resource management ソフトウエア資源管理
 virus protection software ウイルス対策ソフト
 word processing software ワープロ・ソフト
▸Sony's technology center in Shanghai is its base for the development of *software* in China. ソニーの上海のテクノロジー・センターは，中国国内でのソフトウエア開発拠点である．

software program コンピュータのソフトウエア・プログラム
▸ABC hereby grants to XYZ and XYZ accepts the exclusive nontransferable right and license to promote, market and sublicense the *Software Program* within the territory under the terms

set forth herein.　本契約によりABCは，本契約に定める条件により許諾地域内で本ソフトウエア・プログラムの販売促進と販売，サブライセンスを行う譲渡不可の独占的権利とライセンスをXYZに付与し，XYZはこれを承諾する．

solar cell 太陽電池
▶Mitsubishi Electric Corp. plans to invest $70 million to boost production of *solar cells*. 三菱電機は，太陽電池の生産を拡大するため，7,000万ドルの投資を計画している．

solicit 動 勧誘する，募集する，強く求める，…するように要請する，〈資金などを〉集める，訪問販売する
　solicit clients 顧客を勧誘する
　solicit funds from …に資金提供を要請する，…に出資を勧誘する，…から資金を集める
　solicit orders 注文をとる
　solicit proxies 委任状を取り付ける，議決権代理行使の勧誘をする
▶As initial capital to establish an intellectual property fund, the bank plans to *solicit* between ¥5 billion and ¥6 billion from financial institutions and enterprises. 知的財産ファンドを創設するための当初資金として，同行は金融機関や事業会社から50億〜60億円を集める計画だ．
▶During the business suspension, the company will not be allowed to extend new loans, *solicit* new customers or call in loans. 業務停止の期間中，同社は新規融資や新規顧客の勧誘，貸出［貸金］の回収業務ができなくなる．

solicitation 名 勧誘，募集，要請，訪問販売
　insurance solicitation 保険募集（= insurance soliciting）
　solicitation of clients 顧客の勧誘
　solicitation of proxies 議決権代理行使の勧誘，委任状勧誘（= proxy solicitation）
▶*Solicitation* of proxies is being made through the mail, in person, and by telecommunications. 議決権代理行使の勧誘は，郵便，経営陣により直接，または電信・電話などの通信手段で行われています．

solicitor 名 事務弁護士，法務官

solid 形 着実な，堅実な，底堅い，強固な，健全な，安定した
　solid demand 堅実な需要，需要の安定
　solid economic growth 底堅い経済成長，着実な景気拡大
　solid growth 着実な伸び，着実な［底堅い］成長
　solid management 堅実な経営，安定した経営
　solid performance 底堅い業績，堅調な値動き
▶*Solid* growth in our U.S. and Canadian markets fueled our largest dollar increases for the quarter. 当四半期は，米国とカナダ市場での着実な伸びが売上増の最大の原動力となりました．
▶The world economy remains *solid*. 世界経済は，引き続き底堅い．

solution 名 解決，問題解決，問題解決策，問題解決手法，解決法，解決策，対策，手段，コンピュータとアプリケーション，ネットワークの組合せによるシステム構築，ユーザーの要求に応じた情報システムの構築，ソリューション（⇒ **production cycle**）
　comprehensive solution 包括的ソリューション
　computing solution service 業務処理・問題解決サービス
　customized solution 顧客の要求に応じて特注化したソリューション，ソリューションの特注化
　electronic commerce solution 電子商取引ソリューション
　payment solution 決済ソリューション
　solution business 問題解決型営業，ソリューション・ビジネス
　Web solution ウェブ・ソリューション
　win-win-win solution 三方一両得の解決策
▶Our goal is to shape and lead the customer information *solutions* market. 当社の目標は，顧客情報ソリューション（解決策）の市場を形成し，そのマーケット・リーダーになることです．

solvency 名 支払い余力，支払い能力，ソルベンシー（支払い期日の到来時点で支払いできる状態にあること）
　solvency margin 支払い余力，支払い余力比率，ソルベンシー・マージン（= solvency margin rate, solvency margin ratio: 大災害時などの場合における生命保険会社の支払い能力のことで，保険会社の経営［財務］の健全性を判断する基準の一つ）
　solvency position 自己資本比率
　solvency ratio 支払い能力比率，自己資本比率，流動性比率
　solvency rule 支払い能力規制

solvency margin ratio [rate] ソルベンシー・マージン（支払い余力）比率
▶*Solvency margin ratios* are the most closely watched gauges in assessing the financial health of an insurance company. ソルベンシー・マージン比率は，保険会社の経営［財務］の健全性を評価する際に特に注目される指標である．

solvent 形 支払い能力のある，名 溶剤，溶媒，解決策

solvent client 支払い能力のある顧客

sophisticated 形 高度の, 高性能の, 最先端技術の, 最新式の, 最新装置の, 精巧な, 精密な, 巧みな, 複雑な, 手の込んだ, 凝った, 洗練された, あか抜けた, しゃれた, おしゃれな, 品のいい, 高級な, 超近代的な, 都会的な, 有能な, 優秀な, 効率的な, 無駄のない, 本格的な (=cutting-edge, leading edge, state-of-the-art, top of the line; ⇒corporate image)

highly sophisticated technology 高度先端技術
most sophisticated technology 最先端技術
sophisticated design 洗練されたデザイン
sophisticated product 高度な製品, 高加工製品
sophisticated technology 高度技術, 先端技術, 先進技術, ハイテク (=advanced technology, high-tech, high technology)

▸Medical treatment has been getting more *sophisticated* and complicated. 医療が高度化, 複雑化している。

▸Telemarketing methods have become more and more *sophisticated*. 電話勧誘商法の手口は, 巧妙化している。

sophistication 名 技術の高度化, 発達, 高水準, 水準, 精密化, 複雑化, 精巧さ, 知的教養, 知識
consumer sophistication 消費者の知識
economic sophistication 経済発展

▸The ASEAN region's technological *sophistication* in manufacturing components is on par with the world standard. ASEAN (アジア諸国連合) 地域の部品製造技術の水準は, 世界標準並みである。

source(s) 名 源泉, 源, 〈利子・配当などの〉支払い者, 情報源, ニュースソース, 筋, 取材源, 関係者, 資料, 出典, 出所 (⇒vendor)
cash sources 資金の源泉
deduction at source 源泉徴収
external sources of cash 外部流動性
financial source 財源
funding source 資金調達源, 資金源
funds from external sources 外部資金
income from sources without the United States 米国外源泉所得
income source 収入源, 所得源泉 (=income producer)
internal sources 内部資金
internal sources of cash 内部流動性 (=internal sources of liquidity)
liquidity sources 資金源
other sources of funds その他の資金の源泉
outside sources of funds 外部流動性
principle of single source 単一性の原則

production supply sources 原材料調達源
renewable energy sources 恒久的エネルギー源
repayment source 返済原資
revenue sources 財源, 歳入源, 収益源, 収入源
second source 二次供給源, セカンド・ソース (部品などを調達するとき, 企業の防衛手段として1社だけでなく他からも供給を受けること)
source and application of funds 資金の源泉と使途, 資金運用表
source of earnings 収益源 (=earnings source, source of income, source of profits)
source of financing 資金調達源 (=source of funding)
source of funds 資金源, 資金の源泉

▸Financial reports and other documents published by companies are the most fundamental *sources* of information for investors and creditors. 企業が公表する有価証券報告書などは, 投資家や債権者にとって最も基幹的な情報源だ。

sourcing 名 調達, 業務委託, 供給, ソーシング (⇒outsourcing)
double sourcing 供給源の分散
global sourcing グローバル・ソーシング
raw material sourcing 原材料の供給
world sourcing 世界市場への製品供給

▸In addition to the segment's factory expansion program, it is actively pursuing additional capacity through the *sourcing* of products from outside vendors. 当事業部門の工場拡張計画のほかに, 当事業部門は外部ベンダーからの製品調達により, 製造能力の強化に積極的に取り組んでいます。

sovereign 名 国家, 国家機関, 政府・政府機関, 〈政府系企業などの〉公的機関, 君主, 元首, 主権者, 主権国, 独立国, ソブリン債, 形 独立した, 最高の, 最上の, 特効の, ソブリン
sovereign borrower ソブリン発行体, 借り手の国家機関
sovereign debt 公的債務, 国債
sovereign immunity 主権免除, 主権免除特権
sovereign issuance ソブリン債の発行
sovereign issuer ソブリン発行体
sovereign loan 国家向けローン, ソブリン融資, ソブリン・ローン
sovereign name ソブリン銘柄
sovereign remedy 特効薬
sovereign risk ソブリン・リスク, カントリー・リスク (対外融資先が公的機関の場合の債権回収リスク)
structured sovereign 仕組みソブリン債

sovereign wealth fund 政府系投資ファンド, 政府系ファンド, ソブリン・ウエルス・ファンド《略 SWF》（＝government-affiliated investment fund, government-run investment fund: 政府が運用するファンドで、その原資の公的資金は主に中央銀行の外貨準備高や国有天然資源で得られる利益であることが多い。⇒**clout**）

世界の主な政府系ファンド：

アラブ首長国連邦	アブダビ投資庁
クウェート	クウェート投資銀行
サウジアラビア	サウジ通貨庁
シンガポール	シンガポール政府投資公社
中国	中国投資有限責任公司
ノルウェー	政府年金基金
ロシア	準備基金

▶For the fund of a *sovereign wealth fund*, the use of foreign currency reserves and public pension reserves is being studied. 政府系ファンドの元手としては、外貨準備と公的年金積立金の活用が現在検討されている。

space industry 宇宙産業
▶Japan's new H-2A rocket is seen as crucial to the future of the Japanese *space industry*. 日本の新型ロケット「H-2A」は、日本の宇宙産業の将来に重要な意味をもつと見られている。

spam 名 迷惑メール, スパム（＝junk mail, spam mail: 受信者に勝手に送られてくる迷惑な宣伝用の電子メールのこと）
　spam mail 迷惑メール, スパム・メール
　spam e-mail スパム・メール（＝junk mail, spam, spam mail）
▶Reviewing communications privacy rules is a key part of the battle against *spam* e-mails. 通信の秘密に関する規則の見直しは、スパム・メール対策のポイントだ。

spamming 名 スパミング（本人の許可なく広告・宣伝メールを送りつけること）

SPC 特定目的会社, 特別目的会社（**special purpose company**の略）

SPE 特別目的事業体（**special purpose entity**の略）

spec 明細, 仕様(書)（**specification**の略）

special benefits 特別給付
▶These *special benefits* are provided to employees accepting early retirement offers. この特別給付は、早期退職案を受諾する従業員に支払われます。

special demand 特需
▶Thanks to the scorching summer weather and *special demand* due to the Beijing Olympics, sales of home electrical appliances and summer clothing remains brisk. 猛暑と北京オリンピックの特需で、家電や夏物衣料の売れ行きは好調に推移している。

special loss 特別損失（＝extraordinary loss）
▶The corporation reported the largest ever after-tax loss for a Japanese company due to group companies' huge *special losses*. 同社は、グループ企業全体の巨額の損失により、日本企業で過去最大の税引き後損失［税引き後赤字］となったことを発表した。

special profit 特別利益
▶In the first half, the firm booked a *special profit* of about ¥400 billion on debt waivers by its key lenders. 上半期に同社は、主要金融機関の債務免除［債権放棄］で、約4,000億円の特別利益を計上した。

special purpose company 特別目的会社, 特定目的会社《略 SPC》（＝special purpose corporation, special purpose entity: 不動産や債権の証券化など、特別の目的を持って設立される会社。有価証券を発行し、小口化して広く資金を調達できるメリットがある）

special resolution 特別決議
▶Approval for a triangular merger should be based on a *special resolution*. 三角合併の承認は、特別決議によらなければならない［三角合併には、特別決議による承認が必要だ］。

specialize 動 特化する,〈手形など〉の支払いを限定する, 支払い先を指定する

specialty 名 専門, 本職, 得意, 特製品, 捺印証書, 捺印契約
　specialty goods 専門品
　specialty store 専門店

Specified Commercial Transactions Law 特定商取引法（訪問販売法が2000年の改正で「特定商取引法」に変更された。その対象は訪問販売や通信販売、電話勧誘販売など六つの取引形態で、クーリングオフや違反があった場合の行政処分や刑事罰も規定されている）

specimen 名 見本, 適例, 例

speculate 動 投機をする, 思惑売買をする

speculation 名 投機, 思惑, 思惑買い, 憶測, 推測, 観測, 相場（投機とは、配当や株価の短期的な値上がりを期待して株式を売買することをいう）
　buy dollars on speculation 思惑でドルを買う
　currency speculation 通貨投機, 為替投機
　exchange speculation 為替投機
　lose money through speculation 相場で損をする

make money through speculation 相場で儲ける
property speculation 不動産投機, 土地投機
speculation by foreign investment funds 海外投資ファンドの投機
speculation stock 仕手株
▶*Speculation* that some major banks may find themselves with capital shortfalls and then nationalized is driving investors to dump the banks' shares. 大手行の一部が自己資本不足に陥って国有化されるとの思惑から, 投資家は銀行株の売りに出ている.
▶The collapse of the firm was the result of *speculation* by foreign investment funds of a dubious nature. 同社の経営破綻は, 実態不明の海外投資ファンドの投機によるものだった.

speculative 形 投機的な, 思惑による, 推測に基づく, 理論的な
  speculative attacks 投機売り, 投機圧力, 投機筋の攻撃
  speculative buy order 投機的な買い注文
  speculative buying 投機的な買い, 投機買い, 思惑買い
  speculative funds 投機資金 (＝speculative money)
  speculative grade bond 投機の格付け債券, 高利回り債
  speculative import 思惑輸入
  speculative interests 思惑筋
  speculative investment 投機的投資, 投機的運用, 投機
  speculative market 投機市場, 思惑市場, 仕手市場
  speculative stock 仕手株 (＝speculative issue, speculative leader)
  speculative trader 投機筋
speculative group 投機集団
▶The stock prices in Tokyo have fallen as a result of buying and selling operations by hedge funds run by U.S. and European *speculative groups*. 欧米の投機集団が運用しているヘッジ・ファンドの売り買い操作で, 東京(株式市場)の株価は下落している.

speculator 名 投機家, 相場師, 仕手
  land speculator 地上げ屋
spend 動 支出する, 投資する, 出資する, 消費する
▶Sales also gained as the company *spent* more on machinery and equipments. 機械設備投資の拡大に伴って, 同社の売上高も増加した.
spending 名 支出, 投資, 出資, 消費 (⇒**capi-**
tal spending, R&D spending)
  consumer spending 個人消費支出, 消費支出, 家計部門の支出
  corporate spending 企業の支出, 設備投資
  current spending 経常支出
  discretionary spending 裁量的経費
  household spending 個人消費
  investment spending 公共投資
  mandatory spending 義務的経費
  private spending 民間支出
  spending on goods and services モノやサービスへの支出
  spending on R&D 研究開発費 (＝R&D spending)
▶A portion of the increase in R&D *spending* was also due to the unfavorable impact of foreign exchange on R&D expenditures most of which are incurred in Canada. 研究開発費の大半はカナダで発生しているため, 米ドル為替相場の下落による影響も研究開発費拡大の一因でした.

spin off 会社を分割する, 分社化する, 分離する, 切り離す
▶Sony and Sharp agreed to set up the joint venture by *spinning off* a factory Sharp is building in Sakai. ソニーとシャープは, シャープが大阪堺市に現在建設中の工場を分社化して, 両社の合弁会社を設立することで合意した.
spinoff [**spin-off**] 名 分社化, 分社, 会社分割, 切り離し, 分離, スピンオフ(企業が事業の一部を切り離して別の会社に移すこと. ⇒**service**)
  spinoff effects 波及効果 (＝spin-off effects)
  spinoff system 会社分割制度, 分社化制度 (＝spin-off system)
▶Troubled Kanebo Ltd. returned to the black for the first time in six years on the back of a *spinoff* of its cosmetics division. 経営不振[経営再建中]のカネボウは, 化粧品事業の分離などで6期ぶりの黒字転換を果たした.

spiral 名 循環的上昇・下降, 悪循環, 連続的変動
  deflationary spiral デフレの悪循環, デフレ的悪循環, デフレ・スパイラル
  land price spiral 地価高騰
split 動 分離する, 分割する, 分裂する, 離脱する, 解散する (⇒**boost**)
▶On October 1, 2008, the Corporation *split* its common stock 4 for 1. 2008年10月1日に当社は, 当社発行の普通株式1株を4株に分割しました.
▶The company had its total marked-to-market value of stocks raised by *splitting* its one share into 100. 同社は, 自社株1株を100株に分割して

株式の時価総額をつり上げていた。

split 名 分裂, 亀裂, 不和, 分割, 株式分割 （⇒ stock split）
    reverse split 株式併合 （＝reverse stock split, stock split-down）
    share split 株式分割
    split-up of stock 株式分割 （＝share split-up, stock split-up）
▸Prior to the *split*, the company had 10,000 shares of $15 par value common stock issued and outstanding. 株式分割前, 同社は額面15ドルの普通株式1万株が発行済みであった。

split off 分離する, 分離独立させる, 分割する
▸The IRCJ hopes to *split off* the real estate business to prevent the company from making up shortfalls in food supermarket earnings with income from retail space rentals. 産業再生機構が不動産事業を分離するのは, 同社が食品スーパーの収益の不足分を小売店舗スペースの賃貸料でかさ上げするのを避けるのが狙いだ。

split up 分割する
▸Our stores and businesses will be *split up* and sold and we will be torn apart. 当社の店舗と事業は分割・譲渡され, 当社は解体されてしまうだろう。

spokesman 名 広報担当者, 報道官, スポークスマン
    company spokesman 広報担当者
    Pentagon spokesman 米国防総省報道官
    White House spokesman ホワイトハウス報道官
▸"Business performance has improved since the latter half of last year," a company *spokesman* said. 「昨年後半から, 業績が向上している」と広報担当者はいう。

sponsor 動 後援する, 主催する, 後押しする, 支持する, 支援する, 〈制度などを〉設ける, 〈法案などを〉主唱する, 保証する, 保証人になる, 協力する, スポンサーになる
    federally sponsored agencies 連邦政府関連機関
    government sponsored agency [enterprise, entity] 政府系機関
▸We *sponsor* savings plans for the majority of our employees. 当社は, 大多数の当社従業員のために貯蓄制度を設けています。

sponsor 名 〈投資信託証券の〉引受人［引受業者］, 〈ベンチャー・ビジネスや慈善事業などへの〉出資者, 〈プロジェクト・ファイナンスの〉実質的推進者, 〈債務などの〉保証人, 原資産保有者, 後援者, 後援会, 主催者, 発起人, 支持者, 広告主, 番組提供者, スポンサー
    corporate sponsors スポンサー企業
    official sponsor 公式スポンサー
    sponsor company スポンサー企業 （＝corporate sponsor）
    sponsors for large advertisements 大口広告主
▸Companies inside and outside Japan expressed a desire to help Daiei's rehabilitation as a *sponsor* company. 国内外の複数企業が, ダイエー再建支援のスポンサー企業として名乗りを上げた。

spot 形 即座の, 現金の, 現金払いの, 現金取引の, 現物の, 名 場所, 地点, 位置, 地位, 職, 現物, 現地品, スポット
    ad spot スポットCM
    merchandise on spot 現場渡し, 現物
    on the spot 即座に, その場で, 現場で, 現物で, 現金で
    price on spot 現物相場, 現金相場, 現金売価
    spot advertising スポット広告
    spot and short selling of shares 株の現物売りと空売り
    spot announcement 差し込み広告放送, スポット・アナウンスメント
    spot basis 現物決済
    spot broker 現物仲買い, 現物仲買人, 現物ブローカー
    spot campaign スポット・キャンペーン
    spot cargo 現物荷
    spot cash 即時現金, 即金
    spot charter 不定期用船
    spot check 現物相場（現金売買の値段）, 抜き取り検査, 抜き打ち点検［検査］
    spot commodity 現物 （＝cash commodity, spot goods）
    spot contract 現物即時渡し約定
    spot crude スポット原油
    spot currency market 直物通貨市場
    spot deal 直物取引, 現物取引, 直物為替取引
    spot dealers 実株筋
    spot dealing 直物取引, 現物取引
    spot delivery 現場渡し, 現物渡し
    spot display スポット・ディスプレー
    spot dollars ドル直物
    spot economy 現物経済
    spot exchange 直物為替
    spot exchange rate 直物為替相場, 現物相場
    spot exchange transaction 直物為替取引, 現物為替取引
    spot firm 現金取引会社
    spot-forward transaction 直売先買取引

spot goods 現物, 現物取引
spot inspection 立入り検査
spot market 現物市場, 直物市場, 現金取引市場, 当用買い市場, スポット市場, スポット・マーケット （＝cash market: 現金の受け払いで商品が即時に受渡しされる市場）
spot needs 急需要
spot news ニュース速報
spot next [spot/next] スポット・ネクスト（受渡し日が約定日から3日後となる取引。2営業日後(スポット)から翌日までの金利やスワップ・レートを意味することもある）
spot operation 直物取引, 現物取引, 直物操作
spot position 現物持ち高, 直物持ち高
spot price 現物価格, 直物価格, 直物商品価格, スポット価格 （＝cash price: スポット市場［現物市場］で取引される商品の現在価格）
spot purchase 当用買い, 現金買い, 即時買い
spot quotation 現物相場, 現場渡し値段
spot rate 直物相場, 直物レート, 直為替相場, 直物為替レート, スポット・レート
spot rate of exchange 直物為替相場, 現物為替相場
spot reproduction cost 時価再生産原価
spot sale 即売, 現金売り, 現物取引, 現場取引
spot selling 現物売り
spot share 実株, 花形株
spot ship 早舟(はやぶね)
spot start スワップの開始日 （一般に約定日から2営業日後を開始日とする）
spot stock 実株, 現株
spot transaction 直物取引, 現物取引, 実物取引, 直物為替取引, 直物為替契約, 直物契約
spot-weld スポット溶接
▶More than 90 percent of *spot transactions* of stocks are conducted on the Tokyo Stock Exchange. 現物株取引の9割以上が, 東京証券取引所(東証)で行われている。
spread 名 利幅, 利ざや, 上乗せ, 金利差, 開き, 売り値と買い値の差, スプレッド, (銀行の調達金利である)預金金利と(運用金利である)貸出金利との差, 〈株や債券, 通貨取引などの〉買い呼び値(bid)と売り呼び値(offer)との差額, 有価証券の発行者の引受業者への引渡し価格と引受業者の一般投資家への売出価格との差額
interest rate spread 金利スプレッド, 利ざや
profit spread 利ざや
yield spread 利回り格差
▶Wider *spreads* were also seen in the market for commercial mortgage-backed securities. 金利差(スプレッド)の拡大は, 商業用不動産証券の市場でも見られた。
spree 名 熱中, 耽溺, 没入
squander 動 浪費する
squeeze 動 締め付ける, 引き締める, 〈予算や経費などを〉切り詰める, 制限する, 圧迫する, 押し下げる, 縮小する, 低下する, 減少する
▶Profits have been *squeezed* as interest rates remain near zero percent and loan demands stalls. 金利はまだゼロに近いし, 借入需要も停滞したままなので, 利益は減少している。
squeeze 名 締付け, 引締め, 切詰め, 制限, 打撃, 圧迫, 縮小, 低下, 減少
margin squeeze 利益率低下, 利益率圧迫, 利ざや縮小 （＝squeeze in margins）
profit squeeze 利益減少, 利益縮小
squeeze on earnings 利益圧迫, 業績悪化
SRI 社会的責任投資 （socially responsible investingの略）
SRI fund 社会的責任投資ファンド, SRIファンド （社会に貢献する企業は消費者や投資家から信頼を得て, 安定した利益が期待できることから, 社会への貢献度の高い企業を選んで投資する投資信託）
stability 名 安定, 安定性
employment stability 雇用の安定 （＝stability of employment）
exchange stability 為替の安定
market stability 市場の安定
price stability 物価安定
stability of the financial system 金融システムの安定性 （＝financial stability）
stability of the stock market 株価の安定
▶Market *stability* is vital. 市場の安定は, 重要である。
stabilization 名 安定化
economic stabilization policy 経済安定政策, 経済安定化政策
stabilize 動 安定する［させる］
▶We will continue working to *stabilize* and diversify our funding activities. 当社は, 今後とも資金調達の安定化と多様性［多角化］を進めてまいります。
stabilizer 名 安定化装置, スタビライザー
stable 形 安定した
stable shareholder 安定株主
▶The company aims to protect itself from takeover attempts by securing more *stable* shareholders through a third-party share allotment. 同社は, 第三者割当て増資で安定株主を増やすことで, 買収防衛策としての効果を狙っている。

staff 名 社員, 従業員, 職員, 人員, 局員, 幹部, スタッフ
- **credit staff** 与信担当者, 与信担当スタッフ, 審査担当者
- **department of staff** スタッフ部門
- **editorial staff** 編集陣
- **engineering staff** 技術スタッフ
- **maintain staff** 事務所を構える
- **managing staff** 経営陣
- **reduce staff numbers** 人員を削減する
- **staff benefits** 従業員福利費
- **staff costs** 人件費 (=staff expenses)
- **staff reduction** 人員削減 (=reduction of staff numbers)

stag 名 スタッグ(短期の利食いが目的で新株買いをする人)

stage 名 期, 段階, 活動範囲, 動 …を呈する, 実施する
▶The program will be implemented in six *stages*, from initial planning and training, and on-site demonstrations, to eventual plant conversions. 計画は, 当初の企画, 研修, 現地実証試験から最終的なプラントの移転まで, 6段階にわたって実施される。

stagflation 名 景気停滞下[不況下]のインフレ, スタグフレーション (stagnationとinflationの合成語。景気の停滞と物価上昇の同時進行を指す)

stagger 動 〈勤務時間などを〉ずらす, 時差制にする, 調整する
- **staggered board** スタガー取締役会 (=staggered board of directors: 会社の取締役の任期期間を全員同じでなくずらして構成されている取締役会。敵対的買収への防衛手段として利用されることがある)
- **staggered directorships** 取締役のずらし任期制
- **staggered working hours** 時差出勤 (=staggered work-hours program)

staging ground 前進基地
▶Mexico can serve as a *staging ground* for Japanese companies making forays into North and South American markets. メキシコは, 北米・南米市場に進出する日本企業の前進基地でもある。

stagnant 形 不景気な, 沈滞した, 不振の, 低迷した
- **stagnant earnings** 収益悪化
- **stagnant economy** 景気低迷, 不景気, 経済の低迷[停滞], 不振の経済
- **stagnant market** 市場低迷, 市場軟調, 沈滞市況, 軟調市況
- **stagnant sales** 売上不振, 販売不振, 販売低迷

stagnate 動 沈滞する, 停滞する, 不振にする

stagnation 名 沈滞, 低迷, 停滞, 景気停滞, 不振, 不況, 不景気, 経済のゼロ成長
- **a phase of stagnation** 停滞局面, 景気停滞局面
- **business stagnation** 事業不振
- **economic stagnation** 経済停滞, 景気の停滞
- **prolonged stagnation of business activity** 長期にわたる景気停滞, 長引く景気停滞
- **secular stagnation** 長期停滞, 長期低迷

stake 名 出資, 出資比率, 投資金, 投資金額, 資本参加, 株式持ち分, 持ち株, 持ち株比率, 株, 株式, 利害関係 (⇒equity stake)
- **acquire [buy] a 50 percent stake in** …の株式の50%を取得する
- **be at stake** 争点になる, 問題になっている, 事業などが危険な状態にある
- **equity stake rate** 持ち分比率, 出資比率
- **hold a 35 percent stake in** …の株式の35%を保有する, …株の35%を保有している
- **increase one's stake in** …の持ち株比率を引き上げる, …の出資比率を引き上げる (=raise one's stake in)
- **joint stake** 共同出資, 共同出資比率
- **reduce one's stake in** …の持ち株比率を引き下げる, …の出資比率を引き下げる
- **take a stake in** …へ出資する

▶General Motors Corp. has reached an agreement to sell a 51 percent *stake* in its finance arm. ゼネラル・モーターズ(GM)は, 金融子会社(GMAC)の株式の51%を売却することで合意した。

▶Japan Airlines will raise its *stake* in Japan Asia Airways to 100 percent from the current 90.5 percent through an equity swap deal. 日本航空システムは, 株式交換取引により, 日本アジア航空への出資比率を現在の90.5%から100%に引き上げる[日本アジア航空を完全子会社化する]。

▶The most advanced technologies are often at *stake* in lawsuits over intellectual property. 知的財産を巡る訴訟では, 最先端技術が争点になることが多い。

stakeholder 名 利害関係者, 株主, ステークホルダー (利害関係者は, 企業の従業員, 退職者, 労働組合や取引先, 地域社会などを指す。⇒trade union)
▶When a company increases profits through wage cuts, the shareholders' value will increase, but its value to *stakeholders* may decrease. 企業が賃金引下げて利益を増やした場合, 株主価値は増えるが, ステークホルダー[利害関係者]に帰属する価値は減る可能性がある。

stalemate 名 膠着状態, 手詰まり状態, 行き詰まりの状態
▸The *stalemate* can be attributed to the Health, Labor and Welfare Ministry's failure to conduct adequate consensus building with the labor and management representatives. この手詰まり状態は, 労使双方の代表との厚労省の根回し不足によるものだ.

stall 名動 時間稼ぎ(をする) (⇒oil consuming country, squeeze 動)

stamp 動 …に印章を押す, 捺印する, 切手[印紙]を貼る, 名 切手, 印紙
　fiscal stamp 収入印紙
　food stamp 食料クーポン, フード・スタンプ (=food coupon: 米政府から生活保護者と失業保険受給者に支給される)

stance 名 姿勢, 態度, 立場, 構え, 政策, 策, スタンス
　credit stance 金融政策のスタンス
　credit-tightening stance 金融引締めのスタンス (=restrictive monetary policy stance)
　fiscal stance 財政政策
　hard-line stance 強硬姿勢, 強気な態度
　negative stance 消極的な態度, 弱気の構え
　pro-growth stance 成長重視の姿勢
　restrictive stance 引締めのスタンス
▸The European Central Bank shifted to a credit-tightening *stance* late last year. 欧州中央銀行は, 昨年末から金融引締めのスタンスに転じた.

stand 動 有効である, 実施中である, 名 台, 小卓, スタンド

stand-alone [standalone] 形 独立型の, 自立型の, スタンド・アロン型の
　stand-alone company 独立企業
　stand-alone entity 特別目的会社
　stand-alone workstation 独立型ワークステーション

standard 名 標準, 基準, 規格, 基準書, スタンダード (⇒accounting standards, ethical, International Financial Reporting Standards)
　capital standards 自己資本比率, 自己資本比率規制
　credit standards 融資基準, 与信基準
　de facto standard 事実上の標準, 事実上の国際基準, 事実上の世界標準, デファクト・スタンダード
　de jure standard 法による基準, 法律上の基準, 公的基準, デジュアリー・スタンダード
　disclosure standards 開示基準
　ethics standards 倫理基準, 倫理規定 (= ethical standards)
　financial standards 財務基準
　general standards 一般基準, 一般原則
　general standards of auditing 監査一般基準
　generally accepted accounting standards 一般に認められた会計基準
　internal auditing standards 内部監査基準
　origination standards 審査基準
　practice standards 業務基準
　product standards 製品基準
　quality control standard 品質管理基準
　quality standard 品質基準, 品質標register, 品質規格
　safety standard 安全基準
　standard accounts 一般投資家
　standard burden rate 標準配賦率, 製造間接費配賦率 (=standard overhead rate)
　standard cost 標準原価
　technical standard 技術標準
　underwriting standards 与信基準, 貸出基準
　universal standard ユニバーサル・スタンダード, 世界標準, 国際標準
　world standard 世界標準, ワールド・スタンダード (=worldwide standard)
▸All companies in the Group pride themselves on maintaining the highest *standards* of integrity in carrying out business activities. 当グループ企業は, すべて事業活動を実施するにあたって最高の倫理基準を維持することを誇りとする.

Standard & Poors 500 S&P500株価指数

standardization 名 標準化, 規格化, 規格統一, 規格統一化
　standardization of products and services 商品とサービスの規格統一化, 商品・サービスの標準化
　standardization of specifications 仕様の標準化
▸International standards have been prepared by the International Electrotechnical Commission (IEC) for electric, electronic and related technologies as well as the International Organization for *Standardization* (ISO) for other industrial developments. 国際標準は, 電気・電子関連技術は国際電気標準会議(IEC)が, またそれ以外の工業製品は国際標準化機構(ISO)が作成している.

standby [stand-by] 形 控の, 予備の, 待機の, 代役の, スタンドバイ
　standby agreement [arrangement] 残額引受契約, 借入予約, スタンドバイ取決め
　standby commitment 銀行の保証, 信用供与

枠，株主割当ての際のスタンドバイ引受業者 (standby underwriter) による残額引受け，スタンドバイ引受け

standby cost 固定費，準備費

standby credit 保証，銀行による企業の借入金の保証，資金引出し信用供与，保証のためのスタンドバイ信用状

standby letter of credit スタンドバイ信用状

standby pay 待機手当

standby ticket キャンセル待ちの切符

standby time 待機時間

standby underwriting 残額引受け，残額引受発行，残額引受け，引受募集

standing 名 地位，立場，状態，状況，体質，身分，名声，順位，持続，存続，ランキング表，信用評価，形 常設の，常置の，常任の，常備の，永続的な

business standing 営業状態，経営の体質

corporate standing 企業体質

financial standing 財政状態，財務状況，財務体質 (＝financial position, financial status)

standing credit 常設の信用枠

▸The company is a customer of good credit *standing*. 同社は，信用度の高い得意先です。

staple 名 主要産物，重要商品，主成分，供給地，専売品

staple merchandise 主力商品

start 動 始める，着手する，名 着手，開始

start-up 始動，開始，開業，開業準備，ベンチャー企業，新興企業，新会社，新規事業，新規企業，新企業，スタートアップ・カンパニー (＝start-up business, start-up company, start-up firm)

start-up business ベンチャー企業

start-up costs 開業費，開業準備費，始動費，運転開始費，初期費用 (＝preoperating costs)

start-up firm 新興企業，ベンチャー企業 (＝start-up company)

▸The gross margins were lower because the segment has experienced higher costs resulting from the *startup* costs associated with adding new manufacturing capacity. 売上利益が減少したのは，製造設備の新設に伴う初期費用に起因して，当部門のコストが増加したからです。

stash 動 隠匿する，隠す，銀行に預け入れる

state 動 明示する，公表する，公開する，表示する，計上する，評価する，指定する，定める，規定する (⇒lower of cost or market)

be stated at cost less accumulated depreciation and amortization 取得原価から減価償却累計額を控除して表示[評価，計上]される

be stated at the lower of standard cost or market 標準原価または時価のいずれか低いほうの金額で評価[計上，表示]される

stated capital 表示資本金，表示資本額，確定資本金

stated in net amounts 純額表示

stated interest rate 表面利率，約定利率

stated value 表示価額，記載金額，表記金額，表記価格

stated value $1 per share 1株当たり額面額1ドル

▸Property, plant and equipment are *stated* at cost less accumulated depreciation. 有形固定資産は，減価償却累計額控除後の取得原価で評価[計上]されています。

state-of-the-art 形 最先端の，最新式の，最新鋭の，最高級の，高度の，最高水準の，最新技術の，最高技術水準の，技術水準 (＝cutting-edge, leading edge, sophisticated, top of the line, up-to-the-minute)

state-of-the-art life science 先端的な生命科学

state-of-the-art systems 最新システム

state-of-the-art technology 最新技術

▸The M-5 solid-fuel rocket carrying a *state-of-the-art* solar observation satellite was successfully launched from Uchinoura Space Center. 最新技術の太陽観測衛星を搭載したM5固体燃料型ロケットが，内之浦宇宙空間観測所(鹿児島県)から打ち上げられ，打上げは成功した。

▸The process of developing a new vaccine should be shortened by taking advantage of such *state-of-the-art* technologies as gene splicing. 新ワクチンの開発期間は，遺伝子組換えなどの最新技術を駆使して短縮しなければならない。

State of the Union address 一般教書演説 (＝State of the Union message, State of the Union speech)

　一般教書とは➡ 米大統領が年頭に連邦議会上下両院合同本会議で表明する，向こう1年間の施政方針。大統領の演説中，最も重要とされている。内政・外交全般にわたる国家の情勢を要訳，政府の基本政策のほか，大統領の抱負や信念，政治哲学なども織り込まれる。予算教書(Budget Message)，経済報告(Economic Report of the President)とともに，米大統領の三大年頭教書の一つ。

▸Bush's final *State of the Union address* reflected the hard reality faced by the United States on its domestic and diplomatic fronts. ブッシュ米大統領の最後の一般教書演説は，内政・外交面で米国が直面する厳しい現実を映し出した。

statement 名 計算書, 財務表, 報告書, 届出書, 声明, コメント, 声明書, 規約, ステートメント (⇒financial statements)
　application of funds statement 資金運用表
　balance of payments statement 国際収支表
　business statement 営業報告書
　cash flow statement 資金収支表, 現金収支計算書, 収支計算書, 現金資金計算書, キャッシュ・フロー計算書 (=statement of cash flows)
　distribution statement 分売届出書
　earned surplus statement 利益剰余金計算書
　earnings statement 損益計算書 (=income statement, profit and loss statement)
　financial position statement 財政状態計算書, 財政状態表, 貸借対照表
　fund [funds] flow statement 資金フロー計算書, 資金計算書, 資金運用表, 資金表 (=funds statement)
　interim statements 中間財務書類, 中間財務諸表 (=interim financial statements)
　issue a statement コメントを発表する
　offering statement 募集届出書, 発行目論見書
　securities statement 有価証券報告書 (=securities report)
　social impact statement 社会影響報告書
　statement of financial condition 財政状態表, 貸借対照表 (=balance sheet, statement of financial position)
　statement of operations 事業報告書
　untrue statement 不実の記載
　▶The Financial Accounting Standards Board adopted *Statement* No. 96, "Accounts for Income taxes" in December 1988. 財務会計基準審議会(FASB)は, 1988年12月, 基準書No.96「税効果会計」を採用した.

statement of accounts 決算報告書
　▶The former president of Livedoor Co. is said to have instructed the firm's *statement of accounts* to include fabricated earnings. ライブドアの前社長は, 同社の決算報告書に架空収益[架空の売上]を計上するよう指示したといわれる.

state-run 形 国有の, 国営の
　▶Nippon Oil and Toyota will jointly develop new diesel fuel made from palm oil, in conjunction with the Malaysian *state-run* petroleum company Petronas. 新日本石油とトヨタが, マレーシアの国営石油会社ペトロナスと連携して, パーム油を原料にした新ディーゼル燃料を共同開発する.

stationery 名 文房具, 便箋
statistics 統計, 指標, 統計学
　business statistics 企業経営, 経営統計
　corporation statistics 法人企業統計
　customs statistics 通関統計
　economic statistics 経済統計, 景気指標
　employment statistics 雇用統計
　export certification statistics 輸出承認統計
　financial statistics 金融統計
　labor market statistics 雇用統計
　population statistics 人口統計
　static statistics 静態統計
　trade quantity statistics 貿易数量統計
　trade value statistics 貿易額統計
　vital statistics 人口動態統計
　wage statistics 賃金統計

stats 名 統計 (statistics の略)
status 名 地位, 状態, 状況, 情勢, 事情, 構造, 資格, ステータス
　corporate status 法人格
　funded status 拠出状態, 供出状況, 積立状況
　preferred creditor status 優先債権者の地位
　tax status 税務上の取扱い
　▶The life insurers' *status* as large stockholders means that when the market dives, their portfolios also take a tumble. 大株主としての生命保険会社の地位は, 株価が大きく下がると資産内容も急激に悪化することを意味する.
　▶This investment fund is a voluntary organization on the Civil Code and does not have corporate *status*. この投資ファンドは, 民法上の任意組合で, 法人格がない.

statute of limitations 出訴期限, 出訴期限法, 消滅時効, 時効
statutory tax rate 法定税率
　▶Apart from the effects of changes in *statutory tax rates*, we do not expect the new accounting to affect future earnings materially. 法定税率変更の影響のほかは, 新会計処理方法が将来の利益に大きな影響を及ぼすことはないでしょう.

steam 名 推進力, 駆動力, 元気, 力, 勢い, 蒸気, スチーム
　gather steam 勢いを増す, 加速する (=build up steam, gain some steam, get up steam, pick up steam)
　go full steam ahead with …に全力で取り組む
　lose steam 勢いを失う, 勢いが弱まる, 勢いがなくなる, 失速する (=lose some of the steam)
　pick up steam 上向く, 景気が上向く, 上昇傾向にある, 上昇する, …の勢いが増す, 勢いが強まる, 次第に速度を上げる, 次第に注目を浴びるようになる, 次第に動きが出る (=get up [build

up] steam)

run out of steam 息切れする, 元気がなくなる, 気力・意欲がなくなる, ブームなどが下火になる
▶If the driving forces for the Japanese economy, namely capital investment and exports, lose *steam*, the economy inevitably will slow down further. 設備投資と輸出という日本経済の牽引役（日本経済の牽引役である設備投資と輸出）に勢いがなくなれば, 景気の一段の減速は避けられないだろう.
▶The rally has run out of *steam*. 強気相場は息切れしている.

step 名 措置, 手段, 対策, 足どり, 歩調, 歩み, 一歩, 足跡, ステップ
▶While we work to sustain growth during the difficult period, we have taken strategic *steps* to position the firm for continued long-term growth. 当社は, この厳しい時期に成長の維持に取り組む一方, 同社の長期的な発展を視座に据えて戦略的な措置を取りました.

step down 辞職する, 辞任する, 退任する, 身を引く, 引退する（＝resign）
▶The committee called for the president to *step down*. 同委員会は, 社長の辞任を要求した.

sterling 形 英貨の, ポンドの, スターリング銀の, 真正の, 確かな

stimulus 名 刺激, 刺激策, 刺激効果, 景気刺激策, 景気対策, 励み
　budgetary stimulus 財政出動
　domestic stimulus 国内景気の刺激, 国内刺激策, 国内景気対策
　economic stimulus 景気対策
　economic stimulus measures [package] 一連の景気刺激策
　emergency stimulus package 緊急景気対策
　financial stimulus 金融面からの刺激効果
　fiscal and monetary policy stimulus 財政・金融政策を使った景気対策
　fiscal stimulus 財政刺激策, 財政出動
　monetary stimulus 金融政策面での景気刺激策, 金融緩和
　stimulus measures 刺激策, 景気刺激策, 景気対策, 促進措置
　stimulus package 景気刺激策

stipend 名 固定給, 給付金

stock 名 株(share), 株式, 株式資本, 証券, 銘柄, 在庫, 在庫品, ストック（⇒capital stock, common stock, preferred stock, tracking stock, treasury stock）
　base stock method 基準棚卸し法（＝base stock, base stock inventory valuation）
　closing stock 棚卸し資産期末有り高
　convertible stock 転換株式（＝convertible share）
　corporate stock 株式
　cycle stock 循環在庫
　excess stock 過剰在庫
　finished product stock 製品在庫（＝finished goods stock）
　income stock 資産株, 採算株
　initial stock 期首在庫, 期首在庫高
　low priced stock 低位株
　management stock 役員株
　minimum stock level 最低在庫水準
　newly issued stock 新規発行株式, 新規公開株
　nonvoting stock 無議決権株, 議決権のない株式（＝nonvoting share）
　optimum stock 最適在庫量
　portfolio stock 投資用株式
　stock appraisal losses 株式評価損, 株式含み損
　stock award plan 株式報償制度, 株式贈与制度, 株式報奨制度
　stock brokerage 証券会社（⇒online stock brokerage）
　stock brokerage service 証券仲介サービス, 証券仲介業, 証券仲介業務（＝stock brokerage business）
　stock bubble 株価バブル（＝stock price bubble）
　stock-buying limit 株式買入れ枠
　stock buyout [buy-out] 株式買取り, 株の買占め
　stock buyup scheme 日銀の株式買取制度, 株式買入れ制度
　stock certificate 株券, 記名株券, 株式証券（＝share certificate）
　stock compensation plan 株式報奨制度, 株式報酬制度, 株式報酬プラン
　stock-for-stock exchange rate 株式交換比率, 株式交換の交換比率（＝stock exchange rate）
　stock holding 株式保有, 株式所有, 保有株式, 持ち株, 出資比率（＝equity holding, shareholding, stockholding; ⇒stockholding）
　stock investing 株式投資（＝stock investment）
　stock investment efficiency 株式投資効率（⇒ROE）
　stock issue 株式発行, 新株発行, 株式銘柄, 銘柄
　stock-related losses 株式等関連損失
　stock trading 株式売買, 株式取引（＝equity

trading, stock trade, stock transaction)
stock trading via the Internet 株のインターネット取引, インターネットでの株式取引
subsidiary stock 子会社株式
transfer of stock 株式の名義書換え, 株式の譲渡
unclaimed stock 失権株
▶The company's main bank will swap ¥40 billion in debt into *stock*. 同社の主力行が, 400億円分の債権の株式化を行う[債務の株式化に応じる]。
▶The increase in investments mainly reflects a $500 million purchase of the company *stock* in February 2008. 投資の増加は, 主に2008年2月の同社株購入の5億ドルを反映しています。
▶Toyota has increased production to ensure the firm has sufficient *stock* to meet demand. トヨタは, 在庫を十分確保して需要に応えられるよう生産を増やしている。

stock appreciation right 株式評価益権, 株式評価受益権, 株式騰貴権, 株式増価差額請求権《略 SAR》
▶We grant stock options, as well as *stock appreciation rights* (SARs), either in tandem with stock options or free-standing, in our long term incentive program. 当社は, 当社の長期勤労奨励制度で, ストック・オプション(自社株購入権)のほかに, ストック・オプションと組み合わせたまたは単独の株式評価受益権(SAR)も付与しています。

stock buyback 株式の買戻し, 自社株発行済み株式の買戻し, 自社株買戻し, 自社株買い, 自社株取得, 自社株の取得（=share buyback, share repurchase, stock repurchase; ⇒**share buyback**)
▶*Stock buybacks* were limited to certain purposes, such as share retirement and stock option schemes, before the revision of the Commercial Code. 自社株買いは, 商法の改正前は, 株式の消却用やストック・オプション制度向けなど特定の目的に制限されていた。

stock buyback plan 自社株取得計画, 株式買戻し計画
▶A company proposal for *stock buyback* and incentive stock option *plans* was approved at an annual meeting. 年次株主総会で, 自社株取得計画と奨励株式オプション制度の会社提案[会社側の議案]が承認された。

stock company 株式会社（=joint stock company, stock corporation)
▶The minimum capital requirements of ¥10 million for the establishment of a *stock company* have been eliminated under the new Corporate Law. 株式会社を設立する場合の1,000万円の最低資本金規制は, 新会社法で撤廃された。

stock dealing 株式取引, 株の売買（=stock deal, stock transaction)
▶In the *stock dealings*, the firm calculated a loss of ¥3.5 billion in its reports to the Tokyo Regional Taxation Bureau. この株売買で, 同社は東京国税局への申告書に35億円の損失を計上した。

stock dividend 株式配当（=capital bonus: 配当を現金でなく株式で交付すること)
▶The board of directors declared a 8% *stock dividend* on April 1, 2009. 取締役会は, 2009年4月1日, 8％の株式配当を宣言した[株式配当の決議を行なった]。

stock exchange 証券取引所, 株式取引所, 株式交換, 株式売買（=securities exchange; ⇒**New York Stock Exchange**)
American Stock Exchange アメリカン証券取引所, アメックス《略 AMEX》
London Stock Exchange ロンドン証券取引所
stock exchange merger ストック・エクスチェンジ・マージャー（企業の買収・合併の手段として, 存続会社が, 合併で吸収される会社の株主に存続会社の株式を交付する方法)
Stock Exchange of Singapore シンガポール証券取引所
stock exchange offer 株式交換公開買付け, ストック・エクスチェンジ・オファー（M&Aの手段として, 買収先の企業の株式を, 株式などの有価証券で公開買付けする方法)
stock exchange ratio [rate] 株式交換比率（=share exchange rate, stock-for-stock exchange rate)
Toronto Stock Exchange トロント証券取引所
▶Nasdaq launched its $5.3 billion hostile bid for the London *Stock Exchange*. 米ナスダックが, ロンドン証券取引所(LSE)に対して53億ドルの敵対的株式公開買付け(TOB)を実施した。
▶When a project plan for new product development or a new business is completed, a company would be established and placed on the *stock exchange*. 新製品の開発や新事業の事業計画に目途が立ったら, 会社を設立して, 株式を上場する。

stock index 株価指数
narrow based stock index 業種別株価指数
Nikkei Stock Index 300 日経株価指数300
stock index futures 株価指数先物, 株価指数先物取引

stock index option 株価指数オプション
stock market 株式市場, 証券市場, 株式相場, 株式市況, 株式売買, 株価 (=equity market; ⇒sluggish)
 rally in the stock market 株式相場の上昇 (=stock market rally)
 stock market collapse 株式相場の下落
 stock market conditions 株式市況
 stock market crash 株式市場の暴落 (=stock market crisis)
▸World *stock markets* are in a deep slump. 世界の株式市場は, 低迷の度を深めている。
stock offering 株式発行, 株式公開, 株式公募, 株式上場 (⇒**public offering**, **public stock offering**)
 initial stock offering 新規株式公開, 新規株式公募 (⇒**initial public offering**)
 public stock offering 公募増資
▸We raised $2.3 billion by this *stock offering*. この株式公募[株式公開]で, 当社は23億ドルを調達しました。
stock option 株式購入選択権, 株式買受権, 自社株購入権, 株式オプション, ストック・オプション (⇒**stock appreciation right**)
 stock option dealing 株式オプション取引, 個別株オプション取引
 stock option income ストック・オプション利益
 stock option plan 株式購入選択権制度, 株式選択権制度, 自社株購入権制度, 株式オプション制度, ストック・オプション制度 (=stock option program, stock option scheme, stock option system; ⇒**employee stock option plan**, **stock buyback plan**)
▸Common stock equivalents are *stock options* that we assume to be exercised for the purpose of this computation of earnings per common share. 準普通株式[普通株式等価物]は, この1株当たり純利益の計算の際, 行使されると仮定したストック・オプションです。
stock option program 株式購入選択権制度, 株式選択権制度, 自社株購入権制度, 株式オプション制度, ストック・オプション制度 (=stock option plan, stock option scheme)
▸*Stock option programs* are seen as leading to financial window-dressing to manipulate share prices. ストック・オプション制度は, 株価操作のための会計操作につながると見られている。
stock price 株価 (=share price)
 stock price adjustment 株価調整
 stock price average 株価平均

stock price inflation 株価急騰
stock price manipulation 株価操作, 株価操縦 (=stock manipulation)
stock price per share 普通株1株当たり時価
▸The company's *stock price* will be depressed if it lists before the subprime-related market turmoil subsides. サブプライム関連の市場混乱が収まらないうちに上場したら, 同社の株価は低迷すると思われる。
stock price disparity 株価格差
▸The *stock price disparity* between Toyota and Honda is considered primarily due to the two companies' return on equity (ROE) ratios. トヨタとホンダの株価格差は, 主に株主資本利益率(ROE)によるものだ。
stock purchase plan 株式購入制度, 株式購入選択権制度, 株式購入権制度, 自社株購入制度 (⇒**employee stock purchase plan**)
▸ABC Inc. raised $100 million of common equity by means of its Dividend Reinvestment and *Stock Purchase Plan* and the Employees' Savings Plan. ABC Inc.は, 株主配当再投資・株式購入制度と従業員社内預金制度により普通株式を発行して1億ドルを調達しました。
stock purchase warrant 新株引受権, 株式買付け権, 株式買取り権, 株式購入権, 新株引受権証書, 株式購入権証書 (=stock-purchasing warrant)
▸On Sept. 30, 2008, the firm redeemed *stock purchase warrants* it issued in September 1997. 2008年9月30日に同社は, 1997年9月に発行した新株予約権付き社債を償還した。
stock repurchase 自社株買戻し, 株式買戻し, 自社株買い (=share buyback, stock buyback)
▸Under our *stock repurchase* programs, 8,611,396,000 shares were repurchased during 2007 at a cost of $992 million. 当社の自社株買戻しプログラムに従って, 2007年度には861万1,396株を9億9,200万ドルで買い戻しました。
stock split 株式分割, 株式の分割・併合, 無償交付 (=share split, share splitting, split-up of stock:「株式分割」は, 1株を分割して, 発行済み株式数を増やすこと。一般に, 投資家を増やして必要な事業資金を集めやすくするために行われる)
 reverse stock split 株式併合
 stock split-down 株式併合 (=reverse split, reverse stock split, share split-down)
 stock split-up 株式分割 (=share split-up)
 two-for-one stock split 1対2の株式分割, 1対2の比率による株式分割, 1株を2株に増やす株式

分割（⇒**paid-in capital**）
▸After the *stock split*, the par value of the stock was reduced by $3 per share. 株式分割後，株式の1株当たり額面は1株3ドル減少した。

stock swap 株式交換（＝share swap, stock swapping; ⇒**share swap**）
▸The firm made the advertising agency a subsidiary through *stock swaps*. 同社は，この広告会社を株式交換で子会社化した。

stock swap deal 株式交換取引（＝equity swap deal, share swap deal）
▸Citigroup's wholesale acquisition of Nikko Cordial Group through a *stock swap deal* was the nation's first instance of a triangular merger scheme. 株式交換によるシティグループの日興コーディアルグループ完全子会社化は，三角合併方式の国内初のケース［国内第1号］だ。

stock transaction 株式取引，株取引，株の売買（＝equity trading, stock trade, stock trading）
▸Top officials of each stock exchange have a management responsibility to guarantee investors smooth *stock transactions*. 各証券取引所のトップには，投資家に円滑な株式取引を保証する経営責任がある。

stock transfer 株式名義書換え，株式譲渡（＝share transfer）
▸The *stock transfer* will be made on Oct. 5 with Mitsui Fudosan paying ¥8,750 per share. この株式譲渡は，三井不動産が1株当たり8,750円を支払って10月5日に行われる。

stockbroker 名 株式仲買人，株式売買の代行業者，株式ブローカー
▸The company fraudulently collected about ¥14 billion in cash and stock certificates from customers by disguising it as a *stockbroker*. 同社は，株式売買の代行業者と偽って，顧客から現金や株券など約140億円を不正に集めていた。

stockholder 名 株主（＝stockowner; ⇒**shareholder**）
　institutional stockholder 法人株主
　preferred stockholder 優先株株主，優先株主（＝preferred shareholder）
　stockholder plan 株主制度，株主プラン
　stockholder rights plan 株主権利制度
　stockholders' meeting 株主総会（＝general meeting, shareholders meeting, stockholders meeting; ⇒**shareholders meeting**）
　stockholders' representative suit 株主の代表訴訟
▸The approval of numerous *stockholders* must be gained for a retirement of 50 percent of common shares. 普通株式の50％消却については，多くの株主の承認を得なければならない。

stockholder of record 登録株主，株主名簿上の株主（＝shareholder of record）
▸Only *stockholders of record* at the close of business on March 15, 2008 are entitled to vote at the annual meeting. 2008年3月15日の営業終了時現在の登録株主だけが，株主総会で投票する権利があります。

stockholders' equity 株主持ち分，株主資本，資本の部，資本勘定，資本，自己資本，純資産，純資産の部（＝net worth, owners' equity, shareholders' equity: 払込み資本金と利益剰余金の合計。⇒**shareholders' equity**）
　average stockholders' equity 平均株主資本
　common stockholders' equity 普通株主持ち分
　consolidated stockholders' equity 連結株主持ち分
　minority stockholders' equity 少数株主持ち分
　preferred stockholders' equity 優先株主持ち分
▸Average invested capital is defined as *stockholders' equity* plus long- and short-term debts less short-term investments (includes short-term investments categorized as cash equivalents). 平均投下資本＝資本＋長期・短期金融債務－短期投資（現預金等価物として表示する短期投資を含む）です。

stockholding 名 株式保有，保有株式，保有株，持ち株（＝shareholding, stock holding）
▸The massive gains in *stockholdings'* latent value will raise the banks' net worth ratios markedly. 保有株式の含み益の大幅増加で，銀行の自己資本比率も大きく向上する見込みだ。

stockpile 名 貯蔵，蓄積，備蓄，備蓄品，蓄え，在庫，保有，保有量
　build up stockpiles 在庫を積み増す
　current stockpile 在庫水準
　cut stockpiles 在庫を削減する，在庫を減らす
　factory stockpiles 製造業在庫
　oil stockpile base 石油備蓄基地
　strategic stockpile 戦略備蓄
▸The U.S. government reported a surprise drop in crude oil *stockpiles*. 米政府は，原油在庫が予想外に減少したことを発表した。

stocktaking 名 在庫調べ，棚卸し，実績評価，現状把握

storage 名 貯蔵，保管，収納，倉庫，保管料，記憶装置

main storage 主記憶装置
offshore oil storage 石油洋上備蓄
store 名 店舗, 商店, 大型店, ストア
　convenience store コンビニエンス・ストア, コンビニ
　directly operated store 直営店
　discount store ディスカウント店, ディスカウント・ストア
　drug store ドラッグ・ストア
　in-store promotion 店内[店頭]プロモーション, 店内販売促進
　in-store sales 店頭売上
　Nippon Electric Big-Stores Association 日本電気大型店協会
　nonstore retailing 無店舗販売
　specialty store 専門店 (＝speciality store)
　unprofitable store 不採算店舗 (＝unprofitable outlet)
　▸Almost half of its sales are earned at its Ikebukuro and Shibuya *stores* in Tokyo. 同社の売上高のほぼ半分は, 東京都内の池袋店と渋谷店が稼ぎ出している。
　▸Wal-Mart's strategy has been to acquire stakes in existing stores rather than opening directly operated *stores*. 直営店を出店しないで, 既存店の株式を取得するのが, 米ウォルマートのこれまでの戦略だ。
storefront 名 店舗の正面, 副 店頭での
straddle 動 両建てにする (株を一方では買い, 他方では売る)
straight 形 連続した, 1年前と比較した, 副 連続して, 1年前と比較して, ぶっ通しで
　straight loan 通常のローン
　straight salary system 固定給制
　▸It is the fifth *straight* month that the unemployment rate has surpassed that of the United States. 完全失業率が米国を上回ったのは, 5か月連続である。
　▸The price of goods fell by 1.4 percent and services fell for the second *straight* year. 財の値段は1.4％下落し, サービスも2年連続下落した。
straight bond 普通社債, 確定利付き社債 (転換社債以外の普通の社債)
　▸The bank will raise about ¥150 billion by issuing *straight bonds* on a quarterly basis. 同行は, 四半期ベースで普通社債を発行して約1,500億円を調達する。
straight line method 定額法 (＝straight line basis: 固定資産の取得原価から残存価額を差し引いた金額を, 耐用年数で割って, 1年分の減価償

却費を計算する方法)
▸Depreciation is calculated generally on the *straight-line method* using rates based on the expected useful lives of the respective assets. 減価償却費は, 原則として個々の資産の見積り耐用年数に基づく減価償却率を用いて, 定額法で計算されています。
strangle 名 ストラングル (オプション取引で原資産の市価よりcallの行使価格が高くputの行使価格が低いもの)
strategic 形 戦略的, 戦略上の, 戦略上重要な, 戦略上役に立つ, 戦略に必要な
　strategic business alliance 戦略的業務提携
　strategic business unit 戦略的事業単位《略 SBU》 (＝business center)
　strategic choice 戦略の選択, 戦略的選択肢
　strategic diversity 戦略的多様性, 戦略的相違点
　strategic growth market 戦略的成長市場
　strategic implication 戦略的意義
　strategic industry 戦略産業
　strategic intent 戦略的意図 (⇒management executive committee)
　strategic management 経営戦略
　strategic marketing planning 戦略的マーケティング計画
　strategic moves 戦略的な動き
　strategic operations 戦略事業
　strategic performance 戦略的成果
　strategic position 戦略上の地位, 戦略的位置
　strategic review 戦略の検討
　strategic target 戦略目標
　strategic technology development program 戦略技術開発事業
　▸Advanced countries proactively assist the production of passenger airplanes as a *strategic* industry. 先進諸国は, 旅客機製造を戦略産業として積極的に支援している。
strategic alliance 戦略提携, 戦略的業務提携, 戦略的同盟, 製販同盟, ストラテジック・アライアンス
　▸Joint venture and *strategic alliance* marked the quarter—joining the Company to partners with complementary strengths. 合弁事業と戦略的提携が当四半期の際立った業績で, 当社は相互補完力のあるパートナーと手を結びました。
strategic investment 戦略的投資
　▸*Strategic investment* increased the potential for the Corporation's growth in worldwide markets. 戦略的投資で, グローバル市場での当社の潜在成長力は高まりました。

strategic planning 戦略計画, 戦略的計画, 戦略計画策定, 戦略計画設定, 戦略企画, 戦略の策定, ストラテジック・プランニング
▸The firm's sales department now handles *strategic planning*, transactions with mass retailers and business with the public sector. 同社の営業部門は現在, 営業戦略の立案や量販店, 官公庁との取引を担当している。

strategy 名 戦略, 策, 手法, 方針, ストラテジー（⇒**business strategy, core strategy, global strategy, management strategy**）
　acquisition strategy 買収戦略
　competitive strategy 競争戦略, 競争優位戦略
　corporate strategy 企業戦略, 経営戦略, 営業戦略
　defensive strategy 防衛戦略
　diversification strategy 多様化戦略, 多角化戦略（＝strategy of diversification）
　e-business strategy eビジネス戦略
　e strategy e戦略
　economies of scale strategy 数量効果追求戦略
　financial strategy 財務戦略
　focused strategy 的を絞った戦略
　growth strategy 成長戦略
　international business strategy 国際企業戦略
　IT strategy IT戦略
　market niche strategy 市場すき間戦略, マーケット・ニッチ戦略
　market strategy 市場戦略, 製品市場戦略
　merchandise strategy 商品戦略
　multibrand strategy マルチブランド戦略, 複数ブランド戦略
　niche strategy すき間戦略, ニッチ戦略
　price-skimming strategy 上層吸収価格戦略, 上澄（うわずみ）吸収価格戦略
　pricing strategy 価格戦略, 価格設定戦略
　proactive strategy 先行型戦略, 事前行動戦略
　product strategy 製品戦略
　pull strategy 引き付ける戦略, プル戦略（広告中心型の販売促進戦略）
　push strategy 押す戦略, プッシュ戦略（販売業者に利益やマージン, リベート, 販促材料などを提供して商品の推奨販売を期待する販売促進戦略）
　reactive strategy 反抗型戦略, 事後行動戦略
　solution strategy ソリューション戦略
　strategy development 戦略開発, 戦略展開
　strategy formulation 戦略形成, 戦略策定（＝strategy formation）
　strategy implementation 戦略実施, 戦略実行
　strategy rights 戦略権
　tax planning strategy 税務戦略, 戦略的税務計画
　top-down strategy 上位下達戦略, 下降型戦略
　user strategy ユーザー戦略
　value strategy バリュー戦略
▸In 2008 we focused on executing our *strategy*. 2008年度は, 当社の戦略実施に焦点を合わせました。
▸Japan's four megabanks are now rebuilding their global business *strategies*. 日本の4大金融グループは現在, グローバル戦略の再構築に取り組んでいる。
▸We can apply a unique management *strategy* that other companies don't have. 当社は, 他社にないユニークな経営戦略をとることができる。

stream 名 流れ, 傾向, 動向, 趨勢, 見通し, キャッシュ・フロー（⇒**upstream**）
　come back on stream 生産を再開する
　come on stream 稼働する
　go on stream 生産を開始する, 稼働する
　interest stream 金利の流れ, 金利のキャッシュ・フロー
　on stream 生産中, 稼動中
　profits stream 収益見通し（＝earnings stream）
　upper end of the production stream 生産の流れ（生産から消費に至る各段階）の上流
　upper stream industries 上流産業, 川上産業
▸Industries at the upper end of the production *stream* have higher increases in recurring profits. 生産の流れ（生産から消費に至る各段階）の上流にある産業のほうが, 経常利益の増加率が高い。

streamline 動 合理化する, 能率化する, 効率化する, 簡素化する, スリム化する, リストラする（⇒**focus on**）
▸Listed companies have improved their balance sheets by *streamlining* facilities, employees and debts. 上場企業は, 設備, 雇用と負債の過剰を解消して, 財務体質を改善した。
▸We *streamlined* development work on telecommunications network systems in 2008. 当社は, 2008年度に, 通信ネットワーク・システム開発作業の効率化［合理化］を進めました。

streamlining 名 合理化, 能率化, 効率化, 簡素化, スリム化, リストラ
▸Financial institutions have no time to lose in enhancing their profitability, *streamlining* and information disclosure. 金融機関の場合, 収益力の向上や一層の合理化, 情報開示は待ったなしだ。
▸Our *streamlining* projects are being imple-

mented through 2009. 当社の効率化プロジェクトは、2009年度末まで実施されます。

street-name account 実質株主名を株主名簿に登録していない株主の口座

strength 名 力, 強さ, 強み, 力強さ, 体力, 勢い, 好調, 活況, 上昇, 勢力, 兵力, 人数, 長所 (⇒ corporate strength, financial strength)
　business strength 経営体力, 経営力, 事業での成功
　competitive strength 競争力
　credit strength 信用力, 信用度, 信用の質
　currency strength 通貨高
　distributive strength 販売力
　economic strength 経済力, 景気の力強さ, 景気の腰の強さ, 景気好調
　financial strength 資金力, 財力, 財政力, 財務体質, 財務面での健全性, 支払い能力
　financial strength rating 支払い能力の格付け
　industrial strength 製造業の好調
　marketing strength 販売力, マーケティング力
　specific pockets of strength 好調な業種
　strength of demand 需要の強さ, 需要の盛り上がり
　strength of the economy 景気の腰の強さ
　strengths and weaknesses 長所と短所, 強さと弱さ
　yen's strength 円高
▸One of Toyota's *strengths* is that it tailors its models to match the preferences of customers around the world. トヨタの強さの一つは、世界各地でユーザーの好みに合った車を丁寧に作るということだ。
▸Return on equity is an indicator believed to show the real *strength* of a company. 株主資本利益率(ROE)は、企業の本当の実力を示すとされる経営指標だ。
▸Whether equity investments, joint ventures or other alliances, we look for partnerships that complement our own *strengths*. 出資であれ合弁その他の提携であれ、提携によって当社の強みを補完できる場合に、当社は提携先を求めます。

strengthen 動 強化する, 高める, 拡大する, 充実させる, 上昇する, 向上する, 改善する
　continue to strengthen 続伸する, 引き続き好調だ
　strengthened capital base 資本基盤の強化
　strengthened capitalization 資本の充実
　strengthening economy 景気の好転
▸As one step toward this corporate goal, we acquired a leading U.K. telecommunications firm to *strengthen* our position in the U.K. この会社目標達成に向けての第一歩として、当社は英国での事業基盤を強化するため、英国の大手通信会社を取得[買収]しました。

strengthening of the yen 円高
▸The recent *strengthening of the yen* may negatively affect exports. 最近の円高が、輸出に悪影響を与えかねない。

stress 名 圧力, 圧迫, 困難, 困難な状況, 厳しい環境, 厳しい経営環境, 経営難, 強調, 力点, 重点, ストレス
　financial stress 経営難, 金融上の困難, 財務状態の悪化, 信用圧迫
　stress conditions [situations] 困難な状況
　under stress 困難な状況下で, 厳しい状況下で, 厳しい環境下で
▸The industry is under a good deal of *stress*, as evidenced by pressure on profitability and decline in stock prices over the last several months. 業界は、収益性の悪化やここ数か月の株価低迷でも明らかなように、かなり厳しい状況下にあります。

stress test 特別検査 (金融安定化策の一環として米連邦準備制度理事会(FRB)が米主要金融機関に対して実施する特別検査)
▸The U.S. Federal Reserve Board issued the results of its *stress tests* for 19 banks in the United States. 米連邦準備制度理事会(FRB)が、米国内の主要金融機関19社に対して実施した特別検査の結果を発表した。

stricken 形 打撃を受けた, 経営危機に陥った, 資金繰り難の
▸JPMorgan Chase & Co. will buy *stricken* Bear Sterns for $2 a share. 米大手銀行のJPモルガン・チェースが、経営危機に陥った(米証券5位の)ベア・スターンズを1株2ドルで買収する。

strike 名 権利行使, スト, ストライキ, 〈鉱脈などの〉発見, 〈石油などの〉掘り当て, 突然の成功
　be (out) on strike スト中, ストをしている
　call a strike ストを決行する
　call off a strike ストを中止する
　come [go] out on strike ストを開始する
　general strike ゼネスト, 総同盟罷業, ゼネラル・ストライキ
　go ahead with a strike ストに突入する
　go on strike ストをする, ストに突入する
　hunger strike ハンガースト
　official strike 公式ストライキ, 組合公認スト
　protest strike 抗議スト
　sitdown strike 座り込みスト

stage a strike ストを決行する
strike action スト
strike ballot スト権投票
strike pay [benefit] スト手当
strike price オプション取引の権利行使価格, 行使価格 （＝striking price）
vote for strike action スト権投票を行う
wildcat strike 山猫スト（組合執行部の指令なしで組合員が勝手に行うスト）
▸Players in the Nippon Professional Baseball league decided to proceed with a *strike*. 日本プロ野球選手会（日本プロ野球連盟の選手）は, スト決行を決めた。
▸U.S. factory employees went on *strike* to put pressure on the biggest U.S. automaker. 米自動車最大手のゼネラル・モーターズ（GM）に圧力をかけるため, 同社の米工場従業員がストに突入した。

stringent 形 厳重な, 厳しい, 逼迫した

strip 名 商店の建ち並ぶ通り, ストリップ（オプション投資で同一行使価格のコールオプションとプットオプションを1:2の比率で買う［売る］戦略）

strong 形 強い, 強力な, 力強い, 強固な, 堅調な, 好調な, 上昇基調の, 優良な
be in a strong position 優位に立っている, 優位に立つ
remain strong 堅調に推移する
strong balance sheet 強固な財務体質, 健全な財務内容
strong demand 需要の急増, 需要の大幅な伸び, 需要の旺盛, 需要が強いこと
strong dollar 強いドル, ドル高
strong earnings growth 利益の大幅な伸び, 力強い利益の伸び
strong management 強力な経営陣
strong outperformance 大幅なアウトパフォーマンス, パフォーマンスが市場平均を大幅に上回ること
strong price competition 激しい価格競争
strong sales increase 売上の急増, 販売の急増
strong shareholder 安定株主
the strong yen and the weak U.S. dollar 円高・ドル安 （＝the yen's appreciation against the dollar）
▸Sales in Asia Pacific were very *strong*. アジア・太平洋地域での販売［売れ行き］が, 好調でした。
▸The balance sheet of the Corporation is *strong*. 当社の財務状態［財務内容］は, 健全です。
▸The company's performance in business areas remained *strong*. 同社の事業部門の業績が, 好調に［堅調に］推移した。

strong performance 好業績, 好調な業績, 業績好調 （＝strong financial performance）
▸Contributions from the telecommunications companies were higher than in the past, underlying their *strong performance*. 通信会社［通信事業会社］の貢献度は, 好調な業績を反映して, 過去の水準を上回りました。

strong player 有力企業
▸The company has returned to the international business scene as a *strong player* with high profitability. 同社は, 収益性の高い有力企業としてビジネスの国際舞台に返り咲いた。

strong sales 販売好調, 好調な売れ行き
▸Sharp Corp's quarterly group net profit rose 27.2 percent on *strong sales* of liquid crystal display televisions and camera-equipped mobile phones. シャープの四半期連結税引き後利益［純利益］は, 液晶テレビやカメラ付き携帯電話などの販売が好調だったことから, 前年同期比で27.2％増加した。

stronger performance 業績の大幅拡大, 業績の大幅の伸び
▸A good order growth of 15 percent and a record order backlog of over $3 billion for the first half of the year bolster our confidence for a *stronger performance* in the second half. 今年度上半期［上期］は受注高が15％の順調な伸び率を示し, 受注残高も30億ドルを超える記録的な水準に達したため, 私ども経営陣は下半期［下期］の業績の大幅拡大に自信を深めています。

stronghold 名 本拠地, 拠点, 中心点
▸Toyota successfully expanded its sales in GM's *stronghold*, the North American market. トヨタは, GMの本拠地の北米市場で販売アップに成功した。

structure 名 構造, 機構, 組織, 構成, 体系, 方式, 体制, 体質, 構築物, 構造物, 建造物 （⇒capital structure, management structure）
earnings structure 収益構造
equity structure 資本構成, 出資構成, 株主所有権構造
fiscal structure 財政体質
income structure 所得構造
internal control structure 内部統制構造
market structure 市場構造, 市場構成
ownership structure 所有構造, 株主構造, 出資構成
price structure 価格体系, 価格構造
rate structure 料金体系
shareholding structure 株主構成, 株主構造

（=shareholder structure）
term structure 期間構造
▶Major banks are forced to review their earnings *structure*. 大手行は、収益構造の見直しを迫られている。
▶The upgrade reflects Moody's expectation that the company will continue to exhibit an excellent operating performance and outstanding capital *structure*. この格上げは、同社が引き続き好業績と際立った財務基盤を示すとのムーディーズの期待感を反映している。

struggle 動 悪戦苦闘する、奮闘する、苦労する、必死になる、取り組む（⇒**turn around**）
▶The company is *struggling* to recover earnings at its core businesses such as laser printers and digital cameras. 同社は、レーザー・プリンターやデジタル・カメラなど同社の中核事業の収益回復に取り組んでいる。

struggle 名 競争、闘争、紛争、戦い、もみ合い、取っ組み合い、攻防戦
　internal struggle 内部闘争、内紛（=internal conflict）
　litigating struggle 法廷闘争
　work-to-rule struggle 順法闘争（=lawabiding struggle）
▶Hokuetsu's shareholders was dragged into the *struggle* between Oji, Hokuetsu and trading house Mitsubishi Corp. 北越製紙の株主は、王子製紙、北越製紙と三菱商事（大手商社）の3社間の攻防戦に巻き込まれた。

struggling 形 経営不振に陥っている、経営再建中の、生き残りに懸命の、生き残りに必死になっている、もたついている、悪戦苦闘の
▶Toyota has smoothly increased its sales, compared with the *struggling* General Motors Corp. and Ford Motor Co. 販売不振のゼネラル・モーターズ（GM）やフォードに対して、トヨタは順調に売上を伸ばしている。

stub 名 控え、台紙、半券
study 名 研究、調査、分析、スタディ
　case study 事例研究、ケース・スタディ
　empirical study 実証研究
　feasibility study 実行可能性［実現可能性］調査、実行可能性研究、企業化調査、事業化調査、フィージビリティ・スタディ
　field study 現地調査、実地調査、フィールド・スタディ
　full-scale study 本格調査
　job [work] study 作業研究
　operation study 作業研究
　plant layout study 工場配置研究、設備配置研究、生産施設配置研究
　process study 工程分析
　research study 調査研究
　time and methods study 時間・方法研究
　time and motion study 時間・動作研究

style 名 方法、方式、手法、様式、…型、…式、…流、モデル、名称、商号、スタイル
　business style 商号、経営スタイル、経営路線
　house style コーポレート・アイデンティティ、企業イメージ統合戦略
　life style 生活様式、ライフ・スタイル
　management style 経営手法、経営姿勢、経営スタイル
　new style 新モデル
　operating style 経営姿勢
　original business style 独自の経営スタイル、独自の経営路線
　U.S.-style current value accounting standard 米国式の時価主義会計基準
▶With little prospect of its original business *style* bringing about a change in fortunes, the firm will accept the merger offer. 独自の経営路線で業績改善の展望が見えないため、同社は買収提案を受諾すると思われる。

subcontract 名 下請、下請契約、動 下請をする、下請契約をする、下請負させる、委託する、丸投げする
　subcontract factory 下請工場
　subcontract worker 下請業者
　subcontracted work 下請仕事
▶The firm *subcontracted* all the works to other companies. 同社は、業務をすべて別会社に委託していた。

subcontracting 下請、丸投げ、下請契約（=farming out, subcontraction）
　subcontracting firm 下請会社
　subcontracting plant 下請工場
▶Obayashi Corp. imposed a complete ban on *subcontracting* starting this business year. 大林組は、今年度から丸投げを全面的に禁止した。

subcontractor 下請、下請企業、下請会社、下請業者、下請人、下請契約者、サブコントラクター
▶Japanese parts and materials-making *subcontractors* have been forced to set up operations in China as a result of their parent companies, such as major electrical appliance makers, shifting production to that country. 日本の部品や素材などの下請企業は、大手家電メーカーなど親会社の中国への生産拠点の移転に伴っ

て，いや応なく中国に進出した［中国での事業を開始した］．

subject to …に服する，…が適用される，…に準拠する，…の対象である，…の影響を受ける，…を必要とする，…を条件とする，…を免れない，…にかぎり，…の場合にかぎって，…に従って，…を条件として，…を前提として，ただし…
▶Proceeds from exercising stock options are regarded as part of a salary and thus *subject to* a higher tax rate than for one-time income. ストック・オプションを行使して得た利益（ストック・オプション利益）は，給与の一部と見なされるため，一時所得より高い税率（約2倍）が課される．

sublease 图 転貸，再賃貸，又貸し
sublet 動 転貸［転借］する，下請けに出す
submission 图 提出，提示，提示案，提出物，報告書，考え，意見，仲裁付託合意
▶The Audit Committee reviews the corporation's financial statements and related data prior to *submission* to the full board. 監査委員会は，当社の財務書類［財務諸表］と関連資料を，取締役会の全体会議に提出する前に検討します．

submit 動 提出する，提示する，意見を述べる，具申する
▶The firm's shareholders *submitted* proposals to disclose individual executive salaries at their general shareholders meetings. 同社の株主からは，株主総会で役員報酬の個別開示を求める案が出された．

subordinate 图 部下，下役，形 従属的な，下位の，二次的な，副次的な，派生的な
　relationship between supervisors and subordinates 上司と部下の関係
　subordinate convention 派生的公準
　subordinate debenture 劣後条項付き社債，劣後債
　subordinate officer 臨時役員，部下

subordinated 形 後順位の，優先順位が低い，劣後の，下位の （＝junior）
　convertible subordinated debenture 転換劣後社債，劣後転換社債
　dated subordinated bond 期限付き劣後債
　perpetual subordinated bond [debt] 永久劣後債
　subordinated capital 劣後資本
　subordinated claims 劣後請求権
　subordinated debenture 劣後債，劣後社債 （＝subordinated bond: 債券発行会社の破産や清算時に，債務弁済が一般の債務返済後に開始される債券のこと）

subordinated debt 劣後債，劣後債務 （＝junior debt）
subordinated debtholder 劣後債権者，後順位の債権者 （＝junior creditor, junior debtholder）
subordinated funding 劣後資金の調達
subordinated liabilities 劣後債務
subordinated loan 劣後ローン
▶The bank plans to provide the money by transferring ¥100 billion in *subordinated* loans to the insurer's foundation fund. 同行は，劣後ローン1,000億円をこの保険会社の基金に振り替えて，その資金を提供する方針です．

subprime 形 貸出条件がプライム・レート以下の，プライムより信用力が低い，信用力が低い，二級品の，サブプライム
subprime lender サブプライム・ローンの融資，信用力が比較的低い低所得者を対象にした住宅融資の融資銀行［融資行］，住宅ローン会社 （＝subprime mortgage lender; ⇒ **default**）
subprime loan 低所得者を対象にした住宅融資，低所得者層向け住宅ローン，サブプライム・ローン （＝subprime mortgage, subprime mortgage loan）

　サブプライム・ローンとは➡サブプライム・ローンのサブプライム（subprime）は，優良な借り手を対象にした「プライム」より信用力が低い，という意味である．サブプライム・ローンと呼ばれる米国の低所得者層や返済能力に問題がある個人向けの住宅ローン［住宅融資］は，ローン返済開始から2年間くらいは金利が低いが，それ以降は一般に金利が高くなるように設定されている．そのため米国では，高金利の返済ができないサブプライム・ローンの焦げ付き問題で，株価の動揺が続いた．また，サブプライム・ローンを証券化した金融商品を販売している欧米や日本の金融機関が，多額の損失を出す事態になった．

▶Nomura booked about ¥72 billion in losses related to the U.S. *subprime loan* business in the January-June period. 野村［野村ホールディングス］は，1－6月期に米国でのサブプライム・ローン事業関連の損失として約720億円を計上した．

subprime loan crisis サブプライム・ローン問題 （＝subprime mortgage crunch, subprime mortgage fiasco, subprime mortgage loan crisis）
▶Our business will in noway be influenced by the *subprime loan crisis*. 当社の事業がサブプライム・ローン問題の影響を受けるようなことは，まったくありません．

subprime mortgage 低所得者［低所得者層］向け住宅ローン, 低所得者向け住宅融資, 信用力が低い個人向け住宅融資, サブプライム・ローン (＝subprime loan, subprime mortgage loan; ⇒ **fiasco, uncertainty**)
 subprime mortgage crunch サブプライム・ローン問題 (⇒**economy**)
 subprime mortgage lender 住宅ローン会社, サブプライム・ローンの融資行
 subprime mortgage woes サブプライム問題
 ▶UBS will post a pretax loss of up to $690 million in the third quarter mainly because of losses linked to the U.S. *subprime mortgage* crisis. スイス最大手銀行UBSの第3四半期税引き前損失は, 主に米国で起きた低所得者向け融資「サブプライム・ローン」問題の関連損失で, 最高で6億9,000万ドルに達する見通しだ.

subprime mortgage loan サブプライム・ローン
 ▶The instability of U.S. stock prices results from problems related to massive number of unrecoverable *subprime mortgage loans* extended to low-income earners in the United States. 米国の株価不安定は, 米国の低所得者向け住宅ローン「サブプライム・ローン」の焦げ付き急増関連問題に起因している.

subscribe 動 寄付する, 申し込む, 購入申し込みをする, 出資する, 応募する, 引き受ける, 予約する, …に賛成(署名)する, 署名する

subscriber 名 〈株式の〉引受人, 〈年金や電話などの〉加入者, 申込人, 署名者, 〈新聞や雑誌の〉(予約)購読者
 broadband subscribers 高速大容量通信の加入者
 cell phone subscriber 携帯電話の加入者
 subscribers' cable network 加入者回線
 ▶Broadband *subscribers* totaled 14.95 millions as of the end of last fiscal year. 高速大容量通信の加入者総数は, 昨年度末現在で1,495万人に達した.
 ▶Shares taken by the outside *subscribers* at the time of incorporation of the new company shall be limited to one share each. 新会社の設立時に外部の引受人が引き受ける株式は, それぞれ1株に限るものとする.
 ▶The *subscribers* changed jobs from a firm that offered the defined-contribution pension plans to one that did not offer the plans. (確定拠出年金)加入者が, 確定拠出年金を導入している企業から導入していない企業に転職した.

subscription 名 株式の引受け, 応募, 加入, 出資, 予約, 寄付, 寄付金, 定期購読, 署名, 同意 (「応募」とは, 株式などの有価証券が新規発行される場合に買付けの申込みをすること)
 capital subscription 出資, 払込み資本金 (＝subscription to the capital)
 oversubscription 応募超過 (＝surplus subscription)
 private subscription 縁故募集 (＝private offering)
 stock subscription 株式応募, 株式公募, 株式の引受け
 stock subscription contract 株式引受契約, 株式引受契約書
 subscription agreement 募集契約, 元引受契約, 買取り契約
 subscription deposits for new stock to be issued 新株申込み証拠金
 subscription price 応募価格, 買取り価格, 引受価格
 subscription right 新株引受権, 引受込み権
 ▶The nation's largest nonlife insurance company was ordered not to accept new *subscriptions* for medical and other third-sector insurance policies. 国内最大手の損害保険会社が, 医療など第三分野の保険商品の新規募集停止命令を受けた.

subscription Web site 有料サイト, 有料ウェブ・サイト
 ▶Four credit card holders received bills for accessing *subscription Web sites* via cell phones even though they had no recollection of doing so. 利用した覚えがないのに, 携帯電話の有料サイトの利用代金請求書が, 4人のクレジット・カード会員に届いた.

subsequent events 後発事象 (＝events occurring after the balance sheet date, post balance sheet events)

subsidiary 名 子会社, 関係会社, 従属会社 (＝subsidiary company, subsidiary corporation; ⇒**consolidated subsidiary, wholly owned subsidiary**)
 local subsidiary 現地子会社
 majority owned subsidiary 過半数所有子会社
 marketing subsidiary 販売子会社 (＝sales subsidiary)
 overseas subsidiary 海外子会社 (＝foreign subsidiary)
 partially owned subsidiary 部分所有子会社
 quasi-subsidiary 準子会社
 subsidiaries and affiliates 子会社と関連会社
 subsidiary industry 補助産業

subsidiary plant 補助プラント
unlisted subsidiary 非上場子会社
▶Mitsubishi UFJ Financial Group Inc. turned its Mitsubishi UFJ Securities a 100% *subsidiary*. 三菱UFJフィナンシャル・グループは、三菱UFJ証券を100%子会社[完全子会社]化した。

subsidy 名 補助金, 助成金, 奨励金, 報奨金, 研究助成金 （＝grant）
　export subsidies 輸出補助金
　government subsidies 政府補助金, 国庫補助金, 政府助成金
　price subsidies 価格補助金
　public subsidies 公的補助金, 補助金
▶Washington and Brussels will conditionally accept an abolition of *subsidies* to farmers in the United States and the EU who grow agricultural products for export. 米国や欧州連合(EU)は、それぞれ国内の輸出用農産物栽培農家に対する補助金の撤廃を条件付きで受け入れる方針だ。

subsistence 名 生活, 存続, 生計の道
substantial 形 かなりの規模の, 大規模の, 莫大な, 大幅な, 大型の, 豊富な, 実質的な, 重要な, 重大な
▶The market opportunity is *substantial*. 市場機会は、かなりのものです。

substitute 名 代替財, 代理人, 代替
　substitute arrangement 代替契約
subtenant 名 転借人
success 名 成功, 発展, 躍進, 成果, 勝利, 大当たり, ヒット, 上首尾, 上出来, 好結果, 盛会, サクセス （⇒employee, reputation）
　economic success 経済発展, 経済の繁栄, 経済の成功, 経済成長
　industrial success 工業化の発展
　success story 成功物語, 成功談, サクセス・ストーリ
▶Our ultimate *success* will depend on how effectively and quickly we respond to the big changes taking place in the external environment. 当社の最終的な成果は、事業環境[外部環境]に起こっている大きな変化にいかに効果的かつ迅速に対応するかにかかっています。
▶While we very much regret losing valuable counselors, we recognize that constant renewal is essential to *success*. 貴重な助言者を失うことは非常に残念なことではありますが、絶えざる刷新は企業の発展に不可欠である、と私どもは認識しております。

successful company 成功している企業, 成功を収めた企業, 優良企業, 勝ち組企業

▶The economic recovery has been enjoyed by a limited number of people such as those in big cities and by a few *successful* large *companies*. 景気回復が見られるのは、大都市圏の限られた人々や数少ない勝ち組の大手企業に偏っている。

sue 動 訴える, 告訴する
　sue for …で訴える, …を告訴する, 訴訟を起こす, …を求める, 請願する
　sue ... for damages …を相手取って損害賠償の訴えを起こす
▶California's Attorney General Bill Lockyer has *sued* the six largest U.S. and Japanese automakers for damages related to greenhouse gas emissions. 米カリフォルニア州のビル・ロッキャー司法長官は、自動車が排出する温室効果ガスについて日米の大手自動車メーカー6社に損害賠償を求める訴訟を起こした。

suffer 動 〈損失などを〉受ける, 損失を計上する, 〈被害などを〉被る, 打撃を受ける, …に見舞われる, …に巻き込まれる, 耐える, 低迷する, 悪材料になる （⇒appraisal loss）
　suffer a loss 損失を被る
　suffer a plunge 下落する
　suffer big [large] losses 大損害を受ける, 巨額の損失を被る, 多額の損失を計上する
▶The firm *suffered* a plunge in its share prices in the wake of an accounting scandal. 会計処理疑惑の結果、同社の株価が下落した。
▶The hedge fund *suffered* a loss of $6 billion this month. 同ヘッジ・ファンドは今月、60億ドルの損失を被った[計上した]。

suffer from …に苦しむ, 打撃を受ける, …に見舞われる, …に巻き込まれる, 損害を受ける, …が重荷になる, …が悪材料になる
　suffer from a high debt load 重い債務負担に苦しむ, 債務負担が重荷になる
　suffer from price competition overseas 海外での価格競争に巻き込まれる
　suffer from swollen inventory 在庫増に見舞われる
▶Pioneer Corp. and Victor Co. of Japan are *suffering from* ever-fiercer market competition. パイオニアや日本ビクターは、市場競争の激化[競争激化]に苦しんでいる。

sum 名 合計, 総額, 総数, 金額
　initial sum 頭金, 一時金, 契約金
　sum insured 保険金額

Superfund Act 有害物質除去基金法, スーパーファンド法（この基金は有害物質の除去費用にあてられるもので、米政府の出資金, 化学・石油産業

部門等への税金と公害外企業の損害賠償金とで構成されている)

Superfund Amendment and Reauthorization Act of 1986 1986年スーパーファンド修正・再承認法

superintendent 名 監督者, 管理者, 部長, 局長, 管理人, 動 監督する, 管理する
 area superintendent 地域担当管理部長

superior 形 上司, 上役, 上官
▸The project team members submitted the documents to their *superiors*. プロジェクト・チームの職員は, これらの資料を上司に提出した。

superior products and services 優れた製品とサービス
▸Our customers can count on us to consistently deliver *superior products and services* that help them achieve their personal or business goals. お客さまの信頼に応えて, 当社は, つねにお客さま個人の目標または企業の目標達成に役立つ優れた製品とサービスを提供します。

supermarket 名 スーパー, スーパーマーケット
▸Leading *supermarket* chain Daiei Inc. will release household products that help keep rooms warm even when room heaters are set lower. 大手スーパーのダイエーが, ルーム・ヒーターを低めに設定しても室温を暖かく保てる効果がある家庭用品を販売する。

supervise 動 監督する, 指図する, 指揮をとる
supervision 名 監督, 指揮, 監視, 管理
supervision fees 監理料
▸Major general construction companies are paid *supervision fees* after lending their names to subcontractors to increase the number of nominal construction completions. 大手ゼネコンは, 下請業者への名義貸しによって監理料が支払われ, 名目上の完工高を増やすことができる。

supervisor 名 管理者, 監督者, 監視員, 主任, 管理人

supplementary 形 補足的, 補完的, 追加の, 補充の, 付属の, 増補の, 補遣の, 付録の
 supplementary agreement 補足契約, 補足契約書
 supplementary budget 補正予算, 追加予算
 supplementary clause 補足条項
 supplementary finance 補足融資, 補完融資
 supplementary financial information 補足財務情報
 supplementary financial measure 補足融資, 補完融資
 supplementary financing facility 補完融資制度

 supplementary information 補足情報
 supplementary order 追加注文
 supplementary pension 補足年金, 補充年金
 supplementary provisions 付則
 supplementary security 増し担保
 supplementary tariff 補償関税

supplier 名 供給者, 供給会社, 供給業者, 供給下請業者, 供給源, 仕入先, 納入業者, 製造業者, メーカー, 供給国, 輸出国, 売り手, サプライヤー
 housing supplier 住宅メーカー
 leading supplier 大手サプライヤー
 local supplier 現地メーカー
 parts supplier 部品メーカー

supply 名 供給, 供給量, 需給, 供給品, 消耗品(複数形), 貯蔵品, 政府の歳出[経費](複数形), サプライ, 動 供給する (⇒ **money supply**)
 construction supplies 建設資材 (= building supplies)
 factory supplies 工場消耗品
 manufacturing supplies 製造用消耗品
 office supplies オフィス用品費
 operating supplies 作業用貯蔵品
 product supplies 製品需給
 productive material, work in process and supplies 原材料, 仕掛品と貯蔵品
 sources of supply 供給源
 supply and demand of funds 資金需給
 supply-demand gap 需給ギャップ
 supply of funds 資金供給, 資金の供給量
 supply price 供給価格
 supply side 供給サイド, 供給側, 供給面, 供給重視, 供給側重視の経済理論, サプライ・サイド
 tight supply conditions 需給の逼迫
▸*Supply* cannot keep up with demand for some popular items. 売れ筋商品は, 需要に供給が追いつけない状態だ。
▸The Corporation's subsidiaries and associated companies are leaders in in the manufacture and *supply* of telecommunications equipment. 当社の子会社と関連会社は, 通信機器の製造・供給の分野で主導的地位を占めています。

supply chain 供給連鎖, サプライ・チェーン (モノやサービスの顧客に届くまでの全体の流れ。原材料の調達から製品の生産・販売にいたるまでの各プロセスに係わる企業のことを指す場合もある)
▸Our *supply chain* will be strengthened further through management integration. 経営統合により, 当社のサプライ・チェーンは一層強化されることになります。

supply chain management 供給連鎖管理,

サプライ・チェーン・マネジメント《略 SCM》(情報技術(IT)を利用して, 受注発注, 資材や部品の調達, 生産, 製品の配達, 在庫などを統合的に管理して, 企業収益を高めるための管理手法)

support 動 支援する, 援助する, 支持する, サポートする (⇒lion's share)
▶It is in our interest to *support* society's needs.
社会のニーズへの支援は, 当社の利益にもつながることです。

support 名 支援, 援助, 支持, サポート (=aid, assistance; ⇒**customer support service, financial support**)
 credit support 信用増強, 信用補塡, 信用補完
 customer support 顧客支援
 group support グループ支援, 系列支援
 technological support 技術支援
▶GM will restructure its business through Toyota's *support*. GMは, トヨタの支援で経営を再建する方針だ。
▶To extend direct customer *support*, we launched the largest retraining and redeployment program in our history. 直接的な顧客支援を行うため, 当社は過去[これまでで]最大規模の社員再研修・配置転換プログラムを開始しました。

support system 支援システム
 decision support system 意思決定支援システム
 executive support system 経営者層支援システム
 management support system 管理者層支援システム
 operational support system 現業部門のライン支援システム

surcharge 名 上乗せ料金, 追加料金, 割増金, 課徴金, 過重, 不当請求, サーチャージ, 動 追加料金を請求する
 export surcharge 輸出課徴金
 import surcharge 輸入課徴金 (=import surtax)
 tax surcharge 付加税, 加算税

surge 動 急増する, 急騰する, 高まる, 殺到する, 押し寄せる
▶The U.S. dollar *surged* to ¥130 level. ドル相場が, 1ドル=130円台まで急騰した。

surge 名 急増, 急騰, 急上昇, 殺到, 大波, ブーム
▶The *surge* in prices of natural resources could ignite fears of inflation, causing countries around the world to implement tight monetary policies. 天然資源の価格急騰がインフレ懸念を呼び, 世界各国が金融引締め政策を実施する可能性がある。

▶The *surge* of DSL subscribers reflects price competition by providers. DSL(デジタル加入者回線)加入者の急増は, プロバイダーの価格競争を反映している。

surpass 動 超える, 上回る, 突破する, …をしのぐ, …より優れている
▶Toyota's group net profit *surpassed* ¥1 trillion for the third consecutive year. トヨタの連結税引き後利益[連結純利益]は, 3年連続で1兆円を突破した。

surplus 名 余剰, 過剰, 剰余金, 積立金, 黒字, 歳入超過額
 common and surplus 普通株式資本および剰余金
 consolidated surplus 連結剰余金
 contribution surplus 払込み剰余金 (=contributed surplus, paid-in surplus)
 funds surplus 資金剰余金
 legal surplus 法定準備金
 moving toward surplus 黒字転換
 other surpluses その他の剰余金
 provision for surplus 積立金繰入れ
 reserve surplus 積立金
 revaluation surplus 再評価剰余金
 statement of surplus 剰余金計算書 (=surplus statement)
 statutory surplus 法定準備金
 structural surplus 黒字体質
 surplus appropriation statement 利益金処分計算書, 剰余金処分計算書
 surplus for redemption fund 償還基金積立金
 surplus from consolidation and merger 合併剰余金
 surplus from reduction of capital stock 減資差益
 surplus profit 利益剰余金, 超過利潤
 surplus reserve 積立金, 過概準備
▶Investment income recorded a *surplus* of ¥2.62 trillion larger than the previous year. 投資収益は, 前年より黒字が2兆6,200億円拡大した。
▶The closure of the money-losing outlets will result in a *surplus* of about 2,000 employees out of about 22,000 on a consolidated basis. 不採算店舗の閉鎖に伴い, 連結ベースで従業員約22,000人のうち約2、000人が余剰になる。

surplus employees 余剰人員
▶We have been able yo retrain *surplus* employees and reemploy them in another area of the business. 当社は, 余剰人員の再訓練と他の事業部門での再活用を実施することができました。

surplus fund 余剰資金, 剰余金（「剰余金」は, 自己資本のうち資本金と資本準備金以外の部分のことで, 過去の利益の蓄積を示す）
▶Banks are running out of *surplus funds*. 銀行は, 剰余金が底をつきかけている。

surrender 動 引き渡す, 明け渡す, 放棄する, 辞職する,〈保険を〉解約する, 名 降伏, 放棄, 権利放棄, 引渡し, 解約
　surrender charge 解約手数料, 解約料, 保険解約金
　surrender of bill 手形の引渡し
　surrender ratio 解約率
　surrender value 解約払戻し金（＝cash surrender value）

surtax 名 付加税
　import surtax 輸入課徴金
　income surtax 所得税付加税

survey 名 調査, 意識調査, 査察, 査定, 測量, 概観, 概説, サーベイ
　business sentiment survey 企業景況感調査
　establishment survey 事業所調査
　fact-finding survey 実情調査, 実態調査
　geophysical survey 地球物理探査
　household survey 家計調査
　labor force survey 労働力調査
　market survey 市場調査, 市場実査, 実態調査
　marketing survey 市場調査, マーケティング・サーベイ
　morale survey 士気調査
　nationwide survey 全国調査
　national purchasing managers survey 全米購買部協会景気総合指数
　ocean survey 海洋探査
　public opinion survey 世論調査
　sampling survey 標本調査, サンプル調査（＝sample survey）
　survey ship 測量船
　Tankan Survey 日銀短観
　telephone survey 電話による聞き取り調査, 電話調査法

surviving company 存続会社, 他の企業を吸収する会社（＝surviving corporation, surviving entity, surviving firm）
▶The current system requires the shareholders of companies absorbed in mergers and acquisitions to be given stocks of *surviving companies*. 現行の制度は, 企業の吸収合併の際, 吸収合併される会社の株主に対して存続会社の株式を交付することを義務付けている。
▶Yamanouchi Pharmaceutical Co. became the *surviving company* in the merger of the company and Fujisawa Pharmaceutical Co. 山之内製薬と藤沢薬品工業の合併では, 山之内製薬が存続会社になった。

survivor 名 生存者

survivorship 名 生存者権（生き残った者が共有財産の権利を取得する権利）

suspend 動 停止する, 一時停止する, 中止する, 差し止める, 中断する, 離脱する, 停職する
　suspend business 業務を停止する, 営業を停止する, 取引を停止する
　suspend operations 営業を停止する, 操業を停止する
　suspend payment 支払いを停止する
　suspend the sales of nonlife insurance products 損保商品の販売を停止する
　suspend trading 取引を停止する, 売買を停止する
　suspended trading 未決取引, 売買の一時停止
▶The Financial Services Agency has ordered ChuoAoyama PricewaterhouseCoopers to *suspend* its auditing services. 金融庁が, 中央青山監査法人に対して監査業務の停止命令を出した。

suspension 名 停止, 取引停止, 取引停止処分, 差し止め
　suspension of business 業務停止, 取引停止, 営業停止（＝business suspension）
　suspension of operation 操業停止
　suspension of sales 販売停止（⇒order 名）
　suspensions on installment plan 割賦売上高
▶The *suspension* of all operations at Nippon Steel Corp.'s Nagoya steelworks, following a gas tank explosion, was a big blow to the motor industry. ガス・タンク爆発事故の直後から新日本製鉄の名古屋製鉄所で行われている操業の全面停止は, 自動車業界に大打撃を与えた。

sustain 動 維持する, 持続させる, 継続する, 支持する, 支援する,〈損害などを〉受ける, こうむる

sustainable 形 持続可能な, 維持可能な, 持ちこたえられる, 継続利用できる, 長期的な, 本格的な
　sustainable growth 持続的成長, 持続可能な経済成長
　sustainable rally 本格的な上げ相場
　sustainable recovery 本格的な回復, 本格的な景気回復
▶The People's Bank of China aims to restrain an excessive use of funds by businesses and lead the economy in the direction of *sustainable* economic growth. 中国人民銀行が目指しているのは, 企業による資金の過剰使用の抑制と中国経済

sustainable development 持続可能な開発, 持続可能な発展, 安定発展, 環境維持開発
▸For the *sustainable development* of Japan's economy, it is extremely important to expand and deepen economic relations, including trade, with Mexico. 日本経済の安定発展のためには、メキシコとの貿易はじめ経済関係の拡大・深化が極めて重要だ.

sustainable economic recovery 持続的な景気回復, 景気の持続的回復
▸Maintaining an easy monetary policy may lead to excessive corporate capital investment and have a negative impact on the *sustainable economic recovery*. 金融緩和政策を続けると、企業の過剰な設備投資を生み、景気の持続的回復を阻害する恐れがある.

swap 動 交換する, 切り替える, 取り替える, 振り替える, 乗り換える, スワップする
　be swapped for yen funds 円資金にスワップされる
　swap convertible bonds into common shares 転換社債を普通株式に切り換える
▸The remaining debt of ¥230 billion will be converted to equity, with ¥220 billion to be *swapped* into preferred shares and ¥10 billion into common shares. 残りの債務2,300億円は株式に振り替えられ、このうち2,200億円分は優先株に、また100億円分は普通株に振り替えられる.
▸Under the triangle merger, a Japanese subsidiary of a foreign company is able to take over a Japanese firm by *swapping* some of the shares of the parent company of the subsidiary for the target's shares. 三角合併では、海外企業の日本子会社が、親会社の株式の一部と買収標的企業の株式を交換して日本企業を買収することができる.

swap 名 交換, スワップ (=swapping; ⇒**equity swap contract, interest rate swap, share swap, stock swap**)
　conduct a debt-for-equity swap 債務の株式化を行う, 債権の株式化を行う
　currency swap 通貨スワップ
　debt-bond swap 債務の債券化 (=debt-for-bond swap)
　equity swap 株式交換, 株式スワップ, 株価スワップ
　equity swap deal 株式交換取引 (=share swap deal, stock swap deal)
　stock swap deal 株式交換取引 (=equity swap deal, share swap deal; ⇒**remaining**)
　swap transaction スワップ取引
▸SMBC extended loans to corporate clients on condition of buying interest rate *swaps*. 三井住友銀行は、金利スワップを購入することを条件に、法人顧客に融資していた.
▸The company grew through a series of mergers and acquisitions by utilizing stock splits and *swaps* and other means. 同社は、株式分割と株式交換などの手法を駆使したM&A（企業の合併・買収）を繰り返して成長した.

swap agreement スワップ契約,〈中央銀行の〉スワップ協定［相互通貨交換協定］(=swap contract:「スワップ契約」とは, 金利スワップと通貨スワップがあって、相互の債務を交換する契約; ⇒**equity swap contract**)
　currency swap agreement 通貨スワップ契約, 通貨スワップ協定
　equity swap agreement 株式交換契約
　interest rate swap agreement 金利スワップ契約
▸The interest rate *swap agreements* mature at the time the related bank loans mature. 金利スワップ契約は、関連銀行借入金の満期日に満了します.

swap ratio 株式の交換比率
▸The *swap ratio* has yet to be decided. 株式の交換比率は、まだ決まっていない.

swaption 名 スワップション（スワップとオプションの組合せ）

sweeten 動 〈契約など〉の条件を魅力的にする,〈担保を〉有価証券を加えて増す

sweetener 名 甘味料, 魅力的付加材料, 賄賂, 鼻薬（「甘味料」は有価証券の魅力を増す材料のことで, kickerともいう）

SWF 政府系投資ファンド, 政府系ファンド (⇒**sovereign wealth fund**)
▸Singapore's *SWFs* are said to have been instrumental in invigorating the financial market by taking advantage of overseas human resources. シンガポールの政府系ファンド（SWF）は、海外の人材を登用して金融市場の活性化につながげたといわれる.

SWIFT 国際銀行間通信協会, 国際銀行通信協会, スイフト (**Society for Worldwide Interbank Financial Telecommunication**の略)
▸Most cross-border money transfers between financial institutions are carried out through the international data communications network provided by the *SWIFT*. 国境を越える海外送金の

大半は，スイフト（国際銀行間通信協会）が提供している国際的な金融データ通信網を介して行われている。

swing 名 動き，活動，〈株価などの〉変動，進行，はかどり
 forex swings 為替変動（＝currency swings）
 get into full swing 本格化する
 in full swing 最高潮の，真っ最中の，最盛期で，急ピッチで進んでいる
 swing line 信用供与枠
 swings in demand 需要の変動
 upward swing of the yen 円高
 ▸Long-term interest rates have been on an upward *swing*, recently rising as high as 2 percent. 長期金利が，一時2％をつけるなど，上昇傾向を強めている。

SWOT スウォット（**strengths, weaknesses, opportunities, and threats**の略。新商品の「強み，弱み，機会［販売機会］と脅威」の意味で，マーケティング用語）

symbol 名 象徴，表象（emblem），印，記号，符号，紋様，略称，信条（credo），シンボル
 chemical symbol 化学記号
 mathematical symbol 数学記号
 rating symbol 格付け記号
 status symbol 地位の象徴，ステータス・シンボル
 symbol color シンボル・カラー
 symbol economy 象徴経済
 symbol mark シンボル・マーク

syndicate 名〈証券発行の〉引受シンジケート団，〈銀行の〉協調融資団，銀行団，シンジケート，動 シンジケートを組織［組成］する，シンジケートで管理する
 banking syndicate 銀行の協調融資団，銀行融資団，銀行シンジケート団，銀行シンジケート
 international syndicate loan 国際協調融資団，国際シンジケート
 issue syndicate 証券発行団
 issuing syndicate of banks 銀行の発行引受団，証券発行銀行団
 syndicate a deal シンジケート団を組成する，シ団を組成する
 underwriting syndicate 募集引受団
 ▸The initial public offering (IPO) was underwritten by a *syndicate* of leading investment banks. 公開株式(IPO)は，大手投資銀行のシンジケート団が引き受けた。

syndicated loan 銀行団による協調融資，国際協調融資，シ・ローン，シンジケート・ローン（＝syndicated bank loan, syndicated lending）
▸The company took out a *syndicated loan* from 20 banks and leasing companies. 同社は，銀行やリース会社など20社から協調融資を受けた。

synergy 名 相乗効果，シナジー効果，シナジー（＝synergy effect）
▸*Synergies* could be expected through our company's knowhow in urban redevelopment. 都市再開発の当社のノウハウによって，シナジー効果が期待できる。

synergy effect 相乗効果，波及効果，相互補完効果，シナジー効果（＝synergistic effect）
▸The mergers and acquisitions many major U.S. companies pursued failed to produce the expected *synergy effect*. 米国の大企業の多くが追求したM&Aは，予想したシナジー（相乗）効果を上げられなかった。

system 名 組織，機構，体系，方式，体制，制度，設備，システム（⇒operating system）
 back-office system 事務処理システム
 business system 企業体系，事業体系，事務機構，企業システム，ビジネス組織，ビジネス・システム
 crisis management system 危機管理システム，危機管理体制
 custom system 特注システム
 customer system 顧客システム，顧客サポート
 delivery system 配送システム
 electronic payment system 電子決済システム
 estimating systems costs システム原価見積り
 expert system 専門家システム，エキスパート・システム
 fail-safe system 障害時安全システム
 fail-soft system 障害時運転可能システム
 knowledge-based system 知識ベース・システム
 logistics system 物流システム
 operating system 基本ソフト《略 OS》
 planning, program(m)ing, budgeting system 企画計画予算方式，企画計画予算制度《略 PPBS》
 predetermined motion time system 予定動作時間方式，予定動作時間法《略 PMTS》
 procurement system 調達システム
 profit sharing system 利益分配制度
 seniority-order wage system 年功序列型賃金体系
 software system ソフトウエア・システム
 strategic management system 戦略的経営システム
 system contract システム契約
 system design システム設計

system developing planning　システム開発設計
system development tools　システム開発ツール, 開発ツール
system implementation　システム開発
system industry　システム産業
system installation　システム導入, システム構築
system [systems] integration　システム統合
system integrator　システム・インテグレーター (＝SI vendor, solution provider: ユーザーに最適のコンピュータ・システムを開発して提供する企業あるいは専門家)
system of personal data protection　個人情報保護制度
system on chip [silicon]　システムLSI, システム・オン・チップ
system operator　システム・オペレーター (ケーブル・テレビ施設の管理・運営業者)
system organizer　システム・オーガナイザー
system overall manual　システム概要説明書
system program　システム・プログラム
system software　システム・ソフト, システム・ソフトウエア
systems construction techniques　システム構築法, システムの構築方法
systems conversion　システム移行
systems engineer　システム設計者, システム・エンジニア
systems engineering　組織工学, システム工学, システム・エンジニアリング
systems industry　システム産業
wage system　賃金体系, 給与体系, 賃金システム

▸The company is a systems integrator that creates optimal information systems by linking software, hardware and networks.　同社は, ソフトウエアとハードウエア, ネットワークを連結して最適な情報システムを創造するシステム・インテグレーターだ。

▸Toyota aims to establish a *system* to produce 10 million cars per year worldwide, including Japan.　トヨタは, 日本を含む世界各地の生産拠点で年間1,000万台の生産体制確立を視野に入れている。

systemic risk　システム・リスク, システミック・リスク (一つの銀行の破綻が連鎖的に他の金融機関に及び, 金融システム全体が機能不全に陥るリスク)

T t

T-account T字型勘定
T-bill 米財務省短期証券, 英財務省証券 (= Treasury bill)
T-bond 米財務省長期証券 (=Treasury bond)
tab 名 付け札, ラベル, 勘定, 勘定書き, 請求書, 借用書, 記録, 伝票, 〈缶の〉キャップ[タブ], 〈コンピュータの〉タブ・キー, 動 …を選ぶ
  be tabbed as a candidate for …の候補者として選ばれる
  keep tabs [a tab] on …を監視する, …に注意する, …に注目しておく, …から目を離さない
  pay [pick up] the tab 費用を全額負担する
  pick up the tab for …の勘定を支払う
table 動 (米国で)〈議案や計画などを〉棚上げする, 延期[無期延期]する, (英国で)〈提案や要求などを〉審議する[審議に付す], 上程する, 提議する (米国と英国で意味が逆になる)
table 名 表, 図表, 一覧表, 目録, 〈本の〉目次, 作業台, 席, 食事, 料理, 碑文, 銘文, テーブル
  balance of payments table 国際収支表
  bring ... to the table …を会議に出す, …を審議する
  correlation table 相関表
  financial tables 財務諸表
  graphic table 図表
  input-output table 投入産出表
  inter-industry relations table 産業連関表
  lay ... on the table …を見送る, …を延期する, …を棚上げする
  lie on the table (議案などが)握りつぶされる
  money flow table 資金循環表, マネー・フロー表
  put one's cards on the table 手の内を明かす
  summary table 総括表
  table of contents 目次
  tariff table 関税表, 関税率表
  turn the tables (on) …に対して形勢[局面, 立場]を逆転させる, 主客転倒する, …にひとあわ吹かせる, …に仕返しをする
  under-the table donation ヤミ献金
  work table 集計表
tacit 形 暗黙の, 黙示の (=implied)
  tacit agreement 黙示の合意
  tacit choice of governing [applicable, proper] law 準拠法の黙示の選択
  tacit consent 暗黙の同意[協定], 黙約
  tacit contract 黙約
  tacit law 慣習法, 暗黙法
tactic(s) 名 作戦, 作戦行動, 手段, 方策, 策, かけ引き, 戦術
  advertising tactics 広告戦術
  marketing tactics マーケティング戦術
  sales tactics 売上作戦
  scorched earth tactics 焦土作戦
  strategies and tactics 戦略と戦術
  ▶The key to our success will depend on the skill with which we manage change and execute our strategies and *tactics*. 当社の成功の鍵は, 変化に対応して, 戦略と戦術をどのように実施していくかにかかっています。
tag 名 標識, 荷札, 宛名札, 付箋, タグ
  IC tag 電子荷札, ICタグ
  inventory tag 棚卸し票
  price tag 正札
  tag sales 正札販売, タグ・セールス
tailor 動 適応させる, 適合させる, …に合わせる, 組み立てる, 仕組む, 仕立てる, 調製する

be tailored to the needs of …のニーズに合わせてある，…の需要に応じて…する
▶Toyota's figures are the fruit of its global business strategy of meticulously *tailoring* its models to satisfy the various needs of customers around the world, coupled with its cost-cutting efforts. トヨタの業績は，合理化努力[コスト削減努力]と，世界各地のユーザーのさまざまなニーズを満たすためにきめ細かな車作りを目指すトヨタのグローバル経営戦略の成果である.

tailor-made 形　注文仕立ての，目的[要求]にぴったり合った

take-home pay 手取り賃金，手取り給与，可処分所得

take off 突然人気が出る，活況を呈する，〈売上などが〉急に伸びる，離陸する，値段を割り引く，値引きする，差し引く，控除する，中止する，削除する

takedown 名　〈証券の〉引受け分，取り分，引受価格，テークダウン

takeoff 名　離陸，出発点，飛躍
　economic takeoff 経済的離陸，経済的飛躍（経済成長の停滞期から自立的成長期に入った状態）
　industrial takeoff 工業の離陸
　make a good economic takeoff 順調に経済が離陸する
　move to economic takeoff 経済が離陸し始める
　takeoff into a new capacity formation period 新生産能力形成期への離陸
　takeoff into sustained growth 持続的成長への離陸
　takeoff option テークオフ・オプション

take out 〈ローンなどを〉組む，〈保険に〉入る[加入する]，保険を付ける，契約する，獲得する，取得する，取り出す，持ち出す，削除する，取り除く，除去する
　take out a loan contract ローン契約を結ぶ
　take out provisions against loan losses 貸倒れ損失に備えて引当金を引き当てる
▶The number of contracts *taken out* on broadband Internet services rose by 3.74 million to 23.3 million in a year-on-year comparison. ブロードバンド（高速大容量通信）・インターネット・サービスの契約件数は，前年比で374万増の2,330万件に達した.

takeout 名　持ち出し，取り出し，〈免許などの〉取得，証券売買益，長期不動産抵当貸付け（テークアウト・ローン），テークアウト
　takeout commitment 抵当証書購入約定
　takeout financing テークアウト・ファイナンス（=takeout loan）
　takeout loan [mortgage] 長期不動産担保融資，長期不動産抵当貸付け，テークアウト・ローン（=takeout, takeout financing）

take over 〈企業を〉買収する，買い取る，取得する，乗っ取る，〈資産，業務などを〉引き継ぐ，継承する，経営権を獲得する，肩代わりする，占拠する
　take over a failed [troubled] business 破綻した企業の経営を引き継ぐ，経営破綻した会社を引き継ぐ
　take over the assets of …の資産を継承する
　take over the operations of …の営業譲渡を受ける
▶Off-hours trading of stocks cannot be used any more to *take over* a company. 株の時間外取引は，企業買収にはもう使えなくなった.
▶The collapsed Long-Term Credit Bank of Japan was *taken over* by Shinsei Bank. 経営破綻した日本長期信用銀行は，新生銀行が引き継いだ.

takeover [take-over] 名　企業買収，乗っ取り，企業取得，買収，吸収合併，債権などの譲り受け，引継ぎ，テイクオーバー（=acquisition, tender offer; ⇒**friendly takeover, hostile takeover**）
　agreed takeover 合意による株式公開買付け
　anti-takeover measures 買収防衛策
　corporate takeover 企業買収
　defend against a hostile takeover 敵対的買収に対抗する，敵対的買収への防衛策をとる
　high-leverage takeover 多額の借入れによる企業買収
　prevent a takeover 乗っ取りを阻止する（=block a takeover）
　takeover attempt 買収劇，買収攻勢，買収の企て，買収
　takeover battle 買収合戦，株式争奪戦，株争奪戦，争奪戦（=takeover war）
　takeover bidder 買収提案者，買収者
　takeover defense 買収防衛手段，防衛手段，乗っ取り防衛手段，買収防衛策
　takeover plan 企業買収案，買収計画
　takeover-target company 買収標的会社
　unsolicited takeover offer 一方的な企業買収提案，敵対的買収提案
▶The two companies will hold extraordinary shareholders meetings to confirm the *takeover*. 両社は今後，それぞれ臨時株主総会を開いて，買収案を正式に承認する.

takeover bid 株式公開買付け，株式公開買付けによる企業買収，買収提案，テイクオーバー・ビッ

ド《略 TOB》（=take-over bid, takeover offer, tender offer）
friendly takeover bid 友好的株式公開買付け，友好的TOB，株式公開買付けによる友好的買収，友好的買収
hostile takeover bid 敵対的株式公開買付け，敵対的TOB，敵対的買収
takeover bid period 株式公開買付けの期間，TOBの期間（=public tender offer period）
takeover bid system 株式公開買付け制度
unfriendly takeover bid 非友好的株式公開買付け，非友好的TOB，株式公開買付けによる非友好的買収，非友好的買収（=unfriendly takeover）
▸The recent stock-swap deal followed a purchase of stock through a *takeover bid*. 今回の株式交換取引は，株式公開買付け（TOB）による株式買取りに続いて行われた．

takeover offer 企業買収提案，買収提案（=takeover bid; ⇒reject）
▸Quantas Airways has accepted an 11.1 billion Australian dollar *takeover offer* from a private equity consortium. カンタス航空が，民間企業連合が提示していた111億豪ドル（約1兆円）の買収案を受け入れた．

talks 名 会談，交渉，協議，話し合い
 alliance talks 提携協議，提携交渉
 bilateral talks 2国間協議
 debt restructuring talks 債務再編交渉
 exploratory talks 事前協議
 Japan-U.S. framework trade talks 日米包括経済協議
 labor management wage talks 労使賃金交渉
 marathon talks 長時間にわたる会談
 multilateral talks 多国間協議
 multilateral trade talks 多角的貿易交渉，多国間貿易交渉
 one-to-one talks 1対1の協議
 preparatory talks 準備協議
 six-nation talks 6か国協議（=six-party talks, six-way talks）
 spring wage talks 春闘，春の賃金交渉，春の賃上げ交渉
 telephone talks 電話会談，電話会議
 the latest round of multilateral trade liberalization talks 新多角的貿易交渉（新ラウンド）（=the new round of WTO talks）
 working-level talks 実務レベル協議，実務協議，実務者協議
▸Nissan Motor Co.'s board of directors gave its approval for exploratory *talks* on a proposal for struggling U.S. auto giant General Motors Corp. 日産自動車の取締役会は，経営再建中の米自動車大手ゼネラル・モーターズ（GM）に対する提携提案の事前協議を承認した．

tally 名 割符，簿記用紙，計算用紙，記録，計算単位
talon 名〈債券の〉利札引換券
tamper 動 不正取引をする，〈人を〉買収する，〈文書を〉改竄する
tandem 名 2人乗り自転車，タンデム
 in tandem with …と並んで，…と協力して，…と提携して
 move in tandem with …と並行して進む，同時進行する
 tandem currency タンデム通貨
 tandem exchange 中継局
 tandem plan 併設プラン
▸To achieve at least 2 percent nominal growth in gross domestic product, the government must take stimulus measures in *tandem* with the BOJ's easy money policy. 2％超の名目GDP成長率を実現するには，日銀の金融緩和政策と並んで，政府は景気刺激策を取らなければならない．

tangible 形 有体の，有形の
 tangible asset 有形資産，有形固定資産（=physical asset）
 tangible fixed asset 有形固定資産
tangibles 名 有形資産
tap 動〈情報などを〉引き出す，開発する，利用する，選ぶ，選出する，盗聴する
 tap into the market 市場を利用する，…市場に乗り出す，市場で起債する
 tap rising demand 需要増に応える
 tap the market 市場を開発［開拓］する，市場に登場する，市場で起債する，市場で資金を調達する
▸Firms have begun to *tap* into the niche metrosexual market. 企業が，メトロセクシャル（都心（メトロ）に住み，オシャレに精を出す男性）のニッチ市場拡大に乗り出した．

target 動 …を目標に定める，目標にする，標的にする，対象にする，狙う，ターゲットにする
▸Seven & I Holdings Co. *targets* 71 percent of operating profit from convenience stores in the year ending February 2009. セブン＆アイ・ホールディングスは，2009年2月期決算のコンビニエンス・ストア部門の目標を営業利益の71％としている．

target 名 目標，標的，目標水準，買収目標企業，買収対象会社，買収標的の会社，ターゲット
 country-by-country target quantified targets

国別総量目標
earnings target 業績目標, 利益目標, 収益目標 (=earnings goal)
growth target 成長目標
market target 市場標的
numerical target 数値目標
operating operation 運営目標, 操作目標
original target 当初の目標
profit target 収益目標, 運用益の目標
takeover target 買収の対象, 買収の標的, 買収の目標, 買収対象会社, 買収目標企業
target profit 目標利益
▸Japanese companies could become *targets* of foreign takeover bids. 日本企業が, 外資による株式公開買付け (TOB) の標的になる可能性がある。
target company 買収対象会社, 買収目標企業, 買収標的の会社, 標的企業, ターゲット企業, ターゲット・カンパニー (=target firm, targeted company)
▸When a hostile takeover bid occurs, its *target company* can ask shareholders to exercise their right to acquire new shares, reducing the voting power of shares held by the party mounting the takeover bid. 敵対的買収者が現われたら, その買収標的の会社は, 株主に新株予約権 (新株を購入できる権利) を行使してもらって, 敵対的買収者が保有する株式の議決権の比率を引き下げることができる。
targeted company 買収の標的企業
tariff 関税, 関税率, 料金表, 運賃表
  ad valorem tariff 従価関税
  antidumping tariffs 反ダンピング (不当廉売) 関税
  common tariff 共通関税
  counter tariff 対抗関税
  customs tariff 関税率, 関税定率
  discriminative tariff 差別的関税
  drug tariff 薬価基準
  emergency tariffs 緊急関税
  General Agreement on Tariffs and Trade 関税貿易一般協定 (ガット)
  internal tariff 域内関税
  non-discriminative tariff 無差別関税
  preferential tariff treatment 特恵関税 (=preference treatment tariff)
  protective tariff 保護関税
  punitive tariffs 制裁関税
  retaliatory tariffs 報復関税 (=punitive tariffs)
  safeguard tariffs セーフガード関税
  tariff barrier 関税障壁 (=tariff wall)
  tariff classification 関税分類
  tariff elimination 関税撤廃
  tariff escalation 傾斜関税
  tariff quota 関税割当て
  tit-for-tat tariffs 報復関税
▸Preferential *tariffs* for ASEAN's automotive industry were reduced to the 0 to 5 percent range in 2003 for key ASEAN member countries except Malaysia. ASEAN (東南アジア諸国連合) の自動車分野の特恵関税率が, マレーシアを除く主要ASEAN加盟国に対して2003年から0-5%に引き下げられた。
task 仕事, 任務, 職務, 業務, 務め, 課業, 作業, 課題, 問題, タスク
  credit analyst's task 信用アナリストの業務
  data gathering task データ収集業務
  main task 主な任務
  task environment 課業環境
  task force 対策委員会, 対策本部, 専門調査団, 特殊任務を持つ機動部隊, タスク・フォース
  task force on financial issues 金融問題委員会
  task management 課業管理, タスク監理
  task method 課業設定法, 目標課題達成法, 課題基準法, タスク法, タスク・メソッド
  task of the board 取締役会の任務
  urgent task 緊急課題
▸One *task* to be tackled is to reestablish the relationship with the company, which was undermined by poor communication. 取り組むべき一つの課題は, 意思疎通が十分とは言えなかった同社との関係の再構築だ。
tax 税, 税金, 租税
  additional tax 加算税
  advertising tax 広告税 (=advertisement tax)
  applicable taxes 租税公課
  business tax 事業税, 営業税
  capital investment tax 資本投資税
  corporate inhabitant tax 法人住民税
  earnings before taxes 税引き前利益
  effective tax 実効税額
  environmental tax 環境税
  estate tax 相続税, 遺産税
  fixed-rate tax reduction 定率減税
  general excise tax 一般消費税
  indirect business tax 間接事業税
  inhabitant tax 住民税
  inheritance tax 相続税
  local corporate tax 法人事業税 (企業活動に対して課される地方税)

local inhabitants tax 住民税
local tax 地方税
luxury tax 物品税
negligence tax 過少申告加算税
office tax 事業所税
operating tax 営業税, 事業税
ordinary tax 経常税
overdue tax 未納の税, 延滞税
payments of estimated tax 予定納税
progressive tax 累進課税, 累進税
property tax 固定資産税, 資産税, 財産税
ratio of direct and indirect taxes 直間比率
real estate tax 固定資産税
real property acquisition tax 不動産取得税
real property tax 固定資産税
registration tax 登録税
regressive tax 逆進税
reserve for tax payment 納税引当金
reserve for taxes 納税引当金 (=reserve for tax payment)
sales tax 売上税, 物品販売税, 取引高税
shifting of tax 租税の転嫁, 税の転嫁 (=tax shifting)
state and local taxes 州税と地方税
state franchise tax 州法人税
stock dividend tax 株式配当課税
tax advantages 税制上の優遇措置 (=tax concessions, tax incentives)
tax allocation within a period 期間内税金配分
tax allowance 控除
tax amount 税額
tax audit 税務監査
tax avoidance 合法的な租税回避, 節税
tax base 課税ベース, 税収基盤
tax basis 申告基準, 税法基準
tax bill 課税通知書
tax bracket 税率区分, 税率等級
tax burden 租税負担, 税負担
tax claim receivable 税金の還付請求額
tax concessions 税制上の優遇措置, 税制優遇措置 (=tax advantages, tax incentives)
tax cut 減税 (=tax reduction)
tax-deferred share exchanges 株式交換の課税繰延べ (三角合併で, 株式交換時に課税しないで, 交換した日本子会社の親会社の株を実際に売却したときに課税すること)
tax evasion 脱税, 課税逃れ, 税金逃れ (=tax fraud)
tax hike 増税 (=tax increase)
tax holiday 免税期間, 免税措置, タックス・ホリデイ

tax implications 税務上の取扱い
tax incentives 税制上の優遇措置 (=tax advantages, tax concessions)
tax inspection 税務調査
tax investigation 税務調査
tax loss 税務上の損失, 税務上の欠損金
tax management 税務管理
tax on business 企業課税
tax paradise 租税天国
tax payable 未払い税金
tax payment 納税, 税金の支払い
tax planning 納税計画, 租税計画, 節税計画, 税務計画の策定, 租税回避
tax planning strategy 税務計画戦略, 税務戦略, 戦略的税務計画, 戦略的納税計画, 税計画戦略
tax point 課税時期
tax provision 納税引当金, 法人税等額
tax receivable 未収税金
tax reductions for corporations 企業減税
tax relief 免税, 減税, 税額免除, 税負担の軽減, 税金の減免
tax repayment 税金還付
tax revenue 税収
tax revenue sources 税収源, 税源
tax saving 節税, 法人税などの軽減額
tax service 税務サービス, 税務
tax shelter 租税回避地, 租税回避国, 租税回避手段, 税金天国, 税金逃れの隠れみの, 会計操作, タックス・シェルター (=tax haven)
tax surcharge 付加税, 加算税
taxes on income 法人税等, 法人所得税
taxes, other than income taxes 租税公課
transaction tax 取引税
transfer tax 譲渡税, 財産移転税
turnover tax 売上税, 取引高税

▶Deferred *tax* assets are taxes we expect to get funded in future periods. 繰延べ税金資産は, 将来に払戻しされる税金のことです。
▶Fifteen banks filed a lawsuit seeking to abolish a local corporate *tax* targeting major banks. 大手金融機関を対象にした法人事業税の取消しを求めて, 15行が提訴した。
▶There are no estate *taxes* or succession duties imposed by Canada or by any province of Canada. カナダまたはカナダ国内のいかなる州でも, 遺産税または相続税を課されることはありません。

tax asset 税金資産
▶The banks' equity capital is inflated by so-called

"deferred *tax assets*." 銀行の自己資本は，いわゆる「繰延べ税金資産」でかさ上げされている。

tax authorities 税務当局，税務署
▸Proposed adjustments from *tax authorities* will not have a material adverse effect on the consolidated financial position, liquidity or results of operations of the Company. 税務当局からの修正要求で，当社の連結財政状態，流動性や経営成績が悪影響を受けることはないようです。

tax benefit 税務上の特典，〈税額控除や所得控除などの〉税制上の優遇措置，税効果，節税益，課税軽減額
　allowance for unrealizable tax benefits 繰延べ法人税資産評価勘定
　income tax benefit of operating loss carry-forward 欠損金繰越しの税務上の恩典
▸After the extraordinary item, a *tax benefit* due to previous tax losses, net income applicable to common shares was $57 million. 異常損益項目〔前期の租税損金計上に伴う課税軽減額〕控除後の普通株式に帰属する純利益が，5,700万ドルでした。

tax break 減税，税額控除，税率軽減措置，租税優遇措置，租税特別措置，税務上の特典，税制上の特典（=tax cuts, tax deduction, tax reduction）
　tax break for capital gains キャピタル・ゲイン減税
　tax break on housing loans 住宅ローン減税
▸The *tax breaks* on capital gains from stock sales and on dividend income will be extended by one year. 株式譲渡益〔株式売却益〕と受取配当金の税率軽減措置の期間が，1年延長される。

tax convention 租税条約，国際租税条約，国際租税協定（=tax treaty, taxation convention, taxation treaty）
▸This withholding tax may be reduced by an applicable international *tax convention*. この源泉所得税〔源泉徴収税〕は，国際租税条約の適用によって軽減される〔引き下げられる〕ことがあります。

tax credit 税額控除，税金控除（=tax deduction）
　deferred tax credit 繰延べ税金
　direct foreign tax credit 外国税額の直接控除
　foreign tax credit 外国税額控除
　investment tax credit 投資税額控除，投資減税
▸The IRS has proposed adjustments to the Company's income and *tax credits* for these years which would result in additional tax. 内国歳入庁（IRS）は，当社のこれらの事業年度の収入と税額控除について，加算税を伴う可能性のある修正を要求しています。

tax effect 税効果
　tax effect of investment credits 投資税額控除の税効果
　tax effect of operating losses 繰越欠損金の税効果
　tax effect of timing differences 期間差異による調整分，期間差異の税効果，税効果当期配分額（⇒**reverse**）
▸The cumulative effects of accounting changes include the *tax effects* of those adjustments. 会計処理の変更による累積的影響額には，その修正による税効果が含まれています。

tax-exempt 形 免税の，無税の，非課税の，課税されない（=tax free）
　tax-exempt bond 免税債，非課税債券
　tax-exempt borrowings 非課税借入金
tax-exempt expense 非課税費用，損金（⇒**depreciation cost**）
▸Firms will be allowed to treat the full amount of capital investment as *tax-exempt expenses*. 企業は今後，設備投資については全額，非課税費用〔損金〕として処理することができるようになる。

tax expense 法人税等計上額，法人税等費用，税金費用，納税額
▸The Company has $380 million of deferred investment tax credits for financial reporting purposes, which will reduce *tax expense* in future years. 当社の繰延べ投資税額控除額は，財務会計上3億8,000万ドルで，これにより将来の納税額は減少します。

tax free [**tax-free**] 非課税の，無税の，免税の（=tax-exempt）
　tax-free amortization 無税償却
　tax-free disposal of bad loans 不良債権の無税償却
　tax-free income 免税所得，非課税所録
▸After privatization of the state-run Japan Post, users have to pay stamp duties for services that were *tax free* in the past. 国営の日本郵政公社が民営化されてから，利用者は，これまで非課税だったサービスに対しても印紙税を支払わなければならない。

tax haven 租税回避地，租税逃避地，租税避税国，税金天国，タックス・ヘイブン（=tax shelter）
▸A *tax haven* provides preferential treatment, such as an exemption from corporate tax, to its registered firm. タックス・ヘイブン（租税回避地）は，そこに本店登記した会社については法人税の免除などの優遇措置がある。

tax liability 税金債務, 納税額
▸Deferred *tax liabilities* are taxes we expect to pay in future periods.　繰延べ税金債務は，将来に支払う予定の税金のことです。
tax rate 税率, 課税率　(=rate of taxation)
　applicable tax rate 適用税率
　average corporate tax rate 平均法人税率
　basic tax rate 基本税率
　corporate income tax rate 法人所得税率
　current income tax rates 当期の所得税率
　effective tax rate 実効税率
　enacted tax rates 法定税率, 施行される税率
　income tax rate 法人税率, 所得税率
　marginal tax rate 限界税率
　maximum income tax rate 所得税の最高税率
　reduced tax rate 税率の軽減, 軽減税率
　standard tax rate 標準税率
　statutory tax rate 法定税率
　withholding tax rate 源泉徴収税率
▸Our new accounting for income taxes uses the enacted *tax rates* to compute both deferred and current taxes.　法人税に関する当社の新会計処理では，繰延べおよび当期税金の計算に法定税率を使用します。
tax refund 税金還付, 納税の返還　(=tax rebate: tax refundsは「還付税額」)
▸The banks are allowed to include expected *tax refunds* in their capital accounts.　銀行は，その資本勘定に税金の還付見込み分を算入できることになっている。
tax return 税務申告, 納税申告, 確定申告, 税務申告書, 納税申告書　(⇒e-tax)
　income tax return 所得税申告書, 法人税申告書
　make one's income tax return 納税申告する
　tax return filing machine 申告書作成機
▸Tax offices will be accepting 2008 income *tax returns* until March 16.　税務署は，3月16日まで2008年度の確定申告を受け付ける。
tax system 税制, 租税体系　(=system of taxation, taxation system)
　land and financial tax systems 土地・金融税制
　preferential tax system 優遇税制
　securities tax system 証券税制　(=securities taxation system)
　simplified tax system 簡易課税制度
taxable 形 課税対象となる, 課税できる, 課税…　(⇒write off)
　taxable losses or expenses 有税処理
　taxable profit 課税利益
　taxable transaction 課税取引
　taxable revenues 益金
　taxable write-off 課税償却, 有税償却
▸Capital gains realized on the Corporation's common shares by individuals who are not resident in Canada for Canadian income tax purposes generally are not *taxable* in Canada.　カナダ所得税法上, カナダ居住者でない [カナダ居住者に該当しない] 個人が実現した当社の普通株式のキャピタル・ゲインは，一般にカナダでは非課税扱いになります。
taxable income 課税所得, 所得金額
▸In computing the *taxable income* for federal income tax purposes, the following timing differences were taken into account.　連邦所得税算定のための課税所得を算定するにあたっては，次の期間差異を考慮しました。
taxation 名 課税, 徴税, 税収　(⇒two-track income taxation system)
　base of taxation 課税標準
　double taxation relief 外国税額控除
　double taxation agreement [treaty] 二重課税防止条約, 租税条約
　dual taxation 二重課税　(=double taxation)
　favorable [favourable] taxation 優遇税制
　progressive taxation 累進所得税
　security taxation system 証券税制
　self-assessed taxation system 申告納税方式
　separate self-assessment taxation 申告分離課税
　separate taxation at source 源泉分離課税
　source of taxation 税源
　taxation formula 課税方式　(=taxation system)
　taxation office 税務署　(=tax office)
　taxation on enterprise 企業課税
　taxation system reform 税制改革　(=taxation reform)
　taxation treaty 租税条約　(=tax treaty, taxation convention)
　taxation upon total income 総合課税
　thin capitalization taxation 過小資本税制
　transfer pricing taxation system 移転価格税制 (「移転価格税制」は，国内企業が海外に所得を移して, 国内での納税額を意図的に減らすのを防ぐ制度。日本では1986年に導入された)
　unitary taxation 合算課税, ユニタリー課税, ユニタリー・タックス　(=unitary tax)
▸The introduction of a tax system advantageous to banks exclusively would run counter to the principle of fairness in *taxation*.　銀行だけに有

利な税制の導入は，課税の公平原則に反することになる．

taxation bureau 国税局
　a taxation bureau's tax inspection 税務調査
　Tokyo Regional Taxation Bureau 東京国税局
▸The *taxation bureau* did not permit the company to report the money as a loss. 国税局は，同社に対してこの金の損金計上を認めなかった．

taxpayers' money 納税者の金，国民の税金，税収，公的資金，公金
▸The Article 102 of the Deposit Insurance Law seeks to protect all deposits at a collapsing bank through injections of *taxpayers' money* and other public funds. 預金保険法第102条は，税金などの公的資金の注入を通じて破綻しつつある[破綻寸前の]銀行預金の全額保護を求めている．

team 名 団，組，班，チーム
　cross-functional team 機能横断チーム，クロス・ファンクショナル・チーム
　engineering team 研究開発チーム，エンジニアリング・チーム
　management team 経営陣，マネジメント・チーム
　project team プロジェクト・チーム
　research team 研究班，研究チーム
　self-directed team 自主管理チーム，セルフ・ディレクテッド・チーム
▸We have reinforced our management *team* with a mix of newcomers who bring proven track records and rich experiences. 当社は，実績と豊富な経験を兼ね備えた一時的な新メンバーを迎えて，当社の経営陣を強化しました．

team up with …と協力する，…と提携する，…とチームを組む（＝join forces）
▸Sun Microsystems Inc. is *teaming up with* longtime partner Fujitsu Ltd. of Japan to jointly develop the next generation of Sun systems. 米サン・マイクロシステムズは，長年のパートナーである富士通との提携関係を強化して，企業向けの次世代サーバー「サン・システムズ」を共同開発する．

teaser 名 ティーザー広告（商品を小出しにして興味を煽る広告）

tech [Tech] 名 〈英国の〉テクニカル・カレッジ（工業専門学校），〈米国の〉工科大学（institute of technology）

-tech …技術，…テク（＝technology）
　high-tech 先端技術，高度技術，ハイテク
　low-tech 低技術，低レベルの工業技術，ローテク

technical 形 技術の，技術的な，工業技術の，科学技術の，専門的な，技巧上の，実務上の，実用的な，

市場の内部要因による，人為的な，操作的な，テクニカル

technical analysis テクニカル分析，テクニカル・アナリシス（株式や外国為替などの相場や出来高の推移をチャートで示して，変化の傾向を読み取ったり将来の相場を予想したりする手法）

technical assistance 技術協力，技術援助，技術支援，技術指導（＝technical aid, technical cooperation）

technical bulletin 技術公報，実務公報

technical change アヤ（やや長期的な相場のなかでの特に理由のない小さい変動のことを「アヤ」という）

technical collaboration 技術提携，技術協力

technical conditions テクニカル要因（＝technical factors, technical forces）

technical development 技術開発

technical disparity 技術格差

technical documentation 技術書類，技術文書（＝technical documents）

technical efficiency 技術的効率，技術効率

technical expert 技術専門家

technical factors テクニカル要因，市場内部要因（信用取引残高，投資家の売買動向，新株発行による資金調達状況，株価規制など，動向株価を動かす要因のうち株式の需給に直接かかわる要因を「市場内部要因」とか「内部要因」という）

technical forces テクニカル要因

technical guidance 技術指導

technical hitch 機械の一時的な故障，一時的中断［停止］

technical information 技術情報

technical instruction 技術指導

technical interface 技術の提示

technical knowhow 技術的ノウハウ，技術ノウハウ，ノウハウ（⇒field）

technical knowledge 技術知識

technical license 技術実施権，技術ライセンス

technical personnel 技術要員

technical picture 需給関係

technical position 取組み，内部要因，内部要因相場，不自然な人為相場

technical progress 技術の進歩，技術進歩，技術の発展

technical rally アヤ戻し（＝technical correction, technical rebound, temporary correction: 株式相場が下げ基調のとき，一時的に少し高くなる場合のことを「アヤ戻し」という）

technical reaction アヤ押し（株式相場が上げ基調のとき，一時的に少し下がる場合のことを

「アヤ押し」という）
technical reserves 総責任準備金
technical results 技術的成果, 技術成果
technical review 技術調査
technical service 技術役務, 技術サービス, テクニカル・サービス
technical skill 技術的能力, 技術力, ノウハウ
technical specification 技術仕様
technical support 技術援助, 技術サポート, テクニカル面からの下支え, テクニカル・サポート
technical term 専門用語, 術語, テクニカル・ターム
technical tie-up 技術提携
technical training 技術訓練, 技術研修（=technological training, technology training）
technical writer 技術文書作成者, テクニカル・ライター
▶Many *technical* problems remain in implementing the new payoff system. 新しいペイオフ制度の実施には, 実務上の問題点が多い。

technical expertise 技術の専門意見, 技術的知識, 専門技術, 技術鑑定
▶Besides *technical expertise*, we have the skills to provide customized, integrated offers either alone or in concert with partners. 技術的な専門知識のほかに, 当社は, 顧客の要求に応じて特注化した提案や統合化した提案を単独で, もしくはパートナーとともに提供することができます。

technical improvement 技術の改良, 改良技術
▶The Japanese people's tireless efforts in *technical improvement* and innovation have been a driving force in beating the competition both at home and abroad. 日本人の改良技術と創意工夫の面での精力的な努力が, 国内外の競争に勝つ原動力になってきた。

technical standard 技術標準, 技術水準
▶ISDN is a set of *technical standards* worked out by the telecommunications industry internationally. ISDN（総合デジタル通信網）は, 通信業界が国際的に設定した一連の技術標準です。

technicals 名 テクニカル要因, 需給要因, 要因
  bullish technicals 強気のテクニカル要因
  favorable technicals 内部要因の良さ, 好調なテクニカル要因
  good [strong] technicals 好調なテクニカル要因, 好調な需給関係
  supply technicals 供給面の要因

technological 形 科学技術の, 技術的な, テクノロジカル

technological advance 科学技術の進歩
technological assistance 技術援助, 技術支援, 技術指導（=technical assistance）
technological breakthrough 技術の画期的躍進, 技術革新（=technical innovation）
technological capability 技術力
technological capacity 技術能力
technological change 技術革新, 技術変化（=technological innovation, technological renovation），
technological cooperation 技術協力
technological development 技術開発, 科学技術の進歩[発展], 技術の進歩
technological drive 技術志向
technological fluidity 技術の変化
technological forecasting 技術予測, 技術予想
technological friction 技術摩擦
technological innovation 技術革新, 技術開発（=technical innovation）
technological obsolescence 技術の陳腐化, 技術的陳腐化
technological progress 技術の進歩, 技術の発展
technological renovation 技術革新
technological revolution 技術革命, 技術革新
technological risk 技術的リスク
technological support 技術支援（⇒technological development）
technological transfer 技術譲渡, 技術供与, 技術移転
technological unemployment 技術的失業, 生産技術の進歩に伴う失業

technology 名 技術, 科学技術, 工業技術, テクノロジー（⇒**nanotechnology**）
biotechnology 生命技術, バイオテクノロジー
cutting-edge technology 最先端技術, 最新技術, 先進技術
data transmission technology データ伝送技術, データ通信技術
electronic technology 電子技術, コンピュータ技術
energy-saving technology 省エネ技術, 省エネルギー技術
environmental technology 環境技術
financial technology 金融技術, 金融テクノロジー, 財テク
high technology 高度先端技術
most sophisticated technology 最先端技術（=most advanced technology）
pollution control technology 環境保全技術
process technology プロセス技術

product technology　製品技術
state-of-the-art technology　最新技術
system technology　システム技術
technology assessment　技術評価, 技術の事前評価, 技術開発事前評価, テクノロジー・アセスメント《略 TA》
technology drain　技術流出
technology driver　技術牽引者, テクノロジー・ドライバー
technology import　技術輸入, 技術導入
technology licensing organization　技術移転機関《略 TLO》
technology shares　ハイテク株
transfer of technology and know-how　技術・ノウハウの移転
technology transfer　技術移転
video technology　ビデオ技術
wearable technology　ウエアラブル技術
▶Kao plans to sell cosmetics products based on its own *technology* under the Molton Brown brand.　花王は, 独自の技術に基づく化粧品をモルトン・ブラウンのブランドで販売する方針だ。

techno-mart 名　技術取引場, テクノマート
technophobia 名　技術恐怖症, 科学技術恐怖症
technosphere 名　科学技術活動
technostress 名　テクノストレス（コンピュータ作業によるストレス）
TEFL　外国語としての英語教育, テフル (Teaching English as a Foreign Language の略)
telco 名　情報通信会社, 電気通信事業者, 通信株 (telecommunications company の略)
　international telcos　国際電気通信事業者
　telco supplier　通信機器メーカー
telecom 名　通信, 電気通信, 通信事業, テレコム (=telecommunication, telecommunications)
　mobile telecoms　移動通信
　telecom carrier　通信事業者
　telecom firm　通信会社
　telecom group　通信事業グループ
　telecom market　通信市場, 電気通信市場
　telecoms services　通信業務, 通信サービス
　telecom and broadcasting facilities　通信・放送設備
▶We concluded a contract with 90 *telecom* carriers for the construction of a new network of submarine cable connecting Asia and Europe.　当社は, 通信事業者90社と, アジアとヨーロッパを結ぶ新海底ケーブル網の建設に関する契約に調印しました。
telecommunication 名　電気通信, 遠隔通信,

通信, テレコム (=telecom, telecommunications)
　broadband telecommunications　広帯域通信
　convergence of telecommunications and broadcasting　通信と放送の融合
　digital telecommunications network　デジタル通信網
　satellite and line telecommunications　衛星・有線通信
　special telecommunications base facilities　特定電気通信基盤施設
　Telecommunications Act of 1996　米国の1996年通信法
　telecommunications and information industry　通信・情報産業, 情報通信産業
　telecommunications business　通信事業, 電気通信事業
　Telecommunications Business Law　電気通信事業法
　telecommunications facilities　通信設備, 通信施設
　telecommunications industry　通信業界
　telecommunications market　通信市場
　telecommunications equipment　通信機器, 電気通信機器
　telecommunications sector　通信業界, 通信分野, 通信部門
　wire telecommunications equipment　有線電気通信機器
telecommunication [telecommunications] company　通信会社, 通信事業会社, 情報通信会社
▶Major electric appliance manufacturers and 10 *telecommunication companies* turned profits for the year ended March 31.　3月期決算では, 大手電機と情報通信10社が, 黒字に転換した。
telecommunications network　通信網, 電気通信網, 通信ネットワーク
▶With a personal computer linked to a high-speed, large-capacity *telecommunications network* such as a fiber-optic network, one can watch images as clear as those broadcast on TV.　光ファイバー網のような高速大容量通信網に接続したパソコンであれば, テレビで放映される映像と同じくらい鮮明な映像を見ることができる。
telecommuting 名　在宅勤務, 通信勤務, コンピュータ勤務, テレコミューティング (=remote work, telework, teleworking)
▶Other initiatives, like flexible work schedules, *telecommuting* and job-sharing, meet the di-

verse needs of individuals and the company. フレックス・タイムや在宅勤務，ジョブ・シェアリング[ワークシェア]などの他の新しい試みも，個々の社員と会社のさまざまなニーズを満たしています．

telecoms services 通信サービス，通信業務
▶The report calls for new regulation of *telecoms services* and broadcast businesses. この報告書は，通信サービスと放送事業に新しい規制の導入を求めている．

teleconference 形 電話会議
teleconference meeting 電話会議，テレビ会議
▶In a *teleconference meeting*, the GM's board authorized the company's management to consider the proposal by Kirk Kerkorian. 電話会議[テレビ会議]で，米ゼネラル・モーターズ(GM)の取締役会は，カーク・カーコリアン(大株主の米投資会社トラシンダを率いる投資家)の提携案を検討する権限を，同社の経営陣に与えた．

telemarketing 名 テレマーケティング (=telephone shopping, teleshopping: 電話での商品販売ш，または電話での各種調査や案内，コールセンター構築のサポートなどを行う会社のこと)
▶On its Web site and through *telemarketing*, the company advertised that it was engaged in investments and trading stocks. 自社のホームページや電話勧誘を通じて，同社は株の売買や運用業務を宣伝した．

telematics 名 情報・通信複合分野，高度情報社会，テレマティックス

television 名 テレビ，テレビ放送，テレビ映像，テレビ受像機《略 **TV**》(⇒campaign, durable product, electrical, emerging Internet company, liquid crystal display panel, strong sales)
 digital TV デジタル・テレビ，デジタル・テレビ放送
 flat-panel TV set 薄型テレビ
 high definition TV 高精細度テレビ，高品位テレビ，ハイビジョン (=HDTV, high-resolution TV)
 LCD television 液晶テレビ，LCDテレビ (=liquid crystal display television)
 plasma display TV プラズマ・テレビ
▶Hitachi, Ltd. is the leading maker of plasma *TV* sets in the country. 日立製作所は，プラズマ・テレビの国内トップメーカーだ．

temporary 形 一時的な，臨時の，暫定的，仮の
 temporary borrowings 一時借入金
 temporary employment 一時雇用
 temporary layoff 一時解雇，一時帰休

 temporary suspension of trading 取引の一時停止
 temporary transfer 出向
 temporary worker 派遣社員
 temporary worker services 労働者派遣サービス

temporary cash investments 短期投資，一時投資，短期的資金運用投資
▶We reduced our balance of cash and *temporary cash investments* over the last two years. 当社は，過去2年間にわたって現金と短期投資の残高を圧縮しました．

temporary differences 一時差異，一時的差異(貸借対照表上の資産・負債の金額と課税所得計算上の資産・負債の金額との差額)
▶Deferred income taxes reflect the impact of *temporary differences* between the amount of assets and liabilities recognized for financial reporting purposes and such amounts recognized for tax purposes. 繰延べ法人所得税は，財務会計上で認識された資産および負債の金額と税務上で認識された当該金額との一時的差異の影響を反映しています．

temporary employee 期間従業員，派遣社員
▶The number of *temporary employees* at Toyota Motor Corp.'s domestic factories is likely to reach a record high of 7,000 within the year. トヨタ自動車の国内工場で働く期間従業員は，年内に過去最高の7,000人に達する見込みだ．

temporary staffing firm 人材派遣会社 (=temporary staffing agency)
▶A *temporary staffing firm* is trying to find skilled workers. 人材派遣会社が，熟練工を探し求めている．

Temporary Staffing Services Law 労働者派遣法
▶Temporary workers have been increasing as regulations under the 1986 *Temporary Staffing Services Law* have gradually been relaxed. 1986年に施行された労働者派遣法の規制が段階的に緩和されるに従って，派遣社員は増えている．

tenant 名 借地人，借家人，賃借人，借主，現住者，土地保有者，不動産権保有者，出店者，テナント
 key tenant 核店舗，核テナント
 tenant right 借地権
 tenants of online shopping mall 仮想商店街の出店者
▶The company will collect fees from the *tenants* of its online shopping mall. 同社は今後，仮想商店街の出店者から手数料収入が得られる．

tender 動 入札する, 請け負う, 申し出る, 提出する, 提供する, 支払う
▸We *tendered* a bid on a new three-year contract with the government of Saudi Arabia. 当社は, サウジアラビア政府との新規3年契約の入札に応じました.

tender 名 入札, 応募入札, 入札書, 申込み, 提出, 提供, 提出物, 提供物, テンダー
  competitive tender 競争入札
  make a tender for …の入札をする
  open tender 一般競争入札
  public tender 公開入札, 一般競争入札, 競争入札, 公売, 株式公開買付け
  put out to tender 入札に付す, 入札を募る
  self tender 株式の自己買付け, 自己株の買戻し, 自社株の買戻し提案 (買収を仕掛けられた場合などに, 会社が株主に対して行う自社株の買戻し提案のこと)
  tender on the Internet ネット入札, インターネットでの入札
  tender price 株式公開買付けの価格, TOB価格, テンダー価格
  the first round of tenders 一次入札
  win a tender for …を落札する
▸Local governments are promoting fair open bidding for public works projects by offering *tenders* on the Internet. 地方自治体は, インターネットでの入札により, 公共工事[公共事業]の公正な一般競争入札を推進している.
▸The firm will invite open *tenders* for each project. 同社は今後, 個々の事業ごとに一般競争入札を実施する.

tender offer 株式公開買付け, テンダー・オファー (=public tender offer, takeover bid, takeover offer, TOB: 一般の証券取引市場の外で行われる大口証券購入の申込みのこと. ⇒**public tender offer**)
  cash tender offer 現金公開買付け, 現金による株式公開買付け, キャッシュ・テンダー・オファー (買収先の会社の株式を現金で公開買付けする方法)
▸The firm will extend the period during which its *tender offer* is valid to March 2 from the initial expiry date of Feb. 21. 同社は, 同社の株式公開買付けの有効期限を, 当初の有効期限である2月21日から3月2日まで延長する.

tenement 名 保有財産, 借地, 自由保有権
tenor 名 写し, 写本, 謄本, 手形期間, 債券期間
term 名 期間, 契約期間, 専門用語, 用語, 定期不動産権, 条件(複数形で用いられることが多い), 条項, 規定, 約定, 合意 (⇒**business term**)
  accounting term 会計期間
  business year term 決算期 (=business term)
  credit terms 支払い条件
  dollar terms 金額ベース, ドル・ベース, ドル表示 (=dollar-denominated terms)
  in real terms 実質ベースで, 実質で, 実勢価格で
  in terms of voting rights 議決権ベースで, 議決権比率で
  in value terms 名目ベースで, 金額ベースで (=in terms of value)
  in volume terms 実質ベースで, 台数ベースで
  issue terms 発行条件 (=terms of issue)
  long term contract 長期契約
  on equal terms 同じ条件で
  profit for the term 当期利益, 当期利益金
  profits and losses for the term 期中損益
  settlement term ending in March 3月期決算, 3月終了の決算期
  short term debt 短期債務, 短期借入金
  term of payment 支払い期限, 支払い期間
  terms and conditions 条件
  trade terms 貿易条件, 貿易支払い条件, 貿易用語, 取引用語
▸The *terms* and conditions of this agreement may be changed, amended or modified only by a written instrument. 本契約の条件・条項は, 書面でのみ変更, 修正できるものとする.
▸Toyota's group sales and profits hit a record high in the settlement *term* ending in March. トヨタの3月期決算で, 連結売上高と利益はともに過去最高を更新した.

terminal 名 端末, 端末機, 端末装置, 終点, ターミナル (「端末」は, 通信回線でホスト・コンピュータと接続して, データの入力と出力を行うための装置)
  air cargo terminal 航空貨物ターミナル
  combined transport terminal 複合ターミナル
  computer terminal コンピュータの端末, コンピュータ端末装置
  data terminal データ端末, データ通信端末
  intelligent terminal インテリジェント端末
  information terminal 情報端末
  job-oriented terminal ジョブ向き端末
  multimedia terminal マルチメディア端末
  terminal equipment 端末機器, 端末装置
  terminal unit 端末装置, 端末機器, 端末機
  terminal user 端末利用者
▸Cell phone handsets and information *terminals* with highly sophisticated functions are widely

terminal | test

used in Japan.　日本では，かなり高機能の携帯電話や情報端末が普及している。
terminal 形　期末の，最終の，終点の，末期の，末端の，一定期間の，定期の，毎期の
　terminal accounts　期末決算
　terminal cancer　末期がん
　terminal care　末期医療
　terminal date　決算日，期末日
　terminal funding　年金現価積立て方式，年金現価充足方式　（＝terminal funding method）
　terminal market　定期市場
　terminal medical care　終末期医療　（＝terminal care）
　terminal operation　港湾事業
　terminal payment　最終の支払い
　terminal station　終着駅，始発駅
　terminal value　最終価値
　terminal wage　退職給与
▶In *terminal* medical care, it is said to be a basic principle that a team of doctors and nurses takes care of a patient.　終末期医療では，複数の医師や看護婦らが患者の世話をするのが基本とされる。
terminate 動　終わらせる，解雇する，期限切れになる，終結する，決着する　（⇒covenant, notice）
termination 名　〈契約の〉終了，解約，〈期間の〉満了，解除，〈権利の〉消滅，解散　（⇒abandonment, notice）
　account termination　口座解約
　early termination　期限前解約
　lease termination　リース解約
　termination benefit　退職給付
　termination of employment　退職
　termination of office　任期満了
▶Provisions for business restructuring in 2008 covered $130 million for special *termination* benefits.　2008年度の事業再編成引当金には，特別退職給付の1億3,000万ドルが含まれています。
territory 名　領域，分野，区域，領域，ゾーン，領土，販売区域，販売地域，販売領域，担当区域，〈商標やソフトウエア・プログラムなど〉知的財産権の使用許諾地域，許諾地域，契約地域，レベル，テリトリー　（⇒negative territory）
　business territory　商圏，商勢圏
　distribution territory　販売区域
　junk territory　投資不適格のレベル　（⇒junk territory）
　manufacturing territory　製造地域
　negative territory　マイナス，マイナス基調
　neutral territory　中立ゾーン
　positive territory　プラス，プラス基調
　sales territory　販売領域，販売区域，販売地域
　service territory　サービス区域，サービス・エリア
▶*Territory* means the countries set forth in Schedule attached hereto.　「販売区域」は，本契約書に添付する付属書類に明記する国を意味する。
tertiary 形　第三次産業の，サービス部門の
tertiary industry　第三次産業　（サービス産業とほぼ同じで，商業，運輸・通信業，金融業，公務・自由業，有給の家事サービス業などのこと）
　tertiary industry activity index　第三次産業活動指数　（＝index of tertiary industry activity, tertiary industry index）
▶The nation's *tertiary industry* activity index rose 1.5 percent from the previous year.　日本の第三次産業活動指数は，前年度比で1.5％増加した。
test 動　試験する，探る，試す，検定する
　test resistance　抵抗線を試す
　test skills　技能を検定する
　test the market　市場の反応を探る
test 名　試査(test check, test checking, testing)，会計記録の試査，調査，検定，試験，実験，基準，試練，テスト　（⇒examination）
　試査とは➡「試査」は試験的照査の略称で，財務諸表監査の場合は，会計記録の一部を監査対象として検査し，その検査結果から全体としての会計記録[財務諸表]の適否を検討する方法をいう。
　Compliance test　準拠性テスト
　debt test　負債基準
　goodness of fit test　適合度検定
　joint test　結合テスト
　leverage test　負債比率
　market test　市場テスト
　on a test basis　試査により，試査による
　product test　商品テスト
　role-playing test　役割演技法　（セールスマンや従業員の訓練手法の一つ）
　sample test　試供品テスト，サンプル・テスト
　stress test　ストレス・テスト　（⇒stress test）
　test delivery　テスト配信
　test drilling　試掘
　test market　試験市場，テスト市場，テスト・マーケット
　test marketing　試験販売，テスト・マーケティング
　test production　試験生産
　test run　試運転，試験運転，テスト・ラン
　test specification　テスト仕様書
　the test of accounting records　会計記録[会

計報告書]の試査, 財務諸表の試査
transaction test 取引調査
▸Our examinations included such *tests* and other procedures as we considered necessary in the circumstances. 私どもの監査は, 私どもが状況に応じて必要と認めた会計記録の試査とその他の監査手続きを含んでいます。

thermal 形 熱の, 火力発電の, 保温用の
　solar thermal conversion 太陽熱利用
　solar thermal electric generation 太陽熱発電（＝solar thermal power generation）
　thermal fusion 熱融合
　thermal generator 火力発電所（＝thermal power plant, thermal power station）
　thermal pollution 熱公害, 熱汚染

thermal efficiency 熱効率
▸As for the development of gas turbines with higher *thermal* efficiency, the United States and countries in Europe have launched national projects. 熱効率の高いガスタービンの開発については, 欧米諸国は国家プロジェクトをスタートさせている。

thermal power 火力発電
▸*Thermal power* is generated by turbines that are driven by steam generated from the combustion of fossil fuels such as oil. 火力発電は, 石油などの化石燃料を燃やしてできた蒸気で蒸気タービンを回して発電する。

thin market 薄商い市場, 閑散市場, 手薄な市場, 市場低迷, 閑散（活況市場＝active market）
thin trading 薄商い（＝thin volume）
thin margin 薄利, 低い利益率
third party 第三者（＝third person）
　third party beneficiary 第三受益者（契約当事者ではないが, 契約によって直接利益を受ける者）
　third party claims 第三者請求
　third party contractor 第三者請負人
　third party infringement 第三者侵害, 第三者による侵害
　third party organization 第三者機関
third-party allotment [allocation] 第三者割当て, 第三者割当て増資（＝allocation of new shares to a third party, allotment to third parties, third-party share allotment:「第三者割当て」とは, 役員や従業員, 取引先, 提携先, 金融機関など発行会社と特別な関係にあるものに新株の引受権を与えて, 新株を発行すること）
　increase one's capital through a third-party allotment 第三者割当てで増資する
　issue new shares through a third-party allotment 第三者割当てで新株を発行する
　third-party share allotment 第三者株式割当て, 第三者割当て増資（＝third party equity allotment [allocation], third-party allotment of shares）
▸The company is to float new shares under a *third-party* share *allotment* scheme. 同社は, 第三者割当て増資計画に基づいて新株を発行する。

threshold 名 敷居, 戸口, 出発点, 門出, 発端, 閾（いき）, 境界, 限界点,〈賃金の〉物価スライド制
　boom-bust threshold 景気判断の分かれ目
　cognitive threshold 認知閾
　drop below the threshold of …の水準を割り込む
　exposure threshold リスク限度額
　threshold agreement 賃上げを消費者物価指数に連動させる協定, 敷居契約, 敷居協定, 閾値協定
　threshold element しきい値素子, 閾値素子
　threshold level 閾水準
　threshold price 農産物最低価格, 敷居価格
　threshold worker 初心者

thrift 名 倹約, 節約, 貯蓄金融機関, 貯蓄貸付け機関
　paradox of thrift 節約[倹約]のパラドックス
　thrift account 貯蓄性預金勘定
　thrift crisis 貯蓄金融業界の危機
　thrift encouragement 貯蓄奨励
　thrift industry 貯蓄金融業界, S&L業界
　thrift institution 貯蓄金融機関
　thrift savings account 定期積立預金
　thrift shop 中古衣料販売店
　thrifts 米貯蓄金融機関（米国の貯蓄貸付け組合(Savings and Loan Association)と信用組合(credit union), 貯蓄銀行(savings bank)の総称）

throughput 名 処理能力, 処理高, 処理量, 効率, スループット

throwaway age of mass consumption 大量消費の使い捨て時代
▸Our Society is shifting itself from the *throwaway age of mass consumption* to a resource-conserving one. われわれの社会は, 大量消費の使い捨て時代から省資源社会に移行している。

throwaway product 使い捨て製品
▸*Throwaway products* account for much of the garbage we produce. 使い捨て製品が, われわれが生み出すゴミの大半を占めている。

thrust 名 推進, 推進力, 推力, 前進, 攻勢, 厳しい批評, 酷評, 主眼, 主旨, 要点
　global thrust グローバル志向
　make a thrust into …に進出する, …に攻勢を

かける
▶Executive changes to increase the pace of growth and globalization accelerate a global *thrust*. 成長速度とグローバル化を促進するための役員入替えで、グローバル志向を推進しています。

TICAD アフリカ開発会議 (Tokyo International Conference on African Developmentの略)(アフリカの経済・社会開発問題を協議する国際会議で、日本や国連などの主催で1993年から5年ごとに東京で開催。アフリカ諸国に対する経済援助のほかに、アフリカ諸国のオーナーシップ[自助努力]を提唱している)
▶On the closing day, the conference will adopt the *TICAD* 10th Anniversary Declaration. 最終日に、会議では「TICAD10周年宣言」を採択する。

tick 名 信用、掛け、信用売り、掛売り、勘定

tie-in 形 抱き合わせ販売の、抱き合わせの、名 つながり、関係、結びつき、関連、提携、タイアップ、抱き合わせ販売、抱き合わせ広告
　capital tie-in 資本提携
　promotional tie-ins 販促タイアップ
　tie-in advertising 抱き合わせ広告、タイ・イン広告
　tie-in promotion 関連販売促進
　tie-in sale 抱き合わせ販売、関連販売
　tie-in ship 仕組み船

tie up 提携する、連携する、協力する
▶The two companies are aiming to *tie up* in the hotel and resort facilities business. 両社は、ホテル・リゾート施設事業での提携を視野に入れている。
▶MFG, the nation's largest financial group, *tied up* with two major U.S. banks to strengthen its earning power. 国内金融グループ最大手のみずほフィナンシャルグループが、収益力の強化を図るため、米銀大手2行と提携した。

tie-up 名 提携、合併、統合、経営統合、協力、結びつき、〈業務の〉一時停止、タイアップ (=alliance; ⇒**business tie-up, capital tie-up**)
　capital and operational tie-up 資本・業務提携
　capital and strategic tie-up 資本・戦略提携
　comprehensive tie-up 包括提携
　equity tie-up 資本提携
　strategic tie-up 戦略的提携
▶Both companies can enjoy synergies in terms of product development and procurement of materials by the *tie-up*. 提携によって、両社は商品開発や原材料の調達などで相乗効果を見込める。
▶The *tie-up* created the world's largest banking group, with total assets of ¥190 trillion. 統合によって、総資産が190兆円の世界最大の銀行[金融]グループが誕生した。

tier 名 段、段階、層、階層、ティア
　first-tier bank 大手行、上位行
　lower tier-two capital ロワー Tier 2資本
　primary (Tier 1) capital 自己資本の基本的項目
　second-tier bank 準大手行
　second-tier life insurer 中堅生命保険
　supplementary (Tier 2) capital 自己資本の補完的項目
　Tier 1 capital guideline 自己資本の基本的項目基準、基本的項目基準
　Tier 1 capital ratio Tier 1自己資本比率
　two-tier bid 二重価格買付け
　two-tier exchange system 二重為替相場制
　two-tier price 二重価格
　upper tier two capital アッパー Tier 2資本
▶Cases of bankruptcies have been particularly high in fiscal 2007 among small-sized and second-*tier* publishers. 2007年度は、中小の出版社の倒産件数が特に高かった。

tight lending 貸し渋り、貸出の抑制 (=credit crunch)
▶The remaining ¥2 trillion or so will be spent to support small and medium-sized companies and help loosen the *tight lending* policy implemented by private-sector financial institutions. 残りの約2兆円は、中小企業支援と民間の金融機関が行っている貸し渋りへの対策に充てられる。

tight money 金融引締め、金融引締めの状態、金融逼迫、資金需要の逼迫 (=monetary restraint, monetary tightening)

time 名 時、時間、期間、時期、時代、時勢、機会、期限、タイム
　available time 納期
　break-even time 損益分岐期間
　cooling time 冷却期間
　floor-to-time 加工時間
　labor time 作業時間
　lead time 先行期間、準備期間、生産準備期間、企画段階から生産開始までの所要時間、発注から納品までの期間、調達期間、納期、リード・タイム
　predetermined motion time system 予定動作時間法、予定動作時間方式《略 PMTS》
　setup time 設定時間、段取り時間
　time bill 期限付き手形、期限付き為替手形
　time charge 時間報酬制
　time cost 時間費用
　time deposit 定期性預金、定期預金、貯蓄性預金(期限付き預金の総称)

time discount 期間割引
time draft 定期払い手形
time loan 定期貸付け
time money 定期借入れ
time of circulation 流通期間
time of closing 実行時, クロージング時
time policy 期間保険
time series analysis 時系列分析
time table 時刻表, 予定表, 時間割
time ticket 作業時間報告書
time value 時間価値, 期間価値, タイム・バリュー
time wage 時間賃金, 時間給

▶Some information that is transmitted in real *time* globally creates a trend in a very short time. リアルタイムでグローバルに伝達される情報は, 極めて短時間に一つのトレンドを作り出す。

time frame 表示期間, 時間の制限, 時間枠, 期間, タイムリミット

▶The company will reduce the interest-bearing liabilities to a maximum ¥900 billion from ¥1.57 trillion in the same *time frame*. 同社は, 上記期間に有利子負債を1兆5,700億円から最高9,000億円に削減する方針だ。

time horizon 運用期間, 将来展望, タイム・ホライゾン
　investment time horizon 投資資産の運用期間
　investors with a time horizon of 10 years 10年の運用期間を設定している投資家

▶Generally investments involve a longer *time horizon* than speculations. 一般に投資は, 投機より運用期間が長くなる。

time is of the essence 期日厳守, 期限厳守, 期限は絶対条件

▶*Time is of the essence* in this Agreement and in each and every provision thereof. 時間は, 本契約とそのあらゆる規定の絶対条件である[本契約とその各規定において, 期限は厳守することとする]。

timeline 名 工程表, 日程 (＝time line)

timing 名 時期, 時間[時期, 速度]の調整・選択, 好機の選択, 潮時, 頃合い, タイミング

▶Should the Fed misjudge the *timing* or level of its next rate hike, it may interrupt the economic recovery and even bring about rapid inflation. 米連邦準備制度理事会(FRB)が追加利上げの幅やタイミングを誤ると, 景気回復の腰を折り, 急激なインフレを招く可能性もある。

▶The company concealed taxable income by manipulating the *timing* of the calculation in its reports to the tax authorities. 同社は, 税務申告書の計上時期を操作して, 課税所得を隠していた。

timing differences 〈費用収益の〉期間差異, 時間差異, 年度間差額, 期間帰属差異 (⇒**reverse**)

▶The disparity between book income and taxable income is attributable to *timing differences*. 帳簿上の利益と課税所得との差は, 期間差異に起因している。

tip 名 内部情報, 未公開の重要情報, インサイド情報

title 名 役職, 肩書, 所有権, 権利, 権原, 〈不動産などの〉権利証書, 証券, 〈契約書の〉表題, 名称, 称号
(「権原」は資産を使用, 享受, 処分できる権利のこと)

▶The first preferred shareholders are entitled to cumulative annual dividends per share in the amount set out in the *titles* of each series and have one vote per share. 第一優先株式の株主には, 各シリーズの証券に記載されたレート[各シリーズの権利として規定された額]で1株当たり年間累積配当を受ける権利と1株につき1個の議決権が与えられています。

TLO 技術移転機関 (**technology licensing organization**の略。大学で生まれた発明や技術を, 研究者に代わって特許申請して, 民間企業に使用許可[ライセンス]を与えて産業に生かそうという組織)

TM 商標 (**trademark** の略)

TOB 株式公開買付け (**take-over bid [takeover bid]**の略。「株式公開買付け(TOB)」で応募が取得目標の株式数に達しない場合, TOBは不成立となり, 応募された株式を返さなければならない。 ⇒ **takeover bid**)

TOEFL 外国語としての英語の学力テスト, トーフル (**Test [Testing] of English as a Foreign Language**の略)

TOEIC 国際コミュニケーションのための英語力テスト, トーイック (**Test [Testing] of English for International Communication**の略)

toehold purchase トーホールド・パーチェス (「トーホールド・パーチェス」とは, M&Aで買収対象会社(ターゲット・カンパニー)の発行済み株式を5%まで買い集めて, 買収の足がかり(toehold)にすること)

token 名 代用硬貨, トークン, 証拠, 象徴

Tokyo Stock Exchange 東京証券取引所, 東証《略 **TSE**》

Tokyo Stock Price Index 東証株価指数《略 **TOPIX**》 (＝Tokyo stock price index, Tokyo stock price index and average; ⇒**TOPIX**)

toll 名 使用料, 料金, 送信料, 長距離電話料金, 租税, 動 〈物の一部を〉料金として取る

toll-free 名 無料電話, フリーダイヤル
　toll-free dialing service 無料電話サービス

toll-free 800 numbers　800番の無料電話サービス
toll-free telephone inquiries　フリーダイヤルでの問い合わせ
▸The firm is accepting *toll-free telephone inquiries* about the leaked customer data.　同社は，流出した顧客情報についてのフリーダイヤルでの問い合わせに応じている．
tool 名　道具，用具，工具，工作機械，手段，方法，手法，ツール
　debt management tool　債務管理手段，債務管理の手法
　management tool　管理手法，管理の手段，経営手法
　system development tool　システム開発ツール
　tools and furnitures　工具・備品，工具・器具
　tools, furniture and fixtures　工具・器具・備品，工具器具備品
▸Our customers look to us for the *tools* for improving productivity.　当社のお客さまは，生産性向上の切り札として当社に期待を寄せております．
tooling 名　工作，細工，仕上げ細工，段取り，工作機械一式，装備，生産設備，製本の型押し
　blind tooling　空押し
　tooling change　段取り換え，ライン切換え
▸Engineering, *tooling*, manufacturing and applicable overhead costs are charged to costs and expenses when they are incurred.　設計，工作，製造および適用可能な間接費は，その発生時に原価と費用に計上されます．
top 動　上回る，突破する，…を越える，首位になる，首位を占める，トップになる
▸Strong overseas performance helped Toyota's group sales *top* ¥20 trillion for the first time in the year through March.　海外の好業績で，トヨタの3月期決算は，連結売上高が（日本の製造業で）初めて20兆円を上回った．
top 形　最高の，最高位の，最大の，最大限の，最上の，頂上の，最上位の，首位の，筆頭の，最優先の，上部の，トップの，名　最高位，頂上，首位，最優先課題，最優先事項，トップ
　be at the top of the list [agenda]　最優先事項である，最優先課題である
　top brass　幹部，高級幹部，高級将校
　top cadre　最高幹部
　top companies　大手企業
　top copy　原本
　top executive　最高経営者，最高執行者，最高経営幹部，経営幹部，経営首脳，経営者，経営トップ
　　(**top executives**は「首脳陣，経営幹部」の意)
top grossing　興行成績がよい
top-hat scheme　高位者割増年金
top-heavy　資本過大の，幹部［管理職，役職者］が多すぎる，逆三角形の
top line　経常利益，売上高，最高レベル
top manager　経営者
top management　最高経営者，最高経営責任者，最高管理層，最高経営管理者層，経営首脳陣，首脳部，トップ・マネジメント
top player　最大手
top secret　極秘
top shareholder　筆頭株主
top-down 形　上意下達の，上意下達方式の，トップダウン型の，トップダウン　(⇒bottom-up)
　top-down approach　天下り方式，中央集権的な管理方法，トップダウン・アプローチ
　top-down decision making　トップダウン型の意思決定
　top-down society　上意下達社会，トップダウン型社会
　top-down strategy　上意下達戦略，下降型戦略，トップダウン戦略
top priority　最優先課題，最優先事項
▸*Top priority* is to replace the top management of the company.　最優先事項は，同社首脳陣の一新だ．
TOPIX　東証株価指数，トピックス　(**Tokyo Stock Price Index**の略．東証一部の時価総額を加重平均して算出する)
total capital　総資本
▸The ratio of total debt to *total capital* (total debt plus total equity) increased to 56% at December 31, 2008.　総負債額に対する総資本（負債総額と総株主持ち分の合計）の比率は，2008年12月31日現在で増加しています．
total cost　総原価，総費用，原価合計，総コスト
▸Procurement costs are an automaker's greatest expense and account for up to 60 percent of *total costs*.　調達コストは自動車メーカー最大の経費で，最大で総コストの60％を占めている．
▸*Total costs* of telecommunication services declined this past year.　電気通信サービスの総原価は，当年度は低下しました．
total customer satisfaction　顧客の完全な満足［満足度］，顧客の100％満足，トータル・カスタマー・サティスファクション
▸*Total customer satisfaction* remains our fundamental objective.　顧客の100％満足は，今でも当社の基本目標です．

total liabilities 負債合計, 負債総額, 責任総額, 総責任額, トータル・ライアビリティ
▶The company has *total liabilities* of ¥125 billion on a consolidated basis. 同社の負債総額は, 連結ベースで1,250億円に達している。

total operating expenses 総営業費用
▶*Total operating expenses* declined because of restructuring and other charges in 2008. 2008年度は, 事業再編その他の費用を計上したため, 総営業費用は減少しました。

total revenues 総収益, 総売上高, 営業収益合計 (⇒**backdrop, record**)
▶Selling, general and administrative (SG&A) expenditures in the third quarter of 2008 were 18.8 percent of *total revenues*. 2008年第3四半期の販売費および一般管理費(SG&A)は, 総売上高の18.8%でした。

TQM 総合品質経営, 総合[総合的]品質管理, 全社的品質管理 (=total quality control: **total quality management**の略)

traceability 名 追跡可能性, 生産履歴管理, 履歴管理, 〈測定器の〉標準追遡性, トレーサビリティ (商品の生産情報から製造, 加工, 流通などの過程をさかのぼって参照できる仕組み)

tracking stock トラッキング・ストック
▶*Tracking stock* refers to shares whose dividends are paid in accordance with the performance of a company's specific subsidiary or division. 「トラッキング・ストック」とは, 企業の特定の子会社や事業部門の業績に従って配当金を支払う株式のことをいう。

tracking stock in a subsidiary 子会社連動株, トラッキング・ストック (子会社の業績や配当に経済価値を連動させることを意図した株式)

trade 動 売買する, 取引する, 交換する
▶In commodity futures trading, precious metals, petroleum products and other goods are *traded*. 商品先物取引では, 貴金属や石油製品などの商品が取引されている。

trade 名 貿易, 交易, 通商, 取引, 商売, 売買, 下取り, 交換, トレード
　accounts payable (principally trade) 支払い債務(主に営業債務)
　compared trade summary 総括精算表
　day trade デイ・トレード (=day trading: インターネットでの株や債券などの取引のこと)
　gains from trade 貿易利益
　non-trade note 非営業手形
　non-trade receivables 非営業受取債権
　stock in trade 在庫品

trade accounts payable 買掛金, 営業支払い勘定
trade accounts receivable from subsidiaries 子会社売掛金
Trade Act of 1974 米国の1974年通商法
trade asset 営業資産, 棚卸し資産
trade barrier 貿易障壁
trade cycle 景気循環 (=business cycle)
trade discount 営業割引, 営業値引き, 業者割引, 割引
trade expense 営業費
trade insurance 貿易保険
trade notes payable to affiliates 関係会社支払い手形
trade notes receivable from subsidiaries 子会社受取手形
trade payable [payables] 買掛金, 支払い手形, 仕入債務, 買掛債務
trade receivable [receivables] 売掛金, 売上債権, 営業債権, 営業上の未収入金, 受取手形

trade deficit 貿易赤字 (⇒**deficit**)
▶The U.S. *trade deficit* with China jumped by 10.2 percent to $256.3 billion in 2007. 2007年の米国の対中貿易赤字は, 10.2%増の2,563億ドルとなった。

trade friction 貿易摩擦, 通商摩擦 (=trade conflict, trade dispute)
▶Toyota is set to further expand its production overseas, partly to avoid *trade friction*. トヨタは, 貿易摩擦を回避するためにも, 引き続き海外での生産能力を拡充する方針だ。

trade imbalance 貿易不均衡
▶Japan and European countries should keep trying to adjust *trade imbalances* with the United States. 日欧は, 対米貿易不均衡を是正する努力を続ける必要がある。

trade intermediation 売買の仲介
▶Leading trading houses have shifted their main lines of businesses to investment from *trade intermediation*. 大手商社が, 事業の主力を売買の仲介から投資に転換した。

trade secret 企業秘密, 営業秘密, 業務上の秘密, トレード・シークレット
▶We are mindful of our *trade secrets*, our copyrighted material and those things that we can patent. 当社のトレード・シークレットや著作権の対象, 特許化の可能性については, 当社は慎重に検討しています。

trade surplus 貿易黒字, 貿易収支の黒字
▶*Trade surplus* fell 32.2 percent from the pre-

vious year to ¥8.52 trillion. 貿易収支の黒字は，前年比32.2%減の8兆5,200億円となった。

trade union 労働組合, 同業組合 (=labor union)
▸Stakeholders include employees, trading partners, and customers as well as family members of the employees, retirees, *trade unions* and even members of a community near its office or factory. ステークホルダー（利害関係者）には，従業員や取引先，顧客のほかに，従業員の家族や退職者，労働組合，さらには営業所や工場などの近郊の地域社会も含まれる。

trademark 商標, 商標権, トレードマーク
  licensed products bearing the trademark 商標を付した許諾品
  registered trademark 登録商標
  the owner of the trademark 商標の商標権者
  the use of the trademark 商標の使用
  trademarks and other intangible assets, net 商標権およびその他の無形固定資産（純額）
▸The term IBM is a *trademark* of International Business Machines Corporation. IBMは，インターナショナル・ビジネス・マシーンズ・コーポレーションの商標です。

trading 取引, 売買, 商業, 貿易, 営業, トレーディング (⇒foreign exchange trading, insider trading, margin trading)
  algorithm trading アルゴリズム取引（コンピュータのアルゴリズム（問題解決のための処理手順）を株式売買の執行に応用したもので，あらかじめ組み込まれたプログラムに基づいて，株の値動きに応じてコンピュータが自動的に大量の売買注文を実行する）
  bond trading 債券取引, 債券売買取引, 債券トレーディング
  foreign exchange trading 外国為替取引
  heavy trading 大商い
  home trading ホーム・トレーディング (=Net trading, online stock trading, online trading)
  off-hours trading 時間外取引 (=after-hours trading)
  online stock trading 株のインターネット取引
  public trading 公募取引
  short term trading by day traders デイ・トレーダーによる短期売買
  trading assets 販売資産, 事業資産
  trading balances 営業上の債権・債務残高
  twenty-four-hour trading 24時間トレーディング
▸In FX margin *trading*, investors can trade around the clock via the Internet. 外国為替証拠金取引の場合，投資家はインターネットで24時間取引できる。
▸The Tokyo stock market has recently been roaring, with record heavy *trading* seen. 東京株式市場が，記録的な大商いを続けて，活況を呈している。

trading house 商社
▸Hokuetsu Paper Mills Ltd. has completed its planned new share issuance worth about ¥30 billion to major *trading house* Mitsubishi Corp. 北越製紙は，予定していた大手商社の三菱商事を引受先とする約300億円の新株発行［第三者割当て増資］を完了した。

trading profit 売買益, 取引利益, 営業利益, 総利益, 投機利益

trading unit 取引単位
▸Even if the company conducts a reverse stock split, it will safeguard shareholders' interest by changing the minimum *trading unit* from 1,000 shares to 500. 同社が株式併合をしても，最低取引単位を1,000株から500株に変更して株主の権利は守る方針だ。

trading volume 売買高, 売買額, 出来高, 売買株数, 売上高, 取引量
▸The bank's stock ended Monday's trading at ¥827 on a *trading volume* of 247.23 million shares. 同行株は，終値827円，出来高2億4,723万株で月曜日の取引を終えた。

traffic 交通, 運輸, 交通量, 交通機関, 運賃収入, 通話量, 通信流量, 貿易, 取引, 取引量, 顧客数, 顧客規模, トラヒック

tranche 分割発行される証券［融資］の1回分, 〈IMFの〉融資区分, 優先的外貨引出し権, トランシュ
  commercial tranche 民間トランシュ
  credit tranche IMFの条件付き一般貸出, クレジット・トランシュ
  gold tranche ゴールド・トランシュ
  senior tranche 上位トランシュ
  the first tranche of the emergency loan 緊急融資の第1回トランシュ

transaction 取引, 取扱い, 業務処理, 業務, 商取引, 売買, 和解, 示談, 法律行為
  accounting transaction 会計取引, 会計上の取引, 簿記上の取引
  B2B transaction 企業対企業取引 (B2B=b to b, business to business)
  B2C transaction 企業対消費者の取引 (B2C=b to c, business to consumer)
  backlogged transaction 未決済取引

book transaction 帳簿取引
business transaction 商取引, 企業取引
capital transaction 資本取引
capital transactions 資本等取引
financial transaction 金融取引, 財務取引, 資金取引
financing transaction 資金調達取引
interbranch transaction 支店間取引
internal transaction 内部取引
noncash transaction 非現金取引, 現金決済を伴わない取引
nonmonetary transaction 非金銭取引, 非貨幣取引, 非金融取引
nonrecurring transactions 非経常損益
recurring transactions 経常損益
security transaction 証券取引
transaction between affiliated enterprises 系列取引
transaction cost 取引コスト, 売買コスト
transaction gain or loss 為替差損益
transaction in conflict of interest 利益相反取引
transaction value 取引高, 売買高 (=value of transaction)
value of transaction 売買高, 取引高
▶The company will restate its financial results as there were the problems with the way it accounted for a number of *transactions*. 同社は, 一部取引の会計処理方法に問題があったため, 同社の財務成績[業績]を修正再表示することになった。

transaction date 取引日
▶Other assets and other liabilities are translated at rates prevailing at the respective *transaction dates*. その他の資産とその他の負債は, 各取引日の実勢為替レートで換算されています。

transaction 動 移転する, 移す, 移し替える, 振り替える, 転送する, 譲渡する, 名義を書き換える, 振り込む, 送金する, 繰り入れる, 配置転換する (⇒**paid-in capital**)
▶A smaller amount of loan-loss provisions was *transferred* to profits, compared with a year before. 前年と比べて, 貸倒れ引当金の戻り益が少なかった[前年と比べて, 利益に振り替えた貸倒れ引当金の金額が少なかった]。
▶The firm's business was *transferred* to a new company. 同社の営業は, 新会社に譲渡された。

transfer 名 〈財産などの〉譲渡, 移転, 〈権限などの〉委譲, 継承, 〈名義の〉書換え, 転送, 転任, 配属, 配置換, 出向, 振替え, 振込み, 送金, 繰入れ (⇒**stock transfer**)

asset transfer 資産の譲渡, 資産のシフト
automatic transfer 自動決済, 自動振替え
bulk transfer 一括譲渡, 大量譲渡, 包括譲渡 (=bulk sale)
business transfer 営業譲渡, 事業譲渡, 企業移転 (=transfer of business)
capital transfer 資本移転, 資本移動
capital transfer tax 資本移転税, 資産譲渡税, 贈与税 《略 **CTT**》
cash transfer 送金 (=cash remittance, money transfer)
fund transfer 資金移動, 資金のシフト, 口座振替え, 送金 (=the movement of funds)
income transfer 所得移転 (国内企業が商品を通常の取引価格より安い価格で海外の関連会社 (子会社や親会社) に輸出すれば, 国内での所得が減る一方, 商品を安く仕入れた関連会社は, 所得を増やすことができる。これを, 国内から海外への所得移転という)
money transfer 資金の移動 (=transfer of money)
operational transfer 業務移管
ownership transfer 所有権の移転 (=transfer of ownership)
share transfer 株式の名義書換え, 株式譲渡 (=stock transfer, transfer of stocks)
the transfers of officials 公務員の配置転換
transfer agent 名義書換え取扱機関, 名義書換え代理人, 証券代行機関, 株式代行機関 (⇒**shareowner services**)
transfer book 株式名簿, 株主名簿, 名義書換え名簿, 名義書換え台帳
transfer book closed 名義書換え停止
transfer day 名義書換え日
transfer of funds 資金移動, 資金のシフト, 口座振替え (=fund transfer)
transfer of management rights 経営権の譲渡, 経営権の移動・移行
transfer of patent rights 特許権の移転, 特許権の譲渡
transfer of shares 株式の譲渡, 株式移転, 株式の名義書換え (=share transfer, stock transfer, transfer of stakes)
transfer of technology 技術移転
transfer price 振替価格, 内部振替価格, 移転価格 (「振替価格」は, 企業の一部門が他の部門に販売するときに用いる企業内部価格)
transfer pricing 移転価格, 移転価格の決定, 移転価格税制, 振替価格操作
transfer profit 振替利益

▶Misuzu Audit Corp. will begin discussions with three accounting firms over its operational *transfer*. みすず監査法人が，同法人の業務移管について3監査法人と協議を開始することになった。
▶The cost and service charges that relate to fixed asset *transfers* are capitalized and depreciated or amortized by the importing area. 固定資産振替えに関連する原価とサービス料が，輸入地域で資産計上され，減価償却または償却される。
▶The sharp drop in sales was largely due to the spinoff of the company's cosmetics business and the *transfer* or liquidation of 22 businesses. 売上高が大幅に落ち込んだのは，主に同社が化粧品事業を分離し，22事業を譲渡・清算したためだ。

transfer of golden shares 黄金株の譲渡
▶A company is allowed to set restrictions on the *transfer of golden shares*. 企業は，黄金株(拒否権付き種類株式)に譲渡制限を付けることができる[黄金株の譲渡に制限を設けることができる]。

transfer of technical skills 技能継承
▶With the massive retirement of this baby-boom generation, the *transfer of technical skills* from veteran workers to younger ones within their companies may not go smoothly. この団塊の世代の大量引退[退職]で，ベテラン社員から若い社員への社内の技能継承がうまく進まないかもしれない。

transfers between geographic areas 地域区分間の移動，地域間の振替え
▶*Transfers between geographic areas* are made at prices based on total cost of the product to the supplying segment. 地域別区分間の移動は，供給部門にいたるまでに要する製品の総原価に基づく価格で行われます。
▶*Transfers between geographic areas* are on terms and conditions comparable with sales to external customers. 地域間の振替えは，社外顧客への売上と同様の条件で行われています。

transformation 名 変化，変形，変換，転換，転化，変革，改革，事業再編
corporate transformation 企業改革
distribution transformation 流通改革
political transformation 政権交代
▶We are engaged in a comprehensive *transformation* to ensure its competitiveness through the years ahead. 来るべき将来に備えて当社の競争力を強化するため，当社は全力を挙げて改革に取り組んでいます。

tranship 動 積み替える[換える] (⇒transship)
transition 名 移行，推移，変遷，経過，移行時，移行期間，過渡期

net transition amounts 移行時差額 (⇒service cost)
transition obligation 移行時債務，経過債務
transition provisions 経過規定
▶Second quarter performance was unfavorably affected by new product *transitions* and the strength of the U.S. dollars. 第2四半期の業績は，新製品への移行とドル高の悪影響を被りました。

transition asset 移行時資産 (=transitional asset)
▶We are amortizing a *transition asset* related to our change in pension accounting over 15 years. 当社は，年金会計変更関連の移行時差額資産を15年にわたって償却中です。

transitional pension 経過年金
translate 動 換算する，変換する，調整する，解釈する，翻訳する (⇒monetary assets, transaction date)
▶The results are *translated* into U.S. dollars. 業績は，米ドルに換算してあります。

translation 名 換算，変換，調整，解釈，翻訳
accounting translations 会計原則の調整
accumulated foreign currency translation adjustments —— as reported 外貨換算調整[修正]——公表額
effects of foreign currency translation adjustments 外貨換算修正損益
exchange and translation gains (losses) 為替差益(損)
foreign currency translation 外貨換算 (=currency translation, translation of foreign currencies)
translation adjustments 換算調整額，外貨換算調整額，外貨換算修正，為替調整額 (=foreign currency translation adjustments)
translation of foreign balances 外貨建て残高の換算
translation of foreign exchange 外国為替換算
translation of net assets 純資産の換算
▶We show the adjustments from balance sheet *translation* as a separate component of shareowners' equity. 貸借対照表から生じる換算差損額は，株主持ち分の独立した構成要素[独立した一項目]として計上しています。

translation differences 換算差額
▶*Translation differences* are credited to, or charged against, income in the year in which they arise. 換算差額は，発生年度の損益として認識されています。

translation gain or [and] loss 為替換算

差損益, 換算差損益, 為替差損益, 為替換算差額
▸The unrealized *translation gains and losses* on the parent company's net investment in these operations are accumulated in a separate component of shareholders' equity. これらの事業に対する親会社の純投資額にかかわる未実現為替換算差損益［未実現為替差損益］は，株主持ち分の独立項目に累計［累積計上］されています。

transmission 名 伝送, 送信, 伝達, 伝導, 伝動, トランスミッション
  electric transmission 送電
  transmission access 送電能力
  transmission facility 送電施設, 変電設備
  transmission grids 送電系統
  transmission wires 送電線
▸When problems occur at a power generation plant or *transmission* facility, each electric power company can isolate the affected area from the rest of the network to prevent it from spreading. 発電, 送電設備に問題が起きた場合, 電力各社はその影響が出た地域を送電ネットワークから切り離して他地域に広がるのを防ぐことができる。

transmit 動 送信する, 伝送する, 送る, 伝える, 放送する, 知らせる
▸Information on enemy forces obtained by spy satellites and unmanned reconnaissance planes was *transmitted* through digital communication systems. 偵察衛星や無人偵察機が集めた敵軍の情報は, デジタル通信システムで伝送された。

transnational company 超国籍企業, トランスナショナル企業
▸*Transnational companies* are at the highest level of organizational complexity. グローバル市場で企業活動を展開しているトランスナショナル（超国籍）企業は, 極めて複雑な組織で運営されています。

transparency 名 透明性 （⇒current value accounting standard, trend）
  transparency and accountability of business management 経営の透明性と説明責任
  transparency in decision-making 意思決定の透明性
▸Major subsidiaries have each appointed outside directors as a means of actively stimulating objective discussion at board meetings and promoting greater *transparency* of business management. 主要子会社各社は, 取締役会の活性化と経営の透明性向上を図る手段として, 社外取締役を任用しています。

transport 名 運送, 輸送, 運輸, 運搬, 輸送機関, 交通機関, 輸送手段, 交通手段, 移動手段
  air transport 航空輸送, 航空運送
  air transport industry 航空運送業
  bulk transport バルク輸送
  chilled transport チルド輸送
  international multimodal transport 国際複合一貫輸送
  maritime transport 海上交通, 海洋交通, 海上輸送 （=ocean transport, water transport）
  overland transport 陸上輸送
  road transport 道路輸送システム
  transport capacity 輸送能力, 輸送力 （=capacity for transport）
  transport cost 輸送費
  transport efficiency 運送効率
  transport equipment 輸送機器
  transport facility 交通機関
  transport insurance 運送保険
  transport machinery sector 輸送機器セクター, 輸送機械部門
  transport of goods 貨物輸送
  transport sector 運輸部門
  transport service 輸送サービス
  transport system 交通網, 輸送システム, 輸送施設
  urban transport 都市交通
  water transport 水上輸送
▸The basic marine development plan includes the development and utilization of marine resources and securing the safety of maritime *transport*. 海洋開発基本計画には, 海洋資源の開発・利用と海洋交通の安全確保なども含まれている。

transportation 名 輸送, 運送, 運輸, 輸送機関, 輸送料金, 輸送料, 運賃, 輸送許可書
  conveyer [conveyor] transportation コンベア輸送
  intermodal transportation 複合一貫輸送
  land transportation 陸上輸送
  transportation business 運送業
  transportation charge 運賃, 運送料, 運搬費
  transportation claim 運送クレーム
  transportation control 輸送管理, 運搬管理
  Transportation Department 米運輸省
  transportation documents 運送書類
  transportation entry 運送申告
  transportation facility 輸送施設
  transportation goods 積送貨物
  transportation in 運賃着払い
  transportation in bond 保税運送

transportation operation 運送業務, 運送作業
transportation out 発送運賃
Transportation Secretary 米運輸長官
transship 動 積み替える, 別の船に移す, 乗り換える (=tranship)
trans-shipping 名 商品の転売, 貨物の積替え
travel 動 行く, 旅行する, 通う, 外交員をする, 名 旅行, 交通費
treasurer 名 会計役（米国では会社役員の1人）, 財務担当役員, 財務部長, 財務官, 経理部長, 会計係, 金銭出納係, トレジャラー （米大手企業の「トレジャラー（treasurer）」は, 会社の資金調達や運用などの財務部門を統括する役員。⇒**controller**）
  corporate treasurer 企業の財務担当者
  treasurer's department 財務部門
treasurership 名 財務管理, 財産管理
Treasury 名 米財務省, 英大蔵省《略 T》
  Treasuries 米財務省証券 (=Treasury securities)
  Treasury bill 米財務省短期証券, Tビル （通称T-billで, 単にbillとも呼ばれる）
  Treasury bond 米政府長期証券, 財務省長期証券, 財務省証券, 米国債 （=T-bond: 利息が年2回支払われる利付き証券（coupon issues））
  Treasury note 米財務省証券, 財務省中期証券, 中期国債, Tノート （「米財務省中期証券」は, 利息が年2回支払われる利付き証券）
  Treasury Secretary 米財務長官
treasury 名 金庫, 資金, 基金, 財源
  treasury bill 英大蔵省証券
  treasury investment and loan 財政投融資
  treasury purchases 自己株式購入
  treasury stock 金庫株, 自社株, 自己株式 (=reacquired shares, reacquired stock, repurchased shares, repurchased stock, treasury shares: 「金庫株」は, 株価の低迷や乱高下を防ぐため, 企業が自社株を買い戻して, 買い取った株を保有し, 相場が持ち直したときに売ることができる株のこと）
  accounting for treasury stock 自己株式の処理, 自己株式の会計処理
  gain on sale of treasury stock 自己株式売却益
  treasury stock system 金庫株制度
▸In connection with the merger, the company sold 6.5 million shares of common stock held as *treasury stock*. この合併に伴って, 同社は自己株式として保有していた普通株式650万株を売却しました。
treatment 名 処理, 取扱い, 待遇, 措置, トリートメント

accounting treatment 会計処理
favorable tax treatment 税制上の優遇措置, 優遇税制, 優遇税制措置 (=generous tax treatment)
hedge accounting treatment ヘッジ会計処理
off-balance-sheet treatment オフ・バランスシート取引
tax treatment 税務上の取扱い, 税務上の扱い, 税務処理, 税制
treatment of goodwill 営業権[のれん]の取扱い
treatment of waste 減損処理
▸The most significant factors causing these differences between Canadian and U.S. GAAP are the *treatment* of unrealized foreign currency gains and losses. カナダ会計基準と米国会計基準の間でこれらの差異が生じている最大の要因は, 未実現為替差損益の取扱いです。
treaty 名 条約, 条約議定書, 盟約, 盟約書, 協約, 協定, 取決め, 約束, 契約, 約定, 交渉, 協議
  climate change treaty 気候変動条約
  double taxation treaty 二重課税防止条約
  Maastricht Treaty マーストリヒト条約
  Patent Cooperation Treaty 特許協力条約
  private treaty 私的協議
  tax treaty 租税条約
  treaty of commerce 通商条約
  treaty shopping 租税回避, 節税行為, トリーティ・ショッピング
trend 名 傾向, 動向, 基調, 趨勢, 大勢, 流れ, 潮流, 流行, 波, 環境, トレンド
  be above trend トレンドを上回る
  competitive trends 競争環境
  downward trend 下落基調, 下落傾向, 低下傾向
  economic trends 経済動向, 景気動向, 景気
  inflationary trend インフレ動向
  prospective trends 今後のトレンド
  rising trend 上昇基調, 上昇傾向 (=upward trend)
  trend toward service economy サービス経済化, サービス化
  weak trend 減少傾向
▸Another driving force behind the spinoff *trend* is mounting criticism of the lack of transparency at large corporations in the wake of Enron Corp.'s collapse. 分社化傾向の陰のもうひとつの推進力は, エンロンの経営破綻を受けて大企業の透明性[透明性欠如]に対する批判の高まりである。
▸If the current downward *trend* of stock prices

continues, banks' financial resources that could be used to dispose of bad loans will decrease drastically. 株価の下落基調がこのまま続くと，金融機関の不良債権処理の原資は激減する。

trend rate 潜在成長率，傾向率，傾向値
▶Increasing the assumed *trend rate* by 1% in each year would raise our accumulated postretirement benefit obligation at December 31, 2008 by $750 million. 予想傾向値が毎年1％上昇すると，当社の累積退職後給付債務は，2008年12月31日現在で7億5,000万ドル増加します。

trendsetter 先導役，トレンドセッター
▶Unions of major automakers and consumer electronics companies are *trendsetters* in the spring wage negotiations. 春闘［春の賃金交渉］では，大手自動車メーカーや家電メーカーの労組が先導役を務める。

triangular merger 三角合併 (＝triangle merger；⇒**swap** 動)
　forward triangular merger 順三角合併
　reverse triangular merger 逆三角合併
▶The two agreed on a stock-swap deal to realize a *triangular merger*. 両社は，株式交換取引で三角合併を実現することで合意した。

triangular merger scheme 三角合併方式，三角合併制度（2007年5月から解禁となった企業買収の仕組みで，合併の対価として現金でなく，買収する側の企業の親会社の株式が使えるようになった）
▶Under the *triangular merger scheme*, Citigroup absorbed Nikko Cordial Group through its local unit Citigroup Japan Holdings Ltd. 三角合併制度に基づき，シティグループは，同社の日本法人のシティグループ・ジャパン・ホールディングスを通じて日興コーディアルグループを吸収した。

trigger 名 引き金，きっかけ，誘因，起爆剤，トリガー回路，トリガー
　program termination trigger プログラム終了事由
　rating trigger 格付け基準
　trigger effect 引き金効果
　trigger event 解約事由，清算事由
　trigger industry トリガー産業
　trigger price 指標価格，輸入最低基準価格，トリガー価格

trigger 動 引き起こす，…のきっかけを作る，…のきっかけとなる，…の引き金となる，…を誘発する，触発する，…を促す，発射する，発砲する，発動する，動かす
▶The sharp plunge in stock prices was *triggered*

by the Bank of Japan's announcement that it would not implement additional monetary easing policies. 株価急落のきっかけを作ったのは，追加的な金融緩和策は実施しない旨の日本銀行の発表だ。

trilemma 名 三重苦，トリレンマ

trim 動 削減する，縮小する，切り詰める，〈人員などを〉整理する，引き下げる，減額する (⇒**resize**)
▶Efforts made by the corporate sector to *trim* three excesses of debt, workforces and facilities are the second factor propelling the economy forward. 企業が債務，人員，設備という三つの過剰の削減に取り組んだことが，景気回復を推進した第二の要因だ。
▶The company will drastically *trim* its existing affiliates. 同社は，既存の関連会社を抜本的に整理する方針だ。

triple 動 3倍になる，3倍増となる，3倍にする
▶TBS's mainstay broadcasting division *tripled* operating profit to ¥7.45 billion. TBSの主力の放送事業部門は，営業利益が3倍増の74億5,000万円となった。

triple 形 3倍の，3重の，トリプル
　triple A issuer トリプルA格の発行体
　triple A rating トリプルAの格付け
　triple low トリプル安 (＝triple decline)

triple decline トリプル安 (＝triple fall, triple low: 株式，債券と為替が同時に下がること)
▶This *triple decline* has further slowed the economy. このトリプル安が，景気をさらに減速させている。

triple rise トリプル高
▶Japan appears to be climbing out of a crisis situation as a result of recent *triple rises* in stocks, bonds and the yen. 日本は，株価，債券と円の最近のトリプル高で，危機的状況から脱しつつあるようだ。

trouble 名 経営不振，経営破綻，経営難，経営危機
▶GM has been in *trouble* since last year, due to declining profits in its North America operation. GMは，北米事業の減益で昨年来，経営不振に陥っている。

troubled 形 経営不振の，経営破綻した，経営難の，経営難に陥った，経営危機に陥った，問題のある，問題の多い (⇒**financially troubled**)
　troubled business 経営の行き詰まり，経営難，行き詰まった経営，経営危機の企業，経営不振企業
　troubled company 経営不振企業，経営破綻した企業 (⇒**reorganize**)
　troubled loan 不良債権

▶*Troubled* highly leveraged companies have found it necessary to attempt to restructure their existing debt.　負債比率が高い経営不振の企業は，既存の債務を再構築する必要に迫られている。

troubleshooter 名　苦情処理機関，紛争調停人，紛争解決人，仲裁人，故障検査員

troubleshooting 名　仲裁，調停，故障の検査・修理

trough 名　景気の谷，景気の底，最悪期
　cyclical trough　景気の底，景気サイクルの底，景気の谷
　fall to a trough　底を打つ
　get out of a trough　底から抜け出る，最悪期を脱出する
　reach a trough　底を打つ
▶Inventory has just got out of a *trough*.　在庫は，最悪期を脱したばかりだ。

true 形　本物の，正真正銘の，適法の，正当な
　true amount　実際金額
　true and complete books and records　真正かつ完全な会計帳簿と記録
　true and correct copy　真正かつ正確な写し
　true and fair view　真正かつ公正な概観
　true five-day workweek　完全週休2日制

trust 名　信託，委託，信頼，信用，トラスト
　balance of loan trust　貸付け信託の残高
　bond investment trust　公社債投資信託
　deed of trust　信託証書　(＝trust deed)
　employee retirement benefit trust　退職給付信託
　loan trust　貸付け信託
　pension trust　年金信託
　trust business　信託業，信託業務　(＝fiduciary business)
　trust cash fund　金銭信託
　trust estate　信託財産
　trust fee　信託手数料，信託報酬，受託手数料
　trust fund product　信託商品
　trust of shareholders　株主の信頼
　trust principal　信託元本
　trust services　信託業務
　un-incorporated investment trust　非会社型投資信託
　unit investment trust　単位型投資信託，ユニット型投資信託
　voting trust　議決権信託
▶A portion of this accumulated liability was provided for by group life insurance benefits and *trusts* for health care benefits funded before 2008.　この累積債務の一部は，団体生命保険給付と2008年以前に資金拠出した医療給付のための信託によって引き当てられています。

trust bank　信託銀行
▶UFJ Holdings Inc. has agreed to sell UFJ *Trust Bank* Ltd. to Sumitomo Trust & Banking Co., Ltd. for about ¥300 billion to raise its capital adequacy ratio.　UFJホールディングスが，自己資本比率を引き上げるため，UFJ信託銀行を約3,000億円で住友信託銀行に売却することで合意した。

trust fund　信託基金，信託資金，投資信託，トラスト・ファンド
▶Pension contributions are primarily made to *trust funds* held for the sole benefit of plan participants.　年金拠出額は，主に年金加入者の利益を唯一の目的とする信託基金に拠出される。

trust of customers　顧客の信頼
▶Companies cannot do business without the *trust of customers*.　企業は，顧客からの信用を失っては営業できない。

trustee 名　信託機関，管財人，破産管財人，金融整理管財人，受託者，受託会社，幹事会社被信託人，理事，評議員
　board of trustees　理事会
　bond trustee　債券受託者，受託銀行
　indenture trustee　信託証書受託者
　trustee bank　受託銀行
　trustee in bankruptcy　破産管財人　(＝bankruptcy trustee)
　trustee or receiver　管財人，受託者または管財人
▶It is the Corporation's practice to fund amounts for postretirement benefits, with an independent *trustee*, as deemed appropriate from time to time.　随時適切と思われる退職後給付額を，独立した信託機関に積み立てるのが，当社の慣行となっています。

TSE　東京証券取引所，東証　(Tokyo Stock Exchangeの略)
▶Companies listed on the First Section of the *TSE* have registered increases both in income and profit.　東証一部上場企業は，増収増益となった。

TSE-listed companies　東証上場企業
▶A decade ago, 96 percent of *TSE-listed companies* held shareholders meetings on the same day.　10年前は，東証上場企業の96％が，同じ日に株主総会を開いた。

tumble 動　〈物価［株価］が〉下落する，暴落する，急落する，減少する
　tumble across the board　全面安となる，全銘柄にわたって急落［暴落］する
　tumbling dollar　ドルの下落

▶The U.S. dollar *tumbled* for the second straight day against major currencies.　米ドルが, 主要通貨に対して2日連続下落した。

turmoil 名　混乱, 動揺, 騒動, 騒ぎ, 不安, 危機 (⇒market turmoil)
 credit market turmoil　金融市場の混乱 (= turmoil in the financial markets)
 credit turmoil　信用不安
 currency turmoil　通貨危機, 為替市場の混乱
 financial turmoil　金融危機, 金融不安
▶The collapse of the subprime mortgage market and related credit market *turmoil* have resulted in $45 billion of write-downs at the world's biggest banks and securities firms.　サブプライム・ローン市場の悪化や関連金融市場の混乱で, 世界の大手銀行と証券会社の評価損計上額は, これまでのところ450億ドルに達している。

turn around　好転する, 改善する, 回復する, 方向転換する, 方針を変える, 考えを変える, 〈企業[事業]を〉再生する, 再建する
 turn around corporate management　企業の経営を再建する
 turn around the performance of the division　同事業部門の業績を回復する
 turn around the struggling manufacturer　この経営不振のメーカーの事業を再生する
▶GM struggles to *turn around* its North American business as the economy weakens.　GMは, 景気低迷に伴って北米事業の立て直しに懸命に取り組んでいる。
▶Private-sector businesses specializing in *turning around* corporate management have been established one after another.　企業経営の再建[企業再生]を専門にする民間企業が, 相次いで設立されている。

turnabout　方向転換, (方針の180度)転換, 〈会社などの〉再建 (=turnaround)

turnaround 名　転換, 方向転換, 好転, 業績改善, 〈経営戦略や営業・販売, 財務などの〉改善, 企業再生, 事業再生, ターンアラウンド (⇒sharp)
 a sharp turnaround from a loss　赤字から大幅黒字への転換
 corporate turnaround　企業再生
 corporate turnaround fund　企業再生ファンド
 earning turnaround　業績回復
 economic turnaround　景気回復
 major profit turnaround　利益の大幅改善, 利益の大幅回復
 turnaround management business　企業再生ビジネス, 事業再生ビジネス, 事業再生会社
 turnaround situation　業績回復
 turnaround time　業績回復, 応答時間, 往復所要時間, ターンアラウンド・タイム
▶Our business in 2008 showed a *turnaround* as earnings improved quarter by quarter.　2008年度の業績は, 四半期毎の増益にともなって, 改善しています。

turnaround effort　事業再生策
▶Ford is accelerating its North American *turnaround effort*.　フォードは現在, 北米事業部門の事業再生策を推進している。

turnaround plan　企業再生計画, 事業再生計画, 企業再生案
▶The U.S. rating agencies lowered Ford Motor Co,'s rating after the automaker announced a revised *turnaround plan*.　米国の格付け機関は, フォードの企業再生修正案を受けて, 同社の信用格付けを引き下げた。

turnkey 形　完成品引渡し方式の, ターンキー方式の

turnkey contract　完成品受渡し契約, ターンキー契約 (=package deal contract: パッケージ・ディール契約)

turnover 名　売上, 売上高, 総売上高, 取引高, 取引成立額, 出来高, 売買高, 回転, 回転率, 就労率, 転職率
 account receivable turnover　売掛金回転率
 asset turnover　資産回転率 (=asset turnover ratio)
 average daily turnover　1日当たり平均取引高, 1日当たり平均売買高
 capital turnover　資本の回転, 資本回転率
 capital turnover point　資本回収点
 consolidated turnover　連結売上高
 equity turnover　資本回転率 (=sale to net worth)
 gross turnover　総売上高
 labor turnover　労働回転率, 離職率
 merchandise turnover　商品回転率 (=merchandise turnover rate)
 net-worth turnover　自己資本回転率 (純売上高÷自己資本)
 sales turnover　売上高
 stock turnover　在庫回転率, 棚卸し資産回転率, 商品回転率
 total assets turnover　総資産回転率, 総資本回転率
 total turnover　総売上高
 turnover of net worth　自己資本回転率, 株主資本回転率

turnover of total capital employed　使用総資本回転率
turnover of total liabilities and net worth　総資本回転率
turnover of total operating assets　経営資本回転率
working capital turnover　運転資本回転率
▶Revenues rose 2.6 percent on higher *turnover* from property development projects.　不動産開発事業［開発プロジェクト］の売上高の増加で，売上高は2.6％伸びた。

turnover ratio　回転率　(＝turnover rate)
　turnover ratio of assets　資産回転率
　turnover ratio of capital　資本回転率
　turnover ratio of receivables　売上債権回転率，受取勘定回転率　(＝turnover of receivables)
▶A *turnover ratio* of 50% means that it was traded once every two years.　売買回転率50％とは，2年に1回売買されたことを意味する。

turnover ratio of trading　売買回転率
▶A *turnover ratio of trading* refers to a year's trading volume divided by an average number of listed stocks.　売買回転率は，1年間の出来高を平均上場株式数で割った数値を指す。

TV conference　テレビ会議，テレビ・コンファレンス
TV rating　テレビ視聴率
TV spot commercial　テレビ・スポット・コマーシャル
TWI　企業内訓練　(**training within industry**の略)
twin deficits　双子の赤字
▶The *twin deficits*—fiscal and trade—that haunted the United States in the 1980s have returned.　1980年代のアメリカを苦しめた「双子の赤字」(財政と貿易の二つの赤字)が，再燃している。

two-track income taxation system　二元的所得課税方式
▶If the *two-track income taxation system* is introduced, taxpayers will be allowed to offset losses from stock investments from income earned from interest and dividends.　二元的所得課税方式を導入すると，納税者は，利子・配当収入から株式投資による損失を相殺することができるようになる。

U u

UAW 全米自動車労働組合，全米自動車労組（*United Auto Workers*の略）
▶GM is offering a new round of buyouts to all 74,000 of its U.S. hourly workers who are presented by the *UAW*. GMは現在，全米自動車労組（UAW）に加盟している時間給労働者（工場労働者）を対象に，早期退職勧奨制度を新たに実施している。

ubiquitous computing ユビキタス・コンピューティング（あらゆる所にコンピュータやコンピュータ機器が設置される環境）
　ubiquitous computing society ユビキタス社会

ubiquitous information networks ユビキタス情報ネットワーク，ユビキタス情報通信ネットワーク
▶The market for *ubiquitous* information networks will grow to about ¥88 trillion in 2010. ユビキタス情報ネットワークの市場は，2010年には約88兆円に拡大する。

ultimate consumer 最終消費者（＝ultimate customer）

ultra-easy money policy 超低金利政策，超金融緩和政策（＝ultra-easy monetary policy, ultraeasy money policy, ultra-loose monetary policy）

ultra-easy [ultra-loose] monetary policy 超金融緩和政策，金融の量的緩和政策（＝ultra-easy money policy）
▶The Bank of Japan lifted the *ultra-easy monetary policy* in March 2006. 日銀は，2006年3月に金融の量的緩和政策を解除した。

umbrella 名 傘，傘下，保護，包括的組織，形 包括的な（＝wing）
　place ... under one's umbrella …を傘下に置く，…を傘下に収める
　umbrella group 包括団体
　umbrella master agreement 包括標準契約書
　umbrella payments 包括支払い，包括支払い制
　under the umbrella of …傘下の，…に保護[援護]されている
▶The two banks are under the *umbrella* of the financial group. 両行は，同金融グループの傘下にある。
▶Under the *umbrella* of holding company Japan Post Holdings, joined Japan Post Service Co., Japan Post Network Co., Japan Post Bank Co. and Japan Post Insurance Co. 持ち株会社の日本郵政グループ[日本郵政株式会社]の傘下に，郵便事業会社，郵便局会社，郵貯銀行，かんぽ生命保険の4社が加わった。

U.N. Commission on the Limits of the Continental Shelf 国連大陸棚限界委員会

U.N. Convention on the Law of the Sea 国連海洋法条約

unaffiliated 形 関連のない，非関連の，非関連会社の
　sales to unaffiliated customers 関連のない得意先に対する販売
　unaffiliated common stock 非関連会社普通株
　unaffiliated company 非関連会社，非系列会社

unamortized 形 未償却の，償却されていない
　unamortized balance 未償却残高
　unamortized goodwill 未償却営業権
　unamortized obligation 未償却債務
▶The net change during the year in *unamortized* service charges has been eliminated in consoli-

dation. 未償却サービス料の当期の正味増減額は，連結決算上，消去されています。

unanimous 形 満場[全員]一致の，異議のない，意見が一致している，同意見である，同意の，合意の
- **be unanimous for** …に賛成である，…に異議はない
- **be unanimous on** …については意見が一致している
- **unanimous action** 全会一致の決議，満場一致の決議
- **unanimous decision** 満場一致の決定
- **unanimous vote** 満場一致の票決

unauthorized 形 公認されていない，未承認の，無認可の，無許可の，無断での，独断での，不正な
- **unauthorized moneylender** ヤミ金融業者
- **unauthorized moneylending business** ヤミ金融
- **unauthorized use** 不正使用
- **unauthorized vaccine** 未承認ワクチン
▶ Nippon Meat Packers affiliates gave *unauthorized* vaccines to pigs over the past eight years. 日本ハムの子会社が，過去8年間にわたって豚に未承認ワクチンを投与していた。

unbundling 名 〈独占企業の〉強制分割，価格分離，ハードウエアの価格とソフトウエアの価格の切り離し販売，アンバンドリング

uncertain 形 不確実な，不確定な，不安定な，不確かな，不明確な，不透明な
- **uncertain factor** 不確定要因
- **uncertain market conditions** 不透明な市場環境，市場環境の不安定性
- **uncertain outlook** 先行きの不透明感
▶ We continue to operate in a difficult *uncertain* global economic environment. 当社は依然，困難かつ不確実な世界の経済環境のなかで営業活動を続けています。

uncertainty 名 不確実性，不確定，不確定要因，波乱要因，不透明，不透明性，先行き不透明感，不安，不安要因
- **increase the uncertainty about future profitability** 将来の収益性に対する不確実性を高める
- **interest rate uncertainty** 金利の先行き不透明感
- **remove the uncertainty** 不確実性を払拭[排除]する，不透明感を払拭(ふっしょく)する
- **uncertainties in the market** 市場の不確定要因，市場の波乱要因
- **uncertainty over the global economy** 世界経済の不透明感
▶ One of major *uncertainties* for the Corporation is exchange rate fluctuations. 当社にとって最大の不安要因は，為替変動です。
▶ *Uncertainty* about the global economy is increasing due to the U.S. subprime mortgage crisis. 米国のサブプライム・ローン(低所得者向け住宅融資)の焦げ付き問題で，世界経済の不確実性が増大している。

unchanged 形 据え置かれた，変わらない
- **be left unchanged** 据え置かれる，据え置きになる
- **be unchanged** 変わっていない，変わらない，横ばいである，ゼロ成長の
- **keep monetary [credit] policy unchanged** 金融政策を据え置く，金融政策を維持する
- **leave ... unchanged at** …を…に据え置く
- **remain unchanged** 横ばいである，…と変わらない

UNCITRAL 国連国際商取引法委員会 (the United Nations Commission on International Trade Lawの略)

UNCITRAL RULES 国連国際商取引法委員会(UNCITRAL)規則

uncollateralized overnight call rate 無担保コール翌日物 (⇒unsecured)

uncollected 形 回収されない，未収の，未回収の
- **uncollected balance** 未収金
- **uncollected commission** 未収手数料
- **uncollected interest** 未収利息
- **uncollected money** 未回収金
- **uncollected premium** 未収保険料
▶ The firm has about ¥2 billion in nonperforming credits in *uncollected* money owed from construction projects. 工事に伴う同社の未回収金のうち，約20億円が不良債権化している。

uncollectible 形 回収不能の，貸付け金の取立てができない，焦げ付いた (=uncollectable)
- **allowance for uncollectible accounts** 貸倒れ引当金
- **become uncollectible** 回収不能になる，徴収不能になる
- **uncollectible accounts receivable** 回収不能債権
- **uncollectible loan** 不良債権，不良貸付け，貸倒れ，回収不能の融資，焦げ付き融資 (=bad loan, nonperforming loan, uncollectible receivable)
▶ Most of the loans to the dummy companies were *uncollectible*. ダミー会社向け融資の大半は，回収不能だった。

uncollectibles 名 回収不能金，徴収不能料金
▶ The decrease in other costs was mainly due to

lower *uncollectibles*. その他の原価[コスト]の減少は、主に徴収不能料金の減少によるものです。

unconsolidated 形 連結から除外された、連結の範囲に含まれない、連結対象外の、連結されていない、非連結の、単独ベースの
 unconsolidated affiliates 連結対象外の関連会社
 unconsolidated debt 単独ベースの借入金、非連結子会社の負債
 unconsolidated financial statements 単独財務諸表、単独財務書類
 unconsolidated operating profit 単独ベースの営業利益、非連結営業利益
 unconsolidated subsidiary 非連結子会社（= unconsolidated subs.）
▸The firm plans to cut its *unconsolidated* interest-bearing debt by 40 percent by the end of March 2009 under a new business plan. 同社は、新経営計画に基づいて2009年3月末までに非連結有利子負債を40%圧縮する計画だ。

undated 形 償還日の定めのない、償還期日のない、期日のない、日付のない
 undated bill 無日付手形
 undated check 無日付小切手
 undated issue [stock] 永久債
 undated securities 永久債券、永久公債、無償還債券
 undated type 無日付式

underbid 動 〈競争相手より〉安い値を付ける[安く入札する]

undercapitalized 形 過小資本の、資本不足の
undercapitalized bank 過小資本銀行
underground bank 地下銀行
▸China is cracking down on *underground banks* used for illegally remitting money overseas. 中国は現在、海外への違法送金に使われる地下銀行を厳重に取り締まっている。

underlying 形 基礎となる、基礎的、基本的な、根本的な、構造的な、裏付けとなる、担保となる、根底にある、優先する
 underlying asset 原資産、対象資産、担保となる資産
 underlying collateral 担保物件
 underlying demand 基本的な需要
 underlying forces 構造的要因
 underlying inflation (rate) 基礎インフレ率
 underlying principle 基本的な原則
 underlying receivables 裏付けとなる債権
 underlying securities 原証券
 underlying shares 現物株、現物の株式
 underlying trends 基調、根底にあるトレンド
▸Any transaction gains and losses on these financial instruments are generally expected to offset losses and gains on the *underlying* operational cash flows or investments. これらの金融商品取引の損益に期待するのは、一般にその対象となっているキャッシュ・フローや投資から生じる損失および利益との相殺です。
▸The interest rate swap agreements generally involve the exchange of fixed or floating interest payments without the exchange of the *underlying* principal amounts. この金利スワップ契約は、一般的に元本の交換は行わず、固定金利または変動金利による支払い利息を交換することになっています。

underperform 動 下回る、〈市場平均を〉下回る、〈平均を〉下回る、アンダーパフォームする、…を下回るパフォーマンスを示す、…よりパフォーマンスが悪い
 underperform the industry 業界平均を下回る
 underperform the market 市場平均を下回る、パフォーマンスが市場平均を下回る

underperformance 名 市場平均を下回ること、株価パフォーマンスが市場平均を下回ること、低迷、低調、アンダーパフォーマンス

underpin 動 下から支える、下支えする、支持する、補強する
▸Private consumption has so far *underpinned* the overall economy. これまでは、個人消費が景気全般を下支えしてきた。

underpriced stock 割安株、割安な株式（= undervalued stock）

underreport 動 過少申告する（= understate）
▸The firm has *underreported* the ratio of stakes held by major shareholders. 同社は、これまで大株主の株式保有比率を過少申告していた。

underreporting 名 過少申告、過少記載
▸The company announced the *underreporting* of its stake in the financial statement. 同社は、有価証券報告書に同社株式について過少記載していたことを発表した。

undersell 動 …より安値で売る、実際の価値より安く売る、控えめに売り込む

understaffed 形 人員不足の
understanding 名 了解、了解事項、合意、合意事項、同意、協定、協約、取決め、約定条件
 come to an understanding with …と合意に達する
 on the understanding that …という条件で、…を了承した上で、…を承知の上で

on this understanding この条件で，これを承知の上で
reach an understanding with …と合意に達する，…と折り合いがつく
reach an understanding on …に関して取決めをする，…に関する協定を結ぶ
understandings and agreements 了解事項と合意事項，了解と合意
▸This agreement sets forth the entire *understanding* and agreement between the parties as to the matters covered in this Agreement. 本契約書は，本契約で取り扱った事項に関する当事者間の完全な了解と合意事項を定めたものである。

understate 動 過小表示する，過小計上する，実際より少なく計上する，過小評価する （⇒Freddie Mac）
▸The company *understated* its affiliates' stock evaluation losses for two fiscal years until March 2008. 同社は，2008年3月までの2年間の決算で，保有する子会社株の評価損を過小計上していた。

understatement 名 過小表示，過小評価

undertake 動 引き受ける，請け負う，約束する，着手する，乗り出す，進める，取り組む，保証する
undertake an acquisition 買収に乗り出す
undertake investment 投資を進める，投資に踏み切る
▸Our alliance will *undertake* joint projects and marketing efforts. 両社の提携は，共同のプロジェクトやマーケティング活動を約束するものです。

undertaking 名 仕事，事業，会社，企業
nonabandonment undertaking 出資維持保証
parent undertaking 親会社
subsidiary undertaking 子会社

underutilization of the plants 設備の遊休化

undervaluation 名 過小評価，割安な株価評価
undervalue 動 過小評価する
undervalued asset 含み資産，割安な資産
undervalued real estate 過小評価されている不動産
undervalued securities 含み益のある有価証券，割安の有価証券
▸Microsoft's takeover offer substantially *undervalues* Yahoo. 米マイクロソフトの買収提案は，ヤフーをかなり過小評価している。

underweight 名 重量不足，量目不足，不足重量，〈株式などの〉組入れ比率が低いこと，組入れ比率の引下げ，本来保有すべき比率を下回った状態，アンダーウエイト［アンダーウエート］

underwrite 動 〈株式や社債，保険などを〉引き受ける
▸Funds collected through postal savings and kampo postal life insurance were tapped to *underwrite* the fiscal investment and loan program bond. 郵便貯金や簡易保険を通じて集められた資金は，財投債の引受けに充てられていた。

underwriter 名 証券引受人，引受業者，引受証券会社，引受行，保険業者，保険会社，保険代理業者，資金提供者，スポンサー，後援者，アンダーライター
co-underwriter 共同引受行
letters to underwriters 証券引受人への書簡，証券引受業者へのレター
managing underwriter 幹事会社，引受主幹事
principal underwriter 元引受人
underwriter syndication 引受業者の組成，引受団の組成 （=syndication of underwriters）
underwriters' allocations 引受行の割当額
underwriters' fees and commissions 証券引受会社に対する報酬と手数料
▸Big firms may switch to other securities houses as their lead managing *underwriters*. 大企業が，主幹事会社を他の証券会社に切り替える可能性もある。
▸One of the largest *underwriters* of corporate bonds is the investment bank. 社債の最大の引受業者には，この投資銀行も入っている。

underwriting 名 〈保険や証券の〉引受け，引受業務
firm underwriting 確定引受け
stand-by underwriting 引受募集，残額引受発行
underwriting syndicate 引受団，引受シンジケート団
underwriting agreement 引受契約
underwriting amount 引受額
underwriting business 引受業務
underwriting fee 引受手数料
underwriting of corporate bonds 社債の引受け
underwriting spread 引受手数料，引受スプレッド
underwriting standards 貸出審査基準，与信基準，引受基準
underwriting syndicate 募債引受団，引受シンジケート団，引受団，引受シ団，シ団 （=investment banking group, purchase group, underwriting group）
▸We must boost our capital to further expand our core business, including mergers and

acquisitions and the *underwriting* of corporate bonds. 企業の合併・買収(M&A)や社債の引受けなど当社の中核業務をさらに拡充するには，資本の増強が必要である。

undistributed earnings 留保利益，内部留保利益，未分配利益，未処分利益剰余金 （⇒foreign tax credit）
▸*Undistributed earnings* of non-U.S. subsidiaries included in consolidated retained earnings amounted to $13,000 million at December 31, 2008. 連結利益剰余金に含まれている米国外子会社の未処分利益剰余金は，2008年12月31日現在で130億ドルでした。

unemployment 名 失業，失職，失業者，失業率
chronic unemployment 慢性的失業
cyclical unemployment 景気的失業
in-house unemployment 企業内失業，企業内失業者
insured unemployment 保険受給失業者
involuntary unemployment 非自発的失業
latent unemployment 潜在的失業
seasonal unemployment 季節的失業
structural unemployment 構造的失業
technological unemployment 技術的失業
unemployment benefits 失業手当，失業給付
unemployment compensation 失業給付
unemployment rate 失業率，完全失業率
voluntary unemployment 自発的失業
▸*Unemployment* and deflation are visibly deteriorating. 失業率もデフレも，目に見える形で悪化している。

unemployment insurance 失業保険，雇用保険
unemployment insurance program 失業保険
Unemployment Insurance Law 雇用保険法
unemployment insurance system 失業保険制度，雇用保険制度
▸The *unemployment insurance* system is supported by premiums paid by labor and management. 失業保険[雇用保険]制度は，労使が負担する保険料で支えられている。

unexpired 形 消滅しない，期限内の，未満了の，未費消の，未経過の
fixed percentage on unexpired cost method 定率法
unexpired cost 未費消原価，未経過原価
unexpired expense 未経過費用
unexpired interest 未経過利子
unexpired lease term 未満了の賃貸借期間
unexpired period 残期

unfair 形 不当な，不正な，不公正な
unfair business practices 不公正な取引慣行
unfair competition 不正競争，不当競争，不公正競争，不正競業
Unfair Competition Prevention Law 不正競争防止法
unfair profits 不当な利益
unfair labor practices 不当労働行為
unfair trade practices 不公正貿易慣行
▸The *Unfair* Competition Prevention Law bans the bribing of foreign government officials to gain unfair advantage in business deals. 不正競争防止法は，不正な取引上の優位性を得るため[営業で不正な利益を得るため]，外国公務員に利益を供与することを禁じている。

unfavorable 形 不利な，好ましくない，悪い，マイナスの
unfavorable balance 支払い超過
unfavorable effects on earnings per share 普通株式1株当たり利益に対する不利な影響額
unfavorable factor 不利な材料，マイナス要因，悪材料
unfavorable impact 不利な影響，マイナス影響，悪影響
unfavorable market conditions 市況の悪化，市場環境の悪化，不利な市場環境
▸A portion of the increase in R&D spending was due to the *unfavorable* impact of foreign exchange on R&D expenditures. 研究開発費(R&D)増加の一部は，研究開発費に対する為替相場の不利な影響額によるものです。
▸The company attributed the expected net profit decline to the possible *unfavorable* effects of the yen's rise against the dollar and the euro. 同社は，予想される純利益[税引き後利益]減少の理由として，同社に不利な円高・ドル安，ユーロ安の影響を挙げた。

unfavorably affected 不利な影響を受ける，マイナス影響が出る，悪影響を受ける
▸Revenue and earnings were *unfavorably affected* by a stronger U.S. dollar. 収益と利益は，ドル高[米ドル為替相場の上昇]のマイナス影響を受けました。

unforeseen loss 不測の損害
▸Solvency margin rates indicate an insurer's ability to pay out policy obligations in the event of a disaster or *unforeseen loss*. ソルベンシー・マージン比率は，災害時や不測の損害が発生した場合の保険会社の保険契約債務支払い能力を示す。

unfriendly 形 非友好的，友好的でない，敵対的，

厳しい （⇒friendly, hostile）
defensive measures against unfriendly takeover attempts 非友好的買収への防衛策
lender-unfriendly 貸し手に厳しい
unfriendly takeover 非友好的買収，敵対的買収
unfriendly takeover bid 非友好的株式公開買付け，非友好的TOB，株式公開買付けによる非友好的買収，非友好的買収（＝unfriendly takeover）

Uniform Commercial Code 統一商事法典，統一商法典《略 U.C.C》（米国各州の商事取引法を統一するために作成された法案で，1951年に成立）

Uniform Customs and Practice for Documentary Credits 荷為替信用状統一規則

Uniform Trade Secrets Act 統一トレード・シークレット法

uninvited spam e-mail 迷惑なスパム・メール，勝手に送られてくる迷惑な電子メール

union 名 労働組合，組合，ユニオン（⇒represent, wage negotiation）
　Confederation of Japan Automobile Workers' Union 自動車総連
　Federation of All Nissan and General Workers Union 日産労連
　Japan Council of Metalworkers' Union 全日本金属産業労働組合協議会
　Japan Federation of Service and Distributive Workers Union サービス・流通連合
　Japanese Electric, Electronic and Information Union 電機連合
　Japanese Federation of Textile, Chemical, Service and General Workers' Unions UIゼンセン同盟
　Japanese Trade Union Confederation 連合
　National Confederation of Trade Unions 全労連，全国労働組合総連合
　National Trade Union Council 全労協，全国労働組合協議会
▸The *unions* submitted written demands for pay rises and better working conditions against a background of improved corporate performance and a recovering economy. 各労組は，企業業績の改善や景気回復を背景に，賃上げや職場改善の要求書を提出した。

unissued check 未発行小切手
unissued shares 未発行株式（会社が発行できる株式の上限である授権株式（authorized shares）のうち，まだ発行されていない株式の総数）
unit 名 単位，構成単位，部門，事業部門，会社，支社，支店，子会社，設備一式，台，基，装置，セット，ユニット
　business unit 事業部門，事業部，事業単位
　cost unit 原価単位
　credit card unit クレジット・カード会社
　current purchasing power unit 現在購買力単位
　economic unit 経済主体
　finance unit 金融子会社
　headquarters units 本社
　operating unit 事業体
　organizational unit 組織単位
　prefabricated units プレハブ住宅
　research unit 研究所
　single unit depreciation 個別償却
　unit: billion yen 単位: 10億円
　unit cost 単位原価，個別原価，単価
　unit credit 単位給付，単位積増し，単位年金積増し
　unit depreciation 個別償却
　unit kilometers 走行台キロ
　unit method 個別償却法，個別法（＝unit depreciation method: 棚卸し資産の評価方法の一つで，個々の資産ごとに減価償却費を計算する方法。これに対して複数の固定資産を一括して減価償却費を計算する方法を総合償却（composite-life method）という）
　unit sales 販売数量
　unprofitable unit 不採算部門
　wholly owned units of the holding company 持ち株会社の全額出資子会社
▸Each business *unit* is responsible for its own markets. 事業部は，それぞれ各事業部門の市場に関して責任を負っています。
▸NTT DoCoMo has already tied up with Sumitomo Mitsui Financial Group Inc.'s credit card *unit*. NTTドコモは，三井住友フィナンシャルグループのクレジット・カード会社とすでに提携している。

unitary tax 合算課税，ユニタリー課税，ユニタリー・タックス
unitize 動 ユニット化する
universal 形 普遍的な，万国の，世界の，共通の，一般的な，総合的，ユニバーサル
　universal bank 証券業務兼営銀行，総合銀行
　universal banking ユニバーサル・バンキング（銀行の証券業兼営）
　universal partnership 共同組合
　universal pension 一律給付年金
　Universal Product Code 統一商品コード
　universal service 全国均一サービス，ユニバー

サル・サービス（郵便事業の場合は，全国同一料金でサービスを提供すること）

universal shelf registration statement 普遍的一括登録届け出書，普遍的一括登録書類
▸After privatization, the nationwide network of postal offices is maintained to offer *universal services* nationwide. 民営化後も，全国的にユニバーサル・サービスを提供するため，全国の郵便局網は維持されている。

unless otherwise stated [indicated] 別段の記載がないかぎり，特段の記載がないかぎり，とくに他の記載がないかぎり
▸All dollar amounts in this document are in U.S. dollar *unless otherwise stated*. この報告書では，別段の記載がないかぎり，金額はすべて米ドルで表示されています。

unlisted 形 上場されていない，非上場の，未上場の
  unlisted company 非上場会社，非上場企業
  unlisted joint-stock company 株式を上場していない非公開会社（＝unlisted stock company）
  unlisted stock [share] 未上場株，非上場株，場外株，店頭株，未公開株
  unlisted stock company 株式を上場していない非公開会社，非上場会社（＝unlisted joint-stock company）
▸The management of both firms purchased shares from ordinary shareholders in order to withdraw from the stock market to become *unlisted* companies. 両社の経営陣は，株式市場から撤退して非上場企業になるために，普通株主から株を買い取った。

unload 動 処分する，売り払う，売却する
▸In the April-September period, JAJ managed to secure a group net profit of ¥1.5 billion by *unloading* its shareholdings. 4－9月期の中間決算で，日航は保有株を売却してかろうじて15億円の連結差引き後利益を確保した。

unopened package 未開封のパッケージ
unopened product 未開封の商品
unpaid overtime allowance サービス残業代，不払い残業手当，不払い時間外手当
▸The Toyota Labor Standards Inspection Office has ordered Toyota Motor Corp. to pay *unpaid overtime allowances* to some of its employees by the end of the month. 豊田労働基準監督署は，今月末までにトヨタの社員の一部にサービス残業代［不払い時間外手当］を支払うよう命じた［勧告した］。

unprofitable 形 採算の合わない，不採算な，儲からない，利益を生じない，無駄な
  unprofitable division 不採算の事業部門，不採算部門（＝unprofitable operation）
  unprofitable operation 不採算事業（＝unprofitable business）
  unprofitable outlet 不採算店舗（＝unprofitable store；⇒**restructuring plan**）
▸In September 2008, we divested our *unprofitable* outlets. 2008年9月に，当社は不採算店舗を売却しました。

unrealized 形 未実現の
  unrealized equity profits 株式含み益
  unrealized exchange gains and losses 未実現の為替差損益
  unrealized income 未実現利益
  unrealized intercompany profits 未実現内部利益
  unrealized loss 未実現損失，含み損，評価損（＝appraisal loss, latent loss）
  unrealized profits and losses 含み損益（＝appraisal profits and losses, latent profits and losses）
  unrealized revenue 未実現収益
▸Any related *unrealized* exchange gains and losses are allocated to currency translation adjustment. これに関連する未実現為替差損益は，すべて為替換算調整勘定に配賦されています。

unrealized foreign currency losses 未実現為替差損
▸General corporate expenses are principally cash, temporary cash investments and deferred *unrealized foreign currency losses*. 全社共通費は，主に現金預金と短期的資金運用投資と繰延べ未実現為替差損です。

unrealized gain 未実現利益，未実現益，未実現利得，含み益，評価益（＝appraisal gains, latent profits, unrealized profit）
▸Thanks to the increases in *unrealized gains* in their stocks, many banks expect to see their net worth increase. 株式含み益の増加で，多くの銀行は自己資本の上昇を見込んでいる。

unrealized profit 未実現利益，含み益，評価益（＝appraisal profit, latent gain, unrealized gain；保有資産の値上がりによる計算上の利益）
▸Many of the banking groups are running out of *unrealized profits* in their shareholdings. 銀行グループの多くは現在，持ち株の含み益が涸渇している。

unrealized value 未実現評価額，未実現損益，含み損益

▶The bullish stock market in the past six months has led the *unrealized value* of bank-held stocks to swell by about ¥3 trillion. 株式市場が過去半年間，堅調に推移したことで，銀行保有株式の含み損益が約3兆円増加した。

unrecoverable loan 不良債権，不良貸付け，焦げ付き，貸倒れ （＝bad debt, irrecoverable loan）

unrecovered cost 未回収原価，回収不能原価

unreported earnings 収益の申告漏れ，申告漏れ額

unsecured 形 安全でない，無担保の，抵当のない，無保証の，保証のない
　unsecured bond 無担保債券
　unsecured call loan 無担保コール・ローン
　unsecured corporate debenture 無担保社債
　unsecured credit 無担保債権
　unsecured debt 無担保債
　unsecured loan 無担保融資，無担保貸付け，無担保貸付け金，無担保ローン，無担保債権 （＝unsecured credit）
　unsecured overnight call money 無担保コール翌日物
　unsecured overnight call rate 無担保コール翌日物の金利 （⇒money market）
▶The Policy Board of the Bank of Japan voted unanimously to keep the target rate for *unsecured* overnight call money on hold at its policy meeting. 日銀政策委員会は，金融政策決定会合で，（政策金利である）無担保コール翌日物金利の誘導目標を現状のまま据え置くことを全会一致で決めた。

unused patent 休眠特許
▶This intellectual property fund would purchase the rights for the *unused patents* and technologies and store them in a database. この知的財産ファンドは，休眠している特許や技術の権利を買い取って，それをデータベース化する。

unusual 形 異常な，異例の，特別の，前例のない
　unusual dividend 特別配当
　unusual gain and loss 特別損益，異常損益 （＝unusual profit or loss）
　unusual item 異常項目，異常損益項目，特別項目，非正常項目
▶The per share effects of *unusual* items in a quarter may differ from the per share effects of of those same items for the year. ある四半期の特別損益項目による1株当たりの影響額は，事業年度の同じ特別損益項目による1株当たりの影響額と異なる場合があります。

unsolicited 形 頼みもしない，おせっかいな，余計な，頼まれない，自発的な，敵対的な （⇒reject）
　unsolicited bidding 直接入札
　unsolicited offer 敵対的提案
　unsolicited takeover bid 敵対的買収提案 （＝unsolicited takeover offer）
▶Microsoft made an *unsolicited* offer to buy Yahoo Inc. for $44.6 billion. 米マイクロソフトが，米ヤフーに対して446億ドルでの敵対的買収を提案した。

unveil 動 明らかにする，発表する，公にする，公表する，初公開する，公開する，除幕する，打ち明ける
▶Fuji TV *unveiled* a plan to make Nippon Broadcasting System a subsidiary. フジテレビは，ニッポン放送を子会社化する計画を発表した。

upbeat 名 上昇傾向，景気回復ムード，活発化，形 景気のいい，上昇傾向の，盛り上がりのある，楽観的な
▶Japan has become somewhat *upbeat* about the economy. 日本は，景気回復ムードが見られるようになった。

UPC 統一商品コード （**Universal Product Code**の略）

update 動 更新する，最新のものにする，最新式にする，改訂する，アップデートする
　fully update 全面改良する
　update a file ファイルを更新する
　update one's Web site …のホームページを更新する
▶It took an hour to get the information *updated*. 情報を更新するのに，1時間かかった。
▶The firm fully *updated* its pickup truck produced in Thailand last year. 同社は昨年，タイで生産しているピックアップ・トラックを全面改良した。

update 名 更新，改訂，最新情報，最新版
▶All such *Updates* shall become part of Licensor's Products and shall remain in the sole property of Licensor. この最新版は，すべてライセンサーの製品の一部をなし，ライセンサーの単独財産としてとどまるものとする。

upgrade 動 昇格させる，高める，向上させる，底上げする，格上げする，格付けを引き上げる，上方修正する，グレードアップする，名 高度化，機能拡張，格上げ，上方修正，グレードアップ
▶Standard & Poor's *upgraded* the outlooks on its ratings to stable from negative on five insurance companies. スタンダード＆プアーズは，保険会社5社の格付け見通しを「ネガティブ（弱含み）」から「安定的」に上方修正した。

upgrading 名 格上げ, 上方修正, 引上げ, 昇進, 昇格, イメージ・アップ (=rating upgrade)

upload 動 データを送信する, アップロードする (⇒**download**)

upmarket 形 高級な, 上流指向の (=upscale)
▸*Upmarket* supermarket chain Kinokuniya Co. and Takashimaya Co. have reached a basic agreement on a comprehensive business tie-up to jointly create upscale, new-style stores.　高級スーパーの紀ノ国屋と高島屋は, 包括的業務提携をして富裕消費者向けの新店舗を共同開発することで基本合意に達した.

upscale 形 高級な, 上流指向の, 富裕消費者向けの (=upmarket)
▸The Japan unit of *upscale* U.S. department store Saks Fifth Avenue opened its first Japanese outlet in Tokyo.　米国の高級百貨店「サックス・フィフス・アベニュー」の日本法人が, 東京に日本1号店を出店した.

upside 名 上昇, 上昇傾向, 上昇気味, 上値(うわね)の余地, 上昇余地, 有利, 有利な点, メリット, 良い面 (⇒**downside**)
　further upside 相場の一層の上昇, 一層の上値余地
　stock price's upside 株価上昇, 株価上昇の余地, 株価の上値余地
　upside potential 上値余地, 上昇の余地, 値上りの余地 (上値は「現在の株価より高い株価」のこと)
　upside profit potential 収益増加の可能性
　upside risk 上昇のリスク, 上振れリスク
▸The global economy is facing both downside and *upside* risks.　世界経済は, 下振れ, 上振れ両サイドのリスクに直面している.

upstream 名 川上産業, 上流部門, 石油採掘部門, 子会社から親会社への販売, 上り, アップストリーム (「アップストリーム(上り)」は, 回線の信号の流れが利用者から電話局の方向のこと. ⇒**downstream**)
▸The firm is transforming itself into a seamless oil company engaged in both *upstream* and downstream operations.　同社は現在, 原油の採掘[原油生産]から精製・販売まで一貫して手がける石油会社への脱皮を図っているところだ.

uptrend 名 上昇, 上昇傾向, 上昇基調
　the current uptrend in the stock market 現在の株高, 現在の株価上昇
　the recent uptrend in the stock 最近の株価上昇

upturn 名 上昇, 上昇傾向, 上向き, 向上, 好転, 増加に転じること, 回復, 景気回復, 景気拡大局面 (⇒**downturn**)
　cyclical upturn 景気回復 (=cyclical upturn in the economy)
　economic upturn 景気回復, 景気の上向き, 景気拡大局面, 景気回復期
　employment upturn 雇用回復, 労働市場の回復
　market upturn 市場の好転, 市場が上向いていること
　strong upturn 力強い回復, 力強い景気回復
　upturn cycle 上昇サイクル
　upturn in business barometers 景気指標の回復
　upturn in production 生産の回復
▸There are serious concerns that the strong yen and the weak U.S. dollar could hurt the current economic *upturn* led by exports.　大きな懸念材料は, 円高・ドル安の進行で現在の輸出主導の景気回復が打撃を受けることだ.

upward 形 上向きの, 上昇する, 副 上方へ, さかのぼって, …以上, …以来 (⇒**downward**)
　slow upward trend 穏やかな上昇傾向[上昇基調], 緩やかな増加傾向[増加トレンド]
　upward adjustment 上方修正, 増額修正
　upward bias 上昇傾向
　upward earnings revision 業績の上方修正, 業績予想の上方修正
　upward mobility 昇進, 昇級, 出世, 立身出世, 栄達, 上方志向[志向性]
　upward of …以上
　upward path 上昇基調, 増加傾向, 増加基調
　upward pressure on wages 賃金上昇圧力, 賃金の上昇傾向
　upward trajectory 上昇軌道
▸The result of this sale was an *upward* adjustment of $30 million ($19.5 million recorded in June) in the Corporation's investment in the firm.　この売却に伴い, 同社に対する当社の投資額は, 6月に計上した1,950万ドルから3,000万ドルに上方修正されています.

U.S. Commerce Department 米商務省 (⇒**retail sales**)

U.S. Environmental Protection Agency 米環境保護庁《略 EPA》

U.S.-style board structure 米国型の取締役会制度
▸Under the revised Commercial Code, only large companies with capital of more than ¥500 million would be qualified to adopt the *U.S.-style board structure*.　今回の商法改正では, 資

本金5億円以上の大企業だけが米国型の取締役会制度を導入することができる。

U.S. Treasuries 米国債

米国債について➡米国の財務省(U.S. Treasury)が発行する市場性証券(marketable securities)で，償還期限が1年以内の財務省短期証券(Treasury bill, T-bill)と1年超10年以内の財務省中期証券(Treasury note, T-note)，10年超の財務省長期証券(Treasury bond, T-bond)の3種類がある。このうち短期証券は割引発行，中期証券と長期証券は利付き発行となっている。発行方法としては競争入札と非競争入札があり，入札者は公示で募集する。

▸The Bank of Japan would purchase some government holdings in *U.S. Treasuries* as a means of providing the government with funds for market intervention. 政府が保有する米国債の一部を，政府に市場介入資金を供給する手段として日銀が購入する。

U.S. Treasury Department 米財務省

usage history data 〈パソコンなどの〉利用履歴データ

▸Japan Complex Cafe Association requires cafes to install functions that automatically erase *usage history data* by the previous users when a new user logs on the computer. 日本複合カフェ協会は，新規利用者がパソコンを起動すると前の利用者の利用履歴データを自動的に消去する機能の導入を，ネット・カフェに義務付けている。

use 動 使用する，使う，用いる，…に充てる，採用する，利用する，活用する，運用する，投入する

be used for repaying long-term indebtedness 長期債務の返済に充てる

financial resources used 資金の運用

net cash used for acquisition 企業買収に使用した現金純額

net cash used in investing activities 投資活動に投入した正味現金

use the straight line method for financial reporting 財務会計上，定額法を用いる［採用する］

▸This $300 million of 9% Series 7 Notes was *used* to repay the same amount of 10% Series 3 Notes, which matured in May 2008. この利率9％のシリーズ7ノート3億ドルは，2008年5月に満期が到来した利率10％のシリーズ3ノート3億ドルの償還に充当しました。

use 名 使用，使用量，使用法，利用，活用，運用，採用，使途，用途，効用，有用，収益権

cash use 資金の使途

efficient use of resources 資源の効率的活用，資源の効率的利用

land use planning 土地利用計画

limited use 制限的使用，使用の制限

sales and use taxes 売上税と使用税

sources and uses of funds 資金収支表

sources of funds and uses of funds 資金の源泉と資金の運用

use of funds 資金の運用，資金の使用，資金の使途

use of proceeds 資金の使途

uses of financial resources 資金源泉の運用

▸European and U.S. companies established R&D bases in China and put their energy into developing products for *use* by Chinese consumers. 欧米の企業は中国に研究開発拠点を設けて，中国仕様の製品開発に力を注いだ。

useful 形 有効な，効果をあげる

▸Canon's cell production system was particularly *useful* in inventory control. キヤノンのセル生産方式は，在庫管理の面でとくに効果をあげた。

useful life 耐用年数，有効期間

useful life of a depreciable asset 減価償却資産の耐用年数

useful life table 耐用年数表

▸The equipment was estimated to have a *useful life* of 8 years with salvage value estimated at $5,000. この設備の耐用年数8年で，残存価格を5,000ドルと見積もられた。

user 名 使用者，利用者，顧客，加入者，会員，投資家，ユーザー （⇒heavy user）

end user 最終使用者，一般使用者，最終利用者，最終消費者，最終投資家，エンド・ユーザー （＝ultimate purchaser）

industrial user 産業使用者，実需筋

innocent user 善意の使用者

internal user 内部情報利用者

major user 大口ユーザー，大口利用者 （＝large user, substantial user）

Net user ネット利用者 （＝Internet user）

user agreement 利用規約

user card 顧客カード，ユーザー・カード

user-hostile 使いにくい，使いづらい，使い勝手がよくない，ユーザーに親しみにくい，分かりにくい，不便

user lawsuit ユーザー訴訟

user management ユーザー管理

user-to-user signaling ユーザー間情報通知サービス

user-unfriendly 使いにくい，使いづらい，利用しづらい，ユーザー・フレンドリーでない （＝

user-hostile)
users of blog service ブログ・サービスの会員
wrongful user 不法使用者
▸With Rakuten declaring its entry to the banking business, competition to win funds from Net *users* is set to accelerate. 楽天が銀行業への参入を宣言したことで，ネット利用者の資金獲得を狙った競争が加速しそうだ．
user-friendly 形 使いやすい，ユーザーに親しみやすい，ユーザーに分かりやすい，利用者に親切，操作が簡単，便利
▸The consortium of the two companies would bring such benefits as reduced costs in research and development and more *user-friendly* services under a combined brand image. 両社の連合で，研究開発費の削減効果やブランド・イメージを融合した利便性の高いサービスが期待される．
USTR 米国通商代表部 (**Office of the United States Trade Representative**の略称．米国通商代表は**U.S. Trade Representative**)
utility 名 効用，有用，実用，実用性，実用品，公益事業，公共事業，公共事業体，公共事業株 (⇒**liberalization of the electricity market**)
electrical utilities 電力会社 (=power utilities)
housing and utilities 住宅・光熱費
marginal utility 限界効用
public utility 公益事業，公共事業
utilities company 公益企業
utility charges 公共料金 (=utilities, utility rates)
utility model 実用新案，実用新案権，新案特許権
utility output 電力・ガスの生産高
utility rates 公共料金 (=utility charges)
utility vehicle 多目的車，多用途車，ユーティリティ・ビークル
▸Under the new system of postal services, the flat ¥30 fee for paying *utility* charges at post offices or transferring them through ATMs is ¥240 for bills more than ¥30,000. 郵便事業の新制度では，公共料金を郵便局の窓口やATM（現金自動預け払い機）で振り込む場合の手数料は一律30円だったが，3万円以上の場合は240円になった．
utility program ユーティリティ・プログラム (=software tool, utility: ソフトウエアや開発などの支援プログラム，ソフトウエア・メーカーなどが提供する補助的プログラム)

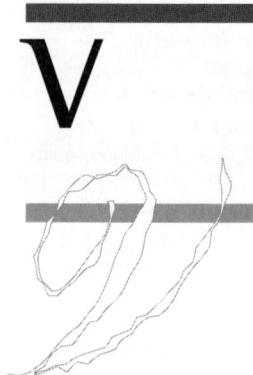

V

vacancies-to-applications ratio 有効求人倍率
▶The seasonally adjusted *vacancies-to-applications ratio* for March stood at 0.77, little changed from February. 3月の有効求人倍率（季節調整値）は0.77倍で、前月と同じだった。

vacancy 图 欠員, 空位, 空室, 空席, 空き地, 空間
　fill the vacancy 欠員を埋める, 欠員を満たす
　office vacancies オフィスの空室, オフィス空室率
　unfilled vacancy 未充足空席
▶Tokyo office *vacancies* fell in January after rising in December 2007. 東京のオフィス空室率が、昨年12月に上昇した後、1月に低下した。

vacancy rate 欠員率, 空室率, 空白率
　commercial office vacancy rate 賃貸オフィスの空室率
　unfilled vacancy rate 未充足求人率
　vacancy rate of commercial office space 賃貸用オフィス・ビルの空室率

vacant 图 空席の, 欠員の, 空いている, 借り手のいない, 遊休の, 相続人[現住者]のいない
　fall vacant 空席になる, 地位が空く
　situation vacant column 求人広告欄
　vacant estate 相続人のいない財産
　vacant hours [time] 暇な時間, 空き時間
　vacant job 就職口
　vacant ground [lot] 空き地
　vacant office [post] 空位, 空いている地位[ポスト]
　vacant possession 無占有
　vacant succession 相続人不存在, 無主相続
▶The post of president has been *vacant*. 社長のポストは、空席になっている。

vacation allowance 休暇手当（＝vacation pay）

Valdez principles バルディーズの原則（環境問題に関する倫理基準）

valid asset 有価値資産, 価値のある資産
▶Revenue is recognized by the conversion of a product into cash or other *valid assets*. 収益は、製品の現金またはその他の有価値資産への転化により認識される。

valuation 图 評価, 査定, 見積り, 評価価格, 査定価格
　actuarial valuation 保険数理上の評価
　hidden valuation 含み資産
　inventory valuation 棚卸し資産評価
　investment valuation allowance 長期投資評価引当金
　market valuation 時価総額（＝aggregate market value, total market value: 株価による企業の価値を示す「時価総額」は、株価に発行済み株式数を掛けて算出する）
　projected benefit valuation method 予測給付評価方式
　stock valuation 株価評価
　taxable valuation 課税評価額
　valuation allowance 評価引当金, 評価性引当金
　valuation basis 評価基準
　valuation profit or loss 評価損益
　valuation reserve 評価性引当金
　valuation surplus 評価剰余金
▶At current prices, the firm's market *valuation* is more than $1.5 billion. 現在の株式でみた同社の時価総額は、15億ドルを超えている。

valuation losses 評価損,保有株の評価損を損失として計上する減損処理額 (＝appraisal losses, evaluation losses)
▸Companies are required to post *valuation losses* on fixed assets whose market value has fallen sharply from their book value. 固定資産の時価が簿価から大幅に下落した場合の固定資産の評価損計上を,企業は義務付けられている。

value 動 評価する,評価換えする,値洗いする,重視する,
  be present valued 現在価値に直す
  be valued at market 時価で評価する
  fairly value 適正に評価する
  value the book at historical cost 原価で計上する
  value the book at market 時価で計上する
▸Our advanced telecommunications equipment is *valued* at approximately $130 million. 当社の先進的通信施設は,約1億3,000万ドルと評価されています。

value 名 価値,価格,評価,評価額,金額,相場,バリュー (⇒book value, corporate value, create, market value, par value, shareholders' value)
  added value 付加価値
  cash value 時価
  capital value 資本価値,資本金
  create value 価値を高める,収益を生み出す
  estimated value 見積り額,見積り価額
  franchise value フランチャイズ価値,営業権
  increase value for our shareholders 当社株主の価値[利益]を高める
  notional principal value 額面
  price book-value ratio 株価純資産倍率
  reported value 簿価
  share value 株価,株式の評価
  simple mean value 単純平均
  the rapid [sharp] surge in the yen's value 急激な円高
  the yen's value against the dollar 円の対米ドル相場
  utility value 利用価値
  value-creative economy 価値創造経済
  value declared 表記価額
  value in use 使用価値
  value of a corporation 企業の価値,企業価値 (＝corporate value)
  value-oriented management 価値重視の経営
  value stock バリュー株 (株式市場で過小評価されている株のこと)
  value strategy バリュー戦略
  value to business 企業価値
▸Financial institutions are required to report latent losses if the *value* of their stock investments falls more than 50 percent below their purchase prices. 保有株の株価が取得価格より50％以上下落した場合,金融機関は評価損を計上しなければならない。
▸One of our principal strategies is to offer customers the best *value*. 当社の主な戦略の一つは,お客さまに最高の価値を提供することです。
▸The *value* of yen continued to drop. 円安が進行した。

value-added 形 付加価値の,付加価値のある,付加価値の高い,高付加価値の
  high value-added operations 付加価値の高い事業,高付加価値事業
  higher value-added specialty end of the business 高付加価値製品分野
  value-added entity 付加価値事業体
  value-added network 付加価値通信網,高度技術情報通信網《略 VAN》
  value-added process manufacturing 委託加工
  value-added product 付加価値のある商品,付加価値製品 (＝value-added goods)
  value-added reseller 付加価値再販業,付加価値再販業者《略 VAR》
  value-added tax 付加価値税《略 VAT》
  value-added technology 付加価値の高い技術,高付加価値技術
▸Japanese firms face the task of developing innovative *value-added* goods and services. 日本企業は,課題として革新的な付加価値商品とサービスの開発が求められている。

value added 名 付加価値 (＝added value)
  increase value added 付加価値を高める
  productivity of value added 付加価値生産性
  ratio of value added to equipment investment 設備投資効率
  tax on value added 付加価値税
  value added analysis 付加価値分析

value to the shaheholders 株主にとっての価値,株主に帰属する価値
▸The value of a corporation is divided between *value to the shareholders* and value to stakeholders. 企業価値は,株主に帰属する価値とステークホルダー (利害関係者) に帰属する価値に二分される。

vanity publisher 自費出版社,自費出版専門の出版社

▶Major *vanity publisher* filed for bankruptcy. 大手の自費出版社が，破産を申し立てた。

variable 形 変わりやすい，不安定な，変動する，可変の，変動できる
  variable annuity 変額年金, 可変年金
  variable cost 変動費, 可変費用, 変動減価
  variable expense 変動費 （＝variable charge）
  variable factory cost 変動製造原価
  variable insurance 変額保険
  variable pension system 変額年金制度
  variable rate 変動金利 （＝variable rate interest）
▶The Company has entered into several transactions which reduce financing costs and exposure to *variable* rate debt. 最近実施した数件の取引で，当社の資金調達コストと変動金利負債に係わるリスクは軽減されています。

variable 名 不確定要素, 変数
  continuous variable 連続変数
  decision variable 意思決定変数
  financial variable 金融指標
  macro economic variables マクロ経済変数
  random variable 確率変数
  target variable 目標変数

variance 名 差異, 差額, 分散
  administration cost variance 一般管理費差異
  cost variance 原価差異, 原価差額 （＝variance of cost）
  overhead variance 製造間接費差異
  market share variance 市場占有率差異
  market size variance 市場規模差異
  material variance 材料費差異
  production variance 製造差異
  quality variance 品質差異
  shrinkage variance 減耗差異
  volume variance 製造量差異, 操業度差異

VAT 付加価値税 （value-added tax の略）

veep 名 副会長, 副社長, 副頭取, 副総裁, 副大統領 （＝vice-president）

vehicle 名 乗り物, 自動車, 車両, 輸送手段, 手段, 媒介物, 商品, 子会社, ビークル （⇒recall 動）
  corporate vehicles 所有企業
  finance vehicle 金融子会社
  funding vehicle 資金調達手段
  investment vehicle 投資商品, 投資子会社, 投資手段
  launch vehicle 打上げ用ロケット
  lunar roving vehicle 月面車, 月面移動車
  methanol-fueled vehicle メタノール車
  motor vehicle tonnage tax 自動車重量税
  off-road vehicle オフロード車
  on-road vehicle 陸上車両
  public vehicle 公共の乗り物
  recreational vehicle RV車
  space vehicle 宇宙船
  special purpose vehicle 特別目的会社
  sports utility vehicle スポーツ・ユーティリティ・ビークル
  utility vehicle 多用途車, ユーティリティ・ビークル
  vehicle excise duty 自動車税
  vehicle industry 自動車産業
  vehicle navigation system 車両用ナビゲーション・システム
  vehicle producer 自動車メーカー
  vehicle security devices 車両安全装置

velocity 名 速度, 速力, 速さ, 高速, 急速, 流通速度
  data transfer velocity データ伝送速度
  income velocity 所得速度, 所得流通速度
  income velocity of money 貨幣の流通速度
  transaction velocity 取引速度, 流通速度
  velocity of circulation 流通速度
  velocity of money 通貨[貨幣]の流通速度

vendor [**vender**] 名 仕入先, 納入業者, 機材調達先, 供給元, メーカー, 販売業者, 販売会社, 売り主, 売り手, 売却元, ベンダー （⇒sourcing）
▶With assured long-term sources for these components from North American *vendors*, it is not economically prudent for us to produce all of these components internally. これらの部品については北米の納入業者から長期供給が保証されているため，これらのコンポーネントをすべて自社工場で生産するのは，もはや経済的に得策ではありません。

venture 名 冒険的事業, 投機の事業, 危険性の高い事業, 事業, 合弁事業, 業務, ベンチャー （⇒joint venture）
  cooperative ventures ジョイント・ベンチャー
  corporate joint venture 合弁会社
  domestic ventures 国内事業
  new ventures 新規事業
  overseas ventures 海外事業
  venture capital firm ベンチャー・キャピタル投資会社, ベンチャー・キャピタル
  venture capitalist ベンチャー・ビジネスへの出資者[投資家], 危険資本家, 危険投資家, 危険負担本家, ベンチャー・キャピタリスト
  venture firm ベンチャー企業 （＝start-up, start-up business）

venture fund ベンチャー・ファンド（投資ファンドの一種で，創業間もない企業の未上場株式に投資して，売却益を狙う）

venture management ベンチャー・マネジメント（＝venture business）

▶The two firms launched projects together, including a joint production *venture* in Canada. 両社は，カナダでの共同生産事業などの共同事業を開始した。

venture business ベンチャー企業，ベンチャー・ビジネス，新ビジネス，投機的事業，研究開発型企業，開拓型新興小規模企業《略 **VB**》（＝startup business, venture company）

▶In the United States, universities and research institutes have direct links with *venture businesses*. 米国では，大学と研究機関がベンチャー企業と直結している。

venture capital 危険資本，危険負担資本，ベンチャー資本，リスク資金，ベンチャー企業に投資する会社，ベンチャー・キャピタル投資会社，ベンチャー・キャピタル《略 **VC**》（＝risk capital）

▶Some of the oil corporation's functions, such as supplying *venture capital* for oil development and conducting R&D, were consolidated into the Metal Mining Agency of Japan. 石油開発のためのリスク資金供給機能や研究開発機能など，石油公団の機能の一部が，金属鉱業事業団に統合された。

venture into …に進出する，…に乗り出す，…に手を広げる（⇒**entity**）

▶The new company reportedly is planning to *venture into* operating hotels and tourism-based businesses. 新会社は，ホテル経営や旅行業に進出する計画だという。

venue 名 開催地，行為地，会場，裁判地

vertical 形 垂直的，同業同種の，縦割りの，縦の（⇒**horizontal**）

  administered vertical marketing system 流通系列化

  vertical channel system 垂直的経路システム

  vertical communication 垂直的コミュニケーション

  vertical competition 垂直的競争

  vertical conflict 垂直的衝突，垂直的コンフリクト（製造業者と小売業者，小売業者と卸売り業者間の競争的闘争）

  vertical diversification 垂直的多角化

  vertical influence 垂直的競争

  vertical integration 垂直統合

  vertical market 垂直的市場

  vertical marketing system 垂直的マーケティング・システム《略 **VMS**》（＝vertically integrated marketing system）

  vertical merger 垂直的合併（＝vertical amalgamation）

  vertical organization 垂直的組織

  vertical publication 業界専門誌

  vertical specialization 垂直的国際分業

  vertical trade 垂直的貿易

vest 動 〈権利，権限を〉与える，付与する，〈権利を〉帰属させる，〈権利が〉帰属する

▶Responsibility for the management and direction of the new company shall be *vested* in the board of directors of the new company. 新会社の経営と指揮に対する責任は，新会社の取締役会に帰属する。

vested 形 確定した，受給権の発生した，既得の

  vested accumulated plan benefits 受給権確定［受給権の発生した］累積年金給付額

  vested benefit obligation 確定給付債務

  vested benefits 受給権確定給付［給付額］，受給権の発生した年金給付，確定給付

  vested interest 既得権，既得権益，確定権利（＝vested right）

veto 動 拒否権を行使する，拒否する，差し止める

▶Acquiring a 35 percent stake in the company would give shareholders the right to *veto* key matters at shareholders meetings. 同社株を35％取得すると，株主総会で重要事項の決議を拒否する権利が株主に与えられる。

veto 名 拒否権

▶Some leading companies may issue certain classes of stock, such as preferred shares, which give shareholders a *veto* when a hostile acquirer proposes a merger or acquisition. 敵対的買収者が合併や買収を提案した場合，主要企業の一部は，株主に拒否権を与える優先株などの種類株を発行する場合もある。

veto power 拒否権（＝veto right, the power of a veto）

▶Golden shares are special shares that give designated shareholders *veto power* at shareholders meetings. 黄金株は，指定株主に株主総会での拒否権を与える特殊な株だ。

vice president [**vice-president**] 副社長（日本企業の部長や次長に相当する職位），副頭取，副会長，副理事長，副総裁，副学長，副大統領《略 **VP**》（＝veep）

  corporate vice-president 本社副社長

  executive vice-president 執行副社長，業務執

行副社長, 副社長, 副理事長
financial vice-president 財務担当副社長
senior vice president 上級副社長, 上席副社長
▸The firm named its senior *vice president* as president. 同社は, 上級副社長を社長に指名した。

vicious cycle 悪循環 (=vicious circle; ⇒ **virtuous cycle**)
▸Large simultaneous sell-offs of banks' shareholdings on the market would lead to a *vicious cycle* of plunging share prices and worsening bank finances. 銀行の保有株を市場で大量に同時に売却すれば, 株価下落と銀行の財務内容の悪化という悪循環つながる。

video 名 映像, 画像, テレビ, ビデオ
　video cassette recorder ホームビデオ, ホームVTR, ビデオ《略 **VCR**》
　video computing ビデオ・コンピューティング（アナログ形式の動画をデジタル形式にして処理するコンピュータでの画像処理）
　video game テレビ・ゲーム, テレビ・ゲーム機
　video on demand ビデオ・オン・デマンド《略 **VOD**》（視聴者のリクエストに応じて見たい映画や番組が配信されるシステム）
　video phone テレビ電話
　video software ビデオ・ソフト
▸*Video* maker Sega Corp. will focus on its software operations. テレビ・ゲーム機メーカーのセガは, 同社のソフトウエア事業に特化する方針だ。

virtual 形 事実上の, 実質的な, 仮想の, バーチャル
　virtual bank 仮想銀行
　virtual branch 仮想支店, バーチャル支店
　virtual company 仮想会社, バーチャル・カンパニー（=virtual corporation）
　virtual corporation 仮想企業, 仮想事業体, バーチャル・コーポレーション
　virtual mall 仮想商店街, バーチャル・モール（=virtual shopping mall）
　virtual manufacturing 仮想生産, バーチャル・マニュファクチュアリング
　virtual money 仮想通貨[貨幣], バーチャル・マネー
　virtual reality 仮想現実, 仮想現実感, 仮想世界, 人工現実感, バーチャル・リアリティ《略 **VR**》
　virtual shop 仮想商店
　virtual shopping バーチャル・ショッピング（インターネットを通じた通信販売）
　virtual space 仮想空間 (=cyberspace)
　virtual university バーチャル大学, サイバー大学
virtual engineering 仮想エンジニアリング, バーチャル・エンジニアリング
▸This new manufacturing process has come to be called *virtual engineering*, as the whole process occurs on computer displays and with the use of peripheral devices. この新しい製造工程は, 工程作業全体がコンピュータの画面と周辺装置を使って行うので, 仮想エンジニアリング[バーチャル・エンジニアリング]と呼ばれるようになった。

virtual marketplace 仮想電子取引市場, 電子商取引市場, バーチャル市場
▸Rakuten's profit increased at its *virtual marketplace*, travel and financial services businesses. 楽天の利益は, 電子商取引市場や旅行事業, 金融サービスで増加した。

virtual owner 実質的な所有者, 実質的な保有者
▸Kokudo Corp. was found to have been the *virtual owner* of a large number of shares in Seibu Railway held in the name of 1,100 individuals. コクドは, 1,100人の個人名義で保有していた大量の西武鉄道株の実質的な保有者であることが分かった。

virtual shopping mall 仮想商店街, 仮想モール, バーチャル・ショッピング・モール（=virtual mall）
▸With the unified standard, a number of *virtual shopping malls* and financial institutions can be directly linked, enabling the purchaser to make on-the-spot payments through various institutions. 規格を統一することで, 複数の仮想モール（仮想商店街）と金融機関を直接接続することができ, 購入者は各種金融機関を通じて即時決済することができる。

virtuous cycle [circle] 好循環, 良循環
▸The *virtuous cycle* of growth in production, income and spending has been basically maintained. 生産・所得と支出の伸びの好循環[好循環メカニズム]は, 基本的に維持されている。

visionary company 未来志向型企業, 先見的な企業, ビジョンを持っている企業, ビジョナリー・カンパニー

vocation 名 職業, 家業, 生業, 天職, 使命, 適性, 才能

vocational 形 職業上の, 就職指導の （⇒**professional regulation**）
　vocational aptitude 職業上の適性
　vocational bureau 職業相談所
　vocational counselor 就職[職業]カウンセラー, 職業[就職]相談員
　vocational court 職業裁判所
　vocational disease [sickness] 職業病 (=oc-

cupational disease)
vocational education 職業教育
vocational guidance 職業指導, 就職指導
vocational test 職業適性検査
vocational training 職業訓練
voice mail 留守番電話, 音声メール, ボイスメール (=voicemail)
▶Today, most offices are automated and *voice mail* has become an obstacle to connecting with someone in real time. 今日, 大半の事務所は自動化され, ボイスメールの出現によってリアルタイムで話し合うことが困難になっている。
void 形 無効な, 効果がない, 欠員の
▶Once the auditing services are suspended, auditing contracts become *void* under the Corporate Law. 監査業務がいったん停止されると, 会社法の規定で監査契約は無効になる。
volatile 形 変わりやすい, 乱高下する, 変動が激しい, 変動が大きい, 変動性が高い, 不安定な, 左右されやすい
 less volatile 変動性が小さい
 volatile market 変わりやすい市場, 乱高下する市場, 変動が激しい市場
 volatile pricing 価格変動, 価格の変動 (=volatile prices)
volatility 名 変動, 変化, 乱高下, 変動性, 変動率, 将来の価格変動性, 価格変動率, 予測変動率, ボラティリティ
 excess volatility in exchange rates 為替相場の過度の変動
 exchange rate volatility 為替の乱高下, 為替相場の変動, 為替変動 (=forex volatility)
 expected income volatility 予想収益変動幅
 historical volatility 過去の変動性, ヒストリカル・ボラティリティ
 implied volatility 予想変動率, インプライド・ボラティリティ
 market volatility 市場変動性, 相場変動性, 市場の乱高下, 市場のボラティリティ
 price volatility 価格変動性, 価格変動
 stock market volatility 株式相場の変動, 株式市場の乱高下, 株式市場のボラティリティ
▶Tokyo will continue to intervene in the foreign exchange market to stem excessive *volatility*. 日本は, 為替相場の極端な変動(円高急伸)を阻止するため, 今後も引き続き市場介入する方針だ。
volume 名 出来高, 取引高, 売上高, 販売高, 操業度, 数量, 量 (「出来高」は株式市場全体の売買株数を示し, 売買高ともいわれる。一般に, 株価が上昇して, 出来高も多いときは, 相場が強いとされている)

break-even volume 損益分岐売上高
haulage volume 輸送数量
in volume terms 実質ベースで, 台数ベースで, 数量ベースで (=in terms of volume)
loan volume 融資高
low-margin, high volume strategy 薄利多売戦略
new issue volume 起債総額
production volume 製造高, 製造量
profit volume ratio 限界利益率, PV比率, 売上高純利益率 (=PV ratio)
retail volume 実質小売売上高
sales volume 売上高, 販売高, 販売数量, 販売量, 売上数量, 取扱い高 (⇒like-for-like basis)
trading volume 出来高, 売買高, 売上高, 売買株数 (=volume of trading)
volume discount 数量割引, 大口割引
volume on the First Section of the Tokyo Stock Exchange 東証第一部の出来高
volume of business 取引高, 売買高
voluntary 形 任意の, 自主的な, 自発的な, 自由意志による, 無償の
 voluntary closure 自主廃業
 voluntary conveyance of estate in land 無償不動産譲渡
 voluntary dissolution 任意解散 (=voluntary winding up)
 voluntary partnership 任意組合
 voluntary reserves 任意積立金
 voluntary retirement 希望退職
 voluntary work 無料奉仕活動, ボランティア
▶Investors who purchased the leasing rights became members in four *voluntary* partnerships. 持ち分権[リース権]を購入した出資者は, 四つの任意組合のメンバーになった。
voluntary cash payment 任意現金支払い
▶Common shares may also be purchased at the average market price by *voluntary cash payments* of as little as US $40 to a maximum of US $4,000 during a quarter. 当社の普通株式は, 1四半期に最低40米ドルから最高4,000米ドルまでの範囲で, 任意現金支払いにより平均市場価格で購入することもできます。
voluntary liquidation 任意清算, 任意整理
▶Shareholders did not approve of *voluntary liquidation* of the company. 株主は, 同社の任意整理を承認しなかった。
voluntary retirement program 希望退職制度, 任意定年退職制度
▶The firm has been in talks with its labor union

about planned job cuts through a *voluntary retirement program*.　同社は, 同社労組と希望退職制度による人員削減計画について協議している。
voluntary separation　自発的退職, 希望退職
　voluntary separation package　自発的退職案, 希望退職案
　voluntary separation program　任意退職計画, 希望退職計画, 自発的退職プログラム
vote 動　投票する, 票決する, 投票で決定する, 議決する,〈株式の〉議決権を行使する　(⇒**participant**)
　vote against　…に反対の投票をする
　vote down　否決する
　vote for　…に賛成の投票をする
　vote one's share　議決権を行使する
▸Shares cannot be *voted* unless the signed proxy form is returned.　署名した委任状［委任状用紙］が返送されない場合, 株式の議決権を行使することはできません。
vote 名　投票, 投票用紙, 票, 得票, 票決, 決議, 投票権, 議決権, 票決権, 選挙権
　affirmative vote　賛成投票
　one vote for each share　1株につき1議決権
▸Each stockholder of record at the close of business on March 10, 2009 is entitled to one *vote* for each share held.　2009年3月10日の営業終了時に株主名簿に記載された株主は, それぞれ所有する株式1株に付き1票の議決権を行使することができます。
voting 名　投票, 投票権行使, 議決権行使
　audience response voting　聴衆反応投票
　cross voting　交差投票
　cumulative voting　累積投票
　electronic voting　電子投票
　multiple choice voting　マルチ選択投票
　nonvoting redeemable preferred stock　無議決権償還優先株式
　nonvoting share　無議決権株　(＝nonvoting stock)
　online voting　電子投票
　parliamentary voting　議会式投票
　stockholder's voting right　株主議決権
　voting bond　議決権付き社債
　voting by proxy　代理人による議決権の行使
　voting right　議決権, 投票権　(＝voting power; ⇒**shareholders list**)
　voting security　議決権付き証券, 議決権のある証券
　voting stock　議決権株式, 議決権株, 議決権付き株式　(＝voting share)
　voting upon stocks　株式に基づく投票
▸The firm's stake in NBS has exceeded 50 percent in terms of *voting* rights, or 46 percent in terms of shareholding ratio.　同社が保有するニッポン放送株が, 議決権比率で［議決権ベースで］50％(持ち株比率で46％)を超えた。
voting power　議決権, 投票権　(＝voting right: 株主が会社の総会で各種の重要な決議に参加できる権利のこと。一般に, 普通株式1株につき1個の議決権が与えられている)
voting share [stock]　議決権株式, 議決権株, 議決権付き株式　(議決権が付いている株式のこと)
▸Citigroup Japan currently owns 67.2 percent of Nikko Cordial's outstanding shares, or 68 percent in terms of the number of *voting* shares.　シティの日本法人, シティグループ・ジャパンは現在, 日興コーディアルの発行済み株式の67.2％(議決権比率で68％)を保有している。
voucher 名　取引証票, 証憑, 引換券, 商品券, バウチャー, 保証人, 証拠書類, 証明書
vulnerable 形　…の影響を受けやすい, …に弱い, …にさらされやすい, …になりやすい, …にもろい, …に無防備な, …の攻撃を受けやすい, …に圧迫される, 軟調の, …に狙われやすい　(⇒**makeup**)
　be vulnerable to criticism　批判を受けやすい
　be vulnerable to economic slowdown　景気低迷の影響を受けやすい
▸Floating shares are *vulnerable* to a hostile takeover bid.　浮動株は, 敵対的TOBに狙われやすい。
vulture fund　ハゲタカ・ファンド

W

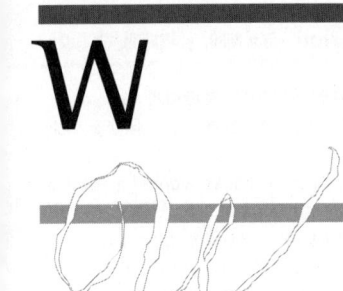

WACC 加重平均資本コスト（weighted average cost of capitalの略。株主資本と銀行などから借りている負債を合わせた資本の平均調達コストのこと）

wage 名 賃金, 給料
  accrued wage 未払い賃金
  daily wage 日給
  efficiency wage 能率給
  hourly wage 時間給
  incentive wage 奨励給
  minimum wage 最低賃金
  nominal wage 名目賃金
  prepaid wage 前払い賃金
  real wage 実質賃金
  salaries and wages 賃金・給与
  seniority order wage system 年功序列型賃金制, 年功序列型賃金体系
  spring wage offensive 春闘
  wage advance 賃金前払い, 賃金前貸し
  wage assignment 給与天引き, 給与[給料]控除
  wage-base increase ベースアップ, ベア
  wage compression 賃金格差縮小
  wage demand 賃上げ要求, 賃金のベースアップ要求（=wage claim）
  wage disparity 賃金格差（=wage differential, wage gap）
  wage dispute 賃金紛争
  wage drift 協定外賃金, 賃金ドリフト, 賃金の上乗せ分, 賃金動向
  wage earner 賃金労働者, 賃金所得者, 勤労者（=wageworker）
  wage-earning households サラリーマン世帯（=households of salaried workers）
  wage freeze 賃金凍結
  wage goods industry 賃金財産業
  wage increase 賃上げ, 賃金引上げ（=wage hike）
  wage level 賃金水準
  wage on job evaluation 職能給
  wage policy 賃金政策
  wage-price spiral 賃金・物価の悪循環
  wage rate 賃金率（1時間当たりの賃金額）
  wage regulations 賃金規定, 賃金調整
  wage scale 賃金率, 賃金体系, 賃金スケール, 給与表
  wage settlement 賃上げ妥結額
  wage structure 賃金構造, 給与構成
  wages and benefits 賃金・諸手当
  wages based on job evaluation 職能給
  wages for job classification 資格給
▶Shuntou spring *wage* talks between corporate management and labor unions started amid weak stocks and yen rise. 株安と円高のなかで, 企業の経営者と労組の春闘[春の賃金交渉]がスタートした。

wage cuts 賃金引下げ, 賃下げ, 賃金カット
▶Members of the current working generation who sustain the pension system are enduring the pain of corporate restructuring and *wage cuts*. 年金制度を支えている現役世代は, リストラや賃下げの痛みに耐え忍んでいる。

wage growth 賃金の伸び, 賃金上昇率
▶Personal consumption has been in the doldrums because of slack *wage growth*. 個人消費は, 賃金の伸び悩みで低迷している。

wage hike 賃上げ, 賃金引上げ（=wage in-

crease)
- The union of Toyota Motor Corp. will demand a ¥1,500 monthly *wage hike* in the spring wage talks. 春闘で，トヨタ自動車労組[労働組合]は，月1,500円の賃上げを要求する。

wage negotiation 賃金交渉，賃上げ交渉 (=wage talks)
- In the conventional style of *wage negotiations*, unions uniformly seek higher wages for workers. 従来の賃金交渉の方式では，労働組合側が横並びで高めの賃上げを目指してきた。

wage restraint 賃金抑制
- Companies have been absorbing the rising cost of fuel and materials through *wage restraint* and increases in productivity, resulting in flat consumer prices. 賃金抑制と生産性向上により，企業は燃料や原材料の値上り分を吸収して，消費者物価の上昇を抑えている。

wage system 賃金体系，給与体系，賃金システム
- It seems likely that the *wage system* itself will be taken up for discussion by management and labor. 今後は，賃金体系そのものが労使の論議の対象になりそうだ。

wages and salaries 賃金・俸給，賃金・給与，賃金給与所得
- The increase in operating expenses was due primarily to increases in *wages and salaries* and to higher depreciation expenses. この営業費用の拡大は，主に賃金・給与の支払い額と減価償却費の増加によるものです。

Wagner Act ワグナー法 (=Wagner Labor Act：National Labor Relations Act (全米労働関係法)の通称)

Wagner-Peyser Act of 1933 1933年ワグナー＝ペイサー法

wagon distributor ワゴン積み流通業者

wagon jobber ワゴン卸売り業者，車配卸売り業者 (=truck jobber, wagon wholesaler)

wagon retailer ワゴン小売業者，車配小売業者，ワゴン・リテイラー

wait and see 様子見，模様眺め，静観，見送り
　take a wait-and-see outlook 模様眺めに回る，模様眺めの展開となる
　wait-and-see attitude 様子見，模様眺めの姿勢 (=wait-and-see stance)
　wait-and-see stance 模様眺めのスタンスを取る
- Investors were generally adopting a *wait-and-see* stance on mainstay issues. 主力銘柄については，投資家は全般に模様眺めのスタンスを取った[模様眺めの展開となった]。

waiting period 待ち期間，待機期間，クーリングオフ期間

waiting time 待ち時間，待機期間

waive 動 〈権利などを〉放棄する，〈債務を〉免除する
- The company's main banks *waived* a total of ¥110.9 billion in company debt. 同社の主力取引銀行が，総額1,109億円の債権を放棄した。

waiver 名 権利の放棄，債務の免除，権利放棄の意思表示，権利放棄証書 (⇒debt waiver, loan waiver)
- Companies must be generating operating profits from their main businesses to seek debt *waivers* from the creditor banks. 取引銀行に債権放棄を求めるには，企業はその主要な事業部門で営業利益を上げていなければならない。

walk-out [walkout] 名 ひやかし客，職場放棄，ストライキ，スト

Wall Street 米国の証券市場，米ニューヨークの株式市場，ニューヨーク株，ウォール街の証券市場，米ニューヨークの株式中心街，米金融街，米金融市場，米金融界，ウォール・ストリート
　a Wall Street economist 市場エコノミスト
　the Wall Street stock market ウォール街の証券市場
　Wall Streeters 米証券市場関係者 (=Wall Street watchers)
- Goldman Sachs results topped *Wall Street* projections for a profit of $4.35 per share. 米証券大手ゴールドマン・サックスの業績は，米金融街の1株当たり4.35ドルの利益予想を上回った。
- *Wall Street* plunged, driving the Dow Jones industrials down 370 points. ニューヨーク株は急落し，ダウ平均株価(工業株30種)は370ドル下落した。

wannabe 名 志望者

want 名 必要，入用，要求，願望，不足，欠乏，欠如
　consumers' wants 消費者の要求
　want ad 求人[求職]広告 (=classified, classified ad)
　want satisfaction 要求充足
　want-slip system 顧客要求伝票システム

wanted 名 募集，求人

wanton development 乱開発

ward off 避ける，防ぐ，かわす
- The firm has scrapped its plan to invoke the nation's first poison pill scheme to *ward off* hostile takeover bids. 同社は，敵対的TOB(株式公開買付けによる企業買収)を防ぐための日本で最初

のポイズン・ピル防衛策の実施計画を白紙撤回した。

warehouse 名　倉庫,〈税関の〉上屋(うわや), 卸売り店, 問屋
- **bonded warehouse**　保税倉庫
- **distribution warehouse**　流通倉庫
- **ex warehouse**　倉庫渡し
- **storage warehouse**　貯蔵倉庫
- **store and warehouse inventories**　流通在庫
- **Warehouse Act**　倉庫法
- **warehouse certificate**　倉庫証券
- **warehouse charge**　倉敷料
- **warehouse club**　会員制の倉庫型ディスカウント店
- **warehouse entry**　税関の入庫申告書
- **warehouse equipment**　倉庫設備
- **warehouse facilities**　倉庫施設
- **warehouse financing**　倉庫金融
- **warehouse industry**　倉庫業
- **warehouse operation**　倉庫運営
- **warehouse receipt**　倉庫証券, 倉荷(くらに)証券
- **warehouse replenishment time**　倉庫補充時間
- **warehouse retailing**　倉庫運営型小売業, ウエアハウス・リテイリング
- **warehouse sales**　倉出し販売
- **warehouse stock**　製品在庫
- **warehouse store**　倉庫運営型店舗, 大型安売り店, ウエアハウス・ストア
- **warehouse storage and handling**　倉庫の保管と取扱い

warehousing 名　倉庫, 倉庫業務, 保管, 保管業務, 入庫
- **warehousing business**　営業倉庫
- **warehousing cost**　保管料
- **warehousing expense**　保管費
- **warehousing system**　倉庫運営システム

wares 名　商品, 売り物

warrant 名　新株引受権, 新株予約権, 株式買取り請求権, 倉庫証券, 権利証券, 権利証書, 権限証書, 証明書, ワラント
- **bond with stock purchase warrant**　株式買取り権付き社債, 新株引受権付き社債, ワラント債
- **bond with warrant**　ワラント付き社債, ワラント債
- **bond with warrants attached**　新株引受権付き社債 (＝warrant bond)
- **detachable warrant**　分離型ワラント, 分離新株引受権付き証書
- **equity warrant**　新株予約権
- **exercise of warrant**　新株引受権の行使, ワラントの行使
- **issue warrants for new shares to**　…への新株予約権を発行する
- **stock [share] warrant**　新株引受権, 新株予約権, 株式引受権, 新株引受権付き証券[証書], 新株引受保証書, 株式ワラント
- **warrant bond**　ワラント債, 新株引受権付き社債《略 **WB**》

▶The company plans to issue share *warrants* on May 20.　同社は, 5月20日に新株予約権の発行を予定している。

▶The market price of the stock *warrants* was $10 per warrant on April 10.　4月10日の新株引受権付き証券の市場価格は, 1単位10ドルであった。

warranty 名　保証, 保証責任, 担保, 担保責任, 瑕疵(かし)担保
- **breach of warranty**　保証違反
- **express or implied warranty**　明示・黙示の保証
- **full warranty**　完全保証
- **no warranty**　無担保
- **product warranty**　製品保証
- **warranties and indemnities**　保証と補償
- **warranty and claim**　保証とクレーム
- **warranty and liability**　保証と責任
- **warranty claim**　保証債務, 品質保証に基づくクレーム
- **warranty costs**　保証コスト, 製品保証費
- **warranty in materials**　製品材料の保証
- **warranty in workmanship**　製造責任に対する保証, 製造工程に対する保証
- **warranty of merchantability**　商品性の保証
- **warranty of performance**　性能保証
- **warranty reserve**　製品保証引当金

▶There shall be no *warranties* which extend beyond the description on such specifications.　当該仕様書の記載事項の範囲を越える保証は, 一切ないものとする。

warranty period　保証期間

▶The *warranty period* of this product shall be 12 months after the date of delivery.　本製品の保証期間は, 引渡しの時点から12か月とする。

Washington 名　米国, 米国政府, ワシントン

▶There is little reason for *Washington* to impose the safeguard tariffs.　米国のセーフガード関税(緊急輸入制限のための関税)発動には, 根拠が乏しい。

waste 名　廃棄, 廃棄物
- **agricultural wastes**　農業廃棄物
- **domestic wastes**　一般廃棄物
- **hazardous wastes**　有害廃棄物
- **industrial wastes**　産業廃棄物, 工場廃棄物

pollution wastes 公害廃棄物
radioactive wastes 放射性廃棄物
solid wastes 固形廃棄物
waste disposal 廃棄物処理
Waste Management Law 廃棄物処理法
waste of loss 廃棄ロス
waste oil disposal 廃油処理
waste water 下水, 廃水
waste water treatment facilities 廃水処理施設

wastage 名 消耗, 毀損, 損耗, 損耗高, 労働力の目減り

watchdog organization 監視団体

water 名 水, 飲料水, 水道, 海, 川, 水域[海域] (複数形), 立場[状況] (複数形), 水質, 品質, 品位, 純度
international waters 公海
territorial waters 領海
water carrier 水上輸送業者, 海運業者
water development 水資源開発
water discharges 排水, 排水量
water jet cutter 超高圧水流切断, ウォータージェット切断
water pollution 水質汚濁, 水質汚染 (＝water contamination)
water purification plant 浄水場
water quality 水質
water quality control 水質管理, 水質保全
water rate 水道料金
water rationing 給水割当制限
water resources development 水資源開発
water service facilities 水道設備
water softener 浄水装置, 軟水化装置, 硬水軟化剤
water storage facilities 貯水施設
water supply system 水道施設
water transportation 水上輸送 (＝water transport)
water treatment business 水処理事業
▸The Corporation's *water* discharges are mostly inorganic in nature and consist of substances such as sodium, chlorides, and sulfates. 当社の排水の大部分は現に無機物質で, その構成物質はナトリウム, 塩化化合物や硫酸塩などです.

watered capital 水増し資本, 水割り資本 (＝watered capital stock)

watered stock 水増し株式, 水割り株式, 水増し資本, 水割り資本

waterfront industrial areas 臨海工業地域

WATS ワッツ (月決め定額料金で長距離通話が何回でもできる電話契約; wide area telecommunications service の略)

way 名 方法, 手段, 様式, 方向, 方針, 路線, 進路, 道筋, 規模, 点, 観点, 要因
be on the way down 減速軌道に乗る
get under way 始まる
one-way market 買い一色, 売り一色
seek ways to …する手段を講じる
three-way intervention 3極の市場介入
way bill 運送状
▸Consultations on management integration between the two firms got under *way*. 両社の経営統合に関する協議が, 始まった.

weak 形 弱い, 弱小の, 中小の, 低迷する, 軟調の, 落ち込んだ, 低下した, 減少した, 冷え込んだ, 厳しい, 悪化した (⇒**strong**)
weak confidence 消費者マインドの冷え込み
weak consumer spending 消費減退
weak demand 需要の低迷, 需要の軟化
weak economic environment 厳しい経済環境, 経済環境の悪化, 景気低迷
weak economy 景気低迷, 景気の悪化, 景気減速, 景気後退, 景気回復が遅いこと, 経済の低迷
weak performance 伸び悩み
weak sales 販売低迷
weak stock market 株式市場の低迷, 軟調な株式市場
weak supply 供給薄
weak yen 円安 (＝weakened yen)
weaker economic activity 景気の減退
weaker oil prices 原油価格の軟化, 原油価格の軟調
weaker operating income 営業収益[営業利益]の減少[低下, 落ち込み]
weaker sales 売上の減少, 販売の悪化, 販売の落ち込み, 販売低迷
▸The *weak* yen is a threat to U.S. economic recovery. 円安は, アメリカの景気回復を脅かす要因だ.

weaken 動 弱くなる, 弱まる, 軟化する, 弱化する, 弱体化する, 低迷する, 悪化する, 下落する, 低下する, 減少する
weaken the balance sheet 財務内容[バランス・シート]を悪化させる
weakened asset quality 資産の質の悪化
weakened profitability 収益性の低下
weakened service quality サービスの質の低下
weakening demand 需要の減退, 需要の軟化, 需要低迷
weakening economy 景気低迷, 景気鈍化

▸The nation's virtuous cycle of growth is *weakening*. 日本の成長の好循環は，弱まっている。

weaker yen 円安
▸The *weaker yen* until recently had been the only lifesaver for the export-reliant economy and stock prices. これまでの円安は，輸出頼みの景気と株価の「唯一の救命ボート」だった。

weakness 名 弱み, 短所, 弱点, 弱含み, 低下, 落ち込み, 減少, 軟化, 下落, 低迷
cyclical weakness 景気後退による低迷
economic weakness 景気低迷, 景気減速
share price weakness 株価低迷, 株価の軟化［下落］
weakness in output 生産低下, 生産の低迷

wealth 名 富, 資産, 財産, 富裕, 資源, 価値のある産物 (⇒sovereign wealth fund)
beginning-of-period wealth 期首の財産額 (=initial wealth)
expected wealth value 期待資産価値
financial wealth 金融資産
income and wealth 所得と資産, 所得と富
maximization of wealth 富の極大化 (=wealth maximization)
mineral wealth 鉱物資源
national wealth statistics 国富統計
negative wealth effect 逆資産効果
real wealth 実質資産
shareholder wealth 株主の富
terminal wealth 期末の財産額 (=end-of-period wealth)
vast wealth 巨万の富, 豊富な資産・財産
wealth effect 資産効果, 富効果
wealth maximization 資産の極大化, 富の極大化
wealth tax 富裕税

▸*Wealth* has been boosted by rallies in stock and bond markets. 株式相場と債券相場の急騰［上昇］で，資産が増加している［資産が膨らんでいる］。

Web 名 ネット上の情報通信網, ホームページ, ウェブ (=homepage, web, WWW: **World Wide Web**の略)
Web account ウェブ口座, ホームページ上の口座
Web advertisement ウェブ広告
Web bank ウェブ・バンク (=virtual bank)
Web-based stock trading 株のネット取引, 株のオンライン取引
Web-based training ウェブ・ベースト・トレーニング《略 WBT》
Web development service ウェブ作成サービス
Web marketing ウェブ・マーケティング (=Internet marketing)
Web sales ホームページ販売, ネット販売
Web shop 電子商店, 仮想店舗 (=EC site, Internet shop, online shop)

Web advertising business ウェブ広告事業
▸Yahoo Japan's quarterly net profit grew 29 percent, helped by its online auction and *Web advertising business*. ヤフーの四半期税引き後利益は，ネット・オークション（競売）とウェブ広告事業に支えられて29％増加した。

Web retailer ネット販売業者
▸*Web retailer* Amazon.com Inc. launched its digital music store, Amazon MP3, with nearly 2.3 million songs without copy protection. 米ネット販売大手のアマゾン・ドット・コムが，コピー制限のない楽曲を約230万曲揃えて，ネット音楽配信サービス［デジタル・ミュージック・ストア］の「アマゾンMP3」を始めた。

Web site ホームページ, ウェブ・サイト, サイト (=homepage, Web page, website; ⇒shopping)
access the Web site ホームページにアクセスする
create a Web site サイトを立ち上げる
investment Web site 投資情報サイト, 投資サイト
launch a Web site ホームページ［ウェブ・サイト］を開設する
live Web site 中継ホームページ
set up a Japanese-language Web site 日本語のホームページを設ける
subscription Web site 有料サイト, 有料ウェブ・サイト
visit the Web site ホームページを訪れる, ホームページを訪問する
Web site advertisement ホームページ広告, ネット広告 (=Web advertising)
Web site operator サイト運営業者

▸The company expects the sales of its own products to increase as more customers visit its *Web site*. 同社は，自社サイトを訪れる客の増加に伴う自社製品の売上増を期待している。

WEF 世界経済フォーラム (**World Economic Forum**の略)

weighted average 加重平均, 総平均, 等価率
weighted average common shares outstanding 発行済み普通株式の加重平均株式数
weighted average discount rate 加重平均割引率
weighted average interest rates on short-term borrowings 短期借入金の加重平均金利

weighted average life 加重平均償還期間
weighted average method 加重平均法, 総平均法
weighted average number of common shares outstanding 発行済み株式数の加重平均, 社外流通普通株式の加重平均株式数
weighted average number of shares outstanding 発行済み株式数の加重平均, 発行済み株式の加重平均株式数
weighted average price 加重平均価格
weighted average time 加重平均期間
▶Earnings per common share are based on the *weighted average* number of shares outstanding. 普通株1株当たり純利益は, 発行済み株式数の加重平均に基づいて計算されています。

weighted mean 加重平均 (= weighted average)

weighting 名 ウエイト付け, 加重付け, 〈株式・債券の〉組入れ比率, 構成比率, 調整比率, 加算手当, リスク・ウェート
bond weighting 債券の組入れ比率
index weighting 指数の組入れ比率
risk weighting リスク・ウェート
weighting allowance 地域手当, 地域調整手当

weights and measures 度量衡

welfare 名 福祉, 厚生, 福利厚生, 福祉事業
community welfare 地域福祉
employee welfare fund 従業員福利厚生基金
social welfare 社会福祉
welfare expense 福利厚生費
welfare facilities for workers 勤労者福祉施設
welfare-to-work program 「福祉から就労」プログラム, 「福祉から仕事へ」プログラム

well 名 井戸, 油井(ゆせい), ガス井, ウエル
development well 開発井
exploratory well 試掘井, 探鉱井
gas well ガス井
injection well 圧入井
oil well 油井
stripper well 零細井, ストリッパー・ウエル

well-capitalized bank 自己資本が充実した銀行

well-developed market 成熟した市場

well-established 確立した, 定着した, 定評のある, 有名な
well-established brand 有名ブランド
well-established company 大手企業

well-informed sources 消息筋

well-known in the art 技術上周知の

well positioned 好位置にある, 有利な立場にある

▶We are *well positioned* in one of the outstanding global growth industries. 際立った世界の成長産業のなかで, 当社は確固たる地位を占めています。

wellhead price 〈原油や天然ガスの〉井戸元価格, 油田渡し価格

wellness 名 健康, ウエルネス
wellness market ウエルネス・マーケット
wellness program 健康増進計画, ウエルネス・プログラム

West Texas Intermediate ウェスト・テキサス・インターミディエート《略 WTI》

whaling 捕鯨, 捕鯨業
aboriginal whaling 先住民生存捕鯨
antiwhaling nation 反捕鯨国
coastal whaling 沿岸捕鯨
commercial whaling 商業捕鯨
International Convention for the Regulation of Whaling 国際捕鯨取締条約
International Whaling Commission 国際捕鯨委員会《略 IWC》
pro-whaling nation 捕鯨容認国
research whaling 調査捕鯨
whaling nation 捕鯨国
whaling resources 捕鯨資源
▶Iceland may resume commercial *whaling* outside the International Whaling Commission. アイスランドは, 国際捕鯨委員会の枠外で国際商業捕鯨を再開するかもしれない。

when-issued 形 発行日取引の

whistleblower [whistle-blower] 内部告発者, 密告者
▶*Whistleblowers* remain insufficiently protected. 内部告発者の保護は, 未だに不十分な状況だ。

whistleblowing [whistle-blowing] 内部告発, 密告
▶*Whistleblowing* by employees continued in the case of the major confectioner which shipped and sold cakes made with expired milk. 消費期限切れの牛乳を使って製造した洋菓子を出荷, 販売した大手菓子メーカーの場合は, 従業員からの内部告発が相次いだ。

white-color job cuts 事務職の削減
▶Ford Motor Co. announced a revised turnaround plan that calls for 10,000 more *white-collar job cuts* and additional plant closures. フォードは, 事務職1万人の追加削減と工場閉鎖の拡大を求める企業再生修正案を発表した。

white knight 白馬の騎士, 友好的買収者, 善意

の買収者，友好的な支援者，友好的な第三者，友好的企業，友好的株主，ホワイト・ナイト（「ホワイト・ナイト」は，敵対的なM&A（企業の合併・買収）にさらされている企業に対して，より好条件での買収を申し出る別の友好的な関係にある企業）

white squire 純白の従者，ホワイト・スクワイア（敵対的買収を未然に防ぐため，相当数の株式を買い取って株の買占めを封じたり，不振な株取引が行われていないかチェックしたりする者を指す）

whole life [**whole-life**] 終身の （＝whole term）
　whole life annuity 終身年金
　whole life insurance 終身保険

wholesale 形 卸売りの，大企業向けの，機関投資家向けの，大口の，大量の，大規模な，無制限の，一網打尽の，無差別な，ホールセール，名 卸売り（⇒retail）
　retail and wholesale markets 小口投資家向け市場と機関投資家向け市場
　retail and wholesale sector 流通業
　wholesale bank 法人向け銀行，大企業向け銀行，ホールセール・バンク
　wholesale banking 卸売銀行業務，大口金融
　wholesale deposits 大口預金
　wholesale investor 機関投資家
　wholesale price index 企業物価指数(旧卸売物価指数)
　wholesale trade 卸売り，卸売業
　▶*Wholesale* prices rose 1.3 percent from the previous year, reflecting a jump in prices of steel and oil products.　企業物価(旧卸売物価)指数は，鉄鋼や石油製品の価格の上昇を反映して，前年比で1.3%上昇した。

wholesale prices 卸売物価，日本の企業物価指数
　▶The Bank of Japan corporate goods price index, designed to gauge *wholesale prices*, hit 105.6 against a base of 100 for 2005.　企業の卸売り段階での商品価格を示す日銀の企業物価指数(2005年＝100)は，105.6となった。

wholesaler 名 卸売業者，卸し企業，問屋，元売り
　▶Nippon Oil Corp., the nation's biggest oil *wholesaler*, and Japan Energy Corp. have agreed to enter into a broad-based tieup, including on developing fuel cell technology.　石油元売り国内最大手の新日本石油とジャパンエナジーは，燃料電池技術の開発などの分野で包括的な業務提携を結ぶことで合意した。

wholly own 完全所有する，全部所有する，完全子会社化する，全額出資する
　▶Citigroup Inc. *wholly owned* Nikko Cordial Corp. through a stock swap deal in January 2008.　シティグループが，株式交換取引で2008年1月に日興コーディアルグループを完全子会社化した。

wholly owned subsidiary 完全所有子会社，完全子会社，全部所有子会社，全額出資子会社，100%所有子会社，100%出資子会社，100%子会社（＝fully owned subsidiary, fully owned unit, totally held subsidiary, wholly owned affiliate）
　put ... under one's wing as a wholly owned subsidiary …を完全子会社として…の傘下に収める
　turn ... into a wholly owned subsidiary …を完全子会社化する
　wholly owned finance subsidiary 完全所有金融子会社，全額出資金融子会社，100%所有の金融子会社
　▶Maruha will put Nichiro under its wing as a *wholly owned subsidiary* through a share swap.　株式交換方式で，マルハはニチロを完全子会社としてマルハの傘下に収める。

widen 動 拡大する，広げる，大きくする，規模拡大する，広がる，大きくなる
　▶The firms' group loss *widened* to ¥70 billion in the six months through September.　同社の連結赤字は，9月中間決算で700億円に拡大した。

wider loss 損失拡大，赤字拡大
　▶The company expects a *wider loss* for fiscal 2009.　同社は，2009年度は赤字拡大を見込んでいる。

wildcat 名 試掘井 （石油やガスが生産されていなかった地域に掘られる試掘井）

win a bidding competition 競争入札で落札する
　▶We *won a bidding competition* for the second telecommunications license in Australia.　当社は，オーストラリアで第二種通信事業者の免許を競争入札で落札しました。

win a contract 契約を獲得する，受注する
　▶A joint venture including Penta-Ocean *won a contract* for about ¥2.6 billion in this construction project.　この建設工事では，五洋建設などの共同事業体(JV)が約26億円で受注した。

win-win-win solution 三方一両得の解決策

wind 名 風，風力
　wind energy potential 風力エネルギーの潜在能力
　wind-generating potential 風力発電能力
　wind generation 風力発電

wind resource 風力資源
wind-riched 風力の豊かな
wind turbine 風力タービン (⇒**assembly line**)
wind farm 発電用風車の列, 風力発電施設
▶The U.S. 28 states now have utility-scale *wind farms* feeding electricity into the local grid. 米国の28州は現在, 公益事業体規模の風力発電施設をもって, 地元の送電線網に電力を供給している.
wind-generated electricity 風力発電
▶The cost of *wind-generated electricity* continues to fall. 風力発電のコストは, 下がり続けている.
wind power 風力
▶*Wind power* can meet all domestic electricity needs as well as all domestic energy needs. 風力は, 国内の総電力需要と国内の総エネルギー需要を満たすことができる.
wind up 解散する, 清算する, 整理する, 事業停止する, 企業を閉鎖する
▶Directors of the company decided at an extraordinary board meeting to *wind up* the ailing company. 同社の取締役は, 臨時取締役会で経営不振に陥っている同社を解散することを決めた.
windfall 名 タナボタ利益, 思わぬ利益, 思いがけない利益, 望外の利益, 臨時利益, 偶発利益, 過剰利得, タナボタ[棚ぼた], 思いがけない幸運, 追い風 (=windfall profit), 形 意外の, 一時的な, 一回かぎりの, 臨時の
▶The firm concealed its real intention of boosting its share price and realizing a handsome *windfall* through a sell-off of its own shares. 同社は, 自社株の株価つり上げと自社株の売り抜けで大幅な利益を得ることが, 同社の本当の目的であることを隠していた.
windfall profit tax 超過所得税
winding up 解散, 清算, 整理, 事業停止, 企業閉鎖
　　compulsory winding up 強制解散
　　voluntary winding up 任意解散
window-dress 動 粉飾する, 粉飾決算する (「粉飾決算」は, 有価証券報告書の虚偽記載などで, 企業の経営を実態以上に良く見せかける行為)
▶The company may have *window-dressed* accounts over three years up to March 2007. 同社は, 2007年3月期までの3年間にわたって, 決算を粉飾していた疑いがある.
window dressing 粉飾, 粉飾決算 (= window-dressed accounts, window-dressing accounts, window dressing settlement)
　　be involved in the window dressing 粉飾に関与する, 粉飾決算に関与する

financial window-dressing 会計操作
window-dressing of accounts 粉飾決算 (= window dressing settlement)
▶Lax internal controls at the auditing firm allowed the *window dressing* of the company's accounts to go unnoticed. この監査法人の甘い内部チェック体制が, 同社の粉飾決算を見過ごした.
wing 名 一翼, 分派, 保護, 活動下
　　spread [stretch] one's wings 能力を十分に発揮する
　　under one's wing …の保護下に, …の傘下に
▶Maruha will put Nichiro under its *wing* as a wholly owned subsidiary through a share swap. 株式交換方式で, マルハはニチロを完全子会社としてマルハの傘下に収める.
winner 名 勝ち組, 勝ち組企業, 成功企業, 勝者, 値上がり銘柄
　　winners and losers 勝ち組と負け組, 値上がり銘柄と値下がり銘柄
winner of a contract 元請業者, 契約獲得企業, 受注者, 施行業者, 落札者 (= contract winner)
▶The *winner of a contract* must be periodically monitored by an independent institution. 落札者に対しては, 独立した第三者機関が定期的にチェックしなければならない.
winner of the bidding 落札業者, 受注者, 受注業者
▶The company's executives told the preselected *winners of the bidding* that the construction project would be divided into seven parts. 同社の複数の役員は, この建設工事を7つの工区に分けることを, 事前に選定した受注業者に知らせていた.
winning product ヒット商品
▶The company needs to produce *winning products* to restore shareholder and consumer confidence. 同社が株主や消費者の信頼を回復するには, ヒット商品を送り出さなければならない.
WIP 仕掛品 (**work in progress, work in process** の略)
WIPO 世界知的所有権機関 (**World Intellectual Property Organization** の略)
wireless communications 無線通信, 無線通信機器
▶An IC tag consists of a microchip and a tiny antenna for *wireless communications*. ICタグは, マイクロチップ(微細な半導体片)と無線通信用のアンテナを組み合わせた構造だ.
wireless telecommunications 無線通信

▶The use of *wireless telecommunications* would allow the development of a high-speed network at a speed of 156 megabits per second (Mbps)—the same as for fiber optic lines—at about 10 percent the cost of developing a fiber-optic network.　無線通信を使うと，光ファイバー網の整備に比べて約10分の1の費用で，光ファイバー回線並みの最大通信速度毎秒156メガビットの高速通信網の整備ができる。

withdraw 動　〈預金などを〉引き出す，〈預金などを〉引き揚げる，〈通貨などを〉回収する，〈市場などから〉撤退する，取り消す，打ち切る，撤回する
　withdraw deposits　預金を引き出す，預金を引き揚げる
　withdraw from the market　市場から撤退する（=pull out of the market）
　withdraw money　金を引き出す，金を下ろす，払い戻す，通貨などを回収する，解約する
▶The company *withdrew* from textile and food production under its revival plan.　同社は，同社の事業再生計画に基づいて，繊維と食品の生産事業から撤退した。

withdrawal 名　撤退，脱退，離脱，撤回，回収，〈預金の〉引出し，引落し，払戻し，取消し，解約，〈出資者や株主に対する〉利益の分配，資本の減少
　bank withdrawal　銀行預金引出し
　double withdrawal　二重引落し（=double deduction）
　partial withdrawal　一部撤退，部分撤退
　withdrawal before maturity　期日前解約
　withdrawal from the core business　中核事業からの撤退，主力事業からの撤退
　withdrawal of deposits　預金の引出し，預金の流出
▶The bank made 30,000 double *withdrawals* for transfers from customer accounts.　同行は，顧客の口座振替えで3万件の二重引落しをした。
▶The *withdrawal* of the company from Japan has yet to be confirmed.　同社の日本からの撤退は，まだ確認されていない。

withhold 動　源泉徴収する，天引きする，保留する，抑える，差し控える，避ける，公表しないでおく
　withheld amounts　源泉徴収による預り金
　withhold at source　源泉徴収する，源泉課税する
▶Persons receiving dividends subject to Canadian withholding taxes, and who are also subject to U.S. income tax on these dividends will be entitled to either a credit or deduction with respect to the Canadian taxes *withheld* when computing their domestic tax.　カナダの源泉所得税が課される配当金の受取人が，その配当金についてさらに米国の所得税を課されるときは，受取人の国内税額を計算する際にカナダの源泉所得税について控除（税額控除もしくは所得控除）を受けることができます。

withholding 名　源泉徴収，〈給料の〉天引き，売り惜しみ
　income tax withholding　源泉所得税預り金（=income tax withheld of source）
　withholding at source　源泉徴収，源泉課税
　withholding income tax　源泉徴収所得税，源泉徴収に係る所得税，源泉所得税
　withholding tax　源泉徴収税，源泉課税，源泉所得税，源泉税，源泉徴収税額，源泉課税税額（=withholding）
▶Dividends paid to owners of the Corporation's common shares who are not residents of Canada, within the meaning of the Canadian Income Tax Act, are subject generally to a 25 percent *withholding* tax.　配当金がカナダ所得税法で規定されているカナダの居住者でない当社の普通株主に社払われた場合，その配当金には，一般に25%の源泉所得税［源泉徴収税］が課されます。

work 動　働く，仕事をする，…を担当する，…を仕事場とする，動かす，操作する，加工する，効果がある，影響する，作動する
▶Toyota and Nissan agreed to *work* together on hybrid vehicle developments in 2002.　トヨタと日産は，2002年にハイブリッド車の開発で提携することに合意した。

work 名　仕事，事業，作業，工事，労働，職，工場（複数形），製作所（複数形），ワーク
　clerical work　事務職，事務的な仕事
　long-term construction work　長期請負工事
　partly finished work　半成工事
　place of work　職場
　spoiled work　仕損じ品
　standards of field work　実施基準
　temporary work　臨時雇用
　work flow　仕事の流れ，作業の流れ，ワーク・フロー
　work in process　仕掛（しかけ・しかかり）品《略 WIP》（=goods in process, work in progress）
　work opportunity tax credit　職業機会減税
　work order　業務委託，業務委託書，製造指図書
　work permit　労働許可証
　work rules　就業規則
　work simplification　作業単純化，業務の簡素化
　work-to-rule　順法闘争（=work-to-rule struggle）

work visa 就労ビザ
works charge 工場経営
works committee 職場委員会
works council 労使協議会, 工場協議会
▸More than two-thirds of our employees face a growing strain in balancing *work* and family demands.　当社従業員の3分の2以上は, 仕事と家族の要求との間のバランスをとるのが重荷, と感じるようになっています。
▸The unions of Nippon Steel Corp. and JFE Steel Corp. demanded hikes in payments for late-night *work* as part of their requests.　新日本製鉄やJFEスチールの労組は, 要求の一部として残業代の引上げを要求した。

work sharing system ワーク・シェアリング, ワークシェア, ワーク・シェアリング・システム (1人当たりの労働時間を短縮して雇用を分かち合う制度)
▸The *work sharing system* may lead to a decline in productivity.　ワーク・シェアリングは, 生産性の低下につながる可能性がある。

workday 名 就業日, 勤務日, 平日
worker 名 労働者, 勤労者, 就労者, 就業者, 働き手, 従業員, 人材
　commitment of workers 社員の帰属意識
　excess workers 余剰人員
　extra worker 臨時雇い労務者
　full time worker フルタイム従業員
　illegal worker 不法就労者
　lower skilled worker 未熟練労働者
　more educated workers 高学歴労働者
　non-union workers 未組織労働者
　part-time worker パート, パート従業員, パート社員, パートタイマー
　public sector worker 公務員
　regular worker 常用労働者
　semi-skilled worker 半熟練労働者
　skilled worker 熟練労働者
　time worker 時間給労働者
　worker buyout 従業員の経営権買取り
　Worker Dispatching Law 人材派遣法
　Worker Profiling and Reemployment Services 労働者選別・再就職支援サービス《略 WPRS》
　workers compensation insurance system 労災保険制度, 労災保険
　workers household 勤労者世帯, サラリーマン世帯
▸The standstill in wages is a result of structural employment factors, including the increasing rate of nonregular *workers* such as part-timers. 賃金が上昇しないのは, パートといった非正規社員の比率の高まりなど, 雇用をめぐる構造的要因が原因だ。

workforce 名 就業者, 労働力, 労働人口, 従業員, 社員, 人員, 全従業員, 全社員 (=labor force, work force)
　workforce development 労働力開発
　Workforce Investment Act of 1998 1998年労働力投資法
　workforce reduction 人員削減
▸GM is forced to make large cuts to its *workforce* due to annual sales fall.　GMは, 年間販売台数の減少で, 大規模な人員整理を余儀なくされている。
▸Japanese firms initially advanced into the Chinese market mainly due to the cheaper *workforce* there.　日本企業は当初, 主に中国の安価な労働力を目当てに中国市場に進出した。

working 形 経営の, 運転する, 運用している, 営業の, 仕事上の, 作業の, 労働の, 職場での, 実用の, 実際の役に立つ, 機能している, 実動の
　working assets 運用資産
　working capital 運転資本, 運転資金 (=operating capital)
　working capital ratio 流動比率
　working conditions 労働条件, 労働環境
　working expense 営業費 (=operating expense, working cost)
　working environment 労働環境, 作業環境, 職場の環境
　working fund 運転資金, 運転資本, 営業資金
　working-level negotiation 事務レベルの折衝, 事務レベルの交渉
　working life 勤続期間
　working relationship 職場の人間関係, 職場での付き合い
　working rules 就業規則
　working team 特別調査班, 作業班, ワーキング・チーム
▸Capital stock was sold to provide additional *working* capital.　追加的運転資金の調達のため, 株式を発行しました。

working committee 作業委員会
▸Wal-Mart Stores Inc., the world's largest retailer, and trading house Sumitomo Corp. plan to establish a *working committee* within this year to study Wal-Mart's entry into Japan.　世界最大の小売業である米ウォルマート・ストアーズと住友商事は, 年内に作業委員会を設けて, ウォルマートの日本進出について検討する方針だ。

working day 営業日, 労働日, 作業日

▶The company has doled out the extra bonus of ¥500 to all employees for 41 *working days* in a row. 同社では，41営業日連続で500円の特別ボーナスを全社員に支給[配布]している。

working group 作業部会, 作業委員会, 作業班, ワーキング・グループ
▶A *working group* of the Financial System Council put together a report concerning capital adequacy requirements. 金融審議会の作業部会が，自己資本比率規制に関する報告書をまとめた。

working hours 就業時間, 勤務時間, 作業時間, 労働時間
▶Reducing *working hours* and increasing childcare leave are essential to help husbands and wives raise their children. 夫婦が協力してこどもを育てられるようにするには，勤務時間の短縮や育児休業の拡大などが欠かせない。

workmen's accident compensation 労働者災害補償, 労災補償

workout 名 トレーニング, 訓練, 体調調整, 〈機械などの〉点検, 適性試験, 処理, 整理, 〈事業部ごとの〉問題点改善, ワークアウト

workplace 名 職場, 仕事場, 作業場 (=worksite)
 bullying in the workplace 職場でのいじめ, 職場のいじめ, 職場いじめ
 workplace bullying 職場のいじめ (=bullying in the workplace)
 workplace training 現場訓練
▶Abusive language, shouting or intimidation was cited as the most common form of bullying in the *workplace*. 職場でのいじめの形態として，「ののしる，どなる，威嚇する」が挙げられた。

workshop 名 仕事場, 作業場, 工場, 研究会, 講習会, 討論会, ワークショップ

workstation 名 個人用高性能パソコン, 作業端末, ワークステーション《略 WS》 (=work station)

workweek 名 週労働時間, 週平均労働時間
 factory workweek 製造業の週平均労働時間 (=workweek in manufacturing)
 five-day workweek 週5日制
 statutory workweek 法定労働時間
 true 5-day workweek 完全週休2日制
▶The segment was able to meet a portion of the demand for additional volume through expanded production lines and expanded *workweeks*. 当部門は，生産ラインの増設や週労働時間の延長などで，製品の需要増の一部に対応することができました。

World Bank 世界銀行 (国際復興開発銀行 (IBRD)の通称。⇒**yuan**)
▶The *World Bank* enjoys a triple-A credit rating. 世界銀行は，トリプルAの格付け(信用格付け)を受けている。

World Economic Forum 世界経済フォーラム《略 **WEF**》(世界各国の政財界人や学識経験者が集まって，毎年1月にスイスのリゾート地ダボスで開かれる世界経済フォーラム年次総会は，ダボス会議(Davos Conference)と呼ばれる)
▶In his speech at the *World Economic Forum* in Davos, Prime Minister Fukuda proposed a plan under which each country would cut greenhouse gas emissions by a quantified target. ダボスの世界経済フォーラム(ダボス会議)の演説で，福田首相は，温室効果ガス排出削減について国別総量目標を設定する構想を示した。

world economy 世界経済 (=global economy)
▶The *world economy* has seen a slowing in growth. 世界経済は，成長が減速している。

world market 世界市場, グローバル市場 (=global market, international market)
▶The company announced a provision of U.S. $200 million in view of a major corporate reorganization to improve its competitiveness in *world markets*. 同社は，グローバル市場での競争力を高めるための大規模な企業再編を視野に入れて，2億米ドルの引当金設定を発表した。

World Trade Organization 世界貿易機関《略 **WTO**》
▶The *World Trade Organization* issued its official condemnation of Chinese commercial practices in a dispute over car parts. 世界貿易機関(WTO)は，自動車部品をめぐる紛争で，中国の商慣習[商慣行]に対する公式の非難声明を出した。

writ 名 令状

write a policy 保険を引き受ける, 保険証券に署名する (=write an insurance policy)
▶Bond insurers *write policies* that promise to cover payments to bondholders if the entity that issued the bonds defaults. 金融保証会社[債券保険会社]は，債券発行体がデフォルト(債務不履行)になった場合に，債券保有者への(元本と利息の)支払い補償を約束する保険を引き受けている。

write down 〈帳簿価格を〉引き下げる, 〈評価を〉引き下げる, 評価減を計上する, 評価損を計上する, 貸倒れ引当金を計上する, 償却する, 再評価する, 記録する (⇒**market value, one-time charge**)
 inventory written down 棚卸し評価損

write down the assets to market value 資産を時価ベースで再評価する

▶Merrill Lynch & Co. will *write down* $5.5 billion for bad bets on subprime mortgages and leveraged loans. 米大手証券のメリルリンチは，低所得者向け住宅融資「サブプライム・ローン」とレバレッジド・ローンの見通しが暗いため，55億ドルの評価損を計上する。

write-down [writedown] 名 評価減，評価損，評価引下げ，減損

　asset write-down 資産評価損，資産の簿価格引下げ

　inventory write-down 棚卸し評価減 (＝inventory written down)

　original write-down 当初の評価損

▶Subprime mortgage-related *write-downs* across the banking industry were more than $40 billion in the third quarter. 銀行業界全体で，米国のサブプライム・ローン(低所得者向け住宅融資)関連の評価損計上額は，第3四半期決算で400億ドルを上回った。

write off 〈債権を〉帳消しにする，〈債権を〉処理する［償却する，放棄する］，〈評価額を〉引き下げる，〈価格を〉引き下げる，減価償却する，〈費用などを〉経費として申告する

　write off a production plant 生産設備を償却する

　write off a 10 million yen debt 1,000万円の借金を帳消しにする

　write off bad debts 貸倒れ損失を計上する

▶Losses incurred by *writing off* nonperforming loans are not generally taxable in the United States. 不良債権処理で生じた損失額は，米国では一般に課税の対象とはならない。

write-off 名 〈債権の〉帳消し，〈債権の〉処理［放棄］，消却，評価減，評価引下げ，償却，貸倒れ償却，貸倒れ損失，減価償却，〈資産の〉除却［切捨て］，削除，〈帳簿の〉締切り (＝writeoff; ⇒delinquent balances)

　account write-offs 貸倒れ損失

　credit write-offs 不良債権の償却

　debt write-off 債務の帳消し

　equity write-offs 株式評価損

　net write-off 正味貸倒れ償却

　loan write-off 債権放棄，債務免除 (＝debt forgiveness, loan forgiveness, loan waiver)

　loan write-off costs 債権処理費用，不良債権処理費用

　nontaxable write-off 無税償却

　write-off interval 償却期間

　write-off of bad loans 不良債権処理，不良債権の償却 (＝bad loan write-off, write-off of nonperforming loans)

　write-off of costs 特別損失

　write-offs of appraisal losses in fixed assets 固定資産の減損処理

▶In leading economies abroad, the disposal of nonperforming loans is made in most cases through a nontaxable *write-off*. 海外の主要国では，不良債権処理は多くの場合，無税償却で行われている。

write-up 名 〈新聞・雑誌などの〉記事，評価増，評価益，評価引上げ，〈資産の〉過大評価

wrongful 形 不法な，不当な，違法な

　wrongful act [conduct] 不法行為

　wrongful dismissal 不当解雇

　wrongful interference 不法妨害

　wrongful use 不正使用

　wrongful user 不正使用者

WTI テキサス産軽質油，ウェスト・テキサス・インターミディエート(**West Texas Intermediate**の略。米テキサス州西部とニューメキシコ州東南部で産出される軽質の原油。米国の市況動向を示す代表銘柄)

WTO 世界貿易機関(**World Trade Organization**の略。⇒**World Trade Organization**)

　the new round of WTO talks 新ラウンド，新多角的貿易交渉

　WTO General Council WTO一般理事会

　WTO panel WTO紛争処理小委員会(パネル)

▶After both China and Taiwan became *WTO* members in 2002, Taiwan's investment in China, led by information technology firms, increased rapidly. 中国と台湾が2002年に世界貿易機関(WTO)に加盟してから，IT(情報技術)産業を中心に台湾の対中投資が急増した。

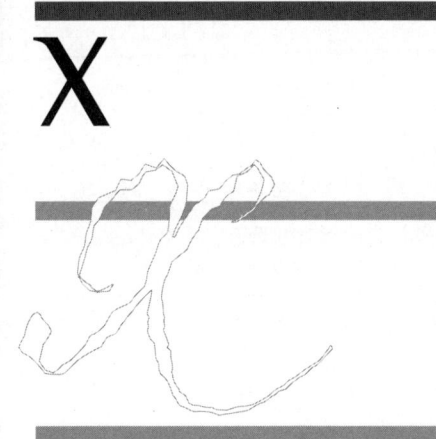

X

X chart X管理図
X factor 不確定要素 (=uncertain factor, uncertainty)
X in 利息落ち (=ex interest)
X-inefficiency X非効率
X pr 優先権利落ち (=ex privileges)
x.a. 諸権利落ち,全権利落ち (=ex all)
XBRL 拡張的財務報告言語 (財務報告用のコンピュータ言語)
XC 利落ち (=ex coupon)
XD 配当落ち (=ex div., ex dividend)
Xenocurrency 国外流通通貨,ユーロダラー
XI 利息落ち,利落ち (=ex interest, x-int.)
Xinhuashe 新華社 (=New China News Agency: 中国の国営通信社)
XR 権利落ち (=ex rights, xr, x-rts.)
XW 権利証落ち,新株引受権落ち,ワラント落ち (=ex warrants, x-warr., xw: 新株引受権利証書が付いていないこと)

Y y

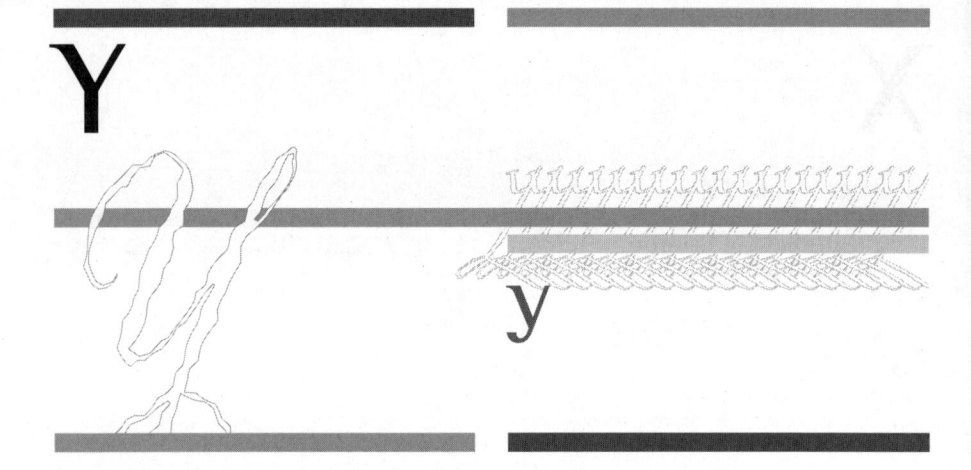

year 名 年, 年度, 事業年度, 期 (⇒business year, current fiscal year, current year, fiscal year, full year, half year)

> 年度と年について➡一般に年次報告書で「年度」とは事業年度(営業年度: business year), 会計年度(企業の会計期間: fiscal year)のことで,「年」は暦年のことである。事業年度と暦年は基本的に違うが, 一般に4月1日から始まって翌年の3月31日に終了する日本企業の事業年度と比べて, 米国企業の場合には事業年度の開始時期と終了時期が暦年と同じで1月1日から12月31日までの1年間となっているのが普通である(6月末, 9月末や10月末をもって終了する1年間を事業年度とする企業もある)。つまり, 事業年度＝暦年の関係にある。そこで, この関係にある12月期決算企業の場合には, とくに原文がfiscal yearとかbusiness yearとなっていなくても, 翻訳上「年度」を用いることも「年」を用いることもできる。

average exchange rates for the year 事業年度の平均為替レート (⇒income statement amounts)
base year 基準年, 基準年度
both on the month and on the year 前月比, 前年同月比ともに
during fiscal year or quarter 年度・期中
during the course of the current (fiscal) year 今期
during the year to come 年初来
each of the years in the three-year period ended December 31, 2008 2008年12月31日に終了した3年間の各事業年度
first half of the year 上半期, 上期
for the fourth year running 4期連続, 4年連続 (＝for the fourth straight year)
for the year as a whole 通年で
from a year ago 前年比, 前年比で, 前年同期比
in the first half of current fiscal year 今年度上半期
in the year-on-year comparison 前年同期比で, 前年同月比で
insurance year 保険年度
on a full year basis 通年で
over a year ago 前年同期比で, 前年同月比
over the past year 前年同月比で
tax year 課税年度, 税務年度, 納税年度, 会計年度, 事業年度, 会計年度 (＝fiscal year, taxable year, year of assessment)
taxable year 課税年度
the preceding year 前年度, 前期
the third straight year 3年連続, 3期連続
the year just ended 前期
the year then ended 同日をもって終了した事業年度
the year to Dec. 31, 2009 2009年12月期
the year under review 当年度, 当期 (＝the period under review)
working year 営業年度, 会計年度, 決算年度
year ending in March 3月終了事業年度, 3月期
year just ended 前期
year-on-year 前年同期比, 前年同月比, 前年比 (＝over a year ago, year-over-year)
year to March 2010 2010年3月期
year to date 年初[期首]から現在までの
year-to-year 前年同期比, 前年同月比 (＝year-on-year)
year through next March 来年3月期, 来年3月

までの事業年度
years in business 業歴

year earlier 前年, 前年比, 前年同期比 （＝year ago）
▸Sales of the overseas subsidiaries of Japanese companies grew 17.3 percent in U.S. dollar terms in the January-March quarter from a *year earlier*. 1—3月期は、日本企業の海外子会社の売上高が、米ドル・ベースで前年同期比17.3％伸びた。

year end 年末, 年度末, 期末, 決算期末 （⇒yearend）
  year-end balance 期末残高
  year-end current rates 決算日の為替レート［為替相場］
  year-end dividend 期末配当
  year-end tax adjustment 年末調整

year ended December 31 12月31日終了事業年度, 12月31日終了年度, 12月31日をもって終了した事業年度, 12月31日に終了した事業年度, 12月期, 12月期決算
▸We have audited the consolidated statements of income and cash flows for the *years ended December 31*, 2008, 2007 and 2006. 私どもは、2008年、2007年および2006年12月31日をもって終了した各事業年度の連結損益計算書と連結キャッシュ・フロー計算書について監査しました。

year-on-year 前年同期比, 前年同月比, 前年比 （＝over a year ago, year-over-year）
▸Sales at existing stores marked *year-on-year* drops of 17 percent in October from a year earlier. 既存店の10月の売上高は、前年同月比で17％減少した。

year-to-date highs 今年最高値, 今年の最高値
▸The firm has seen its share price plummet to about one-third of the *year-to-date highs* it recorded in January. 同社の株価は、1月につけた今年最高値の3分の1程度に急落した。

year under review 当期, 当年度
▸We further improved the service for business customers in the *year under review*. 当期は、法人顧客サービスをさらに改善しました。

yearend 名 年末, 年度末, 期末 （⇒**year end**）
▸Book value of the Corporation's common shares rose to $11 at *yearend* 2008. 当社普通株式1株当たり純資産［純資産額］は、2008年末現在で11ドルに上昇しています。

yearling 名 1年物(債券), 形 1年満期の
yearly 形 年に1度の, 1年の, 年間の

half-yearly report 半期報告, 半期報告書
yearly earnings 年間利益 （＝annual earnings）
yearly installment 年賦（ねんぷ）
yearly order 包括注文, 一括注文, 年度見越し注文 （＝blanket order）
yearly sales 年間売上, 年間売上高
▸Rakuten boasts *yearly sales* of ¥18 billion from a virtual shopping mall and online securities brokerage. 楽天は、仮想商店街やオンライン証券などで180億円の年間売上を誇る。

yellow pages 職業別電話帳, 業種別企業案内, インターネットの情報源の出所・分野をまとめたホームページ, イエロー・ページ

yen 名 円, 円相場
  appreciating yen 円高 （＝rise in the yen's value, yen's appreciation）
  depreciation of the yen 円安 （＝depreciating yen, yen depreciation）
  exchange value of the yen 円の為替相場
  in yen terms 円表示で, 円表示の （＝in yen-denominated terms）
  long dollar positions against the yen 円売りドル買い
  yen-dollar exchange rate 円ドル相場, 円・ドル相場, 円・ドルレート, 円の対ドルレート, 円とドルの為替レート
  yen exchange 円為替
  yen-selling and dollar-buying operations 円売り・ドル買い, 円売り・ドル買い操作, 円売り・ドル買いオペ, 円売り・ドル買いの動き （＝yen-selling, dollar-buying operations）
  yen's value 円相場, 円価値
  yen's value against the dollar 円の対米ドル相場
▸The strong *yen* during this period has been referred to as a crisis for Japan. この時期の円高は、日本の危機として語られている。

yen-buying, dollar-selling operation 円買い・ドル売り操作, 円買い・ドル売りオペ, 円買い・ドル売りの動き （＝yen-buying and dollar-selling operation）

yen credits 円借款
▸Japan will terminate the provision of new *yen credits* to China by 2008. 日本は、中国に対する新規円借款供与を2008年までに停止する。

yen-denominated government bond 円建て国債
▸Moody's Investors Service Inc. cut its rating on *yen-denominated government bonds* by two

notches to A2 from Aa3. ムーディーズ・インベスターズ・サービスは，円建て国債の格付けをAa3からA2に二段階引き下げた．

yen-denominated profits 円建て利益
▸The exchange rate of about ¥115 to the dollar has pushed up the firm's *yen-denominated profits*. 1ドル＝115円前後の為替相場が，同社の円建て利益を押し上げた．

yen loans 円借款 （＝yen-based loans, yen-denominated loans）
▸*Yen loans* are offered to developing countries as part of Japan's official development assistance. 円借款は，日本の政府開発援助（ODA）の一環として発展途上国に供与される．

yen-selling, dollar-buying operation 円売り・ドル買い，円売り・ドル買い操作，円売り・ドル買いオペ，円売り・ドル買いの動き （＝yen-selling and dollar-buying operations）
▸The government and the Bank of Japan implemented a *yen-selling, dollar-buying operation* for their fifth market intervention this year. 政府・日銀は，今年5回目の市場介入として円売り・ドル買いに踏み切った．

yield 動 〈利益，利子などを〉生む［もたらす］，〈権利などを〉譲る，譲渡する，委譲する，〈政権などを〉明け渡す，〈借金などを〉返済する
▸The bonds were sold to *yield* a rate of 10%. 社債発行の利回り率は，10%であった．

yield 名 〈株式・債券などの〉利回り，歩留（ぶど）まり，収益，イールド
　bond yield 債券利回り，長期国債利回り，長期債利回り
　earnings yield 収益率，利益率，株式利回り，益回り
　expected yield 期待利回り
　maturity yield 最終利回り，償還利回り
　redemption yield 償還利回り
　stock dividend yield 株式の配当利回り，配当利回り，株式の利回り
　stock yield 株式利回り
　the yield of the 10-year government bond 10年物国債の利回り
　yield adjustment 利回り調整 （⇒amount receivable）
　yield gap 利回りギャップ
　yield on investment 運用利回り
　yield on securities 有価証券利回り
　yield rate 歩留まり，利回り
　yield to call 繰上げ償還利回り（「繰上げ償還」は，債券を償還期限がこないうちに償還すること）
　yield to maturity 最終利回り，満期利回り《略 YTM》（「最終利回り」は，債券を購入して満期日まで債券を保有した場合の利回りのこと）
▸The *yield* on our stock at the current price is about 4 percent—the highest in our industry. 当社の株式の時価による投資収益率は約4%で，当業界では最高です．

yield curve 利回り曲線，イールド・カーブ
　イールド・カーブについて➡右上がりのイールド・カーブ（順イールド・カーブ）は，長期証券の利回り（長期金利）のほうが短期証券の利回り（短期金利）よりも高い状態を示し，景気下降期の後半から景気拡大期の前半にかけて生じることが多い．また，右下がりのイールド・カーブ（逆イールド・カーブ）は，短期証券の利回り（短期金利）のほうが長期証券の利回り（長期金利）よりも高い状態（長短金利の逆転現象）を示す．これは，中央銀行が金融引締めを行い，短期金利の高め誘導をした場合などに生じることが多い．
　coupon yield curve 債券のイールド・カーブ，国債のイールド・カーブ
　flattening of the yield curve 利回り曲線の平坦化，イールド・カーブのフラット化
　inverted yield curve 右下がりの曲線 （＝negative yield curve）
　negative yield curve 逆イールド，逆イールド・カーブ，右下がりの曲線
　positive yield curve 順イールド，順イールド・カーブ，右上がりの曲線 （＝normal yield, normal yield curve）
　steepening of the yield curve 利回り曲線のスティープ化，長短金利格差の拡大
　yield curve differential 利回り格差 （＝yield differential）
　yield curve inversion 逆イールド，長短金利の逆転，右下がりの曲線 （＝inverted yield curve）
　yield curve play イールド・カーブ裁定
　yield curve slope 利回り曲線の勾配，利回り曲線の傾き
　yield curve swap イールド・カーブ・スワップ（長期と短期の変動金利の交換取引）

young adult ヤング・アダルト （十代後半の人または成年に達したばかりの成人）

yr 年，年度 （＝year）

YTD 年初［期首］から現在までの （**year to date** の略）

yuan 名 〈中国の〉人民元 （＝the Chinese yuan; ⇒benchmark, revaluation）

Z

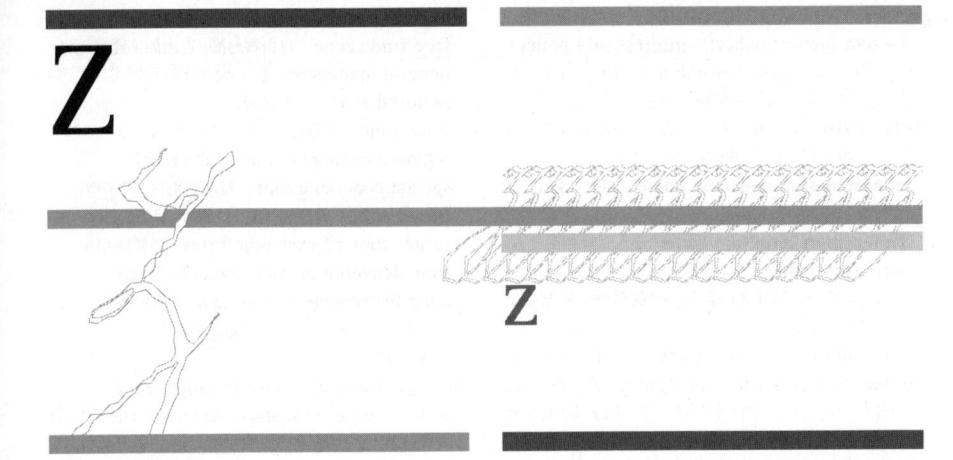

Z chart ゼット図表, Z図表
Z-score Z値 （企業の安全度を示す数値）
zaitech 財テク （＝financial technology）
ZD 無欠点運動, 無欠陥運動 （zero defectsの略）
ZEG 経済のゼロ成長 （zero economic growth の略）
zero 名 零, ゼロ
  zero-base budget ゼロベース予算, ゼロベース予算管理《略 ZBB》（＝zero-base budgeting, zero-based budget: 前年度の実績に関係なく, 採用された業務計画に対してだけ予算をつける方式）
  zero economic growth ゼロ経済成長《略 ZEG》
  zero gravity 無重力
  zero growth ゼロ成長, 開発抑止政策
  zero hour 予定行動開始時刻, 決定的瞬間
  zero option ゼロの選択, ゼロ選択, ゼロ・オプション
  zero profit ゼロ利潤
  zero rate ゼロ税率, 課税率ゼロ
  zero-rating ゼロ税率での課税, 非課税売買
  zero recovery 全額回収不能
  zero tolerance 不寛容主義, 例外なしの法規適用, 厳しい態度で臨むこと, ゼロ・トレランス
  zero-zero plan ゼロ・ゼロ計画, ゼロ選択
  zeros ゼロ・クーポン債 （＝zero coupon bonds）
zero-based 形 ゼロベースの
  zero-based budget ゼロベース予算, ゼロベース予算管理《略 ZBB》
zero coupon ゼロ・クーポン
  serial zero-coupon bond [issue] 連続ゼロ・クーポン債
  zero coupon bond ゼロ・クーポン債 （＝zero coupon issue: 券面にクーポン（利札）がなく表面利率がゼロの債券で, 定期的な利息の支払いがない代わりに発行時に額面の大幅割引価格で売り出される長期割引債）
  zero coupon convertible (bond) ゼロ・クーポン転換社債, ゼロ・クーポンCB
  zero coupon issue ゼロ・クーポン債
  zero coupon note ゼロ・クーポン債
  zero coupon securities ゼロ・クーポン証券
  ▶As of December 31, 2008, the outstanding *zero coupon* notes due 2015 had a face value at maturity of $130 million. 2008年12月31日現在, 2015年満期の発行済みゼロ・クーポン債の満期時の額面総額は, 1億3,000万ドルです。
zero defects 無欠点, 無欠陥, 無欠点運動, ゼロ・ディフェクト運動, ZD運動《略 ZD》（＝zero defects movement）
  ▶Thanks to continuous improvement efforts and an evolving culture that makes quality the top priority, our switching product has *zero defects*. 不断の改善努力と品質を最優先課題とする企業文化を通じて, 当社の交換機は無欠点を達成しました。
zero financing ゼロ金利ローン （＝free financing, no-interest loan, zero-interest loan, zero-interest rate loan, zero-percent financing）
  ▶GM ended *zero financing* and introduced other sales incentives. GMは, ゼロ金利ローンを止めて別の販売促進策を導入した。
zero-interest policy ゼロ金利政策 （＝zero-interest rate policy）
  ▶The lifting of the *zero-interest policy* does not result in better business performance. ゼロ金利政策の解除は, 企業の業績改善につながっていない。

zero-interest rate policy ゼロ金利政策 (=zero-interest policy; ⇒**interest rate policy**)
▶The BOJ lifted the *zero-interest rate policy*. 日銀が, ゼロ金利政策を解除した。

zero sum ゼロ和, ゼロサム (一方が得をすると, その分だけ他方が損をすること)
　non-zero-sum n-person game 非ゼロ和n人ゲーム
　two-person zero-sum game 2人ゼロ和ゲーム
　zero-sum game ゼロ和ゲーム, ゼロサム・ゲーム (ゲーム参加者の得失・損益がつねにゼロになるゲーム)
　zero-sum two persons game ゼロ和2人ゲーム
▶Power politics is a *zero-sum* game. 武力外交[力の外交]は, (片方が得すれば片方が損する)ゼロサム・ゲームだ。

zip code 郵便番号 (=zip, ZIP Code, ZIP code: 5桁の数字のうち最初の3桁は州・市, 後の2桁は郵便区)

zone 名 地域, 地区, 地帯, 範囲, 層, 圏, 区, ゾーン
　bonded zone 保税地区
　business zone 商業地区
　designated industrial zone 指定工業地域
　divisional management zone 部門管理層
　economic development zone 経済開発区
　enterprise zone 企業地区
　exclusive economic zone 排他的経済圏, 排他的経済水域, 排他的経済ブロック
　export processing zone 輸出加工区
　free trade zone 自由貿易圏, 自由加工貿易地域
　general management zone 全般管理層
　polluted zone 汚染地帯
　price zone 価格帯, プライス・ゾーン
　regional economic zone 局地経済圏
　special economic zone 経済特別区, 経済特区
　target zone 目標相場圏, 目標圏, 目標範囲
　target zone of exchange rates 目標圏相場
　zone delivered pricing 地域別輸送価格
　Zone Improvement Plan code 郵便番号, ZIPコード, ジップコード (=ZIP code)
　zone rate 区間運賃率
▶It is generally said that the danger *zone* for the publishing business starts when returns hit 40 percent. 出版事業の危険水域は返品率が4割に達した時点, と一般にいわれている。

zone pricing 地域別価格制, 地帯価格制, 地帯引渡し価格制度
　zone pricing policy 地域価格政策
　zone pricing system 地域価格制, 地帯価格制

zoning 名 地域制, 地区制, 売り場区分, ゾーニング
　commercial zoning 商業地区指定
　zoning regulations 地区規制

zoom 名 〈景気, 物価などが〉急上昇する, 急騰する, 急増する

ZPG 人口増加率ゼロ (**zero population growth** の略)

和英索引

あ

アーキテクチャー　architecture
アーンアウト契約　earn-out
IR活動　investor relations
相容れない　incompatible
愛顧　custom
アイコン　icon
ICタグ　IC tag
間柄　footing
愛着　attachment
相次ぐ　back-to-back
アイデア　concept
アイデア　idea
アイデア商品　novelty
空いている　vacant
相手方当事者　counterparty
相手先商標製造業者　OEM
相手先商標製造業者　original equipment manufacturer
相手先ブランド製造業者　OEM
相手先ブランド製造業者　original equipment manufacturer
アイテム　item
アイデンティティ　identity
iPS細胞　induced pluripotent stem sell
iPS細胞　iPS cell
あいまいな　gray
アウトソーシング　outsourcing
アウトプット　output
アウトフロー　outflow
アウトライト　outright
アウトレット　outlet
アカウンタビリティ　accountability
赤字　deficit
赤字　loss
赤字　red
赤字　red ink
赤字会社　below-par company
赤字額　loss
赤字拡大　wider loss
赤字決算　net loss
赤字店舗　money-losing store
赤字などを補塡する　fund
赤字の　money-losing
赤字の　negative
赤字の事業　money-losing operation
赤字予想　projected loss
赤字を出す　lose
あか抜けた　sophisticated
赤身の　lean
あからさまな　outright
上がり気味の　bullish
上がり気味の　buoyant
上がり下がり　fluctuation
上がり下がりする　fluctuate
上がる　gain

明るい　favorable
明るい　positive
明るい材料　good news
空き　clearance
空き　opening
空き地　vacancy
アキュムレーション　accumulation
明らかにする　define
明らかにする　reveal
明らかにする　unveil
悪影響　adverse effect
悪影響　negative effect
悪影響を与える　negative
悪材料　adverse effect
悪材料　negative
悪材料　negative effect
悪材料　negative factor
…が悪材料になる　suffer from
悪材料になる　suffer
悪循環　spiral
悪循環　vicious cycle
悪状況　plight
アクション　action
アクセス　access
アクセス　hit
アクセス料金　access charge
悪戦苦闘する　struggle
悪戦苦闘の　struggling
アクチュアリー　actuary
アクティブ　active
アグリビジネス　agribusiness
上げ相場　rally
明け渡す　quit
明け渡す　surrender
明け渡す　yield
アジア欧州会議　ASEM
アジア欧州首脳会議　ASEM
アジア太平洋経済協力会議　APEC
アジア太平洋経済協力会議　Asia-Pacific Economic Cooperation
アジア通貨単位　AMU
足跡　step
アジェンダ　agenda
アジオ　agio
足がかり　foothold
足がかり　footing
足がかり　platform
足かせ　drag
足どり　step
足取り　pace
足どりが重い　sluggish
足取りが鈍い　lackluster
足並み　coordination
足並み　pace
足場　foothold
足場　footing
足場　platform
足場　position
味わう　experience
預ける　lodge

預ける　put
アセアン自由貿易圏　AFTA
アセアン自由貿易地域　AFTA
アセスメント　assessment
アセット　asset
アセットバック証券　ABS
与える　assign
与える　award
与える　extend
与える　grant
与える　impose
与える　provide
アタッチメント　add-on equipment
頭金　down payment
新しい　innovative
新しい　new
新しくする　renovate
…に当たる　equivalent to
…に当たる　represent
悪化　collapse
悪化　decline
悪化　deterioration
悪化　downturn
悪化　drop
悪化　pressure
悪化した　weak
悪化している　ailing
悪化する　decline
悪化する　deteriorate
悪化する　weaken
圧縮　cutback
圧縮　reduction
圧する　press
斡旋　conciliation
斡旋業者　agent
圧倒的な　dominant
圧迫　press
圧迫　pressure
圧迫　squeeze
圧迫　stress
…に圧迫される　vulnerable
圧迫する　squeeze
アップストリーム　upstream
アップデートする　update
アップロードする　upload
集まり　session
集める　attract
集める　solicit
あつらえる　customize
圧力　pressure
圧力　stress
圧力団体　lobby
軋轢　friction
宛先　destination
宛名札　tag
あてにならない　incalculable
当てはめる　apply
…に充てる　use
当てる　earmark
当てる［充てる］　appropriate

後入れ先出し法 last-in, first out	亜流 follower	安定した fixed
後入れ先出し法 LIFO	あるいは付け値に非常に近い最高額 ovno	安定した solid
後押し boost		安定した stable
…が後押しする -backed	アルゴリズム取引 algorithm trading	安定状態 plateau
後押しする help		安定水準 plateau
後押しする sponsor	荒れ模様の dirty	安定する even
アドオン金利 add-on rate	…に合わせる tailor	安定する stabilize
後から加わった者 latecomer	合わせる fit	安定性 stability
後からついてくる follow	…案 initiative	安定操作 pegging
後順位の junior	案 formula	アンデス共同市場 ANCOM
後順位の subordinated	案 idea	アンテナ・ショップ antenna shop
後処理 back end	案 package	案内 advice
…に後の日付を書き込む postdate	案 plan	案内 manual
アドバイザー adviser	案 proposal	案内 profile
後回し back burner	案 scheme	案内 prospectus
後回しにする defer	アンカー・テナント anchor tenant	案内役 road map
…の穴埋めをする make up for	アンカーマン anchorman	アンバランス imbalance
アナリシス analysis	安価な downscale	按分に pro rata
アナリスト analyst	アングラ市場 black market	暗黙の tacit
アニュアル・レポート annual report	アンケート questionnaire	
	案件 deal	**い**
アバブ above	案件 project	
アフィリエイト affiliate	案件 question	イアタ IATA
アフター・サービス aftercare	暗号 code	イー… e-
アフター・サービス after-sales service	暗号 encryption	言い争う haggle
	暗号化 encryption	ES細胞 embryonic stem cells
脂 grease	暗号化する encrypt	ES細胞 ES cells
アフリカ開発会議 TICAD	暗号方式 encryption	言い換え restatement
アフリカ統一機構 OAU	アンコム ANCOM	eコマース EC
アプリケーション application	暗証番号 PIN	EU経済通貨統合 EMU
アプリケーション・ソフト application	安全 safety	イールド yield
	安全 security	委員会 board
アプローチ approach	安全機能 fail safe	委員会 commission
アベンド abend	安全性 safety	委員会 panel
アポイントメント appointment	安全性 security	委員団 panel
余り plus	安全性の原則 conservatism	委員長 chairman
余り remainder	安全装置 fail safe	委員長 president
余りの residual	安全装置 safeguard	イエロー・ページ yellow pages
網 network	安全装置 safety	意外の windfall
アメリカ自動車協会 AAA	安全対策の盲点 security holes	いかさま fix
アメリカ生命保険協会 ACLI	安全でない unsecured	いかさまの fake
アモチゼーション amortization	安全な clean	いかさまをする fix
誤り error	安全な safe	生かす capitalize on
歩み step	安全な場所 haven	生かす leverage
粗い crude	安全港 safe harbor	遺棄 abandonment
争い contention	安息地 haven	閾 threshold
争い dispute	アンダーウエート underweight	異議 challenge
争う compete	アンダーパフォーマンス underperformance	勢い momentum
改める reform		勢い steam
アラブ共同市場 ACM	アンダーパフォームする underperform	勢い strength
アラブ石油輸出国機構 OAPEC		勢いをつける pick up
粗利 gross profit	アンダーライター underwriter	域外の offshore
粗利益 gross margin	安定 safety	生き方 lifestyle
粗利益 gross profit	安定 stability	行き詰まった ailing
粗利益率 gross margin	安定化 stabilization	行き詰まり impasse
…を表す represent	安定化装置 stabilizer	行き詰まりの状態 stalemate
表す register	安定期 plateau	域内通信網 LAN
有体財産 property	安定させる even	生き残りに懸命の struggling
有体の tangible	安定させる peg	生き残りに必死になっている struggling
ありのまま bare	安定させる stabilize	

異議のない	unanimous	…以上	upward	一時的な	interim
異議申立て	challenge	委譲	transfer	一時的な	one-time
異議申立て	protest	異常	glitch	一時的な	temporary
…に異議を唱える	question	異常終了	abend	一時的な	windfall
行く	travel	委譲する	yield	一時的に介在する	mezzanine
育成	development	異常損益項目	below the line	一時持込み許可証	carnet
育成する	develop	異常停止	abend	一勝負	deal
育成的便益	incubator facility	異常な	extraordinary	著しい	robust
行く手	horizon	異常な	unusual	著しい	significant
意見	attitude	…以上の	above	著しい変貌	sea change
意見	contention	移植可能な	portable	著しく膨張した	inflated
意見	feedback	威信	prestige	一族	family
意見	idea	威信のある	prestigious	一段と強固にする	reinforce
意見	judgment	…以前	o/b	一段の	further
意見	opinion	遺贈	endowment	一地域に制限する	localize
意見	sentiment	遺贈財産	legacy	位置づける	rank
意見	submission	依存している	dependent	1日	day
意見が一致している	unanimous	委託	commission	1日当たりの	daily
意見書	letter	委託	commitment	1日当たりの取引高	daily turnover
意見上申	bottom-up	委託	consgt	1日のうちの	intraday
意見聴取	hearing	委託	consignment	位置につける	position
意見の一致	accord	委託	mandate	一任勘定の	discretionary
意見の一致	consensus	委託	reference	一任された	discretionary
意見の相違	dispute	委託	trust	一人前の	full-fledged
意見の対立	contention	委託証拠金	margin	1年以内返済予定額	current
意見の発表	delivery	委託する	assign	1年の	yearly
意見表明	opinion	委託する	bail	1年分	full year
意見を述べる	submit	委託する	commit	1年前と比較した	straight
…以後	after	委託する	consign	1年前と比較して	straight
…以降	after	委託する	delegate	1年満期の	yearling
移行	move	委託する	entrust	1年物(債券)	yearling
移行	shift	委託する	subcontract	一番おいしいところ	lion's share
移行	transition	委託取引	broking	一部	fraction
移行期間	transition	委託販売	consgt	1ポンドあたりの税金	poundage
移行時	transition	委託販売	consignment	1ポンドあたりの料金	poundage
意向表明	commitment	委託販売業者	broker	一網打尽の	wholesale
イコール	equal	委託販売品	consgt	一翼	wing
遺産	legacy	委託販売品	consignment	一覧	sight
維持	maintenance	委託保証金	margin	一覧表	list
維持	retention	市	fair	一覧表	schedule
維持可能な	sustainable	位置	fix	一覧表	table
維持管理	maintenance	位置	location	一律の	across-the-board
意識	identity	位置	position	一律の	flat
意識	sentiment	位置	slot	一流株	leader
維持基金	foundation	位置	spot	一流企業向け最優遇貸出金利	prime rate
意識調査	survey	位置確認	fix	一流の	good
意思決定	decision	位置決定	fix	一流の	leading
維持する	keep	一元化	coordination	一流の	master
維持する	maintain	一元化	integration	1回限りの	one-time
維持する	retain	一元化した	consolidated	一回かぎりの	windfall
維持する	sustain	一元化した	integrated	一回限りの	one-off
意思疎通	communication	一元化する	consolidate	1回限りの意思決定	one-shot decision making
意思の疎通	communications	一元化する	coordinate	1か月物資金	one-month money
意思表明状	memorandum of understanding	一元化する	integrate	一括して	across the board
いじめ	bullying	一時解雇	layoff	一括すること	packaging
慰謝料	compensation	一時解雇	redundancy	一括登録	shelf registration
意匠	design	一時帰休	layoff	一括登録制度	shelf registration
意匠	device	一時停止	tie-up	一括	across-the-board
意匠	logo	一時停止する	suspend		
		一時的	one-off		

一括の	blanket
一括返済	maturity
一括法案	package
一括募集	shelf offering
一貫した	seamless
一貫生産する	integrate
一貫生産の	integrated
一見	sight
1,000兆	quadrillion
一掃	clearance
一層の	further
一体化	integration
一体化した	integrated
一体化する	consolidate
一体化する	integrate
一体感	integration
一体性	identity
一致	correspondence
一致	identity
一致させる	reconcile
一致指数	coincident index
一致した意見	consensus
…と一致する	match
一致する	fit
一定期間の	terminal
一定ドル	constant dollar
一定にさせる	peg
一定の	fixed
一定の	regular
一定の割合に従って	pro rata
一手販売権	franchise
一手販売権者	franchisee
一点集中の	one-stop
一般会計基準	GAAP
一般会計基準	generally accepted accounting principles
一般会計原則	GAAP
一般教書演説	State of the Union address
一般薬	ethical
一般公開	exhibition
一般市場	open market
一般市民の	civil
一般社員	rank-and-file employee
一般従業員	rank-and-file employee
一般職員	rank-and-file employee
一般賃金	prevailing rate
一般賃率	prevailing rate
一般的な	general
一般的な	universal
一般に公開されていない	official
一般に公正妥当と認められた会計基準	generally accepted accounting principles
一般に公正妥当と認められた会計原則	GAAP
一般に公正妥当と認められた会計原則	generally accepted accounting principles
一般に公正妥当と認められた監査基準	GAAS
一般に使われなくなった	obsolete
一般に認められた会計基準	GAAP
一般に認められた会計基準	generally accepted accounting principles
一般に認められた会計原則	GAAP
一般に認められた会計原則	generally accepted accounting principles
一般に認められた監査基準	GAAS
一般に認められた監査基準	generally accepted auditing standards
一般に認められている	acceptable
一般の	general
一般の	generic
一般の	regular
一般の人々	public
一般物価変動	inflation
一般名の	generic
逸品	choice
一歩	step
一本化	integration
一本化された	integrated
一本化された	consolidated
一本化する	integrate
移転	flow
移転	move
移転	relocation
移転	transfer
遺伝子	gene
遺伝子組換えの	genetically modified
遺伝子組換えの	GM
遺伝子工学	genetic engineering
遺伝子試料	genetic material
遺伝子の利用技術	bioengineering
移転する	grant
移転する	relocate
移転する	transfer
意図	idea
意図	purpose
井戸	well
異動	move
移動	flow
移動	motion
移動	move
移動	movement
移動	redeployment
移動	relocation
移動	shift
移動式	portable
移動式電話	mobile phone
移動手段	transport
移動する	import
移動する	redeploy
移動する	relocate
移動する	shift
移動性の	movable
移動電話	mobile phone
移動平均	moving average
移動平均線	moving average
意図的欠勤者	absentee
営む	ply
井戸元価格	wellhead price
イニシアチブ	initiative
委任	authorization
委任	commission
委任	commitment
委任	mandate
委任	request
委任契約	mandate
委任された	mandatory
委任状	authorization
委任状	commission
委任状	proxy
委任する	commit
委任する	delegate
委任する	entrust
委任統治	mandate
委任の	mandatory
命綱	lifeline
イノベーション	innovation
違反	breach
…に違反する	infringe on
違反する	renege
委付	abandonment
委付する	abandon
委付保険	abandonment
イベント	event
イベント広場	park
違法貸金業者	illicit loan operator
違法行為	injury
違法行為	malfeasance
違法な	illegal
違法な	wrongful
いま話題の	hot
意味	effect
意味	import
意味する	represent
イメージ	image
イメージ	reputation
イメージ・アップ	upgrading
イメージ・チェンジ	makeover
嫌がらせ	harassment
違約金	fine
違約金	penalty
医薬事業	drug business
遺譲	demise
意欲	drive
意欲	motivation
…以来	upward
依頼	recourse
依頼	request
依頼者	client
依頼書	request
依頼人	client
イラスト	figure

医療	care	引退者	retiree	エート	West Texas Intermediate
医療	health	引退する	retire	ウェスト・テキサス・インターミ	
医療	health care	引退する	step down	ディエート	WTI
医療サービス	medical services	インダストリアル	industrial	…より上の	above
医療費	medical expenses	インダストリアル・エンジニアリン		…より上の	prior
医療保険	care	グ	IE	ウェブ	Web
医療保険	health care	インタビュー	interview	ウェブ偽装詐欺	phishing
医療用薬品	ethical	インタラクティブ	interactive	ウェブ・サイト	Web site
異例の	unusual	インタレスト・カバレッジ比率		ウェブログ	blog
入れ替える	reverse		interest coverage ratio	ウォール街の証券市場	Wall Street
入れ替える	shift	インタレスト・カバレッジ・レシオ		ウォール・ストリート	Wall Street
…に入れ込む	committed to		interest coverage ratio	迂回路	diversion
いわれのない	gratuitous	インディケーター	indicator	請け合う	guarantee
印	symbol	インデックス	index	請け合う	insure
院外活動	lobbying	インテリジェンス	intelligence	受け入れる	accept
院外団	lobby	インテリジェント	intelligent	受け入れる	receive
因果応報の	punitive	インテリジェント機能を備えた		請負	contract
印鑑	seal		intelligent	請負業者	provider
インキュベーション・ビジネス		隠匿する	cover up	請負仕事	piecework
	incubation business	隠匿する	stash	請け負う	tender
インキュベーター	incubator	院内総務	leader	請け負う	undertake
イングランド銀行	B of E	インパクト	impact	受け継ぐ	inherit
イングランド銀行	Bank of England	インフォームド・コンセント		受け付ける	receive
インクリメント	increment		informed consent	受取り	receipt
インコタームズ	Incoterms	インフォマーシャル	infomercial	受取勘定	account receivable
インサイダー	insider	インフォメーション	information	受取金純額	net proceeds
インサイダー取引	insider trading	インプット	input	受取債権	account receivable
インサイド情報	tip	インフラストラクチャー		受取債権	receivable
印刷	print		infrastructure	受取証	receipt
印刷機	press	インフラ整備	infrastructure	受取証	scrip
印刷する	print	インフレ	inflation	受取人	beneficiary
印刷物	print	インフレーション	inflation	受取人	recipient
印紙	stamp	インフレの	inflationary	受け取る	incoming
因子	element	インフレ率	inflation	受け取る	receive
因子	factor	インフレを起こす	overheat	受け取るべき	receivable
印章	seal	インフレを引き起こす	inflationary	受け身の	passive
…に印章を押す	stamp	インフレを誘発する	inflationary	受ける	incur
印紙を貼る	stamp	インフロー	inflow	受ける	suffer
インスタントの	instant	隠蔽	cover-up	受ける	sustain
インストア	in-store	隠蔽工作	cover-up	受渡し	delivery
インストール	set-up	隠蔽する	cover up	動いていない	inactive
インストールする	install	インベスター	investor	…を動かす	drive
印税	royalty	インベスター・リレーションズ		動かす	run
インセンティブ	incentive		investor relations	動かす	trigger
インターネット	Internet	インベスター・リレーションズ	IR	動かす	work
インターネット	net	インボイス	invoice	動かせない	immovable
インターネット関連企業	dot-com	陰謀	plot	動かせる	movable
インターネット上の場所	site	インポート	import	動かない	immovable
インターネット接続業者	provider	引用	quotation	動き	action
インターネットで	online	引用	quote	動き	activity
インターネットの通信規約	IP	飲料水	water	動き	behavior
インターバンク	interbank			動き	development
インターバンク・オファード・レー		う		動き	effort
ト	IBOR			動き	event
インターバンク・ビッド・レート		ウイルス駆除ソフト	antivirus	動き	fluctuation
IBBR			software	動き	motion
インターフェース	interface	ウイルス対策ソフト	antivirus	動き	move
インターンシップ	internship		software	動き	movement
引退	retirement	ウエイト付け	weighting	動き	sign
引退	retreat	ウェスト・テキサス・インターミディ		動き	swing

動きが鈍い	lackluster	生む	earn	売り惜しみ	withholding
動きが鈍い	sluggish	生む	generate	売掛金	account receivable
動く	function	生む	yield	売掛金	open account
動く	run	埋め合わせ	offset	売掛債権	account receivable
牛海綿状脳症	BSE	…を埋め合わせる	make up for	売掛債権	receivable
失う	lapse	埋め合わせる	finance	売り方	bear
失う	lose	埋め合わせる	recoup	売り崩し	raid
失われた10年	lost decade	埋め合わせる	redeem	売り子	salesman
薄商い	thin trading	埋め合わせをする	offset	売り越し	net selling
薄商い市場	thin market	埋める	bridge	売り越し	selling
薄める	dilute	裏書	endorsement	売込み	selling
薄れる	flag	裏書き	backing	売り込む	promote
疑い	misgiving	裏書条項	endorsement	売り込む	sell
疑う	question	裏書譲渡する	endorse	売り材料	negative factor
打上げ	blastoff	裏書譲渡人	endorser	売出し	floatation
打ち明ける	unveil	裏書きする	endorse	売出し	offer
打ち上げる[発射する]	launch	裏書人	backer	売出し	offering
打ち合せ	conference	裏書人	endorser	売出し	placement
打合せ	arrangement	裏金	kickback	売出し	public offering
打ち合わせる	arrange	裏側の	reverse	売出価格	offer price
打ち切る	scrap	裏口金融	backdoor financing	売出価格	offering price
打ち切る	withdraw	裏口資金調達	backdoor financing	売り出す	introduce
内金	deposit	…を裏付けとする	-backed	売り出す	issue
打ち消す	offset	裏付けとなる	underlying	売り出す	launch
打ち出す	come up with	占取する	enter	売り出す	market
打ち歩	premium	裏の	reverse	売り出す	offer
打ち歩	agio	裏舞台	back room	売りつける	impose
宇宙航空研究開発機構	Japan Aerospace Exploration Agency	裏目に出る	backfire	売りつなぎして損失を防ぐ	hedge
宇宙産業	space industry	裏面の	reverse	売り手	supplier
宇宙船の燃料	software	売り	selling	売り手	vendor
内訳	breakdown	売り	sell-off	売り手独占	monopoly
内訳	component	売上	proceeds	売り主	vendor
打つ	hit	売上	revenue	売主	seller
美しい	fair	売上	sales	売り場	department
写し	copy	売上	turnover	売り場	floor
写し	duplicate	売上債権	account receivable	売り場区分	zoning
写し	tenor	売上債権	receivable	売り払う	unload
移し替える	transfer	売上債権回収期間	days sales outstanding	売申込み	offer
写しの	duplicate	売上債権回転日数	days sales outstanding	売戻し選択権	put
移す	relocate	売上債権の買取り業務	factoring	売り物	wares
移す	shift	売上純利益率	profit margin	売り優勢の展開	bearish
移す	transfer	売上総利益	gross income	売り渡す	sell
訴え	action	売上総利益	gross margin	売る	sell
訴える	accuse	売上総利益	gross profit	売る	serve
訴える	claim	売上総利益	margin	売れ筋の	hot-selling
訴える	sue	売上高	figure	売れ残り	plug
訴えること	resort	売上高	proceeds	…で売れる	fetch
うつ病	depression	売上高	revenue	売れるもの	seller
移る	shift	売上高	sales	うわさによると	reportedly
…を促す	trigger	売上高	turnover	上値の余地	upside
うまく行く	pay off	売上高	volume	上乗せ	premium
うまく行っている	going	売上高純利益率	net margin on sales	上乗せ	spread
うまく処理する	manage	売上利益	gross margin	上乗せする	inflate
うまく処理する	meet	売上利益率	gross margin	上乗せ料金	surcharge
うまくはまる	fit	売上利益率	net margin on sales	…を上回る	above
海	water	売上利益率	profit margin	上回る	outweigh
生み出す	create	売り浴びせ	raid	上回る	surpass
生み出す	generate			上回る	top
生む	draw			上向き	upturn
				上向きの	bull

上向きの upward	運搬する haul	営業項目 line of business
上向く pick up	運搬人 bearer	営業している企業 going concern
上屋 shed	運搬人 porter	営業収益 revenue
上屋 warehouse	運搬量 haul	営業収益合計 total revenues
上役 superior	運搬量 haulage	営業純利益 net operating profit
運 fortune	運命 fortune	営業所 office
運 hazard	運輸 traffic	営業上の operating
運営 administration	運輸 transport	営業上の operational
運営 charge	運輸 transportation	営業スタッフ salespeople
運営 conduct	運用 application	…に影響する affect
運営 management	運用 implementation	影響する work
運営会社 operator	運用 investment	営業する do business
運営者 operator	運用 management	営業する operate
運営上の administrative	運用 operation	営業責任者 AE
運営する manage	運用 performance	営業損失 deficit
運営する operate	運用 use	営業地域 franchise
運営する organize	運用管理する manage	営業中の going
運営する run	運用期間 time horizon	営業中の open
運営方法 conduct	運用基準 guideline	営業年度 FY
運航する serve	運用している working	営業の operational
運勢 fortune	運用収益 return	営業の working
運送 conveyance	運用上の operational	影響の範囲 incidence
運送 transport	運用する administer	営業日 working day
運送 transportation	運用する invest	営業秘密 trade secret
運送業 haulage	運用する manage	営業品目 line of business
運送業 porterage	運用する run	営業マン salesman
運送業者 carrier	運用する use	営業免許 franchise
運送業者 dispatch	運用成績 performance	営業免許権 franchise
運送証券 bill of lading	運用成績 return	営業免許権 license
運送店 dispatch	運用の operational	営業免許を与える franchise
運送人 carrier		営業利益 net revenues
運送料 freight	**え**	影響力 clout
運賃 fare		影響力 force
運賃 haulage	エア air	影響力 leverage
運賃 porterage	エアバッグ airbag	影響力 presence
運賃 rate	英貨の sterling	影響を与える affect
運賃 transportation	映画を封切る release	影響を与える impact
運賃・保険料込み値段 CIF	永久的 permanent	…の影響を受けやすい vulnerable
運賃・保険料渡し CIF	永久の permanent	…の影響を受ける subject to
運賃収入 traffic	影響 effect	影響を及ぼす affect
運賃表 tariff	影響 impact	影響を及ぼす impact
運転者 operator	影響 results	英国国債 gilt
運転上の operational	営業 business	英国首相 Downing Street
運転する working	営業 operation	英国政府 Downing Street
運転中の going	営業 practice	英国の公開有限会社 PLC
運転中の running	営業 trading	映写幕 screen
運動 campaign	営業網 franchise	エイジング aging
運動 effort	営業網 presence	衛星 satellite
運動 front	影響額 effect	衛星放送 satellite
運動 motion	影響額 results	映像 image
運動 move	営業活動 operation	映像 video
運動 movement	営業活動を行う do business	映像走査機 scanner
運搬 conveyance	営業科目 line of business	映像の鮮明度 resolution
運搬 handling	営業基盤 franchise	永続 perpetuity
運搬 haul	…を(営業)基盤とする -based	永続的な standing
運搬 haulage	営業区分 segment	永続物 perpetuity
運搬 porterage	営業権 franchise	永代所有権 perpetuity
運搬 transport	営業権 goodwill	営利化 commercialization
運搬経路 haul	営業権の取得 buyout	営利主義 commercialism
運搬経路 haulage	営業行為 doing business	営利性 profitability

営利的な	productive
鋭利な刃物	cutting edge
営利の	commercial
営利目的の	for-profit
英ロンドンのロンバード街	Lombard Street
エージェント	agent
液化	liquefaction
液化天然ガス	liquefied natural gas
液化天然ガス	LNG
エキシビション	exhibition
液状化現象	liquefaction
液晶ディスプレー	LCD
液晶ディスプレー・パネル	liquid crystal display panel
液晶テレビ	LCD TV
液晶テレビ	liquid crystal screen TV
液晶パネル	liquid crystal display panel
液晶表示装置	LCD
役務	service
エクイップメント	equipment
エクイティ	equity
エクスポージャー	exposure
エグゼクティブ	executive
1988年通商法のエクソン・フロリオ条項	Exon-Florio provision of the 1988 trade law
エコ管理監査要項	eco-management and audit scheme
エコツーリズム	ecotourism
エコハウス	ecohouse
えこひいき	discrimination
エコ表示	ecolabeling
エコ・ファクトリー	eco-factory
エコロジー	ecology
エシカル・ドラッグ	ethical
餌食	prey
S&P500株価指数	Standard & Poors 500
エスクロー	escrow
エスタブリッシュメント	establishment
X管理図	X chart
X非効率	X-inefficiency
エッジ	edge
閲覧	access
閲覧	review
閲覧	sight
閲覧可能な	available
閲覧する	access
NYSEユーロネクスト	NYSE Euronext
エネルギー	energy
エネルギー	fuel
エネルギー	power
エネルギー省エネルギー情報局	EIA
絵表示統計図	pictogram
FF金利	key interest rate
MOX燃料	MOX fuel
エム・スリー	M3
エム・ツー	M2
エム・ワン	M1
絵文字	icon
エラー	error
…を選ぶ	tab
選ぶ	elect
選ぶ	name
選ぶ	tap
エリア	area
エリサ法	ERISA
得る	draw
得る	earn
得る	gain
得る	land
得る	notch
エルゴノミクス	ergonomics
エルシー	L/C
エレクトロニクス	electronics
エレクトロニック・コマース	EC
エレメント	element
円	yen
遠因	background
演繹	deduction
遠隔制御	remote control
遠隔操作	remote control
遠隔操作による	remote
遠隔操縦	remote control
遠隔通信	telecommunication
遠隔の	remote
延期	deferment
延期	delay
延期された	deferred
延期する	carry over
延期する	defer
延期する	delay
延期する	postpone
延期する	remit
延期する	reserve
演算記号	operator
演算子	operator
エンジェル	angel
エンジニアリング	engineering
円借款	yen credits
円借款	yen loans
炎暑	heat wave
援助	backing
援助	cooperation
援助	help
援助	support
援助する	help
援助する	support
援助の手	helping hand
エンジン	engine
円相場	yen
延滞	arrears
延滞	delinquency
延滞金	arrears
延滞金	penalty
延滞の	overdue
円建て外債	Samurai bond
円建て国債	yen-denominated government bond
円建て利益	yen-denominated profits
演壇	platform
延着	delay
延長	extension
延長	raising
延長する	extend
延長できる	renewable
遠慮する	forgo

お

オアペック	OAPEC
追い風	windfall
追い風になる	favorable
…に追いつかない	lag
…に追いつく	keep up with
オイル	oil
お色直し	makeover
負う	incur
奥義	knowhow
黄金株	golden share
黄金の落下傘	golden parachute
欧州委員会	EC
欧州委員会	European Commission
欧州開発銀行	EBRD
欧州銀行間取引金利	Euribor
欧州経済通貨同盟	EMU
欧州自由貿易地域	EFTA
欧州証券規制委員会	CESR
欧州第1審裁判所	European Court of First Instance
欧州中央銀行	ECB
欧州中央銀行	European Central Bank
欧州中央銀行制度	European System of Central Banks
欧州中銀	European Central Bank
欧州通貨制度	EMS
欧州店頭株式市場	EASDAQ
欧州ビジネス協会	EBC
欧州復興開発銀行	EBRD
欧州預託証券	EDR
欧州連合	EU
欧州連合	European Union
欧州連合統計局	Eurostat data agency
…に応じる	respond to
旺盛な	massive
応答	response
往復文書	correspondence
応募	subscription
応募者	applicant
応募する	sign up
応募する	subscribe
応募入札	tender

応用	application	大手メーカー	majors	押し上げる	boost
応用システム	application	オートメーション化する	automate	押し上げる	increase
応用する	apply	オーナー	owner	押し上げる	inflate
応用ソフト	application	オーナー	proprietor	押し下げ要因	drag
応用できる	applicable	大ナタを振るう	ax	押し下げる	reduce
横領	raid	大波	surge	押し下げる	squeeze
横領する	appropriate	オーバーアロットメント		押しつける	impose
終える	close		overallotment	押しつける	press
終える	conclude	オーバーウェイト	overweight	押し問答する	haggle
終える	fulfill	オーバーヒート	overheating	おしゃれな	sophisticated
大当たり	success	オーバーヒートする	overheat	汚職	bribery
大改変	shakeout	オーバーファンディング		汚職	malfeasance
大がかりな	massive		overfunding	汚職の	corrupt
大型店	store	オーバーワーク	overwork	押し寄せる	surge
大型の	heavy	大幅な	good	お知らせ	announcement
大型の	large	大幅な	large	押す	press
大型の	massive	大幅な	massive	押す戦略	push strategy
大型の	significant	大幅な	robust	おせっかいな	unsolicited
大型の	substantial	大幅な	sharp	汚染	pollution
大型汎用機	host computer	大幅な	significant	恐れ	fear
大株主	largest shareholder	大幅な	substantial	…する恐れがある	set to
大株主	major shareholder	大幅に減少する	plummet	オゾン層	ozone layer
…より大きい	outweigh	オープニング	opening	…落ち	ex
大きい	massive	オープン	open	落込み	dilution
大きい取り分	lion's share	オープンエンド型	open-end	落込み	drop
大きいほうの	major	おおよその	approximate	落込み	plunge
大きく上回る	soar	オールドエコノミー	old economy	落込み	setback
大きくする	widen	オールファイナンス	allfinanz	落込み	slump
大きく取り上げる	feature	沖合いの	offshore	落込み	weakness
大きくなる	widen	置く	locate	落込み	decline
大きさ	bulk	置く	put	落込み	downturn
大きさ	proportion	憶測	speculation	落ち込む	decline
大きさ	size	遅らせる	delay	落ち込む	drop
…の大きさを変える	resize	送り状	invoice	落ち込む	sag
大きな	high	贈り物	gratuity	落ち込む	slip
大きな	significant	送る	feed	落ち込んだ	weak
大きな影響力のある	material	送る	send	…落ちの	ex
大きな変化	sea change	送る	transmit	落ち目に	downward
オークション	auction	遅れ	delay	落ち目の	downward
大口株主	major shareholder	遅れ	disadvantage	負っている	owe
大口の	major	遅れがちな	laggard	音	audio
大口の	wholesale	…に遅れないようにする	keep up	お得意	client
大蔵省	Treasury		with	おとり商品	leader
大刷新	shake-up	遅れる	delay	踊り場	leveling off
大雑把な	crude	…を怠る	fail	踊り場	plateau
大騒ぎ	scene	行う	deliver	衰える	flag
多すぎる	excessive	行う	effect	同じ	equal
大筋合意	basic agreement	行う	perform	己自身	identity
大底	rock bottom	行う	run	オピニオン	opinion
大底	bottom	行われる	run	オフJT	off the job training
大底に達する	bottom out	抑えて	back	オフJT	off-JT
大底の	rock-bottom	抑える	contain	オファー	offer
オーダー	order	抑える	control	オファー	proposal
オーダーメードの	customized	抑える	curb	オフィサー	officer
…の大台	mark	抑える	moderate	オフィス	office
オーディオ	audio	抑える	quash	オフィス・オートメーション	OA
大手企業	leading company	抑える	withhold	オブ・カウンセル	of counsel
大手の	large	収める	notch	オブジェクト	object
大手の	leading	押し	press	オフショア	offshore
大手の	major	押し上げ	boost	オフショアリング	offshoring

オプション	option
オプション取引	option
オプション料	premium
オフ・バジェット予算	off-budget spending
オフ・バランス	off-balance-sheet
オフ・バランスシート	off-balance-sheet
オフライン	offline
オペ	operation
オペック	OPEC
オペレーション	operation
オペレータ	operator
覚書	agenda
覚書	memorandum
覚書	minutes
覚書	note
オムニバス法案	omnibus bill
重い	heavy
思いがけない幸運	windfall
思いがけない利益	windfall
思い出す	recall
思いつき	idea
思いつく	come up with
表向きの	front
表向きの	official
主な	chief
主な	main
主に	predominantly
重荷	burden
…が重荷になる	suffer from
思惑	speculation
思惑買い	speculation
思惑による	speculative
思惑売買をする	speculate
思わぬ利益	windfall
思わぬ悪い結果を生む	backfire
親会社	parent
親会社から子会社への販売	downstream
親会社専用の	captive
親子会社間取引	intercompany transaction
親子会社間の	intercompany
および／または	and/or
及ぼす	exercise
オリエンテーション	orientation
折り紙をつける	hallmark
織り込む	adjust
織り込む	discount
織り込む	reflect
オリジネーション	origination
織物	fabric
卸売り	wholesale
卸売り業者	distributor
卸売業者	wholesaler
卸売り店	warehouse
卸売りの	wholesale
卸し企業	wholesaler
おろす	draw
下す	deliver
下す	pass
下ろす	clear
降ろす	discharge
降ろす	disembark
…を負わせる	entail
負わせる	impose
終わらせる	conclude
終わらせる	terminate
終値	close
終値	closing
音響・映像の	audiovisual
恩恵を受ける	benefit
穏健派	center [centre]
温室	greenhouse
温室効果ガス	greenhouse
音声	audio
音声メール	voice mail
オンライン	online

か

課	department
課	division
課	office
課	section
カード	card
カード会員	cardholder
カーネル	kernel
カーボン	carbon
カーボンナノチューブ	carbon nanotube
…界	circles
…界	community
…界	public
…界	scene
会	meeting
…街	park
買い上がりすぎた	overbought
害悪	hazard
買上げ	buyback
買い上げる	buy out
海域	water
買入れ	purchase
買入れ債務	account payable
会員	holder
会員	member
会員	user
会員権	seat
会員費	due
外貨	foreign currency
開会	opening
開会	session
海外移住者	expat
海外移住者	expatriate
海外からの	overseas
開会式	opening
海外代理店	factory
海外駐在員	expat
海外駐在員	expatriate
開会中の	open
海外調達	outsourcing
海外投資資金の引揚げ	repatriation
海外取引先	correspondent
海外の	foreign
海外の	offshore
海外の	overseas
海外の輸入者	buyer
海外への	overseas
海外への業務委託	offshoring
海外向けの	overseas
改革	change
改革	improvement
改革	innovation
改革	overhaul
改革	reform
改革	reorganization
改革	reshuffle
改革	restructuring
改革	transformation
改革する	improve
改革する	reform
改革する	reorganize
改革する	reshuffle
買掛金	account payable
買掛金	payable
絵画図表	pictogram
買い方	bull
買い方の	bull
快活な	resilient
下位から上位への	bottom-up
外観	attitude
外観	form
外観	showing
概観	configuration
概観	survey
会期	session
会議	board
会議	conference
会議	conferencing
会議	consultation
会議	convention
会議	meeting
会議	session
会議室	boardroom
階級	rank
開業	inception
開業	practice
開業	start-up
概況・状況説明	briefing
改行キー	return
開業準備	start-up
開業する	locate
買切り	outright purchase
買切りオペ	outright purchase
買切りオペレーション	outright purchase
会議録	proceedings
解禁する	liberalize
会計	account

会計 accounting	介護 nursing care	開始 opening
外形 configuration	会合 session	開始 origination
外形 form	外交員をする travel	開始 start
会計学 accounting	外交慣習 protocol	開始 start-up
会計監査 auditing	外交文書 protocol	開示 disclosure
会計監査役 controller	介護休業制度 nursing leave system	開示する launch
会計期間 period	外国からの直接投資 FDI	開示する disclose
会計基準 GAAP	外国為替 forex	開示する present
会計記録 accounts	外国為替 FX	開示する reveal
会計記録の試査 test	外国為替証拠金取引 FX margin trading	買占め buyout
会計検査 audit		買占め corner
会計検査院 GAO	外国語としての英語教育 TEFL	買占め同盟 ring
会計検査役 controller	外国通貨 foreign currency	買占め屋 raider
会計検査官 auditor	外国の foreign	買い占める buy out
会計検査する audit	外国の overseas	買い占める buy up
会計士 accountant	介護サービス care service	買い占める corner
会計上の fiscal	買い越し capital inflow	会社 business
会計処理 accounting	買い越し額 net buying	会社 company
会計処理する account for	解雇する ax	会社 concern
会計処理する book	解雇する dehire	会社 corporation
会計処理方法 accounting	解雇する dismiss	会社 enterprise
会計責任 accountability	解雇する fire	会社 establishment
会計専門家 accountant	解雇する lay off	会社 firm
会計担当者 accountant	解雇する terminate	会社 house
会計年度 FY	解雇手当 parachute	会社 incorporation
会計年度 period	開催国 host	会社 institution
会計の fiscal	開催する organize	会社 operator
外形標準課税 pro forma standard tax	開催団体 organizer	会社 organization
	開催地 host	会社 undertaking
会計簿 book	開催地 venue	会社 unit
会計役 treasurer	買い支える prop up	会社案内 About Us
解決 arrangement	解散 dismissal	会社概要 About Us
解決 determination	解散 dissolution	会社間取引 intercompany transaction
解決 resolution	解散 liquidation	
解決 settlement	解散 severance	会社間の intercompany
解決 solution	解散 termination	会社間利益 intercompany profit
解決策 fix	解散 winding up	解釈 construction
解決策 formula	改竄 fabrication	解釈 translation
解決策 solution	概算 estimate	解釈する construe
解決策 solvent	解散させる discharge	解釈する translate
解決手段 solution	解散させる dismiss	会社更生 reorganization
解決する arrange	改竄した fake	会社再建 reorganization
解決する decide	概算書 estimate	会社重役の高額の退職手当 golden handshake
解決する determine	解散する close	
解決する fix	解散する dissolve	会社相互間利益 intercompany profit
解決する resolve	解散する liquidate	
解決する settle	解散する split	会社組織にする incorporate
解決法 approach	解散する wind up	会社(組織)の incorporated
解決法 solution	改竄する fabricate	会社の corporate
解決方法 formula	改竄する fake	会社の設立 incorporation
買い気配 bid	改竄する falsify	会社の設立趣意書 prospectus
会見 interview	改竄する tamper	会社乗っ取り raid
解雇 ax	概算する approximate	会社分割 demerger
解雇 discharge	概算する estimate	会社分割 spinoff
解雇 dismissal	概算の approximate	会社役員 executive
解雇 layoff	概算の estimated	会社役員 officer
解雇 redundancy	概算要求基準 ceiling	会社を経営する head
解雇 restructuring	開始 inception	会社を分割する spin off
解雇 sack	開始 launch	回収 collection
介護 day care	開始 launching	回収 payoff

回収 payout	改善する pick up	改訂する revamp
回収 recovery	改善する redeploy	改訂する revise
回収 withdrawal	改善する reform	改訂する update
改修工事 improvement	改善する strengthen	回転 revolving
回収されない uncollected	改善する turn around	回転 rotation
回収する collect	回線接続中 online	回転 turnover
回収する recall	回線網 network	開店 opening
回収する recover	改組 reorganization	回転率 turnover
回収する repossess	改組 shakeout	会頭 president
回収する retire	開祖 founder	解答 resolution
回収する service	回想 recall	回答 response
回収する withdraw	改装 makeover	回答 ruling
回収遅延残高 delinquent balances	改装 renovation	該当項目 hit
回収不能金 uncollectibles	階層 bracket	該当なし N/A
回収不能原価 unrecovered cost	階層 tier	害毒 hazard
回収不能の irrecoverable	改造 makeover	解読する decode
回収不能の uncollectible	改造 reorganization	回読による pass-along
解除 cancelation	外装 packing	買い唱え bid
解除 termination	階層削減 delayering	ガイドライン guideline
解消 dissolution	回想する recall	買取り acquisition
会場 venue	改装する renovate	買取り buyback
開場 opening	改造する convert	買取り buyout
解消する absorb	改造する reorganize	買取り forfeiting
解消する dissolve	改造する revamp	買取り purchase
解消する lay off	海賊版 piracy	買取り purchasing
解消する offset	改組する reorganize	買取り価格 offer price
解消する reduce	海損 average	買取り金融 forfeiting
下意上達 bottom-up	解体 disintegration	買取り請求権 put
会場提供者 host	解体 dissolution	買取り手 acquirer
解職する recall	解体する dissolve	買取り人 purchaser
解除する cancel	快諾 goodwill	買い取る buy
解職権 recall	開拓者 pioneer	買い取る buy back
害する prejudice	開拓する reclaim	買い取る buy out
害すること prejudice	買いだめ hoarding	買い取る buy up
改正 change	買いだめする hoard	買い取る purchase
改正 reform	会談 conference	買い取る take over
改正 revision	会談 interview	買い取ることができる negotiable
改正する reform	会談 session	海難救助 salvage
改正する revise	会談 talks	介入 engagement
開設 launch	改築 makeover	介入 intervention
概説 survey	改築 reconstruction	介入された dirty
解説機能 help	改築する reconstruct	介入する intervene
解説者 analyst	外注 outsourcing	介入操作 operation
解説書 manual	外注する outsource	解任 discharge
開設する locate	買い注文 bid	解任 dismissal
開設する open	会長 chairman	解任権 recall
開設する set up	会長 president	解任する dismiss
回線 channel	開通 opening	解任する recall
回線 line	買付け acquisition	解任請求権 recall
改善 enhancement	買付け purchase	買い主 buyer
改善 improvement	買付け価格 offer price	買い主 purchaser
改善 makeover	買付け選択権 call	概念 concept
改善 pickup	買い付ける purchase	概念 idea
改善 reform	買いつなぎして損失を防ぐ hedge	下位 junior
改善 turnaround	買い手 buyer	下位 subordinate
改善する develop	買い手 purchaser	下位 subordinated
改善する enhance	改訂 restatement	買い乗せをする pyramid
改善する fix	改訂 revision	開発 development
改善する help	改訂 update	開発 engineering
改善する improve	改定する revise	開発 exploration

開発 implementation	外務員 representative	科学技術 technology
開発 innovation	解明 resolution	科学技術活動 technosphere
開発 origination	買戻し buyback	科学技術恐怖症 technophobial
開発 search	買戻し repurchase	科学技術の technical
開発会社 developer	買戻し short-covering	科学技術の technological
開発業者 developer	買戻し条件付き売却契約 repo	価格計算 pricing
開発事業 project	買戻しできない irredeemable	価格形成する price
開発する create	買戻しできる redeemable	価格決定 pricing
開発する develop	買い戻す buy back	価格修正因子 deflator
開発する exploit	買い戻す redeem	価格政策 pricing
開発する originate	買い戻す repurchase	化学製品 chemicals
開発する reclaim	買い物 shopping	価格設定 pricing
開発する tap	解約 cancelation	科学捜査の forensic
会費 due	解約 disinvestment	化学的な chemical
会費 fee	解約 redemption	価格に上乗せする pyramid
回避する lay off	解約 surrender	価格に準じた ad valorem
外部委託 outsourcing	解約 termination	化学の chemical
外部委託する outsource	解約 withdrawal	価格の引下げ markdown
外部化する externalize	解約可能な cancelable	化学物質 chemicals
回復 improvement	解約する cancel	価格分離 unbundling
回復 pickup	解約する surrender	価格変動率 volatility
回復 rally	解約できない noncancelable	価格見積り書 quotation
回復 rebound	解約不能の noncancelable	化学薬品 chemicals
回復 recovery	概要 profile	価格を決める price
回復 rehabilitation	概要 scheme	価格をつける price
回復 revitalization	概要報告 briefing	価格を提示する quote
回復 revival	買い呼び値 bid	価格を引き下げる write off
回復 upturn	回覧する circulate	輝かしい成果 breakthrough
回復させる recuperate	概略的な general	かかる cost
回復させる revitalize	概略の general	カギ bottom line
回復する rally	改良 enhancement	かき集める claw
回復する rebound	改良 improvement	書換え renewal
回復する rebuild	改良 makeover	書換え transfer
回復する recover	改良 reform	書換え継続 renewal
回復する repossess	改良工事 improvement	書き換える roll over
回復する resume	改良する develop	書き込み posting
回復する revive	改良する improve	書き記す keep
回復する turn around	改良する reform	書留にする register
回復不能の irrecoverable	改良する revamp	下級の junior
外部資源の活用 outsourcing	改良費 improvement	下級の lower
外部資源を活用する outsource	回路網 network	家業 vocation
外部取締役 outside director	会話型 interactive	課業 task
外部の external	下院議員 representative	限られた close
改編 reorganization	買う buy	…にかぎり subject to
改編する restructure	買う権利 call	核 core
会報 journal	カウンセラー counselor	家具 fittings
会報 proceedings	カウンターパーティー counterparty	家具 movable
回報 newsletter	返す return	格上げ upgrade
回報 newsletter	変える convert	格上げ upgrading
開放 liberalization	変える shift	格上げする upgrade
開放式の open-end	家屋 premises	架空の会社 dummy company
開放式の open-ended	…する覚悟だ poised to	
解放する discharge	顔ぶれ lineup	格差 difference
解放する dishoard	加害企業 offending enterprise	格差 disparity
解放する release	…を抱えて saddled with	格差 gap
開放する liberalize	抱える experience	格下げ downgrade
開放する open	価格 figure	格下げする decruit
開放的な open	価格 price	格下げする downgrade
開幕 opening	価格 pricing	隠された hidden
買い待ちの long	価格 value	…隠し cover-up

格式　prestige	格付けを引き上げる　upgrade	格安の　knockdown
学識　education	格付けを引き下げる　downgrade	格安品　bargain
隠し所得　skim	確定　determination	確立　establishment
隠し立て　cover-up	確定給付制度　defined benefit plan	確立した　well-established
確実性　assurance	確定給付年金制度　defined benefit plan	確立する　establish
確実性　reliability	確定した　fixed	学歴　background
確実な　reliable	確定した　vested	隠れた　hidden
隠して　back	確定申告　tax return	隠れた　invisible
学習意欲　motivation	確定する　determine	隠れた　latent
拡充する　beef up	…を確定的にする　clinch	隠れた瑕疵　latent defect
拡充する　boost	確定利付き社債　straight bond	隠れた欠陥　latent defect
拡充する　expand	核店舗　magnet store	隠れ場所　harbor
確証　confirmation	獲得　collection	掛け　tick
核心　core	獲得　procurement	家計　household
確信　assurance	獲得　purchase	家計の　economic
革新　advance	獲得する　achieve	掛売り　tick
革新　innovation	獲得する　chalk up	掛け金　annuity
革新　reform	獲得する　clinch	掛け金　contribution
革新　renovation	獲得する　collect	賭け事をする　gamble
革新する　renovate	獲得する　earn	可決する　adopt
革新性　innovation	獲得する　gain	可決する　pass
核心的な　core	獲得する　generate	掛けつなぎする　hedge
革新的な　groundbreaking	獲得する　land	掛けつなぎ売買　hedge
革新的な　innovative	獲得する　net	掛けつなぐ　hedge
隠す　cover up	獲得する　notch	陰で指揮する　mastermind
隠す　skim	獲得する　obtain	掛け値のない　net
隠す　stash	獲得する　procure	駆け引き　tactic(s)
…の拡大　increased	獲得する　secure	駆け引き　game
拡大　addition	獲得する　take out	駆け引き　power game
拡大　expansion	核となる　core	下限　bottom
拡大　extension	確認　confirmation	下限　floor
拡大　gain	確認書　confirmation	下限に近い　marginal
拡大　improvement	確認書　letter	過去　legacy
拡大　increase	核燃料　nuclear fuel	過誤　error
拡大　pickup	確保　availability	過誤　fault
拡大　rise	確保する　achieve	囲い込み　enclosure
拡大する　boost	確保する　insure	下降　downturn
拡大する　diversify	確保する　lock in	下降　lapse
拡大する　expand	確保する　rack up	下降　slide
拡大する　extend	確保する　retain	加工　conversion
拡大する　grow	確保する　secure	加工　fabrication
拡大する　improve	…（の確保）に努める　committed to	加工　machining
拡大する　increase		加工　manufacturing
拡大する　rise	核保有国　nuclear power	加工　processing
拡大する　strengthen	革命　revolution	下降気味　downside
拡大する　widen	額面　face	下降局面　downturn
拡張　enhancement	額面　par value	下降傾向　downside
拡張　expansion	額面価格　par value	加工していない　crude
拡張　extension	額面額　par value	下降する　downward
学長　president	額面金額　par value	加工する　convert
拡張可能な　open-ended	額面超過額　premium	加工する　fabricate
拡張工事　extension	確約　assurance	加工する　work
拡張する　expand	確約　engagement	加工品　finished goods
拡張する　extend	確約　pledge	加工品　finished product
拡張的財務報告言語　XBRL	確約する　commit	過去勤務　past service
格付け　classification	確約する　guarantee	過去勤務　prior service
格付け　grade	確約する　pledge	過酷な　punitive
格付け　grading	格安価格　bargain-basement price	過去最高　record
格付け　ranking	格安の　budget	過去最高の　record
格付け　rating		過去最大　record

過去にさかのぼる	retroactive	貸付け	loan	課税する	impose
過去の	historical	貸付け	loan facility	課税対象となる	taxable
かさ	bulk	貸付け金	indebtedness	課税できる	taxable
傘	umbrella	貸付け金	loan	課税率	tax rate
かさ上げする	inflate	貸付金額を固定した	closed-end	稼ぎ手	earner
家財	movable	貸付け先	borrower	化石燃料	fossil fuels
かさばる	bulk	貸付け実行	drawing	稼ぐ	earn
加算	addition	貸し付ける	finance	架設	installation
加算手当	weighting	貸し付ける	lend	画像	image
瑕疵	defect	貸し付ける	loan	画像	video
瑕疵	fault	貸し手	lender	仮想移動通信事業者	MVNO
瑕疵	flaw	貸主	creditor	下層から上層への	bottom-up
貸方	credit	貸主	lender	下層の	lower
貸方	creditor	貸主	lessor	仮想の	virtual
貸方に記入する	credit	瑕疵のない	clean	数え切れない	incalculable
貸金	credit	貨車で運ぶ	piggyback	家族	family
貸金業者	lender	貨車渡し	FOR	加速させる	accelerate
貸し渋り	tight lending	過重	surcharge	加速する	accelerate
貸倒れ	bad debt	加重付け	weighting	可塑性のある	plastic
貸倒れ	bad loan	加重平均	weighted average	ガソリン	gas
貸倒れ	credit loss	加重平均	weighted mean	ガソリン	gasoline
貸倒れ	default	加重平均資本コスト	WACC	ガソリン電気自動車	hybrid car
貸倒れ	loan loss	過重労働	overwork	型	model
貸倒れ	nonperforming loan	箇条	clause	型	pattern
貸倒れ	unrecoverable loan	過剰	excess	型	size
貸倒れ額	credit loss	過剰	surplus	…型	style
貸倒れ準備金	loan loss reserves	過少記載	underreporting	硬い[堅い, 固い]	hard
貸倒れ償却	write-off	過小計上する	understate	課題	agenda
貸倒れ損失	bad debt	過剰雇用	overmanning	課題	challenge
貸倒れ損失	loan loss	過剰在庫	overstock	課題	needs
貸倒れ損失	write-off	過剰債務	massive debts	課題	problem
貸倒れ損失額	loan loss charge	過少資本の	undercapitalized	課題	task
貸倒れ引当金	loan loss charge	過剰人員配置	overmanning	過大計上	overstatement
貸倒れ引当金	loan loss provisions	過少申告	underreporting	過大な	exorbitant
貸倒れ引当金	loan loss reserves	過少申告する	underreport	過大評価	overstatement
貸倒れ引当金を計上する	write down	過剰生産能力	overcapacity	過大評価	write-up
貸倒れ予想額	credit loss	過剰設備	overcapacity	過大評価する	overvalue
貸出	lending	過剰な	excessive	過大表示	overstatement
貸出	loan	過小評価	understatement	がた落ち	setback
貸出金の劣化	impaired loans	過小評価	undervaluation	肩書	title
貸出金利	lending rate	過小評価する	understate	肩代わり	assumption
貸出金利の上限	maximum lending rate	過小評価する	undervalue	肩代わりする	assume
貸出限度額	line of credit	過小表示	understatement	肩代わりする	take over
貸出債権	loan	過小表示する	understate	型式	model
貸出先	borrower	過剰利得	windfall	型にはまったやり方	lockstep
貸出資産	loan assets	可処分所得	take-home pay	過多の	excessive
貸出の実行	drawdown	…を課す	entail	…型の	-based
貸出の実行[実施]	disbursement	貸す	lend	片方	counterpart
貸出の抑制	tight lending	ガス	gas	過多量	overage
貸し出す	lease	ガス井	well	カタログ・ショッピング	catalog shopping
貸し出す	lend	課する	charge	カタログ請求書	catalog request form
貸し出す	loan	課する	impose	カタログ請求フォーム	catalog request form
瑕疵担保	warranty	風	wind	価値	value
過失	commission	課税	assessment	…より価値がある	outweigh
過失	defect	課税	taxation	価値が下がる	depreciate
過失	fault	課税…	taxable	家畜	livestock
過失	negligence	課税可能な	ratable	勝ち組	winner
貸付け	lending	課税金	charge		
		課税控除	exemption		
		課税されない	tax-exempt		

価値低下 depreciation	活動の最前線 front	稼得者 earner
勝ち取る clinch	活動範囲 activity	稼得する earn
価値のある産物 wealth	活動範囲 stage	門出 threshold
価値のある資産 valid asset	活動範囲を広げる branch out	過度の excessive
価値の下落 impairment	活動力 energy	過度の exorbitant
価値の低下 devaluation	活動力 wing	過度の労働 overwork
価値のない null	活発化 pickup	かなりの good
課徴金 fine	活発化 upbeat	かなりの healthy
課徴金 surcharge	活発な active	かなりの significant
かつ／または and/or	活発な brisk	かなりの規模の substantial
活気 activity	活発な heavy	かなりの収入 competence
活気が乏しい lackluster	活発な high	カニバリズム cannibalism
活気がない dull	活発な robust	加入 access
活気がない lackluster	活発になる intensify	加入 induction
活気づかせる boost	割賦金 installment	加入 participation
活気づかせる buoy	割賦償還 amortization	加入 penetration
活気づけ boost	割賦償還する amortize	加入 subscription
画期的な innovative	割賦適用業務 application	加入させる affiliate
画期的な事件 landmark	割賦払い installment	加入者 affiliate
画期的な新製品 innovation	カップリング coupling	加入者 customer
画期的な出来事 breakthrough	合併 amalgamation	加入者 participant
画期的な出来事 landmark	合併 combination	加入者 subscriber
画期的な発見 landmark	合併 incorporation	加入者 user
活気のある brisk	合併 merger	加入する access
活気のない passive	合併 tie-up	加入する affiliate
活況 activity	合併・買収 M & A	加入する participate
活況 strength	合併会社 merged firm	加入する take out
活況の brisk	合併協議書 merger deal	金 money
活況の buoyant	合併計画 merger plan	金貸し Lombard
活況の robust	合併交渉 merger talks	過熱 overheating
活況を呈している active	合併させる affiliate	過熱する overheat
活況を呈する take off	合併する affiliate	金で手を引かせる buy out
確固たる地位を占める well positioned	合併する consolidate	金を貸す lombard
…の合算 combined	合併する incorporate	金を借りすぎた overborrowed
合算 footing	合併する merge	金を融通する lombard
合算課税 unitary tax	活用 use	可能性 capability
合算した combined	活用する capitalize on	可能性 opportunity
合算する average	活用する exploit	可能性 potential
活性化 revitalization	活用する use	可能性 prospects
活性化する boost	活力がなくなる flag	可能性 scope
活性化する help	仮定 assumption	可能性がある potential
活性化する revitalize	家庭 family	カバーする cover
カット cut	家庭 home	カバーする offset
活動 action	家庭 household	ガバナンス governance
活動 activity	過程 process	カバレッジ coverage
活動 campaign	…と仮定する assume	過半数 majority
活動 conduct	家庭内の domestic	過半数株式 majority stake
活動 effort	家庭の domestic	過半数所有子会社 majority owned subsidiary
活動 life	家庭用電気器具 home appliance	過半数の major
活動 movement	カテゴリー category	株 interest
活動 operation	カテゴリー・キラー category killer	株 issue
活動 swing	家電 home appliance	株 sector
活動期 season	過度 excess	株 share
活動期間 life	稼働する run	株 stake
活動基準管理 ABM	可動性 movable	株 stock
活動基準原価計算 ABC	稼動中の going	株価 stock price
活動停止中の dormant	稼動中の onstream	株価指数連動型上場投資信託 ETF
活動的な active	下等の lower	株価収益率 P/E
活動度 activity	稼働率 availability	株価収益率 PER
	過渡期 transition	

株価純資産倍率 PBR	株式の買い乗せ pyramid	下方への downward
株価純資産倍率 price-to-book value	株式の額面価額 principal	構え stance
株価操作 market manipulation	株式の時価総額 market capitalization	…する構えを見せている poised to
株価のつり上げ kiting		紙 paper
株価を下げる hammer	株式の市場外買付け off-market purchase of shares	かみ合わせ engagement
株券 certificate of share [stock]		上期 first half
株券 share	株式の消却 retirement	上半期 first half
加符号 plus	株式の新規発行 floatation	加盟 induction
下部構造 infrastructure	株式配当 allotment	加盟権 franchise
株式 capital stock	株式売買益 capital gain	加盟国 member state
株式 equity	株式売買の代行業者 stockbroker	加盟する affiliate
株式 share	株式発行可能枠 authorized capital	加盟する enter
株式 stake	株式引受手数料 commission	画面 screen
株式 stock	株式非公開社 privately held company	画面の背景 desktop
株式売付け選択権 put		画面表示 display
株式オプション stock option	株式評価益権 SAR	科目履修案内 orientation
株式買受権 stock option	株式評価受益権 SAR	貨物 cargo
〈オランダ，ベルギーの〉株式会社 N.V.	株式ブローカー stockbroker	貨物 freight
	株式分割 split	貨物 goods
〈ドイツの〉株式会社 AG	株式保有 shareholding	貨物運送 freight
株式会社 corporation	株式保有 stockholding	貨物運送 freightage
株式会社 S.A. [SA]	株式保有率 shareholding	貨物運送料 freightage
株式会社の incorporated	株式未公開企業 privately held company	貨物の積替え trans-shipping
株式買取り請求権 warrant		貨物引換証 bill of lading
株式決済引取り猶予金 contango	株式持ち合い crossholding	貨物便 cargo
株式決済猶予金 contango	株式持ち合い interlocking stockholding	貨物便 freight
株式公開 floatation		貨物列車 freight
株式公開 initial public offering	株式持ち分 stake	貨物を積載した laden
株式公開 IPO	下部組織 infrastructure	通う travel
株式公開 public offering	株主 holder	可用性 availability
株式公開買付け bid	株主 owner	可用度 availability
株式公開買付け public tender offer	株主 shareholder	空売り short selling
	株主 shareowner	体の部分 region
株式公開買付け takeover bid	株主 stockholder	空手形 kite
株式公開買付け tender offer	株主資本 stockholders' equity	…からの ex
株式公開買付け TOB	株主資本比率 capital-to-asset ratio	空の bare
株式公開買付け価格 offer price		借り上げる charter
株式公開企業 publicly held company	株主資本利益率 ROE	借り上げる lease
	株主名簿 list of shareholders	借入れ advance
株式公開企業 publicly owned company [corporation]	株主名簿上の株主 stockholder of record	借入れ borrowing
		借入れ debt
株式公開する float	株主名簿登録機関 registrar	借入れ financing
株式購入選択権 stock option	株主持ち分 net worth	借入れ leverage
株式公募 public offering	株主持ち分 stockholders' equity	借入れ loan
株式市況 bourse	下部の lower	借入金 advance
株式資本 capital stock	買い越し net buying	借入金 borrowing
株式資本 stock	壁 barrier	借入金 debt
株式資本化 capitalization	貨幣 mintage	借入金 indebtedness
株式資本金 capital stock	貨幣 money	借入金 loan
株式上場 public listing	貨幣購買力 purchasing power	借入金残高 outstanding debt
株式所有 shareholding	貨幣項目 monetary items	借入金で企業などを買い取る leverage
株式数 number of shares	貨幣性項目 monetary items	
株式相場 bourse	貨幣性資産 monetary assets	借入金で投機をする leverage
株式投資収益率 ROE	貨幣鋳造 mintage	借入金による leveraged
株式登録機関 registrar	貨幣的ベース monetary base	借入金の定期返済 service
株式仲買い broking	貨幣の monetary	借入金を利用した leveraged
株式仲買人 stockbroker	貨幣流通高 cash in circulation	借入限度額 line of credit
株式の売り乗せ pyramid	可変の variable	借入限度額 loan values
株式の買付け buyout	下方修正する downgrade	借入債務 debt
	下方修正する slash	借入残高 outstanding debt

借入資金による	leveraged
借入資金による企業買収	LBO
借入資金による企業買収	leveraged buyout
借入資本	leverage
借入比率	leverage
借入余力	leverage
借り入れる	borrow
借入枠	line of credit
借入枠中未借入額	line of credit
借換え	conversion
借換え	prepayment
借換え	refinance
借換え	refinancing
借換え	refund
借換え	refunding
借換え	rollover
借換え	shifting loan
借り換える	flip
借り換える	refinance
借り換える	refund
借り換える	roll over
借方	debit
借方	debtor
借方記入	charge
借方に記入する	charge
仮株券	scrip
仮採用期間	probation
仮証券	scrip
借りつなぎ	rollover
借り手	borrower
借り手のいない	vacant
借主	debtor
借主	lessee
借主	tenant
仮の	interim
仮の	preliminary
仮の	temporary
仮払い金	advance
カリフォルニア州公務員退職年金基金	CalPERS
カリブ共同体	CARICOM
仮目論見書	red herring
下流部門	downstream
火力発電の	thermal
…を借りる	piggyback
カルチャー	culture
カルテル	cartel
カルテル	pool
カルネ	carnet
カルパース	CalPERS
加齢	aging
ガレージ起業家	garage entrepreneur
ガレージ・セール	garage sale
過労	overwork
過労死	death from overwork
辛うじて採算が取れる	break even
川	water
…側	interest
川上産業	upstream
川下部門	downstream
かわす	ward off
為替	currency
為替	exchange
為替	foreign currency
為替	forex
為替相場	currency
為替相場	exchange
為替相場	foreign currency
為替手形	b/e
為替手形	draft
為替取組み先	correspondent
為替平価	par value
為替平価	parity
為替リスクの防止・軽減	hedge
…の側に立つ	side with
…の側につく	side with
変わらない	unchanged
変わりやすい	variable
変わりやすい	volatile
変わる	shift
…観	outlook
勘	savvy
考え	idea
考え	submission
考え方	attitude
考え方	idea
考え出す	come up with
考え直す	reinvent
考えを変える	turn around
間隔	clearance
換価した	realized
換価する	realize
管轄	demarcation
管轄区域	jurisdiction
管轄権	competence
管轄権	jurisdiction
カンガルー債	kangaroo bonds
カンガルー方式	kangaroo system
…を喚起する	drive
喚起する	boost
環境	background
環境	climate
環境	condition
環境	environment
環境	framework
環境	opportunity
環境	situation
環境	trend
環境維持開発	ecodevelopment
環境共生住宅	ecohouse
環境経営	eco management
環境経営	ecocentric management
環境中心経営	ecocentric management
環境に配慮した	green
環境にやさしい	ecological
環境にやさしい	ecologically-friendly
環境にやさしい	environmental
環境にやさしい	green
環境にやさしい材料	ecomaterial
環境の	environmental
環境の	green
環境の大量破壊	ecocide
環境破壊	ecocide
環境への適応	integration
環境保護	ecology
環境保護局	EPA
環境保護庁	U.S. Environmental Protection Agency
環境保護に関する	environmental
環境保護の	green
環境保全ラベル	ecolabeling
環境問題	ecology
環境問題に関心のある	ecological
環境問題を意識した	eco-conscious
環境を意識した	eco-conscious
環境を害さない	environmental
換金	liquidation
換金	realization
元金	capital
元金	principal
換金しにくい	illiquid
換金する	cash
換金する	negotiate
関係	affair
関係	concern
関係	footing
関係	framework
関係	link
関係	reference
関係	relations
関係	relationship
関係	tie-in
関係会社	affiliate
関係会社	associate
関係会社	associated company
関係会社	operation
関係会社	subsidiary
関係会社間取引	intercompany transaction
関係者	affiliate
関係者	insider
関係者	interest
関係者	official
関係者	participant
関係者	party
関係者	player
関係者	source(s)
…に関係する	concern
歓迎する	receive
…関係の	related
関係のある	related
関係を築く	establish
簡潔な指示を与える	brief
還元	recycling
還元	return
還元する	return

看護	care	感情	sentiment	観点	way
刊行	issuance	勘定書	account	感度	sensitivity
慣行	convention	勘定書	bill	監督	charge
慣行	practice	勘定書	tab	監督	oversight
慣行	procedure	勘定残高	account balance	監督	supervision
刊行する	publish	勘定残高	balance	監督者	superintendent
勧告の	advisory	官職	appointment	監督者	supervisor
監査	audit	官職	office	監督する	govern
監査	auditing	幹事を務める	manage	監督する	manage
監査	examination	関心	concern	監督する	superintendent
監査	inspection	関心事	affair	監督する	supervise
完済	payoff	関心事	care	観念	concept
監査意見	opinion	関心事	concern	観念	idea
完済する	pay off	完遂	accomplishment	完納	delivery
管財人	manager	関数	function	感応度	sensitivity
管財人	trustee	関数の	functional	完敗	debacle
監査依頼会社	client	慣性	inertia	かんばん方式	just-in-time
監査機関	auditor	関税	customs	かんばん方式	JIT
監査する	audit	関税	duty	幹部	manager
監査する	examine	関税	tariff	幹部	official
監査する	review	完成財	finished goods	幹部	staff
監査人	accountant	完成財	finished product	還付金	rebate
監査人	auditor	完成する	execute	幹部社員	manager
監査法人	auditor	関税なしで	duty-free	幹部職員	ranking official
監査役	auditor	完成品	finished goods	還付する	refund
換算	commutation	完成品	finished product	幹部退職金	golden parachute
換算	conversion	完成品引渡し方式の	turnkey	願望	want
換算	equivalent	関税率	tariff	元本	principal
換算	translation	間接的な	implied	甘味料	sweetener
閑散	thin market	間接的な	indirect	勧誘	inducement
換算額	equivalent	間接的な	secondary	勧誘	solicitation
閑散市場	thin market	間接の	indirect	勧誘する	canvass
換算する	convert	間接費	burden	勧誘する	lure
換算する	translate	間接費	overhead	勧誘する	solicit
閑散とした	quiet	間接部門	overhead	関与	engagement
監視	monitoring	完全子会社化する	wholly own	関与	hand
監視	oversight	完全下請の	in-shop	関与	participation
監視	supervision	完全失業率	jobless rate	関与する	participate
幹事	organizer	完全失業率	joblessness	監理	monitoring
監視員	supervisor	完全所有する	wholly own	管理	administration
幹事会社被信託人	trustee	完全操業度	full capacity	管理	care
監視活動	monitoring	完全な	absolute	管理	charge
がんじがらめの配列	lockstep	完全な	full	管理	conduct
監視官	regulators	完全な	in-depth	管理	control
鑑識眼	discrimination	完全な	outright	管理	custody
幹事行	lead manager	完全な	plenary	管理	governance
幹事銀行	lead manager	完全に	fully	管理	government
監視する	monitor	完全に一体化した	seamless	管理	hand
監視団体	watchdog organization	完全に打ち負かす	hammer	管理	management
幹事(引受会社)	manager	簡素化	streamlining	管理	regulation
患者	case	簡素化する	streamline	管理	supervision
患者数	incidence	観測	speculation	管理運営する	govern
慣習	custom	簡素な	basic	元利合計	amount
慣習	practice	歓待	entertainment	管理者	manager
願書	application	缶詰工業	packing	管理者	superintendent
干渉	intervention	鑑定	appraisal	管理者	supervisor
勘定	account	鑑定	assessment	管理上の	administrative
勘定	accounts	鑑定	opinion	管理職	executive
勘定	tab	鑑定額	assessment	管理する	administer
勘定	tick	観点	level	管理する	control

管理する controlling	keyhole investment	機関誌 journal
管理する keep	キーマン keyman	期間従業員 temporary employee
管理する manage	キーワード keyword	既刊書目録 backlist
管理する monitor	起因 origination	機関投資家 institutional investor
管理する run	記憶 retention	機関投資家向けの wholesale
管理する superintendent	記憶装置 storage	基幹の key
管理的 administrative	記憶素子 chip	期間の periodic
管理人 custodian	記憶力 retention	期間配分 allocation
管理人 superintendent	キオ・プラン Keogh	危機 crisis
管理人 supervisor	器械 instrument	危機 crunch
管理の custodial	機会 opening	危機 difficulties
管理の managerial	機会 opportunity	危機 juncture
管理引受け adoption	機会 scope	危機 turmoil
管理部長 controller	機会 time	機器 equipment
管理法 governance	機械 hardware	機器 hardware
還流 recycling	機械 machine	機器 instrument
還流する return	機械 machinery	機器 machine
完了 accomplishment	議会 session	機器 machinery
完了 fulfillment	機械加工 machining	機器 maker
完了する achieve	議会工作 lobbying	機器構成 configuration
完了する conclude	機械受注 machinery orders	機器調達 procurement
完了する fulfill	機械受注額 machinery orders	危機的状況 crunch
慣例 convention	機械装置 machinery	棄却 dismissal
慣例 routine	機械停止時間 downtime	棄却する dismiss
慣例 rule	機械に送り込む feed	棄却する reject
関連 correspondence	機械類 gadgetry	危急の事態 juncture
関連 reference	企画 enterprise	企業 b
関連 relations	企画 organization	企業 business
関連 relationship	企画 planning	企業 company
関連 tie-in	企画 project	企業 concern
関連会社 affiliate	企画 proposal	企業 corporation
関連会社 associate	企画 scheme	企業 employer
関連会社 associated company	規格 standard	企業 enterprise
関連した related	企画運営者 organizer	企業 firm
関連性 combination	規格化 standardization	企業 institution
関連付ける link	規格境界面 interface	企業 interest
…関連の -focused	企画者 planner	企業 organization
関連のない unaffiliated	企画する project	企業 player
緩和 relief	企画する propose	企業 producer
緩和する reduce	企画段階から生産開始までの所要時間 lead time	企業 provider
	規格統一 standardization	企業 undertaking
き	企画立案 planning	起業 entrepreneurship
…期 period	企画力 organization	企業育成機関 incubator
…期 season	旗艦 flagship	企業育成施設 incubator
期 stage	期間 horizon	企業育成施設 incubator facility
期 year	期間 life	企業イメージ統合戦略 CI
基 unit	期間 period	企業家 entrepreneur
ギア gear	期間 term	起業家 entrepreneur
ギアリング gearing	期間 time	企業改革法 Sarbanes-Oxley Act
議案 items of business	期間 time frame	企業会計改革法 Sarbanes-Oxley Act
議案 resolution	機関 establishment	企業化可能性 feasibility
起案する draw	機関 institution	企業家精神 entrepreneurship
議案提出権 initiative	機関 organization	起業家精神 entrepreneurship
議案の通過を促す promote	帰還 feedback	起業家精神が旺盛な entrepreneurial
議案の読会 reading	期間延長 extension	
キー key	基幹回線 backbone	企業家の entrepreneurial
キーキャプチャー・ソフト key-capture software	期間帰属差異 timing differences	起業家の entrepreneurial
キーホール・インベストメント	既刊号 back number	起業家マインド enterprise
	期間差異 timing differences	企業間 B2B

企業間株式保有 intercorporate stockholding	企業を閉鎖する wind up	記号 mark
企業間の取引 B2B	基金 basic fund	記号 symbol
企業幹部 keyman	基金 capital	起工式 groundbreaking
企業官僚主義 corpocracy	基金 foundation	起工(式)の groundbreaking
企業グループ conglomerate	基金 fund	技巧的な technical
企業グループ group	基金 treasury	気候変動に関する政府間パネル IPCC
企業経営内容の公開 disclosure	基金拠出 capital injection	記載 entry
企業結合 combination	基金設立 funding	記載事項 entry
企業合理化 shakeout	基金増資 capital increase	記載上の clerical
企業再生 turnaround	基金増資 capital injection	記載する enter
企業再編 repositioning	貴金属 metal	記載する include
企業資源管理 ERP	基金を寄付する endow	記載する list
企業資源計画 ERP	器具 instrument	記載する maker
企業市民 corporate citizen [citizenship]	器具 maker	記載する reflect
企業主 owner	ぎくしゃく感がない seamless	記載する report
企業集団 group	議決権 vote	起債する issue
企業取得 acquisition	議決権行使 voting	機材調達先 vendor
企業取得 takeover	議決権行使委任状 proxy	起債発表 launch
企業取得と合併 M & A	議決権のない株式 nonvoting share	兆し evidence
企業情報 BI	議決権を行使する vote	兆し sign
企業情報の開示 disclosure	議決する vote	記事 write-up
企業責任 accountability	危険 hazard	議事 items of business
企業体 concern	危険 jeopardy	…を基軸とする -based
企業体 entity	危険 peril	基軸の key
企業対企業の取引 B2B	危険 risk	議事進行 proceedings
企業対従業員の取引 B2E	期限 day	期日 day
企業担保借入買取り LBO	期限 maturity	期日が到来する mature
企業担保借入買取り leveraged buyout	期限 time	期日のない undated
	期限延長 renewal	記事にする feature
企業対消費者の取引 B2C	期限が切れる expire	記者 correspondent
企業統合 consolidation	期限切れになる terminate	記者会見 news conference
企業内訓練 TWI	危険事情 hazard	記者会見 press conference
企業内情報通信網 LAN	危険資本 venture capital	希釈化 dilution
企業内組織の満足 ES	危険性 hazard	希釈化する dilute
企業内の in-house	危険性 risk	期首 opening
企業内容の開示 disclosure	危険性の高い事業 venture	機種 line
企業認識 CI	期限付き契約 prompt	機種 model
企業の corporate	危険な long	期首から現在までの YTD
企業の entrepreneurial	期限内の unexpired	機種構成 lineup
企業の合併・買収 mergers and acquisitions	期限の経過した overdue	…技術 -tech
	危険負担 risk	技術 capability
企業の吸収合併 M & A	危険負担資本 venture capital	技術 engineering
企業の系列化 integration	危険物 hazard	技術 skill
企業の社会的責任 CSR	期限前償還 prepayment	技術 technology
企業の生存領域 domain	期限前償還する prepay	技術移転機関 TLO
企業の存続可能性 going concern	期限前の advanced	技術援助契約 license agreement
企業の本業 domain	期限前返済 early retirement	技術革新 innovation
企業買収 acquisition	期限前返済 prepayment	技術恐怖症 technophobial
企業買収 takeover	期限前弁済する prepay	既述事項 premises
企業買収家 raider	危険要因 hazard	技術実施許諾者 licenser
企業秘密 trade secret	危険要素 hazard	技術上周知の well-known in the art
企業分割 divestiture	機構 fabric	
企業閉鎖 winding up	機構 machinery	技術情報 knowhow
企業連合 cartel	機構 organization	技術水準 state-of-the-art
企業連合 combination	機構 scheme	技術知識 knowhow
企業連合 consortium	機構 structure	技術的な technical
企業連合 pool	機構 system	技術的な technological
企業連合体 consortium	気候 climate	技術取引場 techno-mart
	起工 groundbreaking	技術の technical
	記号 designation	技術の高度化 sophistication

技術秘訣 knowhow	規制責任者 regulators	気体 gas
技術秘密 knowhow	規制撤廃 decontrol	議題 agenda
期首の initial	規制撤廃 deregulation	議題 matter
基準 base	規制当局 regulators	議題 question
基準 basis	規制を緩和する deregulate	期待される prospective
基準 benchmark	規制を撤廃する deregulate	期待する anticipate
基準 code	季節 season	期待する expect
基準 concept	季節ごとの seasonal	期待値 expectation
基準 criterion	季節調整後の seasonally adjusted	期待できる市場 promising market
基準 gauge	季節調整済みの seasonally adjusted	期待できる分野 promising area
基準 guideline		期待どおりの reliable
基準 method	季節調整値 seasonally adjusted	期待にこたえられない fall flat
基準 principle	季節的な seasonal	期待外れに終わる backfire
基準 requirement(s)	季節の seasonal	期待外れの disappointing
基準 rule	基礎 base	期待利益 expectancy
基準 scale	基礎 basis	…の期待を裏切る disappointing
基準 scheme	基礎 fabric	北大西洋自由貿易地域 NAFTA
基準 standard	基礎 foundation	基地 base
基準 test	基礎 fundamentals	基地 platform
規準 norm	競う compete	既知の known
規準 rule	寄贈 donation	帰着 incidence
基準株 barometer stock	偽造 fabrication	期中 during the period
基準金利 key interest rate	起草作業 drafting work	期中の interim
基準金利 key rate	起草する draw	基調 keynote
基準指数 benchmark	寄贈する donate	基調 trend
基準書 standard	偽装する falsify	記帳 entry
基準測定値 measure	偽造する fabricate	議長 chairman
基準値 benchmark	偽造する fake	議長 president
…の基準となる govern	偽造する falsify	議長国 host
基準にする benchmark	偽造の counterfeit	記帳する book
…基準の -based	偽造の fake	記帳する record
基準銘柄 benchmark	偽造の false	きっかけ trigger
基準量 norm	偽装表示 mislabeling	…のきっかけとなる trigger
規準労働量 norm	寄贈品 donation	…のきっかけを作る trigger
議場 floor	偽造文書 fabrication	拮抗 rivalry
机上型の desktop	規則 bylaws	木づち hammer
議事要旨 minutes	規則 code	切手 stamp
希少の scarce	規則 regulation	切手を貼る stamp
議事録 journal	規則 rule	キット kit
議事録 minutes	帰属意識 identity	規定 clause
議事録 proceedings	帰属計算する impute	規定 establishment
議事録 protocol	帰属させる impute	規定 policy
築く form	帰属させる vest	規定 protocol
築く set up	帰属する vest	規定 provision
傷口 cut	基礎化粧品 foundation	規定 regulation
傷つける prejudice	基礎資料 database	規定 requirement(s)
傷物の irregular	起訴する accuse	規定 rule
…に帰する attribute	起訴する litigate	議定書 pact
帰する impute	起訴する prosecute	議定書 protocol
規制 control	基礎的 underlying	規定する define
規制 regulation	基礎的条件 fundamentals	規定する establish
規制 restriction	基礎的な basic	規定する govern
犠牲 prey	基礎となる underlying	規定する state
規制緩和 deregulation	基礎利益 fundamental profit	起点 origination
規制緩和 liberalization	毀損 wastage	既得の vested
規制緩和する liberalize	既存店ベースの like-for-like	危難 peril
規制機関 regulators	既存の債務 outstanding debt	記入 entry
規制機関 regulatory body	期待 expectancy	記入する book
既成社会 establishment	期待 expectation	記入する enter
規制する regulate	期待 prospects	記入する keep

記入する	put	寄付金	subscription	期末整理	adjustment
疑念	misgiving	寄付する	donate	期末の	terminal
機能	capability	寄付する	subscribe	気味	sign
機能	feature	規模	proportion	機密扱いにする	classify
機能	function	規模	scale	機密扱いの	classified
機能	mode	規模	size	機密性	confidentiality
帰納	induction	規模	way	機密の	sensitive
技能	accomplishment	希望退職	early retirement	機密ルート	pipeline
技能	skill	規模拡大する	widen	義務	accountability
機能拡張	extension	規模縮小	downsizing	義務	charge
機能拡張	upgrade	規模を縮小する	downscale	義務	duty
機能している	operational	基本	base	義務	liability
機能している	working	基本	fabric	義務	obligation
機能障害	malfunction	基本	fundamentals	義務	responsibility
機能する	function	基本	nuts and bolts	義務付ける	mandate
機能する	perform	基本金	foundation	義務的な	mandatory
帰納する	induce	基本契約	basic agreement	義務的な	obligatory
機能停止	failure	基本契約	master agreement	義務として課される	incumbent
機能の	functional	基本合意	basic agreement	義務の履行	performance
機能不全	malfunction	基本合意書	basic agreement	義務不履行者	defaulter
帰納法	induction	基本合意書	memorandum of understanding	義務履行の委託	delegation
…の機能を果たす	serve			記名株券	certificate of share [stock]
機能を果たす	function	基本構造	fabric		
希薄化	dilution	基本財産	endowment	決める	close
希薄化する	dilute	基本財産	principal	決める	decide
希薄化前	primary	基本システム	platform	決める	determine
起爆剤	trigger	基本施設	infrastructure	決める	elect
揮発油	gasoline	基本思想	concept	決める	fix
気晴らし	diversion	基本資料	database	決める	govern
規範	code	基本政策	keynote	決める	name
規範	conduct	基本設計	architecture	疑問	query
規範	law	基本設計	core	規約	bylaws
規範	norm	基本設備	infrastructure	規約	code
基盤	base	基本定款	articles of association	規約	contract
基盤	fabric	基本定款	articles of incorporation	規約	rule
基盤	foothold	基本定款	charter	規約	statement
基盤	footing	基本定款	memorandum of association	客観性	objectivity
基盤	foundation			客観的な	objective
基盤	infrastructure	基本的	primary	客観的目標に基づく	objective
基盤	platform	基本的指標	fundamentals	逆効果	adverse effect
忌避	challenge	基本的な	basic	逆効果になる	backfire
厳しい	hard	基本的な	central	逆ざや	negative spread
厳しい	intensive	基本的な	core	逆資産効果	negative wealth effect
厳しい	poor	基本的な	net	逆転	reversal
厳しい	punitive	基本的な	nuts and bolts	逆転させる	reverse
厳しい	stringent	基本的な	underlying	逆にする	reverse
厳しい	unfriendly	基本的な考え方	concept	逆の	negative
厳しい	weak	基本的な考え方	philosophy	逆の	reciprocal
厳しい環境	stress	基本的な機能に限定した	no-frills	逆の	reverse
厳しい経営環境	stress	基本的な設計思想	architecture	逆風	adverse wind
厳しい批判	thrust	基本的問題	nuts and bolts	逆境	setback
機敏な	prompt	基本の	basic	逆方向の	reverse
寄付	contribution	基本の	master	脚本	scenario
寄付	donation	基本方針	keynote	却下	dismissal
寄付	subscription	基本モデル	core	却下する	dismiss
寄付活動	philanthropy	基本理念	keynote	却下する	quash
寄付金	contribution	期末	closing	逆行	reaction
寄付金	donation	期末	end	逆行	setback
寄付金	endowment	期末	year end	キャッシュ	cash
寄付金	purse	期末	yearend	キャッシュ・カード	cash card

キャッシュ・ディスペンサー	CD	吸収	absorption	急騰	appreciation
キャッシュ・フロー	cash flow	吸収・合併計画	merger plan	急騰	boom
キャッシュ・フロー	stream	吸収合併	absorption	急騰	rally
キャッシュ・フロー割引	discount cash flow	吸収合併	merger	急騰	surge
キャッシュ・マージャー	cash merger	吸収合併	takeover	急騰する	rally
キャッシュレス	cashless	吸収合併する	absorb	急騰する	skyrocket
キャッチオール規制	Catch-all or End-use Controls	吸収合併する	merge	急騰する	soar
キャップ	cap	急襲者	raider	急騰する	surge
キャップ	tab	吸収する	absorb	急騰する	zoom
ギャップ	gap	吸収する	offset	急な	sharp
キャパシティ	capacity	救出	rescue	急に伸びる	take off
キャピタル・ゲイン	capital gain	救出する	rescue	急場	crunch
キャピタル・リース	capital lease	救助	relief	給付	benefit
キャピタル・ロス	capital loss	救助	rescue	給付額	benefit
キャプション	caption	窮状	plight	給付金	benefit
キャリア	career	求償権	contribution	給付金	relief
キャリア	carrier	急上昇	boost	給付金	stipend
キャリー取引	carry trade	急上昇	run	給付費	payout
キャリー・トレード	carry trade	急上昇	surge	休眠中の	dormant
キャルス	CALS	急上昇する	leap	休眠特許	unused patent
キャルス	CALS	急上昇する	skyrocket	休眠の	inactive
キャンセルする	cancel	急上昇する	zoom	給与	compensation
キャンペーン	campaign	休職	separation	給与	salary
キャンペーン	drive	求職	job opening	休養期間	layoff
キャンペーン	effort	求職広告	classified	給与外給付	fringe benefit
級	notch	求職者	job seeker	給与支払い簿	payroll
救援	relief	求職者	jobseeker	給与支払い用経常負担(金)	payload
救援	rescue	休職手当の支払い	separation payments	給与総額	payroll
休暇	layoff	救助する	rescue	給与表	payroll
休暇	leave	求人	job offer	急落	collapse
休会	closing	求人	job opening	急落	downfall
休暇期間	leave	求人	job opportunity	急落	meltdown
休暇許可	leave	求人	opening	急落	meltdown
急拡大	boom	求人	recruitment	急落	plunge
急拡大する	leap	求人	wanted	急落	sell-off
急激な	sharp	求人広告	classified	急落	slump
急減	collapse	求人市場	job market	急落する	nosedive
急減する	collapse	急成長	boom	急落する	plummet
急減する	nosedive	急成長産業部門	fast-growing segment	急落する	plunge
旧号	back number	急成長分野	fast-growing segment	急落する	tumble
急降下	plunge	急増	boom	給料	hire
急行の	express	急増	boost	給料	pay
救済	bailout	急増	sharp increase	給料	paycheck
救済	relief	急増	surge	給料	remuneration
救済	rescue	急増する	leap	給料	salary
救済	salvage	急増する	skyrocket	給料	wage
救済手段	help	急増する	soar	給料小切手	paycheck
救済する	bolster	急増する	surge	給料支払い小切手	paycheck
救済する	rescue	急増する	zoom	給料日	payday
救済措置	bailout	急送の	express	寄与	contribution
急使	courier	急速	velocity	…業	industry
旧式化	obsolescence	急速な	sharp	脅威	challenge
旧式の	obsolete	急速に悪化する	nosedive	教育	development
旧式のもの	back number	窮地	corner	教育	education
休止状態の	dormant	窮地	fix	供応	entertainment
休止中の	dormant	窮地	impasse	強化	beef-up
休止の	idle	窮地	distressed	強化	consolidation
		急転換	about-face	強化	enhancement
				協会	association

境界	demarcation
境界	threshold
業界	community
業界	industry
業界	interest
業界	scene
業界	sector
境界画定	demarcation
業界最大手	majors
境界設定	demarcation
境界線	landmark
強化する	beef up
強化する	bolster
強化する	boost
強化する	consolidate
強化する	enhance
強化する	improve
強化する	increase
強化する	intensify
強化する	reinforce
強化する	strengthen
恐喝	blackmail
恐喝者	racketeer
競技	game
協議	bargain
協議	communication
協議	conference
協議	consultation
協議	deal
協議	negotiation
協議	talks
協議	treaty
協議会	consultation
協議事項	agenda
協議書	deal
競技場	park
協議する	negotiate
供給	export
供給	feed
供給	injection
供給	sourcing
供給	supply
供給会社	supplier
供給過剰	glut
供給過剰	oversupply
供給業者	supplier
供給源	resource(s)
供給源	supplier
供給国	supplier
供給下請業者	supplier
供給者	producer
供給者	supplier
供給する	distribute
供給する	feed
供給する	furnish
供給する	inject
供給する	provide
供給する	serve
供給する	supply
供給地	staple

供給独占	monopoly
狂牛病	bovine spongiform encephalopathy
狂牛病	BSE
供給品	supply
供給元	purveyor
供給元	vendor
供給量	supply
供給ルート	pipeline
供給連鎖	supply chain
競業	competition
協業	cooperation
業況の悪化	contraction
業況判断指数	diffusion index
教訓を得る	profit
狂言の	fake
恐慌	crisis
競合	competition
競合する	compete
競合他社	competitor
競合他社	peer
強豪チーム	powerhouse
強行着陸	hard landing
強固な	solid
強固な	strong
教材	resource(s)
共済事業	mutual relief operations
共済年金	mutual aid pension plan
共済年金制度	mutual aid pension plan
行事	event
業者	house
業者	provider
業種	industry
業種	line of business
供述	showing
業種別企業案内	yellow pages
共進会	fair
強制	pressure
矯正	reform
行政	administration
行政	government
行政機関	agency
行政規則	regulation
行政権や徴税権などを行使できる国家や地方自治体	jurisdiction
行政上の処分	action
強制する	mandate
強請する	extort
矯正する	redress
矯正する	reform
強制的な	cramdown
強制的な	mandatory
行政の	administrative
行政府	government
強制分割	unbundling
業績	accomplishment
業績	achievement
業績	bottom line
業績	business

業績	earnings
業績	figure
業績	performance
業績	results
業績悪化	downside
業績悪化の	distressed
業績改善	turnaround
業績好調	good performance
業績連動型の報酬制度	merit-based pay plan
競争	competition
競争	competitiveness
競争	race
競争	rivalry
競争	struggle
競争相手	competition
競争相手	competitor
競争相手	contender
競争相手	rival
競争相手国	rival
競争条件	playing field
競争上の	competitive
競争する	compete
競争的	competitive
競争の場	playing field
競争力	advantage
競争力	competitiveness
競争力のある	competitive
共存	compatibility
業態超え統合	cross-sectoral tie-up
業態を超えての統合	cross-sectoral tie-up
供託	lodgement
供託所	depository
協調	cooperation
協調	coordination
強調	stress
協調介入	intervention
…を強調する	focus on
協調する	coordinate
協調融資団	consortium
協調融資団	syndicate
協調路線	cooperative approach
共通点がある	comparable
共通の	common
共通の	corporate
共通の	joint
共通の	mutual
共通の	universal
協定	accord
協定	agreement
協定	arrangement
協定	bargain
協定	contract
協定	convention
協定	deal
協定	protocol
協定	treaty
協定	understanding
協定覚書	memorandum of

協定書					拠出制年金制度
	understanding	業務	function	許可	leave
協定書	contract	業務	job	許可	license
協定する	negotiate	業務	occupation	許可	permission
協定を結ぶ	sign up	業務	operation	許可	permit
協同	cooperation	業務	practice	許可	recognition
共同運航	code-sharing	業務	service	巨額	mint
共同海損分担金	contribution	業務	task	巨額の	heavy
共同管理	pool	業務	transaction	巨額の	large
共同企業	joint venture	業務	venture	巨額の	massive
共同企業体	joint venture	業務委託	outsourcing	巨額の介入	massive intervention
共同企業体	JV	業務委託	sourcing	巨額の債務	massive debts
共同経営	partnership	業務委託する	outsource	許可された	green
共同経営者	partner	業務革新	BPR	許可者	licenser
共同計算する	pool	業務革新	reengineering	許可書	license
共同事業	joint venture	業務隔壁	firewall	許可書	permit
共同事業体	consortium	業務活動	activity	許可証	permit
共同事業体	joint venture	業務規則	bylaws	許可する	approve
共同事業体	JV	業務規定	manual	許可する	authorize
共同資金	pool	業務執行	management	許可する	grant
共同社会	community	業務執行役員	officer	許可する	license
共同出資	partnership	業務上の	operational	許可する	recognize
共同出資	pool	業務上の	professional	許可料	fine
共同出資会社	joint venture	業務処理	transaction	許可を与える	license
共同出資事業	joint venture	業務日誌	log	許可を受けた者	licensee
共同出資者	partner	業務の	operating	虚偽記載	misstatement
共同出資する	jointly own	業務の根本的革新	reengineering	虚偽記載する	falsify
共同所有	partnership	業務を革新する	reengineer	虚偽の	false
…が共同所有している	equally	業務を根本的に革新する		虚偽の	misleading
	owned by		reengineer	虚偽の表示	misrepresentation
共同所有者	partner	業務を変革する	reengineer	虚偽表示	misstatement
共同所有する	jointly own	協約	agreement	局	board
共同体	community	協約	convention	局	bureau
共同の	common	協約	covenant	局	department
共同の	corporate	協約	deal	局員	staff
共同の	joint	協約	engagement	局所の	regional
共同の	mutual	協約	pact	極大化	maximization
共同の利権とする	pool	協約	protocol	極端な	excessive
共同負担	sharing	協約	treaty	局地化	localization
共同負担する	pool	協約	understanding	局地の	regional
共同負担する	share	共有する	share	局長	director
共同分担	sharing	共有の	common	局長	superintendent
共同分担する	share	共有の	joint	極度	limit
共同保険	co-insurance	強要	pressure	局部限定	localization
共同連合体	consortium	教養	education	局部的な	regional
京都議定書	Kyoto pact	業容	business	局面	environment
京都議定書	Kyoto Protocol	強要する	extort	局面	period
競売	auction	供与する	extend	局面	phase
競売人	auctioneer	協力	contribution	寄与したもの	contributor
脅迫者	racketeer	協力	cooperation	居住している	resident
共謀	collusion	協力	front	居住者	resident
共謀する	collude	協力	partnership	拠出	contribution
興味を引く	attract	協力	tie-up	拠出	disbursement
興味を持つ	attract	協力する	contribute	拠出	funding
業務	activity	協力する	sponsor	拠出	provision
業務	administration	協力する	tie up	拠出型制度	contributory plan
業務	affair	強力な	strong	拠出型年金制度	contributory plan
業務	business	許可	allowance	拠出金	contribution
業務	concern	許可	approval	拠出する	contribute
業務	engagement	許可	authority	拠出する	fund
業務	execution	許可	authorization	拠出制年金制度	contributory plan

…に寄与する	help	気力	drive	銀行間相場	market rate
寄与する	contribute	ギルト債	gilt	銀行間出し手金利	IBOR
拒絶証書	protest	切れ味が悪い	dull	銀行間の	interbank
拒絶する	reject	儀礼書	protocol	銀行休業日	bank holiday
巨大企業	giant	亀裂	split	銀行業	banking
巨大銀行	megabank	切れる	lapse	銀行業務	banking
巨大銀行グループ	megabank	記録	entry	銀行兼保険業務	allfinanz
巨大な	large	記録	file	銀行口座	bank account
巨大な	massive	記録	record	銀行口座の残高	account balance
巨大複合企業	conglomerate	記録	register	銀行団	syndicate
許諾	license	記録	registry	銀行団による協調融資	syndicated loan
許諾者	grantor	記録	tab		
許諾する	grant	記録	tally	銀行通帳	bankcard
許諾する	license	記録係	registrar	近郊都市	satellite
許諾地域	territory	記録されていない	off-the-book	銀行に預け入れる	stash
許諾料	royalty	記録事項	registration	均衡のとれた	in-depth
虚脱感	burnout	…を記録する	chalk up	銀行間取り手金利	IBBR
拠点	base	記録する	book	均衡レート	equilibrium
拠点	center [centre]	記録する	hit	金庫株	treasury stock
拠点	fab	記録する	list	僅差の	close
拠点	hub	記録する	notch	禁止	ban
拠点	location	記録する	record	禁止	embargo
拠点	presence	記録する	write down	禁止する	ban
拠点	site	記録的な	record	禁止する	prohibit
拠点	stronghold	記録簿	register	禁止する	prohibitive
…を拠点とする	base	記録簿	registry	禁止する	restrict
拠点を置く	base	キロバイト	KB	均質の	homogeneous
許認可	licensing	キロビット／秒	kilobits per second	近似の	approximate
拒否	challenge	キロビット毎秒	kilobits per second	禁止命令	injunction
拒否権	veto	議論	contention	緊縮財政	austere fiscal policy
拒否権を行使する	veto	疑惑	fear	緊縮財政	austerity
拒否する	reject	疑惑	misgiving	緊縮財政政策	austere fiscal policy
拒否する	veto	際立った	significant	緊縮政策	belt-tightening policy
許容	admission	際立った業績	outstanding performance	禁止令	ban
許容できる	acceptable			禁制の	prohibitive
許容できる	allowable	均一価格小売店	one-price retailer	金銭	money
許容範囲の	acceptable	均一価格制	one-price policy	金銭	obligation
キラー・ビーズ	killer bees	均一価格店	one-price retailer	金銭	purse
切り上げる	revalue	均一の	flat	金銭債権	monetary assets
切替え	conversion	金額	amount	金銭債務	debt
切り換える	refinance	金額	sum	金銭債務訴訟	debt
切り替える	convert	金額	value	金銭的	financial
切り替える	swap	金額未記入の白紙小切手	blank check	金銭の	monetary
ぎりぎりの線	bottom line			金銭の	pecuniary
切下げ	cut	緊急	emergency	金銭の引出し	drawing
切下げ	devaluation	緊急援助	bailout	金銭面での	financial
切り下げる	depreciate	緊急事態	contingency	金属	metal
切捨て	write-off	緊急事態	emergency	勤続中の	active
紀律	conduct	緊急輸入制限	safeguard	勤続年数	length of service
切詰め	curtailment	緊急輸入制限措置	safeguard	筋肉質の	lean
切詰め	squeeze	金庫	treasury	吟味	acid test
切り詰め	curtail	均衡	balance	勤務	duty
切り詰める	squeeze	均衡	equilibrium	勤務	service
切り詰める	trim	均衡	proportion	勤務時間	working hours
切り抜ける	manage	銀行	bank	勤務する	serve
切り離し	spinoff	銀行	commercial bank	勤務日	workday
切り離す	demerge	銀行	lender	禁輸	embargo
切り離す	separate	銀行	Lombard	金融	banking
切り離す	spin off	銀行家	Lombard	金融	credit
技量	hand	銀行勘定	bank account	金融	finance

金融	financing
金融	money
金融安定化フォーラム	FSF
金融界	Wall Street
金融緩和	easy money policy
金融緩和策	easy monetary policy
金融緩和策	easy money policy
金融緩和政策	easy monetary policy
金融緩和政策	easy money policy
金融機関	factor
金融機関	institution
金融機関	lender
金融機関の業務純益	net operating profit
金融業者	factor
金融業者	financier
金融債務	debt
金融債務	net debt
金融支援	bailout
金融資産	portfolio
金融市場	money market
金融市場	Wall Street
金融政策	monetary policy
金融整理管財人	trustee
金融仲介	intermediation
金融仲介機関利用	intermediation
金融の	financial
金融の	monetary
金融の証券化	securitization
金融の量的緩和政策	ultra-easy monetary policy
金融派生商品	derivative
金融引締め	tight money
金融引締めの状態	tight money
金融逼迫	tight money
金融保証会社	bond insurer
金融保証会社	monoline
金融保証専門会社	bond insurer
金融保証専門会社	monoline
金融保証保険	bond insurance
金融保証保険会社	monoline
金利	interest
金利	rate
金利減免	ease
金利差	spread
金利体系	scale
金利の誘導目標	key interest rate
金利変動幅固定の	cap and collar
…の金利を下げる	ease
勤労意識	morale
勤労意欲	morale
勤労者	worker
金を払う	hire
金を払って退職させる	buy out
金を払って退職させること	buyout
金を払って引き取らせること	buyout

区	zone
区域	territory
食い違い	discrepancy
食い止める	curb
空位	vacancy
空間	vacancy
空気	air
空気	climate
空気袋	airbag
空港	port
空室	vacancy
空車標識	flag
空席	opening
空席	vacancy
空席の	vacant
偶然	hazard
空前の	record
空洞化	hollowing-out
空白	gap
偶発事項	contingency
偶発事象	contingency
偶発の	contingent
偶発利益	windfall
クーポン	coupon
クーリング・オフ	cooling off
クーリングオフ期間	waiting period
クール・マネー	cool money
クオリティ	quality
区画	lot
くぎ	nail
釘付け	pegging
釘付け政策	pegging
釘付けにする	peg
苦境	corner
苦境	difficulties
苦境	fix
苦境	plight
区切る	segment
草分け	pioneer
草分けの	groundbreaking
くじ引き	drawing
苦情	claim
苦情	complaint
苦情	grievance
苦情処理機関	troubleshooter
苦情の申立て	claim
苦情の申立て	complaint
具申する	submit
下り	downstream
掘削	drilling
掘削の足場	platform
…に屈しない	keep up with
駆動装置	drive
駆動力	drive
駆動力	steam

国	economies
首切り	ax
工夫	device
区分	bracket
区分	category
区分	classification
区分	demarcation
区分	distribution
区分	scope
区分	section
区分上の	divisional
区分する	lot
区分する	segment
区分単位	segment
区別	demarcation
区別	differentiation
区別	discrimination
…を区別する	earmark
区別する	differentiate
組	team
組合	association
組合	consortium
組合	partnership
組合	union
組合員	partner
組合規約	articles of partnership
組合定款	articles of partnership
組合費	due
組合費の天引き	checkoff
組合せ	combination
組合せ	mix
組合せ	packaging
組入れ比率	weighting
組入れ比率が高いこと	overweight
組入れ比率が低いこと	underweight
組入れ比率の引下げ	underweight
組み入れる	include
組み入れる	incorporate
組み入れる	reflect
組替え	reclassification
組替え	realignment
組替え再表示	reclassification
組替え再表示する	reclassify
組み替える	reclassify
組込み	incorporation
組み込む	incorporate
組み込む	install
組立て	fabrication
組立て	makeup
組立て方	fabric
組立工場	assembly plant
組立工程	line
組立作業ライン	assembly line
組立部品一式	kit
組立方式の	knockdown
組立ライン	assembly line
組立ラインを離れる	roll off the assembly line
組み立てる	assemble

組み立てる fabricate	グレードアップする upgrade	経営側 management
組み立てる set up	クレーム claim	経営管理 administration
組み立てる tailor	クレーム complaint	経営管理 management
組む take out	クレジット credit	経営管理学修士 Master of Business Administration
クラウン・ジュエル crown jewels	クレジット・カード card	
暮らし life	クレジット・カード plastic	経営管理学修士 MBA
暮らしぶり lifestyle	クレジット・カードで買う charge	経営管理上の administrative
クラス・アクション class action suit	クレジット・ライン line of credit	経営危機 crisis
	クレディター creditor	経営危機 trouble
倉荷証券 warrant	黒い騎士 black knight	経営危機に陥った stricken
グラフ chart	苦労する struggle	経営危機に陥った troubled
クランチ crunch	玄人 professional	経営基盤 position
繰上げ償還 call	クローズドエンド型の closed-end	経営基盤 presence
繰上げ償還可能な callable	クローナ krona	経営権 control
繰上げ償還時に支払われる割増金 call premium	クローニング cloning	経営権 ownership
	クローネ krone	経営権の取得 buyout
繰上げの advanced	グローバリゼーション globalization	経営権の変更 change of control
繰り上げる advance		経営権を獲得する take over
繰り上げる shift	グローバル global	経営権を握る control
クリアランス clearance	グローバル化 globalization	経営合理化 downsizing
クリアリング clearing	グローバル市場 world market	経営再建 rehabilitation
グリース grease	グローバルな global	経営再建 restructuring
繰入れ transfer	クローン作製術 cloning	経営再建中の struggling
繰り入れる convert	黒字 black	経営資源 resource(s)
繰り入れる set aside	黒字 profit	経営支配権 control
繰り入れる transfer	黒字 surplus	経営支配権を得る control
クリーン clean	黒字の positive	経営者 entrepreneur
グリーン green	グロス gross	経営者 executive
グリーン・ベルト運動 Green Belt Movement	クロス・セリング cross selling	経営者 head
	クロス・ライセンス契約 cross licensing agreement	経営者 leader
クリエイティビティ creativity		経営者 manager
繰越金残存価額 balance	クロス・ライセンス契約 cross licensing contract	経営者 official
繰越し価額 carrying value		経営者 operator
繰越し日歩 contango	黒幕 mastermind	経営者 proprietor
繰り越す carry forward	くわ入れ式 groundbreaking	経営者側 management
繰り越す carry over	…を加えた plus	経営者による営業権取得 management buyout
繰り越す roll over	…を加えて plus	
クリック click	詳しい full	経営者による営業権取得 MBO
クリックする click	詳しく fully	経営者による自社買収 management buyout
クリック・ラップ・アグリーメント click wrap agreement	企て enterprise	
	軍 force	経営者による自社買収 MBO
クリティカル・マス critical mass	君主 sovereign	経営者の entrepreneurial
繰延べ deferment	群衆 mass	経営者の managerial
繰延べ forward	軍隊 force	経営上の administrative
繰延べの deferred	訓練 workout	経営上の managerial
繰り延べる defer		経営上の operating
繰り戻す carry back	け	経営上の operational
グループ bracket		経営陣 leader
グループ circles	ケア care	経営陣 management
グループ group	ケア・サービス care service	経営陣と従業員による企業買収 MEBO
グループウェア groupware	経緯 experience	
苦しい立場 corner	経営 administration	経営陣による企業買収 management buyout
苦しい立場 fix	経営 business	
…に苦しむ suffer from	経営 CAMEL	経営陣による自社株式の公開買付け management buyout
苦しんでいる distressed	経営 management	
車 car	経営 operation	経営する keep
車配卸売り業者 wagon jobber	経営委員会 EC	経営する manage
車配小売り業者 wagon retailer	経営学修士 Master of Business Administration	経営する operate
グレード grade		経営する run
グレードアップ upgrade	経営革新 innovation	経営多角化 diversification

経営統合	integration
経営統合	merger
経営統合	tie-up
経営統合案	merger proposal
経営統合交渉	merger talks
経営統合する	merge
経営統合する	merge operations
経営統合提案	merger proposal
経営統合の契約	merger deal
経営統合の契約書	merger deal
経営統合の合意書	merger deal
経営統合の提案書	merger proposal
経営難	stress
経営難	trouble
経営難に陥った	troubled
経営難に陥っている	distressed
経営難の	distressed
経営難の	troubled
経営の	managerial
経営の	operational
経営の	working
経営破綻	bankruptcy
経営破綻	collapse
経営破綻	failure
経営破綻	trouble
経営破綻した	bankrupt
経営破綻した	troubled
経営破綻する	collapse
経営破綻する	fail
経営不振	trouble
経営不振に陥っている	struggling
経営不振の	ailing
経営不振の	distressed
経営不振の	troubled
経営法	governance
経営方針	policy
経過	transition
警戒	precaution
警戒感	fear
経過期間	aging
計画	deal
計画	device
計画	game
計画	idea
計画	package
計画	plan
計画	planning
計画	program
計画	project
計画	proposal
計画	schedule
計画	scheme
計画案	scenario
計画策定	planning
計画する	map out
計画する	plan
計画する	plot
計画する	project
計画性	foresight
計画的販売促進	merchandising
計画法	programing
計画立案者	mastermind
計画立案者	planner
計画を立てる	plan
経過年金	transitional pension
経過報告	briefing
経過利息	accrued interest
契機	momentum
景気	activity
景気	boom
景気	economy
計器	gauge
景気一致指数	coincident index
景気回復	recovery
景気回復	upturn
景気回復の局面	incipient recovery
景気回復ムード	upbeat
景気拡大	expansion
景気拡大局面	upturn
景気過熱	overheating
景気景気サイクル	cycle
景気後退	contraction
景気後退	downturn
景気後退	recession
景気後退	setback
景気サイクルの	cyclical
景気刺激	boost
景気刺激策	pump priming
景気刺激策	reflationary policy
景気刺激策	stimulus
景気縮小	contraction
景気循環	cycle
景気循環の	cyclical
景気振興策	pump priming
景気先行指数	leading index
景気先行指標総合指数	leading index
景気対策	stimulus
景気対策の	countercyclical
景気沈滞	slump
景気づく	pick up
景気停滞	stagnation
景気停滞下のインフレ	stagflation
景気動向指数	DI
景気動向指数	diffusion index
景気などが回復する	pick up
景気などの押し下げ効果	drag
景気に敏感な	cyclical
景気の悪化	contraction
景気のいい	upbeat
景気の落込み	downturn
景気の底	trough
景気の谷	bottom
景気の谷	trough
景気の冷やしすぎ	overkill
計器盤	panel
景気浮揚策	reflationary policy
景気変動に敏感な	cyclical
景気持ち直しの局面	incipient recovery
景況感	sentiment
景気を過熱する	overdrive the economy
経験	experience
軽減	commutation
軽減	reduction
軽減	relief
経験[知識]の豊富な	savvy
経験させる	expose
経験する	experience
軽減する	decrease
軽減する	reduce
傾向	climate
傾向	pattern
傾向	propensity
傾向	sentiment
傾向	stream
傾向	trend
経済	economies
経済	economy
経済学の	economic
経済危機	crunch
経済機構	economy
経済協力開発機構	OECD
経済車	econobox
経済群	economies
経済国	economies
経済国	economy
経済上の	economic
経済上の引締め	crunch
掲載する	include
掲載する	list
掲載する	publish
掲載する	run
経済性	economies
経済性	economy
経済成長	growth
経済組織	economy
経済域	economies
経済的付加価値	EVA
経済統合協定	EIA
経済同友会	Japan Association of Corporate Executives
経済の	economic
経済のゼロ成長	stagnation
経済のゼロ成長	ZEG
経済の溶解	meltdown
経済連携協定	EPA
計算	account
計算	accounting
計算	determination
計算	figure
計算	measurement
計算書	account
計算書	statement
計算書類	accounts
計算する	reckon
計算単位	tally
計算できない	incalculable
計算用紙	tally

形式	configuration	継続期間	life	契約条項の分離独立性	severance
形式	form	継続企業	going concern	契約商品	contract
形式	pattern	継続企業	ongoing concern	契約書作成	documentation
掲示板	board	計測する	gauge	…と契約する	sign
掲示板	hoarding	継続する	follow	契約する	bargain
傾斜	focus	継続する	sustain	契約する	take out
傾斜	shift	継続的調達と製品のライフサイクル		契約対象製品	licensed product
芸術・科学支援活動	mecenat	の支援	CALS	契約地域	territory
継承	assumption	継続できる	renewable	契約で取り決める	bargain
継承	transfer	継続利用できる	sustainable	契約当事者	party
形状	configuration	形態	form	契約に適合しない商品	
形状	feature	携帯型の	handheld		nonconforming goods
形状	form	携帯情報端末	PDA	契約に適合しない物品	
計上	provision	携帯電話	cell phone		nonconforming goods
計上	recognition	携帯電話	handset	契約の一部とする	incorporate
計上…	reported	携帯電話	mobile phone	契約の解除	dissolution
経常勘定	current account	携帯電話の番号持ち運び制度		契約の約因	consideration
計上された	reported		number portability system	契約品	contract
経常支出	above the line	携帯ネット・サービス	mobile Net	契約不履行者	defaulter
経常収益	current income		services	契約文書	documentation
経常収支	above the line	携帯メール	EMS	契約を解除する	dissolve
経常収支	current account	携帯用の	handheld	契約を結ぶ	enter
経常収入	current income	携帯用の	portable	契約を結ぶ	sign up
継承する	assume	系統	chain	経理	accounting
継承する	take over	系統立てる	organize	経理担当者	accountant
計上する	account for	系統的な	organic	経理部長	comptroller
計上する	accrue	…系の	related	経理部長	controller
計上する	appropriate	刑罰	penalty	計略	game
計上する	book	刑罰の	punitive	計量	measurement
計上する	chalk up	経費	burden	軽量化	downsizing
計上する	charge	経費	cost	軽量化する	downsize
計上する	credit	経費	expenditure	計量経済学モデル	econometric
計上する	declare	経費	expense		model
計上する	earmark	経費	outlay	計量経済分析	econometric
計上する	earn	経費削減	ax		analysis
計上する	generate	経費として申告する	write off	計量経済モデル	econometric
計上する	include	経費として認められる	deductible		model
計上する	list	景品	giveaway	計量モデル	econometric model
計上する	post	景品	premium	経歴	background
計上する	provide	景品引換え券	coupon	経歴	career
計上する	recognize	契約	agreement	系列	series
計上する	record	契約	arrangement	系列会社	affiliate
計上する	report	契約	bargain	系列会社	associate
計上する	state	契約	contract	系列会社	associated company
経常損益計算	above the line	契約	covenant	系列化された	integrated
経常的	current	契約	deal	系列化する	integrate
経常的	ordinary	契約	engagement	系列に置く	affiliate
経常的な	recurring	契約	pact	系列の	serial
継承破産人	DIP	契約	treaty	経路	channel
経常利益	line	契約違反	infringement	ケース	case
係数	factor	契約期間	term	ケータリング・サービス	catering
係数	parameter	契約義務	commitment		service
計数型	digital	契約義務	responsibility	ケーブル	cable
形成	establishment	契約債務	commitment	ゲーム	game
形成	formation	契約者	holder	ケオ・プラン	Keogh
形成	generation	契約者	policyholder	激化する	increase
形成	making	契約書	agreement	激化する	intensify
形成する	establish	契約書	contract	激化する	intensify
形成する	form	契約書	documentation	激減	plunge
形成の	plastic	契約書	indenture	激減させる	deplete

激烈な競争	cutthroat competition
景色	scene
化粧	makeup
化粧の	cosmetic
化粧品	makeup
決意	determination
決意	drive
決意	purpose
決意	resolution
決意する	determine
…する決意である	committed to
欠員	job opening
欠員	opening
欠員の	vacancy
欠員の	vacant
欠員の	void
結果	event
結果	product
結果	results
欠陥	defect
欠陥	deficiency
欠陥	disadvantage
欠陥	fault
欠陥	flaw
欠陥	glitch
欠陥	shortage
欠陥車	lemon
欠陥車の回収	recall
欠陥商品	lemon
欠陥品の回収	recall
決議	action
決議	decision
決議	declaration
決議	resolution
決議	vote
決議案	resolution
決議する	decide
決議する	resolve
決議する	settle
月給	salary
月給制従業員	salaried employee
結局の	net
決議録	proceedings
欠勤	absence
欠勤	leave
結語	closing
結合	combination
結合	coupling
結合	link
結合させるもの	link
結合した	combined
決済	clearing
決済	closing
決済	liquidation
決済	payment
決済	payoff
決済	settlement
決済する	liquidate
決済する	settle
決済引取り猶予金	contango

決算	account
決算	account settlement
決算	accounts
決算	book-closing
決算	closing
決算	earnings
決算	figure
決算	results
決算	settlement
決算期末	year end
決算書	account
決算処理	accounting
決算整理	adjustment
決算内容	results
決算報告書	statement of accounts
決算報告上の	reported
…に結集する	focus on
傑出した	outstanding
傑出した知性	mastermind
傑出した知能	mastermind
欠如	deficiency
欠如	want
決心	determination
決心する	resolve
結成する	form
結成する	organize
欠席	absence
欠席者	absentee
欠損	defect
欠損	deficiency
欠損	deficit
欠損	loss
欠損金	deficit
欠損金	loss
結託	collusion
結託する	collude
決断	decision
決断	determination
決断	resolution
決断する	determine
決断力	determination
決着	resolution
決着	settlement
決着する	terminate
決着をつける	conclude
決定	action
決定	decision
決定	determination
決定	formation
決定	making
決定	matching
決定	resolution
決定	ruling
決定	settlement
決定者	arbiter
決定する	conclude
決定する	decide
決定する	determine
決定する	settle
…を決定的にする	clinch

欠点	defect
欠点	deficiency
欠点	fault
欠点	flaw
月賦払い	installment
欠乏	deficiency
欠乏	shortage
欠乏	want
月報	newsletter
決裂	breakdown
結論	bottom line
結論づける	conclude
結論に達する	conclude
懸念	concern
懸念	fear
懸念	misgiving
懸念材料	concern
懸念材料	negative factor
気配値	quote
気配値	run
下落	collapse
下落	decline
下落	decrease
下落	downside
下落	downturn
下落	drop
下落	fall
下落	meltdown
下落	plunge
下落	pressure
下落	retreat
下落	setback
下落	shrinkage
下落	slide
下落	weakness
下落気味の	bearish
下落傾向	downside
下落させる	depress
下落した	depressed
下落する	decline
下落する	decrease
下落する	depreciate
下落する	downward
下落する	drop
下落する	fall
下落する	lose
下落する	lower
下落する	plunge
下落する	sag
下落する	tumble
下落する	weaken
…兼	cum
券	certificate
圏	area
圏	bloc
圏	zone
原案	protocol
権威	arbiter
権威	authority
権威	clout

権威者 authority	研究助成金 grant	権限 power
牽引車 driving force	研究助成金 subsidy	権限 right
…を原因とする attribute	研究法 approach	権限証書 warrant
牽引役 driver	献金 donation	権の委譲 delegation
牽引役 driving force	献金 offering	権限の委任 delegation
牽引力 engine	現金 cash	権限の付与 empowerment
…の牽引力となる drive	現金 ready	権原要約書 abstract of title
権益 interest	現金および現金同等物 cash and	権限を与える authorize
現役 downside	cash equivalents	権限を与える mandate
現役の active	現金化 liquidation	権限を与える qualify
原価 cost	現金化 realization	権限を委譲する delegate
減価 depreciation	現金回収 payback	権限を委譲する empower
減価 impairment	現金化する encash	権限を付与する empower
現価 present value	現金化する liquidate	健康 health
見解 judgment	現金合併 cash merger	健康 wellness
見解 opinion	現金残高 cash balance	原稿 copy
限界 ceiling	現金資金 cash flow	健康維持機構 HMO
限界 demarcation	現金自動預け払い機 ATM	健康医療 health care
限界 edge	現金自動預け払い機 automated	健康管理 health care
限界 horizon	teller machine	健康と環境重視の生活様式
限界 limit	現金自動支払い機 CD	Lifestyles Of Health And
限界 range	現金収支 cash flow	Sustainability
限界質量 critical mass	現金純額 net cash	健康と環境に配慮したライフスタイ
限界収益点の marginal	現金所要量 cash requirements	ル Lohas
限界設定 demarcation	現金注文 cwo	現行の going
限界点 threshold	現金通貨 cash in circulation	健康保険 health insurance
限界の marginal	現金で受け取る encash	言語能力 competence
限界量 critical mass	現金等価物 cash equivalents	検査 check
減額 deduction	現金同等物 cash equivalents	検査 examination
減額 dilution	現金取引の spot	検査 inspection
減額 downsizing	現金等価物 cash equivalents	検査 screening
減額する dilute	現金に換える cash	検査 search
減額する trim	現金に換える realize	現在価値 present value
原価計算をする cost	現金の hard	減債基金 sinking fund
現価計上する capitalize	現金の spot	…現在で as of
原価合計 total cost	現金の入出金 cash withdrawals	…現在の as of
減価して見積もる depreciate	and deposits	現在の current
減価償却 amortization	現金配当 cash dividend	現在の going
減価償却 depreciation	現金払い主義 pay-as-you-go	現在の immediate
減価償却 write-off	現金払いの spot	現在の running
減価償却する depreciate	現金払い方式 pay-as-you-go	原材料 basic material
減価償却する write off	現金必要見込み額 cash	原材料 feed
減価償却できる depreciable	requirements	原材料 ingredient
減価償却の対象となる depreciable	現金必要量 cash requirements	原材料 raw material
減価償却費 depreciation	現金不要の cashless	原材料の調達 material
減価する depreciate	現金預金 cash	procurement
原価配賦 allocation	現金預金および現金等価物 cash	検索 search
原価法 cost	and cash equivalents	検索エンジン engine
原価を見積もる cost	現金預金残高 cash balance	検索語 keyword
元気 steam	現金預金同等物 cash equivalents	検索専門家 searcher
研究 approach	現金割戻し rebate	検索対象語 keyword
研究 exploration	原型 prototype	検査する examine
研究 research	減刑 commutation	検察側 prosecutors
研究 study	権原 title	検察当局 prosecutors
言及 reference	権限 authority	検査を通る clear
研究会 workshop	権限 authorization	減産 slowdown
研究開発 R＆D	権限 brief	減算 amortization
研究開発 research	権限 commission	原産国 country of origin
研究開発 research and	権限 competence	原産地 country of origin
development	権限 mandate	検事 attorney

献辞 dedication	減じる impair	現地生産 local production
減資 capital reduction	原子炉 reactor	現地生産システム local production system
原始過去勤務 past service	原子炉の炉心 core	
見識 judgment	献身 dedication	現地生産体制 local production system
原始原価 original cost	件数 case	
原資産保有者 sponsor	減税 tax break	現地生産能力 local assembly capacity
現実 fact	牽制行動 diversion	
現実全損 ATL	牽制作戦 diversion	現地生産方式 local production system
堅実な solid	建設 construction	
現実の real	建設 foundation	現地調査 on-the-spot inspection
元首 sovereign	建設・運営・所有 BOO	現地調達 local procurement
検収 acceptance	建設契約 construction contract	現地通貨 local currency
現住者 occupant	建設工事 construction project	現地通貨建て local currency
現住者 tenant	建設する engineer	現地の local
現住者のいない vacant	源泉 resource(s)	現地品 spot
厳重な stringent	源泉 source(s)	堅調な good
検証 examination	健全化 rehabilitation	堅調な healthy
減少 contraction	健全化 revitalization	堅調の strong
減少 decline	源泉課税 PAYE	顕著な dominant
減少 decrease	源泉課税方式 pay-as-you-go	顕著な outstanding
減少 deterioration	健全性 health	検定 authorization
減少 dilution	健全性に劣るもの lemon	検定 probation
減少 drawdown	源泉徴収 PAYE	検定 test
減少 drop	源泉徴収 withholding	献呈 dedication
減少 fall	源泉徴収する withhold	限定 determination
減少 lapse	源泉徴収方式 pay-as-you-go	検定する authorize
減少 loss	健全な healthy	検定する test
減少 plunge	健全な solid	限定する narrow
減少 pressure	現像する develop	限定する qualify
減少 setback	建造物 construction	限定する restrict
減少 shrinkage	建造物 structure	限定付き qualified
減少 slump	原則 principle	減点主義 demerit system
減少 squeeze	原則 rule	限度 ceiling
減少 weakness	減速 slowdown	限度 limit
減少額 deduction	減速効果 drag	検討 review
検証刻印 hallmark	減速する moderate	検討する evaluate
減少させる diminish	減速する slow down	検討する review
減少させる reduce	減損 impairment	原動力 drive
減少した weak	減損 loss	原動力 driver
検証する examine	減損 shrinkage	原動力 driving force
減少する decline	減損 write-down	原動力 dynamics
減少する decrease	減損会計 asset impairment accounting	原動力 engine
減少する dilute		原動力 factor
減少する diminish	現存する de facto	原動力 powerhouse
減少する drop	現存する going	…の原動力になる drive
減少する fall	減退 contraction	限度額 limit
減少する lower	現地 field	限度のない open-end
減少する plunge	現地 scene	…の限度を超える exceed
減少する shrink	言質 assurance	兼任重役 interlocking directorate
減少する squeeze	建築 architecture	兼任役員 interlocking directorate
減少する tumble	建築学 architecture	権能 authority
減少する weaken	建築技術 architecture	権能 competence
懸賞付き番組 giveaway	建築物 architecture	権能 mandate
減少の downward	建築物 fabric	権能 power
現状把握 stocktaking	建築物の定礎式 cornerstone laying ceremony	現場 field
減少へ downward		現場 scene
現職の active	現地組立方式の knockdown	現場 site
現職の incumbent	建築様式 architecture	現場検証 on-the-spot inspection
原初原価 original cost	現地実証試験 on-site demonstration	現場修理サービス on-site service
原子力 nuclear power		現物 kind

現物	spot	…の権利を失う	forfeit	効果	effectiveness
現物どおりの	duplicate	権利を行使する	exercise	効果	impact
現物の	spot	権利を保有する	reserve	効果	results
現物引換え払い	POD	権利を留保する	reserve	硬貨	hard currency
原簿	ledger			公開	disclosure
原本	protocol			公開	exhibition
券面	face			公開	introduction
券面額の変更	redenomination	…後	after	公開	marketing
減耗	consumption	コア	core	公開	offering
減耗	obsolescence	項	clause	公開	presentation
減耗	shrinkage	考案	device	更改	rollover
減耗償却	depletion	考案	origination	公害	pollution
減耗損	shrinkage	考案する	originate	公開会社	listed company
減耗費	shrinkage	好意	goodwill	公開会社	publicly held company
倹約	thrift	行為	act	公開会社	publicly owned company [corporation]
原油	crude	行為	action		
原油	crude oil	行為	agency	公開企業	listed company
原油	oil	行為	behavior	公開企業会計監視委員会	PCAOB
現預金	cash	行為	conduct	公開競技	exhibition
現預金および現金同等物	cash and cash equivalents	行為	deed	公開公募	IPO
		行為	practice	公開市場	open market
現預金残高	cash balance	合意	accord	公開市場操作	operation
権利	claim	合意	agreement	公開する	disclose
権利	patent	合意	arrangement	公開する	introduce
権利	right	合意	consensus	公開する	publish
権利	title	合意	engagement	公開する	release
原理	fundamentals	合意	understanding	公開する	state
原理	principle	合意事項	agreement	公開する	unveil
権利落ち	XR	合意事項	understanding	公開性	disclosure
権利金	premium	合意書	accord	公開討論会	forum
権利行使	strike	合意書	agreement	航海日誌	log
権利者	owner	後遺症	legacy	公開の	open
権利証落ち	XW	行為地	venue	公開の	patent
権利証券	warrant	好位置にある	well positioned	公開有限責任会社	PLC
権利証書	securities	合意の	unanimous	…への効果がある	impact
権利証書	title	合意文書	accord	効果がある	work
権利証書	warrant	行員	clerk	高価格品	high-priced product
権利譲渡	demise	幸運	fortune	効果がない	void
権利侵害	injury	好影響を与える	positive	工学	engineering
権利設定	demise	交易	exchange	工学技術	engineering
権利などを放棄する	release	交易	trade	高額商品	high-priced product
権利の移転	negotiation	公益事業	utility	光学繊維	fiber optics
権利の行使	exercise	校閲者	anchorman	高額の退職金契約	golden handshake
権利の行使可能な	exercisable	校閲する	revise		
権利の主張	claim	後援	backing	高額の退職手当	golden parachute
権利の侵害	infringement	公園	park	効果的な	effective
権利の付与	grant	後援会	sponsor	高価なフル装備の	high-end
権利の放棄	waiver	講演会	exhibition	硬貨の	hard
権利放棄	surrender	後援者	backing	硬貨の差入れ口	slot
権利放棄証書	waiver	後援者	backup	効果をあげる	useful
権利放棄の意思表示	waiver	後援者	benefactor	交換	commutation
原料	ingredient	後援者	sponsor	交換	conversion
原料	material	後援者	underwriter	交換	exchange
原料	raw material	後援者団体	backing	交換	replacement
原料を送る	feed	後援する	-backed	交換	swap
権力	authority	後援する	prop up	交換	trade
権力	clout	後援する	sponsor	高官	ranking official
権力	power	効果	benefit	交換可能通貨	hard currency
権力奪取競争	power game	効果	edge	交換可能の	convertible
権力闘争	power game	効果	effect	抗がん剤	cancer treatment drug

交換する barter	航空路線 airline	行使 exercise
交換する exchange	光景 scene	講師 panelist
交換する swap	…の合計 combined	公示 notice
交換する trade	合計 aggregate	工事 construction
交換できる redeemable	合計 footing	工事 engineering
高感度の sensitive	合計 sum	工事 installation
交換取扱い者 operator	…の合計額 combined	工事 work
交換要員 replacement	好景気 activity	合資会社 LP
好機 breakdown	好景気 boom	公式 formula
好機 opening	合計検算 footing	公式の official
好機 opportunity	後継者 replacement	公式の行事 function
抗議 complaint	合計の aggregate	公式報告書 blue book
抗議 protest	攻撃 offensive	工事契約 construction contract
高機能の intelligent	…の攻撃を受けやすい vulnerable	講師団 panel
好機の選択 timing	好結果 success	行使できる exercisable
高級 quality	貢献 contribution	公示の official
高級志向の high-end	貢献 participation	公社債 bond
高級市場向けに転換する gentrify	公言 profession	公衆 public
恒久的 permanent	高原 plateau	高収益 high performance
高級な high	貢献額 contribution	講習会 workshop
高級な sophisticated	高原現象 plateau	公準 assumption
高級な upmarket	貢献したもの contributor	公準 concept
高級な upscale	…に貢献する benefit	好循環 virtuous circle
高級の high-end	…に貢献する help	控除 allowance
高級ブランド luxury brand	貢献する contribute	控除 deduction
工業 industry	貢献する serve	控除 exemption
鉱業 mining	貢献要因 contributor	控除 rebate
工業化 industrialization	鉱工業の industrial	控除 relief
工業会 industry	公告 notification	交渉 bargain
工業化する industrialize	広告 advertisement	交渉 bargaining
公共機関 authority	広告 advertising	交渉 negotiation
工業技術 technology	広告 notice	交渉 talks
工業技術の technical	広告 publicity	交渉 treaty
鉱業権 license	広告板 hoarding	考証 documentation
工業権使用料 royalty	広告する advertise	鉱床 deposit
公共事業 utility	広告宣伝 advertisement	向上 advance
公共事業株 utility	広告宣伝 advertising	向上 boost
公共事業計画 project	広告宣伝費 advertising	向上 enhancement
公共事業体 utility	広告主 advertiser	向上 gain
公共施設 establishment	広告主 sponsor	向上 improvement
興行主 entrepreneur	広告放送 commercial	向上 pickup
公共職業紹介所 jobcentre	交互実施許諾契約 cross licensing agreement	向上 rise
工業生産の industrial	口座 account	向上 upturn
好業績 good performance	交際 entertainment	工場 fab
好業績 high performance	公債利子 service	工場 facility
公共投資 capital investment	好材料 good news	工場 factory
公共の public	好材料 positive	工場 plant
工業の industrial	好材料の beneficial	工場 shop
工業の発達した industrial	好材料の good	工場 site
工業用の industrial	工作 tooling	工場 work
公金 public funds	耕作 culture	工場 workshop
工具 tool	工作員 agent	向上させる beef up
航空会社 airline	工作機械 tool	向上させる bolster
航空会社 carrier	工作機械一式 tooling	向上させる boost
航空会社などの営業利益 sales	口座残高 account balance	向上させる enhance
航空機 aircraft	口座振替え money transfer	向上させる improve
航空機隊 fleet	口座振替未処理部分 backlogged money transfer	向上させる upgrade
航空日誌 log		工場施設の移動 redeployment
航空便 flight		工場施設の改善 redeployment
航空路 airline	鉱山業 mining	公称資本 authorized capital

工場主	manufacturer	構成	structure	構造物	architecture
交渉する	bargain	構成員	member	構造物	structure
交渉する	negotiate	構成会社	constituent company	高速	velocity
向上する	advance	公正価格	fair value	高速型	high-end
向上する	gain	公正価額	fair value	拘束する	curb
向上する	grow	公正価値	fair value	高速増殖炉	fast breeder reactor
向上する	strengthen	構成機器	hardware	高速大容量通信	broadband
工場設備	plant	公正市価	fair market value	高速の	express
工場設備	plant and equipment	公正市場価格	fair market value	拘束力	force
恒常ドル	constant dollar	公正市場価値	fair market value	拘束力のない	null
工場なしの	fabless	合成樹脂業界	plastics industry	後退	downturn
工場の移動	redeployment	合成樹脂製の	plastic	後退	setback
交渉の切り札	bargaining chip	合成樹脂製品	plastic	後退	slowdown
工場の自動化	FA	校正する	revise	交替	rotation
交渉力	bargaining power	公正妥当と認められている		交替	shift
工場を持たない企業	fabless		acceptable	広帯域	broadband
控除額	deduction	構成単位	unit	広帯域通信網	broadband
控除額	exemption	公正取引委員会	Fair Trade	交替勤務時間	shift
控除可能な	deductible		Commission	交替させる	rotate
公職	office	公正取引委員会	FTC	後退する	slow down
…控除後	after	公正な	arm's length	交替で勤務させる	rotate
…控除後	net of	公正な	clean	後端	back end
控除項目	deduction	公正な	fair	後端部	back end
…を控除したうえで	after	公正な	reasonable	構築	architecture
控除する	credit	公正な評価額	fair value	構築	formation
控除する	deduct	厚生年金保険法	Japanese Welfare	構築	implementation
控除する	recoup		Pension Insurance Law	構築する	create
控除する	reduce	合成の	composite	構築する	form
控除する	take off	合成の	compound	構築物	construction
…控除前	before	高性能	high performance	構築物	structure
更新	renewal	高性能の	sophisticated	公知の	known
更新	restatement	構成比率	weighting	膠着状態	stalemate
更新	rollover	構成物質	material	好調	strength
更新	update	構成部品	component	好調な	brisk
更新する	restate	構成部品	element	好調な	favorable
更新する	update	構成要素	component	好調な	good
更新できる	renewable	構成要素	element	好調な	healthy
構図	form	構成要素	ingredient	好調な	robust
構図	paradigm	公正労働基準法	Fair Labor	好調な	strong
高水準	plateau		Standards Act	好調な	buoyant
高水準	sophistication	功績	deed	交通	traffic
高水準の	high	交戦	engagement	交通機関	traffic
公正	right	口銭	commission	交通機関	transport
厚生	welfare	公然と売り出す	expose	交通手段	transport
攻勢	offensive	公然の	bare	交通の便	communications
攻勢	thrust	公然の	outright	交通量	traffic
更正	assessment	構想	concept	交通量	travel
更生	rehabilitation	構想	idea	好都合な	favorable
構成	breakdown	構想	initiative	工程	fab
構成	configuration	構想	plan	工程	fabrication
構成	fabric	構想	proposal	工程	process
構成	fabrication	構造	architecture	工程表	timeline
構成	form	構造	fabric	行程表	road map
構成	formation	構造	makeup	公的	public
構成	makeup	構造	organization	公的機関	sovereign
構成	mix	構造	profile	公的資金	public funds
構成	organization	構造	status	好敵手	rival
構成	profile	構造	structure	公的な	official
構成	scope	構造上の	organizational	更迭	reshuffle
構成	set-up	構造的な	underlying	更迭する	reshuffle

好転 improvement	公認会計士 certified public accountant	降伏 surrender
好転 rebound		交付する deliver
好転 turnaround	公認会計士 CPA	鉱物資源の開発契約 lease
好転 upturn	公認されていない unauthorized	公文書 dispatch
好転させる improve	後任者 replacement	公平な equal
好転する rebound	公認する authorize	公平な equal
好転する turn around	後任の incoming	公平な even
高騰 boom	公認の official	公平な fair
高騰 rise	公の official	抗弁 defense
行動 act	公の public	合弁 joint venture
行動 action	高濃縮ウラン highly enriched uranium	合弁会社 joint venture
行動 agency		合弁事業 joint venture
行動 behavior	公売 auction	合弁事業 venture
行動 conduct	購買 purchase	…に抗弁する plead
行動 deed	購買 purchasing	合弁の joint
行動 move	購買 shopping	候補 contender
行動 movement	光背効果 halo effect	公募 public offering
強盗 raid	購買後サービス after-sales service	公報 newsletter
強盗 raider	購買時点の POP	広報 flack
行動規範 code of conduct	購買者 buyer	広報 publicity
行動計画 scenario	購買者 purchaser	広報 relations
合同した incorporated	購買動機 motivation	後方業務 logistics
行動準則 code of conduct	購買取引力 bargaining power	後方支援技術 logistics
口頭で説明する present	購買力 purchasing power	合法性 legality
口頭でなく文書による同意 informed consent	後発 latecomer	攻防戦 struggle
	後発医薬品 generic drug	広報担当者 flack
高等の advanced	後発組 latecomer	広報担当者 spokesman
合同の joint	後発組 latecomer	合法的な legal
行動の規範 ethics	後発事象 post-balance sheet event	合法的に偽装する launder
高度化 upgrade	後発事象 subsequent events	合法な allowable
高度科学技術 high-tech	後半 latter half	合法の due
高度技術 high technology	公判 hearing	後方部門 back office
高度技術 high-tech	広範囲の global	公募価格 offering price
高度情報社会 telematics	広範囲の large	公募価格 public offering price
高度先端技術 high technology	広範な comprehensive	候補者 nominee
高度な advanced	公費 public funds	公募増資 public offering
高度な high	公表 announcement	公募入札 auction
高度な high-end	公表 declaration	候補被指名者 nominee
高度の intelligent	公表 disclosure	巧妙な professional
高度の sophisticated	公表 publicity	公務 service
高度の state-of-the-art	公表… reported	公務員 official
豪ドル A$	公表された reported	公務上の official
構内 premises	公表する announce	被る incur
構内交換 PBX	公表する bare	被る receive
構内通信網 LAN	公表する declare	被る suffer
公にする unveil	公表する disclose	被る sustain
購入 acquisition	公表する issue	合名会社 partnership
購入 procurement	公表する name	合名会社定款 articles of partnership
購入 purchase	公表する publish	
購入 purchasing	公表する release	項目 category
購入債務 account payable	公表する report	項目 component
購入者 acquirer	公表する reveal	項目 element
購入する acquire	公表する roll out	項目 item
購入する buy	公表する state	公約 commitment
購入する procure	公表する unveil	公約 platform
購入する purchase	交付 delivery	公約 pledge
購入選択権 option	交付 distribution	公約する commit
購入申し込みをする subscribe	交付 issue	公約する pledge
公認 adoption	高付加価値の value-added	公有地譲渡証書 patent
公認 authorization	交付金 grant	効用 use

効用	utility
公用の	official
公用前渡し金	imprest
小売り	retail
小売り	retailing
合理化	downsizing
合理化	rationalization
合理化	streamlining
高利貸し	loan shark
高利貸し	shark
合理化する	downsize
合理化する	resize
合理化する	streamline
小売活動	retailing
小売企業	retailer
小売業	retailer
小売業	retailing
小売業者	retailer
小売商	retailer
効率	effectiveness
効率	efficiency
効率	throughput
効率化	efficiency
効率化	rationalization
効率化	streamlining
効率化する	streamline
効率性	efficiency
効率的消費者対応	ECR
効率的な	effective
効率的な	efficient
効率的な	sophisticated
効率的物流システム	logistics
効率のよい	efficient
合理的な	due
合理的な	reasonable
小売店	outlet
小売店	retailer
小売店	shop
小売物価指数	RPI
高利回り債	high yield bond
高利回りの	high-yield
交流	exchange
交流の場	forum
交流広場	forum
考慮	account
考慮	assumption
考慮	consideration
網領	platform
網領宣言	platform
効力	availability
効力	effect
効力	effectiveness
効力をもつ	effective
考慮する	allow
考慮する	assume
…考慮前	before
小売零細店	ma-and-pa store
高齢化	aging
高齢化	aging population
高齢化社会	aging society

高齢化社会	aging society
高齢者医療保険	Medicare
高齢者医療保障制度	Medicare
高齢社会	aged society
高齢者の	gray
航路	route
口論	contention
港湾	harbor
港湾荷役	shipping
声	feedback
越えがたい障壁	Chinese wall
…を越える	top
越える	pass
超える	surpass
ゴーイング・コンサーン	going concern
ゴースト	ghost
コード	code
コード	code of conduct
コーポレーション	corporation
コーポレート	corporate
コーポレート・アイデンティティ	CI
コーポレート・シティズン	corporate citizen [citizenship]
コール	call
ゴール	goal
コール・オプションを買うときに支払うオプション料	call premium
コール市場	call market
コール・センター	call center
ゴールデン・ハンドカフ	golden handcuffs
コール・プレミアム	call premium
コール・ローン	call
子会社	affiliate
子会社	arm
子会社	holding
子会社	operation
子会社	subsidiary
子会社	unit
子会社	vehicle
誤解を招きやすい	misleading
互角の	close
互角の	equal
互角の	even
小型化	downsizing
小型化する	downsize
小型株	small-cap
小型集積回路	chip
小型の	handheld
枯渇	depletion
枯渇させる	deplete
涸渇させる	exhaust
互換性	compatibility
互換性がある	compatible
互換性のない	incompatible
誤記	error
誤記	irregularity
小切手	check
小切手	draft

顧客	client
顧客	custom
顧客	customer
顧客	public
顧客	user
顧客関係維持	CRM
顧客関係管理	CRM
顧客基盤	customer base
顧客規模	traffic
顧客熟知	know your customer
顧客熟知規則	know-your-customer rule
顧客熟知の原則	know-your-customer rule
顧客情報の流出	leakage of client information
顧客情報の漏洩	leakage of client information
顧客数	traffic
顧客層	customer base
顧客の完全な満足	total customer satisfaction
顧客の要求に応じて特注化した	customized
顧客の要求に応じて特注化する	customize
顧客満足	CS
顧客満足	customer satisfaction
国営化する	nationalize
国営の	state-run
国外に追放する	expatriate
国外の	external
国外流通通貨	Xenocurrency
国債	government bond
国際IR連盟	IIRF
国際宇宙ステーション	ISS
国際エネルギー機関	IEA
国際化	globalization
国際化	liberalization
国際会計基準	IAS
国際海事機関	IMO
国際開発協会	IDA
国際開発局	AID
国際間の	international
国際間の協定	pact
国際協調融資	syndicated loan
国際協力銀行	Japan Bank for International Cooperation
国際銀行間通信協会	SWIFT
国際銀行通信協会	SWIFT
国際金融公社	IFC
国際経営者団体連盟	IOE
国際決済銀行	BIS
国際原子力機関	IAEA
国際工業所有権保護協会	AIPPI
国際航空輸送協会	IATA
国際裁判	arbitration
国際財務報告基準	IFRS
国際湿地条約	Ramsar Convention
国際借款団	consortium

国際商工会議所	ICC
国際商事仲裁	ICA
国際上の	international
国際石油資本	majors
国際租税協定	tax convention
国際租税条約	tax convention
国際仲裁裁判所	ICA
国際通貨基金	IMF
国際的	international
国際的な	global
国際電気通信連合	ITU
国際電気標準会議	IEC
国債入札	refunding
国際熱核融合実験炉	ITER
国際ビジネス郵便	EMS
国際標準化機構	IOS
国際標準化機構	ISO
国際標準逐次刊行物番号	ISSN
国際標準図書番号	ISBN
国際復興開発銀行	IBRD
国際民間航空機関	ICAO
国際労働機関	ILO
国産の	domestic
告示	announcement
告示	notice
告示	notification
酷使する	punish
告示する	announce
極上の	prime
国籍離脱者	expat
国籍離脱者	expatriate
告訴	complaint
告訴する	accuse
告訴する	sue
告知	announcement
告知	disclosure
告知	notice
告知	notification
小口現金	float
告知書	notice
告知する	announce
小口投資家	retail
国土	land
国内企業	local businesses
国内業界	local businesses
国内事業	on shore business
国内生産	local production
国内総生産	GDP
国内総生産	gross domestic product
国内通貨	local currency
国内通貨建て	local currency
国内の	domestic
国内の	internal
告発	charge
告発する	accuse
告発する	charge
極秘の	classified
酷評	thrust
国民性	identity
国民的な	national
国民投票	plebiscite
国民の	national
国有化する	nationalize
国有の	national
国有の	state-run
国立の	national
国連気候変動枠組み条約締約国会議	COP
固形化燃料	RDF
互恵的な	reciprocal
焦げ付いた	uncollectible
焦げ付き	bad debt
焦げ付き	unrecoverable loan
後光効果	halo effect
個々の	individual
試査	test
心づけ	gratuity
試み	effort
試みの	probationary
誤差	error
誤作動	glitch
誤作動	malfunction
古参	seniority
50%削減する	halve
故障	breakdown
故障	failure
故障	fault
故障	malfunction
故障検査員	troubleshooter
故障時間	downtime
故障付きの	dirty
故障のある	dirty
故障の検査・修理	troubleshooting
個人企業	proprietorship
個人広告	personal
個人識別法	biometrics
個人消息	personal
個人消費	consumption
個人情報	personal
個人情報の流出	leaked personal information
個人的	individual
個人的	personal
個人的自由	privacy
個人の	private
個人投資家	retail
個人年金積立奨励制度	Keogh
個人の	individual
個人の	personal
個人向け取引	retail
個人用高性能パソコン	workstation
コスト	cost
コストを固定する	lock in
個性	identity
小銭	change
固体	object
誇大広告	hype
…に応える	respond to
誇張する	inflate
コツ	knowhow
国家	sovereign
国会議事録	journal
国家機関	sovereign
国家主席	president
国家的な	national
国家の	national
国旗	flag
国庫収入の	fiscal
こつこつ仕事をする	grind
こつこつ働く	plug
国庫の	fiscal
骨子	keynote
凝った	sophisticated
固定型	fixed
固定給	stipend
固定させる	lock
固定させる	peg
固定式の	fixed
固定資産	fixed asset
固定資産	property
固定資産処分損	capital loss
固定した	fixed
固定した	noncurrent
固定資本化する	immobilize
固定する	clinch
固定する	fix
固定する	freeze
固定する	secure
固定相場制	peg
固定費	overhead
固定負債	long term debt
事柄	affair
事柄	event
事柄	matter
今年最高値	year-to-date highs
今年の最高値	year-to-date highs
…ごとに	per
断る	reject
粉にする	grind
好ましい	favorable
好ましくない	unfavorable
好み	preference
好み	propensity
コバンザメ商法	baby sharks retailing
コピー	copy
コピーする	copy
コピー人間作製術	cloning
誤謬	error
誤表示	misstatement
五分五分になる	break even
個別化	customizing
個別化する	customize
個別控除	itemized deductions
個別項目化する	itemize
個別の	independent
個別の	individual
戸別	door-to-door
戸別配達の	door-to-door

戸別訪問	door-to-door
コマーシャリズム	commercialism
コマーシャル	commercial
コマーシャル	pitch
コマーシャル・ペーパー	commercial paper
コマース	commerce
…をごまかして金を巻き上げる	bilk
ごまかして避ける	evade
ごまかす	skim
ごみ固形燃料	RDF
コミッション	commission
コミットメント	commitment
コミットメント・ライン	commitment line
…込みで	inclusive
ゴミなどの投げ捨て	dumping
コミューター	commuter
コミュニケーション	communication
コミュニティ	community
コメント	statement
顧問	adviser
顧問	consultant
顧問	counselor
顧問医師	consultant
顧問会社	adviser
顧問業	adviser
顧問業務	adviser
顧問の	advisory
顧問弁護士	counselor
顧問弁護士	of counsel
コモン・ロー	law
固有資産	identifiable asset
雇用	employment
雇用	engagement
雇用	hiring
雇用	job
雇用	job market
雇用確保	job security
雇用過剰	overmanning
雇用機会	job opportunity
雇用期間	engagement
雇用契約解除	severance
雇用後給付	postemployment benefits
雇用されうる能力	employability
雇用市場	job market
雇用者	employer
雇用者数	payroll
雇用条件にかなう	employable
雇用情勢	job market
雇用する	hire
雇用促進	job development
雇用調整	layoff
雇用調整する	lay off
雇用適性	employability
雇用できる(人)	employable
雇用主	employer
雇用の安定	job security
雇用の増加	job increase
雇用の伸び	job increase
雇用不安	job worries
雇用保険	unemployment insurance
娯楽	diversion
娯楽	game
コルレス先	correspondent
コレポン	correspondence
頃合い	timing
壊す	break
今回	latest
今期	during the year
困窮している	distressed
根拠	authority
根拠	basis
根拠	foundation
根拠	premises
根拠	reason
…を根拠に据える	base
根拠のある	reasonable
根拠のない	gratuitous
根拠を置く	base
コングロマリット	conglomerate
今月	Inst.
今月	instant
今月の	instant
根源	parent
混合	mix
混合の	compound
今後の	prospective
混載輸送	consolidation
コンサルタント	consultant
コンサルティング	consulting
コンサルティング・サービス	consultation
混成の	composite
混成の	compound
コンセプト	concept
コンセンサス	consensus
コンソーシアム	consortium
コンソル公債	consol
コンソル公債	Consols
コンタンゴ	contango
根底にある	underlying
コンテンツ	content
コントローラー	comptroller
コントローラー	controller
コントロール	control
困難	difficulties
困難	stress
困難な	hard
困難な	lean
困難な状況	stress
今年度	during the year
今年度の	latest
コンパクト・ディスク	CD
コンパチビリティ	compatibility
コンパチブル	compatible
コンパラブル	comparable
コンピュータ	computer
コンピュータ	machine
コンピュータ援用エンジニアリング	CAE
コンピュータ援用生産	CAP
コンピュータ援用製造	CAM
コンピュータ援用設計	CAD
コンピュータ化	computerization
コンピュータ回線で	online
コンピュータ回線を使って	online
コンピュータ化された	e-
コンピュータ化する	automate
コンピュータ化する	computerize
コンピュータ勤務	telecommuting
コンピュータ支援生産	CAP
コンピュータ支援製造	CAM
コンピュータ支援設計	CAD
コンピュータ支援ソフトウエア技術	CASE
コンピュータ処理する	computerize
コンピュータで集中管理された	intelligent
コンピュータ統合生産	CIM
コンピュータ統合生産システム	CIM
コンピュータによる工程設計	CAPP
コンピュータによる製造	CAM
コンピュータの運用操作技術	software
コンピュータの画面	desktop
コンピュータのネットワークで	online
コンピュータの普及	computerization
コンピュータ・プログラム	program
コンピュータ・プログラム	software
コンピュタリゼーション	computerization
コンピュータ利用訓練	CBT
コンピュータを使った訓練	CBT
コンピュータを利用した製造自動化システム	CAM
コンフォート・レター	comfort letter
コンプライアンス	compliance
コンベアによる流れ作業	conveyer system
コンベア方式	conveyer system
梱包	package
梱包	packaging
梱包	packing
梱包材料	packaging
根本原理	basis
根本原理	fundamentals
根本的な	underlying
混乱	hazard
混乱	turmoil

さ

差　difference
差　discrepancy
差　disparity
差　gap
差　imbalance
サークル　circles
サーチ　search
サーチャージ　surcharge
サービサー　servicer
サービス　service
サービス残業代　unpaid overtime allowance
サービス産業の　invisible
サービス部門の　tertiary
サーベイ　survey
サーベンス・オクスレー法　Sarbanes-Oxley Act
差異　difference
差異　discrepancy
差異　disparity
差異　variance
財　commodity
財　goods
最悪期　trough
再位置付け　repositioning
最大手　leader
財貨　commodity
財貨　goods
再開　renewal
災害　casualty
再開する　resume
在外代理店　factory
再開発　redevelopment
再開発　renewal
再開発して高級化する　gentrify
再活性化　revitalization
再教育　retraining
最近参入した企業　latecomer
細工　tooling
採掘　mining
採掘料　royalty
サイクル　cycle
再訓練　retraining
裁決　decision
裁決　determination
裁決　judgment
裁決　resolution
裁決者　arbiter
裁決する　decide
債券　bond
債券　debt
債券　note
債券　paper
債券　securities
債券　security
債権　credit
債権　debt

債権　loan
債権　payment
債権　receivable
再建　reconstruction
再建　recovery
再建　rehabilitation
再建　reorganization
再建　restructuring
再建　revival
再建　turnabout
再現　reconstruction
財源　finance
財源　resource(s)
財源　treasury
債権回収　loan collection
債権回収　servicing
債権回収会社　servicer
債権買取り　factoring
債権買取り業者　factor
債権額　exposure
債券期間　tenor
債権国　creditor
債権国会議　consortium
債権債務関係　obligation
債権者　creditor
再研修　retraining
再建　rebuild
再建する　reconstruct
再建する　rehabilitate
再建する　reorganize
再建する　restructure
再建する　revive
再建する　turn around
再現する　reconstruct
再検討する　reinvent
債権取立て　factoring
債券などの発行　launching
債権に対する引当金　loan reserves
債券によって保証された　bonded
債権の現在価値　loan values
債権の査定　loan assessment
債券の短期物　front end
債権の届出　claim
債券発行　loan
債権表示証書　note
債権放棄　debt waiver
債権放棄　loan forgiveness
債権放棄　loan waiver
債券保険　bond insurance
債権保有者　creditor
債権を帳消しにする　write off
在庫　backlog
在庫　inventory
在庫　stock
在庫　stockpile
在庫あり　in-stock
再興　rehabilitation
再考　review
最高　cap
最高　ceiling

最高　high
最高　maximum
採鉱　mining
最高位　top
最高位の　chief
最高位の　top
最高価格先出し法　HIFO
最高価格帯の　high-end
最高価格払出し法　HIFO
最高技術水準の　state-of-the-art
最高技術責任者　CTO
最高級船　flagship
最高級の　prime
最高級の　state-of-the-art
最高業務運営責任者　COO
最高業務執行役員　CEO
最高業務執行理事　CEO
最高記録　high
最高記録　record
最高経営責任者　CEO
最高原価先出し法　HIFO
最高限度　cap
最高財務責任者　CFO
最高財務担当役員　CAO
最高執行責任者　COO
最高情報責任者　CIO
最高情報担当役員　CIO
最高水準の　state-of-the-art
再興する　rebuild
再構成　restructuring
再構成する　restructure
最高責任者　head
再構築　reconstruction
再構築する　rebuild
再構築する　reconstruct
再構築する　restructure
最高知識担当役員　CKO
最高の　maximum
最高の　optimal
最高の　sovereign
最高の　top
催告　notification
在庫調べ　stocktaking
在庫として持つ　keep
在庫のない品　backorder item
在庫のない商品　backorder item
在庫品　inventory
在庫品　stock
在庫目録　backlist
再雇用　reemployment
最先出願者特許主義　first-to-file principle
最先発明者特許主義　first-to-invent principle
財産　asset
財産　estate
財産　fortune
財産　goods
財産　possession

和英

財産 property	最上等 prime	再生利用する recycle
財産 wealth	最小の minimum	最前線 cutting edge
財産移転 conveyance	最上の optimum	最前線 forefront
財産移転証書 conveyance	最上の sovereign	最前線 front line
財産永久拘束 perpetuity	最上の top	最前線 leading edge
採算がとれる lean	在職の incumbent	最前線の cutting-edge
採算が取れる pay	最初の initial	最先端 cutting edge
財産管理 treasurership	最初の premier	最先端 forefront
財産権 property	再処理 recycling	最先端 leading edge
財産権 property right	最新鋭 cutting edge	最先端技術の sophisticated
財産所有権 property right	最新鋭 leading edge	最先端の advanced
採算性 feasibility	最新鋭の advanced	最先端の cutting-edge
採算性 profitability	最新鋭の state-of-the-art	最先端の latest
財産的価値のある proprietary	最新型 cutting edge	最先端の state-of-the-art
採算点 break-even (point)	最新型 leading edge	最善の optimum
採算の合わない unprofitable	最新技術の state-of-the-art	最善の努力をする条件の best-efforts
財産の移転 grant	最新式 cutting edge	最前部 forefront
財産の譲渡 settlement	最新式 leading edge	最前部 leading edge
採算の取れる規模 critical mass	最新式にする update	最前列 front
財産分与 endowment	最新式の cutting-edge	催促 demand
財産目録 inventory	最新式の sophisticated	細則 bylaws
採算ライン break-even (point)	最新式の state-of-the-art	最大 maximum
採算ラインになる break even	最新情報 update	最大化 maximization
財産を譲渡する release	最新設備の導入 renovation	最大数 maximum
催事 event	最新装置の sophisticated	最大限の maximum
材質 material	最新の advanced	最大限の top
最終 back end	最新の emerging	最大限有効に使う economize
最終赤字 net loss	最新の hot	最大の chief
最終黒字 net profit	最新の innovative	最大の dominant
最終結果[成果] bottom line	最新の latest	最大の key
最終決定 bottom line	最新のものにする update	最大の main
最終産物 end-product	最新版 update	最大の maximum
最終消費者 ultimate consumer	再審理 review	最大の top
再就職 reemployment	サイズ size	最大のシェア lion's share
再就職斡旋 outplacement	…のサイズを変える resize	最大の比率 lion's share
再就職する reenter the workforce	再生 rehabilitation	最大の部分 lion's share
再修正する reverse	再生 renewal	最大量 maximum
最終製品 end-product	再生 reorganization	最高値 high
最終製品 finished product	再生 revitalization	採択 adoption
最終損益 bottom line	再生 revival	採択可能な acceptable
最終的な net	財政 budget	在宅勤務 telecommuting
最終手続き closing	財政 finance	採択する adopt
最終の latest	財政援助 funding	在宅でできる in-home
最終の terminal	財政家 financier	在宅の in-home
最終目的 destination	最盛期 season	財団 foundation
最重要事項 bottom line	再生事業 recycling	最短コース fast track
最重要製品 flagship	財政資金過調達 overfunding	再調査 review
最重要な high	財政上の economic	再調整 realignment
最重要な leading	財政上の fiscal	再調整する realign
最重要な master	財政上の monetary	再調達 replacement
最重要な prime	再生する rebuild	再調達 repurchase
最終利益 net profit	再生する rehabilitate	再陳述 restatement
再取得 replacement	再生する reorganize	再賃貸 sublease
再循環 recycling	再生する revitalize	最低 bottom
最小 minimum	再生する revive	最低 low
最上位機種 flagship	再生する turn around	最低 minimum
最上位の top	財政難 crunch	最低 rock bottom
最小限 minimum	財政の fiscal	裁定 arbitrage
最小限の minimum	再整理する reverse	裁定 arbitration
最小値 minimum	再生利用 recycling	

裁定　award	maintenance	債務国　debtor
裁定　rule	再販売価格維持　RPM	債務再編　rescheduling
裁定　ruling	再販売価格維持制度　resale price	債務残高　outstanding debt
裁定額　award	maintenance	債務支払い不能者　bankrupt
最低記録　low	最低値　low	債務者　borrower
裁定金　award	再評価　revaluation	債務者　debtor
再提携　realignment	再評価する　revalue	財務省　Treasury
再提携する　realign	再評価する　write down	財務省　U.S. Treasury Department
最低限の経済規模　critical mass	再表示　restatement	財務状況　balance sheet
裁定する　award	再表示する　restate	債務証券　debt
裁定取引　arbitrage	最頻値　mode	債務証書　bond
最低取引単位　lot	財布　purse	債務証書　obligation
最低の　knockdown	細分化する　segment	財務省証券　T-bill
最低の　minimum	再分配　redistribution	財務状態　balance sheet
最低の　rock-bottom	再分類　reclassification	財務省短期証券　T-bill
最低レベル　rock bottom	再分類する　reclassify	財務省長期証券　T-bond
最低レベルに達する　bottom out	再編　consolidation	財務上の　financial
最低レベルの　rock-bottom	再編　overhaul	財務諸表　accounts
最適化　optimization	再編　realignment	財務書類　accounts
最適の　optimal	再編　reorganization	財務体質　balance sheet
最適の　optimum	再編　reshuffle	債務棚上げ　bailout
財テク　zaitech	再編　restructuring	債務担保証券　CDO
サイト　site	再編　shakeout	債務超過　deficiency
サイト　Web site	再編　shake-up	債務超過　deficit
再統合　realignment	再編する　realign	債務超過　insolvency
再統合する　realign	再編する　reorganize	債務超過　negative net worth
再投資　reinvestment	再編する　reshuffle	債務超過額　negative net worth
再投資する　reinvest	再編する　resize	債務超過の　insolvent
サイドライン　sideline	再編成　divestiture	財務統括役員　CAO
歳入　revenue	再編成　realignment	財務内容　balance sheet
再入手する　repossess	再編成　reorganization	財務内容　finance
歳入超過額　surplus	再編成　shakeout	債務などの不履行　failure
在任期間　length of service	再編成する　realign	財務の　financial
在任期間　office	再編成する　reorganize	債務の支払いにあてる　obligate
再燃　revival	再編成する　reshape	債務の支払いを繰り延べる
再燃する　revive	再編成する　restructure	reschedule
才能　capability	再保険　reinsurance	債務の転付　delegation
才能　vocation	再保険をかける　reinsure	債務の免除　waiver
財の輸出入　merchandise trade	再ポジショニング　repositioning	債務の履行　performance
サイバービジネス　cyberbusiness	再保証　reinsurance	財務表　statement
栽培する　grow	再保証する　reinsure	債務負担　obligation
再配置　redeployment	債務　borrowing	財務部長　controller
再配置　relocation	債務　debt	債務不履行　default
再配置する　redeploy	債務　engagement	債務不履行者　defaulter
再配置する　relocate	債務　indebtedness	債務返済　debt servicing
再配備　redeployment	債務　liability	債務返済　servicing
栽培品種　agrotype	債務　loan	債務返済繰延べ　rescheduling
再配分　redeployment	債務　obligation	債務返済を繰り延べる　reschedule
再配分　redistribution	債務　responsibility	債務法　liability method
再配分する　redeploy	財務　balance sheet	財務報告上の　reported
再発明する　reinvent	財務　finance	債務方式　liability method
裁判員制度　lay judge system	財務　financing	債務免除　debt waiver
再販価格維持　resale price	財務会計基準審議会　FASB	債務免除　loan forgiveness
再販価格維持　resale price	債務過多　over-indebtedness	債務免除　loan waiver
maintenance	財務官　financier	債務履行　servicing
裁判管轄　jurisdiction	財務管理　treasurership	財務レバレッジ　leverage
裁判管轄権　jurisdiction	財務基盤　balance sheet	債務を負った　encumbered
裁判権　competence	財務基盤　capital structure	債務を抱えた　indebted
裁判権　jurisdiction	財務広報　investor relations	債務を再編する　reschedule
裁判所　forum	財務広報　IR	債務を免除する　discharge
再販売価格維持　resale price		

細目 item	詐欺行為 fraud	削減する contain
最安値 low	詐欺師 racketeer	削減する curtail
再融資 refinance	…に先立つ ante-date	削減する cut
再融資 refinancing	詐欺的な fraudulent	削減する downsize
再融資する refinance	先の prior	削減する lay off
最優先課題 top	詐欺の fraudulent	削減する liquidate
最優先課題 top priority	先のことを考えて proactively	削減する reduce
最優先事項 top	先日付 postdate	削減する slash
最優先の top	先物 forward	削減する trim
最優先問題 top priority	先物 futures	搾取する exploit
最有力候補者 front runner	先物為替 futures	削除 write-off
最有力の dominant	先物契約 futures	削除する take off
採用 adoption	先物取引 futures	削除する take out
採用 hiring	先行き outlook	作成 execution
採用 recruiting	先行き prospects	作成する execute
採用 use	先行き不透明感 uncertainty	作成する prepare
採用する adopt	作業 effort	作成する present
採用する govern	作業 operation	作成する produce
採用する hire	作業 task	サクセス success
採用する recruit	作業 work	作戦 campaign
採用する use	作業委員会 working committee	作戦 tactic(s)
再利用 recycling	作業委員会 working group	作戦行動 tactic(s)
材料 factor	作業時間 working hours	作戦上の operational
材料 force	作業所 shop	策定 formation
材料 ingredient	作業場 shop	策定する come up with
材料 material	作業場 workplace	策定する map out
材料 point	作業場 workshop	作品 fare
材料 raw material	作業台 table	策略 game
材料 reason	作業端末 workstation	策略 plot
再利用する recycle	作業手順書 manual	探る test
財力 finance	作業の working	下げ相場の downmarket
財力 purse	作業班 working group	下げ止まり bottoming out
サインする exchange	作業日 working day	下げ止まる bottom out
差益 capital surplus	作業票 job order	避ける ward off
差益 gain	作業部会 working group	避ける withhold
差益 gross profit	先渡し契約 forward	下げる cut
査閲 inspection	先渡し取引 forward	下げる lower
査閲 review	策 effort	下げる reduce
査閲する review	策 exercise	ささいな cosmetic
さえない dull	策 measure	支え mainstay
差額 balance	策 package	支える bolster
差額 difference	策 plan	支える buoy
差額 spread	策 program	支える help
差額 variance	策 scheme	支える prop up
さかのぼって upward	策 shift	査察 inspection
遡って日付を入れる backdate	策 stance	査察 survey
下がり気味の bear	策 strategy	差し入れる post
下がり気味の bearish	策 tactic(s)	差押さえ attachment
下がる lower	作為 action	差し押さえ通告を受けた人
下がる moderate	作為 commission	garnishee
下がる retreat	索引 index	差し押さえる garnish
盛んな売行き run	削減 curtailment	差し押さえる garnishee
詐欺 fraud	削減 cut	差し押さえる levy
詐欺 rig	削減 cutback	指図書 job order
先入れ先出し法 first-in, first-out	削減 downsizing	指図する order
basis	削減 drawdown	指図する supervise
先入れ先出し法 FIFO	削減 drawdown	差出人 mailer
先送り back burner	削減 layoff	差し止め suspension
先買権を得るために占有する	削減 reduction	差止請求 injunction
preempt	削減する ax	差止命令 injunction

差し止める	suspend	査定価格	valuation	参加する	participate
差し止める	veto	査定額	assessment	参加する	share
差し伸べる	extend	査定する	assess	参加する	sign up
差し引いたうえで	after	査定する	award	参加調印した	signatory
差し控える	forgo	作動する	function	参加登録する	enter
差し控える	withhold	作動する	perform	傘下に置く	affiliate
差引	deduction	作動する	run	参加呼びかけ	challenge
差引額	deduction	作動する	work	産業	industry
差引勘定	offset	サブプライム	subprime	残業	overtime
…差引き後	after	サプライ	supply	産業化	commercialization
…差引き後	net of	サプライ・チェーン	supply chain	産業化	industrialization
…差引後純額	net of	サプライ・チェーン・マネジメント		産業界	industry
差引残高	account balance		SCM	産業空洞化	deindustrialization
…差引き前	before	サプライヤー	supplier	産業工学	IE
差し引く	credit	差別	differentiation	産業の	industrial
差し引く	deduct	差別	discrimination	産業用の	industrial
差し引く	recoup	差別化	differentiation	残金	balance
差し引く	take off	差別化する	differentiate	参考	consultation
差し戻す	remit	差別制の	preferential	参考	reference
…から詐取する	bilk	差別待遇	discrimination	参考書	manual
詐称する	falsify	差別をしない	fair	参考人	reference
座席	place	サポート	support	参考文献	reference
座席の一括予約	block booking	サポートする	support	残差	residual
挫折	setback	妨げる	prohibit	参事官	counselor
誘い込む	lure	サムライ・ボンド	Samurai bond	算式	formula
誘い水	pump priming	鞘取り売買	arbitrage	三重苦	trilemma
誘って…させる	induce	左右されやすい	sensitive	3重の	triple
定める	appoint	左右されやすい	volatile	産出	generation
定める	determine	左右する	determine	産出する	deliver
定める	establish	作用	agency	算出する	gauge
定める	fix	作用物質	agent	産出高	output
定める	include	サラ金	loan shark	産出地帯	field
定める	provide	サラ金業者	loan shark	算術平均	arithmetic mean
定める	state	さらけだす	bare	産出量	output
座談会	panel	…にさらされやすい	vulnerable	参照	consultation
サチュレーション	saturation	さらす	expose	参照	reference
…冊	copy	サラダ・ボウル	salad bowl	参照番号	reference
札	bill	騒ぎ	turmoil	斬新	innovation
雑	misc.	傘下	umbrella	斬新さ	novelty
雑	miscellaneous	参加	access	斬新性	novelty
雑誌	journal	参加	entry	斬新な	innovative
雑誌	magazine	参加	hand	賛成	approval
刷新	innovation	参加	participation	酸性試験	acid test
刷新	renewal	参加意思表示	commitment	酸性試験比率	acid test ratio
刷新	renovation	傘下入りする	affiliate	…に賛成(署名)する	subscribe
刷新	shakeout	参加型の	bottom-up	賛成する	approve
刷新する	renovate	参加勧誘	challenge	山積	backlog
刷新する	reshape	参加企業	participant	残存価格	salvage value
刷新する	reshuffle	参加行	participant	残存価格	scrap value
刷新する	revamp	三角合併	triangular merger	残存価額	salvage value
殺到	flood	3か月ごとに	quarterly	残存価額	scrap value
殺到	influx	参加国	member state	残存する	remaining
殺到	surge	参加国	participant	残高	backlog
殺到する	flood	参加者	affiliate	残高	balance
殺到する	surge	参加者	entrant	残高	outstanding balance
査定	adjustment	参加者	entry	残高	outstanding debt
査定	appraisal	参加者	participant	産地直送	drop shipment
査定	assessment	参加者	player	算定	accounting
査定	survey	参加する	access	算定	assessment
査定	valuation	参加する	enter	算定	determination

算定	measurement	仕入書	invoice	時間	time
算定する	assess	仕入担当者	buyer	時間外取引	off-hours trading
算定する	determine	仕入れる	procure	時間外の	after-hours
算定する	gauge	仕入れる	purchase	時間外労働	overtime
算定する	provide	シーン	scene	時間稼ぎ(をする)	stall
暫定的	temporary	シェア	market share	時間差異	timing differences
暫定的な	interim	シェア	share	志願者	applicant
暫定的な	preliminary	シェアリング	sharing	時間の制限	time frame
賛同	approval	Jカーブ	J-curve	時間の調整・選択	timing
賛同する	approve	自営業者	proprietorship	時間枠	time frame
参入	access	自営業者	self-employed people	…式	style
参入	entrance	自営業者退職年金制度	Keogh	士気	morale
参入	entry	市営の	municipal	指揮	leadership
参入	participation	ジェネリック	generic	指揮	supervision
参入	penetration	ジェネリック医薬品	generic drug	式	form
算入	inclusion	ジェネレーション	generation	時期	juncture
参入機会	access	シェルフ登録	shelf registration	時期	period
算入して	inclusive	支援	contribution	時期	point
参入する	access	支援	help	時期	season
参入する	participate	支援	rescue	時期	time
算入する	include	支援	support	時期	timing
3倍増となる	triple	支援者	backer	敷居	threshold
3倍にする	triple	支援する	contribute	敷金	deposit
3倍になる	triple	支援する	help	次期繰越し	cf, c/f
3倍の	triple	支援する	rescue	次期繰越し	C/D [c/d]
産物	architecture	支援する	sponsor	磁気情報	magnetic information
産物	product	支援する	support	指揮する	run
サンプル	pattern	支援する	sustain	敷地	location
三方一両得の解決策	win-win-win solution	支援の手	helping hand	敷地	lot
残務	backlog	潮時	timing	時期の調整・選択	timing
残価	remainder	しおれる	flag	識別	differentiation
残余	remainder	市価	market price	識別	discrimination
残余	residual	市価	market value	識別	identification
残余権	remainder	時価	fair market value	識別可能資産	identifiable asset
残余の	remaining	時価	fair value	識別する	differentiate
残余の	residual	時価	market price	識別番号	ID
残留物	residual	時価	market value	識別番号	identification
		時価	quotation	識別符号	ID
		視界	horizon	識別力	discrimination
		司会者	chairman	支給	issuance
試合	game	司会者	host	支給する	allow
試合場	park	仕掛品	WIP	至急の	express
地上げ	land sharking	資格	capacity	支給日	payday
地上げ行為	land sharking	資格	competence	自給率	self-sufficiency rate
仕上げ細工	tooling	資格	requirement(s)	死去	going
地上げ屋	land shark	資格	status	市況	market
示威運動	demonstration	資格取得の	qualifying	市況	market conditions
シーズン	season	資格認可	licensing	事業	activity
シームレス	seamless	…に資格を与える	qualify	事業	affair
シーリング	ceiling	資格を与える	qualifying	事業	business
シール	seal	資格を持たせる	fit	事業	concern
仕入れ	procurement	シカゴ・マーカンタイル取引所	CME	事業	enterprise
仕入れ	purchase	自家商標	private brand	事業	game
仕入れ	purchasing	時価総額	aggregate market value	事業	operation
仕入原価	original cost	時価総額	market valuation	事業	project
仕入れ債務	payable	地固め	consolidation	事業	scheme
仕入債務	account payable	時価で評価する	mark to market	事業	service
仕入先	creditor	時価評価額	market value	事業	undertaking
仕入先	supplier	時間	hour	事業	venture
仕入先	vendor			事業	work

事業家	entrepreneur	事業を行う	do business	資金を出す	finance
事業会社	operator	事業を展開する	do business	資金を調達する	borrow
事業活動領域	domain	事業を展開する	operate	資金を調達する	finance
事業環境	playing field	事業を統合する	merge operations	資金を調達する	fund
事業機会	opportunity	支局	branch	資金を提供する	fund
事業基盤	position	指揮をとる	supervise	資金を補充する	refinance
事業基盤	presence	資金	capacity	資金を賄う	fund
事業基盤の強化	repositioning	資金	capital	軸	focus
事業基盤の再構築	repositioning	資金	cash	試掘井	wildcat
事業区分	segment	資金	finance	軸となる	core
事業再生	revival	資金	financing	仕組み	fabric
事業再生	turnaround	資金	fund	仕組み	framework
事業再生融資	DIP finance	資金	liquidity	仕組み	practice
事業再編	reorganization	資金	money	仕組み	scheme
事業再編	transformation	資金	proceeds	仕組む	engineer
事業者	operator	資金	resource(s)	仕組む	tailor
事業主	employer	資金	treasury	刺激	impact
事業主	operator	市銀	commercial bank	刺激	incentive
事業主	proprietor	資金化	funding	刺激	inducement
事業所	establishment	資金供給	money supply	刺激	stimulus
事業所	site	資金供与	funding	刺激効果	stimulus
事業所で内製化した	in-shop	資金供与者	creditor	刺激策	stimulus
事業所内の	in-shop	資金繰り	cash flow	刺激する	boost
事業所レベルの	in-shop	資金繰り	liquidity	刺激する	revive
事業体	enterprise	資金繰り難の	stricken	刺激誘因	motivation
事業体	entity	資金繰りの問題	cash flow problem	試験	probation
事業団	foundation	資金源	funding	試験	test
事業単位	entity	資金交付	disbursement	資源	raw material
事業提携先	partner	資金収支	cash flow	資源	resource(s)
事業停止	winding up	資金需要	capital requirements	資源	wealth
事業停止する	wind up	資金需要の逼迫	tight money	事件	affair
事業展開	doing business	試金石	acid test	事件	case
事業統合	merger	資金洗浄	laundry	事件	deal
事業年度	FY	資金洗浄	money laundering	事件	event
事業年度	period	資金調達	access to financing	資源開発	mining
事業年度	year	資金調達	borrowing	資源循環	recycling
事業の再構築	restructuring	資金調達	finance	試験する	test
事業の再編成	restructuring	資金調達	financing	試験的	pilot
事業の種類	line of business	資金調達	fund raising	志向	orientation
事業の詳細な計画・実行	logistics	資金調達	funding	志向	preference
事業の新規性	novel business	資金調達計画	fund-raising plan	指向	drive
事業廃止部門	discontinued operation	資金提供	funding	施行	effect
事業買収	acquisition	資金提供者	underwriter	施行	execution
事業費	funding	資金投下	investment	施行	implementation
市況品	commodity	資金などを還流する	recycle	事項	affair
試供品	sample	資金難	cash flow problem	事項	clause
事業部	division	…の資金に充てる	finance	事項	event
事業部の	divisional	資金の移動	money transfer	事項	fact
事業部門	division	資金の運用・調達	cash flow	事項	item
事業部門	line	資金の回転調達	rollover	事項	matter
事業部門	line of business	資金の再調達	refinancing	事項	point
事業部門	segment	資金の出し手	lender	…志向型	-oriented
事業部門	unit	資金の調達	raising	施行する	implement
事業分野	line of business	資金の必要額	capital requirements	…志向の	driven
事業分野	segment	資金の流出入	cash flow	…志向の	-minded
事業免許	franchise	資金の流入	capital inflow	…志向の	-oriented
事業要綱	prospectus	資金引出し	drawdown	自己株式	treasury stock
事業ライン	line of business	資金引出し実行	drawdown	自国通貨	local currency
事業領域	domain	資金必要額	cash requirements	自国の	domestic
		資金を供給する	finance	自己資金	net worth

自己資本					
自己資本	capital	資産	property	時事通信	newsletter
自己資本	equity	資産	wealth	事実上存在する	de facto
自己資本	net worth	資産・負債承継	P&A	事実上の	de facto
自己資本	proprietorship	資産運用	asset management	事実上の	effective
自己資本	stockholders' equity	資産運用サービス	asset management services	事実上の	virtual
自己資本が充実した銀行	well-capitalized bank	資産化	capitalization	事実に基づく	objective
自己資本規制	capital requirements	資産価格	asset value	事実の開示	disclosure
自己資本比率	capital ratio	資産化する	capitalize	支社	branch
自己資本比率	capital-to-asset ratio	資産型リース	capital lease	支社	unit
		資産価値	asset value	自社株	treasury stock
自己資本比率規制	capital requirements	資産管理	asset management	自社株買い	buyback
自己資本利益率	ROE	資産管理	portfolio	自社株買戻し	buyback
事後処理	aftercare	資産管理業務	custody service	自社株購入権	stock option
事後的	after	資産基盤	asset base	自社株取得	buyback
仕事	affair	持参金	dowries	自主管理	self-management
仕事	career	資産計上	capitalization	自主企画商品	private brand
仕事	effort	資産権利	property right	自主再建	self-rehabilitation
仕事	engagement	資産構成	asset base	自主性	independence
仕事	game	資産構成	portfolio	自主性	initiative
仕事	gig	資産譲渡益	capital gain	支出	disbursement
仕事	job	資産譲渡損	capital loss	支出	expenditure
仕事	labor	試算する	estimate	支出	expense
仕事	task	資産担保コマーシャル・ペーパー	asset-backed commercial paper	支出	outlay
仕事	undertaking	資産担保証券	ABS	支出	payout
仕事	work	資産担保証券	asset-backed securities	支出	spending
自己同一性	identity			支出額	disbursement
自己投下資本	down payment	資産と負債の継承	P&A	支出金	payout
仕事上の	working	資産と負債の承継	P&A	支出する	appropriate
仕事のない	jobless	資産内容	CAMEL	支出する	defray
仕事場	office	資産内容	portfolio	支出する	disburse
仕事場	workplace	資産に計上する	capitalize	支出する	pay
仕事場	workshop	持参人	bearer	支出する	spend
…を仕事場とする	work	持参人	carrier	自主的な	free
仕事量	load	資産売却益	capital gain	自主的な	independent
仕事を請け負わせる	farm out	資産売却損	capital loss	自主的な	voluntary
仕事をする	serve	指示	brief	地所	estate
仕事をする	work	支持	approval	地所	lot
仕事をまかせる	farm out	支持	backing	市場	field
自己認識	identity	支持	backup	市場	market
事後の	after	支持	endorsement	市場	marketplace
自己売買	dealing	支持	support	市場	outlet
自己破産	self-declared bankruptcy	時事開設	newsletter	市場	sector
事後日付	postdate	指示器	display unit	事象	event
自己持ち分	equity	支持者	backer	事情	backdrop
市債	municipal	支持者	sponsor	事情	scene
施策	measure	…が支持する	-backed	事情	situation
試作品	prototype	…を支持する	side with	事情	status
時差出勤	flextime	指示する	order	市場アクセス	access
時差出勤制	flextime	支持する	approve	市場荒し	raider
時差制にする	stagger	支持する	bolster	市場外取引	off-market trading
視察	inspection	支持する	prop up	市場介入	intervention
試算	estimate	支持する	share	市場開放	deregulation
資産	asset	支持する	sponsor	市場開放する	deregulate
資産	balance sheet	支持する	support	市場価格	market price
資産	competence	支持する	sustain	市場価格	market value
資産	equipment	支持する	underpin	市場価値	market value
資産	fortune	事実	deed	市場環境	market conditions
資産	holdings	事実	fact	市場環境	market environment
				市場関係者	market player
				市場関連資産価格方式	market-

市場金利				731		質を置く	

	related asset value method	指針	indicator	事態	event
市場金利	market rate	自信	assurance	事態	juncture
市場金利	prevailing rate	自信	confidence	事態	matter
市場経済	market economy	指数	factor	事態	scenario
市場原理	market principles	指数	figure	事態	scene
市場原理に基づく	market-driven	指数	index	事態	situation
市場参加者	market player	指数	indicator	時代	time
市場参加者	marketer	指数	key gauge	時代遅れの	obsolete
市場シェア	market share	指数	reading	時代遅れのもの	back number
市場志向の	market-driven	指数	series	次第に高める	pyramid
市場商人	marketeer	指数化方式にする	index	時代に取り残された	obsolete
市場筋	market player	指数関数的な	exponential	下請	subcontract
市場性	merchantability	指数の	exponential	下請	subcontracting
市場性ある	marketable	システミック・リスク	systemic risk	下請	subcontractor
市場占拠率	market share	システム	system	下請け	delegation
市場占拠率	share	システム・リスク	systemic risk	下請負させる	subcontract
市場占有率	market share	鎮める	quash	下請契約	subcontract
市場占有率	share	姿勢	approach	下請契約	subcontracting
市場操作	manipulation	姿勢	attitude	下請契約者	subcontractor
市場操作	market manipulation	姿勢	commitment	下請契約をする	subcontract
市場操作	rig	姿勢	presence	下請けに出す	sublet
市場相場	market rate	姿勢	stance	下請に出す	farm out
市場調査	marketing research	時勢	time	下請をする	subcontract
事情聴取	debriefing	私生活	privacy	従う	follow
事情聴取する	debrief	市制の	municipal	従う	fulfill
事情通の	savvy	施政方針	policy	…に従って	subject to
市場低迷	thin market	施設	equipment	下から上に向かっている	bottom-up
市場特性	characteristics of the market	施設	establishment	下からの意見具申	bottom-up
		施設	facility		
市場取引	marketing	施設	installation	自宅でできる	in-home
市場などに参入する	enter	施設	institution	下支えする	underpin
市場に出す	launch	施設	plant	親しい	close
市場に出す	market	施設	premises	仕立てる	tailor
市場に出す	pitch	施設	site	下取り	trade
市場の拡大	market growth	私設の	private	下回る	lag
市場の気配	run	慈善	philanthropy	下回る	underperform
市場の混乱	market turmoil	慈善市	fair	…を下回るパフォーマンスを示す	
市場の地合い	sentiment	慈善活動	philanthropy		underperform
市場の実勢金利	prevailing rate	自然環境	ecology	下向きに	downward
市場の需要	market demand	自然減	attrition	下向きの	bear
市場の状況	market conditions	慈善行為	philanthropy	下向きの	downward
市場の状態	market conditions	事前行動の	proactive	下役	subordinate
市場の成長	market growth	慈善事業	philanthropy	示談	settlement
市場の動揺	market turmoil	慈善団体	philanthropy	示談	transaction
市場の内部要因による	technical	事前に対策を講じて	proactively	質	hock
市場の伸び	market growth	事前の	pilot	質	pawn
市場の崩壊	meltdown	事前の	prior	質入れする	pledge
市場の暴落	debacle	事前の	proactive	質権設定	pledge
市場優先の	market-driven	次善の策	lesser of two evils	質店営業者	pawnbroker
市場リスク	market risk	事前販売期間	premarketing period [phase]	質流れ	foreclosure
市場レート	market rate			質屋	Lombard
辞職	resignation	事前評価	assessment	質屋	pawnbroker
辞職する	quit	思想	idea	市中	market
辞職する	resign	死蔵	hoarding	支柱	mainstay
辞職する	step down	…しそうだ	poised to	市中銀行	commercial bank
辞職する	surrender	持続	standing	思潮	climate
私書箱	post-office box	持続可能な	sustainable	視聴覚教材	software
指針	conduct	持続させる	sustain	視聴覚の	audiovisual
指針	guideline	持続する	maintain	視聴率	rating
指針	index	事態	affair	質を置く	pledge

質 quality	実行する implement	実証 demonstration
実演 demonstration	実行する originate	実情 case
実演 exhibition	実行する perform	実情 fact
実演宣伝 demonstration	実行する phase in	失職 unemployment
実演販売 demonstration	実行する run	実施料 fee
しっかりした savvy	実効税率 effective tax rate	実施料 license fee
質疑 question	執行部 executive	実施料 royalty
失脚 downfall	執行役員 executive	実勢価格 market price
失業 joblessness	実査 inspection	実勢相場 prevailing rate
失業 redundancy	実際 deed	叱責(する) reprimand
失業 unemployment	実際 fact	実績 experience
実業 business	実際的な知識 savvy	実績 figure
実業界 business	実際の effective	実績 performance
失業者 unemployment	実際の real	実績 results
失業者の jobless	実在の objective	…の実績がある experience
失業中の jobless	実際の役に立つ working	実績評価 stocktaking
失業保険 unemployment insurance	実際面 nuts and bolts	実践 practice
失業率 jobless rate	実際より多く計上すること overstatement	実践的な nuts and bolts
失業率 joblessness	実際より少なく計上する understate	実装 implementation
失業率 unemployment	実際より前の日付を付ける ante-date	実体の real
シックス・シグマ six sigma		実体のない intangible
失権 forfeiture	失策 oversight	実地 field
実験 test	実施 conduct	実地細目 nuts and bolts
実現 fulfillment	実施 execution	失墜 fall
実現 implementation	実施 implementation	失墜する fall
実現 realization	実施 launch	質的な qualitative
実現可能性 feasibility	実施 launching	実店舗 offline
実現した realized	実施額 disbursement	ジット JIT
実現済みの realized	実時間 real time	ジット just-in-time
実現する realize	実時間処理 real time	実動の effective
実現する secure	実施義務 accountability	実動の working
実験的 pilot	実施許諾 grant	失敗 failure
実験店舗 antenna shop	実施許諾 license	失敗 setback
実現の要件を満たした realized	実施許諾 licensing	失敗企業 loser
執行 administration	実施許諾する license	失敗する fail
執行 execution	実施許諾製品 licensed product	失敗する fall flat
失効 expiration	実施権 license	実物宣伝 demonstration
失効 forfeiture	実施権許諾契約 license agreement	実務 business
失効 lapse	実施権許諾者 licenser	実務 practice
実行 action	実施権契約 license agreement	実務上の technical
実行 deed	実施権者 licensee	実務知識 savvy
実行 execution	実施されている effective	実務面での細部 nuts and bolts
実行 exercise	実施する adopt	質問 query
実行 fulfillment	実施する effect	質問 question
実行 implementation	実施する execute	質問事項 questionnaire
実行 origination	実施する implement	質問する inquire
実行 practice	実施する stage	実用 utility
執行委員会 EC	実施中である stand	実用化 commercial utilization
実行可能性 feasibility	実施中の effective	実用化 commercialization
執行機関 executive	実質上の real	実用上の economic
失効させる extinguish	実質的推進者 sponsor	実用性 utility
執行する administer	実質的な de facto	実用的な economic
執行する execute	実質的な substantial	実用の technical
失効する expire	実質的な virtual	実用の working
失効する lapse	実質の real	実用品 utility
実行する deliver	実質簿価 effective book value	実利的な economic
実行する draw	実質本位の no-frills	実利本位の no-frills
実行する execute	実習 probation	質量 mass
実行する exercise		実力 clout
実行する fulfill		実例 paradigm

仕手	operator	指導力	leadership	支払い拒絶	dishonor
仕手	speculator	市内の	local	支払い金	disbursement
指定	appointment	シナジー効果	synergy	支払い金額	payment
指定	designation	品ぞろえ	lineup	支払い繰延べ	rollover
指定する	appoint	品揃え	range	支払い債務	account payable
指定する	assign	品物	item	支払い先を指定する	specialize
指定する	earmark	品物	kind	支払い者	source(s)
指定する	list	品物	merchandise	支払い準備金	reserve
指定する	name	シナリオ	scenario	支払い済みの	prepaid
指定する	state	シニア	senior	支払い請求	call
私的自由	privacy	ジニー・メイ	Ginnie Mae	支払い遅延	delinquency
指摘する	accuse	ジニ係数	Gini coefficient	支払い遅延の	overdue
私的な	personal	ジニ係数	Gini Index	支払い停止	default
私的な	private	辞任	resignation	支払い能力	responsibility
支店	arm	辞任する	resign	支払い能力	solvency
支店	branch	辞任する	step down	支払い能力以上に購入する	
支店	unit	地主	lessor		overtrade
時点	juncture	市の	municipal	支払い能力のある	solvent
時点	point	…をしのぐ	surpass	支払い日	maturity
支店長	manager	支配	control	支払い不能	insolvency
…の時点で	as of	支配	governance	支払い不能者	insolvent
使途	application	支配	government	支払い不能の	bankrupt
使途	disposition	支配	hand	支払い不能の	insolvent
使途	use	支配	rule	支払い保険金	payout
始動	start-up	支配下の	captive	支払い保証契約	bond
指導	guideline	支配機構	establishment	支払い満期になる	endow
指導	leadership	支配権	possession	支払い満期の	payable
自動化	automation	支配している	controlling	支払猶予	grace
自動化	robotization	支配する	control	支払い猶予期間	credit
自動化する	automate	支配する	controlling	支払い余力	solvency
自動機器	automation	支配する	govern	支払い利息・税金・営業権償却費控
指導基準	guideline	支配層	establishment	除前利益　EBITA
指導教官	counselor	支配的な	controlling	支払いを拒絶する	dishonor
自動継続	renewal	支配的な	dominant	支払いを限定する	specialize
自動式の	automatic	支配できる	controlling	支払いを待っている	receivable
指導者	bellwether	支配人	manager	支払う	clear
指導者	center [centre]	支配力	clout	支払う	defray
指導者	head	支配力	power	支払う	disburse
指導者	leader	支配力獲得競争	power game	支払う	foot
指導者	mastermind	地場産業	local businesses	支払う	fork
指導者	official	自発的な	unsolicited	支払う	match
自動車	car	自発的な	voluntary	支払う	meet
自動車	machine	支払い	disbursement	支払う	pay
自動車	vehicle	支払い	payment	支払う	pay out
指導者の資質	leadership	支払い	payoff	支払う	reckon
自動車乗り入れ[自動車通り抜け]	支払い	payout	支払う	service
式の店　drive-through store	支払い	payout	支払う	tender
指導性	leadership	支払い委託	mandate	支払うべき	payable
自動制御機能	feedback	支払い勘定	account payable	支払わせる	charge
自動操作	automation	支払い期限	maturity	支払われる	payable
自動装置	automation	支払い期限に達した	payable	支払われるべき	receivable
自動装置	robot	支払い期限の過ぎた	overdue	市販	marketing
自動装置の	automatic	支払い期日	maturity	地盤	footing
自動的な	automatic	支払い期日	prompt	市販可能性	merchantability
自動登録機	register	支払い期日になる	mature	四半期	quarter
…の指導による	-led	支払い期日のきた	due	四半期ごとに	quarterly
自動の	automatic	支払い期日の到来した	payable	四半期ごとの	quarterly
自動引落しシステム	direct debit	…の支払い義務がある	owe	四半期の	quarterly
system		支払い義務額	expenditure	四半期ベースの	quarterly
指導部	leader	支払い義務のある	due	四半期別	quarterly

市販性 merchantability	資本基盤 capitalization	資本流入 capital inflow
市販の commercial	資本金 capital	資本をかけすぎた overcapitalized
自費出版社 vanity publisher	資本金 capital stock	資本を再編する recapitalize
自費出版専門の出版社 vanity publisher	資本金 common share	資本を投入する capitalize
	資本金 common stock	市民の civil
指標 benchmark	資本金の欠損 impairment	事務 administration
指標 data	資本組入れ capitalization	事務 affair
指標 evidence	資本組入れ recapitalization	事務員 clerk
指標 figure	資本構成 capital structure	事務員の clerical
指標 gauge	資本構成 capitalization	事務改善活動 O & M
指標 guideline	資本構成を修正する recapitalize	事務官 clerk
指標 index	資本構成を変更する recapitalize	事務官 clerk
指標 indicator	資本構造 capital structure	事務管理 administration
指標 key gauge	資本拘束 change of control	事務局 bureau
指標 measure	資本再編 recapitalization	仕向け先 destination
指標 measurement	資本参加 stake	仕向け地 destination
指標 proxy	資本支出 capex	仕向け地持込み渡し(関税込み[済み])条件 DDP
指標 ratio	資本主 investor	
指標 reading	資本主 proprietor	仕向け地持込み渡し(関税抜き)条件 DDU
指標 series	資本主 proprietorship	
指標 statistics	資本集約型 capital-intensive	事務作業の機械化 OA
辞表 resignation	資本集約的 capital-intensive	事務所 office
指標金利 key interest rate	資本主勘定 proprietorship	事務所 representative
指標金利 key rate	資本準備金 capital reserve	事務上の clerical
指標となる pilot	資本準備金 capital surplus	事務処理 back office
指標銘柄 bellwether	資本剰余金 capital reserve	事務処理 paperwork
指標銘柄 benchmark	資本剰余金 capital surplus	事務処理 processing
指標銘柄 on-the-run issue	資本ストック capital stock	事務処理 servicing
支部 branch	資本総額 capitalization	事務机共用制 hot-desking
私物化する appropriate	資本増強 capital increase	事務の仕事 paperwork
シフト flight	資本損失 capital loss	事務部門 back office
シフト shift	資本調達 capitalization	事務弁護士 solicitor
シフトさせる shift	資本調達 financing	事務量測定 CWM
シフトする shift	資本調達 fund raising	使命 mission
自分自身 identity	資本積立金 capital surplus	使命 vocation
紙幣 bill	資本的支出 capex	指名 appointment
紙幣 note	資本的支出 net capital expenditures	指名 designation
次ページに続く PTO		指名権 power
紙片 slip	資本的支出純額 net capital expenditures	指名する adopt
死亡 demise		指名する appoint
司法行政 jurisdiction	資本的支出総額 gross capital expenditures	指名する name
司法権 jurisdiction		指名する propose
司法権 jurisdiction	資本投下 capital investment	締切り closing
志望者 wannabe	資本投資 capital investment	締切り footing
脂肪の少ない lean	資本として使用する capitalize	締切り write-off
司法の場での legal	資本に組み入れる capitalize	締切日 cutoff
資本 CAMEL	資本に組み入れる recapitalize	締め切る close
資本 capacity	資本燃焼率 burn rate	締めくくる conclude
資本 capital	資本の減少 withdrawal	…を示す experience
資本 net worth	資本の再構成 recapitalization	…を示す post
資本 stockholders' equity	資本の削減 capital reduction	示す define
資本化 capitalization	資本の増強 capital injection	示す present
資本回収 payback	資本の注入 capital injection	示す record
資本が過大評価された overcapitalized	資本の引上げ disinvestment	示す reflect
	資本の部 stockholders' equity	示す register
資本額固定の closed-end	資本不足の undercapitalized	示す represent
資本化する capitalize	資本変更 recapitalization	示す reveal
資本株式 capital stock	資本リース capital lease	締付け squeeze
資本化リース capital lease	資本利益率 ROI	締め付ける squeeze
資本勘定 stockholders' equity	資本利得 capital gain	…を占める account for

…を占める	generate	尺度	measurement	首位の	prime
占める	occupy	尺度	scale	首位の	top
締める	lock	尺度とする	benchmark	首位を占める	top
下期	last half	借家契約	lease	主因	agent
下期	latter half	借用	drawdown	主因	driver
下期	second half	借用書	tab	主因	driving force
地元企業	local businesses	借用証書	bond	事由	event
地元の	local	社債	bond	事由	reason
下半期	last half	社債	debenture	週5日制	five-day week
下半期	latter half	社債担保証券	CBO	自由意志による	voluntary
下半期	second half	社債保険	bond insurance	周囲の	environmental
諮問	adviser	奢侈品	luxury	収益	CAMEL
諮問	consultation	車種	model	収益	earning
諮問	consulting	車種構成	lineup	収益	earnings
諮問	advisory	写真説明文	caption	収益	income
視野	horizon	ジャスダック	Jasdaq	収益	proceeds
ジャーナル	journal	ジャストインタイム	just-in-time	収益	profit
社印	seal	社説	leader	収益	return
社員	employee	社団	association	収益	revenue
社員	hire	社団	company	収益	yield
社員	member	社長	chairman	収益権	use
社員	partner	社長	head	収益性	performance
社員	people	社長	president	収益性	profitability
社員	staff	借家人	lessee	収益性がある	profitable
社員	workforce	借家人	tenant	収益性が高い	profitable
…社会	circles	借款	loan	収益の資本還元	capitalization
社会	community	借金	borrowing	収益の申告漏れ	unreported earnings
社会	economy	借金	charge		
社会	public	借金	debt	収益率	profitability
社会還元	reinvestment	借金	hock	収益率	ratio
社会資本	infrastructure	借金	liability	収益率	return
社外調達	outsourcing	…に借金がある	owe	収益力	profitability
社外調達する	outsource	借金がある	indebted	収益力がある	profitable
社会的	public	借金しすぎた	overborrowed	収益を上げる	chalk up
社会的生産基盤	infrastructure	借金する	borrow	収益を受けるべき	beneficial
社会的責任投資	SRI	借金を返す	pay off	収益を生む	perform
社外取締役	independent director	射程	range	10億	bn
社外取締役	outside director	射程距離	range	自由化	decontrol
社会復帰	rehabilitation	社内の	in-house	自由化	deregulation
謝金	honorarium	社内の	internal	自由化	liberalization
弱化する	weaken	社内の職業訓練	on the job training	集会	convention
借記	charge	社内留保	retained earnings	集会	session
借記する	charge	社内留保利益金	retained earnings	自由化する	deregulate
弱小の	weak	ジャパン・マネー	Japan money	自由化する	liberalize
弱体化する	weaken	遮蔽する	screen	従価方式の[で]	ad valorem
借地	leasehold	遮蔽物	screen	習慣	custom
借地	tenement	社報	newsletter	習慣的な	regular
借地契約	lease	写本	tenor	周期	cycle
借地権	leasehold	邪魔物	drag	什器	facility
借地人	lessee	車両	vehicle	周期的な	cyclical
借地人	tenant	謝礼	fee	周期的な	periodic
弱点	defect	謝礼	honorarium	週休2日制	five-day week
弱点	deficiency	謝礼	remuneration	従業員	employee
弱点	disadvantage	謝礼	reward	従業員	help
弱点	flaw	しゃれた	sophisticated	従業員	manpower
弱点	weakness	ジャンク	junk	従業員	people
尺度	benchmark	ジャンク債	junk	従業員	personnel
尺度	criterion	首位	top	従業員	staff
尺度	gauge	首位になる	top	従業員	worker
尺度	measure	首位の	leading	従業員	workforce

従業員株式購入選択権制度	ESOP
従業員支援制度	EAP
従業員支援プログラム	EAP
従業員数	manpower
従業員の満足	ES
従業員引き抜き	raid
従業員満足	ES
従業員名簿	payroll
従業員持ち株制度	ESOP
就業機会	job opportunity
就業時間	working hours
就業者	worker
就業者	workforce
就業体験	internship
就業のチャンス	job opportunity
就業日	workday
集金	collectible
集金	collection
自由勤務時間	flextime
集計的	aggregate
襲撃	raid
終決	determination
終結する	terminate
集合教育	off the job training
集合体	aggregate
自由行動権	blank check
自由裁量権	disposition
自由裁量の	discretionary
収支	account
収支	balance
従事	engagement
従事	occupation
収支がとんとんになる	break even
自由市場	open market
…を重視する	focus on
重視する	value
充実	adequacy
充実させる	strengthen
充実した	full
充実した	massive
充実度	adequacy
重質の	heavy
収支とんとん	break-even (point)
…重視の	-focused
…重視の	-minded
…重視の	-oriented
収集資料	documentation
収縮	contraction
就職口	job
就職口	opening
就職困難者	job seeker
就職指導の	vocational
終身雇用	lifetime employment
終身年金	perpetuity
終身の	whole life
修正	adjustment
修正	restatement
修正	revision
修正再表示	restatement
修正再表示する	restate

修正する	adjust
修正する	restate
修正する	revamp
修正する	revise
集積回路	IC
集積回路	integration
修繕	renovation
修繕する	renovate
集線装置	hub
習俗	practice
従属会社	subsidiary
充足する	fulfill
従属的な	subordinate
従属の	dependent
醜態	scene
重大局面	crisis
重大時期	juncture
重大な	heavy
重大な	major
重大な	real
重大な	significant
重大な	substantial
重大発見	breakthrough
住宅	home
住宅	house
住宅市場	housing market
住宅地の中流階級化	gentrify
住宅着工	housing starts
住宅着工件数	housing starts
住宅着工戸数	housing starts
住宅投資	housing investment
住宅融資証券	mortgage-backed security
住宅融資証券事業	mortgage-backed securities business
住宅ローン	housing loan
住宅ローン	mortgage
住宅ローン債権担保証券	RMBS
住宅ローン担保証券	RMBS
収奪する	plunder
集団	aggregate
集団	family
集団	group
集団	mass
集団訴訟	class action suit
集団代表訴訟	class action suit
集団の	mass
私有地	estate
周知の	known
周知の	open
…に執着する	focus on
集中	focus
集中化	focus
集中キャンペーン	saturation
集中させる	concentrate
…に集中する	focus
集中する	concentrate
集中的	intensive
終点	terminal
重点	stress

重点地区	center [centre]
終点の	terminal
…に重点を置く	-oriented
充当可能な	available
充当金	reserve
充当する	appropriate
周到な	close
周到な準備	foresight
習得	experience
自由な	free
自由な	open
柔軟な	flexible
柔軟な	plastic
12月期決算	calendar year
自由になる	disposable
収入	earnings
収入	proceeds
収入	receipt
収入	revenue
収入金額	receipt
収入高	receipt
収入などを申告する	return
就任	assumption
就任する	assume
私有の	private
収納	receipt
収納	storage
修復	rehabilitation
修復	renovation
修復作業	renovation
修復する	recycle
修復する	renovate
十分位数(の)	decile
十分体制が整っている	well positioned
十分な	due
十分な	full
十分な	good
十分な情報提供に基づく同意	informed consent
十分な説明に基づく同意	informed consent
十分に	fully
十分に発達した	in-depth
週平均労働時間	workweek
周辺機器	device
周辺機器	peripheral
周辺資産	noncore assets
周辺装置	peripheral
周辺の	peripheral
自由貿易協定	FTA
自由貿易圏	FTA
自由貿易地域	FTA
自由保有権	freehold
自由保有権	tenement
自由保有不動産	freehold
終末処理	back end
住民数	population
住民投票	plebiscite
重役	executive

集約化 integration	主眼点 keynote	主催者 sponsor
重役会 board	主眼点 nuts and bolts	主催する organize
…集約型 intensive	主義 approach	主催する promote
…集約型 -oriented	主義 basis	主催する sponsor
集約する consolidate	主義 concept	取材する cover
…集約性の高い intensive	主義 method	主債務者 principal
…集約的 intensive	主義 philosophy	主旨 thrust
重要 matter	主義 principle	趣旨 effect
重要語 keyword	…主義の -based	趣旨 point
重要商品 staple	需給 supply	樹脂業界 plastics industry
重要人物 keyman	受給権の発生した vested	主軸 core
収用する expropriate	受給資格がある eligible	樹脂産業 plastics industry
重要性 account	受給者 beneficiary	種々雑多な miscellaneous
重要性 concern	受給者 recipient	首相 premier
重要性 import	需給要因 technicals	首唱者 pioneer
重要である concern	祝祭日 bank holiday	主唱する sponsor
重要な basic	縮小 ax	受信する download
重要な central	縮小 contraction	主成分 basis
重要な key	縮小 curtailment	主成分 staple
重要な large	縮小 cut	主席の chief
重要な material	縮小 cutback	首席の senior
重要な prior	縮小 decline	受贈 donation
重要な sensitive	縮小 decrease	受贈金 donation
重要な significant	縮小 drawdown	主題 matter
重要な substantial	縮小 drawdown	主体性 identity
重要な役割を演じる feature	縮小 pressure	主体的な proactive
収容能力 capacity	縮小 reduction	…を主体とする -centered
重要部分 forefront	縮小 shrinkage	受諾 compliance
重要ポスト office	縮小 squeeze	受託会社 trustee
重要要素 backbone	縮小する cut	受託者 depository
収容力 capacity	縮小する decline	受託者 trustee
修理 renovation	縮小する decrease	受託者の fiduciary
修理する fix	縮小する diminish	受託所 depository
修理する renovate	縮小する downsize	受諾する accept
修理点検 maintenance	縮小する moderate	受託製造会社 EMS
終了 close	縮小する narrow	手段 device
終了 determination	縮小する recede	手段 instrument
終了 end	縮小する shrink	手段 leverage
終了 exit	縮小する squeeze	手段 measure
終了 expiration	縮小する trim	手段 medium
終了 termination	熟成 aging	手段 move
終了する end	熟知 knowledge	手段 resort
終了する expire	熟練 skill	手段 resource(s)
重量不足 underweight	熟練技術 accomplishment	手段 shift
就労 employment	熟練工 craftsman	手段 solution
就労機会 job opportunity	熟練した professional	手段 step
就労 worker	熟練した skilled	手段 tactic(s)
就労体験 internship	熟練を要する skilled	手段 tool
週労働時間 workweek	授権 authorization	手段 vehicle
就労不能 invalidity	授権 commission	手段 way
就労率 turnover	授権株式 authorized capital	…の手段として機能する serve
収録する include	授権株式数 authorized capital	受注／出荷比 book-to-bill ratio
収賄 bribery	主権国 sovereign	受注確約書 confirmation
受益 benefit	授権資本 authorized capital	受注残 back order
受益金 benefit	主権者 sovereign	受注残 order backlog
受益者 beneficiary	受験準備 fit	受注残高 backlog
主演させる feature	受講者 participant	受注残高 order backlog
主眼 keynote	取材源 source(s)	受注残高 orders on hand
主眼 thrust	主催者 host	受注仕様生産 CTO
主幹事 lead manager	主催者 organizer	受注生産 BTO

受注生産	build to order	出世コース	fast track	首脳	leader
受注生産方式	BTO	出世第一主義	careerism	首脳陣	leader
受注生産方式	build to order	出世第一主義者	careerist	守秘義務	confidentiality
受注高	order	出張修理サービス	on-site service	手法	approach
受注品	order	出張所	branch	手法	engineering
主張	allegation	出廷等担保金証書	bail bond	手法	knowhow
主張	attitude	出典	source(s)	手法	method
主張	case	出店	outlet	手法	practice
主張	contention	出展者	exhibitor	手法	strategy
主潮	mainstream	出店者	tenant	手法	style
主張する	claim	出店する	open	手法	tool
主張する	plead	出発	going	首謀者	mastermind
出演	gig	出発点	takeoff	首謀者として指揮する	mastermind
出演契約	gig	出発点	threshold	寿命	life
出荷	delivery	出版する	publish	寿命	life cycle
出荷	shipment	出版物	press	種目	item
出荷	shipping	出費	outlay	主役を演じる	feature
出荷する	ship	出品者	exhibitor	授与	commission
出荷台数	shipment	出品する	exhibit	授与	presentation
出荷量	shipment	出品物	entry	需要	demand
出願	application	出品物	exhibition	需要	needs
出向	attachment	出力	output	主要8か国	G8
出向	transfer	主導	drive	主要8か国首脳会議	G8
出港禁止	embargo	主導	initiative	需要家	customer
出港手続き	clearance	…主導型	driven	主要株主	major shareholder
出国	exit	…主導型	-led	主要企業	leading company
出国手続き	clearance	受動喫煙	second-hand smoke	主要債権国会議	Paris Club
出資	capital investment	主導権	initiative	主要産物	staple
出資	contribution	主導者	bellwether	主要事実	matter
出資	disbursement	主導者	mastermind	主要政策金利	key interest rate
出資	funding	主導的	leading	主要でない	side
出資	investment	主導的地位	cutting edge	主要取引銀行	main bank
出資	participation	主導的地位	leading edge	主要な	central
出資	spending	主導的地位	leading position	主要な	chief
出資	stake	受動的な	passive	主要な	dominant
出資	subscription	…主導の	driven	主要な	key
出資企業	investor	…主導の	-led	主要な	large
出資金	annuity	取得	acquisition	主要な	leading
出資金	capital	取得	procurement	主要な	main
出資金	capital investment	取得	purchase	主要な	major
出資者	investor	取得	purchasing	主要な	master
出資者	owner	取得	takeout	主要な	prime
出資者	proprietor	取得価格	book value	需要の多い	hot
出資者	sponsor	取得価額	original cost	主要銘柄	blue chip
出資者持ち分	proprietorship	取得原価	original cost	需要予測と在庫補充のための共同事業	CPFR
出資する	capitalize	取得原価基準	historical cost basis	授与者	investor
出資する	contribute	取得原価主義	historical cost basis	授与する	award
出資する	finance	取得原価法	historical cost basis	樹立	establishment
出資する	fund	取得時の	historical	樹立する	establish
出資する	invest	取得者	acquirer	樹立する	notch
出資する	spend	取得する	acquire	主流	mainstream
出資する	subscribe	取得する	buy	狩猟	game
出資比率	capital ownership	取得する	obtain	受領	receipt
出資比率	ownership	取得する	procure	受領額	receipt
出資比率	shareholding	取得する	purchase	受領者	recipient
出資比率	stake	取得する	take out	受領する	receive
出所	source(s)	取得する	take over	受領できる	receivable
出世	career	ジュニア	junior	主力	backbone
出世街道	fast track	主任	supervisor	主力	core
出席者	participant	主任の	chief		

主力　mainstay	純資産　stockholders' equity	venture
主力株　leader	純資産価値　NAV	ジョイント・ベンチャー　JV
主力機種　flagship	純資産額　book value	省　board
主力行　main bank	純資産価値　equity	省　department
主力事業　main business	純資産の部　stockholders' equity	省　office
主力商品　flagship	純資産利益率　RONA	仕様(書)　spec
主力商品　mainline products	瞬時電子取引　CALS	使用　employment
主力商品　mainstay	順次の　serial	使用　use
主力製品　flagship	遵守[順守]　compliance	…上　purpose
主力製品　mainline products	純収益　net revenues	条　section
主力取引銀行　main bank	純収支　net cash	掌握する　control
主力の　leading	純収入　cash flow	上位　precedent
主力の　main	純収入　net income	小委員会　panel
種類　category	遵守性　compliance	上意下達の　top-down
種類　form	順序　method	上位の　senior
種類　kind	順序　order	上映　showing
種類　line	純所得　net income	上演　presentation
種類　range	純粋な　absolute	上演　showing
手腕　capability	純粋な　clear	上演される　run
手腕　savvy	純粋の　net	商会　firm
手腕　skill	純増　net increase	照会　inquiry
順位　notch	準則　bylaws	照会　reference
順位　rank	純損益　bottom line	紹介　introduction
順位　ranking	純損失　net loss	障害　barrier
順位　standing	純損失収益性　bottom line	障害　casualty
…の順位を決める　rank	潤沢な資金　ample liquidity	障害　failure
純売上高　net sales	順調な　going	障害　fault
純運転資本　net working capital	順調な　healthy	障害　glitch
純営業収益　net operating revenues	準通貨　quasi money	障害　hazard
純営業利益　net operating profit	純度　water	生涯　career
純益　net	順応　fit	障害時の安全性　fail safe
純益を上げる　net	順応指導　orientation	障害時の運転可能性　fail soft
準大手の　second-tier	順応する　fit	照会状　inquiry
巡回キャンペーン　roadshow	順応性のある　flexible	紹介する　introduce
巡回説明会　roadshow	純売却益　net proceeds	照会人　reference
純額　net	純白の従者　white squire	照会番号　reference
瞬間　instant	準備　arrangement	昇格　promotion
循環　cycle	準備　provision	昇格　upgrading
循環　flow	準備完了の　green	奨学基金　foundation
循環　rotation	準備期間　lead time	奨学金　exhibition
循環させる　circulate	準備金　provision	奨学金　grant
循環使用　recycling	準備金　reserve	小額債券　baby bond
循環使用する　recycle	準備させる　fit	昇格させる　promote
循環処理する　recycle	準備する　arrange	昇格させる　upgrade
循環的上昇・下降　spiral	準備する　organize	奨学資金　exhibition
循環的な　cyclical	準備する　prepare	小額の　fractional
純キャッシュ　net cash	準備する　set up	使用可能度　availability
…に準拠する　subject to	順日歩　contango	使用可能な　available
準拠性　compliance	純費用　net charge	償還　amortization
純金融負債　net financial liabilities	純負債　net debt	償還　redemption
準子会社　quasi subsidiary	純負債比率　gearing	償還　refunding
純債務　net debt	純利益　bottom line	償還　reimbursement
順次　series	純利　earnings	償還　repayment
純資金　net proceeds	純利益　earnings	償還　retirement
純資産　asset value	純利益　net earnings	召喚　recall
純資産　book value	純利益　net income	上官　superior
純資産　capital	純利益　net profit	償還可能な　callable
純資産　equity	純利益　proceeds	償還可能な　redeemable
純資産　net asset	純量　net	償還期限　maturity
純資産　net worth	ジョイント　joint	償還期日のない　undated
	ジョイント・ベンチャー　joint	

償還されない	irredeemable	商業化	commercialization	証券会社	brokerage
償還する	call	商業界	marketplace	証券化する	securitize
償還する	pay off	商業価値なし	NCV	証券監督者国際機構	IOSCO
償還する	redeem	商業銀行	commercial bank	証券規制監督者国際機構	IOSCO
償還する	refund	商業者商標	private brand	証券業	brokerage
償還する	repay	商業主義	commercialism	使用権許諾者	licenser
償還する	retire	商業証券	commercial paper	上限金利	cap
召喚する	recall	商業上の	commercial	証券広報	investor relations
償還請求	recourse	商業地区	center [centre]	使用権者	licensee
償還請求権	put	商業地区	downtown	証券代行業務	custody service
償還請求権	recourse	商業手形	commercial paper	条件付き捺印証書	escrow
償還できる	callable	商業的な	commercial	条件付きの	qualified
償還日の定めのない	undated	商業取引所	mercantile exchange	…を条件として	subject to
償還プレミアム	call premium	商業の	commercial	…を条件とする	contingent
商機	opportunity	商業の	mercantile	…を条件とする	subject to
蒸気	steam	商業ベースの	arm's length	証券取引委員会	SEC
試用期間	probation	商業ベースの	commercial	証券取引委員会	Securities and Exchange Commission
上記事項	premises	商業用不動産証券	asset-backed securities		
上記の	aforesaid			証券取引自動通報システム	SEAQ
小規模の	junior	商業利用	commercial utilization	証券取引所	bourse
償却	amortization	消極的な	negative	証券取引所別途売買サービス	SEATS
償却	depreciation	消極的のれん	negative goodwill		
償却	write-off	消極のれん	negative goodwill	証券取引等監視委員会	Securities and Exchange Surveillance Commission
消却	cancelation	使用許諾	license		
消却	write-off	使用許諾	licensing		
乗客	fare	使用許諾者	grantor	証券取引法	Securities and Exchange Law
償却額	amortization	使用許諾する	license		
償却可能な	depreciable	使用許諾製品	licensed product	証券仲買会社	brokerage
償却基金	sinking fund	使用許諾地域	territory	証券の発行	float
償却されていない	unamortized	賞金	award	証券売買益	takeout
償却する	amortize	賞金	premium	証券売買取引	broking
償却する	cancel	小区画	plot	証券引受人	underwriter
償却する	depreciate	承継銀行	bridge bank	証券保管機関	custodian
償却する	extinguish	衝撃	blow	証券保有高	position
償却する	write down	衝撃	impact	証券や商品の取引所	exchange
償却する	write off	衝撃を与える	impact	条件を魅力的にする	sweeten
消却する	cancel	証券	bill	証拠	confirmation
消却する	retire	証券	equity	証拠	evidence
償却性の	depreciable	証券	instrument	証拠	token
償却積立金	sinking fund	証券	investment	商号	style
償却費	depreciation	証券	issue	照合	adjustment
昇級	promotion	証券	note	照合	check
昇給	award	証券	paper	照合	identification
上級	senior	証券	securities	照合	matching
上級レベルの	advanced	証券	security	称号	title
商業	business	証券	stock	条項	clause
商業	commerce	証券	title	条項	feature
商業	trading	使用権	license	条項	feature
状況	affair	証言	evidence	条項	provision
状況	climate	条件	climate	条項	section
状況	condition	条件	condition	商行為	doing business
状況	experience	条件	offer	商工会議所	chamber of commerce and industry
状況	going	条件	requirement(s)		
状況	scenario	条件	reserve	証拠金	margin
状況	scene	条件	term	証書類	document
状況	situation	上限	cap	証書類	documentation
状況	standing	上限	ceiling	証書類	voucher
状況	status	上限	guideline	証書類提出	documentation
状況	water	上限	maximum	証拠資料	evidence
商業化	commercial utilization	証券化	securitization	証拠能力のない	incompetent

証拠物件 evidence	上昇基調の strong	装束 outfit
証拠文書 instrument	上昇気味 upside	消息筋 knowledgeable sources
詳細 particulars	上昇局面 rally	消息筋 well-informed sources
詳細な in-depth	上昇傾向 upbeat	正体 identity
詳細な計画を立てる map out	上昇傾向 upside	状態 condition
詳細な段取り nuts and bolts	上昇傾向 uptrend	状態 going
詳細に fully	上昇傾向 upturn	状態 position
詳細に示す map out	上昇傾向にある positive	状態 situation
上司 superior	上昇傾向の buoyant	状態 standing
使用した employed	上昇傾向の upbeat	状態 status
使用資本利益率 ROI	上昇させる increase	…の状態になる run
勝者 winner	上昇させる inflate	小卓 stand
商社 firm	上場されていない unlisted	承諾 acceptance
商社 house	上場される list	承諾 approval
使用者 employer	上昇した increased	承諾 authorization
使用者 user	上昇する advance	承諾 compliance
成就 accomplishment	上昇する appreciate	承諾する accept
成就 fulfillment	上昇する gain	承諾する approve
上首尾 success	上昇する rally	承諾する grant
…に照準を合わせる concentrate	上昇する rise	商談 negotiation
証書 bill	上昇する strengthen	承知 knowledge
証書 certificate	上昇する upward	常置人員 establishment
証書 deed	上場する debut	常置の standing
証書 document	上場する introduce	省庁 government
証書 indenture	上場する launch	象徴 attribute
証書 letter	上場する list	象徴 symbol
証書 receipt	上場する quote	象徴 token
証書 securities	上場停止 delisting	上出来 success
仕様書 document	上場投資信託 ETF	使用できる disposable
…の上昇 increased	清浄な clean	使用できる operational
上昇 advance	上場廃止 delisting	商店 establishment
上昇 appreciation	上昇余地 upside	商店 outlet
上昇 backup	上場を停止する delist	商店 shop
上昇 boost	上場を廃止する delist	商店 store
上昇 enhancement	生じる accrue	焦点 focal point
上昇 expansion	昇進 career	焦点 focus
上昇 gain	昇進 promotion	商店街 mall
上昇 hike	昇進 upgrading	商店の建ち並ぶ通り strip
上昇 improvement	昇進させる promote	…に焦点を当てる focus on
上昇 increase	正真正銘の true	…に焦点を合わせる focus on
上昇 pickup	昇進する leap	焦点を合わせる focus
上昇 rally	少数 minority	…に焦点を置く focus on
上昇 rise	少数派 minority	…に焦点を絞る focus
上昇 strength	少数民族 minority	譲渡 assignment
上昇 upside	使用する use	譲渡 conveyance
上昇 uptrend	情勢 affair	譲渡 disposition
上昇 upturn	情勢 climate	譲渡 grant
上場 debut	情勢 condition	譲渡 negotiation
上場 IPO	情勢 development	譲渡 transfer
上場 launching	情勢 environment	小道具類 gadgetry
上場 listing	情勢 run	譲渡可能定期預金証書 CD
上場 offering	情勢 situation	譲渡可能な assignable
上場会社 listed company	情勢 status	譲渡可能な negotiable
上場会社 publicly held company	情勢分析家 analyst	仕様と構成 architecture
上場企業 listed company	常設の permanent	焦土作戦 scorched-earth defense
上場企業 publicly held company	常設の standing	譲渡証書 assignment
上場企業 publicly owned company [corporation]	仕様説明書 manual	譲渡証書 conveyance
	商戦 shopping	譲渡証書 deed
上場企業会計監視委員会 PCAOB	上層部 establishment	譲渡所得 capital gain
上昇基調 uptrend	消息 information	譲渡する amortize

譲渡する assign	消費の少ない lean	情報開示 disclosure
譲渡する grant	商標 brand	情報開示を受けた者 recipient
譲渡する negotiate	商標 label	情報隔壁 firewall
譲渡する pass	商標 TM	情報化する computerize
譲渡する remit	商標 trademark	情報管理 documentation
譲渡する sell	証憑 voucher	情報機関 intelligence
譲渡する transfer	商標権 trademark	情報技術 IT
譲渡する yield	商標登録による保護を受けていない	情報源 source(s)
譲渡性預金 CD	generic	情報検索 IR
譲渡損失 capital loss	商標文字 logo	情報検索 search
衝突 collision	消費量 consumption	情報検索代行業者 searcher
衝突 conflict	消費量 expenditure	情報庫 database
譲渡抵当 mortgage	商品 commodity	情報コマーシャル infomercial
譲渡人 grantor	商品 goods	情報収集 intelligence
商取引 commerce	商品 instrument	上方修正 upgrade
商取引 transaction	商品 item	上方修正 upgrading
私用に供する appropriate	商品 media	上方修正する raise
承認 acceptance	商品 merchandise	上方修正する upgrade
承認 admission	商品 product	情報集積体 database
承認 allowance	商品 vehicle	情報処理能力が付加してある
承認 approval	商品 wares	intelligent
承認 authorization	賞品 award	情報処理能力を持つ intelligent
承認 confirmation	商品化 commercialization	情報戦略統括役員 CIO
承認 endorsement	商品化計画 merchandising	情報操作 intelligence
承認 permission	商品群 line of products	情報通信会社 telco
承認 recognition	商品計画 merchandising	情報の公開 disclosure
昇任 promotion	商品券 coupon	情報の障壁 Chinese wall
使用人 employee	商品券 voucher	情報の内容 content
承認する appropriate	商品構成 lineup	情報の中身 content
承認する approve	商品先物 commodity futures	情報番組 magazine
承認する recognize	商品先物契約 commodity futures	上方へ upward
商人の mercantile	商品性 merchantability	情報ルート pipeline
常任の standing	商品性 merchantable quality	情報漏洩防止システム firewall
正念場 acid test	商品戦略 merchandising	情報を転送する download
商売 business	商品としての品質 merchantable	抄本 copy
商売 deal	quality	正味 net
商売 game	商品取引 commodity exchange	正味運転資本 net working capital
商売 trade	商品取引所 commodity exchange	正味価額 equity
商売の mercantile	商品取引所 mercantile exchange	賞味期限 shelf life
商売をやめる fold up	商品の受領 acceptance	賞味期限 best-before date
消費 consumption	商品の転売 trans-shipping	正味キャッシュ net cash
消費 spending	商品の有料付属品 option	正味現金 net cash
消費額 consumption	商品売買 merchandising	正味財産 capital
消費支出 consumption	商品貿易 merchandise trade	正味財産 net asset
消費者 c	商品ライン line of products	正味財産 net worth
消費者 consumer	上部の top	正味財産 proprietorship
消費者物価指数 CPI	使用不能時間 downtime	正味資産 net asset
消費者物価指数にスライドさせる	小部分 fraction	正味資産 net worth
index	障壁 barrier	正味収入保険料 net premium
消費者物価指数に連動させる	商法 sales	revenues
index	商法 selling	正味増加 net increase
消費者マインド confidence	使用法 use	正味入金額 net proceeds
消費者向けの commercial	情報 code	正味の clear
消費する spend	情報 content	正味の net
常備する keep	情報 data	正味簿価 NBV
消費税 consumption tax	情報 information	正味保険料収入 net premium
消費税 excise	情報 intelligence	revenues
…に消費税を課す excise	情報 knowledge	商務省 U.S. Commerce Department
消費高 consumption	情報・通信複合分野 telematics	証明 demonstration
常備の standing	情報化 computerization	証明書 certificate

証明書　letter	条令　act	触診　exploration
証明書　voucher	条例　bylaws	職責　duty
証明書　warrant	奨励金　premium	職責　responsibility
…に証明印を押す　hallmark	奨励金　rebate	食肉処理　beef-up
照明する　seal	奨励金　subsidy	食肉処理する　beef up
証明する　certify	奨励する　promote	職人　craftsman
消滅　demise	使用を禁止する　freeze	職人　hand
消滅　determination	除外する　foreclose	職人気質　professionalism
消滅　expiration	除外する　set aside	職の安全　job security
消滅　lapse	初回の　maiden	職能　function
消滅　termination	所感　sentiment	職能の　functional
消滅しない　unexpired	書簡　correspondence	職能法人　P.C.
消滅する　expire	書簡　letter	職場　job
消滅する　lapse	書記官　clerk	職場　shop
正面の　front	初期の　initial	職場　workplace
消耗　consumption	書記の　clerical	職場外訓練　off the job training
消耗　depletion	除却　abandonment	職場研修　on the job training
消耗　wastage	除却　disposal	触発する　trigger
消耗させる　deplete	除却　retirement	職場での　working
消耗する　exhaust	除却　write-off	職場内訓練　on the job training
消耗品　supply	除却する　retire	職場放棄　walk-out
条約　convention	除去　clearance	食品　food
条約　pact	除去　clearing	食品医薬品局　FDA
条約　treaty	除去　relief	食品スーパー　grocery store
条約議定書　protocol	除去する　take out	食品の製法　formula
賞与　award	職　employment	食品包装　packing
賞与　bonus	職　job	植物　plant
譲与　grant	職　place	植民地　mandate
乗用車　car	職　position	職務　business
剰余金　retained earnings	職　post	職務　duty
剰余金　surplus	職　spot	職務　function
譲与人　grantor	職　work	職務　job
将来起こりそうな　potential	職員　clerk	職務　office
将来財産権　expectancy	職員　employee	職務　task
将来性　capability	職員　office	職務上の　functional
将来性　potential	職員　official	職務促進　job development
将来性　prospects	職員　personnel	職務の交替要員　relief
将来展望　time horizon	職員　staff	職務保障　job security
将来の　prospective	職員定数　payroll	職務離脱者　absentee
将来の価格変動性　volatility	職員録　blue book	…の職務を果たす　serve
将来を見越した　forward-looking	職業　business	職務を果たす　function
将来を見据えた　forward-looking	職業　career	食料　foodstuff
将来を見通した　forward-looking	職業　game	食糧　food
勝利　success	職業　occupation	食糧　foodstuff
上流指向の　upmarket	職業　profession	食料品　foodstuff
上流指向の　upscale	職業　vocation	助言　advice
上流部門　upstream	職業斡旋　placement	助言　consulting
少量　fraction	職業開発　job development	助言者　adviser
使用料　due	職業訓練　job training	助言者　counselor
使用料　fee	職業紹介　job referral	助言の　advisory
使用料　hire	職業紹介　placement	諸権利落ち　x.a.
使用料　royalty	職業上の　professional	諸国　economies
使用料　toll	職業上の　vocational	所在地　location
使用量　use	職業人　professional	所持　possession
省力化　automation	職業の　professional	書式　document
省力化する　automate	職業能力　skill	書式　form
奨励　incentive	職業別電話帳　yellow pages	書式　formula
奨励　inducement	食材　food	所持人　bearer
奨励　promotion	食事　table	所持人　holder
症例　case	職掌上の　functional	所持品　possession

書状 correspondence	署名者 signatory	助力 help
書状 letter	署名者 subscriber	処理量 throughput
徐々に上げる pyramid	署名する execute	書類 document
徐々に取り入れる phase in	署名する sign	書類 documentation
初心者 newcomer	署名する subscribe	書類 paper
助成 furtherance	署名調印する sign	書類 paperwork
助成金 bonus	書面 deed	書類事務 paperwork
助成金 grant	所有 hand	書類の不備 discrepancy
助成金 subsidy	所有 holding	序列 ranking
所属させる attach	所有 ownership	知らせる announce
所帯 household	所有 possession	知らせる transmit
除隊 discharge	所有 property	調べる inquire
処置 disposition	所有期間 horizon	シリーズ series
処置 move	所有権 fee	シリーズの serial
助長 furtherance	所有権 ownership	知りうる範囲 knowledge
助長 promotion	所有権 possession	自力再建 self-rehabilitation
助長する facilitate	所有権 property	シリコン・チップ chip
助長する help	所有権 property right	退く retreat
助長する promote	所有権 right	退ける reject
助長する serve	所有権 title	自立 independence
ショック blow	所有権者 owner	自立型の stand-alone [standalone]
職権 commission	所有権者の proprietary	自立した independent
職工 hand	所有財産 holding	自律的な成長 self-sustainable
ショッピング shopping	所有者 holder	growth
ショッピング・センター mall	所有者 owner	資料 data
ショップ shop	所有者 ownership	資料 file
所得 earnings	所有者 proprietor	資料 material
所得 income	所有者の proprietary	資料 paper
所得 melon	所有主 proprietor	資料 resource(s)
所得 proceeds	所有する own	資料 source(s)
所得隠し skim	所有する possess	資力 purse
所得勘定 income account	所有地 land	指令 mandate
所得控除項目 itemized deductions	所有地 property	事例 case
所得収支 income account	所有比率 ownership	熾烈な intensive
所得税 income tax	所有物 possession	熾烈な競争 cutthroat competition
初日 opening	所有物 property	試練 test
初の maiden	所有持分 holding	試練の probationary
処罰 penalty	所有有価証券 portfolio	白物 home appliance
処罰する punish	処理 charge	仕訳帳 journal
序盤 opening	処理 conduct	新… new
ジョブ job	処理 disposal	芯 core
処分 disposal	処理 disposition	新案 model
処分 disposition	処理 handling	新案品 novelty
処分 liquidation	処理 liquidation	人為的な technical
処分 penalty	処理 processing	新入り latecomer
処分 retirement	処理 treatment	人員 manpower
処分 settlement	処理 workout	人員 personnel
処分可能な available	処理 write-off	人員 staff
処分する liquidate	処理されていない crude	人員 workforce
処分する punish	処理する account for	人員過剰 redundancy
処分する sell	処理する administer	人員削減 ax
処分する settle	処理する include	人員削減 downsizing
処分する unload	処理する liquidate	人員削減 job cut
初歩的な basic	処理する settle	人員削減 layoff
除幕式 dedication	処理する write off	人員削減する downsize
除幕する unveil	処理高 throughput	人員整理する rightsize
署名 execution	処理手順 procedure	人員漸減 attrition
署名 hand	処理の managerial	人員の入れ替え reshuffle
署名 sign	処理能力 throughput	人員配置 placement
署名 subscription	処理方法 formula	人員不足の understaffed

人員補充 recruitment	進行 swing	真実 fact
人員を入れ替える reshuffle	人口 population	人事部 HR
侵害 breach	人工衛星 satellite	人事部 human resources
侵害 prejudice	信号化 digitalization	斟酌する allow
新会員 recruit	新興企業 start-up	人種差別撤廃 integration
新会社 start-up	人口構成 demographics	人種差別をしない integrated
…を侵害する infringe on	振興する promote	進出 advance
新華社 Xinhuashe	進行する run	進出 entrance
新型商品 novelty	人口増加率ゼロ ZPG	進出 participation
新加入者 entrant	人口増殖 cloning	進出 penetration
新株先買権 preemptive right	人工多能性幹細胞 induced pluripotent stem sell	進出 presence
新株引受権 preemptive right		…に進出する venture into
新株引受権 right	人口統計 demographics	進出する advance
新株引受権 warrant	人口統計学の demographic	進出する branch out
新株引受権落ち XW	人口統計上の demographic	進出する participate
新株優先引受権 preemptive right	人口動態 demographics	人種統合 integration
新株予約権 preemptive right	人口動態に関する demographic	進取の気性 enterprise
新株予約権 warrant	新興の emerging	新手法 innovation
新株割当て抽選 ballot	人工の plastic	信条 symbol
シンガポール取引所 Singapore Exchange Ltd.	申告 declaration	紳士録 blue book
	申告 return	新人 newcomer
審議 consultation	申告書 report	心身の衰弱 burnout
審議会 board	申告書 return	進水させる launch
審議会 consultation	申告する declare	申請 application
審議会 panel	申告する report	申請者 applicant
新規株式公開 initial public offering	深刻な状況 plight	申請者 application
新規株式公開 IPO	申告漏れ額 unreported earnings	申請する enter
新規株式公募 IPO	審査 assessment	申請する file
新規企業 start-up	審査 inquiry	新制度 innovation
新企業 start-up	審査 review	新生の emerging
新規公募 IPO	審査 screening	真正の sterling
新規採用 recruitment	人材 human resources	新製品の紹介 rollout
新規採用する recruit	人材 manpower	新製品の発売 launch
新規参入企業 entrant	人材 worker	新生面開拓の groundbreaking
新規参入企業 newcomer	人材開発 recruitment	新生面を開く reshape
新規参入業者 newcomer	人材スカウト headhunting	新設合併 consolidation
新規参入組 entrant	人材スカウト会社 headhunter	新設住宅着工戸数 housing starts
新規参入組 newcomer	人材スカウト係 headhunter	新設する create
新規参入者 entrant	人材スカウト業 headhunter	親切な good
新規参入者 latecomer	人材登用 recruitment	親善 goodwill
新規参入者 newcomer	人材派遣会社 temporary staffing firm	真相 case
新規事業 start-up		真相 fact
新規事業開発者 pioneer	人材をスカウトする headhunt	心像 image
新規事業者 newcomer	人材を引き抜く headhunt	深層の in-depth
新機軸 innovation	審査会 panel	人造の false
新機軸の innovative	審査する assess	迅速 dispatch
新規資本 fresh capital	審査する review	迅速な prompt
新規上場 debut	審査する screen	迅速な quick
新規上場する debut	審査団 panel	信託 trust
新規上場する float	診察 consultation	信託機関 trustee
新規性 novelty	診察 exploration	信託基金 trust fund
新規に発行する float	診察 interview	信託資金 trust fund
新規の new	人事 personnel	信託の fiduciary
新記録 high	シンジケート syndicate	診断 consulting
新工夫 innovation	シンジケートで管理する syndicate	診断 evaluation
震源地 focus	シンジケートを組織[組成]する syndicate	慎重性の原則 conservatism
人件費 payroll		進捗させる expedite
振興 incentive	人事刷新 personnel change	進捗状況 progress
振興 promotion	人事刷新 reshuffle	進呈 presentation
進行 movement	新事態 development	人的 human

人的資源	human resources	陣容	makeup	水域	water
人的資源	manpower	信用売り	tick	随意の	discretionary
人的な	personal	信用供与	facility	推計	estimate
進展	advance	信用供与限度	line of credit	推計	projection
進展	development	信用供与枠	credit facilities	推計する	estimate
進展	move	信用供与枠	line of credit	遂行	accomplishment
進展	movement	信用限度	line of credit	遂行	conduct
進度	rate	信用状	credit	遂行	discharge
浸透	penetration	信用状	L/C	遂行	fulfillment
侵入	penetration	信用状	letter of credit	遂行	implementation
進入	approach	信用状開設依頼書	application	遂行する	execute
新入会員	entrant	信用状未使用残高	outstanding	遂行する	fulfill
新入社員	entrant		letters of credit	遂行する	implement
新入社員	hire	信用できる	reliable	遂行する	perform
新入社員	hiring	信用度	creditworthiness	遂行する	prosecute
新入社員	newcomer	信用度	rating	随時償還	call
新入社員	recruit	信用等級が最高の	prime	水質	water
新入社員募集	recruitment	信用度の高い	creditworthy [credit-	水準	level
新入生	entrant		worthy]	水準	mark
新入生	recruit	信用の	fiduciary	水準	norm
信任	confidence	信用の質	creditworthiness	水準	point
信認	confidence	信用評価	standing	水準	sophistication
新任	newcomer	信用保証	credit guarantee	水準から外れる	slip
心配	concern	信用保証制度	credit guarantee	推奨する	recommend
心配	misgiving	信用力	creditworthiness	水上輸送する	navigate
新発明	innovation	信用力がある	creditworthy [credit-	推進	furtherance
侵犯	infringement		worthy]	推進	improvement
審判	hearing	信用力が低い	subprime	推進	promotion
審判	judgment	信用力の高い	creditworthy	推進	thrust
審判を下す	decide		[credit-worthy]	推進する	accelerate
信憑性	reliability	信用枠	credit facilities	推進する	boost
人物	figure	信用枠	facility	推進する	improve
新聞	journal	信頼	confidence	推進する	promote
新聞	paper	信頼	goodwill	推進する	serve
新聞のトップ見出し	leader	信頼	reliability	推進力	drive
新分野に発展する	branch out	信頼	trust	推進力	driver
進歩	advance	信頼性	reliability	推進力	driving force
進歩	development	信頼できる	reliable	推進力	steam
進歩	improvement	信頼できる	safe	推進力	thrust
進歩	progress	信頼度	confidence	推薦	plug
信望	prestige	信頼度	loyalty	推薦する	propose
信望	reputation	信頼度	reliability	推薦する	recommend
信奉者	follower	審理	hearing	推測	speculation
進歩した	advanced	心理	sentiment	推測する	extrapolate
進歩する	advance	侵略	penetration	推測に基づく	speculative
進歩的な	forward-looking	尽力	effort	衰退	downturn
シンボル	symbol	森林伐採	deforestation	衰退	obsolescence
人民元	renminbi	進路	way	衰退して	downward
人民元	yuan	進路指導	orientation	衰退する	downward
人民幣	renminbi			垂直的	vertical
新メンバー	newcomer	**す**		推定	estimate
審問	hearing			推定	expectation
尋問	hearing	図	chart	推定	projection
信用	claim	図	figure	推定する	assume
信用	confidence	図案	device	推定する	estimate
信用	credit	図案	figure	推定する	expect
信用	goodwill	吸い上げる	offset	推定する	extrapolate
信用	tick	推移	development	推定値	estimate
信用	trust	推移	transition	推定に用いる	extrapolate
陣容	lineup	水位	level	推定の	estimated

推定量 estimate	スケジュール schedule	素早い prompt
水道 water	助変数 parameter	素早い quick
水平線 horizon	…筋 authority	素晴らしい fab
水平的 horizontal	筋 source(s)	スピード pace
水平になる level off	筋書き scenario	図表 chart
水平飛行をする level off	筋道 channel	図表 table
水面下の behind-the-scenes	筋道 method	スピンオフ spinoff
推力 thrust	素性 identity	ずぶの素人 newcomer
推論する conclude	進み具合 going	スプレッド spread
スウォット SWOT	進む run	スポークスマン spokesman
数字 figure	勧める recommend	スポット spot
数字化 digitalization	進める advance	スポンサー sponsor
数字表示式の digital	進める facilitate	スポンサー underwriter
趨勢 run	進める undertake	スポンサーになる sponsor
趨勢 stream	進んだ advanced	図面 drawing
趨勢 trend	スターリング銀の sterling	スライド方式にする index
数値 figure	スタイル figure	ずらす stagger
数値 level	スタイル style	スランプ slump
数値 reading	スタグフレーション stagflation	すり合わせ coordination
…の数値を求める evaluate	スタッグ stag	刷りたての紙幣 mint
スーパー retailer	スタッフ staff	スリム化 streamlining
スーパー supermarket	スタディ study	スリム化する streamline
スーパーファンド法 Superfund Act	スタビライザー stabilizer	スループット throughput
スーパーマーケット supermarket	すたれた obsolete	ずれ discrepancy
枢要な key	すたれること obsolescence	スロット slot
数量 figure	スタンス stance	スワップ swap
数量 quantity	スタンダード standard	スワップション swaption
数量 volume	スタンダード＆プアーズ総合500種	スワップする swap
据え置かれた unchanged	株価指数 S & P 500	図をかく plot
据え置き deferment	スタンド stand	寸法 size
据え置き型の deferred	スタンド・アロン型の stand-alone	
据え置き期間 grace period	[standalone]	**せ**
据え置きの deferred	スタンドバイ standby	
据え置く defer	スチーム steam	税 duty
据え置く keep	すっぱ抜く expose	税 tax
据え置く maintain	ステータス status	成果 accomplishment
据え付け installation	ステートメント statement	成果 achievement
据え付ける install	ステップ step	成果 effectiveness
据える position	すでに発生している outstanding	成果 payoff
スキーム scheme	素手の bare	成果 performance
…好きの -minded	捨てる scrap	成果 product
すき間 clearance	捨てる set aside	成果 results
すき間 niche	ストア store	成果 reward
スキャナー scanner	ストック pool	成果 success
スキル skill	ストック stock	正価 net
救いの手 helping hand	ストック・オプション stock option	盛会 success
救う rescue	スト破り監視員 picket	成果が上がらない negative
すぐ現金化できる quick	ストライキ strike	性格 identity
少なくとも fully	ストライキ walk-out	税額控除 credit
すぐに操業できる onstream	ストラテジー strategy	税額控除 tax break
スクラップにする scrap	ストラテジック・アライアンス	税額控除 tax credit
スクリーン screen	strategic alliance	正確に fully
スクリップ scrip	ストラテジック・プランニング	成果主義型の賃金制度 merit-based pay plan
優れた master	strategic planning	
優れた知性の持ち主 mastermind	ストラングル strangle	成果主義型の報酬制度 merit-based pay plan
優れた知能の持ち主 mastermind	ストリップ strip	
…より優れている surpass	ストレス pressure	青瓦台 Blue House
図形 figure	ストレス stress	生活 life
スケール scale	スパイ agent	生活 subsistence
スケールの大きい massive	スパム spam	生活手段 career

生活循環	life cycle	整合	matching	生産が開始される	roll off the assembly line
生活物資補給路	lifeline	税効果	tax effect		
生活保護手当	relief	成功企業	winner	生産がスタートする	roll off the assembly line
生活様式	lifestyle	精巧さ	sophistication		
静観	wait and see	精巧な	sophisticated	精算勘定	open account
税関	customs	精査	search	生産工学	IE
請願運動	lobbying	制裁	penalty	生産効率	productivity
正規の	full	制裁	sanctions	生産国	producer
正規の	regular	制裁金	fine	生産者	producer
請求	call	制裁金	penalty	生産者価格指数	PPI
請求	claim	制裁措置	sanctions	生産者直送	drop shipment
請求	demand	制裁の	punitive	生産者直送で送る	drop-ship
請求	request	制作	creativity	生産準備期間	lead time
請求金額	bill	制作	making	生産上の	productive
請求金額	charge	制作	production	清算する	clear
請求権	claim	政策	agenda	清算する	close
請求事項	claim	政策	approach	清算する	liquidate
請求書	bill	政策	deal	清算する	reckon
請求書	invoice	政策	drive	清算する	settle
請求書	tab	政策	effort	清算する	wind up
請求書を送る	bill	政策	initiative	生産する	assemble
請求する	bill	政策	measure	生産する	come up with
請求する	charge	政策	package	生産する	fabricate
請求する	claim	政策	plan	生産する	manufacture
請求する	demand	政策	policy	生産する	produce
制御	control	政策	program	生産する	roll out
制御する	curb	政策	stance	生産性	efficiency
制御する	harness	製作	fabrication	生産性	productivity
制御盤	panel	製作	manufacture	生産制限要求	featherbedding
税金	charge	製作	manufacturing	生産設備	factory
税金	tax	製作	output	生産設備	plant
税金還付	tax refund	製作	production	生産設備	plant and equipment
税金控除	tax credit	制作会社	maker	生産設備	tooling
税金債務	tax liability	政策金利	key interest rate	生産第1号が工場出荷される	roll off the assembly line
税金などの還付	refunding	政策金利	key rate		
税金の還付	refund	政策綱領	platform	生産高	output
税金費用	tax expense	製作者	maker	生産中	on stream
生計の道	subsistence	製作者	manufacturer	生産調整	output adjustment
政権	administration	製作所	work	生産停止	off stream
政権	government	製作する	fabricate	生産的な	productive
政権	leadership	製作する	manufacture	生産能力	capacity
制限	limit	製作する	produce	生産品	product
制限	rationing	政策方針	platform	生産物	commodity
制限	reserve	精査する	scan	生産量	output
制限	restriction	清算	clearing	生産力	productivity
制限	squeeze	清算	liquidation	生産力のある	productive
制限解除	decontrol	清算	settlement	生産履歴管理	traceability
税減額効果	benefit	清算	winding up	生産枠	output ceiling
制限する	curb	生産	fabrication	生産を中止する	fold up
制限する	qualify	生産	generation	政治	government
制限する	restrict	生産	manufacture	正式記録	registration
制限する	squeeze	生産	manufacturing	正式に記録する	register
制限のない	open	生産	output	正式に記録にのせる	enter
制限を受けない	free	生産	production	正式に登録する	enter
…に制限を設ける	determine	生産	rollout	正式の	due
性向	propensity	精算	adjustment	正式の	full
成功	career	精算	reimbursement	正式の	official
成功	making	生産・調達・運用支援統合情報システム	CALS	正式の	plenary
成功	success			政治資金	barrel
整合	coordination	生産委託契約	OEM	制止する	restrict

税収	taxation
成熟化	saturation
成熟した市場	well-developed market
青書	blue book
政治要項	program
精神疾患	mental problems
精神障害	mental illness
精神障害	mental problems
精神障害者	mentally ill people
精神障害の	mentally disturbed
精神病	mental illness
精神病	mental problems
製図	drawing
正数	plus
生成	generation
精製	refining
税制恩典燃え尽き	burnout
精製していない	crude
精製していない	raw
税制上の特典	tax break
生成する	generate
成績	achievement
成績	mark
成績	record
成績	results
成績	showing
生鮮食品	perishable food
生鮮食品	perishable goods
生鮮食料品	perishable food
生鮮食料品	perishable goods
製造	fabrication
製造	making
製造	manufacture
製造	manufacturing
製造	production
製造間接費	burden
製造間接費	overhead
製造技術	knowhow
製造業	factory
製造業者	maker
製造業者	manufacturer
製造業者	producer
製造業者	supplier
製造工程請負工場	EMS
製造指図書	job order
製造者	manufacturer
製造する	fabricate
製造する	manufacture
製造する	produce
製造設備を持たない	fabless
製造を禁止する	freeze
生存者	survivor
生存者権	survivorship
生態	ecology
生態学	ecology
生態学の	ecological
生態環境	ecology
生態環境	ecotop
生態系	ecology

生態系	ecosystem
生態系の	ecological
生体工学	bioengineering
生体認証	biometrics
生態の	ecological
贅沢品	luxury
精出して働く	ply
成長	expansion
成長	growth
成長	progress
成長が止まる	level off
成長市場	promising market
成長する	grow
成長の原因	making
成長の要因	making
成長分野	promising area
成長率	growth
精通	knowledge
精通した	savvy
制定	establishment
制定する	establish
制定法	act
制定法	legislation
制度	establishment
制度	facility
制度	framework
制度	package
制度	plan
制度	program
制度	requirement(s)
制度	scheme
制度	system
正当	right
精糖所	refinery
正当な	de jure
正当な	due
正当な	true
正当な評価	appreciation
正当な理由のない	gratuitous
政党の綱領	program
制度などを導入する	establish
正の	plus
正の	positive
製販同盟	strategic alliance
整備	development
整備	enhancement
整備	improvement
整備	maintenance
税引き後赤字	net loss
税引き後営業利益	NOPAT
税引き後金額	net
税引き後で	after tax
税引き後の	after-tax
税引き後の	net
税引き後利益	net income
税引き後利益	net profit
税引き後利益の赤字	negative net worth
税引き前の	pretax
整備する	develop

整備する	maintain
製品	development
製品	equipment
製品	finished goods
製品	finished product
製品	goods
製品	manufacture
製品	merchandise
製品	product
製品一覧表	lineup
製品群	family
製品群	range
製品系列	line of products
製品構成	line of products
製品種目	line of products
製品特性	feature
製品のライフサイクル	life cycle
製品品目	line of products
製品ライフサイクル	PLC
製品ライン	line of products
政府	administration
政府	government
政府	sovereign
政府	Washington
政府開発援助	ODA
政府機関	sovereign
政府系ファンド	SWF
政府住宅抵当金庫	GNMA
税負担率	effective tax rate
政府調達	B2G
生物現存量	biomass
生物工学	bioengineering
生物工学	biotechnology
生物資源	biomass
生物体総量	biomass
生物統計学	biometrics
生物量	biomass
政府の介入を受けた	dirty
政府の歳出・経費	supply
政府の補助金	grant
成分	component
成分	element
成分	ingredient
成分表示	ingredient
製法	process
製本の型押し	tooling
精密化	sophistication
精密機械	precision
精密機器	precision
精密な	close
精密な	sophisticated
税務上の特典	tax break
税務申告	tax return
税務申告書	tax return
生命	life
声明	announcement
声明	statement
生命維持装置	life support
生命技術	biotechnology
生命工学	biotechnology

声明書 statement	世界経済フォーラム World Economic Forum	セグメント segment
生命情報科学 bioinformatics	世界市場 world market	セグメント帰属資産 identifiable asset
生命情報工学 bioinformatics	世界測位衛星システム global positioning system	セグメント固有資産 identifiable asset
生命線 lifeline		
生命保険 life insurance	世界的位置決定システム global positioning system	施主 owner
生命保険会社 life insurer		是正する correct
生命倫理 bioethics	世界的規模の global	是正する redress
制約 barrier	世界の global	世帯 family
制約 restriction	世界の universal	世帯 household
誓約 commitment	世界貿易機関 World Trade Organization	世代 generation
誓約 covenant		節 clause
誓約 engagement	世界貿易機関 WTO	接岸する land
誓約 pledge	セカンダリー市場 secondary market	積極的な active
制約する impair		積極的な bullish
誓約する pledge	席 platform	積極的な positive
制約を受けない free	席 table	接近 approach
製油所 refinery	積置き配当 cumulative dividend	接近する access
整理 adjustment	積載量 load	設計 architecture
整理 consolidation	積送品 consgt	設計 design
整理 divestiture	積送品 consignment	設計 engineering
整理 liquidation	石炭 coal	設計自動化 DA
整理 winding up	責任 accountability	設計者 planner
整理 workout	責任 charge	設計する engineer
整理公債 consol	責任 duty	設計する plan
整理する close	責任 liability	…の設計図を作る plot
整理する consolidate	責任 office	節減 curtailment
整理する divest	責任 responsibility	節減 cut
整理する liquidate	…する責任がある accountable	説示 charge
整理する trim	責任がある responsible	接触面 interface
整理する wind up	責任者 head	セッション session
整理するもの organizer	責任者 manager	接戦の close
成立 execution	責任者 official	接続 access
税率 tax rate	責任生産量 norm	接続技術 interface
税率軽減措置 tax break	責任総額 total liabilities	接続する access
成立しない fall flat	責任の重い responsible	接続装置 interface
整理統合した consolidated	…の責任を負う foot	接続料金 access charge
整理統合する consolidate	責任を負う assume	接待 entertainment
整理箱 organizer	責任を負う responsible	絶対安全性 fail safe
整理保管する file	責任をとる assume	絶対的な absolute
整流 commutation	責務 commission	絶対的な outright
勢力 force	責務 concern	絶対の absolute
勢力 strength	責務 responsibility	切断 severance
精力 energy	石油 oil	設置 establishment
精錬所 refinery	石油 petroleum	設置 installation
セーフガード safeguard	石油化学製品 petrochemical	設置先 site
セーフガード措置 safeguard	石油採掘部門 upstream	設置する establish
セーフ・ハーバー safe harbor	石油精製・販売部門 downstream	設置する install
セール sale	石油輸出国機構 OPEC	設定 configuration
セールス sales	石油輸出国機構 Organization of Petroleum Exporting Countries	設定 establishment
セールスマン AE		設定水準 peg
セールスマン agent		設定する create
セールスマン representative	セキュリタイゼーション securitization	設定する establish
セールスマン salesman		設定する fix
…を背負う piggyback	セキュリティ security	設定する form
…を背負って saddled with	セキュリティ・システム firewall	設定する post
世界化 globalization	セキュリティ・ホール security holes	設定する provide
世界銀行 IBRD		設定する secure
世界銀行 World Bank	赤裸々 bare	設定する set aside
世界経済 world economy	セクション section	設定する set up
世界経済フォーラム WEF	セクター sector	

セット kit	競り bid	全国店頭銘柄気配自動通報システム NASDAQ
セット unit	競り bidding	
セットアップ set-up	競り売り auction	全国店頭銘柄建値自動通報システム NASDAQ
Z図表 Z chart	競り手 bidder	
Z値 Z-score	セル生産方式 cell production system	全国民の national
ZD運動 zero defects		潜在成長率 potential
セット販売 bundle	ゼロ zero	潜在的な dormant
…が折半出資している equally owned by	ゼロ金利政策 zero-interest rate policy	潜在的な latent
		潜在的な potential
設備 capacity	ゼロ金利ローン zero financing	潜在能力 capability
設備 equipment	ゼロ・クーポン zero coupon	潜在能力 potential
設備 facility	ゼロサム zero sum	潜在力 potential
設備 hardware	ゼロ・ディフェクト運動 zero defects	漸次的移行 gradation
設備 installation		漸次導入する phase
設備 plant and equipment	ゼロベース zero-based	全社員 workforce
設備 system	ゼロ和 zero sum	全社的 across-the-board
設備一式 unit	世話 agency	全社的品質管理 TQM
設備拡張 expansion	世話 care	船主 owner
設備過剰 overcapacity	栓 plug	全従業員 workforce
設備装置 plant and equipment	善意 goodwill	全住民 population
設備貸与 leaseback	善意の買収者 white knight	船主責任保険 P&I insurance
設備投資 capex	全員一致の unanimous	選出 election
設備投資 capital investment	全員出席の plenary	戦術 tactic(s)
設備の移動 redeployment	全額出資する wholly own	選出する adopt
説明 account	先願主義 first-to-file principle	選出する elect
説明会 briefing	前記事項 premises	選出する tap
説明会 presentation	前期比 quarterly	前述の aforesaid
説明書 document	選挙 election	先取権 preference
説明する account for	選挙 poll	先取権 priority
説明責任 accountability	全業種一律の across-the-board	先取権のある preferential
説明を受けた上での承諾［同意］ informed consent	選挙運動 campaign	先取特権 lien
	選挙権 vote	先取特権 preemptive right
節約 economy	占拠者 occupant	専心 dedication
節約 thrift	占拠する take over	前身 forerunner
節約する economize	選挙民の信任 mandate	前進 advance
節約する save	先駆 forerunner	前進 breakthrough
設立 establishment	先駆者 forerunner	前進 thrust
設立 float	先駆者 pioneer	先進7か国会議 G7
設立 formation	前月比 month-on-month	先進7か国財務相・中央銀行総裁会議 G7
設立 foundation	前月比で month-on-month	
設立時の initial	宣言 declaration	漸進主義 incrementalism
設立者 founder	宣言 profession	…に専心する committed to
設立者 organizer	宣言する declare	前進する advance
設立する create	先見性 foresight	先制する preempt
設立する establish	全権の plenary	全世界一体化 globalization
設立する float	先見の明 foresight	全世界的 global
設立する form	全権利落ち x.a.	全世界の global
設立する incorporate	先行 precedent	船籍 registry
設立する organize	選好 preference	前線 front
設立する set up	選好 propensity	全船舶 fleet
設立定款 articles of incorporation	…先行型 -led	船倉 bulk
瀬戸際 edge	先行型の proactive	漸増する pyramid
背中合わせの back-to-back	先行期間 lead time	船側 ship
是認 approval	全航空機 fleet	専属の captive
狭まる narrow	先行指数 leading index	専属の exclusive
狭める narrow	先行指標 forerunner	全速力 career
狭域通信網 LAN	先行条件 prerequisite	センター center [centre]
セミナー briefing	先行の pilot	船隊 fleet
…の責に帰す impute	先行の proactive	全体 pie
責める accuse	宣告 declaration	全体的な global

選択 choice	専念する commit	専門的職業 career
選択 election	前年同期比 year earlier	専門的職業 profession
選択 option	前年同期比 year-on-year	専門的な professional
選択 preference	前年同月比 year-on-year	専門的な technical
選択科目 option	前年比 year earlier	専門店 shop
選択権 choice	前年比 year-on-year	専門用語 term
選択権 election	前納する prepay	占有 assumption
選択権 option	専売 monopolization	占有 holding
選択肢 alternative	専売所 staple	占有 occupation
選択肢 option	専売の proprietary	占有 possession
選択手段 option	船舶隊 fleet	占有期間 occupation
選択する elect	選抜する screen	占有権 occupation
選択的な preferential	先発明主義 first-to-invent	占有者 occupant
選択の余地 option	principle	占有する appropriate
先端 edge	前半 first half	占有する assume
船団 fleet	全般的な general	占有する occupy
先端技術 high-tech	全般的な large	占有する possess
先端的な emerging	全般的に across the board	専有する foreclose
先端の advanced	全部 fully	専有の exclusive
全地球位置把握システム global	潜伏期間 incubation period	戦略 strategy
positioning system	潜伏中の dormant	戦略企画 strategic planning
全地球測位システム global	全部原価 full cost	戦略計画 strategic planning
positioning system	全部所有する wholly own	戦略計画策定 strategic planning
全地球測位システム GPS	全部の full	戦略計画設定 strategic planning
前兆 forerunner	前文 premises	戦略上重要な strategic
選定 choice	全米供給管理協会 Institute for	戦略上の operational
前提 assumption	Supply Management	戦略上の strategic
前提 premises	全米供給管理協会 ISM	戦略情報 intelligence
前提条件 prerequisite	全米自動車労働組合 UAW	戦略上役に立つ strategic
…を前提として subject to	全米証券業協会 NASD	戦略提携 strategic alliance
宣伝 commercial	全米消費者同盟 Consumers Union	戦略的 strategic
宣伝 flack	全米投資家協会 NAIC	戦略的業務提携 strategic alliance
宣伝 plug	全米保険監督官協会 NAIC	戦略的計画 strategic planning
宣伝 publicity	全米保険業協会 ACLI	戦略的財務広報 investor relations
宣伝する advertise	前方の front	戦略的投資 strategic investment
宣伝する exploit	全面回復 full-scale recovery	戦略的同盟 strategic alliance
宣伝する promote	全面的 across-the-board	戦略に必要な strategic
宣伝の promotional	全面的 full	戦略の策定 strategic planning
宣伝文 blurb	全面的な absolute	全力を挙げる commit
宣伝用の promotional	全面的な global	全力を傾ける concentrate
前途 horizon	全面的な回復 full-scale recovery	先例 authority
先頭 cutting edge	全面的に across the board	先例に従う follow suit
先頭 forefront	全面安の展開 bearish	前例に倣う follow suit
先頭 front	専門 specialty	前例のない unusual
先頭 leading edge	専門家 authority	洗練された sophisticated
戦闘 engagement	専門家 player	洗練されていない crude
先導企業 leading company	専門家 professional	…に栓をする plug
先導者 bellwether	専門外取扱品 sideline	
先導役 trendsetter	専門家気質 professionalism	そ
選任 election	専門家集団 panel	
先任権 seniority	専門型大量販売店 category killer	…層 public
前任者 predecessor	専門家の報告書 expertise	層 bracket
先任順 seniority	専門技術 expertise	層 tier
選任する appoint	専門技術 knowhow	層 zone
選任する elect	専門誌 journal	総… general
先任の senior	専門職 profession	添う meet
専任の resident	専門職の professional	相違 discrepancy
専念 dedication	専門法人 P.C.	相違 disparity
前年 year earlier	専門知識 expertise	総意 consensus
…に専念する committed to	専門知識 knowhow	相違点 gap

総売上高	total revenues	創業する	set up	操作	manipulation
総売上高	turnover	操業する	operate	操作	operation
総営業費用	total operating expenses	増強する	beef up	相殺	compensation
		増強する	bolster	相殺	offset
総益金	gross income	増強する	boost	総裁	president
…の増加	increased	増強する	intensify	相殺額	offset
増価	appreciation	増強する	reinforce	相殺勘定	contra account
増加	accumulation	操業短縮	slowdown	相殺関税	countervailing duty
増加	addition	操業中	on stream	相殺する	average
増加	advance	操業中の	onstream	相殺する	net
増加	enhancement	操業停止	off stream	相殺する	offset
増加	gain	操業度	capacity	操作が簡単	user-friendly
増加	growth	操業度	volume	捜査官	agent
増加	improvement	送金	money transfer	走査機	scanner
増加	increase	送金	transfer	創作	origination
増加	increment	送金する	remit	捜索	search
増加	pickup	送金する	transfer	造作	fittings
増加	rise	送金手数料	remittance fees	創作する	create
総会	convention	総崩れ	debacle	創作性	creativity
総会	meeting	総計	aggregate	操作された	dirty
増加額	accrual	総計	gross	操作上の	operational
増加額	appreciation	総計…に達する	amount	操作する	control
総額	aggregate	総計する	reckon	操作する	manipulate
総額	amount	総計…になる	aggregate	操作する	operate
総額	figure	総計の	aggregate	操作する	run
総額	gross	総経費	overhead	操作する	work
総額	pie	総決算	bottom line	走査する	scan
総額	sum	増減	change	走査装置	scanner
増額	increment	総原価	full cost	操作的な	technical
総額の	full	総原価	total cost	操作の	managerial
増加させる	boost	倉庫	depository	増資	capital increase
増加した	increased	倉庫	magazine	増資	capital increment
増加する	accrue	倉庫	storage	増資	capital injection
増加する	advance	倉庫	warehouse	増資	fresh capital
増加する	gain	倉庫	warehousing	増資	recapitalization
増加する	grow	総合司会者	anchorman	総資産	identifiable asset
増加する	increase	総合施設	center [centre]	総資産利益率	ROA
増加する	rise	総合的	general	創始者	founder
総括原価	full cost	総合的	integrated	創始者	pioneer
総括的	across-the-board	総合的	universal	喪失	forfeit
総括的法案	omnibus bill	総合的な	comprehensive	喪失した	forfeit
総株式数	capital stock	総合的な	global	喪失する	forfeit
増加部分	accrual	総合的品質管理	TQM	総資本	total capital
相加平均	arithmetic mean	総合の	composite	総資本利益率	ROA
増加量	increment	総合品質管理	TQM	総収益	gross income
早期採用者	early adopter	総合品質経営	TQM	総収益	total revenues
早期是正措置	early corrective measures	総合保険	allfinanz	総従業員数	payroll
		倉庫業務	warehousing	操縦する	manipulate
早期退職	early retirement	相互作用の	interactive	総収入	gross income
早期退職勧奨	buyback	総コスト	total cost	贈賄	bribery
早期定年	early retirement	相互に情報を交換できる	interactive	創出	generation
創業	formation	相互の	mutual	創出する	create
創業	foundation	相互の	reciprocal	創出する	provide
操業	activity	相互利益協定	combination	送受話器	handset
操業	operation	相互理解	communication	相乗効果	synergy
増強	beef-up	相互利用する	share	装飾する	garnish
増強	boost	捜査	raid	総所得	gross income
増強	increment	操作	device	送信	transmission
創業者	founder	操作	handling	増進	enhancement
創業者会長	founder chairman			増進	gain

増進　increment	装置　equipment	ゾーン　zone
増進　promotion	装置　hardware	阻害要因　disincentive
送信する　transmit	装置　installation	阻害要因　drag
増進する　gain	装置　package	阻害要因　hazard
送信料　toll	装置　unit	遡求　recourse
総数　sum	増築　addition	遡求権なし　nonrecourse
造成する　develop	総長　president	遡及して適用する　backdate
総責任額　total liabilities	想定　assumption	遡及する　retroactive
創設　establishment	想定　projection	遡及力のある　retroactive
創設　origination	贈呈　presentation	即座の　immediate
創設　promotion	想定する　assume	即座の　instant
増設　addition	贈呈する　present	即座の　outright
創設者　founder	争点　issue	即座の　prompt
創設する　establish	騒動　turmoil	即座の　quick
創設する　originate	相当額　equivalent	即座の　spot
増設する　expand	…に相当する　equivalent to	即時　instant
創造　origination	…に相当する　represent	即時　real time
創造する　create	相当する　comparable	即時決済　on-the-spot payment
創造する　generate	相当な　healthy	即時処理　real time
創造する　originate	相当な　reasonable	即時の　immediate
創造性　creativity	相当な　significant	即時の　instant
創造力　creativity	相当の　due	即時の　prompt
相続　inheritance	贈答品　novelty	即時の　quick
相続権　inheritance	相当分　equivalent	即時払い　prompt
相続財産　inheritance	相場　market	即時払いの　prompt
相続財産権　fee	相場　market price	促進　furtherance
相続する　inherit	相場　quotation	促進　improvement
相続人のいない　vacant	相場　quote	促進　promotion
総体　aggregate	相場　rate	促進策　incentive
増大　boost	相場　speculation	促進する　accelerate
増大　enhancement	相場　value	促進する　advance
増大　gain	相場師　operator	促進する　bolster
増大　growth	相場師　speculator	促進する　expedite
増大　increase	相場操作　rig	促進する　facilitate
増大　increment	相場操縦　manipulation	促進する　help
相対応する　reciprocal	相場操縦　market manipulation	促進する　improve
増大した　increased	相場の回復　recovery	促進する　promote
増大する　bulk	装備　tooling	促進する　serve
増大する　gain	総費用　total cost	属性　attribute
増大する　grow	送付する　serve	属性　property
増大する　increase	増分　increment	即席簡易食品　fast food
増大する　incremental	造幣局　mint	即席の　instant
総体的な　generic	総平均　weighted average	側線　sideline
総体(の)　gross	双方向通信機能　conferencing	速達の　express
総体の　aggregate	双方向の　interactive	速達便　dispatch
送達　delivery	増補　supplementary	測定　determination
送達　service	総務部長　secretary	測定　measurement
送達する　deliver	総輸入元　distributor	測定基準　benchmark
送達する　remit	贈与　donation	測定する　determine
相談　conference	贈与　endowment	測定する　gauge
相談　consultation	贈与財産　settlement	測定値　measurement
相談　consulting	創立　establishment	測定用器具　gauge
相談相手　consultant	創立　formation	測度　measure
相談員　counselor	創立　foundation	速度　pace
相談者　client	創立　promotion	速度　rate
相談役　adviser	創立する　establish	速度　velocity
相談役　consultant	贈賄　bribery	速度の調整・選択　timing
相談役　counselor	ソーシング　sourcing	束縛する　curb
装置　device	ゾーニング　zoning	側面の　side
装置　drive	ゾーン　territory	測量　survey

速力　velocity	訴訟　case	損害　injury
底　bottom	訴訟　lawsuit	損害　loss
底　floor	訴訟　legal action	損害　prejudice
底　low	訴訟　proceedings	損害額　loss
底上げする　upgrade	訴訟記録　minutes	損害塡補　indemnity
底入れ　bottom	訴訟実務　practice	損害賠償　damage
底入れ　bottoming out	訴訟手続き　practice	損害保険会社　nonlife insurance company
底入れする　bottom out	訴訟手続き　proceedings	損害保険会社　nonlife insurer
底打ち　bottoming out	訴訟手続き　process	損害を与える　prejudice
底打ちする　bottom out	訴訟を起こす　litigate	損害を受ける　suffer from
底堅い　robust	素数　prime	損金　deduction
底堅い　solid	素数の　prime	損金算入　deduction
損なう　dilute	租税　tax	損金算入できる　deductible
損なう　impair	租税　toll	存在　presence
損なう　prejudice	租税回避地　tax haven	存在感　presence
損なうこと　prejudice	租税条約　tax convention	損失　deficit
底に届く　bottom	組成する　form	損失　disadvantage
底値　bottom	租税逃避地　tax haven	損失　loss
底値　floor	租税特別措置　tax break	損失拡大　wider loss
底値　low	租税避難国　tax haven	損失金　deficiency
底値に達する　bottom out	租税優遇措置　tax break	損失金　deficit
底離れ　bottoming out	措置　action	損失の穴埋めをする　cover
底を打つ　bottom out	措置　device	損失補償　indemnity
底をつく　bottom out	措置　feature	損失補償契約　indemnity
底をつく　exhaust	措置　measure	損失補塡規定　keep-harmless clause
素材　basic material	措置　move	
素材　material	措置　proceedings	損失予防をとる　hedge
素材　raw material	措置　program	損失予防手段　hedge
粗雑な　crude	措置　step	損失を被る　lose
素子　device	措置　treatment	損失を計上する　suffer
素子　element	訴追する　prosecute	損傷　prejudice
組織　establishment	即刻　immediate	存続　life
組織　fabric	率先　initiative	存続　standing
組織　institution	率先者　pioneer	存続　subsistence
組織　machinery	備え　hedge	存続会社　surviving company
組織　makeup	その筋　authorities	存続期間　life
組織　organization	その筋　authority	損得なしになる　break even
組織　scheme	その他　AOB [a.o.b.]	損耗　impairment
組織　structure	その他　misc.	損耗　wastage
組織　system	その他　miscellaneous	損耗高　wastage
組織化　organization	その割合に応じて　pro rata	
組織替えする　restructure	ソフト　software	**た**
組織化する　organize	ソフトウエア　software	
組織再編　reorganization	ソフトウェアなどのセット販売　bundling	ターゲット　target
組織者　organizer		ターゲットにする　target
組織上の　organizational	ソブリン　sovereign	ダーティ　dirty
組織する　form	ソブリン債　sovereign	ターミナル　terminal
組織全体の　organizational	粗末な　crude	ターンアラウンド　turnaround
組織体　entity	ソリューション　solution	ターンキー方式の　turnkey
組織体　organization	ソルベンシー　solvency	…台　mark
組織的運動　drive	ソルベンシー・マージン比率　solvency margin ratio	台　stand
組織的な　organic		台　unit
組織的な　organizational	損益　income	第1位の　premier
組織内の　in-house	損益　P&L	第1四半期　Q1
組織変更　reorganization	損益勘定　income account	第2四半期　Q2
組織変更する　reorganize	損益計算書　income account	第2四半期　second quarter
阻止する　contain	損益分岐点　break-even (point)	第3四半期　Q3
素質　capability	損害　casualty	第4四半期　Q4
素質　potential	損害　damage	タイアップ　tie-in
訴訟　action	損害　disadvantage	

タイアップ tie-up	待機の standby	大失態 fiasco
代案 alternative	大規模 size	大失敗 debacle
代案 backup	大規模な heavy	大失敗 fiasco
第一級の fab	大規模な large	大失敗する fall flat
第一順位の primary	大規模な major	貸借 lending
第一世銀 IBRD	大規模な massive	貸借勘定 balance
第一等の prime	大規模な substantial	貸借勘定 balance
第一人者 front runner	大規模な wholesale	貸借契約(書) charter
第一の chief	退却 retreat	貸借対照表 balance sheet
第一面 front	退却する retreat	貸借対照表に計上されない off-balance-sheet
第一面の front	耐久財 durables	
第一線 forefront	退去 exit	貸借対照表に表示されない off-balance-sheet
第一線 front line	怠業 slowdown	
退院 discharge	大恐慌 depression	台車輸送 piggyback
対売上高純利益率 net margin on sales	大競争 megacompetition	大衆 mass
	大金 bundle	大衆迎合的な経済保護主義 populist protectionism
ダイエット食品 diet aid	大金 fortune	
対応 action	代金 charge	大衆の mass
対応 fit	代金 consideration	大衆向けの downmarket
対応 matching	代金 proceeds	大衆向けの downscale
対応 measure	代金取立て collection	退出 exit
対応 move	待遇 treatment	対象 center [centre]
対応 parity	体系 framework	対象 matter
対応 reaction	体系 scheme	対象 object
対応 response	体系 structure	対象 objective
…に対応する keep up with	体系 system	退場 exit
…に対応する respond to	体系化する organize	代償 commutation
対応する applicable	体験 experience	代償 compensation
対応する meet	体験する experience	代償 remuneration
…対応の compatible	代行業者 agent	対照勘定 contra account
対価 compensation	代行者 proxy	代償金 commutation
対価 consideration	代行者 relief	退場する exit
対価 fee	代行者 representative	…の対象である subject to
対価 remuneration	…を代行する represent	…を対象とする affect
対価 reward	対抗馬 contender	…を対象とする cover
退化 deterioration	大国 giant	対象にする target
退化 obsolescence	大黒柱 mainstay	退職 going
代价 charge	太鼓判を押す hallmark	退職 retirement
大会 convention	対策 effort	退職 separation
大会 meeting	対策 measure	退職 severance
対外 foreign	対策 move	退職勧奨金 golden handshake
対外 overseas	対策 package	退職給付債務 projected benefit obligation
大改革 shake-up	対策 policy	
対外純資産残高 net creditor position	対策 program	退職金契約 golden parachute
	対策 project	退職後 postretirement
大改造 shakeout	対策 protection	退職者 retiree
大改造 shake-up	対策 solution	退職奨励金 buyback
対外直接投資 FDI	対策 step	退職する resign
対外的な external	第三債務者 garnishee	退職する retire
対外投資資金の本国送金 repatriation	第三次産業 tertiary	退職補償金 golden parachute
	第三者 third party	対処する manage
代替え commutation	第三者間取引にかかわる arm's length	退陣 exit
退化した obsolete		退陣する exit
退化する deteriorate	第三者寄託金 escrow	対人の personal
大気 air	第三世銀 IFC	体制 establishment
待機期間 waiting period	台紙 stub	体制 leadership
待機期間 waiting time	大事業 enterprise	体制 scheme
大企業の官僚的体質 corpocracy	体質 culture	体制 structure
大企業向けの wholesale	体質 standing	体制 system
代議士 representative	体質 structure	大勢 trend

体制側	establishment
堆積物	deposit
退蔵	hoarding
退蔵する	hoard
代替	backup
代替	commutation
代替	replacement
代替	substitute
代替財	substitute
代替策	alternative
代替策	fall-back position
代替投資市場	AIM
代替燃料供給所	eco-station
代替品	replacement
大多数	majority
大多数の意見	consensus
台地	plateau
台帳	ledger
体調調整	workout
態度	attitude
態度	orientation
態度	presence
態度	stance
対等	coordination
対等関係	coordination
対投資家関係	investor relations
対等の	equal
対等の	even
大統領	president
大統領経済諮問委員会	CEA
大統領補佐官	adviser
対内直接投資	FDI
ダイナミクス	dynamics
第二位の	secondary
第二世界銀行	IDA
退任	resignation
退任する	resign
退任する	retire
退任する	step down
対の	duplicate
滞納	arrears
滞納	default
滞納金	arrears
大発見	breakthrough
大半	bulk
大半	majority
大半	mass
代表者	representative
代表者を任命する	delegate
…を代表する	represent
代表する	representative
代表団	delegation
代表的な	representative
代表として派遣する	delegate
代物弁済	accord
大部分	lion's share
大部分	majority
大部分	mass
大部分の	major
太平洋地域経済協力機構	OPEC
大変化	sea change
大変革	sea change
大変革	shake-up
大変金になる	lucrative
耐乏生活	austerity
台本	scenario
怠慢	negligence
タイミング	timing
タイム	time
タイム・ホライゾン	time horizon
タイムリミット	time frame
代役	backup
代役	standby
耐用期間	life
代用硬貨	token
太陽電池	solar cell
耐用年数	life
耐用年数	useful life
代理	agency
代理	deputy
代理委任状	proxy
代理関係	agency
代理機関	agent
代理業	agency
代理業務	commission
代理権	agency
代理権	authority
代理権	proxy
代理権の授与	delegation
代理行為	agency
代理行為	proxy
対立	conflict
対立	friction
対立	impasse
代理店	agency
代理店	agent
代理店	distributor
代理人	agent
代理人	attorney
代理人	proxy
代理人	representative
代理人	substitute
代理人を任命する	delegate
代理の	representative
大量	bulk
大量	mass
大量	mint
大量	quantity
大量	size
大量売り	sell-off
大量売りによる急落	sell-off
大量需要	run
大量消費社会	mass-consumption society
大量生産	mass production
大量生産	rollout
大量生産型の	commercial
大量生産する	mass-produce
大量生産する	roll out
大量の	heavy
大量の	large
大量の	mass
大量の	massive
大量の	significant
大量の	wholesale
大量の売り	massive selling
大量の資金	ample liquidity
大量発行	massive issuance
大量利用者	heavy user
体力	strength
…の代理をつとめる	represent
対話式の	interactive
対話処理	interactive
対話性	interactive
ダウ	Dow
ダウ工業株平均	Dow Jones
ダウ・ジョーンズ工業株平均	Dow Jones
ダウ・ジョーンズ社	Dow Jones
ダウニング・ストリート	Downing Street
ダウンサイジング	downsizing
ダウンスケール	downscale
ダウンストリーム	downstream
ダウンタウン	downtown
ダウンマーケティング	downmarketing
ダウンロードする	download
絶え間ない	running
耐える	suffer
高い	good
高い	high
打開	breakthrough
…よりも高い値を付ける	outbid
高い流動性	ample liquidity
高入先出し法	HIFO
高いレベルの知能を持つ	intelligent
多角化	diversification
多角化	diversity
多角化	expansion
多角化企業	conglomerate
多角化する	diversify
多角経営	pentagon management
多角式の	multiple
多角的貿易交渉	multilateral trade talks
多額の	heavy
多額の	massive
多額の	significant
多額の利益配当	melon
高く評価する	appreciate
高さ	level
高値	high
高値安定の	hard
…の高値を呼ぶ	fetch
高まり	increase
高まる	grow
高まる	intensify
高まる	rise

高まる	surge	多重アクセス・コンピュータ	host computer	達成する	secure
高める	boost	多重の	multiple	脱退	withdrawal
高める	create	多種多様な	multiple	脱同調化	decoupling
高める	enhance	多数	majority	…建て	denominated
高める	improve	多数	mass	立替え	disbursement
高める	increase	多数の	major	立替え金	disbursement
高める	intensify	多数の	mass	建て替える	rebuild
高める	serve	多数の	multiple	建具類	fittings
高める	strengthen	タスク	task	立て直し	reconstruction
高める	upgrade	助け	help	立て直し	rehabilitation
抱き合わせ広告	tie-in	助ける	help	立て直し	shakeout
抱き合わせの	tie-in	惰性	inertia	立て直す	fix
抱き合わせ販売	bundle	惰性	momentum	立て直す	rebuild
抱き合わせ販売	bundling	多大の	massive	立て直す	reconstruct
抱き合わせ販売	tie-in	戦い	race	立て直す	rehabilitate
抱き合わせ販売の	tie-in	戦い	struggle	立て直す	reshape
抱き込む	fix	たたき売り	dumping	立て直す	restructure
多岐にわたる	general	ただし…	subject to	立て直す	revamp
多極分散する	decentralize	正しい	fair	立て直す	revive
タグ	tag	正す	redress	建て値	quotation
卓越した	fab	立会い	ring	建て値	quote
卓上型	desktop	立会い	session	縦の	vertical
卓上の	desktop	立会所	boardroom	…建ての	-based
託送	consgt	立会場	boardroom	建物	premises
託送	consignment	立会場	floor	縦割りの	vertical
宅地開発業者	developer	立会場	ring	妥当性	adequacy
宅地造成業者	developer	立ち上げる	enter	妥当な	applicable
宅配の	door-to-door	立ち上げる[起動する]	launch	妥当な	fair
宅配便	home delivery	立入り検査	on-the-spot inspection	妥当な	reasonable
巧みな	sophisticated	立入り権者	licensee	棚上げ状態	back burner
巧みに操る	manipulate	立入り考査	on-the-spot inspection	棚上げする	set aside
巧みに運営する	engineer	立入り調査	on-the-spot inspection	棚卸し	inventory
巧みに管理する	engineer	立ち入る	access	棚卸し	stocktaking
巧みに計画する	engineer	立ち直りの早い	resilient	棚卸し資産	inventory
巧みに処理する	engineer	立ち退く	quit	棚卸し高	inventory
たくらむ	plot	立場	capacity	棚卸し表	inventory
蓄え	hoarding	立場	footing	棚卸し品	inventory
蓄え	stockpile	立場	presence	棚ざらし期間	shelf life
蓄えておく	set aside	立場	stance	店ざらし品	plug
蓄える	hoard	立場	standing	棚ぼた	windfall
蓄える	save	立場	water	タナボタ利益	windfall
蓄える	set aside	立場を強める	bolster	他の企業を吸収する会社	surviving company
打撃	blow	タックス・ヘイブン	tax haven	頼まれない	unsolicited
打撃	squeeze	脱工業化	deindustrialization	頼みの綱	mainstay
打撃を与える	hammer	脱工業化	postindustrialism	頼みの綱	recourse
打撃を与える	hit	脱出	flight	頼みの綱	resort
打撃を受けた	stricken	…に達する	hit	頼みもしない	unsolicited
打撃を受ける	suffer	達成	accomplishment	束	bundle
打撃を受ける	suffer from	達成	achievement	束	packet
打撃を加える	land	達成	execution	打破	breakthrough
妥結	settlement	達成	fulfillment	束ねる	bundle
多国間合意	multilateral accord	達成基準	norm	タブ	tab
多国間貿易交渉	multilateral trade talks	達成する	achieve	タブ・キー	tab
打算	convenience	達成する	chalk up	だまし取る	bilk
確かな	reliable	達成する	deliver	ダミー会社	dummy company
確かな	sterling	達成する	execute	試す	test
出し物	fare	達成する	gain	ためになる	profitable
他社に配置換えする	decruit	達成する	meet	だめになる	fold up
他社に負けない	competitive	達成する	rack up	ためる	hoard

| 和英 |

保つ	maintain	談合	collusion	担保権行使	foreclosure
多様化	diversification	談合する	collude	担保権実行	foreclosure
多様化する	diversify	探査	exploration	担保財産	collateral
多様性	diversity	探査	search	担保責任	warranty
多様性	productivity	短縮	curtailment	担保付き債券	mortgage bond
頼っている	dependent	短縮	cutback	担保付き社債	mortgage bond
頼ること	resort	短縮	reduction	担保付き融資	mortgage
堕落した	corrupt	短縮語	contraction	担保提供者	mortgagor
多量の	massive	短縮する	reduce	…を担保とする	-backed
だれ気味の	dull	単純作業化する	deskill	担保となる	underlying
団	team	短所	defect	…を担保に入れる	cover
段	tier	短所	flaw	担保に入れる	pledge
単位	entity	短所	weakness	担保に供する	pledge
単位	unit	炭素	carbon	担保の供与	posting
単一価格制	one-price policy	団体	association	担保の差し入れ	posting
単一価格政策	one-price policy	団体	circles	担保範囲	coverage
単一の	flat	団体	community	担保品	collateral
単一の事業	monoline	団体	corporation	担保品	pledge
段階	echelon	団体	group	担保物	guarantee
段階	gradation	団体	organization	担保物件	collateral
段階	grade	団体規約	articles of association	担保不動産	mortgage
段階	level	団体交渉	bargaining	端末	terminal
段階	notch	団体などに加入する	enter	端末機	handset
段階	phase	断定する	conclude	端末機	terminal
段階	process	耽溺	spree	端末装置	terminal
段階	scale	タンデム	tandem	弾薬庫	magazine
段階	stage	担当記者	hand	弾力のある	resilient
段階	tier	担当区域	territory		
段階的移行	gradation	担当者	agent		
段階的な金利調整	incrementalism	担当者	official	**ち**	
段階的に解消する	phase out	担当者	representative	地位	appointment
段階的に削減する	phase out	…を担当する	work	地位	capacity
段階的に実行する	phase	…担当の	i/c	地位	position
段階的に撤廃する	phase out	単独ベース	parent	地位	post
段階的に取り入れる	phase in	単独ベースの	unconsolidated	地位	presence
段階的に廃止する	phase out	段取り	organization	地位	profile
段階的に閉鎖する	phase out	段取り	plan	地位	rank
団塊の世代	baby boomers	段取り	tooling	地位	reputation
嘆願する	plead	単なる	bare	地位	slot
短期借入金純額	net short-term borrowings	断念する	forgo	地位	spot
短期金融市場	money market	単発の	one-time	地位	standing
短期金融市場	secondary market	単発プロモーション	one-shot promotion	地位	status
短期資金	call	ダンピング	dumping	地域	area
短期資金計画	short-run fund planning	ダンピングする	dump	地域	corner
短期資金市場	call market	ダンピング防止	antidumping	地域	region
短期市場	call market	断片	fraction	地域	sector
短期的な	immediate	断片の	fractional	地域	zone
短期投資資金	hedge fund	担保	charge	地域間の売掛金	interarea accounts receivable
短期の	current	担保	collateral	地域間振替え	interarea transfer
短期の	short-term	担保	guarantee	地域協定	regionwide agreement
探求	search	担保	mortgage	地域市場	geographic market
短期利益計画	short-range profit planning	担保	pledge	地域社会	community
タンク集積所	harbor	担保	security	地域社会ベースの	community-based
探検	exploration	担保	warranty	地域制	zoning
探鉱	exploration	担保掛け目	haircut	地域全体の	regional
断交	severance	担保金	margin	地域的集中	localization
談合	bid-rigging	担保権	charge	地域的な	regional
		担保権	lien	地域特化	localization
		担保権が付いていない	clean		

地域の regional	知識 savvy	着手する start
地域別売上高 geographic revenues	知識 sophistication	着手する undertake
地域密着型の community-based	知識エンジニア KE	着想 idea
小さな包み packet	知識管理 KM	着々と進める pyramid
チーム team	知識統括役員 CKO	着服する appropriate
地位を占める rank	知識ベース・マシーン KBM	着陸許可 clearance
チェーン・ストア multiple	知性 intelligence	着陸させる land
チェーン店 chain	地政学的リスク geopolitical risks	着陸する land
チェーン店 chain store	地帯 climate	チャネル channel
チェーン店 franchisee	地帯 land	チャプター・イレブン Chapter 11
地役権 easement	地帯 zone	チャレンジ challenge
チェック check	遅滞 arrears	チャンス opportunity
チェックオフ checkoff	遅滞 delay	注意 care
チェックする monitor	地代 rent	注意 note
遅延 arrears	縮める narrow	中位数 median
遅延 delay	秩序 order	注意義務 care
遅延金利 contango	チップ chip	注意せよ NB [nb]
地価 land price	チップ gratuity	中位の median
違い difference	チップ perquisite	中位の second-tier
地下銀行 underground bank	知的教養 sophistication	中央 center [centre]
近づく approximate	知的財産 intellectual property	中央銀行 central bank
近づける approximate	知的財産権 intellectual property	中央処理装置 chip
力 ability	知的資産 intellectual asset	中央値 median
力 capability	知的資産 knowledge	中央の central
力 dynamics	知的障害 mental handicap	中央の median
力 force	知的障害者 mentally handicapped	仲介 agency
力 leverage	people	仲介 arbitrage
力 power	知的職業 profession	仲介 brokerage
力 steam	知的職業法人 P.C.	仲介化 intermediation
力 strength	知的所有権 intellectual property	仲介機関 intermediary
力強い strong	知的な intelligent	仲介業 brokerage
力強さ strength	知的範囲 competence	仲介業者 agent
…に力を注ぐ focus on	地点 point	仲介業者 intermediary
力を注ぐ concentrate	地点 spot	仲介者 intermediate
…の力を弱める depress	知能 intelligence	仲介者 middleman
地球温暖化 global warming	知能的な intelligent	仲介手数料 brokerage
地球規模の global	地平線 horizon	仲介人 broker
地球全体の global	地歩 footing	仲介の intermediary
地球的規模化 globalization	地歩 position	中核 core
地球にやさしい材料 ecomaterial	地方 climate	中核 hub
地球の大気 greenhouse	地方債 municipal	中核事業 main business
地区 park	地方自治体の municipal	…を中核事業にする focus on
地区 zone	地方の local	中核的な core
畜牛界 cattle industry	地方の regional	…を中核に据える focus on
畜牛産業 cattle industry	地方分権 decentralization	中核の key
蓄財 accumulation	地方分散 decentralization	中型車 intermediate
逐次の serial	地方法 bylaws	中間 half
地区制 zoning	知名度 name	中間 half year
蓄積 accumulation	知名度 name recognition	中間 midterm
蓄積 backlog	知名度 reputation	中間会計期間の interim
蓄積 stockpile	チャージ charge	中間管理者 middle manager
蓄積した accumulated	チャーター charter	中間管理職 middle manager
地区連銀経済[景況]報告書 beige	チャーターする charter	中間生成物 intermediate
book	チャート chart	中間製品 semifinished goods
地形 configuration	着実な solid	中間的に介在する mezzanine
遅行指数 lagging index	着手 launch	中間に位置する intermediate
遅行する lag	着手 launching	中間に位置する mezzanine
知識 idea	着手 start	中間の half-yearly
知識 information	着手資金 seed capital	中間の interim
知識 knowledge	着手する launch	中間の intermediary

中間の	intermediate	中心相場	prevailing rate	超大型合併	megamerger
中間の	median	中心地	center [centre]	超大型チェーン店	megastore
中間派	center [centre]	中心的存在	backbone	超過	excess
中間領域	interface	中心的な	central	懲戒(する)	reprimand
中期	midterm	中心的な	core	超過額	excess
注記	note	中心的な	dominant	超過勤務	overtime
中期国債	medium	中心点	center [centre]	超過勤務	overwork
中期	intermediate	中心点	stronghold	超過所得税	windfall profit tax
中期物	intermediate	…中心の	-centered	超過担保	haircut
中級の	intermediate	…中心の	driven	長期	long term
中級レベルの	intermediate	…中心の	-focused	長期請負契約	long term contract
中継の	intermediary	…中心の	-led	長期受取勘定	long-term receivable
中堅幹部	middle manager	…中心の	-oriented	長期受取債権	long-term receivable
中堅の	second-tier	中心の	central	長期格付け	long-term debt rating
忠告	advice	中心の	key	長期貨幣性資産	long-term monetary assets
中国	Beijing	中心の	master		
中国人民銀行	People's Bank of China	中心レート	prevailing rate	長期借入金	long term debt
		中枢	center [centre]	長期借入債務	long term debt
中国政府	Beijing	中枢	core	長期金融売掛債権	long-term finance receivables
中古品販売	garage sale	中枢	hub		
仲裁	arbitration	忠誠心	loyalty	長期金融債権	long-term finance receivables
仲裁	intervention	中性の	neutral		
仲裁	troubleshooting	抽選	drawing	長期金利	long-term interest rate
駐在員	representative	抽選会	drawing	長期勤労奨励制度	long-term incentive program
駐在員事務所	liaison office	中断	abandonment		
駐在員事務所	representative	中断	breakdown	長期経営計画	long-term planning
仲裁機関	arbitration	中断	cut	長期計画	long-term planning
仲裁裁定	award	中断する	suspend	長期契約	long term contract
駐在している	resident	中途解約不能の	noncancelable	長期欠勤者	absentee
仲裁する	mediate	中途退職金の支払い	separation payments	長期工事契約	long term contract
仲裁人	arbiter			長期国債の借換え	funding
仲裁人	arbitrator	中南米8か国グループ	G8	長期優化	funding
仲裁人	troubleshooter	注入	infusion	長期債券	longs
…駐在の	-based	注入	injection	長期債権	long-term receivable
仲裁判断	award	注入する	inject	長期債務	long term debt
仲裁付託合意	submission	中米共同市場	CACM	長期資金調達	long-term financing
中止	abandonment	…に注目する	focus on	長期資本	capitalization
中止	cancelation	注目の的	focus	長期奨励報酬制度	long-term incentive program
中軸	backbone	注文	order		
中止事業	discontinued operation	注文殺到	run	長期的な	permanent
中止する	cancel	注文残高	backlog	長期的な	sustainable
中止する	scrap	注文時支払い条件	cwo	長期にわたる	prolonged
中止する	suspend	注文仕立ての	tailor-made	長期の	long
中止する	take off	注文書	order	長期の	long-dated
忠実性	loyalty	注文する	order	長期の	noncurrent
忠実度	loyalty	注文生産した	customized	長期の	prolonged
中止になる	fold up	注文生産する	customize	長期負債	long term debt
注釈	note	注文生産方式	build to order	長期負債対総資本比率	long-term debt-to-total capital
中小企業	small business	注文に応じて作る	customize		
中小企業庁	SBA	注文品	order	長期不動産抵当貸付け	takeout
中小の	weak	中立	neutral	長期目標	project
抽象モデル	automation	…帳	book	超巨大合併	megamerger
中心	center [centre]	庁	board	超巨大銀行	megabank
中心	core	庁	office	長距離電話料金	toll
中心	focus	調印	execution	超近代的な	sophisticated
中心	forefront	調印式	closing	超金融緩和政策	ultra-easy monetary policy
中心	hub	調印者	signatory		
中心街	downtown	調印する	execute	超金融緩和政策	ultra-easy money policy
中心人物	center [centre]	調印する	seal		
中心人物	keyman	調印する	sign	帳消し	write-off

帳消しにする　make up for	調達先　purchase	直接投資　direct investment
帳消しにする　offset	調達資金　proceeds	直接利回り　current yield
兆候　evidence	調達手段　funding	勅選弁護士　Q.C.
兆候　sign	調達する　obtain	直利　current yield
超高速の　high-end	調達する　procure	著作権　copyright
超国籍企業　transnational company	調達する　provide	著作権所有の　copyright
調査　consultation	調達する　raise	著作権侵害　piracy
調査　examination	調達する　receive	著作権侵害者　pirate
調査　exploration	調達人　purveyor	著作権を取得する　copyright
調査　inquiry	調停　conciliation	著作権を侵害する　pirate
調査　research	調停　intervention	…の著作権を保護する　copyright
調査　review	調停　settlement	著作物　content
調査　search	調停　troubleshooting	著作隣接権　neighboring right
調査　study	超低金利政策　ultra-easy money policy	貯蔵　hoarding
調査　survey		貯蔵　stockpile
調査　test	調停者　arbiter	貯蔵　storage
調査する　examine	調停する　mediate	貯蔵所　magazine
調査する　inquire	調停する　reconcile	貯蔵する　hoard
調査する　monitor	頂点に達する　peak	貯蔵品　supply
調査する　review	調度　fittings	貯蓄　savings
調査団　panel	懲罰的な　punitive	貯蓄貸付け機関　thrift
調査票　questionnaire	超微細加工・計測技術　nanotechnology	貯蓄貸付組合　S&L
調子　fix		貯蓄金融機関　thrift
徴収　collection	超微細加工技術　nanotechnology	貯蓄する　save
徴収する　collect	超微小技術　nanotechnology	直結　online
徴収する　levy	帳票　document	直結した　cum
徴収不能料金　uncollectibles	重複　overlap	貯留岩　reservoir
長寿社会　aged society	重複関係　overlap	チルド輸送　chilled transport
調書　file	重複上場する　dual-list	賃上げ　pay hike
長所　strength	重複の　duplicate	賃貸しする　hire
頂上　top	重複部分　overlap	賃貸しする　lease
頂上の　top	貼付する　attach	沈下する　sag
帳尻　balance	長編映画　feature	賃借りする　hire
調整　adjustment	帳簿　book	賃借りする　lease
調整　arrangement	諜報　intelligence	賃金　hire
調整　coordination	帳簿外の　off-the-book	賃金　pay
調整　matching	帳簿価格　book value	賃金　wage
調整　translation	帳簿価額　book value	賃金制度　pay plan
徴税　collectible	帳簿価額　carrying amount	賃金引上げ　pay hike
徴税　taxation	帳簿価額　carrying value	賃借資産　leasehold
調整局面　setback	帳簿上の価格　book value	賃借人　lessee
調整する　adjust	帳簿に手を加える　cook books	賃借人　tenant
調整する　coordinate	帳簿に載せる　book	賃借不動産　leasehold
調整する　correct	帳簿の閲覧　inspection	賃借料　hire
調整する　discount	帳簿を改竄する　cook books	賃借料　rent
調整する　regulate	帳簿をごまかす　cook books	賃借料　rental
調整する　stagger	帳面　book	陳述　allegation
調整する　translate	聴聞会　hearing	陳述　case
調製する　tailor	凋落　downfall	陳述　delivery
調整手当　weighting	調理法　formula	陳情運動　lobbying
調節　coordination	潮流　trend	陳情団　lobby
調節する　adjust	調和　correspondence	沈滞　doldrums
調節する　regulate	調和[協調]を図る　harmonize	沈滞　slowdown
挑戦　challenge	調和させる　coordinate	沈滞　stagnation
調達　funding	調和させる　harmonize	沈滞気味の　dull
調達　procurement	…と調和する　match	沈滞した　dull
調達　purchase	調和する　fit	沈滞した　stagnant
調達　sourcing	貯金　savings	賃貸　lease
調達可能な　available	直接支払い制　direct disbursement system	賃貸　leasing
調達期間　lead time		賃貸借契約(書)　lease

沈滞する stagnate	通貨単位の呼称変更 redenomination	通則 rule
賃貸人 lessor		通達 communication
賃貸料 rental	通貨の monetary	通達 ruling
陳腐化 obsolescence	通貨の変動 float	通知 advice
陳腐化した obsolete	通貨膨張 inflation	通知 notice
賃料 rent	通貨安 devaluation	通知 notification
陳列 display	通関申告 entry	通知書 note
陳列 exhibition	通関手続き clearance	通知書 notice
陳列許容期間 shelf life	通関手続き entry	通知書 notification
陳列する exhibit	通関港 port	通知方法 notice
陳列する expose	通期 full year	通年 full year
陳列する order	通期の annual	通念 attitude
陳列する pitch	通勤 commutation	通風装置 register
	通勤者 commuter	通報 notification
つ	通告 notice	通用を廃止する demonetize
	通告 notification	ツール tool
追加 addition	通告書 notice	通例 rule
追加機器 add-on equipment	通算可能な年金制度の portable	通話 call
追加資本 fresh capital	通商 commerce	通話量 traffic
追加出資義務のない nonassessable	通商 trade	通話路 channel
追加的な additional	通常定款 articles of association	使いこなす manage
追加投資 addition	通常定款 bylaws	使い捨ての disposable
追加の further	通常定款 memorandum of association	使い果たす deplete
追加の supplementary		使い果たす exhaust
追加払込み義務を負わない nonassessable	通商停止 embargo	…が使いやすい -friendly
	通常取引前の時間外取引 premarket trading	使いやすい user-friendly
追加払込み請求がない nonassessable		使う use
	通商の commercial	…につき per
追加料金 surcharge	通常の common	突合せ footing
追加料金を請求する surcharge	通常の general	突合せ matching
追加割当て overallotment	通常の generic	…付きで cum
追求 search	通常の ordinary	継ぎ手 coupling
…追求型の -oriented	通常の regular	継ぎ手 fittings
追及する prosecute	通称名 doing business as	月中平均 daily average for a month
追求する follow	通信 communication	
追随者 follower	通信 communications	…付きの cum
追随する follow	通信 correspondence	つきまとう ghost
追随する follow suit	通信 telecom	継ぎ目のない seamless
追跡可能性 traceability	通信 telecommunication	就く assume
追跡する follow	通信員 correspondent	机 bureau
追徴金 assessment	通信株 telco	償い reparation
追徴金 forfeit	通信機器 communications	償う recoup
追徴不能の nonassessable	通信機器本体 mainline	作り変える reshape
…について行く keep up with	telecommunications equipment	作り出す create
…についていけない lag	通信機能 capability	作り直す form
追認 confirmation	通信規約 protocol	作り直す reinvent
追放 dismissal	通信業者 carrier	作り直す reshape
追放する dismiss	通信業務 telecoms services	作る fix
…通 copy	通信勤務 telecommuting	ツケ negative legacy
通貨 cash	通信サービス telecoms services	つけ込む capitalize on
通貨 currency	通信事業 telecom	付け札 tab
通貨 money	通信事業者 carrier	付ける put
通貨供給量 M	通信事業者間接続料金 access charge	伝えられるところによれば reportedly
通貨供給量 money supply		
通貨切下げ devaluation	通信手段 communications	伝える pass
通学 commutation	通信情報 message	伝える transmit
通学者 commuter	通信文 message	続けざまの back-to-back
通貨下落 devaluation	通信網 network	続ける keep
通貨収縮 deflation	通信流量 traffic	突っ込んだ in-depth
通貨収縮の deflationary	通信路 channel	包む bundle

勤め	employment	強み	advantage	低下させる	reduce
務め	task	強み	edge	低下した	weak
勤め口	position	強み	strength	低下して	downward
務める	serve	強める	intensify	低下する	decline
つながり	tie-in	強める	reinforce	低下する	decrease
つなぎ銀行	bridge bank	釣合い	balance	低下する	depreciate
つなぎ金融	bridge loan	釣合い	proportion	低下する	deteriorate
つなぎとめる	retain	つり上げる	inflate	低下する	diminish
つなぎ融資	bridge financing	釣銭	change	低下する	downward
つなぎ融資	bridge loan			低下する	drop
つなぐ	bridge			低下する	fall
潰れる	fold up	て		低下する	lower
積み換える	tranship	…で	per	低下する	moderate
積み替える	tranship	手当たり次第の	random	低下する	plunge
積み替える	transship	手当	allowance	低下する	sag
積立て	funding	手当	benefit	低下する	shrink
積立金	deposit	手当	bonus	低下する	slip
積立金	fund	手当	compensation	低下する	squeeze
積立金	reserve	手当	pay	低下する	weaken
積立金	surplus	手当てする	administer	ディカップリング	decoupling
積立金を払い戻す	pay out	手荒く扱う	punish	定款	articles of incorporation
積み立てる	fund	ティア	tier	定款	settlement
積み立てる	set aside	提案	bid	提議	motion
積み荷	cargo	提案	initiative	定期市	fair
積み荷	shipment	提案	motion	定期刊行物	journal
積荷	bulk	提案	offer	定期刊行物	magazine
積荷	freightage	提案	plan	定期航空便	flight
積荷	load	提案	presentation	定期航空路	airline
積み荷証	bill of lading	提案	proposal	定期購読	subscription
積み荷証券	B/L	提案する	come up with	提起する	enter
積み荷証券	bill of lading	提案する	float	定義する	define
積み荷明細書	invoice	提案する	offer	定期性預金	fixed deposit
積み増し	accumulation	提案する	propose	定期船	packet
積み増す	book	TOB価格	offer price	定期大会	convention
積み増す	boost	ティーザー広告	teaser	定期賃借権	leasehold
積み増す	rebuild	T字型勘定	T-account	定期的な	periodic
積む	gain	ディーラー	dealer	定期的な	recurring
爪	nail	ディーラー	dealership	定期的な	regular
詰め込む	load	ディーリング	dealing	定期的に往復する	ply
詰め物	plug	ディーリング管理業務	back office	定期的に返済する	amortize
強い	high	ディール	deal	定期の	regular
強い	strong	定員	opening	定期の	terminal
強い影響を与える	determine	低下	decline	定期不動産権	term
…に強い関心がある	-minded	低下	decrease	低級の	downmarket
強気	bull	低下	deterioration	提供	availability
強気材料	positive	低下	drawdown	提供	cooperation
強気筋	bull	低下	drop	提供	donation
強気筋	longs	低下	fall	提供	offering
強気筋の	bull	低下	pressure	提供	provision
強気相場	rally	低下	reduction	提供	tender
強気の	bullish	低下	shrinkage	提供可能性	availability
強気の	good	低下	slowdown	提供者	provider
強気の	hard	低下	squeeze	提供者	purveyor
強気の	long	低下	weakness	提供する	advance
強気の	positive	低価格・低品質の	downscale	提供する	barter
強くなる	intensify	低価格の	downscale	提供する	deliver
強く求める	solicit	定額償却	amortization	提供する	extend
強さ	strength	定額法	straight line method	提供する	furnish
強含みの	positive	低下させる	depress	提供する	offer
		低下させる	moderate	提供する	present

提供する	provide	停止する	suspend	抵当	security
提供する	run	提示する	float	抵当銀行協会	MBA
提供する	serve	提示する	offer	抵当権	mortgage
提供する	service	提示する	post	抵当権設定	mortgage
提供する	tender	提示する	present	抵当権設定者	mortgagor
提供物	tender	提示する	propose	抵当権付き債権	secured mortgage
定期預金	fixed deposit	提示する	submit	抵当権付き社債	mortgage bond
定期預金証書	CD	定時総会	annual meeting	抵当権の請戻し権喪失	foreclosure
定期旅客機	airliner	提出	presentation	抵当証券担保付き証券	MBS
低金利化	ease	提出	submission	抵当証書	mortgage
テイクオーバー	takeover	提出	tender	抵当証書担保付き債券	CMO
テイクオーバー・ビッド	takeover bid	提出する	come up with	…を抵当とする	cover
デイケア	day care	提出する	enter	抵当流れ	foreclosure
提携	alliance	提出する	file	抵当流れにする	foreclose
提携	cooperation	提出する	lodge	抵当に入れる	pledge
提携	front	提出する	present	抵当のない	unsecured
提携	networking	提出する	produce	抵当品	pledge
提携	partnership	提出する	propose	抵当物	pawn
提携	tie-in	提出する	submit	デイ・トレーダー	day trader
提携	tie-up	提出する	tender	定年退職者	retiree
提携相手	alliance partner	提出物	submission	低燃費の小型車	econobox
提携関係	alliance	提出物	tender	停泊	keel
提携企業	partner	提唱する	propose	低評価	devaluation
提携先	alliance partner	抵触	conflict	定評のある	well-established
提携先	partner	停職する	suspend	ディフェクト	defect
提携作業	collaborative work	低所得者層向け広告戦略	downmarketing	ディマーケティング	demarketing
提携させる	affiliate	低所得消費者の	downmarket	低迷	decline
提携者	affiliate	低所得の	downscale	低迷	difficulties
提携者	partner	定時を過ぎた	after-hours	低迷	doldrums
提携する	affiliate	ディスカウント	discount	低迷	downturn
提携する	tie up	ディスクロージャー	disclosure	低迷	drop
締結	execution	ディストリビュータ	distributor	低迷	plunge
低減	layoff	ディスプレー	display	低迷	slowdown
低減する	diminish	ディスプレー装置	display unit	低迷	slump
低減する	lay off	…を呈する	stage	低迷	stagnation
低減する	lower	訂正する	correct	低迷	underperformance
低減する	reduce	定性的な	qualitative	低迷	weakness
低減する	slash	提訴	charge	低迷した	poor
逓減する	diminish	定足数	quorum	低迷した	sluggish
抵抗	friction	停滞	deterioration	低迷した	stagnant
抵抗	opposition	停滞	inertia	低迷する	decline
低コストの	competitive	停滞	plateau	低迷する	flag
体裁	showing	停滞	stagnation	低迷する	plunge
停止	ban	停滞期	plateau	低迷する	slow down
停止	suspension	停滞した	lackluster	低迷する	suffer
提示	offer	停滞する	deteriorate	低迷する	weak
提示	presentation	停滞する	slow down	低迷する	weaken
提示	submission	停滞する	stagnate	低迷の	dull
提示案	submission	定着した	well-established	締結国	signatory
提示価格	asking price	低調	underperformance	低落する	downward
提示価格	offer price	…で手いっぱい	saddled with	出入り口	gate
提示価格	quotation	停電	cut	低利長期の	soft
提示額	offer	程度	extension	手入れ	raid
定時株主総会	AGM	程度	level	定例株主総会	AGM
定時株主総会	annual general meeting of shareholders	程度	notch	定例株主総会	annual general meeting of shareholders
定時株主総会	annual meeting	程度	rate	定例の	regular
停止する	ban	抵当	guarantee	手薄な市場	thin market
停止する	shut down	抵当	mortgage	テークアウト	takeout
		抵当	pledge	テークダウン	takedown

データ data	適合度 fit	適用する reflect
データ figure	出来事 affair	適用対象とはならない exempt
データコップ datacop	出来事 event	適用できる applicable
データ処理能力を持っている intelligent	出来事 scene	適用範囲 coverage
テキサス産軽質油 WTI	摘要を作成する brief
データの記憶場所 location	適した地位 niche	適例 specimen
データベース database	適した場所 niche	…テク -tech
データベースによる知識発見 KDD	適したものにする fit	出口 exit
データ・マイニング data mining	適所 niche	テクニカル technical
データを送信する upload	適商品質 merchantable quality	テクニカル・カレッジ tech
データを電子化した digital	敵性 competence	テクニカル要因 technicals
テーブル table	適性 vocation	テクノストレス technostress
テーマ・パーク park	適正 adequacy	テクノマート techno-mart
出遅れ株 laggard	適正価値 fair value	テクノロジー technology
出遅れる lag	適正規模にする rightsize	テクノロジカル technological
手落ち oversight	適性試験 workout	テコ leverage
手形 bill	適正市場価格 fair market value	テコ入れする reinforce
手形 draft	適正な appropriate	テコ入れをする prop up
手形 instrument	適正な due	テコの作用 leverage
手形 note	適正な fair	デコンストラクション deconstruction
手形 paper	適正 optimum
手形期間 tenor	適切性 adequacy	デコンストラクター deconstructor
手形交換 clearance	適切 applicable	デザイン design
手形交換 clearing	適切な appropriate	デザイン pattern
手形交換高 clearance	適切な due	デザイン・オートメーション DA
手形所持人 noteholder	適切な reasonable	手先 agent
手形名宛人 drawee	敵対する hostile	出先 field
手形などを譲渡できる negotiable	敵対的 hostile	デジタル digital
手形の期限が来る fall	敵対的 unfriendly	デジタル化 digitalization
手形の提示 presentation	敵対的M&A hostile takeover	デジタル著作権管理 DRM
手形の振出し drawing	敵対的な unsolicited	デジタル方式の digital
手形の振出し issue	敵対的買収 hostile takeover	手じまい clearance
手形振出人 drawer	敵対的買収者 raider	デジュアリー de jure
手紙 communication	敵対的買収に対する防衛手段 poison pill	手順 method
手紙 correspondence	手順 procedure
手紙 letter	出来高 turnover	デシル(の) decile
出来 showing	出来高 volume	手数料 charge
適応させる fit	出来高払い incentive	手数料 commission
適応させる tailor	出来高払いの仕事 piecework	手数料 fee
適応指導 orientation	適当な applicable	手数料 fine
…に適応する keep up with	出来栄え showing	手数料 premium
適応する fit	摘発する expose	手数料 rebate
適応性 adequacy	適法性 legality	デスクトップ型コンピュータ desktop
適格 competence	適法な de jure
適格特別目的事業体 QSPE	適法の due	デスクトップ型の desktop
適格な applicable	適法の legal	テスト test
適格にする qualify	適法の true	手助け helping hand
適格年金制度 approved pension scheme	てき屋 racketeer	手近の ready
摘要 brief	撤回 recall
適格の eligible	適用 application	撤回 repeal
適格の qualified	適用 implementation	撤回 withdrawal
適格の qualifying	適用可能な applicable	撤回する recall
出来具合 fit	適用業務 application	撤回する recede
適合 compliance	…が適用される govern	撤回する repeal
適合 fit	…が適用される subject to	撤回する rescind
適合させる tailor	適用される applicable	撤回する retract
適合する fit	適用除外 exemption	撤回する scrap
適合性 compatibility	適用除外の exempt	撤回する withdraw
適合性 fit	適用する apply	哲学 philosophy
適合性がある compatible	適用する implement	撤去 clearance

手付け金	consideration
手付け金	deposit
手付け金	down payment
手付け金	margin
デッサン	drawing
撤収	retreat
撤収する	retreat
…に徹する	driven
鉄製配管	pipeline
撤退	exit
撤退	withdrawal
…から撤退する	pull out of
撤退する	exit
撤退する	retire
撤退する	withdraw
でっち上げ	fabrication
でっち上げる	fabricate
手続き	procedure
手続き	proceedings
手続き	process
手続き	processing
徹底的な	in-depth
徹底的な	intensive
徹底的な	outright
鉄道会社	carrier
鉄道で運ぶ	piggyback
撤廃する	liberalize
撤廃する	scrap
手詰まり状態	stalemate
手で持てる	handheld
手取り給与	take-home pay
手取金	proceeds
手取り賃金	take-home pay
手取りで	after tax
手取りの	after-tax
出直す	reinvent
テナント	tenant
手に入れる	buy out
手に入れる	land
手に入る	going
手抜かり	negligence
手抜かり	oversight
手抜き	negligence
手の込んだ	sophisticated
デノミ	redenomination
デノミネーション	redenomination
手配	arrangement
デバイス	device
手配する	arrange
手配する	effect
手配する	organize
手はずを整える	arrange
手放す	divest
手引書	manual
デビット	debit
デビュー	debut
デビューする	debut
デファクト	de facto
デフォルト	default
デフレ	deflation

デフレーション	deflation
デフレーター	deflator
デフレの	deflationary
デフレの再燃	recurrence of deflation
デベロッパー	developer
手本	pattern
手本	role model
出前サービス	catering service
手間仕事	piecework
手間取る	delay
出回る	circulate
デマンド	demand
デメリット	diseconomy
デメリット	downside
デモ	demonstration
手持ち	hand
手持ち注文	backlog
手持ちの	ready
手持ちの受注分	orders on hand
手元	hand
デモンストレーション	demonstration
デラウエア一般会社法	Delaware Corporation Law
テリトリー	territory
デリバティブ	derivative
デルタ	delta
デルファイ法	delphi method
テレビ	television
テレビ	video
テレビ映像	television
テレビ会議	TV conference
テレビ視聴率	TV rating
テレビ受像機	television
テレビ番組編成予定表	lineup
テレビ放送	television
テレホン・サービス	answering service
テレマーケティング	telemarketing
テレマティックス	telematics
手を引く	recede
…に手を広げる	venture into
手を広げる	branch out
…店	outlet
点	way
店員	clerk
店員	salesman
店員	salespeople
転化	transformation
転嫁	shift
展開	development
展開	environment
展開	rollout
展開する	break
展開する	develop
転嫁する	impute
転嫁する	shift
転換	conversion
転換	diversion

転換	reversal
転換	rotation
転換	shift
転換	transformation
転換	turnabout
転換	turnaround
転換可能な	convertible
転換社債型新株予約権付き社債	moving strike convertible bond
転換社債型新株予約権付き社債	MSCB
転換社債の第三者割当て発行	multiple private offering
転換する	convert
転換する	divert
転換する	return
転換性のある	convertible
転換できる	convertible
転記	posting
電気	electricity
電気器具類	gadgetry
転記する	post
電気通信	telecom
電気通信	telecommunication
電気通信事業者	carrier
電気通信事業者	operator
電気通信事業者	telco
電機の	electrical
電気の	electric
電気の	electrical
電気部品	device
典型	norm
典型	paradigm
典型的な	representative
点検	check
点検	inspection
点検	workout
伝言	conveyance
伝言	message
電算化	computerization
電算化した	digital
電算化する	computerize
電算機	computer
電算機化	computerization
電算機使用	computerization
展示	demonstration
展示	display
展示	exhibition
展示	showing
電子	electron
電子化	computerization
展示会	exhibition
展示会	fair
電子機器	electronics
電子技術	electronics
電子計算機	computer
電子計算機で自動化する	computerize
電子決済	EFT
電子決済	ETF

電子工学 electronics	店頭取引の over-the-counter	問合せ reference
電子工学の e-	店頭取引ブローカーの手数料	問合せ先 reference
電子工学の electronic	markdown	問い合わせる inquire
電子式 e-	店頭の in-store	…に問う question
電子資金取引 ETF	店頭の over-the-counter	同意 accord
電子資金振替え ETF	店頭売買の over-the-counter	同意 agreement
電子市場 EM	店頭銘柄自動通報システム	同意 approval
電子証券取引ネットワーク ECN	NASDAQ	同意 consensus
電子商取引 EC	店内 floor	同意 permission
電子情報 elint	店内の in-store	同意 subscription
電子情報処理 EDP	転任 transfer	同意 understanding
展示する expose	天然ガス natural gas	同意見である unanimous
電子データ交換 EDI	天然ガス・ハイドレート NGH	同意語 equivalent
電子データ処理 EDP	天然資源の埋蔵地帯 field	同意した consent
電子的手段による digital	天然の crude	同意書 agreement
電子取引市場 EM	天然のままの crude	同意する accept
電子荷札 IC tag	転売する flip	同意する approve
電子の e-	天引き withholding	同意する arrange
電子の electronic	天引きする withhold	統一 coordination
展示品 exhibition	伝票 note	統一 integration
電子モニターによる情報収集活動	伝票 slip	同一 identity
elint	伝票 tab	同一区内の local
転写 copy	添付する attach	統一された integrated
転借する sublet	添付ファイル attachment	同一条件の like-for-like
転借人 subtenant	テンポ pace	統一商事法典 Uniform Commercial
天井 ceiling	填補 absorption	Code
天職 vocation	店舗 office	統一商品コード UPC
転職斡旋 outplacement	店舗 outlet	統一商法典 Uniform Commercial
転職者 job hopper	店舗 store	Code
転職防止のための社員に対する特別	展望 outlook	統一する integrate
優遇措置 golden handcuffs	填補する absorb	同一性 identity
転職防止優遇措置 golden	店舗の正面 storefront	統一体 entity
handcuffs	店舗レベルの in-store	統一ドル constant dollar
転職率 turnover	転用 diversion	統一トレード・シークレット法
転進 redeployment	転用 redeployment	Uniform Trade Secrets Act
電線 cable	転用価額 salvage value	同意の unanimous
転送 transfer	転用する divert	動因 agent
伝送 transmission	転落する plunge	動因 drive
転送する import	展覧 demonstration	投下 infusion
転送する transfer	展覧 exhibition	等価 parity
伝送する transmit	展覧会 exhibition	倒壊 breakdown
伝送路 line	電力 electricity	同格 parity
転貸 sublease	電力 power	動学 dynamics
転貸する sublet	電力の electric	投下した employed
伝達 communication	電力の electrical	投下資本利益率 ROI
伝達 conveyance	電話 call	投下する invest
伝達 transmission	電話会議 audiographic conference	…と同価値 equivalent to
伝達事項 message	電話会議 teleconference	…を統括する head
店頭 front end	電話交換手 operator	統括する manage
店頭 OTC	電話線 line	統括本部 headquarters
店頭 shop front	電話での顧客対応窓口業務 call	等価物 equivalent
伝統 identity	center	等価率 weighted average
伝動 transmission	電話取次ぎ代行業 answering	投函する mail
伝導 transmission	service	登記 entry
店頭株式市場 NASDAQ		登記 posting
店頭市場 OTC		登記 record
店頭市場の over-the-counter	と	登記 register
伝動装置 gear		登記 registration
店頭で storefront	問合せ inquiry	登記 registry
店頭取引市場 off-exchange	問合せ query	投機 speculation

当期 during the year	投機をする speculate	倒産 bankruptcy
当期 year under review	道具 device	倒産 collapse
騰貴 advance	道具 gear	倒産 failure
騰貴 appreciation	道具 tool	倒産 insolvency
騰貴 enhancement	道具一式 kit	動産 goods
動機 incentive	統計 data	動産 movable
動機 inducement	統計 figure	倒産した bankrupt
動議 motion	統計 results	倒産した insolvent
道義 morality	統計 statistics	倒産する collapse
道義 principle	統計 stats	倒産する fail
投機家 speculator	同系会社 associate	動産の movable
登記官 registrar	統計学 statistics	動産の personal
当期純損失 net loss	凍結させる peg	投資 capitalization
当期純利益 line	凍結する freeze	投資 exposure
当期純利益 net earnings	統合 alliance	投資 investment
当期純利益 net income	統合 consolidation	投資 spending
当期純利益 net profit	統合 formation	同時 real time
当期剰余金 net profit	統合 integration	投資家 account
登記する record	統合 merger	投資家 investor
登記する register	統合 tie-up	投資家 player
騰貴する appreciate	動向 behavior	投資家 user
道義性 morality	動向 condition	投資会社 investor
動機づけ motivation	動向 cycle	投資額 investment
投機的事業 venture	動向 development	投資家説明会 briefing
投機的な speculative	動向 dynamics	投資家説明会 roadshow
動機となる力 dynamics	動向 environment	投資家説明会を行う roadshow
当期に during the period	動向 event	投資家向け広報 investor relations
同期に during the period	動向 experience	投資家向け広報 IR
道義にかなった ethical	動向 move	投資家向け広報活動 investor relations
当期の current	動向 movement	
投機売買 gamble	動向 pattern	投資家向け広報活動 IR
当期分 current	動向 performance	投資家向け情報公開 investor relations
登記簿 register	動向 record	
登記簿 registry	動向 stream	投資家向け説明会 briefing
等級 bracket	動向 trend	投資家向け説明会 roadshow
等級 grade	統合化 dovetailing	投資家向け説明会を行う roadshow
等級 rank	統合基幹業績システム ERP	投資側 investor
等級 rate	統合基幹業務システム ERP	投資勘定 investment
等級格付け grading	統合業務システム ERP	投資金 stake
等級に分ける classify	統合計画 merger plan	投資金額 stake
等級をつける rank	統合交渉 merger talks	投資銀行 investment bank
同業異種間の horizontal	統合された integrated	投資国 investor
同業組合 trade union	統合した combined	投資顧問 asset management
同業者 competitor	統合した consolidated	投資顧問 manager
同業者 counterpart	統合する consolidate	投資顧問の advisory
同業者 interest	統合する integrate	投資事業 investment
同業者 peer	統合する merge	投資資産 investment
東京証券取引所 Tokyo Stock Exchange	同梱する bundle	投資資産 portfolio
	同梱ソフトウェア bundle	投資者 investor
東京証券取引所 TSE	踏査 exploration	当事者 counterparty
同業他社 peer	当座貸越し overdraft	当事者 party
同業他社 rival	当座借越し overdraft	投資信託 investment trust fund
同業他社に対する優位性 leadership	当座勘定 open account	投資信託 trust fund
	等差中項 arithmetic mean	投資信託基金 investment trust fund
同業同種間の vertical	洞察力 foresight	
当局 authorities	当座の current	投資する capitalize
当局 authority	当座の quick	投資する invest
当局者 official	当座比率 acid test ratio	投資する spend
当期利益 bottom line	当座預金 current account	等質の homogeneous
当期利益 current income	当座預金 current deposit	当日の same-day

同質の	homogeneous	道徳上の	ethical	同僚	peer
同日の	same-day	道徳性	morality	動力装置	power plant
同時の	simultaneous	道徳的な	ethical	登録	entry
当四半期	reporting quarter	頭取	president	登録	record
投資引上げ	disinvestment	東南アジア諸国連合	ASEAN	登録	register
投資物	investment	投入	infusion	登録	registration
投資不適格	junk	投入	injection	登録	registry
投資不適格レベル	junk territory	投入	input	登録株主	stockholder of record
同時並行的	parallel	導入	establishment	登録機関	registrar
投資見送り	disinvestment	導入	import	登録事項	registration
党首	head	導入	induction	登録事務官	registrar
党首	leader	導入	innovation	登録する	record
同種の	homogeneous	導入	installation	登録する	register
同種の	like-for-like	導入	introduction	登録物件	registration
同種の	related	導入	launch	登録簿	register
頭書	premises	導入	launching	登録簿	registry
登場	entrance	投入する	inject	道路地図	road map
東証株価指数	Tokyo Stock Price Index	投入する	invest	討論会	panel
		投入する	launch	討論会	workshop
東証株価指数	TOPIX	投入する	phase in	討論者	panelist
当初の	initial	投入する	put	討論の	forensic
投資利益	earnings	投入する	use	トークン	token
投資利益	payback	導入する	introduce	トータル物流管理	logistics
投資利益率	ROI	導入する	launch	トーホールド・パーチェス	toehold purchase
投資利益を上げるまでの期間	payback	導入する	phase in		
		当年度	year under review	都会的な	sophisticated
投じる	cast	統廃合する	consolidate	時	time
統制	control	逃避	flight	ドキュメンテーション	documentation
統制解除	decontrol	逃避先	haven		
統制経済政策	dirigism	投票	election	ドキュメント	document
統制する	regulate	投票	poll	都銀	commercial bank
統制撤廃	decontrol	投票	vote	得	percentage
当然支払われるべき	due	投票	voting	研ぐ	grind
逃走	flight	投票結果	return	得意	specialty
闘争	struggle	投票権	vote	得意客	client
同族	family	投票権行使	voting	得意客	customer
同族の	related	投票所	poll	得意先	client
統率する	manage	投票数	poll	得意先	custom
統率力	leadership	投票する	vote	得意先	customer
動態	dynamics	投票で決定する	vote	得意先	goodwill
党大会	convention	投票用紙	vote	得意先	purchaser
動態学	dynamics	同文の	duplicate	特使	courier
到達	reach	答弁する	plead	独自性	identity
到達数	reach	謄本	copy	独自性	initiative
統治	governance	謄本	duplicate	特質	attribute
統治能力	governance	謄本	tenor	特質	hallmark
到着地変更	diversion	同盟	alliance	特質	quality
盗聴する	tap	同盟関係	alliance	特集記事	feature
…の統治を委任する	mandate	同盟国	alliance	特集する	feature
…と同等	equivalent to	透明性	transparency	特殊化する	differentiate
同等	coordination	当面の	immediate	特殊技術を持った	skilled
同等	parity	動揺	instability	特殊技術を要する	skilled
同等にする	even	動揺	turmoil	特殊技能を持った	skilled
同等の	comparable	盗用する	appropriate	特殊法人	quango
同等の	even	騰落	fluctuation	特色	feature
同等の	like-for-like	騰落単位	point	…を特色にする	feature
同等物	counterpart	動力学	dynamics	特性	attribute
同等物	equivalent	等量	parity	特性	feature
道徳	ethics	…と同量	equivalent to	特性	profile
道徳	morality	同僚	colleague	特性	property

特性 quality	特別目的会社 SPC	特許証 patent
特製品 specialty	特別目的事業体 SPE	特許状 charter
独占 corner	特報 dispatch	特許請求の範囲 claim
独占 monopolization	毒薬条項 poison pill	特許相互利用契約 cross licensing agreement
独占 monopoly	特約店 outlet	
独占体 monopoly	特有の appropriate	特許の proprietary
独占企業体 monopoly	独立 independence	特許物件 patent
独占禁止の antitrust	独立型の stand-alone [standalone]	…に特許を与える charter
独占禁止法 Antimonopoly Law	独立企業間の arm's length	特許を与える license
独占事業体 monopoly	独立系 independent	取っ組み合い struggle
独占する corner	独立系発電事業者 IPP	特恵 preference
独占的 exclusive	独立国 sovereign	特恵的な preferential
独占の proprietary	独立国家共同体 CIS	特権 franchise
独占販売権 franchise	独立採算制 pay-as-you-go	特権 patent
独占販売権を与える franchise	独立採算制 self-supporting accounting system	特権株 golden share
特選品 choice		特効の sovereign
独創性 creativity	独立採算の事業部 self-funding department	突然人気が出る take off
独創力 creativity		突然の故障 glitch
独創力 initiative	独立した arm's length	突然の成功 strike
独断での unauthorized	独立した independent	どっちつかずの gray
特段の記載がないかぎり unless otherwise stated [indicated]	独立した sovereign	どっと押し寄せる flood
	独立性 independence	ドットコム dot-com
戸口 threshold	独立第三者間の arm's length	突入 plunge
特注化 customizing	独立当事者間の arm's length	突破 breakthrough
特注化する customize	独立取締役 independent director	突破する surpass
特注の customized	独立の free	突破する top
特徴 feature	独立発電事業者 IPP	突発事故 emergency
特徴 hallmark	…すると言明する committed to	突発事故 glitch
…を特徴にする feature	都市 center [centre]	トップ leading edge
特定商取引法 Specified Commercial Transactions Law	都市銀行 commercial bank	トップ top
	閉じる lock	トップ企業 front runner
特定する fix	都心部 downtown	トップダウン型の top-down
特定の場所に置く position	土台 basis	トップになる top
特定の銘柄品 brand	土台 foundation	トップの top
特定分野 niche	土台 nuts and bolts	トップランナー front runner
特定目的会社 SPC	土台 platform	届く範囲 reach
特定目的適合性 fitness for any particular purpose	土壇場 crunch	届け先 destination
	土地 land	届出 notification
特定目的への適合性 fitness for any particular purpose	土地 premises	届出書 statement
	土地, 建物および設備 property	届け出る register
特に優れた outstanding	土地価格 land price	届ける deliver
特に他の記載がないかぎり unless otherwise stated [indicated]	土地税制 land tax system	届ける send
	土地賃借権 leasehold	滞って back
特売品 leader	土地取引 land deal	ドネーション donation
特売品 loss leader	土地に立ち入る enter	ドネーションウェア donationware
特派員 correspondent	土地の local	賭博 gamble
得票 vote	土地への立ち入り entry	とび抜けた outstanding
特別検査 stress test	土地保有者 tenant	土俵 playing field
特別注文に応じて作った customized	特化する specialize	飛ぶように売れる hot
	特価の knockdown	乏しい lean
特別注文に応じて作り変える customize	特価品 bargain	乏しい poor
	突貫工事 fast track	乏しい scarce
特別の additional	特許 franchise	富 fortune
特別の extraordinary	特許 license	富 wealth
特別の unusual	特許 patent	ドミノ効果 knock-on effect
特別配当 bonus	特許技術 proprietary technology	ドメイン domain
特別配当 melon	特許権 patent	留め置き商品 layaway
特別番組 feature	特許権実施契約 license agreement	共食い cannibalism
特別引出し権 SDR	特許権使用料 license fee	…を伴う entail
特別報酬 golden parachute	特許権侵害 piracy	ドライブ drive

ドライブ・スルー店　drive-through store	取り消す　dissolve	取引先　account
トラスト　trust	取り消す　recall	取引先　client
トラスト・ファンド　trust fund	取り消す　recede	取引先　customer
トラストを規制する　antitrust	取り消す　rescind	取引先　relationship
トラッキング・ストック　tracking stock	取り消す　retract	取引される　quote
	取り消す　reverse	取引所　bourse
トラック会社　carrier	取り消す　withdraw	取引所　house
トラフィック　traffic	取り込む　attract	取引証票　voucher
トラブル　glitch	取り込む　download	取引所外取引　off-market trading
トランシュ　tranche	取り込む　import	取引数量　lot
トランスミッション　transmission	取り込む　lure	取引する　bargain
取扱い　deal	取下げ　abandonment	取引する　do business
取扱い　disposition	取り下げる　abandon	取引する　play
取扱い　handling	取り下げる　rescind	取引する　trade
取扱い　management	取締役　director	取引成立額　turnover
取扱い　transaction	取締役会　board	取引高　sales
取扱い　treatment	取締役の地位　seat	取引高　turnover
取扱い説明書　manual	取り締まる　regulate	取引高　volume
取り扱う　cover	取り出し　takeout	取引停止　suspension
取り扱う　manage	取り出す　take out	取引停止処分　suspension
鳥インフルエンザ　bird flu	取立て　collectible	取引店　correspondent
トリガー　trigger	取立て中の手形・小切手類　float	取引などをまとめる　clinch
トリガー回路　trigger	取り立てる　levy	取引の切り札　bargaining chip
取替え　replacement	取り立てる　recover	取引の収支　bottom line
取り返す　recuperate	取次ぎサービス　drop-off service	取引発生日の　historical
取り返せない　irrecoverable	取次店　distributor	取引量　traffic
取り替える　exchange	取り次ぐ　mediate	取引量の多い　active
取り替える　swap	取付け　installation	取引を拡大して利ざやを稼ぐ　pyramid
…に取り掛かろうとしている　set to	取付け　run	
取り交わす　exchange	取付け品　fittings	トリプル　triple
取決め　agreement	取り付ける　attach	トリプルA　AAA
取決め　appointment	取り付ける　furnish	取り分　cut
取決め　arrangement	取り付ける　install	取り分　takedown
取決め　bargain	取り除く　divest	取りまとめ　arrangement
取決め　deal	取り除く　set aside	取りまとめる　arrange
取決め　engagement	取り除く　take out	取戻し不能の　irrecoverable
取決め　treaty	取引　activity	取り戻す　recoup
取決め　understanding	取引　bargain	取り戻す　redress
取り決める　arrange	取引　bargaining	取り戻す　resume
取り決める　close	取引　business	度量衡　weights and measures
取り決める　fix	取引　deal	努力　effort
取り決める　negotiate	取引　dealing	努力　exercise
取り崩す　reverse	取引　exchange	努力の成果　effort
取組み　approach	取引　negotiation	トリレンマ　trilemma
取組み　commitment	取引　ring	ドル　dlrs
取組み　drive	取引　trade	ドル　dollar
取組み　effort	取引　trading	ドル相場　dollar
取組み方　approach	取引　traffic	取るに足らない　cosmetic
…に取り組む　committed to	取引　transaction	取るに足らないほどの　fractional
取り組む　commit	取引相手　counterpart	トレーサビリティ　traceability
取り組む　struggle	取引相手　counterparty	トレーダー　player
取り組む　undertake	取引相手方　counterparty	トレーディング　trading
取消し　dissolution	取引確認通知　confirmation	トレード　trade
取消し　recall	取引関係　account	トレードマーク　trademark
取消し　repeal	取引慣行　code of conduct	トレーニング　workout
取消し　reversal	取引完了　closing	トレンド　trend
取消し　withdrawal	取引銀行　creditor	トレンドセッター　trendsetter
取消し不能　noncancelable	取引金融機関　creditor	鈍化する　moderate
取り消す　cancel	取引契約　bargain	鈍化する　slow down
	取引契約　commitment	どん底　rock bottom

どん底の	rock-bottom	長引く	prolonged	軟化	weakness
どん底まで下がる	bottom out	仲間	peer	軟化する	weaken
どんでん返し	reversal	中身	mix	難関突破	breakthrough
トンネル会社	dummy company	眺め	scene	難局	difficulties
問屋	distributor	流れ	flow	難局	impasse
問屋	warehouse	流れ	movement	難題	challenge
問屋	wholesaler	流れ	process	軟着陸	soft landing
		流れ	run	軟調な	sluggish
な		流れ	stream	軟調の	soft
		流れ	trend	軟調の	vulnerable
内閣	government	流れ込み	influx	軟調の	weak
内閣改造	reshuffle	流れ作業で完成する	roll off the assembly line	難のある	irregular
内規	bylaws			軟派	
内国歳入庁	Internal Revenue Service	投げ売り	dumping	難問	challenge
		投げ売り	sell-off	難問	problem
内国歳入庁	IRS	投げ売りする	sell off		
内国歳入法	Internal Revenue Code	投げる	cast	**に**	
内国歳入法典	Internal Revenue Code	名残	legacy		
		なし崩し償却	amortization	荷揚げする	discharge
内国の	domestic	成し遂げる	effect	ニーズ	needs
内職	sideline	…になじみやすい	-friendly	ニート	NEET
内製の	in-house	ナスダック	NASDAQ	似通った	comparable
内線	extension	捺印	seal	荷為替信用状統一規則	Uniform Customs and Practice for Documentary Credits
内装	packaging	捺印契約	covenant		
内部化	internalization	捺印契約	specialty		
内部会計統制	internal accounting control	捺印証書	covenant	荷為替手形の買取り	negotiation
		捺印証書	deed	賑やかな盛り場	downtown
内部告発	whistleblowing [whistle-blowing]	捺印証書	specialty	二級品の	subprime
		捺印する	seal	二桁台の	double-digit
内部告発者	whistleblower [whistle-blower]	捺印する	stamp	二元的所得課税方式	two-track income taxation system
		納得診察	informed consent		
内部者	insider	7か国蔵相会議	G7	二元的な	dual
内部者取引	insider trading	ナノ技術	nanotechnology	二酸化炭素	carbon dioxide
内部情報	tip	ナノテク	nanotechnology	二酸化炭素の回収・貯留	CCS
内部成長	organic growth	ナノテク製品	nanotech product	二次的…	pass-along
内部調達	internalization	ナノテクノロジー	nanotechnology	二次的支払い義務	recourse
内部調達資金	internally generated funds	ナノメートル	nanometer	二次的請求	recourse
		ナビゲーション・システム	navigation system	二次的な	indirect
内部取引	intercompany transaction			二次的な	secondary
		ナフサ	naphtha	二次的な	subordinate
内部の	in-house	名前	name	二重為替相場	dual exchange rate
内部の	intercompany	…の名前を挙げる	name	二重相場	dual exchange rate
内部の	internal	生の	raw	二重相場制	dual exchange rate
内部利益	intercompany profit	波	trend	二重取り	double dip
内部留保	retained earnings	並数	mode	二重の	double
内部留保利益	undistributed earnings	滑らかな	seamless	二重の	dual
		並ぶ	rank	二重の収入	double dip
内密	confidence	並べる	order	二重払い	double dip
内容	matter	…になりやすい	vulnerable	24時間営業	round-the-clock service
内容	mix	成り行き	event		
内容	quality	成り行き	run	偽の	fake
内容の特定	disclosure	生業	vocation	偽の	false
内容見本	prospectus	…になる	experience	偽ブランド品	counterfeit brand product
直す	fix	…になる予定の	prospective		
長い	long	なれ合い	collusion	偽物の	fake
仲卸業者	middleman	ナレッジ	knowledge	日銀の剰余金	net income
仲買	brokerage	ナレッジ・エンジニア	KE	日時	date
仲買業	brokerage	ナレッジ統括役員	CKO	日常業務	daily business
仲買人	middleman	ナレッジ・マネジメント	KM	日常業務	routine
中だるみ	doldrums	名を挙げる	list	日常の	daily

日米財界人会議	Japan-U.S. Business Conference	入荷高	receipt	任意償還プレミアム	call premium
日用雑貨・食料品店	grocery store	入漁料	fishing fee	任意の	discretionary
日用品	commodity	入庫	warehousing	任意の	free
日量…バレル	bpd	入港	keel	任意の	gratis
日録	journal	入港禁止	embargo	任意の	random
日課	routine	入国	entry	任意の	voluntary
日刊の	daily	入札	auction	認可	approval
日記	journal	入札	bid	認可	authorization
荷造り	packaging	入札	bidding	認可	license
日経平均	Nikkei index	入札	issuance	認可	licensing
日経平均株価	Nikkei index	入札	offering	認可	permission
日産…バレル	bpd	入札	tender	認可	permit
日誌	journal	入札業者	bidder	認可	recognition
日商連	Japan Independent Stores Association	入札参加企業	bidder	認可者	licenser
		入札者	bidder	認可する	approve
ニッチ	niche	入札書	tender	認可する	authorize
日中の	intraday	入札する	tender	認可する	clear
日程	timeline	入札談合	bid-rigging	認可する	recognize
		入札の付け値	bid	認可薬品	ethical
日本経済団体連合会	Japan Business Federation	入質	hock	認可を与える	license
日本経団連	Japan Business Federation	入質	pawn	認可を受けた者	licensee
		入質	pledge	人気	sentiment
日本商工会議所	Japan Chamber of Commerce and Industry	入質する	pledge	人気のある	hot
		入社	entrance	人間環境工学	ergonomics
日本商店連盟	Japan Independent Stores Association	入社	induction	人間工学	ergonomics
		入手	procurement	人間的	human
日本消費者協会	Japan Consumers' Association	入手可能な	available	人間の	human
		入手経路	pipeline	認識	idea
日本農林規格	Japanese Agricultural Standards	入手する	access	認識	knowledge
		入手する	gain	認識	notice
日本弁護士連合会	Japan Federation of Bar Associations	入手する	obtain	認識	realization
		入手する	possess	認識	recognition
日本貿易振興機構	Japan External Trade Organization	入手する	procure	認識する	recognize
		入手できる	going	認証	authentication
二等分する	halve	入場	admission	認証	confirmation
二度の下降	double dip	入場	entrance	認証する	certify
二度の下落	double dip	入場	entry	人数	strength
荷主	owner	入場者	gate	認知	recognition
二の次	back burner	入場者数	footfall	認定	authorize
2倍になる	double	入場者数	gate	認定	establishment
2倍の	double	入場料	admission	認定	recognition
鈍い	dull	入場料	fee	認定する	certify
荷札	label	入場料	gate	認定する	establish
荷札	tag	入場料総額	gate	認定する	recognize
日本型レバレッジド・リース(JLL)方式による資金調達	JLL financing	ニュース	information	任務	brief
		ニュースキャスター	anchorman	任務	challenge
日本の合同会社	LLC	ニュースソース	source(s)	任務	charge
荷役	handling	ニューズレター	newsletter	任務	commission
荷役口	port	ニュートラル	neutral	任務	concern
入会	admission	入門書	manual	任務	duty
入用	want	任務	function
入会	entrance	ニューヨーク商業取引所	NYMEX	任務	job
入会	entry	ニューヨーク証券取引所	NYSE	任務	mission
入会	induction	入力	entry	任務	office
入会金	fee	入力	input	任務	post
入会金	footing	入力する	enter	任務	task
入会する	enter	二流の	secondary	任務報告	debriefing
入荷期間	lead time	二流の	second-tier	…の任務を果たす	serve
入学	admission	…に荷を積む	load	任命	appointment
入学許可	admission	任意償還	call	任命	commission

任命					
任命	posting	ネットで	online		meeting of shareholders
任命書	commission	ネット取引	Net trading	年次株主総会	annual meeting
任命する	appoint	ネット配信	Net distribution	年次決算	annual accounts settlement
任命する	assign	ネット販売	Net trading		
任命する	name	ネットワーキング	networking	年次決算報告書	annual report
		ネットワーク	network	年次社員総会	AGM
		ネットワーク化	networking	年次社員総会	annual general meeting of shareholders
ぬ		ネットワーク構成	network configuration		
抜け目のない	savvy	ネットワーク作り	networking	年次総会	annual meeting
布地	fabric	ネットワーク利用料金	access charge	年次の	annual
				年次報告書	annual report
ね		熱の	thermal	年初	BOY
		熱波	heat wave	年初から現在までの	YTD
値上がり	advance	根抵当	fixed collateral	年数	life
値上がり	hike	値入れ	markup	年数	period
値上がり益	capital gain	値入れ率	markup	年数調べ	aging
値上がりする	advance	値引き	allowance	年代物の	obsolete
値上がり銘柄	winner	値引き	cut	年長	seniority
値上げ	hike	値引きする	take off	年度	calendar year
値上げ	markup	ねらい	idea	年度	FY
値上げ	raising	ねらい	object	年度	period
値洗い	mark-to-market	狙う	target	年度	year
値洗いする	mark to market	…に狙われやすい	vulnerable	年度	yr
値洗いする	value	練り直し	makeover	年度間差額	timing differences
値入れ額	markup	…の値を付ける	fetch	年度末	end
値動き	performance	値を付ける	quote	年度末	year end
ネーム	name	年	year	年度末	yearend
ネガティブ	negative	年	yr	年に1度の	yearly
値切る	haggle	年1回の	annual	年賦金	annuity
値崩れ	slide	年2回の	biannual	年賦償還	amortization
ネゴシエーション	negotiation	年4回	quarterly	年報	annual report
値下がり確率	risk	年4回の	quarterly	年報	newsletter
値下がり株	loser	年換算	annualized terms [basis]	年俸制	annual salary system
値下がり銘柄	loser	年換算の	annualized	年末	year end
値下げ	markdown	年間の	annual	年末	yearend
値下げする	downscale	年間の	during the year	年利	per annum rate
値下げ幅	markdown	年間の	yearly	年率	annualized rate
値段	figure	年間フレックス制	flexyear	年率	annualized terms [basis]
値段	price	年間フレックス・タイム制	flexyear	年率換算	annualized terms [basis]
値段	rate	年金	annuity	年率換算の	annualized
値段[相場]をいう	quote	年金	benefit	年率の	annualized
値段の安い	economic	年金	pension	燃料	feed
値段を決める	price	年金	savings	燃料	fuel
値段をつける	price	年金受給権者	annuitant	燃料電池	fuel cell
熱意	energy	年金受給者	annuitant	年齢調べ	aging
値付け	pricing	年金受給者	pensioner		
値付け	quote	年金受給者	retiree	**の**	
…に熱心な	-minded	年金受領権	annuity		
捏造	fabrication	年金数理計算上の	actuarial	納期	lead time
捏造する	fabricate	年金数理上の	actuarial	農業	agriculture
捏造する	fake	年金数理人	actuary	農業関連産業	agribusiness
捏造する	falsify	年金生活者	pensioner	農業技術	agrotechnology
熱中	spree	年金生活者	retiree	農業経営	agronomics
ネット	Internet	年金保険制度	annuity	農業経済学	agronomics
ネット	net	年功	seniority	農業信用局	Farm Credit Administration
ネット関連企業	dot-com	年功序列	seniority		
ネット・キャシュ	net cash	年間営業報告書	annual report	農業大国	agri-power
ネット上で	online	年次株主総会	AGM	農業の	agricultural
ネット上の情報通信網	Web	年次株主総会	annual general	農耕地	land
ネット接続会社	provider			農産物	agricultural

納税額	tax expense	伸び	growth	パートナーシップ定款	articles of partnership
納税額	tax liability	伸び	improvement	バード法	Byrd Amendment
納税申告	tax return	伸び	increase	パート法	PERT
納税申告書	tax return	伸び	pace	ハードランディング	hard landing
納税の返還	tax refund	伸び	pickup	ハーバー	harbor
農地	land	伸び	rise	バーン・レート	burn rate
納入	delivery	伸び悩み	plateau	パイ	pie
納入	payment	伸び悩み	pressure	廃案にする	scrap
納入期間	delivery interval	伸び悩みの	flat	灰色の	gray
納入業者	supplier	伸び悩みの	lackluster	灰色の	neutral
納入業者	vendor	伸び悩みの	poor	ハイエンド	high-end
納入する	deliver	伸び悩む	level off	バイオインフォマティクス	bioinformatics
納入する	sell	伸び率	growth	バイオエンジニアリング	bioengineering
ノウハウ	expertise	伸びる	grow	バイオテクノロジー	biotechnology
ノウハウ	knowhow	伸びる	increase	パイオニア	pioneer
納品	delivery	伸びる	rise	バイオ燃料	biofuel
納品引受書	confirmation	ノベルティ	novelty	バイオマス	biomass
納付金	contribution	上り	upstream	バイオメトリクス	biometrics
納付金	fee	乗り換える	roll over	売価	market price
納付する	contribute	乗り換える	swap	売価	retail
農法	agriculture	乗り換える	transship	媒介	medium
能率	efficiency	乗り切る	manage	媒介物	vehicle
能率化	streamlining	乗り越える	bridge	媒介変数	parameter
能率化する	streamline	…に乗り出す	venture into	排ガス	emission
能率的な	efficient	乗り出す	undertake	倍加する	double
能力	ability	乗り物	conveyance	廃家電	discarded home electronics products
能力	capability	乗り物	vehicle		
能力	capacity	ノルマ	norm	廃棄	abandonment
能力	competence	のれん	goodwill	廃棄	dissolution
能力	power			廃棄	repeal
能力	savvy	## は		廃棄	retirement
能力	skill			排気	emission
能力以上の取引をする	overtrade	刃	edge	排気ガス	emission
能力の高さ	competence	場	meeting	排気ガス	exhaust
逃れる	evade	場	opportunity	廃棄する	dissolve
軒並み	across the board	場	platform	廃棄する	quash
残り	balance	場	scene	廃棄物の投棄	dumping
残り	remainder	場	session	売却	disposal
残りの	remaining	場合	case	売却	disposition
載せる	load	…の場合にかぎって	subject to	売却	divestiture
載せる	run	パーク	park	売却	factoring
…を除いて	net of	把握する	monitor	売却	liquidation
望ましい成果を十分得るための確固たる基盤	critical mass	バーゲン	bargain	売却	sale
		バーコード	bar code	売却	sales
ノックダウン	knockdown	パーセンテージ・ポイント	percentage point	売却	sell-off
ノックダウン方式の	knockdown			売却益	proceeds
ノッチ	notch	パーセント	percent	売却先	buyer
乗っ取り	buyout	パーセント	percentage	売却収入	proceeds
乗っ取り	takeover	パーセント・ポイント	percentage point	売却する	divest
乗っ取り行為	raid			売却する	sell
乗っ取り屋	raider	パーソナル・コンピュータ	PC	売却する	sell off
乗っ取る	buy out	バーター	barter	売却する	unload
乗っ取る	take over	パーチェス	purchase	売却する	liquidate
延ばす	delay	バーチャル	virtual	売却元	vendor
延ばす	extend	ハード	hard	配給	distribution
伸ばす	bolster	パート	PERT	配給	issuance
伸ばす	create	ハードウエア	hardware	配給	marketing
伸ばす	grow	バード修正法	Byrd Amendment		
伸ばす	increase	パートナー	partner		
伸び	gain	パートナーシップ	partnership		

配給 rationing	賠償金 compensation	売買 trade
配給業者 distributor	賠償金 indemnity	売買 trading
配給する distribute	賠償金 reparation	売買 transaction
配給停止 cut	賠償責任 liability	売買可能な marketable
廃業する fold up	排除する foreclose	売買契約 bargain
背景 backdrop	配信 distribution	売買契約 commitment
背景 background	配信する distribute	売買する trade
背景 scene	倍数 multiple	売買選択権 option
背景説明 briefing	胚性幹細胞 ES cells	売買高 turnover
肺結核 consumption	胚性幹細胞 embryonic stem cells	売買取引 dealing
背後事情 background	廃絶 ban	売買報告書 confirmation
廃材価額 scrap value	敗走 flight	売買約定 commitment
廃止 repeal	配送 delivery	廃品にする scrap
廃止事業 discontinued operation	配送可能な available	配布 distribution
廃止する ax	配送する distribute	配賦 absorption
廃止する repeal	倍増する double	配賦 allocation
廃止する rescind	配属 attachment	配賦 application
敗者 loser	配属 transfer	配賦 apportionment
買収 acquisition	媒体 media	配賦 distribution
買収 bid	配達 delivery	配賦 proration
買収 buyout	配達する deliver	パイプ pipeline
買収 fix	配達人 distributor	配賦可能な applicable
買収 purchase	配達路 route	配布する circulate
買収 takeover	排他的 exclusive	配布する distribute
買収案件 bid	排他的経済水域 EEZ	配賦する absorb
買収会社 acquirer	配置 configuration	配賦する allocate
買収企業 acquirer	配置 disposition	配賦する apply
買収者 acquirer	配置 location	配賦する prorate
買収する acquire	配置替え redeployment	パイプライン pipeline
買収する bribe	配置する position	パイプライン pipeline
買収する buy	配置転換 diversion	ハイブリッド車 hybrid car
買収する buy out	配置転換 redeployment	配分 allocation
買収する fix	配置転換 relocation	配分 allotment
買収する purchase	配置転換 shift	配分 distribution
買収する take over	配置転換 transfer	配分 sharing
買収する tamper	配置転換する redeploy	配分する allocate
買収対象会社 target	配置転換する relocate	配分する apportion
買収提案 bid	配置転換する transfer	敗北 setback
買収提案 bidding	入ってくる incoming	バイヤー buyer
買収提案 takeover bid	ハイテク high technology	培養 culture
買収提案 takeover offer	ハイテク high-tech	売呼び値 offer
買収標的会社 target	ハイテクノロジー high technology	配慮 care
買収防衛策 antitakeover measure	配当 allocation	配慮 concern
買収防衛策 antitakeover method	配当 apportionment	入る enter
買収防衛策 poison pill	配当 distribution	入る take out
買収目標企業 target	配当 dividend	配列 configuration
排出 discharge	配当 payout	配列 disposition
排出 emission	配当落ち XD	パイロット pilot
排出 exhaust	配当金 cash dividend	バウチャー voucher
排出権 allowance	配当金 dividend	はかどり swing
排出権 ecoright	配当金 payout	端株 fraction
排出する exhaust	配当する apportion	端株の fractional
排出物 emission	配当を行う issue	破棄 cancelation
排出量取引制度 cap-and-trade system	背任行為 malfeasance	破棄 reversal
排出割当て allowance	売買 deal	破棄する reverse
賠償 compensation	売買 dealing	波及効果 ripple effect
賠償 indemnity	売買 market	博識の savvy
賠償 reimbursement	売買 marketing	白紙の請求書 blank bill
賠償 reparation	売買 sale	拍車をかける accelerate
	売買 sales	莫大な substantial

剥奪 divestiture	パソコン PC	発行株式数 issued shares
剥奪 forfeit	破損 breakage	発光技術 lighting technology
白馬の騎士 white knight	破損箇所 breakage	発行債 issue
博覧会 fair	破損賠償高 breakage	発行したばかりの貨幣 mint
薄利 thin margin	破損物 breakage	発行条件 scale
歯車 gear	旗 flag	発行済み outstanding
暴露する bare	パターン pattern	発行済み株式 issued shares
暴露する expose	裸の bare	発行済み株式数 issued shares
激しい keen	果たす fulfill	発行済み株式の時価総額
激しい競争 cutthroat competition	果たす perform	capitalization
激しく攻撃する hammer	働き activity	発行済み資本金 paid-in capital
激しく非難する hammer	働き agency	発行する float
ハゲタカ・ファンド vulture fund	働き function	発行する issue
パケット packet	働き口 job	発行する offer
パケット単位に区切る packet	働き手 worker	発行する publish
励み incentive	働く function	発行する sell
励み stimulus	働く serve	発行体 borrower
派遣 dispatch	働く work	発行体 name
派遣 posting	破綻 collapse	発光ダイオード LED
派遣社員 temporary employee	破綻 failure	発光ダイオード light-emitting
派遣する dispatch	破綻 insolvency	diode
バザー fair	破綻した bankrupt	発行登録 shelf registration
ハザード hazard	破綻した insolvent	発行人 issuer
はさみ込み広告 insert	破綻者 bankrupt	発行日取引の when-issued
破産 bankruptcy	破綻する collapse	発行部数 issue
破産 failure	破綻する fail	発行前取引 premarket trading
破産 liquidation	8か国蔵相会議 G8	発行目論見書 prospectus
破産管財人 trustee	発案 idea	パッシブ passive
破産した bankrupt	発案 initiative	発射 blastoff
破産した broke	発議 initiative	発射 discharge
破産者 bankrupt	発議 motion	発射する trigger
破産者 insolvent	発揮する exercise	発祥地 home
破産する bust	はっきりした outright	発信者番号 ID
破産する fail	罰金 fine	発信者番号 identification
破産する fold up	罰金 forfeit	罰する punish
破産する liquidate	罰金 forfeiture	発生 accrual
破産宣告を受けた者 bankrupt	罰金 penalty	発生 generation
破産手続き bankruptcy	ハッキング hacking	発生 origination
初め inception	パッキング packing	…発生器 generator
初めての maiden	バックアップ backup	発生させる create
初めの initial	バックアップ機能 backup	発生させる import
始める set up	バックイン back-in	発生させる incur
始める start	バックエンド back end	発生事項 event
場所 land	バックグラウンド background	発生済み利息 accrued interest
場所 location	バック・ナンバー back number	発生する accrue
場所 place	バック・リベート kickback	発生する generate
場所 platform	バックログ backlog	発生する provide
場所 scene	パッケージ package	発生利息 accrued interest
場所 slot	パッケージング packaging	発生率 incidence
場所 spot	発見 strike	発想 idea
パス・アロングの pass-along	発言権 floor	発送 dispatch
端数の fractional	発効 effect	発送 shipment
バス会社 carrier	発行 issuance	発送する dispatch
はずみ momentum	発行 issue	発送する ship
はずみをつける pick up	発行 offering	罰則 penalty
派生商品 derivative	発行 sale	発達 sophistication
派生的 subordinate	初公開 rollout	発達した advanced
派生的な secondary	初公開する roll out	発注から納品までの期間 lead time
派生物 derivative	初公開する unveil	発注者 owner
派生物質 derivative	発行価額 offer price	発注する order

発展	advance	パテント	patent	バルディーズの原則	Valdez principles
発展	boost	歯止め効果	ratchet effect	バレル	barrel
発展	development	歯止めをかける	contain	ハロー効果	halo effect
発展	making	花形	center [centre]	パワー	power
発展	progress	鼻薬	sweetener	パワー・ゲーム	power game
発展	success	話し合い	talks	班	team
発電	generation	跳ね上がる	leap	番	size
発電	power generation	跳ね上がる	skyrocket	範囲	coverage
発電機	generator	跳ね返る	rebound	範囲	domain
発展させる	develop	パネラー	panelist	範囲	extension
発展させる	improve	パネリスト	panelist	範囲	horizon
発電所	power plant	パネル	panel	範囲	range
発電所	powerhouse	幅	level	範囲	scope
発展する	advance	幅	range	範囲	zone
発展する	grow	幅広い	comprehensive	範囲外	below the line
発電設備	power plant	ハブ	hub	範囲内	above the line
発電装置	power plant	パフォーマンス	performance	繁栄	fortune
発展途上国	LDC	…よりパフォーマンスが悪い	underperform	反映させる	reflect
発電の	electric			反映する	reflect
発電用風車の列	wind farm	パブリシティー	publicity	繁華街	center [centre]
発電容量	capacity	パブリック・プライベート・パートナーシップ	PPP	繁華街	downtown
初登場	debut			半額にする	halve
初登場する	debut	バブル	bubble	半期	half
発動する	trigger	破片	fraction	半期	half year
初値を付ける	open	場面	scene	半期の	half-yearly
発売	debut	場面	situation	半期の	interim
発売	introduction	速さ	pace	反響	feedback
発売	launching	速さ	velocity	反響	reaction
発売	rollout	払込み	payment	番組	content
発売する	debut	払込み資本	paid-in capital	番組	program
発売する	introduce	払込み資本金	paid-in capital	番組提供者	sponsor
発売する	launch	払込み請求	call	番組の内容	content
発売する	release	払込み猶予期間	grace period	番組編成	programing
発売する	roll out	払い込む	contribute	反撃	opposition
発売する	ship	払戻し	payoff	判決	action
発表	announcement	払戻し	rebate	判決	decision
発表	launch	払戻し	refund	判決	determination
発表	launching	払戻し	refunding	判決	judgment
発表	presentation	払戻し	reimbursement	判決	ruling
発表	rollout	払戻し	repayment	判決する	decide
発表する	announce	払戻し	withdrawal	判決を下す	decide
発表する	bare	払い戻す	refund	半券	stub
発表する	come up with	払い戻す	repay	版権	copyright
発表する	declare	ハラスメント	harassment	半減させる	halve
発表する	disclose	パラダイム	paradigm	版権所有の	copyright
発表する	issue	ばらにする	break	版権を取得する	copyright
発表する	provide	パラメーター	parameter	犯行	fact
発表する	release	パラレル	parallel	番号持ち運び制度	Mobile Number Portability (MNP) system
発表する	reveal	バランス	balance		
発表する	roll out	バランス	proportion	万国の	universal
発表する	unveil	バランス・シート	balance sheet	犯罪資金の洗濯	laundering
発表の場	outlet	バランスト・スコアカード	balanced scorecard	反射的な	automatic
発病率	incidence			繁盛している	brisk
初舞台	maiden	波乱要因	uncertainty	半数所有会社	associate
発砲する	trigger	バリア	barrier	半製品	semifinished goods
抜本的改革	shake-up	張り合う	compete	半製品	semimanufactured goods
抜本的改組	shake-up	パリ・クラブ	Paris Club	ハンセン指数	Hang Seng index
発明	origination	パリティー	parity	販促キャンペーン	campaign
発明する	originate	バリュー	value		
発明の開示	disclosure	パルシング	pulsing	反則金	penalty

反対 opposition	販売業者 vendor	P&A方式 P&A
反対の negative	販売区域 territory	PFI方式 PFI
反対の reverse	販売権 dealership	BOO方式 BOO
判断 assessment	販売後サービス after-sales service	ビークル vehicle
判断 attitude	販売後の保証・修理 aftercare	PDCAサイクル PDCA cycle
判断 award	販売先 placement	ヒート・アイランド現象 heat island phenomenon
判断 decision	販売奨励金 incentive	
判断 determination	販売奨励金 push money	BBレシオ book-to-bill ratio
判断 estimate	販売スタッフ salespeople	冷え込み downturn
判断 judgment	販売する distribute	冷え込んだ weak
判断 opinion	販売する market	被害 damage
判断 ruling	販売する offer	被解雇者 redundancy
判断する assess	販売する provide	控え stub
判断する decide	販売する release	控えの duplicate
判断する determine	販売する sell	控えの standby
判断する evaluate	販売促進 promotion	控えめに売り込む undersell
判断する gauge	販売促進員 marketer	比較可能な comparable
反ダンピング antidumping	販売促進運動 campaign	比較対象 proxy
判断力 judgment	販売促進活動 promotion	非課税の nontaxable
範疇 category	販売促進担当者 merchandiser	非課税の tax free
番付け ranking	販売促進のための promotional	非課税の tax-exempt
判定 decision	販売促進用の promotional	光コンピュータ optical computer
判定 evaluation	販売代理店 distributor	光磁気ディスク optical magnetic disk
判定 resolution	販売高 volume	
判定 ruling	販売妥当期限 sell-by date	光の解像 resolution
判定する decide	販売地域 territory	光ファイバー技術 fiber optics
反転 reversal	販売手数料 load	光ファイバー fiber optics
反騰 rally	販売店 dealer	光ファイバー optical fiber
反動 reaction	販売店 dealership	被監査会社 client
反騰する rally	販売店 distributor	悲観的な negative
半導体 chip	販売人 seller	悲観的な見方の bearish
半導体 semiconductor	販売費および一般管理費 SG&A	非関連会社の unaffiliated
半導体製造業者 chipmaker	販売領域 territory	非関連の unaffiliated
半導体メーカー chipmaker	販売路 route	引合い inquiry
ハンドセット handset	販売を禁止する freeze	引合書 inquiry
反トラストの antitrust	販売を促進する promote	引き合う pay off
ハンドリング handling	反発 opposition	引上げ hike
バンドリング bundling	反発 pressure	引上げ increase
反応 feedback	反発 rally	引上げ upgrading
反応 reaction	反発 reaction	引揚げ salvage
反応 response	反発 rebound	引き上げる boost
万能細胞 embryonic stem cells	反発する rebound	引き上げる increase
万能細胞 ES cells	パンフレット brochure	引き上げる land
万能細胞 induced pluripotent stem sell	半分 half	引き上げる raise
	半分に引き下げる halve	引き揚げる withdraw
…に反応する respond to	半分に減らす halve	引当金 accrual
販売 marketing	汎用の大型コンピュータ mainframe	引当金 allowance
販売 placement		引当金 provision
販売 retailing	反落 setback	引当金 reserve
販売 sale	氾濫 flood	引当金繰入れ provision
販売 sales	氾濫する flood	引当金繰入れ額[充当額] provision
販売 selling	判例 case	引当金計上 provision
販売員 representative	範例 paradigm	引当金を繰り入れる provision
販売員 salesman	販路 market	引当金を計上する provision
販売員 salespeople	販路 outlet	引当金を積む reserve
販売外交員 salesman		引当計上する provide
販売開始 launching	**ひ**	引き当てる set aside
販売会社 vendor		ピギーバック piggyback
販売係 salesman	日 day	…を率いる head
販売業者 dealer	PR誌 newsletter	引受け acceptance

引受け assumption	引き出す tap	company
引受け purchase	引き出す withdraw	非上場の unlisted
引受け subscription	引継ぎ assumption	被譲与者 grantee
引受け underwriting	引継ぎ takeover	秘書役 secretary
引受価格 takedown	引き継ぐ assume	ビジョナリー・カンパニー visionary
引受行 underwriter	引き継ぐ carry over	company
引受業者 sponsor	引き継ぐ take over	被信託人の fiduciary
引受業者 underwriter	引きつける attract	被推薦人 nominee
引受業務 underwriting	引取り猶予金 contango	非正規雇用者 nonregular
引受業務の依頼[委任] mandate	引き取る repossess	employee
引受拒否 dishonor	引き伸ばす defer	非製造業 nonmanufacturer
引受先 buyer	被許可者 grantee	非製造業 nonmanufacturing
引受主幹事 lead manager	非拠出 noncontributory	sector
引受証券会社 underwriter	被許諾者 grantee	非製造業者 nonmanufacturer
引受シンジケート団 syndicate	被許諾者 licensee	非製造業セクター
引受済み手形 acceptance	引渡し abandonment	nonmanufacturing sector
引受人 guarantee	引渡し delivery	非製造部門 nonmanufacturing
引受人 sponsor	引渡し surrender	sector
引受人 subscriber	引き渡す consign	非政府機関 NGO
引受け分 takedown	引き渡す deliver	非政府組織 NGO
引き受ける accept	引き渡す surrender	非政府団体 NGO
引き受ける acquire	低いほうの lower	非専属的 nonexclusive
引き受ける assume	低い利益率 thin margin	非戦略的業務部門 nonstrategic
引き受ける buy	引く戦略 pull strategy	business
引き受ける commit	ピクトグラム pictogram	非戦略的事業 nonstrategic
引き受ける incur	引くプロモーション戦略 pull	business
引き受ける purchase	promotion strategy	非戦略的事業部門 nonstrategic
引き受ける subscribe	引け close	business
引き受ける undertake	非継続事業 discontinued operation	非戦略的事業部門 nonstrategic
引き受ける underwrite	ピケ隊員 picket	division
引受けを拒絶する dishonor	秘訣 knowhow	非戦略部門 nonstrategic division
引き起こす create	否決する reject	秘蔵 hoarding
引き起こす generate	引け値 close	非相互会社化 demutualization
引き起こす incur	引ける close	非相互会社化する demutualize
引き起こす induce	飛行 flight	秘蔵する hoard
引き起こす procure	非公開会社 private company	非遡求 nonrecourse
引き起こす trigger	非公開会社 privately held	非対称デジタル加入者回線 ADSL
引落し debit	company	非対称デジタル加入者回線
引落し withdrawal	非公開の classified	asymmetrical digital subscriber
引き落とす deduct	非公開の close	line
引換券 voucher	非合法な illegal	非弾力的な inelastic
引き金 trigger	非国有化する privatize	備蓄 stockpile
…の引き金となる trigger	被雇用者の employed	備蓄品 stockpile
引き下がる retire	被実施者 licensee	非中央集権化 decentralization
引下げ cut	ビジネス business	非中核事業 noncore business
引下げ deduction	ビジネス街 downtown	非中核的事業資産 noncore assets
引下げ reduction	ビジネス活動 doing business	非中核的資産 noncore assets
引き下げる cut	ビジネス活動をする do business	日付 date
引き下げる decrease	ビジネス・チャンス opportunity	…の日付で as of
引き下げる lower	ビジネスピープル businesspeople	…の日付に as of
引き下げる reduce	ビジネス・プロセスの再設計 BPR	日付のない undated
引き下げる slash	ビジネス文書交換 EDI	日付を実際より遅らせる postdate
引き下げる trim	ビジネスマン businesspeople	引っ越し move
引き下げる write down	ビジネス・モデル BM	必死である likely
引き下げる write down	被指名者 nominee	必死になる struggle
引締め squeeze	非主力事業 noncore business	必需品 needs
引き締める squeeze	批准 confirmation	ぴったり合う fit
引出し drawer	費消 expenditure	…に匹敵する equal
引出し withdrawal	非常事態 emergency	匹敵する comparable
引き出す draw	非上場会社 privately held	ヒット hit

ヒット success	否認する reject	評価減 impairment
ビッド bid	被任命者 nominee	評価減 write-down
筆頭株主 largest shareholder	非排他的 nonexclusive	評価減 write-off
筆頭の top	日日の intraday	評価減を計上する write down
ヒット商品 hit product	日々の daily	評価下げ markdown
逼迫 pressure	備品 fittings	評価する assess
逼迫した stringent	非武装の open	評価する estimate
必要 needs	被扶養者 dependent	評価する evaluate
必要 want	碑文 table	評価する gauge
必要額 needs	疲弊させる exhaust	評価する monitor
必要最小限の basic	備忘録 agenda	評価する put
必要資金 cash requirements	秘密 confidence	評価する rank
必要条件 prerequisite	秘密 privacy	評価する record
必要条件 requirement(s)	秘密遵守[順守] confidentiality	評価する review
…を必要とする subject to	秘密性 confidentiality	評価する state
必要とする cost	秘密保持 confidence	評価する value
必要とする demand	秘密保持 confidentiality	評価増 appreciation
必要とする entail	秘密裏の behind-the-scenes	評価増 write-up
必要な条件 ingredient	秘密漏洩 giveaway	評価損 appraisal loss
必要量 needs	罷免 dismissal	評価損 latent loss
否定する reject	罷免する dismiss	評価損 write-down
否定的な negative	ひやかし客 walk-out	評価損を計上する write down
否定的な側面 downside	飛躍 takeoff	評価できる ratable
ビデオ video	百分率 percent	評価引上げ write-up
非適格年金 nonqualified plan	百分率 percentage	評価引下げ write-down
非適合品 nonconforming goods	非友好的 unfriendly	評価引下げ write-off
秘伝 knowhow	票 vote	評議員 trustee
非転換社債 nonconvertible bond	表 list	表記する list
非転換優先株式 nonconvertible preferred stock	表 listing	票決 vote
	表 table	票決権 vote
非同期転送モード ATM	費用 charge	票決する vote
1株当たり per share	費用 cost	表現形式 form
1株当たり純資産 BPS	費用 expense	病後保護 aftercare
1株当たり純資産額 BPS	費用・収益の対応 matching	表示 demonstration
1株当たり純利益 EPS	評価 appraisal	表示 designation
1株当たり純利益 net profit per share	評価 assessment	表示 disclosure
	評価 estimate	表示 display
1株当たり配当金 DPS	評価 evaluation	表示 exhibition
1株当たり利益 EPS	評価 mark	表示 label
非独占的 nonexclusive	評価 opinion	表示 labeling
…に等しい contain	評価 rating	表示 notice
等しい equal	評価 reputation	表示 presentation
人手 hand	評価 valuation	表示 reporting
人手 manpower	評価 value	表示 showing
人にやさしい技術 ergonomics	評価益 appraisal gain	標識 logo
人のまねをする follow suit	評価益 appreciation	標識 mark
人々 people	評価益 latent gain	標識 sign
…に一役買う contribute	評価益 latent profit	標識 tag
1人当たり per capita	評価益 write-up	表示期間 time frame
雛型 role model	評価替え mark-to-market	表示形式 presentation
避難 retreat	評価替え revaluation	表示する cover
避難所 harbor	評価換える value	表示する include
避難所 haven	評価替えする mark to market	表示する list
非難する accuse	評価価格 valuation	表示する present
避難場所 haven	評価額 assessment	表示する record
避難場所 safe harbor	評価額 value	表示する report
避難港 harbor	評価額を引き下げる write off	表示する represent
避難港 safe harbor	評価勘定 contra account	表示する state
ビニール plastic	評価切上げ appreciation	表示装置 display
ビニール製の plastic	評価切下げ devaluation	表示装置 display unit

表示端末装置 display	比率 proportion	ファクタリング factoring
…表示の denominated	比率 ratio	ファクタリング業者 factor
表示方法 presentation	非流動的 noncurrent	ファクト fact
標準 criterion	比例 proportion	ファクトリー・オートメーション FA
標準 level	比例した ratable	ファシリティ facility
標準 mark	比例して pro rata	ファニー・メイ Fannie Mae
標準 norm	比例配分 proration	ファブレス fabless
標準 standard	比例配分する prorate	ファミリー family
標準化 standardization	卑劣な dirty	不安 concern
標準契約 master agreement	非連結 nonconsolidated	不安 crisis
標準契約書 master agreement	非連結 offline	不安 fear
標準追遡性 traceability	非連結の unconsolidated	不安 instability
標準的な master	非連結ベースの nonconsolidated	不安 misgiving
標準的方式 norm	非連動 decoupling	不安 turmoil
表象 attribute	非連動性 decoupling	不安 uncertainty
表象 symbol	広がる widen	不安材料 concern
…を表章する represent	広げる widen	不安定 disequilibrium
費用処理する expense	広さ proportion	不安定 instability
費用処理する recognize	広場 forum	不安定性 instability
表題 title	広める circulate	不安定な uncertain
標的 mark	秘話化 encryption	不安定な variable
標的 target	品位 quality	不安定な volatile
標的にする target	品位 water	不安定要因 instability
平等な equal	敏感な quick	ファンデーション foundation
平等な fair	敏感な sensitive	ファンド fund
費用として計上する expense	品質 quality	不要因 uncertainty
費用として控除される deductible	品質 water	フィー fee
費用に計上する expense	品質管理 QC	フィージビリティ feasibility
表の作成 listing	品質管理 quality control	フィードバック feedback
評判 reputation	品質証明 hallmark	フィールド field
評判では reportedly	品質低下 deterioration	フィッシング phishing
費用負担 burden	品質保持期限 freshness date	不一致 conflict
費用便益分析 CBA	品質保証 hallmark	不一致 discrepancy
標本 sample	品質保証 QA	不一致 disparity
表明 announcement	…に品質保証印を押す hallmark	不一致 division
表明する announce	貧弱な lean	不一致 friction
表明する represent	…に便乗する piggyback	不一致 gap
表面 face	便箋 stationery	フィランソロピー philanthropy
表面 front	品のいい sophisticated	フィランソロピー活動
表面記載事項 face	品評会 fair	philanthropy
表面伝導型電子放出ディスプレー	品目 item	部員 member
SED	便覧 manual	封印 seal
表面に出ない latent		風景 scene
表面利率 coupon		封鎖 closure
評論 review	ふ	風潮 climate
開かれた open	…部 copy	風土 climate
開き disparity	部 board	風土 culture
開き gap	部 department	フード food
開き spread	部 division	ブーム boom
開く open	部 section	ブーム surge
開く set up	ファースト・フード fast food	風力 wind
平社員 rank-and-file employee	ファーム firm	風力 wind power
ピラミッド pyramid	歩合 percentage	風力発電 wind-generated
ピラミッド型組織 pyramid	歩合 rate	electricity
ピラミッド式価格[賃金]の決定	ファイアウォール firewall	風力発電施設 wind farm
pyramid	歩合制 percentage	プール pool
ピリオド period	ファイナンス finance	プールする pool
比率 measure	ファイバー光学 fiber optics	フェア fair
比率 mix	ファイル file	フェア fair
比率 percentage	ファクター factor	フェース face

フェール・セーフ fail safe	不況 downturn	副大統領 vice president
フェール・ソフト fail soft	不況 recession	復調する pick up
増えた increased	不況 slump	副頭取 veep
増える increase	不況 stagnation	副頭取 vice president
増える pick up	不況下のインフレ stagflation	副本 copy
フォーカス focus	不況期 depression	副本 counterpart
フォーミュラ formula	不況の ailing	副本 duplicate
フォーム form	部局 arm	含み益 appraisal gain
フォーメーション formation	不均衡 discrepancy	含み益 latent gain
フォーラム forum	不均衡 disequilibrium	含み益 latent profit
フォールト fault	不均衡 disparity	含み損 appraisal loss
フォロワー follower	不均衡 imbalance	含み損 latent loss
フォワード forward	副会長 veep	含みを持つ latent
付加 addition	副会長 vice president	含む contain
賦課 absorption	副学長 vice president	含む cover
賦課 assessment	副業 sideline	含む include
部下 subordinate	副業をする moonlight	服務 service
付加価値 added value	復元 reconstruction	…を含めて incl.
付加価値 value added	復元する rebuild	含めて inclusive
付加価値額 added value	復元する reconstruct	膨らませる inflate
付加価値税 VAT	複合一貫輸送 intermodal transportation system	福利厚生 welfare
付加価値の value-added		福利厚生費 fringe benefit
付加価値のある value-added	複合企業 conglomerate	副理事長 vice president
付加価値の高い value-added	複合企業体 conglomerate	袋小路 impasse
孵化期間 incubation period	復号する decode	不景気 depression
付加給付 fringe benefit	複合体 conglomerate	不景気 doldrums
賦課金 assessment	複合の composite	不景気 recession
賦課金 due	複合の compound	不景気 slump
不確実性 uncertainty	複合の multiple	不景気 stagnation
不確実な uncertain	複雑化 sophistication	不景気な slack
不確定 uncertainty	複雑な sophisticated	不景気な sluggish
不確定な uncertain	福祉 welfare	不景気な stagnant
不確定の contingent	服地 material	不景気の depressed
不確定要因 uncertainty	複式の compound	不経済 diseconomy
不確定要素 variable	複式の double	符号 code
不確定要素 X factor	複式の multiple	符号 correspondence
付加する accrue	福祉事業 welfare	符号 mark
賦課する levy	副次的な side	符号 symbol
付加税 surtax	副次的な subordinate	不公正な unfair
不活発 inertia	複写 copy	負債 borrowing
不活発な dull	複写 duplicate	負債 charge
不活発な inactive	複写する copy	負債 debit
不活発な lackluster	複写する download	負債 debt
不活発な passive	複写する fake	負債 engagement
不活発な quiet	副社長 veep	負債 gearing
不活発な slack	副社長 vice president	負債 indebtedness
不活発な sluggish	服従 compliance	負債 leverage
付加的機能 option	復職 recall	負債 liability
付加的な additional	復職 rehabilitation	負債 obligation
付加的な side	復職 replacement	不在 absence
付加料 load	復職させる reinstate	部材 element
不完全 fault	…に服する subject to	負債がある indebted
武器 hardware	複製 backup	負債額 indebtedness
不規則性 irregularity	複製 copy	負債合計 total liabilities
不規則な irregular	複製 duplicate	不採算事業 money-losing operation
普及する circulate	複製する copy	
普及率 penetration	複製の duplicate	不採算店舗 money-losing store
不況 contraction	副総裁 veep	不採算な unprofitable
不況 depression	副総裁 vice president	不採算の money-losing
不況 doldrums	副大統領 veep	負債・自己資本比率 d/e ratio

不在者	物質的な

不在者　absentee
負債総額　total liabilities
負債に陥る　incur
負債比率　gearing
負債比率　leverage
負債法　liability method
負債方式　liability method
不実表示　misstatement
節目　benchmark
不出頭　absence
不首尾　fiasco
部署　post
不祥事　irregularity
不振　doldrums
不振　downturn
不振　impasse
不振　inertia
不振　slack
不振　slump
不振　stagnation
布陣　lineup
不振で　slack
不振にする　stagnate
不振の　depressed
不振の　dull
不振の　lackluster
不振の　poor
不振の　sluggish
不振の　stagnant
不信の念　misgiving
付随して起こる　incidental
付随書　protocol
…に付随する　contingent
付随する　peripheral
付随的な　incidental
付随費用　incidentals
不正　collusion
不正　fix
不正アクセス　hacking
不正確な　false
不正行為　irregularity
不正行為　malfeasance
不正工作　bid-rigging
不正資金の出所偽装工作　laundering
不正資金の出所を隠す　launder
不正資金の洗浄　laundering
不正資金の洗浄　money laundering
不正資金を洗浄する　launder
不正侵入防止機能　firewall
不正侵入防止装置　firewall
不正操作　manipulation
不正操作する　fix
不正取引をする　tamper
不正な　dirty
不正な　false
不正な　illegal
不正な　unauthorized
不正な　unfair
不正入札　bid-rigging

不正の　corrupt
不正表示　mislabeling
不正利得　pie
不正利得　racketeering
防ぐ　defend
防ぐ　ward off
敷設　installation
敷設　mining
付箋　tag
不足　crisis
不足　deficiency
不足　deficit
不足　shortage
不足　want
付則　bylaws
不足額　balance
不足額　deficiency
不足額　deficit
不足額　shortage
不足額　shortfall
付属器具　fittings
付属させる　attach
不足している　scarce
不足重量　underweight
付属書類　schedule
付属設備　add-on equipment
付属設備　improvement
付属装置　attachment
不足高　shortage
付属定款　bylaws
付属電話機　extension
付属の　supplementary
不測の事態　contingency
不測の損害　unforeseen loss
付属品　fittings
付属部品　attachment
不足分　difference
不足分　shortfall
付属文書　attachment
不足量　shortfall
舞台　platform
舞台　scene
舞台裏の　behind-the-scenes
付帯費用　incidentals
付託　reference
二桁の　double
二桁の　double-digit
不確かな　contingent
不確かな　uncertain
再び活性化する　revive
再び膨張させる　reflate
負担　assumption
負担　burden
負担　encumbrance
負担　liability
負担　responsibility
負担額　liability
負担金　contribution
負担金　due
負担させる　charge

負担する　absorb
負担する　assume
負担する　defray
負担する　foot
負担する　incur
負担する　pay
負担能力　coverage
負担範囲　incidence
負担部分　contribution
負担分　share
不注意　negligence
部長　manager
部長　superintendent
不調の　ailing
普通株　capital stock
普通株　common share
普通株　common stock
普通株式　common share
普通株式　common stock
普通株式に帰属する純利益　net income applicable to common shares
普通株式に帰属する当期純利益　net earnings applicable to common shares
普通株式に帰属する当期純利益　net income applicable to common shares
普通株資本金　common share
普通株資本金　common stock
普通社債　straight bond
普通の　common
普通の　ordinary
物価　price
物価下落　deflation
物価下落の　deflationary
物価高騰　inflation
物価上昇　inflation
物価上昇率　inflation
物価スライド制　sliding scale system
物価スライド制　threshold
復活　renewal
復活　revival
復帰させる　reinstate
復帰する　return
ブック　book
ブックビルディング方式　book building method
ブック・ランナー　book runner
復権　rehabilitation
物件　property
復興　reconstruction
復興　recovery
復興　rehabilitation
復興　revitalization
不都合　disadvantage
復興させる　revitalize
物質　material
物質的な　material

プッシュ・プル技術	push/pull technology	浮動する	afloat	不法侵入	raid
プッシュ型サービス	push technology	不当請求	surcharge	不法侵入者	raider
プッシュ技術	push technology	浮動的な	floating	不法取引	giveaway
プッシュ戦略	push strategy	不当な	excessive	不法な	false
プッシュ販売戦略	push distribution strategy	不当な	unfair	不法な	illegal
物体	object	不当な	wrongful	不法な	wrongful
払底	shortage	不当な手数料	kickback	付保する	insure
物的	material	不動の	immovable	付保範囲	coverage
物的担保	lien	不当表示	mislabeling	付保割合条件付き保険	co-insurance
物的担保実行手続き	foreclosure	不当表示	misrepresentation	不満	complaint
物的な	physical	不透明	uncertainty	不満	grievance
プット	put	不透明性	uncertainty	踏み込み	raid
ぶっ通しで	straight	不透明な	dull	踏み倒す	bilk
プット・オプション	put	不透明な	uncertain	不明確な	uncertain
物品	commodity	不当廉売	dumping	不毛な	lean
物品	goods	不当廉売する	dump	部門	area
物品	kind	歩留まり	yield	部門	arm
物品	merchandise	船積み	shipment	部門	branch
物品税	excise	船積み	shipping	部門	category
物々交換	barter	船積み品	shipment	部門	department
物々交換する	barter	船積み量	shipment	部門	division
不釣り合い	disparity	船荷	shipment	部門	function
物理的な	physical	船荷証券	B/L	部門	operation
物流管理	logistics	船荷証券	bill of lading	部門	process
不適格な	incompetent	船荷の容積を評価する	bulk	部門	section
浮動株数	float	船で送る	ship	部門	sector
不動産	estate	負の	negative	部門	unit
不動産	premises	負の遺産	negative legacy	部門間の	intersegment
不動産	premises	負の効果	negative effect	部門の	divisional
不動産	real estate	負の側面	negative effect	部門の	functional
不動産	realty	負の投資	disinvestment	増やす	enhance
不動産開発業者	developer	負ののれん	negative goodwill	増やす	expand
不動産価格に占める負債比率	LTV	腐敗性商品	perishable goods	増やす	increase
不動産業者	realtor	腐敗性商品	perishables	富裕	wealth
不動産権設定者	grantor	不働の	idle	富裕消費者向けの	upscale
不動産権保有者	tenant	不払い	nonpayment	扶養家族	dependent
不動産権利証書	deed	不払い残業手当	unpaid overtime allowance	扶養家族	dependents
不動産・工場設備	property	不払い時間外手当	unpaid overtime allowance	浮揚させる	bolster
不動産証券	mortgage-backed security	不備	defect	浮揚させる	buoy
不動産証券化事業	mortgage-backed securities business	不備	deficiency	不要人員採用要求	featherbedding
不動産証券事業	mortgage-backed securities business	不備	disadvantage	付与する	accrue
不動産譲渡	conveyance	不備	flaw	付与する	grant
不動産使用料	rent	不必要な	gratuitous	付与する	provide
不動産担保債	mortgage bond	不平等	disparity	付与する	vest
不動産担保付き債券	debenture	部品	component	プライス	price
不動産仲介	listing	部品	fittings	フライチャイジング	franchising
不動産仲介契約	listing	部品	module	フライト	flight
不動産抵当証書担保債券	CMO	部分	component	プライバシー	privacy
不動産投資信託	REIT	部分	percentage	プライベート	private
不動産の	real	部分	proportion	プライベート・ファイナンス・イニシアチブ	PFI
不動産の立ち入り権	license	部分	section	プライベート・ブランド	private brand
不動産物件	premises	不平	complaint	プライマリー	primary
浮動して	afloat	普遍的な	universal	プライム・レート	prime rate
不当人員要求	featherbedding	不便な点	disadvantage	プラグを差し込む	plug
		不法行為	irregularity	ブラケット	bracket
		不法行為	malfeasance	プラザ合意	Plaza Accord
				プラスアルファ	plus

プラス記号　plus	振出日後　A/D [a/d]	プロ意識　professionalism
プラスチック　plastic	振り出す　draw	フロー　flow
プラスチック産業　plastics industry	振り出す　issue	ブローカー　broker
プラスチック製の　plastic	ブリッジ・バンク　bridge bank	ブローカー　brokerage
…のプラスになる　benefit	ブリッジ・ローン　bridge loan	フロート　float
プラスの　beneficial	不利な　poor	ブロードバンド　broadband
プラスの　plus	不利な　unfavorable	プロキシ　proxy
プラスの　positive	不利な影響　adverse effect	ブログ　blog
プラズマ　plasma	不利な立場　disadvantage	プロクシー　proxy
プラス要因　positive	不利な点　downside	ブログに記事を書く　blog
ブラックナイト　black knight	プリペイド　prepaid	付録の　supplementary
ブラック・マーケット　black market	振り戻す　reverse	プログラミング　programing
プラットフォーム　platform	不良　defect	プログラム　program
プラン　package	不良貸出　bad loan	プログラムの修正　fix
プラン　plan	不良貸付け　bad debt	ブログを運営する　blog
フランチャイザー　franchisor	不良貸付け　bad loan	プロ根性　professionalism
フランチャイズ　franchise	不良貸付け　loan loss	プロジェクト　project
フランチャイズ加盟店　franchisee	不良貸付け　nonperforming loan	プロセス　process
フランチャイズ契約　franchise agreement	不良貸付け　unrecoverable loan	プロダクション　production
	不良債権　bad debt	プロダクティビティ　productivity
フランチャイズ契約書　franchise agreement	不良債権　bad loan	プロダクト　product
	不良債権　impaired asset	プロダクト・ライン　line of products
フランチャイズ主宰者　franchisor	不良債権　impaired loans	
フランチャイズ本部　franchisor	不良債権　loan loss	プロトコル　protocol
ブランディング　branding	不良債権　nonperforming loan	プロトタイプ　prototype
ブランド　brand	不良債権　unrecoverable loan	プロの　professional
ブランド　label	不良債権　loan loss charge	プロバイダー　provider
プラント　plant	不良債権残高　delinquent balances	プロフィール[プロファイル]　profile
ブランド商品　brand	不良債権処理額　loan loss charge	
ブランド戦略　branding	不良債権処理損　loan loss charge	プロフィット　profit
ブランド店　brand	不良債権比率　bad loan ratio	プロフェッショナル　professional
ブランド品　brand	不良資産　impaired asset	プロポーション　figure
プラント輸出契約の注文者　owner	不良品　lemon	プロモーショナル　promotional
プランナー　planner	不良融資　bad loan	プロモーション　promotion
プランニング　planning	不慮の事故　casualty	プロモーション用具　promotools
不利　disadvantage	フリンジ・ベネフィット　fringe benefit	フロント　front
不利　downside		フロント係　clerk
フリーソフトウエア財団　FSF	プリント回路基板　card	不和　friction
フリーダイヤル　toll-free	プリント基板　card	不和　split
フリート　fleet	部類　category	不渡り　dishonor
不利益　downside	ふるいにかける　screen	不渡りとして戻ってくる　bounce
不利益　prejudice	ブルートゥース　Bluetooth	不渡りにする　dishonor
振替え　commutation	ブル・ブック　blue book	不渡りにする　float
振替え　money transfer	プル戦略　pull strategy	雰囲気　climate
振替え　reclassification	プル販売戦略　pull distribution strategy	分化　differentiation
振替え　transfer		文化　culture
振り替える　convert	振るわない　dull	分解　disintegration
振り替える　reclassify	プレーヤー　player	分解　separation
振り替える　swap	フレキシブル　flexible	分解する　resolve
振り替える　transfer	プレス　press	文化活動への貢献・寄与　mecenat
不履行　breach	プレスする　press	文化産業　pop industry
不履行の債務　delinquency	プレゼンス　presence	文化支援　mecenat
振込み　money transfer	プレゼンテーション　presentation	文化支援事業　mecenat
振込み　payment	フレックス・タイム　flextime	文化商品　cultural product
振込み　transfer	フレックスプレース　flexplace	文化商品　pop item
振込み手数料　remittance fees	プレッジ　pledge	分化する　differentiate
振り込む　transfer	フレディ・マック　Freddie Mac	分割　divestiture
プリセール　presale	プレミアム　premium	分割　division
振出人　drawer	プロ　professional	分割　separation
振出人　issuer	フロア　floor	分割　severance

分割 split	分担 quota	平価 parity
分割上の divisional	分担金 contribution	閉会 closure
分割する split	分担する share	平価切上げ appreciation
分割する split off	分担量 load	平価切上げ revaluation
分割する split up	奮闘する struggle	平価切下げ depreciation
分割発行 series	分派 wing	平均 average
分割発行される証券の1回分 tranche	分配 apportionment	平均 norm
	分配 distribution	平均売掛債権滞留日数 days sales outstanding
分割払い installment	分配 division	
分割払い購入 HP	分配 marketing	平均化する level off
分権化 decentralization	分配 sharing	平均して…になる average
分権する decentralize	分配金 dividend	…の平均値を出す average
文献調査 documentation	分売する distribute	平均の average
粉砕する grind	分配する allot	…の平均をとる average
分散 diversification	分配する distribute	平衡 equilibrium
分散 diversity	分配する share	平衡 parity
分散 variance	分布 distribution	併合 merger
分散化 diversification	分別 fraction	平衡させる even
分散する decentralize	分別 judgment	平行の parallel
分散する diversify	文房具 stationery	並行の parallel
分散投資 diversification	文面 face	米国銀行協会 ABA
分散投資して損失リスクを少なくする hedge	文面 message	米国国家規格協会 ANSI
	分野 area	米国債 U.S. Treasuries
分散投資する diversify	分野 branch	米国仲裁協会 AAA
分枝系 cloning	分野 category	米国通商代表部 USTR
分社 spinoff	分野 corner	米国法曹協会 ABA
分社化 spinoff	分野 division	米国預託証券 ADR
分社化する spin off	分野 domain	閉鎖 closing
文書 data	分野 field	閉鎖 closure
文書 document	分野 front	閉鎖会社 private company
文書 documentation	分野 niche	閉鎖式の closed-end
文書 letter	分野 scene	閉鎖する close
文書 paper	分野 sector	閉鎖する shut down
文書化 documentation	分野 territory	平日 workday
文書管理 documentation	分離 demarcation	米州開発銀行 IDB
文書業務 paperwork	分離 separation	米州機構 OAS
粉飾 window dressing	分離 spinoff	米州際通商委員会 ICC
粉飾決算 window dressing	分離する demerge	平準化する harmonize
粉飾決算する window-dress	分離する resolve	平坦化 flat
粉飾する cook books	分離する separate	閉幕 closure
粉飾する dress up	分離する sever	平面図 plan
粉飾する window-dress	分離する spin off	兵力 force
文書作成 documentation	分離する split	兵力 resource(s)
文書事務 paperwork	分離する split off	兵力 strength
文書の提供 documentation	分離独立させる split off	並列の parallel
文書の利用 documentation	分類 breakdown	ベーシス・ポイント basis point
文書を渡す serve	分類 category	ベーシス・ポイント bp
分数 fraction	分類 classification	ベーシック basic
分数の fractional	分類 distribution	ベージ・ブック beige book
分析 analysis	分類 labeling	ベース base
分析 breakdown	分類した classified	ベース basis
分析 evaluation	分類する classify	ベース pace
分析 search	分裂 disintegration	…をベースにした -based
分析 study	分裂 division	…をベースにする base
分析家 analyst	分裂 split	ベータ係数 beta
分析する monitor	分裂する split	ペーパー paper
紛争 dispute		北京 Beijing
紛争 struggle		隔たり gap
紛争解決者 troubleshooter		ペッグ peg
紛争調停人 troubleshooter	ヘアカット haircut	別計画 backup

ヘッジ hedge	変更 revision	incubation business
別紙 schedule	変更自由な open-end	ベンチャー・キャピタル venture capital
ヘッジ資金 hedge fund	変更する customize	
ヘッジ・ファンド hedge fund	変更する realign	ベンチャー資本 venture capital
別段の記載がないかぎり unless otherwise stated [indicated]	変更する shift	…偏重の -oriented
	弁護士 attorney	変動 behavior
別途資金 sinking fund	弁護士 counselor	変動 change
ヘッドハンティングする headhunt	弁護士 of counsel	変動 fluctuation
別の船に移す transship	弁護士の意見書 opinion	変動 move
別表 schedule	弁護士の鑑定 consultation	変動 movement
別方針 backup	弁護する defend	変動 shift
ベテランの savvy	弁護する plead	変動 swing
ペテン師 racketeer	返済 discharge	変動 volatility
ペナルティ penalty	返済 payback	変動が大きい volatile
ペネトレーション penetration	返済 payment	変動が激しい volatile
ベネフィット benefit	返済 refund	変動金利型抵当貸付け adjustable rate mortgage
ベビー・バスター世代 baby busters	返済 reimbursement	
ベビー・ブーマー baby boomers	返済 repayment	変動金利型抵当貸付け ARM
ヘビー・ユーザー heavy user	返済 replacement	変動しない fixed
減らす cut	返済 retirement	変動する floating
減らす decrease	弁済 payment	変動する fluctuate
減らす diminish	弁済 refund	変動する variable
減らす reduce	弁済 reimbursement	変動性 volatility
減らす slash	弁済期限 maturity	変動性が高い volatile
減る decrease	返済金 refund	変動相場制 float
ヘルス health	弁済金 refund	変動相場制である float
ヘルスケア health care	返済する pay	変動相場制に移行する float
ベルト・コンベア方式 conveyer belt system	返済する pay off	変動相場制にする float
	返済する refund	変動できる variable
ヘルプ help	返済する repay	変動率 volatility
便益 benefit	返済する retire	変動利付き転換社債 adjustable rate convertible note
便益 convenience	返済する service	
変化 change	返済する yield	編入 incorporation
変化 fluctuation	弁済する discharge	編入した incorporated
変化 movement	弁済する liquidate	返品 return
変化 shift	弁済する pay	弁明 allegation
変化 transformation	弁済する refund	便利 convenience
変化 volatility	返済遅延 delinquency	便利 user-friendly
変化がない flat	返済不能の insolvent	便利さ convenience
変革 innovation	弁償 refund	弁理人 attorney
変革 transformation	弁償 reimbursement	便利な小型機器 gadgetry
変化の shift	変身 makeover	弁論 proceedings
変換 commutation	変数 variable	弁論の forensic
変換 transformation	編成 lineup	
変換 translation	編成 set-up	**ほ**
返還 reimbursement	編成する organize	
変換可能な convertible	変遷 transition	保育 day care
変換する translate	変造する customize	保育施設 incubator facility
返還する repay	変造する fake	保育所 day-care center
返還する return	変造する falsify	保育的便益 incubator facility
便宜 convenience	変則 irregularity	ボイスメール voice mail
便宜 facility	ベンダー vendor	ポイズン・ピル poison pill
返却 replacement	ペンタゴン(五角形)経営 pentagon management	補遺の supplementary
返却 return		ポイント percentage point
返金 rebate	ベンチマーク benchmark	ポイント point
返金 repayment	ベンチャー venture	法 code
返金する repay	ベンチャー企業 start-up	法 law
変形 transformation	ベンチャー企業育成事業 incubation business	法 rule
弁護 defense		法案 bill
変更 change	ベンチャー企業支援事業	法医学の forensic

法域権限　jurisdiction	方向　way	報酬　remuneration
防衛　defense	方向性　orientation	報酬　reward
防衛策　defense	方向性　pattern	報酬　salary
防衛策　defensive measure	方向づけ　orientation	報酬制度　pay plan
防衛策を取る　defend	方向転換　about-face	法主体　entity
防衛する　defend	方向転換　turnabout	放出　emission
防衛力　defense	方向転換　turnaround	放出する　release
貿易　commerce	方向転換する　turn around	放出物　emission
貿易　trade	報告　account	放出量　emission
貿易　trading	報告　advice	報償　compensation
貿易　traffic	報告　report	報償　remuneration
貿易外収支　invisibles	報告　reporting	報償　reward
貿易外の　invisible	報告　review	報奨　incentive
貿易黒字　trade surplus	報告義務がある　responsible	報償金　compensation
貿易取引　merchandise trade	報告された　reported	報償金　rebate
貿易の　mercantile	報告四半期　reporting quarter	報奨金　award
貿易保護政策　protectionist policy	報告書　certificate	報奨金　incentive
崩壊　breakdown	報告書　letter	報奨金　premium
崩壊　collapse	報告書　newsletter	報奨金　push money
崩壊　debacle	報告書　report	報奨金　reward
崩壊　disintegration	報告書　return	報奨金　subsidy
崩壊　fall	報告書　review	褒賞金　reward
崩壊する　collapse	報告書　statement	報奨金で奨励する　incentivize
崩壊する　fall	報告書　submission	方針　basis
法外な　excessive	報告書を提出する　report	方針　initiative
法外な　exorbitant	報告する　report	方針　line
法外な　prohibitive	報告責任　accountability	方針　orientation
望外の利益　windfall	報告を求める　debrief	方針　philosophy
包括　inclusion	防護策　hedge	方針　policy
包括的　generic	方策　device	方針　principle
包括的　global	方策　instrument	方針　profile
包括的組織　umbrella	方策　measure	方針　strategy
包括的な　blanket	方策　resource(s)	方針　way
包括的な　comprehensive	方策　tactic(s)	法人　corporation
包括的な　inclusive	方式　approach	法人　firm
包括的な　umbrella	方式　basis	法人　institution
包括法　omnibus bill	方式　formula	法人格の付与　incorporation
包括法案　package	方式　method	方針決定　orientation
包含　inclusion	方式　mode	法人事業税　corporate tax
包含する　include	方式　plan	法人所得税　income tax
放棄　abandonment	方式　procedure	法人税　corporate tax
放棄　forgiveness	方式　scheme	法人税等計上額　tax expense
放棄　surrender	方式　structure	法人税等費用　tax expense
放棄　write-off	方式　style	法人組織　incorporation
法規　regulation	方式　system	…する方針だ　poised to
法規　rule	奉仕する　serve	…する方針だ　set to
放棄する　abandon	防止する　curb	方針転換　about-face
放棄する　divest	放射　radiation	法人の　corporate
放棄する　quit	放射エネルギー　radiation	法人の　incorporated
放棄する　surrender	放射性物質　radioactive materials	方針を変える　turn around
放棄する　waive	放射線　radiation	…する方針を固める　set to
放棄する　write off	放射熱　radiation	包装　package
俸給　salary	放射能　radiation	包装　packaging
防御　defense	放射能漏れ　radiation	包装　packing
防禦壁　firewall	放射能漏れ　radioactive leak	放送　air
冒険する　gamble	報酬　commission	放送　broadcasting
冒険的事業　venture	報酬　compensation	包装材料　packaging
宝庫　mint	報酬　fee	放送する　transmit
方向　channel	報酬　pay	放送番組の時間帯　slot
方向　orientation	報酬　payoff	法則　law

法廷 forum	暴落する plummet	北米自由貿易協定 NAFTA
法定休日 bank holiday	暴落する tumble	捕鯨 whaling
法定公告 legal notification	法律 act	捕鯨業 whaling
法定実効税率 effective tax rate	法律 law	保健 health
法定資本 capital stock	法律 legislation	保険 assurance
法定の legal	法律家 attorney	保険 insurance
法廷の forensic	法律行為 transaction	保険 security
法的権限 competence	法律顧問 counselor	保険案内書 prospectus
法的権限 power	法律事務 practice	保険委付 abandonment
法的効力 force	法律上の de jure	保険外交員 agent
法的措置 legal action	法律上の legal	保険会社 carrier
法的存在者 entity	法律上の訴え legal action	保険会社 insurer
法的手続き legal action	法律の legal	保険会社 underwriter
法的手続き proceedings	法律の付則 schedule	保険が付けられる insurable
法的な legal	法律文書 instrument	保険加入者 policyholder
報道 report	暴力団員 racketeer	保険業者 carrier
冒頭 opening	法令 regulation	保険業者 insurer
報道官 spokesman	飽和 saturation	保険業者 underwriter
報道機関 communications	飽和感 saturation	保険金 claim
報道機関 media	飽和させる saturate	保険金 insurance
報道機関 medium	飽和状態 saturation	保険金 premium
報道機関 press	飽和度 saturation	保険金額 insurance
暴騰した inflated	ボード board	保険契約 insurance
報道する cover	ポートフォリオ portfolio	保険契約 policy
報道する report	ボーナス bonus	保険契約者 policyholder
冒頭陳述 opening	ホーム home	保険契約する insure
報道によると reportedly	ホームページ Web site	保険契約を結ぶ insure
冒頭部分 front	ホールセール wholesale	保険計理士 actuary
法に適った de jure	保温用の thermal	保険者 carrier
報復関税 retaliatory tariffs	簿価 book value	保険者 insurer
報復措置 retaliatory measures	簿価 carrying amount	保険証券 policy
報復的な punitive	簿価 carrying value	保険条件 insurance
報復の punitive	簿価 original cost	保険証券を発行する insure
豊富な in-depth	簿外の hidden	保険証書 policy
豊富な substantial	簿外の off-balance-sheet	保険数理士 actuary
豊富な資金 ample liquidity	簿外の off-the-book	保険数理上の actuarial
方便 instrument	他に負けない keen	保険数理専門家 actuary
方法 approach	他よりすぐれる exceed	保険代理業者 underwriter
方法 method	保管 charge	保険付きの insured
方法 plan	保管 retention	保険つなぎ hedge
方法 shift	保管 storage	保険に適する insurable
方法 style	保管 warehousing	保険に入っている insured
方法 tool	保管業務 warehousing	保険の担保 coverage
方法 way	保管所 depository	保険料 contribution
泡沫 bubble	保管する file	保険料 insurance
法務官 attorney	保管する keep	保険料 premium
法務官 solicitor	補完的 supplementary	保険をかけていない bare
法務担当者 legal representative	保管人 custodian	保険をかける cover
方面 front	保管人 depository	保険をかける insure
訪問 call	保管文書 data on file	保険を付ける cover
訪問販売 solicitation	保管料 storage	保険を付ける effect
訪問販売する solicit	補強 beef-up	保険を付ける insure
暴落 collapse	補強 enhancement	保険を付ける take out
暴落 crisis	簿記用紙 tally	保険を引き受ける insure
暴落 meltdown	補強する beef up	保護 care
暴落 meltdown	補強する bolster	保護 custody
暴落 slump	補強する reinforce	保護 defense
暴落する break	補強する underpin	保護 protection
暴落する collapse	募金運動 drive	保護 umbrella
暴落する nosedive	保菌者 carrier	保護 wing

保護観察期間 probation	保証金 bond	母体 parent
保護主義 protectionism	保証金 deposit	歩調 step
保護手段 safeguard	補償金 compensation	…と歩調を合わせる keep up with
保護する defend	補償金 indemnity	発起 promotion
保護する protect	保証契約 guarantee	発起する promote
保護する(もの) protective	保証書 caution	発起人 founder
保護政策 protectionist policy	保証書 guarantee	発起人 sponsor
保護貿易主義 protectionism	保証状 guarantee	没収 forfeiture
保護貿易主義に基づく protective	保障条項 safeguard	没収された forfeit
保護貿易政策 protectionist policy	保証証書 bond	没収する forfeit
保持 holding	保証する certify	没収物 forfeit
保持 retention	保証する endorse	没収物 forfeiture
ポジション position	保証する guarantee	発端 inception
ポジション presence	保証する hallmark	発端 threshold
ポジションの再設定 repositioning	保証する insure	ホットデスキング hot-desking
保持する keep	保証する protect	ホットな hot
保持する retain	保証する seal	没入 spree
ポジティブ positive	保証する secure	没落 downfall
保釈 bail	保証する sponsor	ポテンシャル potential
保釈金 bail	保証する undertake	…を補填する make up for
保釈金 bond	補償する insure	補填する cover
保釈する bail	保証責任 warranty	補填する finance
保守 maintenance	保証人 backer	補填する redeem
補充 recruiting	保証人 caution	ボトム bottom
補充 replacement	保証人 guarantee	ボトムアップ bottom-up
募集 effort	保証人 guarantor	ボトムアップ型の bottom-up
募集 offer	保証人 insurer	ボトムアップ経営 bottom-up
募集 offering	保証人 security	骨組み framework
募集 placement	保証人 sponsor	保有 holding
募集 raising	保証人 voucher	保有 possession
募集 recruiting	保証人になる sponsor	保有 retention
募集 solicitation	保証の fiduciary	保有 stockpile
募集 wanted	保証のない unsecured	保有数 inventory
募集価格 asking price	保証保険 bond insurance	保有株 holding
募集価格 offer price	補助金 subsidy	保有株 holdings
募集価格 offering price	補助の pilot	保有株 shareholding
補充する recruit	母数 parameter	保有株 stockholding
募集する recruit	ホスト host	保有株式 portfolio
募集する solicit	ポスト post	保有株式 shareholding
募集説明会 roadshow	ホスト計算機 host computer	保有株式 stockholding
補充の supplementary	ポスト工業化 postindustrialism	保有財産 holding
保守主義 conservatism	ホスト・コンピュータ host computer	保有財産 tenement
保守する maintain	補正されていない crude	保有者 holder
保守の custodial	補正する adjust	保有する own
保証 assurance	補正する correct	保有する retain
保証 backing	保税倉庫に預けられた bonded	保有全車両 fleet
保証 bond	保税品の bonded	保有高 holdings
保証 guarantee	保全 maintenance	保有量 stockpile
保証 protection	保全 protection	ホライズン horizon
保証 security	保全する maintain	ボラティリティ volatility
保証 warranty	保全する protect	掘り drilling
保障 protection	保蔵する hoard	掘り当て strike
保障 security	補足協約 protocol	掘り下げた in-depth
補償 compensation	補足的 supplementary	ポリシー policy
補償 indemnity	保存 reserve	掘り出し物 bargain
補償 protection	保存 retention	ポリプロピレン polypropylene
補償 reimbursement	保存する keep	保留 back burner
補償 reparation	保存する save	保留 reserve
保証額 guarantee	保存品 reserve	保留 retention
保障規約 safeguard		保留する reserve

保留する withhold	マーケット・プレーヤー market player	前向きの forward-looking
ホワイト・スクワイア white squire		前渡し advance
ホワイト・ナイト white knight	マーケットメーカー marketmaker	前渡し金 advance
本格回復 full-scale recovery	マーケティング marketing	前渡し金 down payment
本格的な full-fledged	マーケティング・販売費 marketing and sales expenses	前渡しする advance
本格的な significant		前渡しの advanced
本格的な sophisticated	マーケティングおよび販売費 marketing and sales expenses	マガジン magazine
本格的な sustainable		任せる consign
本格的な回復 full-scale recovery	マーケティング研究 marketing research	任せる entrust
本拠 head office		賄う cover
本業 main business	マーケティング専門家 marketeer	巻き返し戦略 rollback strategy
本業の core	マーケティング調査 marketing research	…に巻き込まれる suffer
本拠地 home		…に巻き込まれる suffer from
本拠地 stronghold	マーケティング・リサーチ marketing research	紛らわしい misleading
本拠地占有権 franchise		まぎれもない outright
本国 home	マージン margin	マグヌソン・モス保証法 Magnuson-Moss Warranty Act
本腰を入れた full-fledged	マーチャンダイジング merchandising	
本質 identity		マグヌソン・モス連邦取引委員会修正法 Magnuson-Moss FTC Improvement Act
本質 kind	マーチャント・システム merchant system	
本社 head office		
本社 headquarters	毎季に quarterly	マクロの aggregate
本社を置く -based	毎期の terminal	負け組 loser
本職 professional	マイクロチップ製造工場 fab	負け組企業 loser
本職 specialty	埋蔵量 deposit	負ける lose
本職の professional	毎年の annual	マザーズ Mothers
本船 ship	マイナス disadvantage	摩擦 friction
本店 head office	マイナス negative territory	マシニング machining
本店 headquarters	マイナス影響 negative effect	マシン machine
本店を置く -based	マイナス基調 negative territory	マス mass
ポンド pound	マイナス効果 negative effect	マス mass
本当の objective	マイナス成長 contraction	増す enhance
ポンドの sterling	マイナスになる decline	増す gain
本人 identity	マイナスの negative	マスクワーク mask work
本人 principal	マイナスの unfavorable	マスコミ media
本人確認 identification	マイナスの営業権 negative goodwill	マスター master
本人証明技術 biometrics		マスター契約 master agreement
本人自らの personal	マイナスの投資 disinvestment	マスター契約書 master agreement
本音 bottom line	マイナス要因 drag	マスプロ mass production
ほんの bare	マイナス要因 negative	又貸し sublease
ほんの僅かの fractional	マイナス要因 negative factor	待ち期間 waiting period
本場 center [centre]	毎日の daily	待ち行列 queue
本部 franchisor	マインド sentiment	待ち時間 waiting time
本部 head office	…前 before	末期の terminal
本部 headquarters	前受金 advance	抹消 cancelation
…に本部を置く -based	前貸し advance	まったく同様の duplicate
本元 home	前貸し金 advance	末端の terminal
本物の true	前金 advance	マッチング matching
翻訳 translation	前倒しする front-load	マテリアル material
翻訳する translate	前段階 front end	的 center [centre]
本流 mainstream	…より前に起こる ante-date	まとめ役 organizer
	前の prior	まとめる conclude
ま	前払い advance	まとめる map out
	前払い prepayment	まとめる organize
マーカンタイル取引所 mercantile exchange	前払い金 advance	…に的を絞った -focused
	前払いする advance	…に的を絞る focus on
マーク mark	前払いする prepay	マニュアル manual
マークアップ markup	前払いの prepaid	マニュファクチュアリング manufacturing
マークダウン markdown	前販売 presale	
マーケット market	前日付 ante-date	…を免れない subject to
マーケット・シェア market share	前向きに proactively	免れる evade

まね copy	見送り wait and see	未償却の unamortized
マネー money	見送る forgo	未上場の unlisted
マネー・サプライ M	見落とし oversight	未承認の unauthorized
マネー・サプライ money supply	未解決の open	未使用の maiden
マネー・サプライM1 M1	未解決の outstanding	未処分利益剰余金 undistributed earnings
マネー・サプライM2 M2	未回収原価 unrecovered cost	未処理 backlog
マネー・サプライM3 M3	未回収の uncollected	未処理の outstanding
マネージャー manager	未開発の dormant	未処理の raw
マネー・マーケット money market	未開封の商品 unopened product	未処理の口座振替え backlogged money transfer
マネー・ロンダリング laundering	未開封のパッケージ unopened package	未処理部分 backlog
マネー・ロンダリング money laundering	見返り信用状の back-to-back	ミシン machine
マネー・ロンダリングをする launder	磨く grind	ミス error
招く incur	未加工の raw	水 water
マネジメント management	見方 case	水鳥湿地保全条約 Ramsar Convention
マネジメント・バイアウト management buyout	…に味方する side with	水増し株式 watered stock
マネジメント・バイアウト MBO	見切り品として処分する sell off	水増し雇用要求 featherbedding
マネジメント・バイイン MBI	見極める evaluate	水増し小切手 watered capital
マネタリー monetary	未経過の unexpired	水増し資本 watered stock
マネタリー・ベース monetary base	未決済小切手 float	ミスマッチ discrepancy
マネタリー・ベースの残高 monetary base balance	未決済取引 backlogged transaction	ミスマッチ mismatch
幻 ghost	未決済の outstanding	店 establishment
摩滅 attrition	未決算勘定 open account	未整備 defect
磨滅 obsolescence	未決算の open	店先 shop front
磨耗 attrition	未決定の open	店じまいする fold up
守る defend	未決定の outstanding	見出し headline
守る keep	未公開の重要情報 tip	満たす fulfill
守る maintain	見越し額 accrual	満たす meet
マルチ商法詐欺 pyramid scam	見越し計上する accrue	みだらな crude
丸投げする farm out	見越し項目 accrual	みだらな dirty
回す pass	見越し負債 accrued liabilities	道筋 way
回り道 diversion	見越す anticipate	ミックス mix
回れ右 about-face	見越す capitalize on	見つける come up with
満期 expiration	見込み breakdown	密告 whistleblowing [whistle-blowing]
満期 maturity	見込み expectancy	
満期一括償還型債券 bullet	見込み prospects	密告者 whistleblower [whistle-blower]
満期書替え rollover	見込み額 allowance	
満期全額一括償還 bullet	見込み薄の long	密接行進法 lockstep
満期になる expire	見込みのある likely	密接な close
満期になる mature	見込みのある prospective	密造 racketeering
満期の経過した overdue	見込む allow	…密着型の -based
満期の過ぎた due	見込む anticipate	密売 racketeering
満期を迎える expire	見込む assume	見積り appraisal
満場一致 unanimous	見込む expect	見積り estimate
慢性的な prolonged	見込む foresee	見積り expectation
マンデート mandate	未婚の maiden	見積り projection
マンデートを獲得する mandate	ミサイル関連技術規制 Missile Technology Control Regime	見積り quotation
マンパワー manpower		見積り quote
万引き shoplifting	未成工事 progress	見積り valuation
満了 expiration	未実現の unrealized	見積り価格 quotation
満了 termination	未収金 account receivable	見積り額 accrual
	未収入金 account receivable	見積り額 quotation
み	未収の uncollected	見積り給付債務 projected benefit obligation
	未収の債権 claim	
…に見合う match	未収利息 accrued interest	見積り書 estimate
ミーティング meeting	未熟な crude	見積りの estimated
	未償還の outstanding	見積もる estimate
	未償還負債 outstanding debt	見積もる expect
	未償却残高 carrying value	

見積もる project	身分証明 identity	無形の invisible
見積もる put	未分配利益 undistributed earnings	無形貿易収支 invisibles
見積もる quote	見本 pattern	無欠陥 zero defects
密約 deal	見本 sample	無欠陥運動 ZD
密輸 racketeering	見本 specimen	無欠点 zero defects
密輸商 courier	見本市 fair	無欠点運動 ZD
見通し expectation	…に見舞われる experience	無欠点運動 zero defects
見通し forecast	…に見舞われる suffer	…向けの -oriented
見通し forecasting	…に見舞われる suffer from	無効 invalidity
見通し foresight	未満了の unexpired	無効化する extinguish
見通し outlook	身元 identity	無効な null
見通し profile	身元確認 identification	無効な void
見通し projection	身元保証 reference	無効にする quash
見通し prospects	ミューチュアル mutual	無効にする repeal
見通し stream	未来志向型企業 visionary company	無効にする rescind
見通しが明るい bullish	未来志向の forward-looking	無効にする reverse
見通しが暗い bearish	未来の prospective	無作為の random
…する見通しだ poised to	未履行債務 commitment	無差別な wholesale
…する見通しだ set to	未履行の outstanding	無資格の incompetent
認められている acceptable	魅力的な fair	無視する set aside
認める accept	魅力的付加材料 sweetener	無借金の pay-as-you-go
認める claim	見分ける differentiate	矛盾 conflict
認める grant	身を引く step down	矛盾 discrepancy
認める receive	実を結ぶ pay off	矛盾する incompatible
見直し overhaul	民営化 privatization	無償還公債 irredeemable
見直し revaluation	民営会社 private company	無償還社債 irredeemable
見直し review	民営化支援金 dowries	無償給付 grant
見直し revision	民営化する privatize	無条件購入 outright purchase
見直す revamp	民営の private	無条件信用取引勘定 open account
見直す revise	民間活動団体 NGO	無条件の absolute
港 harbor	民間企業 private company	無条件の clean
港 haven	民間資金による社会資本整備 PFI	無条件の outright
港 port	民間の civil	無償資金 grant
源 source(s)	民間の commercial	無償修正 recall
見習い probation	民間の private	無償で gratis
見習い中の probationary	民事の civil	無償の free
身につける gain	民族性 identity	無償の gratuitous
ミニマム minimum	民放の commercial	無償の voluntary
未納金 arrears		無償のサービス契約 mandate
未発行株式 unissued shares	**む**	無職の jobless
未発行小切手 unissued check		無人化 robotization
未払い額見越し accrual	無意識の automatic	無人探査車 robotic rover
未払い勘定 payable	ムーディーズ Moody's Investors Service	結びつき relationship
未払い給料 back pay	ムーディーズ・インベスターズ・サービス Moody's Investors Service	結びつき tie-in
未払い金 account payable	ムーディーズ投資等級 Moody's Investment Grade	結びつき tie-up
未払い金 accrual	向かい風 adverse wind	無制限の open-end
未払い金 arrears	無額面 nonpar	無制限の wholesale
未払い債務 accrued liabilities	無関税の duty-free	無税で duty-free
未払い残高 outstanding balance	無議決権株 nonvoting share	無税の duty-free
未払い残高 outstanding debt	むきだしの bare	無税の nontaxable
未払いの deferred	無記名方式の bearer	無税の tax free
未払いの outstanding	無業者 NEET	無税の tax-exempt
未払い費用 accrual	無許可の unauthorized	無線通信 wireless communications
未払い費用 accrued liabilities	…に報いる recompense	無線通信 wireless telecommunications
未払い負債 accrued liabilities	無形財産 intangible	無線通信機器 wireless communications
未払い負債額 outstanding debt	無形の intangible	無体の intangible
未払い利息 accrued interest		無駄の unprofitable
未費消の unexpired		
身分 rank		
身分 standing		

無駄のない sophisticated	名匠 craftsman	目立った outstanding
無断欠勤 absenteeism	名称 name	目立った significant
無断での unauthorized	名称 style	目玉 flagship
無担保コール翌日物の金利 uncollateralized overnight call rate	名称 title	目玉商品 feature
	命じる mandate	目玉商品 flagship
	命じる order	目玉商品 leader
無担保債券 debenture	名人の master	目玉商品 loss leader
無担保の unsecured	名声 prestige	目玉商品にする feature
無認可添加物 banned ingredient	名声 reputation	メタル metal
無認可の unauthorized	名声 standing	メタンハイドレート methane hydrate
無能な incompetent	名声のある prestigious	
無能力の incompetent	明白な express	メッセージ message
無配当の passive	明白な patent	メッセージ posting
無報酬の gratuitous	銘文 table	メディア media
…に無防備な vulnerable	名簿 book	メディアン median
無防備の open	名簿 file	メディケア Medicare
無保証の as is, where is	名簿 list	メディケイド Medicaid
無保証の unsecured	名簿 listing	目処 prospects
無利息の passive	名簿 register	目に見えない invisible
無理やり詰め込む grind	名簿業者 name-list broker	メニュー menu
無料回収・修理 recall	命名する name	メモ memorandum
無料回収・修理する recall	名目上の front	メモランダム条項 memorandum
無料で gratis	名目上の nominal	目盛り scale
無料電話 toll-free	名目の nominal	メリット advantage
無料の free	名目ベースの nominal	メリット upside
無料の gratis	盟約 treaty	メルトダウン meltdown
無料の gratuitous	盟約書 treaty	メロン melon
	名誉 reputation	面 front
め	命令 bidding	面 level
	命令 mandate	免許 license
目新しい商品 novelty	命令 order	免許 licensing
目新しさ novelty	命令 rule	免許 permit
明確な clear	命令の mandatory	免許権保持者 licensee
明確な express	命令を出す order	免許証 permit
明確にする define	迷惑メール nuisance e-mail	免許状 letter
銘柄 brand	迷惑メール spam	免許状 license
銘柄 issue	メイン main	免許状 permit
銘柄 name	メインバンク main bank	免許手数料 license fee
銘柄 security	メインフレーム mainframe	免許保有者 licensee
銘柄 stock	メーカー factory	免許料 license fee
名義 name	メーカー industry	免許を与える license
名義書換え registration	メーカー maker	免許を受けた者 licensee
名義書換え機関 registrar	メーカー manufacturer	免除 cancelation
名義書換え代理人 registrar	メーカー producer	免除 exemption
名義貸し name lending	メーカー supplier	免除 forgiveness
名義上の nominal	メーカー vendor	免職 discharge
名義上の株式保有 nominee	メーカー特約店 dealer	免職 dismissal
名義人 nominee	メーキング making	免職 sack
名義を書き換える transfer	メーリング・リスト mailing list	免除された exempt
明言する committed to	メール mail	免除された free
名工 craftsman	メガバンク megabank	免除された機関 exempt
明細 spec	女神 fortune	免除された人 exempt
明細書 bill	目先の immediate	免除されたもの exempt
明細書 document	メザニン型の mezzanine	免除する dispense
明細書 list	目覚しい robust	免除する exempt
明細書 particulars	メジャー major	免除する forgive
明細表 schedule	目印 landmark	免除する release
明示された express	珍しい scarce	免除する remit
明示する disclose	メセナ mecenat	免除する waive
明示する state	目立つ dominant	免税 exemption

免税者	exempt
免税で	duty-free
免税の	duty-free
免税の	tax free
免税の	tax-exempt
免責	discharge
免責	exemption
面接	interview
面接法	interview
面談	interview
メンテナンス	maintenance
メンバー	member
綿密な	in-depth
綿密に計画する	map out
儲かっている	going
儲からない	unprofitable
もうかる	pay
儲かる	economic
儲かる	lucrative
儲かる	profitable
儲かる仕事	earner
設ける	create
設ける	establish
設ける	impose
設ける	locate
設ける	sponsor
申し入れ	lodgement
申込み	application
申込み	bid
申込み	bidding
申込み	offer
申込み	proposal
申込み	tender
申込みが発行数を上回った	oversubscribed
申込みが募集額を上回った	oversubscribed
申込み国	bidder
申込み者	application
申込み者	subscriber
申込者	applicant
申し込む	enter
申し込む	offer
申し込む	subscribe
申立て	allegation
申立て	case
申立て	fact
申立て	motion
申立て	showing
申立て書	demand
申し立てられた事実	fact
申し立てる	file
申し立てる	lodge
申し立てる	plead
申し立てる	present
申し出	offer
申し出る	enter

申し出る	propose
申し出る	tender
申し開き	allegation
申し分のない	optimal
網状組織	network
燃え尽き	burnout
燃え尽き症候群	burnout
モーゲージ	mortgage
モーゲージ証券	mortgage-backed security
モーゲージ担保債務証書	CMO
モーゲージ担保証券	MBS
モーゲージ担保証券	mortgage-backed security
モーゲージ・バンカーズ協会	MBA
モード	mode
モール	mall
目次	table
黙示の	implied
黙示の	tacit
目前の	immediate
目的	destination
目的	end
目的	goal
目的	object
目的	objective
目的	purpose
目的地	destination
目的地	objective
…の目的にかなう	serve
目的にぴったり合った	tailor-made
目的の	objective
目標	goal
目標	horizon
目標	mark
目標	object
目標	objective
目標	target
目標水準	target
…を目標に定める	target
目標にする	target
目標の	objective
目録	file
目録	indenture
目録	inventory
目録	list
目録	table
目論見書	prospectus
模型	model
模写する	fake
モジュール	module
模造する	fake
模造の	counterfeit
模造品	piracy
もたついている	struggling
…をもたらす	drive
…をもたらす	entail
もたらす	achieve
もたらす	earn
もたらす	net

もたらす	yield
持ち合い株	crossheld shares
持ち合い株式	crossheld shares
持ち合わせの	ready
用いる	use
持ち株	holdings
持ち株	shareholding
持ち株	stake
持ち株	stockholding
持ち株会社	holding company
持ち株会社	holdings
持ち株制度	intercorporate stockholding
持ち株比率	holding
持ち株比率	holdings
持ち株比率	ownership
持ち株比率	shareholding
持ち株比率	stake
持ち越す	carry over
持ちこたえられる	sustainable
持ち込み	introduction
持ち込む	import
持ち高	position
持ち出し	takeout
持ち出す	take out
持ち直し	rally
持ち直し	rebound
持ち直し	recovery
持ち直す	rebound
持ち場	post
持ち運びできる	portable
持ち分	equity
持ち分	interest
持ち分	quota
持ち分株	share
持ち分権	equity
持ち分資本利益率	ROE
持ち分プーリング	pooling of interest
持ち分プーリング法	pooling of interest
持ち分法適用会社	associate
モチベーション	motivation
持つ	own
目下の	immediate
最も基本的な	bare
最も重要な	main
最も重要なもの	flagship
最も代表的なもの	flagship
もてなし	entertainment
モデル	model
モデル	pattern
モデル	style
元売り	wholesaler
基近物	front end
戻し入れる	reverse
戻し関税	kickback of duty
戻し税	rebate
戻す	return
元帳	ledger

…に基づく	-based	問題解決策	solution	…にやさしい	-friendly
戻ってくる	bounce	問題解決手法	solution	安い	budget
元手	seed capital	問題点	issue	安い	competitive
元になる	master	問題のある	troubled	安い値を付ける	underbid
求める	demand	問題の多い	troubled	安く売り払う	sell off
戻り益	return	問題の核心	bottom line	安くする	downscale
戻る	return	紋様	symbol	安く入札する	underbid
モニターする	monitor			保蔵	hoarding
モニタリング	monitoring			安値	bargain-basement price
物	merchandise	**や**		安値	low
物	deal			…より安値で売る	undersell
もの言う株主	outspoken shareholder	八百長	fix	安値を付ける	plunge
物知りの	savvy	八百長をする	fix	安物の	downmarket
物の取引	merchandise trade	野外撮影場	location	やせた	lean
物の貿易	merchandise trade	夜間アルバイトをする	moonlight	家賃	rent
もの珍しさ	novelty	夜間市場	night mart	約款	clause
モノライン	monoline	夜間取引市場	night mart	約款	covenant
模範	model	焼く	burn	薬効	effectiveness
模範	paradigm	役員	director	雇い入れる	recruit
模範	pattern	役員	officer	雇い人	employee
模範生	role model	役員	official	雇い人	help
模倣	copy	役員室	boardroom	雇い主	employer
模倣者	follower	薬剤	agent	雇う	hire
模倣する	copy	約定	commitment	家主	lessor
模倣品	piracy	約定	covenant	破る	renege
もみ合い	struggle	約定	treaty	ヤミ市	black market
もみ消し	cover-up	約定条件	understanding	ヤミ金融業者	illicit loan operator
もみ消し工作	cover-up	約定品	contract	ヤミ金融業者	illicit moneylender
もみ消す	cover up	役職	appointment	ヤミ金融業者	loan shark
燃やす	burn	役職	place	ヤミ金融業者	shark
模様	device	役職	position	ヤミ市場	black market
模様	pattern	役職	title	ヤミ取引	black market
模様替え	makeover	役職員	executive	やめる	quit
模様眺め	sideline	役職員	ranking official	やめる	forgo
模様眺め	wait and see	躍進	breakthrough	病める	ailing
モラール	morale	躍進	success	やり合う	haggle
モラル	morality	躍進する	leap	やりがいのある仕事	challenge
盛り上がりのある	upbeat	約束	appointment	やり手の	savvy
盛り上がる	pick up	約束	commitment	やり取り	communication
盛り返す	rally	約束	covenant	やり取りする	exchange
盛り込む	include	約束	engagement	やり残し	backlog
…にもろい	vulnerable	約束	obligation	ヤング・アダルト	young adult
門	gate	約束	pact		
文言	clause	約束	treaty	**ゆ**	
文言	face	約束事	convention		
モンタージュの	composite	約束する	commit	優位	advantage
問題	affair	約束する	undertake	優位	edge
問題	barrier	約束手形	note	優位性	advantage
問題	case	約束不履行者	defaulter	優位性	edge
問題	concern	役得	perquisite	優位な立場	leadership
問題	crisis	役に立たない	incompetent	優位に	predominantly
問題	difficulties	…に役に立つ	-friendly	誘因	incentive
問題	issue	…の役に立つ	serve	誘因	inducement
問題	matter	役に立つ	beneficial	誘因	trigger
問題	point	役に立つ	profit	誘引する	attract
問題	problem	役に立つ	profitable	有益な	beneficial
問題	question	薬品	chemicals	有益な	healthy
問題	task	役目	function	有益な	profitable
問題解決	solution	役目を果たす	function	遊園地	park
		役割	function	有害な	negative
		焼ける	burn		

有害物質除去基金法 Superfund Act	友好的買収者 white knight	郵政事業 postal business
有価証券 securities	有効な available	優勢な dominant
有価証券担保貸付けの掛け目 haircut	有効な effective	優勢に predominantly
	有効な efficient	優先 preference
有価証券の分売 distribution	有効な useful	優先 priority
有価証券の保有状態 position	有効保存期間 shelf life	優先… preferred
有価証券報告書 annual report	有効利用 redeployment	有線 cable
有価証券報告書 portfolio	有効利用する redeploy	優先株式の発行 issuance of preferred shares
有価証券明細表 portfolio	ユーザー client	
有価証券を加えて増す sweeten	ユーザー customer	優先権 precedent
有用価値資産 valid asset	ユーザー user	優先権 preference
遊戯 game	ユーザーに親しみやすい user-friendly	優先権 priority
有機ELディスプレー organic electroluminescent screen		優先権利落ち X pr
	ユーザーに分かりやすい user-friendly	優先権を与えられた preferred
有機体の organic		優先権を持つ preferred
有機的成長 organic growth	融資 advance	優先事項 priority
有機的成長率 organic growth	融資 credit	優先順位 priority
有機的な organic	融資 exposure	優先順位が低い subordinated
有機物質の organic	融資 facility	優先順位の senior
遊休 idle	融資 finance	優先する controlling
遊休の inactive	融資 financing	優先する govern
遊休の vacant	融資 funding	優先する underlying
優遇 discrimination	融資 lending	優先的 preferred
優遇 preference	融資 loan	優先的外貨引出し権 tranche
優遇する preferential	有事 emergency	優先的選択権 option
優遇措置 advantage	有資格の eligible	優先的な preferential
有形固定資産 plant and equipment	有資格の qualified	…優先の driven
有形固定資産 property	融資行 lender	…優先の -minded
有形資産 tangibles	融資業務 lending service	…優先の -oriented
有形の material	融資金 loan facility	優先の senior
有形の tangible	融資区分 tranche	郵送係 mail
有限会社 limited liability company	融資限度 line of credit	郵送係 mailer
	融資先 borrower	郵送先名簿 mailing list
有限責任会社 LLC	融資先 commitment	郵送する mail
有限責任組合 LLP	融資先 debtor	有体動産 goods
有限責任組合 LP	融資先 loan recipient	誘致する attract
有限責任事業組合 limited liability partnership	融資先企業 borrower	誘導 induction
	融資先企業 loan recipient	誘導する engineer
有限責任事業組合 LLP	融資者 lender	誘導する induce
有限責任パートナーシップ limited liability partnership	融資承認 commitment	優等生 role model
	融資する finance	誘導目標 bellwether
有限責任パートナーシップ LLP	融資する loan	有能な efficient
融合 merger	融資総額 exposure	有能な sophisticated
友好関係を結ぶ affiliate	融資の1回分 tranche	…を誘発する trigger
有効期間 useful life	優秀 good	誘発する generate
有効求人倍率 vacancies-to-applications ratio	優秀 sophisticated	郵便 mail
	有償荷重 payload	郵便事業 postal business
有効性 availability	優勝候補 front runner	郵便制度 mail
有効性 effectiveness	有償重量 payload	郵便船 packet
有効性 efficiency	有償搭載量 payload	郵便番号 zip code
有効である force	融資枠 credit facilities	郵便物 packet
有効である run	融資枠 facility	郵便利用者 mailer
有効である stand	融資枠 loan facility	有望市場 promising market
友好的な株主 white knight	融資枠の設定 commitment line	有望な likely
友好的企業 white knight	融資を受ける borrow	有望な分野 promising area
友好的でない unfriendly	融資をする lend	有名な well-established
友好的な支援者 white knight	融通手形 kite	猶予 delay
友好的な第三者 white knight	融通のきく flexible	有用 use
友好的買収 friendly offer	優勢 advantage	有用 utility
友好的買収 friendly takeover	優勢 edge	猶予期間 grace period

有利 advantage	輸送機関 transport	要求 call
有利 upside	輸送機関 transportation	要求 challenge
有利子の interest-bearing	輸送許可書 transportation	要求 demand
…に有利な -friendly	輸送手段 transport	要求 mandate
有利な beneficial	輸送手段 vehicle	要求 needs
有利な economic	輸送する ship	要求 request
有利な favorable	輸送船団 fleet	要求 want
有利な lucrative	輸送料 transportation	要求書 request
有利な profitable	輸送料金 transportation	要求水準 norm
有利な立場 leverage	委ねる consign	要求する charge
有利な立場にある well positioned	委ねる entrust	要求する claim
有利な点 upside	委ねる pass	要求する demand
有利な取引材料 bargaining chip	委ねる put	要求する extort
ユーリボー Euribor	油田渡し価格 wellhead price	…の要求などを満たす serve
優良 quality	ユニオン union	要求にぴったり合った tailor-made
優良株 blue chip	ユニット unit	用具 tool
優良刻印 hallmark	ユニット化する unitize	用具ひと揃い kit
優良な creditworthy [credit-worthy]	ユニバーサル universal	要件 requirement(s)
優良な prime	輸入 import	擁護 defense
優良な strong	輸入する import	用語 term
優良の good	輸入製品 import	養護 day care
優良品 quality	輸入代理店 distributor	擁護する defend
有力企業 leading company	輸入品 import	溶剤 solvent
有力とされる likely	ユビキタス・コンピューティング ubiquitous computing	要旨 keynote
有力な dominant	許される allowable	用事 engagement
有力な leading	許し permission	様式 form
有力な likely	許す allow	様式 mode
幽霊 ghost		様式 pattern
ユーロ euro		様式 style
ユーロカレンシー eurocurrency		様式 way
ユーロ圏 eurozone	よい結果を生む pay off	要職 office
ユーロ債 Eurobond	よい知らせ good news	養殖 culture
ユーロダラー euro-dollars	良い面 upside	要人 keyman
ユーロダラー Xenocurrency	用意 provision	様子見 sideline
ユーロノート euronotes	…する用意[準備]ができている poised to	様子見 wait and see
ユーロボンド Eurobond	…する用意ができている set to	要する cost
ユーロマネー eurocurrency	用意する come up with	要する demand
床 floor	用意する fix	要請 request
行き悩み impasse	用意する organize	要請 solicitation
輸出 export	用意する prepare	要請書 request
輸出 shipment	用意する set aside	…するように要請する solicit
輸出国 supplier	用意する set up	要請する plead
輸出する ship	容易にする enhance	容積 bulk
輸出製品 export	容易にする facilitate	用船 freight
輸出品 export	要員 personnel	用船契約(書) charter
ゆすり blackmail	要因 agent	要素 element
ゆすり racketeer	要因 element	要素 factor
ゆすり racketeering	要因 factor	要素 ingredient
譲り受け takeover	要因 force	要素 momentum
譲受人 grantee	要因 ingredient	要素 parameter
ゆすり屋 racketeer	要因 parameter	様相 pattern
譲り渡す resign	要因 player	様相 sign
譲る yield	要因 reason	様態 form
油井 well	要因 technicals	用地 land
輸送 conveyance	要因 way	用地 location
輸送 haul	…の要因となる help	用地 site
輸送 transport	…の要因になる contribute	要注意の sensitive
輸送 transportation	容疑 allegation	要点 bottom line
輸送機関 conveyance		要点 point
		要点 thrust

用途		801			寄り付き

用途	purpose	余剰	excess	予定	plan
用途	use	余剰	redundancy	予定	program
陽動	diversion	余剰	surplus	予定	schedule
陽動作戦	diversion	余剰人員	redundancy	予定案	agenda
容認する	accept	余剰高	overage	予定給付債務	projected benefit obligation
容認できる	acceptable	余剰利益	melon		
溶媒	solvent	与信	credit	予定行動開始日	D-day
用品	equipment	与信限度額	line of credit	予定されている	due
用品	item	与信残高	exposure	予定する	anticipate
用務	engagement	与信枠	credit facilities	予定する	assume
要約書	briefing	与信枠	facility	予定通り進行しない	lag
要約する	brief	予想	assumption	予定通りに進んだ	green
要約する	resume	予想	estimate	予定の計画	scenario
予想される	prospective	予想	expectancy	予定配賦	application
預金	account	予想	expectation	予定表	agenda
預金	bank account	予想	forecast	予定表	chart
預金	banking	予想	forecasting	予定表	schedule
預金	cash	予想	outlook	予定利率	promised yield rate
預金	credit	予想	projection	余波	momentum
預金	deposit	予想	prospects	予備	backup
預金	savings	予想赤字	projected loss	予備措置の	proactive
預金額	deposit	予想される	likely	予備知識	background
預金通帳	bankcard	予想される	prospective	予備貯蔵	backlog
預金保険機構	Deposit Insurance Corporation	予想する	anticipate	予備的合意書	memorandum of understanding
		予想する	assume		
抑圧された	depressed	予想する	estimate	予備的な	preliminary
よく聞かれる質問事項とその答え FAQ		予想する	expect	呼び値	quote
		予想する	forecast	予備の	pilot
翌日返済証券担保貸付け	overnight loan	予想する	foresee	予備の	preliminary
		予想する	project	予備の	standby
翌日物	overnight loan	予想できない	incalculable	予備品	reserve
抑制	control	予想を裏切った	disappointing	呼び水	pump priming
抑制因子	disincentive	装い	outfit	呼び水経済政策	pump priming
抑制する	contain	予測	estimate	呼び水的支出政策	pump priming
抑制する	control	予測	forecast	呼び水用の財政支出	pump priming
抑制する	curb	予測	forecasting	予備目論見書	red herring
抑制する	depress	予測	outlook	呼び戻し	recall
抑制的マーケティング demarketing		予測	profile	呼び戻す	recall
		予測	projection	呼び物	feature
抑留	embargo	予測	scenario	呼び物にする	feature
余計な	unsolicited	予測給付債務	projected benefit obligation	呼び寄せる	attract
予見	forecast			余分なサービスを提供しない	no-frills
予見する	forecast	予測給付債務制度	projected benefit obligation		
予見する	foresee			余分なサービスを省いた	no-frills
予告	notice	予測数量	expectancy	予報	forecast
横の	horizontal	予測する	estimate	予報	outlook
横ばい状態	leveling off	予測する	forecast	予防手段	preventive
横ばい状態	plateau	予測する	project	予防手段	safeguard
横ばい状態になる	level off	予測単位給付	projected unit credit	予防措置	precaution
横ばい状態の	flat	予測単位年金積増し	projected unit credit	予防の	preventive
横ばいの	flat			読み込む	load
汚れた	dirty	予測変動率	volatility	読取り機	scanner
汚れのない	fair	預託	deposit	予約	appointment
横割りの	horizontal	予知	forecast	予約	subscription
予算	budget	余地	potential	(予約)購読者	subscriber
予算外支出	off-budget spending	余地	scope	予約する	book
予算に合った	budget	予知する	forecast	予約する	reserve
予算に計上する	budget	予兆	forerunner	予約する	subscribe
予算ばらまき	pump priming	…によって	per	予約取引	forward
予算を組む	earmark	予定	agenda	寄り付き	opening

拠り所 mainstay	落差 gap	リーダー性 leadership
余力 potential	落札価格 bid	リーチ reach
…による -led	楽な soft	リート REIT
…によれば per	楽にする facilitate	リード・タイム lead time
世論調査 poll	楽に儲かる soft	利益 advantage
…に弱い vulnerable	ラチェット効果 ratchet effect	利益 benefit
弱い weak	楽観的な upbeat	利益 bottom line
弱い者いじめ bullying	楽観的見方 bullish	利益 credit
弱気材料 negative	…から手を引く pull out of	利益 earning
弱気筋 bear	ラベリング labeling	利益 earnings
弱気の bear	ラベル label	利益 gain
弱気の bearish	ラベル tab	利益 income
弱気の negative	ラベルの貼付 labeling	利益 increment
弱気含みの bearish	ラベル表示 labeling	利益 interest
弱くなる weaken	ラムサール条約 Ramsar Convention	利益 melon
弱含み weakness		利益 payoff
弱含みの negative	欄外の marginal	利益 percentage
弱まる weaken	乱開発 wanton development	利益 plus
弱み weakness	ランキング ranking	利益 profit
弱める dilute	ランキング表 standing	利益 return
弱める impair	ランク rank	利益が得られる lucrative
弱める moderate	乱高下 fluctuation	利益が発生する benefit
4極通商会議 quadrilateral trade talks	乱高下 volatility	利益供与 payoff
	乱高下する fluctuate	利益剰余金 retained earnings
4倍増にする quadruple	乱高下する volatile	利益処分 below the line
4倍増になる quadruple	LAN接続ケーブル backbone	利益などを生む return
4倍にする quadruple	ランダム random	利益などを還元する recycle
4倍になる quadruple	ランド land	…の利益になる benefit
四分位数 quartile	ランドマーク landmark	利益になる pay
四分位の quartile	乱売 dumping	利益になる profit
	乱売する dump	利益の大きい lucrative
## ら	乱脈経営 irregularity	利益の分配 withdrawal
	乱脈融資 irregularity	利益配当 dividend
ライセンサー licenser		利益目当ての mercantile
ライセンシー licensee	## り	利益や価格を確定する lock in
ライセンシング licensing		利益率 margin
ライセンス license	リアクション reaction	利益率 profit margin
ライセンス供与 licensing	リアクター reactor	利益率 profitability
ライセンス供与する license	リアル real	利益率 ratio
ライセンス許諾者 grantor	リアルタイム real time	利益率 return
ライセンス許諾者 licenser	リーエン lien	利益を上げる earn
ライセンス契約 license agreement	リーガル legal	利益を与える benefit
ライセンス契約 licensing	リース lease	利益を受ける beneficial
ライセンス製品 licensed product	リース leasing	利益を生み出すもの earner
ライセンス料 license fee	リース rental	利益を生む profitable
ライバル competition	リース契約 lease	利益を得る benefit
ライバル competitor	リース契約 lease obligation	利益を得る profit
ライバル contender	リース債権 lease receivable	利益を生じない unprofitable
ライバル peer	リース債務 lease obligation	リエンジニアリング reengineer
ライバル rival	リース支払い額 lease payments	リエンジニアリング reengineering
ライフ life	リースする lease	利落ち XC
ライブ gig	リース取引 lease	利落ち XI
ライフサイクル life cycle	リースによる借戻し leaseback	理解 fix
ライフ・サイクル・アセスメント LCA	リースバック leaseback	理解 knowledge
	リース物件 leasehold	理解 realization
ライフスタイル lifestyle	リース料 lease payments	利害関係 concern
ライフライン lifeline	リース料の支払い lease payments	利害関係 interest
ライボー LIBOR	リーダー leader	利害関係 stake
ライン line	リーダーシップ clout	利害関係がある concern
ラインアップ lineup	リーダーシップ leadership	利害関係者 interested parties

利害関係者 stakeholder	リスク危険度 exposure	リニューアル renewal
理解力 intelligence	リスク資金 venture capital	理念 concept
理解力 savvy	リスク資産総額 exposure	理念 philosophy
力学 dynamics	リスクを回避する hedge	利乗せ pyramid
力作 effort	リスケジューリング rescheduling	利乗せする pyramid
力点 stress	リステートメント restatement	利幅 profit margin
力量 competence	リスト list	利幅 spread
陸 land	リストラ overhaul	リハビリ rehabilitation
陸揚げする discharge	リストラ restructuring	利払い servicing
陸揚げする disembark	リストラ streamlining	利払い余力率 interest coverage ratio
陸揚げする land	リストラする downsize	リファイナンス refinance
リクエスト request	リストラする restructure	リファイナンス refinancing
陸上一貫輸送効率化法 Intermodal Surface Transportation Efficiency Act	リストラする streamline	リフォーム reform
	リセッション recession	リベート kickback
陸地 land	理想郷 pie	リベート rebate
陸標 landmark	理想像 role model	利便 convenience
リクルート recruit	理想の姿 role model	利便性 convenience
リクルートメント recruitment	利息 coupon	リボルビング revolving
利権 interest	利息 interest	利回り return
履行 discharge	利息落ち X in	利回り yield
履行 execution	利息落ち XI	リミット limit
履行 fulfillment	利息条件付きの interest-bearing	リモート・コントロール remote control
履行 implementation	利息払い debt servicing	
履行義務のある due	利息を生まない passive	リモコン remote control
履行する execute	リターン return	略号 code
履行する fulfill	リターン reward	略称 symbol
履行する meet	離脱 withdrawal	略奪する plunder
履行する service	離脱する split	略奪品 plunder
履行能力 responsibility	離脱する suspend	…流 style
履行利益 expectancy	リチウムイオン充電池 lithium ion rechargeable battery	理由 account
リコール recall		理由 reason
リコール recall	…率 factor	留意せよ NB [nb]
リサーチ research	率 percent	流行 currency
リサイクル recycle	率 rate	流行 trend
利下げ ease	立案 planning	粒子 plasma
利札 coupon	立案者 mastermind	粒子状物質 particulate matter
利札引換券 talon	立案者 organizer	流出 discharge
利ざや margin	立案する draw	流出 flow
利ざや profit margin	立案する plan	流出 outflow
利ざや scalp	利付きの interest-bearing	流出額 outflow
利ざや spread	立証 establishment	流出した個人情報 leaked personal information
利子 interest	立証する establish	
理事 director	立身出世主義 careerism	留置権 lien
理事 manager	立身出世主義者 careerist	流通 currency
理事 trustee	立地 location	流通 distribution
理事会 board	立地条件 location	流通 marketing
理事会 meeting	立地変更 relocation	流通 negotiation
利子支払い保証倍率 interest coverage ratio	立派な full-fledged	流通 retailing
	立派な演説 effort	流通可能の negotiable
利潤 earnings	立法 legislation	流通業 distributor
利潤 gain	リテーラー retailer	流通業者 distributor
利潤 profit	リテール retail	流通させる circulate
利潤をもたらす pay	利点 advantage	流通させる dishoard
利殖 accumulation	利点 benefit	流通させる distribute
離籍 separation	利点 incentive	流通市場 aftermarket
離職 severance	利点 percentage	流通市場 secondary market
リスク crisis	利得 benefit	流通して afloat
リスク risk	利得 gain	流通する afloat
リスク・ウェート weighting	利得 payoff	流通する circulate
	利得 profit	

流通する	floating		understanding	旅客輸送	passenger transportation
流通性	liquidity	了解事項	understanding	旅行	travel
流通性のある	negotiable	両替	conversion	旅行する	travel
流通速度	velocity	両替	exchange	リリースする	release
流通停止にする	immobilize	両替する	convert	離陸	takeoff
流通量	float	両替する	exchange	離陸許可	clearance
流通ルート	pipeline	利用可能度	availability	離陸する	take off
流動	current	利用可能な	available	利率	coupon
流動化	liquidation	利用技術	software	リレーション	relations
流動資産	current assets	料金	bill	履歴	career
流動資産の換金性	liquidity	料金	charge	履歴管理	traceability
流動資産の換金能力	liquidity	料金	due	理論的な	speculative
流動する	floating	料金	fare	理論的枠組み	paradigm
流動性	CAMEL	料金	fee	厘	percentage point
流動性	current	料金	rate	臨界	critical mass
流動性	liquidation	料金	toll	臨界質量	critical mass
流動性	liquidity	料金徴収荷重	payload	臨界量	critical mass
流動性がある	liquid	料金として取る	toll	輪郭	profile
流動性に乏しい	illiquid	料金表	tariff	リンク	link
流動性の高い	liquid	良好な	favorable	リンクさせる	peg
流動性の高い投資	liquid investment	良好な	good	リンクする	link
		量産	mass production	リンケージ	linkage
流動性の高さ	ample liquidity	量産	rollout	臨時雇用	short-hour
流動性の高さ	liquidity	量産する	mass-produce	臨時収入	perquisite
流動性のない	illiquid	量産する	roll out	臨時の	contingent
流動的	current	量産的な	commercial	臨時の	current
流動的	floating	利用した	employed	臨時の	extraordinary
流動比率	current ratio	良質	quality	臨時の	one-time
流入	inflow	利用者	user	臨時の	temporary
流入	influx	利用者に親切	user-friendly	臨時の	windfall
流入額	inflow	利用者認証	authentication	臨時費用	contingency
流入資金	capital inflow	領収	receipt	臨時利益	windfall
留分	fraction	領収書	receipt	隣接した	immediate
留保	reserve	良循環	virtuous circle	輪番	rotation
留保	retention	…を利用する	leverage	倫理	ethics
留保する	retain	利用する	access	倫理	morality
留保利益	retained earnings	利用する	apply	倫理規程	code of conduct
留保利益	undistributed earnings	利用する	capitalize on	倫理綱領	code of conduct
流用	diversion	利用する	exploit	倫理綱領	ethics
流用する	convert	利用する	play	倫理性	morality
流用する	divert	利用する	reclaim	倫理体系	ethics
猟	game	利用する	tap	倫理的	ethical
量	amount	利用する	use	倫理の	ethical
量	quantity	稜線	edge		
量	volume	両建てにする	straddle	る	
利用	access	量的緩和	quantitative easing		
利用	employment	量的生物資源	biomass	累加配当	cumulative dividend
利用	hit	量的な	quantitative	類型	pattern
利用	use	利用できる	disposable	類似	correspondence
領域	area	利用できる	serve	類似	identity
領域	domain	領土	domain	類似	parity
領域	field	領土	territory	類似の	comparable
領域	niche	量の	quantitative	類似物件	comparables
領域	range	両方またはいずれか一方	and/or	類似例	identity
領域	region	利用明細書	bill	累積	accumulation
領域	scope	量目不足	underweight	累積した	accumulated
領域	territory	両用の	dual	累積配当	cumulative dividend
領域	territory	料理	table	類別	classification
了解	understanding	両立	compatibility	ルール	rule
了解覚書	memorandum of	両立性	compatibility	ルビコン川	Rubicon

れ

例	paradigm
例	specimen
零	zero
レイオフ	layoff
レイオフ	redundancy
レイオフを進める	lay off
例外	exemption
冷却期間	cooling off
冷却効果	air-cooling effects
零細小売店	ma-and-pa store
令状	writ
0.1ポイント	notch
0.25%	quarter point
レーザー	laser
レース	race
レート	rate
レーベル	label
歴史的	historical
歴史的原価	original cost
歴史的建造物	landmark
暦年	calendar year
レギュラー	regular
レギュレーション	regulation
レコード会社	label
レスキュー	rescue
レター	letter
列	queue
劣位	disadvantage
劣化	deterioration
劣化	impairment
劣化した貸出金	impaired loans
劣化する	impair
れっきとした	full-fledged
劣後の	junior
劣後の	subordinated
レッテル	label
レッド・ヘリング	red herring
レバレッジ	leverage
レバレッジド・バイアウト	leveraged buyout
レビュー	review
レビューする	review
レベル	echelon
レベル	level
レベル	rank
レベル	territory
レポート	report
レポ取引	repo
廉価な	downscale
廉価な	knockdown
連環	link
連関	linkage
連携	alliance
連携	coordination
連携	partnership
連携させる	coordinate
連携する	coordinate
連携する	tie up
連携を取る	coordinate
連結	combination
連結	consolidation
連結	coupling
連結	group
連結会社間取引	intercompany transaction
連結器	coupling
連結計上する	consolidate
連結決算	consolidation
連結した	combined
連結した	consolidated
連結する	consolidate
連結する	link
連結装置	attachment
連結対象外の	unconsolidated
連結対象にする	consolidate
連結対象の	consolidated
連合	alliance
連合	association
連合体	association
連合の	joint
連鎖	chain
連鎖効果	knock-on effect
連鎖店	chain
連鎖店	chain store
連鎖反応	knock-on effect
レンジ	range
連続	series
連続した	serial
連続した	straight
連続して	straight
連続している	running
連続する	running
連続的変動	spiral
連続の	back-to-back
連帯の	joint
レンタル	rental
連動	link
連動化	coupling
連動させる	link
連動させる	peg
連動する	gear
連邦住宅貸付抵当公社	Freddie Mac
連邦住宅抵当金庫	Fannie Mae
連邦準備制度理事会	Fed
連邦準備制度理事会	FRB
連邦調達規則	FARs
連邦取引委員会	FTC
連邦の	federal
連邦の	national
連邦破産法11章	Chapter 11
連絡	communication
連絡事務所	liaison office
連絡する	report
連絡網	network

ろ

ロイヤルティ	loyalty
ロイヤルティ	royalty
老化	aging
老朽	aging
老朽化	aging
老朽化	deterioration
老朽化	obsolescence
老朽化した	obsolete
老朽化する	deteriorate
労災補償	workmen's accident compensation
労作	effort
労使協約	deal
労働	labor
労働	work
労働意欲	morale
労働組合	trade union
労働組合	union
労働時間	working hours
労働市場	job market
労働者	labor
労働者	worker
労働者側	labor
労働者災害補償	workmen's accident compensation
労働者派遣法	Temporary Staffing Services Law
労働人員	manpower
労働人口	workforce
労働生活の質	QWL
労働総同盟産業別組合会議	AFL-CIO
労働の	working
労働日	working day
労働力	labor
労働力	manpower
労働力	workforce
浪費する	squander
労務	labor
労務	service
労力	manpower
老練な	skilled
ローカライズする	localize
ローカリゼーション	localization
ローカル	local
ローカル・エリア・ネットワーク	LAN
ローテーション	rotation
ロードショー	roadshow
ロードする	load
ロード・マップ	road map
ロールオーバー	rollover
ローン	financing
ローン	loan
ローン担保証券	CLO
ローンチ	launch
ローンによる資金の調達	

	drawdown	group
ログ	log	ワーク work
…にログインする enter	ワークアウト workout
録音 audio	ワークシェア work sharing system
ロケーション location	ワーク・シェアリング work sharing system
ロケット rocket	
ロケットの燃料 software	ワークショップ workshop
ロゴ logo	ワークステーション workstation
ロジスティクス logistics	わいせつな dirty
露出する bare	わいろ pie
ロス loss	賄賂 bribe
路線 approach	賄賂 kickback
路線 formula	賄賂 payoff
路線 line	賄賂 sweetener
路線 route	賄賂のきく corrupt
路線 way	賄賂を贈る bribe
路線価 roadside land price	賄賂を使う grease
ロハス Lohas	和解 accord
ロビー lobby	和解 conciliation
ロビーイング lobbying	和解 settlement
ロビー活動 lobbying	和解 transaction
ロビー団体 lobby	和解させる mediate
ロフト・ビジネス loft business	和解させる reconcile
ロボット automation	和解する settle
ロボット robot	枠 quota
ロボット robotics	枠組み framework
ロボット化 robotization	枠組み paradigm
ロボット技術 robotics	枠組み scope
ロボット工学 robotics	ワグナー法 Wagner Act
ロボットの導入 robotization	分け前 cut
論及 reference	分け前 lot
論拠 basis	分け前 percentage
論拠 case	分け前 proportion
論証 demonstration	ワゴン卸売り業者 wagon jobber
論争 contention	ワゴン小売業者 wagon retailer
論争 dispute	ワゴン積み流通業者 wagon distributor
論点 contention	
論点 issue	ワゴン・リテイラー wagon retailer
論点 point	ワシントン Washington
論点 question	…渡し ex
ロンドン銀行間オファー・レート LIBOR	私会社 private company
	渡す deliver
ロンドンの銀行間取引金利 LIBOR	渡り合う compete
ロンドンの金融街 Lombard Street	ワッツ WATS
ロンドンの金融市場 Lombard Street	ワラント warrant
	ワラント落ち XW
論文 paper	割合 percent
	割合 percentage
	割合 proportion
	割合 rate
輪 link	割合 ratio
ワーキング・グループ working	割当て apportionment

割当て allocation
割当て allotment
割当て assignment
割当て proportion
割当て quota
割当て rationing
割当金 allotment
割当数量 quota
割当量 assignment
割り当てる allocate
割り当てる allot
割り当てる allow
割り当てる apportion
割り当てる assign
割り当てる consign
割り当てる lot
割り当てる prorate
割高な excessive
割付け makeup
割り引いて売る[買う] discount
割引 discount
割引 rebate
割引額 discount
割引現在価値 discount cash flow
割引する discount
割引率 discount
割引料 discount
割り引く discount
割り引く take off
割符 tally
割振り allocation
割り振る allocate
割増価格 premium
割増金 premium
割増金 surcharge
割増退職金 golden parachute
割増退職金 redundancy
割戻し rebate
割戻し金 kickback
割安株 underpriced stock
割安な株式 underpriced stock
悪い poor
悪い unfavorable
悪い面 downside
湾岸協力会議 GCC
ワンストップの one-stop
ワンセグ one-segment broadcasting
ワン・トゥ・ワン・マーケティング one-to-one marketing
ワンプライス店 one-price retailer

2009年7月10日　初版発行

ビジネス実務総合英和辞典

2009年7月10日　第1刷発行

著者	菊地義明（きくち・よしあき）
発行者	株式会社三省堂　代表者八幡統厚
印刷者	三省堂印刷株式会社
発行所	株式会社三省堂

〒101-8371
東京都千代田区三崎町二丁目22番14号

電話　編集　（03）3230-9411
　　　営業　（03）3230-9412

振替口座　00160-5-54300
http://www.sanseido.co.jp

〈ビジネス総合英和・816pp.〉

落丁本・乱丁本はお取替えいたします

ISBN 978-4-385-11030-1

Ⓡ本書を無断で複写複製（コピー）することは，著作権法上の例外を除き，禁じられています。
本書をコピーされる場合は，事前に日本複写権センター（JRRC）の許諾を受けてください。

http://www.jrrc.or.jp　　　　　eメール: info@jrrc.or.jp　　　　　電話: 03-3401-2382

財務情報英和辞典

菊地義明 [著]　A5 判　544 頁

英文の四半期・年次財務報告書を読み・書くことに特化した、初めての英和辞典。約1万3千項目を収録。ビジネスパーソンや経営学・経済学を学ぶ学生にとって必携の一冊！

グランドコンサイス英和辞典

三省堂編修所 [編]　A5 変型判　3,024 頁

あらゆる分野の専門語までを幅広く網羅し、携帯版英和で最大の 36 万項目を収録。

グランドコンサイス和英辞典

三省堂編修所 [編]　A5 変型判　2,528 頁

和英辞典では最大級の、見出し語・複合語・派生語 21 万項目、用例 11 万項目を収録。

ウィズダム英和辞典 第 2 版

井上永幸・赤野一郎 [編]　B6 変型判　2,144 頁

コーパスを全面利用した初の英和辞典。ビジネスユースにも十分な約 9 万項目を収録。

ウィズダム和英辞典

小西友七 [編修主幹]　B6 変型判　2,112 頁

総合的英語発信力が身につく和英辞典。ビジネスユースにも十分な約 8 万 8 千項目を収録。